ST. JAMES PRESS

Gay & Lesbian

ALMANAC

ST. JAMES PRESS

Gay & Lesbian
ALMANAC

Editor

Neil Schlager

With Foreword by

R. Ellen Greenblatt

ST. JAMES PRESS

AN IMPRINT OF GALE

DETROIT • NEW YORK

Neil Schlager, *Editor*

Michael J. Tyrkus, *Project Coordinator*

Laura Standley Berger, Joann Cerrito, Dave Collins, Nicolet V. Elert,
Miranda Ferrara, Kristin Hart, Margaret Mazurkiewicz
St. James Press Staff

Peter M. Gareffa, *Managing Editor, St. James Press*

Mary Beth Trimper, *Production Director*
Deborah Milliken, *Production Assistant*

Cynthia Baldwin, *Product Design Manager*
Pamela A. E. Galbreath, *Art Director*
Pamela A. Reed, *Photography Coordinator*
Randy Bassett, *Image Database Supervisor*
Robert Duncan, Mike Logusz, *Imaging Specialists*

The St. James Press gay & lesbian almanac / editor, Neil Schlager.
        p.   cm.
   Includes bibliographical references and index.
   ISBN 1-55862-358-2
   1. Gay men—Biography. 2. Lesbians—Biography. 3. Gay men—
History. 4. Lesbians—History   I. Schlager, Neil, 1966- .
   II. Gay & lesbian biography.
HQ76.3.U5S75 1998
305.9'0664'09--dc21   98-6156
                                                             CIP

Printed in the United States of America

St. James Press is an imprint of Gale

10 9 8 7 6 5 4 3 2

CONTENTS

FOREWORD

A theme that surfaces repeatedly throughout lesbian and gay autobiographical accounts is the authors' search for information on their awakening identities. For many, the first stop on this journey is their local library. Coming-out literature abounds with descriptions of individuals surreptitiously, yet expectantly, surveying library shelves, searching for answers to their many questions about homosexuality.

But until relatively recently, few reference books dealing exclusively with lesbian and gay topics were available. A 1988 article on gay and lesbian reference materials listed only 40 publications, half of which were travel guides or periodicals, with the rest being indexes, directories, guides, and bibliographies (Malinowski, 1988). No encyclopedias or almanacs were cited. The only books that existed along those lines were compilations of trivia, such as Leigh Rutledge's *Gay Book of Lists* (1987). While these types of books may be interesting reading, they most likely provided little help or comfort to those seeking tangible answers to their queries.

It is only within the last decade that popular almanacs began to appear. The first of these, the *Alyson Almanac*, published in 1989, resembles its predecessors in that it consists largely of lists. The editors of this almanac relied heavily on articles in the *Advocate* and *Washington Blade* for information, and, in later editions, on clippings and other information sent in by readers. Other popular almanacs such as *Out in All Directions* and the companion volumes the *Gay Almanac* and the *Lesbian Almanac* have appeared in more recent years.

What sets the *St. James Press Gay & Lesbian Almanac* apart from these is that here for the first time is an almanac that is not a frothy concoction of trivia, but a comprehensive, substantive volume written in a scholarly tone throughout. Like the other almanacs, it stands up to quick consultation, but it is also great for browsing or more sustained study. Comprising almost two dozen chapters written by experts in the field, this reference source provides a broad, multifaceted overview of lesbian and gay history, culture, and communities in the United States. An extensive bibliography including articles, books, and, most notably, Internet resources accompanies each chapter in addition to the sizable general bibliography at the end of the book. A comprehensive general index of names, titles, events, organizations, and concepts rounds out the volume, providing full access to its rich contents.

The *St. James Press Gay & Lesbian Almanac* explores the significant issues facing gays and lesbians today, including marriage, military service, employment, law, and health. Examining the full gamut of lesbian and gay culture ranging from the arts to travel and leisure, this volume strives to give a balanced voice to the concerns and interests of both lesbians and gay men.

One of the highlights of the *St. James Press Gay & Lesbian Almanac* is the section on historical documents. Here is the pageant of gay and lesbian history in the making, illustrated by such reports as the "New Years Eve Drag," the "Woman-Identified Woman" by the Radicalesbians, and the Colorado Amendment 2 decision. Another feature that sets the *St. James Press Gay & Lesbian Almanac* apart from its predecessors is its inclusion of local and regional history and information.

With the publication of the *St. James Press Gay & Lesbian Almanac*, library shelves will offer those searching for information on lesbianism and homosexuality a comprehensive place to start searching for answers to their many questions.

—R. Ellen Greenblatt
University of Colorado at Boulder, 1998

EDITOR'S NOTE

Welcome to the *St. James Press Gay & Lesbian Almanac,* a comprehensive reference source covering gay and lesbian history and culture.

As R. Ellen Greenblatt notes in her foreword to the book, previous encyclopedias and almanacs covering gay and lesbian culture, with their collections of brief articles, lists, quotes, and statistical information, have served primarily as ready reference entertainment. Our goal with the *St. James Press Gay & Lesbian Almanac* has been to create a more in-depth reference source that provides substantive surveys of most aspects of gay and lesbian history and culture. By collecting these broad surveys in a single source, we hope to offer readers not only a reliable place to access information about the gay and lesbian experience, but also a useful starting point to additional serious research about the topics discussed herein.

Scope, Organization, and Content

Reference sources rarely have airtight inclusion criteria and scopes, and our almanac is no exception. In general, it focuses on the gay and lesbian experience in the United States, both historically and in the present. Because of the invisibility of gays and lesbians in the U.S. prior to the 1920s, most of the chapters restrict their coverage to the twentieth century. While Americans and American issues are at the heart of the *Almanac,* some chapters include discussions of non-U.S. events and people whose influence on the U.S. gay rights movement is too great to ignore. Examples include the "Music" chapter, where both Elton John (English) and k. d. lang (Canadian) are profiled, and the "Literature" chapter, where seminal writers Oscar Wilde (Irish) and Virginia Woolf (English) are discussed. Finally, readers should note that although the "gay and lesbian" experience is the primary focus of the *Almanac,* bisexual and transgender issues also receive coverage.

Organizationally, the *Almanac* is divided into 23 chapters, the majority of which include a general discussion of the topic at hand followed by profiles of prominent individuals in that field. All chapters except the "Significant Documents" chapter end with a "References" section that identifies books, periodical articles, Internet sites, and occasionally organizations where readers can find more information about the topic. Most of the chapters cover specific spheres of human activity (e.g. "Politics," "Family," "Sports," "Labor and Employment," "Religion and Spirituality"), but a handful serve a somewhat different purpose. "Chronology," for instance, contains brief descriptions of key twentieth-century events arranged in chronological order; "Organizations" contains similarly brief overviews of influential groups in the history of the gay rights movement; and "Significant Documents" includes the full or partial text of important primary documents—speeches, articles, legal cases, and government texts. Because these three chapters touch on virtually all of the spheres that are covered in other chapters, they are placed at the beginning of the book. Finally, readers will note the existence of a separate chapter covering "AIDS," in addition to one devoted to "Health," an organizational division that reflects that enormous impact AIDS has had on virtually every aspect of gay and lesbian culture.

Other comments about specific content decisions are also in order, because of the broad nature of most of the chapters. For instance, readers should be aware that "Performing Arts" covers the fields of theater, dance, and performance art, while opera is treated in "Music"—along with classical and pop/rock music. In addition, "Visual Arts" comprises art, photography, and architecture. Inevitably, there is overlap in these chapters as well as others; performance art, for instance, often straddles the line between "high" art and performance, while certain writers have achieved renown both as playwrights (treated in "Performing Arts") and as novelists and/or poets (treated in "Literature"). Lastly, readers should note that some chapters contain a simple chronological discussion of a topic, while others are divided by genre and/or gender; "Performing Arts," as an example, includes discrete discussions of the three fields, and each field is further divided into a discussion of lesbian and gay male issues. Readers seeking information on specific individuals, events, or topics should refer first to the index at the back of the book.

In addition to the subject-specific reference lists at the end of each chapter, readers will find an annotated general bibliography at the back of the book that lists general books of interest about the gay and lesbian experience.

Writers

The chapters in the *St. James Press Gay & Lesbian Almanac* were written by a collection of professors, journalists, librarians, and freelance writers. Owing to the length and research demands of each chapter, writers were given significant latitude to determine the specific content and arrangement of their essays. In addition, writers were given the freedom to use the terminology that they felt was most appropriate; thus, readers will find varying uses of several presently accepted terms in gay and lesbian studies, from "homosexual" to "gay and lesbian" to "queer." In most chapters, readers will find text near the beginning of the chapter that discusses issues of terminology, organization, and content. Bylines at the end of each chapter identify the author(s) of the chapter, and the "Notes on Contributors" section at the back of the book contains brief biographical comments about all contributors.

Acknowledgments

I would like to thank the following individuals for their help in creating the *St. James Press Gay & Lesbian Almanac:* my editor at St. James Press, Mike Tyrkus, for his thoughtfulness, responsiveness, and patience, even in the face of often-overwhelming deadline pressure; the members of the advisory board, for their assistance in identifying the chapter list, advice on matters of content and organization, and help in finding writers; R. Ellen Greenblatt, for compiling the book's foreword; Jill Posener, who worked tirelessly to acquire and gain permission to use the photographs in the book; my partner, Jeffery, for his constant encouragement and support throughout this project; and all of the writers, without whose expertise, energy, commitment, and hard work the book would never have come into being.

—Neil Schlager
Editor

ADVISORY BOARD

Acknowledgments

The editor gratefully acknowledges the following individuals and organizations for allowing use of photographs and text:

Photographs, charts, and tables:

Cover photograph courtesy of **Michael Bettinger.**

Peter Aaron/Esto: Photo of Robert F. Wagner Park, designed by Rodolfo Machado and Jorge Silvetti, Boston. **Barry Adam:** Photo of Barry Adam. **Dina Alfano:** Photos of Melissa Etheridge (1994); k. d. lang (1997). **Luis Alfaro:** Photo of Luis Alfaro. **Wayne Andrews/Esto:** Photos of Hearst Castle, San Simeon, designed by Julia Morgan; National Farmer's Bank, Owatonna, Minn., designed by Louis H. Sullivan. **AP/Worldwide Photos:** Photos of Carson McCullers (1941); Margarethe Cammermeyer (photographer Matt Todd, 1992); Gianni Versace (photographer Dave Cheskin, 1997); Senators Nunn and Warner visiting submarine during military debate (photographer Steve Helber, 1993); Elton John (photographer Don Edgar, 1997); Glenn Burke (photographer Mark Hundley, 1993); David Kopay (1977); Lorraine Hansberry; James Baldwin. **Beth Armitage:** Photo of George Mason University (Virginia) students demonstrating. **Artists Rights Society:** "Triple Elvis," silkscreen on canvas by Andy Warhol (1964). **Arthur Aviles:** Photo of Bill T. Jones. **K. C. Bailey, courtesy of Amy Pivar:** Photo of Amy Pivar. **Michael Bettinger:** All photos in the Family chapter. **Christopher Bierlein, courtesy of Random House:** Photo of Andrew Tobias. **Donna Binder, Impact Visuals:** Photos of Allen Schindler's mother with a gay naval escort; David Mixner; Rep. Steve Gunderson with Rob Morris. **Chandler Burr:** All charts and tables in the Science chapter. **Cathy Cade:** Photos of military veterans at March on Washington (1993); Christopher Street West parade, Los Angeles (1972); Minnesota family at March on Washington (1993); Youth Empowerment Speakout at March on Washington (1993); "Living Sober" marchers, San Francisco Freedom Day Parade (1986); "Lesbianas Latinas" marchers at March on Washington (1993); "Bi-Anna Ross" marcher, San Francisco Freedom Day Parade (1986); P-FLAG at March on Washington (1993); Lesbian Elders Dance, organized by GLOE (1985). **Phyllis Christopher:** Photos of Jewelle Gomez; B. Ruby Rich. **Cleveland Museum of Art:** "Dancing Sailors," watercolor by Charles Demuth (1917). **Collection Whitney Museum of American Art, New York:** "The Fleet's In" by Paul Cadmus (1934). **Tee A. Corinne:** Photo of Bonnie Zimmerman. **Paula Court:** Photo of John Kelly. **Louie Crew:** Photo of Louie Crew. **Current Medicine:** "How HIV retrovirus works at the cellular level," illustration on p. 170. Reprinted from Mandell, G.L., and Mildvan, D., eds. *AIDS: Atlas of Infectious Diseases Volume I.* Philadelphia, PA: Current Medicine, 1995. Figure 2-15, "Viral Replication," page 2.7. **David Danelski:** Photo of Doric Wilson. **Darlene/Photo Graphics:** Photos of ice skaters winning gold at the Gay Games; women's softball game. **Mark Darley/Esto:** Photo of Drager House, Los Angeles, designed by Franklin D. Israel. **David Geffen Company:** Photo of David Geffen. **Donna Deitch:** Photo of Donna Deitch. **Arthur Elgort, courtesy of Mark Morris Dance Company:** Photo of Mark Morris. **Lillian Faderman:** Photo of Lillian Faderman. **Frameline:** Photos of Marlon Riggs; Gus Van Sant. **Ken Friedman, courtesy of American Conservatory Theatre:** Photo of scene from *Angels in America.* **Garland Publishing:** Figure 5 in Military chapter; reprinted from Rimmerman, Craig, ed., *Gay Rights, Military Wrongs.* Garland Publishing, 1996. "State Military Personnel Policies on Sexual Orientation," Table 3. **Gay and Lesbian Historical Society of Northern California:** Photos of Leonard Matlovich on the cover of *Time* (1975); cover of a lesbian pulp novel; Walt Whitman; cover of *Giovanni's Room* by James Baldwin; Cover of the *Ladder* depicting homophile pickets in Washington, D.C. (1965); Anti-Briggs Initiative advertisement; *Crimes against Nature* flyer, Gay Men's Theater Collective; *White Captive* by George Quaintance (1951); from the "Youths in the Grotto" series by Baron Wilhelm von Gloeden; the Village People on the cover of *US* magazine (1979); cover of *ONE* magazine on p. 618 (1958); cover of *Time* ("The Homosexual in America"); cover of *Time* ("Ellen: Yep, I'm Gay," 1997); cover of *National Enquirer* (Rock Hudson); gay periodicals shown on p. 403; cover of *Newsweek* ("Gay in America"); cover of *San Francisco Focus* ("Gay and Lesbian Power"). **Marc Geller:** Photos of Keith Meinhold (1993); Thom Gunn (1988); John Waters (1997); Harry Britt (1986); Roberta Achtenberg, Harry Britt, and Carole Migden; Larry Kramer. **Rick Gerharter:** Photos of Troy Perry; Cherrie Moraga; Vito Russo; Todd Haynes; Morris Kight with the ashes of Harvey Milk (1988); Karen Thompson and Sharon Kowalski. **John Glines:** Photo of John Glines. **James D. Gossage:** Joe Cino at Caffe Cino (1965). **Morgan Gwenwald:** Photo of Stonewall 25, March on the United Nations (1994); AIDS protestors (p. 20); Lesbian Avengers protest (1995). **John Hall:** Photo of Catherine Saalfield. **Jorjet Harper, courtesy of Toni Armstrong, Jr.:** Robin Tyler with Wanda Henson. **David Harsany, courtesy of Lou Harrison:** Photo of Lou Harrison. **Billy Howard, from the book *Epitaphs for the Living: Words and Images in the Time of AIDS*, SMU Press (1989):** Photos on pages 173, 193, and 196. **Human

Rights Campaign: Photo of Elizabeth Birch. **JEB (Joan E. Biren):** Photos of Rita Mae Brown (1973); Audre Lorde; Adrienne Rich; New York Gay Pride Parade (Local and Regional Views, p. 635; 1989); David Scondras; Franklin Kameny at 1979 March on Washington (1979); Del Martin and Phyllis Lyon; Michigan Womyn's Music Festival (1977). **Deborah Kass:** "Triple Silver Yentl (My Elvis)" (1993). **Mary Levin, courtesy of Marieka Klawitter:** Photo of Marieka Klawitter. **Kelly Linvil:** Photo of Jan Oxenberg (1996). **Lippincott-Raven:** "History and progression of HIV," illustration on p. 171. Reprinted from DeVita, V.T.; Hellman, S.; and Rosenberg, S.A., eds. *AIDS: Etiology, Diagnosis, Treatment, and Prevention.* Philadelphia, PA: Lippincott-Raven, 1997. Figure 5-1, "Representative Course of Progression to Acquired Immunodeficiency Syndrome (AIDS) in Three Types of Progressors," p. 90. **T. L. Litt:** Photo of Paul Monette (1991). **Patsy Lynch:** Photos of Mel White being arrested at White House (p. 557, 1996); Leonard Matlovich's grave (1993); Urvashi Vaid at AIDS rally near White House (1989); Urvashi Vaid protesting at George Bush speech (1990); AIDS protestors at Department of Health and Human Services (1988). **Paul Margolies/The Names Project:** Photo of the AIDS Memorial Quilt in Washington, D.C. (1996). **Mariah Wilderness Expeditions:** Photo of river rafting. **Michael Marsland, courtesy of Yale University:** Photo of Art and Architecture Building at Yale University, designed by Paul Rudolph. **Dona Ann McAdams:** Photos of *Dress Suits for Hire,* WOW Café; Carmelita Tropicana; Tim Miller (1987); Ishmael Houston-Jones; John Fleck. **Ann P. Meredith:** Photo of Thomas Waddell with daughter Jessica. **Moorland-Spingarn Research Center, Howard University:** Photo of Angelina Grimke (from Grimke Collection). **David Morgan:** Photo of John Corigliano and William Hoffmann. **Carol L. Newsom:** Photo of Martina Navratilova. **Daniel Nicoletta:** Photos of Harry Hay (1994); Allen Ginsberg (1997); Harvey Milk (1976); White Night Riots (1979); Charles Ludlam (1981). **Michael James O'Brien:** Photo of protest sign, "ACT UP Is Watching." **Outlook Records:** Photo of Pansy Division. **Richard Payne AIA:** Photos of the Glass House in Connecticut, designed by Philip Johnson (1986); the AT&T Building in New York, designed by Philip Johnson. **Performing Arts Library and Museum, San Francisco:** Engraving of Charlotte Cushman (engraver Alonzo Chappell; 1875); photo of Nance O'Neill. **Jill Posener:** Photos of Rosemary Curb and Nancy Manahan; Janie Spahr; Dorothy Allison (1989); Pomo Afro Homos; Robert Patrick (1974); Judy Dlugacz (1997). **Brenda Prager:** Photo of Axis Dance Theatre Company. **Rink Foto:** Photos of Randy Burns; Joe Steffan; Perry Watkins; Academy Sex Club in San Francisco, with warning notices about AIDS; Christopher Isherwood with Don Bachardy; "Oppose Anti-Asian Discrimination" protestors (1980); Robert Chesley; Ned Rorem; line dancing cowboys; Folsom Street Fair; men at Fire Island (1977); Gore Vidal (1982). **Michael Rogol:** Photo of the model for the Cathedral of Hope, designed by Philip Johnson (1996). **Jennifer Roper:** Photo of Cheryl Dunye. **Steve Rosenthal, courtesy of Williams College Museum of Art:** Photo of rotunda of Williams College Museum of Art, renovation designed by Charles Moore. **Tracey Russo, Boston University School of Medicine:** Photo of Richard Pillard. **Albert Sanchez, courtesy the Press Network:** Photo of Ani DiFranco. **Ronni L. Sanlo:** Photo of Ronni L. Sanlo. **Sue Schaffner:** Photo of the Five Lesbian Brothers. **Servicemembers Legal Defense Network:** Charts in the Military chapter, "Lesbian Baiting: The Disproportionate Impact of the Gay Policies on Women"; "Total Discharges and Rate of Discharge Under Gay Policies"; "Violations of 'Don't Ask, Don't Tell, Don't Pursue, Don't Harass' for All Services"; "Costs of Training Replacements for Servicemembers Discharged Under Gay Policy." Reprinted from SLDN's Third Annual Report. Reprinted by permission of SLDN. **Bruce Talbot, courtesy of Marga Gomez:** Photo of Marga Gomez. **Tom of Finland Foundation, Los Angeles:** Drawing by Tom of Finland. **Janet Van Ham/HBO:** Photo of scene from HBO production, *And the Band Played On.* **Mel White:** Photo of Mel White protesting to end the ban on gays in the military (page 272). **Millie Wilson:** "White Girl" (1995). **Susan Wilson:** Photo of Sanford Sylvan. **Xochitl Films, San Francisco:** Photo of Lourdes Portillo making *Columbus on Trial* (1992).

Text:

"I Am Your Sister: Black Women Organizing Across Sexualities," by Audre Lorde. From *A Burst of Light,* by Audre Lorde. Ithaca, New York: Firebrand Books, copyright 1988 by Audre Lorde. **Reprinted by permission of Firebrand Books.**

"The New Year's Eve Drag," by Myler Vollmer. Unpublished, undated paper, circa 1930. **Reprinted by permission of the Burgess Collection, University of Chicago Archives.**

"Homosexual Outlet" from *Sexual Behavior in the Human Male,* by Alfred Kinsey. W. B. Saunder Co., 1948. **Reprinted by permission of the Kinsey Institute for Research in Sex, Gender, and Reproduction, Inc.**

"Statement of Purpose," Daughters of Bilitis, from *The Ladder.* **Reprinted by permission of Barbara Grier.**

"Civil Liberties: A Progress Report," speech by Franklin E. Kameny, July 22, 1964. **Reprinted by permission of Franklin E. Kameny.**

"A Gay Manifesto," by Carl Wittman, and "The Woman-Identified Woman," by Radicalesbians. Reprinted from *Out of the*

1

Chronology

THE LATE 1940s AND EARLY 1950s

The Flourishing of a Drag Ball Culture

Drag balls developed in the black working-class neighborhoods of major U.S. cities in the late nineteenth century, bringing together thousands of black and white men in well-publicized social extravaganzas that both reflected and reinforced the growing visibility of gay communities. In the 1940s and 1950s, between two and three thousand people came to see or be seen at the balls in New York and Chicago, with nearly equal numbers of blacks and whites, and a mixture of working-class and middle-class gays. According to *Ebony* magazine, which provided extensive and largely favorable coverage of the Harlem balls in the early 1950s, "Park Avenue rubbed shoulders with 125th Street and bankers laughed gaily with artists from Greenwich Village." The police, who otherwise arrested crossdressers, gave "official sanction for one night of the year to men dressing as women in public" and even provided crowd control to keep back straight onlookers.

Attending drag balls could be dangerous, however. Onlookers sometimes jeered participants, and not all cities permitted such events to be held. The police in Atlantic City and Washington, D.C., for example, banned balls in the 1930s; in the latter case, officers took no action when straight passersby began to beat and chase the crossdressing men who showed up. Thereafter Washingtonians had to travel to Baltimore or New York to attend balls.

Many made such trips because drag balls were sites where the participants themselves were in control and could celebrate themselves, if just for an evening, without fearing arrest or feeling like they were "the only one." As a result, these events affirmed the gay community and provided gay and bisexual men with a sense of empowerment and belonging. This empowerment was especially significant for black gay and bisexual men, who were able to exer-cise a measure of authority that was frequently denied to them elsewhere in society.

The popularity of drag balls during the 1940s and 1950s challenged the traditional depiction of lesbigay life during the period as severely limited by the federal government's anti-gay witch hunts and the rise of a Cold War-era ideology of conformity and domesticity. The fact that balls attracted large numbers of black men and were held in black neighborhoods also called into question the common perception that African Americans who pursued same-sex relationships could not be open in their own communities for fear of being rejected by straight friends and family members.

Sources: Beemyn, "A Queer Capital"; Chauncey, *Gay New York*; Drexel, "Before Paris Burned."

The Impact of World War II on Gay Community Formation

By uprooting millions of young women and men and often placing them in nonfamilial, sex-segregated environments, World War II fostered the process of lesbigay identity formation and the development of lesbigay communities. More than at any previous time, those attracted to people of the same sex had opportunities to find each other and to socialize publicly together. As large numbers of men—and some women—left home to join the armed forces, others migrated to urban areas to work in the burgeoning defense industries and to take the jobs of those who had been sent overseas. The paid female work force rose by more than six million, as many white middle-class women entered the labor market for the first time. African-American women, who had been limited largely to domestic and agricultural work in the past, were also able to obtain factory jobs due to the shortage of male laborers, but only after protests against their exclusion.

The dearth of young men greatly increased the number of work and social environments where women predominated, thereby providing greater opportunities for lesbians and bisexual women to find each other while ensuring that these all-female spaces avoided the "taint of deviance." Similarly, the millions of men serving in the military lived side by side and had to depend upon each other for survival. As a result, men of all sexualities formed close emotional bonds, and gay and bisexual men could often act on their feelings without raising the suspicions of others. The fact that the military quickly had to assemble a vast army meant that lesbians, gay men, and bisexuals typically had little difficulty entering and remaining in the service, provided they did not disrupt military life by aggressively pursuing relationships with uninterested companions.

As lesbians, gay men, and bisexuals flooded into urban areas during the war, the number of bars, restaurants, and other establishments that catered to them dramatically increased, particularly in the coastal cities that served as centers of military production and points of embarkment for U.S. troops. Following the war, many lesbigay women and men from small towns and rural areas stayed in these large cities so that they could lead an active, more open lesbigay life. Consequently, the end of the fighting did not reverse the changes that resulted from World War II, and urban gay cultures continued to develop and grow in the late 1940s and beyond.

Sources: Bérubé, *Coming Out under Fire*; D'Emilio, *Sexual Politics, Sexual Communities*.

Mattachine Society Founding

The Mattachine Society was a male-dominated organization founded in Los Angeles in 1951. The primary founder was Harry Hay, who suggested the organization's name and did much of the initial recruitment. The Mattachine Society was named for medieval jesters, called Mattachines, who wore masks and whom Hay thought may have been gay. Hay and the other founders were either Communists or those sympathetic to Marxist thought, and this was reflected in the structure, political philosophy, and goals of the organization. The Mattachine Society was structured in a way that concealed the identities of the leaders and the total membership of the organization from both outsiders and other members of the group. Politically, the society's early leaders saw "homosexuals" as an oppressed minority group similar to racial/ethnic minorities, with their own distinct culture. Homosexual oppression was not simply based on prejudice, but was an integral part of society's basic institutions. To end this oppression, homosexuals themselves had to be active agents in changing the status quo. Their goals were to bring homosexuals together, educate them on their status as an oppressed minority, and get them to do political work to end their oppression and form an "ethical homosexual culture."

To achieve these goals, the early Mattachine held discussion groups, in which members talked about what it meant to be gay and debated theoretical issues. They became more politically active after one member, Dale Jennings, was arrested in February 1952 for allegedly soliciting an undercover cop. The Mattachine saw the case as an example of police entrapment and publicized it as such. Thanks to their efforts, the charges against Jennings were eventually dropped. The publicity the Mattachine Society received from the case resulted in new members and additional chapters in other parts of California.

Members began to engage in other activities to achieve their goals. In January 1953, several became involved in publishing the first major journal devoted to lesbigay issues, *ONE*. Mattachine members also sent letters to politicians running for office asking for their position on issues affecting lesbigays. This attracted unfavorable publicity and caused dissension within the organization. Anxiety about Communist infiltration of American life was at its height during the early 1950s, and some Mattachine members feared being the target of a witch hunt. In addition, they questioned the leadership and goals of the organization. Communists and their sympathizers were forced out. Kenneth Burns emerged as one of Mattachine's new leaders, and led the effort to reshape the organization.

The original organizational structure was replaced with one in which members and leaders were known to each other, though members' identities were still kept secret from outsiders. In their political theory, they adopted an accommodationist perspective that was typical of what came to be known as the homophile movement. Instead of seeing themselves as an oppressed minority group with a distinct culture, they saw themselves as being just like heterosexuals except for their sexuality. They engaged in social service work, such as blood drives, to show they were good citizens and established a dialogue with members of the medical and academic communities to solicit their support, establish legitimacy, and educate the public about same-sex sexuality. They also provided support for lesbigays and tried to educate them on how to fit into mainstream society by conforming to dominant cultural ideas of respectability and appropriate gender behavior. The editors of the journal, *ONE*, an entity independent of Mattachine, attacked the new agenda, and continued to promote the organization's original goals and political strategy. A particular target was the reliance on professionals as "experts" on same-sex sexuality, since many of those experts believed lesbigays were mentally ill. Mattachine leaders refused to take a stand on the issue, while *ONE* editors saw lesbigay identity positively. In 1955, Mattachine began publishing the *Mattachine Review*, whose editorial content better reflected the new orientation of the organization.

The Mattachine Society's accommodationist perspective was also adopted by other lesbigay organizations of the late 1950s, such as the mostly female Daughters of Bilitis. Although Mattachine grew in membership and developed chapters nationally, its numbers remained small, due mostly to fear of exposure and the lack of interaction with the most significant lesbigay institution at the time, the bars. Accommodationist leaders dominated lesbigay political thought until the early 1960s, when East Coast homophile leaders would advocate a return to Mattachine's original vision.

Sources: D'Emilio, *Sexual Politics, Sexual Communities*; Miller, *Out of the Past*.

1950s Lesbian Subcultures

The scarcity of men and the sex-segregated environments during World War II provided a context for many women to find others with lesbian desires. After the war, many stayed in port cities and further developed the emerging lesbian subcultures. They did so because mainstream society saw them as sick, sinners, or criminals, and they wanted spaces where they could formulate affirmative self-conceptions. However, they also wanted an accessible pool of social and sexual contacts. These subcultures were divided primarily along race/ethnicity, class, and age lines.

For working-class and young lesbians, the bars were the center of lesbian life. It was one of the few spaces where many felt they could be themselves and find kindred spirits for friendship, romance, sex, and networking. Bars were not entirely safe spaces, however. The specter of the police was ever present. The bars were sometimes raided, especially when city officials felt the need to "clean up" the city, such as during election campaigns. Women also faced entrapment by police officers and harassment by heterosexuals. Fear of arrest—and the possibility of having one's name in the paper or an employer or family member contacted—kept some from going to the bars.

The primary indicator of membership in the working-class lesbian bar scene was the degree to which one conformed to the polarities of masculine and feminine in terms of dress, demeanor, sexuality, and style. In this world, one was either butch or femme. Butches generally had short hair, wore men's clothes, and were sexually aggressive. Femmes had longer hair, wore women's clothes and cosmetics, and were sexually passive. Those known to frequently switch between or who refused to choose one of these identities, often referred to as kikis or AC/DCs, were viewed negatively. For some, butch or femme identities were the core of their being, while for others, they were identities adopted simply to fit in. Butch/femme identities were a two-edged sword. On the one hand, they allowed those with some level of lesbian desire to identify and feel a sense of community with each other. But it also made them potential targets for harassment and violence. This was especially the case with butches, since their style readily marked them as "lesbian."

The lives of wealthy and older middle-class lesbians did not center around either butch/femme identities or bars. These women were also far more likely to include gay men in their lives. They were more assimilationist in their outlook, and saw butch/femme identities as reinforcing negative stereotypes about lesbians. Hence, disagreements sometimes arose regarding which lesbian identity was most appropriate. One arena where this conflict manifested itself was in print. For example, between 1957 and 1967, the *Ladder*, a journal of the mostly middle-class homophile organization Daughters of Bilitis, stated that one of the organization's goals was to promote among lesbians "a mode of behavior and dress acceptable to society."

Because wealthy and middle-class lesbians were more likely to have the space and financial resources to entertain at home, much of their social lives centered around dinner parties and private events. Because of their social standing, many felt they had a lot to lose by not being discreet, so they generally did not go to bars due to the possibility of raids. Many also felt that besides sharing lesbian desires, they had little in common with the working-class lesbians who dominated the bar scene. Some did go occasionally because it was one of the few lesbian-centered spaces outside their friendship networks. Those most likely to go were women who lived in cities with bars that had a mostly middle-class clientele.

Except for black women, little is known about lesbian life among women of color. Lesbian life was, for the most part, segregated by race/ethnicity. As was the case in the larger culture, however, some African Americans began to integrate white-dominated bars in the 1950s. Although there was some racial/ethnic tension, it rarely erupted into open conflict. Some commentators, such as author/activist Audre Lorde, have noted that relatively speaking, there was more interracial contact within lesbian culture than was the case elsewhere. This contact was most likely to occur, however, in mostly white spaces, and only among a small subgroup of African Americans, whites, and other women of color.

If Elizabeth Kennedy and Madeline Davis's study of Buffalo, New York, is any indication, black lesbians differed from their white counterparts in several ways. For example, working-class black lesbian life was less centered around bars and more focused on socializing in each other's homes. House parties were common. Some also went to those mostly straight black clubs that tolerated a lesbigay presence. Black lesbians tended to be more integrated in their communities of origin than were white lesbians, and were more likely to include heterosexual African Americans and gay men in their social lives.

The 1950s were a critical time in lesbian and bisexual history. More so than at any other time previously, women with lesbian desires were able to form communities that were relatively safe havens from an increasingly oppressive heterosexual world.

Sources: Faderman, *Odd Girls and Twilight Lovers*; Kennedy and Davis, *Boots of Leather, Slippers of Gold*; Miller, *Out of the Past*.

McCarthyism and the Postwar Sex Crime Panic

Reflecting fears over the increasing visibility of lesbians, gay men, and bisexuals and the changing gender roles precipitated by World War II, a sex crime panic swept the U.S. in the late 1940s and early 1950s, fueled by sensational media accounts of the murders of children by "sexual psychopaths." Such attacks were no more frequent proportionately than in earlier decades, but caught up in the Cold War's emphasis on sexual conformity, newspapers and magazines throughout the country gave extensive coverage to any sex-related crime and successfully mobilized public support for increased police and government action.

While lesbians, gay men, and bisexuals were not the only ones regarded as "sexual perverts and degenerates"—indeed, anyone failing to adhere to the sexual conventions of the dominant society risked being considered psychopathic—they often became the focus of campaigns against sex criminals. This targeting resulted in part from the rise of the stereotype of gay men as compulsive child molesters. Despite the fact that most reported child sex murders involved heterosexual men attacking young girls, the media drew particular attention to cases of men assaulting little boys to support the contention that gay men by nature could not inhibit their sexual desires and had to be controlled by the police and psychiatrists. Between 1947 and 1955, twenty-one states and the District of Columbia passed sexual psychopath laws that generally classified "practicing homosexuals"—even those whose relationships were with other consenting adults—as mentally ill and subject to institutional confinement.

The fear that a "homosexual menace" was sweeping the U.S., combined with the anti-Communist fervor of the Cold War, led to the perception that homosexuality was being spread by Communists to undermine the country. Right-wing ideologues in Congress, most notably Senator Joseph McCarthy, stirred up this paranoia, charging that "sex perverts" were rampant in the national government in an attempt to discredit the Truman administration. The witch hunt that followed resulted in the dismissal of thousands of federal workers simply on the suspicion that they were gay, including 381 people who lost their jobs at the State Department between 1950 and 1953. An executive order in 1953 explicitly directed federal agencies to fire and not hire employees because of "sexual perversion," thereby ensuring that all government bodies would continue to discriminate against people suspected of being lesbigay even when the anti-lesbigay hysteria died down. At the same time, the military intensified its dismissal of lesbians, gay men, and bisexuals; discharges for homosexuality, which had averaged about 1,000 per year in the late 1940s, jumped to 2,000 per year in the early 1950s, and to over 3,000 by the end of the decade.

The widespread stereotyping of lesbians, gay men, and bisexuals as sexual psychopaths and risks to national security in the 1950s gave local police forces a free reign to crack down on people whom they suspected of being lesbigay. Across the country, vice squads were established to harass and arrest men in cruising areas such as parks and public rest rooms, and both women and men faced the threat of raids in bars known for their lesbigay clientele. In Washington, D.C., for example, more than 1,000 people were apprehended each year in the late 1940s and early 1950s under a "sexual perversion elimination program," and in Philadelphia, an average of 100 people were arrested each month during the 1950s on misdemeanor sex charges. Large-scale police actions also occurred in San Francisco, Baltimore, New Orleans, Boise, and many other cities. Often the number of arrests increased dramatically during local electoral campaigns, as officials sought to show voters that they were "tough on crime."

Sources: Beemyn, "A Queer Capital"; Chauncey, "The Postwar Sex Crime Panic"; D'Emilio, "The Homosexual Menace" and *Sexual Politics, Sexual Communities*; Freedman, "Uncontrolled Desires."

Christine Jorgensen Raises Public Awareness of Transsexuality

Sometimes a child is born and to all outward appearances seems to be of a certain sex. During childhood, nothing is noticed; but at the time of puberty, where the sex hormones come into action, the chemistry of the body seems to take an opposite turn and chemically the child is not of the supposed sex, but rather of the opposite sex.... I was one of those people.

So wrote Christine (née George) Jorgensen, an ex-GI from the Bronx, explaining to her parents why she was undergoing sex reassignment surgery in Denmark in 1952—the first person from the United States to undergo the newly developed medical procedures.

When accounts of her "sex change" reached the international press, Jorgensen became an instant celebrity—"the most talked-about girl in the world." In the U.S., the mainstream media was fascinated by her transformation into "a beautiful blonde with silken hair," and initially provided mostly sympathetic coverage, even reporting favorably on her relationship with a male Air Force sergeant. However, when it was revealed that she had not completely transformed her physical appearance (the limits of medical technology prevented her from having a surgically constructed vagina until 1954), and thus no longer adhered to traditional gender expectations, Jorgensen lost her status as "a glamour girl" and became what *Newsweek* called "a castrated male." While she had previously appeared on a number of television programs, mingled with Hollywood celebrities and prominent media figures, and even rode in the Easter Parade, her entertainment career quickly became limited to performing as a novelty act in Las Vegas. Jorgensen remained in the public spotlight, but largely because she was the subject of constant ridicule. According to transgender rights activist Leslie Feinberg, "in the years that followed, just the mention of her name provoked vicious laughter."

But for Feinberg and others who grew up not fitting into either gender category, "[Jorgensen's] dignity and courage set a proud example." As she states: "I had no other adult role model who crossed the boundaries of sex or gender. Christine Jorgensen's struggle beamed a message to me that I wasn't alone. She proved that even a period of right-wing reaction could not coerce each individual into conformity."

Sources: Feinberg, *Transgender Warriors*; Serlin, "Christine Jorgensen and the Cold War Closet."

Kinsey's Studies on Human Sexuality

In the post–World War II era, the discussion of sexuality, which had previously been seen as something done in private, exploded into the public sphere. This is largely because of sexologist Alfred Kinsey. His studies on white sexuality in the U.S., *Sexual Behavior in the Human Male* (1948) and *Sexual Behavior in the Human Female* (1953), received national attention and changed the way Americans looked at themselves sexually. The results of his interviews with more than 18,000 white Americans during the 1930s and 1940s challenged much of the conventional thinking about sexuality. This included the view that most in the U.S. were sexually conservative, that what made something "natural" or "normal" was what was promoted in the dominant culture (as opposed to what people actually did), and that sexuality (particularly in terms of sexual object choice) was rigid.

Kinsey's studies also had a major impact on the way Americans viewed same-sex sexuality. He argued that, particularly among working-class men, same-sex sexual behavior was more widespread than had been believed. He found that more than 50 percent of the men and 28 percent of the women surveyed told interviewers they had been attracted to others of the same sex at some point in their lives; 13 percent of the women and 37 percent of men in the study had had at least one post-adolescent same-sex sexual experience to orgasm; and 4-5 percent of men and about 3 percent of women had engaged in same-sex sexual behavior exclusively. On the basis of these numbers and the cross-cultural research he examined, which showed considerable variations in attitudes toward same-sex sexuality, Kinsey concluded that same-sex sexual behavior "would appear in the histories of a much larger portion of the population if there were no social constraints." He also argued that most gays and lesbians did not fit popular stereotypes of gender inversion. Finally, Kinsey concluded that in terms of their sexual behavior and psychological responses, people did not fit neatly into the conventional sexual categories of "homosexual," "heterosexual," and "bisexual." Rather, sexuality was a continuum, with most people falling somewhere between exclusive heterosexuality and exclusive homosexuality.

Responses to Kinsey's conclusions varied. Some criticized the results of his studies on methodological and moral grounds. For people like Senator Joseph McCarthy, who had already been trying to purge Communists and those suspected of engaging in same-sex sexual activity out of government positions, the studies only showed that the "homosexual menace" was far more widespread and harder to eradicate than previously thought, since those who engaged in it were not always easily identifiable. For others, such as Harry Hay and those involved in the homophile movement, it provided ammunition in their quest to abolish sodomy laws. The studies also started a debate within academic and medical communities over whether same-sex sexuality was a sickness. Other researchers, most notably Evelyn Hooker, would also challenge this view. Finally, Kinsey's research allowed lesbigays to see they were not alone in their desires, and at least one "expert" believed they were not sinful, sick, or criminal. They were simply part of the normal mix of human sexuality.

Sources: Bullough, *Science in the Bedroom*; Chauncey, *Gay New York*; D'Emilio, *Sexual Politics, Sexual Communities*; Irvine, *Disorders of Desire*.

THE MID-1950s

The Founding of the Daughters of Bilitis and the Publication of *The Ladder*

Formed in 1955 as a private social club in San Francisco for middle-class lesbians seeking an alternative to the gay bar culture, the Daughters of Bilitis quickly became more political, taking its lead from, and serving as a counterpoint to, the male-dominated Mattachine Society. Like its predecessor, DOB largely took an accommodationist approach; members emphasized social conformity and respectability in order to counter the negative image of homosexuality and argued that they were no different from heterosexuals beyond what they did in bed—a distinction they considered a strictly private matter. DOB's stated objectives included "educat[ing] the variant" to "understand herself and make an adjustment to society" and "advocating a mode of behavior and dress acceptable to society."

Given the hostile climate toward lesbigays represented by the McCarthyite witch hunts, it is not surprising that members would try to modify their own behavior as much as they would attempt to change the dominant culture. At the time, even belonging to the group was too much of a threat for many of the educated, middle-class women whom it sought to attract, despite a name—taken from Pierre Louys's "Song of Bilitis," a narrative about a lesbian poet said to have lived on the isle of Lesbos in ancient Greece with Sappho—designed to mask the nature of the organization. Membership thus remained small, never exceeding a couple hundred, although other chapters were formed in New York, Los Angeles, Chicago, Boston, New Orleans, San Diego, Cleveland, Denver, Detroit, Philadelphia, and Portland, Oregon.

But the impact of the Daughters of Bilitis was much greater than its limited membership might indicate. Responding to the near total absence of positive information about lesbians, it began publishing *The Ladder*, a monthly magazine consisting of news reports, research findings, literary works, book reviews, and political and social commentaries, in 1956. Not only did *The Ladder* counter the dominant images of homosexuality and provide readers with a better self-image of themselves, but it also gave lesbians a voice and a common language to describe their experiences and helped build self-identified lesbian communities on both local and national levels. As a result, DOB laid the groundwork for the development of lesbian feminism in the late 1960s and early 1970s.

Yet, ironically, it was the rise of the women's liberation movement and the growing militancy of many young lesbians that led to the dissolution of DOB. Members of the group had always resented the patriarchal attitude of male leaders within the Mattachine Society and *ONE*, but saw the need to work with them to build a homophile rights movement. However, with the founding of feminist organizations and the gradual welcoming of lesbian participation in them in the late 1960s and early 1970s, lesbians increasingly became involved in the women's movement. This resulted in a split within DOB between old guard homophiles and a militant wing energized by lesbian feminism. At the same time, while tremendous numbers of young lesbians were coming out and becoming politically active, they were forming or joining more radical lesbian-feminist organizations, making the Daughters of Bilitis increasingly irrelevant, despite attempts to make it more confrontational. The national structure of DOB was dismantled in 1971, and *The Ladder* folded the following year.

Sources: Blumenfeld and Raymond, *Looking at Gay and Lesbian Life*; D'Emilio, *Sexual Politics, Sexual Communities*; Witt, Thomas, and Marcus, *Out in All Directions*.

THE LATE 1950s AND EARLY 1960s

Lesbian Pulp Fiction

The 1950s and much of the 1960s were times of intense scrutiny about same-sex sexuality. While there was fear that "sex deviates" were threatening the established social order—and hence, needed to be repressed and purged from various social institutions—there was also curiosity about them. One manifestation of this was in literature. Hundreds of cheap paperback novels that purported to tell the "truth" about lesbian life proliferated in drugstores and newsstands throughout the country. Their intended audience was heterosexual men, and many of them were written by men who published under female pseudonyms. Most presented sensationalized accounts of lesbian life. The audience was to get a titillating peek at a life they presumably knew nothing about. Titles like *Strange Sisters*, *Twilight Girl*, and *Odd Girl Out* beckoned them, as did the sexually suggestive illustrations and copy on the covers. The intimate lives of blonde and brunette white women awaited. But while these novels provided a peek into an exciting other world, they also reaffirmed the rightness of the heterosexual one. The medical model of homosexuality as a sickness reigned supreme, and the typical lesbian in these novels lived a tortured existence. The copy from one novel read, "Happy and miserable at once, they were wracked by feelings neither could fully understand." As one feminist critic, Kate Adams, put it, lesbian characters were "fated to end up by novel's end heterosexual, unhappy, and/or dead."

While the intended audience for these novels was straight men, they also attracted the attention of women with same-sex desires. These books were one way in which they discovered there were others like themselves. The characters often had experiences lesbian and bisexual readers could relate to: coming to terms with sexual identity, trying to fit into a community of lesbians and bisexual women, experiencing sex with a woman for the first time. In addition, women reading these novels discovered there were environments where there were others like themselves. Many of these novels were set in places where lesbians and bisexual women were most likely to meet, such as all-female environments, bars, and areas known as lesbigay hangouts, such as New York City's Greenwich Village. They also discovered ways of being a lesbian—for better or worse. For example, many could identify with the butch/femme role-playing and the ambivalent feelings about lesbianism that were typical in these novels. There were also novels such as *The Price of Salt* by Patricia Highsmith (under the pseudonym Claire Morgan), which challenged compulsory heterosexuality. Women met, fell in love, had conflicts, survived them, and lived happily ever after.

Finally, women with same-sex sexual desires used the novels to discover others like themselves in real life. They passed them on to others as a way of finding out whether they were "kindred spirits." But the possession of these novels was a double-edged sword, for while it allowed these women to seek others like themselves, it also marked them as sexually different. The consequences could be devastating if the wrong person caught them.

Lesbians and bisexual women had complex and often contradictory relationships with these novels. For some, the representations reinforced the self-loathing they already felt. Others, however, were able to use them as a stepping stone to create a positive sense of self at a time when there were few avenues in which they could do so.

Sources: D'Emilio, *Sexual Politics, Sexual Communities*; Faderman, *Odd Girls and Twilight Lovers*; Koski and Tilchen, "Some Pulp Sappho."

The Publication of James Baldwin's *Giovanni's Room* and *Another Country*

James Baldwin's *Giovanni's Room* (1956) and *Another Country* (1962) were among the first novels to provide a realistic depiction of the lives of gay and bisexual men, despite the anti-lesbigay hostility of the publishing industry, literary critics, and society in general. *Giovanni's Room*, in fact, initially had to be printed in England because Baldwin's U.S. publisher found it "repugnant" and "feared legal action over the homosexual content." The editor warned that the novel "would ruin his reputation as a leading young black writer" and even suggested that Baldwin burn the manuscript. *Another Country* was likewise the target of harsh anti-lesbigay criticism; both the liberal white press and black militants such as Eldridge Cleaver, who had previously praised Baldwin for his treatment of racial themes, denounced the book for presenting a positive portrait of homosexuality and attacked Baldwin himself for being bisexual.

For many black lesbians, gay men, and bisexuals, though, the novels, along with Baldwin's openness about his sexuality, were inspirational and paved the way for the development of a black lesbigay literary tradition. "I loved James Baldwin," remembered essayist and publisher Barbara Smith, "not only because he made me want to shape prose with a clarity and fire that gave it the power to make people change, but because his life showed me a way out." Writer Joseph Beam agreed, "as I look back on Baldwin's writing, I admire most his wisdom and courage in dealing sensitively with male relationships and the richness with which he drew black culture."

Sources: Beam, "James Baldwin"; Campbell, *Talking at the Gates*; Smith, "We Must Always Bury Our Dead Twice"; Weatherby, *James Baldwin*.

The Beat Generation

In most of 1950s America, same-sex sexuality was considered a sin, sickness, or crime. But in some places, it was a symbol of nonconformity, of rebellion. Such was the case with a group of mostly young, white, male writers and artists who populated San Francisco's North Beach section. Among other things, they challenged what they saw as the post-World War II white middle-class values of conformity, consumerism, and marital heterosexuality.

After the 1957 publication of *On the Road*, Jack Kerouac's portrait of what he dubbed the "Beat generation," other writers and artists, disaffected youth, and tourists came to North Beach from around the country. They also got national media coverage. The same year Kerouac's novel was published, poet Lawrence Ferlinghetti was arrested, tried, and later acquitted on obscenity charges for selling fellow-Beat Allen Ginsberg's *Howl and Other Poems* in his bookstore, City Lights.

The media often enhanced the Beats' reputation as nonconformists by publishing sensational accounts of their lives, emphasizing their drug use and sexual experimentation. Some Beats, such as Allen Ginsberg, William Burroughs, Robert Duncan, and Jack Spicer, were gay. Others saw themselves as bisexual or predominantly heterosexual but "bi-curious." In San Francisco, the Beat and lesbigay communities partly overlapped. Several lesbigay bars, for example, were located in North Beach.

Many Beats included same-sex sexuality as a theme in their work. Because of this, lesbigays had access to one of the few discourses during the 1950s that portrayed their sexuality as a viable alternative to the heterosexual norm. Allen Ginsberg, for example, noted that parts of his poem "Howl" were "an acknowledgement of the basic reality of homosexual joy."

Sources: D'Emilio, *Sexual Politics, Sexual Communities*; D'Emilio and Freedman, *Intimate Matters*; Miller, *Out of the Past.*

THE MID- AND LATE 1960s

The Homophile Movement's Shift from Accommodation to Protest

Inspired in part by the sit-ins and freedom rides of the black civil rights movement, homophile organizations began to shift their dominant political strategy beginning in the early 1960s. More activists were challenging the emphasis on (1) providing support networks for lesbigays; (2) educating them on fitting into mainstream American society so they could be seen as "respectable" and no different from heterosexuals; and (3) relying on the medical and academic communities to give them legitimacy and educate the general public about same-sex sexuality. East Coast chapters of the Mattachine Society led the way in demanding equal rights for lesbigays rather than sympathy and understanding, advocating the use of direct action protest, and rejecting the sickness model of lesbigay identity. Franklin Kameny of Mattachine-Washington, D.C., and Randy Wicker of Mattachine-New York emerged as leaders of the more activist homophiles.

In their goals and political strategy, the militant factions of these groups more closely resembled the original vision of the Mattachine Society promoted by founder Harry Hay. They initiated letter writing campaigns and picketed government buildings to draw attention to and confront government officials over employment and immigration policies that discriminated against lesbigays, protested Cuba's policy of imprisoning lesbigays, and challenged police harassment and bar raids. Wicker also persuaded some in the press to write sympathetic stories about lesbigay life and politics. The pickets, particularly one in front of the White House in 1965, garnered national media attention, even though there were never more than a few dozen people involved in any protest action. In January 1963, the activists established East Coast Homophile Organizations (ECHO) to coordinate these efforts regionally.

The growing number of militants led to conflicts with accommodationists, particularly over the issue of adopting resolutions rejecting the idea that lesbigays were mentally ill. Eventually, the militants took over the leadership of most East Coast homophile organizations. Like the accommodationists, however, they had little contact with lesbigays who were part of the bar scene and were never able to mobilize the lesbigay masses.

San Francisco was one of the few areas that had some success in integrating social and political lesbigays during this time, due in

THE LADDER Adults Only .50
Oct. 1965

a LESBIAN review

QUARTER MILLION
HOMOSEXUAL
FEDERAL EMPLOYEES
PROTEST
CIVIL SERVICE COMMISSION
POLICY

HOMOPHILE
GROUPS PICKET
IN NATION'S CAPITAL

Cover of *The Ladder* depicting homophile pickets in Washington, D.C., 1965.

part to the so-called "Beat generation" of artists and writers who made the city their home. For many Americans, the Beats came to symbolize a rejection of the post-war white middle-class ethic of conformity and consumerism. One of the ways in which some were nonconformists was in their sexuality. Some, such as poet Allan Ginsberg, were openly gay and created affirming images of same-sex sexuality in their work. For many Beats, same-sex sexuality signified rebellion rather than perversion.

Several scandals and police crackdowns in the late 1950s and early 1960s also played a role in unifying social and political lesbigays. San Francisco's emerging reputation as a homosexual mecca became an issue during the 1959 mayoral election campaign. Although the incumbent was reelected in spite of the charges, he initiated a crackdown on the city's lesbigay bars and male cruising areas. This, along with an investigation of the city's police and liquor licensing agencies for extorting money from lesbigay bar owners, led to increased media scrutiny of lesbigay life.

It was not the San Francisco chapters of the established homophile organizations that initiated a response to the attacks on lesbigay institutions. Instead, it was people such as Black Cat bar

employee José Sarria, who in 1961 became the first openly gay man to run for public office. Although he lost, he received significant support from, and became a symbol of pride for, many in the city's lesbigay community. Bar owners and employees formed the Tavern Guild in 1962 to fight police harassment of bar patrons and efforts of the liquor licensing agency to shut them down. Two years later, activists formed the Society for Individual Rights (SIR) to foster a sense of community and encourage/engage in political action. They established what is believed to be the first lesbigay community center in the country, mounted voter registration drives, held forums at which candidates expressed their views on lesbigay issues, and endorsed candidates they felt served the community's needs. Because they tried to reach multiple segments of the lesbigay community, they quickly became the country's largest lesbigay organization.

The growing number of homophile organizations with a direct action, civil rights focus led to the formation in 1966 of a national coalition to coordinate their efforts: the North American Conference of Homophile Organizations (NACHO). Through litigation and protest, the coalition challenged bar closings, medical and academic experts who promoted the sickness model of lesbigay identity, police harassment, and government policies excluding lesbigays from employment, immigration, and the military. Inspired by the Black Power movement and its celebration of black culture, NACHO at its 1968 convention adopted the slogan, "Gay Is Good," a term generally credited to Franklin Kameny.

Though the homophile movement's leadership continued to be primarily bi-coastal throughout the 1960s, growing numbers of organizations were being established in other areas as well. Despite this, the movement remained small, involving some 5,000 people. Many were closeted. San Francisco's success at mobilizing the masses would generally not be repeated elsewhere until after the June 1969 Stonewall Riots in New York City.

Sources: D'Emilio, *Sexual Politics, Sexual Communities*; Miller, *Out of the Past*.

The Rise of Lesbigay Churches and Groups

While some—both lesbigay and heterosexual—see religion and same-sex sexuality as being antithetical to one another, others have tried to reconcile the two. Central to this effort have been attempts to challenge the anti-lesbigay doctrines of many mainstream religious organizations and provide non-oppressive spaces where lesbigays can practice their religious beliefs.

The earliest known attempt to establish a predominantly lesbigay church in the U.S. was in 1946, when George Hyde founded the Eucharistic Catholic Church in Atlanta. Nine years later, Chuck Rowland created the Church of ONE Brotherhood. Both efforts were short-lived. The lesbigay church movement took off in 1968 under the leadership of Reverend Troy Perry, who founded the Metropolitan Community Church (MCC) in Los Angeles after being excommunicated from the Church of God because he was gay. Today, the Universal Fellowship of MCC, as it is now called, has more than 300 churches internationally. African Americans have also been in the forefront of establishing predominantly lesbigay churches. Bishop Carl Bean has established the Unity Fellowship in several cities with large black lesbigay populations. And the late Dr. James Tinney founded the Faith Temple in Washington, D.C. In addition to establishing separate churches, lesbigays have carved out non-oppressive spaces within mainstream churches through groups such as Dignity (Catholic), Affirmation (Methodist), and Integrity (Episcopalian). These churches and groups have not only provided affirming spaces for lesbigays to worship, they have also been actively involved in various social issues, ranging from AIDS to sponsoring Cuban refugees.

Lesbigay churches and groups have had to deal with heterosexism on two fronts. One, they have often been the targets of anti-lesbigay violence. In 1972, for example, MCC churches in Los Angeles and San Francisco were destroyed by arson fires. Two, lesbigay churches and groups have challenged the doctrines of and fought to be recognized by mainstream religious organizations. Beth Chazim Chadashim, a Los Angeles lesbigay Jewish synagogue founded in 1972, was the first to receive mainstream recognition when it was accepted into the Union of American Hebrew Congregations in 1974. MCC has failed in its efforts to be recognized by the National Council of Churches. There are, however, a growing number of mainstream churches and church leaders, such as the United Church of Christ and Reverend Jesse Jackson, who support lesbigays in various ways. Together with lesbigay churches and groups, they are fighting the traditional religious discourse on same-sex sexuality.

Sources: Blumenfeld and Raymond, *Looking at Gay and Lesbian Life*; Comstock, *Unrepentant, Self-Affirming, Practicing*; Miller, *Out of the Past*; Nonas and LeVay, *City of Children*; Thompson, *Long Road to Freedom*; Tinney, "Why a Black Gay Church?"

Lesbigay Involvement in Other Social Movements

Many lesbigays who were part of the early liberation movement were also involved in other social movements of that era. Their efforts to incorporate the goals of these other movements into lesbigay organizations and add lesbigay issues to the agendas of New Left and feminist organizations met with limited success. Within lesbigay organizations, the primary problem was a growing emphasis on single-issue politics and a lack of support for some issues, particularly if the leaders of the movements being supported were anti-lesbigay. Within the other social movements, lesbigays either had problems having their agenda taken seriously or were hostilely rejected.

Perhaps the most successful integration of lesbigay issues within other movements has been in the feminist movement. Early on, feminists such as Betty Friedan feared that lesbian involvement in the movement would provide an excuse for others to discredit it. Because of this, some tried to purge lesbians from feminist organizations. However, they faced stiff challenges from lesbians and bisexual women such as Rita Mae Brown. As a result, groups such as the National Organization for Women began to adopt resolutions recognizing lesbian oppression and its importance as a feminist issue. In some circles, lesbians were even celebrated as the ideal feminists because they symbolized independence from men.

Lesbigays who were part of other social movements were less successful in having their issues addressed. Often, their efforts to raise lesbigay concerns were met with laughter or hostility. An exception was Huey Newton, leader of the Black Panther Party, a "Black" nationalist organization. In a letter published in the group's periodical, *Black Panther*, Newton urged other revolutionaries to put aside their negative feelings about women and lesbigays, stop using lesbigay slurs as a way of attacking enemies of the movement, accept the idea that women and lesbigays can be revolutionaries, recognize the oppression of lesbigays and women, and include the right of people to use their bodies as they wish as part of the movement's agenda. He even went so far as to say that lesbigays "might be the most oppressed people in society" and "the most revolutionary." Most in the Black Power and New Left movements did not share Newton's view, leading many lesbigays to end their involvement with them. They did, however, incorporate some of the Left's political analyses and practices into lesbigay liberation organizations.

Although lesbigays continue to have problems building coalitions with leaders of other social movements, there have been some successes. Links with the feminist movement continue to be strong. Some labor leaders, such as the late Cesar Chavez, have endorsed lesbigay rights. So have a number of civil rights leaders, including Coretta Scott King, Jesse Jackson, and the Congressional Black Caucus. Lesbigays and activists from other movements have also worked together on specific issues, such as federal hate crimes legislation.

Sources: Faderman, *Odd Girls and Twilight Lovers*; Lane, "Newton's Law"; Marotta, *The Politics of Homosexuality*; Miller, *Out of the Past*.

The Stonewall Riots

Police attacks on bars with a predominantly lesbigay clientele occurred frequently in New York and other U.S. cities, so officers had no reason to expect anything unusual when they raided the Stonewall Inn, a Greenwich Village bar patronized primarily by black and Latino drag queens, on 27 June 1969. But instead of passively accepting harassment and arrest, as the police expected, customers fought back. When the bar's employees and some of its clientele were taken into custody, other patrons and bystanders began to throw bottles and cobblestones at the officers, who barricaded themselves inside the Stonewall for protection. The crowd attempted to break down the door, and when this failed, they set fire to the bar. Police reinforcements rescued the officers, but could not stop the uprising. The following night, a crowd of more than two thousand—consisting of black and Latino drag queens, along with street people, butch and femme lesbians, and young white radicals—resumed the protest, urged on by chants of "Gay Power" and "We Want Freedom Now." A police riot squad with more than four hundred officers responded by savagely beating anyone they could reach with their nightsticks, seriously injuring many demonstrators.

The Stonewall Riots were not the first time that lesbigays fought back against a police crackdown, but the uprising was arguably the most dramatic act of resistance. In the words of Joan Nestle, a lesbian activist who witnessed the rioting on the second night, "it was done by the most marginal of our people, who had no thought that there would be anyone to protect them.... [T]hose who had been ridiculed the most risked the most—their lives—to fight back." The riots were also important because they led to the coalescing of a national lesbigay liberation movement. In the months after Stonewall, activists in New York formed the Gay Liberation Front and Street Transvestite Action Revolutionaries, organizations styled after Black Power, radical feminist, and leftist groups. By the next year, lesbigay liberation organizations existed on college campuses and in cities throughout the country.

Sources: D'Emilio, *Sexual Politics, Sexual Communities*; Duberman, *Stonewall*; Nestle, "Those Who Were Ridiculed the Most Risked the Most."

THE EARLY AND MID-1970s

Lesbigay Liberation vs. Lesbigay Rights: Early Post-Stonewall Politics

The aftermath of the 1969 Stonewall Riots in New York signaled the dawn of a new era in the struggle to end lesbigay oppression. Soon after the riots, activists formed groups such as the Gay Liberation Front. Like other social movements of the late 1960s and early 1970s, their goal was to change society, not integrate into or reform it. This represented a shift from the integrationist emphasis of the groups that were part of the homophile movement. Gay liberation leaders wanted to transform traditional sexual and gender identities and relationships into ones that were non-oppressive. They also wanted to change some aspects of lesbigay communities. This included institutions such as bars and bathhouses, which they felt were exploitive, ghettoizing, and emphasized objectification and predatory sexuality. New York City and San Francisco emerged as the centers of this new radicalism.

There were several ideas that were central to the new movement. One was the concept of "coming out." Before, coming out meant acknowledging one's sexuality to other lesbigays, becoming part of their world, and leading a double life. Now, it was a political act in which one's sexuality was acknowledged to heterosexual friends, family members, co-workers, etc. Also central was the use of the word *gay* to refer to men and women with a same-sex sexual identity. It signified a rejection of the ambivalence many who were part of the homophile movement felt about their sexuality and their insistence that they were "just like heterosexuals." It was also a rejection of dominant constructions of lesbigays as sick, sinners, or criminals. Gays were oppressed minorities. They were different, proud, and had their own cultural norms and institutions. Third, there was the use of consciousness-raising groups, which provided a forum for people to discuss the personal and political aspects of being gay. Finally, there was a change in the leadership structure of these organizations. In their quest to be democratic and egalitarian, everything was done by consensus.

The gay liberation movement's attempt to change the world had limited success. Within lesbigay communities, it instilled a sense of pride in being different, created alternatives to the bars and baths by, for example, holding dances and dinners, and prompted explosive growth in the number of lesbigay organizations and publications. In the larger society, it publicly confronted leaders about their positions on lesbigay issues, picketed institutions with anti-lesbigay policies, held dances in defiance of laws against same-sex dancing, and publicized its agenda using political theater and other tactics. Perhaps its most significant accomplishment was fundamentally changing the discourse on same-sex sexuality, so affirming voices could challenge traditional anti-lesbigay views. However, it lacked a concrete plan for large-scale social change, and like other revolutionary movements, was losing support as the country grew more conservative.

The gay liberation movement also had internal problems. For example, it had difficulty negotiating its relationship with other revolutionary movements, of which many gay liberationists were also a part. Some people wanted to support these other groups and show solidarity with them, while others felt they should focus just on lesbigay issues. Some were also uncomfortable supporting certain causes or

organizations, such as the Black Panther Party. This was both because they did not agree with the cause or group and because many of these organizations were anti-lesbigay. They also had problems dealing with diversity within the lesbigay movement. Charges of racism, sexism, and other forms of oppression led some to leave the movement or form their own organizations.

Finally, there were those who questioned the movement's goal of revolutionary social change. They saw lesbigay oppression as systemic, but felt the best solution was to insist on integrating into mainstream society on their own terms. They wanted to change the social context in which they were lesbigay, but not change society in other ways. Hence, groups formed that reflected this more reformist, cultural pluralist orientation such as the Gay Activist Alliance (GAA). Instead of "gay liberation," such groups wanted lesbigay "rights," which they sought to achieve through the strategies used in the black civil rights movement—direct action protest, litigation, legislation, and education—to force various social institutions to rethink and change their anti-lesbigay policies. These emerging groups, which came to dominate the lesbigay political scene by the mid-1970s, did retain some of the liberationists' ideas, including the construction of positive lesbigay identities and the use of coming out as a political strategy. The latter has been turned into an annual celebration by the Human Rights Campaign, a lesbigay rights organization founded in 1980. Since 1988, it has sponsored National Coming Out Day on 11 October, the anniversary of the 1987 March on Washington.

Unlike previous attempts at politicizing lesbigay oppression, the lesbigay rights movement had national organizations to promote its agenda. By adopting a traditional leadership style, a clear reformist agenda, and proven political strategies, the GAA and its successors, such as the National Gay and Lesbian Task Force and the Lambda Legal Defense and Education Fund, were responsible for making lesbigays a potent force in U.S. politics.

Sources: Adam, *The Rise of a Gay and Lesbian Movement*; D'Emilio, *Making Trouble*; Faderman, *Odd Girls and Twilight Lovers*; Miller, *Out of the Past*.

Lesbian, Gay, Bisexual, and Transgender Pride Celebrations

Each 4th of July from 1965 to 1969, homophile groups sponsored a picket line in front of Philadelphia's Independence Hall to remind Americans that lesbigays continued to face discrimination in a supposedly free country. These "Annual Reminder" demonstrations stressed decorum and civility in an attempt to show that lesbigays deserved civil rights because they were no different than heterosexuals. In contrast, the commemorations of the Stonewall riots were more festive, broad-based, and lesbigay-affirming. At the Eastern Regional Conference of Homophile Organizations (ERCHO) in the fall of 1969, lesbigay liberation activists succeeded in passing a resolution that called for the Reminders to be replaced by a more inclusive yearly demonstration that could "encompass the ideas and ideals of the larger struggle ... [for] fundamental human rights." The proposal also urged homophile groups throughout the country to celebrate the event on the last Saturday in June. The New York City commemoration, known as the Christopher Street Liberation Day after the location of the Stonewall Inn, drew an estimated 10,000 participants, who marched from Greenwich Village to Central Park on 28 June 1970, carrying signs such as "Homosexual Is Not a Four-Letter Word," "I Am a Lesbian and I Am Beautiful," "Gay Power," and "We Are the Dykes Your

Gay Freedom Day Celebration in San Francisco, 1986.

Mother Warned You About." Marches also occurred in Chicago, San Francisco, and Los Angeles.

Over the next few years, "Gay Freedom Day" celebrations spread to nearly every large urban area in the U.S., and the number of participants grew exponentially. By the late 1970s, what had become "Gay and Lesbian Pride Week" was held in dozens of cities, with more than half a million people participating. Today, close to four million people in over three hundred cities and more than twenty countries worldwide take part in Pride activities, which frequently occur throughout the month of June and include not only rallies and parades, but also picnics, film festivals, concerts, talent shows, town meetings, and government lobbying. Reflecting a desire to be inclusive of all members of the queer community, many local commemorations are now referred to as lesbian, gay, bisexual, and transgender celebrations.

Sources: Blumenfeld and Raymond, *Looking at Gay and Lesbian Life*; D'Emilio, *Sexual Politics, Sexual Communities*; Scott, "It Was June, It Was Hot, It Was Different."

Lesbian Nationalism

During the late 1960s and early 1970s, there were a number of social movements that followed in the footsteps of the black civil rights movement. Lesbians and bisexual women, mostly younger and college-educated, were a part of many of them. However, they often felt their acceptance within these movements was tenuous. They faced sexism within the gay liberation and lesbigay rights movements, heterosexism within the feminist movement, and both in New Left and other social movements. When feminist organizations such as NOW began to see heterosexism as an issue and became more open to those with same-sex desires, many lesbians and bisexual women left the other movements and carved out spaces for themselves within feminism. It is within these spaces that the movement known as lesbian feminism flourished.

Lesbian feminism was born out of two impulses that are common in other nationalist movements, such as the Black Power movement: pessimism that the oppressor can change and an affirmation of the oppressed social identity. In the case of lesbian feminism, they generally felt men would never give up their power over women and treat them as equals. However, they also wanted to create spaces where they could be with other women and construct non-oppressive definitions of womanhood.

Central to lesbian feminism was the idea that a lesbian represented the ultimate feminist: one who was socially, psychologically, economically, and sexually independent of men; who resisted male dominance; and who put her primary energies into loving and supporting other women. A lesbian was what one lesbian-feminist group, Radicalesbians, called a "woman-identified woman" (see p. 70). "Lesbian" was not simply a label for women with a same-sex sexual identity. It was also a political identity. Women could (and should) choose to be lesbians because what author/activist Adrienne Rich called the institution of "compulsory heterosexuality" was a major way in which men oppressed women.

Another central part of lesbian feminism was establishing communities with other women. This generally took one of two forms. Women either created living and working collectives within urban spaces (particularly college towns), or they formed rural communes. When a woman became part of a lesbian feminist community, she made a commitment to change both herself and the world. Changing the first meant making a commitment to unlearning those beliefs and behaviors that were considered male or that men used to oppress women, and learning to value those ideas and practices that affirmed feminist womanhood. This included changing the language used to reinforce male dominance (such as changing "history" to "herstory"), and devaluing violence, competitiveness, and social hierarchies. It also meant valuing attributes the movement associated with women, such as spirituality, egalitarianism, communalism, cooperative economics and leadership, acceptance of diversity, and the matriarchal past. Consciousness raising groups were a key part of this process. In these spaces, women examined the gender politics of their lives. Changing the world generally did not involve transforming male-dominated institutions. Instead, women created alternative institutions where they could be self-sufficient, supportive of each other, and free of male values. This included creating food co-ops, credit unions, health clinics, resource centers, and businesses. These communities were linked to each other through institutions such as the press and music. In songs, periodicals, and books produced by the likes of Olivia Records, *The Lesbian Connection,* and Naiad Press, these women distributed information on and created dialogues about the Lesbian Nation.

Feminist nationalism had a number of problems, which led to its decline by the end of the 1970s. Many ventures did not last long due to poor management and lack of resources. In the attempt to create the ideal feminist, many women felt left out or were shut out. For example, lesbians who faced other oppressions, such as those based on race/ethnicity, were reluctant to abandon their communities of origin. For these women, doing so meant losing allies in their battles against the other ways they were oppressed. Lesbian feminists and those who wanted to have access to the same opportunities men had and integrate into mainstream society viewed each other with disdain. So did lesbian feminists and women who continued to have sexual relationships with men, who worked and socialized with gay men, or who engaged in sexual practices in which power imbalances were a key component, such as butch/femme relationships and sadomasochism. Within lesbian-feminist communities, there were conflicts over how committed one was to the principles of the Lesbian Nation. This manifested itself in what was commonly known as political correctness, in which women were pressured to adhere to community ideals and practices. Women often criticized each other for not going far enough in either ridding themselves of male-centered ideas and behaviors or in valuing diversity. Women who dressed in traditionally feminine ways, such as wearing dresses, were rebuked. And women who were of color, older, differently abled, fat, and so forth, frequently accused their "sisters" of oppressing them.

Although lesbian nationalism had essentially collapsed by the 1980s, it had a major impact on both the cultural pluralist lesbian community that became the dominant visible lesbian community

and U.S. culture as a whole. Although the goals of complete separation and becoming the ideal feminist were replaced with carving out spaces within mainstream society and allowing for multiple feminist identities, diversity and independent institutions continued to be valued. Also, as mainstream businesses such as publishers and music companies discovered they could profit from marketing their goods and services to specific social groups, they began to target lesbians and bisexual women.

Sources: Adam, *The Rise of a Gay and Lesbian Movement*; Faderman, *Odd Girls and Twilight Lovers*; Miller, *Out of the Past.*

Lesbigay Music

Lesbigays have always had a special relationship with music. Since at least the early twentieth century, artists such as Gladys Bentley took the lyrics to popular songs and changed them to reflect lesbigay sensibilities. Music continues to be an integral part of the cultural fabric of post-Stonewall lesbigay America, albeit in different ways.

For those involved in lesbian feminism, "women's music" was, for a while, one of the more-successful attempts at building institutions and creating community. Lesbian and closeted bisexual artists such as Cris Williamson, Holly Near, and Meg Christian sang about love, politics, and community between women. Most of this music was initially grounded in European folk traditions, but it later expanded to include the styles of people of color, such as soul, salsa, and blues. As was the case in the pre-Stonewall era, lesbian artists sought to empower and create a sense of community. The women's music of the 1970s, however, was different in that it had much more of a political consciousness. In that respect, it had more in common with the social protest songs popular in the late 1960s.

For lesbian feminists, it was essential that the production and distribution of the music remain true to their woman-identified vision. They formed record companies owned and collectively run by women. Employees were paid according to need, artists were expected to project a working-class image, and lyrics were expected to be non-oppressive and promote lesbian-feminist worldviews. Olivia Records, founded in 1973, was the most influential and successful. Record companies sold their records in women's spaces, and female promoters booked and marketed the artists. Typical venues included coffee houses and concerts. Music festivals, which began in the mid-1970s, were also popular, particularly the annual Michigan Womyn's Music Festival, which continues to draw large crowds.

Women's music did enjoy limited success outside of lesbian-feminist communities. Some FM radio stations played it, and some mainstream record stores sold it. However, the success of women's music declined by the early 1980s, as did lesbian nationalism generally. Many enterprises suffered from financial troubles and/or mismanagement. Many also had problems practicing their commitment to diversity and engaging in non-oppressive behavior. Finally, younger lesbians and bisexuals, who tended to be more pluralist than nationalist in their outlook, were beginning to take advantage of changes in the mainstream music industry. Although lyrics specifically about women loving women continued to be rare—as were openly lesbian or bisexual artists—there were more women who reflected the sensibility of lesbians and bisexual women. Younger women were more likely to seek out either mainstream female artists who exhibited strength and independence, such as Tina Turner, or the growing number of lesbian and bisexual crossover artists, such as k.d. lang and Melissa Etheridge. Although these crossover artists were known within women's communities to be lesbian or bisexual and often dressed in ways that were popular within those communities, they generally downplayed their sexuality in both their music and public personae.

The music most popular among gay and bisexual men during the community building of the 1970s was a stark contrast to women's music. It was mainly a product of the mainstream recording industry, produced and performed mostly by heterosexuals. It had its roots in black musical traditions, rather than European. And it usually lacked gay-specific content, political or otherwise.

Disco, which emerged as the dominant musical form, originated in New York City clubs frequented by black gay and bisexual men in the late 1960s, where soul and Philly tunes were mixed with an up tempo, continuous bass beat. Divas such as Gloria Gaynor and Donna Summer wailing about love, sex, and heartache typified disco. The sound migrated to mostly white gay and bisexual men's clubs by the mid-1970s. Out of this music, a different kind of bar was born, the discotheque, where glamour and spectacle reigned supreme. Men showed off their stylish clothes, buffed bodies, and/or dancing skills, usually in hopes of attracting someone for love or sex. Disco achieved mainstream popularity in the mid-to-late 1970s, and reached its peak with the 1977 release of the film, *Saturday Night Fever*. By the end of the decade, however, disco was declared dead.

With the 1980s came other forms of dance music, such as club, house, and techno. As was the case with disco, much of this music was rooted in black musical traditions, began in clubs frequented by black gay and bisexual men, and featured black artists and producers. Although this music has been less successful in reaching mainstream audiences, producer/artists such as Frankie Knuckles, the openly gay "godfather of house," have remixed songs by popular artists such as Michael Jackson and Toni Braxton that have become staples in clubs and on dance-oriented radio stations across the country.

Although disco was rarely explicitly gay, it did reflect the sensibilities of many gay and bisexual men in that it featured strong women singing about sexual relationships. There was the occasional openly gay or bisexual male artist, such as Sylvester, who had mainstream hits. There were also groups like the Village People, who incorporated gay imagery and themes into their act, such as macho drag and the joys of male bonding in sex-segregated environments such as the YMCA or the navy. But the lyrics and imagery could easily have been (and often were) read in non-gay ways. This continued to be the case with the various forms of dance music that proliferated in the post-disco era, with artists such as Jimmy Sommerville being the exception. Music companies continued to see gay and bisexual men as a major market for dance music, however, and have even produced music compilations that were "gay" in their packaging, if not in the artists' lyrics or public personae.

Sources: Faderman, *Odd Girls and Twilight Lovers*; Miller, *Out of the Past*; Paoletta, "The Godfather of House Knuckles Down"; Stein, "Androgyny Goes Pop"; Thomas, "The House the Kids Built."

The Rise of Lesbigay Institutions

One of the most visible manifestations of post-1960s lesbigay America has been the proliferation of businesses, social and po-

litical groups, and other institutions catering to them. This growth began in earnest in the early 1970s. For example, in 1969, there were only about 50 lesbigay political organizations. By 1973, there were well over 1,000. Activists created such national political organizations as the National Gay and Lesbian Task Force, the National Latino/a Lesbian and Gay Organization, and the National Center for Lesbian Rights. Traditional lesbigay institutions such as bars and (in the case of men) baths grew in number and became more specialized in the type of clientele they sought to attract. And rather than being controlled by the Mafia, as had sometimes been the case in the past, many were lesbigay owned and operated. The number of alternatives to traditional institutions grew, too. Many cities with large lesbigay populations developed community centers, bowling leagues, choruses, professional associations, college student organizations, social groups for people with a shared race/ethnicity, gender, and leisure interest, and so on.

The number of lesbigay writers, artists, musicians, and institutions distributing their creative output also grew. The Los Angeles based *Advocate* began in 1967 and quickly became one of the most popular nationally distributed lesbigay news and consumer magazines. More recent efforts include *Girlfriends* and *SBC*. A number of cities have lesbigay newspapers that provide local and regional coverage. Lesbigay literature and music have flooded lesbigay and mainstream book and music stores. They were issued by both mainstream presses and record companies, as well as by lesbigay businesses, such as Alyson Publications and Olivia Records. By the mid-1980s, lesbigays began to see more images of themselves in films and videos made by and for them.

To foster a sense of community on international, national, and local levels, lesbigays have created events and annual celebrations. These include the annual lesbigay and black Pride celebrations, academic conferences, music and film festivals, sporting events, leather and drag contests, and National Coming Out Day. The Gay Games, founded by Tom Waddell and first held in 1982, attracts athletes and sports fans from around the world every four years. These institutions and events have made lesbigays a major cultural and political force, as well as increased lesbigay visibility and community diversity.

Sources: D'Emilio, *Making Trouble*; LeVay and Nonas, *City of Friends*; Miller, *Out of the Past*.

Homosexuality Is No Longer Classified as a Psychological Disorder, Although Transsexuality Continues to Be

Historically, theories to explain sexuality, particularly same-sex sexuality, have tended to reflect societal attitudes at a given time and have been used to justify discrimination against lesbians, gay men, and bisexuals. During the early nineteenth century, homosexuality was characterized as either a grave sin or a depraved social behavior—a form of vice linked to insanity and crime. Later in the century, when men and women attracted to others of the same sex were starting to be recognized as having a specific identity, homosexuality began to be viewed as a pathological condition resulting from both biological and environmental factors. Physicians in the early twentieth century such as Sigmund Freud had a more enlightened view, believing that same-sex attraction was a natural feature of human existence rather than a degeneracy or illness; nevertheless, they still felt that homosexuality was due to arrested psychosexual development. Given this history of antagonism toward lesbigays, and the fact that lesbians, gay men, and bisexuals lacked a strong voice of their own, it is not surprising that homosexuality was listed as a mental disorder when the American Psychiatric Association (APA) published its first *Diagnostic and Statistical Manual* in 1952.

But the homophile movement in the 1950s and 1960s, along with a growing number of studies by sex researchers such as Alfred Kinsey and Evelyn Hooker that showed that lesbigay people were no less well-adjusted than heterosexuals, began to challenge the dominant psychiatric perspective. Protests from lesbigay activists and supportive mental health professionals led the APA in 1973 to remove homosexuality from the group's nomenclature of disease, since being lesbigay did not "regularly cause emotional distress" or generally result in "impairment of social functioning." The move was historic; not only did it mean that the leading psychiatric organization was on record recognizing that homosexuality was a normal, healthy identity, but it also served to strengthen the self-image of lesbigay youth. No longer would people attracted to others of the same sex be forced to grow up with most medical authorities telling them that they were sick or perverted. In more-recent years, the APA has refuted renewed claims by a handful of psychiatrists that homosexuality can be cured.

But while the APA has become more educated about the lives of lesbians, gay men, and bisexuals, the organization continues to hold stereotypical attitudes toward transgendered people, and transsexuality is still listed as a mental disorder in the latest *Diagnostic and Statistical Manual* (1994). Like lesbigay activists twenty-five years earlier, transgender leaders are working to change this classification, noting that the pathologizing of transsexuality has been used to justify attempts to "treat" children who display "gender-variant behavior."

Sources: Bayer, *Homosexuality and American Psychiatry*; Blumenfeld and Raymond, *Looking at Gay and Lesbian Life*; Johnson, "Transgender Activists Focus on the Long Journey Ahead"; Thompson, *Long Road to Freedom*.

THE LATE 1970s

New Right Challenges to Lesbigay Rights: Anita Bryant and John Briggs

By the mid-1970s, it seemed as if the lesbigay rights movement was on a roll. Eighteen states had repealed their sodomy laws. Many areas had ordinances forbidding discrimination on the basis of sexual identity, including Los Angeles, Seattle, Minneapolis, and the District of Columbia. More educators were incorporating lesbigay issues into school curricula. And lesbigays were becoming a major political force within the Democratic Party. Beginning in 1977, however, a serious challenge to these gains was being mounted. The New Right, a loose but well-organized and financed coalition of religious and secular social conservatives, as well as anti-regulation business interests, sought to fight many of the social changes brought on by political movements of recent decades. Not only was this coalition opposed to civil rights protections for lesbigays, it was also variously against abortion, the Equal Rights Amendment, and pornography. Although the groups often differed in their agendas and did not always agree, they generally believed that the country's growing permissiveness and the government's increasing regulatory powers were threats to traditional social arrangements regarding the family, gender relations, reproduction, sexuality, and capitalism. In their campaigns,

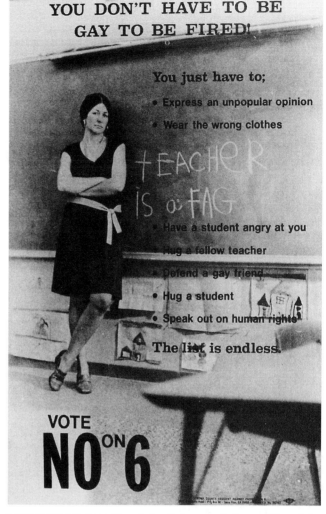

Advertisement targeting John Briggs and Proposition 6 in California.

lesbigays—particularly men—were portrayed as predators and child molesters. A common slogan was that lesbigays "don't reproduce, they recruit." New Right activists also resurrected the argument used by racial segregationists during the black civil rights movement that business people had the right to refuse to hire or sell goods and services to certain groups.

The first major anti-lesbigay campaign was in Dade County, Florida, which includes Miami. In January 1977, the county passed an ordinance forbidding discrimination based on sexual identity. Evangelical singer and Florida citrus growers' spokesperson Anita Bryant campaigned to have the law repealed. Through her organization, Save Our Children, Inc., she got enough signatures to force a referendum. The campaign revived national attention, and a number of conservative groups endorsed Bryant's efforts. In June, voters overwhelmingly sided with Bryant, and the law was repealed. This was the start of an increasingly hostile political climate for lesbigays.

Bryant's success led to other repeal campaigns across the country. In 1978, voters in St. Paul, Minnesota; Wichita, Kansas; and Eugene, Oregon also repealed their anti-discrimination ordinances. Efforts were underway to do the same in Seattle. There were also attempts to pass laws prohibiting public schools from promoting same-sex sexuality as a viable alternative to heterosexuality, either through their hiring or teaching practices. Such a law was passed in Oklahoma. California became the next battleground, as state senator John Briggs led a campaign to persuade voters to pass an amendment to the state constitution called Proposition 6.

Lesbigays felt besieged, not only by attempts to take away their civil rights, but by the increasing level of violence against them. Although lesbigay communities and political groups had been split by gender, class, and race/ethnicity, they came together against common enemies. They used the media to persuade voters that lesbigays deserved equal rights, confronted opponents in public forums, built coalitions with labor, civil rights, and other groups, and canvassed door to door to get their message out. They also boycotted Florida citrus products and held protests. As a result, Proposition 6 was defeated, as was Seattle's repeal campaign. Anita Bryant's contract with Florida citrus growers was canceled, and the Oklahoma law was eventually overturned by the Supreme Court. The momentum of the New Right had been halted—at least temporarily. However, the conflict between lesbigay activists and social conservatives would continue into the 1980s and 1990s.

Sources: Adam, *The Rise of a Gay and Lesbian Movement*; Faderman, *Odd Girls and Twilight Lovers*; Miller, *Out of the Past*.

The Election and Assassination of Harvey Milk

Although Harvey Milk was not the first openly lesbigay person to be elected to public office when he won a seat on the San Francisco Board of Supervisors in 1977 (Kathy Kozachenko and Elaine Noble had been elected to Ann Arbor, Michigan's City Council and the Massachusetts House of Representatives respectively in 1974), he quickly became a folk hero to many lesbigay people because of the way he used his prominent position to increase the visibility and power of lesbigays in San Francisco and throughout the country. "I was elected by the people of this district," he said, "but I also have a responsibility to gays—not just in this city, but elsewhere." Milk was one of the leaders of the successful campaign against the Briggs Initiative, a referendum that would have barred anyone suspected of being lesbian, gay, or bisexual from teaching in California's public schools. He also sponsored a lesbigay rights bill for San Francisco, which, showing Milk's ability to build coalitions with people of color, labor activists, and other groups, passed with the opposition of only one supervisor, Dan White, a former police officer who had referred to gays as "social deviates."

On 27 November 1978, just weeks after the resounding defeat of the Briggs Initiative, White killed Milk and liberal San Francisco Mayor George Moscone, apparently because he was angered by Moscone's refusal to re-appoint him to the Board of Supervisors after he had briefly resigned. Milk had strongly supported the mayor's decision. Many lesbigay activists considered Milk's murder to be the result of the hostile atmosphere created for lesbians, gay men, and bisexuals by the Briggs referendum and efforts to overturn lesbigay rights ordinances around the country. Rather than just the actions of an unstable individual, the assassinations represented the extreme of an organized movement that sought to force lesbigay people back into the closet and stop the migration of lesbigays to San Francisco in the 1970s.

On the night of the shootings, more than 25,000 San Franciscans marched in a silent candle-lit procession to City Hall. Six months later, this mourning turned to rage when White received the lightest possible penalty; a jury from which lesbigay people had been excluded sentenced him to less than eight years in jail after psychiatrists argued that he had a "diminished capacity" because of a junk-food diet, what the gay press scornfully dubbed the "Twinkies defense." Under California law, White could have received the death penalty; instead, he served slightly more than five years in prison. The decision was seen as declaring "an open season on gay people."

If lesbigay activists were concerned that many residents of San Francisco's predominantly lesbigay Castro district had become complacent, the White Night Riots proved otherwise. Following the verdict, 5,000 people marched to City Hall, where they smashed the building's front doors and fought with the police, many of whom had openly supported White during the trial. Ordered not to attack the protesters, the police responded instead by destroying a gay bar and beating up its patrons, some severely. By the end of the night, an estimated 100 lesbigays and at least 61 police officers were hospitalized. For many lesbians, gay men, and bisexuals in San Francisco and around the country, justice and a sense of closure did not occur until White committed suicide in 1985.

Sources: Adam, *The Rise of a Gay and Lesbian Movement*; Cruikshank, *The Gay and Lesbian Liberation Movement*; Shilts, *The Mayor of Castro Street*.

The Marches on Washington

The lesbian, gay, bisexual, and transgender rights movement has grown enormously in the past twenty years, perhaps best demonstrated by the success of the three national marches held in Washington, D.C., each of which has been larger and more diverse than the previous one. Coming in the wake of the lenient jail sentence given to Dan White for the assassination of openly gay San Francisco supervisor Harvey Milk, the 1979 March on Washington for Lesbian and Gay Rights, the first national demonstration of its kind, drew more than 100,000 people from around the country. Despite the fear of established lesbian and gay groups that the march would spawn a right-wing backlash similar to Anita Bryant's "Save Our Children" campaign, it had the opposite effect, helping to solidify a national lesbigay rights movement. The march also featured the first National Third World Gay and Lesbian Conference, which was attended by hundreds of people of color and helped give rise to the National Coalition of Black Lesbians and Gays.

On 11 October 1987, more than a half million people (between 500,000-650,000 according to organizers) descended on Washington to participate in the second national March on Washington for Lesbian and Gay Rights. Many were angry over the government's slow and inadequate response to the AIDS crisis and the Supreme Court's 1986 decision to uphold sodomy laws in *Bowers v. Hardwick*. The march succeeded in bringing national attention to the impact of AIDS on lesbigay communities with the first display of the NAMES Project AIDS Memorial Quilt; in the shadow of the U.S. Capitol, a tapestry of nearly 2,000 fabric panels offered a powerful tribute to the lives of some of those who had been lost in the pandemic. The march also drew unprecedented media coverage to anti-lesbigay discrimination, as approximately 800 people were arrested in front of the Supreme Court two days later in the largest civil disobedience action ever held in support of the rights of lesbians, gay men, bisexuals, and

White Night Riots in San Francisco, 1979.

transgendered people. Although the 1987 March on Washington sparked the creation of BiNet U.S.A. and the Latino/a Lesbian and Gay Organization, the first national groups for bisexuals and lesbigay Latinos respectively, the most lasting effect of the weekend's events might have been felt on the local level. Energized and inspired by the march, many activists returned home and established social and political groups in their own communities, providing even greater visibility and strength to the struggle for lesbian, gay, bisexual, and transgender rights.

The resulting growth of the movement was shown six years later when close to a million people attended the 1993 March on Washington for Lesbian, Gay, and Bi Equal Rights and Liberation, making it the largest demonstration in U.S. history to that time. The event was also groundbreaking for receiving the unanimous endorsement of the board of the NAACP—the first time that direct institutional ties had been made between the lesbigay rights movement and the civil rights movement—and for explicitly including bisexuals. In addition to the march, participants could take part in more than 250 related events, including conferences, work-shops, protests, congressional lobbying, dances, readings, and religious ceremonies.

Sources: Thompson, *Long Road to Freedom*; Vaid, *Virtual Equality.*

THE EARLY AND MID-1980s

Lesbigays of Color Community Building

Most of what is known about efforts to build community among various lesbigay groups of color before the late 1960s has focused on African Americans. Among them, separate institutions and events go back at least to the late nineteenth century, when they held large drag queen balls that drew thousands. Before the late 1960s, these efforts were primarily social in nature, and were borne out of the desire to find and socialize with others like themselves. It was also a way of dealing with racial/ethnic and sexual oppression from white lesbigays and heterosexual African Americans respectively. With the arrival of the civil rights movement and the drive for racial integration in the 1950s, this situation began to change. Although some integrated into or formed race/ethnicity-based coalitions with mostly white lesbigay and heterosexual people of color organizations, the desire for separate institutions and events did not die. Primary reasons were the combination of continued white lesbigay racism, heterosexism within racial/ethnic communities, and the need to be in spaces where both their racial/ethnic and sexual identities were validated.

As was the case within larger, predominantly white lesbigay communities, the ways in which lesbigays of color tried to create community expanded in the early 1970s. Until the late 1970s, bars and various social events remained the primary ways in which lesbigays of color created community. New forms were emerging, however, such as churches and health care organizations—the latter particularly since the AIDS epidemic began to affect lesbigays of color significantly and health awareness grew among women. The media became a major part of the community building effort on both local and national levels, particularly among African Americans. For example, black gay and bisexual men developed various dance music forms such as disco and house. There have also been efforts to document and examine the lives of lesbigays of color in print and on film/video. Since the late 1970s, several periodicals

have come out, though most were short lived or published irregularly. More successful have been the several anthologies featuring the poetry, fiction, and essays of lesbigays of color. And Richard Fung, Marlon Riggs, and Michelle Parkerson are among the lesbigays of color who have been part of the emerging lesbigay independent film and video movement.

Lesbigays of color have also been organizing politically. As early as the late 1960s, there were Third World caucuses within mostly white lesbigay or feminist groups such as the Gay Liberation Front and the National Organization for Women, as well as separate local groups. There were also organizations such as the Combahee River Collective, in which women of color of all sexual identities united around feminist issues, some of which dealt with same-sex sexuality. Separatist political organizing accelerated during the late 1970s, when many lesbigays of color became disillusioned with organizations dominated by white lesbigays and heterosexual people of color because they refused to address the multiple ways in which many people were oppressed, deal with discrimination and other forms of oppression within their respective communities, or integrate their leadership.

Sources: Chauncey, *Gay New York*; D'Emilio, *Beyond Trouble*; LeVay and Nonas, *City of Friends*.

The 1993 March on Washington drew close to one million people.

The AIDS Pandemic and the
U.S. Government's Slow Response

The first AIDS cases were reported in 1981, although studies of unexplained deaths subsequently identified cases dating back to the 1970s and earlier. The initial cases were discovered in Los Angeles and New York among a small cluster of young gay men, all of whom had severely impaired immune systems that made them susceptible to rare forms of cancer and pneumonia. Because these first cases seemed to be limited to gay men, the medical establishment originally referred to the syndrome as Gay-Related Immune Deficiency (GRID)—until gay activists protested the naming of a chronic illness after an already stigmatized group. Changing the name of the syndrome, though, did not prevent the mainstream media from viewing AIDS as a "gay plague" that gays had brought on themselves through irresponsible sex. In contrast, hemophiliacs, children, and the wives of infected men were considered "innocent victims."

The initial linking of AIDS with gay men—and, to a lesser extent, with intravenous drug users—meant that the federal government did not give a high priority to the funding of prevention programs or research. In the words of Randy Shilts, a reporter on AIDS for the *San Francisco Chronicle* who later died from the syndrome, "No one cared because it was homosexuals who were dying.... [They] didn't seem to warrant the kind of urgent concern another set of victims would engender." For example, the U.S. Centers for Disease Control and Prevention, which had primary responsibility for tracking AIDS, was slow to do so, and then categorized cases by "risk groups" rather than "risk behavior." This classification system increased the pariah status of gay and bisexual men while failing to offer critical information that could prevent additional transmissions. At the same time, the Food and Drug Administration, the agency responsible for certifying new drugs, had an extremely cumbersome approval process and, according to a federal AIDS panel, less than half the staff it needed to review experimental treatments.

Elected officials were often no more responsive to the crisis. Ronald Reagan did not even mention AIDS until more than five years into his presidency, after fellow actor Rock Hudson died from the syndrome in 1985. During his silence, more than 15,000 people in the U.S. lost their lives to AIDS, and tens of thousands were infected. Congress was also culpable in the spread of AIDS by banning educational materials that were sexually explicit or that presented homosexuality in a positive light, thereby making it extremely difficult to reach some of the people most likely to engage in unsafe sexual practices.

The lack of effective educational programs also meant that the general public had little understanding of AIDS and how it was transmitted, leading to irrational fears about casual contact and numerous incidents of discrimination against those who were believed to be infected. At times during the 1980s, people with AIDS were forced out of their homes and schools, denied medical treatment, and prevented from flying on airlines, eating in restaurants, and swimming in public pools. Not until well-known figures such as Magic Johnson, Arthur Ashe, and Greg Louganis revealed that they were HIV-positive did many people in the U.S. begin to show compassion for people with AIDS and not treat them as outcasts.

Sources: Blumenfeld and Raymond, *Looking at Gay and Lesbian Life*; Patton, *Sex and Germs*.

The "Lesbian Sex Wars" and the Rise of S/M Communities

Among lesbians in the 1970s, the dominant voice belonged to cultural feminists, who considered pornography to be inherently exploitive of women, dismissed power differences and role playing in lesbian relationships, and promoted an androgynous appearance that downplayed women's bodies. But, by the end of the decade, lesbians who identified as sex radicals, including many butches, femmes, and s/m dykes, had begun asserting their right to sexual pleasure beyond the confines of "vanilla sex" and encouraging women to fight what they saw as the anti-sexual stance prevalent among lesbian feminist leaders. Like cultural feminists before them, lesbian sex radicals created their own forms of entertainment in the 1980s, such as sexually explicit videos and magazines, lesbian burlesque shows, sex clubs, and stores and mail-order businesses specializing in sex toys for women. These sexual institutions aimed to do more than titillate; for example, the lesbian sex magazine *On Our Backs* stated in its premiere issue in 1984 that its mission was to promote "sexual freedom, respect and empowerment for lesbians."

Some of the most visible sex activists—and the ones most vociferously attacked by cultural feminists—were lesbians who identified as sadomasochists. They formed social and support groups throughout the country in the 1980s, both to explore their sexuality and to counter claims that s/m perpetuated violence and the oppression of women. The most well-known of these organizations, SAMOIS, a lesbian-feminist s/m group in San Francisco, edited *Coming to Power*, one of the first books to give a voice to s/m lesbians, in 1981. Many of the anthology's contributors argued that, rather than violating basic feminist tenets, as some antipornography activists had charged, s/m sex furthered feminism, since it challenged gender hierarchies and allowed women to find and use their power in consensual ways, thereby giving them a healthy means to acknowledge differences and work out conflicts.

With both cultural feminists and lesbian sex radicals asserting that the other was betraying the ideals of feminism, confrontations were inevitable, and heated conflicts occurred at women's music festivals, academic conferences, and political demonstrations throughout the 1980s.

One of the most contentious moments in the "lesbian sex wars" developed around the Ninth Scholar and Feminist Conference, "Towards a Politics of Sexuality," held at Barnard College in 1982. A group led by Women Against Pornography condemned the conference for "promoting patriarchal values" and for including women whom they labeled as engaging in deviant sexual practices. Wearing t-shirts that said "For a Feminist Sexuality" on the front and "Against s/m" on the back, they passed out leaflets during the conference that attacked individual participants by name. This created a chilling atmosphere that prevented any meaningful feminist dialogue about sex and, in the words of a petition signed by the event's supporters, obscured "the diversity of the conference and the broad issues it raised." Today, lesbian communities in general seem more accepting of a range of sexual identities and practices, although pornography, butch/femme roles, and s/m remain contentious issues at times, and bisexuals and transgendered people still face discrimination from some lesbians.

Sources: Duggan and Hunter, *Sex Wars*; Faderman, *Odd Girls and Twilight Lovers*; SAMOIS, *Coming to Power*; Vance, *Pleasure and Danger*.

Sharon Kowalski and Karen Thompson's
Struggle to Be Together

In 1983, Sharon Kowalski, a high school physical education teacher, was involved in a car accident that left her unable to walk or communicate beyond short words and gestures. At the time, Kowalski and her lover, Karen Thompson, had been partners for nearly four years and considered themselves married, having exchanged rings and bought a house together near St. Cloud, Minnesota. However, they were not open about their sexuality, especially to Kowalski's parents, who, when they learned of the couple's relationship, denied that their daughter was a lesbian and went to court to prevent Thompson from visiting her and being involved in her rehabilitation. In 1985, a district court judge awarded unconditional guardianship of Kowalski to her father, despite his lack of involvement in her life before the accident, and he immediately denied visitation rights to Thompson and moved Kowalski to a nursing home that a court had previously ruled as unable to provide for her medical needs.

Kowalski had consistently stated that she wanted to live in St. Cloud with Thompson, but reflecting how women with disabilities are often treated as children, the legal system questioned her ability to make such a decision for herself, and Thompson had to

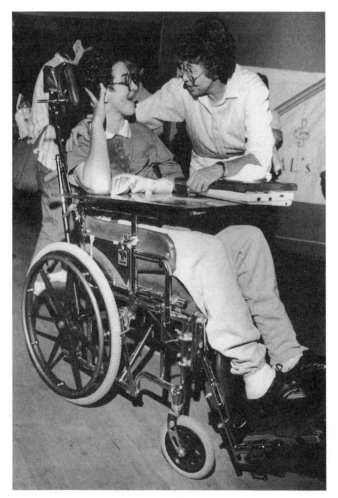

Sharon Kowalski (left) and Karen Thompson

fight just to have judges consider Kowalski's wishes and ensure that she was given proper medical treatment. Finally, in December 1991, after an eight-year struggle, a Minnesota appeals court granted Thompson guardianship, enabling Kowalski to move back to their home and to continue to make progress in her rehabilitation. However, as Thompson noted at the time, the outcome was bittersweet. "I don't view this as a victory. This is what's right. This is what's just. This should have happened a long time ago."

Kowalski and Thompson's struggle to be together vividly demonstrates the precarious position of lesbians, gay men, and bisexuals in a deeply heterosexist society and the importance of fighting for equal rights for both lesbigay families and people with disabilities. According to Thompson, it also shows the critical need for same-sex couples to file durable powers of attorney and living wills and to be open about their sexuality in order to dispel the kinds of myths that kept her and Kowalski's relationship from being recognized.

Sources: Schmitz, "Kowalski and Thompson Win!"; Thompson and Andrzejewski, *Why Can't Sharon Kowalski Come Home?*

Gay and Lesbigay Cultures Go Mainstream

In the post-Stonewall era, lesbigays have made inroads into mainstream U.S. culture in several ways. One is the influence of lesbigay political philosophy. Increasingly, those with a same-sex sexual identity are described with the labels they use to define themselves such as "gay," "lesbian," or "bisexual," rather than terms with negative connotations, such as "homosexual." Related to this are lesbigay challenges to the meanings of their identities. Rather than being seen as sick, sinful, or criminal, they are increasingly being seen as oppressed minorities. Finally, the discourse on "coming out" has become part of the national consciousness. This perhaps has especially been the case since the Human Rights Campaign started sponsoring National Coming Out Day in 1988, as some in the media have held special events in conjunction with it. Television talk show host Oprah Winfrey, for example, has had shows in which lesbigays have come out to friends and relatives on that day.

Various aspects of gay male culture have also had an impact on the U.S. mainstream, though not always in their original forms. One example is camp. Although there is disagreement over exactly what camp is, authors Simon LeVay and Elisabeth Nonas argue it generally includes "parody, excess, deliberate artificiality, and sexual suggestiveness or gender confusion." Drag has been the most prominent aspect of camp that has migrated to the mainstream. During the 1960s and 1970s, "bisexual chic" rock musicians such as David Bowie (via his Ziggy Stardust alter ego), Mick Jagger, and Alice Cooper incorporated drag and homo-eroticism into their acts. Numerous films and television shows have featured men in drag, including *To Wong Foo, Thanks for Everything, Julie Newmar* and the "Men on Film" sketch on the FOX television show, *In Living Color.* Another aspect of camp, "gay" humor—that witty, sometimes bitchy repartee—has found its way into comedies such as NBC's *Frasier,* thanks in large part to the growing number of lesbigay comedy writers.

Other aspects of gay male culture that have made their way into the mainstream include black gay dance music and styles, of which disco and vogueing are the most prominent. There is also the eroticization of the male body, particularly in coffee table books, calendars, and advertising. Underwear ads by designers like

Calvin Klein (who started the trend), Structure, and Versace, and exotic dance groups such as the Chippendales have become cultural staples. Increasingly, male actors such as Sylvester Stallone and Mel Gibson have bared their backsides and buffed bodies in their films. The influence of lesbigays on mainstream culture has been limited, but their presence has been unmistakable and continues to grow.

Sources: Bronski, *Culture Clash*; LeVay and Nonas, *City of Friends*; Rutledge, *The Gay Decades*; Thomas, "The House the Kids Built."

THE LATE 1980s

Bowers v. Hardwick

In 1982, an Atlanta police officer went to Michael Hardwick's home to serve a warrant for alleged outstanding tickets. He saw him having sex with another man and arrested him for violating Georgia's sodomy law, which prohibits oral and anal sex. Those convicted can get up to 20 years in prison. At the time, 26 states and the District of Columbia had laws on the books criminalizing either oral and/or anal sex regardless of the participants' gender, or just same-sex oral and/or anal sex. Before 1961, all states had such laws. Penalties varied considerably. Michigan had the toughest punishment: repeat offenders could get life in prison. Although the charges against Hardwick were dropped, he decided to sue the state and have the law declared unconstitutional. That set the stage for the infamous 1986 Supreme Court decision, *Bowers v. Hardwick*. In a 5-4 vote, the Court reaffirmed the right of a state to regulate private sexual conduct between consenting adults.

Hardwick's lawyers argued that sodomy laws violated the "right to privacy" in sexual matters, which had been interpreted in previous Supreme Court cases as being protected by the due process clause of the 14th Amendment. This clause prevents governments from depriving someone of "life, liberty, or property" without having a compelling reason for doing so. Hardwick's lawyers argued that sex between consenting adults should be protected, just as women's reproductive rights, the right to own and use pornographic materials, and the right to marry outside one's race/ethnicity had been in previous cases where the privacy doctrine had been invoked. Similar reasoning had been used to persuade supreme courts in several states to strike down their sodomy laws. However, Justice White, writing for the majority, disagreed. The majority believed the right to consensual sex had little in common with privacy rights involving procreation, marriage, and family. Furthermore, the state did have a legitimate interest in controlling sexual behavior, even between consenting adults, since the acts in question had a long history in Western culture of being regulated. They noted the state also had the right to regulate other kinds of sexual acts between consenting adults, such as adultery and incest.

Justice Blackmun and the three other justices who dissented agreed with the reasoning presented by Hardwick and argued that the majority defined the case too narrowly. From their perspective, the issue was not whether someone had "a fundamental right to engage in homosexual sodomy," but whether they had the broader right "to be let alone." They argued that certain decisions were best left to the individual and certain places should be protected from state intrusion except in extraordinary circumstances. Like family and marriage, sexuality is a key part of human existence, and decisions regarding it should be left up to the individual.

The decision had tremendous implications for the lesbigay rights movement, since it justified various forms of lesbigay oppression. Why protect from discrimination someone whose behavior was illegal in many areas? Hence, opponents argued that lesbigays should continue to be discriminated against in jobs and housing, and barred from serving in the military, immigrating to this country, getting custody of children, and legally marrying. The decision also helped fuel a climate in which people could justify harassment and violence against lesbigays. Although the Hardwick decision (and the AIDS epidemic) made it more difficult for lesbigays to fight heterosexism, progress has been made. The 26 states with sodomy laws in 1986 have been reduced to 18, with most of the remaining states in the South and Rocky Mountains. Cities such as New Orleans have passed lesbigay anti-discrimination laws even though oral and/or anal sex is still a crime under state law. And 11 states have passed lesbigay anti-discrimination laws.

Sources: Adam, *The Rise of a Gay and Lesbian Movement*; *Bowers v. Hardwick*, 106 S.Ct. 2841 (1986); Cudnik, "Two More States Pass Gay Civil Rights Laws"; Keen, "Hardwick Revisited"; Leonard, "The Legal Position of Lesbians and Gay Men in the United States."

Responses to AIDS: The Development of ACT UP and the NAMES Project

Disproportionately affected by AIDS during the first decade of the pandemic, gay and bisexual men did not sit by idly, but sought to keep the memory of those who had died alive and to increase public awareness and government action to prevent others from becoming infected. The most visible and powerful symbol of the impact of AIDS has been the NAMES Project AIDS Memorial Quilt, which has served as both a tribute to the people who have lost their lives and an important part of the grieving process for their friends, lovers, and family members.

Conceived by longtime San Francisco gay activist Cleve Jones in 1985, the Quilt was first unveiled at the second March on Washington for Lesbian and Gay Rights in October 1987. At that time, it consisted of 1,920 panels and was larger than a football field. Since then, it has been displayed four more times in its entirety in the nation's capital, growing tremendously with each unveiling. At the showing in October 1996, the Quilt included more than 50,000 panels and was more than 29 football fields long. Beyond these full-size displays, portions of the Quilt are shown more than a thousand times each year to millions around the country. Although the NAMES Project originally focused on the impact of AIDS on largely white lesbigay communities, it has since grown to encompass all segments of the U.S. population, reflecting the changing demographics of the pandemic and the effect it has had on all our lives.

Another response promulgated by the AIDS crisis is direct action protest. In 1987, more than two hundred protesters, angered by what they saw as the country's business-as-usual attitude toward the deaths of thousands of gay and bisexual men, staged a demonstration in New York City that blocked rush-hour traffic on Wall Street. The group, which became known as the AIDS Coalition to Unleash Power, or ACT UP, inspired many people living with AIDS to become actively involved in their own treatment—such as by fighting for faster approval of and lower prices for AIDS drugs —rather than accepting the passive victim role

Protesters demonstrating for increased AIDS education.

expected of them. Within just a few years, activists across the country had formed dozens of new chapters, using similar confrontational tactics to draw attention to the AIDS crisis and the slow reaction of the Reagan and Bush administrations.

ACT UP played an instrumental role in changing how the federal government responded to AIDS and other diseases. For example, it succeeded in greatly accelerating the Food and Drug Administration's process for approving experimental drugs, vastly expanded access to clinical trials, helped secure housing assistance for people living with AIDS, and strengthened the position of AIDS service organizations in their efforts to obtain much-needed government funding. Moreover, ACT UP restored a sense of militancy to the lesbigay rights movement, inspiring the formation of Queer Nation, the Lesbian Avengers, and other radical groups in the late 1980s and early 1990s. ACT UP itself, though, began to decline in the 1990s, as AIDS received greater attention and funding and as activists were more frequently given a voice in policy decisions. Inevitably, some members also burned out, but many others still remain involved in AIDS education and advocacy today.

Sources: Freiberg, "After 10 Years, ACT UP Now Fights Dwindling Membership"; Stoesen, "A Decade of Rage and Remembrance"; Witt, Thomas, and Marcus, *Out in All Directions*.

The Tremendous Impact of AIDS on People of Color

Although AIDS at first largely affected only white gay and bisexual men, the pandemic quickly impacted on people of color in the 1980s because of two main reasons: racism and class bias on the part of health officials, service providers, and the mainstream media, and the lack of prevention programs specifically targeted to African Americans and Latinos. The initial silence of most black leaders and the black press about AIDS—because of a reluctance to address homosexuality and a fear of reinforcing the historical association of African Americans with drug use and sexually transmitted disease—contributed to the vulnerability of black communities and enabled the tremendous impact of AIDS on people of color to remain underreported. For example, African Americans and Latinos accounted for more than 40 percent of AIDS cases by 1987, even though they constituted only about one-fifth of the U.S. population. In 1995, they represented nearly 60 percent of reported AIDS cases, and for the first time the number of new cases among African Americans began to exceed the number of new cases among whites. The prevalence of AIDS is now six times greater among blacks by proportion than among whites.

AIDS has had a particularly devastating impact on women of color and black gay and bisexual men. Today, the majority of African American men living with AIDS are gay and bisexual, and many leading black gay writers have been lost to the pandemic, including Joseph Beam, Essex Hemphill, Melvin Dixon, Craig Harris, Marlon Riggs, and Assotto Saint. At the same time, more than half of the women in the U.S. with AIDS are now African American and about one-fourth are Latina. Compounding this crisis is the fact that people of color often have less access to medical care than whites, and as a result, are diagnosed later, receive less extensive treatment, and die sooner. While new drug therapies offer hope for longer and healthier lives for some people with HIV and AIDS, the high cost of the drugs and the lack of adequate federal support for treatment programs mean that they are beyond the reach of many women and men of color.

Sources: Hammonds, "Race, Sex, AIDS"; O'Connell, "AIDS Rate for Blacks Is Six Times that of Whites."

The Development of a National Bisexual Movement

Bisexual women and men have long been involved in the struggle for sexual liberation. Many members of the Mattachine Society and Daughters of Bilitis, for example, were out bisexuals, and sexual fluidity was an underlying principle of the Gay Liberation Front and other radical gay groups that arose during the early 1970s. In the decade following Stonewall, bisexuals also developed their own organizations in New York City, San Francisco, Chicago, Los Angeles, Detroit, and Minneapolis. Most of these groups, though, were predominantly male, and all had disbanded by the mid-1980s, as bisexual men devoted more of their time to AIDS activism.

While male-dominated bisexual organizations were beginning to fold, bisexual women were creating groups to support each other and to counter the hostility they received from lesbian communities. Most had been active themselves in lesbian groups until being excluded for their involvement with men, as lesbian separatism and a dichotomous view of sexuality became more entrenched in the late 1970s. Yet, despite rejecting an exclusive lesbian politic, these women remained committed to feminism, and feminist principles were central to groups such as the Boston Bisexual Women's Network, Chicago Action Bi-Women (both formed in 1983), and the Seattle Bisexual Women's Network (founded in 1986).

A national bisexual movement began to take shape when a call for a bisexual contingent for the 1987 March on Washington for Lesbian and Gay Rights brought together 75 people from around the country and laid the groundwork for the establishment of the North American Bisexual Network. The movement further took shape at the first national bisexual conference, which was held in San Francisco in 1990. The following year, the name was changed to BiNet U.S.A., and reflecting the influence of feminism, it developed a consensus decision-making process and a leadership structure consisting of a team of six national coordinators and thirty regional organizers. In direct contrast to the male-dominated groups of the 1970s, the organization has had about equal numbers of women and men in leadership roles. During its first ten years, BiNet has fought biphobia in the dominant society and increased the visibility of bisexuals, with members appearing on television talk shows and being quoted in the mainstream and lesbian and gay press. The organization has also educated national lesbian and gay rights organizations about the importance of using bi-inclusive language and recognizing the involvement of bisexuals in the

sexual liberation struggle. One major victory was convincing lesbian and gay organizers to include bisexuals explicitly in the 1993 March on Washington, the first time that bisexuals have been acknowledged in a national political action.

But perhaps the bisexual movement's most significant progress has been on the local level. In the 1990s, the number of bisexual organizations in the U.S. has grown tremendously, from several dozen groups established primarily on the coasts to more than 300 located in every region of the country. At the same time, the names and charters of many lesbian and gay organizations, newspapers, and conferences have been changed to include bisexuals, as more bi-identified individuals have come out and, mirroring the national political scene, sought to have their involvement recognized. As a result, bisexuals have created supportive communities throughout the U.S., not just in major cities or at traditionally liberal universities.

Sources: Donaldson, "The Bisexual Movement's Beginnings in the 70s"; Highleyman, "A Brief History of the Bisexual Movement"; Ochs, *The Bisexual Resource Guide*; Udis-Kessler, "Identity/Politics."

Bisexual marcher at a San Francisco Freedom Day parade.

Queer Nationalism

Toward the end of the 1980s, militant, direct-action protest had become part of the lesbigay political landscape again. The group ACT UP (AIDS Coalition To Unleash Power), which focused on AIDS issues, started the trend. However, there were other groups, most notably Queer Nation, which used street theater and various forms of confrontational protest to increase public awareness of a broader range of lesbigay issues. These young militants were tired of politely asking the world for justice. Now, they were demanding it. This was evident in their rhetoric: "We're here! We're Queer! Get used to it!" Queer Nation began in New York City, and chapters quickly spread to other parts of the country, mostly on the East and West Coasts. Members were mostly white males, but they made a commitment to inclusion and diversity.

Some of their tactics were controversial. They confronted heterosexual privilege and anti-lesbigay violence by, for example, holding kiss-ins in straight bars and marches in neighborhoods where lesbigays had been the targets of harassment and/or violence. The tactic that caused the most controversy was "outing," in which activists would expose various public figures as lesbigay. The purpose was to show that lesbigays were everywhere and expose the hypocrisy of closeted lesbigays who publicly took anti-lesbigay stances. However, critics argued that outing was an invasion of privacy, harmed those targeted, and had little political effectiveness.

Although Queer Nation spawned other militant groups such as the Lesbian Avengers, this new radicalism was short lived. The election of the more-moderate Clinton administration was a major reason for this. The groups also suffered from internal problems similar to those that befell the gay liberation movement: chaotic organizational structure and the inability to deal effectively with issues of difference. Their legacy is the reclamation of the word "queer," which they used to describe lesbigays and other sexual/gender minorities. They took what had been a derogatory word and turned it into a symbol of rebellion and inclusiveness.

Sources: Bérubé and Escoffier, "Queer/Nation"; Chee, "A Queer Nationalism"; Faderman, *Odd Girls and Twilight Lovers*; LeVay and Nonas, *City of Friends*; Miller, *Out of the Past*.

THE EARLY AND MID-1990s

The Emergence and Growth of Queer Studies

The pioneering research in lesbian and gay studies that was conducted in the 1970s and early 1980s received little institutional support, either from academia or the publishing industry. Many scholars had to do their studies "after-hours"—in addition to their regular workloads—and then had difficulty finding outlets to present and publish their work. Some lesbian scholars became a part of women's studies programs, where they often found a safe space to come out and conduct research, but tensions sometimes developed because of heterosexism and the scarce resources of these programs, and obviously women studies could not accommodate gay male scholars unless their research focused on women or they approached the study of gay men from a feminist perspective.

Because of the general hostility of academia and the grassroots development of lesbian and gay studies, much of the early work in the field was conducted by independent scholars who published their findings in community newspapers and journals such as *Con-*

ditions, Sinister Wisdom, Gay Community News, Body Politic, Heresies, and *The Advocate*, or in books by small independent presses such as Firebrand, Kitchen Table, Alyson, Cleis, Crossing, Seal, and Spinsters. The first historical archives were also community efforts, including the Lesbian Herstory Archives, the San Francisco and Boston Lesbian and Gay History Projects, and the Sexual Minorities Archives.

The groundbreaking works in lesbian and gay studies, along with the emergence of a post-Stonewall generation of openly lesbian and gay scholars, helped give academic legitimacy to courses and research in the field and encouraged additional work. Among the important early texts addressing the experiences of lesbians, gay men, and bisexuals were Jonathan Ned Katz's *Gay American History* (1976) and *Gay/Lesbian Almanac* (1983); Michel Foucault's *A History of Sexuality* (1978); John Boswell's *Christianity, Social Tolerance, and Homosexuality* (1980); Cherríe Moraga and Gloria Anzaldúa's *This Bridge Called My Back* (1981); Lillian Faderman's *Surpassing the Love of Men* (1981); Audre Lorde's *Zami* (1982); Evelyn Torton Beck's *Nice Jewish Girls* (1982); Barbara Smith's *Home Girls* (1983); and John D'Emilio's *Sexual Politics, Sexual Communities* (1983).

These and other books paved the way for the tremendous growth of the field in the 1990s, which began to be called queer studies in order to reflect the influence of new, gay-specific theories and the inclusion of bisexuals and transgendered people in many of the emerging discourses. Today, many university presses and large commercial houses publish books in queer studies, with some having extensive lists and titles such as the University of Chicago, NYU, Columbia, and Routledge. Scholars now also have many more outlets for presenting their work, with the major conferences of more traditional disciplines offering panels on queer subjects, and lesbigay caucuses being formed in academic organizations such as the Modern Language Association, the American Historical Association, the American Sociological Association, and the American Psychological Association. In addition, scholars in queer studies have begun their own conferences. To date, there have been six national, multidisciplinary queer studies conferences, as well as numerous regional and graduate student conferences in the field.

With the amount of research in queer studies burgeoning and increasing the field's academic legitimacy, the number of courses that focus on lesbians, gay men, and/or bisexuals has proliferated. By the early 1990s, most large universities and colleges offered such classes, with a number developing queer studies programs, departments, or centers. The best known of these is the Center for Lesbian and Gay Studies (CLAGS), founded at the City University of New York in 1991.

Sources: de Lauretis, "Queer Theory"; Escoffier, "Inside the Ivory Closet."

The Creation of a National Transgender Movement

While bisexuals successfully lobbied to be included in the name of the 1993 March on Washington for Lesbian, Gay, and Bi Equal Rights and Liberation, a similar campaign to recognize transgendered people failed; they had to settle for trans-inclusive language in the march's list of demands. But the effort helped bring together transsexuals, crossdressers, drag queens, butch kings, intersexed people, and others who cross traditional boundaries of sex and gender into a national political movement that could fight ignorance and discrimination in both lesbian and gay communities and the larger society. Also playing a critical role in the movement's development in the 1990s has been the proliferation of transgender interest groups and chat rooms on the Internet, which have connected people from around the country and afforded them a level of safety as they "came out," and the publication of an increasing number of books by transgendered people themselves. Leslie Feinberg's *Stone Butch Blues* (1993) and *Transgender Warriors: Making History from Joan of Arc to RuPaul* (1996) and Kate Bornstein's *Gender Outlaw: On Men, Women and the Rest of Us* (1994) have been particularly important in providing visibility to transgendered people and educating others about their lives.

"There's finally a voice saying, 'Enough,'" argues Riki Anne Wilchins, a New York City transgender activist. "When you have people in isolation who are oppressed and victimized and abused, they think it's their own fault, but when ... they see it happening to other people, they realize it's not about them. It's about a system, and the only way to contest a system is with an organized response." This response has included forming GenderPAC, a political advocacy group, to lobby Congress to include transgendered people in hate crimes reporting legislation and the Employment Non-Discrimination Act being proposed by lesbian and gay groups. It has also involved the creation of Transsexual Menace, a direct-action group with more than 40 chapters across the U.S., to call attention to the frequency with which transgendered people are still attacked and killed and to protest the fact that the American Psychiatric Association continues to classify transsexualism as a mental disorder, much like it once considered homosexuality to be a sickness. Already transgendered people have made important progress in gaining civil rights protection, with Minnesota and cities such as Seattle, Santa Cruz, San Francisco, Iowa City, and Cambridge passing laws outlawing discrimination based on someone's gender identity. On a national level, history was made in May 1997 when ten members of Congress signed a letter at the urging of GenderPAC deploring violence against the differently gendered—the first time that legislators have publicly supported transgendered people.

Sources: Feinberg, *Transgender Warriors*; Goldberg, "Shunning 'He' and 'She,' They Fight for Respect"; Johnson, "Transgender Activists Focus on the Long Journey Ahead."

Lesbigay Art Controversies

In the 1980s and early 1990s, lesbigay artists and others who created works that were sexually explicit, overtly political, or represented unpopular ideas, as well as the institutions that exhibited them, became the center of controversy. Public artworks with lesbigay themes were vandalized. State and federal arts funding agencies were forced to defend projects to which they awarded grants. And institutions such as public broadcasting, museums, and galleries became embroiled in political and/or legal battles over the kinds of art they funded or presented.

Ongoing controversies over government funding of art and whether works that were sexually explicit or overtly political should be defined as "art" came to a head in 1990, and the funding practices of the National Endowment for the Arts (NEA), became a focal point of the debate. In Congress, Senator Jesse Helms and other conservatives tried to either abolish the NEA or restrict the kinds of projects the agency could fund, with varying degrees of success. For the 1990 fiscal year, for example, they prohibited

the NEA from funding art that fit the Supreme Court's most recent definition of "obscenity." Those receiving funds had to sign documents in which they agreed to follow the new guidelines. A number of artists and institutions refused to sign, returned their grants in protest, or sued. Artists and institutions also protested attempts to censor their work and displays by deliberately creating or exhibiting work they believed would violate NEA guidelines, artistically satirizing Senator Helms and others who tried to censor them, holding demonstrations and other public events in support of controversial art, and mounting campaigns to defeat public officials in elections.

Lesbigay artists and institutions unknown outside of the art world suddenly became household names. Images from Marlon Riggs's documentary of black gay life, *Tongues Untied*, were used in a Pat Buchanan presidential primary ad attacking then President George Bush and the NEA. Washington, D.C.'s Corcoran Gallery of Art canceled a retrospective exhibit of the late photographer Robert Mapplethorpe, which featured, in addition to still lifes and celebrity portraits, photos depicting sadomasochism, homoeroticism, interracial sexuality, and nude children. Cincinnati's Contemporary Arts Center became the first museum in U.S. history to be tried on (and later acquitted of) obscenity and child pornography charges, also in connection with a Mapplethorpe exhibit. Ironically, the controversies often increased interest in and the value of these artists' work.

Sources: Bronski, "It's Not the Flesh, It's the Flowers"; Dubin, *Arresting Images*; Segrest, "Visibility and Backlash"; Zeh, "Mapplethorpe Trial Ends in Acquittal."

The New Right's Ballot Initiatives

In the early 1990s, the New Right mounted another offensive against the gains made by the lesbigay rights movement. Again, their target was legislation and government policies prohibiting discrimination based on sexual identity. And again, their primary strategy was to go directly to the voters. Instead of simply campaigning to repeal the legislation, however, they also tried to get voters to approve initiatives preventing state and local governments from instituting such laws or policies in the future. Also different this time around was the dominant rhetoric used to secure passage of these ballot measures. Although the New Right continued to demonize lesbigays in various ways, this was not the primary thrust of their campaigns. Instead, they focused on the idea that lesbigays were trying to get "special rights," and tried to convince voters that discrimination against lesbigays was not the same as discrimination based on other social categories such as race/ethnicity or religion. Lesbigays campaigning against these initiatives typically responded by arguing that they were seeking equal rights, not special rights.

The 1992 elections were the first major battleground. Voters in Oregon, Colorado, and Tampa, Florida were asked to support anti-lesbigay referendums. Measure 9 in Oregon was the most restrictive. In addition to having provisions repealing ordinances that protected lesbigays from discrimination and preventing such laws or policies from being instituted in the future, it also included language that claimed same-sex sexuality was "perverse," mandated that this claim be taught in public schools, and prevented government funds from being used to present lesbigay sexuality as a viable alternative to heterosexuality. The statewide Oregon measure failed, as did the attempt to repeal Portland's lesbigay rights ordinance. The New Right's biggest success was the passage in Colorado of Amendment 2.

Similar campaigns were waged in the 1994 elections. Oregon and Florida were again battlegrounds. They were joined by Idaho. The statewide measures in Oregon and Idaho failed in close races. Although local measures in Florida and rural Oregon passed, those in the two Oregon counties were not enforceable because they were preempted by state law.

Lesbigay activists mounted challenges to the New Right's successes. When Amendment 2 was passed in Colorado, they organized a consumer boycott of the state. They also challenged the amendment's legality in the courts. The case, *Romer v. Evans*, eventually made its way to the U.S. Supreme Court. In May 1996, the New Right was dealt a severe blow when the Court, in a 6-3 decision, ruled that Amendment 2 was unconstitutional because it violated the equal protection clause of the 14th Amendment. Justice Kennedy, writing for the majority, argued that the state could only deny someone equal protection if it had a legitimate end and "neither burdens a fundamental right nor targets a suspect class." Amendment 2 did not meet this test because Colorado failed to provide an adequate rationale for it. The state argued that the amendment's primary purposes were to deny special rights to lesbigays and respect other citizens' freedom of association. The Court majority, however, believed the amendment as written was inconsistent with the reasons the state used to justify it. They concluded the Amendment's real intent was animosity toward lesbigays, which was not a legitimate state interest.

The ruling was a major victory for lesbigays, but its effect was limited. The Court did not rule that lesbigays as a group had constitutional protections. Instead, the Court made it difficult for state and local governments to place broad-based restrictions on lesbigays. The New Right could still fight to have existing lesbigay anti-discrimination laws repealed. And more importantly, the New Right could propose future ballot initiatives like Amendment 2, as long as the initiatives were written in accordance with the Court's guidelines.

Sources: Freiberg, "Colorado Gays: 'We're Ecstatic, We're Elated'" and "Gays Jubilant about Supreme Court Decision"; Keen, "High Court's Decision 'Levels the Playing Field,'" "High Court Ruling Is 'Revolutionary,'" "Maine Is Third State to Reject Similar Anti-Gay Ballot Measures," "Initiatives in Oregon, Idaho Appear Defeated," and "Gays Win in Oregon, But Lose in Colorado"; Miller, *Out of the Past*; "*Romer v. Evans*: Excerpts from the Majority."

Lesbigays and the Military

During the early days of the Clinton administration, the issue of whether lesbigays should be allowed to serve in the military became a hotly debated issue. Since the military formally instituted a policy keeping lesbigays out of the armed services in 1943, more than 80,000 people have been discharged. And the cost has been enormous. For example, a General Accounting Office study concluded that between 1982 and 1992, implementing the policy cost taxpayers half a billion dollars. President Clinton planned to end the ban by executive order, but encountered considerable opposition from those within the military and from groups of social conservatives. They argued that lifting the ban would threaten unit cohesiveness, promote violence against lesbigay service members, hurt morale, compromise heterosexuals' privacy, and lead to legal

problems, as performing oral and anal sex is a crime in the military. Supporters, however, claimed lesbigays have already shown they can effectively serve in the military, a conclusion supported by several studies conducted by the Defense Department itself.

Since the initial controversy, a total ban has been replaced with various forms of a "Don't Ask, Don't Tell" policy. In the most recent version, lesbigays can serve in the military as long as they remain celibate and do not disclose their sexual identity. The military will no longer ask recruits about their sexuality, conduct witch hunts of suspected cases of same-sex sexuality, or allow the harassment of those suspected of being lesbigay. Since the various policies have taken effect, however, the percentage of discharges has remained constant, and there have been reports of widespread abuses of the policy.

A number of lesbigay service people have fought the military's ban in the courts, including Leonard Matlovich, Perry Watkins, Margarethe Cammermeyer, Joe Steffan, and Keith Meinhold, with varying degrees of success. Some have also challenged the current policy. Since the lower courts have issued contradictory rulings on the constitutionality of the military's policies, it seems the Supreme Court will ultimately decide the issue.

Sources: Chibbaro, "Debate Over Ban Ignites"; Johnson, "Secretary of Defense Asks for Probe of Policy Abuse" and "Under DOD 'Don't Ask' Policy, Twice as Many Tell"; Keen, "DOD's Evidence in Favor of Gays"; LeVay and Nonas, *City of Children*; Miller, *Out of the Past*.

The Landmark Victory for Same-Sex Marriage in Hawaii and the Resulting Government Backlash

Although a number of cities and the states of Vermont and New York have extended limited health and insurance benefits to the "domestic partners" of municipal employees, no states permit same-sex marriages, and until 1993, it seemed as if such a right was unlikely to be won anytime soon. But in that year, the Hawaii Supreme Court ruled in *Baehr v. Miike*, a lawsuit brought by three same-sex couples who had been denied marriage licenses, that preventing them from marrying constituted gender discrimination and violated the state's guarantee of equal protection under the law. The court issued a preliminary finding that Hawaii had to issue marriage licenses to same-sex couples unless it could show a "compelling" reason not to, and remanded the case back to the trial court to give the Hawaiian government a chance to prove such a compelling need. In 1996, this court ruled that the state did not have just cause, and *Baehr v. Miike* was returned to the Hawaii Supreme Court for final disposition. It is likely that the case will ultimately be decided in favor of the lesbian and gay plaintiffs and, unless opponents can pass a constitutional amendment, Hawaii will set a tremendous precedent in the struggle for equal rights for lesbians, gay men, and bisexuals.

But, in an attempt to minimize the potential impact of the decision, more than half of the state legislatures have enacted laws in the last few years that explicitly ban same-sex couples from marrying in their states and prohibit the recognition of same-sex marriages performed in other states. Similarly, Congress overwhelmingly passed and President Clinton signed the so-called Defense of Marriage Act in 1996, which enabled all states to ignore same-sex marriages that might become legal in other states. The law also limited the federal definition of marriage to a union between one man and one woman. Thus, if Hawaii or another state does legalize same-sex marriage, any same-sex couples choosing to wed would be ineligible for numerous federal benefits that are granted automatically to married other-sex couples, including veterans and Social Security survivor benefits, income tax breaks, and the right to have a foreign-born spouse migrate to the U.S.

Sources: Chibbaro, "House Vote Angers Many Gays"; Keen, "Victory Declared in Hawaii Case."

Lesbigay Images on Television and in the Movies

Throughout much of television and movie history, lesbians and gays have generally been portrayed in one of two ways—when they were represented at all. Either they were a problem or a source of comic relief. Until recently, the media has rarely presented same-sex sexuality as something people accepted without question. And people with same-sex sexual identities were rarely presented as anything other than white and male. If lesbians and gays were seen as a problem, they were sick, sinful, criminals, or oppressed minorities, and needed to be dealt with in some way by society, friends, relatives, or themselves. If they were presented as funny, the humor stemmed from the problem of same-sex sexuality, gender-bending, or gay male characters doling out witty/bitchy lines. In addition, lesbianism has often been presented as exotic and titillating to heterosexual male characters and audiences. The ways in which same-sex sexuality has been seen as a problem or as being funny has changed over time, however, and has clearly been influenced by lesbigay political movements. For example, many post-1960s representations of same-sex sexuality have focused on coming out and straight prejudices and fears of homo-eroticism.

Bisexuality has also usually been viewed as a problem, though in different ways. It has been seen as something that did not "really" exist, a transitional stage to a "true" same-sex sexual identity, situational (such as in prison), inherently promiscuous, the result of an abusive heterosexual relationship (in the case of married women having relationships with other women), or exploitative (such as hustling). Because of this, representations of people with bisexual identities—as opposed to those who are behaviorally bisexual—have been rare. This continues to be the case, even in recent representations produced by lesbians and gays.

Beginning in the early 1980s, Hollywood began to produce more mainstream movies that reflected the influence of lesbigay culture and politics. However, these movies were primarily in the form of gender-bending comedies such as *Victor/Victoria* and problem dramas on coming out or AIDS such as *Philadelphia*. Although representations of lesbigays have been on the silver screen virtually since its inception in the early twentieth century, television has focused on them only since the late 1960s. Lesbigay characters typically appeared only sporadically before the late 1970s; they were guests in episodes of shows in which they were the focus, or they were the subjects of made-for-television movies. Since then, there have been several television series featuring recurring lesbigay characters, including *Soap* and *Dynasty*. However, their sexuality was rarely portrayed as something that was casually accepted. Notable exceptions include the "Francesca" segments on *The Tracy Ullman Show* and the Showtime comedy *Brothers*. The 1990s witnessed a proliferation of shows with recurring lesbigay characters, including *Friends*, *Cybil*, and *Northern Exposure*. In the spring of 1997, ABC's *Ellen* became the first network prime-time show to feature a lesbigay central character.

The changing cultural climate, in which there has been greater acceptance of same-sex sexuality among some segments of society, has played a role in this proliferation of images. Another factor has been the influence of media watchdogs such as GLAAD, the Gay and Lesbian Alliance Against Defamation. GLAAD has served as consultants on various productions and has organized protests against representations it found to be harmful, such as *Basic Instinct*.

Whether on television or in the movies, this increased representation has resulted in somewhat more diverse images. Lesbian and bisexual women have been featured, for example, in the television show *Heartbeat* and the film *Higher Learning*. Lesbigay characters of color have been featured in such shows as *Spin City* and *My So Called Life*, as well as films such as *Get on the Bus* and *Boys on the Side*.

Since the late 1980s, lesbigays have played a greater role in representing themselves on television and in the movies. Lesbigay writers and producers have worked on such shows as *Friends* and *Frasier* and mainstream movies such as *To Wong Foo, Thanks for Everything, Julie Newmar*. They have been limited in how they can represent same-sex sexuality, however. In spite of the much talked about "lesbian kiss" episodes of *L.A. Law* and *Roseanne*, representing same-sex intimacy in mainstream movies and television—especially among men—has generally remained taboo. It has largely been lesbigay independent film producers who have been in the forefront in representing same-sex sexuality as something people take for granted. Films such *as My Beautiful Launderette* and *Go Fish* have explored various aspects of lesbigay life or have featured lesbigay characters even though their sexuality was not a central element of the story. Unfortunately, few of these films have played in mainstream movie theaters. They tend to be shown in theaters and film festivals that specialize in independent cinema.

Sources: Bryant, *Bisexual Characters in Film*; Ehrenstein, "More Than Friends"; Kielwasser, "Lots of Gays in TV Shows, But They Can't Even Hold Hands"; Russo, *The Celluloid Closet*; Weiss, *Vampires and Violets*.

ACKNOWLEDGMENTS

Brett Beemyn would like to thank Warren Blumenfeld, Lani Ka'ahumanu, Amanda Udis-Kessler, and Riki Anne Wilchins for their feedback on entries.

REFERENCES:

Adam, Barry D. *The Rise of a Gay and Lesbian Movement*. Boston: Twayne Publishers, 1987.

Avicolli, Tommi. "Images of Gays in Rock Music," in *Lavender Culture,* edited by Karla Jay and Allen Young. New York: New York University Press, 1994: 182-94.

Bayer, Ronald. *Homosexuality and American Psychiatry: The Politics of Diagnosis*. New York: Basic Books, 1981.

Beam, Joseph. "James Baldwin: Not a Bad Legacy, Brother," in *Brother to Brother: New Writings by Black Gay Men,* edited by Essex Hemphill. Boston: Alyson Publications, 1991: 184-86.

Beemyn, Brett. "A Queer Capital: Lesbian, Gay, and Bisexual Life in Washington, D.C., 1890-1955." Ph.D. diss., University of Iowa, 1997.

Bérubé, Allan. *Coming Out under Fire: The History of Gay Men and Women in World War Two.* New York: Plume, 1990.

Bérubé, Allan and Jeffrey Escoffier. "Queer/Nation," in *OUT/LOOK,* vol. 11, Winter 1991: 12-14.

Blumenfeld, Warren J., and Diane Raymond. *Looking at Gay and Lesbian Life.* Boston: Beacon Press, 1988.

Bornstein, Kate. *Gender Outlaw: On Men, Women and the Rest of Us.* New York: Routledge, 1994.

Bronski, Michael. *Culture Clash: The Making of a Gay Sensibility.* Boston: South End Press, 1984.

———. "It's Not the Flesh, It's the Flowers," in *Gay Community News,* 12-18 August 1990.

Bryant, Wayne M. *Bisexual Characters in Film: From Anaïs to Zee.* Binghamton, New York: Harrington Park Press, 1997.

Bullough, Vern. *Science in the Bedroom: A History of Sex Research.* New York: Basic Books, 1994.

Campbell, James. *Talking at the Gate: A Life of James Baldwin.* New York: Viking, 1991.

Chauncey, George. *Gay New York: Gender, Urban Culture, and the Making of the Gay Male World, 1890-1940.* New York: HarperCollins, 1994.

———. "The Postwar Sex Crime Panic," in *True Stories from the American Past,* edited by William Graebner. New York: McGraw Hill, 1993: 160-78.

Chee, Alexander. "A Queer Nationalism," in *OUT/LOOK,* vol. 11, Winter 1991: 15-19.

Chibbaro, Lou, Jr. "Debate Over Ban Ignites," in *Washington Blade,* 20 November 1992.

———. "House Vote Angers Many Gays: Many Supporters of the Community Vote for Marriage Bill," in *Washington Blade,* 19 July 1996.

Comstock, Gary. *Unrepentant, Self-Affirming, Practicing: Lesbian/Bisexual/Gay People within Organized Religion.* New York: Continuum, 1996.

Cruikshank, Margaret. *The Gay and Lesbian Liberation Movement.* New York: Routledge, 1992.

Cudnik, Doreen. "Two More States Pass Gay Civil Rights Laws," in *Gay People's Chronicle,* 16 May 1997.

de Lauretis, Teresa. "Queer Theory: Lesbian and Gay Sexualities—An Introduction," in *differences,* vol. 3, Summer 1991: iii-xviii.

D'Emilio, John. "The Homosexual Menace: The Politics of Sexuality in Cold War America," in *Passion and Power: Sexuality in History,* edited by Kathy Peiss and Christina Simmons. Philadelphia: Temple University Press, 1989: 226-40.

———. *Making Trouble: Essays on Gay History, Politics, and the University.* New York: Routledge, 1992.

———. *Sexual Politics, Sexual Communities: The Making of a Homosexual Minority in the United States, 1940-1970.* Chicago: University of Chicago Press, 1983.

D'Emilio, John, and Estelle B. Freedman. *Intimate Matters: A History of Sexuality in America.* New York: Harper and Row, 1988.

Donaldson, Stephen. "The Bisexual Movement's Beginnings in the 70s: A Personal Retrospective," in *Bisexual Politics: Theories, Queries, and Visions,* edited by Naomi Tucker. New York: Harrington Park Press, 1995: 31-45.

Drexel, Allen. "Before Paris Burned: Race, Class, and Male Homosexuality on the Chicago South Side, 1935-1960," in *Creating a Place for Ourselves: Lesbian, Gay, and Bisexual Community Histories,* edited by Brett Beemyn. New York: Routledge, 1997: 119-44.

Duberman, Martin. *Stonewall.* New York: Plume, 1993.

Dubin, Steven. *Arresting Images: Impolitic Art and Uncivil Actions.* New York: Routledge, 1992.

Duggan, Lisa, and Nan D. Hunter. *Sex Wars: Sexual Dissent and Political Culture.* New York: Routledge, 1995.

Ehrenstein, David. "More Than Friends," in *Los Angeles Magazine,* May 1996: 60-67+.

Escoffier, Jeffrey. "Inside the Ivory Closet: The Challenges Facing Lesbian and Gay Studies," in *OUT/LOOK,* vol. 3, Fall 1990: 40-48.

Faderman, Lillian. *Odd Girls and Twilight Lovers: A History of Lesbian Life in Twentieth-Century America.* New York: Penguin, 1991.

Feinberg, Leslie. *Stone Butch Blues.* Ithaca, New York: Firebrand Books, 1993.

———. *Transgender Warriors: Making History from Joan of Arc to RuPaul.* Boston: Beacon Press, 1996.

Freedman, Estelle B. "'Uncontrolled Desires': The Response to the Sexual Psychopath 1920-1960," in Peiss and Simmons: 199-225.

Freiberg, Peter. "After 10 Years, ACT UP Now Fights Dwindling Membership: Protest Group Had Remarkable Influence on U.S. AIDS Policy," in *Washington Blade,* 14 March 1997.

———. "Colorado Gays: 'We're Ecstatic, We're Elated,'" in *Washington Blade,* 24 May 1996.

———. "Gays Jubilant About Supreme Court Decision," in *Washington Blade,* 24 May 1996.

Goldberg, Carey. "Shunning 'He' and 'She,' They Fight for Respect," in *New York Times,* 8 September 1996.

Hammonds, Evelynn. "Race, Sex, AIDS: The Construction of 'Other,'" in *Race, Class, and Gender: An Anthology,* edited by Margaret L. Andersen and Patricia Hill Collins. Belmont, California: Wadsworth Publishing, 1992: 329-40.

Highleyman, Liz A. *A Brief History of the Bisexual Movement.* Cambridge, Massachusetts: Bisexual Resource Center, 1993.

Irvine, Janice. *Disorders of Desire: Sex and Gender in Modern American Sexology.* Philadelphia, Pennsylvania: Temple University Press, 1990.

Johnson, Wendy. "Secretary of Defense Asks for Probe of Policy Abuse," in *Washington Blade,* 1 March 1996.

———. "Transgender Activists Focus on the Long Journey Ahead: Job Protections, Hate Crime Protections on the Agenda," in *Washington Blade,* 21 February 1997.

———. "Under DOD 'Don't Ask' Policy, Twice as Many Tell," in *Washington Blade,* 10 May 1996.

Keen, Lisa. "Gays Win in Oregon, But Lose in Colorado," in *Washington Blade,* 6 November 1992.

———. "Hardwick Revisited," in *Washington Blade,* 5 July 1996.

———. "High Court Ruling is 'Revolutionary,'" in *Washington Blade,* 24 May 1996.

———. "High Court's Decision 'Levels the Playing Field,'" in *Washington Blade,* 31 May 1996.

———. "Initiatives in Oregon, Idaho Appear Defeated," in *Washington Blade,* 11 November 1994.

———. "Maine Is Third State to Reject Similar Anti-Gay Ballot Measures," in *Washington Blade,* 10 November 1995.

———. "Victory Declared in Hawaii Case: No Marriages Likely Until Case Is Appealed to State Supreme Court," in *Washington Blade,* 6 December 1996.

Kennedy, Elizabeth Lapovsky, and Madeline D. Davis. *Boots of Leather, Slippers of Gold: The History of a Lesbian Community.* New York: Penguin Books, 1994.

Kielwasser, Al. "Lots of Gays in TV Shows, But They Can't Even Hold Hands," in *Gay People's Chronicle,* 29 August 1997.

Koski, Fran, and Maida Tilchen. "Some Pulp Sappho," in Lavender Culture, edited by Karla Jay and Allen Young. New York: New York University Press, 1994: 262-74.

Lane, Alycee. "Newton's Law," in *BLK,* March 1991: 11-15.

Leonard, Arthur. "The Legal Position of Lesbians and Gay Men in the United States," in *Second ILGA Pink Book,* edited by the Pink Book Editing Team. Utrecht: Interdisciplinary Gay and Lesbian Studies Department, Utrecht University, 1988: 99-108.

LeVay, Simon, and Elisabeth Nonas. *City of Friends: A Portrait of the Gay and Lesbian Community in America.* Cambridge, Massachusetts: MIT Press, 1995.

Marotta, Toby. *The Politics of Homosexuality.* Boston: Houghton Mifflin Company, 1981.

Miller, Neil. *Out of the Past: Gay and Lesbian History from 1869 to the Present.* New York: Vintage Books, 1995.

Nestle, Joan. "Those Who Were Ridiculed the Most Risked the Most," in *Gay Community News,* 11-17 June 1989.

Ochs, Robyn, ed. *The Bisexual Resource Guide.* Second Edition. Cambridge, Massachusetts: Bisexual Resource Center, 1996.

O'Connell, Brian. "AIDS Rate for Blacks Is Six Times that of Whites," in *Washington Blade,* 3 May 1996.

Paoletta, Michael. "The Godfather of House Knuckles Down," in *Out,* June 1994: 62, 64.

Patton, Cindy. *Sex and Germs: The Politics of AIDS.* Boston: South End Press, 1985.

"*Romer v. Evans*: Excerpts from the Majority," in *Washington Blade,* 24 May 1996.

Russo, Vito. *The Celluloid Closet: Homosexuality in the Movies.* Revised Edition. New York: Harper and Row, 1987.

Rutledge, Leigh. *The Gay Decades.* New York: Penguin Books, 1992.

SAMOIS, ed. *Coming to Power: Writings and Graphics on Lesbian S/M.* Boston: Alyson, 1981.

Schmitz, Dawn. "Kowalski and Thompson Win!," in *Gay Community News,* 22 December 1991-4 January 1992.

Scott, Kim. "It Was June, It Was Hot, It Was Different," in *Washington Blade,* 1994 Pride Guide.

Segrest, Mab. "Visibility and Backlash," in *The Question of Equality: Lesbian and Gay Politics in America since Stonewall,* edited by David Deitcher. New York: Scribner, 1995: 84-122.

Serlin, David Harley. "Christine Jorgensen and the Cold War Closet," in *Radical History Review,* vol. 62, Spring 1995: 136-65.

Shilts, Randy. *The Mayor of Castro Street: The Life and Times of Harvey Milk.* New York: St. Martin's Press, 1982.

Smith, Barbara. "We Must Always Bury Our Dead Twice," in *Black/Out,* vol. 2, no. 1, Fall 1988: 40, 42-43, 45.

Stein, Arlene. "Androgyny Goes Pop: But Is It Lesbian Music?," in *Sisters, Sexperts, Queers: Beyond the Lesbian Nation,* edited by Arlene Stein. New York: Plume, 1993: 96-109.

Stoesen, Lyn. "A Decade of Rage and Remembrance: The NAMES Project AIDS Memorial Quilt Is Now the Size of 29 Football Fields, But Its Power Remains in Each of the Panels," in *Washington Blade,* 11 October 1996.

Thomas, Anthony. "The House the Kids Built," in *Out/Look,* vol. 5, Summer 1989: 24-33.

Thompson, Karen, and Julie Andrzejewski. *Why Can't Sharon Kowalski Come Home?* San Francisco: Spinsters/Aunt Lute, 1988.

Thompson, Mark, ed. *Long Road to Freedom: The Advocate History of the Gay and Lesbian Movement.* New York: St. Martin's Press, 1994.

Tinney, James. "Why a Black Gay Church?," in *In the Life: A Black Gay Anthology,* edited by Joseph Beam. Boston: Alyson, 1986: 70-86.

Udis-Kessler, Amanda. "Identity/Politics: Historical Sources of the Bisexual Movement," in *Queer Studies: A Lesbian, Gay, Bisexual, and Transgender Anthology,* edited by Brett Beemyn and Mickey Eliason. New York: New York University Press, 1996: 52-63.

Vaid, Urvashi. *Virtual Equality: The Mainstreaming of Gay and Lesbian Liberation.* New York: Anchor Books, 1995.

Vance, Carole S., ed. *Pleasure and Danger: Exploring Female Sexuality.* Boston: Routledge and Kegan Paul, 1984.

Weatherby, W. J. *James Baldwin: Artist on Fire.* New York: Dell, 1989.

Weiss, Andrea. *Vampires and Violets: Lesbians in Film.* New York: Penguin Books, 1993.

Witt, Lynn, Sherry Thomas, and Eric Marcus, eds. *Out In All Directions: The Almanac of Gay and Lesbian America.* New York: Warner Books, 1995.

Zeh, John. "Mapplethorpe Trial Ends in Acquittal," in *Gay Community News,* 14-20 October 1990.

—Brett Beemyn and Gregory Conerly

2

Organizations

Considering that the lesbian and gay movement in the United States has fought so assiduously to disrupt the homophobic nomination of gay men and lesbians as "unnatural," and by extension has found the very logic of the natural to be a corrupt strategy that is antithetical to progressive politics, it is with a sense of risk that I suggest that perhaps nothing seems more natural to those active in Lesbian, Bisexual, Gay, Transgender (LBGT) organizing and organizations than the genre of the list. Lists of voters, lists of enemies, lists of drag kings who will "man" the Pride parade booth, lists of people who have died from AIDS related complexes, lists of people who have volunteered the 10 p.m. to 2 a.m. shift to wheat paste the city with newly printed posters, Leigh Rutledge's *The Gay Book of Lists*—all are examples of the profusion of lists within LBGT organizing. But the list of LBGT organizations that is contained in this chapter is a slightly new phenomenon. Certainly, multiple lists of lesbian and gay organizations have been written in the past—the North American Conference of Homophile Organizations (NACHO), founded in 1966, is only one example of early listing activities and documentation of gay and lesbian organizations throughout the U.S.—and this present list of LBGT organizations, in a way, follows in that tradition. But not until recently, about the last decade, have lists of LBGT organizations become available for mass consumption. And never before has the compilation of a complete list of organizations been such a complete impossibility.

While a list, a survey of LBGT organizations in the U.S. offers a kind of tangible and definitive affirmation of the historical longevity and sheer intensification of coordination efforts within the scene of the U.S. gay rights movement, it can offer only an imperfect and limited sketch of the lineaments of the constitution and distribution of lesbian, bisexual, gay, transgendered, and otherwise queer people in the U.S. Any examination of the LBGT movement will necessarily privilege some objects of knowledge over others, and a survey of LBGT organizations is no different in this respect—at best, it can produce a robust, but always incomplete and partial, view of the profusion of LBGT culture and

will probably, and ironically, produce more exclusions than inclusions. The documentation of every single LBGT group in the U.S., for example, is something of an impossibility, at least right now, given the fact that much of the information about older, non-dominant organizations lies in archives, attics, and probably even old FBI files as well as the fact that new organizations are constantly constituted, reconstituted, and terminated on a daily basis. A serious and near exhaustive account of LBGT organizations in the U.S. could easily consume the entirety of this almanac. The June 1996 edition of the *New York Metropolitan Area Lesbian and Gay Directory of Services and Resources*, for example, contains alone more than 500 listings of current organizations and service groups ranging from Wall Street lunch clubs to ACT UP. While the concentration of LBGT organizations will be higher in metropolitan centers, the more than 500 listings represent probably only a slight fraction of the true scene of organizing and activism in the New York area and an even more infinitesimal fraction of the organizational work on both coasts—the loci usually privileged by LBGT history—as well as across the interior of the U.S., Hawaii, Alaska, and Puerto Rico.

The explosion of recognizable groups—that is, groups institutionalized with names, phone numbers, addresses, tax ID numbers, etc.—is complemented and complicated by the fact that multitudes of affinity groups and coalitions have been, and increasingly in the last decade, are, integral to LBGT organizing. Writing specifically about the tactics of the AIDS activist group ACT UP, Douglas Crimp and Adam Rolston explain, "A tradition of Left organizing, affinity groups are small associations of people within activist movements whose mutual trust and shared interests allow them to function autonomously and secretly, arrive at quick decisions by consensus, protect one another at demonstrations, and participate as units in coordinated acts of civil disobedience" (Crimp and Rolston, p. 20). Similarly, Judith Butler points out that an open coalition "will affirm identities that are alternately instituted and relinquished according to the purpose at hand; it will be an open assemblage that permits of multiple convergences and divergences without obedience to a normative telos of definitional closure" (Butler, p. 16). Affinity groups and coalitions, sometimes operating under the aegis of larger organizations such as ACT UP and sometimes operating independently of any other groups, account for an enormous and certainly under-remarked volume of the work of activism and organizing.

To give one example, which is not listed in this almanac, Queer Cosmos, a loose assemblage of white, queer activists in Boulder, Colorado, was created in May 1990 when a few people on the Boulder National Coming Out Day Committee heard about the formation of a new group called Queer Nation in New York. As co-founder Jim Davis-Rosenthal recounts, "We were troubled by the notion of a nation, and since Boulder's claims have always extended to the Cosmos, we wouldn't be satisfied with anything less than the cosmic" (e-mail correspondence 7 April 1998). So Queer Cosmos was founded; its logo was, "If you were queer, you'd be homo by now." The core group of activists within Queer Cosmos that had long been active in Boulder queer politics—Kat Morgan, Christopher DeWinter, Rob Glovier, Sue Larson, and Jim Davis-Rosenthal—began fabricating multiple new organizations to feign the appearance of an enormous, politically mobilized LBGT constituency in Boulder. Certainly a proportion of Boulder gays were in fact politically active and many others actually participated in Queer Cosmos organizing, but Queer Cosmos' strategic production of multiple events—protests against schools, churches, businesses, Bill McCartney (Colorado University-Boulder's football coach and founder of the religious right men's group Promise Keepers), in short, protests against any organization or person who had uttered a homophobic remark or had a discriminatory policy—suggested the presence of an adamantly radical LBGT population that was taking over Boulder in the early part of the 1990s. In fact, the Left response to the Gulf War in Boulder was largely orchestrated by Queer Cosmos which, through its "Dykes and Fags Against Body Bags" campaign, organized a demonstration in front of the city's army recruitment facility. The demonstration, led by drag queens, culminated in a march that shut down Boulder's streets for several hours.

"The organization was completely ad hoc and only met when necessary to put on an action or an activity," remarks Davis-Rosenthal. "We were mostly anarchists in philosophy, so the idea was to provide a minimal structure to create the most visibility. We were pretty successful at doing that and a lot of the visibility we created helped other movements and organizations to form." Of course, the political mobilization of LBGT people in Boulder in the late 1980s and early 1990s cannot be entirely encapsulated in a history of Queer Cosmos—Queer Cosmos was just one of the organizations doing LBGT political work in Boulder at the time—but the example of Queer Cosmos does indicate the challenges within the project of understanding the production of LBGT organizations. Queer Cosmos was an ad hoc coalition very different in form and purpose from, for example, the Human Rights Campaign (HRC), the country's largest gay and lesbian organization. But Queer Cosmos, lacking HRC's 200,000-plus membership, hefty budget and placement in Washington, D.C., has done very significant work that has probably benefited HRC. In the narrativizing of the history of LBGT organizations, it is generally, however, HRC and other larger groups that—because of their pure size, or because of a coast-focused inclination to examine LBGT organizing efforts primarily in the metropolitan centers of California, New York, and Washington, D.C.—get documented within LBGT histories.

The challenge for those working on the history of LBGT organizations as well as for those doing LBGT activism and organizing in the future will be to research the diversity of not only smaller regional organizational elaborations that get eclipsed in LBGT organization histories but also the collaborative, coalitional efforts that seek to provisionally ally LBGT organizations with other social justice movements and organizations. Queer Cosmos is only one organization among many throughout the U.S. whose history is not widely known. LBGT organizations without access to dominant gay and lesbian culture, with its historical predilection for whiteness, and until very recently its marginalization of bisexual

and transgendered people, still remain largely hidden within the perimeters of historical accounts. Much activism and research currently being pursued by historically marginalized groups—African Americans, Asian Americans, Latinos/as, immigrants, bisexuals, and transgendered people—is increasingly, if slowly, changing the current picture of LBGT organizational efforts in the U.S. At its best, this chapter offers an incredibly blurry snapshot of LBGT organizations from 1924 to the present, giving brief synopses of dominant organizations that, because of their size or political or media impact, have effected substantial changes in LBGT communities and self-determination. It is not a synthetic history, but seeks to offer the reader a few of the major touchstones with an emphasis on contemporary organizations. Nor is it an account of all LBGT organizational efforts. The lack of recognizable organizations in the 1920s, 1930s, and 1940s, for example, should not necessarily be read as a sign that no LBGT organizational efforts were occurring. The discursive formation of LBGT identities and politics took place, although in a less distinguishable manner, in the cultural productions of the Harlem Renaissance, in the publications of Radclyffe Hall's *The Well of Loneliness* and Djuna Barnes's *Nightwood,* and, as Lillian Faderman has documented, in the formation of lesbian military communities during World War II, to name just a few instances of early lesbian and gay organizing that does not proceed under the banner of particular organizations.

Readers interested in more synthetic historical accounts of U.S. LBGT organizations are referred to the bibliography of this chapter. For accounts of early organizations, see in particular Jonathan Ned Katz's *Gay American History: Lesbians and Gay Men in the U.S.A.* and John D'Emilio's indispensable and seminal *Sexual Politics, Sexual Communities: The Making of a Homosexual Minority in the United States, 1940-1970.* Martin Duberman's *Stonewall* is an excellent starting point for researching 1960s efforts, and Eric Marcus's *Making History: The Struggle for Gay and Lesbian Equal Rights, 1945-1990* chronicles the oral histories of some of the key figures within the history of LBGT organizations and activism. This present listing, unlike most of those that have preceded it, has benefited enormously from the invention of the World Wide Web. While web sites are certainly not replacements for libraries and are useful only to the extent that people with access to on-line computers can access those web sites, the internet has enabled organizations not only to disseminate their materials more efficiently but also to document their work and histories in the present tense. All non-cited references are derived from organizations' web sites, the addresses of which are listed in the headers of each listing.

EARLY ORGANIZATIONS

Society for Human Rights
Founded: 1924
Founder: Henry Gerber

While the Mattachine Society and the Daughters of Bilitis are generally credited as the first homosexual emancipation organizations in the U.S., the first organization was actually the Society for Human Rights (SHR), conceived of by Henry Gerber, an American soldier who, while in Germany during World War I, discovered the homosexual emancipation movement of German sexologist Magnus Hirschfeld (Duberman, 1993, p. 76). Naming the organization after the largest gay German group, Bund für

Menschenrecht (Katz, p. 336), Gerber, along with Rev. John T. Graves and Al Meininger and four other friends, founded the Society for Human Rights on 10 December 1924, in Chicago with the following charter declaration:

> To promote and to protect the interests of people who by reasons of mental and physical abnormalties [sic] are abused and hindered in the legal pursuit of happiness which is guaranteed them by the Declaration of Independence, and to combat the public prejudices against them by dissemination of facts according to modern science among intellectuals of mature age. The Society stands only for law and order; it is in harmony with any and all general laws insofar as they protect the rights of others, and does in no manner recommend any acts in violation of present laws nor advocate any matter inimical to the public welfare (Katz, p. 385).

Directing its energies at laws criminalizing homosexual acts in Illinois and narrowing its purview by excluding bisexuals, despite the fact that Al Meininger, unbeknown to the others, was in fact a bisexual with a wife and two children, SHR managed to produce two issues of its publication, *Friendship and Freedom*, the first homosexual liberation magazine in the U.S., before all three men were arrested in 1925 without warrants. The *Examiner* reported in its article, "Strange Sex Cult Exposed," that Meininger had committed "strange sex acts" with other men and that police had found a pamphlet in Meininger's house that "urged men to leave their wives and children." Although Gerber's case was eventually dismissed, Gerber was discharged from his job at the post office for "conduct unbecoming a postal worker." According to Gerber, "That definitely meant the end of the Society for Human Rights" (Katz, pp. 391-93).

While the Society for Human Rights experienced some success with organizing homosexual men in 1924, its rapid termination one year later in 1925 underscored and dramatized the very real dangers of activism that was explicitly organized. That homophile activism in the U.S. did not take recognizable form in the guise of major organizations with names attached to them again until 1950 with the appearance of the Mattachine Society suggests not so much that LBGT people did not engage in activist work around homosexual issues between 1925 and 1950 as it punctuates the reality that to call attention to oneself as homosexual during this period was tantamount to an invitation of criminal persecution. Gerber, writing a historic account of SHR in a 1962 edition of *One*, 37 years after SHR's end, suggested that homosexuals themselves were at fault for the failure of homosexuals to organize themselves coherently:

> What was needed was a Society, I concluded.... The first difficulty was in rounding up enough members and contributors so the work could go forward. The average homosexual, I found, was ignorant concerning himself. Others were fearful. Still others were frantic or depraved. Some were blasé. Many homosexuals told me that their search for forbidden fruit was the real spice of life. With this argument they rejected our aims. We wondered how we could accomplish anything with such resistance from our own people (Katz, p. 388).

Fear, depravity, and the spice of forbidden fruit—in short, those things that make the organization of a coherent

and mutually intelligible community extremely difficult. Gerber's prescient words cannot help but point to the way in which the divisions that seem to tear apart "the gay community" today are not necessarily exceptional problems but constitutive of the process of organizing people of different backgrounds and experiences under the rubric of homosexuality. While the Mattachine Society and the Daughters of Bilitis had their own particular organizational problems, Gerber's difficulties were certainly not unrecognizable as these two organizations continued the work of homophile emancipation.

The Mattachine Society
Founded: 1951
Founder: Harry Hay

Although the Mattachine Society was officially founded in April 1951 in Los Angeles with its Statement of Mission and Purposes, the idea of forming a society that would organize itself around the issue of homosexuality came three years earlier at a beer bust at the University of Southern California. At this all-gay gathering, Harry Hay, a music teacher at the People's Education Center and long-time Communist party member, began discussing the presidential campaign of Henry Wallace of the Progressive party with the others (D'Emilio, p. 60). According to an interview, Hay remembers, "I came up with the idea that we should start a group called 'Bachelors for Wallace.' With the help of a couple of quarts of beer, we worked up quite a case for what the Bachelors for Wallace would do, what we would ask for—constitutional amendments, etc. It sounded like a great idea" (Katz, p. 408). Eager to begin the organizational work the next day after the party, Hay called the men with whom he had discussed the idea, but as Hay recalls, "I found out that the only one who remembered anything except his hangover was me." Not dissuaded by this collective failure of homosexual men's memory, Hay pressed on and began collecting "influential people, like ministers and sympathetic sociologists, and psychologists to condone it, to sponsor it." Realizing that the anti-Communist witch hunts as well as the House Un-American Activities Committee were taking aim at subversive elements within the U.S., Hay remarks: "It was obvious McCarthy was setting up the pattern for a new scapegoat, and it was going to be us—Gays. We had to organize, we had to move, we had to get started."

By July 1950, Hay had written up three versions of a prospectus, the last one for a group called the "International Bachelors Fraternal Orders for Peace and Social Dignity sometimes referred to as Bachelors Anonymous," which described itself as "a service and welfare organization devoted to the protection and improvement of Society's Androgynous Minority" (Katz, p. 409). Working "in the spirit ... of the United Nations Charter, for the full-class citizen participation of Minorities everywhere, including ourselves," the organization dedicated itself to the "enlightened ... ethics of the standard community" and outlined a project "to understand ourselves and then demonstrate this knowledge to the community" and "to regulate the social conduct [such as "the violation of public decency"] of our minority" (Katz, p. 410). The 1950 prospectus outlines the following guiding mission:

We, the androgynes of the world, have formed this responsible corporate body to demonstrate by our efforts that our physiological and psychological handicaps need be no deterrent in integrating 10 percent of the world's population towards the constructive social progress of mankind (Katz, p. 410).

While Hay's idealist vision of a homosexual community as a minority was certainly radical, his commitment to regulating that minority and enrolling the psychological establishment to sanction the community mark the rudimentary beginnings of a shift within an organization, initially Marxist in principal, that would become more assimilationist by 1953.

It was not until 1951—after Hay had in August 1950 given Bob Hull, a gay man in Hay's Labor School music theory class, an envelope with a copy of his prospectus enclosed, and Hull had subsequently introduced Chuck Rowland and Dale Jennings to Hay—that the Mattachine Society was born. They took their name from the medieval Société Mattachine, a secret fraternity of men who never appeared unmasked. As Hay recalls, "we felt that we 1950s Gays were also a masked people, unknown and anonymous" (Katz, p. 413). They soon initiated a series of semi-public discussions to which only chosen friends, overwhelmingly male, were invited to discuss topics such as "Sense of Value" and "Social Directions of the Homosexual." In April, they drafted their statement of "Mission and Purposes" in which they outlined three purposes: "to unify" homosexuals "isolated from their own kind"; "to educate" both homosexuals and heterosexuals by developing an "ethical homosexual culture ... paralleling the emerging cultures of our fellow-minorities—the Negro, Mexican, and Jewish Peoples"; and "to lead." Accordingly, the "more ... socially conscious homosexuals [are to] provide leadership to the whole mass of social deviates" (Katz, p. 412). What developed was a complex and secretive guild system that was responsible for leading multiple discussion groups and attending to political action (D'Emilio, pp. 69-70). Feeling more of a commitment to Mattachine, Hay revealed his activities to the Communist party, suggesting that they expel him. "They rejected 'expulsion,'" recalls Hay, "and, in honor of my eighteen years as a teacher and cultural innovator dropped me as 'a security risk but [recognized me] as a lifelong friend of the people'"(Katz, p. 413).

When Mattachine member Dale Jennings was arrested in a Los Angeles park and charged with lewd and dissolute behavior in 1952, Mattachine's ad hoc Citizens Committee to Outlaw Entrapment mobilized the previously unorganized gay community to respond to Jennings's entrapment by a plainclothes officer. "Mattachine's membership distributed the leaflets, probably the first in America to raise the homosexual issue, in areas frequented by homosexuals—at gay beaches in Santa Monica and bars in Los Angeles, in restrooms known to be cruised by gay men, and at park benches and bus stops in homosexual areas of the city" (D'Emilio, p. 70). Although Jennings admitted his homosexuality, the charges were eventually dropped. This mobilization generated not only financial contributions to cover the costs of Jennings's trial which helped generate an early legal victory for the homophile movement and which served as a catalyst that helped to rapidly increase Mattachine's membership. By 1953, Mattachine groups had formed throughout southern California and Berkeley, with membership reaching 2,000 and nearly 100 discussion groups by May (D'Emilio, p. 71). Wanting to use its increased visibility productively, the Mattachine Society incorporated in the summer of 1952

as a not-for-profit educational organization whose professional status would, it was hoped, appeal to the psychological establishment and public officials (D'Emilio, p. 73).

Although the Mattachine Society was committed to appealing to heterosexuals through professional organizations in its initial years, its argument that homosexuals were a distinct minority and were therefore patently different from heterosexuals, as well as the fact that its founders had had long associations with the Communist party, made the Mattachine Society in fact quite radical. Certainly, it was too radical to its growing and perhaps more conservative membership, which, in the height of McCarthyism in 1953 and the activities of the House Un-American Activities Committee, found Mattachine's emergence out of Communist ideals decidedly perilous. In a series of conventions in the early part of 1953, a core group of Mattachine members—Kenneth Burns, Hal Call, and Marilyn Rieger—opposed Hay and Rowland and articulated a political program antithetical to that of its founders (D'Emilio, pp. 75-79). If the initial Mattachine was invested in a minoritizing view based on a radical idealism, what Hay later referred to as "a great transcendent dream of what being Gay was all about" (Katz, p. 419), the new Mattachine that emerged in 1953 held the belief that, as Rieger put it: "We know we are the same, no different than anyone else. Our only difference is an unimportant one to the heterosexual society, *unless we make it important*" (D'Emilio, p. 79). By August, Rowland's call for an "ethical homosexual culture" had become completely eclipsed by an assimilationist stance perhaps best articulated by the Los Angeles group's statement: "Homosexuals are not seeking to overthrow or destroy any of society's existing institutions, laws or mores, but to be assimilated as constructive, valuable, and responsible citizens" (D'Emilio, p. 84). Working with "persons, institutions, and organizations which commanded the highest possible public respect," the new Mattachine went so far as to disassociate itself from homosexuality per se, but with the notable consequence that membership dropped dramatically (D'Emilio, p. 85).

With the publication of its new magazine, the *Mattachine Review*, in 1955, its founding of its national headquarters in 1956, and establishment of small chapters in New York, Chicago, Boston, Denver, Philadelphia, Detroit, and Washington, D.C., Mattachine's membership began to grow again after 1955 (D'Emilio, pp. 89, 115). In 1959, Mattachine held its sixth annual convention, its first convention outside of California, in Denver and received excellent media coverage in the *Denver Post* (D'Emilio, pp. 119-21). And by 1960, the *Mattachine Review* had a monthly circulation of about 2,200, small in comparison to the more radical *ONE Magazine*'s monthly circulation of 5,000 (D'Emilio, p. 110). But by 1960, Mattachine's membership had also dropped down again to a low 230 (D'Emilio, p. 115). Mattachine's national structure was eventually dissolved in 1961, and by 1964, the *Review*, a monthly publication, saw only sporadic printings that contained more reprints of old stories and fewer news stories (D'Emilio, p. 185). Although the 1960s saw the dissolution of the Mattachine Society, it was Frank Kameny, founder of its Washington, D.C. chapter in 1961, who, according to Barbara Gittings—founder of the New York Daughters of Bilitis chapter—"articulated a complete, coherent philosophy of the Gay movement" with his controversial insistence that homosexuality was not a sickness (Katz, p. 427). As D'Emilio observes, the Mattachine Society did its work under excruciatingly difficult social constraints, including police harassment and job discrimination:

Fear, along with a lack of confidence in their own ability to speak with authority about homosexuality, [also] created a crippling dependency. In their search for allies and their quest for legitimacy in the eyes of the establishment, movement leaders often bowed to an apparently superior professional wisdom that was part of the problem they needed to confront.... [T]he movement took upon itself an impossible burden—appearing to a society that defined homosexuality as beyond respectability (D'Emilio, p. 125).

ONE, Incorporated. *See* **Libraries, Archives, and Educational Organizations.**

The Daughters of Bilitis
Founded: 1955
Founders: Del Martin and Phyllis Lyon

In many ways following in the tradition set out by Hay's Mattachine Society, the Daughters of Bilitis (DOB), recognized

as the first lesbian organization in the U.S., defined itself as "A Woman's Organization for the Purpose of Promoting the Integration of the Homosexual into Society." Despite the fact that it was an organization created by and for lesbians, nowhere does the word "lesbian" appear in its statement of purpose, which looks remarkably similar to that of the Mattachine Society. According to the statement, DOB had four purposes, "Education of the variant ... to enable her to understand herself and make her adjustment to society"; "education of the public"; "participation in research projects by duly authorized and responsible psychologists, sociologists, and other such experts directed towards further knowledge of the homosexual"; and finally, "investigation of the penal code as it pertains to the homosexual ... proposal of changes ... and promotion of these changes through the due process of law in the state legislature" (Katz, p. 426). Clearly, the missions of Mattachine and DOB converged, but Mattachine remained an overwhelmingly male establishment with a few token lesbians holding leadership positions within the organization, a situation that reflected not only the profound marginalization of lesbians within the emerging homophile movement but also the general invisibility of lesbians in American society in the 1950s.

The Daughters of Bilitis was formed when Del Martin, a San Francisco woman divorced from her husband, moved to Seattle in 1949 and met Phyllis Lyon, a co-worker whom Martin believed

Del Martin and Phyllis Lyon (l-r), founders of The Daughters of Bilitis.

to be heterosexual. By 1953, they were lovers and had moved back to San Francisco, where they both found the gay bar scene less than desirable. Meeting together with three other lesbian couples on 21 September 1955, the eight women formed what was initially a social group, the Daughters of Bilitis, the name derived from Pierre Louÿs' erotic poem "Songs of Bilitis." Deciding to incorporate education into DOB's mission, which caused the blue-collar lesbians in the group to leave DOB and form their own social group, DOB members began in 1956 attending ONE's educational seminars and promoting their own discussions. A small group of roughly 12 women, they published 200 copies of the first edition of *The Ladder*, the group's magazine, in October 1956 (D'Emilio, pp. 101-03). Although its circulation was small, *The Ladder* indicated DOB's commitment to serving specifically lesbian needs to which neither ONE nor Mattachine were attending. *The Ladder*, remarked editor Helen Sanders, "was never meant to be a political journal" and included much poetry, fiction, history, and biography (D'Emilio, p. 104). But despite DOB's focus on lesbianism, many lesbians did not join. "Class prejudice also compromised DOB's ability to attract larger numbers of lesbians. The founders and leaders of DOB were for the most part white collar semiprofessionals disenchanted with a bar subculture, whose population included many women who labored in factories and appeared butch in dress and behavior." *The Ladder* also suggested to its members that "their attire should be that which society will accept" (D'Emilio, p. 106).

Establishing chapters in New York, Los Angeles, Chicago, and Rhode Island, DOB grew very slowly in the 1950s, and by 1960, DOB's membership stood at 110, about one half that of Mattachine in the same period (D'Emilio, p. 115). During the 1950 and 1960s, ONE, Mattachine, and DOB all held ongoing dialogues in their magazines and conferences in which DOB was constantly scrutinized. Dorr Legg, editor of *ONE Magazine*, for example, remarked in 1961 that all lesbians were "brainwashed" (D'Emilio, p. 123). DOB was also always quick to—rightfully—scrutinize Mattachine and ONE for their consummate and continuing failure to address lesbianism. At Mattachine's 1959 conference in Denver, Del Martin castigated her fellow homophile groups:

> At every one of these conventions I attend, year after year, I find I must defend the Daughters of Bilitis as a separate and distinct women's organization. First of all, what do you men know about Lesbians? In all of your programs and your "[Mattachine] Review," you speak of the male homosexual and follow this with—oh, yes, and incidentally there are some female homosexuals, too, and because they are homosexual all this should apply to them as well. *ONE [Magazine]* has done little better. For years they have relegated the Lesbian interest to the column called "Feminine Viewpoint." So it would appear to me that quite obviously neither organization has recognized the fact that Lesbians are *women* and that this twentieth century is the era of emancipation of women. Lesbians are not satisfied to be auxiliary members or second-class homosexuals. So if you people do with to put DOB out of business, you are going to have to learn something about the Lesbian, and today I'd like to give you your first lesson (Katz, p. 431).

DOB was clearly an intransigent presence within the homophile movement, constantly critiquing Mattachine and ONE for their

androcentrism, but DOB did successfully work in coalition with Mattachine in the 1960s to attack organized religion through the newly formed Council on Religion and the Homosexual (Faderman, pp. 192-93).

Even so, with the rise of militancy during the 1960s, DOB, in its traditional assimilationist stance, found itself unable to sustain the shock of direct action activism and effectively appeared conservative in the face of a decade whose activists favored confrontation over appearing respectable and appealing to heterosexual society for their acceptance. The orientation of DOB's leadership did, however, begin to shift—Del Martin involved herself in feminist politics, writing in 1967 in *The Ladder*, "The Lesbian is first of all a *woman*.... It is time that the Daughters of Bilitis and the Lesbian find and establish a much broader identification than that of the homosexual community or homophile movement" (D'Emilio, p. 228). Barbara Gittings, founder and president of the New York DOB chapter, dared to place the word "Lesbian" on the cover of *The Ladder* for the first time in January 1964, and Rita Laporte, DOB women's liberationist, remarked, "As I see it, when you've accomplished your aims in the homophile movement, you can proudly point to the fact that now lesbians have *full* second class citizenship, along with all women. That's nowhere near enough for me" (D'Emilio, p. 229). Del Martin shifted her energies away from the homophile movement in order to join NOW (National Organization for Women) in 1967, and Gittings and Laporte, as D'Emilio puts it, "transformed [*The Ladder*] into a publication that blazed a distinctly lesbian-feminist trail." Longtime DOB members felt women's liberation was an assault on the lesbian homophile movement. "The women's lib movement was coming very much to the fore [with] a whole new bunch of people who were talking a language that we didn't understand.... DOB was dying. It took from 1968 to 1970 to pound the nails into the coffin" (D'Emilio, pp. 229-30).

East Coast Homophile Organizations
Founded: 1963

A type of crossover organization between earlier homophile groups and the new activism of the 1960s, East Coast Homophile Organizations (ECHO) formed in January 1963 when four organizations—Daughters of Bilitis, New York Mattachine Society, Janus Society of Philadelphia, and Washington Mattachine Society—converged on Philadelphia to "explore ways of closer intergroup cooperation" (D'Emilio, p. 161). One of their more significant achievements, protesting the Cuban government's confinement of homosexuals in labor camps, produced a shift in homophile political strategies that placed ECHO-affiliated members not in a conference hall listening to medical professionals speak about homosexuals but on picket lines at the Civil Service Commission building, the State Department, the Pentagon, the White House, and Independence Hall in Philadelphia. The picket lines were very small, with anywhere from 7 to 45 picketers in comparison to the enormous Students for a Democratic Society antiwar demonstrations, but as D'Emilio notes: "Picketing implicitly involved an open avowal of one's homosexuality, and though many might applaud it, few were prepared to risk the possible consequences of a public stand. That some did, however, signaled a change and provided a model for others to emulate" (D'Emilio, p. 165).

ECHO's decision to picket, for example, led to DOB's resignation from ECHO, suggesting the beginnings of a shift that would witness the functional end of the homophile movement committed to assimilationist political strategies.

Society for Individual Rights. *See* **Community Centers.**

North American Conference of Homophile Organizations
Founded: 1966

Formed in August 1966 at a meeting in Kansas City that brought together representatives of 15 organizations on both coasts, North American Conference of Homophile Organizations (NACHO, pronounced NAY-ko) represents—in the hope of some of its more radical, East Coast constituents—the first attempt of the gay movement to create a national body that would serve as the voice of a militant, unified homophile movement. At the meeting, Frank Kameny brazenly argued: "Homophile organizations must be radical....We must demand the right to cruise, the right to work, the right to public accommodations, and the other rights the homosexual lacks," and he encouraged those present to adopt the strategies of the black civil rights movement. Although a national body per se was not formed at the meeting, NACHO did serve as the venue for homophile groups to convene annually to discuss the movement's issues. NACHO also created a national legal fund, sponsored several protests, and produced studies examining the relationship of homosexuals to the law. At the 1968 Chicago conference, participants adopted the slogan "gay is good," a radical departure from the conciliatory and deferential attitude taken by the homophile movement to the medical establishment in years past (D'Emilio, pp. 197-99).

Yet, for all of its radical potential, NACHO's "assimilationist civil rights goals," Duberman argues, "seemed old-fashioned" and NACHO itself seemed to younger gays and lesbians "hopelessly bourgeois." As he points out:

A fair percentage of the radical young who were gay or lesbian had not yet come to terms with their own sexuality. Some of them steered clear of NACHO not—or not simply—because of its centrist political views, but because they felt unready and threatened in the one area where NACHO did take a radical stance: namely, in its insistence that homosexuality was neither abnormal nor natural. Here was irony aplenty. The members of NACHO, centrist in all else, were raising one radical standard under which the nonconforming young did not dare to rally (Duberman, 1993, pp. 170-71).

Radical, not radical at all, too radical—NACHO has been understood as occupying all of these degrees of radicality, sometimes simultaneously. While the present debates about the radical and assimilationist politics of contemporary LBGT national bodies such as the Human Rights Campaign and the National Gay and Lesbian Task Force are perhaps much more complicated than these earlier debates, it is clear, at least, that charges of assimilation and unnecessary militancy have been and continue to be constitutive of the production and form of LBGT organizations within the U.S.

Student Homophile League. *See* **Student Organizations.**

Metropolitan Community Church. *See* **Religious Organizations.**

CONTEMPORARY POLITICAL/LEGAL/ACTIVIST ORGANIZATIONS

National Gay and Lesbian Task Force
2320 17th Street NW
Washington, D.C. 20009-2702
ED: Kerry Lobel
Founded: 1973
http://www.ngltf.org
ngltf@ngltf.org
p: 202-332-6483
f: 202-332-0207

The same year that witnessed the Supreme Court's landmark decision in *Roe v. Wade*, guaranteeing a woman's constitutional right to an abortion, the formation of the nascent Lambda Legal Defense Fund, and the beginning of Joan Nestle and Deborah Edel's Lesbian Herstory Archives, also witnessed the formation of the National Gay Task Force by activists Dr. Howard Brown, Martin Duberman, Barbara Gittings, Ron Gold, Frank Kameny, Nathalie Rockhill, and Bruce Voeller. Later renamed the National Gay *and Lesbian* Task Force, NGLTF has been at the forefront of demonstrating its commitment to widening the boundaries of inclusion within the gay community, actively including lesbians and, more recently, transgendered people in its mission statement. According to the *Washington Blade* (12 December 1997, p. 27), NGLTF remains, with the exception of the National Latino/a Lesbian & Gay Organization (LLEGO) and the National Black Lesbian and Gay Leadership Forum (NBLGLF), the only major national gay organization to include transgendered people in its mission statement, a move seen by some as potentially politically dangerous. In a time of slow but steady mainstreaming of gay and lesbian politics—a process seemingly obsessed with presenting palatable images to something called "the general public" and based on the belief that transgendered people do not substantively constitute part of the gay community—NGLTF's inclusive support of transgendered people is a move that actively interrogates the foundational presuppositions from which gay politics charts its future.

Among its successes, NGLTF can be credited with being the first gay group to secure a meeting in the White House, doing so in 1977. While Jimmy Carter was notably absent, NGLTF's meeting with Carter's presidential staff was a national media event (Marcus, pp. 269-71). NGLTF was also integral in persuading the American Psychiatric Association to declassify homosexuality as a mental disorder in 1973. Securing offices in Washington in 1986, NGLTF became the nation's leading gay rights organization, working simultaneously on multiple fronts, everywhere and anywhere it was needed. While the early 1990s was perhaps the nadir of this organization, with the executive director's office door seeming like a revolving door, NGLTF has since regrouped under the leadership of former and present executive directors Melinda Paras and Kerry Lobel. Poised to celebrate its eleventh annual Creating Change conference in 1998, arguably the largest LBGT activist conference in the country, featuring speakers, workshops, and panel discussions, NGLTF now serves as a conduit between national and grassroots politics, offering pragmatic organizational training and advice to activists and organizers working at the local level.

NGLTF's formidable commitment to get LBGT people talking to one another can be seen in its recent inception of a roundtable series, one bringing together the executive directors of all the country's major, national gay organizations. In 1997, NGLTF also created the Federation of Statewide Gay, Lesbian, Bisexual, and Transgendered Political Organizations, a group of 32 states dedicated to working strategically and coalitionally across state lines. Their resources extend beyond their ability to organize and train activists, however. NGLTF's array of publications such as *Beyond the Beltway: State of the States 1995*, *LGBT Campus Organizing: A Comprehensive Manual,* and *To Have & To Hold: Organizing for Our Right to Marry*, as well as multiple pamphlets and fact sheets, are all available through its web site.

Lambda Legal Defense and Education Fund
120 Wall Street, Suite 1500
New York, New York 10005
ED: Kevin Cathcart
Founded: 1973
http://www.lambdalegal.org
general@lambdalegal.org
p: 212-809-8585

Celebrating its twenty-fifth anniversary in 1998, Lambda has fought many hard legal battles to get to where it is today as the nation's most influential legal advocate of civil rights for lesbians, gay men, and people with HIV/AIDS. Not surprisingly, Lambda's first case hinged on Lambda's right to exist as a non-profit organization dedicated to providing legal assistance to lesbian and gay men. In 1972, a New York court denied Lambda's request for non-profit status, arguing curiously that Lambda's "stated purposes are on their face neither benevolent nor charitable, nor, in any event, is there a demonstrated need for this corporation." With this decision overturned in 1973, Lambda inaugurated itself as the "first organization in the country (and probably the world) to establish itself principally to fight for lesbians and gay men in the courts and within the legal profession."

Initially an entirely volunteer-based organization, Lambda made the shift to a paid staff in 1977 and opened its first offices in 1979 in New York. With regional offices now in Los Angeles, Chicago, and Atlanta, Lambda's attorneys and staff work to combat discrimination wherever the law affects lesbians, gays, and people with HIV/AIDS. Taking on major test cases in which there exists the possibility for a legal precedent or for which a ruling could affect a large majority of the gay and lesbian or HIV/AIDS populations, Lambda pursues litigation in areas such as:

> discrimination in employment, housing, public accommodations, and the military; HIV/AIDS-related discrimination and public policy issues; parenting and relationship issues; equal marriage rights; equal employment and domestic partnership benefits; "sodomy" law challenges; immigration issues; anti-gay initiatives; and free speech and equal protection rights.

To date, Lambda's most far-reaching victory is doubtlessly the 1996 Supreme Court ruling that overturned Amendment 2, Colorado's 1992 anti-gay initiative, but Lambda is constantly chipping away at discriminatory legislation and public policy across the country. In a 1997 case, *Able v. USA*, Lambda won a decisive victory with the ACLU in which a district court judge ruled the military policy of "Don't Ask, Don't Tell" unconstitutional. While this case is currently being appealed, it remains the substantive first step in what promises to be a long, protracted battle. Lambda's representation of three same-sex couples denied marriage licenses in Hawaii in one of the most closely watched legal cases in years, *Baehr v. Miike*, forms one of the principal cornerstones of Lambda's marriage project, which seeks to illustrate that, according to Lambda, "Once lesbian and gay couples marry legally, people will see that the sky does not fall."

National Center for Lesbian Rights
870 Market St., Suite 570
San Francisco, California 94102
ED: Kate Kendell
Founded: 1977
http://www.nclrights.org
nclrsf@aol.com
p: 415-392-6257
f: 415-392-8442

Beginning as the Lesbian Rights Project within a public interest law firm, Equal Rights Advocates, the National Center for Lesbian Rights (NCLR) incorporated in 1989 to become what is now a "progressive, feminist, multicultural legal center devoted to advancing the rights and safety of lesbians and their families." As such, NCLR remains the only legal organization in the U.S. devoted primarily to advancing lesbian rights. NCLR now focuses its energies on issues revolving around "child custody and visitation, adoption, alternative insemination, same-gender marriage, domestic partnership, immigration and asylum, youth and lesbian health." Under the directorship of its founder, Donna Hitchens, now a superior court judge in San Francisco, and its second executive director, former Assistant Secretary of Housing and Urban Development, Roberta Achtenberg, NCLR has had some real successes. Notably, in 1986, NCLR represented Anne Affleck and Rebecca Smith, the first lesbian couple in the U.S. to adopt a child together. In 1988, NCLR brought attention to the importance for lesbians of securing partner protection documents, citing an important case in which Karen Thompson was denied hospital visitation rights by the parents of her partner, Sharon Kowalski, who became disabled in a car accident.

At present, NCLR is active in multiple areas of advocacy. Offering free information and legal counseling to lesbians, gay men, bisexuals, and transgendered individuals and technical assistance to attorneys, it serves a purpose analogous to the Lambda Legal Defense and Education Fund. Yet, its services remain quite wide ranging, and its title proclaiming dedication to "lesbian rights" would seem to insufficiently call attention to its work on multiple projects that intersect with lesbian rights. Through its Mary Ward Project, NCLR advocates on behalf of lesbian parents seeking custody and visitation rights. In 1998, NCLR helped to win a landmark victory for lesbian mothers when the Missouri Court of Appeals adopted the non-discriminatory "nexus" standard put forth by NCLR's amicus brief, which argued that custody decisions should not be based "on a parent's sexual orientation when there is no evidence that the parent's sexual orientation has harmed the child in any way." Through its Youth Project, NCLR works both on a policy level, recently vigorously lobbying the American Psychological Association "to eliminate Gender Identity Disorder (GID) as a legitimate diagnostic disorder," and on a more immediate level, setting up a toll free number (800-528-NCLR) to provide free support to youth who are being harassed due to either their sexual orientation or their gender identity.

NCLR's Immigration and Asylum Rights Task Force provides information to LBGT immigrants and asylum seekers as well. Under its auspices, NCLR successfully organized an Emergency Asylum Campaign to provide free legal representation for LBGT and HIV-positive asylum seekers. Working on the lesbian health front, NCLR recently secured grants from the Gay and Lesbian Medical Association's Lesbian Health Fund and the Astraea National Lesbian Action Foundation to recruit lesbians to take part in the Women's Health Initiative, the largest study of women's health in the U.S. With a staff of only five, NCLR has grown and spread its sphere of influence considerably since its inception.

Human Rights Campaign
1101 14th Street NW
Washington, D.C. 20005
ED: Elizabeth Birch
Founded: 1980
http://www.hrc.org
hrc@hrc.org
p: 202-628-4160
f: 202-347-5323

Originally called the Human Rights Campaign Fund, Human Rights Campaign (HRC) has moved from figuring itself as an organization that only provides monetary support for pro-gay candidates to being the largest and certainly one of the most influential national lesbian and gay political organizations in the U.S. According to its mission statement, HRC "envisions an America where lesbian and gay people are ensured of their basic equal rights—and can be open, honest and safe at home, at work, and in the community." To this end, HRC raised $11.1 million in 1997 to educate the public, organize and train volunteers at both the state and local level, participate in election campaigns, sponsor the National Coming Out Project, and lobby the federal government on issues pertaining to lesbians and gays as well as AIDS. With more than 200,000 members, HRC is a substantial lobbying force in Washington; in 1996 alone, HRC's PAC contributed more than $1 million to elect candidates—Republican, Democrat, and independent—to federal offices.

The HRC has played a significant role in fighting anti-lesbian and -gay state ballot measures in recent years, helping both Oregon and Idaho in 1994 and Maine in 1995 to defeat state bills that would have put lesbians and gays in further political peril. HRC also gave the largest single contribution that aided in the legal battle that resulted in the Supreme Court overturning Amendment 2 in 1996. Further accomplishments include increasing federal AIDS funding; helping the passage of key legislation such as the Ryan White Comprehensive AIDS Resources Emergency (CARE) Act, the Americans with Disabilities Act, the Hate Crimes

Statistics and Hate Crimes Sentencing Enhancement Acts, and supporting issues pertaining particularly to lesbian health such as programs for breast and cervical cancer research and screening. Among the many items on its list of achievements, HRC can claim an unprecedented first—the appearance of President Clinton at an HRC dinner, the first time a U.S. president has ever appeared at a gay event while in office.

HRC maintains an active presence in all of the key arenas in Washington and is now perhaps the principal gay and lesbian organization setting the agenda and charting the trajectory of future national gay and lesbian politics. For 1997, HRC targeted six primary focal points to which they contributed their resources: 1) ending workplace discrimination by lobbying Congress to pass the Employment Non-Discrimination Act (ENDA), which would prohibit workplace discrimination on the basis of sexual orientation; 2) continuing the fight against AIDS by influencing federal AIDS policy, maintaining the Office of AIDS Research as an integral part of the National Institutes of Health (NIH), and participating in the AIDS policy coalition and National Organizations Responding to AIDS; 3) punishing hate crimes against lesbians and gays by advocating for the reform of federal hate crimes laws; 4) increasing awareness of lesbian health issues by pushing the Centers for Disease Control and Prevention to increase outreach to lesbians in cancer screening and prevention programs and by requesting the NIH to include lesbian health issues in its research; 5) protecting lesbian and gay families by supporting the right of lesbians and gays to marry, by protecting gay and lesbian parents from having their children taken away from them, and by securing other rights for lesbians and gays that inhere in the marriage contract, such as the right to visit a sick or injured partner in the hospital; 6) advocating for moderate approaches to securing lesbian and gay rights by educating what HRC refers to as "fair-minded Americans" and by supporting "fair-minded candidates." HRC is committed to getting the entire spectrum of the American electorate involved in the political process of securing lesbian and gay equal rights in the U.S. and helps to make this goal possible through its Action Center on its web site, which allows anybody with access to a computer to almost effortlessly send a letter to her or his congressperson.

Gay and Lesbian Alliance Against Defamation
150 West 26th Street, #503
New York, New York 10001
ED: Joan Gerry
Founded: 1985
http://www.glaad.org
glaad@glaad.org
p: 212-807-1700
f: 212-807-1806

Originally conceived of in 1985 as a New York-based operation, Gay and Lesbian Alliance Against Defamation (GLAAD) took on the *New York Post*, publicly critiquing its sensational news reporting on AIDS. Its stated mission was "to improve the public's attitudes toward homosexuality and put an end to violence and discrimination against lesbians and gay men." Essentially concerned with issues of representation—in particular, the negative stereotypes and derogatory portrayals of lesbians and gay men in the media—GLAAD has since concerned itself with targeting and pressuring media giants such as the *New York Times* in its continued use of the term "homosexual" to describe gays. In 1988, another chapter of GLAAD was formed on the West Coast in Los Angeles to combat what many lesbians and gays saw as Hollywood's fascination with portraying lesbians and gays as serial killers and otherwise socially dysfunctional psychopaths, but it was not until 1990 that GLAAD finally secured meetings with studios and television producers. In the same year, GLAAD successfully pressured CBS-TV to reprimand and eventually suspend Andy Rooney for a homophobic comment he made on a news piece during the show *60 Minutes*.

With chapters in the bi-coastal media centers of the U.S., Los Angeles and New York, GLAAD had successfully positioned itself to react quickly to any media crisis to which they were alerted. Unifying itself as a national organization in 1994, GLAAD became the most influential and listened-to lesbian and gay media watchdog organization in the U.S. With chapters housing Media Resource Centers now located in San Francisco; Washington, D.C.; Atlanta; and Kansas City, GLAAD's resources are distributed regionally across the country. As a national organization, GLAAD concentrates its efforts on four strategies. Through its Monitoring and Mobilization program and its Outreach to Media Professionals program, GLAAD works on two fronts, respectively, organizing the LBGT community to respond to both negative and positive portrayals of LBGT people, and working directly with media professionals to educate and offer them accurate information pertaining to LBGT people. GLAAD's Community Skills Building and Outreach program offers training and technical assistance in media to LBGT organizations and individuals, but more generally and as overarching agenda, GLAAD believes that promoting LBGT visibility should be perhaps the primary means through which LBGTs will gain acceptance. To that end, GLAAD implements public education campaigns representing positive images of LBGTs. (It should be noted that while GLAAD refers to transgendered people in its literature, it does not include them in its mission statement.)

Some of GLAAD's more famous, notable achievements include successfully lobbying Hallmark Cards to withdraw the word "lesbian" from its list of banned words, launching a successful campaign to ensure the airing of the lesbian kiss episode of *Roseanne*, and leading a six-month "Let Ellen Out" campaign that eventuated in the title character of *Ellen* declaring on national television that she was gay, hence inaugurating the first television show in which the lead character was lesbian or gay.

National Latino/a Lesbian and Gay Organization
1612 K Street NW, Suite 500
Washington, D.C. 20006
ED: Martín Ornelas-Quinterop
Founded: 1987
http://llego.org
aquiLGBT@llego.org
p: 202-466-8240
f: 202-466-8530

At the 1987 March on Washington for Gay and Lesbian Rights, Enlace, the Washington, D.C., Metropolitan Coalition of Latino/a Lesbians and Gay men, hosted a meeting called the Primer Encuentro for Latino/a activists. At this meeting, attended by more

than 70 people from 13 states as well as Puerto Rico, the National Latino Lesbian and Gay Activists (NNLGA) was formed. Troubled with the lack of HIV/STD prevention programs concentrating on gay and bisexual Latino men, NNLGA set the foundation for a national organization whose mission now "is to strengthen Latina Lesbian, Latino Gay, bisexual, and transgender communities at local, national and international levels by facilitating access to cultural, political, and community development resources." This organization is now called, appropriately enough, LLEGO, or translated, "I arrive, I am equal to."

Since 1992, LLEGO has hosted an annual conference called the Encuentro Nacional that brings together Latino/a community activists, government officials, students, artists, educators, and scholars. Conference topics range from youth empowerment, lesbian health, spirituality, and mental health to crossing borders, leadership/infrastructure development, fund-raising, and creating a national Latino/a LGBT Agenda. While the conference has taken place in the past in Washington, D.C.; San Jose; and Houston, 1997 marked the conference's first appearance outside of the continental U.S., when it convened in Puerto Rico. The 1998 conference will be held in Chicago and is entitled "Acción, Orgullo y Poder" ("Action, Pride and Power"). Other programming that LLEGO oversees includes the Cultura Es Vida/Culture is Life (CEV) weekend workshop retreats in the U.S. and Puerto Rico as part of its national health campaign; the Visibility Organization Leadership Action and Revolution (VOLAR); a Latina lesbian visibility program; the Youth, Empowerment and Support (YES) caucus; and a transgender summit planned for the summer of 1998. While LLEGO has worked successfully at the local level, its 1993 grant from the Centers for Disease Control and Prevention (CDC) has allowed it to work on a national level as well and develop the Technical Assistance and Training on AIDS (TATA) Project, a program that has provided technical assistance and training and has dispersed "over $200,000 in seed funding to over 40 AIDS prevention service organizations and socio-cultural groups in the U.S. and Puerto Rico."

National Black Lesbian and Gay Leadership Forum
1436 U Street NW, Suite 200
Washington, D.C. 20009
ED: Keith Boykin
Founded: 1988
http://www.nblglf.org
nblglf@aol.com
p: 202-483-6786
f: 202-483-4970

With its headquarters based initially in Los Angeles, National Black Lesbian and Gay Leadership Forum (NBLGLF) became a national organization in 1995 when it convened its first national Board of Directors and subsequently opened a new office in Washington in 1996. Established by Phill Wilson and Ruth Waters, the Forum was created in 1988 out of the concern that the gay rights movement remained a largely white affair that primarily addressed the needs of white lesbians and gay men. Beginning as an annual conference, the Forum developed an AIDS Prevention Team in 1991, dedicated to providing services such as treatment advocacy, HIV support groups, and counseling to African Americans in South Central Los Angeles. With programs in place such as its Brother-

2-Brother Program, which "empowers Black men by providing a safe space to explore issues of identity, sexuality, health and masculinity" and convenes an annual conference for black men "of all sexual orientations"; its Women's Health Program, an education program for black women; and its new—and also what is the first ever—Black Lesbian and Gay Community Center in Washington, which houses a black lesbian and gay archive, the Forum advocates not only for black lesbians and gay men, but also for transgender communities as well. NBLGLF is actually only one of three national groups that includes transgendered people in its mission statement, along with LLEGO and NGLTF.

Its annual conference, which celebrated its 10-year anniversary in 1997 with nearly 1,000 participants, concentrates on imparting leadership training to the conference participants with the support of notable participants such as Cornel West, Alice Walker, former Surgeon General Joycelyn Elders, Rev. Jesse Jackson, bell hooks, Angela Davis, and Congressional Black Caucus Chair Maxine Waters. With a new National Field Program in development, the Forum hopes to extend the work of its annual conference and operate as a training resource providing skills and technical assistance to black activists and organizations across the country. Its focus on black gay youth, with its new Youth Program, which will be giving annual scholarships to promote leadership and a National Mentoring Project, which will provide youths with adult role models, is also a centerpiece of its future plans.

Testifying before Congress and securing meetings with black churches as well as the White House, the Forum has become perhaps the leading voice and advocate of African-American GLBT people. Nearly doubling its 1996 annual budget of $450,000 to $850,000 in 1997, 41 percent of which came from grants from the Centers for Disease Control (*Washington Blade*, 12 December 1997, p. 22) to support the group's expanding AIDS/HIV prevention programs, the Forum has successfully begun the admittedly arduous task of filling in a critical fissure in the uneven fabric of the gay rights movement.

Queer Nation/Dyke Action Machine!
Founded: 1990
http://www.echonyc.com/~dam

Most often associated with the activist chant "We're here, we're queer, get used to it," which was soon quickly taken up by lesbian and gay activists around the U.S. at marches and other direct action events, Queer Nation was formed in April 1990 at an ACT UP New York meeting out of a desire to apply the radical direct action tactics developed within AIDS activism to broader gay and lesbian issues. Although "Queer Nation" and "Queer Theory" were officially created at roughly the same time, Teresa de Lauretis notes in her Introduction to the "Queer Theory: Lesbian and Gay Sexualities" issue of *differences*, an event which installed the term "queer" into academic lexicons and established queer theory as a formal intellectual enterprise: "The term 'queer' was suggested to me by a conference [that took place in 1989 called 'How do I look? Queer Film and Video'] in which I had participated.... My 'queer,' however, had no relation to the Queer Nation group, of whose existence I was ignorant at the time" (de Lauretis, p. xvii). Although De Lauretis goes on to suggest that "there is in fact very little in common" between the two, Queer Nation's activist work has done much to trouble queer theory's disaffiliation from

Queer Nation. As Lauren Berlant and Elizabeth Freeman have remarked, Queer Nation's enterprise is a complicated one whose work is theoretically inflected:

> Queer Nation's outspoken promotion of a national sexuality not only discloses that mainstream national identity touts a subliminal sexuality more official than a state flower or a national bird but also makes explicit how thoroughly the local experience of the body is framed by laws, policies, and social customs regulating sexuality. Queer Nation's tactics of invention appropriate for gay politics both grass roots and mass-mediated forms of countercultural resistance from left, feminist, and civil rights movements of the sixties.... [Queer Nation] redeploys these tactics in a kind of guerilla warfare that names all concrete and abstract spaces of social communication as places where "the people" live and thus as national sites ripe both for transgression and legitimate visibility. Its tactics are to cross borders, occupy spaces, and to mime the privileges of normality—in short, to simulate "the national" with a camp inflection (Berlant and Freeman, "Queer Nationalities," p. 152).

As Berlant and Freeman suggest, Queer Nation—as well as ACT UP, Lesbian Avengers, and other direct action groups—has done a great deal to disrupt the theory/practice distinction that has unproductively bifurcated academic and activist discourses and has effectively helped to reconfigure the contours of queer theoretical work as much as it has constructed a distinctively queer form of resistance within the U.S. Queer Nation, however, "does not look for a theoretical coherence to regulate in advance all of its tactics: all politics in the Queer Nation are imagined on the street" (Berlant and Freeman, p. 156).

In the same way that ACT UP groups spread quickly across the country after ACT UP's initial formation in New York, a quick proliferation of the Queer Nation model into other urban and suburban spaces within the U.S. promptly put Queer Nation onto the map. This map imagined the nation as a queer space that was dramatically seized and redistributed by queers for queer modes of living. Perhaps the group's primary modus operandi, the confrontational gay and lesbian kiss-in within heterosexual spaces such as straight bars and government buildings, suggested that urbane, more assimilationist strategies would not do justice in the context of increasing marginalization of and violence against lesbian and gay people. Queer Nation's "I Hate Straights" broadside, distributed at the Chicago and New York Gay Pride parades in 1990, is exemplary in its categorical refusal to engage the liberal logic that would have gays and lesbians building bridges with their would-be heterosexual allies. Pointing to the multiple ways in which straight people continually fail to understand the privilege of heterosexuality, the broadside announces, "I hate straights on behalf of the gay people who have to emotionally 'take care' of the straights who feel guilty for their privilege; I hate straights for requiring the sublimation of gay rage as the price of their beneficent tolerance." Its imperative was to "BASH BACK ... LET YOURSELF BE ANGRY ... THAT THERE IS NO PLACE IN THIS COUNTRY WHERE WE ARE SAFE" (Berlant and Freeman, p. 158).

While Queer Nation successfully articulated a national space within gay and lesbian politics for the articulation of queer rage by bringing together affinity groups such as HI MOM (Homosexual Ideological Mobilization against the Military), UNITED COLORS, a queers of color group, and QUEER PLANET, an environmental group, as well as numerous others under the auspices of the term "queer," many activists grew leery of a queer politics that proceeded under the aegis of the nation, no matter how queer that nation was. And while the "Queer" of Queer Nation promised an activism that would attend to all queer constituents, Queer Nation had difficulty delivering. As Queer Nationalist Carrie Moyer remarks, "Not surprisingly, Queer Nation, the group that was supposed to unite gay *and* lesbian activists to agitate for an agenda common to both, rarely—if ever—focused on lesbian issues. So Dyke Action Machine! (DAM!) began as the lesbian working group of Queer Nation" (Moyer, pp. 439-40). DAM! eventually mutated to become DAM!, the lesbian graphics project, with a membership of two, Carrie Moyer and Sue Schaffner. But the ubiquity of their graphic work in New York and other places around the world where lesbians congregate testifies to the fact that an LBGT organization need not be enormous or well-funded in order to do effective work.

In 1994, DAM! produced and wheat pasted all over New York City a film poster for Stonewall 25 featuring a multi-racial, lesbian triumvirate who would appear in the faux film, *Straight to Hell*. In Lesbo/Rambo-style fashion, the poster humorously proclaims, "She came out. So the Army kicked her out. Now she's out for blood." Placed next to other posters around the city advertising films such as *The Lion King*, DAM!'s *Straight to Hell* poster served to affirm lesbian resistance by quickly and strategically queering public spaces. In 1995, DAM! invaded the World Wide Web when it launched the world's first fantasy lesbian television network, The Girlie Network" (http://www.echonyc.com/~dam), which would feature shows such as "Leave us the beaver," "Bring us your children," and its season premiere, "OB-GYN." While the web site television network has enjoyed much success, DAM! is troubled by its homogeneous audience and so has recently re-focused its energies on its widespread promotion through matchbooks, wallet cards, and other media of a phone line for a lesbian militia equipped with self-defense products geared to the "separatist on-the-go." "Our next challenge as a public art/agitprop outfit," suggests Moyer, "is to find a new way of surprising our viewers into action. What uncharted media avenues remain for making an impact within image-saturated urban sites?" (Moyer, p. 446). Although Queer Nation as a formal collective has died out in recent years, the fraught concept of queer nationality remains in currency, and its multiple affinity groups, which either came to it preformed or formed under its auspices, continue to engage in the arduous work of re-visioning the constitution of a queer nation whose borders are constantly and necessarily in flux.

Gay and Lesbian Victory Fund
1012 14th Street NW, Suite 1000
Washington, D.C. 20005
ED: Brian Bond
Founded: 1991
http://www.victoryfund.org
VictoryF@aol.com
p: 202-842-8679

Based conceptually on EMILY's List, a donor network supportive of pro-choice, female, Democratic candidates that has provided the financial means for women to run for, but more impor-

tantly, win political office at all levels of government, the Gay and Lesbian Victory Fund functions as a fundraising body that donates money to openly gay and lesbian candidates who have a chance at winning an election and who actively work to secure lesbian and gay civil rights. Originally conceived of by gay activists Terry Bean and Vic Basile, the Victory Fund is a non-partisan Political Action Committee (PAC) that disburses nearly $1 million annually and has made profitable returns on its investments. In the November 1997 elections, 10 of 15 Victory Fund-supported candidates were voted into office.

Lesbian Avengers
Founded: 1992
http://www.lesbian.org/chicago-avengers/

"Ask About Lesbian Lives." Such was the simple entreaty printed on 300 lavender balloons that the Lesbian Avengers distributed in the fall of 1992 to children entering a Queens public school in a district that had refused to implement New York City's gay-positive Rainbow curriculum. The Lesbian Avengers' first direct action, this distribution of balloons, accompanied by a full marching band playing "We Are Family," set the audaciously imaginative tone for a lesbian group about which many people, especially those in this right-to-life Queens school district they were confronting, had never heard. As lesbian author and activist Sarah Schulman remembers:

> Some parents let their kids keep the balloons. Some refused. But every child who attended school that day heard the word "lesbian," and for some, it just might have been the most important day of their lives. It certainly forced the teachers to discuss the existence of lesbians, regardless of what restrictions had been placed on them by Mary Cummins, the bigoted chair of the local school board (Schulman, p. 281).

But this was only the first action that culminated as a result of a meeting earlier that spring in which six lesbian friends—Ana Maria Simo, Anne-Christine D'Adesky, Maxine Wolfe, Marie Honan, Ann Maguire, and Sara Schulman—many of whom had been active in AIDS, feminist, and other progressive politics, sat down in Simo's New York apartment to discuss starting a specifically lesbian group that would get more lesbians doing direct action political work on the streets.

With the word "lesbian" firmly ensconced in the minds of Queens school district school children, the Lesbian Avengers took to the streets again. Deploying similar direct action tactics to ACT UP and its forerunners, the Lesbian Avengers continued their work in New York when Denver's Mayor, Wellington Webb, came to New York to promote Colorado tourism shortly after the passage of the anti-gay initiative, Amendment 2. The Lesbian Avengers quickly procured their logo—"Lesbian Avengers, We Recruit"—when Mary Cummins accused one of the Lesbian Avengers with that very act at a school forum, and soon thereafter, they became associated with eating fire (Schulman, p. 284). While certainly a useful media tactic, the Lesbian Avengers' fire eating actually memorializes the deaths of Hattie Cohens and Brian Mock, an African-American lesbian and a disabled white gay man living in Oregon who burned to death in 1992 in their apartment when Neo-

A Lesbian Avengers protest.

Nazi skinheads threw a molotov cocktail into their apartment. The fire eating tradition started at a Take Back the Night March in New York when about 10 Lesbian Avengers ate fire while others chanted, "Their fire will not consume us; we take it and we make it our own" (Wolfe, pp. 431-32).

But more than their logo and fire eating, the Lesbian Avengers are perhaps best known for their uproarious and disorderly Dyke Marches, which have always taken place without a permit. Their first march took place at the 1993 Gay and Lesbian March on Washington. After much planning in advance and distribution of 8,000 flyers on the days leading up to the alternative dyke march, the Lesbian Avengers amassed about 20,000 dykes for what Sarah Schulman has called "the largest lesbian event in the history of the world" (Schulman, p. 286). Although the Dyke March received scant media attention, it remains one of the most electrifying moments in the history of lesbian direct action. At the Stonewall 25 celebration, the Lesbian Avengers organized another nonpermitted International Dyke March. As Maxine Wolfe, longtime ACT UP activist and Lesbian Avenger co-founder, recalls, "Although the March was not slated to begin until 5:30, by 3:30 dykes were already showing up at the park, and by 5 P.M., it was totally a dyke space—dykes chatting in groups, sitting on benches reading, a dyke saxophone quartet playing music" (Wolfe, p. 434). Engaging in such radical direct action work, the Lesbian

Avengers remain a virtual storehouse of practical organizational advice for revolutionary lesbian activists and have produced *The Lesbian Avenger Handbook*, an indispensable guide for lesbian grassroots organizing and activism that is available at the Chicago chapter's web site. With more than 55 chapters, 5 of which are international, the Lesbian Avengers remain a vital and consequential component of the LBGT movement today.

Log Cabin Republicans
1633 Q Street NW
Washington, D.C. 20009
ED: Richard Tafel
Founded: 1993
http://www.lcr.org
p: 202-347-5306
f: 202-347-5224

A *non sequitur* to many lesbians and gays, the Log Cabin Republicans (LCR) inhabit a perplexing and somewhat bewildering position within the present lesbian and gay political scene. With many gays, a large majority of whom identify as Democrat or at least non-Republican, finding LCR members' dedication to the Republican party frustrating, and many Republicans figuring homo-sexuality as anathema to a conservative political agenda, the Log Cabin organization escapes easy classification and would seem to have very few friends. With more than 50 chapters across the country, however, LCR is fast becoming more palatable, if only a bit, in an age of bi-partisan politics. Evidence of the Republican party's softened stance toward its gay constituency can be found in presidential candidate Bob Dole's acceptance, albeit grudgingly, of a $1000 contribution that his campaign had initially returned to Log Cabin during the 1996 presidential race.

Initially convening in 1978 to fight California's Proposition 6, the first anti-gay initiative in the U.S., the group has steadily built up its clubs, which require a minimum of 10 members, ultimately establishing itself as a Washington-based national organization in 1993. Log Cabin is something of an anomaly in D.C., since the Democratic party has no such national gay and lesbian organiza-tion, although it does have many local gay and lesbian Democratic clubs across the county. LCR's Political Action Committee (PAC) donates money to Republican candidates who support gay issues as well as AIDS legislation. In 1996, the PAC donated $76,000 to candidates at all levels of government.

With its full-time staff of five, Log Cabin works to fulfill its stated mission "to educate the Republican party about the con-cerns and the issues facing the gay and lesbian community." Log Cabin calls itself "the home for mainstream gay and lesbian Ameri-cans" and remains committed to "Republican views on crime, fis-cal responsibility and foreign policy ... individual groups rather than group rights ... limited government rather than big govern-ment." Ironically, though, LCR maintains that its top legislative priority for 1997 was increasing the federally sponsored AIDS Drug Assistance Program (ADAP), a key component of the Ryan White CARE Act that makes expensive drugs more affordable to people living with AIDS/HIV. Indeed, as the only lesbian and gay organization to testify before a House Appropriations subcom-mittee on AIDS funding within the last two congresses, LCR suc-cessfully lobbied for a $118.5 million increase in federal ADAP funding, a victory that LCR maintains was a result of Republican efforts. Log Cabin Republicans also asserts its support of ENDA (Employee Non-Discrimination Act), the congressional legislation prohibiting workplace discrimination on the basis of sexual orien-tation.

Servicemembers Legal Defense Network
1612 K Street NW, Suite 308
Washington, D.C. 20006
ED: Michelle M. Benecke and C. Dixon Osburn
Founded: 1993
http://www.sldn.org
sldn@sldn.org
p: 202-328-3244

All LBGT organizations respond to specific needs and prob-lems, but it is perhaps the Servicemembers Legal Defense Net-work (SLDN) that exemplifies this fact most profoundly. SLDN was founded in 1993 in direct response to President Clinton's establishment of a new policy regarding gays in the military, the so called "Don't Ask, Don't Tell, Don't Pursue" policy, which was intended to stop the military from asking its mem-bers about their sexual orientation. While Clinton had initially

planned to overturn the existing policy explicitly banning gays and lesbians from military service, his administration ultimately produced a compromise policy on 19 July 1993, which would ostensibly allow lesbians and gays to serve in the military as long as they do not divulge their sexual orientation. Producing probably more loopholes and problems than workable solutions, the "Don't Ask, Don't Tell" policy remains the inhospitable *domus* that SLDN both inhabits and tries to tear down on a daily basis. With its nine staff members and a nationwide net-work of more than 200 attorneys, SLDN operates as both a watchdog, documenting the multiple abuses of the policy, and an advocate of servicemembers being investigated.

In its 1998 *Fourth Annual Report*, SLDN documents the fact that total command violations have increased 27 percent for the fourth year in a row. Reported also are the 124 "Don't Ask" vio-lations in 1997, up 39 percent over 89 reported violations in 1996; 235 "Don't Pursue" violations, an increase of 23 percent over last year's 191; and 182 new "Don't Harass" violations—including death threats and physical assaults—a 38 percent increase over the 132 reported incidents in 1996. In response to the overwhelm-ing annual increases of violations of the new policy, SLDN has developed an impressive *Survival Guide*, available on its web site, extensively detailing the provisions of the policy, its uneven imple-mentation, and useful information for lesbian and gay servicemembers. The *Guide* explains that the new policy is no different from the previous one in that "servicemembers still face discharge based on the same grounds: statements, acts or marriage." Significant is the fact that the assertion of one's homosexuality constitutes a "homosexual act," along with kissing and handholding. While the *Guide* outlines specifically what constitutes grounds for dismissal, it also provides arguments used successfully to avoid discharge. One of the more humorous arguments, the Queen for A Day argument, has been used to persuade the military that a servicemember's homosexual conduct signaled a temporary depar-ture from usual and customary behavior.

While SLDN continues to dedicate its resources to intervening on behalf of servicemembers accused of committing homosexual acts—since its inception, SLDN has helped more than 700 servicemembers negotiate the simple yet multiply interpreted policy—it also takes aim at the policy itself in order to substan-tively change it. According to its "Solution" web site page,

> In their first year, SLDN secured three significant changes to the policy on homosexuals and launched efforts to change twelve additional areas. These efforts will not make the new policy on homosexuals constitutional, but they will make life for lesbian and gay servicemembers slightly less intolerable and will help erode the pillars undergirding the new policy.

Among its recent successes, SLDN can claim two substantial vic-tories. With the Department of Defense having ordered a replace-ment of the 1989 recruiting form that asks recruits if they are gay, one officially sanctioned avenue of discrimination in the military has been effectively bulldozed. No less important is a memoran-dum circulated by Former Under Secretary of Defense Edwin Dorn that, according to SLDN, states that "commanders should inves-tigate perpetrators of anti-gay harassment and lesbian-baiting, not their victims."

Sex Panic!
Lesbian and Gay Community Services Center
208 West 13th Street
New York, New York 10011
ED: None
Founded: 1997
http://www.geocities.com/~sexpanicnyc/
mail@sexpanic.org
p: 212-252-4925

One of the most recent—and most vocal—LBGT organizations on the scene of queer activism in the U.S., Sex Panic! calls itself a pro-queer, pro-feminist, anti-racist direct action group based in New York City that seeks "to defend public sexual culture and safer sex in New York City from police crackdowns, public stigma, and morality crusades." Formed in May 1997 by a group of queer academics, journalists, artists, and others concerned about the increasing harassment of LBGT people and shutting down of queer spaces such as theaters, sex clubs, dance clubs, and bars in New York, Sex Panic! takes aim not only at the politically conservative Giuliani administration whose quality of life programming has rightfully been associated with the Disneyfication of Times Square and the concomitant increased policing of LBGT people in New York City, but also at well-known figures within the gay community such as Andrew Sullivan and Bruce Bawer for their explicitly conservative opposition to non-normative LBGT politics, and even at less centrist figures such as Larry Kramer. Arguing that queer sex and sexuality are increasingly marginalized by both people outside of and within LBGT communities, Sex Panic! notes in its "Declaration of Sexual Rights," created at the National Sex Panic! Summit in San Diego during November 1997

> The LBGT movement, feminism, and AIDS activism all include long histories of advocating the principles of sexual self-determination. These principles are under attack. In the name of "mainstream" acceptance, many are increasingly willing to embrace regulation and stigma for more marginal groups.

Sex Panic! therefore affirms the following sexual rights: 1) the right to sexual and reproductive self-determination; 2) the rights to publicly accessible sexual culture; 3) the right to a sexual life free from shame and stigma; and 4) freedom from government intervention.

As Douglas Crimp, Ann Pellegrini, Eva Pendleton, and Michael Warner, a group of long-time activists and academics discussing Sex Panic's formation, point out:

> This is not the first time that officials have launched repressive measures against sex in the name of the public good. Since the nineteenth century, it has been a recurrent pattern: public morals and health have been invoked; scapegoats have been found in homosexuals, sex workers, and others who are unlikely to fight back, and a fantasy of purity is held up as the norm. Historians have come to call this pattern a "sex panic." We have taken this name, with a sense of irony, to publicize our belief that we are in the middle of one.

Although Sex Panic!, a sort of queer, unapologetic prodigal intersexed son of Queer Nation, has only been in existence for about a year, it has garnered much media attention around the U.S., and while its multiple publications (available on its web site) and features in the media have driven it into a place of prominence, rivaled only by that of ACT UP in the 1980s, Sex Panic!'s tenure on the scene of LBGT activism has been a short one as of yet. As a direct action LBGT organization lacking both rules and formal membership, Sex Panic's purpose is to voice concerns that other dominant LBGT and AIDS/HIV organizations do not discuss. With signs that read "Gay Men's Health Compromise" and "Gay Men Hoarding Contracts," Sex Panic! recently, for example, joined ACT UP New York in a demonstration at GMHC (Gay Men's Health Crisis), criticizing GMHC for its stance on HIV names reporting. As an alternative to the liberal establishment of the relatively resource rich LBGT organizations, Sex Panic! does not worry about appeasing centrist supporters and is effectively one of the few resources available to radical activists worried by the increasing normativization of LBGT politics and its attendant privatization of queer sex, privileging of traditional households and relationships, and scapegoating of HIV-positive, sexually active people. While activist groups such as ACT UP and Queer Nation may not still receive the same attention they received in the 1980s, the creation of Sex Panic! confirms the continuing need for direct action activist groups that attend to concerns of marginalized constituencies within LBGT and other sexual communities.

FAMILY ORGANIZATIONS

Senior Action in a Gay Environment
305 7th Avenue
New York, New York 10001
ED: Terry Kaelber
Founded: 1978
sageusa@aol.com
p: 212-741-2247
f: 212-366-1947

While it is a simple fact that lesbians and gay men have always grown older, this fact has remained one of the least discussed and least confronted issues within both LBGT communities and gerontology professional groups. Constantly confronting the double bind of ageism within LBGT communities and the failure of gerontologists to take seriously and understand the issues and problems specific to non-heterosexual aging populations, many older LBGT people find themselves lacking sufficient support networks. Realizing these significant problems, a group of social workers, gerontologists, and lesbian and gay community members formed Senior Action in a Gay Environment (SAGE) in 1978. Today, as "the nation's oldest and largest community based intergenerational social service agency dedicated to honoring, caring for, and celebrating the lesbian and gay community's senior members," SAGE has a membership of more than 3,000 men and women of all ages and provides services to more than 1,500 people, including 300 homebound seniors, each month. With a full-time staff of 6,350 volunteers, and an annual budget of $465,000, SAGE offers direct services to clients in the New York City area and offers information, education, and advocacy on lesbian and gay aging throughout the United States.

Through its Social Services programming, SAGE offers case management and counseling on all government entitlement programs for seniors; visits to homebound seniors; individual, family, and group psychotherapy; support services specifically geared to the

This lesbian elders dance, organized by GLOE, is an example of the kinds of activities promoted by SAGE.

needs of older lesbians; and AIDS assessment services and clinic treatment. Vigorously combating the widely held belief within LBGT communities that gay and lesbian life, be it sexual, social, or psychological, ends somewhere between the ages of 40 and 50, SAGE has developed a Social and Support Program that seeks to provide an extensive community support network. SAGE's drop-in center, the country's only gay and lesbian senior center, is housed in the New York Gay and Lesbian Community Services Center and remains a vibrant social space for older and elderly LBGT people in New York City. Multiple ongoing health care seminars keep SAGE's members apprised of the latest developments in the fast-changing, complex world of managed care and Medicare, and SAGE's multiple weekend trips, socials, rap groups, and Broadway theater excursions also keep its members in constant contact with each other. With programming including painting, Italian, creative writing, and Tai Chi classes, a reading and discussion group, Morning at the Opera group, bereavement group, and multiple other discussion groups such as Men over 40 who are into S&M, and monthly dances, SAGE offers an alternative model for aging lesbians and gays who would rather not stop being lesbian or gay simply because they are no longer young. SAGE, in fact, has more than a dozen independent affiliates in cities across the U.S. and Canada, a testament to the need for support services of aging lesbians and gays.

While the organization remains committed to its New York members, SAGE also provides consultation to groups all over the U.S. and Canada to help them develop and create similar LBGT senior groups based on the SAGE model. SAGE works at both the local and national level, advocating on behalf of senior gays and lesbians and ensures that their voices are heard and their faces are seen in Washington or anywhere else SAGE's buses might deposit Pride Parade marches. In 1998, SAGE convened its first annual conference, entitled "Gays and Lesbians Growing Older." Featuring Del Martin and Phyllis Lyon, the founders of the Daughters of Bilitis, the conference addressed such topics as discrimination in mainstream health care and senior housing and the invisibility of gay seniors, among other issues. Considering the unique situation of the present historical moment, which has witnessed an inordinate number of LBGT people coming out and the fact that these people will become older, and the relative lack of a substantial network of support services for LBGT seniors across the country, SAGE's work with and advocacy for senior lesbians and gays today is setting the necessary groundwork for thinking through the challenges, benefits, and expectations of the next, arguably larger, post-Stonewall generation of LBGT people who may have lived the majority of their lives out of the closet.

Gay and Lesbian Parents Coalition International
PO Box 34337
San Diego, California 92163
ED: C. Ray Drew
Founded: 1979
http://www.glpci.org
glpci@glpci.org
p: 619-296-0199
f: 619-296-0699

As is increasingly recognized, LBGT people are not only born into families—they produce them as well. While Gay and Lesbian Parents Coalition International (GLPCI) was established initially as the Gay Fathers Coalition at the first March on Washington for Gay and Lesbian Rights in 1979, the coalition changed its name to its present appellation in 1986 to reflect both its international reach as well as its expanded scope, the inclusion of lesbian mothers within its mission. In its nascent formation, GLPCI's focus was two-fold: it initiated an annual conference in 1981, which in 1983 expanded to include a workshop for children of gay parents, and also, like many other national groups, worked to develop local support networks for gay parents in a period in which there existed no seriously formalized infrastructure recognizing the specific needs and challenges of gay parents. Today, with a member base of 4,000 individuals and 100 local parenting groups based primarily in the U.S. and Canada, GLPCI concentrates on providing programming dedicated to advocacy, education, and support—the same tenets of P-FLAG's mission statement.

In order to educate and advocate on behalf of the growing population of LBGT parents, GLPCI publishes a weekly electronic newsletter, *The Parent's Network*, the archive of which is accessible through GLPCI's web site, and in addition to providing information about the numerous possibilities and alternatives for raising children such as surrogacy, adoption, lesbian and gay men parenting, and alternative insemination, GLPCI has also compiled an extensive directory, *Resources for Gay Men & Lesbians Interested in Parenting*, available free through its web site. GLPCI has also produced, in conjunction with the Lesbian and Gay Parents Association of San Francisco, a workshop training guide and accompanying 10-minute video entitled "Both of My Moms' Names Are Judy: Children of Lesbians and Gays Speak Out" for educators and administrators. In addition to its own local parents groups, GLPCI provides and sponsors support groups such as Children of Lesbian and Gays Everywhere and the Straight Spouse Network (SSN), a group for non-gay people formerly or presently married to LBGT people.

———————

Parents, Families and Friends of Lesbians and Gays
1101 14th Street NW, Suite 1030
Washington, D.C. 20005
ED: Vacant
Founded: 1981
http://www.pflag.org
info@pflag.org
p: 202-638-4200

While you may not have heard of any of the largest lesbian and gay organizations in the U.S., there is a good chance that you prob-ably have heard of Parents, Families and Friends of Lesbians and Gays (P-FLAG), and for good reason. With more than 400 local chapters and more than 69,000 members in the U.S., Puerto Rico, and now five other countries, P-FLAG is the largest network of people where affiliation to the group is based solely on having a family member or friend who is gay or lesbian. Since the early 1980s, P-FLAG has been and continues to be the first place many parents will call when faced with the news of their child's homosexuality. P-FLAG's network is so far reaching that it will almost invariably extend into the community—and sometimes not surprisingly, the same neighborhood—of the parents who have just learned, for example, that their child, attending college across the country, is gay or lesbian. Dating its official inception in 1981 when it organized itself as a national group, the same year that the occurrence of Kaposi's sarcoma in 41 gay men was first reported in the *New York Times*, P-FLAG locates its roots much earlier, when in 1972, Jeanne Manford marched in New York's gay pride parade after her gay son Morty had been beaten earlier that year in public while police officers looked on. Carrying a sign proclaiming her love and support of her gay son, Manford was greeted with a profound and overwhelming enthusiasm from participants. With this public declaration, Manford had clearly spoken what had previously been unmentionable. P-FLAG later had its first meeting in 1973 with about 20 people in attendance. Helping Larry and Adele Starr set up a second group in Los Angeles, Manford successfully put P-FLAG on both coasts, initiating the slow but steady proliferation of P-FLAG support groups across the country.

As a national organization, P-FLAG does its work under the aegis of a three-point mission statement: "Parents, Families and Friends of Lesbians and Gays promotes the health and well-being of gay, lesbian and bisexual persons, their families and friends through: support, to cope with an adverse society; education, to enlighten an ill-informed public; and advocacy, to end discrimination and to secure equal civil rights." Realizing that it is sometimes one of the only—and sometimes, the only—support available for families, P-FLAG operates a wide range of support groups at the level of the local chapter, including groups for new families coming to terms with their feelings about a family member's coming out and groups for parents of lesbian, gay, bisexual, and transgendered teens, but also groups for straight spouses with gay partners, children of lesbian or gay parents and family AIDS support groups. P-FLAG also distributes multiple publications such as *Be Yourself, Beyond the Bible,* and *Our Daughters & Sons*. In 1995, as part of its mission to educate, P-FLAG initiated Project Open Mind, a nationwide public education campaign that "seeks to reach the 'moveable' middle to affirmatively change their attitudes about gay, lesbian and bisexual Americans" through television ads and other media. According to P-FLAG, "the message is simple: hate speech creates a climate where it is unsafe to be gay." As an example, P-FLAG members have been active in supporting Disney for its inclusive employment practices despite the heavy criticism and pressures of the Southern Baptist boycott. P-FLAG's campaign has been so successful that it now has formidable competition in PFOX, Parents and Friends of Ex-Gays, a group dedicated to steering gay and lesbian children into reparative therapy.

Beyond the work of support and education, P-FLAG has moved into the more politically charged arena of advocacy, making its presence known throughout Washington, D.C. In 1997, P-FLAG "was the only gay-identified group represented at the President's

Summit for America's Future" and made sure that a parent's voice was heard at a historic meeting of a dozen gay and lesbian activists with President Clinton. P-FLAG members have recently also actively urged the U.S. Congress to pass the Employment Non-Discrimination Act (ENDA) and testified before the House and the Senate, urging them to defeat the anti-gay federal Defense of Marriage Act (DOMA), legislation that did eventually pass. As an organization that places the family at the center of the gay rights movement, P-FLAG has made fighting for equal marriage rights a top advocacy priority. Simultaneously focusing its energies on both local and national levels, however, has strained P-FLAG in recent years and led in 1997 to the resignation of its Executive Director, Sandra Gillis. Managing the turbulent oscillation between the national and local levels has been a skill that many LBGT organizations have had to learn, and P-FLAG is clearly no exception.

Children of Lesbians and Gays Everywhere
2300 Market Street, #165
San Francisco, California 94114
ED: Felicia Park Rogers
Founded: 1990
http://www.colage.org
colage@colage.org
p: 415-861-KIDS (5437)
f: 415-255-8345

An autonomous program of the Gay and Lesbian Parents Coalition International, Children of Lesbians and Gays Everywhere (COLAGE) is the product of one of the most typical family dramas in the U.S., the parent/child altercation. In 1990, GLPCI parents organized several workshops for their children at their annual conference. Of the organized workshops, COLAGE remarks: "though the parents got full credit for trying ... they didn't go over very well. A group of two dozen of the kids at the conference got together half way through to discuss their problems with the workshops." Approaching the conference committee about taking on the production of the youth conference in the future, the parents, acquiescing to their children's demands, agreed to let the children develop their own program. They took on the name, Just for Us, the title of a newsletter that a gay father and his daughter had been publishing, and agreed to take over the publication of the newsletter as well. Still publishing the newsletter under that title, Just for Us became COLAGE in 1993, after a conference in 1992 when it met for the first time outside of the annual GLPCI conference for three days and drafted a mission statement and set long-term goals.

In 1995, COLAGE opened a national office in San Francisco run entirely by volunteers, and in 1997, COLAGE hired its first paid director and a few paid staff. With an annual operating budget of approximately $75,000, received primarily from small private donations, COLAGE has 1,500 members and approximately 20 affiliated groups across the U.S. and other countries and works at both the local and international levels, providing outreach and advocacy for children of lesbians and gays as well as bisexual and transgendered parents. Among its many interesting services, COLAGE sponsors a pen pal program that puts children of LBGT parents in contact with others, and also awards the Lee Dubin Memorial Scholarship to children of LBGT parents attending an

accredited post-secondary institution, including trade school. While COLAGE kids have declared their autonomy from the GLPCI parent group and now have their own autonomous annual conference, they still meet in conjunction with GLPCI's conference and organize an entire spectrum of kid-specific workshops that meet the needs of kids of LBGT parents.

LIBRARIES, ARCHIVES, AND EDUCATIONAL ORGANIZATIONS

ONE Institute/International Gay and Lesbian Archives
PO Box 69679
West Hollywood, California 90069
Founded: 1952
http://www.usc.edu/Library/oneigla
oneigla@usc.edu
p: 310-854-0271

One Institute/International Gay and Lesbian Archives (ONE/GLA), a nonprofit educational corporation situated on the University of Southern California's campus, is the result of a 1994 merger between two organizations central to the pre-Stonewall lesbian and gay movement. Locating its pre-history in 1942, when 19-year-old Jim Kepner entered the San Francisco Public Library in search of information on his newly discovered homosexuality, found nothing, and subsequently began searching for and finding used books about homosexuality in used book stores, ONE/IGLA prides itself on being "the oldest ongoing Gay/Lesbian organization in the Western Hemisphere." Since 1942, this collection has been transformed and re-located several times, moving to Los Angeles in 1951 with Jim Kepner; becoming the Western Gay Archives in 1977; the National Gay Archives in 1979, when Kepner incorporated the collection, moving it from his home to a storefront in Hollywood; and then the Natalie Barney/Edward Carpenter Library of the International Gay & Lesbian Archives in 1986, when its overflowing materials were moved to a building in West Hollywood that still could not hold the entirety of the collections. IGLA's 1994 merger with ONE once again uprooted the archives to the USC campus, the newest home of IGLA.

But that is only half of the story. In 1952, a year after Jim Kepner's move to Los Angeles, Dorr Legg, also in Los Angeles, founded with several others ONE, Incorporated, an organization devoted initially to the publication and distribution of ONE Magazine, a notoriously brazen and irreverent periodical produced by and directed at a gay and lesbian minority as a supplement to the relative lack of positive coverage of the rising homophile movement. The first issue of ONE, at the direction of its first editor, Dale Jennings, and its board, composed primarily of Mattachine Society members, was published in January 1953. "[T]he movement's first full-time worker," according to John D'Emilio, Dorr Legg also played a significant role within the Mattachine Society, the homophile emancipation group founded by Harry Hay and others in 1950, as well as the Knights of the Clock, a Los Angeles interracial social club that he joined with his lover, who was black (D'Emilio, pp. 72, 88). With a growing readership, One Magazine sought to target a primarily homosexual audience and left the work of appealing to and dialoguing with potential heterosexuals allies to the Mattachine Society and Daughters of Bilitis (D'Emilio, p. 108). ONE Magazine's initial circulation of 2,000 throughout the country grew to a monthly 5,000 in 1954, a significant increase over the estimated Mattachine Review's 2,200 and the DOB *Ladder*'s 500 (D'Emilio, pp. 73, 110). A legal setback in 1954, the U.S. Post Office's confiscation of copies of *ONE* and subsequent declaration that it was "obscene, lewd, lascivious and filthy," ultimately led to a Supreme Court victory for ONE, Inc. in 1958, which significantly changed the lesbian and gay publishing landscape in the U.S., making it more habitable.

While both IGLA and ONE maintained separate organizational identities, Kepner and Legg both benefited mutually from the relationship. Kepner wrote articles for *ONE Magazine* and helped ONE, Inc. start its own library and develop its new additional services for the lesbian and gay community such as peer counseling, legal referrals, and travel. In 1958, as part of its dedication to the new "homophile studies," Kepner helped teach some of ONE's homophile classes, and ONE began to publish the *ONE Institute Quarterly of Homophile Studies*, the first scholarly journal dedicated to the study of homosexuality (it ceased publication in 1972). When it first began offering annual educational conferences in 1950 and graduate seminars in the field of the emerging lesbian and gay studies in 1981, ONE may not have been planning to find a warm—and fiscally robust—affiliation at USC thirteen years later in 1994, when ONE and IGLA merged to form the largest gay and lesbian library and archive in the world, housing more than two million items. But with a building dedicated by USC and continued community and corporate support, ONE Institute/International Gay & Lesbian Archives remains one of the most important resources for LBGT communities today.

At present, ONE/IGLA is active in four distinct areas. First, the merged library and archives contain more than 20,000 books and 4,000 periodical titles in a variety of languages and from countries outside of the U.S., 800 films and videos, files with more than one million clippings, newsletters, and ephemera, the papers of Dignity and the Mattachine Society, and audio recordings. Included in this collection is the Lesbian Legacy Collection, a special collection within ONE/IGLA that is "the world's largest known Lesbian collection" of lesbian materials and projects including the *ALA Guide to Lesbian Materials*, *The Southern California Lesbian Oral History Project,* and a slide show, "Lesbian Activism in Los Angeles, 1970-1990." While maintaining the computerized archive collection catalogue continues to be an ongoing process, ONE/IGLA's staff has recently begun a digital image processing and archiving project that will digitize fragile materials that are beginning to deteriorate. Second, since archives are most effective when they are being used, the ONE Institute Center for Advanced Studies, headed by gay USC professor Walter Williams, brings in leading scholars doing LBGT studies. With infrastructural support including USC's nearby Center for Scholars in Residence and a growing fellowship fund for Center Scholars, the Center for Advanced Studies is quickly developing a reputation as an LBGT think tank ensuring that the archive remains a bustling site of queer scholarly activity. Third, continuing its long tradition of publishing lesbian and gay related materials, the ONE Institute Press has begun publishing on the world wide web. *The International Gay & Lesbian Review*, edited by Williams, which provides abstracts and reviews of LBGT Studies books, and *Overcoming Heterosexism: International Perspectives*, edited by Williams and James Spears, are both available through the archives' web site, allowing its editors to provide up-to-date information. Finally, ONE/IGLA uses its vast store of resources to provide educational outreach through its ONE Forum, which sponsors a monthly series of seminars bringing together writers, artists, academics, and community leaders. With ONE/IGLA's dedication to moving queer

history into the digital age, its web site remains probably one of the best resources for anyone embarking on a queer research project.

Lesbian Herstory Archives
LHEF, Inc.
PO Box 1258
New York, New York 10116
Coordinators: Joan Nestle, Deborah Edel, and Judith Schwarz
Founded: 1973
http://www.datalounge.net/network/pages/lha//
p: 718-768-DYKE (3953)
f: 718-768-4663

Incorporated in 1980 as The Lesbian Herstory Educational Foundation, Inc., a not-for-profit foundation, Lesbian Herstory Archives (LHA) has grown to be the largest and oldest lesbian archive in the world while still maintaining the impressive commitment to the community that made its collection possible. Staffed completely by volunteers and funded by multiple small donations, the Lesbian Herstory Archives now houses more than 20,000 volumes, 12,000 photographs, 300 special collections, 1,600 periodical titles, 1,300 organizational and subject files, and countless other materials such as film and video footage, records and tapes, posters and T-shirts, and buttons and personal memorabilia. According to LHA: "The range of material is astonishing—from medical texts to steamy 1950s pulp novels to short-lived Lesbian publications, from rhinestone pasties worn by a lesbian stripper to a team-autographed softball to a lambda-emblazoned hard hat." Located in a Brooklyn, Park Slope brownstone owned by LHA, a location specifically not in an academic institution, the Lesbian Herstory Archives remains dedicated to the grassroots values on which its project has been predicated since its initial inception. Departing from the stringent requirements of most academic archives, LHA declares, "All Lesbian women must have access to the archive; no academic, political or sexual credentials may be required for usage of the collection; race and class must be no barrier for use or inclusion."

Opened in 1976 in the pantry of the Upper West Side New York apartment of Joan Nestle and Deborah Edel, the Lesbian Herstory Archives was the result of three years of planning beginning in 1973, when a lesbian consciousness-raising group at the Gay Academic Union began to grow "concerned about the failure of mainstream publishers, libraries, archives and research institutions to value Lesbian culture." After Judith Schwarz became a co-coordinator of the LHA with Nestle and Edel, all three developed a traveling slide show in order to bring the archive to others, a practice completely consistent with their deep commitment to the entire lesbian community. This slide show continues to be shown in churches, bars, houses, and other places lesbians gather all around the world. Realizing that lesbians actually live in places outside of the greater New York metropolitan area, LHA remains dedicated not only to getting visitors into the archive to see lesbian history, but also to getting the archive out to researchers all over the world. To that end, LHA's volunteers will gladly (if perhaps slowly) fill requests for specific materials to those unable to make it to New York. Requests can be sent directly to its address, and more specific directions can be found at its web site.

With its liberal dedication to collecting "any materials that are relevant to the lives and experiences of Lesbians" as well as continuing to build the collection, LHA has produced for itself a formidable challenge for the future. With the entirety of its collection—a portion of which had been stored off-site for a long time—now under one roof, the LHA volunteer staff is focusing its efforts on making the collection as accessible as possible, and producing an on-line computerized catalogue. At present, the LHA also provides performance and exhibition space and plans on providing facilities for photography and filmmaking in the future.

The National Museum & Archive of Lesbian and Gay History
The Pat Parker/Vito Russo Center Library
The Lesbian and Gay Community Services Center
208 West 13th Street
New York, New York 10011
Founded: 1988/1990
http://www.gaycenter.org
p: 212-620-7310
f: 212-924-2657

Housed in the Gay and Lesbian Services Center in New York City, the National Museum & Archive of Lesbian and Gay History is one of the largest repositories of lesbian and gay culture in the U.S.

The National Museum, showing its first exhibit in 1988, provides "space for artwork investigating the diversity and depth of gay and lesbian life." While a permanent exhibition space finally opened in 1995 with "Nuestras Vidas, Nuestras Familias, Nuestras Communidad," a photography exhibit curated by Las Buenas Amigas, the Museum's lack of a permanent space prior to 1995 did not significantly interfere with the Museum's "Center Show" in 1989, which featured site-specific installations by more than 50 artists including Keith Haring's second-floor men's room homoerotic mural as well as others by Kenny Scharf, Nancy Spero, and Leon Golub. Since then, the Museum has exhibited such shows as: *Mariette Allen Transformations: Cross-Dressers and Those Who Love Them; Keepin On: Images of Afro-American Women from the Lesbian Herstory Archives; Graphic Facts: AIDS Posters from Around the World; A Memorial Dew Cloth: Celebrating 500 Years of Native American Survival; Center Kids and AIDS: How Our Children See AIDS; Our Eyes: A Multimedia Exhibit by Lesbian and Gay Families;* and *ACT UP Tenth Anniversary: An Exhibition Marking the Founding of ACT up at the Center*, among multiple others.

The National Archive, founded in 1990 through the coordination of archivist Rich Wandel, houses thousands of papers, periodicals, correspondences, and photographs donated by lesbian and gay individuals and organizations. Some of the more notable items in the collection include papers of the Christopher Street Liberation Day Committee; the papers of performer and activist Michael Callen; the first gay cable show; the papers of the 1979 and 1987 National Marches on Washington for Lesbian and Gay Rights; and the FBI files, obtained by Martin Duberman, on the Mattachine Society, the Gay Liberation Front, and the Gay Activists Alliance. Among other activities conducted by the archive are the annual "Inqueery" lecture series; photo exhibits; New York City walking tours including "Homo Harlem," "Lesbian Ladies: Homo High Society," and "Bisexual Bystanders of the East 80s"; and

the compilation of materials for *The Lesbian Almanac* and *The Gay Almanac*. Still welcoming donations, the archive now has a computerized card catalogue and a paid part-time staffer to document the growing collection thanks to a grant from the New York State Documentary Heritage Program.

Founded in 1991, one year after the opening of the National Archive of Lesbian and Gay History, The Pat Parker/Vito Russo Center Library is named in honor of the late lesbian poet Pat Parker and the late gay film historian Vito Russo, author of the groundbreaking book *The Celluloid Closet*. Built to "encourage and facilitate the reading and research of lesbian and gay literature in a comfortable gay-affirmative space," and recently moved in 1994 to a permanent location within the Center, the Library maintains a growing collection of more than 12,000 titles of LBGT fiction and non-fiction, dozens of periodicals, and videos, the collection of which was named in honor of Michael Janik, a film professor who died of an AIDS-related illness in 1992. Thanks to volunteer efforts beginning in 1994, the Library's card catalogue became accessible through an efficient computer database in 1996.

Gay and Lesbian Historical Society of Northern California
PO Box 424280
San Francisco, California 94142
Founded: 1985
http://www.glhs.org
glhsnc@aol.com
p: 415-777-5455

A community-based, nonprofit, educational organization, Gay and Lesbian Historical Society of Northern California (GLHS) houses a collection of works of writers, artists, and photographers, as well as community organization records, posters, buttons, and anything else that documents the history of "lesbians, gay men, bisexuals, transgendered people, and queers of all kinds." As such, its collection includes: more than 80 collections from individuals and more than 40 organizational records; more than 2,300 periodical titles; a collection of erotica dating from the 1940s; subject files of both published and non-published papers; and tapes and transcriptions from its Oral History Project. The collection is unique in its focus on Northern California and the San Francisco Bay Area. A full-time professional archivist works with the assistance of community volunteers to catalogue the growing collection, which is now housed both at GLHS's Market Street Reading Room and the San Francisco Public Library (SFPL). In a joint effort to make the archive more accessible to the public, GLHS and the San Francisco Public Library agreed in 1996 to place part of the archive on permanent deposit at the James C. Hormel Gay and Lesbian Center at the main branch of the SFPL. Despite its marked enthusiasm for this new alliance, GLHS remains circumspect with regard to its collection being housed in a governmental institution. As the archive is, in part, a testament to the inability of governmental institutions to accommodate adequately the needs of LBGT people, GLHS has reserved through a legal contract the right to remove its collection from the San Francisco Public Library.

In addition to the activities of the archive, GLHS also publishes a newsletter and sponsors multiple programs and exhibits. Past exhibits include: *History on Fabric: 20 Years of T-Shirts; The Lesbian Erotic: Pictures from 1975-1995; Shedding a Straitjacket: Homophile Civil Rights/Homosexual Liberation 1961-66; Found-*

ing a Dynasty: José Sarria, the Black Cat, & the San Francisco Imperial System; and, most recently, *Queer & Kinky Danger: Artists Relating to Leather, SM, Kink.* GLHS's web site also features a links page of other LBGT archives and libraries in the U.S., Canada, and Europe.

Center for Lesbian and Gay Studies
The Graduate School and University Center of the City
    University of New York
33 West 42nd Street, Room 404N
New York, New York 10036
ED: Jill Dolan
Founded: 1991
clags@broadway.gc.cuny.edu
p: 212-642-2924

Founded formally in 1991 by Martin Duberman, gay historian and author of 16 books including *Hidden from History* and *Stonewall,* Center for Lesbian and Gay Studies (CLAGS) actually began taking form much earlier, in 1985 in Duberman's living room, when he invited a few other scholars to discuss "possibilities for establishing a research institute that would encourage and disseminate reliable scholarship on gender and sexual nonconformity" (Duberman, 1997, p. 1). Unlike the independent ONE Institute, CLAGS' placement in the Graduate School at CUNY makes it "the first university-affiliated research center in the United States devoted to the study of gay and lesbian subjects" (CLAGS *Directory*). Receiving only a small portion of its funding today from CUNY, though, CLAGS remains an organization driven by membership contributions from its more than 2,000 members. According to Duberman: "CLAGS went through a protracted struggle to come into existence and a difficult journey of survival and growth. Its many public successes were matched by periodic internal strife over how best to implement the feminist and multicultural values on which it had been founded. But that history must be left for future telling" (Duberman, 1993, p. 1). While that future remains to be told officially, the profitable consequences of those earlier conflicts can be seen in CLAGS' ongoing commitment to sometimes boisterous but always intellectually engaging programming, as it continues its perennial negotiation of the problem of what it means to work at the intersection of feminist and multicultural concerns within a lesbian and gay organization.

Its first public event, "New York City Lesbian and Gay History and Culture," in 1987, was the first of many following conferences, symposia, and colloquia. Operating as a venue for work-in-progress, CLAGS has most recently brought scholars such as Nayan Shah speaking on "Asian Men, White Boys, and the Policing of Sex in Early Twentieth-Century California" and Sasha Torres on "The Epistemology of the Toaster Oven." Always inhabiting the porous boundaries of LBGT studies, CLAGS has recently sponsored such conferences as "Black Nations?/Queer Nations?"; "Identity/Space/Power: Lesbian, Gay, Bisexual and Transgender Politics"; "Queer Globalization/Local Homosexualities: Citizenship, Sexuality, and the Afterlife of Colonialism"; and "Anxious Pleasures: A Symposium on the Erotics of Pedagogy," bringing together Jane Gallop, David Eng, Jim Kincaid, and Ann Pellegrini. In addition to producing and sponsoring multiple conferences, CLAGS also awards Rockefeller Humanities Fellowship annually to scholars doing consequential work in the field of LBGT

studies. Its annual David R. Kessler Endowed Lectureship also honors scholars who have made a significant impact in gay and lesbian scholarship and communities. Past honorees include French feminist and activist Monique Wittig and writer and professor Samuel Delany.

COMMUNITY CENTERS

Society for Individual Rights
Founded: Organization, 1964/community center 1966

While the Mattachine Society, Daughters of Bilitis, and ONE certainly provided the initial articulations of the emerging homophile movement throughout the late 1950s and early 1960s, it was the Society for Individual Rights (SIR) that established the first U.S. gay community center, a center that most resembles the community center that is so integral to the cohesion of LBGT communities across the country today. What made SIR so different from the other dominant homophile groups in San Francisco was its refusal to separate politics from social life and its belief that the "community" was, in fact, the site of political mobilization. As SIR's first president, William Berdemphl, wrote in SIR's magazine *Vector*: "There is not now, and never has been, a 'Homophile Movement.' Our work is to create a Community feeling that will bring a 'Homophile Movement' into being." As John D'Emilio notes, the founding members of SIR, many of whom ran gay bars—like Bill Plath who ran the D'Oak Room bar and was president of the Tavern Guild, an association of gay bar proprietors and employees that published the legal guide "Pocket Lawyer"—understood the centrality of gay bars to the emerging gay community and effectively used these spaces to politically mobilize their patrons through social functions (D'Emilio, pp. 189-91). "[SIR] held dances, parties, brunches, and drag entertainments. It sponsored bridge clubs, bowling leagues, outings in the country, meditation groups, and art classes. With goods collected from the gay male community, it operated a thrift shop, staffed by volunteers, that provided a regular source of income for the organization. In April 1966, it opened a gay community center in San Francisco, the first of its kind in the country." By 1967, SIR counted almost 1,000 gays among its membership, becoming at that time the largest homophile organization in the country (D'Emilio, pp. 190-91).

As Hal Call, who took over the Mattachine Society in 1953, recalls: "Mattachine was going into eclipse by the late 1960s. In fact, it went downhill from the time the Society for Individual Rights came into being in 1964. A lot of the people who worked with Mattachine in the early days became involved in SIR because it was more strongly a membership-participation and volunteer service-type group" (Marcus, p. 68). Nancy May, a heterosexual woman married to a gay man and the only female founding member of SIR, recalls that SIR began after Guy Strait's gay rights group, the League for Civil Education, dissolved (Marcus, p. 138). Coming from various backgrounds, SIR's members certainly had much political experience, and that experience led them to produce a democratically based organization that was very much unlike earlier attempts to organize gays. "I wanted SIR to be everything for everybody," recalls Nancy May. "It was to be for the grass-roots people, unlike Mattachine, which was an elitist kind of thing. SIR was for the people who wanted to have places where people could go to further their interests" (Marcus, p. 139). While the history of the rise of LBGT community centers across the country is a discontinuous one that reflects the particular needs of the communities that have created and continue to create them, May's vision of what SIR was to become has served as the silent template for the creation of LBGT community centers since 1966.

National Association of Lesbian and Gay Community Centers
c/o Lesbian and Gay Community Services Center
2088 West 13th Street
New York, New York 10012
Conveners: Dallas, Los Angeles, Minneapolis, New York, and Denver
Founded: 1994
webmaster@gaycenter.org
p: 212-620-7310

Today, more than three decades after the establishment of the SIR Community Center in San Francisco, the National Association of Lesbian and Gay Community Centers (NALGCC) operates as a network that enables community centers throughout the U.S. to exchange ideas and program models. Although community center representatives have been meeting annually since 1987 at the National Lesbian & Gay Health Association, they did not convene as a formal body until 1994, when representatives from more than 30 community centers from around the country met at the New York City Lesbian & Gay Community Services Center in preparation for Stonewall 25. Presently, NALGCC organizes a nationwide Promote the Vote project and has produced an on-line *National Directory of Lesbian & Gay Community Centers* (http://www.gaycenter.org/natctr), maintained by the New York City Lesbian & Gay Community Services Center. The sixteenth edition of the *Directory* lists more than 75 separate organizations, 5 of which—located in Santa Barbara, San Diego, Los Angeles, Chicago, and New York—have annual budgets that exceed $1 million.

Los Angeles Gay & Lesbian Center
1625 N. Schrader Boulevard
Los Angeles, California 90028-6213
ED: Lorri L. Jean
Founded: 1971
http://www.gay-lesbian-center.org
p: 213-993-7400

The oldest community center in the U.S., offering services since 1971, the Los Angeles Gay & Lesbian Center maintains the largest annual budget of all the LBGT community centers. With an annual budget of approximately $20 million, 65 percent of which is derived from government grants with the remaining coming from individual donors, corporate, and foundation donations, and fundraising events, the Los Angeles Gay & Lesbian Center maintains three satellite locations in addition to its McDonald/Wright Headquarters. It is also planning to open a Community Education Center at another location in June 1998 that will offer not only much needed space, including a 200-seat multimedia auditorium, multiple community meeting rooms, and offices for non-profit gay and lesbian organizations, but also self-enrichment courses and educational opportunities. The Education Center will be the new home for the Center's HIV-prevention programs.

Its substantial budget has enabled the Los Angeles Gay & Lesbian Center to hire more than 240 full-time staff and provide an incredible array of social services to the community. The Center's Health Services Program comprises the Jeffrey Goodmam Special Care Clinics in Hollywood and Century City, which, according to the Center, offer the most comprehensive system for HIV/AIDS care in Los Angeles; the Pedro Zamora Youth HIV Clinic, the country's first peer care clinic; the Audre Lorde Lesbian Health Clinic; as well as a broad range of mental health services at low cost. Its California AIDS Clearinghouse (CAIN) produces and distributes all AIDS educational materials on behalf of the state of California and also funds the production of other educational materials as well. In addition to its multiple health-related services, the Center maintains an extensive Community Outreach & Education Department, soon to be housed in the new Education Center; Legal Services; Youth Services, including the Jeff Griffith Gay & Lesbian Youth Center, serving primarily homeless and runaway youth; and the Department of Policy and Public Affairs, which seeks to fulfill the Center's mission of "increasing the public understanding of gay and lesbian lives." While no other community center's budget surpasses that of Los Angeles', the majority of others throughout the U.S. are able to operate within their communities with significantly smaller budgets, serving not only as social outlets, but as the organizational structure that coheres and serves often radically diverse constituencies within the LBGT community.

STUDENT ORGANIZATIONS

Student Homophile League
Columbia-Barnard Lesbian Bisexual Gay Coalition
106 Earl Hall, Mail Code 2000
Columbia University
New York, New York 10027
Founded: 1967
http://www.columbia.edu/cu/lbgc/home.html
lbgc@columbia.edu
p: 212-854-1488

The institutional site where many American college-bound teenagers come out, the university lesbian and gay group has become an indispensable territory on many college campuses where queer family drama, political activism, rap groups, and frank talk of safer sex practices all happen simultaneously. The first such group was Columbia University's Student Homophile League (SHL), a group of 12 students that met in secrecy for the first time in 1967 to form a support and discussion group for its members. Deciding they wanted to be recognized as an official student group, the group's leader, Robert Martin, a.k.a. "Steven Donaldson," approached the university and was granted recognition for the group on 19 April. Both the *Columbia Spectator*, the student newspaper, and the *New York Times* reported the group's formation and caused a tumultuous argument both on and off campus. According to the Columbia-Barnard Lesbian Bisexual Gay Coalition, the descendent of SHL: "Then-Dean of Columbia College David Truman called the group 'quite unnecessary,' and the director of counseling services, Dr. Anthony Philip, feared that the group would encourage 'deviant behavior.' It was only with the support of University Chaplain Rev. John Cannon that the group was able to continue, and even then it was forbidden to serve a social function for fear that this would lead to violations of New York State sodomy laws." Undeterred by SHL's problems, other student groups took root at New York University, Cornell, and Stanford that same year (D'Emilio, p. 210).

By 1968, with its students critical of the university's plan to place an athletic facility in neighboring Harlem's Morningside Park, Columbia had become a veritable battleground for student uprisings. On the same day in April that student protests erupted, eventually closing down the university, SHL members picketed a medical school-sponsored forum on homosexuality that had failed to include a homosexual on the panel and distributed a flyer that read, "It is time that homosexuality be pulled out of the morass of psychiatry, 'abnormality' and 'emotional disturbance' ... and placed into its proper setting as a sociological problem of deeply entrenched prejudice and discrimination against a minority group" (quoted in D'Emilio, p. 216). After several more years of SHL campus activism, Columbia's administration established in 1971—in the basement of Furnald Hall—the "Furnald Gay Lounge," today called the "Steven Donaldson Queer Lounge," and instituted the First Friday Dance, a monthly event that to this day ensures that the Morningside Heights neighborhood is filled with gay men at least one night per month.

Today, the Columbia-Barnard Lesbian Bisexual Gay Coalition operates as an umbrella group for the multiple and diverse campus groups including GABLES (Gay, Bisexual, and Lesbian Employees and Supporters), Queergrads, Queers of Color, Queer Studies Group, Campus Queers for Christ, Gayava (GLB Jewish students), BIONIC (Bisexuality discussion group), and LABIA (Lesbians and Bisexuals in Action), as well as many others. Since 1968, LBGT people on Columbia's campus have certainly and increasingly encountered a supportive community as well as a modicum of institutional support; Columbia extended domestic partner benefits in 1993 to university employees. Yet, as with all campus LBGT organizing, the fight is a continuing and arduous one. As GABLES' Stephen Davis points out, "Although Columbia is credited with having the first campus gay and lesbian *student* organization ... many gay, lesbian and bisexual faculty and staff at the University have until recently considered the general social and political environment of Columbia to be 'closeted' and unaccepting of them." Although the genealogy of Columbia's LBGT student groups will seem familiar to most people who have been or are active in campus LBGT politics and activism, every campus poses its own particular challenges, which each different LBGT group must confront according to the needs of its constituents. Columbia's Student Homophile League, the first gay student group to exist, may be an excellent example of the making of a campus LBGT movement, but it remains only one narrative among many campus movements that have and continue to respond differently according to the particular circumstances—inflected by differences in class, race, gender, region, etc.—that those groups inhabit.

RELIGIOUS ORGANIZATIONS

Although religion has received relatively little attention from historians of LBGT organizing, many LBGT people in the U.S. have looked precisely to churches and other kinds of spirituality for support. Harry Hay's Radical Faeries, a gay spirituality group established in 1979, is perhaps the most "queer" religious group in existence today. But most denominations in the U.S. have divi-

sions that attend to the needs of their LBGT congregations. Some of the larger groups include: Affirmation/Gay & Lesbian Mormons, Affirmation (United Methodist), Dignity (Catholic), Emergence International (Christian Science), Honesty (Southern Baptist), Integrity (Episcopal), Maitri Dorje (Buddhist), National Gay Pentecostal Alliance, Presbyterians for Lesbian/Gay Concerns, and the World Congress of Gay and Lesbian Jewish Organizations. The Unitarian Universalists, "a liberal religion born of the Jewish and Christian traditions," organized in 1961 by consolidating two religious denominations, has concerned itself with gay issues since 1971, when Reverend Richard Nash and Elgin Blair co-founded the UU Gay Caucus to lobby for the creation of an Office of Gay Affairs. By 1973, the UU General Assembly resolved to create that office, now named The Office of Bisexual, Gay, Lesbian and Transgender Concerns. As early as 1984, the Unitarian Universalists began allowing clergy to perform "Services of Union" between same-gender couples. (UU Queer History, http://uua.org) While the Unitarian Universalists have been overwhelmingly accommodating of LBGT congregations, the church is not necessarily a "gay church."

Metropolitan Community Church
UFMCC World Center
8704 Santa Monica Blvd., 2nd Floor
West Hollywood, California 90069
Moderator: Rev. Elder Troy D. Perry
Founded: 1968
http://www.ufmcc.com
info@ufmcchq.com
p: 310-360-8640
f: 310-360-8680

Although other attempts to form gay churches preceded its formation, the Metropolitan Community Church (MCC), now a fellowship of more than 32,000 members and 300 Christian congregations in 19 countries, remains the largest LBGT church in the world today. Realizing that most LBGT people have been raised to believe that religion is antithetical to homosexuality, MCC seeks to provide a space that will allow for its congregations to be LBGT and spiritual at the same time. The idea for this church, in fact, arose out of the fact that its founder, Revered Troy D. Perry, then 27, was "defrocked by his Pentecostal church for homosexuality and recovering from a suicide attempt." A few months after his removal, on 6 October 1968, Perry held a worship service for 11 men and one woman, a small congregation composed of Protestants, Catholics, and one Jewish person. This was the Metropolitan Community Church's first service. Since the congregation's first meeting, MCC has become the Universal Fellowship of Metropolitan Community Churches. Although the 1994 Los Angeles earthquake destroyed its "mother" church, UFMCC's ongoing capital campaign has enabled it to purchase a new space in the middle of West Hollywood. Today, many LBGT people still feel that religion is antithetical to homosexuality, but UFMCC's rapid growth, along with the work of other LBGT religious concerns, has effected a substantial change within LBGT communities and has functionally ensured that religion will continue to play a significant role in the determination of LBGT identities in the future.

HIV/AIDS ORGANIZATIONS

Gay Men's Health Crisis
119 West 24th Street
New York, New York 10011
Founded: 1981
http://www.gmhc.org
p: 212-807-6664

In July 1981, a *New York Times* article announced boldly "Rare Cancer Seen in 41 Homosexuals." Gay author Larry Kramer responded to this news by inviting 80 men to his apartment to hear a doctor speak about this "gay cancer," what was eventually diagnosed as Kaposi's sarcoma. That night, Kramer raised $6,635 for biomedical research when a hat was passed around. By October, the CDC had declared the disease—soon to be known as GRID (Gay Related Immune Deficiency) and later AIDS (Acquired Immunodeficiency Syndrome)—an epidemic. Six months after this initial meeting, six gay men—Nathan Fain, Larry Kramer, Larry Mass, Paul Popham, Paul Rapoport, and Edmund White—met in Kramer's apartment and officially named themselves Gay Men's Health Crisis (GMHC). In 1982, they started the world's first AIDS Hotline (212-807-6665), and opened their first office in a donated space on West 22nd Street in New York City. By 1984, when the CDC had isolated HIV (Human Immunodeficiency Virus), the infectious agent believed to cause AIDS, GMHC had published its first safe-sex pamphlet, *Healthy Sex Is Great Sex*, and by 1985 it had expanded its Education Department to include an AIDS Prevention program and opened an Ombudsman's Office to deal with complaints that people with AIDS were being met by health care professionals who refused to examine them. Throughout the 1980s and 1990s, GMHC continued to develop its resources, producing, among other educational media, the *GMHC Safer Sex Comix*, which Senator Jesse Helms labeled "disgusting," advocated for AIDS patient confidentiality, helped the passage of the Ryan White Comprehensive AIDS Resources Emergency (CARE) Act, and served as a model for other AIDS services organizations across the U.S.

Today, GMHC is the oldest and largest not-for-profit AIDS organization in the United States. With more than 8,500 clients, 6,500 volunteers, 291 staff, and an annual budget of $31 million, 80 percent of which comes from private donors, GMHC seeks through its mission to provide compassionate care to New Yorkers with AIDS, educate to keep people healthy, and advocate for fair and effective public policies. Offering everything from individual and group therapy, nutritional counseling, recreational classes, and baby-sitting to legal assistance on landlord/tenant disputes, estate planning, debt/credit problems, discrimination, insurance, immigration, and custody matters, GMHC remains the largest service provider to people with AIDS/HIV in New York City. While it is the largest, it is important to remember that it is, however, certainly not the only AIDS services organization in New York City. Nonetheless, GMHC's monetary resources do allow it to distribute annually more than one million educational brochures, fact sheets, and publications such as *Treatment Issues* and to produce multiple seminars and workshops to educate gay men, lesbians, bisexuals, and drug users about AIDS/HIV. While GMHC's work has been essential to the passage of the Americans with Disabilities Act and New York State's confidentiality law, fundamental challenges still present themselves with regards to AIDS advocacy. Among the formidable tasks that GMHC sees for itself are

assuring explicit AIDS education for communities at risk, more HIV prevention behavioral studies, streamlined research to speed AIDS drugs and a cure, and improving managed care for people with HIV, and protecting Medicaid Programs.

———————

The NAMES Project Foundation
310 Townsend Street, Suite 310
San Francisco, California 94107
ED: Anthony Turney
Founded: 1985
http://www.aidsquilt.org/names/
info@aidsquilt.org
p: 415-882-5500
f: 415-882-6200

Perhaps the most awesome testimonial to the AIDS pandemic to date, the AIDS Quilt, as the NAMES Project is colloquially known, is a symbol of mourning for those who have died of AIDS-related illnesses that insists that the lives of people with AIDS must always be remembered. The idea for an AIDS quilt was conceived by San Francisco gay rights activist Cleve Jones in 1985 at a candlelight march commemorating the assassinations of Mayor George Moscone and San Francisco Supervisor Harvey Milk. During the march's planning stages, the number of AIDS-related deaths in San Francisco had passed 1,000, and so Jones asked the marchers to write the names of those who had died on placards. As Jones remembers: "It was a startling image. The wind and rain tore some of the cardboard names loose, but people stood there for hours reading names. I knew then that we needed a monument, a memorial" (Sturken, p. 185). About two years later, in February 1987, Jones and Joseph Durant made the first two panels, measuring 3 by 6 feet—about the size of a human grave—to commemorate the lives of Marvin Feldman and Ed Mock. On 28 January, the Quilt, now with 40 sections, was shown publicly for the first time at San Francisco's City Hall. On 11 October, 1,920 memorial panels were exhibited at the March on Washington for Lesbian and Gay Rights. Steadily, the size of the AIDS Memorial Quilt grew as it began touring the country and raising money for local AIDS service organizations.

During its first national tour in 1988, the Quilt visited 20 cities and grew by 6,000 panels as visitors added memorial panels. Although the enormity of the Quilt prohibits it from being shown in its entirety most of the time it is displayed, the complete Quilt has been shown in Washington, D.C. in 1987, 1988, 1989, 1992, and, most recently, in 1996 on the mall. The Quilt was nominated for a Nobel Peace Prize in 1989, and parts of it were carried by marchers in President Clinton's 1993 inaugural parade. With almost 50 national chapters and 37 international affiliates, The NAMES Project continues to expand, but not without contention. The project of graphically remembering diverse individuals from multiple communities raises divisive issues and remains a work in process that continually interrogates the questions of how to remember the dead. A kind of anti-memorial, one that is constantly moving, constantly in the making, and constantly growing, the Quilt marks the inability to completely mourn the deaths of people with AIDS until the final panel is stitched to the Quilt. At present, the quilt is comprised of more than 43,000 panels.

———————

ACT UP
332 Bleecker St., Suite G5
New York, New York 10014
Founded: 1987
http://www.actupny.org
actupny@panix.com
p: 212-966-4873

Embattled, fierce, and "in your face," the AIDS Coalition To Unleash Power (ACT UP) can be credited with literally forcing AIDS onto the national agenda in the U.S. With President Reagan only publicly speaking the word "AIDS" for the first time in May 1987, six years after Kaposi's sarcoma and pneumocystis carinii pneumonia (PCP) had been identified in a growing number of gay men, gay men and lesbians realized that the federal government would not make AIDS a priority unless it was forced to do so. On 10 March 1987, Larry Kramer, author of *Faggots* and *The Normal Heart* and co-founder of the Gay Men's Health Crisis, was asked to replace Nora Ephron at the New York Lesbian and Gay Community Services Center's speaker's series. Instead of speaking about his writing, he made a plea for the need of a community organization that would mobilize politically around the AIDS epidemic. Within a few days, ACT UP was formed. Call-ing itself a "diverse, nonpartisan group of individuals united in anger and committed to direct action to end the AIDS Crisis," ACT UP not only inspired a contentious national dialogue on AIDS/HIV, but also helped to produced a model for a new genera-tion of LBGT direct action activism. As gay film historian Vito Russo recalls: "This is a new kind of activism. It's a coalition that we were never able to achieve in the 1970s. Back then the idea and the dream were that gay people would come together with other oppressed groups like blacks and Asians and women to form a coalition. That didn't happen because we had too many differences" (Marcus, pp. 415-16).

Seeing the productivity of differences within a group and rec-ognizing the necessity of allowing for those differences to exist, ACT UP specifically figured itself as a coalition whose member-ship was loosely comprised of affinity groups. As Douglas Crimp and Adam Rolston point out: "A tradition of Left organizing, af-finity groups are small associations of people within activist move-ments whose mutual trust and shared interests allow them to func-tion autonomously and secretly, arrive at quick decisions by con-sensus, protect one another at demonstrations, and participate as units in coordinated acts of civil disobedience. ACT UP's affinity groups function in all of these ways, but our affinities, like our identities, are complexly constituted" (Crimp and Rolston, p. 21).

Members of ACT UP protest at the Department of Health and Human Services.

The Silence=Death Project, a group of six gay men who created the now famous graphic of a pink triangle on a black background printed above the slogan, "Silence=Death," is one such affinity group. Although they had been active several months before ACT UP's formation, their work soon came to emblematize ACT UP, and sales of Silence=Death T-shirts, pins, and stickers soon became ACT UP's primary source of revenue. Other affinity groups include: Gran Fury, an artist collective recognized as "ACT UP's unofficial propaganda ministry and guerrilla graphic designers" (Crimp and Rolston, p. 16), which produced many of the stunning graphics associated with ACT UP; Little Elvis; Testing the Limits; DIVA TV (Damned Interfering Video Activist Television; and LAPIT (Lesbian Activists Producing Interesting Television).

ACT UP's first action, a demonstration on Wall Street "to protest the alliance between the FDA and Burroughs Wellcome," the pharmaceutical company that had been granted a monopoly on the newly announced and incredibly costly drug AZT, took place on 24 March, 14 days after Kramer's speech. More than 250 ACT UP protesters showed up, and 17 were arrested for civil disobedience. The demonstration was reported on national news, and a few weeks later the FDA sped up its drug approval process. Soon thereafter, autonomous ACT UP chapters began appearing all around the country. Although ACT UP does not today generally receive as much media attention as it initially received when, for example, its women's caucus overtook New York's Shea Stadium in 1988 with banners reading "AIDS Kills Women" and "No Glove, No Love," or when, in 1989, ACT UP members stormed New York's St. Patrick's Cathedral in a massive die-in to criticize Cardinal John O'Connor's repudiation of safe-sex practices such as condom use, ACT UP has chapters in major cities around the U.S. as well as in Europe that continue to fight, using direct action tactics, for an end to AIDS. Its New York web site offers a plenitude of resources for starting an ACT UP group, researching ACT UP, or simply learning about the current AIDS crisis. Although ACT UP is far from finished with its work, ACT UP/NY's archive, located in the New York Public Library's Rare Manuscript Division, holds many of its documents from the years 1987 to 1995 and is accessible to anyone doing research on this group, which has mobilized many into action in the fight against AIDS.

REFERENCES:

Berlant, Lauren and Elizabeth Freeman. "Queer Nationalities," in *National Identities & Post-Americanist Narratives,* edited by Donald Pease. Durham: Duke University Press, 1994.

Butler, Judith. *Gender Trouble: Feminism and the Subversion of Identity.* New York: Routledge, 1990.

Crimp, Douglas and Adam Rolston. *AIDS DEMO GRAPHICS.* Seattle: Bay Press, 1990.

Davis-Rosenthal, Jim. Internet interview with Elliott R. Trice, 7 April 1998.

De Lauretis, Teresa, ed. "Queer Theory: Lesbian and Gay Sexualities, An Introduction," in *differences,* vol. 3, no. 2, 1991.

D'Emilio, John. *Sexual Politics, Sexual Communities: The Making of a Homosexual Minority in the United States, 1940-1970.* Chicago: University of Chicago Press, 1983.

Duberman, Martin. *A Queer World: The Center for Lesbian and Gay Studies Reader.* New York: New York University Press, 1997.

―――. *Stonewall.* New York: Plume, 1993.

Faderman, Lillian. *Odd Girls and Twilight Lovers: A History of Lesbian Life in Twentieth-Century America.* New York: Penguin, 1991.

Hevesi, Alan C. *Lesbian and Gay Directory of Services and Resources: New York Metropolitan Area.* New York: Office of the Comptroller, June 1996.

Katz, Jonathan Ned. *Gay American History: Lesbian and Gay Men in the U.S.A.* New York: Meridian, 1992.

"A Look at the Largest Gay Political Organizations," in the *Washington Blade,* vol. 28, no. 50, 12 December 1997.

Marcus, Eric. *Making History: The Struggle for Gay and Lesbian Equal Rights, 1945-1990.* New York: HarperPerennial, 1992.

Moyer, Carrie and Dyke Action Machine! "Do You Love the Dyke in Your Face?" in *Queers in Space: Communities, Public Spaces, Sites of Resistance,* edited by Gordon Brent Ingram, Anne-Marie Bouthillette, and Yolanda Retter. Seattle: Bay Press, 1997.

Rutledge, Leigh. *The Gay Book of Lists.* Boston: Alyson Publications, 1987.

Schulman, Sarah. *My American History: Lesbian and Gay Life During the Reagan/Bush Years.* New York: Routledge, 1994.

Sturken, Marita. *Tangled Memories: The Vietnam War, The AIDS Epidemic, and the Politics of Remembering.* Berkeley and Los Angeles: University of California Press, 1997.

Wolfe, Maxine. "This Is about People Dying: The Tactics of Early ACT UP and Lesbian Avengers in New York City," in *Queers in Space: Communities, Public Spaces, Sites of Resistance,* edited by Gordon Brent Ingram, Anne-Marie Bouthillette, and Yolanda Retter. Seattle: Bay Press, 1997.

—Elliott R. Trice

3

Significant Documents

- Chicago Vice Commission, "The Social Evil in Chicago: A Study of Existing Conditions" (Chicago: Gunthorp-Warren Printing, 1911)
- Myler Vollmer, "The New Year's Eve Drag," Unpublished, undated paper, circa 1930, from Burgess Collection, University of Chicago Archives
- Alfred Kinsey, *Sexual Behavior in the Human Male* (Philadelphia: W.B. Saunder Company, 1948). Excerpts from Chapter 21, "Homosexual Outlet" (excluding tables)
- United States Senate, *Employment of Homosexuals and Other Sex Perverts in Government*, Senate Document # 241, 81st Congress, 2nd session, 15 December 1950
- Ralph Major, "New Moral Menace to Our Youth," *Coronet*, September 1950
- Statement of Purpose, Daughters of Bilitis (1955)
- Franklin Kameny, "Civil Liberties: A Progress Report," speech delivered on 22 July 1964, to The Mattachine Society of New York
- Carl Wittman, "A Gay Manifesto," (1969)
- Radicalesbians, "The Woman-Identified Woman," 1970
- Harvey Milk, "That's What America Is," speech, 25 June 1978
- Audre Lorde, "I Am Your Sister: Black Women Organizing across Sexualities," 1980
- Larry Kramer, "1,112 and Counting," *The New York Native*, 14-27 March 1983
- Supreme Court of the United States, *Bowers v. Hardwick*, 30 June 1986
- *Baehr v. Lewin*, Supreme Court of Hawaii, May 1993
- Pentagon Policy Guidelines on Homosexuals in the Military, 19 July 1993
- Colorado's Amendment 2, 1992
- The Employment Non-Discrimination Act (ENDA)

The following chapter consists of several documents that pertain significantly in some way to gay and lesbian culture. The title of each piece is followed by a brief introduction (in italics), and then the text of the article, speech, court case, etc.

CHICAGO VICE COMMISSION, "THE SOCIAL EVIL IN CHICAGO: A STUDY OF EXISTING CONDITIONS" (CHICAGO: GUNTHORP-WARREN PRINTING, 1911)

Evidence of a visible homosexual subculture in the United States dates back to at least the turn of the twentieth century. Long be-fore the formation of any organized political movement, a gay and lesbian subculture flourished in large American cities and was noted and recorded by professionals from a variety of fields. The psychiatric literature from the end of the nineteenth and beginning of the twentieth centuries is replete with studies and observations of persons variously labeled "inverts," "perverts," "members of the third sex," or "homosexual." Police and judicial records are another source of information, since homosexual acts were against the law in all states until 1961, and places where gays and lesbians congregated were subject to periodic raids. Perhaps the most interesting observations of a burgeoning gay subculture were made by moral reformers during the Progressive Era. In their efforts to eliminate vice from America's fast-growing cities—particularly female prostitution, which they referred to as "the social evil"—they often discovered commercial establishments in urban "red-light" districts that catered to gay men. The Chicago Vice Commission, established by Mayor Busse in 1910 under pressure from the Chicago church federation, was typical of these moral reform organizations. In its final report, the Commission included a description of "whole groups and colonies" of gay men it had unexpectedly encountered. The Commission was able to identify these groups because of their tendency to use gender inversion as a way to announce their homosexuality. Although not all gay men adopted this mode of self-presentation, the fact that many did suggests a degree of openness about homosexuality not generally associated with this period.

* * *

At the very outset of the Commission's investigation, its attention was called by several persons to a condition of affairs with regard to sexual perversion which was said to be enormously prevalent and growing in Chicago. In reporting their impressions of their work on the Municipal bench at the Harrison street court, Judges X and Y said that the most striking thing they had observed in the last year was the great increase of sex perversion in Chicago. Police officers state the same thing. The testimony of others and the results of investigations by the Commission corroborate these statements. The Commission already had considerable information, including estimates which seemed incredible before an investigator was put in the field to find out the nature and extent of this form of vice.

The Commission's investigator was, of course, unable to gain entrance into those circles of the very well-to-do which are engaged in these practices, nor did he concern himself with the lowest stratum of society, which is the class most observable in our courts. Nor did he gain any information about the much more occasional cases among women, of which the Commission heard something from other sources. He most readily, however, became acquainted with whole groups and colonies of these men who are sex perverts, but who do not fall in the hands of the police on account of their practices, and who are not known in their true character to any extent by physicians because their habits do not, as a rule, produce bodily disease. It is noteworthy that the details of information gained from a police officer, who was once detailed on this work, and from a young professional student, who himself, for a time, has been partially engaged in this practice, were completely substantiated by the Commission's investigator.

It appears that in this community there is a large number of men who are thoroughly gregarious in habit; who mostly affect the carriage, mannerisms, and speech of women; who are fond of many articles ordinarily dear to the feminine heart; who are often people of a good deal of talent; who lean to the fantastic in dress and other modes of expression, and who have a definite cult with regard to sexual life. They preach the value of non-association with women from various standpoints and yet with one another have practices which are nauseous and repulsive. Many of them speak of themselves or each other with the adoption of feminine terms, and go by girls' names or fantastic application of women's titles. They have a vocabulary and signs of recognition of their own, which serve as an introduction into their own society. The cult has produced some literature, much of which is incomprehensible to one who cannot read between the lines, and there is considerable distribution among them of pernicious photographs.

In one of the large music halls recently, a much applauded act was that of a man who by facial expression and bodily contortion represented sex perversion, a most disgusting performance. It was evidently not at all understood by many of the audience, but others wildly applauded. Then, one of the songs recently ruled off the stage by the police department was inoffensive to innocent ears, but was really written by a member of the cult, and replete with suggestiveness to those who understood the language of this group.

MYLER VOLLMER, "THE NEW YEAR'S EVE DRAG," UNPUBLISHED, UNDATED PAPER, CIRCA 1930, FROM BURGESS COLLECTION, UNIVERSITY OF CHICAGO ARCHIVES

By the 1920s and 1930s, another group of professionals began to take note of the gay subculture. Sociologists doing field work in the neighborhoods and commercial establishments of American cities encountered gay men frequently and often incorporated them into their work. The following document was written by students of sociologist Ernest Burgess at the University of Chicago. It describes a phenomenon that had become a regular fixture of the social calendar in most major American cities by this time—gay drag balls. Prior to the advent of gay and lesbian pride marches, they were probably the largest gatherings of gays and lesbians in most cities. As evidenced by the presence of police officers, they were sanctioned by the city and in fact frequented by many of the city's non-gay elite. These drag balls suggest that although homosexuals were not generally accepted in American society at this time, their existence was not nearly as marginal as once thought.

*   *   *

Twice a year, with the knowledge and protection of Chicago's officialdom, do the homosexuals of the city gather in great num-

bers for their semi-annual costume ball, at which conventions and repressions are flung to the winds. New Year's Eve and Halloween mark the occasions for the celebrations of the "shadow world."

Picking our way carefully down south Wabash Avenue last New Year's Eve ... we arrived at the Coliseum Annex. The sidewalks and entrance to the hall were crowded with men hanging around, joking at the arrival of each newcomer in costume, overly eager to enter into conversation with you. Our guides told us that they were all "wise" and curious, some just looking on, others there for a possible pick-up with some homosexual at the Drag, some there to prey on the less experienced boys who were inside cavorting to the music. We were soon to discover that where homosexuals congregate, there also are the racketeers, black-mailers, jackrollers, and all their ilk who prey on another's misfortunes—made possible because a hypocritical society insists on calling homosexuality a "crime"—as though the poor unfortunates could help themselves!

Entering the hall, one recognized at once uniformed guards from the Chicago Stadium, very much in evidence, and also noted that they were selected for their size and physique. The Drag was well guarded by them, as well as by numerous uniformed policeman, and several plain-clothes-men—for this was one occasion when official Chicago put its approval on the public appearance of its intermediate sex.

Despite the rundown appearance of the Annex, it was an unusual and colorful sight to see some five hundred persons dancing and standing about, swaying to the music of a colored jazz orchestra. It was a strange and unconventional sight, however, because here we see two young men in street clothes dancing together, cheek to cheek, holding one another in close embrace, as any girl and boy would at any dance, save, perhaps, that the two youths were much more intense in their forbidden roles.

Here are two persons, both dressed in gorgeous evening gowns, one with a tiara, both in slim high French heeled satin slippers, and heavily jewelled, dancing together gracefully, without any suggestive movements. And both are men! Heavily powdered, with eyebrows pencilled and rouged lips and cheeks, their arms and hands taking effeminate gestures, it is difficult to discern their true sex.

Here is something else. Two young men, very slender, in sack suits well tailored, with ties and shirts well matched, are dancing together. But they seem different from the other men in street clothes who are dancing together. This couple is too graceful for masculine movements. Then we see that they are two girls—both Lesbians, finely featured, with boyish bobbed haircuts, playing the role of young manhood.

There are also the men in street clothes, lacking courage to come in Drag, who are dancing with other men, occasionally embracing and kissing them in moments of abandon. Young effeminate lads, older men of more masculinity, and the old men, paunchy with bald heads and lustful expressions.... There are some pitiful creatures there; homosexuals who have been unable to make the adjustment to society's conventions, and are beaten. Lads who in bitterness and resentment have resorted to promiscuity, alcohol, and narcotics, as escape mechanisms....

Falsetto voices sound in our ears. We hear expressions such as "Maude," "dearie," "fannie." There are shrill exclamations of glee and merriment as the men in women's clothing frequent the toilet marked plainly "Women...." Physically all types are there. Homosexuals thin and wasted, others slender and with womanish curves, others overfed and lustfully fat. Negroes mingle freely with whites. There seemingly is no race distinction between them.

It is a garish affair, with a hollow, mocking ring about it all. Many homosexuals of better class, who have succeeded in making some adjustment to society by bluffing the public, looked in, to leave at once in disgust. The group of onlookers are too dangerous to be seen with—blackmail is a common racket; and the homosexuals participating are going the limit too freely in careless abandon. Discretion is flung to the winds, as they "let themselves go" on one of the two nights of the year when they can openly "be themselves," reveal their true natures, and be with others of their kind, without fear of arrest or public censure. All the pent up longings and desires of months are being given free rein on this rare occasion.

ALFRED KINSEY, *SEXUAL BEHAVIOR IN THE HUMAN MALE* (PHILADELPHIA: W.B. SAUNDER COMPANY, 1948). EXCERPTS FROM CHAPTER 21, "HOMOSEXUAL OUTLET" (EXCLUDING TABLES)

In the 1930s, Alfred Kinsey, a Harvard-trained professor of zoology at Indiana University, began to turn his scientific gaze from the North American gall wasp to the sexual lives of human beings. Such a scientific investigation of sexual behavior had never before been conducted in the United States. With funding from the National Research Council, Kinsey and his colleagues interviewed tens of thousands of American men and women, using a standardized list of questions designed to elicit truthful responses about very personal information. In compiling a subject's sexual history, for example, they would ask a subject when he had his first homosexual experience rather than if he had ever had a homosexual experience, subtly suggesting that they did not judge such behavior abnormal. Published in two monumental volumes, Sexual Behavior in the Human Male *(1948) and* Sexual Behavior in the Human Female *(1953), Kinsey's findings suggested that the actual behavior of Americans was greatly at odds with prevailing sexual mores.*

In addition to uncovering high rates of masturbation and adultery, Kinsey found that 37 percent of the male population had engaged in at least one homosexual encounter to the point of orgasm since the onset of adolescence. He found that 4 percent of the men he interviewed were exclusively homosexual throughout their lives. Contradicting popular opinion, his study of women revealed that half as many females as males were exclusively homosexual in any age group. Although often cited as the source for the figure that 10 percent of the population is homosexual, Kinsey's study never cited such a statistic. Moreover, Kinsey did not use the term "homosexual" to apply to persons, only to behavior. Nevertheless, the Kinsey report was interpreted by many as suggesting that people attracted to members of their own sex were not isolated misfits but part of a huge segment of the population.

Kinsey propelled sex into the public discourse to an unprecedented degree and made his name a household word. Denounced from many pulpits and on the floor of Congress, the studies were widely indicted for somehow causing, rather than reflecting, changes in sexual activity. Although criticized for their sampling technique, which relied on word-of-mouth referrals rather than a random selection, Kinsey's studies remain among the most comprehensive examinations of the sexual habits of the American population. Although funding for the studies was cut off in 1954, and Kinsey died soon thereafter, the Kinsey Institute for Research in

Sex, Gender, and Reproduction at Indiana University continues his legacy.

*   *   *

In the total male population, single and married, between adolescence and old age, 24 percent of the total outlet is derived from solitary sources (masturbation and nocturnal emissions), 69.4 percent is derived from heterosexual sources (petting and coitus), and 6.3 percent of the total number of orgasms is derived from homosexual contacts. It is not more than 0.3 percent of the outlet which is derived from relations with animals of other species.

Homosexual contacts account, therefore, for a rather small but still significant portion of the total outlet of the human male. The significance of the homosexual is, furthermore, much greater than the frequencies of outlet may indicate, because a considerable portion of the population, perhaps the major portion of the male population, has at least some homosexual experience between adolescence and old age. In addition, about 60 percent of the pre-adolescent boys engage in homosexual activities, and there is an additional group of adult males who avoid overt contacts but who are quite aware of their potentialities for reacting to other males.

The social significance of the homosexual is considerably emphasized by the fact that both Jewish and Christian churches have considered this aspect of human sexuality to be abnormal and immoral. Social custom and our Anglo-American law are sometimes very severe in penalizing one who is discovered to have had homosexual relations. In consequence, many persons who have had such experience are psychically disturbed, and not a few of them have been in open conflict with the social organization.

It is, therefore, peculiarly difficult to secure factual data concerning the nature and the extent of the homosexual in Western European or American cultures, and even more difficult to find strictly objective presentations of such data as are available. Most of the literature of the homosexual represents either a polemic against the heinous abnormality of such activity, or as biased argument in defense of an individual's right to choose his patterns of sexual behavior.

Until the extent of any type of human behavior is adequately known, it is difficult to assess its significance, either to the individuals who are involved or to society as a whole; and until the extent of the homosexual is known, it is particularly impossible to understand its biologic or social origins. It is one thing if we are dealing with a type of activity that is unusual, without precedent among other animals, and restricted to peculiar types of individuals within the human population. It is another thing if the phenomenon proves to be a fundamental part, not only of human sexuality, but of mammalian patterns as a whole. The present chapter is, therefore, wholly confined to an analysis of the data which we now have on the incidence and the frequency of homosexual activity in the white male population in this country.

Definition

For nearly a century the term homosexual in connection with human behavior has been applied to sexual relations, either overt or psychic, between individuals of the same sex. Derived from the Greek root *homo* rather than from the Latin word for man, the term emphasizes the *sameness* of the two individuals who are involved in a sexual relation. The word is, of course, patterned after and intended to represent the antithesis of the word heterosexual, which applies to a relation between individuals of different sexes.

The term homosexual has had an endless list of synonyms in the technical vocabularies and a still greater list in the vernacular. The terms homogenic love, contrasexuality, homo-erotism, similisexualism, uranism, and others have been used in English. The terms sexual inversion, intersexuality, transsexuality, the third sex, psychosexual hermaphroditism, and others have been applied not merely to designate the nature of the partner involved in the sexual relations, but to emphasize the general opinion the individuals engaging in homosexual activity are neither male nor female, but persons of mixed sex. These latter terms are, however, most unfortunate, for they provide an interpretation in anticipation of any sufficient demonstration of the fact; and consequently they prejudice investigations of the nature and origin of homosexual activity.

The term Lesbian, referring to such female homosexual relations as were immortalized in the poetry of Sappho of the Greek Isle of Lesbos, has gained considerable usage within recent years, particularly in some of the larger Eastern cities where the existence of female homosexuality is more generally recognized by the public at large. Although there can be no objection to designating relations between females by a special term, it should be recognized that such activities are quite the equivalent of sexual relations between males....

In studies of human behavior, the term inversion is applied to sexual situations in which males play female roles and females play male roles in sex relations. Most of the data on "homosexuality" in the animal studies actually refer to inversion. Inversion, of course, may occur in either heterosexual or homosexual relations, although there has been a widespread opinion, even among students of human psychology, and among some persons whose experience has been largely homosexual, that inversion is an invariable accompaniment of homosexuality. However, this generalization is not warranted. A more elaborate presentation of our data would show that there are a great many males who remain as masculine, and a great many females who remain as feminine, in their attitudes and their approaches in homosexual relations, as the males and females who have nothing but heterosexual relations. Inversion and homosexuality are two distinct and not always correlated types of behavior.

If the term homosexual is restricted as it should be, the homosexuality or heterosexuality of any activity becomes apparent by determining the sexes of the two individuals involved in the relationship. For instance, mouth-genital contacts between males and females are certainly heterosexual even though some persons may think of them as homosexual. And although one may hear of a male "who has sex relations with his wife in a homosexual way," there is no logic in such a use of the term, and analyses of the behavior and of the motivations of the behavior in such cases do not show them necessarily related to any homosexual experience.

On the other hand, the homosexuality of certain relationships between individuals of the same sex may be denied by some persons, because the situation does not fulfill other criteria that they think should be attached to the definition. Mutual masturbation between two males may be dismissed, even by certain clinicians, as not homosexual, because oral or anal relations or particular levels of psychic response are required, according to their concept of homosexuality. There are persons who insist that the active male in an anal relation is essentially heterosexual in his behavior, and that the passive male in the same relation is the only one who is

homosexual. These, however, are misapplications of terms, which are often unfortunate because they obscure the interpretations of the situation which the clinician is supposed to help by his analysis.

These misinterpretations are often encouraged by the very persons who are having homosexual experience. Some males who are being regularly fellated by other males without, however, ever performing fellation themselves, may insist that they are exclusively heterosexual and that they have never been involved in a truly homosexual relation. Their consciences are cleared and they may avoid trouble with society and with the police by perpetrating the additional fiction that they fantasy themselves in contact with a female. Even clinicians have allowed themselves to be diverted by such pretensions. The actual histories, however, show few if any cases of sexual relations between males which could be considered anything but homosexual.

Many individuals who have had considerable homosexual experience, construct a hierarchy on the basis of which they insist that anyone who has not had as much homosexual experience as they have had, or who is less exclusively aroused by homosexual stimuli, is "not really homosexual." It is amazing to observe how many psychologists and psychiatrists have accepted this sort of propaganda, and have come to believe that homosexual males and females are discretely different from persons who merely have homosexual experience, or who react sometimes to homosexual stimuli. Sometimes such an interpretation allows for only two kinds of males and two kinds of females, namely those who are heterosexual and those who are homosexual. But as subsequent data in this chapter will show, there is only about half of the male population whose sexual behavior is exclusively heterosexual, and there are only a few percent who are exclusively homosexual. Any restriction of the term homosexuality to individuals who are exclusively so demands, logically, that the term heterosexual be applied only to those individuals who are exclusively heterosexual; and this makes no allowance for the nearly half of the population which has had sexual contacts with, or reacted psychically to, individuals of their own as well as the opposite sex. Actually, of course, one must learn to recognize every combination of heterosexuality and homosexuality in the histories of various individuals.

It would encourage clearer thinking on these matters if persons were not characterized as heterosexual or homosexual, but as individuals who have had certain amounts of heterosexual experience and certain amounts of homosexual experience. Instead of using these terms as substantives which stand for persons, or even as adjectives to describe persons, they may better be used to describe the nature of the overt sexual relations, or of the stimuli to which an individual erotically responds.

Previous Estimates of Incidence

Many persons have recognized the importance of securing specific information on the incidence of the homosexual. The clinician needs to know how far the experience of his patient departs from norms for the remainder of the population. Counselors, teachers, clergymen, personnel officers, the administrators of institutions, social workers, law enforcement officers, and still others who are concerned with the direction of human behavior, may completely misinterpret the meaning of the homosexual experience in an individual's history, unless they understand the incidence and frequency of such activity in the population as a whole....

There are many persons who believe the homosexual to be a rare phenomenon, a clinical curiosity, and something which one may never meet among the sorts of persons with whom he would associate. On the other hand, there are some clinicians and some persons who have had first-hand contacts in the homosexual, who have estimated that something between 50 and 100 percent of the population has such experience.

In this country, three investigators have obtained data on the incidence of the homosexual in our American male population. It is notable that all three of them have secured figures which are remarkably higher than the European studies have given—not because there is any likelihood that the American picture is particularly different from that in Europe, but because all of these studies have come nearer satisfying the demands of a population survey. All of them involved a more thorough coverage of particular groups, and all of them were based on direct interviews with persons with whom the interviewer had had enough contact to have developed some rapport. Hamilton (1929) found that 17 percent of the hundred men in his study had had homosexual experience after they were eighteen years old. Ramsey (1943), in a study of 291 younger boys, one-half of whom constituted a hundred percent sample of a seventh and eighth grade group in a junior high school, found that 30 percent had adolescent homosexual experience to the point of orgasm. More recently (1947), Finger has reported 27 percent of a college class of 111 males admitting "at least one overt homosexual episode involving orgasm." These figures come remarkably close to those which we have obtained in the present study.

One other source of data on the extent of "homosexuality" among American males has recently become available through statistics gathered by Selective Service Boards and at induction centers during the last war. Theoretically, this should have been a splendid opportunity to gain information that would have been of considerable scientific use and of considerable practical use to the armed forces. From these sources, the overall figures show that about one-tenth of 1 percent of all the men were rejected by draft boards, about 0.4 percent were turned down at induction centers, and about as many more were subsequently discharged for homosexual activity while they were in active service. The total gives about 1 percent officially identified as "homosexual." These figures are so much lower than any which case history studies have obtained that they need critical examination.

The most obvious explanation of these very low figures lies in the fact that both the Army and Navy had precluded the possibility of getting accurate data on these matters by announcing at the beginning of the war that they intended to exclude all persons with homosexual histories. The American Army and Navy have always been traditionally opposed to homosexual activity, and in the last war, for the first time, they turned to psychiatrists to provide expert help in eliminating individuals with such histories.

Incidence Data in Present Study

The statistics given throughout this volume on the incidence of homosexual activity, and the statistics to be given in the present section of this chapter, are based on those persons who have had physical contacts with other males, and who were brought to orgasm as a result of such contacts. By any strict definition such contacts are homosexual, irrespective of the extent of the psychic stimulation involved, of the techniques employed, or of the relative importance of the homosexual and the heterosexual in the his-

tory of such an individual. These are not data on the number of persons who are "homosexual," but on the number of persons who have had at least some homosexual experience—even though sometimes not more than one experience—up to the ages shown in the tables and curves....

In these terms (of physical contact to the point of orgasm), the data in the present study indicate that at least 37 percent of the male population has some homosexual experience between the beginning of adolescence and old age. This is more than one male in three of the persons that one may meet as he passes along a city street. Among the males who remain unmarried until the age of 35, almost exactly 50 percent have homosexual experiences between the beginning of adolescence and that age. Some of these persons have but a single experience, and some of them have much more or even a lifetime of experience; but all of them have at least some experience to the point of orgasm.

These figures are, of course, considerably higher than any which have previously been estimated; but as already shown they must be understatements, if they are anything other than the fact.

We ourselves were totally unprepared to find such incidence data when this research was originally undertaken. Over a period of several years we were repeatedly assailed with doubts as to whether we were getting a fair cross section of the total population or whether a selection of cases was biasing the results. It has been our experience, however, that each new group into which we have gone has provided substantially the same data. Whether the histories were taken in one large city or another, whether they were taken in large cities, in small towns, or in rural areas, whether they came from one college or from another, a church school or a state university or some private institution, whether they came from one part of the country or from another, the incidence data on the homosexual have been more or less the same....

Those who have been best acquainted with the extent of homosexual activity in the population, whether through clinical contacts with homosexual patients, through homosexual acquaintances, or through their own firsthand homosexual experience, will not find it too difficult to accept the accumulative incidence figures which are arrived at here. There are many who have been aware of the fact that persons with homosexual histories are to be found in every age group, in every social level, in every conceivable occupation, in cities and on farms, and in the most remote areas in the country. They have known the homosexual in young adolescents and in persons of every other age. They have known it in single persons and in the histories of males who were married. In large city communities they know that an experienced observer may identify hundreds of persons in a day whose homosexual interests are certain. They have known the homosexuality of many persons whose histories were utterly unknown to most of their friends and acquaintances....

Scientific and Social Implications

In view of the data which we now have on the incidence and frequency of the homosexual, and in particular on its co-existence with the heterosexual in the lives of a considerable portion of the male population, it is difficult to maintain the view that psychosexual reactions between individuals of the same sex are rare and therefore abnormal or unnatural, or that they constitute within themselves evidence of neuroses or even psychoses.

If homosexual activity persists on as large a scale as it does, in the face of very considerable public sentiment against it and in spite of the severity of the penalties that our Anglo-American culture has placed upon it through the centuries, there seems some reason for believing that such activity would appear in the histories of a much larger portion of the population if there were no social restraints. The very general occurrence of the homosexual in ancient Greece and its wide occurrence today in some cultures in which such activity is not as taboo as it is in our own, suggests that the capacity of an individual to respond erotically to any sort of stimulus, whether it is provided by another person of the same or of the opposite sex, is basic in the species. That patterns of heterosexuality and patterns of homosexuality represent learned behavior which depends, to a considerable degree, upon the mores of the particular culture in which the individual is raised, is a possibility that must be thoroughly considered before there can be any acceptance of the idea that homosexuality is inherited, and that the pattern for each individual is so innately fixed that no modification of it may be expected within his lifetime.

The opinion that homosexual activity in itself provides evidence of a psychopathic personality is materially challenged by these incidence and frequency data. Of the 40 or 50 percent of the male population which has homosexual experience, certainly a high proportion would not be considered psychopathic personalities on the basis of anything else in their histories. It is argued that an individual who is so obtuse to social reactions as to continue his homosexual activity and make it any material portion of his life, therein evidences some social incapacity; but psychiatrists and clinicians in general might very well re-examine their justification for demanding that all persons conform to particular patterns of behavior. As a matter of fact, there is an increasing proportion of the most skilled psychiatrists who make no attempt to re-direct behavior, but who devote their attention to helping an individual accept himself, and to conduct himself in such a manner that he does not come into open conflict with society....

There are those who will contend that the immorality of homosexual behavior calls for its suppression no matter what the facts are concerning the incidence and frequency of such activity in the population. Some have demanded that homosexuality be completely eliminated from society by a concentrated attack upon it at every point, and the "treatment" or isolation of all individuals with any homosexual tendencies. Whether such a program is morally desirable is a matter on which a scientist is not qualified to pass judgement; but whether such a program is physically feasible is a matter for scientific determination.

The evidence that we now have on the incidence and frequency of homosexual activity indicates that at least a third of the male population would have to be isolated from the rest of the community, if all those with any homosexual capacities were to be so treated. It means that at least 13 percent of the male population would have to be institutionalized and isolated, if all persons who were predominately homosexual were to be handled in that way. Since about 34 percent of the total population of the United States are adult males, this means that there are about six and a third million males in the country who would need such isolation.

If all persons with any trace of homosexual history, or those who were predominately homosexual, were eliminated from the population today, there is no reason for believing that the incidence of the homosexual in the next generation would be materially reduced. The homosexual has been a significant part of human sexual activity ever since the dawn of history, primarily because it is an expression of capacities that are basic in the human animal.

UNITED STATES SENATE, *EMPLOYMENT OF HOMOSEXUALS AND OTHER SEX PERVERTS IN GOVERNMENT*, SENATE DOCUMENT # 241, 81ST CONGRESS, 2ND SESSION, 15 DECEMBER 1950

Beginning during World War II, the federal government began a policy of excluding gay men and lesbians from the military. By the 1950s, as America entered a Cold War with the Soviet Union, that policy spread to the entire federal work force. In the spring of 1950, a veritable panic over the presence of homosexuals in government service swept the nation when a State Department official revealed that 91 homosexuals had been fired from the department. Over the course of the next decade, thousands more throughout the federal government were either fired or quietly asked to resign. Officially, gays and lesbians were considered "security risks" because they were vulnerable to blackmail, and therefore subject to coercion by enemy agents. Unofficially, many people assumed a natural affinity between Communists and homosexuals, since both comprised invisible subcultures that seemingly posed a threat to proper, middle-class notions of American life.

The following report made to the Senate Committee on Expenditures in the Executive Departments by its Subcommittee on Investigations was the result of a series of closed-door hearings held in the fall of 1950. It was the first full-scale investigation into homosexuality ever conducted by the federal government. Psychiatrists, security personnel, military officers, public health professionals, police officers, and other government officials testified concerning their knowledge of homosexuals. No gay men or lesbians were consulted. The Hoey committee report, named after the chairman of the committee, Senator Clyde Hoey (D-North Carolina), makes two overall conclusions about gay and lesbian government employees. First, it asserts that they can be coerced into revealing state secrets through blackmail, without ever offering a single incidence in American history where that had occurred. Second, it suggests that they are undesirable because they are emotionally unstable and exert a corrosive, immoral influence on their fellow workers. Widely circulated and reprinted, the report has been used for nearly half a century as the basis for the notion that gays and lesbians are undesirable employees who pose a risk to national security.

*   *   *

Introduction

An investigation on a Government-wide scale of homosexuality and other sex perversions is unprecedented. Furthermore, reliable, factual information on the subject of homosexuality and sex perversion is somewhat limited. In the past, studies in this field, for the most part, were confined to scientific studies by medical experts and sociologists. The criminal courts and the police have had considerable experience in the handling of sex perverts as law violators, but the subject as a personnel problem until very recently has received little attention from Government administrators and personnel officers.

The primary objective of the subcommittee in this inquiry was to determine the extent of the employment of homosexuals and other sex perverts in Government; to consider reasons why their employment by the Government is undesirable; and to examine into the efficacy of the methods used in dealing with the problem.

Because of the complex nature of the subject under investigation it was apparent that this investigation could not be confined to a mere personnel inquiry. Therefore, the subcommittee considered not only the security risk and other aspects of the employment of homosexuals, including the rules and procedures followed by Government agencies in handling these cases, but inquiries were also made into the basic medical, psychiatric, sociological, and legal phases of the problem. A number of eminent physicians and psychiatrists, who are recognized authorities on this subject, were consulted and some of these authorities testified before the subcommittee in executive session. In addition, numerous medical and sociological studies were reviewed. Information was also sought and obtained from law-enforcement officers, prosecutors, and other persons dealing with the legal and sociological aspects of the problem in 10 of the largest cities in the country.

The subcommittee, being well aware of the strong moral and social taboos attached to homosexuality and other forms of sex perversion, made every effort to protect individuals from unnecessary public ridicule and to prevent this inquiry from becoming a public spectacle. In carrying out this policy it was determined at the outset that all testimony would be taken by the subcommittee in executive session.... In the conduct of this investigation the subcommittee tried to avoid the circus atmosphere which could attend an inquiry of this type and sought to make a thorough factual study of the problem at hand in an unbiased, objective manner.

It was determined that even among the experts there existed considerable difference of opinion concerning the many facts of homosexuality and other forms of sex perversion. Even the terms "sex pervert" and "homosexual" are given different connotations by the medical and psychiatric experts. For the purpose of this report the subcommittee has defined sex perverts as "those who engage in unnatural sexual acts" and homosexuals are perverts who may be broadly defined as "persons of either sex who as adults engage in sexual activity with person[s] of the same sex." In this inquiry the subcommittee is not concerned with so-called latent sex perverts, namely, those persons who knowingly or unknowingly have tendencies or inclinations toward homosexuality or other types of sex perversion, but who, by the exercise of self-restraint or for other reasons do not indulge in overt acts of perversion. This investigation is concerned only with those who engage in overt acts of homosexuality or other sex perversion.

The subcommittee found that most authorities agree on certain basic facts concerning sex perversion and it is felt that these facts should be considered in any discussion of the problem. Most authorities believe that sex deviation results from psychological rather than physical traits that are positive as identifying marks of sex perversion. Contrary to a common belief, all homosexual males do not have feminine mannerisms, nor do all female homosexuals display masculine characteristics in their dress or actions. The fact is that many male homosexuals are very masculine in their physical appearance and general demeanor, and many female homosexuals have every appearance of femininity in their outward behavior....

Psychiatric physicians generally agree that indulgence in sexually perverted practices indicates a personality which has failed to reach sexual maturity. The authorities agree that most sex deviates respond to psychiatric treatment and can be cured if they have a genuine desire to be cured. However, many overt homosexuals have no real desire to abandon their way of life and in such cases cures are difficult, if not impossible. The subcommit-

tee sincerely believes that persons afflicted with sexual desires which result in their engaging in overt acts of perversion should be considered as proper cases for medical and psychiatric treatment. However, sex perverts, like all other persons who by their overt acts violate moral codes and laws and the accepted standards of conduct, must be treated as transgressors and dealt with accordingly.

Sex Perverts as Government Employees

Those charged with the responsibility of operating the agencies of Government must insist that Government employees meet acceptable standards of personal conduct. In the opinion of this subcommittee homosexuals and other sex perverts are not proper persons to be employed in Government for two reasons; first, they are generally unsuitable, and second, they constitute security risks.

General Unsuitability of Sex Perverts

Overt acts of sex perversion, including acts of homosexuality, constitute a crime under our Federal, State, and municipal statutes and persons who commit such acts are law violators. Aside from the criminality and immorality involved in sex perversion, such behavior is so contrary to the normal accepted standards of social behavior that persons who engage in such activity are looked upon as outcasts by society generally. The social stigma attached to sex perversion is so great that many perverts go to great lengths to conceal their perverted tendencies. This situation is evidenced by the fact that perverts are frequently victimized by blackmailers who threaten to expose their sexual deviations....

In further considering the general suitability of perverts as Government employees, it is generally believed that those who engage in overt acts of perversion lack the emotional stability of normal persons. In addition there is an abundance of evidence to sustain the conclusion that indulgence in acts of sex perversion weakens the moral fiber of an individual to a degree that he is not suitable for a position of responsibility.

Most of the authorities agree and our investigation has shown that the presence of a sex pervert in a Government agency tends to have a corrosive influence upon his fellow employees. These perverts will frequently attempt to entice normal individuals to engage in perverted practices. This is particularly true in the case of young and impressionable people who might come under the influence of a pervert. Government officials have the responsibility of keeping this type of corrosive influence out of the agencies under their control. It is particularly important that the thousands of young men and women who are brought into Federal jobs not be subjected to that type of influence while in the service of the Government. One homosexual can pollute a Government office.

Another point to be considered in determining whether a sex pervert is suitable for Government employment is his tendency to gather other perverts about him. Eminent psychiatrists have informed the subcommittee that the homosexual is likely to seek his own kind because the pressures of society are such that he feels uncomfortable unless he is with his own kind. Due to this situation the homosexual tends to surround himself with other homosexuals, not only in his social, but in his business life. Under these circumstances if a homosexual attains a position in Government where he can influence the hiring of personnel, it is almost inevitable that he will attempt to place other homosexuals in Government jobs.

Sex Perverts as Security Risks

The conclusion of the subcommittee that a homosexual or other sex pervert is a security risk is not based upon mere conjecture. That conclusion is predicated upon a careful review of the opinions of those best qualified to consider matters of security in Government, namely, the intelligence agencies of the Government. Testimony on this phase of the inquiry was taken from representatives of the Federal Bureau of Investigation, the Central Intelligence Agency, and the intelligence services of the Army, Navy and Air Force. All of these agencies are in complete agreement that sex perverts in Government constitute security risks.

The lack of emotional stability which is found in most sex perverts and the weakness of their moral fiber, makes them susceptible to the blandishments of the foreign espionage agent. It is the experience of intelligence experts that perverts are vulnerable to interrogation by a skilled questioner and they seldom refuse to talk about themselves. Furthermore, most perverts tend to congregate at the same restaurants, night clubs, and bars, which places can be identified with comparative ease in any community, making it possible for a recruiting agent to develop clandestine relationships which can be used for espionage purposes.

As has been previously discussed in this report, the pervert is easy prey to the blackmailer. It follows that if blackmailers can extort money from a homosexual under the threat of disclosure, espionage agents can use the same type of pressure to extort confidential information or other material they might be seeking. A classic case of this type involved one Captain Raedl who became chief of the Austrian counterintelligence service in 1912. He succeeded in building up an excellent intelligence net in Russia and had done considerable damage to the espionage net which the Russians had set up in Austria. However, Russian agents soon discovered that Raedl was a homosexual and shortly thereafter they managed to catch him in an act of perversion as the result of a trap they had set for that purpose. Under that threat of exposure Raedl agreed to furnish and he did furnish the Russians with Austrian military secrets....

Other cases have been brought to the attention of the subcommittee where Nazi and Communist agents have attempted to obtain information from employees of our Government by threatening to expose their abnormal sex activities. It is an accepted fact among intelligence agencies that espionage organizations the world over consider sex perverts who are in possession of or have access to confidential material to be prime targets where pressure can be exerted. In virtually every case despite protestations by the perverts that they would never succumb to blackmail, invariably they express considerable concern over the fact that their condition might become known to their friends, associates, or the public at large....

Extent of Sex Perversion in Government

It is not possible to determine accurately the number of homosexuals and other sex perverts in the Government service. The only known perverts are those whose activities have been brought to the attention of the authorities as the result of an arrest or where some other specific information has resulted in the disclosure of their perversions.

Not even the experts are in agreement as to the incidence of homosexuality and other sex perversion among the general population and to attempt to arrive at an estimated figure as to the number of perverts in the Federal Government would be sheer speculation and serve no useful purpose. While most authorities agree that the incidence of sex perversion follows a rather constant pattern throughout our entire social structure, regardless of education, wealth, or social position, it clearly does not follow that the same relative number of perverts should be found in the Federal service as are found outside of the Government. In this regard we must consider the fact that homosexuals and other persons with arrest records or other known indications of unsavory character are largely eliminated from a great many sensitive jobs where all applicants are thoroughly investigated prior to employment. Furthermore, some check is made of all Government employees prior or soon after their appointment and this would tend to eliminate many undesirables....

The subcommittee has attempted to arrive at some idea as to the extent of sex perversion among Government employees by obtaining information from the personnel records of all Government agencies and the police records in the District of Columbia.... An individual check of the Federal agencies revealed that since 1 January 1947, the armed services and civilian agencies of Government have handled 4,954 cases involving charges of homosexuality or other types of sex perversion. It will be noted that the bulk of these cases are in the armed services as is indicated by the fact that 4,380 of the known cases in Government involved military personnel and 574 involved civilian employees....

Handling of the Sex Perversion Problem in Government: The Rules of Government

The regulations of the Civil Service Commission for many years have provided that criminal, infamous, dishonest, immoral or notoriously disgraceful conduct, which includes homosexuality or other types of sex perversion, are sufficient grounds for denying appointment to a Government position or the removal of a person from the Federal service....

In reviewing the methods and procedures in the handling of the problem of sex perversion in the Government, two factors must be considered. First, consideration must be given to preventing such persons from obtaining Government employment and, second, the methods used in detecting and removing perverts who are already in the Government service should be examined. Under present procedures all applicants for Government positions are screened by the Civil Service Commission soon after their appointment. While these applicants are not subject to a so-called full field investigation, their fingerprints are checked against the files of the FBI to determine whether they have a prior arrest record, and other name checks are also made. As a result of this screening process, the Civil Service Commission is notified in the event the applicant has a police record of sex perversion; and, if such a record does exist, further investigation is conducted to determine the complete facts. A spot check of the records of the Civil Service Commission indicates that between 1 January 1947 and 1 August 1950, approximately 1,700 applicants for Federal positions were denied employment because they had a record of homosexuality or other sex perversion.

The subcommittee has found that many civilian agencies of government have taken an entirely unrealistic view of the problem of sex perversion and have not taken adequate steps to get these people out of government. Known perverts and persons suspected of such activities have been retained in some Government agencies, or have been allowed to leave one agency and obtain employment in another, notwithstanding the regulations of the Civil Service Commission and the rules of the agencies themselves.... Some officials undoubtedly condoned the employment of homosexuals for one reason or another. This was particularly true in those instances where the perverted activities of the employee were carried on in such a manner as not to create public scandal or notoriety. Those who adopted that view based their conclusions on the false premise that what a Government employee did outside of the office on his own time, particularly if his actions did not involve his fellow employees or his work, was his own business. That conclusion may be true with regard to the normal behavior of employees in most types of Government work, but it does not apply to sex perversion.

Conclusion

There is no place in the United States Government for persons who violate the laws or the accepted standards of morality, or who otherwise bring disrepute to the Federal service by infamous or scandalous personal conduct. Such persons are not suitable for Government positions and in the case of doubt the American people are entitled to have errors of judgement on the part of their officials, if there must be errors, resolved on the side of caution. It is the opinion of this subcommittee that those who engage in acts of homosexuality and other perverted sex activities are unsuitable for employment in the Federal Government. This conclusion is based upon the fact that persons who indulge in such degraded activity are committing not only illegal and immoral acts, but they also constitute security risks in positions of public trust.

RALPH MAJOR, "NEW MORAL MENACE TO OUR YOUTH," *CORONET,* SEPTEMBER 1950, PP. 101-08

In the post-World War II period, homosexuals were no longer stereotyped as effete males or masculine females who enjoyed dressing in drag but were increasingly portrayed as an invidious threat both to national security and to America's children. Sensationalist press coverage of a number of brutal child murders gave rise to a nation-wide fear that "sexual deviates" were preying on children. Since homosexuality was commonly assumed to be the manifestation of a mental illness, many assumed this psychopathology could degenerate further to drug addiction, sadism, and murder. In this atmosphere, the public began to conflate all types of sexual non-conformity and criminality. Increased media attention to the presence of gay people and a willingness to discuss sexual subjects in print contributed to a virtual public panic over "sex crimes." Cities and states initiated campaigns against sex criminals that frequently became campaigns against homosexuals. This article from Coronet, *a popular magazine of the decade, was typical in its dire tone and explicit warning to parents about the dangers homosexuals allegedly posed to children. Its central thesis, the myth of the homosexual as child molester, has been repeatedly cited by opponents of gay and lesbian civil rights, and was the organizing principal behind Anita Bryant's anti-gay campaign in the 1970s called "Save our Children."*

*   *   *

Behind a wall erected by apathy, ignorance, and a reluctance to face facts, a sinister threat to American youth is fast developing. Unlike disease and crime, this threat, until very recently, was sel-

dom discussed in public; its existence was acknowledged only in whispers—and in sordid police and prison records. Not since the see-no-evil-hear-no-evil attitude toward syphilis has there been such an example of public refusal to grapple with a serious problem—in this case, the problem of homosexuality.

Although more than 8,000,000 Americans today are actual or potential homosexuals, it took a ballyhooed Congressional investigation to put homosexuality in the headlines, however inadequately.... Despite the awareness of doctors and social workers to this danger to American youth, prejudice and prudery have conspired to keep the truth from the public.... So little has been written about this subject that many people are unaware a danger exists, or even more significant, that homosexuality is rapidly increasing throughout America today.... In the most recent and widespread survey, conducted by Dr. Alfred C. Kinsey and published in his celebrated work *Sexual Behavior in the Human Male*, it is reported that "37 percent of the total male population has had at least some overt homosexual experience ... between adolescence and old age."

Most Americans assume either a scornful or a tolerant attitude toward these perverts. On one hand, the hip-swinging, falsetto-voiced men can excite such fury in other men as to provoke brutal attacks. Disgust and gutter humor thus characterize the reactions of the majority toward the "fairy." On the other hand, many are inclined to regard the sex pervert merely as a "queer" who never harms anyone but himself. This is an extremely dangerous and shortsighted attitude, according to those who have studied the problem. For instance, Eugene D. Williams, Special Assistant Attorney General of the State of California, declares: "All to often, we lose sight of the fact that the homosexual is an inveterate seducer of the young of both sexes, and that he presents a social problem because he is not content with being degenerate himself; he must have degenerate companions, and is ever seeking younger victims."

Therein lurks the hidden danger of homosexuality. No degenerate can indulge his unnatural practices alone. He demands a partner. And the partner, more often than not, must come from the ranks of the young and innocent. Each year, literally thousands of youngsters of high-school and college age are introduced to unnatural practices by inveterate seducers. Irreparable mental and psychological damage is only one side of the story. The other is even more reprehensible. Some male sex deviants do not stop with infecting their often-innocent partners: they descend through perversions to other forms of depravity, such as drug addiction, burglary, sadism, and even murder. Once a man assumes the role of homosexual, he often throws off all moral restraints. While thumbing his nose at society through his sexual perversions, at the same time he indulges in other vices that society brands as immoral.

In some people, homosexuality may represent a passing phase in emotional development—a temporary protest against conservative morals or a craving for self-expression carried to bizarre extremes. In other cases, it eventually becomes a way of life, a fraternal comradeship which, to its zealots, is infinitely superior to normal human relations. To these members of a publicly scorned inner circle, homosexuality offers a refuge from the rigid pattern of normal society.

While the appearance of most of these unfortunates may betray them to watchful persons, other sex aberrants look, act, and dress like anyone else. It is they who are the real threat. For until an overt action is committed, their victims sense no danger.

"There is a widespread theory among psychologists and psychiatrists," writes Dr. Kinsey, "that the homosexual is a product of an effete and over-organized urban civilization. The failure to make (normal male-female) adjustments is supposed to be consequent on the complexities of life in modern cities." Psychiatrists explain the city phenomenon this way: relationships in metropolitan areas tend to minimize family life in favor of business life. Office associates, fellow-workers, and friends of the same sex assume exaggerated emotional influence. Likewise, most large cities boast taverns, night clubs, and restaurants which cater almost exclusively to perverts and thereby become scenes of conversation (sic) for innocents seeking companionship.

Steps must be taken now to protect American youth from an ever-growing peril. Every psychiatrist, sociologist and educator queried in *Coronet's* survey stressed one point: "More than anyone else, parents are responsible for erasing the threat of homosexuality." Since parental attitudes and home environment are fundamental to healthy adolescent development, mothers and fathers should combat homosexuality through vigilance, kindness, and sympathetic understanding.

Here are some suggestions from experts on how parents may protect their children against homosexuality and its converts: (1) Instruct boys and girls as early as possible in the knowledge of normal sex practices. (2) Encourage your children to bring their sex problems and questions to you. (3) Know your children's friends. (4) Urge children to exercise caution in speaking to strangers. (5) Investigate your children's schools, camps, social clubs, and athletic organizations.

In the history of modern society, there have been few menaces that frank and open discussion, coupled with intelligent action, have failed to eliminate. Once venereal disease was finally placed under the spotlight of public scrutiny, doctors found their task easier. Now a new menace—homosexuality—has arisen. And again, the primary challenge is to mothers and fathers. Through knowledge of the facts, plus a concerted attack, the sinister shadow of sexual perversion can be removed from the pathway of America's youth.

STATEMENT OF PURPOSE, DAUGHTERS OF BILITIS (1955)

The first lesbian organization in the nation was founded in San Francisco in 1955 by Del Martin and Phyllis Lyon. Formed as a social club, an alternative to the bars, the Daughters of Bilitis functioned as a self-help group for gay women. It took its name from the erotic poem "Song of Bilitis" by French author Pierre Louy, but also invoked the names of many mainstream women's groups, such as the Daughters of the American Revolution (DAR). It worked closely with chapters of the Mattachine Society, which were predominately male. As part of the homophile movement, it focused on education and research by straight professionals to change societal attitudes toward the homosexual. The title of its monthly publication, The Ladder, *referred to the organization's belief that lesbians needed to improve themselves in order to climb the ladder of respectability and thereby achieve acceptance in mainstream society. The group's conservative focus on getting the lesbian to conform to societal standards of proper female behavior, rather than trying to change societal attitudes, is reflected in the following statement of purpose, which appeared on the inside cover of* The Ladder *throughout the 1950s and 1960s.*

* * *

A Women's Organization for the Purpose of Promoting the Integration of the Homosexual Into Society By:

1. Education of the variant [compiler's note: variant was another term used to describe homosexuals or lesbians], with particular emphasis on the psychological, physiological, and sociological aspects, to enable her to understand herself and make her adjustment to society in all its social, civic and economic implications—this to be accomplished by establishing and maintaining as complete a library as possible of both fiction and non-fiction literature on the sex deviant theme; by sponsoring public discussions on pertinent subjects to be conducted by leading members of the legal, psychiatric, religious, and other professions; by advocating a mode of behavior and dress acceptable to society.

2. Education of the public at large through acceptance first of the individual, leading to an eventual breakdown of erroneous taboos and prejudices; through public discussion meetings aforementioned; through dissemination of educational literature on the homosexual theme.

3. Participation in research projects by duly authorized and responsible psychologists, sociologists and other such experts directed towards further knowledge of the homosexual.

4. Investigation of the penal code as it pertains to the homosexual, proposal of changes to provide an equitable handling of cases involving this minority group, and promotion of these changes through due process of law in the state legislatures.

FRANKLIN KAMENY, "CIVIL LIBERTIES: A PROGRESS REPORT," SPEECH DELIVERED ON 22 JULY 1964, TO THE MATTACHINE SOCIETY OF NEW YORK

In the early 1960s, Franklin Kameny spearheaded a new militancy in the homophile movement. Dismissed from the federal government in 1957, Kameny was one of thousands of suspected gay men and lesbians purged from the federal payroll during the 1950s. Kameny, however, was the first to fight his dismissal all the way to the Supreme Court. He lost his individual legal suit, but went on to found the Mattachine Society of Washington, D.C. (MSW) in 1961. Unlike its predecessor gay organizations that had focused on education and self-help, MSW took an activist approach. As the group's president, Kameny insisted that homosexuality was not a moral or a mental health problem but a civil liberties issue. With an eye on the black civil rights movement, he championed the cause that gays are a political minority group. He charged that the government's anti-gay policies were analogous to discrimination based upon religious or racial grounds. Dubbing his organization the "NAACP of the homosexual minority," he adopted traditional reform movement tactics to end the treatment of gays and lesbians as second-class citizens. This included the first sustained public picketing by gay men and lesbians, including the now famous protests in front of the White House in 1965. Confronting the psychiatric profession's insistence that homosexuality was a mental illness, Kameny coined the slogan "Gay is Good" in 1968, a self-conscious emulation of the African-American motto "Black is Beautiful." In the following speech, Kameny articu-

lates the philosophy behind his new militancy, one that by the late 1960s would become part of the core beliefs of the gay movement.

*   *   *

My approach is one of strong and definite positions, unequivocally held. I feel that the nurture and presentation of controversy are not as virtuous as many in the movement would have them be, nor is the cultivation of an outward neutrality on questions upon which we should be taking a firm, clear, no-nonsense stand.

It seems to me that there are three primary directions in which a homophile organization can go—social service, information and education, and civil liberties-social action. These are complementary, of course, neither mutually exclusive nor competitive, and usually become matters of a difference of emphasis from one organization to another—the placing of the emphasis resulting from a mixture of the setting in which the organization finds itself and the interests and personalities of those leading the particular group.

As I understand it, the Daughters of Bilitis, for example, devotes itself primarily to social services; the Mattachine Society of New York, in the well-established Mattachine tradition, emphasizes the information and education role. The Mattachine Society of Washington, from the outset has placed its emphasis in the area of civil liberties and social action. It is as an exponent of that emphasis that I speak this evening.

My reasons for placing emphasis where I do are the following. In regard to social services: No *lasting* good can be accomplished by administration of social service *alone*. Let me give an example by analogy. One can supply virtually unlimited amounts of money, food, clothing, and shelter to the poor, but unless one gets to the roots of poverty—the economic system which produces unemployment, the social system which produces lack of education, and the one which over-produces people, etc.—one will accomplish little of lasting value. Similarly, we can refer homosexuals to lawyers, we can find jobs for those who have lost jobs, or have been denied them because of homosexuality, and we can assist them in other ways, but unless and until we get at and eliminate the discrimination and prejudice which underlies—and, in fact, which *are*—the homosexuals' problem, we will accomplish nothing of lasting value, either, and our jobs will go on literally without end.

Obviously we cannot easily turn away people now in need with the argument that we are working in order that those in the future will not need; so there is clearly a place in the homophile movement for the social services, but only, I feel, to supplement work of a more fundamental nature, dealing with changes of attitudes, prejudice and policy.

We come next to the area of information and education. While this is important, I feel that any movement which relies solely upon an intellectually-directed program of information and education, no matter how extensive, to change well-entrenched, emotionally-based attitudes, is doomed to disappointment. The Negro tried for 90 years to achieve his purposes by a program of information and education. His achievements in those 90 years, while by no means nil, were nothing compared to those of the past 10 years, when he tried a vigorous civil liberties, social action approach and gained his goals thereby.

The prejudiced mined, and that is what we are fighting, is not penetrated by information and is not educable. This has been shown in a number of studies of the mental processes associated with prejudice, and has been confirmed by a recent study which showed that tolerance is only slightly promoted by more information; that communication of facts is generally ineffectual against predispositions; that prejudices, opinions, attitudes, and beliefs, usually change only when people are forced to change.

The prejudice against homosexuality is primarily one of an emotional commitment, not an intellectual one; and appeals based upon fact and reason will, for the most part, not be effective.

Where a program of information and education *will* be useful and very important is in presenting our position to that minority of the majority who are potentially our allies anyway, but who have not thought about the matter before—such as the clergy, as just one of a number of examples—who are looked to as leaders by the masses of people.

Even there, however, a vigorous and outgoing program is necessary. Let me illustrate this point with an anecdote. Late in 1962, when the Mattachine Society of Washington was about a year old and had begun to establish itself in the homophile movement by more than its mere existence, I wrote letters to all of the other homophile organizations in the country introducing our group and describing some of the endeavors in which we were then engaged. I mentioned our dealings with the Washington chapter of the ACLU [American Civil Liberties Union]. One of the organizations wrote back, saying that they too had contacted their local ACLU affiliate, and that ACLU representatives had spoken to their membership on several occasions. I replied by saying that representatives of the ACLU had never addressed our membership, but representatives of the Mattachine Society of Washington had addressed the ACLU's membership. I think the difference is illustrative of my point and is important. It has served us exceedingly well.

Information and education yes, but *not* to inform and educate us. The homophile movement does not, I feel, exist in any major degree for the edification of its own members. In its information and education role, it exists primarily to inform and to educate the public. We should appear before the public in the role of authorities on questions of homosexuality—as indeed we are. I am truly pleased to see growing, particularly on the East Coast, a strong trend toward the bringing of the talks, the lectures, the discussions, outside our own group, and before other groups—before the heterosexual public.

This brings us to the area of civil liberties and social action. Here, we get into an area in which we are engaging in what is fundamentally down-to-earth, grass-roots, occasionally tooth-and-nail politics. We are dealing with emotions of people, and the policies of officialdom, and our methods must be in accord with this.

Official policies—laws, regulations, etc., on the one hand and popular opinion and prejudice on the other hand, interact strongly and circularly. It is obvious that if we work almost infinitely long to change public attitudes and are successful in doing so then after another long wait, we might see laws and official policies change. The reverse process is much faster, and much more efficient and is especially suitable to a group located, as mine is, in Washington. Prejudiced official attitudes and policies reinforce private discrimination. The private employer, for example, may or may not hire homosexuals, if the government *does* hire them; he will *not* hire them if the government does *not*.

For these reasons, I feel that the primary direction of endeavor and the one likely to be most fruitful should be the changing of the attitudes and policies of those who are, or to whom the community looks, as constituted authority. Wherever discrimination is officially sponsored, it is amenable to attack within the framework of administrative and judicial procedure. This has been the backbone of our approach in Washington.

I would suggest that here in New York you have at least one beautiful example of the kind of situation which needs this sort of approach. I refer to the continued closing of gay bars. This seems to me to be an obvious infringement upon the right of the homosexual citizen to freely associate, to assemble, and to make use of public accommodations of his own choice. I have suggested that this is a matter which a group such as Mattachine Society of New York might well take up. I am told that it is difficult to get a bar owner who will cooperate. *This is not a matter for the bar owners. This is a matter for homosexuals.* The lawsuits which brought an end to school segregation were not initiated by schools which wished to integrate; they were brought by Negro school children who wished to attend.

Returning, however to matters of rationale of approach—I feel that in going before the public, it is absolutely necessary to be prepared to take definite, unequivocal positions upon supposedly controversial matters. We should have a clear, explicit, consistent viewpoint and we should not be timid in presenting it.

There are those in the movement who seem to feel that whenever controversy exists, we should be impelled to impartially present both or all sides of the question. I disagree. We should certainly not sponsor the presentation of opposing views. The Democrats don't present the views of the Republicans as having equal merit with theirs. Our opponents will do a fully adequate job of presenting their views, and will not return us the favor of presenting ours; we gain nothing in virtue by presenting theirs, and only provide the enemy—and let us not think of them as less than an enemy—with ammunition to be used against us.

We are not dealing with scientists; let us not employ the scientific method where it is not applicable. To do so is naive and unrealistic to an almost suicidal degree.

As our dealings with some of the government officials in Washington have indicated, we are dealing with an opposition which manifests itself as a ruthless, unscrupulous foe who will give no quarter and to whom any standards of fair play are meaningless. Let us respond realistically. We are not playing a gentlemanly game of tiddly-winks or croquet or chess. An impractical, theoretical intellectualism is utterly unrealistic and can be completely self-destructive in this context.

Now, a few particulars. My starting point is one now well accepted among the homophile organizations, although still novel elsewhere—that the homosexuals make up a minority group comparable to other, what might be called sociological minorities, such as the Negro, the Jews, etc.... With this as a starting point, I look upon the homophile organizations as playing for the homosexual minority the same role as is played by the NAACP or CORE for the Negro minority.

We cannot ask for our rights as a minority group from a position of inferiority or from a position, shall I say, as less than whole human beings. I feel that the entire homophile movement ... is going to stand or fall upon the question of whether or not homosexuality is a sickness, and upon our taking a firm stand on it.

Suffice it to say for the moment that a reading of the so-called authorities on this matter shows an appalling incidence of loose reasoning, of poor research, of supposedly generally applicable conclusions being derived from an examination of non-representative samplings, of conclusions being incorporated into initial assumptions, and vice versa, with the consequent circular reasoning.

There seems to be no valid evidence to show that homosexuality, *per se*, is a sickness. Accordingly, I take the position unequivocally that, until and unless valid, positive evidence shows otherwise, homosexuality *per se* is neither a sickness, a defect, a disturbance, a neurosis, a psychosis, nor a malfunction of any sort. I will go further and say that I feel so strongly that the rationale for the homophile movement rests, and rests heavily upon this position, that should evidence arise to show conclusively that this position is in error, I shall give serious thought to leaving the movement. I do not anticipate that I shall ever need to do so.

Another question which has a way of intruding itself upon any general discussion of homosexuality is that of morality and immorality. It is a point upon which I have rarely heard a straight, direct statement of position from persons in the homophile movement—even when expressing publicly their own views. I take the stand that not only is homosexuality, whether by mere inclination or by overt act, not immoral, but that homosexual acts engaged in by consenting adults are moral, in a positive and real sense, and are right, good and desirable, both for the individual participants and for the society in which they live.

There is another point which comes up frequently in discussions of homosexuality: the matter of the origins of homosexuality and the possibility of re-orientation to heterosexuality. While, as a person dealing with all aspects of homosexuality, I find that these questions are ones of some passing interest; from the viewpoint of civil liberties and social rights, these questions interest me *not at all.*

I do not see the NAACP and CORE worrying about which chromosome and gene produces a black skin or about the possibility of bleaching the Negro. I do not see any great interest on the part of the B'nai B'rith Anti-Defamation League in the possibility of solving problems of anti-Semitism by converting Jews to Christianity.

In all of these minority groups, we are interested in obtaining rights for our respective minorities *as* Negroes, *as* Jews, and *as* homosexuals. Why we are Negroes, Jews, or homosexuals is totally irrelevant, and whether we can be changed to whites, Christians, or heterosexuals is equally irrelevant.

There is one final point of basic approach and that is the somewhat subtle one, one which is difficult to express clearly. In reading through many statements put out by the homophile movement, there is easily perceptible a defensive tone—a lightly-veiled feeling that homosexuality really is inferior to heterosexuality but that, since we have to live with it, it must be made the best of. I am unwilling to grant even the slightest degree of inferiority: I look upon homosexuality as something in no way shameful or intrinsically undesirable.

Now, from the civil liberties and social rights viewpoint, just what do we want? I feel that we want, basically, what all other minority groups want and what every American citizen has the right to request and to expect—in fact, to demand: To be judged and to be treated, each upon his own merits as an individual and only on those criteria truly relevant to a particular situation, not upon irrelevant criteria, as homosexuality always is, having to do only with the harmless conduct of our private lives. We wish, AS HOMOSEXUALS to be rid of the contempt directed against us by our fellow citizens.... In short, as homosexuals we want "the right, as human beings, to develop our full potential and dignity, and the right, as citizens, to be allowed to make our maximum contribution to the society in which we live."

I feel that with due regard for strategy and tactics, we must take a bold, strong, uncompromising initiative in working for these rights; that the established framework of authority, constituted and otherwise, must be challenged directly by every lawful means at hand. There will, of course, be reactions to any such attempts. Such backlash, too, must be faced squarely and responded to fully. Most important, that such backlash may occur must not be allowed to act as a deterrent to further action.

Time is getting on, and my topic of major concern is the Washington homophile scene, so I'll proceed to the second part of my talk. [Mattachine of Washington's] first major project was the sending of a letter to every member of Congress, to the President and his Cabinet, to other members of the Executive Branch, and to members of the Judicial Branch of the Federal Government, as well as to officials of the Government of the District of Columbia. This letter informed the recipients of our existence and goals. It was accompanied by a news release asking for changes in Federal policy toward homosexuals, in the areas of Federal Civil Service employment, the issuance of security clearances, and policies of the Armed Forces....

In March of 1963 we presented to the US Civil Rights Commission a 9-page statement entitled "Discrimination Against the Employment of Homosexuals" and we testified at hearings held at that time by the Commission. At our instigation, the Washington ACLU's Committee on Discrimination has devoted a considerable portion of its time to the problems of homosexuals.... We have done our best to encourage the bringing of test court cases against the Government in the areas of U.S. Civil Service employment, security clearances, and military discharges.... We have several cases now in progress.

In May of 1963, for the first time within the memory of anyone, a gay bar in Washington was raided. I spent much of the month of June last year collecting affidavits from those arrested. A formal complaint was filed by the Mattachine Society of Washington against the Police Department. A conference was held involving high police officials and Mattachine Society of Washington officials. As a consequence, I don't think that any more gay bars in Washington will be raided....

We have formed a Research Committee now engaged in a number of projects related to the gathering of published information for the Society's own internal use. By far the most important project has to do with blackmail. One of the most successful brainwashing jobs in history has been that done by our Federal Government on the American public—including all too many in the homosexual community—in convincing them, to the point that it has become part of American folklore, that (1) all homosexuals are poor security risks because of susceptibility to blackmail; and (2) that exclusion is the only remedy. We don't believe either of these. We are thus preparing a survey of the homosexual community on various aspects of the question of blackmail, its prevalence, and the susceptibility of individual homosexuals to it.

We come now to the last of our current areas of major endeavor, religion. Our Committee on Approaches to the Clergy has informally approached perhaps two dozen clergymen of several faiths and denominations, with a considerable and gratifying degree of favorable response. The Committee's bases of approach are two—of equal emphasis. First, we feel that the homosexual finds himself rejected by almost every religious body to the loss and detriment both of the religious bodies and of the homosexuals. We seek to remedy this by working for closer integration of the homo-

sexuals with the religious life of their communities. Second, we wish to enlist the aid of clergy in our battle for civil rights.

I feel that these activities with religious leaders are of the utmost importance because the commitment of most people to their religion and to the leaders thereof is an emotional one. They will follow the lead taken by a minister where they will not follow the intellectual lead set by other leaders and person in positions of constituted authority. If we can get any substantial portion of the clergy to support us openly and actively, we can go a very long way, very quickly, toward remedying some of the situations in our regard which are so badly in need of remedy.

That completes a quick account of our activities, past, present, and proposed, in all three areas—civil liberties and social rights; information and education; and social services.

CARL WITTMAN, "A GAY MANIFESTO," (1969)

In June 1969, a routine raid on The Stonewall Inn in New York's Greenwich Village turned into a riot when for the first time the gay, lesbian, and transvestite patrons of a gay bar fought back. The Stonewall Riots have become a legend in gay and lesbian history, often credited with inaugurating the gay rights movement, something that had been developing for almost 20 years at that point. What it did symbolize was a shift to a new period of gay liberation, with tactics and philosophies that differed markedly from those of the homophile movement, even in its later activist manifestation. Influenced by the counter-culture and the black nationalist movement, gay liberationists were not interested in assimilating homosexuals into mainstream America but in transforming mainstream values and behaviors. Rather than fighting for the right to marry, they attacked the patriarchal and capitalist basis of marriage and promoted new, more egalitarian relationships. They insisted on the natural bisexuality of all humans and fought against not only homophobia but sexism and racism. Gay Liberation Fronts (GLFs), which sprang up in many cities, shunned hierarchical structures and rules of order in favor of egalitarian decision making based on consensus. Their meetings often took the form of a consciousness raising session, helping individuals realize how they were being oppressed by the conservative traditions of the dominant culture.

Like many gay liberationists, Carl Wittman was actively involved in other 1960s social movements, such as Students for a Democratic Society (SDS). "A Gay Manifesto," which he wrote in San Francisco in 1969, captures the substance and tone of the gay liberationist philosophy that proliferated in activist circles throughout the country around the time of the Stonewall Riots.

*   *   *

San Francisco is a refugee camp for homosexuals. We have fled here from every part of the nation, and like refugees elsewhere, we came not because it is so great here, but because it was so bad there. By the tens of thousands, we fled small towns where to be ourselves would endanger our jobs and any hope of a decent life; we have fled from blackmailing cops, from families who disowned or "tolerated" us; we have been drummed out of the armed services, thrown out of schools, fired from jobs, beaten by punks and policemen.

And we have formed a ghetto, out of self-protection. It is a ghetto rather than a free territory because it is still theirs. Straight cops patrol us, straight legislators govern us, straight employers keep us in line, straight money exploits us. We have pretended everything is OK, because we haven't been able to see how to change it—we've been afraid.

In the past year there has been an awakening of gay liberation ideas and energy. How it began we don't know; maybe we were inspired by black people and their freedom movement; we learned how to stop pretending from the hip revolution. Amerika in all its ugliness has surfaced with the war and our national leaders. And we are revulsed by the quality of our ghetto life.

Where once there was frustration, alienation, and cynicism, there are new characteristics among us. We are full of love for each other and are showing it; we are full of anger at what has been done to us. And as we recall all the self-censorship and repression for so many years, a reservoir of tears pours out of our eyes. And we are euphoric, high, with the initial flourish of a movement.

We want to make ourselves clear: our first job is to free ourselves; that means clearing our heads of the garbage that's been poured into them. This article is an attempt at raising a number of issues, and presenting some ideas to replace the old ones. It is primarily for ourselves, a starting point of discussion. If straight people of good will find it useful in understanding what liberation is about, so much the better.

It should also be clear that these are the views of one person, and are determined not only by my homosexuality, but my being white, male, middle-class. It is my individual consciousness. Our group consciousness will evolve as we get ourselves together—we are only at the beginning.

I. On Orientation

1. *What homosexuality is:* Nature leaves undefined the object of sexual desire. The gender of the object is imposed socially. Humans originally made homosexuality taboo because they needed every bit of energy to produce and raise children: survival of species was a priority. With overpopulation and technological change, that taboo continued only to exploit us and enslave us.

   Homosexuality is *not* a lot of things. It is not a makeshift in the absence of the opposite sex; it is not hatred or rejection of the opposite sex; it is not genetic; it is not the result of broken homes except inasmuch as we could see the sham of American marriage. Homosexuality is the capacity to love someone of the same sex.

2. *Bisexuality:* Bisexuality is good; it is the capacity to love people of either sex. The reason so few of us are bisexual is because society made such a big stink about homosexuality that we got forced into seeing ourselves as either straight or non-straight. Also, many gays got turned off to the ways men are supposed to act with women and vice-versa, which is pretty fucked-up. Gays will begin to turn to women when 1) it's something that we do because we want to, and not because we should and 2) when women's liberation changes the nature of heterosexual relationships.

3. *Heterosexuality:* Exclusive heterosexuality is fucked up. It reflects a fear of people of the same sex, it's anti-homosexual, and it is fraught with frustration. Heterosexual sex is fucked up, too; ask women's liberation about what straight guys are like in bed. Sex is aggression for the male chauvinist; sex is obligation for the traditional woman. For us to become heterosexual

in the sense that our straight brothers and sisters are is not a cure, it is a disease.

II. Women

1. *Lesbianism:* It's been a male-dominated society for too long, and that has warped both men and women. So gay women are going to see things differently from gay men; they are going to feel put down as women, too. Their liberation is tied up with both gay liberation and women's liberation.

2. *Male chauvinism:* All men are infected with male chauvinism—we were brought up that way. It means we assume that women play subordinate roles and are less human than ourselves. It is no wonder that so few women have become active in our groups. Male chauvinism, however, is not central to us. We can junk it much more easily than straight men can. For we understand oppression. We have largely opted out of a system which oppresses women daily—our egos are not built on putting women down and having them build us up. But we need to purge male chauvinism, both in behavior and in thought among us. Chick equals nigger equals queer. Think it over.

3. *Women's liberation:* They are assuming their equality and dignity and in doing so are challenging the same things we are: the roles, the exploitation of minorities by capitalism, the arrogant smugness of straight white male middle-class Amerika. They are our sisters in struggle.

III. On Roles

1. *Mimicry of straight society:* We are children of straight society. We still think straight: that is part of our oppression. One of the worst of straight concepts is inequality. Straight thinking views things in terms of order and comparison. A is before B, B is after A. This idea gets extended to male/female, on top/on bottom, spouse/not spouse, heterosexual/homosexual, boss/worker, white/black, and rich/poor. Our social institutions cause and reflect this verbal hierarchy. This is Amerika.

2. *Marriage:* Marriage is a prime example of a straight institution fraught with role playing. Traditional marriage is a rotten, oppressive institution. Those of us who have been in heterosexual marriages too often have blamed our gayness on the breakup of the marriage. No. They broke up because marriage is a contract which smothers both people, denies needs, and places impossible demands on both people.

   Gay people must stop gauging their self-respect by how well they mimic straight marriages. To accept that happiness comes through finding a groovy spouse and settling down, showing the world that "we're just the same as you" is avoiding the real issues, and is an expression of self-hatred.

3. *Alternatives to marriage:* People want to get married for lots of good reasons, although marriage won't often meet those needs or desires. We're looking for security, a flow of love, and a feeling of belonging and being needed.

   These needs can be met through a number of social relationships and living situations. Things we want to get away from are:

1) exclusiveness, propertied attitudes toward each other, a mutual pact against the rest of the world; 2) promises about the future, which we have no right to make and which prevent us from, or make us feel guilty about, growing; 3) inflexible roles, roles which do not reflect us at the moment but are inherited through mimicry and inability to define egalitarian relationships.

We have to define for ourselves a new pluralistic, role free social structure for ourselves. It must contain both the freedom and physical space for people to live alone, live together for a while, live together for a long time, either as a couple or in larger numbers; and the ability to flow easily from one of these states to another as our needs change.

Liberation for gay people is defining for ourselves how and with whom we live, instead of measuring our relationships in comparison to straight ones, with straight values.

4. *Gay "stereotypes":* The straights' image of the gay world is defined largely by those of us who have violated straight roles. There is a tendency among "homophile" groups to deplore gays who play visible roles—the queens and nellies. As liberated gays, we must take a clear stand. 1) Gays who stand out have become our first martyrs. They came out and withstood disapproval before the rest of us did. 2) If they suffered from being open, it is straight society whom we must indict, not the queen.

5. *Closet queens:* This phrase is becoming analogous to "Uncle Tom." To pretend to be straight sexually, or to pretend to be straight socially, is probably the most harmful pattern of behavior in the ghetto. The married guy who makes it on the side secretly; the guy who will go to bed once but who won't develop any gay relationships; the pretender at work or school who changes the gender of the friend he's talking about; the guy who'll suck cock in the bushes but who won't go to bed. If we are liberated we are open with our sexuality. Closet queenery must end. Come out.

IV. On Oppression

It is important to catalog and understand the different facets of our oppression. There is no future in arguing about degrees of oppression. A lot of "movement" types come on with a line of shit about homosexuals not being oppressed as much as blacks or Vietnamese or workers or women. We don't happen to fit into their ideas of class or caste. Bull! When people feel oppressed, they act on that feeling. We feel oppressed. Talk about the priority of black liberation or ending imperialism over and above gay liberation is just anti-gay propaganda.

1. *Physical attacks:* We are attacked, beaten, castrated and left dead time and again. Cops in most cities have harassed our meeting places: bars and baths and parks. They set up entrapment squads. Cities set up "pervert registration," which if nothing else scares our brothers deeper into the closet.

2. *Psychological warfare:* Right from the beginning we have been subjected to a barrage of straight propaganda. Since our parents don't know any homosexuals, we grow up thinking that we're alone and different and perverted. Our school friends identify "queer" with any non-conformist or bad behavior. Our elementary school teachers tell us not to talk to strangers or accept rides. Television, billboards, and magazines put forth a false ide-

alization of male/female relationships, and make us wish we were different, wish we were "in."

3. *Self-oppression:* As gay liberation grows, we will find our uptight brothers and sisters, particularly those who are making a buck off our ghetto, coming on strong to defend the status quo. This is self-oppression: "don't rock the boat," "things in SF are OK," "gay people just aren't together," "I'm not oppressed." These lines are right out of the mouths of the straight establishment. A large part of our oppression would end if we stop putting ourselves and our pride down.

4. *Institutional oppression:* Discrimination against gays is blatant, if we open our eyes. Homosexual relationships are illegal, and even if these laws are not regularly enforced, they encourage and enforce closet queenery. The bulk of the social work/psychiatric field looks upon homosexuality as a problem, and treats us as sick. Employers let it be known that our skills are acceptable only as long as our sexuality is hidden. Big business and government are particularly notorious offenders.

V. On Sex

1. *What sex is:* It is both creative expression and communication: good when it is either, and better when it is both. Sex can also be aggression, and usually is when those involved do not see each other as equals; and can also be perfunctory, when we are distracted or preoccupied. These uses spoil what is good about it.

I like to think of good sex in terms of playing the violin: with both people on one level seeing the other body as an object capable of creating beauty when they play it well; and on a second level the players communicating through their mutual production and appreciation of beauty. As in good music, you get totally into it—and coming back out of that state of consciousness is like finishing a work of art or coming back from an episode of an acid or mescaline trip. And to press the analogy further: the variety of music is infinite and varied, depending on the capabilities of the players, both as subject and as objects. Solos, duets, quartets are possible.

2. *Objectification:* In this scheme, people are sexual objects, but they are also subjects, and are human beings who appreciate themselves as object and subject. This use of human bodies as objects is legitimate only when it is reciprocal. If one person is always object and the other subject, it stifles the human being in both of them.... Gay liberation people must understand that women have been treated exclusively and dishonestly as sexual objects. A major part of their liberation is to play down sexual objectification and to develop other aspects of themselves which have been smothered so long.... For us, sexual objectification is a focus of our quest for freedom. Learning how to be open and good with each other sexually is part of our liberation. And one obvious distinction: objectification of sex for us is something we choose to do among ourselves, while for women it is imposed by their oppressors.

3. *On positions and roles:* Much of our sexuality has been perverted through mimicry of straights, and warped from self-hatred. These sexual perversions are basically anti-gay:

"I like to make it with straight guys"
"I'm not gay, but I like to be 'done'"
"I like to fuck, but don't want to be fucked"
"I don't like to be touched above the neck"

This is role playing at its worst; we must transcend these roles. We strive for democratic, mutual, reciprocal sex. This does not mean that we are all mirror images of each other in bed, but that we break away from roles which enslave us.

4. *Chickens and studs:* Face it, nice bodies and young bodies are attributes, they're groovy. They are inspiration for art, for spiritual elevation, for good sex. The problem arises only in the inability to relate to people of the same age, or people who don't fit the plastic stereotypes of a good body. At that point, objectification eclipses people, and expresses self-hatred.

VI. On Our Ghetto

We are refugees from Amerika. So we came to the ghetto—and as other ghettos, it has its negative and positive aspects. Refugee camps are better than what preceded them, or people never would have come. But they are still enslaving, if only that we are limited to being ourselves there and only there. Ghettos breed self-hatred. We stagnate here, accepting the status quo.

San Francisco—ghetto or free territory: Our ghetto certainly is more beautiful and larger and more diverse than most ghettos, and is certainly freer than the rest of Amerika. That's why we're here. But it isn't ours. Capitalists make money off us, cops patrol us, government tolerates us as long as we shut up, and daily we work for and pay taxes to those who oppress us.

To be a free territory we must govern ourselves, set up our own institutions, defend ourselves, and use our own energies to improve our lives. The emergence of gay liberation communes and our own paper is a good start. The talk about a gay liberation coffee shop/dance hall should be acted upon. Rural retreats, political action offices, food cooperatives, a free school, unalienating bars—they must be developed if we are to have even the shadow of a free territory.

VII. On Coalition

Right now the bulk of our work has to be among ourselves—self educating, fending off attacks, and building free territory. Thus basically we have to have a gay/straight vision of the world until the oppression of gays is ended.

But not every straight is our enemy. Many of us have mixed identities, and have ties with other liberation movements: women, blacks, other minority groups; we may also have taken on an identity which is vital to us: ecology, dope, ideology. And face it: we can't change Amerika alone. Who do we look to for coalition?

1. Women's liberation
2. Black liberation
3. Chicanos
4. White radicals and ideologues
5. Hip and street people
6. Homophile groups

Conclusion: An Outline of Imperatives for Gay Liberation

1. *Free ourselves:* come out everywhere; initiate self defense and political activity; initiate counter community institutions.
2. *Turn other gay people on:* talk all the time; understand, forgive, accept.
3. *Free the homosexual in everyone:* we'll be getting a good bit of shit from threatened latents: be gentle, and keep talking and acting free.
4. We've been playing an act for a long time, so we're consummate actors. Now we can begin *to be*, and it'll be a good show!

RADICALESBIANS, "THE WOMAN-IDENTIFIED WOMAN," 1970

In the late 1960s and early 1970s, many lesbians began to identify more with the values and tenants of the newly revitalized women's movement than with the largely male-dominated gay liberation movement. But within the women's movement lesbians were often denounced as the "Lavender Menace" that gave women's liberation a bad name. At the second Congress to Unite Women in 1970, a group of lesbian demonstrators took over the proceedings and confronted the women's movement with its own homophobia. Out of this Congress came a position paper by a group calling itself the Radicalesbians that redefined lesbianism as an act of political solidarity with other women. In order to appeal to non-gay women, they de-emphasized the sexual elements of lesbianism and borrowed the language of feminist separatism. Rejecting the notion that lesbians were more masculine than other women, the Radicalesbians asserted that their almost complete rejection of men and patriarchal standards made them the most "women-identified" of women. The Radicalesbians' position paper, "The Woman-Identified Woman," which appears below, captures the sentiments of many lesbian feminists in the early 1970s. During this period, many lesbian-feminists, most notably author Rita Mae Brown, pursued their separatist agenda by living together in lesbian collectives, such as the Furies in Washington, D.C. They continued to confront the gay movement with its sexism and the women's movement with its homophobia.

*   *   *

What is a lesbian? A lesbian is the rage of all women condensed to the point of explosion. She is the woman who, often beginning at an extremely early age, acts in accordance with her inner compulsion to be a more complete and freer human being than her society—perhaps then, but certainly later—cares to allow her. These needs and actions, over a period of years, brings her into painful conflict with people, situations, the accepted ways of thinking, feeling, and behaving, until she is in a state of continual war with everything around her, and usually with her self. She may not be fully conscious of the political implications of what for her began as personal necessity, but on some level she has not been able to accept the limitations and oppression laid on her by the most basic role of her society—the female role. The turmoil she experiences tends to induce guilt proportional to the degree to which she feels she is not meeting social expectations, and/or eventually drives her to question and analyze what the rest of her society, more or less accepts. She is forced to evolve her own life pattern, often living much of her life alone, learning usually much earlier than her "straight" (heterosexual) sisters about the essential aloneness of life (which the myth of marriage obscures) and about the reality of illusions. To the extent that she cannot expel the heavy socialization that goes with being female, she can never truly find peace with herself. For she is caught somewhere between accepting society's view of her—in which case she cannot accept herself—and coming to understand what this sexist society has done to her and why it is functional and necessary for it to do so. Those of us who work that through find ourselves on the other side of a tortuous journey through a night that may have been decades long. The perspective gained from that journey, the liberation of self, the inner peace, the real love of self and of all women, is something to be shared with all women—because we are all women.

It should be understood that lesbianism, like male homosexuality, is a category of behavior possible only in a sexist society characterized by rigid sex roles and dominated by male supremacy. Those sex roles dehumanize women by defining us as a supportive/serving caste in relation to the master caste of men, and emotionally cripple men by demanding that they be alienated from their bodies and emotions in order to perform their economic/political/military functions effectively. Homosexuality is a by-product of a particular way of setting up roles (or approved patterns of behavior) on the basis of sex; as such it is an inauthentic (not consonant with "reality") category. In a society in which men do not oppress women, and sexual expression is allowed to follow feelings, the categories of homosexuality and heterosexuality would disappear.

But lesbianism is also different from male homosexuality, and serves a different function in the society. "Dyke" is a different kind of put-down from "faggot," though both imply you are not playing your socially assigned sex role—are not therefore a "real woman" or a "real man." The grudging admiration felt for the tomboy and the queasiness felt around a sissy boy point to the same thing: the contempt in which women—or those who play a female role—are held. And the investment in keeping women in that contemptuous role is very great. Lesbian is the work, the label, the condition that holds women in line. When a woman hears this word tossed her way, she knows she is stepping out of line. She knows that she has crossed the terrible boundary of her sex role. She recoils, she protests, she reshapes her actions to gain approval. Lesbian is a label invented by the man to throw at any woman who dares to be his equal, who dares to challenge his prerogatives, who dares to assert the primacy of her own needs. To have the label applied to people active in women's liberation is just the most recent instance of a long history; older women will recall that not so long ago, any woman who was successful, independent, not orienting her whole life about a man, would hear this word. For in this sexist society, for a woman to be independent means she *can't* be a *woman*—she *must* be a *dyke*. That in itself should tell us where women are at. It says as clearly as can be said: women and person are contradictory terms. For a lesbian is not considered a "real woman." And yet, in popular thinking, there is really only one essential difference between a lesbian and other women: that of sexual orientation—which is to say, when you strip off all the packaging, you must finally realize that the essence of being a "woman" is to get fucked by men.

"Lesbian" is one of the sexual categories by which men have divided up humanity. While all women are dehumanized as sex objects, as the objects of men, they are given certain compensations: identification with his power, his ego, his status, his pro-

tection (from other males), feeling like a "real woman," finding social acceptance by adhering to her role, etc. Should a woman confront herself by confronting another woman, there are fewer rationalizations, fewer buffers by which to avoid the stark horror of her dehumanized condition. Herein we find the overriding fear of many women towards exploring intimate relationships with other women: the fear of her being used as a sexual object by a woman, which not only will bring no male-connected compensations, but also will reveal the void which is woman's real situation. This dehumanization is expressed when a straight woman learns that a sister is a lesbian; she begins to relate to her lesbian sister as her potential sex object, laying a surrogate male role on the lesbian. This reveals her heterosexual conditioning to make herself into an object when sex is potentially involved in a relationship, and it denies the lesbian her full humanity. For women, especially those in the movement, to perceive their lesbian sisters through this male grid or role definitions is to accept this male cultural conditioning and to oppress their sisters much as they themselves have been oppressed by men. Are we going to continue the male classification system of defining all females in sexual relation to some other category of people? Affixing the label lesbian not only to a woman who aspires to be a person, but also to any situation of real love, real solidarity, real primacy among women is a primary form of divisiveness among women: it is the condition which keeps women within the confines of the feminine role, and it is the debunking/scare term that keeps women from forming any primary attachments, groups, or associations among ourselves.

Women in the movement have in most cases gone to great lengths to avoid discussion and confrontation with the issue of lesbianism. It puts people up-tight. They are hostile, evasive, or try to incorporate it into some "broader issue." They would rather not talk about it. If they have to, they try to discuss it as a "lavender herring." But it is no side issue. It is absolutely essential to the success and fulfillment of the women's liberation movement that this issue be dealt with. As long as the label "dyke" can be used to frighten women into a less militant stand, keep her separate from her sisters, keep her from giving primacy to anything other than men and family—then to that extent she is controlled by the male culture. Until women see in each other the possibility of a primal commitment which includes sexual love, they will be denying themselves the love and value they readily accord to men, thus affirming their second-class status. As long as male acceptability is primary, the term lesbian will be used effectively against women.

It should also be said that some younger, more radical women have honestly begun to discuss lesbianism, but so far it has been primarily as a sexual "alternative" to men. This, however, is still giving primacy to men, both because the idea of relating more completely to women occurs as a negative reaction to men, and because the lesbian relationship is being characterized simply by sex, which is divisive and sexist. On one level, which is both personal and political, women may withdraw emotional and sexual energies from men, and work out various alternatives for those energies in their own lives. On a different political/psychological level, it must be understood that what is crucial is that women begin disengaging from male-defined response patterns. In the privacy of our own psyches, we must cut those cords to the core. For irrespective of where our love and sexual energies flow, if we are male-identified in our heads, we cannot realize our autonomy as human beings.

But why is it that women have related to and through men? By virtue of having been brought up in a male society, we have internalized the male culture's definition of ourselves. That definition views us as relative beings who exist not for ourselves, but for the servicing, maintenance and comfort of men. That definition consigns us to sexual and family functions, and excludes us from defining and shaping the terms of our lives. In exchange for our psychic servicing and for performing society's non-profit-making functions, the man confers on us just one thing: the slave status which makes us legitimate in the eyes of the society in which we live. This is called "femininity" or "being a real woman" in our cultural lingo. We are authentic, legitimate, real to the extent that we are the property of some man whose name we bear. To be a woman who belongs to no man is to be invisible, pathetic, inauthentic, unreal. He confirms his image of us—of what we have to be in order to be acceptable by him—but not our real selves; he confirms our womanhood—as he defines it, in relation to him—but cannot confirm our personhood, our own selves as absolutes. As long as we are dependent on the male culture for this definition, for this approval, we cannot be free.

The consequence of internalizing this role is an enormous reservoir of self-hate. This is not to say the self-hate is recognized or accepted as such; indeed most women would deny it. It may be experienced as discomfort with her role, as feeling empty, as numbness, as restlessness, a paralyzing anxiety at the center. Alternatively, it may be expressed in shrill defensiveness of the glory and destiny of her role. But it does exist, often beneath the edge of her consciousness, poisoning her existence, keeping her alienated from herself, her own needs, and rendering her a stranger to other women. Women hate both themselves and other women. They try to escape by identifying with the oppressor, living through him, gaining status and identity with the oppressor, living through him, gaining status and identity from his ego, his power, his accomplishments. And by not identifying with other "empty vessels" like themselves, women resist relating on all levels to other women who will reflect their own oppression, their own secondary status, their own self-hate. For to confront another woman is finally to confront one's self—the self we have gone to such lengths to avoid. And in that mirror we know we cannot really respect and love that which we have been made to be.

As the source of self-hate and the lack of real self as rooted in our male-given identity, we must create a new sense of self. As long as we cling to the idea of "being a woman," we will sense some conflict with that incipient self, that sense of I, that sense of a whole person. It is very difficult to realize and accept that being "feminine" and being a whole person are irreconcilable. Only women can give each other a new sense of self. That identity we have to develop with reference to ourselves, and not in relation to men. This consciousness is the revolutionary force from which all else will follow, for ours is an organic revolution. For this we must be available and supportive to one another, give our commitment and our love, give the emotional support necessary to sustain this movement. Our energies must flow toward our sisters, not backwards towards our oppressors. As long as women's liberation tries to free women without facing the basic heterosexual structure that binds us in one-to-one relationship with our own oppressors, tremendous energies will continue to flow into trying to straighten up each particular relationship with a man, how to get better sex, how to turn his head around—into trying to make the "new man" out of him, in the delusion that this will allow us to be the "new

woman." This obviously splits our energies and commitments, leaving us unable to be committed to the construction of the new patterns which will liberate us.

It is the primacy of women relating to women, of women creating a new consciousness of and with each other which is at the heart of women's liberation, and the basis for the cultural revolution. Together we must find, reinforce and validate our authentic selves. As we do this, we confirm in each other that struggling incipient sense of pride and strength, the divisive barriers begin to melt, we feel this growing solidarity with our sisters. We see ourselves as prime, find our centers inside of ourselves. We find receding the sense of alienation, of being cut off, of being behind a locked window, of being unable to get out what we know is inside. We feel a realness, feel at last we are coinciding with ourselves. With that real self, with that consciousness, we begin a revolution to end the imposition of all coercive identifications, and to achieve maximum autonomy in human expression.

HARVEY MILK, "THAT'S WHAT AMERICA IS," SPEECH DELIVERED ON GAY FREEDOM DAY, 25 JUNE 1978

By the 1970s, openly gay men and women were not only demanding equal rights, they were increasingly getting elected to public office. Elaine Noble, a Massachusetts State Representative, was the first. But the most famous and influential was Harvey Milk, elected to the San Francisco Board of Supervisors in 1977, after two previous unsuccessful runs. He was elected not only by gays and lesbians who had made San Francisco's Castro one of the nation's largest gay neighborhoods, but through alliances with labor unions and other progressive groups. Charismatic and outspoken, he was an indefatigable defender of human rights. In California, he lead the successful opposition to Proposition 6, "the Briggs Initiative," which sought to ban lesbians and gay men from teaching in public schools. As a national figure, he was a principal opponent of Anita Bryant in her campaign to overturn the gay rights ordinance in Dade County, Florida.

In 1978, he and San Francisco's mayor George Moscone were assassinated in city hall by Dan White, a former police officer and political opponent of Milk's on the Board of Supervisors. When White, who confessed to the murders, was found guilty only of "voluntary manslaughter," riots erupted in San Francisco's civic center. Aware that his prominence as a militant gay politician put him in danger, Milk had recorded a tape to be played in the event he was assassinated. "I have never considered myself a candidate," he said. "I have always considered myself part of a movement, part of a candidacy." He asked that people use his death as an opportunity to come out of the closet, a strategy he had always insisted could change the world. Though he did not live to see it, his call for a gay and lesbian march on Washington, D.C., was fulfilled in 1979, and repeated in 1987 and 1993.

*   *   *

My Name is Harvey Milk—and I want to recruit you. I want to recruit you for the fight to preserve your Democracy from the John Briggs and the Anita Bryants who are trying to constitutionalize bigotry.

We are not going to allow that to happen. We are not going to sit back in silence as 300,000 of our gay brothers and sisters did in Nazi Germany. We are not going to allow our rights to be taken away and then march with bowed head into the gas chambers. On this anniversary of Stonewall I ask my gay sisters and brothers to make the commitment to fight for themselves, for their freedom, for their country.

Gay people, we will not win their rights by staying quietly in our closets ... we are coming out! We are coming out to fight the lies, the myths, the distortions! We are coming out to tell the truth about gays!

For I'm tired of the conspiracy of silence.

I'm tired of listening to the Anita Bryants twist the language and the meaning of the Bible to fit their own distorted outlook. But I'm even more tired of the silence from the religious leaders of this nation who know that she is playing fast and loose with the true meaning of the Bible. *I'm tired of their silence more than of her Biblical Gymnastics!*

And I am tired of John Briggs talking about false role models. He's lying in his teeth and he knows it. But I'm even more tired of the silence from educators and psychologists who know that Briggs is lying and yet say nothing. *I'm tired of their silence more than of Briggs' lies!*

I'm tired of the silence. So I'm going to talk about it. And I want *you* to talk about it.

Gay people, we are painted as child molesters. I want to talk about that. I want to talk about the *myth* of child molestations by gays. I want to talk about the *fact* that in this state some 95 percent of child molestations are heterosexual and usually the parent....

I want to talk about the *fact* that all child abandonments are heterosexual.

I want to talk about the *fact* that all abuse of children is by their heterosexual parents.

I want to talk about the *fact* that some 98 percent of the six million rapes committed annually are heterosexual.

I want to talk about the *fact* that one out of every three women who will be murdered in this state this year will be murdered by their husbands.

I want to talk about the fact that some 20 percent of all marriages contain domestic violence.

And finally, I want to tell the John Briggs and the Anita Bryants that you talk about the *myths* of gays but today I'm talking about the *facts* of *heterosexual violence* and what the hell are you going to do about that?????

Clean up your own house before you start telling lies about gays. Don't distort the Bible to hide your own sins. Don't change facts to lies. Don't look for cheap political advantage in playing upon people's fears! Judging by the latest polls, even the youth can tell you're lying!

And like the rest of you, *I'm tired* of our so-called friends who tell us that we must set standards. What standards?

The Standards of the rapist? The wife beaters? The child abusers? The people who ordered the bomb to be built? The people who ordered it to be dropped? The people who pulled the trigger? The people who gave us Vietnam? The people who built the gas chambers? The people who built the concentration camps?—Right *here*, in California, and then herded all the Japanese-Americans into them during World War II.... The jew baiters? The Nigger knockers? The corporate thiefs? The Nixons? The Hitlers?

What standards do *you* want *us* to set? Clean up your act, clean up your violence before you criticize lesbians and gay men because of their sexuality.... It is *madness* to glorify killing and violence on one hand and be ashamed of the sexual act, the act that conceived you, on the other....

Well, I'm tired of the lies of the Anita Bryants and the John Briggs.

I'm tired of their myths.

I'm tired of their distortions.

I'm speaking out about it.

Gay brothers and sisters, what are *you* going to do about it? You must *come out.* Come out ... to your parents.... I know that it is hard and will hurt them but think about how they will *hurt you* in the voting booth! *Come out ... to your relatives.* I know that is hard and will upset them but think of how they will upset you in the voting booth. *Come out to your friends ...* If indeed they are your friends. *Come out* to your neighbors ... to your fellow workers ... to the people who work where you eat and shop.... *Come out* only to the people you know, and who know you. Not to anyone else. But once and for all, break down the myths, destroy the lies and distortions.

For your sake.

For their sake.

For the sake of the *youngsters* who are becoming scared by the votes from Dade [County, Florida] to Eugene [Oregon].

If Briggs wins he will not stop. They never do. Like all mad people, they are forced to go on, to *prove* they were right! There will be no safe "closet" for any gay person.

So break out of yours today—tear the damn thing down once and for all!

And finally, most of all, *I'm tired* of the *silence* from the White House.

Jimmy Carter: You talked about Human Rights a lot.... In fact, you want to be the world's leader for human rights. Well, *damn it, lead!!* There are some fifteen to twenty million lesbians and gay men in this nation listening and listening very carefully.

Jimmy Carter: When are you going to talk about *their* rights? Until you speak out against hatred, bigotry, madness, you are just Jimmy Carter. When you do, then and only then, will some twenty million lesbians and gay men be able to say Jimmy Carter is *Our* President, too!

Jimmy Carter, you have the choice:

How many more years?

How much more damage?

How much more violence?

How many more lives?

History says that, like all groups seeking their rights, sooner or later we will win. The question is: When?

Jimmy Carter, you have to make the choice—it's in your hands: it is up to you. Now, before it becomes too late, come to California and speak out against Briggs....

If you don't—then we will come to you!!! If you do not speak out, if you remain silent, if you do not lift your voice against Briggs, then I call upon lesbians and gay men from all over the nation ... your nation ... to gather in Washington ... one year from now ... on that national day of freedom, the fourth of July ... to gather in Washington on that very same spot where over a decade ago Dr. Martin Luther King spoke to a nation of his dreams....

I call upon all minorities and especially the millions of lesbians and gay men to wake up from their dreams ... to gather on Washington and tell Jimmy Carter and their nation: "Wake up.... Wake up, America.... No more racism, no more sexism, no more ageism, no more hatred ... no more!"

Jimmy Carter: Listen to us today ... or you will have to listen to lesbians and gay men from all over this nation as they gather in Washington next year.... [compiler's note: President Carter did come to California and did ask voters to defeat the Briggs Initiative, but only when it became clear that the Initiative was going to lose anyway.]

And to the bigots ... to the John Briggs ... to the Anita Bryants ... and all their ilk.... Let me remind you what America is ... listen carefully:

On the Statue of Liberty it says: "Give me your tired, your poor, your huddled masses yearning to be free...." In the Declaration of Independence it is written: "All men are created equal and they are endowed with certain inalienable rights...." And in our National Anthem it says, "Oh, say does that star-spangled banner yet wave o'er the land of the free."

For Mr. Briggs and Mrs. Bryant and all the bigots out there: That's what America is. No matter how hard you try, you cannot erase those words from the Declaration of Independence. No matter how hard you try, you cannot chip those words from off the base of the Statue of Liberty. And no matter how hard you try, you cannot sing the "Star Spangled Banner" without those words.

That's what America is.

Love it or leave it.

AUDRE LORDE, "I AM YOUR SISTER: BLACK WOMEN ORGANIZING ACROSS SEXUALITIES," 1980

One of the speakers at the first March on Washington for gay rights in 1979 was Audre Lorde. In a movement dominated by white men, Lorde became a powerful voice for women and African Americans. As a black lesbian feminist, Lorde drew connections between the racism, sexism, and homophobia she experienced, reminding the black community that it was not entirely heterosexual and the gay community that it was not entirely white. As a writer, poet, and teacher, Lorde questioned the universalizing tendency in notions such as "gay community" or "sisterhood," and expressed the particularity of who she was—a black woman, lesbian, feminist, mother of two, daughter or Caribbean immigrants, cancer survivor, and activist. As Lorde wrote, "community must not mean a shedding of our differences, nor the pathetic pretense that these differences do not exist." Like much of her writing, teaching, and activism, the speech reprinted below from 1980 explores this central theme of how to organize across difference. The author of more than a dozen books of poetry and prose, Lorde served as poet laureate of New York State before her death from cancer in 1992.

*   *   *

Whenever I come to Medgar Evers College I always feel a thrill of anticipation and delight because it feels like coming home, like talking to family, having a chance to speak about things that are very important to me with people who matter the most. And this is particularly true whenever I talk at the Women's Center. But, as with all families, we sometimes find it difficult to deal constructively with the genuine differences between us and to recognize that unity does not require that we be identical to each other. Black women are not one great vat of homogenized chocolate milk. We have many different faces, and we do not have to become each other in order to work together.

It is not easy for me to speak here with you as a Black Lesbian feminist, recognizing that some of the ways in which I identify myself make it difficult for you to hear me. But meeting across difference always requires mutual stretching, and until you can hear me as a Black Lesbian feminist, our strengths will not be truly available to each other as Black women.

Because I feel it is urgent that we not waste each other's resources, that we recognize each sister on her own terms so that we may better work together toward our mutual survival, I speak here about heterosexism and homophobia, two grave barriers to organizing among Black women. And so that we have a common language between us, I would like to define some of the terms I use: *Heterosexism*—a belief in the inherent superiority of one form of loving over all others and thereby the right to dominance; *Homophobia*—a terror surrounding feelings of love for members of the same sex and thereby a hatred of those feeling in others.

In the 1960s, when liberal white people decided that they didn't want to appear racist, they wore dashikis, and danced Black, and ate Black, and even married Black, but they did not want to feel Black or think Black, so they never even questioned the textures of their daily living (why should flesh-colored Band-Aids always be pink?) and then they wondered, "Why are those Black folks always taking offense so easily at the least little thing? Some of our best friends are Black...."

Well, it is not necessary for some of your best friends to be Lesbian, although some of them probably are, no doubt. But it is necessary for you to stop oppressing me through false judgement. I do not want you to ignore my identity, nor do I want you to make it an insurmountable barrier between our sharing of strengths.

When I say I am a Black feminist, I mean I recognize that my power as well as my primary oppressions come as a result of my Blackness as well as my womanness, and therefore my struggles on both these fronts are inseparable.

When I say I am a Black Lesbian, I mean I am a woman whose primary focus on loving, physical as well as emotional, is directed to women. It does not mean I hate men. Far from it. The harshest attacks I have ever heard against Black men come from those women who are intimately bound to them and cannot free themselves from a subservient and silent position. I would never presume to speak about Black men the way I have heard some of my straight sisters talk about the men they are attached to. And of course that concerns me, because it reflects a situation of noncommunication in the heterosexual Black community that is far more truly threatening than the existence of Black Lesbians.

What does this have to do with Black women organizing?

I have heard it said—usually behind my back—that Black Lesbians are not normal. But what is normal in this deranged society by which we are all trapped? I remember, and so do many of you, when being Black was considered *not normal*, when they talked about us in whispers, tried to paint us, lynch us, bleach us, pretend we did not exist. We called that racism.

I have heard it said that Black Lesbians are a threat to the Black family. But when 50 percent of children born to Black women are born out of wedlock, and 30 percent of all Black families are headed by women without husbands, we need to broaden and redefine what we mean by a *family*.

I have heard it said that Black Lesbians will mean the death of the race. Yet Black Lesbians bear children in exactly the same way other women bear children, and a Lesbian household is simply another kind of family. Ask my son and daughter.

The terror of Black Lesbians is buried in that deep inner place where we have been taught to fear all difference—to kill it or ignore it. Be assured: loving women is not a communicable disease. You don't catch it like the common cold. Yet the one accusation that seems to render even the most vocal straight Black woman totally silent and ineffective is the suggestion that she might be a Black Lesbian.

If someone says you're Russian and you know you're not, you don't collapse into stunned silence. Even if someone calls you a bigamist, or a childbeater, and you know you're not, you don't crumple into bits. You say it's not true and keep on printing the posters. But let anyone, particularly a Black man, accuse a straight Black woman of being a Black *Lesbian*, and right away that sister becomes immobilized, as if that is the most horrible thing she could be, and must at all costs be proven false. That is homophobia. It is a waste of woman energy, and it puts a terrible weapon into the hands of your enemies to be used against you to silence you, to keep you docile and in line. It also served to keep us isolated and apart.

I have heard it said that Black Lesbians are not political, that we have not been and are not involved in the struggles of Black people. But when I taught Black and Puerto Rican students writing at City College in the SEEK program in the sixties I was a Black Lesbian. I was a Black Lesbian when I helped organize and fight for the Black Studies Department of John Jay College. And because I was fifteen years younger then and less sure of myself, at one crucial moment I yielded to pressures that said I should step back for a Black man even though I knew him to be a serious error of choice, and I did, and he was. But I was a Black Lesbian then.

When my girlfriends and I went out in the car one 4 July night after fireworks with cans of white spray paint and our kids asleep in the back seat, one of us staying behind to keep the motor running and watch the kids while the other two worked our way down the suburban New Jersey street, spraying white paint over the black jockey statues, and their little red jackets, too, we were Black Lesbians.

When I drove through the Mississippi delta to Jackson in 1968 with a group of Black students from Tougaloo, another car full of redneck kids trying to bump us off the road all the way back into town, I was a Black Lesbian.

When I weaned my daughter in 1963 to go to Washington in August to work in the coffee tents along with Lena Horne, making coffee for the marshalls because that was what most Black women did in the 1963 March on Washington, I was a Black Lesbian.

When I taught a poetry workshop at Tougaloo, a small Black college in Mississippi, where white rowdies shot up the edge of campus every night, and I felt the joy of seeing young Black poets find their voices and power through words in our mutual growth, I was a Black Lesbian.

When Yoli and I cooked curried chicken and beans and rice and took our extra blankets and pillows up the hill to the striking students occupying buildings at City College in 1969, demanding open admissions and the right to an education, I was a Black Lesbian. When I walked through the midnight hallways of Lehman College that same year, carrying Midol and Kotex pads for the young Black radical women taking part in the action, and we tried to persuade them that their place in the revolution was not ten paces behind Black men, that spreading their legs to the guys on the tables in the cafeteria was not a revolutionary act no matter what the brothers said, I was a Black Lesbian. When I picketed for Welfare Mothers' Rights, and against the enforced sterilization of young Black girls, when I fought institutionalized racism in the New York City schools, I was a Black Lesbian.

But you did not know it because we did not identify ourselves, so now you can say that Black Lesbians and Gay men have nothing to do with the struggles of the Black Nation.

And I am not alone.

When you read the words of Langston Hughes you are reading the words of a Black Gay man. When you read the words of Alice Dunbar-Nelson and Angelina Weld Grimke, poets of the Harlem Renaissance, you are reading the words of Black Lesbians. When you listen to the life-affirming voices of Bessie Smith and Ma Rainey, you are hearing Black Lesbian women. When you see the plays and read the words of Lorraine Hansberry, you are reading the words of a woman who loved women deeply.

Today, Lesbians and Gay men are some of the most active and engaged members of Art Against Apartheid, a group which is making visible and immediate our cultural responsibilities against the tragedy of South Africa. We have organizations such as the National Coalition of Black Lesbians and Gays, Dykes Against Racism Everywhere, and Men of All Colors Together, all of which are committed to and engaged in antiracist activity.

Homophobia and heterosexism mean you allow yourselves to be robbed of the sisterhood and strength of Black Lesbian women because you are afraid of being called a Lesbian yourself. Yet we share so many concerns as Black women, so much work to be done. The urgency of the destruction of our Black children and the theft of young Black minds are joint urgencies. Black children shot down or doped up on the streets of our cities are priorities for all of us. The fact of Black women's blood flowing with grim regularity in the streets and living rooms of Black communities is not a Black Lesbian rumor. It is sad statistical truth. The fact that there is widening and dangerous lack of communication around our differences between Black women and men is not a Black Lesbian plot. It is a reality that is starkly clarified as we see our young people becoming more and more uncaring of each other. Young Black boys believing that they can define their manhood between a sixth-grade girl's legs, growing up believing that Black women and girls are the fitting target for their justifiable furies rather than the racist structures grinding us all into dust, these are not Black Lesbian myths. These are sad realities of Black communities today and of immediate concern to us all. We cannot afford to waste each other's energies in our common battles.

What does homophobia mean? It means that high-powered Black women are told it is not safe to attend a Conference on the Status of Women in Nairobi simply because we are Lesbians. It means that in a political action, you rob yourselves of the vital insight and energies of political women such as Betty Powell and Barbara Smith and Gwendolyn Rogers and Raymina Mays and Robin Christian and Yvonne Flowers. It means another instance of the divide-and-conquer routine.

How do we organize around our differences, neither denying them nor blowing them up out of proportion?

The first step is an effort of will on your part. Try to remember to keep certain facts in mind. Black Lesbians are not apolitical. We have been a part of every freedom struggle within this country. Black Lesbians are not a threat to the Black family. Many of us have families of our own. We are not white, and we are not a disease. We are women who love women. This does not mean we are going to assault your daughters in an alley on Nostrand Avenue. If does not mean we are about to attack you if we pay you a compliment on your dress. It does not mean we only think about sex, any more than you only think about sex.

Even if you do believe any of these stereotypes about Black Lesbians, begin to practice *acting* like you don't believe them. Just as racist stereotypes are the problem of the white people who believe them, so also are homophobic stereotypes the problem of the heterosexuals who believe them. In other words, those stereotypes are yours to solve, not mine, and they are a terrible and wasteful barrier to our working together. I am not your enemy. We do not have to become each other's unique experiences and insights in order to share what we have learned through our particular battles for survival as Black women....

There was a poster in the 1960s that was very popular: HE'S NOT BLACK, HE'S MY BROTHER! It used to infuriate me because it implied that the two were mutually exclusive—he couldn't be both brother and Black. Well, I do not want to be tolerated, nor misnamed. I want to be recognized.

I am a Black Lesbian, and I *am* your sister.

LARRY KRAMER, "1,112 AND COUNTING," *THE NEW YORK NATIVE*, 14-27 MARCH 1983

One of the first written accounts of the disease that would become known as Acquired Immune Deficiency Syndrome (AIDS) appeared in the New York Times *in July 1981. It announced that a rare cancer, Kaposi sarcoma, had been diagnosed in over 40 gay men. Knowing that many of his friends were sick and fearing that a burgeoning epidemic was threatening the gay community, Oscar-nominated screen writer and novelist Larry Kramer held a meeting in his apartment to help organize a response. In time the group formalized as the Gay Men's Health Crisis (GMHC), the first grassroots AIDS services organization in the country. With mainstream healthcare facilities unwilling or unable to respond to the needs of the growing epidemic, GMHC and similar community organizations in other cities became the primary caregivers and advocates for those suffering from AIDS. Never before had any community constructed such an extensive and sophisticated alternative healthcare network in response to a crisis affecting its members. Because the AIDS epidemic affected the gay community in disproportionate numbers, hospitals, drug trials, and medical research became new venues in the fight for gay and lesbian rights.*

As the crisis grew, Kramer and others became more impatient with government intransigence. The indifference and neglect of many existing institutions towards the AIDS epidemic is best exemplified by the silence of President Ronald Reagan, who did not mention the word AIDS in public until the end of 1987, after more than 25,000 people had already died. In 1987, Kramer called a meeting at the New York Lesbian and Gay Community Center that led to the formation of the AIDS Coalition to Unleash Power (ACT UP). Chapters of this direct action AIDS group quickly formed in other cities around the nation. ACT UP became known for its well-orchestrated and provocative acts of civil disobedience at such venues as the New York Stock Exchange, the National Institutes of Health, and St. Patrick's Cathedral. The anger and frustration that fueled ACT UP's acts of civil disobedience are evident in the following essay by Larry Kramer. A call to action to the gay and lesbian community, the essay was reprinted in most gay newspapers around the country. It became a catalyst to a new political movement centered around the AIDS epidemic.

*   *   *

If this article doesn't scare the shit out of you, we're in real trouble. If this article doesn't rouse you to anger, fury, rage, and action, gay men may have no future on this earth. Our continued existence depends on just how angry you can get.

I am writing this as Larry Kramer, and I am speaking for myself, and my views are not to be attributed to Gay Men's Health Crisis.

I repeat: Our continued existence as gay men upon the face of this earth is at stake. Unless we fight for our lives, we shall die. In all the history of homosexuality we have never before been so close to death and extinction. Many of us are dying or already dead.

Before I tell you what we must do, let me tell you what is happening to us.

There are now 1,112 cases of serious Acquired Immune Deficiency Syndrome. When we first became worried, there were only 41. In only twenty-eight days, from 13 January to 9 February [1983], there were 164 cases—and 73 more dead. The total death tally is now 418. Twenty percent of all cases were registered this January alone. There have been 195 dead in New York City from among 526 victims. Of all serious AIDS cases, 47.3 percent are in the New York metropolitan area.

These are serious cases of AIDS, which means Kaposi sarcoma, *Pneumocystis carinii* pneumonia, and other deadly infections. These numbers do not include the thousands of us walking around with what is also being called AIDS: various forms of swollen lymph glands and fatigues that doctors don't know what to label or what they might portend.

The rise in these numbers is terrifying. Whatever is spreading is now spreading faster as more and more people come down with AIDS.

And, for the first time in this epidemic, leading doctors and researchers are finally admitting they don't know what's going on. I find this terrifying too—as terrifying as the alarming rise in numbers. For the first time, doctors are saying out loud and up front, "I don't know."

For two years they weren't talking like this. For two years we've heard a different theory every few weeks. We grasped at the straws of possible cause: promiscuity, poppers, back rooms, the baths, rimming, fisting, anal intercourse, urine, semen, shit, saliva, sweat, blood, blacks, a single virus, a new virus, repeated exposure to a virus, amoebas carrying a virus, drugs, Haiti, voodoo, Flagyl, constant bouts of amebiasis, hepatitis A and B, syphilis, gonorrhea.

I have talked with the leading doctors treating us. One said to me, "If I knew in 1981 what I know now, I would never have become involved with this disease." Another said, "The thing that upsets me the most in all of this is that at any given moment one of my patients is in the hospital and something is going on with him that I don't understand. And it's destroying me because there's some craziness going on in him that's destroying him." A third said to me, "I'm very depressed. A doctor's job is to make patients well. And I can't. Too many of my patients die."

After almost two years of an epidemic, there still are no answers. After almost two years of an epidemic, the cause of AIDS remains unknown. After almost two years of an epidemic, there is no cure.

Hospitals are now so filled with AIDS patients that there is often a waiting period of up to a month before admission, no matter how sick you are. And, once in, patients are now more and more being treated like lepers as hospital staffs become increasingly worried that AIDS is infectious.

Suicides are now being reported of men who would rather die than face such medical uncertainty, such uncertain therapies, such hospital treatment, and the appalling statistic that 86 percent of all serious AIDS cases die after three years' time.

If all of this had been happening to any other community for two long years, there would have been, long ago, such an outcry from that community and all its members that the government of this city and this country would not know what had hit them.

Why isn't every gay man in this city so scared shitless that he is screaming for action? Does every gay man in New York *want* to die?

Let's talk about a few things specifically.

* Let's talk about which gay men get AIDS

No matter what you've heard, there is no single profile for all AIDS victims. There are drug users and non-drug users. There are the truly promiscuous and the almost monogamous. There are reported cases of single-contact infection.

All it seems to take is the one wrong fuck. That's not promiscuity—that's bad luck.

* Let's talk about AIDS happening in straight people

We have been hearing from the beginning of this epidemic that it was only a question of time before the straight community came down with AIDS, and that when that happened AIDS would suddenly be high on all agendas for funding and research and then we would finally be looked after and all would then be well.

I myself thought, when AIDS occurred in the first baby, that would be the breakthrough point. It was. For one day the media paid an enormous amount of attention. And that was it, kids.

There have been no confirmed cases of AIDS in straight, white, non-intravenous-drug-using, middle-class Americans. The only confirmed straights struck down by AIDS are members of groups just as disenfranchised as gay men: intravenous drug users, Haitians, eleven hemophiliacs (up from eight), black and Hispanic babies, and wives or partners of IV drug users and bisexual men.

If there have been—and there may have been—any cases in straight, white, non-intravenous-drug-using, middle-class Americans, the Centers for Disease Control isn't telling anyone about them. When pressed, the CDC says there are "a number of cases that don't fall into any of the other categories." The CDC says it's impossible to fully investigate most of these "other category" cases; most of them are dead. The CDC also tends not to believe living, white, middle-class male victims when they say they're straight, or female victims when they say their husbands are straight and don't take drugs.

Why isn't AIDS happening to more straights? Maybe it's because gay men don't have sex with them.

Of all serious AIDS cases, 72.4 percent are in gay and bisexual men.

* Let's talk about "surveillance"

The Centers for Disease Control is charged by our government to fully monitor all epidemics and unusual diseases.

To learn something from an epidemic, you have to keep records and statistics. Statistics come from interviewing victims and getting as much information from them as you can. Before they die. To get the best information, you have to ask the right questions.

There have been so many AIDS victims that the CDC is no longer able to get to them fast enough. It has given up. (The CDC also had been using a questionnaire that was fairly insensitive to the lives of gay men, and thus the data collected from its early study of us have been disputed by gay epidemiologists. The National Institutes of Health is also fielding a very naive questionnaire.)

Important, vital case histories are now being lost because of this cessation of CDC interviewing. This is a woeful waste with as terrifying implications for us as the alarming rise in case numbers and doctors finally admitting they don't know what's going on. As each man dies, as one or both sets of men who had interacted with each other come down with AIDS, yet more information that might reveal patterns of transmissibility is not being monitored and collected and studied. We are being denied perhaps the easiest and fastest research tool available at this moment.

It will require at least $200,000 to prepare a new questionnaire to study the next important question that must be answered: *How is AIDS being transmitted?* (In which bodily fluids, by which sexual behaviors, in what social environments?)

For months the CDC has been asked to begin such preparations for continued surveillance. The CDC is stretched to its limits and is dreadfully underfunded for what it's being asked, in all areas, to do.

* Let's talk about various forms of treatment

It is very difficult for a patient to find out which hospital to go to or which doctor to go to or which mode of treatment to attempt.

Hospitals and doctors are reluctant to reveal how well they're doing with each type of treatment. They may, if you press them, give you a general idea. Most will not show you their precise numbers of how many patients are doing well on what and how many failed to respond adequately.

Because of the ludicrous requirements of the medical journals, doctors are prohibited from revealing publicly the specific data they are gathering from their treatments of our bodies. Doctors and hospitals need money for research, and this money (from the National Institutes of Health, from cancer research funding organizations, from rich patrons) comes based on the performance of their work (i.e. their tabulations of their results of their treatment of our bodies); this performance is written up as "papers" that must be submitted to and accepted by such "distinguished" medical publications as the *New England Journal of Medicine*. Most of these "distinguished" publications, however, will not publish anything that has been spoken of, leaked, announced, or intimated publicly in advance. Even after acceptance, the doctors must hold their tongues until the article is actually published. Dr. Bijan Safai of Sloan-Kettering has been waiting over six months for the *New England Journal*, which has accepted his interferon study, to publish it. Until that happens, he is only permitted to speak in the most general terms of how interferon is or is not working.

Priorities in this area appear to be peculiarly out of kilter at this moment of life or death.

* Let's talk about hospitals

Everybody's full up, fellows. No room in the inn.

Part of this is simply overcrowding. Part of this is cruel.

Sloan-Kettering still enforces a regulation from pre-AIDS days that only one dermatology patient per week can be admitted to that hospital. (Kaposi's sarcoma falls under dermatology at Sloan-Kettering.) But Sloan-Kettering is also the second-largest treatment center for AIDS patients in New York. You can be near death and still not get into Sloan-Kettering.

Additionally, Sloan-Kettering (and the Food and Drug Administration) requires patients to receive their initial shots of interferon while they are hospitalized. A lot of men want to try interferon at Sloan-Kettering before they try chemotherapy elsewhere.

It's not hard to see why there's such a waiting list to get into Sloan-Kettering.

Most hospital staffs are still so badly educated about AIDS that they don't know much about it, except that they've heard it's infectious. (There still have been no cases in hospital staff or among the very doctors who have been treating AIDS victims for two years.) Hence, as I said earlier, AIDS patients are often treated like lepers.

For various reasons, I would not like to be a patient at the Veterans Administration Hospital on East 24th Street or at New York Hospital. (Incidents involving AIDS patients at these two hospitals have been reported in news stories in the *Native*.)

I believe it falls to this city's Department of Health, under Commissioner David Sencer, and the Health and Hospitals Corporation, under Commissioner Stanley Brezenoff, to educate this city, its citizens, and its hospital workers about all areas of a public health emergency. Well, they have done an appalling job of educating our citizens, our hospital workers, and even, in some instances, our doctors. Almost everything this city knows about AIDS has come to it in one way or another, through Gay Men's Health Crisis. And that includes television programs, magazine articles, radio commercials, newsletters, health-recommendation brochures, open forums, and sending speakers everywhere, including—when asked—into hospitals. If three out of four AIDS cases were occurring in straights instead of in gay men, you can bet all hospitals and their staffs would know what was happening. And it would be this city's Health Department and Health and Hospitals Corporation that would be telling them.

* Let's talk about what gay tax dollars are buying for gay men

Now we're arriving at the truly scandalous.

For over a year and a half the National Institutes of Health has been "reviewing" which from among some $55 million worth of grant applications for AIDS research money it will eventually fund.

It's not even a question of NIH having to ask Congress for money. It's already there. Waiting. NIH has almost $8 million already appropriated that it has yet to release into usefulness.

There is no question that if this epidemic were happening to the straight, white, non-intravenous-drug-using middle class, that money would have been put into use almost two years ago, when the first alarming signs of this epidemic were noticed by Dr. Alvin Friedman-Kien and Dr. Linda Laubenstein at New York University Hospital.

During the first *two weeks* of the Tylenol scare, the United States Government spent $10 million to find out what was happening.

Every hospital in New York that's involved in AIDS research has used up every bit of the money it could find for researching AIDS while waiting for NIH grants to come through. These hospitals have been working on AIDS for up to two years and are now desperate for replenishing funds. Important studies that began last year, such as Dr. Michael Lange's at St. Luke's-Roosevelt, are now going under for lack of money. Important leads that were and are developing cannot be pursued. (For instance, few hospitals can afford plasmapheresis machines, and few patients can afford this experimental treatment either, since few insurance policies will cover the $16,600 bill.) New York University Hospital, the largest treatment center for AIDS patients in the world, has had its grant application pending at NIH for a year and a half. Even if the application is successful, the earliest time that NYU could receive any money would be late summer.

The NIH would probably reply that it's foolish just to throw money away, that that hasn't worked before. And, NIH would say, if nobody knows what's happening, what's to study?

Any good administrator with half a brain could survey the entire AIDS mess and come up with twenty leads that merit further investigation. I could do so myself. In any research, in any investigation, you have to start somewhere. You can't just not start anywhere at all.

But then, AIDS is happening mostly to gay men, isn't it?

All of this is indeed ironic. For within AIDS, as most researchers have been trying to convey to the NIH, perhaps may reside the answer to the question of what it is that causes cancer itself. If straights had more brains, or were less bigoted against gays, they would see that, as with hepatitis B, gay men are again doing their suffering for them, revealing this disease to them. They can use us as guinea pigs to discover the cure for AIDS before it hits them, which most medical authorities are still convinced will be happening shortly in increasing numbers.

Gay men pay taxes just like everyone else. NIH money should be paying for our research just like everyone else's. We desperately need something from our government to save our lives, and we're not getting it.

* Let's talk about health insurance and welfare problems

Many of the ways of treating AIDS are experimental, and many health insurance policies do not cover most of them. Blue Cross is particularly bad about accepting anything unusual.

Many serious victims of AIDS have been unable to qualify for welfare or disability or social security benefits. There are increasing numbers of men unable to work and unable to claim welfare because AIDS is not on the list of qualifying disability illnesses. (Immune deficiency is an acceptable determining factor for welfare among children, but not adults. Figure that one out.) There are also increasing numbers of men unable to pay their rent, men thrown out on the street with nowhere to live and no money to live with, and men who have been asked by roommates to leave because of their illnesses. And men with serious AIDS are being fired from certain jobs.

The horror stories in this area, of those suddenly found destitute, of those facing this illness with insufficient insurance, continue to mount. (One man who'd had no success on other therapies was forced to beg from his friends the $16,600 he needed to try, as a last resort, plasmapheresis.)

* Finally, let's talk about our mayor, Ed Koch

Our mayor, Ed Koch, appears to have chosen, for whatever reason, not to allow himself to be perceived by the non-gay world as visibly helping us in this emergency.

Repeated requests to meet with him have been denied us. Repeated attempts to have him make a very necessary public announcement about this crisis and public health emergency have been refused by his staff.

I sometimes think he doesn't know what's going on. I sometimes think that, like some king who has been so long on his throne he's lost touch with his people, Koch is so protected and isolated by his staff that he is unaware of what fear and pain we're in. No *human* being could otherwise continue to be so useless to his suffering constituents. When I was allowed a few moments with him at a party for outgoing Cultural Affairs Commissioner (and Gay Men's Health Crisis Advisory Board Member) Henry Geldzahler, I could tell from his response that Mayor Koch had not been well briefed on AIDS or what is happening in his city. When I started to fill him in, I was pulled away by an aide, who said, "Your time is up."

I could see our mayor relatively blameless in this shameful secreting of himself from our need of him in this time of epidemic—except for one fact. Our mayor thinks so little of us that he has assigned as his "liaison" to the gay community a man of such appalling insensitivity to our community and its needs that I am ashamed to say he is a homosexual. His name is Herb Rickman, and for a while our mayor saw fit to have Rickman serve as liaison to the Hasidic Jewish community, too. Hasidic Jews hate gays. Figure out a mayor who would do that to you.

To continue to allow Herb Rickman to represent us in City Hall will, in my view, only bring us closer to death.

When I denounced Rickman at a recent gay Community Council meeting, I received a resounding ovation. He is almost universally hated by virtually every gay organization in New York. Why, then, have we allowed this man to shit on us so, to refuse our phone calls, to scream at us hysterically, to slam down telephones, to threaten us, to tease us with favors that are not delivered, to keep us waiting hours for an audience, to lie to us—in short, to humiliate us so? He would not do this to black or Jewish leaders. And they would not take it from him for one minute. Why, why, why do we allow him to do it to us? And he, a homosexual!

One can only surmise that our mayor wants us treated this way.

My last attempt at communication with Herb Rickman was on 23 January [1983], when, after several days of his not returning my phone calls, I wrote to him that the mayor continued to ignore our crisis at his peril. And I state here and now that if Mayor Ed Koch continues to remain invisible to us and to ignore us in this era of mounting death, I swear I shall do everything in my power to see that he never wins elective office again.

Rickman would tell you that the mayor is concerned, that he has established an "Inter-Departmental Task Force"—and, as a member of it, I will tell you that this Task Force is just lip service and a waste of everyone's time. It hasn't even met for two months. (Health Commissioner David Sencer had his gallstones out.)

On 28 October 1982, Mayor Koch was implored to make a public announcement about our emergency. If he had done so then, and if he was only to do so now, the following would be put into action:

1. The community at large would be alerted (you would be amazed at how many people, including gay men, still don't know enough about the AIDS danger.)

2. Hospital staffs and public assistance offices would also be alerted and their education commenced.

3. The country, President Reagan, and the National Institutes of Health, as well as Congress, would be alerted, and these constitute the most important ears of all.

If the mayor doesn't think it's important enough to talk up AIDS, none of these people is going to, either.

The Mayor of New York has an enormous amount of power—when he wants to use it. When he wants to help his people. With the failure yet again of our civil rights bill, I'd guess our mayor doesn't want to use his power to help us.

With his silence on AIDS, the Mayor of New York is helping to kill us.

I am sick of our electing officials who in no way represent us. I am sick of our stupidity in believing candidates who promise us everything for our support and promptly forget us and insult us after we have given them our votes. Koch is the prime example, but not the only one. Daniel Patrick Moynihan isn't looking very good at this moment, either. Moynihan was requested by gay leaders to publicly ask Margaret Heckler at her confirmation hearing for Secretary of Health and Human Services if she could be fair to gays in view of her voting record of definite anti-gay bias. (Among other horrors, she voted to retain the sodomy law in Washington, D.C., at Jerry Falwell's request.) Moynihan refused to ask this question, as he has refused to meet with us about AIDS, despite our repeated requests. Margaret Heckler will have important jurisdiction over the CDC, over the NIH, over the Public Health Service, over the Food and Drug Administration—indeed, over all areas of AIDS concerns. Thank you, Daniel Patrick Moynihan. I am sick of our not realizing we have enough votes to defeat these people, and I am sick of our not electing our own openly gay officials in the first place. Moynihan doesn't even have an openly gay person on his staff, and he represents the city with the largest gay population in America.

I am sick of closeted gay doctors who won't come out to help us fight to rectify any of what I'm writing about. Doctors—the very letters "M.D."—have enormous clout, particularly when they fight in groups. Can you image what gay doctors could accomplish, banded together in a network, petitioning local and federal governments, straight colleagues, and the American Medical Association? I am sick of the passivity or nonparticipation or half-hearted protestation of all the gay medical associations (American Physicians for Human Rights, Bay Area Physicians for Human Rights, Gay Psychiatrists of New York, etc., etc.), and particularly our own New York Physicians for Human Rights, a group of 175 of our gay doctors who have, as a group, done *nothing*. You can count on one hand the number of our doctors who have really worked for *us*.

I am sick of the *Advocate*, one of this country's largest gay publications, which has yet to quite acknowledge that there's anything going on. That newspaper's recent AIDS issue was so innocuous you'd have thought all we were going through was little worse than a rage of the latest designer flu. And their own associate editor, Brent Harris, died from AIDS. Figure that one out.

With the exception of the *New York Native* and a few, very few, other gay publications, the gay press has been useless. If we can't get our own papers and magazines to tell us what's really happening to us, and this negligence is added to the negligent non-interest of the straight press (*The New York Times* took a leisurely year and a half between its major pieces, and the *Village Voice* took a year and a half to write anything at all), how are we going to get the word around that we're dying? Gay men in smaller towns and cities everywhere must be educated, too. Has the *Times* or the *Advocate* told you that twenty-nine cases have been reported from Paris?

I am sick of gay men who won't support gay charities. Go give your bucks to straight charities, fellows, while we die. Gay Men's Health Crisis is going crazy trying to accomplish everything it does—printing and distributing hundreds of thousands of educational items, taking care of several hundred AIDS victims (some of them straight) in and out of hospitals, arranging community forums and speakers all over this country, getting media attention, fighting bad hospital care, on and on and on, fighting for you and us in two thousand ways, and trying to sell 17,600 Circus tickets, too. Is the Red Cross doing this for you? Is the American Cancer Society? Your college alumni fund? The United Jewish Appeal? Catholic Charities? The United Way? The Lenox Hill Neighborhood Association, or any of the other fancy straight charities for which faggots put on black ties and dance at the Plaza? The National Gay Task Force—our only hope for national leadership, with its new and splendid leader, Virginia Apuzzo—which is spending more and more time fighting for the AIDS issue, is broke. Senior Action in a Gay Environment and Gay Men's Health Crisis are, within a few months, going to be without office space they can afford, and thus will be out on the street. The St. Mark's Clinic, held together by some of the few devoted gay doctors in this city who aren't interested in becoming rich, live in constant terror of even higher rent and eviction. This community is desperate for the services these organizations are providing for it. And these organizations are all desperate for money, which is certainly not coming from straight people or President Reagan or Mayor Koch. (If every gay man within a 250-mile radius of Manhattan isn't in Madison Square Garden on the night of 30 April to help Gay Men's Health Crisis make enough money to get through the next horrible year of fighting against AIDS, I shall lose all hope that we have any future whatsoever.)

I am sick of closeted gays. It's 1983 already, guys, when are you going to come out? By 1984 you could be dead. Every gay man who is unable to come forward now and fight to save his own life is truly helping to kill the rest of us. There is only one thing that's going to save some of us, and this is numbers and pressure and our being perceived as united and a threat. As more and more of my friends die, I have less and less sympathy for men who are afraid their mommies will find out or afraid their bosses will find out or afraid their fellow doctors and professional associates will find out. Unless we can generate, visibly, numbers, masses, we are going to die.

I am sick of everyone in this community who tells me to stop creating a panic. How many of us have to die before you get scared off your ass and into action? Aren't 195 dead New Yorkers enough? Every straight person who is knowledgeable about the AIDS epidemic can't understand why gay men aren't marching on the White House. Over and over again I hear from them, "Why aren't you guys doing anything?" Every politician I have spoken to has said to me confidentially, "You guys aren't making enough noise. Bureaucracy only responds to pressure."

I am sick of people who say, "it's no worse than statistics for smokers and lung cancer" or "considering how many homosexuals there are in the United States, AIDS is really statistically affecting only a very few." That would wash if there weren't 164 cases in twenty-eight days. That would wash if case numbers hadn't jumped from 41 to 1,112 in eighteen months. That would wash if cases in one city—New York—hadn't jumped to cases in fifteen countries and thirty-five states (up from thirty-four last week). That would wash if cases weren't coming in at more than four a day nationally and over two a day locally. That would wash if the mortality rate didn't start at 38 percent the first year of diagnosis and climb to a grotesque 86 percent after three years. Get your stupid heads out of the sand, you turkeys!

I am sick of guys who moan that giving up careless sex until this blows over is worse than death. How can they value life so little and cocks and asses so much? Come with me, guys, while I visit a few of our friends in Intensive Care at NYU. Notice the looks in their eyes, guys. They'd give up sex forever if you could promise them life.

I am sick of guys who think that all being gay means is sex in the first place. I am sick of guys who can only think with their cocks.

I am sick of "men" who say, "We've got to keep quiet or *they* will do such and such." *They* usually means straight majority, the "Moral" Majority, or similarly perceived representatives of *them.* Okay, you "men"—be my guests: You can march off now to the gas chambers; just get right in line.

We shall always have enemies. Nothing we can ever do will remove them. Southern newspapers and Jerry Falwell's publications are already printing editorials proclaiming AIDS as God's deserved punishment on homosexuals. So what? Nasty words make poor little sissy pansy wilt and die?

And I am very sick and saddened by every gay man who does not get behind this issue totally and with commitment—to fight for his life.

I don't want to die. I can only assume you don't want to die. Can we fight together?

For the past few weeks, about fifty community leaders and organization representatives have been meeting at Beth Simchat Torah, the gay synagogue, to prepare action. We call ourselves the AIDS Network. We come from all areas of health concern: doctors, social workers, psychologists, psychiatrists, nurses; we come from Gay Men's Health Crisis, from the National Gay Health Education Foundation, from New York Physicians for Human Rights, the St. Mark's Clinic, the Gay Men's Health Project; we come from the gay synagogue, the Gay Men's Chorus, from the Greater Gotham Business Council, SAGE, Lambda Legal Defense, Gay Fathers, the Christopher Street Festival Committee, Dignity, Integrity; we are lawyers, actors, dancers, architects, writers, citizens; we come from many component organizations of the Gay and Lesbian Community Council.

We have a leader. Indeed, for the first time our community appears to have a true leader. Her name is Virginia Apuzzo, she is head of the National Gay Task Force, and, as I have said, so far she has proved to be magnificent.

The AIDS Network has sent a letter to Mayor Koch. It contains twelve points that are urged for his consideration and action.

This letter to Mayor Koch also contains the following paragraph:

> It must be stated at the outset that the gay community is growing increasingly aroused and concerned and angry. Should our avenues to the mayor of our city and the members of the Board of Estimate not be available, it is our feeling that the level of frustration is such that it will manifest itself in a manner heretofore not associated with this community and the gay population at large. It should be stated, too, at the outset, that as of 25 February, there were 526 cases of serious AIDS in New York's metropolitan area and 195 deaths (and 1,112 cases nationally and 418 deaths) and it is the sad and sorry fact that most gay men in our city now have close friends and lovers who have either been stricken with or died from this disease. It is against this background that this letter is addressed. It is this issue that has, ironically, united our community in a way not heretofore thought possible.

Further, a number of AIDS Network members have been studying civil disobedience with one of the experts from Dr. Martin

Luther King's old team. We are learning how. Gay men are the strongest, toughest people I know. We are perhaps shortly to get an opportunity to show it.

I'm sick of hearing that Mayor Koch doesn't respond to pressures and threats from the disenfranchised, that he walks away from confrontations. Maybe he does. But we have tried to make contact with him, we are *dying,* so what other choice but confrontation has he left us?

I hope we don't have to conduct sit-ins or tie up traffic or get arrested. I hope our city and our country will start to do something to help start saving us. But it is time for us to be perceived for what we truly are: an angry community and a strong community, and therefore a *threat.* Such are the realities of politics. Nationally we are 24 million strong, which is more than there are Jews or blacks or Hispanics in this country.

I want to make a point about what happens if we don't get angry about AIDS. There are the obvious losses, of course: Little of what I've written about here is likely to be rectified with the speed necessary to help the growing number of victims. But something worse will happen, and is already happening. Increasingly, we are being *blamed* for AIDS, for this epidemic; we are being called its perpetrators, through our blood, through our "promiscuity," through just being the gay men so much of the rest of the world has learned to hate. We can point out until we are blue in the face that we are not the cause of AIDS but its victims, that AIDS has landed among us first, as it could have landed among them first. But other frightened populations are going to drown out these truths by playing on the worst bigoted fears of the straight world, and send the status of gays right back to the Dark Ages. Not all Jews are blamed for Meyer Lansky, Rabbis Bergman and Kahane, or for money-lending. All Chinese aren't blamed for the recent Seattle slaughters. But all gays are blamed for John Gacy, the North American Man/Boy Love Association, and AIDS.

Enough. I am told this is one of the longest articles the *Native* has ever run. I hope I have not been guilty of saying ineffectively in five thousand words what I could have said in five: we must fight to live.

I am angry and frustrated almost beyond the bound my skin and bones and body and brain can encompass. My sleep is tormented by nightmares and visions of lost friends, and my days are flooded by the tears of funerals and memorial services and seeing my sick friends. How many of us must die before *all* of us living fight back?

I know that unless I fight with every ounce of my energy I will hate myself. I hope, I pray, I implore you to feel the same.

I am going to close by doing what Dr. Ron Grossman did at GMHC's second Open Forum last November at Julia Richman High School. He listed the names of the patients he had lost to AIDS. Here is a list of twenty dead men I knew:

Nick Rock
Rick Wellikoff
Jack Nau
Shelly
Donald Krintzman
Jerry Green
Michael Maletta
Paul Graham
Toby
Harry Blementhal
Stephen Sperry

Brian O'Hara
Barry
David
Jeffrey Croland
Z.
David Jackson
Tony Rappa
Robert Christian
Ron Doud

And one more, who will be dead by the time these words appear in print. If we don't act immediately, then we face our approaching doom.

SUPREME COURT OF THE UNITED STATES, *BOWERS V. HARDWICK*, 30 JUNE 1986

On 3 August 1982, Michael Hardwick was arrested in his own bedroom for engaging in oral sex with another man. The arresting police officer, who was let into the apartment by Hardwick's roommate, was there to serve a warrant involving an earlier citation of Hardwick for having an open can of beer on a public street. Hardwick, who worked as a bartender at a gay bar in Atlanta, Georgia, had been seen by the officer exiting the bar with the beer can. Due to some confusion over the court date on his initial citation, Hardwick had failed to show up in court and the officer had gone to extraordinary measures to obtain and serve a warrant for Hardwick's arrest. As a result of the arrest for sodomy, Hardwick and his lover spent ten hours in jail. Although the district attorney did not choose to prosecute the case, Hardwick, aided by gay rights advocates, filed a federal civil rights challenge to the Georgia sodomy statute, alleging that it violated his fundamental right to privacy.

In June 1986, in the case of Bowers v. Hardwick, *the United States Supreme Court upheld in a 5-4 decision the constitutionality of the Georgia sodomy law. The court in effect ruled that gay men and lesbians have no right to privacy, even while having sex in their own bedrooms. In his majority opinion, Justice White cited the long tradition of anti-sodomy legislation dating back to the seventeenth century and concluded that "no connection between family, marriage, or procreation on the one hand and homosexual activity on the other has been demonstrated." As the dissenting opinion pointed out, the court's "almost obsessive focus" on homosexuality obscured the fact that the Georgia sodomy law outlaws both heterosexual and homosexual sodomy. Although many states began in 1961 to repeal their anti-sodomy laws, about half the states still retain them. Historically enforced much more aggressively against gay men and lesbians, anti-sodomy laws criminalize gay sex and serve as the justification for much anti-gay discrimination.*

Bowers *was the most important judicial case in the history of the gay and lesbian rights movement up to that time, and a major defeat. Many gay rights advocates compared it to other Supreme Court decisions that stymied civil rights struggles but were eventually overturned, such as* Dred Scott v. Sandford *(1857), which declared blacks were not citizens, and* Plessy v. Ferguson *(1896), which declared "separate but equal" facilities to be constitutional. At the National March on Washington in 1987, thousands of gays and lesbians engaged in a mass sit-in outside the Supreme Court to express their outrage over the* Bowers *decision. In one of the largest acts of civil disobedience since the Vietnam war, nearly 600 protesters were arrested. After his retirement in 1990, Justice Lewis Powell, who had sided with the majority in* Bowers v. Hardwick *made an unprecedented admission that he "probably made a mistake in that one." The decision, however, still stands.*

*   *   *

JUSTICE WHITE delivered the opinion of the Court, in which Justices BURGER, POWELL, REHNQUIST, and O'CONNOR joined:

In August 1982, respondent Hardwick was charged with violating the Georgia statute criminalizing sodomy by committing that act with another adult male in the bedroom of respondent's home. After a preliminary hearing, the District Attorney decided not to present the matter to the grand jury unless further evidence developed.

Respondent then brought suit in the Federal District Court, challenging the constitutionality of the statute insofar as it criminalized consensual sodomy. He asserted that he was a practicing homosexual, that the Georgia sodomy statute, as administered by the defendants, placed him in imminent danger of arrest, and that the statute for several reasons violates the Federal Constitution. The District Court granted the defendants' motion to dismiss for failure to state a claim.

A divided panel of the Court of Appeals for the Eleventh Circuit reversed. The court went on to hold that the Georgia statute violated respondent's fundamental rights because his homosexual activity is a private and intimate association that is beyond the reach of state regulation by reason of the Ninth Amendment and the Due Process Clause of the Fourteenth Amendment. The case was remanded for trial, at which, to prevail, the State would have to prove that the statute is supported by a compelling interest and is the most narrowly drawn means of achieving that end.

Because other Courts of Appeals have arrived at judgments contrary to that of the Eleventh Circuit in this case, we granted the Attorney General's petition for certiorari questioning the holding that the sodomy statute violates the fundamental rights of homosexuals. We agree with petitioner that the Court of Appeals erred, and hence reverse its judgment.

This case does not require a judgment on whether laws against sodomy between consenting adults in general, or between homosexuals in particular, are wise or desirable. It raises no question about the right or propriety of state legislative decisions to repeal their laws that criminalize homosexual sodomy, or of state court decisions invalidating those laws on state constitutional grounds. The issue presented is whether the Federal Constitution confers a fundamental right upon homosexuals to engage in sodomy, and hence invalidates the laws of the many States that still make such conduct illegal, and have done so for a very long time. The case also calls for some judgment about the limits of the Court's role in carrying out its constitutional mandate.

We first register our disagreement with the Court of Appeals and with respondent that the Court's prior cases have construed the Constitution to confer a right of privacy that extends to homosexual sodomy and, for all intents and purposes, have decided this case. The reach of this line of cases was sketched in *Carey v. Population Services International. Pierce v. Society of Sisters* and *Meyer v. Nebraska,* were described as dealing with childrearing and education; *Prince v. Massachusetts,* with family relationships; *Skinner v. Oklahoma,* with procreation; *Loving v. Virginia,* with marriage; *Griswold v. Connecticut,* with contraception; and *Roe v. Wade,* with abortion. The latter three cases were interpreted as construing the Due Process Clause of the Fourteenth Amendment to confer a fundamental individual right to decide whether or not to beget or bear a child.

Accepting the decisions in these cases and the above description of them, we think it evident that none of the rights announced in those cases bears any resemblance to the claimed constitutional right of homosexuals to engage in acts of sodomy that is asserted in this case. No connection between family, marriage, or procreation, on the one hand, and homosexual activity, on the other, has been demonstrated, either by the Court of Appeals or by respondent. Moreover, any claim that these cases nevertheless stand for the proposition that any kind of private sexual conduct between consenting adults is constitutionally insulated from state proscription is unsupportable.

Precedent aside, however, respondent would have us announce, as the Court of Appeals did, a fundamental right to engage in homosexual sodomy. This we are quite unwilling to do. It is true that, despite the language of the Due Process Clauses of the Fifth and Fourteenth Amendments, which appears to focus only on the processes by which life, liberty, or property is taken, the cases are legion in which those Clauses have been interpreted to have substantive content, subsuming rights that to a great extent are immune from federal or state regulation or proscription. Among such cases are those recognizing rights that have little or no textual support in the constitutional language.

Striving to assure itself and the public that announcing rights not readily identifiable in the Constitution's text involves much more than the imposition of the Justices' own choice of values on the States and the Federal Government, the Court has sought to identify the nature of the rights qualifying for heightened judicial protection. In *Palko v. Connecticut,* it was said that this category includes those fundamental liberties that are "implicit in the concept of ordered liberty," such that "neither liberty nor justice would exist if [they] were sacrificed." A different description of fundamental liberties appeared in *Moore v. East Cleveland,* where they are characterized as those liberties that are "deeply rooted in this Nation's history and tradition."

It is obvious to us that neither of these formulations would extend a fundamental right to homosexuals to engage in acts of consensual sodomy. Proscriptions against that conduct have ancient roots. Sodomy was a criminal offense at common law, and was forbidden by the laws of the original 13 States when they ratified the Bill of Rights. In 1868, when the Fourteenth Amendment was ratified, all but 5 of the 37 States in the Union had criminal sodomy laws. In fact, until 1961, all 50 States outlawed sodomy, and today, 24 states and the District of Columbia continue to provide criminal penalties for sodomy performed in private and between consenting adults. Against this background, to claim that a right to engage in such conduct is "deeply rooted in this Nation's history and tradition" or "implicit in the concept of ordered liberty" is, at best, facetious.

Nor are we inclined to take a more expansive view of our authority to discover new fundamental rights imbedded in the Due Process Clause. The Court is most vulnerable and comes nearest to illegitimacy when it deals with judge-made constitutional law having little or no cognizable roots in the language or design of the Constitution. There should be, therefore, great resistance to expand the substantive reach of those Clauses, particularly if it requires redefining the category of rights deemed to be fundamental. Otherwise, the Judiciary necessarily takes to itself further authority to govern the country without express constitutional authority. The claimed right pressed on us today falls far short of overcoming this resistance.

Respondent, however, asserts that the result should be different where the homosexual conduct occurs in the privacy of the home. He relies on *Stanley v. Georgia,* where the Court held that the First Amendment prevents conviction for possessing and reading obscene material in the privacy of one's home:

> If the First Amendment means anything, it means that a State has no business telling a man, sitting alone in his house, what books he may read or what films he may watch.

Stanley did protect conduct that would not have been protected outside the home, and it partially prevented the enforcement of state obscenity laws; but the decision was firmly grounded in the First Amendment. The right pressed upon us here has no similar support in the text of the Constitution, and it does not qualify for recognition under the prevailing principles for construing the Fourteenth Amendment. Its limits are also difficult to discern. Plainly enough, otherwise illegal conduct is not always immunized whenever it occurs in the home. Victimless crimes, such as the possession and use of illegal drugs, do not escape the law where they are committed at home. *Stanley* itself recognized that its holding offered no protection for the possession in the home of drugs, firearms, or stolen goods. And if respondent's submission is limited to the voluntary sexual conduct between consenting adults, it would be difficult, except by fiat, to limit the claimed right to homosexual conduct while leaving exposed to prosecution adultery, incest, and other sexual crimes even though they are committed in the home. We are unwilling to start down that road.

Even if the conduct at issue here is not a fundamental right, respondent asserts that there must be a rational basis for the law, and that there is none in this case other than the presumed belief of a majority of the electorate in Georgia that homosexual sodomy is immoral and unacceptable. This is said to be an inadequate rationale to support the law. The law, however, is constantly based on notions of morality, and if all laws representing essentially moral choices are to be invalidated under the Due Process Clause, the courts will be very busy indeed. Even respondent makes no such claim, but insists that majority sentiments about the morality of homosexuality should be declared inadequate. We do not agree, and are unpersuaded that the sodomy laws of some 25 States should be invalidated on this basis.

Accordingly, the judgment of the Court of Appeals is Reversed.

I.

JUSTICE BLACKMUN, wrote a dissenting opinion, with whom Justices BRENNAN, MARSHALL, and STEVENS joined:

This case is no more about "a fundamental right to engage in homosexual sodomy," than *Stanley v. Georgia,* (1969), was about a fundamental right to watch obscene movies, or *Katz v. United States,* (1967), was about a fundamental right to place interstate bets from a telephone booth. Rather, this case is about "the most comprehensive of rights and the right most valued by civilized men," namely, "the right to be let alone." *Olmstead v. United States,* (1928) (Brandeis, J., dissenting).

The statute at issue denies individuals the right to decide for themselves whether to engage in particular forms of private, consensual sexual activity. The Court concludes that the statute is valid essentially because "the laws of ... many States ... still make such conduct illegal and have done so for a very long time." But the fact that the moral judgments expressed by statutes like this may be "natural and familiar ... ought not to conclude our judgment upon the question whether statutes embodying them conflict with the Constitution of the United States." *Roe v. Wade,* (1973). Like Justice Holmes, I believe that [i]t is revolting to have no better reason for a rule of law than that so it was laid down in the time of Henry IV. It is still more revolting if the grounds upon which it was laid down have vanished long since, and the rule simply persists from blind imitation of the past.

I believe we must analyze respondent Hardwick's claim in the light of the values that underlie the constitutional right to privacy. If that right means anything, it means that, before Georgia can prosecute its citizens for making choices about the most intimate aspects of their lives, it must do more than assert that the choice they have made is an "'abominable crime not fit to be named among Christians.'"

In its haste to reverse the Court of Appeals and hold that the Constitution does not "confe[r] a fundamental right upon homosexuals to engage in sodomy," the Court relegates the actual statute being challenged to a footnote, and ignores the procedural posture of the case before it. A fair reading of the statute and of the complaint clearly reveals that the majority has distorted the question this case presents.

First, the Court's almost obsessive focus on homosexual activity is particularly hard to justify in light of the broad language Georgia has used. Unlike the Court, the Georgia Legislature has not proceeded on the assumption that homosexuals are so different from other citizens that their lives may be controlled in a way that would not be tolerated if it limited the choices of those other citizens. Rather, Georgia has provided that [a] person commits the offense of sodomy when he performs or submits to any sexual act involving the sex organs of one person and the mouth or anus of another.

The sex or status of the persons who engage in the act is irrelevant as a matter of state law. In fact, to the extent I can discern a legislative purpose for Georgia's 1968 enactment of § 16-6-2, that purpose seems to have been to broaden the coverage of the law to reach heterosexual as well as homosexual activity. I therefore see no basis for the Court's decision to treat this case as an "as applied" challenge to § 16-6-2, or for Georgia's attempt, both in its brief and at oral argument, to defend § 16-6-2 solely on the grounds that it prohibits homosexual activity. Michael Hardwick's standing may rest in significant part on Georgia's apparent willingness to enforce against homosexuals a law it seems not to have any desire to enforce against heterosexuals. But his claim that § 16-6-2 involves an unconstitutional intrusion into his privacy and his right of intimate association does not depend in any way on his sexual orientation.

II.

Our cases long have recognized that the Constitution embodies a promise that a certain private sphere of individual liberty will be kept largely beyond the reach of government.

In construing the right to privacy, the Court has proceeded along two somewhat distinct, albeit complementary, lines. First, it has recognized a privacy interest with reference to certain decisions that are properly for the individual to make. Second, it has recognized a privacy interest with reference to certain places without regard for the particular activities in which the individuals who occupy them are engaged. The case before us implicates both the decisional and the spatial aspects of the right to privacy.

The Court concludes today that none of our prior cases dealing with various decisions that individuals are entitled to make free of governmental interference "bears any resemblance to the claimed constitutional right of homosexuals to engage in acts of sodomy that is asserted in this case." While it is true that these cases may be characterized by their connection to protection of the family, the Court's conclusion that they extend no further than this boundary ignores the warning in *Moore v. East Cleveland,* (1977) against clos[ing] our eyes to the basic reasons why certain rights associated with the family have been accorded shelter under the Fourteenth Amendment's Due Process Clause.

We protect those rights not because they contribute, in some direct and material way, to the general public welfare, but because they form so central a part of an individual's life. "[T]he concept of privacy embodies the 'moral fact that a person belongs to himself, and not others nor to society as a whole.'" *Thornburgh v. American College of Obstetricians & Gynecologists.* And so we protect the decision whether to marry precisely because marriage is an association that promotes a way of life, not causes; a harmony in living, not political faiths; a bilateral loyalty, not commercial or social projects.

We protect the decision whether to have a child because parenthood alters so dramatically an individual's self-definition, not because of demographic considerations or the Bible's command to be fruitful and multiply. And we protect the family because it contributes so powerfully to the happiness of individuals, not because of a preference for stereotypical households. The Court recognized in Roberts that the "ability independently to define one's identity that is central to any concept of liberty" cannot truly be exercised in a vacuum; we all depend on the "emotional enrichment from close ties with others."

Only the most willful blindness could obscure the fact that sexual intimacy is "a sensitive, key relationship of human existence, central to family life, community welfare, and the development of human personality." The fact that individuals define themselves in a significant way through their intimate sexual relationships with others suggests, in a Nation as diverse as ours, that there may be many "right" ways of conducting those relationships, and that much of the richness of a relationship will come from the freedom an individual has to choose the form and nature of these intensely personal bonds.

The Court claims that its decision today merely refuses to recognize a fundamental right to engage in homosexual sodomy; what the Court really has refused to recognize is the fundamental interest all individuals have in controlling the nature of their intimate associations with others.

The behavior for which Hardwick faces prosecution occurred in his own home, a place to which the Fourth Amendment attaches special significance. The Court's treatment of this aspect of the case is symptomatic of its overall refusal to consider the broad principles that have informed our treatment of privacy in specific cases. Just as the right to privacy is more than the mere aggregation of a number of entitlements to engage in specific behavior, so too protecting the physical integrity of the home is

more than merely a means of protecting specific activities that often take place there.

"The right of the people to be secure in their ... houses," expressly guaranteed by the Fourth Amendment, is perhaps the most "textual" of the various constitutional provisions that inform our understanding of the right to privacy, and thus I cannot agree with the Court's statement that "[t]he right pressed upon us here has no ... support in the text of the Constitution." Indeed, the right of an individual to conduct intimate relationships in the intimacy of his or her own home seems to me to be the heart of the Constitution's protection of privacy.

III.

The Court's failure to comprehend the magnitude of the liberty interests at stake in this case leads it to slight the question whether petitioner, on behalf of the State, has justified Georgia's infringement on these interests. I believe that neither of the two general justifications for § 16-6-2 that petitioner has advanced warrants dismissing respondent's challenge for failure to state a claim.

First, petitioner asserts that the acts made criminal by the statute may have serious adverse consequences for "the general public health and welfare," such as spreading communicable diseases or fostering other criminal activity. Inasmuch as this case was dismissed by the District Court on the pleadings, it is not surprising that the record before us is barren of any evidence to support petitioner's claim. In light of the state of the record, I see no justification for the Court's attempt to equate the private, consensual sexual activity at issue here with the "possession in the home of drugs, firearms, or stolen goods," to which *Stanley* refused to extend its protection. None of the behavior so mentioned in *Stanley* can properly be viewed as "[v]ictimless,": drugs and weapons are inherently dangerous, and for property to be "stolen," someone must have been wrongfully deprived of it. Nothing in the record before the Court provides any justification for finding the activity forbidden by § 16-6-2 to be physically dangerous, either to the persons engaged in it or to others.

The core of petitioner's defense of § 16-6-2, however, is that respondent and others who engage in the conduct prohibited by § 16-6-2 interfere with Georgia's exercise of the "'right of the Nation and of the States to maintain a decent society,'" Essentially, petitioner argues, and the Court agrees, that the fact that the acts described in § 16-6 "for hundreds of years, if not thousands, have been uniformly condemned as immoral" is a sufficient reason to permit a State to ban them today. I cannot agree that either the length of time a majority has held its convictions or the passions with which it defends them can withdraw legislation from this Court's scrutiny.

As Justice Jackson wrote so eloquently for the Court in *West Virginia Board of Education v. Barnette:*

> We apply the limitations of the Constitution with no fear
> that freedom to be intellectually and spiritually diverse,
> or even contrary, will disintegrate the social organization....
> [F]reedom to differ is not limited to things that do not
> matter much. That would be a mere shadow of freedom.
> The test of its substance is the right to differ as to things
> that touch the heart of the existing order.

It is precisely because the issue raised by this case touches the heart of what makes individuals what they are that we should be especially sensitive to the rights of those whose choices upset the majority.

The assertion that "traditional Judeo-Christian values proscribe" the conduct involved cannot provide an adequate justification for § 16-6-2. That certain, but by no means all, religious groups condemn the behavior at issue gives the State no license to impose their judgments on the entire citizenry. The legitimacy of secular legislation depends, instead, on whether the State can advance some justification for its law beyond its conformity to religious doctrine. Thus, far from buttressing his case, petitioner's invocation of Leviticus, Romans, St. Thomas Aquinas, and sodomy's heretical status during the Middle Ages undermines his suggestion that § 16-6-2 represents a legitimate use of secular coercive power. A State can no more punish private behavior because of religious intolerance than it can punish such behavior because of racial animus.

The Constitution cannot control such prejudices, but neither can it tolerate them. Private biases may be outside the reach of the law, but the law cannot, directly or indirectly, give them effect.

It took but three years for the Court to see the error in its analysis in *Minersville School District v. Gobitis,* (1940), and to recognize that the threat to national cohesion posed by a refusal to salute the flag was vastly outweighed by the threat to those same values posed by compelling such a salute. I can only hope that here, too, the Court soon will reconsider its analysis and conclude that depriving individuals of the right to choose for themselves how to conduct their intimate relationships poses a far greater threat to the values most deeply rooted in our Nation's history than tolerance of nonconformity could ever do. Because I think the Court today betrays those values, I dissent.

BAEHR V. LEWIN, MAY 1993
SUPREME COURT OF HAWAII,

In 1990, two lesbian couples and one gay male couple in Hawaii applied for marriage licenses. Since the 1970s, a growing number of gay and lesbian couples around the nation had made similar requests. When, like all the others, they were denied marriage licenses, they filed suit against the state of Hawaii, charging that the denial violated their civil rights. The established gay and lesbian political organizations discouraged the suit, feeling that it was a losing battle that would simply create more opposition for the movement. Many activists also felt that by seeking the right to marry, gays and lesbians would be legitimizing an oppressive, patriarchal institution. But the three gay couples continued the suit on their own, and in May 1993, the Supreme Court of Hawaii declared that the denial of the couples' marriage licenses appeared to violate the equal protection clause of the state constitution, which outlawed discrimination based on sex. It remanded the case back to the lower court, insisting the state prove "a compelling interest" in continuing the ban on same-sex marriage, the highest possible burden of proof.

The prospect that Hawaii might recognize same-sex marriages sent shock waves through the legislatures of the other 49 states and the U.S. Congress. Because the U.S. Constitution's "full faith and credit" clause generally requires one state to honor contracts made in another, same-sex marriages obtained in Hawaii might be valid in other states. Despite substantial legal precedent for the power of a state to deny recognition to marriages performed in another state if they violate its own public policies, the U.S. Con-

gress quickly enacted The Defense of Marriage Act. Signed by President Clinton during the 1996 election campaign, the act explicitly prohibits any state from being required to recognize a same-sex marriage performed in another state. Around the same time, many state legislatures adopted bans on same-sex marriage. Through the legal struggle of three couples in Hawaii, same-sex marriage became one of the most important and controversial issues in the gay movement and mainstream politics throughout the nation. The excerpts below are from the original 1993 decision of the Hawaii Supreme Court, which precipitated the heated debate.

*   *   *

The precise question facing this court is whether we will extend the *present* boundaries of the fundamental right of marriage to include same-sex couples, or, put another way, whether we will hold that same-sex couples possess a fundamental right to marry. In effect, as the applicant couples frankly admit, we are being asked to recognize a new fundamental right....

In the case that first recognized a fundamental right to privacy, *Griswald v. Connecticut* ... the [U.S. Supreme] Court declared that it was "deal[ing] with a right ... older than the Bill of Rights...." And in a concurring opinion, Justice Goldberg observed that judges "determining which rights are fundamental" must look not to "personal and private notions," but "to the 'traditions and [collective] conscience of our people....'"

Applying the foregoing standards to the present case, we do not believe that a right to same-sex marriage is so rooted in the traditions and collective conscience of our people that failure to recognize it would violate the fundamental principles of liberty and justice that lie at the base of all our civil and political institutions. Neither do we believe that a right to same-sex marriage is implicit in the concept of ordered liberty, such as that neither liberty nor justice would exist if it were sacrificed. Accordingly, we hold that the applicant couples do not have a fundamental constitutional right to same-sex marriage arising out of the right to privacy or otherwise....

Marriage is a state-conferred legal status, the existence of which gives rise to rights and benefits reserved exclusively to that particular relationship. This court construes marriage as "'a partnership to which both partners bring their financial resources, as well as their individual energies and efforts....'" So zealously has this court guarded the state's role as the exclusive progenitor of the marital partnership that it declared, over seventy years ago, that "common law" marriages—i.e. "marital" unions existing in the absence of a state-issued license and not performed by a person or society possessing governmental authority to solemnize marriages—would no longer be recognized in the Territory of Hawaii....

The applicant couples correctly contend that the [Hawaii Department of Health's] refusal to allow them to marry on the basis that they are members of the same sex deprives them of access to a multiplicity of rights and benefits that are contingent upon that status. Although it is unnecessary in this opinion to engage in an encyclopedic recitation of all of them, a number of the most salient marital rights and benefits are worthy of note. They include: (1) a variety of state income tax advantages.... (2) public assistance from and exemptions relating to the Department of Human Services.... (3) control, division, acquisition, and disposition of community property.... (5) rights to notice, protection, benefits, and inheritance.... (6) award of child custody and support payments in divorce proceedings....

The equal protection clauses of the United States and Hawaii Constitutions are not mirror images of one another. The fourteenth amendment to the United States Constitution somewhat concisely provides, in relevant part, that a state may not "deny to any person within its jurisdiction the equal protection of the laws." Hawaii's counterpart is more elaborate. Article I, Section 5 of the Hawaii Constitution provides in relevant part that "[n]o person shall ... be denied the equal protection of the laws, *nor be denied the enjoyment of the person's civil rights or be discriminated against in the exercise thereof because of* race, religion, *sex*, or ancestry." (emphasis added). Thus, by its plain language, the Hawaii Constitution prohibits state-sanctioned discrimination against any person in the exercise of his or her civil rights on the basis of sex....

Accordingly, we hold that sex is a "suspect category" for purposes of equal protection analysis under article I, section 5 of the Hawaii Constitution and that HRS§ 572-1 is subject to the "strict scrutiny" test. It therefore follows, and we so hold, that (1) HRS§ 572-1 is presumed to be unconstitutional (2) unless Lewin, as an agent of the State of Hawaii, can show that (a) the statute's sex-based classification is justified by compelling state interests and (b) the statute is narrowly drawn to avoid unnecessary abridgements of the applicant couples' constitutional rights....

As a final matter, we are compelled to respond to Judge Heen's suggestion that denying the appellants access to the multitude of statutory benefits "conferred upon spouses in a legal marriage ... is a matter for the legislature, which can express the will of the populace...." In effect, we are being accused of engaging in judicial legislation. We are not. The result we reach today is in complete harmony with the *Loving [v. Virginia]* Court's observation that any state's powers to regulate marriage are subject to the constraints imposed by the constitutional rights to the equal protection of the laws....

PENTAGON POLICY GUIDELINES ON HOMOSEXUALS IN THE MILITARY, 19 JULY 1993

While campaigning for the presidency in 1992, Bill Clinton told a gay audience at a California fundraiser, "I have a vision for America, and you are a part of it." The gay community raised approximately $3 million towards his campaign. Pollsters estimated that 75 percent of the gay vote went to Clinton. No presidential candidate had ever courted or received such support from the gay and lesbian community. Among the promises he made was that he would end the ban on gays and lesbians from serving in the military. The ban, which dated from World War II, was one of the most egregious examples of official anti-gay discrimination in American society. Over the years, tens of thousands of gays and lesbians had been expelled from the armed forces. In addition to Clinton's promise, a number of court challenges to the ban by gay and lesbian service members and the outing of the Pentagon spokesperson during the Gulf War had put the ban in the media spotlight.

Opposition within the military and in Congress to lifting the ban prevented Clinton, once in office, from fulfilling his pledge. In the ensuing debate, the rationale for the ban shifted from the ability of gays and lesbians to effectively serve their country and the discrimination they suffered to the discomfort straight soldiers would experience if forced to serve with openly gay soldiers. The ban became one of the major political controver-

sies of 1993, and the focus of that year's March on Washington, which drew over half a million gay men and lesbians to the nation's capital. Eventually, what President Clinton billed as a "compromise" was proposed, barring military officials from asking recruits about their sexual orientation, while barring military personnel from disclosing their homosexuality. Under the compromise, dubbed "Don't Ask, Don't Tell, Don't Pursue," gay men and lesbians could theoretically serve in the military as long as they remained in the closet and refrained from homosexual activity. In fact, more gay men and lesbians have been discharged annually from the armed forces since the compromise than before. The following document outlines the Pentagon's "Don't Ask, Don't Tell, Don't Pursue" policy.

*   *   *

Accession Policy

Applicants for military service will no longer be asked or required to reveal if they are homosexual or bisexual, but applicants will be informed of the conduct that is proscribed for members of the armed forces, including homosexual conduct.

Discharge Policy

Sexual orientation will not be a bar to service unless manifested by homosexual conduct. The military will discharge members who engage in homosexual conduct, which is defined as a homosexual act, a statement that the member is homosexual or bisexual, or a marriage or attempted marriage to someone of the same gender.

Investigations Policy

No investigations or inquires will be conducted solely to determine a service member's sexual orientation. Commanders will initiate inquiries or investigations when there is credible information that a basis for discharge or disciplinary action exists. Sexual orientation, absent credible information that a crime has been committed, will not be the subject of a criminal investigation. An allegation or statement by another that a service member is a homosexual alone, is not grounds for either a criminal investigation or a commander's inquiry.

Activities

Bodily contact between service members of the same sex that a reasonable person would understand to demonstrate a propensity or intent to engage in homosexual acts (e.g. hand-holding or kissing in most circumstances) will be sufficient to initiate separation.

Activities such as association with known homosexuals, presence at a gay bar, possessing or reading homosexual publications or marching in a gay rights rally in civilian clothes will not, in and of themselves, constitute credible information that would provide a basis for initiating an investigation or serve as the basis for an administrative discharge under this policy.

The listing by a service member of someone of the same gender as the person to be contacted in case of emergency, as an insurance beneficiary or in a similar context, does not provide a basis for separation or further investigation.

Off-Base Conduct

No distinction will be made between off-base and on-base conduct.

From the time a member joins the service until discharge, the service member's duty and commitment to the unit is a 24 hour-a-day, seven-day-a-week obligation. Military members are required to comply with both the Uniform Code of Military Justice, which is Federal law, and military regulations at all times and in all places. Unacceptable conduct, homosexual or heterosexual, is not excused because the service member is not "at work."

Investigations and Inquiries

Neither investigations nor inquiries will be conducted solely to determine an individual's sexual orientation.

Commanders can initiate investigations into alleged homosexual conduct when there is credible information of homosexual acts, prohibited statements or homosexual marriage.

Commanders will exercise sound discretion regarding when credible information exists, and will evaluate the information's source and all attendant circumstances to assess whether the information supports a reasonable belief that a service member has engaged in proscribed homosexual conduct.

Credible Information

Credible information of homosexual conduct exists when the information, considered in light of its source and all attendant circumstances, supports a reasonable belief that a service member has engaged in such conduct. It requires a determination based on articulable facts, not just a belief or suspicion.

Security Clearances

Questions pertaining to an individual's sexual orientation are not asked on personnel security questionnaires. An individual's sexual conduct, whether homosexual or heterosexual, is a legitimate security concern only if it could make an individual susceptible to exploitation or coercion, or indicate a lack of trustworthiness, reliability, or good judgement that is required of anyone with access to classified information.

The Threat of Extortion

As long as service members continue to be separated from military service for engaging in homosexual conduct, credible information of such behavior can be a basis for extortion. Although the military cannot eliminate the potential for the victimization of homosexuals through blackmail, the policy reduces the risk of homosexuals by making certain categories of information largely immaterial to the military's initiation of investigations.

Extortion is a criminal offense and offenders will be prosecuted. A service member convicted of extortion risks dishonorable discharge and up to three years confinement.

Outing

A mere allegation or statement by another that a service member is a homosexual is not grounds for official action. Commanders will not take official action against members based on rumor, suspicion or capricious allegations.

However, if a third party provides credible information that a member has committed a crime or act that warrants discharge, e.g. engages in homosexual conduct, the commander may, based on the totality of the circumstances, conduct an investigation or inquiry, and take nonjudicial or administrative action or recommend judicial action, as appropriate.

Harassment

Commanders are responsible for maintaining good order and discipline.

All service members will be treated with dignity and respect. Hostile treatment or violence against a service member based on a perception of his or her sexual orientation will not be tolerated.

COLORADO'S AMENDMENT 2, 1992

By the 1990s, ten states and well over a hundred cities had enacted gay civil rights laws. But in many states and municipalities, right-wing groups organized to repeal these laws, often submitting the issue to the voters through referenda. In Colorado, a group called "Colorado for Family Values" succeeded in 1992 in putting on the state ballot a proposed constitutional amendment that would not only repeal the gay rights ordinances in several Colorado cities, but would have barred such laws from ever being enacted in the state. Proponents of the measure claimed that such laws granted gay men and lesbians "special rights" rather than equal rights and would lead to quotas and preferential treatment. Approved by 53 percent of the voters, Amendment 2 spawned a nation-wide boycott of Colorado, organized by gay and lesbian activists with the support of unions, city governments and Hollywood celebrities. Gay organizations immediately filed suit against Amendment 2 in a case that made it all the way to the U.S. Supreme Court.

In Romer v. Evans, *the Supreme Court gave the gay rights movement one of its most significant judicial victories. In his majority opinion, Justice Kennedy chastised Colorado for expressing "animus" towards gays and lesbians. "We must conclude that Amendment 2 classifies homosexuals not to further a proper legislative end but to make them unequal to everyone else," wrote Kennedy. "This Colorado cannot do. A state cannot so deem a class of persons a stranger to its laws." In a symbolic shift that suggested a more liberal attitude, the Supreme Court for the first time used the terms "gay" and "lesbian" rather than "homosexual" in its written opinion. Although it did not reverse or even address its earlier decision in* Bowers v. Hardwick, *the court was clearly moving in a new direction.*

*   *   *

No Protected Status Based on
Homosexual, Lesbian, or Bisexual Orientation

"Neither the State of Colorado, through any of its branches or departments, nor any of its agencies, political subdivisions, municipalities or school districts, shall enact, adopt or enforce any statute, regulation, ordinance or policy whereby homosexual, lesbian or bisexual orientation, conduct, practices or relationships shall constitute or otherwise be the basis of or entitle any person or class of persons to have or claim any minority status, quota preferences, protected status or claim of discrimination. This Section of the Constitution shall be in all respects self-executing."

Supreme Court of the United States, *Romer v. Evans*, 20 May 1996

Majority Opinion, by JUSTICE KENNEDY:

One century ago, the first Justice Harlan admonished this Court that the Constitution "neither knows nor tolerates classes among citizens." *Plessy v. Ferguson* (1896) (dissenting opinion). Unheeded then, those words now are understood to state a commitment to the law's neutrality where the rights of persons are at stake. The Equal Protection Clause enforces this principle and today requires us to hold invalid a provision of Colorado's Constitution.

The enactment challenged in this case is an amendment to the Constitution of the State of Colorado, adopted in a 1992 statewide referendum. The parties and the state courts refer to it as "Amendment 2," its designation when submitted to the voters. The impetus for the amendment and the contentious campaign that preceded its adoption came in large part from ordinances that had been passed in various Colorado municipalities. For example, the cities of Aspen and Boulder and the City and County of Denver each had enacted ordinances which banned discrimination in many transactions and activities, including housing, employment, education, public accommodations, and health and welfare services. What gave rise to the statewide controversy was the protection the ordinances afforded to persons discriminated against by reason of their sexual orientation. Amendment 2 repeals these ordinances to the extent they prohibit discrimination on the basis of "homosexual, lesbian or bisexual orientation, conduct, practices or relationships."

Yet Amendment 2, in explicit terms, does more than repeal or rescind these provisions. It prohibits all legislative, executive or judicial action at any level of state or local government designed to protect the named class, a class we shall refer to as homosexual persons or gays and lesbians.

Soon after Amendment 2 was adopted, this litigation to declare its invalidity and enjoin its enforcement was commenced in the District Court for the City and County of Denver. Among the plaintiffs (respondents here) were homosexual persons, some of them government employees. They alleged that enforcement of Amendment 2 would subject them to immediate and substantial risk of discrimination on the basis of their sexual orientation. Other plaintiffs (also respondents here) included the three municipalities whose ordinances we have cited and certain other governmental entities which had acted earlier to protect homosexuals from discrimination but would be prevented by Amendment 2 from continuing to do so. Although Governor Romer had been on record opposing the adoption of Amendment 2, he was named in his official capacity as a defendant, together with the Colorado Attorney General and the State of Colorado.

The State's principal argument in defense of Amendment 2 is that it puts gays and lesbians in the same position as all other persons. So, the State says, the measure does no more than deny homosexuals special rights. This reading of the amendment's language is implausible. We rely not upon our own interpretation of the amendment but upon the authoritative construction of Colorado's Supreme Court. The state court, deeming it unneces-

sary to determine the full extent of the amendment's reach, found it invalid even on a modest reading of its implications.

Sweeping and comprehensive is the change in legal status effected by this law. So much is evident from the ordinances that the Colorado Supreme Court declared would be void by operation of Amendment 2. Homosexuals, by state decree, are put in a solitary class with respect to transactions and relations in both the private and governmental spheres. The amendment withdraws from homosexuals, but no others, specific legal protection from the injuries caused by discrimination, and it forbids reinstatement of these laws and policies. Amendment 2, in addition, nullifies specific legal protections for this targeted class in all transactions in housing, sale of real estate, insurance, health and welfare services, private education, and employment. Not confined to the private sphere, Amendment 2 also operates to repeal and forbid all laws or policies providing specific protection for gays or lesbians from discrimination by every level of Colorado government.

We cannot accept the view that Amendment 2's prohibition on specific legal protections does no more than deprive homosexuals of special rights. To the contrary, the amendment imposes a special disability upon those persons alone. Homosexuals are forbidden the safeguards that others enjoy or may seek without constraint. They can obtain specific protection against discrimination only by enlisting the citizenry of Colorado to amend the state constitution or perhaps, on the State's view, by trying to pass helpful laws of general applicability. This is so no matter how local or discrete the harm, no matter how public and widespread the injury. We find nothing special in the protections Amendment 2 withholds. These are protections taken for granted by most people either because they already have them or do not need them; these are protections against exclusion from an almost limitless number of transactions and endeavors that constitute ordinary civic life in a free society.

First, the amendment has the peculiar property of imposing a broad and undifferentiated disability on a single named group, an exceptional and, as we shall explain, invalid form of legislation. Second, its sheer breadth is so discontinuous with the reasons offered for it that the amendment seems inexplicable by anything but animus toward the class that it affects; it lacks a rational relationship to legitimate state interests. It identifies persons by a single trait and then denies them protection across the board. The resulting disqualification of a class of persons from the right to seek specific protection from the law is unprecedented in our jurisprudence.

The primary rationale the State offers for Amendment 2 is respect for other citizens' freedom of association, and in particular the liberties of landlords or employers who have personal or religious objections to homosexuality. Colorado also cites its interest in conserving resources to fight discrimination against other groups. The breadth of the Amendment is so far removed from these particular justifications that we find it impossible to credit them. We cannot say that Amendment 2 is directed to any identifiable legitimate purpose or discrete objective. It is a status-based enactment divorced from any factual context from which we could discern a relationship to legitimate state interests; it is a classification of persons undertaken for its own sake, something the Equal Protection Clause does not permit. We must conclude that Amendment 2 classifies homosexuals not to further a proper legislative end but to make them unequal to everyone else. This Colorado cannot do. A State cannot so deem a class of persons a stranger to its laws. Amendment 2 violates the Equal Protection Clause, and the judgment of the Supreme Court of Colorado is affirmed.

JUSTICE SCALIA Dissent: with whom the CHIEF JUSTICE and JUSTICE THOMAS join:

The Court has mistaken a Kulturkampf for a fit of spite. The constitutional amendment before us here is not the manifestation of a "bare ... desire to harm" homosexuals, but is rather a modest attempt by seemingly tolerant Coloradans to preserve traditional sexual mores against the efforts of a politically powerful minority to revise those mores through use of the laws. That objective, and the means chosen to achieve it, are not only unimpeachable under any constitutional doctrine hitherto pronounced (hence the opinion's heavy reliance upon principles of righteousness rather than judicial holdings); they have been specifically approved by the Congress of the United States and by this Court. In holding that homosexuality cannot be singled out for disfavorable treatment, the Court contradicts a decision, unchallenged here, pronounced only 10 years ago, *Bowers v. Hardwick* (1986), and places the prestige of this institution behind the proposition that opposition to homosexuality is as reprehensible as racial or religious bias. Whether it is or not is precisely the cultural debate that gave rise to the Colorado constitutional amendment (and to the preferential laws against which the amendment was directed). Since the Constitution of the United States says nothing about this subject, it is left to be resolved by normal democratic means, including the democratic adoption of provisions in state constitutions. This Court has no business imposing upon all Americans the resolution favored by the elite class from which the Members of this institution are selected, pronouncing that "animosity" toward homosexuality is evil. I vigorously dissent.

The amendment prohibits special treatment of homosexuals, and nothing more. Despite all of its hand-wringing about the potential effect of Amendment 2 on general antidiscrimination laws, the Court's opinion ultimately does not dispute all this, but assumes it to be true. The only denial of equal treatment it contends homosexuals have suffered is this: They may not obtain preferential treatment without amending the state constitution. That is to say, the principle underlying the Court's opinion is that one who is accorded equal treatment under the laws, but cannot as readily as others obtain preferential treatment under the laws, has been denied equal protection of the laws. If merely stating this alleged "equal protection" violation does not suffice to refute it, our constitutional jurisprudence has achieved terminal silliness.

I turn next to whether there was a legitimate rational basis for the substance of the constitutional amendment—for the prohibition of special protection for homosexuals. It is unsurprising that the Court avoids discussion of this question, since the answer is so obviously yes. The case most relevant to the issue before us today is not even mentioned in the Court's opinion: In *Bowers v. Hardwick* (1986), we held that the Constitution does not prohibit what virtually all States had done from the founding of the Republic until very recent years—making homosexual conduct a crime. That holding is unassailable, except by those who think that the Constitution changes to suit current fashions. If it is constitutionally permissible for a State to make homosexual conduct criminal, surely it is constitutionally permissible for a State to enact other laws merely disfavoring homosexual conduct.

The Court's opinion contains grim, disapproving hints that Coloradans have been guilty of "animus" or "animosity" toward ho-

mosexuality, as though that has been established as un-American. Of course it is our moral heritage that one should not hate any human being or class of human beings. But I had thought that one could consider certain conduct reprehensible—murder, for example, or polygamy, or cruelty to animals—and could exhibit even "animus" toward such conduct. Surely that is the only sort of "animus" at issue here: moral disapproval of homosexual conduct, the same sort of moral disapproval that produced the centuries-old criminal laws that we held constitutional in *Bowers*.

The problem is that, because those who engage in homosexual conduct tend to reside in disproportionate numbers in certain communities, and of course care about homosexual-rights issues much more ardently than the public at large, they possess political power much greater than their numbers, both locally and statewide. Quite understandably, they devote this political power to achieving not merely a grudging social toleration, but full social acceptance, of homosexuality. By the time Coloradans were asked to vote on Amendment 2 , three Colorado cities—Aspen, Boulder, and Denver—had enacted ordinances that listed "sexual orientation" as an impermissible ground for discrimination, equating the moral disapproval of homosexual conduct with racial and religious bigotry.... I do not mean to be critical of these legislative successes; homosexuals are as entitled to use the legal system for reinforcement of their moral sentiments as are the rest of society. But they are subject to being countered by lawful, democratic countermeasures as well.

That is where Amendment 2 came in. It sought to counter both the geographic concentration and the disproportionate political power of homosexuals by (1) resolving the controversy at the statewide level, and (2) making the election a single-issue contest for both sides. It put directly, to all the citizens of the State, the question: Should homosexuality be given special protection? They answered no. The Court today asserts that this most democratic of procedures is unconstitutional. Lacking any cases to establish that facially absurd proposition, it simply asserts that it must be unconstitutional, because it has never happened before.

When the Court takes sides in the culture wars, it tends to be with the knights rather than the villains or more specifically with the Templars, reflecting the views and values of the lawyer class from which the Court's Members are drawn.

Today's opinion has no foundation in American constitutional law, and barely pretends to. The people of Colorado have adopted an entirely reasonable provision which does not even disfavor homosexuals in any substantive sense, but merely denies them preferential treatment. Amendment 2 is designed to prevent piecemeal deterioration of the sexual morality favored by a majority of Coloradans, and is not only an appropriate means to that legitimate end, but a means that Americans have employed before. Striking it down is an act, not of judicial judgment, but of political will. I dissent.

THE EMPLOYMENT NON-DISCRIMINATION ACT (ENDA)

The Employment Non-Discrimination Act or "ENDA" is a bill that, if enacted by the U.S. Congress, would forbid employment discrimination based on sexual orientation. Although a gay civil rights bill has been introduced in every Congress since 1977, the scope of ENDA is more modest than previous failed attempts to include gay men and lesbians under federal civil rights protections. ENDA would apply only to discrimination in employment, not to housing or public accommodations, and only to employers with 15 or more employees. ENDA explicitly does not require that fringe benefits be provided to the partners of lesbian and gay workers. ENDA also expressly forbids the uses of quotas or preferential treatment. In addition, ENDA does not apply to the armed forces or religious organizations, including religious schools.

In one of the nationally televised debates during the presidential election of 1996, two private citizens posed questions about ENDA to candidates Bob Dole and Bill Clinton. President Clinton has endorsed ENDA since 1995. In a vote on ENDA in 1996, the Senate came within one vote of passing the legislation. Polling data show that, while most Americans favor preventing job discrimination against gay people, most are not aware that such discrimination is still legal. In committee hearings concerning ENDA, several major corporations that already have their own anti-discrimination policies testified in favor of the federal legislation. Enactment of this bill has been a principal goal of the Human Rights Campaign, a gay and lesbian lobbying group.

*   *   *

S. 869
105th CONGRESS, 1st Session (1997)

A Bill to prohibit employment discrimination on the basis of sexual orientation.

Be it enacted by the Senate and House of Representatives of the United States of America in Congress assembled,

SECTION 1. SHORT TITLE

This Act may be cited as the 'Employment Non-Discrimination Act of 1997.'

SECTION 2. PURPOSES

The purposes of this Act are—

1) to provide a comprehensive Federal prohibition of employment discrimination on the basis of sexual orientation;
2) to provide meaningful and effective remedies for employment discrimination on the basis of sexual orientation; and
3) to invoke congressional powers, including the powers to enforce the 14th amendment to the Constitution and to regulate interstate commerce, in order to prohibit employment discrimination on the basis of sexual orientation.

SECTION 3. DEFINITIONS

In this Act:

COMMISSION—The term 'Commission' means the Equal Employment Opportunity Commission.

COVERED ENTITY—The term 'covered entity' means an employer, employment agency, labor organization, joint labor-management committee, an entity to which section 717(a) of the Civil Rights Act of 1964 applies....

EMPLOYER—The term 'employer' means a person engaged in an industry affecting commerce who has 15 or more employees.

EMPLOYMENT OR AN EMPLOYMENT OPPORTUNITY—Except as provided in section 10(a)(1), the term 'employment or an employment opportunity' includes job application procedures, hiring, advancement, discharge, compensation, job training, or any other term, condition, or privilege of employment, but does not include the service of a volunteer for which the volunteer receives no compensation.

RELIGIOUS ORGANIZATION—The term 'religious organization' means—

A) a religious corporation, association, or society; or
B) a school, college, university, or other educational institution, if—
   i) the institution is in whole or substantial part controlled, managed, owned, or supported by a religion, religious corporation, association, or society; or
   ii) the curriculum of the institution is directed toward the propagation of a religion.

SEXUAL ORIENTATION—The term 'sexual orientation' means homosexuality, bisexuality, or heterosexuality, whether the orientation is real or perceived.

SECTION 4. DISCRIMINATION PROHIBITED

A covered entity shall not, with respect to the employment or an employment opportunity of an individual—

1) subject the individual to a different standard or different treatment, or otherwise discriminate against the individual, on the basis of sexual orientation; or
2) discriminate against the individual based on the sexual orientation of a person with whom the individual is believed to associate or to have associated.

SECTION 5. RETALIATION AND COERCION PROHIBITED

a) RETALIATION—A covered entity shall not discriminate against an individual because the individual opposed any act or practice prohibited by this Act or because the individual made a charge, assisted, testified, or participated in any manner in an investigation, proceeding, or hearing under this Act.
b) COERCION—A person shall not coerce, intimidate, threaten, or interfere with any individual in the exercise or enjoyment of, or on account of the individual's having exercised, enjoyed, assisted in, or encouraged the exercise or enjoyment of, any right granted or protected by this Act.

SECTION 6. BENEFITS

This Act does not apply to the provision of employee benefits to an individual for the benefit of the partner of the individual.

SECTION 7. NO DISPARATE IMPACT; COLLECTION OF STATISTICS

a) DISPARATE IMPACT—The fact that an employment practice has a disparate impact on the basis of sexual orientation does not establish a prima facie violation of this Act.

b) COLLECTION OF STATISTICS—The Commission shall not collect statistics on sexual orientation from covered entities, or compel the collection of such statistics by covered entities.

SECTION 8. QUOTAS AND PREFERENTIAL TREATMENT PROHIBITED

a) QUOTAS—A covered entity shall not adopt or implement a quota on the basis of sexual orientation.

b) PREFERENTIAL TREATMENT—A covered entity shall not give preferential treatment to an individual on the basis of sexual orientation.

SECTION 9. RELIGIOUS EXEMPTION

IN GENERAL this Act shall not apply to a religious organization.

SECTION 10. NONAPPLICATION TO MEMBERS OF THE ARMED FORCES

In this Act, the term 'employment or an employment opportunity' does not apply to the relationship between the United States and members of the Armed Forces (Army, Navy, Air Force, Marine Corps, and Coast Guard).

SECTION 11. CONSTRUCTION

Nothing in this Act shall be construed to prohibit a covered entity from enforcing rules regarding nonprivate sexual conduct, if the rules of conduct are designed for, and uniformly applied to, all individuals regardless of sexual orientation.

SECTION 12. ENFORCEMENT

ENFORCEMENT POWERS—With respect to the administration and enforcement of this Act in the case of a claim alleged by an individual for a violation of this Act—

The Commission shall have the same powers as the Commission has to administer and enforce (A) title VII of the Civil Rights Act of 1964 or (B) sections 302 and 304 of the Government Employee Rights Act of 1991....

A court of the United States shall have the same jurisdiction and powers as the court has to enforce—

A) title VII of the Civil Rights Act of 1964;

B) sections 302 and 304 of the Government Employee Rights Act of 1991;

C) the Congressional Accountability Act of 1995; and

D) chapter 5 of title 3, United States Code.

REFERENCES:

Baehr v Lewin, Supreme Court of Hawaii, May 1993.

Bowers v Hardwick, Supreme Court of the United States, 30 June 1986.

Chicago Vice Commission. "The Social Evil in Chicago: A Study of Existing Conditions." Chicago: Gunthorp-Warren Printing, 1911.

Colorado's Amendment 2, 1992.

Daughters of Bilitis. Statement of Purpose (reprinted in every issue of *The Ladder,* published by the Daughters of Bilits), 1955.

"Don't Ask, Don't Tell, Don't Pursue," Pentagon Policy Guidelines on Homosexuals in the Military, 19 July 1993.

The Employment Non-Discrimination Act (ENDA).

Kameny, Franklin. "Civil Liberties: A Progress Report," speech delivered to Mattachine Society of New York, 22 July 1964; reprinted in New York Mattachine Newsletter.

Kinsey, Alfred. "Homosexual Outlet," in *Sexual Behavior in the Human Male.* Philadelphia: W.B. Saunder Company, 1948.

Kramer, Larry. "1,112 and Counting," in the *New York Native,* 14-27 March 1983.

Lorde, Audre. "I Am Your Sister: Black Women Organizing across Sexualities," in *A Burst of Light,* by Audre Lorde. Ithaca, New York: Firebrand Books, 1988, essay c.1980.

Major, Ralph. "New Moral Menace to Our Youth," in *Coronet,* September 1950: 101-108.

Milk, Harvey. "That's What America Is," speech delivered on Gay Freedom Day, 25 June 1978; reprinted in *The Mayor of Castro Street: The Life and Times of Harvey Milk,* by randy Shilts, New York: St. Martin's, 1982: 364-371.

Radicalesbians. "The Woman-Identified Woman," in *Out of the Closets: Voices of Gay Liberation,* edited by Karla Jay and Allen Young. New York: Pyramid, 1972, essay c.1970.

Romer v Evans, Supreme Court of the United States, 20 May 1996.

United States Senate. *Employment of Homosexuals and Other Sex Perverts in Government.* Senate Document #241, 81st Congress, 2nd session, 15 December 1950.

Vollmer, Myler. "The New Year's Eve Drag," unpublished paper, courtesy of Burgess Collection, University of Chicago Archives, c.1930.

Wittman, Carl. "A Gay Manifesto," in *Out of the Closets: Voices of Gay Liberation,* edited by Karla Jay and Allen Young. New York: Pyramid, 1972, essay c.1969.

—Compiled by David K. Johnson

4

Coming Out

Coming out is a life-altering ritual that lies at the heart of the gay and lesbian experience and the modern gay and lesbian movement. It is also a social and political act that fundamentally challenges traditional ideas about the nature of nature, the structure of family, and the shape of American society.

Coming out is considered by many to be not just a singular act—embodied in the statement, "I am gay or lesbian"—but rather a lifelong process that is enacted again and again, as the gay man or lesbian makes his or her identity known to new people, in new situations, and in new roles not even imagined a generation ago, as in the coming out of lesbian and gay parents.

Ironically, however, this increasingly popular ritual is necessitated chiefly by the erroneous but widely held presumption that everyone is heterosexual. Put another way, when it is more commonly recognized that sexuality truly comes in diverse forms, this act of differentiating oneself from the heterosexual presumption may become a thing of the past.

The following essay discusses the psychological and social processes of coming out; the political significance of coming out from the perspective of the gay and lesbian movement; and the history of coming out and the social forces that have influenced its development during the past century. Among the specific topics considered are: coming out in the media, the military, politics, religion, school, sports, the workplace, and as parents.

THE PROCESS OF COMING OUT

The process of coming out, like any great transition in life, is anything but neat and systematic. Indeed, it often begins in an existential crisis, as Gilbert Herdt, a psychological anthropologist who studies gay and lesbian youth, has written.

The reason for this is not a mysterious one: most Americans are taught to think of themselves as heterosexual; they are not taught to expect that they may grow up lesbian or gay. When they first experience feelings of same-sex attraction, therefore, it shakes their sense of who they are. The heterosexual identity no longer seems to fit, yet the negative prejudices surrounding ho-

mosexuality may make the gay or lesbian identity too frightening to try on. Denial, repression, and all the usual tactics of avoiding unpleasant truths often follow—permanently in the case of those who live their lives in the closet, temporarily for those who eventually come to terms with their identity.

Coming out, Herdt argues, offers a solution to this dilemma of being suspended between feelings of tabooed desire on the one hand, and the pressure to conform to the heterosexual mainstream on the other. In the process, it changes the individual's relationship to the world.

"Like the rites of birth and death, puberty and marriage," he writes, "coming out necessitates transitions from one social role and cultural field to another throughout life; and through these ritual transformations, 'society' recognizes that the change is immutable and irreversible." In the process, he adds, the individual is also thought of as entering gay and lesbian culture.

More specifically, Herdt proposes that the process of coming out occurs in three phases: First, the individual learns that being gay or lesbian is an option. In other words, the individual breaks through what writer Adrienne Rich referred to as "compulsory heterosexuality": the dominant social norm, supported by most religious, political, educational, and cultural institutions, that says one is expected to be heterosexual.

Second, the individual challenges the common stereotypes about homosexuality. That is, the individual sorts through all the false and prejudicial stereotypes associated with this identity. This is a critical stage because if it is not passed through, the internal pressure to resist a negative identity may be so strong as to encourage the gay man or lesbian to stop the coming out process here and continue to pass as (pretend to be) heterosexual.

And, third, Herdt writes, one "must learn how to be gay or lesbian." More specifically, one must restructure one's relationships with other people on the basis of a new gay or lesbian identity.

The Popular Psychology Perspective

From a more "pop psychology" perspective, Rob Eichenberg, author of one of the earliest books on the topic, entitled *Coming Out: An Act of Love*, described the coming out process in these three stages:

First comes the personal phase in which the individual understands the fact that he/she is lesbian or gay and sorts through all the feelings the discovery involves. This stage, Eichenberg notes, can take years, as the negative prejudices associated with homosexuality make it natural for people to resist the realization that they are lesbian or gay.

Second comes what Eichenberg describes as the private phase, when one begins to tell select people that one is lesbian or gay. In most circumstances, people choose to tell friends first, and family members sometime later, since family members tend to have more negative and more involved reactions than friends.

The third and final phase is what Eichenberg describes as the public stage, when one feels free to come out to anyone. At this point, in other words, the individual does not seek to hide or compartmentalize his or her sexual identity but rather integrates it into his or her personal, professional, and family life.

THE POLITICAL SIGNIFICANCE OF THE LESBIAN AND GAY MOVEMENT

Annoyed by all the attention that actress Ellen DeGeneres received in 1997 for coming out, a guest on the *Oprah Winfrey Show* asked the actress: Why should this be such a big deal? You don't see me coming out as straight on the cover of *Time* magazine.

Putting aside the fact that this woman was neither a celebrity, nor as a straight woman did she have a need to come out, she raised a question frequently voiced by many heterosexuals: namely, Why do gay men and lesbians make such a big deal out of coming out?

The psychological need to come out has been suggested above, as only this process allows the gay man or lesbian the chance to live truthfully, by negating the assumption that he or she is straight. But the act also holds great political significance to the lesbian and gay movement: indeed, it is repeatedly spoken of as the most important contribution any gay man or lesbian can make to the movement.

From the perspective of gay and lesbian activists, the political significance of coming out rests on at least two factors: First, coming out to someone you know is thought to be the single most effective way to help combat negative prejudice against gays and lesbians.

And second, the more gay men and lesbians come out, the more political clout the community is thought to harness to influence elected officials and win support for gay and lesbian equal rights, such as the right to marry, to serve in the military, and to not be discriminated against in the workplace on the basis of sexual orientation. Indeed, history seems to attest to this fact, as the section below will demonstrate.

THE HISTORY OF COMING OUT

Beginnings: The Creation of the Homosexual Identity

Coming out rests on what we in the post-modern age would call a social construct: namely, the gay, lesbian, or bisexual identity. This is a notion that a person can be defined by his or sexual orientation, particularly if this orientation places one in the gay or lesbian minority, as opposed to the heterosexual majority. But sex was not always viewed this way.

Neither Sappho nor Plato, for example, came out 2,500 years ago, because people didn't think to categorize themselves by their sexual practices then. They might have felt attracted to men, women, or men and women, but in ancient Greece that didn't make them gay, lesbian, or bisexual. Indeed, homosexuality was considered a behavior, not an identity, throughout most of Western civilization.

But things began to change during the late nineteenth century, as modern science ushered in what journalist Neil Miller has described as a "mania for classification." Sexologists, or medical doctors specializing in the study of sexuality, began to see the world not merely as made up of men and women but also of homosexuals and heterosexuals.

With the new category of homosexuals to study, sexologists sought to discover the causes of homosexuality. Some hoped to improve homosexuals' experience in society by proving, basically, that they could not help themselves. Yet as scientists were wont to do, they defined the characteristics of the people they studied, and, in the process, turned the homosexual identity into something that seemed all-defining.

Philosopher Michel Foucault, writing in *History of Sexuality, Volume One,* put it this way: "The nineteenth-century homosexual became a personage, a past, a case history, and a childhood, in addition to being a type of life, a life form, and a morphology, with an indiscreet anatomy and possibly a mysterious physiology. Nothing that went into his total composition was unaffected by his sexuality."

All of this would, unintentionally, lay the groundwork for coming out.

The Root Obstacles to Coming Out

After the homosexual identity became a part of American culture at the turn of the twentieth century, few people rushed to come out, even though the growth of industrialization made it, technically speaking, increasingly possible to live life as a homosexual. In other words, as the economy changed from one that was farm-centered to one that was urban-centered, people became less dependent upon the family for their work. They could survive by living alone or with someone of the same sex. Yet coming out publicly during the early twentieth century represented more than the breaking of a taboo.

Society's repression of homosexuality, after all, had deep and definite roots, reaching back to the Christian Middle Ages, according to David Greenberg, a New York University sociologist. The church, Greenberg argues, linked attitudes toward homosexuality with attitudes toward procreation, and declared that homosexuality was a sin against God and nature. As the dominant institution in medieval society, the church also turned this declaration into law, one that made sodomy punishable by death at the stake.

A similarly severe antagonism toward homosexuality can be found centuries later among the Puritans who settled in the newly discovered United States. Viewing homosexuality as contrary to their goal of building and populating a new nation, they passed the first sodomy law in 1610 in the Virginia colony. It, too, called for the death penalty.

Yet as the centuries passed, the dominance of the church both in Europe and the United States began to fade under the growing influences of secular disciplines, such as science and medicine, and in the process, the harshness of sodomy laws lessened. For the most part, however, the prejudice against homosexuality continued. Indeed, as numerous observers have pointed out, homosexuality went from being thought of as a sin to being thought of as a sickness.

The enormity of the risks of being seen as a homosexual were perhaps best demonstrated by Oscar Wilde, who, having unwittingly come out, was found guilty of "gross indecency," and sentenced to prison. He died a short time after his release.

The obstacles to coming out, in other words, remained formidable at the turn of the century. Indeed, even by the middle of the twentieth century, sodomy was considered a felony in every state in the nation. To express one's homosexuality publicly invited a prison sentence, unemployment, divorce, and deep and abiding ostracism. And, yet, as with every point in the history of homosexuality, there were those who were ahead of their time.

The Pioneers: 1900-1920

It was "a great advance in civilization," Virginia Woolf wrote, when homosexuality—namely, the homosexuality of Lytton Strachey and others among her circle of friends—became a central topic of conversation for the Bloomsbury writers and artists who met in England around the time of World War I. This openness about homosexuality, Woolf wrote, was one of the things that reflected the welcome transition from the restraints of the Victorian era to the apparent new-found freedom of the modern age.

Meanwhile, in American bohemian communities such as Greenwich Village and Harlem, writers, artists, and liberal intellectuals demonstrated a similar growing openness about homosexuality. Yet in all these places, attitudes about coming out were mixed.

In Bloomsbury, for example, Strachey, the author of *Eminent Victorians,* and the economist John Maynard Keynes came out to their friends—typically by speaking or writing of their love for a particular man—but neither came out publicly. This reticence may have been influenced by the fact that homosexuality and heterosexuality were then, in theory and practice, more fluid concepts than they are today. Both men, for example, spent their later years with female companions. But their reticence to come out almost certainly was also influenced by a calculation of the risks.

The fact that Strachey, Keynes, and others came out in their bohemian circles, nonetheless, remains a step in the history of coming out. As Strachey's biographer, Michael Holroyd, wrote: "[I]n a society which regarded homosexuality as more grave than murder, what Lytton and Keynes were looking for almost as urgently as love itself, was a discreet and sympathetic source of disclosure." It sounds, in other words, like the birth pangs of the yet unnamed impulse to come out publicly.

The Surprising Impact of World War II

For most ordinary gay men and lesbians who lived in small-town America prior to World War II, coming out must have seemed a formidable—if not impossible—challenge, as no place can monitor forbidden practices like a small town. But, for many young men and women, the United States military ironically made coming out possible, with mass recruitment for World War II, according to Allan Berube, author of *Coming Out under Fire.*

In the first place, as Berube argues, the military's conscription of millions of men inspired a significant number of women to move from small towns to cities to take over what were formerly men's jobs. In the process, many came into contact with lesbians for the first time, and came out to themselves.

The development of American cities, after all, had played a key role in making an underground homosexual subculture possible as early as the nineteenth century, as David Greenberg argues in *The Construction of Homosexuality.* This was not only because industrial development made independence from the nuclear family possible but because large urban environments lent the anonymity a small town lacked.

But the home-front was not the only place women came out to each other during the war. The Women's Army Corps, or WAC—

true to its reputation—became a magnet for lesbians, according to Berube. How many knew they were lesbians before they joined, and how many discovered they were lesbian during their years of service, can never be known. But, apparently, enough came out during the war for it to be noticed.

A secret lecture, which Berube uncovered, was delivered to officer candidates in 1943, and spoke to the coming-out experience this way: "Sometimes [a relationship] can become an intimacy that may eventually take some form of sexual expression. It may appear that, almost spontaneously, such a relationship has sprung up between two women, neither of whom is a confirmed active homosexual." Indeed, living and working among only women helped make this experience possible.

Among the men who would serve in the war, military recruiters also unwittingly aided the coming-out process by asking every potential soldier: Have you ever had homosexual feelings or experiences? It was a question they might not previously have thought of themselves, Berube argues, since it is common for people to deny taboo feelings unless directly confronted with them.

But for many, the coming-out experience did not stop there. As with the women who joined the WAC, Berube writes, "many gay soldiers ... did not even know they were homosexual until after they were in the armed forces, where life in the barracks was especially charged with homosexual tension." Because of the common hostility toward homosexuality, the barracks were a dangerous place for coming out. But weekend passes and furloughs in large cities that housed gay and lesbian bars helped make coming out possible. In the end, Berube estimates, a million or more gay men served during World War II. Again, how many came out during the war cannot be known. For many, however, coming together with other men made it more possible.

Going Back In during the 1950s

While the war was going on overseas, the United States government had relied on women to take on what had previously been thought of as men's work. But as the war ended and 12 million American soldiers prepared to come home, leaders of some of the most powerful institutions in the country were not content with letting the changes in the gender game work itself out. They preferred women in what were deemed their places, and men in what were deemed theirs.

Thus, during late 1940s and early 1950s, the government, churches, and the media launched a campaign to turn things back to the way they used to be: with a man as the breadwinner, a woman as the homemaker, and sex as something men and women did strictly to make babies. For those who had come out during the war, the effect was chilling. Coming out was nowhere to be found in the new American dream of marriage, a house in the suburbs, and 2.5 children.

But the resurrection of traditional gender roles was not the only pressure that weighed against gay men and lesbians who might have wished to come out during the 1950s. The American government, which emerged from the war as the world's preeminent democratic power, was newly engaged in an ideological battle with the Soviet Union, the world's chief communist power. Senator Joseph McCarthy, famously, led the battle on the home front, accusing writers, actors, and Hollywood producers alike of having communist ties. Then he hit upon another idea.

Communists, McCarthy argued, were attempting to undermine the United States government by spreading homosexuality within its midst. If the connection seems a spurious one, one must recall that during the war, the U.S. military had enacted a policy declaring that homosexuality represented a security risk—among other reasons, because homosexuals were thought to be unstable. In 1952, the American Psychiatric Association added further fuel to the fire by listing homosexuality as a soiciopathic personality disturbance.

Neither allegation would ever be proven, and the latter would be officially retracted. But this did not stop people from believing them at the time. Consequently, McCarthy, who some suspect was himself a closeted homosexual, contributed to a virtual witch-hunt for homosexuals, in which police went so far as to entrap them.

Coming out in this atmosphere, in other words, was not a wise option for most gay men and lesbians. Underground bars became the chosen retreats, where men and women who dared not come out publicly could at least come out to each other.

Coming Out in Secret Organizations

Despite the enormous social pressures against homosexuality during the 1950s, the decade also saw the establishment of the first organizations that inspired gay men and women to come out, albeit in a manner that is considered inadequate, even shame-based, today.

The Mattachine Society was founded by Harry Hay in Los Angeles in 1951, and the Daughters of Bilitis was founded by Del Martin and Phyllis Lyon in San Francisco in 1955. A world apart from the "We're here, we're queer, get used to it" tactics of Queer Nation in the 1990s, Mattachine and Daughters of Bilitis were formed as secret support groups: publicized by word of mouth and held in private homes.

Even Hay's choice of a name reflected the fact that most homosexuals were then deeply closeted. "Mattachine," he said, referred to a "masked people, unknown and anonymous" who came together and danced, as Jonathan Ned Katz documents in *Gay American History.*

Both groups, nevertheless, represent an early stage in the community's coming out process that closely mirrors the individual's coming out process even today. That is, typically one first comes out to oneself, then to another gay man or lesbian, then to friends and family, and, only finally, publicly.

Similarly, the Mattachine Society and Daughters of Bilitis allowed gay men and lesbians to meet and come out to each other. This was particularly true after one of the founding Mattachine members dared to come out in court in 1952. Charged with soliciting an undercover police officer, Dale Jennings surprised the jury by pleading not guilty. They deadlocked. The Mattachine Society declared victory. And through publicity surrounding the case, according to Neil Miller in *Out of the Past*, Mattachine membership grew to several thousand people nationwide.

Jennings and a few other isolated cases notwithstanding, however, those who spoke publicly on behalf of the Mattachine Society and Daughters of Bilitis typically used pseudonyms—in part, because the FBI was known to infiltrate meetings. In this regard, their contribution to the coming out movement must be seen as limited. Dismissing them as irrelevant, or even an embarrassment, however, would be a failure to recognize the times in which they lived.

The Beat Writers Present Another View

Like the artists, writers and intellectuals who came out to each other in the bohemian enclaves of the 1920s, there were pioneers among the artistic and bohemian enclaves of the 1950s—only, in these times, they dared to come out publicly. Among them, most notably, were poet Allen Ginsberg and novelist William Burroughs.

Ginsberg and Burroughs, along with Jack Kerouac (whom journalist Neil Miller describes as "mainly heterosexual"), were the inspiration of the Beat Generation, a counterculture movement that rejected the conformity and traditionalism of the 1950s. In particular, they rejected the norm that said sexuality could be rightly felt and expressed only as heterosexuality. Personal experience told them that was ludicrous.

Ginsberg especially was open about his homosexuality. Did this inspire other gay men and lesbians among the counterculture movement to come out, as well? The numbers, perhaps, will never be known. But Ginsberg, like other beat writers, helped people have a better attitude about their own homosexuality. As historian John D'Emilio wrote, "Through the beats' example, gays could perceive themselves as nonconformists rather than deviates, as rebels against stultifying norms rather than immature, unstable personalities."

In this regard, the beats can be seen as inspiring an important step in the history of coming out, as they helped people shed inherited negative views about homosexuality, a step that remains a classic stage in the coming out process, even today.

Coming Out behind Potted Plants in the 1960s

By the early 1960s, homosexuality was just beginning to be a topic of public debate. The Kinsey studies on American sex practices, published in 1947 and 1953, had taken people by surprise by asserting, first, that more people had homosexual experiences than was ever imagined, and second, that sexuality was a continuum: on one side was heterosexuality; on the other, homosexuality; and in the middle, bisexuality.

In other words, the Kinsey studies suggested that heterosexuality was not the only "natural" form of sexuality; that homosexuality also could be a natural though different form of sexuality; and that the American Psychiatric Association's classification of it as an illness was wrong.

In challenging a centuries-old rejection of homosexuality, Kinsey (who reportedly was a closeted gay man) contributed to a growing curiosity about it. In 1961, the first TV documentary on the subject was aired. Seven gay men spoke on a WBAI radio broadcast. And *The New York Times* published its first significant report on the topic in 1963.

Yet gay men and lesbians were not coming out—or, in most cases, being asked to come out—in these news reports. Rather, they spoke using pseudonyms, or from behind potted plants. More often, they were merely speculated about by doctors, police officers, and government officials.

The first gay man or lesbian believed to have come out in the news media was Randy Wicker, a young (relatively more radical) Mattachine Society activist who in 1964 appeared on *The Les Crane Show,* a New York call-in talk show.

Then, in 1965, 12 gay men and lesbians dressed up in suits and dresses and came out in front of the U.S. White House. Spurred by the news that Fidel Castro had sentenced homosexuals to work camps in Cuba, they marched to protest and publicize anti-gay American policies. But the news media ignored them. So they returned a second time, and this time they made the news, thus becoming the first people to come out publicly during a march on Washington.

The 1960s Counterculture Movement

While the 1960s was a decade of protests—for black civil rights, against the Vietnam war, for women's rights, against a corrupt government—the banner of lesbian and gay civil rights was not taken up by this first generation of young people to enter college in mass numbers.

Yet as the students of the sixties questioned authority and challenged conventions about sex—especially against premarital sex, contraception, abortion, and sex as an expression of love instead of procreation—they began to shake some of the classic rationales for the condemnation of homosexuality. In other words, they laid the foundation for the question, If sex is not for procreation alone, why shouldn't those who wish to have homosexual sex be permitted to do so?

It would take gay men and lesbians to bring this issue to the fore, beginning with the Stonewall riots in June 1969. But the changes in the nation's attitude regarding sex and conformity that developed throughout the 1960s helped set the context.

The Stonewall Riots

The Stonewall Riots, as historian Martin Duberman has emphasized, did not mark the beginning of the gay and lesbian movement. Nor, as is evident from the history recounted above, did the riots initiate the practice of coming out. Even when every social force in the nation stood against them, there were those who came out—to themselves, another roomful of gay men and lesbians, or the public at-large—before the riots at the Stonewall Inn in New York's Greenwich Village. But the Stonewall Riots were the great turning point in gay and lesbian history because they inspired a mass movement for gay and lesbian liberation, a movement that had at its heart and soul a call to come out.

The riots began, without premeditation, in the early morning hours of 27 June 1969, when the police raided the Stonewall Inn on Christopher Street. Several hundred people were inside. The police ordered them to line up and show proof of age. The police also eyeballed everyone to judge whether they were wearing clothes that the state would deem inappropriate to their gender, an act that could lead to their arrest in New York state.

The Stonewall crowd was used to police raids, as the police were there about an average of once a month, according to Duberman, who recounts the history in his book, *Stonewall.* But because the Stonewall was Mafia-owned, and a number of local police officers were more interested in taking bribes than arresting gay men and lesbians, the bar's management usually got a tip beforehand. Money changed hands. And the raid was canceled, or the police simply made their presence known without taking any action. Bribe-taking only worked, after all, if the bar continued to be a viable business, as Duberman recalls.

But this raid was different. According to Duberman, the Bureau of Alcohol, Tobacco, and Firearms had discovered that the Stonewall was bootlegging its liquor and that local officers were accepting bribes. Thus, the ATF planned this night's raid, keeping local officers out of the loop until the last minute.

As police checked IDs and clothes, those who passed the tests were released and gathered outside. In the process, they created an audience for others who were being led out. Playing to the audience, several people camped up their exit, or entrance, as it were. And the mood grew festive.

When a paddy wagon arrived, the police began to bring out those they had arrested. The people on the street booed and tried to block the paddy wagon. Others started to rock it. Some of the prisoners escaped. A few people threw slaps and punches. The police pushed past the crowd, but the crowd fought back. They shouted "pigs" and "gay power." Others threw bottles, cans, whatever they could find. Surprised by the unusual show of strength, the police retreated inside the Stonewall. But the people on the street attempted to break down the door and threw a garbage can, lighter fluid, and matches inside.

Outside, a riot control unit arrived. The crowd, which was growing larger and angrier, left the scene, but only for a few minutes, as they walked around the block and returned behind the riot officers. They threw more debris. They started fires in garbage cans. And some formed a chorus line and sang, "We are the Stonewall girls."

Two hours later, things quieted down. The police left with a number of people in their custody, and everyone else dispersed. But the next day, word of the riots spread. And that night, a crowd of several thousand people returned. Riots broke out again, and gay men and lesbians, "newly emboldened," held hands on the street, according to Duberman.

This was the moment that represented a shift in the consciousness of gay men and lesbians. As Duberman tells it, "After the second night of rioting, it had become clear to many that a major upheaval, a kind of seismic shift, was at hand." A police officer said, "Suddenly, they were not submissive anymore." Some days later, poet Allen Ginsberg observed, "They've lost that wounded look."

With the spontaneous Stonewall Riots, fighting the tyranny of anti-gay oppression had officially begun. The next challenge would be to fight it daily, in every walk of life, by coming out.

COMING OUT IN THE 1970s

In the weeks after the riots, the New York chapter of the Mattachine Society called a meeting. Appalled by the rioting and worried about how others would now see homosexuals, their goal was to bring the new-found gay spirit under control. But they failed.

The Mattachine Society, which was born of the repressive 1950s, had encouraged coming out to each other, while largely refraining from coming out in public. But the younger generation—many of whom had been involved in the civil rights, feminist, and anti-war movements and who now had been inspired by the Stonewall Riots—wanted more. As one young man said to the Mattachine leaders during that meeting, "We don't want ... acceptance, goddamn it! We want respect."

To that end, the younger generation broke off from the Mattachine Society and formed a new organization, called the Gay Liberation Front. GLF meetings were essentially consciousness-raising sessions. But unlike the support groups of the Mattachine Society and Daughters of Bilitis, the GLF had greater ambitions than helping each other come out in private. The GLF sought to fight oppression on every front, and they expected what they did in private toward this end to change the world. Meanwhile, they inspired the formation of another organization, the Gay Activists Alliance, which focused more narrowly on securing basic rights for gay men and lesbians.

But it was the GLF that gave birth to the idea of coming out as the building block of liberation—an idea that would be taken up by almost every other gay and lesbian organization that would later come into existence. In the months following the Stonewall Riots, GLF leaders called upon gay men and lesbians "to expose themselves for what they are," and not to isolate from society, as Duberman recalls. Their aim, in other words, was "the free and open public expression of homosexual affections." To this end, they began publishing a paper called *Come Out!*

"A Gay Manifesto"

Carl Wittman, an activist in the Students for a Democratic Society (SDS) movement, expressed what would become the predominant theory of coming out and its role in the gay and lesbian liberation movement in what he called "A Gay Manifesto" (see p. 67). It said:

> To pretend to be straight sexually, or to pretend to be straight socially, is probably the most harmful pattern of behavior in the ghetto.... If we are liberated, we are open with our sexuality. Closet queenery must end. Come out. But ... [e]ach of us must make the steps toward openness at our own speed and on our own impulses. Being open is the foundation of freedom; it has to be built solidly.

In other words, coming out, as it was perceived in the late 1960s and early 1970s—and, for the most part, today—was both a personal and a political act. While seen in controversial terms by the original Mattachine members, it was thought of by many among the younger generation as an enormously powerful and promising one on both fronts. Personally, coming out offered the gay man or lesbian a release from the pain of self-hatred and internalized oppression that came as a natural response to being stigmatized by others. It also offered relief from the series of lies and deceptions that were part of the life of anyone who attempted to hide something so central to who they were. (See "The Process of Coming Out.")

Politically, coming out was seen as the key to building a mass movement for gay and lesbian liberation and equal rights. When a closeted gay man or lesbian saw another come out, he or she was encouraged to come out, too. And when people came out in great numbers, there was the promise of political clout.

This was, and remains, the snowball theory of coming out, which soon began to prove itself in practice. As people heard of the Stonewall Riots through the news media, more people came out. As word spread of the Gay Liberation Front, and then the Gay Activists Alliance, still more people came out. As publications like *Come Out!* became available, at first underground and then on newsstands, even more people came out.

But perhaps the best early demonstration of the power, fear, and controversy associated with the new coming-out phenomenon was the Christopher Street Liberation Day March, held in June 1970 to mark the first anniversary of the Stonewall Riots. This was the first of what would come to be known as the annual Gay and Lesbian Pride Parade.

The First Gay and Lesbian Parade

The Christopher Street Liberation Day March, held on 28 June 1970, was a testament to how far the growing community of gay and lesbian activists had traveled since the Stonewall Riots in their belief that coming out was the key to the gay and lesbian movement.

"The main problem holding us back from where we want to get to is that of secrecy or fear, and the failure of homosexuals to get out of the closet," said Jim Foster, one of the parade organizers. The goal of the parade, therefore, was to encourage more gay men and lesbians to come out and join the movement.

But this was not an easy task in 1970, when one could still be arrested for homosexual behavior. There was a real risk of losing one's job, one's friends, one's family—and the American Psychiatric Association still labeled homosexuality as a mental illness. Even the seemingly simple experience of making a parade poster demonstrates this point.

Peter Hujar, a fashion photographer and lover of one of the parade organizers, wanted a picture of Gay Liberation Front members on the street, their arms linked, and smiling for a parade poster that would be headlined, COME OUT!! But one person after another, worried about the consequences, said no.

Finally, Hujar rounded up 15 men and women, a tiny number from among the thousands who had participated in GLF activities. But Hujar tried to make the best of it, printing the photo in such a way that disguises the fact that there are only 15 people representing this parade. But even then, as Duberman recalls, people raised an eyebrow over the poster, as if to say to those who came out for it, "You realize, of course, that your life is finished." To some, that remained a question. To most people, the larger question remained: how many would come out for the parade?

Not many showed up at the official start-time of the parade. The organizers waited to see if more people would come. Then they began to walk, as the police held their line, and a few spectators gathered on the sidelines to watch. To those marching, it appeared as if the people on the sidelines were gay or lesbian and "calculating the risks," Duberman reports. But there was a great excitement in the air, as this marked a moment that people were doing something completely unprecedented and terrifically courageous. And as the marchers winded their way from the small streets of Greenwich Village toward Central Park, where the parade would conclude, more people joined in. Some had signs that proclaimed: "Sappho was a Right-On Woman," "Two, Four, Six, Eight: Gay is Just as Good as Straight," or, simply, "Gay Power." Some just walked. And by the end, some 2,000 people—perhaps as many as 5,000, according to Neil Miller—came out publicly.

It was truly a remarkable event, which *The New York Times* covered on the front page. Shortly after, Jill Johnston, an out lesbian writer for *The Village Voice,* described the significance of the new coming out phenomenon this way:

> A proud (and often public) declaration of one's homosexuality became the first act of joining the new movement—a marked change from the use of pseudonyms by many homophile leaders. The key phrase is COME OUT. Come out of hiding. Identify yourself. Make it clear. Celebrate your sexuality.

The first annual pride parade put that challenge on the map.

Male v. Female Styles of Coming Out

The goal of coming out was liberation. But even a goal as open-ended as liberation can be influenced, or hemmed in, by the styles of the times and the values and priorities of those coming out. In the 1970s, for example, gay men and women came out in different ways and attached different meanings to the act; in the process, different identities became associated with each.

To many gay men, the real joy of coming out was about being sexually open, after decades in which they could have been arrested for it. Some moved to large cities, where they could go to the bars and bathhouses, where promiscuity became something to revel in. As Neil Miller wrote in *Out of the Past,* "It was as if years of repression had suddenly shed its skin, as if every gay man were sixteen again and all the men about whom he had ever fantasized ... were suddenly available for a smile."

But many lesbians had a different take on the coming-out experience. Instead of moving to cities to be with other lesbians, many chose to live in rural areas or areas not yet known for large numbers of homosexuals, such as Northampton, Massachusetts; Boulder, Colorado; Ithaca, New York; and Berkeley and Oakland, California. More significantly, many lesbians emphasized the political more than the sexual significance of coming out. Especially for those lesbians who had roots in the feminist movement, coming out meant challenging the history and traditions of male dominance over women. Traditionally feminine behavior and appearance was seen as undermining to women and something that lesbians should avoid, according to Lillian Faderman, author of *Odd Girls and Twilight Lovers: A History of Lesbian Life in Twentieth-Century America.*

It also followed that lesbians who exhibited this behavior—or, more specifically, who came out while maintaining a traditional feminine appearance—could be roundly ousted from lesbian circles. As writer Joan Nestle has recalled, "At gatherings of the seventies, if a woman walked in wearing makeup, lipstick, nail polish, even heels, she would not be spoken to, or asked to leave."

But even in the midst of these heady times that gave birth to the notion of political correctness, many lesbians were unwilling to allow their coming-out experience to be restricted by a certain brand of feminist—typically, middle-class—politics. And they simply came out their own way.

Coming out, in short, was ultimately too powerful an experience—and too fundamentally a rite of passage—to be restricted to a singular definition. The needs and values of the times and the diversity of the growing population of out gay men and lesbians were bound to leave their mark on the experience.

Coming Out in Politics

Remarkably, the first openly gay person to run for public office did so in 1961. Jose Sarria, a female impersonator, ran for a seat as a San Francisco supervisor. He lost but never really expected to win. His goal, he explained, was to "show gay people that you could do anything."

A decade later, an openly gay person had still failed to win an election, or even to come out after winning election. But in 1972, a gay man and a lesbian came out for the first time in an address before the Democratic National Convention. Not exactly a prime-time event—they spoke at 5 a.m.—it still reached a television audience of approximately one million. The pair also made history by encouraging other gay men and lesbians to come out during a political event broadcast nationwide.

As Madeline Davis of Buffalo, New York, said to the convention: "Twenty million gay Americans are the untouchables in our society.... Now we are coming out of our closets and onto the convention floor to tell you ... and, to tell all gay people throughout America, that we are here to put an end to our fears."

The pioneers who came out in American politics in the 1970s were significant in two regards: first, because they furthered the political goal of coming out, by increasing visibility and, thereby, political clout; and, second, because it marked the penetration of one of the institutions most fiercely and officially opposed to homosexuality. In this way, if only slightly, subtly, and more in spirit than in practice, coming out began to undermine government opposition to homosexuality—particularly when gay and lesbian officials began to do it.

The First to Come out as Elected Officials: City Council members Nancy Wechsler and Jerry DeGrieck came out after a homophobic incident occurred in a restaurant in Ann Arbor, Michigan, in 1972. It was a powerful and original way to show support for gay men and lesbians at a time when they were under attack.

Two years later, Elaine Noble took a still greater risk by coming out as an openly lesbian candidate for the Massachusetts House of Representatives. More impressive yet, she won. *The New York Times* pronounced her "the first avowed lesbian elected to office."

But the most interesting point about Noble's coming out is not simply that she was the first, but that she came out in a district comprised of mainly elderly and low-income voters, who are typically thought to be among those most opposed to homosexuality, and it did not compromise her success as a candidate.

How did she do it? *The New York Times* suggested this answer: "What enabled Miss Noble to win the district was a campaign that stressed her community work and the fact that she had met so many of the voters face to face." Her success, in other words, was in the strategy that has now become a familiar refrain of gay and lesbian activists: come out in person to everyone you can, and you'll do the most you can to overcome anti-gay prejudice.

Gerald Eugene Ulrich's coming out affirmed the solidity of this principle six years later as he became the first openly gay person to be elected mayor—in the Bible Belt small town of Bunceton, Missouri, no less. "Everyone in town knew me," he said. "They knew my parents. I grew up in this area."

Harvey Milk: The Impact of Being an Out Politician: No account of coming out in politics during the 1970s would be complete without mention of the late Harvey Milk, who was elected to the San Francisco Board of Supervisors in 1977 and murdered in 1978.

A man whose attitude toward coming out clearly had been influenced by the times, Milk spent the 1950s and 1960s as a closeted gay man, working as a financial analyst in New York, and supporting Barry Goldwater for president, according to Neil Miller in *Out of the Past.*

But then, as the counterculture swept through the nation in the 1960s, Milk's attitude about coming out changed, and in the early 1970s, he moved to San Francisco, where he ran several times for the Board of Supervisors before winning in 1977. Almost immediately, he showed a strong sense of responsibility about his role as an out elected official, as he helped pass a local gay rights ordinance and addressed numerous gay and lesbian organizations nationwide.

A year later, Dan White, a former supervisor, assassinated both Milk and San Francisco's mayor at the time, George Moscone. Afterward, some 25,000 people marched in vigil. When White was found guilty simply of manslaughter, riots broke out, causing extensive damage and the hospitalization of 61 police officers and more than 100 gay men and lesbians.

Randy Shilts's 1982 biography of Milk, entitled *The Mayor of Castro Street,* and an Academy-Award winning documentary, entitled *The Life and Times of Harvey Milk*, have since memorialized Milk, making a legend of a man who, like John F. Kennedy, had a limited amount of time to prove himself. But his life and death, and the gay and lesbian community's reaction to both, indisputably demonstrated the power and influence—and, in this case, potential danger—of coming out as an elected politician in the first decade of gay and lesbian liberation.

Coming Out in the Military

In 1975, Leonard Matlovich, a 31-year-old sergeant in the United States Air Force, came out to his superior officer by handing him a letter, which declared: "After some years of uncertainty, I have arrived at the conclusion that my sexual preferences are homosexual as opposed to heterosexual. I have also concluded that my preferences will in no way interfere with my Air Force duties, as my preferences are now open." Matlovich's letter then went on to request that on the basis of more than a decade of service, which included three tours of duty in Vietnam, a Purple Heart, and a Bronze star, the military's ban against gays in the military be waived in his case. With this, one one man launched the controversy over the presence—or, more accurately, the coming out—of gay men and lesbians in the military.

Matlovich's challenge and the larger principle it implied was not one that would be settled quickly, as we know from the continuing debate. Yet Matlovich did succeed in bringing the issue of gays and lesbians coming out in the military to public attention as never before, as Neil Miller recounts in *Out of the Past.*

Six months after he submitted his letter, he appeared, wearing his medals, on the cover of *Time* magazine. The cover line said, "I am a Homosexual." Two months later, the Air Force discharged him; three years later, a U.S. Court of Appeals ruled that the discharge was illegal. Two years after that, another judge got around to ordering the Air Force to reinstate him. But the Air Force didn't want a gay man who had publicly come out back in their fold, and they offered him a settlement of $160,000, tax-free, if he would simply stay away. If he didn't take it, they added, they would fight his reinstatement all the way to the U.S. Supreme Court.

Matlovich, who was working as a used car salesman, took the settlement. Six years later, he was diagnosed with AIDS. Two years after that, he died, but he used his death to come out again, to the military and all others who cared to know. Eligible for burial in Arlington National Cemetery, Matlovich had his gravestone engraved with the words, "When I was in the military, they gave me a medal for killing two men, and a discharge for loving one."

While Matlovich's appeal to the Air Force was unsuccessful, his coming out did help spur others to do the same. In the late 1970s, U.S. Navy Ensign Vernon "Copy" Berg III came out and fought a discharge order after he was discovered having a homosexual relationship with a Navy civilian; Women's Army Corps Private Debbie Watson and Private First Class Barbara Randolph came out and declared they would fight any discharge orders. And Army Reserve Drill Instructor Miriam Ben-Shalom came out to her commander by saying, If they kicked out Matlovich, "why don't they kick *me* out?" Apparently thinking it a good question, they did.

But Ben-Shalom challenged the Army Reserves in court, and when she lost, she challenged them again until the Supreme Court heard the case in 1990. The high court upheld the discharge order. But even then, Ben-Shalom continued to speak on behalf of the right of gay men and lesbians to come out in the military.

Coming Out in the Church

Organized religion, it can be argued, is the greatest enemy gay men and lesbians have ever had. As far back as the Middle Ages, the Christian church declared sodomy a sin against God and nature and called for punishment by burning at the stake. It was with no small amount of courage, therefore, that a group of gay men and lesbians came together in California in 1968 to form a non-denominational Christian church where gay men and lesbians could come out and find acceptance. They called themselves the United Fellowship of Metropolitan Community Churches, and two years later, they had more than 500 members.

It was the first successful coming out in the world of religion, but not the only one to take place in the 1970s. In 1972, for example, Rev. Bill Johnson became the first out gay man to be ordained as a clergyman of the United Church of Christ, one of the only Protestant Christian churches to adopt a nondiscriminatory policy regarding sexual orientation.

In the same year, a number of gay men and lesbians came together to form Beth Chayim Chdashim, the first gay and lesbian synagogue. In 1977, Ellen Marie Barrett was ordained as an Episcopal priest in Manhattan, becoming the first out lesbian to be ordained by a major Christian denomination. In 1978, Rabbi Allen Bennett became the first openly gay rabbi in San Francisco.

And in the same year, Jane Adams Spahr, a Presbyterian minister in San Rafael, California, came out after being ordained four years before. She was forced to resign her position. But she has continued to work to support the right of gay men and lesbians to come out in the Presbyterian church.

Coming Out in Sports

In the world of sports, only the rarest of the rare gay men and lesbians were willing to come out in the 1970s. And for good reason: even massaging another player's temples could get a woman kicked out of the International Women's Professional Softball League in the mid-1970s. Extreme macho attitudes in men's sports made it equally difficult to consider coming out, as Lynn Rosellini, a reporter for *The Washington Star,* discovered in 1975 when she wrote a series entitled "Gays in Sports," and was unable to find anyone willing to come out—until finally, one retired player braved it: former NFL running back David Kopay. Sports, then and now, remained "one of the most closeted worlds inhabited by lesbians and gay men," as Lynn Witt and her co-authors observed in *Out in All Directions: The Almanac of Gay and Lesbian America.*

One reason for this is that people have erroneously, but historically, associated homosexuality with gender confusion. Gay men, the stereotype goes, are sissies, and lesbians are manly. By this thinking, gay men cannot compete in the competitive world of sports, and lesbians who are thought of as "too manly" make people uncomfortable because they challenge the role of heterosexual male athletes and the stereotypical image of women as non-competitive.

In short, coming out in sports was made difficult by the failure of people to recognize the diversity inherent in human behavior, not only among gay men and lesbians but within the genders as well.

Coming Out in the Gay and Lesbian Media

It would be a mistake to overlook the role of the gay and lesbian media in fostering coming out during the 1970s, as numerous publications started up around the nation, such as the *Washington Blade,* the *Philadelphia Gay News,* San Francisco's *Bay Area Reporter,* Chicago's *Gay Life,* and the nationally circulated *Advocate.*

Not only did these publications, many of which were sold on newsstands, increase visibility, but they distributed information useful to those who had not yet come out, such as bar happenings and classified ads. Moreover, they served as starting grounds for a number of gay men and lesbians who would go on to become influential in the movement, including writer Randy Shilts; Urvashi Vaid, later head of the National Gay and Lesbian Task Force; Kevin Cathcart, later executive director of the Lambda Legal Defense and Education Fund; and Richard Burns, executive director of New York City's Lesbian and Gay Community Center.

Coming Out in the Workplace

The people who were among the first to come out in the workplace during the 1970s were people who worked in creative fields, such as advertising, communications, art, music, design, architecture, retail, and fashion, according to Annette Friskopp and Sharon Silverstein in *Straight Jobs, Gay Lives.*

Coming out in a white-collar profession was still generally considered "unthinkable," write Friskopp and Silverstein. It would take a new decade for those barriers to be broken.

COMING OUT IN THE 1980s

If a number of the gay men and lesbians who came out in the seventies felt euphoric to be "free at last," coming out in the eighties had a very different, complex, and mature feel to it.

Many gay men began coming out with the explosion of the AIDS epidemic, which then carried as much as a certain death sentence. An unprecedented number of gay men and lesbians came out politically—not only as elected officials, but in far greater numbers as activists, drawn to fight government inaction on AIDS. They also came out to help each other, as they organized support, health, and public education organizations devoted to curbing the spread of the disease.

Beyond the realm of AIDS, meanwhile, a number of lesbians and a lesser number of gay men came out as parents, which spread the coming out phenomenon to entirely new realms, including playgrounds and PTA meetings. Children also began to come out, as the children of gay and lesbian parents.

Finally, the very concept of coming out began to be institutionalized, when in 1988 the Human Rights Campaign Fund (HRC) announced a "National Coming Out Day" program. This program marked 11 October as the official day when gay men and lesbians who had not yet come out were encouraged to do so; those who already had come out were urged to help others do so, through numerous gay and lesbian public education events that were held around the nation.

Coming out in the 1980s, in short, lent a more complex identity to gay men and lesbians than the American public had seen before.

The Age of AIDS

The first news reports about the outbreak of the disease that would later be called AIDS demonstrated confidence about few facts—except, apparently, one: it had been seen in gay men, and thereby was thought to be "related to [the] gay life style," as a

Center for Disease Control epidemiologist told *The Los Angeles Times* in 1981. While that statement left many questions unanswered, the mysterious disease was alternately dubbed "the gay cancer," and "gay related immune deficiency" or GRID.

The news made gay men very anxious, on two counts: the health threat, of course, was one of them; but the other was a fear, held by many activists, that coming out around AIDS would lead to a backlash, as gay men would be seen not only as stigmatized members of society but as carriers of a deadly virus. Some responded by trying to deny or repress the facts, even the number of deaths from AIDS, according to Neil Miller in *Out of the Past.*

But other activists, such as Larry Kramer, whose efforts led to the founding of the Gay Men's Health Crisis in 1982, pushed for publicity about AIDS, even going to mainstream media organizations to ask for it. And by 1983, the facts and, moreover, the image of gay men suffering from this new deadly disease, began to appear in the mainstream media.

Then, for perhaps the first time, the American public began to see images of gay men that many could not help but find sympathetic: as courageous human beings confronting death. But the impact, for the first several years of the disease, was limited.

Rock Hudson—and Company—Come Out: By 1985, the number of AIDS-related deaths had skyrocketed to more than 4,000, and the number of people infected with the disease rose to twice that amount. These were striking numbers by any count. But what really drew America's attention to AIDS was the appearance of a beloved celebrity stricken with the disease: actor Rock Hudson.

Through Hudson, the face of a gay man with AIDS finally became a known and admired one, and the mainstream media were riveted. The number of articles about people with AIDS ran high for two years.

Meanwhile, many ordinary gay men and lesbians also began to come out around the disease, volunteering at and donating money to grassroots service organizations, such as the Gay Men's Health Crisis (GMHC). Indeed, where many middle-class and wealthy gay men and lesbians previously had remained closeted during efforts to repeal sodomy laws or pass anti-discrimination legislation during the 1970s, the concrete reality of AIDS drew them out in the 1980s, according to Miller in *Out of the Past.*

The coming out of numerous lesbians in this regard helped bridge the severed connections that had developed between gay men and lesbians during the 1970s, as a number of lesbians saw gay men as part of the larger male-dominated structure they opposed. In the light of AIDS, the immediate needs of people who were dying overwhelmed the political principles of separatism.

The Rise of ACT UP: By 1987, six years after the first AIDS case was reported in the United States, it became clear that the Reagan administration was treating AIDS as something far less than the epidemic it was. In a position to earmark greater funding for research into treatment and a cure, the administration did not. On at least one occasion, it even reduced the amount of spending proposed by the U.S. Congress.

Indeed, to the conservative Republicans in the White House and the Christian fundamentalists backing them, this disease, which appeared to strike only gay men and drug users, seemed, if not a blessing in disguise, then God's punishment for immoral behavior.

Understandably angry again, playwright Larry Kramer decided it was time to inspire the many young activists who had come out around AIDS to put their energy to work in a new constructive direction. To this end, he appeared before an audience at the New York Lesbian and Gay Community Center one night in 1987 and asked half of them to stand up. "At the rate we are going, you could be dead in less than five years," he said. Then he challenged them to go out and protest as other groups did, complaining and pleading at once, "Why are we so invisible, constantly and forever!"

If the consequences of remaining closeted in the 1970s were self-hatred, internalized oppression and half-lived lives, the consequence in the age of AIDS was, quite simply, an early death. And the only people who could do something about it were gay men and lesbians willing to stand up for themselves and fight back. That was Kramer's message, and it got through.

Two days after the meeting, some 300 gay men and lesbians—many of whom were young and HIV-positive—came together to form ACT UP, the AIDS Coalition To Unleash Power. Their motto, itself a statement on the closet, was, "Silence = Death." Their goal was to fight for the early release of all experimental drugs that could treat AIDS. And their strategy was a 1980s version of Henry David Thoreau's civil disobedience. One of their first events, for example, consisted of lying down like corpses in New York City rush-hour traffic.

ACT UP's tactics proved extremely controversial—and ultimately, alienating, as, for example, they stomped on communion wafers in protest against the Catholic Church. Yet they also proved effective at their stated goal: within two years, the Food and Drug Administration loosened its restrictions on experimental drugs designed to treat AIDS.

They also inspired the rise of another group, Queer Nation, which would apply similar street-theater tactics to the larger goal of increasing gay and lesbian visibility. In the early 1990s, this would take the form of "outing," which turned traditional coming-out theory on its head. (See "The Advent of Outing.")

Lesbian and Gay Parents Come Out

Parenting children, of course, is nothing new to gay men and lesbians. Millions have done it throughout history. But, typically, they were forced to closet their sexual orientation in the process. Indeed, the dual desires to have a same-sex lover and to raise a child seemed an irreconcilable conflict.

But this began to change when donor (also called alternative or artificial) insemination became available to lesbians, and surrogate motherhood became a way for gay men to have a child. Then, coming out as a lesbian or gay man—and being a parent—became a real possibility.

What was first most accurately called artificial insemination is a practice that goes back more than a hundred years. In *Reinventing the Family*, author Laura Benkov cites a case from 1884 when a doctor inseminated an unconscious woman, without her knowledge or consent. Her husband, who was infertile, pleaded with the doctor never to tell her, and neither she, nor the son she gave birth to, ever did find out.

Well into the twentieth century, artificial insemination continued to be thought of as a secret solution to infertility problems in heterosexual couples. A couple simply went to the doctor's office, and the doctor used a syringe to inseminate sperm from another male into the woman.

For lesbians, it was an ideal solution to the parenting dilemma—only most doctors didn't think so throughout most of the twentieth century. Indeed, as late as 1979, a survey showed that 90 percent of doctors said they would refuse to inseminate unmarried women, according to Benkov.

Many explained their decision by saying they believed children needed a mother and a father, and that a single woman (as lesbians might feign be seen, to dodge a doctor's prejudice against them) should not raise a child alone. Some also thought it was illegal, although it wasn't.

But by the end of the 1970s, lesbians began to find ways to get around the doctor's informal guidelines by asking male friends, relatives, or acquaintances to help them by donating sperm, either with or without co-parenting privileges.

Problems, however, soon arose, as some of these men who claimed to have given their sperm freely, simply to help the woman, had a change of heart after the baby was born and decided to fight for custody. This kind of legal challenge left many lesbian mothers with broken hearts, as the courts ruled against them, especially if the man was heterosexual. The rise of AIDS also presented a problem, before the advent of testing.

Then in 1982, a group of women who had been running a feminist health-care organization in California called the Oakland Feminist Women's Health Care Center decided to respond to lesbians' and unmarried women's demands for medically controlled sperm donations. They established the Sperm Bank of California, which made insemination available to all women, regardless of sexual orientation or marital status. A number of other sperm banks later followed suit, and what was dubbed the lesbian baby boom, or "gayby boom," took off.

While the number of children born to lesbian mothers through donor insemination is not known, Benkov reports that more than 1 million American children have been born this way. This, however, is far from a full representation of the growing trend of parenting among gay men and lesbians, as children have also been brought into gay and lesbian families through adoption, surrogate motherhood, prior relationships, foster care, and other means. Indeed, in 1992 there were somewhere between 3 and 8 million gay and lesbian parents raising between 6 and 14 million children, according to a leading gay and lesbian family researcher, Charlotte Patterson.

Children, Baby-sitters, and Grandparents: As more gay and lesbian parents came out in the 1980s, they put their children in the position of needing to do the same. And to some extent, the need to come out, as it were, also was extended to other people involved in the life of the child, including baby-sitters, grandparents, and aunts and uncles.

April Martin, for example, tells the story of the baby-sitter who took her child to the park, where she encountered the usual questions about what the child's father did. In the beginning, the baby-sitter used the old trick of switching pronouns and said simply, "He's a psychologist," referring to Martin. But eventually, and of her own accord, she began to say that the parents of the child in her care were lesbians—in effect, coming out for them.

How the grandparents of the children of gay and lesbian parents answer common questions also reflects on the extended coming out challenge that stems from the rise of gay and lesbian parenting. For example, every time a grandparent is asked about her grandchild's home life; every time a grandparent shows off a picture of a grandchild and is asked what his mommy and daddy do; and every time a grandparent takes a grandchild out and is faced with questions about whether he looks like his mother or father, he or she is put in the position of having to decide whether to come out about the true nature of the grandchild's family.

While this extended family dynamic is a frequently overlooked aspect of the coming-out experience, it remains an important and fundamental aspect of society's larger coming out, or openness, about the presence and increasingly visible role of gay men and lesbians.

But, of course, aside from the lesbian or gay parent, the person put most directly in the position of needing to come out as part of a gay- or lesbian-headed household is the child. The child's experience in this regard may vary, according to Martin, based on a number of factors, ranging from the openness of the parent, to the presence of diversity in school, to the age of the child.

Young children tend to be able to come out most matter-of-factly about their family structures, many child researchers and parents have noted, because they have not yet learned society's prejudices against homosexuality. But as they become adolescents, they often become more reticent to come out about being the children of lesbian or gay parents.

At this stage of development, some young people become angry at their parents for being gay or lesbian because it makes them different from their friends, and adolescence is a time when most young people want above all to fit in. And despite the studies that have shown that children of lesbian and gay parents are no more inclined to grow up lesbian or gay than children of heterosexual parents, a number of children worry that they, too, will grow up gay or lesbian and be subject to a stigma no one willingly embraces.

During adolescence, consequently, children of gay and lesbian parents may refuse to come out by avoiding talking about their parents in school, refusing to bring friends home, or inviting only one parent to school events. These kinds of coming-out issues can require a lot of conversations and patience. But, frequently, most of the difficulties pass with adolescence, and the adult children of gay and lesbian parents become more willing to come out about the people who raised them.

Coming Out in Congress

In the 1980s, two Congressmen broke barriers by becoming the first national politicians to come out: Rep. Gerry Studds (D-Mass.) after being outed, and Rep. Barney Frank (D-Mass.) of his own accord. In addition, several hundred thousand people came out during the 1987 March on Washington. In 1991, Rep. Steve Gunderson (R-Wisc.) also was outed and, afterward, came out.

The path to Studds's coming-out experience began with a congressional investigation, launched after a page alleged that House members used illegal drugs. The drug charges appeared to have been unfounded. Yet, in the process of the investigation, it was found that Studds had engaged in a sexual relationship with a sixteen-year-old page in 1973.

Studds was censured by Congress, then went on with business as usual—but as the first openly gay U.S. congressman. Moreover, he began to speak openly on behalf of gay and lesbian rights. And more significant yet, he was re-elected to his seat.

Meanwhile, Barney Frank, Studds's colleague from Massachusetts, continued to serve as a semi-closeted gay man. "I used the privileges of the closet, which was an eighties' norm," he said during a 1997 interview. "If you didn't get caught doing something illegal, no one would talk about your being gay. So I was out privately, but in public."

But being only half-out was enormously stressful, Frank said, because it required that he lie or hedge about himself in even the most casual of conversations. It also required that he spend a great deal of energy to think of ways not to reveal himself. Being closeted also was stressful because it made it very difficult to have a happy personal life.

So in 1987, Frank began to calculate what would happen if he came out publicly, and what would be the best way to do it. "I assumed that I would be able to survive politically but I would be diminished by it," Frank said.

To his surprise, he was discouraged from coming out by gay and straight people alike. "Some of the best defenders of human rights volunteered to me that I shouldn't do this because they thought I would be diminished," he said. "And straight people couldn't fully understand the emotional need to come out. But I had a strong personal need. I also thought I would be doing a service: You clearly can't beat a prejudice from a hiding place."

Once he resolved to come out, Frank next had to decide how to do it. He did not want to make an announcement of it, because he did not want his sexual orientation to be considered a political issue; announcing it, he thought, would invite people to judge it that way.

"So I decided that, if asked, I would say so," Frank told *The Village Voice* in a 1989 interview. But the privilege of the closet continued to be the norm, and he found even when he wanted them to, journalists would not ask if Frank were gay. "They would ask if they could ask me. But, no [I thought], I'm not giving them permission; that was important to me. Finally, *The Boston Globe* decided they would ask me." He answered, "Yes, so what?"

There were few negative repercussions as a result of his coming out, Frank reports. Indeed, years later, Frank has an increasingly strong reputation as an outspoken and respected voice in Congress.

In 1996, *The New York Times* described Frank this way: "He is Newt Gingrich's nemesis, a pit bull of oratory, the point man of the House Democratic Leadership for floor debates and a star of C-Span. He is also an unofficial adviser to President Clinton and was a force behind the Administration's recently proposed gay rights bill." In the process, he has become a powerful voice for gay rights, even invoking his relationship with his partner, Herb Moses, during a congressional debate on the Defense of Marriage Act.

As of 1997, Frank remained the only out gay man or lesbian who had come out and stayed in Congress.

Coming Out in the News Media

Randy Shilts became one of the first openly gay reporters for a major U.S. daily newspaper when he was hired by *The San Francisco Chronicle* in 1981. And through his groundbreaking reporting on AIDS, which culminated in the book, *And the Band Played On,* as well as through his biography of openly gay San Francisco Supervisor Harvey Milk, who was murdered in 1978, Shilts became one of the most visible gay or lesbian reporters in a decade that would bring out many.

But only after reporting on AIDS exploded in the mainstream news media after actor Rock Hudson came out as HIV-positive in 1985 did a number of gay and lesbian reporters begin to voluntarily or involuntarily come out as a result of having AIDS.

In 1986, for example, Bill Cox of *The Honolulu Star-Bulletin* came out in the last story he wrote as a man dying of AIDS. In 1989, Tom Cassidy, correspondent for CNN Financial News, came out on local CBS, *People Magazine*, the Donahue Show, and the Dick Cavett Show, according to Edward Alwood, author of *Straight News: Gays, Lesbians, and the News Media.*

Other reporters came out, not to their readers but to their colleagues, which later increased coverage of AIDS and other gay and lesbian issues. For example, after a *Chicago Tribune* reporter died of AIDS in 1987, Jean Latz Griffin, a heterosexual, married mother of three, proposed that her editor assign her to a gay beat. And to her surprise, he did.

Other reporters came out, in more or less quiet tones, throughout the rest of the decade, although perhaps the most influential coming out—at *The New York Times*—would not occur until 1990. (See "Coming Out in the Media," below.)

Coming Out on TV Talk Shows

A number of gay men, lesbians, and bisexuals came out to American TV audiences during the 1980s through TV talk shows—most notably, *The Donahue Show.* Among the topics Phil Donahue featured were: "The Bisexual Couple"; "Homosexual Prom Couple"; "Gay Atheists"; "Lesbian Sperm Bank"; and "Gay Senior Citizens."

In 1988, more gay men and lesbians began coming out on other talk shows, including *The Oprah Winfrey Show, Geraldo,* and *Sally Jessy Raphael.* Among their topics: "National Coming Out Day," "Teen Lesbians and Their Moms," and "When 'The Other Man' Is a Woman."

Whether these shows advanced or detracted from an understanding of gay men and lesbians is open to debate. But they clearly demonstrated an increase in the coming out of gay men and lesbians, as the subject was made regular daytime TV fare.

Coming Out in School

In 1980, Aaron Fricke, an 18-year-old from Rockport, Rhode Island, decided to take a same-sex date to his high school prom. The school tried to stop him but Fricke won, securing the right for other gay and lesbian teens. His case received widespread attention, and Fricke became one of the first publicly known gay adolescents.

Later that decade, some of the first gay and lesbian high school teachers began to come out. One of these teachers, Kevin Jennings of Concord Academy in Concord, Massachusetts, took his first steps in 1987 when a student asked about the meaning of the ring he wore to mark his commitment to his partner. Jennings told him about his lover and then, on a case-by-case basis, came out to other students until he decided that wasn't good enough. All his students, he thought, needed out role models. He made the decision to come out publicly, an experience he describes in *One Teacher in Ten* as follows: "On 10 November 1988, I rose to the pulpit of the Concord Academy chapel, my talk in my hands, sweat drenching my button-down shirt and soaking through to my blue blazer." For fifteen minutes, he spoke about his struggle with being gay when he was a teenager, his struggle with substance abuse problems and attempted suicide, and then his realization that it was OK to be gay."

"I didn't expect what happened next," Jennings continued. "Kids literally leapt up from their pews and rushed the pulpit, surrounding me and hugging me, many of them crying as they tried to thank me for what I had done."

When he later returned to his classroom, he found the blackboard covered with graffiti. "I temporarily blanked out, so sure was I that they had written homophobic epithets across the slate. When my vision returned, I read what they actually had written.

'We love you, Kevin, and we're so proud of you,' it read. Each student had signed it."

By the end of the decade, it remained a rarity for a gay or lesbian high school teacher to receive such a warm welcome, let alone risk coming out, when they easily could be fired even for introducing a gay or lesbian text into their class discussions.

But the tide began to shift slightly, as concern grew about the plight of gay and lesbian youth in schools. In 1989, a U.S. Department of Health and Human Services report brought attention to gay and lesbian youth, as it found that they were two to three times more likely to attempt suicide than their heterosexual peers. Gay and lesbian activists used it as evidence of the awful consequences of the anti-gay environment in many schools, a point that Jennings and others would use to foster and support the gay and lesbian youth movement, which would come out in the 1990s.

Coming Out in Sports

Martina Navratilova was one of the first athletes to break the taboo against coming out in sports. She did so during an interview with *The Daily News* in 1981. As a result, her income, though not her career, suffered, as she lost numerous endorsement opportunities. Navratilova went on, however, to win nine Wimbledon tennis singles titles and four U.S. Open championships, making her perhaps the greatest female tennis player of all time.

One year later, Dr. Tom Waddell, a physician and Olympic decathlete, founded the Gay Games, a sports competition modeled after the Olympic games but organized as an event to bring together—and, thereby, bring out—gay, lesbian, and bisexual athletes in a wide range of sports.

The first Gay Games, held in San Francisco, attracted some 1,700 athletes. In 1996, the number of participating athletes in seventeen events doubled, to 3,500. The games, again held in San Francisco, attracted some 10,000 spectators.

Coming Out in the Workplace

In the 1980s, gay men and lesbians began to pioneer coming out not only in the more-creative industries such as advertising, fashion, and music but in health care, government, entertainment, the media, publishing, banking, and financial services, according to Annette Friskopp and Sharon Silverstein, authors of *Straight Jobs, Gay Lives.* But the greatest strides would remain to be made in the 1990s. (See "Coming Out in the Media.")

COMING OUT IN THE 1990s

In 1994, the twenty-fifth anniversary of the Stonewall Riots, *New York* magazine ran a cover story, asking, "Is Everyone Gay?" The question seemed reasonable, with coming out in the military a front-page story; the rise of the "outing" phenomenon; the coming out of an increasing number of gay and lesbian writers, singers, parents, politicians, and activists; and an unprecedented number of appointees in the new Democratic administration in Washington, D.C.

The Advent of "Outing"

After the rise of the nationwide gay and lesbian movement in 1969, coming out was considered something that was both personal and political. It was thought to serve political ends because the more gay men and lesbians came out, the more political clout the community would have to fight for equal rights. And yet coming out was seen to rest on an action that was strictly personal: the desire and the willingness to accept one's own homosexuality and express it to others.

While gay and lesbian activists encouraged more people to come out, most activists never thought it was their place to force anyone to come out. Indeed, as the early "Gay Manifesto" declared: "[E]ach of us must make the steps toward openness at our own speed and on our own impulses. Being open is the foundation of freedom; it has to be built solidly." Through the seventies and well into the eighties, this statement continued to reflect the predominant thinking, repeated by person after person, year after year, as if it were the most solid principle in the history of coming out. Stated plainly, it said, People had to come out when *they* were ready to.

But at the close of the 1980s and early 1990s, two things happened that turned this traditional philosophy on its head and set off a heated controversy both within the gay and lesbian community and in the mainstream media. First, Queer Nation, a new activist organization dedicated to the street theater tactics of ACT UP, but with the broader goal of increasing gay and lesbian visibility, launched what was referred to as the "Absolutely Queer" campaign. In this campaign, Queer Nation identified closeted celebrities whom they judged to have done something antagonistic toward other gays and lesbians, and then printed their pictures on posters headlined "Absolutely Queer"—in essence, forcing them out of the closet.

And in a second related tactic, Michelangelo Signorile, editor of the now defunct *OutWeek*, a New York-based gay and lesbian paper, and author of the paper's "Gossip Watch" column, introduced the practice of identifying closeted public figures, deemed by Signorile to have done something antagonistic toward gay men and lesbians.

Signorile's targets included politicians, publishers, producers, and even fellow gossip columnists. Signorile called the practice "equalizing" and explained it by saying that the news media's refusal to identify a public figure's homosexuality implied shame. Publishing it, he argued, thereby equalized homosexuality with heterosexuality. *Time* magazine later coined the term "outing" to describe the practice of forcing someone out of the closet against their will.

The Signorile Theory of Outing: In 1993, Signorile defended outing in *Queer in America: Sex, the Media, and the Closets of Power*, a book that would become a national bestseller. He wrote:

> There exists in America what appears to be a brilliantly orchestrated, massive conspiracy to keep all homosexuals locked in the closet.... [T]he conspiracy is a relatively unconscious one, ingrained as it is in our culture.... [It] is carried out by three power structures (the media in New York, the political system in Washington, DC, and the entertainment industry, in Hollywood).... In all three power structures, closeted lesbians and gay men themselves are among the most influential people at the very top helping to orchestrate the closet conspiracy.

As an example, Signorile cited the instance of closeted gay and lesbian actors who hired publicists to concoct stories of heterosexual romances and sell them to closeted gossip columnists, who published the stories, even though they knew the stories to be false. Meanwhile, he argued, some of these closeted columnists wrote positively about people who expressed anti-gay attitudes, such as Andrew Dice Clay and William Buckley.

In the case of private individuals who closeted their homosexuality, Signorile agreed, it would be a violation of their privacy to force them to do otherwise. But he saw public figures—who not only chose to stay in the closet, but hypocritically to promote anti-gay causes—as fair game. So did a number of other Queer Nation activists.

In this spirit, Signorile and others outed fellow gossip columnist Liz Smith, Wisconsin Representative Steve Gunderson, and Senator Mark Hatfield, who denied he was gay but changed his voting record on gay issues. Signorile also outed the late multimillionaire publisher Malcolm Forbes shortly after his death in 1990, saying he harassed and coerced male employees into having sex.

Signorile also outed multimillionaire record producer and president of Reprise Records David Geffen, on the grounds that he was hurting gay men and lesbians while benefiting from his production of the band Guns N'Roses, known, among other things, for its anti-gay lyrics. Following his outing, Geffen dropped Guns N'Roses; in 1981, he came out as bisexual in an interview in *Vanity Fair*; and in 1992, he came out as gay.

Geffen has since become a generous supporter of AIDS organizations and other gay and lesbian issues. Through the David Geffen Foundation, he is estimated to have spent an estimated $35 million on these and other civil liberties issues, according to *The Advocate*.

In the fall of 1991, Signorile turned his attention to another target, Assistant Secretary of Defense Pete Williams. Williams was a closeted man who had been the military's spokesman during the Gulf War. Signorile judged this hypocrisy, given the military's ban against gays openly serving in the military, and outed Williams. Subsequently, Secretary of Defense Dick Cheney was asked about his position on the ban against gays in the military. While Cheney didn't speak against the ban, he failed to defend it, a move Signorile credits as another outing victory.

The Impact of Outing: While the advent of outing clearly brought more people out of the closet—some because they were dragged out, some because they were afraid of being dragged out—gay and lesbian organizations and the news media have continued to assess outing in mixed terms.

As anyone who has gone through the process of coming out knows, one must be ready to come out to oneself before one can be ready to come out to anyone else. The alternative is both terrifying and psychologically damaging. Forcing people—even public figures or celebrities—to come out, therefore, seems a violation of privacy, or decency, in the eyes of many people.

And yet what about when those public figures or celebrities use their privileged positions in ways that are harmful to other gay men and lesbians—especially if only to squelch any questions about their own sexual orientation? Here, a number of people would agree with Signorile that outing is justified.

In the years since outing rose to the public's attention, primarily between 1989 and 1991, it has declined. But its legacy continues in a number of regards. First, closeted gay men and lesbians know that what in the 1980s was called "the privilege of the closet"—that is, if you don't speak openly of your homosexuality, no one else will either—is no longer a guarantee. There is now an unspoken and sometimes spoken rule that closeted gay men and lesbians who vote or act against gay and lesbian interests may be outed, as even Rep. Barney Frank has threatened to do to some of his colleagues. Second, as the outing of notable gay and lesbian public figures contributed to the increase in gay and lesbian visibility in the 1990s, it may have added to the traditional snowballing theory of coming out, by inspiring others to do so voluntarily. But to what extent will likely never be known.

Coming Out in the Military

When Bill Clinton, the nation's first baby-boomer presidential candidate, campaigned for office in 1991, he visited the John F. Kennedy School of Government at Harvard University, where a student asked him about his position on gays and lesbians serving in the military. Clinton said he supported their right to serve and that, if elected president, he would lift the military's ban against homosexuality, issued 50 years before.

The military ban, of course, never actually prevented gay men and lesbians from serving: as Allan Berube noted, more than a million had served during World War II alone. But the ban did effectively force gay men and lesbians to stay in the closet. It also gave the military the right to discharge those who dared come out. What candidate Clinton promised, therefore, was to guarantee the right of military personnel to state openly that they were gay or lesbian.

But, as the events of 1993 made all too clear, Clinton greatly underestimated the power of the opposition to gay men and lesbians in the military, especially from Christian fundamentalists and two key figures in Washington, D.C., General Colin Powell, the head of the Joint Chiefs of Staff, and Senator Sam Nunn (D-Georgia) chairman of the Senate Armed Services Committee. All immediately mobilized against any change to the ban with such force that it took not only Clinton but gay and lesbian organizations by surprise.

Indeed, the controversy over whether gay men and lesbians should be allowed to come out in the military dominated the news during the first ten days of Clinton's presidency, although the issue repeatedly was erroneously presented as a debate about whether gays and lesbians should be allowed to serve in the military.

Like family members who respond to a child's coming out by saying, "It's OK if you're gay, but let's not talk about," most opponents of lifting the ban against gays in the military refused to talk about the issue as one that rested on the act of coming out. And yet it would be misleading to overlook the fact that the controversy got America talking about gays and lesbians in a way they never had before: as subjects of a public policy issue, and, at least in some circles, as strong, capable people who defended the country.

Clinton, informed that Congress would overturn any executive order to lift the ban and wishing to avoid failing in his first official move, backpedaled. He announced that he would leave it up to the Pentagon to devise its own method of ending the ban within six months. This was a move that left little promise of change, since the Pentagon was adamantly opposed to lifting the ban. But there was at least a slight political pressure to make it appear as if the department were working toward a compromise.

Into this open space came Sen. Sam Nunn, who, as journalist Neil Miller observed, had just been snubbed by Clinton when the President overlooked Nunn for the position of Secretary of Defense. Nunn introduced the new "Don't Ask, Don't Tell" policy, proposing that the military would no longer ask prospective soldiers if they ever had homosexual feelings or experiences, and

would refrain from witch-hunts meant to uncover and discharge gay and lesbian service people.

But the "Don't Ask, Don't Tell" proposal also required gays and lesbians in the military to closet their sexual orientation and remain celibate. If they did not do so, but either directly came out or were witnessed acting out homosexual feelings or acts, they could be discharged. This would apply equally to military personnel who came out in the news media, and to those who came out simply to a friend.

The proposed policy would permit the military to uphold discharge orders against people who recently had come out during the public debate over the issue, and those who had come out before, out of their own conviction that it was in the service of a just cause.

Among those who had recently come out, for example, were Navy Petty Officer Keith Meinhold, who appeared on *World News Tonight with Peter Jennings*; Tracy Thorne, a guest on *Nightline* with Ted Koppel; and Colonel Margarethe Cammermeyer, chief nurse of the Washington State National Guard, who came out to her superior officers when being considered for the position of chief nurse of the National Guard of the United States. After being discharged, Cammermeyer also came out in a book and as the subject of a TV movie.

The proposed "Don't Ask, Don't Tell" executive order was anything but a guarantee that gay men and lesbians could come out in the military. But Nunn was still not satisfied and proposed that it be stated in an amendment to the defense authorization bill, where he added the alleged justification for the policy by stating that gay men and lesbians represented an "unacceptable risk" to national security.

Then, in one of the longest journeys traveled in the shortest periods of time, Clinton signed the amendment, codifying both the "Don't Ask, Don't Tell" policy and the official statement that gays and lesbians represented an "unacceptable risk" into law. It was a bitter shock for gay men and lesbians, as what began as a presidential candidate's promise to permit them to come out resulted in an official policy that prohibited them from doing so.

Today, the policy—justified on the basis of prejudice, not facts—remains a battleground, as individual gay men and lesbians continue to come out, be discharged, and challenge the policy in the courts.

Coming Out in the Media

In late 1990, Jeffrey Schmalz, deputy national editor of *The New York Times,* collapsed in the newsroom and went into a grand mal seizure. A month later, he learned that he had developed full-blown AIDS, according to Edward Alwood, author of *Straight News: Gays, Lesbians, and the News Media.* While Schmalz had not previously been out at work and had never written as an openly gay man, things changed after this incident. As he said in a 1992 interview with Alwood, "AIDS just sort of blew everything open."

Seeing a known and respected colleague become stricken with AIDS made people in the *Times* newsroom aware of the issue as never before, and when Schmalz returned to work, he was assigned a new beat: covering gays, lesbians, and AIDS. Writing as a newly out gay man who was HIV positive, he reported in a ground-breaking article in 1992, "Two years ago tomorrow, I collapsed at my desk in the newsroom of the *New York Times,* writhed on the floor in a seizure and entered the world of AIDS."

Schmalz died less than a year later, but his impact did not. David Dunlop, another openly gay reporter, took over Schmalz's beat until it was gradually disbanded. But perhaps more important, Schmalz introduced *New York Times* readers to the face of an out gay man dying of AIDS, and that impact could not be forgotten. Having come out at one of the most prestigious papers in the world, Schmalz is also thought to have inspired other reporters to do the same.

Among those who came out in the 1990s were Paul Wynne of KGO-TV in San Francisco, where he broadcast his final segment from a hospital bed in 1990; Robert O'Boyle, who wrote a column entitled "Living with AIDS" in *The Seattle Times* and *Walla Walla Union-Bulletin* from 1990 to 1991; and Juan Palomo, a *Houston Post* columnist who came out in a 1991 column addressing a local gay-bashing murder only to have his editors delete the revelation. Palomo later spoke to an alternative weekly about the incident and was fired. But other media professionals condemned the move, and Palomo was rehired within a week, able to write as an openly gay man.

Other important media figures who made a point of coming out to their colleagues in the 1990s included: Leroy Aarons, vice president of news at the *Oakland Tribune*, who came out before the American Society of Newspaper Editors (ASNE) while revealing results of an ASNE survey of gay and lesbian journalists in 1990; and Helen Zia, former executive editor of *Ms.* magazine, who came out on a live broadcast of C-SPAN during a keynote address to the Asian-American Journalists Association's 1990 national convention.

Others who came out to readers and colleagues on a national level included: Linda Villarosa, who came out in a 1991 *Essence* magazine article entitled "Coming Out," which appeared in the form of a dialogue with her mother (Villarosa, an editor of the magazine, was later promoted to executive editor); Andrew Sullivan, an openly gay man who was named editor of *The New Republic* in 1991, and who went on to write frequently about gay and lesbian issues; and Deb Price, who in 1992 became the first syndicated weekly columnist on lesbian and gay issues in *The Detroit News*, a Gannett-owned newspaper. Price's column was later syndicated in many of the other 83 Gannett papers and the company's national newspaper, *USA Today*.

Finally, in 1994, Steve Gendel, a CNBC reporter, became the first national TV correspondent to come out during a network news story, which aired during *The Today Show*'s coverage of the twenty-fifth anniversary of the Stonewall Riots.

Coming (Further) Out as Parents

Since 1969, gay men and lesbians in every walk of life have balanced the desire to come out with the risks of doing so. But as the number of gay men and lesbians who came out as parents in the 1990s rose, they discovered that the act of parenting removed much of the choice about coming out. When a lesbian has a baby, after all, it's highly unlikely for her to walk through life without being asked, Does your baby look like you or your husband? It's equally unlikely for a gay man not to be asked, Where's your baby's mommy?

Even in the most casual interactions—on the street, in the playground, or at the supermarket—lesbian and gay parents throughout the 1990s routinely faced the question of coming out as a gay or lesbian parent. But it is far from only casual encounters that put them in this position. When gay and lesbian parents take their children to the pediatrician's office, to daycare, or to the emergency room, they routinely are faced with a situation in which they must decide whether to come out.

At the doctor's office, for example, a parent must fill out forms that ask for the name of the mother and father. Should a lesbian mom cross out father, write partner, and fill in a woman's name? In the event of an emergency, such a decision would probably be best for the safety of the child. Consequently, many lesbian moms decide to come out to their doctors, where they previously may never have dreamt of it. Similar situations tend to arise when one enrolls a child in daycare, where the child's co-parent is also best identified in the event of an emergency. Here, again, a lesbian mom might find herself coming out to people she never would have before.

Once a child enters school, the occasions for coming out only increase. If there are two parents, schools want to know the names of both. In parent-teacher conferences, teachers routinely ask lesbian moms about their child's father, and ask gay dads about their child's mother. Answering questions such as these demands a decision about whether to come out. Similarly, attending a child's spelling bee, hockey game, or first school play, or even meeting a child at the school bus, puts one in the company of other parents, who commonly make small-talk by asking questions about one's husband or wife.

Some people try to calculate the open-mindedness of the person they are talking to—whether it is a teacher or another parent—and let that sway how they handle such questions. But with the growth of gay and lesbian parenting, there has been an increasing tendency for parents to come out whenever the occasion arises—not only for their own psychological health, but for their children's. As April Martin, a psychologist and lesbian mother of two, wrote in *The Lesbian and Gay Parenting Handbook,* "Denying or omitting who we are may feel demeaning, and we may worry about the messages it sends our children."

Put another way, children learn from watching their parents: if parents lie about or hide who they are, it teaches the child to feel ashamed of who she/he is. If parents come out, without shame, children learn to feel pride and confidence in themselves, as well.

But, of course, the right decision does not necessarily make coming out as a parent the easiest decision. "On the one hand, there is stress involved in coming out all the time, especially to people who are strangers or only casual acquaintances," Martin writes.

Coming out also can be demanding in that gay and lesbian parenting continues to be unfamiliar to most people and leaves them with numerous questions. Parents who are seeking more understanding of their families, therefore, often end up spending a lot of time explaining things after they come out.

Among the common questions gay and lesbian parents face when they come out are: How did you get the baby? How does donor insemination work? Did you meet the father? What do you know about him? What will you tell your child about her father? What does your child call you, since you are both mommies (or daddies)?

There also are gender-specific questions, such as the one often targeted to gay dads: How will you teach your girl to wear make-up, dresses—in short, to act like a girl? And to lesbian moms comes the question: How will you teach your boy to play ball, shave—in short, not act like a girl? Coming out, in other words, requires that gay and lesbian parents work their way through questions about sexual orientation that are laced with traditional gender assumptions.

And these are the dialogues that arise in the best of situations. In less favorable circumstances, gay and lesbian parents who come out have encountered negative reactions that range anywhere from avoidance to antagonism. Indeed, coming out as gay and lesbian parents ironically represents both one of the most traditional of behaviors—the raising of children—and, in the eyes of many, one of the most radical developments of the past 15 years.

Experience shows that parents tend to develop very definite and passionate ideas about how children should be parented, as if becoming a parent to one child makes one feel like a surrogate parent of all children. Emotions often fly and reason fails.

It is perhaps for this reason that even some of the most liberal and gay-friendly Americans are opposed to the coming out of gay and lesbian parents, at least initially. More specifically, bringing children into the picture elicits strong emotions—what Spinoza called "love-prejudice"—which, in turn, leads to the unearthing of its opposite: "hate-prejudice."

The Challenge to Child Development Theories: Perhaps one of the most widespread consequences of the coming out of gay and lesbian parents is that it has challenged both common and academic schools of psychology that presume normal and healthy child development depends upon the presence of a mother and a father.

Indeed, numerous studies of the children of gay and lesbian parents published since the 1980s have unanimously reported that healthy child development does not require the presence of a mother and a father. More specifically, these studies have shown that children raised by lesbian and gay parents are no more likely to grow up with developmental difficulties than children raised by heterosexual parents. There is no greater incidence of problems in personality development, moral judgment, intelligence, social relationships, gender roles, sexuality, or any other key determinant of child development.

Indeed, some experts argue that children fare better with two lesbian parents than with a mother and father because women frequently tend to try harder to learn good parenting skills; to share household responsibilities more equally; and, therefore, to be happier than a man and woman in a traditional family structure.

The Vulnerability of Coming Out as Parents: Studies, however, are one thing; prejudices are another. And it takes time for studies to penetrate some people's prejudices. As a result, a number of people who have come out as gay and lesbian parents have faced legal battles challenging their custody of their children.

While laws and court precedents vary from state to state, those who have been most vulnerable to custody challenges have been those who have a child who was conceived through a prior heterosexual relationship, or a known sperm donor. Some gay dads and lesbian moms who have adopted a child also have been vulnerable to challenges from biological parents who put their child up for adoption, only to fight for the child back once they discovered he or she was adopted by a gay or lesbian couple.

While results have varied, a number of courts have ruled in favor of a heterosexual suing for custody, in effect ignoring the body of evidence that demonstrates that children can be successfully raised in a gay- or lesbian-headed household, and enforcing the prejudice against the coming out of gay and lesbian parents.

In one of the most highly publicized cases, for example, Sharon Bottoms, a lesbian mother from Virginia, lost custody of her three-year-old son in a challenge from her mother, whom Bottoms claimed allowed her to be raped by a male acquaintance when she was a child. Writing in 1995, a Virginia state supreme court judge

ruled that, as a lesbian, Bottoms was an unfit mother for her son, because her lesbianism might make other people might react prejudicially toward him.

The judge wrote, "We have previously said that living daily under conditions stemming from active lesbianism practiced in the home may impose a burden upon the child by reason of the 'social condemnation' attached to such an arrangement, which will inevitably affect the child's relationship with its [his] peers and with the community."

Yet negative rulings by courts have not stopped the progression of gay and lesbian parents from coming out. In 1993, for example, *The New York Times* published a front-page article headlined, "Gay Parents Become Increasingly Visible." The article went on to describe the breadth of the coming-out trend by noting, "Gay families are going public not only in relatively liberal cities with large gay populations, like New York and San Francisco, but also in Ypsilanti Township, Mich., Salina, Kan., and Tacoma, Wash."

Three years later, *Newsweek* published a front-page story featuring singer Melissa Etheridge and her partner, filmmaker Julie Cypher, headlined, "We're Having a Baby."

Gay men and lesbians also continue to be encouraged to come out as parents through the support of organizations such as Gay and Lesbian Parents Coalition International, which is reported to have some 70 chapters and 1,400 members.

Coming Out in Politics

In the 1990s, gay men and lesbians arrived on the political scene. There were 108 openly gay and lesbian delegates, alternates and party officials at the Democratic National Convention in 1992, according to Neil Miller. An out lesbian public official, San Francisco Supervisor Roberta Achtenberg, spoke at the televised convention, as did Boy Hattoy, an openly gay man with AIDS. For the first time, the gay vote was courted by a presidential candidate, as Bill Clinton promised to end the ban against gays and lesbians in the military and to appoint an AIDS Czar. During his acceptance speech, Clinton became the first elected president to promise to appoint gays and lesbians to his administration. And after he was sworn in, the first-ever Gay and Lesbian Inaugural Ball was held in Washington.

Why the new change in attitude toward gays and lesbians among the political elite? Clinton's national finance campaign director Rahm Emanuel explained it this way during an interview with *The New York Times*: "The gay community is the new Jewish community. It's highly politicized, with fundamental health and civil rights concerns. And it contributes money. All that makes for a potent political force, indeed."

Indeed, the Human Rights Campaign Fund—which used campaign contributions to urge politicians to support gay and lesbian rights—became one of the ten largest political action committees in the country. Meanwhile, the Gay and Lesbian Victory Fund was continuing to train candidates nationwide in how to run a successful campaign as an out candidate.

Coming Out in the Clinton Administration: Clinton's election was celebrated as something of a coming out party, as some 1,700 gay men and lesbians gathered for the first ever Gay and Lesbian Inaugural Ball, held at the National Press Club in Washington. Singer k.d. lang stood before the crowd and said, "The best thing I ever did in my life was come out."

The gay-friendly president, however, would soon disappoint gay men and lesbians as he retreated into a compromise with a hostile Senate over the gays-in-the-military ban and accepted the "Don't Ask, Don't Tell" compromise. But he did succeed in appointing an unprecedented number of out gay men and lesbians to his administration.

In 1993, Clinton nominated Roberta Achtenberg, out lesbian and San Francisco Supervisor, to the post of Assistant Secretary for Fair Housing and Equal Opportunity at the U.S. Department of Housing and Urban Development. This presented the Senate confirmation committee with its first opportunity to vote on an out gay or lesbian official.

The Achtenberg hearing became, naturally enough, a flash point for debate on the role of out gay men and lesbians serving in the administration, as Sen. Jesse Helms and others on the committee spent three days discussing Achtenberg's lesbianism and relationship with Mary Morgan, a San Francisco Municipal Court justice.

But there were some added coming-out surprises during the committee hearings, as when Sen. Claiborne Pell (D-Rhode Island) announced that his daughter was lesbian, and he didn't want to see her barred from holding a government job because of it. It is thought to be the first time a senator publicly announced that a member of his family was gay or lesbian, as Neil Miller reports in *Out of the Past.*

It also was the first time the congressional committee approved the nomination of an out lesbian, voting 58-31 in favor of Achtenberg's appointment.

Clinton would go on to appoint some 25 more out lesbians and gay men to his administration within the next two years in a broad spectrum of offices, including the departments of Commerce, Defense, Energy, Education, Health and Human Services, Housing and Urban Development, Interior, Justice, and Labor.

Then, in 1997, another out lesbian became the highest ranking openly gay or lesbian American to serve in the federal government, as Virginia Apuzzo was named assistant to the president for management and administration. A longtime gay and lesbian activist, Apuzzo previously served as executive director of the National Gay and Lesbian Task Force, president of the New York State Civil Service, and deputy secretary of labor for the U.S. Department of Labor.

1993 March on Washington: In April 1993, hundreds of thousands—some reports say a million—gay men and lesbians came out to march on Washington for the third time. What was different in this case, however, was that the marchers came out not only in Washington but through extensive media coverage.

Unlike in 1979 and 1987, CNN provided live coverage of all six hours of the march and rally. ABC and NBC broadcast their morning shows live from Washington. And almost every major daily newspaper in the country ran headlines about the march the following day, according to the editors of *Out in All Directions.*

This televised coming out was presented in generally favorable terms by most news organizations, and several prominent journalists noted the change in the mood and style of this march, in contrast to earlier marches and demonstrations. Writing in *The Washington Post,* for example, columnist E. J. Dionne, Jr. praised the 1993 march as a "serious and sober celebration of liberty."

Celebrities Begin to Come Out

In the 1990s, celebrities—lesbian singers and actresses, in particular—began to lead the way out of a closet long maintained through fear that the revelation of gay or lesbian sexual orientation would ruin one's career.

Singer k.d. lang was one of the first to come out, doing so in 1992. Singer Melissa Etheridge followed by coming out at the Gay and Lesbian Inaugural Ball in January 1993. Actress Amanda Bearse of the TV series *Married ... With Children* also came out in 1993, after having been outed by *The Globe* tabloid two years before. Singer Janis Ian came out in 1993; the Indigo Girls came out in 1994; and rapper, singer, songwriter Me'Shell Ndegeocello came out as bisexual in 1993 and as lesbian in 1996.

But the most prominent coming out of the 1990s—arguably in any field—was by actress and comedian Ellen DeGeneres, who came out in 1997. After much speculation, it was announced in the spring of that year that the character she plays on the ABC-TV show, *Ellen,* would come out as a lesbian—making her the first openly gay or lesbian lead character on television.

DeGeneres also chose the week that the show would air to come out herself, on the cover of *Time* magazine. The cover line said simply, "Yep, I'm gay." Her humor and girl-next-door appeal attracted enormous attention, as did the special one-hour show, which drew an estimated 42 million viewers and earned DeGeneres an Emmy award.

Meanwhile, despite the significant number of gay men in Hollywood, only a handful came out during the 1990s: Dan Butler, of the NBC sitcom *Frasier;* Mitchell Anderson, of the Fox series, *Party of Five;* and Wilson Cruz, of the highly acclaimed ABC series *My So-Called Life.*

Cruz, a first-generation Puerto Rican, came out publicly at the age of 19 when he agreed to play the part of Rickie Vasquez, a Latino gay high school student on the show, becoming one of the first actors at the beginning of his career to take the chance of doing so.

His reason: "When I was a kid, I always wanted to see someone who was living my life on TV," Cruz said during a 1987 interview, "and I felt that the character and people involved in the show were doing such an incredible job being honest and true to the experience that to have an actor who in his life was denying his truth and reality felt hypocritical to me. And I didn't see any reason why I shouldn't be honest about who and what I am."

The show was later canceled, but Cruz went on to appear in Oliver Stone's *Nixon,* an NBC movie, *On Seventh Avenue,* and a California production of the musical *Rent.*

Coming Out in Sports

The world of sports continued to be one of the most closeted environments for gay men and lesbians in the 1990s, with a few notable exceptions. Martina Navratilova, the world-champion tennis player, who first came out publicly in 1981, came out as a gay and lesbian activist in 1993. Navratilova's first step was to lend her name to a fund-raising event called "A Gay and Lesbian Tribute to Martina." The event raised $250,000 to benefit the Gay Games IV. She later joined an American Civil Liberties Union lawsuit to overturn a Colorado law banning the enactment of gay and lesbian rights ordinances, as Neil Miller reports in *Out of the Past.* She was a speaker at the 1993 March on Washington. And, in 1997, she began speaking up on behalf of gay and lesbian teens.

Greg Louganis, four-time Olympic diving champion, later joined Navratilova by coming out during the Gay Games IV, where he declared during a videotaped welcome, "It's great to be out and proud." And, in 1995, Louganis came out about being HIV-positive during a *20/20* interview with Barbara Walters. Louganis won four Olympic gold medals at the 1984 and 1988 Olympics for platform and springboard diving. He also won a silver medal in 10-meter platform diving in the 1976 Olympics, when he was sixteen.

In 1996, professional golfer Muffin Spencer Devlin came out during a *Sports Illustrated* interview, making her the first member of the Ladies Professional Golf Association to do so.

Meanwhile, thousands more came out during the Gay Games events held in 1990 and 1994. In 1990, 7,000 gay and lesbian athletes came out for Gay Games III in Vancouver, British Columbia, followed by a record 15,000 athletes who came out for Gay Games IV, held in New York in 1994.

Gay Games IV, which coincided with the twenty-fifth anniversary of the Stonewall Riots, also attracted 500,000 spectators and were said to have brought $100 million to New York City.

Coming Out in School

In 1990, a small group of gay, lesbian, and straight teachers in Boston banded together to fight anti-gay discrimination in school. Among their activities was lobbying on behalf of a state bill to outlaw discrimination against gay and lesbian students. The bill was introduced in 1991 and again in 1992 but never came up for a vote. Then, in 1993, things began to change.

Some 1,000 gay, lesbian, and straight high school students from Massachusetts took to the state capitol to lobby and demonstrate on behalf of the bill. Many also testified in statewide hearings organized by the newly formed Governor's Commission on Gay and Lesbian Youth. The students received widespread media coverage, and, in 1993, Massachusetts became the first state to pass a bill outlawing discrimination against students in public schools on the basis of sexual orientation.

Meanwhile, GSAs, or Gay/Straight Alliances, began to be formed in Massachusetts and other states by gay, lesbian, and straight students who wanted a safe place to discuss sexual orientation. Students were not required to come out to participate in GSAs, but many did, first to each other and then, often, to other students and their teachers as they organized gay and lesbian awareness events.

As gay and lesbian youth came out in the 1990s, they lent a new tone to the process, as well, as many refuted the rigid labeling of themselves as gay or lesbian and insisted upon referring to themselves as being open to loving people of any gender. In some circles, coming out also become trendy in the mid-1990s, as some straight students joined GSAs simply because they were thought of as the places where hip people hung out.

But in countless other places, young people who were courageous enough to come out while in high school faced far more serious consequences. In Wisconsin, for example, Jamie Nabozny, who'd come out to his family when he was eleven, started being harassed at school a few years later. He'd never actually come out publicly, but he never denied it either. Harassment and physical attacks escalated until he was forced to drop out of school.

Then, supported by Lambda Legal Defense Fund, Nabozny filed a lawsuit against his school district for its failure to protect him, and in 1996 he was awarded nearly a million dollars in a precedent-setting case that many believe will help other gay and lesbian youth come out safely in school. The publicity surrounding this case also propelled Nabozny into a position as a gay youth spokesperson. In the fall of 1997, he was featured in an MTV special about new youth leaders.

Coming Out in the Workplace

While there remains a long way to go, some tough workplace barriers were leapt in the nineties as people began to come out in large conservative corporations, consulting firms, and investment banks, according to Annette Friskopp and Sharon Silverstein, authors of *Straight Jobs, Gay Lives*, which studies the coming-out experiences of Harvard Business School Graduates.

"Rather than hiding their sexual orientation at work, we learned from our survey, most gay professionals come out at work at least selectively," write Friskopp and Silverstein. "Of those who do not work for themselves, 40 percent are out to a boss, more than half are out to one or more subordinates, and three fourths have come out to at least one coworker in their present job," they added.

But, it should be emphasized, while the Friskopp and Silverstein survey focused on Harvard Business School graduates, coming out in the workplace at-large is far from a universal phenomenon. For example, a 1992 survey of 1,400 gay men and lesbians in Philadelphia found that 76 percent of the men and 81 percent of the women concealed their orientation at work.

Among the reasons why more gay and lesbian professionals came out at the workplace during the nineties were the passage of state and city laws and company policies prohibiting discrimination based on sexual orientation and the publication of public opinion polls that revealed that a majority of Americans believe gay men and lesbians should not be discriminated against in the workplace.

On the other hand, these developments are not reason enough to make everyone feel confident coming out at work, and so many remain closeted for fear of losing their jobs or not being promoted. It is hoped, however, that the proposed federal Employment Non-Discrimination Act, which would prohibit employment discrimination on the basis of sexual orientation, will change that.

REFERENCES:

Books

Alwood, Edward. *Straight News: Gays, Lesbians, and the News Media.* New York: Columbia University Press, 1996.

Benkov, Laura. *Reinventing the Family: The Emerging Story of Lesbian and Gay Parents.* New York: Crown Publishers, 1994.

Bullough, Vern, L. *Homosexuality: A History.* New York: New American Library, 1979.

Duberman, Martin. *Stonewall.* New York: Penguin Books USA Inc., 1993.

Duberman, Martin, Martha Vicinus, and George Chauncey, Jr., eds. *Hidden from History: Reclaiming The Gay and Lesbian Past.* New York: Penguin Books, 1989.

Faderman, Lillian. *Surpassing the Love of Men: Romantic Friendship and Love between Women from the Renaissance to the Present.* New York: William Morrow and Company, Inc., 1981.

Foucault, Michel. *The History of Sexuality: An Introduction, Volume I.* New York: Vintage Books, 1990.

Friskopp, Annette, and Sharon Silverstein. *Straight Jobs, Gay Lives: Gay and Lesbian Professionals, the Harvard Business School, and the American Workplace.* New York: Scribner, 1995.

Greenberg, David F. *The Construction of Homosexuality.* Chicago, Illinois: The University of Chicago Press, 1990.

Herdt, Gilbert, and Andrew Boxer. *Children of Horizons: How Gay and Lesbian Teens are Leading a New Way Out of the Closet.* Boston, Massachusetts: Beacon Press, 1993.

Jennings, Kevin, ed. *One Teacher in Ten: Gay and Lesbian Educators Tell Their Stories.* Boston, Massachusetts: Alyson Publications, Inc., 1994.

Katz, Jonathan Ned. *Gay American History: Lesbians and Gay Men in the U.S.A.* New York: Penguin Books USA Inc., 1992.

————. *The Invention of Heterosexuality.* New York: Penguin Books USA Inc., 1995.

Laird, Joan, and Robert-Jay Green, eds. *Lesbians and Gays in Couples and Families: A Handbook for Therapists.* San Francisco, California: Jossey-Bass Inc., 1996.

Lee, Hermione. *Virginia Woolf.* New York: Alfred A. Knopf, 1997.

Marcus, Eric. *Making History: The Struggle for Gay and Lesbian Equal Rights.* New York: HarperCollins Publishers, Inc., 1992.

Martin, April. *The Lesbian and Gay Parenting Handbook: Creating and Raising Our Families.* New York: HarperCollins Publishers, Inc., 1993.

Miller, Neil. *Out of the Past: Gay and Lesbian History from 1869 to the Present.* New York: Vintage Books, 1995.

The National Museum & Archive of Lesbian and Gay History. *The Lesbian Almanac: The Most Comprehensive Reference Source of Its Kind.* New York: The Berkley Publishing Group, 1996.

Russo, Vito. *The Celluloid Closet: Homosexuality in the Movies.* New York: Harper & Row, Publishers, Inc., 1981.

Sherman, Suzanne, ed. *Lesbian and Gay Marriage: Private Commitments, Public Ceremonies.* Philadelphia, Pennsylvania: Temple University Press, 1992.

Shilts, Randy. *And the Band Played On: Politics, People, and the AIDS Epidemic.* New York: Penguin Books, 1988.

Signorile, Michelangelo. *Queer in America: Sex, the Media, and the Closets of Power.* New York: Anchor Books, 1993.

Witt, Lynn, Sherry Thomas, and Eric Marcus, eds. *Out in All Directions: The Almanac of Gay and Lesbian America.* New York: Warner Books, Inc., 1995.

Periodicals

Jones, James H. "Dr. Yes," in *The New Yorker,* 25 August and 1 September 1997.

Gallagher, John. "The Amazing Invisible Men of Show Business," in *The Advocate,* 13 May 1997.

Moss, J. Jennings. "The Players," in *The Advocate,* 20 August 1996.

Other

1987 interview with Rep. Barney Frank, by Lisa Bennett.
1987 interview with Wilson Cruz, by Lisa Bennett.

—Lisa Bennett

5

Family

It is an almost unchallenged assumption in America today that families are important. The family into which we are born is important and demands our loyalty. It is also assumed that it is the responsibility of almost all adults to either create a family or participate in family life. We are taught to be wary and distrustful of those who reject the family.

Every person who is gay, lesbian, bisexual, or transgender is a member of at least one family, the family into which she/he was born. And while it is not often recognized, most of those individuals also form a diversity of families during their adult lives, much in the way that heterosexual adults form a diversity of families. But because of the prejudice and discrimination this society directs toward people who do not identify as heterosexual, these families are often hidden from public view. This chapter will attempt to cast some light on these families and help the reader to understand the range and depth of the diversity of them.

A word about terminology is appropriate at this point. This chapter is about the families that people who identify as gay, lesbian, bisexual, or transgender are born into or create. That is quite a list and it would be cumbersome to repeat each time it was necessary to identify all who are included. To simplify, I will use several short cuts. At times I might use the term "gay families" or "gay and lesbian families" to denote these families. I wish to make it clear that I am not leaving out people who are bisexual or transgender.

There is a term, though, that is inclusive, though somewhat controversial. The term is "queer." "Queer" was used for many years as a derogatory epithet for people who are homosexual. In recent years the term has been reclaimed by many in this community to be a term that signifies pride in how people who are gay, lesbian, bisexual, or transgender are different from heterosexuals. Therefore, I will also use the term "queer families" to broadly identify the families created by people who are gay, lesbian, bisexual, or transgender.

It is also important to note that families that are identified here as queer families could also contain many people who are not gay,

lesbian, bisexual, or transgender. A lesbian and her heterosexual children will here be called a queer family, though there may also be a heterosexual father in this family. Perhaps at times a better term might be a "mixed heterosexual/homosexual family," but again, that's cumbersome. While the term "queer family" will at times identify families where all the members are queer and at other times families in which some of the members are queer, it will refer generally to families that are headed by one or more queer individuals.

WHAT IS A QUEER FAMILY?

Family does not mean the same thing to all people. The term "family" is not based on any enduring facts or objective truths but rather on what people believe a family to be. In different countries, and at different times in history, family has meant something different to different people.

A narrow definition of family might be two people who are legally married, or parents and their children, or all the descendants of a common ancestor. A wider definition of family might include a man and woman, living as a couple, whether or not they are legally married. A still wider understanding of family is the extended family. Extended families combine people who are descended from common ancestors, together with people who marry into that family (legally or in common law arrangements) along with other individuals who, because of the longevity or importance of their relationship, are considered to be part of the family, even though they are not related by blood or marriage.

Anthropologists had attempted for many years to distinguish between "kin" and "fictive kin." Kin were members of the clan, related by blood or marriage and thus "real" family. Fictive kin were people who were "make believe" family: people who were considered to be family, but really weren't part of the family. Anthropologists no longer use this distinction as they have come to believe that all family is fictive kin. All the relationships that are considered to be family are created.

The U.S. Census bureau tries every ten years to determine how many people there are in America, but it also collects a vast amount of other information about these people, including number of families. In the 1990 census, queer families were not counted as families. To the Census Bureau, in order to be considered a family it was necessary for the individuals in a household to be related by marriage, birth, or adoption (*Statistical Abstract of the U. S.*, pp. 5-6). While such a distinction includes some queer families, such as those composed of a gay man or lesbian women and their biological or adopted children, it misses many queer families, such as

We Are Family. **Sign at protest held in Sacramento, California on 11 October 1991, following a veto by Governor Pete Wilson of Assembly Bill 101, which would have made it illegal to discriminate against homosexuals in employment and housing.**

same-sex couples. Furthermore, queer families do not always reside in the same household and may not legally marry.

The census, though, has made some progress in counting queer families. In the 1990 census, the government did try to determine how many same-sex couples shared a household. For political reasons, however, the Census Bureau did not attempt to list these households as families.

What then is a queer family? A three-part definition will be used here. First, it is a family headed by one or more people who are either gay, lesbian, bisexual, or transgender. Second, the people who are part of these families, either through their words or actions, are committed to each other for emotional support. And third, they demonstrate love and caring for each other. This definition is a concept of family based on love rather than blood or legal contracts. Beyond this broad definition, there are a wide variety of queer families. "Family" does not mean the same thing to all people who are queer.

The basic and most common form of queer family is the committed couple composed of two adults of the same gender. In a few instances, three or more individuals of the same or different genders might form a menage, and consider themselves to all be married. In addition, there are millions of queer families in which there is a queer parent and her/his children (while recognizing the other parent may not be queer). Very often the two forms of families are combined: there is a queer couple and there are children. The children may be a part of these families because of a variety of circumstances that will be discussed later in this chapter.

Another form of family is perhaps unique to the queer community. Lesbians and gays have created diverse forms of "extended families of choice," composed of numerous individuals, who, while often unrelated by blood, consider themselves to be an extended family. These families often begin as friendship networks but because of time, trust, and commitment, become an extended family.

Queer families differ from non-queer families in primarily two ways, the first being the queer family is headed by one or more people who define themselves as lesbian, gay, transgender, or possibly as bisexual rather than by someone who identifies as heterosexual. The second difference is less obvious but no less important.

For the most part, queer families are unrecognized and unsanctioned. Their existence is often dismissed. The lack of legal and societal recognition and sanctioning has significant repercussions on the structure and functioning of queer families. In many ways, queer families are remarkably similar to the families of heterosexuals. On a day-to-day basis, queer families need to accomplish most of the same tasks that heterosexual families need to accomplish. Queer families must successfully negotiate all the relationships within and between the different members of the family. In addition, they need to successfully negotiate the relationship between the family and all those people in the community outside the family.

Because these families are unsanctioned by mainstream America, and because of the widespread prejudice against lesbians and gays and the discrimination that often results from that prejudice, interactions between the queer family and the greater society can have a host of negative consequences for the family members. And, because these families are often created and exist outside of the mainstream, they take on characteristics that differ from mainstream couples, families, and extended families.

This chapter will examine gay and lesbian families, including the families created by gays and lesbians as well as the families into which gays and lesbians were born. A note of caution: not every queer person will agree with the ideas expressed here regarding family. Indeed, for many in the queer community, "family" is an oppressive heterosexual concept from which they wish to distance themselves. Despite this, most of those same people either form committed couple relationships; create multigenerational households; or have a network of friends with whom they celebrate holidays, call when they are happy or sad, and generally fulfill all the same functions as do families in the heterosexual concept. Only a very few exist in isolation from others. They may object to the term "family," but most inevitably create their own version of a family, regardless of what they call it.

History of the Queer Family

The history of queer families is difficult to ascertain. Because in the past, those individuals whose homosexual behavior came to public light were often punished, most people kept their homosexual behavior and relationships a secret. Thus, until the last 30 years, during which the laws and public attitudes concerning homosexual behavior and queer people have changed, little was recorded regarding queer people and the families they created. Yet, it is not an entirely unknown subject. Recorded accounts of criminal proceedings regarding homosexual behavior, personal diaries and letters, medical notes, and other similar sources give us some insight into the evolution of the queer family.

First and perhaps most important to understand is that the queer family in America exists within the context of American society and is modeled, more than anything else, on the traditional American concept of family. Therefore, to understand today's queer family it is necessary to understand not only the overall history of the family but also how the traditional American family differs historically from the family in other times and places.

Family is a fluid concept. It has changed over time and has meant different things to people in different cultures. For example, families in biblical times were quite different from families today. If we believe that the stories in the Old Testament were representative of life in the Middle East several thousand years ago, extended families of several generations lived together and were headed by a patriarch who ruled and made all crucial decisions. The individual family units within the extended families needed to maintain close ties for the physical protection and economic benefits of the members. Polygamy was known, and if a man's brother died without having children, he was expected to marry the widow and have children with her.

While there did not appear to be a place for queer families in those days, there are stories in the Bible that cause a modern reader to wonder if in fact queer families did exist in some context. A modern reader examining the stories of the love between David and Jonathan, or of Ruth and Naomi, may be struck with the allusions to the non-traditional love between those individuals. This is more striking since love is not the basis of many of the traditional marriages in the Bible; protection, politics, and economics all seem to be more important than emotion. Yet one important fact is missing. We do not know if the relationships between David and Jonathan or Ruth and Naomi were intended to represent sexual or asexual romances. Even if these relationships were asexual, however, it does not necessarily disqualify them from being queer relationships or forming queer families. We know that today some queer families are formed with the understanding that the adult partners do not intend to be sexual with each other. A sexual relationship between the adults is not part of the definition being used here for a queer family.

Same-sex couples appeared to form romantic relationships in other European cultures throughout the ages (Boswell, 1994). From Greek and Roman times through the middle ages and into modern times, same-sex couples had commitment ceremonies that were strikingly similar to heterosexual marriage ceremonies. Again, we do not know how many of these couples had sexual relationships, nor is that information essential. We do know that individuals of the same sex publicly affirmed their commitment, love, friendship, and importance to each other. And, perhaps because they were assumed to be asexual, women in 19th-century America were permitted to write passionate letters to each other, hold hands in public, and use all the terminology associated with modern romantic heterosexual love, without risking social, religious, or legal reprisal. Again, the extent to which these relationships were or were not also at times sexual is unknown. Common sense tells us

that some, but not all, of these relationships included a sexual component.

While families have evolved over time, the model of the traditional American family has been remarkably stable for several centuries. During this time, the traditional American family was quite different from families found in many other parts of the world. The basis of the traditional American family has been the nuclear family, based on a married couple who came together, not because of politics, economics, or protection, but because of romantic love. Americans have for the most part never lived in extended family units. Young people were expected to leave the family into which they were born and create another household, headed by a married couple.

Two factors that helped to form the structure of the traditional American family also aided the formation of the modern queer family. The first factor was the Industrial Revolution, which led to the rise of the great American cities. The second factor was the availability of cheap land in the westward expansion across the continent. Both factors made it economically possible for young married heterosexual couples to move from the family into which they were born and create families of their own that lived in separate households. But both factors also made it possible for a person or couple to have anonymity, either in the rural West or in the great cities of the East. That anonymity enabled queer individuals to form couples and family relationships without embarrassing the family into which they were born, and to live a queer life in a society often hostile to nontraditional relationships. This would have been considerably more difficult in many other cultures of the world in which people were expected to live in multigenerational extended families.

While these factors helped in the structural formation of the queer family, an additional factor aided in the development of the concept of the queer family. It is impossible to have a concept of a queer family without a concept of a queer individual. While people have been engaged in homosexual behavior since before recorded history, it is only recently that we have come to understand that while anyone can engage in homosexual behavior, some people are oriented toward members of their own gender. Until about 100 years ago, there was no concept of homosexuality or heterosexuality (Katz, 1990, p. 7). The development of the concept of sexual orientation meant it was now possible to have a family headed by a queer individual or couple, thus enabling us to understand what we now call a queer family. While there have always been such families, they could not comprehend them as we do today without our modern understanding of the nature of sexual orientation.

Queer families appear to have paralleled traditional American families. Not only is the romantic couple the basis for both, but the structure of the traditional family has been the model for the queer family. In the immediate post-World War II years, the traditional American family had strong emphasis on the American father going off to work and earning a living for the family, while the American mother stayed at home and took care of the house and children. Roles were gender based and heavily defined and proscribed. Not surprisingly, this corresponds to a period in queer families when there appeared to have been the greatest emphasis on role division between the "butch" and the "femme" in queer relationships. Though more prevalent perhaps in lesbian than gay male relationships, these divisions began to disappear in the late 1960s with the rise of the women's and gay movements. At the same time, the traditional American family was undergoing great change and upheaval. Wives were demanding more equality. In both queer and non-queer relationships, there was a movement away from gender-based, with the person in the male role being in charge, to more equality. Looking back over the past several hundred years, the past 30 years have been the time of greatest change for both traditional and queer families.

Concurrent with the social changes in the American family in the late 1960s was an event that had a profound effect on changing queer families. The event was the Stonewall Riots in June 1969. A number of queer transvestites, drawn primarily from various ethnic minorities in New York City, sparked a weekend of riot and protest and began what is now known as the modern gay rights movement. As a result, there was a significant change in the attitudes of many queer people. Whereas before the norm was to keep the lifestyle as hidden from public scrutiny as possible, following the Stonewall Riots queer people began to challenge the societal prohibitions against homosexuality and demand public acceptance. Queer individuals, couples, and the families they were creating were being interviewed on television and in the popular media. Queer people began a political and legal challenge to the laws and bureaucratic rules that discriminated against them. Queers came out of the closet. The result was that it became easier to form a queer family and to be open about it.

Queer families began to insist on equal rights. Queers began to meet openly together to support each other and to discuss the problems they were having, in part, in dealing with creating their families. Until this time, stories of lesbians and gay men were mainly filled with details of how they kept their lives secret from the outside world, and of the inhibiting effect that had on the families they created.

These changes, both in the traditional as well as the queer family, have created a backlash that has sought to stop these changes and return to the model of families most familiar during the immediate post-World War II years. Social conservatives, along with right-wing politicians and conservative Christian, Jewish, and Muslim religious fundamentalists have in recent years been calling homosexuals a threat to the family and a threat to traditional marriage. Though this assertion is often repeated, there is no evidence to support it. In fact, the effect of constantly calling queer people a threat to the family may have inadvertently made queer people more pro family and loyal supporters of the family than if queer people had never been accused of being anti-family in the first place.

It can be reasonably argued that queer families are a valuable hidden resource and are potentially of great help to traditional families. At times, when a traditional family discovers that one of its members is queer, contact with queer families can help the members of the traditional family to deal with something they have been taught to fear. Stable queer families are role models for queer youth, whose only alternatives are the pathological role models of queer people long portrayed in the popular media. Queer families can also be a resource for traditional families when the traditional nuclear family needs additional adults to care for children, as is often the case in our busy and demanding society. Finally, queer families are adopting children who are older and have special needs, a circumstance that is becoming more common. Many of these same children would spend their young lives in the foster care system if not for adoption by queer couples and families. Queer couples are now also becoming foster parents.

While homosexuals are not a threat to the traditional family, homophobia—the irrational fear of homosexuality—is a threat. Ho-

mophobia causes families to reject gay and lesbian members, or those gay and lesbian members to separate from families in order not to cause the family embarrassment or pain. Homophobia leads to violence against queer family members. Homophobia causes depression among lesbian, gay, bisexual, and transgender youth, leading to an unusually high rate of suicide, which profoundly affects all surviving members of the family.

But the efforts seeking to portray queer individuals and families as anti-family continues. One argument given is that when a child comes out to the family as gay, lesbian, bisexual, or transgender, she/he is rejecting not only the blood family but also the entire concept of "the family." However, a connection is made that doesn't exist: there is no connection between being queer and whether a person does or does not support the nature and structure of the family. A major reason for "coming out," for a child telling parents of her/his sexual nature, is to repair a growing distance in the family that happens when this information is kept secret.

The argument is also made that queer people are anti-family in part because they do not have children. While this has never been entirely true, it is becoming even less true now. The same argument is not directed at presumably heterosexual individuals who choose not to reproduce. Priests and nuns are one example. Despite vows of celibacy that prevent them from having children, they are never portrayed as a threat to the family. The spinster (and presumably heterosexual) schoolteacher is not considered to be anti-family. Quite the contrary, these individuals are usually seen as important supporters of the family and who help those who reproduce to deal with the stresses that parenting creates. The same argument can be made for queer people. One does not have to create children to be a supporter of the family or to have an important role in helping families deal with the stresses of modern life.

Another argument made is that queer folks are anti-family because it is said that queer folks recruit children into the queer lifestyle. The implication is that if these children had not been recruited, they would have been heterosexual and eventually produce their own children. While there is increasing evidence that there is a genetic or biological component to sexual orientation, the reality is that we still do not know how it is that an individual becomes attracted to a member of her/his own or the opposite gender. What we do know with a fair degree of certainty is that, whatever the mechanism is, it occurs quite early in the person's life. No child, adolescent, or adult is recruited. Queer people do not go out to schools, parks, and playgrounds looking to recruit unwitting children. The opposite is usually true. Most queer individuals fight those feelings inside of them for a long time before accepting them. At that point, the queer person is the one who usually goes looking for other queer folk. Recruitment is never necessary. In fact, queer people often protect and give a home, family, and community to queer children rejected by the families into which they were born, until the families of origin are able to accept and maybe welcome the queer child back into the family.

GAY AND LESBIAN COUPLES

The most common form of family that queer people create is the same-sex couple. While because of the prejudice directed toward queer people, the exact number of queer couples is impossible to obtain, enough research has been done to know with certainty that there are literally millions of lesbian and gay men living as couples in the United States at any one time.

Queer people become part of a couple for the same reasons as do all other people. All people have an inner need to connect with another person, to love and be loved, to care for and be cared for by that person, to have one's life shared and witnessed, to have a friend, to build a life with someone, to have a stable sexuality and to create a family. The greater economic strength of a couple is also a motivating factor for some, as is the physical protection provided by not being alone.

Despite the large number of queer couples that exist, queer couples, and particularly lesbian couples, have only been seriously studied in recent years. Prior to 20 years ago, the fact that queer people formed healthy, long term, committed couple relationships was unknown to most people. A survey examining psychologists' pre-1977 research projects in which lesbians and gays were the subjects showed that investigators almost totally ignored studying gay and lesbian couples. They seemed unaware that these relationships existed, or that they were important to gays and lesbians (Morin, 1977). This, however, is not surprising, if that time in history is understood. Until 1973, psychiatrists and psychologists considered gays and lesbians to be mentally ill. It would have been difficult for those same mental health professionals to consider gays and lesbians to be mentally ill and to also believe that gays and lesbians formed relationships that were worthy of study.

Most of what we do know of queer couples is thus of recent vintage, from interviews and comparative studies completed primarily in the 1980s and 1990s. Our knowledge of queer couples prior to that time is based primarily on anecdotal records, court documents, medical histories, letters, and the oral histories of gays and lesbians who are alive in the late-20th century and can recall how it was during the early part of the century.

There have now been enough studies to see trends in the research. When looked at as a whole, the following trends appear with consistency (Kurdek, 1995):

1. Gays and lesbians do form relationships. Most gay men and lesbians find themselves in committed relationships at some points in their lives, and these relationships are important to them.

2. Sexual relations are handled differently in gay and lesbian relationships. Lesbians tend to have relationships that are monogamous, and gay men tend to have sexually open relationships.

3. Gay and lesbian relationships are structured differently than heterosexual relationships. Queer relationships tend to be based on models of equality, where the partners share power and are best friends. The traditional heterosexual relationship still shows hierarchical structure with the male being more powerful.

4. Gay and lesbian relationships tend to grow and change, in reliable and predictable ways over the years, much in the same manner as do heterosexual relationships.

5. When measuring the overall satisfaction of queer people in their relationships, the results indicate that queer people are about as satisfied with their relationships as are heterosexuals with their marriages.

6. The satisfaction and stability that gays and lesbians have in their relationships are linked to other factors, such as the ability of the couple to solve problems, how interdependent they are, and their individual differences.

The first point, that gays and lesbians do form relationships, is the most important. Queer people, like most others, are basically family-oriented people, and they form family units that mirror the traditional American nuclear family. This usually begins with becoming a couple.

Like most young girls, lesbians were taught to place a high value on relationships. Not surprisingly, studies have indicated that a high number of lesbians are in committed relationships. (A joke that illustrates this goes as follows. Question: What do lesbians do on the second date? Answer: They rent a U Haul!) One estimate is that between 40 and 85 percent of all lesbians are in a committed relationship at any given time (Kurdek, 1995; Peplau and Cochran, 1990). Another estimate, based on a summary of 11 separate studies of lesbian couples, is even higher, indicating that between 60 and 80 percent of lesbians are in committed relationships (Klinger, 1996). For gay men, the results are similar. Estimates are that between 40 and 60 percent are in relationships. It is possible that these figures underestimate the true percentage of queer people in relationships. A large percentage of the people who respond to most research studies are relatively young, and the young tend to be in committed relationships less often than when compared with older gays and lesbians (Peplau et al. 1996). Even more important, perhaps, is that virtually *all* queer people report being in a committed relationship at some time in their lives. This mirrors what we know of heterosexuals regarding marriage and adult relationships.

A 1988 study of lesbian and gay couples (Bryant and Demian, 1990) extensively studied queer couples. Seven hundred six lesbian couples and 560 gay male couples were asked to respond on many aspects of their relationships. The results have helped us to understand much about queer relationships. While the basic problem with this study is a problem similar to many studies of queer people and queer families (the sample tended to be weighted toward those who are Caucasian, better educated, wealthier, and living in urban areas), the results of this study were revealing.

The study reaffirmed that queer people do indeed form stable, committed, long-term relationships. While this study was biased toward those new to relationships (19 percent of the lesbians and 13 percent of the gay male couples replying had been in a relationship for less than one year), one lesbian couple had been in a relationship for 43 years and three gay male couples had been in their relationships for more than 40 years. More than 100 couples (out of the 1,266 couples surveyed) had been in their relationships for more than 15 years.

After it was accepted that same-sex relationships existed and were worthy of study, the area that was first and most acutely investigated was the sexual practices of same-sex couples. More so than heterosexual couples, lesbian and gay couples are defined in terms of their sexual partners and practices. Simply put, lesbian couples tend to be monogamous, and gay male couples tend to be sexually open. This appears to reflect how men and women are raised in our culture. Men, regardless of their sexual orientation, are taught that both recreational and romantic sex are acceptable and desirable. Women are taught that sex should occur in the context of a committed romantic relationship. Even though lesbians and gays differ from straight women and men in other aspects of the relationships they form, lesbians and gay men tend to follow sex role socialization in regards to their sexuality. Regardless, there is no accepted model of exclusivity in same-sex relationships. The rules that apply for male-female couples (monogamy is strongly condoned) do not fit for same-sex couples.

An important study of gay male couples conducted in the late 1970s indicated that monogamy was virtually nonexistent for gay men in relationships, and the longer gay men were in a relationship, the less likely it was to be monogamous (McWhirter and Mattison, 1984), to the point where no gay male couples who were together more than ten years were monogamous. Later studies contradicted this and showed that significant numbers of gay men do have long-term monogamous relationships. It is likely that the times during which these studies were conducted influenced the results. The 1970s were an unusual time for queer people in general. Political and social activism was new and heady. Sexual liberation was chic, and sexually open relationships within the gay male community were glamorized. As a result, regarding monogamy, the 1970s was probably not a representative decade to study gay male relationships. However, even though there are now a significant number of gay male relationships that are monogamous, monogamy still occurs much less frequently among gay men when compared to lesbians or heterosexuals.

Early studies of the types of relationships formed by gay men and lesbians often categorized couples by the sexual practices of the couple. One early model divided queer relationships into those that were "closed-coupled" and "open-coupled," where the closed-coupled were the "happily married" ones and the open-coupled ones were not happy with their relationships and were looking outside of those relationships for excitement (Bell and Weinberg, 1978). Another early model of gay male relationships divided gay men into those who were "home builders" and those who were "excitement seekers" (Silverstein, 1981). While both were adequate early attempts at looking at the couple relationships formed by queer men and women, we now have a more sophisticated picture of how queer relationships work, especially in the sexual arena.

Gay men, in particular, have been able to redefine relationships, particularly on the sexual level. A more recent topology of gay relationships goes far beyond the open/closed dichotomy. In this model (Shernoff, 1995), gay male relationships can be broken down into five distinct kinds of relationships with regards to sexuality. The first is the sexually exclusive couple, in which the pair may have been monogamous from the beginning of their relationship or may have decided at some point to become sexually exclusive. A second type of relationship that gay men form is the sexually nonexclusive relationship, in which the relationship is open but that fact remains unacknowledged. Outside sexual activities are not discussed, but both men assume the other partner is having outside sexual contacts.

A third type of relationship formed by gay men is those that are primarily sexually exclusive relationships (menages). Here, the couple remains sexually active within the relationship but occasionally brings a third person into the relationship for sexual, and possibly emotional, purposes. In these situations, which may go on for years, the third person is rarely sexual with only one person of the couple without the other being there.

A fourth type of gay male sexual couple arrangement is one that is not exclusive sexually, and this fact is acknowledged by the members of the couple. The two members of the couple continue to be sexual with each other but may have various types of outside sexual contact, from affairs with individuals to anonymous sexual encounters. They may engage in group sex as a couple or alone. The key here is that there is acknowledgement that this outside sexual contact is permitted and does occur.

Lastly, there are those relationships that are asexual. These men may have had a sexual relationship with each other at one time, or the relationship may have been asexual from the beginning. They may have sex with others outside the relationship or they may be totally asexual. The key is that despite the lack of an ongoing sexual relationship with each other, they consider themselves to be a committed couple and not merely friends.

With regard to lesbian couples and sexuality, a major issue now being openly discussed in the lesbian community, and one that has been validated by a number of studies, is the issue known as "lesbian bed death." This term refers to a circumstance in which a couple discontinues genital sex a year or two after the relationship begins. Typically, friendship and physical affection remain, but genital sex becomes significantly less frequent or even absent. For many lesbians, this development is not a problem. They value more highly the physical affection, such as touching, kissing, and embracing. For others, however, the demise of genital sex in a relationship is a problem. This issue often becomes a major factor in the dissolution of the relationship, especially when it is accompanied by one of the partners seeking genital sex elsewhere. The origins of this issue may lie with female sexuality in general, both the unknown genetic component as well as the way in which women are socialized with regard to their sexuality. In any case, both lesbian and gay male couples are less successful at maintaining an ongoing sexual relationship within the relationship than are married heterosexuals, and sexual relationships tend to disappear for lesbians more quickly than for gay men.

Queer relationships are structured differently from heterosexual relationships. Gay and lesbian relationships are more similar to each other than they are to heterosexual couples.

People unfamiliar with queer relationships have at times assumed that queer relationships are similar to heterosexual relationships, where one partner is the masculine role partner and assumes the responsibilities usually associated with men, and the other is the feminine role partner, acting out the traditional female responsibilities. However, there has been limited evidence to support this as a model of queer relationships (Bell and Weinberg, 1978; Blumstein and Schwartz, 1983; Harry, 1982). While it might have been true in the post-World War II years when this model of relationships was popularized for heterosexuals by the media, the myth that this is the dominant form of queer relationships stubbornly endures despite considerable evidence to the contrary.

A second model of queer relationships, also believed to exist by people not familiar with gay relationships (though actually not common), is one in which there is a great age difference between the two partners, with the older one dominating the younger one. Hollywood has portrayed this type of queer relationship repeatedly in film. This model is probably derived from two concepts. For gay men in relationships, the public has been taught that there was an idealized ancient Greek model of a relationship between an older and a younger man where an older man becomes the mentor of a younger man, and has a sexual relationship with him. The second reason this idea exists is more pernicious. It is rooted in a deep-seated prejudice that says queer men and women are inherently pedophiles and are intent on seeking out younger people in order to molest them and to convert them to homosexuality. While older-younger queer relationships do exist, they are probably as common as similar heterosexual relationships, and may occur for the same reasons. Youth and beauty are prized in our society by some, both queer and non-queer; they place a high value on youth and beauty when finding a mate.

The dominant form of queer relationships tends to be based on a model of equality, where the partners share power and are best friends. Because queer couples do not have the gender differences of heterosexual couples, it is impossible for queer couples to assign tasks based on gender. While there has been movement away from this in heterosexual couples, it is still fairly common. The man and woman get to do the tasks usually associated with their sex in a relationship, and this tendency increases after the birth of children (Thompson and Walker, 1989). Same-sex couples cannot do this. When it comes to a task such as housework, for example, in heterosexual marriages the woman tends to do the bulk of the work. In same-sex couples, the work is more evenly divided (Blumstein and Schwartz, 1983; Kurdek, 1993). In gay male couples, the housework begins as a shared chore, but as the relationship ages, the tasks are usually assigned to one partner based on skills or availability of time (McWhirter and Mattison). In lesbian couples, the household chores remain evenly divided, even as the relationship ages (Blumstein and Schwartz; Kurdek, 1993). It would appear that both lesbian and gay couples are able to teach us a lot about sharing of decisions and negotiation, something that could perhaps be of great benefit to heterosexual couples.

Lesbian and gay couples are also structured differently from heterosexual relationships in another important way. Both lesbian and gay couples are significantly closer emotionally than are heterosexual couples (Green et al. 1996). Closeness here means asking each other for help, having friends in common, spending time and doing things together, feeling emotionally close to each other, having common interests, making decisions together, and having togetherness be a top priority. While some people might expect this in the case of lesbian couples, because of the assumption that women are relationship oriented, that it is also true for gay male couples is perhaps new and surprising news to many people.

It was, however, believed for years by mental health professionals and others that the closeness of lesbian couples had to be a problem for them. At the same time, it was believed that gay men in relationships would be like heterosexual men in relationships: distant, uninvolved, and needing a woman to make the relationship work. Modern understanding of queer couples has shown both of these beliefs to be incorrect (Green et al. 1996). The closeness of lesbian couples is quite functional, and queer men in couple relationships show the same propensity for closeness as do lesbians. A deeper understanding of queer people involves understanding that the differences between queer and non-queer people is more than the sex of the person to whom one is attracted. Other personality traits tend to be present. Queer people tend to be more androgynous than non-queer people. That difference enables both queer men and women to have relationships that are quite close.

Queer relationships also exhibit significantly more flexibility than traditional heterosexual relationships, with lesbians being more flexible than both gay men and heterosexuals. While heterosexuals' roles in marriage are strongly linked to their sex, gays and lesbians need to determine who does what each time they get into a relationship. Flexibility, thus, is needed for the queer relationship to be able to succeed.

Both queer and heterosexual relationships change over time in predictable ways. The developmental changes of heterosexual relationships are often understood in terms of what is called "The Family Life Cycle." Events, such as the meeting of the couple, the engagement, the marriage, the birth of children, the children leaving home and marrying, and the birth of grandchildren are seen as part of the normal course of the development of most heterosexual families. While not all heterosexual families go through all these stages, enough go through the stages to be able to mark a family's development along the family life cycle.

Similar developmental changes can be seen in queer relationships. Various developmental models of these changes have been proposed over the years. One developmental model of the changes over the years in gay male relationships was developed by two mental health professionals in San Diego by interviewing numerous gay men who were in relationships. It resulted in a six-stage model of the development of gay male relationships (McWhirter and Mattison).

Stage One is known as "Blending." This occurs during the first year of the relationship. It is usually an intense period, characterized by limerance (the state of falling in love or being in romantic love). The men tend to do almost everything together. Differences are dismissed. Sexual activity is high.

Stage Two is known as "Nesting." This usually occurs during the second and third years of the relationship. While in this stage there is an emphasis on creating the home and finding compatible ways to be with each other, in some ways the honeymoon that characterized the first stage is over. Differences begin to emerge and ambivalence about the relationships creeps in.

Stage Three is "Maintaining" and usually takes up years four and five. After the intense joining during the first three years, we see here each queer man begin to emerge as a separate entity once again. Conflict is dealt with, as is the establishment of traditions.

Stage Four is "Building" and takes place from years six through ten. This is a time of high productivity for the couple but also a time of danger. Couples often become complacent during this period and do not communicate or process through problems. Couples tend to collaborate, both in terms of cooperation as well as in terms of avoiding important issues.

Stage Five is "Releasing" and occurs during years 11 through 20. Trust, which develops gradually for most people, is now well established. Finances are often merged by this time. Partners sometimes take each other for granted during this period.

Stage Six is "Renewing" and happens from years 20 onward. The couple have often achieved security, and their perspective shifts. The 20th-anniversary party is often a special event for gay men. Remembering past times together takes on a special meaning. The couple often assumes without question that they will be together till one of them dies.

The developers of this model stress that this is a general model. Not all gay male couples go through this at the times indicated here. Some skip stages. Some go through stages more slowly. Sometimes, one member of a couple is in one stage while the partner is in another stage. The essential point, though, is that gay couples progress through a series of definable and recognizable stages.

The previous model was developed with gay male couples in mind. Lesbian couples also go through their own unique process as a couple. The gay male model would not fit entirely for lesbian couples. While there is some evidence that the beginning stages of the relationship, where there is limerance, merging, and high sexual activity, is the same for both queer men and women

(Kurdek, 1988 and 1989), the initial period of blending appears to last longer with female couples, and the loss of limerance does not occur as soon as with male couples.

Other models of the development of lesbian couple's relationships have been proposed. One model (Clunis and Green, 1988) begins with the women at the pre-relationship stage. During this period, each woman decides whether she wishes to invest the time needed to be in a relationship. This is followed by the romance stage, which is similar to the blending stage of gay male couples (previously described). Next comes the conflict stage, which again is similar to the maintaining stage of gay male couples.

Following this is the acceptance stage, where the members of the couple are aware and accepting of the faults of the other. This is followed by a commitment stage, where trust between the partners has increased and the issue to be worked on is increased acceptance of the other. Following this is the collaboration stage, where now the couple can create something together, such as a multigenerational family, a business, or something outside of the relationship that enhances the relationship. Other theorists have proposed that there is a "lesbian family life cycle" (Slater and Mencher, 1991). Unlike the heterosexual family life cycle, which is centered around children and events supported and validated by the community, the lesbian family life cycle is not child centered and the relationship is not supported or validated by the larger community.

On those rare occasions when Hollywood depicted a queer person or couple in a film, they were generally portrayed as silly, frivolous, criminal, unhappy, or even demented people in a sick relationship, which almost always ended with the rejection, humiliation, arrest, imprisonment, hospitalization, suicide, murder, or death of one or both of the partners. Hollywood seemed to believe that queer people could not have a happy, loving, satisfying relationship. The truth is quite different. Queer people are about as satisfied with their relationships as are married heterosexuals (Bettinger, 1986; Zacks et al. 1988). It is interesting to note that cohabiting but unmarried heterosexuals are less satisfied with their relationships than are queer or married folk.

This does not imply that queer relationships are without problems. Quite the contrary is true. Queer folk have many of the same issues to work out in their relationships as do heterosexuals. What this means, rather, is that queer folk are about as successful as are married heterosexuals in solving problems and having a satisfying relationship.

And when these issues are worked out successfully, the results are often a high level of satisfaction for the couple, regardless of the sexual orientation of the couple. Some issues that affect the satisfaction of the members of the couple are as follows: When the members of the couple feel they share equally in power and control, and when the couple shares decision making, satisfaction is positively affected. When at least one of the couple is emotionally expressive, and when the members of the couple place a high value on the relationship, believe the relationship to have many attractions, and believe that the relationship is better than the alternatives, then again satisfaction and happiness with the relationship is higher. These factors appear to be true for all types of couples. Queer couples appear to be quite "normal" in this regard.

Same-Sex Legal Marriage

A relatively new issue facing many queer families is the question of legal same-sex marriage. During the first 25 years of the modern queer civil rights movement, same-sex marriage was never high on the list of priorities. But because a court case in Hawaii (and now, another serious legal challenge in the state of Vermont) has made it seem possible that same-sex marriage might be legalized, the queer community has had to consider the possibility, impact, and desirability of being able to legally marry someone of the same gender. Many see this as a logical development in the quest for equal rights for queer people, which has paralleled the civil rights movement for African Americans in many ways. Until the 1960s marriage between African Americans and European Americans was illegal in many states.

This quest is not without controversy in the queer community, which has long prided itself on the uniqueness of its relationships and its ability to function and thrive outside the mainstream. The ability to marry someone of the same sex will have a profound impact, both emotional and structural, on queer people as individuals, couples, and multigenerational families.

In society, marriage has many meanings. Culturally, it is the ultimate rite of passage. More than any other event, getting and being married defines one as a responsible adult (having children adds to this but is not essential). Nothing else in our culture marks maturation the way legal marriage does. There is a strong negative connotation to being an adult and not being legally married.

Marriage not only has a cultural context, it also has a highly significant personal meaning. Individuals are conditioned to believe that marriage is the ultimate validation of self worth— "someone wants me." As a result, the person who legally marries feels a sense of accomplishment; he or she has completed the rite of passage. Marriage has been presented as the goal of growing up; people are indoctrinated to believe they should eventually marry. This goal has always been impossible for queer people to fulfill, unless they married someone of the opposite sex. But that would change with legal same-sex marriage.

Legal marriage also has another special personal meaning: it validates us as sexual people. In our sex-phobic society, all expressions of sexuality outside of marriage are officially disapproved of. While for women this standard is virtually absolute, for men there is a double standard. Being legally married, however, frees an individual from almost all constrictions in this area. As long as the sex is within marriage, it is considered acceptable, healthy, and welcomed.

Queer people never get such validation of their sexuality. It is never all right for gays or lesbians to engage in consensual adult sexual activity, whether it is promiscuous anonymous sexual activity or sexual activity within the context of a stable, loving, committed relationship. They are asked, in essence, to live celibate lives. Legal same-sex marriage could change this and acknowledge that the sexual feelings and needs of gays and lesbians are valid.

Marriage also has spiritual meanings. A Jewish wedding is called a "kiddushin," which means "to make holy." The "holy union of matrimony" is a term we have all heard many times. In the Christian and Jewish religions, marriage is necessary to fulfill the commandment to "be fruitful and multiply," since having children outside of marriage is not encouraged. Protestant ministers and Jewish rabbis are expected to refrain from sex unless they are married. Marriage is virtually an expectation in most Western religions.

Legal same-sex marriage will likely be a mixed blessing, having consequences, both positive and negative, for the couples and the individuals involved. Legal marriage will probably have either a stabilizing or a destabilizing effect on different queer couples.

Marriage appears to be a stabilizing force in most relationships, and married couples appear to have a much lower rate of separation than do queer couples (Blumstein and Schwartz). Same-sex marriage could also stabilize couples in other ways. Because marriage is a contract and can only be dissolved legally, the process of dissolving the relationship would take longer than it does now. Couples that might otherwise split might find opportunities to work out their differences. Some might reconsider the results, especially if the decision to split was impulsive. For heterosexuals, the more barriers there are to separating, the more likely it is that a couple will stay together (Levinger, 1979).

Legal marriage could also stabilize and strengthen the extended families of gays. Rejection of gays as individuals and couples by their families is not uncommon. Some cannot bring their partners to family functions or sleep in the same bed with their partners in the homes of other family members because they are not married. Legal marriage could help to defuse this situation and perhaps normalize these relationships within the context of the extended family. The sanctioning of these relationships by the state might be enough to permit some family members to put aside their prejudices and allow full participation by the gay couple in family functions. It could also help queer people to feel that they have taken their rightful place in the adult extended family as a married person and make them less likely to exclude themselves from family gatherings.

Legal marriage also has the possibility of destabilizing relationships that have been stable for a long time. If it were available, some couples who were doing fine without legal marriage might avail themselves of the option if one of them wanted it more than the other. Being coerced into marriage is usually a prescription for failure. The result may be that some of the couples will split up—something that might not have happened if they were never legally married. There is a high divorce rate among stable cohabiting heterosexual couples who eventually marry. Marriage is a powerful and a conservative institution with history, tradition, and rules. There would undoubtedly be pressure on queer couples to conform to the traditional model of heterosexual relationships, both to be married and to imitate heterosexual marriage.

Just as legal marriage would affect queer couples, it would also have a profound impact on queer individuals. Our society is cruel to those who grow up queer. We tell them from the time they are young that they are sick mentally, criminal, sinful, and immoral. For many, the impact will be positive. Simply having this option available, whether or not the individual takes advantage of it, will have a positive impact on the self image of many gay men and lesbians. It will validate internally their feelings; not only is homosexuality good, but wanting a close interpersonal homosexual relationship is valid and healthy.

But just as with couples, the benefits for individuals may not be entirely positive. For some, the rewards of inclusion into adult society that might come with legal same-sex marriage—whether monetary, career, familial, or psychological—might not seem worth the price. Marriage might be seen as another pressure, one they thought they had escaped by being queer. If legal same-sex marriage is available, there will undoubtedly be more pressure on queer people to mate and marry. Not all will welcome the pressure.

Another potential disadvantage of same-sex legal marriage for gay men and lesbians might be the entire matter of legal divorce. All of the problems now associated with legal heterosexual divorce would be a possibility in queer relationships: the lawyers, the mediators, the expenses, the loss of privacy. Without legal same-sex marriage, these problems are minimized. Legal same-sex marriage would involve the state in what many consider to be essentially a private matter. For some who are arguing for getting the state out of the marriage business entirely (with the understanding that there would still be a need to insure parental responsibilities to children) and letting churches bless and sanctify couples, legal same-sex marriage seems like a step backwards.

If there is one area where legal same-sex marriage will most likely have a positive impact, it is the area of multigenerational families that queer people have been and continue to create. Children in families headed by queer individuals or couples do not suffer because of that fact (suffering of children was an argument made by the State of Hawaii, but refuted by the plaintiffs in the case). However, these children could benefit if their queer parents gained the right to legally marry.

It's difficult being a child. Even in the best of situations, where the child has loving parents who can give him or her most of what he or she needs, it can be hard being a child. Children are continually changing and growing—physically, mentally, and emotionally. They have a need for stability around them in order to deal with the changes that they are experiencing.

Legal same-sex marriage would likely help children of queer parents because of the stability and comfort that would be provided by the legal protection, ability for the nonbiological parent to adopt, inheritance rights, and visitation rights should the parents separate. Simply knowing that life would go on if one of the parents died would be a small measure of comfort.

Legal same-sex marriage would also protect the children of these families in another way. Queer couples have used the homophobic laws as they now exist to exclude a nonbiological parent from visitation after a break up, even when there was a written contract agreeing to such visitations. Legal same-sex marriage would stop this. The children would be further protected and would benefit.

Children are also more likely to fit in with their peers. Just as it would be more comforting for a child if the heterosexual parents were married rather than merely cohabiting with their partner, the child in a gay family would also be comforted. It would also allow the parents to demonstrate commitment to the child in relationships, regardless of whether the child turns out to be homosexual or heterosexual.

Queer couples and families are functioning quite nicely without legal same-sex marriage. The option to marry, however, would add another dimension that would likely stabilize and normalize the relationships and families headed by queer couples. However, in other situations it might actually destabilize an otherwise stable relationship. In short, marriage would probably be a mixed blessing. The full impact would only be seen years after it became a reality. Most people in the queer community welcome having the option to marry, regardless of whether they choose to avail themselves of the opportunity.

Commitment Ceremonies and Rituals

Rituals and commitment ceremonies are important to queer people. In one study, 57 percent of the women and 36 percent of the men indicated they wore a ring or some other symbol that represented their commitment to the relationship (Bryant and Demian). While commitment ceremonies may have been occurring for thousands of years (Boswell), there has been an increased focus on such ceremonies in the last few years. In one study (Bryant and Demian) 19 percent of the lesbians and 11 percent of the gay men reported having had a commitment ceremony. Religious institutions, both those in the mainstream religious community and those churches and synagogues with special outreaches to the lesbian and gay community, have seen a steady increase in such commitment ceremonies.

A commitment ceremony is not a legal marriage. Legal marriage is a state-sponsored arrangement that invests the couple with certain responsibilities and entitles the couple to benefits. Couples who have commitment ceremonies may be able to sign legal papers to give the partner various rights, but the state restricts certain privileges, such as social security and pension survivor rights, immigration rights, and other primarily economic benefits to couples who legally marry. Queer couples who have a commitment ceremony are not entitled to any of those benefits and cannot get those benefits by signing any legal papers between them.

Nevertheless, queer commitment ceremonies continue because they are meaningful to the individuals involved. Because they are out of the mainstream, the commitment ceremonies, both religious and secular, that gays are having are extremely varied in form. Sometimes the ceremonies mirror traditional marriage ceremonies. Others are quite creative, incorporating a queer sensibility. For some, the ceremony is a way to announce to the world that the relationship exists. For others, the commitment ceremonies are a celebration of the relationship, a validation of the relationship, and for many, a consecration, fulfilling spiritual and religious needs. And finally, the commitment ceremony may fulfill a family obligation to be married.

The Metropolitan Community Church is a nondenominational Christian church organization serving primarily the queer community. With local churches in most large American cities, MCC has been conducting ceremonies of "holy union" for more than 25 years. In addition, it is not uncommon in more liberal mainstream churches to occasionally have such a ceremony. Ceremonies have been conducted in mainstream Episcopal, United Methodist, and Unitarian Churches. Jewish congregations affiliated with the Reform, Reconstructionist, and Renewal movements have also conducted commitment ceremonies, and ceremonies have appeared even at Quaker Meetings. While the umbrella organizations of these churches may not have an official policy of approval for these ceremonies, queer couples who are interested can find local churches and clergy people who are willing to conduct them. However, what each church or clergy person calls the ceremony can vary. While many members of the clergy will shy away from calling it a marriage, as that is a legal term and many of those same individuals are empowered by the state to perform legal marriages, many queer people simply like calling it a wedding.

The ceremony and accompanying celebrations can vary from the simple to the complex. In the most basic form, the ceremony can include only the two people in the relationship. Or, some feel at least one witness is needed, often someone who in traditional marriages fulfills the role of the minister or judge. At the other end of the spectrum, queer couples are having ceremonies and celebrations as elaborate as any traditional marriage. Fortunately for queer couples contemplating such a ceremony, they no longer need to figure out from scratch how to go about planning a ceremony and how to explain it to friends or relatives who might be unaware of the ceremony's meaning or significance. Guides are now available that can help the couple through the entire process.

Domestic Partner Registrations

It is now possible in some cities and counties for two people to register as domestic partners. West Hollywood, California, became the first city in the United States to permit these registrations when on 21 February 1985, the City Council adopted an ordinance that contained the regulations regarding the creation and termination of domestic partner registrations in that city. Other cities and counties have followed. San Francisco, Berkeley, Oakland, Santa Monica, New York City, New Orleans, and Minneapolis, to name a few, all now have domestic partner registrations. In 1996, West Hollywood once again led the way by becoming the first city to recognize the domestic partner registrations of other cities and accord those couples the same rights that would have been granted if they had registered in West Hollywood.

The benefits accorded to registered domestic partners vary with each city and county. Many grant some of the same benefits that the spouses of city employees who are married are entitled to receive (such as access to health care, life insurance benefits, and bereavement leave). Non-city employees are often granted hospital visitation privileges, which are usually restricted to family. Survivorship rights to apartments are common.

Domestic partner registration also has a strong emotional impact on couples. Many queer people have expressed a need for governmental validation of their relationships, as well as the legal benefits that accompany this registration.

The requirements to become a domestic partner in any given city or county vary. Most require some of the following:

1. Neither individual may be married or in a registered domestic partnership with anyone else.
2. They must not be related by blood.
3. They must be legal adults (usually 18 years of age).
4. They agree to be responsible for the other's welfare.
5. The couple must pay a fee for the processing of the registration.

Some localities insist that one of the persons either live or work in that locality. Others insist that the domestic partners share a common residence (a requirement that does not exist for couples wishing to marry).

In addition to filling out the registration papers, city employees in San Francisco are now permitted to conduct a ceremony in conjunction with the registry. In 1996, Mayor Willie Brown and then-Supervisor (now State Assemblywoman) Carole Midgen of San Francisco presided over a mass domestic partner ceremony where hundreds of gay men and lesbians "married" each other in a joyous celebration. If this were only for the legal benefits that go along with the registry, then no public ceremony would have been needed. But many of those taking part in the ceremony indicated that they had a need for a public declaration of their love and commitment, as well as the need to normalize their lives. With television cameras recording the moment and broadcasting the event on the national evening news, this mass ceremony may have helped to heal some of the damage this society inflicts on queer people.

Domestic Partner Benefits

Along with the increasing recognition of domestic partnerships by governmental bodies, corporations have progressively been extending the same company benefit package usually restricted to married couples to the domestic partners of their queer (and some-times heterosexual) employees. Many of these corporations feel that it is in their interest to provide the benefits, believing it will make them more competitive by allowing them to attract skilled workers.

In areas where there is a governmental domestic partner regis-try, some of these corporations require that the employee and his or her domestic partner register. But most companies appear to accept a statement by the employee that the other person is a domestic partner. Some companies have restricted their domestic partner benefits to same-sex couples, stating that marriage is avail-able to opposite sex couples but not to same-sex couples.

Legal Protections for Queer Couples

While queer couples cannot attain all the legal benefits that are given to heterosexually married couples, there are three legal docu-ments that queer couples can execute that afford them a degree of protection. These documents not only provide the couple with legal protections, but the execution of these documents also often provides the couple with a sense of emotional security and helps the couple to see themselves more as a couple. It is a concrete step that gives them a feeling that their relationship is valid in a society that does not recognize same-sex relationships. Those documents are:

1. A will or revocable trust that names the other partner as the beneficiary of various processions of the deceased partner. Unlike married heterosexual partners, same-sex partners do not automatically inherit from the deceased partner if that person dies without a will. In most states, other relatives of the deceased will inherit the property.
2. A power of attorney naming the partner to manage one's assets if that person becomes incapacitated. Without such a document, the courts will make this decision.
3. A durable power of attorney for health care. This allows the partner to make medical decisions when the other partner is unable to do so. This is especially important in the age of AIDS.

MULTIGENERATIONAL FAMILIES CREATED BY LESBIANS AND GAYS

There is one almost universal expectation and assumption made of people in our culture: that they will marry and have children of their own. Exceptions, such as joining a Catholic religious order, are rare. Part of this rests on the assumptions that all people are heterosexual and that children will be the natural result of most adult relationships.

It has been recognized in the past hundred years that some people, by their nature, are not heterosexual. It has been generally assumed that being queer meant the person would not fulfill the expectation of getting married and having children. While this as-sumption about queer people was and is not entirely true, it has been one of the reasons queer people have been vilified by this society.

Queer people, though, have for the most part been affected by the same expectations as their non-queer siblings. Many queer people have wanted to have children of their own. Some in the

past have found ways of doing this. Others have believed this option was not open to them as a queer person.

With the advent of the modern queer rights movement, options and possibilities previously thought to be impossible have become a reality. Queer people began to live more open lives. Queer people began to press for civil rights. And many queer people began to reconsider the idea that they could or should not have a multigenerational family simply because they were queer.

The major problem that had to be overcome was obvious. Chil-dren are created by the joining of an egg and a sperm. A queer couple or individual is lacking at least one part of the formula. So, having and raising children is not as simple a matter as it can be for non-queer couples. Queer people and couples find it nec-essary to plan for having a family in ways that non-queer couples do not have to consider. And, in increasing numbers, that has been the case. A national news magazine several years ago noted that there was a "gayby" boom going on in America, in which queer couples were openly having and raising children in numbers never before seen. This next section will thus examine the phe-nomena of multigenerational queer families.

How Common Are Queer Families?

The first and perhaps most important fact to note is that mul-tigenerational queer families do exist. This, by itself, may be sur-prising to some, but it is actually not a new phenomenon. It has been happening to some degree probably for all of recorded his-tory. Only a few years ago the concept of multigenerational queer families would have seemed like an oxymoron to most people, an idea so contradictory and impossible by it's nature that it need not be addressed. Yet being a parent has been and continues to be important to both queer and non-queer people. Queer people are now creating families through a variety of means: biologically, as well as through adoption and foster care.

It is difficult, if not impossible, to determine how many multi-generational queer families exist in America. Many queer parents fear drawing attention and attempt to hide the nature of their fam-ily. Additionally, there is a statistical problem. Mark Twain once said "There are lies, damned lies, and statistics." The clever use of statistics can be used to prove, or disprove, many points, in-cluding the existence of queer families. While by no means defini-tive numbers, the following statistics can be used to gain some idea of how many queer families exist in America.

To arrive at any numbers, we have to extrapolate from other data. The first and perhaps most critical question is how many queer people are there in America. Alfred Kinsey, in his famous studies of human sexuality, came up with a multitude of statistics concerning human sexual behavior. These studies, based on ex-tensive interviews with people living in the Midwest, were done in the 1940s (Kinsey et al. 1948 and 1953). From those studies, other people attribute to Kinsey a figure that 10 percent of people living in America are either gay or lesbian. Recent surveys have suggested that the percentage of gay men and lesbians may be somewhat lower. One analysis of the data from many other stud-ies of the number of queer people in America came up with the figure of 5.5 percent of the population (Diamond, 1993).

The correct number is important because it is the starting point for figuring out how many queer families there are in America. If the Kinsey figure of 10 percent is incorrect, and in fact the real number closer to half that, or the 5.5 percent figure, that would still amount to over 14 million Americans who are queer, a huge number.

Colage: Children of Lesbians and Gays Everywhere booth at the San Francisco Lesbian, Gay, Bisexual and Transgender Pride Fair, June 1995.

Observers know fairly accurately how many of the people who identify as lesbian or gay have biological children, and they have derived that number in the following manner. About 20 percent of the men who openly identify as gay indicate on surveys that they have previously been heterosexually married (Bell and Weinberg; Harry, 1983; Jay and Young, 1979; Spada, 1979). A higher percentage of lesbians, between 25 and 42 percent, indicate they were once married (Saghir and Robins, 1973; Bell and Weinberg; Masters and Johnson, 1979; Klein, 1978). Somewhere between a quarter and a half of all gay men who were married indicate they have biological children from those marriages (Bell and Weinberg; Miller, 1979), and between half and three quarters of all lesbians who are married have biological children (Gottman, 1979; Jardine and Whyte, 1971; Rila and Reed, 1980; Kirkpatrick et al. 1976). Additionally, in recent years there has been a trend among lesbians to have children through alternative methods of fertilization (Pies, 1985; Schulenberg, 1985; Hornstein, 1984). Queer individuals and couples are also now adopting children and being foster parents. This results in estimates of the number of between 2 and 8 million queer families and between 4 and 14 million children in those families (Patterson, "Lesbian Mothers," 1995). Clearly, queer families exist, and in great numbers.

The majority of queer families began as heterosexual families, before one of the parents came out and identified as a queer person. Some of the men and women who heterosexually married may have had some idea or may have even known unequivocally that they were queer. They married because of social pressure. Or, they married because they wanted to have a family and had no conception that it was possible for them to be in a same-sex relationship and have children in their lives. The option of being queer and having a multigenerational family is only now being widely recognized. Part of this recent development is that some queer individuals are entering into heterosexual marriage, sometimes with another identified queer person, at other times with a nonidentified queer person, for the intention of creating a family. Though rare, these relationships do exist.

An example of the changes regarding families in the queer community can be seen by looking at one case example. Congregation Sha'ar Zahav, a Jewish synagogue in San Francisco with a special outreach to lesbians and gays, now has 500 adult members and 150 children in the congregation, and the majority of those children are under three years old. Fifteen years ago, there were almost no children in the congregation. Today the congregation has a fully functioning Hebrew school for the children. Similar examples are seen in other cities and other denominations.

Queer families tend to be quite diverse in terms of how the members are related and how the parental responsibilities are divided. If the children are the result of a former heterosexual relationship, they might now be raised by a single parent. The parent might be in a same-sex relationship, in which case the partner may, or may not, be taking a step-parent role. Both partners may have children from former heterosexual relationships, and again they may or may not consider themselves to be a blended or stepfamily. Many lesbians are now having children by alternative means of fertilization, so the fathers of the children may be a mixture of men whose identity to the children is known or not known, or men who may or may not be involved to some degree with the raising of the children.

Custody

For many years the courts have been trying to answer the questions of whether queer people are fit to be parents and whether children will be harmed by the experience of having a queer parent. Several stories, separated by twenty years, illustrate why this is a scary issue for queer families and why many queer families hide the nature of their family.

In 1975, Mary Risher lost custody of her nine-year-old son Richard. A jury decided the son should live with the father because Mary Risher had admitted to being a lesbian (Kirkpatrick, 1996). This case might be easy to dismiss because it happened so long ago, at a time in America when the understanding of homosexuality was just beginning to change within the mental health profession and the community at large. But consider the results in two more recent court cases.

Sharon Bottoms, a lesbian, was living in Virginia with her female partner, and her biological son, Tyler. In 1995 she lost custody of Tyler to her mother, Kay Bottoms, who went to court and convinced a judge that Sharon was unfit to raise Tyler because Sharon was at the time living with a female life partner, April Wade. Buford Parsons, the circuit judge who originally decided the case, called Sharon Bottoms "unfit" and "immoral" because of her homosexuality. The judge said that Sharon Bottoms had violated Virginia's "crimes against nature law," which justified removing her child from her care and placing the child with her mother.

This case is ongoing. Sharon Bottoms is no longer contesting custody of her child but is continuing to appeal the visitation arrangements, particularly the prohibitions against her partner from having any contact with her son. On 29 July 1997, the Virginia Court of Appeals remanded the case back to Judge Buford Parsons. Judge Parsons was given instructions that he was to base his visitation rights decision on what was in the best interest of the child, and not to rely only on the sexual orientation of the mother, in determining visitation.

In Florida, John Andrew Ward was given custody of Cassie Ward, the child of his marriage to Mary Frank Ward, the biological mother and a lesbian. The judge based this decision on the fact that the mother was a lesbian, overlooking the criminal history of the father, who, twenty-two years earlier, had been convicted of murdering his first wife. In a tragic footnote, in the months following the decision Mary Frank Ward gained eighty pounds and died of a heart attack.

The bases for these decisions are the sodomy laws and the laws against homosexuality in the states where these decisions were rendered. Until Illinois decriminalized homosexuality in 1961, ev-

ery state had a law that outlawed sexual relations between consenting adults of the same sex. Today, homosexual behavior is still against the law in 24 states. In 1986, the United States Supreme Court in *Bowers v. Hardwick*, by a five to four vote, upheld the sodomy law in Georgia and thus gave its imprimatur to the sodomy laws in other states.

These laws have generally been the basis by which many queer people have been denied custody of their children and had visitation privileges restricted. The courts have usually held in these states that a parent declaring that they were queer would be breaking the law and would thus be an unfit parent. Though it is quite possible for heterosexuals to violate many of the same laws, heterosexuals are almost never asked about their private sexual practices, and the same standards regarding sodomy are not applied (Ricketts and Achtenberg, 1990).

Research on Queer Families

Much of what we know about families headed by queer mothers and fathers tends to come from two sources (Patterson, "Lesbian Mothers," 1995; Falk, 1989). First is the legal system, which, as a result of custody disputes, has over the years been concerned with the best interest of the children and has been trying to determine if having a queer parent hurts the child in any way. Even in states where homosexuality is no longer illegal, courts have reflected the societal prejudice against queer people and have been reluctant to award custody to a parent who indicates she (or occasionally he) is queer. The other source of knowledge about queer families is research conducted by observers trying to understand how best to raise children in a queer family.

Lesbian Mothers

Of great concern to the courts has been whether lesbian mothers are fit to be mothers, or whether because they are lesbian, the children will suffer. Much research has been done, and from the results researchers have concluded that essentially no differences can be found in the mental health of divorced lesbian mothers and divorced nonlesbian mothers. When the research was reviewed that compared the two groups of mothers in regard to their mental health, psychological functioning, self concept, happiness, or overall adjustment, both groups of mothers scored similarly (Patterson, "Lesbian Mothers," 1995; Falk).

Several differences were found, however. Divorced lesbian mothers were more likely than divorced heterosexual mothers to fear losing their children in custody cases (Lyons, 1983; Pagelow, 1980). It is possible to speculate that the mother living with this fear has a negative effect on the children and that therefore laws that would prevent a queer parent from losing children in a custody case because of sexual orientation would be of benefit to the children in those families. Another difference found was that divorced lesbian mothers were more likely to be members of a feminist organization than were divorced heterosexual mothers (Green et al. 1986).

Another difference is that it is more likely that a divorced lesbian mother will be living with a romantic partner than is the case a with divorced heterosexual mother (Harris and Turner, 1986; Kirkpatrick et al. 1981; Pagelow). The children of a divorced lesbian mother are thus more likely to have more than one parent figure in the home, a possible benefit to the children. There appear to be other benefits as well. Lesbian couples with children report greater satisfaction with their sexual relationship and their relationship in general when compared to lesbian couples who do not have children (Koepke et al. 1992). Since overall lesbians' satisfaction with their relationships is the same as heterosexuals' satisfaction, the higher satisfaction experienced by lesbians with children can only benefit the home life of the children.

The children of lesbian mothers appear not to suffer any loss of support or contact from their fathers. When compared with divorced heterosexual mothers, both groups received financial support from the fathers of the children (only) about one half the time. However, some studies report that fathers have a higher visitation rate in cases in which the mother is a lesbian (Kirkpatrick et al. 1981). This suggests that divorced lesbian mothers and the divorced fathers may be better at working out child care and custody arrangements than divorced heterosexual mothers and the fathers (Golombok et al. 1983; Hare and Richards, 1993).

Children of lesbian mothers have also been extensively studied. Again, the need for much of this research came from the judicial system, where lesbian mothers found it necessary, primarily in custody disputes, to show that their children did not suffer psychosocially from having a lesbian parent.

As queer people have been repeatedly accused of trying to convert innocent children to a life of homosexuality, queer parents have also been challenged in custody disputes with the charge that children raised in a queer family will more likely become queer than children raised in a heterosexual family. So, the courts have had a keen interest, not only in the sexual orientation of children raised in queer families, but also in the children's ability to identify with their gender and the extent to which these children take part in activities normally associated with that gender.

The results of such studies overall indicate very little differences between children raised in queer and heterosexual households. Sexual orientation of the children is unaffected by the mother's lesbian sexual orientation (Golombok et al.; Green, 1978; Huggins, 1989; Paul, 1986; Rees, 1979). Gender identity of the children appears to be the same regardless of the parent's sexual orientation (Golombok et al.; Green, 1978; Green et al. 1986). Nor does having a lesbian mother appear to have any effect on the sex role behavior of the children (Golombok et al.; Green, 1978; Green et al. 1986; Hoeffer, 1981; Kirkpatrick et al. 1981).

Gay Fathers

The concept of a gay father might seem like a contradiction to some. Such people assume that to be a father requires heterosexual sex, and they further assume that gay men do not have heterosexual sex. While it is not required that a gay man actually engage in the act of heterosexual intercourse to become the father of a child (alternative forms of fertilization are possible), many gay and bisexual men have had sexual relations that have produced children. Research done in the 1970s indicated that between a fifth and a quarter of gay men indicate they are fathers (Bell and Weinberg; Weinberg and Williams, 1974). With greater permission in the 1990s for young gay men to come out, the percentage of gay men who are fathers from previous heterosexual marriages might be decreasing, but this is likely being offset to a significant degree by the increasing number of gay men who are choosing to be fathers after they come out as gay men.

Some people will also assume that being a gay father is a new idea. This is not so. While the concepts of homosexuality and heterosexuality are modern, men who we would now define as

homosexual have from the beginning of time also been having heterosexual relations and thus, gay fathers have been around equally as long. It is only in recent years that we have come to understand that men who are homosexual may also produce children.

Compared with what we know about lesbian mothers, little is known about gay fathers. And what we do know is not based on a representative sample of gay men. The research that has been done has consisted primarily of interviews with small, nonrepresentative samples of gay fathers who are usually white, middle class, educated, and who live in urban areas. Gay fathers of color, those who are working class, less educated, and who live in rural areas are under-represented. Nonetheless, the body of research we have, based on the aforementioned nonrepresentative sample, provides the best view we have of gay fathers.

What we do not know about gay fathers is notable by its absence. There have not yet been any studies of the psychological adjustment of gay fathers when compared to heterosexual fathers. This absence is notable, because, as just mentioned, there is a considerable body of knowledge about how lesbian and nonlesbian mothers compare in this regard. It is believed this difference exists because of the interest the judicial system has in information concerning lesbian mothers' fitness to be a custodial parent, and the acknowledgement that very few gay fathers are custodial parents (Patterson, 1996).

While we do not have the same information about gay fathers, researchers have looked at many aspects of the experience of being gay and a parent. They have learned that gay fathers are, for the most part, divorced fathers who started families before they came to realize or accept their gayness. Because today custody of children after divorce is usually awarded to the mother (it was not always so; in the 19th century custody of children of divorced parents was usually awarded to the father), most gay fathers do not live with their children (Bigner and Bozett, 1990; Bozett, 1980 and 1989). In those cases where a gay father has custody of his children after divorce, it is almost always because of unusual circumstances. The same is generally true for heterosexual fathers who have custody of their children after a divorce.

The motivation to be a father essentially appears to be the same for heterosexual men as for gay men, with one exception. Gay men who are fathers tend, more often, to cite the higher status this society confers on fathers than on nonfathers (Bigner and Jacobson, 1989). This might suggest that gay men are trying to compensate for their lower status in society. However, this is only a suggestion, and further research would be needed to confirm it.

We now understand that many gay fathers go through an apparently difficult process of coming to terms with their gayness and of being a gay father. (It should be noted that some, and perhaps many, gay men never go through this transformation process and remain closeted for their entire lives, perhaps even refusing to admit even to themselves the nature of their sexuality.)

One researcher called this process "Integrative Sanctioning" (Bozett, 1981, *American Journal of Orthopsychiatry* and *Alternative Lifestyles*). Here, a father, who also happens to be gay, over a period of time goes through a transformation from an identity anchored in the heterosexual world to an identity anchored in the gay world. In order to accomplish this, the gay man goes through a process of letting non-gay people know he is gay and letting gay people know he is a father. If he receives a positive response to such disclosures, it enables the man to integrate his identity as a gay man and as a father.

Another researcher, B. Miller, writes of this transformation in great detail (Miller, 1979). Gay men go though a four-step process, notes Miller. *Step 1* is called "covert behavior." Here the father might engage in sexual behavior with other men, but to him such behavior is merely a physical act that says nothing about his sexual orientation. *Step 2* involves "marginal involvement" in the gay community. The father at this point has more than occasional contact with others in the gay community and is somewhat ambivalent about his sexual identity. At times he might believe he is a gay man who is married (and possibly considering divorce). Yet at other times, he might deny this and revert back to the belief that these are merely physical acts of a heterosexual father who is having sex with another man.

Step 3 is called "transformed participation," in which the man begins to identify as gay. At this stage, he starts to let others know of his gayness and is concerned that the legal system might negatively affect his rights to see his children. He discloses his gayness to some people (typically to a wife or an ex-wife, but not to his children), while becoming more involved in the gay community. He might still be trying to keep separate his involvement in the gay community and his activities as a father.

Finally, if the process continues, the man arrives at *Step 4,* "open endorsement." Here the identities are integrated. He is a gay man who is also a father and is able to tell many people those two facts about himself. The children, at this point, often know their father is gay and also know some of their dad's friends and almost certainly his partner, if he has one.

This research led Miller to a number of conclusions, as reported by Bozett (Bozett, 1989). He found that the single most important event that propelled a man though these steps was falling in love with another man. Factors that made it more difficult for gay fathers to come out included inability to see the gay world as a viable alternative, a perception that other gays would not be supportive, financial problems, family pressure, homophobia, the dependence of the wife on the gay father, and religious and moral principles. Those gay men who left their wives and began new gay relationships tended to have less tension in those new relationships than the gay men who remained heterosexually married had in their continuing relationships. Also, by coming out, these gay fathers seemed to achieve a greater sense of well being and a contentment they had not known previously in their marriage. Overall, those men who went through this process seemed to feel it was positive and added a valuable dimension to their lives. The gay men who came to believe that being gay and being a father were compatible had an easier time leaving their wives.

When the sum of the literature of what we know concerning gay fathers is examined, the following conclusions appear to be reasonable (Bozett, 1989). While most gay men appeared to father children as a result of marriage, most of these gay men were married just one time. Gay fathers generally perceive their family backgrounds as having been positive, and no differences can be discerned between the relationships gay fathers or non-gay fathers had with their parents. Gay men who do not father children are as masculine as gay men who father children.

Some of those gay men are content to remain married, but many are not and divorce their wives. Gay men who are fathers appear to have a more difficult time coming to terms with being gay than do women who are mothers and lesbian.

In regards to relationships with the families into which they were born, there appear to be few differences between gay and non-gay men. The research does not seem to support that gay men tended to have more difficulty with their relationships with their own parents than did their heterosexual siblings.

Having children appears to be a profound experience for gay men. Fatherhood appears to make it more difficult for gay men to come to terms with their homosexuality; gay men who are married but who do not have children appear to have an easier time coming out. Gay men seem to be more reluctant than lesbian mothers to let their children know of their homosexuality. On measures of masculinity, gay fathers and non-gay fathers score about the same.

Being gay and being a father does not in and of itself appear to be a problem. The research shows that it is possible to be an effective parent and also be gay. It appears to be easier for the children if they are told at an early age of their father's homosexuality, and no long-term problems seem to result from this fact or disclosure. The children of these men tend to have fewer problems with their father's gayness than the fathers feared they would.

While few gay men who are fathers have custody of their children, most maintain consistent contact with their children and indicate they have a positive relationship with them. In fact, gay men appear to try harder to create a positive relationship with their children than one would expect in a traditional heterosexual household.

In some ways, having a gay man for a father appears to give the children a different experience when it comes to growing up. Gay men appear to make a greater effort to be sure the children have opposite-sex role models. Being the economic provider appears to be of greater importance to heterosexual providers, while being a nurturing father appears to be of greater importance to gay fathers. Gay fathers appear to be more responsive to their children and place a greater value on warmth. Gay fathers also appear to be less traditional than non-gay fathers.

In those rare cases where gay men have custody of their children after a divorce, and the father is living with a partner or lover, these families are faced with many of the same challenges as are faced by blended heterosexual families. In one study of 48 blended gay families (Crosbie-Burnett and Helmbrech, 1993), inclusion of the gay father's lover in the parenting increased the likelihood of family happiness.

While most gay men who are fathers had their children before they came to terms with their homosexuality, there have always been some who created biological children of their own after they came to realize they were gay. This trend appears to be increasing significantly in recent years and is happening through a variety of means. Some gay men are using surrogate mothers to birth their biological children. Others are becoming sperm donors, adopting children or becoming foster parents.

Blended Queer Families

Blended families are quite common in America. Because of the high rate of divorce and remarriage among heterosexuals, it is common to have a family where the children are not biologically related. Such families are known as blended families and have as one of their core issues creating a new family with family loyalty from two or more previous separate families. It is easy to have divided loyalties in such families, which often causes additional tension and acting out on the part of the children or the adults.

Blended families are actually quite common among queer families because of the different ways queers create families. The goal is the same: to create a cohesive family unit, where the individuals are committed to creating a family and demonstrating love and caring for each other. Queer families need to recognize this is difficult for the children, who may feel loyal to noncustodial parents and may resist seeing the new adult in the family as a legitimate parent figure. They also may resist bonding emotionally with the children of the other queer parent.

Adoption and Foster Care

A 1988 national survey of queer couples found that four percent of the men and ten percent of the women said they planned to have children (Bryant and Demian). Because of their increasing visibility and the success many queer individuals and couples have had in creating families during the past ten years, it is likely that these numbers would be higher if the survey were repeated today.

Perhaps one of the most controversial issues regarding queer families is the issue of adoption and foster care. Queer people have adopted or been foster parents to the children of relatives, or have become adoptive and foster care parents as single adults without their sexuality becoming known in the process. However, the issue of whether openly queer people should be permitted to adopt or be foster parents to the children of nonrelatives has been quite controversial.

The laws and rules regarding foster care and adoption of children by queer adults vary from state to state. Presently, two states—New Hampshire and Florida—forbid homosexuals from adopting children by law. In other states, there are institutional barriers. Where it has happened, the children queer people and couples are permitted to adopt are children who are difficult to place, children with "special needs," children of minority parentage, or children with behavior problems.

The history of queer foster and adoption care is illustrative of the controversy that surrounds the issue.

1973: Chicago—Children with "homosexual tendencies" are placed with queer foster parents.

1974: Washington State—An attempt is made to exclude queer people from consideration as foster parents through new regulations, even though some children were already being placed with queer foster parents. The proposed regulations were eventually withdrawn. Oregon—Department of Human Resources refuses to permit placing any children in queer foster homes.

1974-1979: Foster placements in queer households take place in New York, New Jersey, Massachusetts, Minnesota, and Pennsylvania.

1975: Vancouver, Washington—A judge orders the removal of a gay youth from foster placement with a gay male couple.

1976: California—It becomes policy to permit queer people with a "clean record" to become foster parents.

1985: A foster child was removed from the care of a gay male couple in Boston after sensational media coverage of the placement (Ricketts and Achtenberg).

One of the primary issues in queer foster care and adoption is whether the parents should be open about their sexual orientation. For a long time, the conventional wisdom was that queer people who wanted to be foster or adoptive parents should not mention this aspect of their lives, unless directly asked.

There are others who now object to this approach. Many want queer people to be open concerning their sexuality throughout the process. They believe that secrecy in this aspect of the family can only lead to a feeling of shame that is detrimental to all involved. If the nature of the sexuality of the parents later becomes known, it might result in the disruption of the placement of the child. It would also make it more difficult to place queer adolescents in the homes of stable queer couples, where they might be exposed to positive role models.

The process of adopting a child can occur in many ways, and the rules related to each option vary. This can have considerable impact for the prospective queer couple that wishes to adopt a child. The following factors may affect the situation.

The adoption can be of a child living abroad or in the United States. In international adoption, the regulations regarding adoption vary with each country. Queers may find it easier to adopt internationally than in America, as some countries are more eager to have their children adopted and may also be less concerned about the sexual orientation of the parent. Older queer people may find their age being a disqualifying factor in America but may find that the same factor might work in their favor in adoptions from China.

The major variable concerning domestic adoption is whether to pursue an independent adoption or go through an agency. Until the recent past, the conventional wisdom in the queer community was that if a queer person wanted to adopt a child, independent adoption was preferable. In independent adoption, a private lawyer arranges the adoption between the birth parent(s) and the adoptive parents. State agencies may be involved to some degree, especially when the adoption is across state lines. The nature of the sexual orientation is usually disclosed to the birth parent, to preempt problems in the future if this information is withheld and later becomes known. Independent adoptions can be costly, however, which can be a drawback for many seeking to adopt a child.

The second option for domestic adoptions is to go through an agency. The agency will investigate the prospective parents and will rate the preferability of the potential homes for placement of children. Prospective queer parents have often been placed low on the lists because of their sexual orientation. Again, this appears to be changing in certain localities, and queer parents have successfully adopted children though public agencies.

In both of these options, the process can be open or closed. In open adoptions, the birth and the adoptive parents may meet or know who each other is. In closed adoptions, the identities of both parties are sealed. Prospective queer parents might prefer one or the other method depending on other factors.

A related variable is one- or two-parent adoption. Married heterosexuals adopt the child as a couple. Until recently, when a queer couple has had a child placed in their home, it has almost always been with only one of the members of the couple being given legal custody of the child. Again, this is changing. In California, a judge who grants the final adoption has wide latitude, and adoption has now been granted in some cases to a queer couple, where both become the legal parents of the child.

Closely related to this is the issue of second-parent adoption, where one parent has legal custody of the child and the second parent applies to also be the legal parent of the child. This is often done to give the child greater protection in the event of the death of the first parent or to give the child access to health or other benefits that only a legal child is entitled to receive.

In most situations where this involves a queer couple, one parent is the biological parent of the child (through either a former heterosexual union or a lesbian who conceived through alternative fertilization) or has adopted the child. When the child was conceived through anonymous alternative fertilization, there is no second parent who can challenge the adoption. When the child has a known biological father, the situation becomes more complicated. If the child was conceived in a former heterosexual relationship, the father may not want to give up his parental rights. If the father became the biological parent as a known semen donor, he may still be a legal parent. These legalities must be addressed. In second-parent adoptions, however, it is the intention that the first parent does not lose any parental rights.

Because this involves the courts and public agencies, a social worker might be required to conduct a home study to determine for the courts if second-parent adoption is in the best interests of the child. Such a study may involve social workers, lawyers, and judges who are not familiar with queer families, and the parents might need to educate them to the realities of queer families and why the legal second parent is needed. Some courts have rejected these requests, and cases have had to be appealed.

A corollary to this has been cases in which a child is conceived to a lesbian through alternative fertilization while the mother is part of a lesbian couple. The couple later separates, and the nonbiological mother then finds it necessary to go to court to secure custody and visitation privileges. Courts have generally sided in these cases with the biological mother.

Adoption after fostering is another possibility. Here many public agencies are, again, usually involved throughout the process. In almost all of these cases, the child is older and has special needs. The child has been living in the home of the prospective adoptive parents for a length of time, and it is generally known that the placement is likely to be in the best interests of the child.

A different form of adoption, more common in the past, has been adult adoption. This has been one method same-sex couples used in the past to legally join themselves to one another. One partner legally adopts the other adult partner. This method insures that the partner is legally considered to be family should the other one die. It protects the assets of the couple and also has emotional value in enabling the partners to feel closer. Usually the older partner adopts the younger partner.

Foster care is another option for queer people wanting to become parents. Sometimes this involves being a foster parent for the child of a relative, but often it means being a foster parent for children who cannot be cared for by their biological parents or who are rejected by their biological parents for many different reasons (such as behavior problems). In a few special situations, queer women and men have been able to be foster parents to children who were rejected by their parents when they told their parents they were queer. In these situations, the queer foster parent has been able to serve as a role model for these adolescents.

Prospective foster parents go through a process of being licensed as foster parents. Since it has been estimated that between 30 and 70 percent of adolescents in need of foster care may be queer (or questioning if they are queer), foster care agencies have in recent years been seeking out queer couples and individuals to be foster parents. However, this is still considered controversial in many areas of the country.

Alternative Fertilization

Also known as artificial insemination, this relatively simple procedure enables a woman to become pregnant without engaging in sexual intercourse. A syringe-like device is used to insert male semen into the vagina of the woman in the hope she will become pregnant. For many lesbians, this is the preferred method for creating a family. It is also of interest to many queer men as it is another method by which they can become fathers. There are a number of factors that need to be considered by anyone contemplating creating a family in this way.

For a woman, the first factor is whether she desires the identity of the father/donor to be known or unknown. If she wishes the identity of the father to be unknown, it is necessary to go through a company, commonly known as a sperm bank, which provides sperm to a woman for a fee. In addition to keeping the name of the donor private, the sperm bank protects the woman by testing the men for HIV (the virus that causes AIDS) and other sexually transmitted diseases. Sperm banks have sperm from men of various ethnic and racial backgrounds, thus enabling the woman to choose physical characteristics of the father that are compatible with her wishes. One major drawback for the woman is that financially this procedure is likely to be quite costly, and multiple attempts are often needed to produce conception.

If a known donor is to be involved in the insemination, there are several possible routes to fertilization, each with a number of relevant factors. Known donors can be done through a sperm bank or through private arrangements.

If there is no sperm bank involved, it is necessary to have the father privately tested for HIV. For maximum safety, the following procedure is recommended. The man produces a number of sperm samples that are then frozen by a private sperm bank. He also takes a blood test that seeks to find antibodies in his blood for HIV. If antibodies are present, the man is eliminated as a donor. Because there is a delay between infection with HIV and production of the antibodies, the man repeats the HIV test six months later. If the test results are negative, the sperm can then be safely used in attempts to inseminate the woman. In extremely rare circumstances, however, a person does not produce antibodies to the HIV virus, so an additional precaution may be to ask the man to take a blood test designed to look specifically for the DNA of the HIV virus in his blood.

While this procedure is the safest for the woman, as already mentioned, it is quite costly. At a minimum, the father should take a series of HIV antibody tests, which are generally available free in most communities. The actual procedure of alternative fertilization is quite simple: a man produces fresh sperm that is then inserted into the woman so fertilization can occur. This scenario occurs quite frequently, especially when the individuals have a previous social relationship and desire to create a family together where there will be some level of paternal involvement in the life of the child.

There are also private sperm banks that will provide a queer woman with a known donor, sometimes a queer man. There are a number of advantages to using this method. The child will know the father and will not wonder who he is, and queer female couples can ask that the same donor inseminate both of them, thus providing the children with a biological relationship.

There are also benefits to the father who uses a known sperm donor bank. In California, the donor who works through this kind of facility is protected from ever having a financial obligation to the child, as he is not legally the father of the child. Donors should check the law in their state or locality. Donors should be aware that without going through such a facility, a court may later decide the father is financially responsible for child support, regardless of what legal papers have been signed to the contrary. Courts have ruled that the mother and father cannot always sign away the legal right of the child to paternal support.

A major question for queer women who are using a known donor, whether privately or through a sperm bank, is the extent to which they wish the father to be involved in the life of the child. Questions regarding legal and physical custody, financial responsibility, and visitation need to be addressed. It is quite common to find gay men donating sperm to lesbian women to create alternative families where the men wish to be involved to some degree in the life of the family. The extent of the involvement varies widely. And, some lesbian women prefer to have a gay man as the sperm donor, believing the father would not be able later to challenge for custody of the child on the grounds that the mother's homosexuality makes her an unfit parent.

Additionally, the lesbian mother may want a man in her child's life, and a gay man as the father might be more willing to be involved, as he would probably not have a competing family interest. The lesbian mother might also feel more comfortable around gay men, believing the gay man would be more knowledgeable concerning the lesbian lifestyle.

It is wise to consult a lawyer when contemplating having a child in a known donor situation. Sample contracts exist (and are available on the World Wide Web) that detail the level of responsibility between the parents, and these contracts are then tailored to the desires of the individuals in the particular case. This process should be completed before any attempts at conception are made.

Surrogacy

Surrogacy involves a pregnant woman who gives birth to a child to be raised by other people. The mother gives up all parental rights to the child. Either she has an egg that was fertilized in vitro and implanted into her uterus, or she has her own egg impregnated by the sperm of a man, usually by means of alternative fertilization. The former situation is rare in queer families and might occur where a lesbian wants to have a biological child but cannot give birth herself. The later case is more common in queer families, when generally a queer man is the father.

Surrogacy usually involves relatively large financial payments to a woman and is thus an option available only to people with great financial resources. Lawyers and contracts are almost always involved from the beginning of the process. This method is a preferred option for some gay men, as the child will be biologically related to the father. This also permits the possibility that the same woman will be a surrogate mother twice, with sperm from each member of a gay male couple, thus enabling the children to be half siblings and biologically related.

Surrogacy is controversial. Some see a moral problem with paying a woman to produce children. Others believe that the mother is always emotionally harmed in the long run by accepting money and then having to give up the child. Some women, despite having signed legal contracts before the conception, and after having accepted and spent the financial benefits, have changed their minds about giving up the child after the child is born. Courts and public opinion appear to be mixed on the legalities and sympathies.

QUEER FAMILIES OF CHOICE

Michael Rowe, a journalist, essayist, and a gay man writes, "I made brothers out of my two oldest friends. I'm not sure where the line between friendship and brotherhood is drawn and crossed, but is has to do with trust and time.... Barney and I are gay. Chris is ebulliently heterosexual. He and his partner, Claire, have a small perfect miracle of a little blond boy named Alex.... Alex is the next generation of my family, but before him there was the three of us" (Preston and Lowenthal, 1995). In this brief description is the essence of a phenomenon known as the queer family of choice. Queer people, often without any conscious trying, can create extended families from their friendship networks.

Another queer writer, Andrew Holleran, author of many novels set in the queer community, noted of gay life in New York City in the 1970s, "eventually you learned that everyone had his little circle of friends, and every circle its central figure. You acquired these units without even trying to, consciously, they accreted, adhered and one day you realized without a word having been spoken, that you belonged to X and Y. A friend used to ask about someone he'd not met: 'Who are his people?'" (Preston and Lowenthal).

Just as queer couples are often unrecognized and invalidated by the greater society, queer families of choice to an even greater extent are both unrecognized and invalidated by the mainstream. Obituaries in newspapers in the queer community, such as San Francisco's *Bay Area Reporter*, regularly note the existence of a queer family of choice of the deceased, and often list those individuals by name as survivors of the deceased. When these same persons' obituaries appear in a mainstream newspaper, the queer family of choice is never mentioned as survivors.

The queer family of choice is often composed of a mixture of friends, lovers, ex-lovers, and blood relations. Queer people have redefined the family to include both friends and relatives. These queer families of choice serve many of the same functions as do extended families of chance—the aunts, uncles, cousins, grandparents, nieces, and nephews that a person gets by being a member of a biological family.

If one were to ask a modern lesbian or gay who was living a life out of the closet, who were members of her/his queer family, the queer person would likely understand the question even if she/he had never heard the words used in that manner before. That is because most queer people today have an extended family that is not composed of biological relatives.

For many queer people, these families of choice are more important than the biological families into which they were born. Biological families have often proved incapable or unwilling to provide support, and as a result many queer people have a negative relationship with their biological family. Most realize they will be tolerated at family gatherings but do not feel accepted or understood. Because of the lack of social approval by the biological families of origin for the intimate adult relationships created by queer people, the queer families of choice created from the friendship network become more important. They are the people that queer people turn to when there is a crisis and support is needed. They are the ones that help queer people to cope.

As with the multigenerational families created by queer people, relatively little is known about the queer families of choice out-

Family Link—a nonprofit organization that provides temporary housing for the members of the family of people with AIDS when they are visiting San Francisco to be with a family member who is ill. "Family" is both the biological family and the family which the person with AIDS has created in her or his life. The photo was taken at the Castro Street Fair in June 1990.

side of the queer community. But the queer family has recently been the subject both of literature and anthropological study.

Much of the history of the queer family of choice has been lost over time. It is possible, however, to trace at least one element in the creation of these families as they applied to gay men. For hundreds of years, masquerade balls were common in America and Europe. Beginning at least by the latter part of the 19th century, gay couples gathered for their own version of these masquerade balls, and these evolved into "drag" balls, which by the 1920s were sometimes attracting thousands of attendees. At these drag balls, some men would dress in elaborate female attire and were accompanied by exceedingly masculine men in suits and tuxedos.

From such drag balls evolved a semi-institutional form of the queer family of choice. Beginning at least in the post-World War II years, and possibly earlier, within the gay male drag community, a number of these gay men formed "houses," loosely based on the couture "houses" of the fashion world. The "House of (insert a female drag name here)" would be headed by an older, more experienced, male drag queen who might respectfully be called the "mother" of the house. Often there would be a "father" of the house, along with members

(or children) of varying ages. The activities of such houses would center on preparation for a series of drag balls. But they were much more than that. They were multigenerational queer families, where younger queer men, relatively new to the queer community, could find a safe place to belong. The recent documentary movie *Paris Is Burning* illustrates how this phenomena still exists in the minority queer community today.

The evolution of queer families of choice probably has also been influenced by another part of the world of drag balls. It was common for many of the participants in that world to at times use "camp" phrases for various communications. Many were based on family metaphors. Close friends became "sisters" (regardless of their gender), while older gay men were referred to as "aunties." These camp family metaphors reinforced that the relationships between these gay men were more than merely friendships, that they were in fact kin.

While less is known about lesbians historically than about gay men, lesbians too began creating families of choice in significant numbers in the 1940s. During this period, World War II created opportunities for lesbians to begin to congregate in bars and homes in a way that they had never been able to previously.

Today, there continues to be a great feeling of kinship between queer people. A new magazine aimed at the queer community is entitled *In the Family*, a variation of an older expression popular within the African-American community, that someone who is lesbian or gay is "in the life." Two people discussing whether another person is perhaps queer might ask "Is (s)he part of the family?"

Just as the Stonewall Riots of June 1969 had a significant effect on the queer community, so did the AIDS crisis in the 1980s. The AIDS epidemic, though, also had profound effects on the queer families of choice. On one hand, the AIDS epidemic brought family members together, to take care of the ill, to bury the dead, to grieve with and support those who lived afterwards. It integrated the lesbian and gay male parts of the community in ways not seen since before Stonewall. But it also had the effect of destroying many queer families of choice. On one hand, it was not uncommon for many members of the same queer family of choice to succumb to the illness. And in other queer families, it killed key family members who previously kept the family together.

Many factors appear to be important in determining the cohesiveness and the quality of the support that these families can give their members. Among them are the following (Green et al., 1996; Weston, 1991).

The first element is *time:* how much time people spend together, and the passage of time. Time is important in creating trust, shared memories, and history. Celebrating holidays, birthdays, and life events together helps to bind the members of a family. It is part of creating a shared history.

Time is also important for building *trust*. Passage of time without major violations of trust enables people to feel closer and trust each other. Queer people have often experienced rejection by biological family members and society. Acceptance by the other members of the queer family builds trust.

The third element is *support*—emotional, practical, and material support. Being there for others helps to create the feeling of family. Emotional support involves being able to listen, not judge, and support other family members through a variety of life's experiences. Practical support means security, knowing there is someone there when a ride is needed, or when someone is needed to watch the children, or pick up the medicine. Material support is also a key factor. Money in our society often defines relationships. Sharing what one has, which is material support, is a function usually associated with family members.

A fourth key element in the creation and maintaining of a queer family is a person who is the *central figure*. This is usually an outgoing person, an individual who likes to organize, a person who will say, "let's all get together for Brenda's birthday" and make sure everyone is called. A great tragedy of the AIDS epidemic occurs when the disease fells this person. The family has to not only cope with the loss of a family member, but must cope with the loss of the individual who was in many ways the central hub around whom most of the other individuals in the family revolved.

Since so many families exist because of the person who is the central figure, a family's strength is also dependent upon the *relationship density*, or how many of the individuals who are the spokes in this wheel eventually get to know each other and have relationships independent of the central figure. Even with the central figure still there, the more individuals who have relationships that do not go through the central figure, the stronger are the family ties, and the more it reminds individuals of a biological family. These ties between the family members also make it possible for the family to survive the loss of the central figure.

A key element of any family is the ability to *integrate new people* (lovers, children, additional friends). The boundaries of the chosen family need to be permeable. The movie *Longtime Companion* not only followed how AIDS affected one queer family over a number of years, but it also showed how new individuals were integrated into the family. Freedom for a person to leave and to have other relationships also strengthens a queer family of choice.

To a notable greater degree, queer people try to maintain some sort of relationship with their ex-lovers, and often (sometimes after an initial period of separation) these individuals remain part of the extended queer family of choice. Queer people appear to try not to "throw away" family members. Queer couples in the process of separation who have undergone couples counseling often indicate that if they can not remain as a couple, they certainly want to remain as friends.

THE FAMILIES INTO WHICH GAYS AND LESBIANS ARE BORN

It is an often-repeated notion that being queer means rejecting "the family," both the family into which the person is born and family life in general. People who are familiar with families in which there are queer members know this is usually not true. While in many cases there is a disruption of some family relationships after an individual initially lets other members of the family know of his or her sexual orientation, it is usually a temporary situation. Families almost always adjust to an individual "coming out." The person who comes out does not stop being a member of the family or interacting with other family members. That person now has a new and more accurate identity within the family. Often, this results in family members feeling closer.

The reason a queer person does not come out, or delays coming out to parents or other individuals in the family, is often out of a desire to prevent what they believe would be a disruption in family relationships. A queer person often fears rejection, losing his or her family by coming out to them.

Queer individuals, whether they are "out" to other family members or "in the closet," have demonstrated a desire to remain integrated in the life and structure of the family into which they were born. In families where there was a temporary cutoff, being thrown out of the family in most cases does not mean losing contact with all family members. While the parents, for a time, might not be talking to the person who came out, that individual almost always stays in contact with other family members, siblings, grandparents, aunts, uncles, cousins, etc. The usual response is for the person who came out to try to enlist these other relatives as allies to stop the continuing disruption of the family. Queer people are quite loyal to the families into which they were born, often more loyal than other family members who would cut them off from the family because of their sexual nature.

One reason for this loyalty is that queer people need the family into which they were born. They know they live in a world that is hostile to those who are sexually different. They know they are more likely to be rejected by individuals whom they hardly know when the nature of their sexuality becomes known or is suspected. Having a solid relationship with the family into which they were born becomes all the more important under those circumstances.

Coming out to one's family of origin is one of the more significant events in the life of a queer person. And usually, a person does not come out to her/his family of origin until after coming out to friends and coworkers. More than any other event, coming out signifies an emotional separation from the family of origin. In effect it says, "I am a separate person from you. I have a life of my own and am (probably) different from what you wanted or expected." Regardless of where the queer person is actually living, coming out is, in effect, leaving home.

For many queer people it is important to come out to their families of origin for other reasons. Not only does it establish them as having a separate identity, it is also usually necessary to enable the queer person to be closer to her/his family. To have such a significant secret distances them from the family into which they were born. Coming out often serves as an attempt to bridge an emotional distance in the family created by the secret.

Queer families of choice might be more important to people who are not out to their families of origin. Within the queer family, they can be who they actually are and do not have to watch what they say or modify how they act. Within their families of origin, however, they have to pretend to be someone they aren't: they must watch the gender of whom they are dating, etc., lest their secret become known. That can be emotionally exhausting.

Rejection by members of the family of origin is one of the concerns of many queer people before they come out. This fear is well grounded. About one third of the people who do come out to their families of origin have a tale that involves significant initial rejection of them by various family members. For some, the rejection is extreme. The queer person may be told that she/he is no longer a member of the family, or that she/he is disowned, or even considered to have died. While these rejections are rarely permanent, they are feared and do have a large emotional impact on the person who is being rejected. By the reaction of family members to the news of coming out, a queer person learns as much about his or her family as the family learns about the queer person. All individuals learn whether the familial love is conditional or unconditional.

Coming out is also an opportunity for integration of the family of choice with the family of chance. Each family now has the opportunity to begin to know each other as important parts of the queer person's entire family. If the person who is coming out has a partner, the coming out is more significant. It says to the family of origin that the queer person has another nuclear family, more so than if he or she were unattached but with a queer family of choice. Straight families understand a lover/partner in ways that telling them about a queer family of choice does not connote.

Holidays such as Christmas and Thanksgiving can be a difficult time for queer people in relation to their families of origin. If they are not out to their families of origin, there is probably an expectation that the queer person will spend the holiday with them, since these are "family" holidays and the queer person is presumed not to have any other family. It can be quite awkward when in fact the queer person does have a queer family and must explain to the family of origin why she or he may not want to come home to spend the holidays with them.

Within the family, a special bond often develops between the queer members of the family. They share a common experience. Even when they have never met, queer people are aware of the uncle who never married and moved away, or the great aunt who was rumored to have been a lesbian, and often feel a special kinship with that other family member. When more than one sibling in the family is queer, common knowledge of that often brings them closer.

CONCLUSION

Queer people are generally family oriented people. Queer people form a diversity of families, ranging from couples and multigenerational families to extended families of friends. Queer people are also loyal members of the families into which they were born. In short, queer people are quite similar to non-queer people in how they relate to the concept of family. The major differences result from the nature of homosexuality. Queer couples have two individuals of the same gender, and the multigenerational families are sometimes headed by a couple of the same gender, or by an individual who prefers a partner of the same gender. This alone produces dynamics that cause queer families to be different from non-queer families. The other major difference is that queer families are unsanctioned by society and are often subject to discrimination and ridicule, resulting in queer families being formed and operating outside the mainstream.

GAY AND LESBIAN FAMILY STORIES

Two Men and Two Children

On a warm summer Saturday afternoon, Mel and Vince sat around a table in their backyard in Oakland, California, while their two sons, Ian and Paul, used their seemingly boundless energy to run around the yard, ride their tricycles, and play "tag," as Mel and Vince recounted how they met and how they came to create the family that was around them.

Vince and Mel met in October 1982 in church. Both were members of Dignity, an organization created for people who are both gay and Catholic. Looking back, Mel commented how an organization such as Dignity provided him with a built-in method of screening people. He said by attending Dignity services while he was also in the process of looking for a life partner, he was aware that he would likely meet men with whom he shared a common history and common values. This was important to him. Two years later, in 1984, Mel and Vince decided to begin living together and bought their home, a California-style bungalow.

For Vince, buying the house was a milestone. "It gave me a sense that a family was possible. The house was almost like a marriage license." For Mel, "the house was binding. It bound us both legally and emotionally." Several years later, Mel commented, in 1988 and 1989, he began to sense a need for something more in the relationship. He described a need for "triangulation," and didn't know how to deal with it. He thought about children but was unsure as to how to proceed.

"I knew there was another person waiting to get in," Mel commented. "That threw me for a loop. I didn't think it was possible for a gay couple to adopt a child." But they had met another gay couple who had adopted a child, and eventually they attended a meeting of a group organized for gay and lesbian parents.

Vince remembered that the biggest issue seemed to be "How?" They considered and rejected the idea of a surrogate mother. They felt there was too great a risk that at some time in the future they could lose their children, having heard of other situations in which the surrogate mother won custody of the child and moved to another city. Vince also said he didn't want to share the children with a third or fourth parent. He felt that such a scenario would be too difficult for both the children and the parents. Mel also nixed the idea of a private adoption through an agency or a law-

Ian Stenger-Morgante (in tree), (bottom, l-r) Mel Stenger, Paul Stenger-Morgante, and Vince Morgante.

yer. He seemed personally offended by the idea, and said it seemed too much like a market where someone "buys" a baby.

Vince commented that "both of us felt a certain calling to help a disadvantaged child who was already born," noting that there were 30,000 children in California at any given time waiting for adoption. Mel commented "These kids needed a home, we needed kids, therefore, a match."

So they began the process of attempting to adopt a child. In May 1989, a friend took them to the Alameda County Social Service Department, where they met with two female social workers. The social workers were not receptive; not nasty, just not receptive. "We don't give kids to gay male couples," they were told. "We just don't do that."

While the social workers were surprised at their request, Mel and Vince decided to fill out a one page application, noting their names, ages, who they were, and what kinds of children they would accept, thus beginning the process of initiating a "home study" of them by the department. Across the top, Mel said, he scrawled the words "Gay Couple," just to make sure no one thought they were trying to mislead the department.

"Within a week we had a call from the department and were assigned a social worker," Mel noted. "The social worker told us that they had *never* given an infant to a gay couple. She said it

was more likely that we could get an older child, perhaps one between the ages of three and five." The social worker was trying to be honest with them. She told them that being a gay couple was considered a negative, but also assured them the department would look at many of the other factors in their favor. They were also told if a child was placed with them, it would most likely be a boy, since most of the girl children in foster care had already been physically or sexually abused by men in their lives, and the department would be reluctant for that reason to place a girl child with two men.

A month later, in June 1989, the social worker called and asked if they would consider taking a five-year-old boy, one who had been rejected by every foster home. This placed Vince and Mel in a quandary. They had long planned a European vacation for that summer. They didn't want to appear to be putting a vacation over a child, but the trip had been long planned. They reluctantly told the social worker they couldn't consider this child.

Over the next year, they spoke with the social worker about three other children. They never got to the point of meeting any of those particular children. In April 1990, the social worker called again and asked if they could also consider accepting an infant. They told the social worker that, yes, they would certainly consider having an infant placed with them.

In June 1990, while Mel, who is an elementary school teacher, was preparing to teach summer school, the social worker called and spoke with Vince and told him of an infant who had just been born. The mother had drank alcohol consistently throughout her pregnancy; she had not had any prenatal care, and one of her previous babies had died of SIDS, better known as crib death. The baby had multiple risk factors. Would they consider this infant? The social worker wanted to meet with them the next day to discuss the possible placement.

Mel and Vince drove downtown, and it was clear immediately that the social worker wanted to place this child with them. The social worker had thought of all the couples available, and had advocated for Mel and Vince. The social worker had met with a panel of social workers at the department and had compared Mel and Vince with three other heterosexual couples also wanting to adopt a child. The panel of social workers all wanted this child placed with Mel and Vince.

"This was very empowering," Vince noted. "It was one of the highlights of this process." Mel noted that "from a political perspective, it was validating to be chosen above straight couples."

The social worker told them this was the first time in the state of California that a newborn baby was being given to a gay male couple. Mel is a singer and a member at the time of the Gay and Lesbian Chorus. Several days later, at a concert that was part of San Francisco's gay pride week, an announcement was made to the audience that such a placement of a baby had happened to a chorus member for the first time. The audience wildly cheered. They too recognized what a momentous event this was.

But there were practical matters to take care of first. They drove to a baby store and told the woman behind the counter, "We are having a baby in one hour. We want to buy everything we will need." After the perplexed and astonished store keeper was explained the details of the strange request, she gave Mel and Vince a crash course on babies and child care, while selling them diapers, blankets, creams, and everything else they would need for the next several days.

Vince headed home with the supplies to await the arrival of the social worker (who they were now calling the stork lady) and their child. Mel went off the supermarket to buy baby formula, only to be confronted by numerous brands; low fat, no fat, dairy, non-dairy, soy, each declaring a superior product. Amid such confusion, he made some choices and headed home to find the stork lady and baby just arriving. And, as was a fitting introduction to parenthood, the baby had just pooped, enabling them to change his diaper for the first time.

They had a surprise as their son arrived. He was connected to an apnea monitor, which measured his heart and breathing and would sound an alarm if the baby stopped breathing. Since the mother's first baby had died of SIDS, the department wanted to be cautious with this child, despite the fact that the department had told them there was no correlation between siblings and SIDS. Mel and Vince had a physician friend immediately come over to evaluate their son, and the physician told them the monitor was probably unnecessary. After numerous false alarms over the next few days, they took the baby to the hospital for an evaluation, and with the permission of the department, removed the apnea monitor.

They named the child Ian, because they were told his ancestry was a combination of Scottish, Irish, and English. With Ian now living with them, life changed radically. Mel noted "it was like hitting a brick wall at 20 m.p.h." Priorities changed. They could no longer just pick up the keys and leave the house. It became a project to go anywhere. "And our sleep became disrupted," Vince noted. "Here was Ian sleeping three feet from our bed, awakening, crying, and with the apnea monitor going off those first few days. The loss of sleep continued for quite awhile."

And having a child also had a profound emotional impact on them individually. Mel noted that when Ian began to speak, he brought up for Mel all the unresolved issues Mel had with his own father. Mel explained how he grew up in an abusive household, and this had left him with considerable rage toward his father, who was and is abusive and rejecting. He thought he had resolved this rage years before but now found that with Ian talking, he was experiencing the rage all over again. Mel began psychotherapy once again in order to figure out how to be a father and deal with his rage.

Over the next two years, the adoption process continued. The social worker told them that because of a State of California policy, she could only recommend the adoption be by one parent. Even though Vince and Mel had applied for and received the child as a couple, the social worker could only recommend, because of this state policy, that the adoption be in Mel's name alone.

In December 1992, they went to court to finalize the adoption. The Superior Court Judge, Ken Kawaichi, told them that he had the power to override state policy and the recommendation of the social worker, if he chose to do so. After reviewing the material, he told them that he was granting the adoption to them jointly. They now had joint legal custody of Ian. Vince felt this action by the judge, more than anything else, gave a legal validation to their relationship. They were both now the legal parents of Ian.

Several months later, in the spring of 1993, they began to talk about the adoption of a second child. "I felt another presence waiting to get in," said Mel as he lifted his left palm indicating that ethereal presence. Vince also very much wanted a second child. Vince was concerned that Ian not grow up alone. He was aware that separation was likely to be an issue for Ian. Ian would not only have to deal with being separated from his biological mother and father, but also from many of his new cousins. Vince noted that his own extended family was living in many distant parts of the country, and Mel's family continued to be rejecting.

Ian would not have close family members around. They felt he would need someone with whom to talk, and they didn't want Ian to be an only child.

They were also aware that being the son of two gay men was an almost unique situation in this society. This they felt could isolate a child. They wanted Ian to have someone near by who understood what that was like. So, in February 1993 they again called the social worker to say they were interested in adopting a second child. This time they did not have to fill out any additional paperwork, since it was all done the first time, but they were told they would have a different social worker, since their former social worker had been given a promotion.

Adopting a second child was again an emotionally difficult task. They met an eleven-month-old baby who had been born to a mother who was addicted to heroin. The baby was lethargic and had delayed motor skills. The baby also seemed to have difficulty focusing on those around him. They went home and had what they described as a "tragic weekend." They worried about the child and what would happen to him. They did not know if they were capable of giving the care this child would need. They cried a lot that weekend. As Mel recounted the story, he cried once again as he remembered the agony of the weekend.

They called the social worker and said they did not know what to do. The social worker told them if this baby had caused them so much pain already, it was probably not a good match. Mel and Vince feared the department would now see them as "too picky."

Several months later they had another phone call saying another child was available. They were told the mother of this child had been addicted to crack and the baby had gone through a drug withdrawal. Nevertheless, they decided to accept the child. On 1 June 1993, Paul came to live with them.

They found that their experience with Paul was significantly different from the experience with the baby who had been addicted to heroin. While both babies had to go through a drug withdrawal after birth, they found they were more relaxed with Paul. They described Paul as a "visual" baby. He did not move around a lot at first, and did not make a lot of sounds, except to cry. But he communicated with his eyes. He has been verbally delayed throughout his first few years. And he shook every time his diaper was changed.

Again they were awarded joint custody in the adoption. They have had little trouble with preschool for the children. Ian attended a preschool run by a local Baptist church that had been thrown out of it's national organization because of a positive and friendly outreach to those in the lesbian and gay community. Ian now attends the elementary school where Mel is a teacher. Mel noted a little concern because now, in the playgrounds, the only derogatory term with which he hears kids taunting each other is "faggot." He knows Ian will have to deal with this. On the other had, Ian has had a coming out to them. Though only seven, Ian is sophisticated in his understanding of concepts. He understands that Daddy Mel and Daddy Vince feel a special way for other men. In a somewhat sheepish way, he told them he feels that way for other little girls, and was relieved to find his parents fully understand and support those feelings.

An Alternative Queer Family

Diana, a lesbian mom, and Mariana, a nonlesbian mom, have known each other for eighteen years. They were both hired in

(From l-r) Vicente Roman, Mariana Valdez, Emma Buchbinder, Diana Buchbinder, Aaron Buchbinder, and Nefertitti the cat.

the late 1970s to work in the Children's Program at the Women's Alcoholism Coalition and have been close ever since. Vicente, age 16, is the son of Mariana. While Mariana and Vicente's father were a couple for three years, they never married. While working together at the Coalition, Mariana and Diana developed a professional relationship. They wrote papers together and presented them at professional conferences. While working together, they found they had a lot in common, and as a result, also became close personal friends. They began to consider themselves to be "family" soon after Vicente was born.

Diana was heterosexually married when she began working at the Coalition. She soon, however, began a relationship with a co-worker named Joyce, who herself was co-parenting another child. Diana agreed to leave her husband and to continue her relationship with Joyce on one condition, that she could have children of her own. Both Diana and Mariana continued to work at the Coalition and later in a foster child/adoption program where they had contact with the Department of Social Services.

At the time, in the early 1980s, Diana found that the Department of Social Services was not receptive to permitting single parents or same-sex couples to be foster parents or to adopt children. Diana confronted the Department, asking them to make clear what their policy was. This led to Diana's first attempt at being

a foster parent, this time of a seven-year-old girl who was later placed in residential care.

Diana finally decided she needed to have a social worker as her advocate and located one who helped her in the process. This led to the adoption of Aaron, who is now 14 years old. The Department of Social Services had at first tried (unsuccessfully) to place Aaron with a more favorable "straight family." After Aaron languished in the bureaucratic system for four and a half months, Diana managed to have Aaron placed with her in foster care with adoption being the goal. This was eventually successful.

As is not uncommon when people are trying to adopt children, as soon as she began the process of adopting Aaron, she became pregnant (through an anonymous sperm donor) with Emma, who is now thirteen. Conception and having a baby had been difficult for Diana. She needed to take fertility drugs under a doctor's care to become pregnant and had previously had three miscarriages. But because she was aware the social worker for Aaron would not be pleased that another child was also coming into the family so soon, and might stop the adoption process, Diana cleverly managed to hide her pregnancy from the social worker. Later, the social worker did acknowledge that she would have taken Aaron from Diana if she had known Diana was pregnant. The social worker said she would have been concerned that because there was a second child on the way, there would not have been enough time for Diana to properly "bond" with Aaron.

Soon after this, Diana, with her family, moved to Seattle for a year before moving back to San Francisco. Mariana also thought of moving with Diana to Seattle, but remained in San Francisco. Upon returning to San Francisco, Diana rented a house Mariana located, but they lived apart. One year ago, with their children entering their teenage years, they bought a two-unit house together. Diana, Aaron, and Emma live downstairs, while Mariana and Vicente live upstairs.

They are happy to report that this arrangement works well for them. They are close but have their separate spaces. They help each other with driving the kids around, they share appliances, and they feed each other's pets when necessary. Mariana said she feels "blessed" by having this arrangement. "This is my fantasy family, it is like having my extended family here," although she notes that she doesn't think her biological extended family would be as helpful as is Diana. Mariana also states that she feels each have a "vested interest in each other's children."

Diana is going to need all the help she can get right now. In addition to being the mother of two teenage children, and working full time, she has recently agreed to become, for the next two years, the president of Congregation Sha'ar Zahav, a synagogue in San Francisco with a special outreach toward lesbians, gays, and bisexuals. Being able to rely on Mariana, as a member of her family, has, in part, made this possible.

Extended Family, Love, and Alternative Fertilization

This is an example of another stable, committed queer alternative family. The history of this family begins in 1977 in St. Louis, when Steve rented a summer sublet in Ora's home. Ora was living in a six-unit building of which four units eventually became occupied by people who considered themselves to be part of a loose, hippie-style collective. The occupants found they got along well and after the summer was over, Steve never moved out. Adults, children, queers, straights, bisexuals, and people who could not be classified lived in the various units. Both Ora and Steve were beginning their own processes of coming out as queer people.

Both soon dropped out of school, Ora to do political work, and Steve to become an electrician. Time passed and the household, which had many people in addition to Ora and Steve, became more cohesive and felt more like a family. But in 1981, when Ora decided she needed to move to San Francisco to attend law school, two of the other house members, Steve and Alex, decided to move with her. In San Francisco they set up a collective household, which enabled Ora to keep her expenses down and not worry about where money for food was going to come from while she attended law school. Steve by this time was working as a journeyman electrician, and Alex worked as a locksmith.

In 1982, Ora met Rena. Ora's significant other at the time was Rena's roommate. The relationship was not working for a number of reasons, and Ora was told the relationship was over. At that point, the relationship between Ora and Rena began to develop, and on 21 April 1983 (the day that they consider to be their anniversary), Ora and Rena decided they were lovers. Problems between Ora, Rena, and Rena's roommate resulted in Rena moving into Ora's home before they had anticipated. Ora had planned on a long trip for the summer of 1983 and took the trip as planned. She discovered that absence did make the heart grow

fonder, and she and Rena had many long romantic phone calls that summer.

Ora returned, and now there were four in the family: Ora, Rena, Steve, and Alex. Rena said she was feeling insecure about what the level of commitment in the relationship actually was. So, in the fall of 1983, Ora and Rena had the first of what was to be three commitment ceremonies. With Alex present, Ora and Rena committed themselves to live together and to work out difficulties, in order that they might be able to live "happily ever after."

The second commitment ceremony was also a casual affair. At the annual Gay Pride celebration, Ora and Rena bought inexpensive rings and privately exchanged them. Though there was almost no ceremony, they considered the event to be significant. Early in their relationship they discussed how long they could envision being together. Because of their own personal histories, neither could envision what the relationship would be like more than five years into the future. At the five-year mark, they bought a down comforter to mark the occasion.

From early in the relationship, they discussed having children. Ora always knew she wanted children in her life, but said she knew from an early age that being a birth mother was not important to her. She had many children in her life in the collective in St. Louis and was close to them. But she felt more like a quasi parent than a parent, and she wanted more.

Timing was an issue. In 1986, Ora, Rena, and Steve bought the first of two houses they would buy together. It was a fixer upper and others were also involved, though not as homeowners. Rena felt a need to own a home for the security it represented. Ora felt ready to have children, as she had now graduated from law school, but Rena was not sure she was ready. It was clear to them, however, that they would want more than one child.

They considered all alternatives—adopting children, being foster parents, alternative fertilization. They also considered combining methods, such as having one child through alternative fertilization and one through adoption.

They decided to have at least one child through alternative fertilization. They wanted a known donor, because they did not want the child to wonder who the father was. They also wanted to make sure the father was a nice person, so they decided to try to choose the donor themselves. They spent two years talking with every man they thought was a reasonable possibility. They considered Steve, their house mate and family member, and Alex, who by now had moved back to St. Louis and was married with a child of his own. Both seriously considered being the donor, but after further discussing it, each decided it was not a good idea, and Ora and Rena continued to look. They considered Ora's brother, who declined to serve as a donor.

After intense, intentional searching, serendipity took over. On a trip to Amsterdam and Israel to attend an international conference of queer Jews, Ora met a man named Ron, who was from Detroit. They had attended a workshop on creating families at the conference, and they became friends and exchanged holiday cards after that. When other choices were not working out, Ora, almost off-handedly in a holiday card, asked Ron if he would consider being the donor, and he immediately replied with an enthusiastic yes.

Ron had several motivations for saying yes. Although comfortable with being a gay man, he felt an obligation as a Jewish man to father a child. He wanted to have children in his life but was not interested in the responsibilities of being a custodial fa-

(Left side, from top to bottom) Rena Frantz, Tsipora Prochovnicn, Ora Prochovnicn, and Shayna Prochovnicn; (right) Steven Neff and Spinoza the dog.

ther. That he was Jewish, and their children would be Jewish, was also important to Ora and Rena. Ron and Rena had never met, so Ron came to San Francisco and spent time with both of them.

They decided to use the services of a sperm bank for several reasons. Because Ron lived in Detroit, they needed a sperm bank to store the semen. Also, all wanted to make sure that Ron was not the legal father of the child, and this could be accomplished by going through a sperm bank. They drew up legal contracts between each of them, putting into writing the understandings they had reached.

Eventually Tsipora was conceived. Steve agreed to baby-sit the child one day per week, and from the beginning, on Sundays, Ora and Rena were able to get away and have time alone together. Though Steve was not enthusiastic about these responsibilities before Tsipora was born, he came to like his role as a significant person in the life of the child. Tsipora and her siblings now consider him their Uncle Stevie.

In addition to undergoing alternative fertilization, Ora and Rena had also been on the Department of Social Service foster care to adoption list. After Tsipora was born, Lyn came to live with them. As an adolescent, she had come out as a lesbian and was rejected by her family. After a traumatic series of events, she

came to live with Rena, Ora, Steve, and Tsipora. Because she was troubled as an adolescent, it was difficult for all, but the relationship lasted until Lyn was eighteen.

Rena and Ora wanted a second child of their own. After becoming frustrated with the Department of Social Service foster care to adoption program, they asked Ron if they could use the remaining frozen sperm samples to inseminate Rena again. He reluctantly agreed, feeling his goal had been fulfilled with the birth of Tsipora. They also told him they would have the remaining sperm samples thrown away if any were left after Rena became pregnant again, assuring him that he would not have more children.

In the quiet of their bedroom, with Ora reading aloud from *Winnie the Pooh* as she used Ron's sperm to inseminate Rena, Shayna was conceived on the first attempt.

Ron sees the children about twice a year. He sends them gifts and cards. The children are full siblings and know their father. Ora has formally adopted the children, making her their legal parent. Ron would like his children to call him Ron. Tsipora, in her impish ways, teases him by calling him Daddy, while Shayna calls him Ron.

In May 1996, with all family and friends present, Ora and Rena had a formal wedding. It was the 13th anniversary of their relationship, and they thought of it as their relationship Bat Mitzvah. They now realize the ceremony was more significant and moving than they had anticipated, and noted that it felt wonderful to have both a public commitment and a Jewish Ceremony.

An Extended Queer Family of Choice

The photo below was taken on 7 September 1997. The occasion was the 20th anniversary of the relationship of Jerry Singer and Donald Dodge (not pictured here as he was elsewhere at the party, as were several other long-time members of the author's queer family of choice). The following is the story of this family's creation and history.

Early in 1972, Michael Bettinger attended a meeting of the Gay Activists Alliance in New York City. At that meeting, he met Arthur Felson (1943-1986). Michael quickly became friends with Arthur and his lover, Jeffrey Katzoff. Soon after that, Michael became lovers with Robert Parker (1936-1992), and all four became close friends.

Jeffrey Katzoff has two close queer friends who were also part of that circle. One was Charlie Hoffman, who was at the party where the photo below was taken, and Jerry Singer, whose anniversary was the occasion for this party. Soon added to the group was another friend, Sam Goldsmith (1951-1993).

In 1974, Arthur and Jeffrey separated as lovers, and by early 1976, the same was true for Michael and Robert. The expectation, though, was that even though these individuals no longer formed couples, they were all expected to remain part of the family. So after a period of difficulty, all the individuals in the separating couples managed to work out friendships.

Over the next two years, the entire family moved to San Francisco. Michael, called the family trailblazer, moved first, in February 1976. Later that year, Jeffrey moved to San Francisco to attend law school. The following summer, Jerry announced he had met a new lover, Donald Dodge, who lived in San Francisco, and he too was moving. Sam then managed to get his company to transfer him to San Francisco. Arthur, Robert, and Charlie Hoffman also moved at the same time. By late 1978, the entire family had been reconstituted in San Francisco.

In 1978, Jeffrey met Ethan, and they have now been together as a couple for nearly 20 years. Sam met Arthur Reed in San Francisco the same year. In 1980, Sam, Arthur Reed, and Arthur Felson moved back to New York. Jeffrey and Ethan moved to Los Angeles for professional opportunities. Though never discussed, everyone assumed, correctly, that the commitment to the family would not be impeded by the different cities in which the people lived. Visits over the years have been common, and family members have traveled to be together for every big family event.

(From l-r) Michael Bettinger, Arthur Reed, Barry Schiller, Jeffrey Katzoff, Ethan Kenny, and Jerry Singer.

In 1986, Arthur Felson died of AIDS. In 1992, Robert Parker passed away from the same disease. In 1993, AIDS claimed Sam Goldsmith. With each death, the family came together to mourn. Though there were losses, additions to the family occurred. The author and Robert Goldstein became life partners in 1987 and celebrated with a commitment ceremony, which occurred in a synagogue officiated by a rabbi. They called it a *kiddushin*, or a ceremony to make their relationship "holy." All available family members flew into San Francisco for the ceremony, with the exception of Jerry and Donald, who were living in France that year.

The 20th-anniversary party for Jerry and Donald had another added bonus. It was an opportunity for the rest of the family to welcome Barry into the family. Arthur and Barry have now been partners for about a year, and while some family members have met Barry before, this was the first family event at which Barry was able to take part as a member of the family and to be welcomed into the family.

A Wedding

Christopher Johnson and Barry Miller met through a personals ad in the *Bay Times*, a San Francisco biweekly newspaper aimed toward the queer community, and have been together for five and a half years. Several months ago, they had a wedding ceremony. Though not recognized by the State of California as a marriage, for them the ceremony had the same meaning.

"I knew I wanted to spend the rest of my life with Barry," Chris said one afternoon in the house they own together in Oakland, California. "I wanted to commemorate our love and have something memorable for us. Both of us have supportive parents and in talking with them, the idea grew. We started small but found it easy to get carried away by the excitement."

"We really enjoy weddings," Barry mentioned. "Lately, we've been going to about ten a year. We travel to New York City for enormous family weddings. We wanted our wedding to be an event like that, to celebrate our love."

Chris noted, "We began by calling it a commitment ceremony, but then as we progressed, we realized it was a wedding. We stopped calling it a commitment ceremony. We tried to prepare our heterosexual guests that a commitment ceremony is every bit a wedding as any other wedding you go to."

"The Unitarian minister who married us said to us, 'You are doing this for all the right reasons.' We were doing it because we wanted to do it, not because it was expected of us," Barry recalled. "We also did it for our friends and our parents. They kept asking us, 'When are you two going to get married?'"

In December 1996, just before the holiday season and six months before their wedding was to take place, Chris and Barry sent their friends and relatives a letter explaining that the following summer they were planning to have a "Commitment Ceremony" at a Napa Valley winery and asked the people to put aside the date. They realized many would have to travel a considerable distance to be there. In the letter, they felt it was necessary to explain what a "Commitment Ceremony" was.

In their words, "Simply put, it's a wedding. It's a chance for us to express our lifetime commitment to each other, and to validate our feeling for each other in the presence of the people who are most important in our lives. In short, we are doing this for pretty much the same reasons that straight people get married: love."

Christopher Johnson (left) and Barry Miller

"The Ceremony," they continued, "is a celebration of our union and a blessing of our future together. The major difference between this wedding and others you've attended is that the 'marriage' is not legally recognized when the ceremony is over—and that there are two grooms and no bride."

When the 150 guests arrived at their wedding, they were handed a program for the event. On the cover were two photographs of the grooms as five-year-old kids. Inside read:

Program
Processional
"The Snowman's Music Box"—George Winston
"Over The Rainbow"—Andre Previn
Opening Words and Welcome
Silence and Prayer
Reading: "A Goose Story"
Words to the audience
Water Pouring Ceremony
Words to each other
"Breathless Taste of Spring"
  Written by Pilar Montaine and Gary Remal Malkin
  Performed today by Pilar Montaine and John Hoy
Candle Lighting Ceremony
Acknowledgement of family

Blessing and congregational affirmation
Vows and Rings
Breaking of the glass
Recessional
"Be My Baby"—The Ronettes

Chris and Barry are also registered as domestic partners in the City of Oakland, but for them, that is more of a political statement than an emotional one. The ceremony, without any official validation, is much more meaningful to them.

REFERENCES:

Books and Articles: Queer Couples

Berzon, Betty. *Permanent Partners: Building Gay and Lesbian Relationships That Last.* New York: Dutton, 1988.

Bettinger, M. *Relationship Satisfaction, Cohesion and Adaptability: A Study of Gay Male Couples.* Unpublished doctoral dissertation, California Graduate School of Marital and Family Therapy, San Rafael, California, 1986.

Blumstein, P. and P. Schwartz. *American Couples: Money, Work and Sex.* New York: William Morrow and Company, 1983.

Boswell, J. *Same-Sex Unions in Premodern Europe.* New York: Vintage Books, 1994.

Bryant, S. and Demian, eds. *Partners: Newsletter for Gay and Lesbian Couples*, May/June, 1990.

Clunis, D. M. and G. D. Green. *Lesbian Couples.* Seattle: Seal Press, 1988.

Curry, H. and D. Clifford. *A Legal Guide for Lesbian & Gay Couples.* Berkeley: Nolo Press, 1988.

Green, R.-J., M. Bettinger, and E. Zacks. "Are Lesbian Couples Fused and Gay Male Couples Disengaged?" in *Lesbians and Gays in Couples and Families: A Handbook for Therapists,* edited by J. Laird and R.-J. Green. San Francisco: Jossey-Bass, 1996.

Harry, J. "Decision Making and Age Differences Among Gay Male Couples." *Journal of Homosexuality 8*, no. 2, 1982: 9-21.

———. "Gay Males and Lesbian Relationships," in *Contemporary Families and Alternative Lifestyles,* edited by E. D. Macklin and R. H. Rubin. Beverly Hills, California: Sage, 1983.

Johnson, S. E. *Staying Power: Long Term Lesbian Couples.* Tallahassee, Florida: Naiad Press, 1991.

Isensee, R. *Love Between Men: Enhancing Intimacy and Keeping Your Relationship Alive.* Los Angeles: Alyson Publications, 1990.

Klinger, R. L. "Lesbian Couples." in *Textbook of Homosexuality and Mental Health,* by R. P. Cabaj and T. S. Stein. Washington, D.C.: American Psychiatric Press, 1996.

Kurdek, L. A. "The Allocation of Household Labor in Homosexual and Heterosexual Cohabiting Couples," in *Journal of Social Issues 49*, 1993: 27-139.

———. "Lesbian and Gay Couples," in *Lesbian, Gay and Bisexual Identities over the Lifespan,* edited by A. R. D'Augelli and C. J. Patterson. New York: Oxford University Press, 1995.

———. "Relationship Quality of Gay Men and Lesbian Cohabiting Couples," in *Journal of Homosexuality 15*, 1988: 93-118.

———. "Relationship Quality of Gay Men and Lesbian Cohabiting Couples, A 1 Year Follow Up Study," in *Journal of Social and Personal Relationships*, vol. 6, 1989: 39-59.

Laird, J. and R.-J. Green, eds. *Lesbians and Gays in Couples and Families: A Handbook for Therapists.* San Francisco: Jossey-Bass, 1996.

McWhirter, D. P. and A. M. Mattison. *The Male Couple: How Relationships Develop.* Englewood Cliffs, New Jersey: Prentice-Hall, 1984.

Peplau, L. A. and S. D. Cochran. "A Relationship Perspective on Homosexuality," in *Homosexuality/Heterosexuality: Concepts of Sexual Orientation,* edited by D. P. McWhirter, S. A. Sanders, and J. M. Reinisch. New York: Oxford University Press, 1990.

Peplau, L. A., R. C. Veniegas, and S. M. Cambell. "Gay and Lesbian Relationships," in *The Lives of Lesbians, Gays and Bisexuals: Children to Adults,* edited by R. C. Savin-Williams and K. M. Cohen. Fort Worth: Harcourt Brace College Publishers, 1996.

Poverny, L. M. and W. A. Finch. "Gay and Lesbian Domestic Partnerships: Expanding the Definition of Family," in *Social Casework 69*, no. 2, 1988: 116-121.

Shernoff, M. "Male Couples and Their Relationships Styles," in *Journal of Gay and Lesbian Social Services 2*, no. 2, 1995.

Silverstein, C. *Man to Man: Gay couples in America.* New York: William Morrow, 1981.

Slater, S. and J. Mencher. "The Lesbian Family Lifecycle: A Contextual Approach," in *American Journal of Orthopsychiatry*, vol. 61, 1991: 372-382.

Sullivan, A. *Same-Sex Marriage: Pro and Con, A Reader.* New York: Vintage, 1987.

Tessina, T. *Gay Relationships: How to Find Them, How to Improve Them, How to Make Them Last.* New York: St. Martin's Press, 1989.

Zacks, E., R.-J. Green, and J. Marrow. "Comparing Lesbian and Heterosexual Couples on the Circumplex Model: An Initial Investigation." *Family Process 27*, 1988: 471-484.

Books and Articles: Multigenerational Queer Families

Achtenberg, Roberta. *Preserving and Protecting the Families of Lesbians and Gay Men.* San Francisco: National Center for Lesbian Rights, 1990.

Bagnall, R. G., P. C. Gallagher, and J. L. Goldstein. "Burdens on Gay Litigants and Bias in the Court System: Homosexual Panic, Child Custody, and Anonymous Parties," in *Harvard Civil Rights and Civil Liberties Law Review 19*, 1984: 497-559.

Barret, R. L. and B. E. Robinson. *Gay Fathers.* Lexington, Massachusetts: Lexington Books, 1990.

Benkov, L. *Reinventing the Family: Lesbian and Gay Parents.* Crown Publishing, New York, 1994.

Bigner, J. J. and F. W. Bozett. "Parenting by Gay Fathers," in *Homosexuality and Family Relations,* by F. W. Bozett and M. S. Sussman. New York: Harrington Park Press, 1990.

Bigner, J. J. and R. B. Jacobson. "The Value of Children to Heterosexual Fathers," in *Homosexuality and the Family,* edited by In F. W. Bozett. New York: Harrington Park Press, 1989.

Bozett, F.W. *Gay and Lesbian Parents.* New York: Praeger, 1987.

———. "Gay Fathers: A Review of the Literature," in *Homosexuality and the Family,* by Bozett. N.p., n.d.

———. "Gay Fathers: Evolution of the Gay-Father Identity," in *American Journal of Orthopsychiatry 51*, 1981: 552-559.

———. "Gay Fathers: How and Why They Disclose Their Homosexuality to Their Children," in *Family Relations 29*, 1980: 173-179.

————. "Gay Fathers: Identity Conflict through Integrative Sanctioning," in *Alternative Lifestyles 4*, 1981: 90-107.

Burke, P. *Family Values: Two Moms and Their Son.* New York: Random House, 1993.

Corley, R. *The Final Closet: The Gay Parents' Guide for Coming Out to Their Children.* Miami: Editech Press, 1990.

Cramer, D. "Gay Parents and Their Children: A Review of Research and Practical Implications," in *Journal of Counseling and Development 64*, 1986: 504-507.

Crosbie-Burnett, M. and L. Helmbrech. "A Descriptive Study of Gay Male Step Families," in *Family Relations*, vol. 42, 1993: 256-262.

Falk, P. J. "Lesbian Mothers: Psychological Assumptions in Family Law," in *American Psychologist 44*, 1989: 941-947.

Gibbs, E. D. "Psychosocial Development of Children Raised by Lesbian Mothers: A Review of Research," in *Women and Therapy 8*, nos. 1-2, 1988: 65-75.

Gil de Lamadrid, M., ed. *Lesbians Choosing Motherhood: Legal Implications of Donor Insemination and Co-parenting.* San Francisco: National Center for Lesbian Rights, 1991.

Gold, M., E. Perrin, D. Futterman, and S. Friedman. "Children of Gay or Lesbian Parents," in *Pediatrics in Review 15*, no. 9, 1994: 354-358.

Golombok, S., A. Spencer, and M. Rutter. "Children in Lesbian and Single Parent Households: Psychosexual and Psychiatric Appraisal," in *Journal of Child Psychology and Psychiatry*, vol. 24, 1983: 551-572.

Gottman-Schwartz, J. "Children of Gay and Lesbian Parents," in *Marriage and Family Review 14*, no. 3, 1989: 177-196.

Gottsfield, R. L. "Child Custody and Sexual Lifestyle," in *Conciliation Courts Review 23*, no. 1, June 1985: 43-46.

Green, R. "Sexual Identity of 37 Children Raised by Homosexual or Transsexual Parents," in *American Journal of Psychiatry 135*, 1978: 692-697.

Green, R., J. B. Mandel, M. E. Hotvedt, J. Gray, and L. Smith. "Lesbian Mothers and Their Children: A Comparison with Solo Parent Heterosexual Mothers and Their Children," in *Archives of Sexual Behavior 7*, 1986: 175-181.

Griffin, C. W., M. J. Wirth, and A. G. Wirth. *Beyond Acceptance: Parents of Lesbians and Gays Talk About Their Experiences.* New York: St. Martin's Press, 1986.

Hanscombe, Gillian E. and Jackie Forster. *Rocking The Cradle— Lesbian Mothers: A Challenge in Family Living.* Boston: Alyson Press, 1987.

Hare, J. and L. Richards. "Children Raised by Lesbian Couples. Does the Context of Birth Affect Father and Partner Involvement?" in *Family Relations 42*, 1993: 249-255.

Harris, M. B. and P. H. Turner. "Gay and Lesbian Parents," in *Journal of Homosexuality 12*, 1986: 101-113.

Hoeffer, B. "Children's Acquisition of Sex-Role Behavior in Lesbian-Mother Families," in *American Journal of Orthopsychiatry 5*, 1981: 536-544.

Hornstein, F. "Children by Donor Insemination: A New Choice for Lesbians," in *Test-tube Women: What Future for Motherhood?*, edited by R. Arditti, R. D. Klein, and S. Minden. London: Pandora Press, 1984.

Huggins, S. L. "A comparative study of self-esteem of adolescent children of divorced lesbian mothers and divorced heterosexual mothers," in *Homosexuality and the Family* by Bozett (also issued simultaneously in *The Journal of Homosexuality 18*, nos. 1/2, 1989).

Kirkpatrick, M. "Lesbians as Parents," in *Textbook of Homosexuality and Mental Health*, edited by R. Cabaj and R. Stein. Washington, D.C.: American Psychiatric Press, 1996.

Kirkpatrick, M., J. Roy, and K. Smith. "A New Look at Lesbian Mothers," in *Human Behavior*, August 1976: 60-61.

Kirpatrick, M., C. Smith, and R. Roy. "Lesbian Mothers and Their Children: A Comparative Survey," in *American Journal of Orthopsychiatry 51*, 1981: 545-551.

Koepke, L., J. Hare, and P. B. Moran. "Relationship Quality in a Sample of Lesbian Couples with Children and Child Free Lesbian Couples," in *Family Relations 41*, 1992: 224-229.

Lyons, T. A. "Lesbian Mothers' Custody Fears," in *Women and Therapy 2*, 1983: 231-240.

Martin, A. *The Lesbian and Gay Parenting Handbook: Creating and Raising Our Families.* New York: HarperPerennial, 1993.

Miller, B. "Counseling Gay Husbands and Gay Fathers," in *Gay and Lesbian Parents*, by Bozett. N.p., n.d.

————. "Gay Fathers and Their Children," in *The Family Coordinator 28*, 1979: 544-552.

Morgen, K. B. *Getting Simon: Two Gay Doctors' Journey to Fatherhood.* New York: Bramble Books, 1995.

Muller, A. *Parents Matter: Parents' Relationship with Lesbian Daughters and Gay Sons.* Tallahassee, Florida: Naiad Press, 1987.

Pagelow, M. D. "Heterosexual and Single Lesbian Mothers: A Comparison of Problems, Coping and Solutions," in *Journal of Homosexuality 5*, 1980: 198-204.

Patterson, C. J. "Adoption of Minor Children by Lesbian and Gay Adults: A Social Science Perspective," in *Duke Journal of Gender LAW and Policy*, vol. 2, 1995: 191-205.

————. "Children of Lesbian and Gay Parents," in *Child Development*, 1992: 1025-42.

————. "Lesbian and Gay Couples Considering Parenthood: An Agenda for Research, Service, and Advocacy," in *Journal of Gay and Lesbian Social Services 1*, no. 2, 1994: 33-55.

————. "Lesbian and Gay Parents and Their Children," in *The Lives of Lesbians, Gays and Bisexuals: Children to Adults*, edited by R. C. Savin-Williams and K. M. Cohen. Fort Worth: Harcourt Brace College Publishers, 1996.

————. "Lesbian Mothers, Gay Fathers and Their Children," in *Lesbian, Gay and Bisexual Identities over the Lifespan*, by D'Augelli and Patterson. N.p., n.d.

Pies, C. *Considering Parenting: A Workbook for Lesbians.* San Francisco: Spinster Ink, 1985.

Pollack, J. S. *Lesbian and Gay Families: Redefining Parenting in America.* New York: Franklin Watts, 1995.

Pollack, Sandra and Jeanne Vaughn. *Politics of the Heart: A Lesbian Parenting Anthology.* Firebrand Books, 1987.

Rafkin, L. *Different Mothers: Sons and Daughters of Lesbians Talk About Their Lives.* Pittsburgh: Cleis Press, 1990.

Rees, R. L. *A Comparison of Children of Lesbian and Single Heterosexual Mothers on Three Measures of Socialization.* Berkeley: California School of Professional Psychology, 1979.

Ricketts, W. *Lesbians and Gay Men as Foster Parents.* Portland: National Child Welfare Resource Center, University of Southern Maine, 1991.

Ricketts, W. and R. Achtenberg. "Adoption and Foster Parenting for Lesbians and Gay Men: Creating New Traditions in Family," in *Homosexuality and Family Relations*, edited F. W. Bozett and M. S. Sussman. New York: Harrington Park Press, 1990.

Schulenberg, J. *Gay Parenting.* Garden City, New York: Doubleday, 1985.

Stein, Terry S. "Homosexuality and New Family Forms: Issues in Psychotherapy," in *Psychiatric Annals 18*, 1988: 12-20.

Books and Articles: Bisexual Queer Family Issues

Jardine, J. and S. Whyte. *The Bisexual Female.* Los Angeles: Centurion Press, 1971.

Klein, F. *The Bisexual Option.* New York: Arbor House, 1978.

Paul, J. P. *Growing up with a Gay, Lesbian or Bisexual Parent: An Exploratory of Experiences and Perceptions.* Unpublished doctoral dissertation, University of California at Berkeley, 1986.

Rila, M. and B. Reed. *100 Bisexual Women.* San Francisco: Institute for the Advanced Study of Human Sexuality, 1980.

Books and Articles: Queer Families of Choice

Ahern, S. and K. G. Bailey. *Family by Choice.* Minneapolis: Fairview Press, 1996.

Nardi, P. M. "That's What Friends Are For: Friends as Family in the Gay and Lesbian Community," in *Modern Homosexualities,* edited by K. Plummer. New York: Routledge, 1992.

Preston, J. and M. Lowenthal, eds. *Friends and Lovers.* New York: Plume, 1995.

Vacha, K. *Quiet Fire: Memoirs of Older Gay Men.* Trumansburg, New York: The Crossing Press, 1985.

Weston, Kath. *Families We Choose.* New York: Columbia University Press, 1991.

Books and Articles: Statistics on Queer Couples and Families

Bell, A. and M. Weinberg. *Homosexualities: A Study of Diversity Among Men and Women.* New York: Simon and Schuster, 1978.

Blumstein, P. and P. Schwartz. *American Couples: Money, Work and Sex.* New York: William Morrow, 1983.

Bryant, S. and Demian, eds. *Partners: Newsletter for Gay and Lesbian Couples.* N.p., May/June 1990.

Jay, K. and A. Young. *The Gay Report.* New York: Summit, 1979.

Saghir, M. T. and E. Robins. *Male and Female Homosexuality: A Comprehensive Investigation.* Baltimore, Maryland: Williams and Wilkins, 1973.

Spada, J. *The Spada Report.* New York: New American Library, 1979.

Weinberg, M. and C. Williams. *Male Homosexuals: Their Problems and Adaptations.* New York: Oxford University Press, 1974.

Books: Commitment Ceremonies

Ayers, T. and P. Brown. *The Essential Guide to Lesbian and Gay Weddings.* San Francisco: Harper San Francisco, 1994.

Books: For Children

Gantz, Joe. *Whose Child Cries: Children of Gay Parents Talk About Their Lives.* Rolling Hills Estates, California: Jalmar Press, 1983.

Newman, L. *Heather Has Two Mommies.* Boston: Alyson Publications, 1990.

Prejudice and Bigotry Are Not Family Values. **Sign at protest held in Sacramento, California on 11 October 1991, following a veto by Governor Pete Wilson of Assembly Bill 101.**

Rafkin, L. *Different Mothers: Sons and Daughters of Lesbians Talk About Their Lives.* Pittsburgh: Cleis, 1990.

Willhoite, M. *Daddy's Roommate.* Boston: Alyson Publications, 1990.

Books and Articles: Other

Diamond, M. "Homosexuality and Bisexuality in Different Populations," in *Archives of Sexual Behavior*, vol. 33, 1993: 291-310.

Gottman, J. M. *Marital Interaction: Experimental Investigations.* Chicago: Academic Press, 1979.

Katz, J. N. "The Invention of Heterosexuality," in *Socialist Review 20*, January-March 1990: 7.

Kinsey, A., W. Pomeroy, and C. Martin. *Sexual Behavior in the Human Male.* Philadelphia: W. B. Saunders, 1948.

Kinsey, A, W. Pomeroy, C. Martin, and P. Gebhard. *Sexual Behavior in the Human Female.* Philadelphia: W. B. Saunders, 1953.

Masters, W. H. and V. E. Johnson. *Homosexuality in Perspective.* Boston: Little, Brown and Company, 1979.

Morin, S. F. "Heterosexual Bias in Psychological Research on Lesbianism and Male Homosexuality," in *American Psychologist 32*, 1977: 629-637.

Thompson, L. and A. J. Walker. "Women and Men in Marriage, Work, and Parenthood," in *Journal of Marriage and the Family 51*, 1989: 845-872.

Organizations

AASK (Adopt A Special Kid) America
657 Mission St., #601
San Francisco, CA 94105-4120
(800) 232-2751 or (415) 543-2275

Adoption Options—Rainbow Kids
Contact: Chuck Smith
(404) 633-6021

Adoption Resource Exchange for Single Parents
P.O. Box 5782
Springfield, VA 22150
Elmy Martinez, Exec. Director
(703) 866-5577

Center Kids
The Family Project
Lesbian/Gay Community Services Center
208 West 13th Street
New York, NY 10011
(212) 620-7310

Colage: Children of Lesbians and Gays Everywhere
2300 Market Street
Box 165
San Francisco, CA 94114
(415) 861-KIDS
E-mail: KIDSOFGAYS@aol.com

Custody Action for Lesbian Mothers (CALM)
P.O. Box 281
Narbeth, PA 19072
(215) 667-7508

Family Fertility Center
1801 Oakland Blvd., Suite 250
Walnut Creek, CA 94596
Voice: (510) 977-4850
Fax: (510) 977-4854

Fenway Community Health Center, Lesbian/Gay Family and Parenting Services
7 Haviland St.
Boston, MA 02115-2608
(617) 267-0900 ext. 282

Future Gay Fathers of America
P.O. Box 43206
Montclair, NJ 07043
Phone: Wayne Steinman (adoption), (718) 987-6747
E-Mail: GLPCI@aol.com
or Tim Fisher (surrogacy), (201) 783-6204 (phone and fax)
E-mail: FamValues@aol.com

Gay and Lesbian Parents Coalition International
P.O Box 50360
Washington, DC 20091
(202) 583-8029

Growing Generations
6310 San Vicente Blvd. Suite 410
Los Angeles, CA 90048
Phone: (310) 475-4770
Fax: (310) 470-7196
E-mail: growinggen@earthlink.net

Lambda Legal Defense and Education Fund
666 Broadway
New York, NY 10012
Phone: (212) 995-8585
E-mail: LLDEF@aol.com

Lavender Families Resource Network
PO Box 21567
Seattle, WA 98111
(206) 325-2643

Lesbian and Gay Parenting Program
1784 Market Street
San Francisco, CA 94102
(415) 565-7674

Lesbian and Gay Parenting Project
c/o Lyon-Martin Clinic
2480 Mission Street, Suite 214
San Francisco, CA 94110
(415) 525-7312

Love Makes A Family Inc.
PO Box 11694
Portland, OR 97211
(503) 228-3892

National Adoption Information Clearinghouse
11426 Rockville Pike, Suite 300
Rockville, MD 20852
(301) 231-6512

National Gay and Lesbian Task Force
Family Issues Project
1517 U Street NW
Washington, D.C. 20009
(202) 332-6483

Pact, An Adoption Alliance
3315 Sacramento Street, Suite 239
San Francisco, CA 94118
(415) 221-6957

PFLAG: Parents, Families and Friends of Lesbians and Gays
1101 14th Street, NW
Suite 1030
Washington, DC 20005
(202) 638-4200

Rainbow Flag Health Services
A Known Donor Sperm Bank
Leland Traiman, RN/FNP, Director
(510) 763-SPERM (763-7737)
E-mail: rainbowf@flash.net

Sperm Bank of California
Reproductive Technologies, Inc.
2115 Milvia Street, 2nd Floor
Berkeley, CA 94704
(510) 841-1858

Straight Spouse Support Network
Amity Pierce Buxton (author of The Other Side of the Closet)
8215 Terrace Drive
El Cerrito, CA 94530
Phone: (510) 525-0200
E-mail: KYUB40C@prodigy.com

Internet Resources

Alternative Family Project: http://www.queer.org/afp
Alternative Family Matters: http://members.aol.com/altfammat
COLAGE (Children of Lesbians and Gays Everywhere) Home Page: http://www.colage.org/
Family Q Home Page: http://www.studio8prod.com/familyq

Gay & Lesbian Parenting: http://www.teleport.com/~dorsieh/info.queer.html
Gaydads: http://userwww.service.emory.edu/~librpj/gaydads.html
GLPCI (Gay and Lesbian Parents Coalition International) HOME PAGE: http://abacus.oxy.edu/QRD/www/orgs/glpci/home.htm
Lesbian Moms Web Page: http://www.lesbian.org/moms
Lesbian Mothers Support Society: http://shell6.ba.best.com/~agoodloe/lesbian-moms/index.html
Partners Task Force for Gay & Lesbian Couples—Parents: http://www.eskimo.com/~demian/parents.html
Prospective Queer Parents: http://www.geocities.com/WestHollywood/3373
Rainbow Families: http://lesbianmoms.org/rainbofamily
Rainbow Flag Health Services: http://www-leland.stanford.edu/~blandon/rainbow.html#sources
We Are Family: http://www.pridemail.com/wearefam/index.html
Yahoo! Lesbians, Gays & Bisexuals—Parenting: http://www.yahoo.com/Society_and_Culture/Lesbians_Gays_and_Bisexuals/Parenting

—Michael Bettinger

6

Health

- **Physical Health**
- **Mental Health**
- **Barriers to Care**
- **Impact on Care**
- **Conclusions**
- **Resources**

In the late 1940s, the World Health Organization defined health as "a state of complete physical, mental, and social well being and not merely the absence of disease or infirmity" (Callahan, 1977, p. 26). While these components of health are often discussed separately, it is crucial that the interaction between the three be acknowledged. The purpose of this article is to describe health care issues specific to gay men and lesbians, including both physical and mental health. However, it is impossible to discuss these aspects of health without also discussing the social context in which gay men and lesbians live. Homophobia and heterosexism have a profound impact on the physical and psychological well-being of homosexuals, and thus any discussion of gay and lesbian health must start with a discussion of these broader issues.

According to Stein (1996, p. 39) "(h)omophobia is a fear or hatred of homosexuality and gay and lesbian persons arising from a variety of societal and intrapsychic sources. Homophobia has been used to refer to a wide variety of negative feelings, attitudes, and behaviors directed toward homosexuality and gay men and lesbians." In contrast, heterosexism is "an ideological system that denies, denigrates, and stigmatizes any nonheterosexual form of behavior, identity, relationship, or community. It operates principally by rendering homosexuality invisible and, when this fails, by trivializing, repressing, or stigmatizing it" (Herek, 1990, p. 316). Heterosexism provides the context in which homophobia flourishes and is sanctioned within society. The overt manifestations of homophobia and heterosexism are discrimination and violence towards gay men and lesbians, or towards those who are perceived as homosexual. Gay men and lesbians may also internalize these negative cultural attitudes and beliefs, resulting in poor self esteem and even self-hatred.

The physical and psychological health risks for gay men and lesbians who live in this homophobic and heterosexist environment include: (1) increased risk of some types of cancer and infectious diseases (Cole, Kemeny, Taylor and Visscher, 1996; Harrison, 1996); (2) Physical and psychological injury resulting from being the victims of hate crimes and biased violence (Herek, 1989; Herek, 1993). At the extreme physical injury may result in the death of the victim (Berrill, 1990), while Post-Traumatic Stress

Disorder (PTSD), depression, withdrawal, and self-blame (Garnets, Herek and Levy, 1990; Hanson, 1996; Otis and Skinner, 1996), along with an increased risk for suicide (Savin-Williams, 1994) are the effects of psychological injury; and (3) an increased risk for alcohol and drug related problems (Anderson, 1996; Bradford, Ryan and Rothblum, 1994).

Heterosexism and homophobia also affect the health care services available to gay men and lesbians. Although the American Psychiatric Association removed homosexuality from its list of mental disorders in 1973, many physicians and other mental health providers continue to see homosexuality as a disease that needs to be cured (Herek, 1990). Because of these provider attitudes, lesbians and gay men may be more hesitant to seek services, not disclose their sexual orientation to providers and thus receive inappropriate services, or disclose their sexual orientation and risk rejection (Peterson and Bricker-Jenkins, 1996; Schwartz, 1996). While it is critical that health care providers understand the personal impact of cultural homophobia and heterosexism on their gay and lesbian clients/patients, it is also critical that sexual orientation not overshadow other needs of the person.

Clearly gay men and lesbians in the United States have not achieved a state of social well-being, and will not as long as homophobia and heterosexism exist. The social context in which lesbians and gay men live has an interactive effect on both their physical and psychological well being. The remainder of this chapter will focus on the physical and psychological health of gay men and lesbians, the barriers they face in receiving care necessary to achieve psychological and physical well-being, and the organizations and services that are committed to developing services that are sensitive to the unique needs of lesbians and gay men.

PHYSICAL HEALTH

The health care concerns of gay men and lesbians are both similar to, and different from, those of heterosexual men and women. Within this arena it is vital to distinguish between sexual behavior and sexual identity, since it is behavior, not identity, that either protects or puts a person at risk for certain health care concerns. For example, while women who have sex exclusively with other women are at decreased risk of being infected with HIV, studies report that as many as 77 percent of women who identify themselves as lesbians have been sexually active with men at some time in their life (Johnson, Smith and Guenther, 1987). Likewise, O'Neill and Shalit (1992, p. 191) note "that the majority of men found to have had 'occasional' or 'fairly frequent' sex with other men were or had been married (Fay, 1989) and that, in an ethically controversial study published in 1970, it was reported that

54 percent of men having sex in public bathrooms were married (Humphreys, 1970)." In addition, both an individual's sexual orientation and her or his behavior may vary over time.

One of the most comprehensive articles concerning the health care concerns of men and women who engage in same-sex behavior was written by the Council on Scientific Affairs of the American Medical Association. This article as well as others note that it is difficult to compare disease morbidity and mortality rates between individuals who engage in same-sex and opposite-sex behavior because of the dearth of studies that use sexual behavior as a variable. In addition, many of the studies done on same-sex samples are not representative of the gay and lesbian populations, but rather are samples of convenience that include an overrepresentation of young, white, well-educated persons (Rothblum, 1994). Without prospective, population-based studies it is impossible to determine the actual incidence of disease among gay men and lesbians. Thus, the unique health care concerns of lesbians and gay men are anticipated based on known risk factors that contribute to certain diseases, and the known incidence of these risk factors in these groups (Council on Scientific Affairs, 1996).

Women

Sexually Transmitted Diseases (STDs). "Women who only have sex with women are at less risk for contracting syphilis, gonorrhea, and chlamydia than women who have intercourse with men" (Robertson and Schachter, 1981; Council on Scientific Affairs 1996, p. 1354-55) and also have a low incidence of Hepatitis A, amebiasis, shigellosis, and helminthism (Johnson, Smith and Guenther, 1987; Robertson and Schachter, 1981). "In contrast, bacterial vaginosis, candidiasis, and *Trichomonas vaginalis* infection do occur in lesbians and appear to be transmissible between women" (White and Levinson, 1995, p. 464). In instances where infection occurs between same-sex partners it is critical that both women be treated.

Women who have sex with other women may also be at risk for contracting the Human Immunodeficiency Virus (HIV). While the most common risk behaviors are either unprotected heterosexual activity or intravenous (IV) drug use, there are also isolated incidences of woman-to-woman transmission reported in the medical literature (Rankow, 1995). While exposure to menstrual and traumatic bleeding is the most likely source of these isolated incidences, HIV has also been found in cervical and vaginal secretions, and thus HIV may theoretically be transmitted by infected women who are not bleeding (White and Levinson, 1995). It is also important to note that recurrent vaginal infections that are resistant to treatment may indicate the presence of HIV.

Rankow (1995) states that due to inadequate research there are no clear guidelines for women who partner with other women regarding safer sex practices to reduce the incidence of sexually transmitted diseases.

> Current recommendations include: household plastic wrap or latex barriers to protect against oral contact with vaginal fluids, menstrual blood, blood resulting from traumatic penetration, HPV or herpes simplex virus (HSV-1 and HSV-2) lesions, fecal-borne pathogens, and breast milk. Only water-based lubricants should be used with latex or plastic wrap, as oil-based products may degrade the integrity of the barrier. If sex toys are shared, they must be well cleaned between partners with one part bleach to

ten parts soapy water, or covered with a fresh condom. Direct genital-to-genital stimulation (tribadism) can be an unsafe practice because it may lead to mucosal exposure to blood or sexual fluids. Intact skin provides a good barrier, and latex gloves or finger cots protect hands in case of cuts or abrasions. Any woman engaging in heterosexual activity should use a condom and spermicide with every encounter (Rankow, 1995, p. 488).

Cancer. There are no prospective, population-based studies comparing the incidence of various cancers between lesbian and heterosexual women. However, White and Levinson (1993) have identified specific risk factors for various types of cancer that are distributed differently in the lesbian and heterosexual populations. Among the risk factors identified for lesbians are never giving birth to children (nulliparity) and lower number of births (oligoparity), older age at birth of first child, never breast feeding an infant, higher incidence of alcohol use and smoking, higher body mass, decreased use of oral contraceptives, lower incidence of sexually transmitted diseases, and less-frequent screening exams. In addition, Rankow (1995) has noted that lesbians may have less access to their family history concerning the incidence of cancer due to estrangement and lack of communication with their biological relatives. Harrison (1996, pp. 13-15) has summarized these risk factors for lesbians and their association with an increased, or decreased risk for specific types of cancers.

Factors That May Indicate an Increase in Risk for Specific Cancers in Lesbians

Disease or Condition	Risk Factors
Breast cancer	Nulliparity, older age at first childbirth, no breast-feeding, smoking, increased alcohol use, high body mass index, and fewer screening exams
Ovarian cancer	No oral contraceptive use, nulliparity, smoking
Endometrial cancer	No oral contraceptive use, nulliparity, oligoparity
Colon cancer	Smoking, increased body mass index, fewer screening exams
Lung cancer	Increased smoking

Factors That May Indicate a Decrease in Risk for Specific Cancers in Lesbians

Disease or Condition	Risk Factors
Cervical cancer	Decreased incidence of Human papilloma virus in lesbian population; this may be mitigated by increased smoking and fewer screening exams

The risk of a woman in the United States being diagnosed with breast cancer in her lifetime is well established at one-in-eight, a figure that has been labeled a national epidemic. While exact figures are unknown, it is believed that the risk of a lesbian developing breast cancer is even greater, based on particular risk factors (Gallagher, 1997). It is imperative that large scale, population-based studies be undertaken to determine the incidence of various types of cancer among lesbians. As mentioned, lesbians have screening exams less frequently, due to barriers to care that will be discussed more fully later in this chapter, which results in delayed diagnosis and treatment (Simkin, 1991; Taravella, 1992). Education and prevention programs need to be developed to inform lesbians about their risk for various forms of cancer, in the hope that such programs could result in earlier detection and treatment.

Reproductive Health Issues. Reproductive health issues are the most common reason why women come in contact with health care providers and the most common access point for preventive health care. It is well documented that lesbians seek routine care less frequently than heterosexual women, with Stevens and Hall (1988) reporting that 84 percent of their sample described a general reluctance to seek health care. Trippet and Bain (1992) reported that 24.7 percent of the lesbians in their sample "failed to seek health care" (p. 148), while Bruenting's (1992) findings supported an earlier study by Smith, Johnson, and Guenther (1985) that found that lesbian women are less likely to seek routine gynecological care. Robertson and Schachter (1981) found the average time between Pap smears for heterosexual women was 8 months, and for lesbians, 21 months, using the same clinic. Moran (1996) found similar results in a Canadian sample, with only 42 percent of lesbians receiving yearly Pap smears compared to 75 percent of all Canadian women aged 25-34 and 64 percent aged 35-44. Thirteen percent of the lesbians in her study had never had a Pap smear.

The reasons for the failure of lesbians to seek routine gynecologic care are multiple, including both a perception of reduced need as well as inappropriate care by providers. Health care providers may misinform their lesbian patients about the need for routine exams (Rankin, 1995; Simkin, 1993), reinforcing the patient's perception of reduced need. However, as Rankin (1995, p. 488) states:

A complete history of past and current sexual behaviors is imperative to accurately assess each patient and devise a screening protocol appropriate to her needs. All women, even those who have never engaged in heterosexual intercourse and who are not currently sexually active, need periodic cervical screening and regular bimanual pelvic examination (Edwards and Thin, 1990; Simkin, 1993).

Many providers routinely ask what form of birth control a woman uses and the frequency of intercourse. Both of these questions are reflective of heterosexist attitudes and constitute a barrier for lesbians seeking care (Robertson, 1992; Stevens and Hall, 1988). At the same time that many lesbians find questions about contraception to be inappropriate and heterosexist, they may have questions about alternative forms of *conception* that are not readily addressed.

Lesbians considering parenthood are faced with important decisions about conception. They must weigh use of alternative insemination, knowledge of the donor versus an unknown donor, and participation of the donor/father in the child's life; these decisions have both personal and legal ramifications. To choose the best for their children

and family, lesbians must have access to information that will help them make informed choices. Lesbians often need access to the health care system for assistance with conception (Levy, 1996, pp. 52-53).

Harvey, Carr, and Bernheine (1989), in a study of lesbian mothers' health care experiences, found that 82 percent of the women conceived through alternative insemination donors. All of the women in this study used the medical system to help them with insemination. While some lesbians have used gay men as donors, this has been discouraged due to the increased risk for HIV as well as potential custody issues (Gentry, 1992; Rankow, 1995; Zeidenstein, 1990). However, Tash and Kenney (1993) found that many lesbians report health care providers who lack knowledge about, and who are not supportive of, lesbian parenting.

Even though most of the lesbians in Harvey, Carr, and Bernheine's (1989) study had not used regular health care providers prior to pregnancy, 100 percent of these women received prenatal care once they had conceived. Levy (1996) attributes this to the fact that lesbians have to face many obstacles to becoming pregnant and because pregnancy requires a conscious choice. Harvey and others (1989) also reported a high rate of satisfaction by these women with the prenatal care they received.

Along with the medical issues that lesbians confront in the reproductive arena, legal issues must also be considered. As stated by Rankow (1995, p. 489):

As is true for all patients, women who partner with women should be encouraged to file a durable power of attorney for health care granting emergency decision making and next-of-kin status to a partner or significant other. A separate document confers medical authority over the couple's children to the nonbiological parent (Curry, 1991). Without this document, partners may be denied access to or information regarding their loved ones in case of illness, hospitalization, or incapacitation (Smith, Heaton and Seiver, 1989).

Gentry (1992) also recommends that any lesbian who is thinking about parenting should seek legal counsel from an attorney who specializes in homosexual and lesbian parenting issues.

Men

Sexually Transmitted Diseases (STDs). Men who have sex with men are susceptible to the entire range of sexually transmitted diseases that are found among heterosexual men. "Because of certain sexual practices (such as oral-anal sexual contact and receptive anal intercourse), gay males may have increased risk for gastrointestinal infections (including those caused by Giardia lamblia, Entamoeba histolytíca, Shigella species, various species of Camphylobacter, and hepatitis A) and sexually transmitted diseases (including gonorrhea, chlamydia, syphilis, herpes, HIV, human papilloma virus [HPV] and hepatitis B virus [HBV])" (Harrison, 1996, p. 13).

HIV is an STD of great importance and is discussed elsewhere in this almanac. However, it is important to note that any incidence of an STD indicates an exposure to HIV. While the incidence of STDs in the gay community showed a marked decrease following the advent of AIDS, there is recent evidence that STDs are again increasing among men who have sex with other men. Thus, it is critical that "counseling regarding safer sexual practices and the appropriateness of HIV antibody testing should be undertaken in all cases of sexually transmitted diseases" (O'Neill and Shalit, 1992, p. 195). O'Neill and Shalit (1992) also recommend that all gay men who do not already test positive for hepatitis receive a full course of the hepatitis vaccine because of the epidemic nature of hepatitis in the gay community.

Cancer. Men who have sex with other men are at increased risk for certain types of cancer due to an increased risk for STDs, higher incidence of smoking and alcohol use, and fewer screening exams (Harrison, 1996). Harrison (1996, pp. 12, 15) summarizes the type of cancer and the associated risk factors.

Factors That May Indicate an Increase in Risk for Specific Cancers in Gay Men

Disease or Condition	Risk Factors
Colon cancer	Increased smoking; decreased frequency of screening
Anal cancer	Higher incidence of HPV, transmitted via anal-receptive sexual intercourse
Hepatocellular carcinoma	HPV, transmitted via anal-receptive sexual intercourse
Lung cancer	Increased smoking

The Council on Scientific Affairs (1996) reports that men who have sex with other men have a significantly higher rate of anal cancer than a matched control of heterosexual men, with a 1982 study conducted by Daling, Weiss, Klopfenstein, Cochran, Chow and Daifuku reporting an incidence 25 to 50 times higher. A retrospective study conducted by Melbye, Cote, Kessler, Gail and Biggar (1994) found the rate of anal cancer in men diagnosed with AIDS to be 84 times greater than found in age- and sex-matched men in the general population.

Giving support to the interaction between physical, psychological, and social states of health are the findings of a study by Cole and his colleagues. Cole and others (1996) studied the incidence of cancer among HIV-seronegative men who participated in the Natural History of AIDS Psychosocial Study. These authors report that men who were more closeted about being gay had a significantly higher incidence of cancer than those who were open about their sexual orientation (odds ratio = 3.18). In addition, the study found that there was an increased incidence of several infectious disease, including pneumonia, bronchitis, sinusitis, and tuberculosis (odds ratio = 2.91) among the men in their sample who concealed their homosexual identity.

Other health concerns. Rectal trauma, including abrasions, fissures, thrombosed hemorrhoids, and lacerations may result from receptive anal intercourse if "it is performed without consent, without proper lubrication, or under the influence of substances that blunt pain responses" (O'Neill and Shalit, 1992, p. 198). These traumas may be associated with sexually transmitted diseases and lead to further complications. O'Neill and Shalit stress the importance of a thorough exam and obtaining an honest history if rectal trauma is diagnosed or suspected, and that "the physician's atti-

tude regarding these behaviors can help or hinder this process" (1992, p. 199).

Women and Men

In addition to the issues discussed above for both men and women who have same-sex relationships, both gay men and lesbians may be at higher risk for other diseases related to the common risk factors of higher incidence of smoking, alcohol use, less-frequent screening exams, and the stress of living in a homophobic and heterosexist society. Harrison (1996, p. 15) again identifies these diseases and the associated risk factors:

Factors That May Indicate an Increase in Risk for Specific Illnesses in Lesbians and Gay Men

Disease or Condition	Risk Factors
Stroke, coronary artery disease	Increased smoking, fewer screening exams
Alcoholism, depression, suicide	Increase stress from living in a homophobic society
Anti-gay violence	Being openly gay/lesbian; being perceived as gay

Alcoholism, depression, and suicide will all be discussed within the context of mental health issues for gay men and lesbians. However, violence has been identified as a major public health issue during the past few years, with increased national attention being given to domestic violence, urban violence, and hate crimes.

Domestic Violence. Much less is known about domestic violence within gay and lesbian communities than anti-gay violence. The dearth of information in this area may be due to the difficulty lesbians and gay men have in accessing domestic violence services, which are designed for heterosexual women (Gentry, 1996). It is also difficult to discuss domestic violence with a provider with whom a gay man or lesbian is not comfortable disclosing his/her sexual orientation (Harrison, 1996). In addition, it is a widely held myth in gay and lesbian communities that domestic violence does not exist, thus making the victim of domestic violence feel more isolated and self-blaming (Gentry, 1992; Hanson, 1996).

According to Hanson (1996, p. 104), "Gay men and lesbians face the same range of violence in their relationships as heterosexuals—physical abuse, economic control, sexual abuse, threats and intimidation, isolation, and property destruction." The same indicators that lead health care professionals to suspect that a woman in a heterosexual relationship is a victim of domestic violence should be used as indicators in same-sex relationships (i.e., unexplained injuries or frequent "accidents"; minimizing physical injuries, vague complaints, or acute anxiety; isolation, reluctance to discuss partner and home life and reference to partner's anger; frequent "fleeing" from home or suicide attempts [Hanson, 1996]). Providers need to be sensitive to the fact that one of the ways perpetrators control their victims in these relationships is by threatening to "out" the victim to persons where disclosure would be devastating to the victim. Health care providers who suspect or know that battering is occurring should encourage the client to seek help (Gentry, 1992; Harrison, 1996).

Anti-gay violence. Anti-gay violence falls within the rubric of either biased crimes (Hanson, 1996) or hate crimes (Herek, 1989; Berrill, 1990). This type of violence is perpetrated against persons who are known to be, or are suspected to be, gay or lesbian. While the most common perpetrators of anti-gay violence are strangers to the victim, intra-familial violence may also occur in response to a child acknowledging, or being suspected of being, homosexual. The range of acts that fall within the category of anti-gay violence range from verbal abuse and threats of violence to physical attacks, sexual assault, and ultimately murder.

While figures vary according to the population studied, Herek (1989) reports that as many as 92 percent of lesbians and gay men surveyed report they have been the targets of anti-gay verbal abuse or threats during their lifetime, and 24 percent report being physically attacked because of their sexual orientation. A study conducted for the U.S. Department of Justice in 1993 suggested that gay men and lesbians may be the most victimized group in the nation (reported in Harrison, 1996), with the number of anti-gay hate crimes increasing each year. From 1988 to 1992 the incidence of hate crimes against gay men and lesbians in five cities in the United States increased from 697 to 1,898 according to figures from the National Gay and Lesbian Task Force (Berrill, 1992). Recent studies also suggest that more than 85 percent of the violent crimes against lesbians and gay men go unreported to the police (Dean, Wu and Marti, 1992; von Schulthess, 1992).

Both gender and racial/ethnic differences have been reported in the type and incidence of biased violence. Berrill (1990, p. 280) summarizes the gender differences found across studies.

Males generally experienced greater levels of anti-gay verbal harassment (by nonfamily members), threats, victimization in school and by police, and most types of physical violence and intimidation (including weapon assaults and being pelted with objects, spat upon, and followed or chased). Lesbians, on the other hand, generally experienced higher rates of verbal harassment by family members and fear of anti-gay violence. In surveys that measured discrimination, lesbians also were found to have encountered significantly more discrimination than gay men (Aurand et al., 1985; Gross et al., 1988). Both gay men and lesbians appear to suffer comparable rates of familial physical abuse.

While these differences may reflect the higher incidence of violent crimes against men in general, they may also reflect the fact that "Like other women, [lesbians] are so conditioned to expect violence in their lives [because of their gender], so trained to accept the threat of violence, that when they are assaulted it may not even occur to question *why* it occurred" (Tallmer, 1984, as reported in Berrill, 1990, p. 282).

Racial and ethnic differences were also reported in a survey by Comstock (1991). In this national survey 68 of the 291 respondents were gay men and lesbians of color, most of whom were black or Hispanic. Comstock found that racial minority respondents were more likely than Caucasian respondents to experience violence and threats of violence, including being chased or followed, pelted with objects, or physically assaulted. The respondents of color were also more apt to be victimized in gay and lesbian identified areas, a fact that suggests double jeopardy created by race and sexual orientation. As with lesbians, it may be difficult for gay men and lesbians of color to know if they are the targets of violence due to their race, ethnicity, or sexual orientation (Berrill, 1990; Hanson, 1996).

Anti-gay and anti-lesbian hate crimes are marked by extreme violence, and victims often report multiple injuries. "(U)se of hand-held and club-like weapons that require excessive use of force (such as golf clubs, baseball bats, hammers, and knives instead of guns); use of bias language during the attack, such as calling the victim a 'dyke' or 'faggot'; and perpetrators outnumbering victims" (Hanson, 1996, p. 98). This is also true of anti-gay murders, where extreme brutality is present. Berrill (1990, p. 280) reports a personal communication with the director of victim services at Bellevue hospital in New York City, who observed that "'attacks against gay men were the most heinous and brutal I encountered. They frequently involved torture, cutting, mutilation, and beating, and showed the absolute intent to rub out the human being because of his [sexual] preference' (M. Mertz, personal communication, 12 March 1986)." While there has been speculation that the increase in hate crimes towards gay men and lesbians is related to the AIDS crisis, Herek (1989, p. 951) suggests the following:

AIDS may be less a cause of antigay sentiment than a focal event that crystallizes heterosexuals' preexisting hostility toward gay people. Other likely contributors to an increase in antigay attacks include the rise of antigay religious fundamentalism, antigay pronouncements from the Catholic Church, and antipathy toward gay people and civil rights issues by the Reagan [and Bush] administration.

Gay and Lesbian Youth. Gay and lesbian youth are at increased risk from anti-gay and lesbian violence. While the actual number of violent incident reports is similar to that of adult populations, the perpetrators of these violent acts are frequently peers or "trusted" adults. D'Augelli (1992) found, in a study of 160 college lesbians and gay men, that 64 percent were abused by fellow students and roommates, while 23 percent reported abuse from faculty, staff, and administrators. Martin and Hetrick (1988) found that nearly 50 percent of the lesbian, gay, and bisexual youth in their study who had been victims of violence reported that the violence was perpetrated by a family member. As summarized by Savin-Williams (1994, p. 263):

Violence against lesbian, gay male, and bisexual youths often takes place in the home and neighborhood, perpetuated not only by peers but also by adults, including family members. After coming out to their family or being discovered as gay, many youth are 'rejected, mistreated, or become the focus of the family's dysfunction' (Gonsiorek, 1988, p. 116). Youths fear retribution more from fathers than from mothers (D'Augelli, 1991).... many intensely feared their father's reactions to their sexual identity. Indeed, nearly 10 percent who disclosed to their fathers were kicked out of their home (Boxer et al., 1991).

Because of the developmental tasks facing these youth, the aftermath of this discrimination and rejection is particularly devastating. While a common response among college-age students is to hide their sexual orientation (i.e., Herek, 1993), this may be more difficult for youth who are still in junior high and high school. A number of problems have been associated with peer and adult harassment of gay and lesbian youth, including school related-problems, homelessness (due either to rejection by family or fleeing abuse), physical and mental health problems, prostitution, and conflict with the law. The actual number of gay and lesbian youth among the homeless is unknown, but some estimates are as high as 40 percent (Savin-Williams, 1994). "If these youths do not find programs that meet their needs within 1 or 2 weeks of their arrival on the street, drugs, prostitution, pregnancy, criminal activity, and HIV will take them" (Savin-Williams, 1994, p. 264).

A review of recent studies on the incidence of drug and alcohol use among gay and lesbian youth suggests a much higher rate among this group than in the general population (Savin-Williams, 1994). Citing Rotheram-Borus, Rosario, and others (1992, p. 17), Savin-Williams (1994, p. 265) states that "The lifetime prevalence rates for our youths are 50 percent higher for alcohol, three times higher for marijuana and eight times higher for cocaine/crack." This is also true for suicide. It is estimated that gay and lesbian youth account for as many as 30 percent of completed youth suicides each year (Harrison, 1996; Savin-Williams, 1994; Council on Scientific Affairs, 1996).

MENTAL HEALTH

Anti-gay and anti-lesbian violence are the overt manifestations of homophobia and heterosexism. The more subtle manifestations occur within the psychological development of gay men and lesbians that occurs within this oppressive social context. This approach to understanding the psychological development of lesbians and gay men is recent. Up until 1973 homosexuality was defined as a mental illness by the American Psychiatric Association in the *Diagnostic and Statistical Manual (DSM)*, and the psychological distress found among gay men and lesbians was attributed to their sexual orientation. The removal of homosexuality as a mental illness from the *DSM* marked a major shift in how psychological distress among gay men and lesbians was viewed. The revolution in thinking about sexual orientation, and the shift to thinking of homosexuality as a normal variation of sexual desire, began with the writings of Alfred Kinsey and his colleagues and of psychologist Evelyn Hooker (Stein, 1996). Erwin (1993) provides a thorough discussion of the different theoretical paradigms that have been used to understand the high rates of suicide among homosexuals, a discussion that gives understanding across gender, age, and race/ethnicity. While her discussion focuses specifically on suicide it provides the foundation to understand the broader mental health issues faced by gay men and lesbians.

Historically, the dominant paradigm used to explain mental health problems among gay men and lesbians focused on the "belief that the inherent psychopathology of gay people" (Erwin, 1993, p. 437) resulted in high rates of suicide, depression, and substance abuse. This belief has its roots in the Judeo-Christian tradition, which sees homosexuality as sinful and immoral, and as a choice that weak and inferior people engage in "due to lasciviousness and immorality" (p. 440). Even though these moral overtones were challenged during the nineteenth century, with the developing emphasis on scientific understanding, the focus on homosexuality as individual deviancy continued. Richard von Krafft-Ebing, an Austrian psychiatrist, "believed a heritable defect resulting in an abnormal nervous system could be traced in sexually 'pathological' individuals. This pathology resulted in higher rates of mental abnormalities, suicide, and violence among sexual 'perverts' than among other men" (p. 441). While Sigmund Freud did

not support the notion that a neurological defect was the cause of homosexuality, and saw all sexuality as "the product of early psychological development and familial relations," his writings formed the "foundation for seeing homosexuality as psychopathological" (p. 442). As noted, this paradigm dominated until 1973, when homosexuality was removed as a category of mental illness from the *Diagnostic and Statistical Manual*.

The removal of homosexuality as a mental illness from the *Diagnostic and Statistical Manual* marked a major shift in how mental health and psychological distress among gay men and lesbians was understood. Rather than problems being viewed as a manifestation of the inherent psychopathology of the homosexual individual, a competing paradigm that is based on the "belief that self-destructive behavior among many gays and lesbians in the United States is due to social isolation and the internalization of negative stereotypes" (Erwin, 1993, p. 437) has emerged. While the contemporary roots of this paradigm come from the gay liberation movement, and an acceptance that many oppressed groups experience psychological distress, the predecessor of this idea can also be found in the nineteenth century. "In the 1860s, the theory of homosexuality as an innate, nonpathological variation was promoted by social reformers such as Karl Ulrichs, Havelock Ellis, Edward Carpenter, Edward Stevenson, and Magnus Hirschfeld." Ulrichs "saw homosexuals as mentally healthy, and believed they not only were harmless, but perhaps even particularly valuable for their combined male and female qualities." Ultimately these men advocated for "the repeal of laws prohibiting homosexual acts" (p. 441). However, these views were seen as "unscientific," and with the adoption of Krafft-Ebing's theories the social climate remained oppressive for homosexuals. While Ulrichs never spoke directly to the question of suicide, this oppressive climate created the social conditions Emile Durkheim wrote of in 1897 in his landmark sociology treatise, *Suicide*, where he posited that suicide was a "social fact ... not an individual phenomenon" (p. 441). Thus, according to this more contemporary theory, mental health problems and psychological distress among gay and lesbian people have their root in the homophobic and heterosexist attitudes in which gay and lesbian people are raised, live and work (Council on Scientific Affairs, 1996). The fact that the incidence of depression and suicide among lesbians is similar to heterosexual women (Bradford, Ryan and Rothblum, 1994), and that gay men and lesbians of color have a higher incidence of mental health problems than their white counterparts (Savin-Williams, 1996), supports this emerging paradigm. Clearly, sexism and racism, as well as homophobia and heterosexism, contribute to psychological distress.

Growing up Gay, Lesbian, or Bisexual

Savin-Williams (1996) discusses the process of sexual identity development and the coming-out models that "have been proposed to describe the movement from first awareness to full disclosure" (p. 154). This process involves first an awareness of feeling different, then the labeling of self as homosexual, and finally disclosure to others.

Feeling Different. According to Bell, Weinberg, and Hammersmith (1981) 70 percent of lesbians and gay men describe feeling different during childhood.

Reasons given in retrospect for feeling different include an early and pervasive captivation with members of one's own sex that feels passionate, intimate, exciting, and mysterious (especially characteristic of 'pre-lesbian' girls; see Golden, 1996); a desire to engage in play activities and to possess traits not typical of their sex; and a disinterest in, or sometimes an aversion toward, the activities socially prescribed for their own sex (Bailey and Zucker, 1995). Not uncommonly, intrapsychic tensions increase for such youths when they doubt their ability to meet the heterosexual obligations that are promulgated by their peers and family members (Savin-Williams, 1996, p. 157-58).

These feelings occur during puberty, before the ability to reflect and label sexual feelings and attractions develops, leaving the youth with feelings of being alone and without support (Gochros and Bidwell, 1995). As noted by Savin-Williams (1996, p. 158), "these experiences have profound repercussions for self-acceptance and self-rejection, which evolve during later adolescence."

Self-labeling. The realization that being different may mean being homosexual *may* start to emerge with the onset of puberty (Remafedi, 1987; Troiden, 1979). The use and acceptance of this label will depend on numerous factors, including both the availability of gay and lesbian role models as well as the youth's psychological defenses. According to Savin-Williams (1996, p. 159) "Defenses are shattered or rendered unnecessary because homoerotically inclined adolescents now have available to them a construct and role models of homosexuality, making it less frightening to recognize and honestly label their same-sex attraction." He also believes that youth are defining their sexual identity at an increasingly early age due to the visibility of homosexuality in the media and in society.

For many gay and lesbian youth psychological defenses may be used to keep same-sex attractions from surfacing. Passing as heterosexual is a common response to the fear and anxiety created by homoerotic feelings, and the belief that if one does not behave as a homosexual that these feelings will change. As noted earlier, as many as 77 percent of adult women who identify themselves as lesbians have been sexually active with men at some time in their lives (Johnson, Smith and Guenther, 1987), and the majority of men who have "occasional" or "fairly frequent" sex with other men are married (O'Neill and Shalit, 1992). Gochros and Bidwell (1996) suggest that gay and lesbian youth may engage in promiscuous heterosexual activity in an attempt to deny these homoerotic feelings, behavior that can increase the risk of contracting sexually transmitted diseases. These defenses can result in awkwardness and shame in interpersonal relationships, as well as feelings of depression.

Savin-Williams (1996, pp. 169-170) discusses other psychological defenses that are commonly used to delay self-labeling:

- Rationalization: "It's something I'll outgrow," "I did it because I was lonely," "It's just a means to earn money," "I was drunk/high."
- Relegation to insignificance: "It's just sexual experimentation or curiosity that is natural at my age," "I did it only as a favor for a friend."
- Compartmentalization of sexual desire: "I mess around with other boys/girls, but that does not make me a faggot/dyke," "I just love this person, not all men/women."
- Withdrawal from provocative situations to remain celibate or asexual: "I'm saving myself for the right girl/boy."

- Denial, frequently engaging in heterosexual dating or sexual behavior: "I can't be gay—I've had a girlfriend/boyfriend for years."
- Sublimation, redirection of energies to other efforts, such as intellectual or work pursuits.

These defensive strategies, used to avoid acknowledging same-sex attraction, may work temporarily but do not totally succeed in blocking the feelings these youth experience. The high incidence of depression, substance abuse, and suicide attempts cited earlier are artifacts of how poorly these defense mechanisms work in helping youth cope with these feelings. While Savin-Williams focuses his discussion on gay, lesbian, and bisexual youth, the process of self-labeling and the defense mechanisms used to ward off the anxiety of same-sex attraction are not bound by age. These strategies would not be needed if homophobia and heterosexism were not so prevalent.

Disclosure to others. Once a person has labeled him/herself as being gay, lesbian, or bisexual, he/she must confront the decision of whether to share this information with other people. This is a process that continues throughout life, regardless of the number of times a gay or lesbian person has self-disclosed to others. Because of the pervasive nature of heterosexism, others assume a person is heterosexual unless the gay man or lesbian tells them otherwise. Cain (1991) discusses the psychological stress of this process as the gay man or lesbian weighs the potential costs and benefits of self-disclosing. However, Savin-Williams (1996, p. 159) notes:

Even though disclosure may invite negative reactions that compromise one's physical safety and psychological security, there are many advantages to publicly proclaiming one's sexuality. Disclosure to others leads to decreased feelings of loneliness and guilt (Dank, 1973); identity synthesis, integration, and commitment (Cass, 1979; Coleman, 1981-1982; Troiden, 1989); healthy psychological adjustment and positive self-esteem (Gonsiorek and Rudolph, 1991; Savin-Williams, 1990); and a positive gay identity (McDonald, 1982). Fitzpatrick (1983) found that those who disclosed their sexual identity had a greater sense of freedom, of being oneself, of not living a lie, and of experiencing genuine acceptance.

There are also physical health consequences related to self-disclosure. As noted earlier Cole and others (1996) found that men who concealed their homosexual identity had a significantly higher incidence of cancer and several types of infectious diseases than men who were open about being gay.

Savin-Williams (1996) also notes some interesting gender differences within the process of coming out to self and others. Specifically, lesbians appear to work through their sexual identity issues through an *internal* process and within the context of an intimate relationship with another woman. They are more discriminating about those to whom they disclose their sexual identity, and more frequently see being lesbian as a choice. On the other hand, gay men are more apt to use an *external* working-through process, "and to use outward social and sexual activity in order to develop self-acceptance as a gay person" (p. 160). They are more public about their sexual identity and believe that being gay is beyond their control. These differences are reflective of the more general gender differences being studied between men and women

153

(Gilligan, 1982; Jordan, Kaplan, Milller, Stiver, and Surrey, 1991; Jordan, 1997).

Along with gender, numerous other factors will influence the process of coming out. While Savin-Williams (1996) suggests that earlier self-labeling as gay or lesbian is due to the availability of role models in society and the media, this availability is recent. The public response to the "coming out" episode of *Ellen* in the spring of 1997 indicates that societal acceptance of homosexuality is increasing, but even then sponsors pulled their ads from this episode in fear that there would be a negative response. Public policy still denies the reality of gay and lesbian relationships (Hartman, 1996), and the U.S. military has a policy of "don't ask, don't tell." Any public acknowledgment of being gay, lesbian, or bisexual in the military will result in dismissal. Thus, while earlier self-labeling may be present among younger gay men and lesbians, age and generational differences may be found in the coming-out process.

Race and Ethnicity. Ethnic and racial differences are also evident in the coming-out process, differences that may be obscured by the dominance of white, middle-class bias in the present research (Rothblum, 1994). Greene (1994) discusses the impact of being a minority within a minority, "the multiple levels of oppression and discrimination that accompanies such status" (p. 248), and the dual challenge of developing a healthy identity as a dual minority. Support of the family is critical in helping youth cope with racism, but this support may be withdrawn if the family discovers the youth is gay or lesbian (Erwin, 1994). Thus, the attitudes of the family and its cultural identity are important to understand. Greene (1994) explores cultural gender roles and the meaning of sexual orientation within various minority cultures, warning that "gross descriptions of cultural practices may never be applied with uniformity to all members of an ethnic group" (p. 244). She then goes on to provide a broad framework from which to look at gay men and lesbians from Latin American, Asian American, African American, and Native American cultures, a framework that is critical to understanding the mental health needs of gay men and lesbians of color. A brief description of how the values of these four cultures *may* affect the process of coming out is important in understanding the mental health concerns of gay men and lesbians of color. However, a note of caution is necessary—every individual and family is different, and it is imperative that these differences be understood and respected.

Latin Americans. This term is used to indicate those people whose families originated in Puerto Rico, Mexico, Central and South America, and those of Spanish ancestry from many Caribbean Islands (Greene, 1994). Dominant norms within the Latino culture include the centrality of family (*familismo*) and well-defined gender roles (*machismo* and *marianismo*) (Morales, 1996). The social roles inherent in the meaning of *machismo* and *marianismo*, coupled with the family as the primary social unit, have resulted in the near invisibility of gay, lesbian, and bisexual people within the Latino community. According to Greene (1994), while same-gender sexual behavior is not uncommon within Latino cultures, adoption of a gay identity is much more complicated.

> Rather than behavior, it is the overt acknowledgment and disclosure of gay or lesbian identity that is likely to meet with intense disapproval in Latino communities (Espin, 1984, 1987; Hidalgo, 1984; Morales, 1992).... To label oneself gay or lesbian implies not only consciously participating in behavior that is condemned but actively

confronting others with your choice to do so, thus violating the injunction to be indirect (Greene, 1994, p. 244).

The paucity of gay and lesbian role models, in conjunction with the importance attached to gender roles, may keep the Latino/a youth who is feeling different from his/her peers from labeling him/herself as gay or lesbian. If this self-labeling occurs, the pressure to remain "closeted" may be intense in order "to avoid the ridicule and outcast status that would result from openly acknowledging their identity" (Greene, 1994, p. 244). Latino gays and Latina lesbians in North American urban settings have very negative reactions to the traditional concepts of *machismo* and *marianismo*, and "among the various subgroups within Latino cultures, lesbians and gays may be the most victimized by Latino gender-role norms and by sanctions for not conforming to those norms" (Morales, 1996, p. 275).

Asian Americans. Using the definition of Asian American to include Americans of Japanese or Chinese ancestry, Greene (1994, p. 245) states that "(T)he most salient feature of Asian-American families is the expectation of unquestioning obedience to one's parents and their demand for conformity, consistent with the respect accorded elders and the sharp delineation of gender roles." Sex is considered a taboo subject and is not openly discussed. "Same-sex sexual behavior, awareness, and identification are shrouded in secrecy, stigma, and the sometimes overwhelming power of cultural expectations" (Liu and Chan, 1996, p. 137). Chan (1989) found that the majority of Asian American gays and lesbians reported a widespread belief that homosexuality is a white, western phenomenon and does not exist within the Asian American community. This belief, coupled with the demand for conformity and lack of discussion about sex, may result in a lack of gay and lesbian role models and hamper the process of self-identification, similar to the Latin American community.

Even if self-identification as gay, lesbian, or bisexual occurs, "(O)pen disclosure that one is gay or lesbian would be seen as threatening the continuation of the family line and a rejection of one's appropriate roles within the culture as well" (Greene, 1994, p. 245). As noted by Liu and Chan (1996, p. 143) the fear of rejection by family goes well beyond that found in the anglo community for several reasons:

> First, when an individual's self-concept is strongly associated with the family, loss of the family may be devastating to self-esteem. Second, when the concept of face is deeply rooted, and maintaining a public appearance that fulfills gender-role expectations is demanded by the family, the psychological experience can be a perception of constant scrutiny by others, leading to vigilance in maintaining the proper image in the eyes of one's family and community. Third, as the East Asian family is often defined by and immersed in traditional culture, rejection by one's family can be experienced as a totalizing disconnection from one's ethnic identity and entire community. Finally, alternative, nonfamily resources for LGBAAs [lesbian, gay, and bisexual Asian Americans] may be limited because of social, cognitive, and emotional isolation, as well as racial discrimination in the predominantly Euro-American LGB community at large (Chan, 1994; Greene, 1994).

Chan (1989) found that the primary identification of the Asian American gay men and lesbians in her study was as a gay man or

Like other minorities, Asian Americans must battle racial discrimination in addition to homophobia.

perceived shortage of marriageable men in African American communities and the perceived importance of continued propagation of the race" (Greene, 1994, p. 246).

Mays, Cochran, and Rhue (1993), in their study of black lesbians, found that "compared to their White counterparts, African American lesbians were more likely to have children, maintain close relationships with their families, and depend more on family members or other African American lesbians for support" (Greene and Boyd-Franklin, 1996, p. 252). These results attest to the prominence of ongoing family of origin relationships in the lives of adult African American lesbians" (Greene and Boyd-Franklin, 1996). Black lesbians were also found to have more contact with men and with their heterosexual peers. The importance of family and community, coupled with homophobia within the African American community, makes the coming out process more difficult. Greene and Boyd-Franklin (1996, p. 259) cite Villarosa, who was interviewed in Brownworth (1993):

> It is harder for us to consider being rejected by our families.... All we have is our families, our community. When the whole world is racist and against you, your family and your community are the only people who accept you and love you even though you are black. So you don't know what will happen if you lose them...and many black lesbians (and gay men) are afraid that's what will happen (p. 18).

While African American families tend to tolerate gay and lesbian members, there is little acceptance. Gay and lesbian relationships may be defined as friendships, with the true nature of the relationship remaining hidden and unnamed. This conflict between sexual identity and family and community norms results in greater levels of tension and loneliness among African American lesbians and gay men (Mays and Cochran, 1988). For African American lesbians and gay men, being African American is their primary source of identification, related not only to the importance of family but also to the racial discrimination that occurs in gay and lesbian communities.

Native Americans. As with other ethnic groups, the term Native American encompasses "hundreds of different tribal groups, cultures, and languages" (Greene, 1994, p. 246). Deviating from the traditional view of only two genders, some Native American cultures have historically included alternatives that have not been defined by dichotomies. "American Indian groups have at least six alternative gender styles: women and men, not-men (biological women who assume some aspects of male roles) and not-women (biological men who assume some aspects of female roles), lesbians and gays" (Brown, 1997, p. 6). The differences between not-men and not-women and gays and lesbians may be more of an artifact of dichotomous western thinking, rather than Native culture, where a range of sexual expression was accepted. According to Brown (1997, p. 9):

> Not-men and not-women are generally discovered to be different during childhood (Callender and Kochems, 1986; Little Crow et al., 1997; Roscoe, 1992; Williams, 1992). These differences are usually encouraged and nurtured. During adolescence these children would experience an initiation ceremony (described in more detail by Little Crow et al., 1997). For example, during the initiation ceremony, if they chose the other biological gender's

lesbian rather than as an Asian American. This shift in primary identification may occur for Asian Americans who disclose their sexual identification to others, but this shift may be costly, exacerbating the psychological distress members of this group experience (Erwin, 1994).

African Americans. Gender roles within the African American community have been much more flexible than those found in Latin American, Asian American, and Anglo communities, due both to their African heritage and adaptation to racism and slavery. Strong family ties are present within the nuclear and extended families, often encompassing "fictive kin," members who are not related by blood or marriage (Greene and Boyd-Franklin, 1996). However, even though African Americans embrace this flexible family structure, "(T)he African-American community is viewed by gay and lesbian members as extremely homophobic and rejecting of gay and lesbian individuals, generating the pressure to remain closeted" (Greene, 1994, p. 246). The intensity of this homophobia appears to come from multiple sources, including the history of sexual objectification of African American men and women related to slavery, the strong Christian religiosity within the African American community, and the belief that heterosexual privilege can raise the status of African American women. "Dyne (1980) suggests that homophobia may also represent a reaction to the implements, they were declared officially not-men and not-women.

All not-men and not-women had roles in their communities. Their roles frequently differed significantly from those of other women and men, but they had very definite places. A colleague once described this by referring to an American Indian table of organization—it has a place for everyone: No one is left out (Little Crow, 1993). Each tribal group varied in how these not-men and not-women functioned, but in most cases they were members of the community. They were rarely ostracized for being different, but if they were they could find another tribal group to accept them. More commonly they were revered and believed to have special powers, such as the gift of prophecy, because of their difference. They were called on frequently for exceptional service to their communities. They often served functions that no one else could do (Williams, 1992).

While this traditional view would suggest that some Native Americans are accepting of homosexuality, perhaps due to colonization, oppression, and loss of traditional values, this is not necessarily true today particularly on reservations. The result is more pressure on Native American gay men and lesbians to remain closeted or to move to urban communities. Such a move may result in a loss of culture and support from family and increased feelings of isolation (Greene, 1994). "Common to many tribes is the importance of spirituality, family support, and continuing the existence of the tribe" (Greene, 1994, p. 246, citing personal communication from Sears, May 1992).

The process of coming out for Native American gay men and lesbians may depend on how the pre-colonial concept of a third sex has been incorporated into their tribal and familial heritage. If the tribe and the family applauds the attributes of a person of the third sex, then forming a healthy self-identity for Native American gay men and lesbians can easily be done within this cultural context. However, if the tribe and family do not have this appreciation, then the Native American lesbian and gay man faces the same conflict as other people of color, where loss of family and tribe results in loss of protection from racist attitudes in the larger society.

The importance of culture and family for gay men and lesbians of color is evident throughout the previous discussion. Not only is family the primary source of support in developing a positive self-identity within a racist environment, this support is often contingent on the adoption of cultural norms that are incongruent with a gay or lesbian identity. While the coming-out process discussed by Savin-Williams (1996) is a complicated process for any individual coming to terms with a homosexual identity, this process is even more complicated for gay men and lesbians of color. Morales has developed an identity model comprised of five psychosocial states of identity integration for ethnic-minority gays and lesbians (1996, pp. 279-81). These states include:

State 1: Denial of Conflicts. "In this state of psychosocial consciousness, individuals tend to minimize the reality of discrimination they may experience" as an ethnic minority gay man or lesbian and may believe they are treated as others. Sexual orientation may not be clearly defined, or it may be repressed or suppressed. In order to deny conflict these individuals may "act straight or act White,

in order to avoid discrimination in certain social contexts" (p. 279). Even though these individuals may engage in homosexual behavior, they do not connect this behavior with their self-identity. They may continue to believe they are heterosexual or refuse to consider the question of sexual orientation.

State 2: Bisexual versus Gay. In this state of psychosocial consciousness individuals "prefer to think of themselves as bisexual rather than gay. Upon examining their sexual and affectional lifestyles, however, there may be no difference between those who identify themselves as gay and those who identify as bisexual." While some individuals in this state "may be genuinely bisexual in orientation, a great many others are predominately gay and are having difficulty bringing their self-definitions in line with their feelings" (p. 279).

State 3: Conflicts in Allegiances. In this state of consciousness the individual is simultaneously aware of being a member of both an ethnic and sexual minority group. This "triggers anxiety about maintaining relationships in the two communities and about whether to keep relationships in the two communities separate" (p. 279). The possibility of losing the connections in either community and how to maintain these dual, and perhaps conflicting, relationships becomes of major concern. "Drawing from both communities, the individual must discover his (her) own blend of values and relationships that support a sense of personal worth and ethics" (p. 280).

State 4: Claiming an Ethnic and Gay/Lesbian Identity. Persons in this state of psychosocial consciousness have claimed both an ethnic identity and an identity as gay or lesbian. Feelings of anger towards both communities may develop—anger towards their ethnic community for being homophobic and towards the gay and lesbian communities for being racist. Connection with other gay men and lesbians who share the person's ethnic heritage is critical to maintaining a positive self image, "and to begin working politically against ethnic discrimination in the gay (and lesbian) community" (p. 280).

State 5: Integrating the Various Communities. Persons in this state of psychosocial consciousness are beginning to develop a multicultural perspective, and "adjusting to the reality of the limited social options currently available for many gay and lesbian people of color becomes a source of anxiety and feelings of isolation and alienation" (p. 280). These people "need reassurance that, indeed, their life does and will require a constantly evolving balancing act, as they attempt to maintain a coherent and authentic identity across two divergent social contexts, each of which is important to their sense of belonging. Also they can, over time, learn to better predict the outcomes of their attempts to integrate members of the two communities" (p. 281).

Morales (1996, p. 276) distinguishes between *acculturation*—"a person learning and adopting the characteristics, language, mannerisms, norms, and style of another culture"; *assimilation*—the person's blending into the other culture until cultural differences are minimized"; and *biculturalism* and *multiculturalism,* which refer "to a person's ability to know and use the characteristics, language, mannerisms, norms, and styles of two or more cultures and to understand the differences between them and know how to apply that knowledge effectively in the appropriate context." Morales (1996, p. 276) relates this to mental health, stating:

> In empirical studies, Latino individuals with greater *bicultural competence* have shown more resiliency and less likelihood of using risky coping mechanisms related to stress, such as substance abuse. By contrast, high- and low-acculturated individuals have been at greater risk for developing mental health problems (Santisteban and Szapocznik, 1982; Marshall, 1993).

Although speaking specifically of Latino individuals, there is good reason to believe that these findings would apply to other ethnic minorities who live within the United States.

Gay men and lesbians of color must deal with the attitudes and beliefs of the dominant culture about their race, and with both the dominant and minority culture about their sexual orientation. Gay men and lesbians from the dominant culture have fewer layers to negotiate, but the stress of being a gay man or lesbian, regardless of race, in a homophobic and heterosexist society still creates enormous psychological stress.

Meyer (1995), in a study of the mental health of 741 gay men (89 percent white and 11 percent men of color), conceptualized psychological *stress* as being rooted in the minority status of gay men and having three major components: *internalized homophobia, stigma,* and *experience. Internalized homophobia* is the adoption of negative societal attitudes about homosexuality in viewing oneself. *Stigma* "relates to expectations of rejection and discrimination" due to being gay. *Experience* is the actual experiences of discrimination and violence experienced by gay men due to their sexual orientation. Meyer looked at the association between these three measures of psychological *stress* and five measures of psychological *distress,* including *demoralization, guilt, suicide, AIDS-related traumatic stress response (AIDS-TSR)* and *sex problems. Demoralization* was assessed using a scale that measured anxiety, sadness, helplessness, hopelessness, psychophysiological symptoms, perceived physical health problems, poor self-esteem, and confused thinking. *Guilt* was measured by asking about rational or irrational feelings of guilt, while *suicide* was measured using both suicidal ideation and/or behavior. The *AIDS-TSR* scales measured symptoms of psychological *distress* in relation to the effects of the AIDS epidemic, and *sex problems* related to inhibited sexual desire, excitement, or orgasm.

Internalized homophobia was significantly related to all five sources of psychological *distress,* while *stigma* and *experience* were significantly related to *demoralization, guilt, suicide* and *AIDS-TSR.* Simply put, this study suggests that the greater the psychological *stress* reported, the greater the psychological *distress* these men experienced. Meyer raises the possibility that a similar minority stress process may apply to lesbians, but cautions against generalizing his results to lesbians and lesbians and gay men of color. Further research is needed to understand the psychological *stress* created through the dual or triple oppression of gender, race, and sexual orientation, and their effects on psychological *distress* and mental health.

In a review of early studies on the overall psychological adjustment of gay men and lesbians in comparison to their heterosexual counterparts, Rothblum (1994, p. 214) reports there were no significant differences on personal adjustment.

> Gay men were found less defensive and less self-confident than heterosexual men; lesbians were found more self-confident than heterosexual women....Given the extremely negative attitudes held by the public and by mental health professionals, it is remarkable that lesbians and gay men have adjusted so well.

Even given this overall positive adjustment, the fact that there is a high incidence of depression, suicide, and substance abuse among gay men and lesbians, as well as among gay and lesbian youth, is well documented in the literature (Bell and Weinberg, 1978; Bradford, Ryan and Rothblum, 1994; Erwin, 1994), and can be understood as a response to gay men and lesbians developing their sexual identity within a society that is homophobic. According to Harrison (1996, p. 14):

> Gay men and lesbians have been found more likely to consider or attempt suicide than heterosexuals (McKirnan and Peterson, 1989b; Pillard, 1988). The risk is considerably greater for blacks than for whites, perhaps because of subcultural attitudes toward homosexuality that may put additional pressure on these individuals. Other studies have suggested that depression and bipolar disorder are more common in gay populations than in heterosexual ones (McKirnan and Peterson, 1989b; Pillard, 1988).

Depression

"Growing up gay means growing up different.... Difference does not preclude the establishment and maintenance of a positive identity as a homosexual" (Bernard, 1992, p. 32). However, for gay men and lesbians, different may mean derogatory labels and internalization of homophobic attitudes that lead to feelings of depression. Depression is characterized by "low self-esteem; ideas of helplessness, hopelessness, worthlessness, failure, guilt, self-blame, at times to the point of delusional thinking; suicidal ideation, which may lead to suicide attempts" (O'Neil, 1984, p. 350). As previously noted, gay men and lesbians who feel they must hide their sexual orientation are often socially isolated, clinically depressed, and potentially suicidal (Savin-Williams, 1996).

Bradford and others (1994) found that more than one-third of the lesbians in their national study "had experienced a 'long depression or sadness' at some point in the past" (p. 231), and that 11 percent were both currently experiencing and being treated for depression. Trippet (1994) reported an even higher rate, with 66 percent of the lesbians in her sample indicating they had experienced depression at some time in their life. Since women in the United States are much more likely to experience depression than men, Bradford and others (1994) question if the incidence for lesbians is higher than found in the overall female population. However, Trippet (1994, p. 321) notes:

> The relationship issues and depression experienced by a lesbian have a different source than those experienced by a heterosexual woman. A lesbian's relationship with another woman may be hidden from family and known

by only a few friends. If the relationship breaks up, the woman has a limited support group to turn to for help in her grief. If the lesbian is depressed because of the difficulty of being a homosexual in a heterosexual world, she may feel limited in trying to find a sensitive counselor to whom she can turn for help. The lesbian either lives in isolation or with a few friends in the heterosexual community or lives within a lesbian community, which tends to be small and rather incestuous in its relationships (Brown, 1989).

Depression is also common among gay men, and has increased within the context of the AIDS epidemic. As noted earlier the AIDS epidemic has given rise to an increase in the expression of societal homophobia, along with the tremendous loss of life within the gay community. Depression may also be caused by HIV infection, or a reaction to a seropositive diagnosis (Winiarski, 1991). Social support is critical to preventing depression among gay men, with Vincke and Bolton (1994) finding that lower levels of social support lead to reduced self-acceptance and higher levels of depression. Otis and Skinner (1996), in their study of the relationship between violence and depression, also found that self-esteem and social support were related to depression. Of particular significance was their finding that "crimes that involved physical harm, threat of harm and verbal abuse, male sexual assault, and multiple victimization proved to significantly affect depression for both gay men and lesbians" (p. 110).

"'Depression' is a term used in everyday language to connote a well-known dysphoric feeling state" (O'Neil, 1984, p. 149). At the extreme, depression may result in the person committing suicide. Alcohol and other drugs may also be used as a temporary way to reduce feelings of depression. Suicide and substance abuse are too often the behavioral manifestations of depression found among gay men and lesbians.

Suicide

In a survey of 575 white gay men, 111 black gay men, 229 white lesbians, and 64 black lesbians, Bell and Weinberg (1978) reported the percentage of individuals in these groups who had attempted or seriously contemplated suicide compared to their heterosexual counterparts. The figures were consistent: 37 percent of white gay men compared to 13 percent of white heterosexual men; 24 percent of black gay men compared to 2 percent of black heterosexual men; 41 percent of white lesbians compared to 26 percent of white heterosexual women; and 25 percent of black lesbians compared to 19 percent of black heterosexual women. Over half of the suicide attempts in this sample occurred before age 20. As noted earlier, the rate of suicide among gay and lesbian youth is startling, accounting for at least 30 percent of all adolescent suicides (Harrison, 1996; Savin-Williams, 1994; Council on Scientific Affairs, 1996). Catalan and Pugh (1995) also report a higher incidence of depression and suicide among men newly diagnosed with HIV infection, which indicates increased risk for gay men (Council on Scientific Affairs, 1996).

Bradford and others (1994) found that among 1,925 lesbians who responded to the National Lesbian Health Care Survey, 18 percent had attempted suicide. This percentage was higher for Latina (28 percent) and African American (27 percent) lesbians than their white counterparts (16 percent), and women 17 to 24 years of age reported more frequent attempts (24 percent) than

did women in other age groups. Less than half of all the women surveyed indicated they had never thought about suicide, with another 35 percent indicating they thought about it rarely. The authors question if the rates for adult lesbians in their sample is higher than the general population of women in the United States, stating:

> Research among heterosexual women has found that the rate of reported suicide attempts is very high among professional women such as physicians, perhaps somewhat comparable to the large percentage of lesbians in professional occupations in the current study. For example, Pitts, Schuller, Rich, and Pitts (1979) found the suicide rate for female physicians to be higher than that of male physicians, and four times higher than White U.S. women of the same age (p. 240).

However, the authors do not address the relative rates of attempted suicide among African American and Latina lesbians in their sample. While there is no question that the rates of suicide contemplated or attempted is high among lesbians, the question that still remains is how gender, race, and sexual orientation interact with and contribute to these statistics.

Substance Abuse

Anderson (1996), in a recent review of the literature on substance abuse among gay men and lesbians, challenges the popular notion that alcoholism among lesbians and gays clusters around 30 percent. According to Anderson these estimates have relied on early studies that had serious methodological limitations. She then goes on to summarize the widely cited study by McKirnan and Peterson (Anderson, 1996, p. 61):

> McKirnan and Peterson (1989a) found that gay men and lesbians in Chicago were less likely than the general population to abstain from alcohol (14 percent vs. 29 percent), more likely to be moderate drinkers (71 percent vs. 57 percent), and likely to be similar in terms of heavy drinking (15 percent vs. 14 percent). Seventeen percent of the gay men and 9 percent of the lesbians were heavy drinkers compared with 21 percent of men and 7 percent of women in the general population. Similar trends characterized the use of other drugs. Gay men and lesbians were more likely than the general population to have used marijuana in the previous year (56 percent vs. 20 percent), but frequent use was similar at 11 percent for gays and lesbians and 9 percent for the general population. Gay men and lesbians were also more likely to use cocaine in the previous year (23 percent vs. 8.5 percent) and frequent cocaine use was 2.3 percent and 0.7 percent respectively. Rates of use of other drugs were extremely low. McKirnan and Peterson concluded that, when compared to those in the general population, lesbians were much more similar to gay men in their use of alcohol and other drugs, and both lesbians and gay men showed far less decline in use with age. They did *not* find the very heavy alcohol and other drug use often ascribed to this population.

However, Hughes and Wilsnack (1997, p. 21) point out an apparently discrepant finding in McKirnan and Peterson's research, stating that "gay women and men, even though they were not over-represented among heavy drinkers, reported rates of alcohol problems almost twice as high as those for heterosexual women and men (23 percent vs. 12 percent)." McKirnan and Peterson (1989a) suggest that this higher rate of alcohol-related problems may be associated with higher overall use of alcohol, not just heavy use.

The high rate of alcohol consumption and alcohol-related problems among gay men and lesbians have been attributed to a number of factors. Anderson (1996) reviews the individual psychological, social, and cultural/political factors associated with the etiology of substance abuse and reports that in relation to psychological and social factors the evidence is inconclusive. However, there is little question that the use of alcohol and other drugs is related to living in a homophobic and heterosexist society. As stated by Anderson (1996, p. 63):

> Because the dominant culture in our society is heterosexist, the "coming out" process may involve abusing substances as one way of dealing with the shame of becoming a member of a stigmatized group (Nicoloff and Stiglitz, 1987). Kus (1988) maintains that "it is the internalized homophobia prior to having reached the stage of Acceptance in the coming out process which is the root of alcoholism in gay men" (p. 27). Conflict or ambivalence about one's gay or lesbian identity has been identified by a number of authors as a risk factor for developing chemical dependency (Coleman, 1981/1982; Glaus, 1988; Weather, 1980).

McKirnan and Peterson (1989b) found that gay men and lesbians who reported more negative affectivity (i.e., feelings of depression, alienation, anxiety, and low self-esteem) were more apt to use alcohol to reduce tension and to experience alcohol-related problems. Conflict over sexual orientation had no apparent relationship with substance abuse.

Depression, suicide, and substance abuse are all serious problems facing the gay and lesbian community. While none of these problems are unique to gay men and lesbians, the factors associated with their development and the extent of the impact are unique. The process of developing a positive identity for gay men and lesbians is made more difficult due to the homophobic and heterosexist nature of our society. For gay men of color, and for all lesbians, this difficulty may be compounded due to societal racism and sexism. Health and mental health providers are in the unique position of being able to help gay men and lesbians overcome some of these negative stereotypes. However, the research indicates that health and mental health professionals may be part of the problem rather than part of the solution.

BARRIERS TO CARE

Provider Attitudes

Health Care Providers: "In 1973, the American Psychiatric Association removed homosexuality per se from its classification of mental disorders.... However, as recently as 1991, one in seven family practice and internal medicine residents still considered homosexuality a mental disorder" (Hayward and Weissfeld, 1993; Harrison, 1996, p. 14). Stevens (1992) reviewed the literature on lesbian health care from 1970 to 1990 and concluded:

This review of the empirical literature on lesbians' health care experiences suggests that deeply entrenched prejudicial meanings about lesbian health remain influential in the education of health care providers, the quality of health care they deliver, their comfort in interacting with clients, and the institutional policies under which they work. Knowledgeable, empathic, and fully accessible care cannot coexist with such conditions. The present findings indicate that many lesbians interpret health care interactions as abusive and perceive high-quality, safe health services to be unavailable to them. Such findings are of serious concern and call for immediate radical changes on the part of educators, practitioners, administrators, and policymakers (p. 114).

Schwartz (1996), reported similar findings within the health care system for gay men.

The attitudes of health care providers towards homosexuality have a major impact on the care that lesbian and gay patients receive. Douglas, Kalman, and Kalman (1985) looked at homophobia in response to the AIDS crisis, surveying physicians and nurses working with AIDS patients. The mean score on the Index of Homophobia (IHP) was 50.84 for physicians and 55.6 for nurses, indicating "low-grade" homophobia. However, the authors state:

> Our results indicate that a disturbingly high percentage of the health professionals we studied acknowledge more negative, even overtly hostile, feelings towards homosexuals than they had before the emergence of the AIDS epidemic (p. 1311).

Nearly 10 percent of the respondents in this study also agreed with the statement that homosexuals who get AIDS are "getting what they deserve."

Taravella (1992) reported the findings of a 1991 survey of physicians conducted by the University of California at San Francisco. The survey found that 35 percent of the respondents "'would feel nervous among a group of homosexuals' and 'believe that homosexuality is a threat to many of our social institutions'" (p. 34).

Finally, a frequently cited study on the attitude of physicians was conducted by Mathews, Booth, Turner, and Kessler (1986), who surveyed members of the San Diego Medical Society. These authors found that 22.9 percent of 930 respondents scored in the homophobia range on the Heterosexual Attitudes Towards Homosexuality (HATH) Scale. Forty percent of the sample scored in the neutral or ambivalent range, with the remaining 37 percent being homophilic (having favorable attitudes towards homosexuals). However, of particular interest was the discrepancy between measured attitudes towards homosexuality and respondents' expressed behavior. Thirty percent of the respondents would not admit a homosexual applicant to medical school, 40 percent would discourage homosexual physicians from training in pediatrics or psychiatry, and 40 percent would cease making referrals to homosexual physicians in these specialties.

These attitudes are clearly manifested in the care received by lesbians. Smith and others (1985) studied 1,921 lesbians and 424 bisexual women and found that only 41.1 percent of the women had disclosed their sexual orientation to a physician. Of the women who had disclosed their sexual orientation, 58 percent responded to a question asking them to describe the reaction of the physician to their self-disclosure. While response varied by sexual orientation of the physician, 30 percent stated that the physicians' responses had been negative. Of these negative responses, 12 percent were further categorized as "cool," 30 percent as embarrassment, 25 percent as inappropriate ("e.g., suggesting referral to a mental health professional, or voyeuristic"), and 22 percent as overt rejection (Smith et al., 1985, p. 1086). Stevens and Hall (1988) found that 72 percent of the respondents in their study who believed they were identifiable to the health provider as a lesbian, reported negative responses from health care providers. "They described being responded to with ostracism, invasive personal questioning, shock, embarrassment, unfriendliness, pity, condescension and fear" (p. 72).

Fear of negative responses keeps many lesbians from disclosing their sexual orientation to their physician. Smith and others (1985) found that while 46.8 percent of the lesbians in their sample had told their physician who provided gynecologic care of their sexual orientation, another 36.4 percent wanted to tell their physician but believed that "physician awareness of their sexual orientation would hinder the quality of health care" (p. 1086). Fear and concern was greatest among lesbians who sought care from a private physician or student health clinic, while those who disclosed their identity were more likely to receive care at a women's clinic.

Heterosexism is also a barrier to lesbians seeking health care, being manifested primarily in attitudes towards sexuality and reproduction.

"I got this survey in the mail, of women professionals. One of the questions was, 'What kind of birth control do you use?' I wrote in, 'Lesbian sex is the best method of birth control there is.' I just wish I could've been there to see the reaction" (Raymond, 1988, p. 18).

Medical history questionnaires and questions asked by providers assume that female clients are heterosexual, focusing on contraception and sexual intercourse (Robertson, 1992; Stevens and Hall, 1988). Planned Parenthood, which provides pap smears and breast exams to women, mandates that birth control is a mandatory part of their services (Simkin, 1991). According to Stevens and Hall (1988, p. 72), "Overwhelmingly, participants found that there was no routine, comfortable way to let health care providers know that heterosexual assumptions were not applicable to them as lesbians." In addition to avoiding irrelevant information, lesbians wanted health information that was pertinent to them.

Schwartz (1996) provides anecdotal evidence that the issues for gay men are similar to those which have been documented for lesbians. Schwartz gives a very poignant example of a gay man with rectal fissures that are causing him great physical pain, and the subsequent psychological pain he encounters as his physician makes homophobic remarks while examining him.

Mental Health Providers: Few studies have been published that assess the attitudes of mental health providers. Harris, Nightengale, and Owen (1995) reviewed the existing literature on the knowledge and attitudes of mental health providers towards gay men and lesbians. Citing Fassinger (1991, p. 166, cited in Harris et al., 1995, p. 93), they conclude:

Mental health professionals hold heterosexist assumptions … are generally uninformed about gay and lesbian life-

styles and issues … and hold many of the societal stereotypes about gay people … leading to distorted judgment about their clinical concerns.

Their research, which compared social workers, psychologists, and nurses on knowledge and attitudes about gay and lesbian clients, found that nurses had a significantly higher score on the Attitudes towards Lesbians (ATL) and Attitudes towards Gay Men (ATGM) scales than either social workers or psychologists, indicating a higher level of homophobia. Nurses also had a significantly lower score on the knowledge test than the other two groups. While there were no gender differences found in either of these areas, the respondents with more advanced degrees were more knowledgeable and less homophobic. Of particular interest was the fact that 51 percent of the respondents stated they had no information related to homosexuality in their professional training, and the mean number of classroom hours was only 3.3 (SD = 5.37).

A national survey of master level social workers by Berkman and Zinberg (1997) found that the vast majority (90 percent) of their sample were not homophobic. These results showed a much lower level of homophobia than earlier studies by DeCrescenzo (1984) and Wisniewski and Toomey (1987). No significant differences were found on level of homophobia based on age, marital status, being a parent, income, MSW vs. Doctorate degree, or primary work capacity. Men tended to be slightly more homophobic than women, and both genders slightly more homophobic towards gay men than lesbians, although these differences did not reach statistical significance.

In contrast to these low levels of homophobia, the authors found that the majority of their respondents had heterosexist attitudes, as measured by a 13-item heterosexist scale. Women were significantly less heterosexist than men, and younger respondents less heterosexist than older respondents. Significant relationships were also found between levels of homophobia and heterosexism and contact with gay men and lesbians, with greater contact corresponding to lower levels of homophobia and heterosexism. Single items were used to measure both religiosity and the respondents prior use of psychotherapy. Respondents who stated that religion was very important in their lives were more homophobic and heterosexist, as were respondents who had never been in psychotherapy. There was also no association between the amount of professional education received on homosexuality and either level of homophobia or heterosexism. This last finding is of particular interest, since both the National Association of Social Workers (NASW) as well as the Council on Social Work Education (CSWE) have emphasized the need for content on sexual orientation to be included in schools of social work. Differences may have been obscured due to the low levels of homophobia found in this study, but the results may point to the need to educate students about heterosexism rather than just focusing on content relevant to gay, lesbian, and bisexual people.

Few studies assessed the level of homophobia among psychiatrists, and none were located that looked at heterosexism. The Council on Scientific Affairs of the American Medical Association warns that despite the removal of homosexuality as a mental illness by the American Psychiatric Association in 1973, "some psychiatrists may continue to regard homosexuality as a disorder, and some mental health practitioners may present homosexuality as abnormal and dysfunctional" (1996, p. 1356). In a small Canadian study, Chaimowitz (1991) found relatively low levels of homophobia among psychiatric residents, family practice residents, and psychiatric faculty of a medical school. However, 25 percent of the psychiatric faculty admitted they were biased against lesbians and gay men, and psychiatric residents underestimated their homophobic responses in comparison with family practice residents and psychiatric faculty. As with other groups of mental health practitioners, women were found to be less homophobic than men.

Psychologists appear to have somewhat lower levels of homophobia when compared to other mental health professionals (DeCrescenzo, 1984), and may be somewhat more knowledgeable about gay and lesbian issues (Harris et al., 1995). This may be due in part to the fact that higher levels of education have historically been required to practice as a psychologist, and studies show an inverse relationship between homophobia and education (Harris et al., 1996). McGuire and others (1995), in a study of the relationship between ethical decision making in working with clients with AIDS and therapist homophobia, found a relatively low level of homophobia among the 643 Florida psychologists who participated in their study. However, the results did indicate a significant relationship between homophobia and the likelihood of breaching confidentiality, with this likelihood increasing the more dangerous the patient was perceived. The American Psychological Association has taken a very proactive stance, issuing its first statement against discrimination of homosexuals in 1975, supporting the action of the American Psychiatric Association (http://www.apa.org/pi/statemen.html). In 1997 the American Psychological Association also "overwhelmingly approved a resolution affirming its longtime position that homosexuality is not a disorder and raising questions about the efficacy and ethics of so-called reparative therapies" (http://psychology.ucdavis.edu/rainbow/html/facts_changing.html). Again, no studies were found that assessed the level of heterosexism among psychologists.

Other Barriers

Financial resources. Not surprisingly, the lack of financial resources is an additional barrier for lesbians seeking health care. Dennenberg (1992) discusses the economic discrimination women face, and the fact that lesbians do not have access to the resources and privileges married heterosexual women have through their husbands. For example, heterosexual women and their children may gain access to health insurance through their husbands' employment, but "lesbians usually cannot place a lover or a partner's children on their health insurance policy. Furthermore, lesbians may be less able to recruit support and resources from their family of origin, who often reserve such favors for their married children" (Dennenberg, 1992, p. 16). Trippet and Bain (1992) reported that the cost of health care and perceived lack of need were the most frequently cited reasons why lesbians in their study did not have a health care provider.

While these issues may also be true for gay men, fewer gay men enter relationships with children, and more have access to health insurance through their own employment. Clearly, the AIDS epidemic has raised critical issues about the financial access of gay men to appropriate health care. Many gay men diagnosed with HIV or AIDS have lost their health insurance coverage when they are no longer able to work. Eligibility for Medicaid is based on income, and Medicare has a two-year waiting period after a candidate is certified as disabled. While Ryan White funding is invaluable in providing funding for persons with AIDS who meet the eligibility guidelines, this funding will not cover other health issues.

Exclusion of family and friends. The final barrier for gay men and lesbians in seeking health care is the exclusion of friends and family in seeking and receiving care. Stevens (1992) reported a number of studies where some lesbians "only felt safe when accompanied by a partner or friend who could act as a witness or advocate" (p. 111). Simkin (1991) discusses how "lesbians are often denied access to their partners in emergency rooms or intensive care units" (p. 1622). These contexts were also perceived as more dangerous by lesbians and gay men due to the reduced opportunity to select their provider, and because they felt cut off from friends and family, resulting in feelings of vulnerability and lack of protection (Stevens, 1992; Schwartz, 1996).

IMPACT ON CARE

Physical Health

All persons seeking medical care want the best care provided by the most competent provider available. For gay men and lesbians this may provide a dilemma not encountered by heterosexuals. Gay men and lesbians must determine not only the professional competency of a potential provider, but also his/her attitudes and beliefs about homosexuality, and hope that the provider is homophilic as well as competent. This dilemma can result in a delay by lesbians and gay men in seeking care.

In a 1988 study, Stevens and Hall reported that 84 percent of their sample of lesbians described a general reluctance to seek health care, and it is well documented that lesbians seek routine care less frequently than heterosexual women. Trippet and Bain (1992) reported that 24.7 percent of the lesbians in their sample "failed to seek health care" (p. 148), while Bruenting's (1992) study was "consistent with the Smith, Johnson and Guenther (1985) finding that lesbian women are less likely to seek routine gynecological care" (p. 169). Robertson and Schachter (1981) found the average time between pap smears for heterosexual women was 8 months, and for lesbians, 21 months, using the same clinic.

The most significant risk faced by lesbians in avoiding routine care is that "lesbians may not receive early warning of abnormal Papanicolaou smears, endometrial cancer, or breast cancer" (Simkin, 1991, p. 1621). In addition, lesbians may not perceive their risk for cervical and breast cancer to be any different than heterosexual women (Trippet and Bain, 1993; Zeidenstein, 1990). Trippet and Bain (1992) reported that the reasons lesbians failed to seek health care were "the lesbians' participation in self-care (as a result of negative experience with health care providers) and the lack of financial resources" (p. 147). The results may be devastating, with lesbians seeking care at later stages of an illness, treatment being more invasive, and with increased risk of death.

O'Neill and Shalit (1992) discuss the impact of provider homophobia, reporting on a study (Davison and Friedman, 1981) in which health professionals evaluated patients identified as homosexual differently from those who were not identified as homosexual. The providers were more apt to interpret problems presented by the patients identified as homosexual in sexual terms, whereas other diagnoses were more frequently considered for patients not identified as homosexual. O'Neill and Shalit (1992) go on to state that gay men seeking care may experience "excessive emotional stress as a result of medical illness if they believe it to be the result of their sexual practices. This stress may cause them to postpone seeking consultation about a symptom and needlessly delay treatment" (p. 192). Schwartz (1996) provides numerous examples of the psychological and emotional distress experienced by gay men when they encounter homophobic health care providers, concluding:

> Blatant homophobia, heterosexism, inadequate knowledge and discrimination within the health care system are common experiences for gay men. Even though these barriers have long been present, the advent of AIDS has pointed out their negative impact on the health care of gay men. In addition to these external barriers which gay men face are the internal barriers of fear and internalized homophobia. In order for gay men to receive adequate health care, both of these issues must be confronted. Health care providers need to become aware and knowledgeable about the unique needs of gay men, while gay men must become comfortable in asserting their right to receive appropriate and gay-affirming health care services (pp. 31-32).

Mental Health

Most gay men and lesbians seek psychotherapy for the same reasons and types of problems as heterosexual men and women. In some instances the issue of sexual orientation will be at the center of the presenting concern, in other instances it will be on the periphery. Regardless, the mental health professional providing care must be cognizant of the unique issues confronted by lesbians and gay men as they attempt to negotiate in a world that discriminates against them due to their sexual orientation.

According to Stein (1996, p. 39), "risk for anti-gay and heterosexist bias in psychotherapy with gay men is high.... Special concerns for gay men in therapy include dealing with coming out, effects of anti-gay prejudice and violence, relationship issues, concerns of gay youth, parenting, and concerns about family of origin. Gay men may also present with problems with sexuality and sexual dysfunction and special health issues, such as HIV infection and alcohol and substance abuse."

Stein (1996, p. 40) states that "the gender and sexual orientation of the therapist do not determine the effectiveness of his or her work with gay men. While that may be true in terms of effectiveness, Bradford and others (1994) in their national survey of lesbians found that 89 percent of the respondents preferred to see a woman therapist, whereas only 1 percent preferred to see a man. Sexual orientation of the therapist was less important than gender, but 66 percent still preferred a counselor who was lesbian or gay. Ethnicity was least important, with 33 percent of Latina lesbians, 31 percent of African American lesbians, and 27 percent of white lesbians preferring a therapist of their own ethnic background.

In contrast to the reluctance of lesbians to seek medical care, Bradford and others (1994) found that nearly three-fourths of the women in their study sought professional counseling. This figure was similar to that found by Morgan (1992), who found that 77.5 percent of the lesbians and 28.9 percent of the heterosexual women in her sample had been in therapy. According to Bradford and others (1994, pp. 240-41), the reasons for this are multiple:

> Morgan and Eliason (1992) asked lesbians who had and those who had never been in therapy for reasons why so

many lesbians seek therapy. Themes mentioned by at least half the sample included the fact that societal oppression causes stress for lesbians, therapy and personal growth are modeled and accepted by the lesbian community, and lesbians are introspective and have practice facing hard issues. Given the results of these studies, it is understandable why lesbians in the current study who were more out were also more likely to have used counseling. Lesbians who were more out also were more likely to have sought counseling for reasons related to being lesbian, such as difficulties with lovers or family, than were more closeted lesbians.

Of particular concern are gay and lesbian youth who are referred to counseling for issues that may be indicative of a struggle with sexual identity. Too often, mental health professionals have either ignored sexual orientation as an underlying issue or have dismissed the intensity of it with platitudes such as "it's just a passing developmental phase." Gochros and Bidwell (1996), along with Slater (1988), outline critical issues that counselors must consider in working with gay and lesbian youth.

No discussion on the impact of homophobia and heterosexism on the mental health care provided to gay men and lesbians would be complete without some mention of reparative or sexual orientation conversion therapies. As noted earlier, the American Psychological Association has recently passed a resolution that raises questions about the efficacy and the ethics of reparative therapies. Haldeman (1994) reviewed the literature on sexual orientation conversion therapies and concluded that the literature on psychotherapeutic and religious conversion therapies showed no evidence indicating that such treatments are effective. These treatments are based in the belief that homosexuality is a mental illness and that homoerotic feelings are undesirable. Given the lack of effectiveness, Haldeman suggests the need for research to determine if there are negative consequences to these therapies. Clearly, the most damaging aspect of this approach is the homophobia that underlies the belief that a homosexual sexual orientation should be changed.

CONCLUSIONS

There are numerous obstacles lesbians and gay men must overcome in order to achieve a state of health as defined by the World Health Organization. The literature reviewed in this article clearly demonstrates that it is impossible to discuss physical, mental, and social well being as separate entities, but that the discussion must focus on the interaction of all aspects of a person's life. The societal conditions that foster homophobia and heterosexism are at the root of the physical and mental health problems that are encountered by lesbians and gay men. The physical health of gay men and lesbians is compromised by their delay in seeking care, a delay that is the result of homophobia and heterosexism by providers. Internalized homophobia may also increase the risk of physical disease. Physical health is also compromised by lack of information, or by misinformation about the unique health care needs of this population. Public health announcements concerning both HIV and breast cancer do not include information specific to gay men and lesbians. Information concerning the spread of HIV does not include information about anal intercourse, and information about the increased risk of breast cancer for lesbians is not in the mainstream press. Public policies that deny gay men and lesbians the right to marry create financial barriers to health and mental health care not encountered by heterosexuals. Institutional policies that do not support gay and lesbian relationships increase the stress already experienced during times of illness.

Homophobia and heterosexism create the social climate in which anti-gay and anti-lesbian violence and hate crimes occur, a climate that makes it difficult for gays and lesbians to develop a positive sense of self. The impact of this social climate is seen most poignantly in the high suicide rate among gay and lesbian youth, as well as the higher incidence of alcohol and drug abuse. The same social climate that fosters homophobia and heterosexism is also responsible for racial and gender discrimination, which exacerbate the difficulties of developing a positive self identity for gay and lesbian people of color. The fact that the majority of lesbians and gay men do not have mental health problems attests to their resiliency and strength.

While these oppressive social conditions continue to exist and are being fostered by conservative religious and political movements, there are a number of recent events that indicate that social change is occurring that may result in a healthier social climate for gay and lesbian youth and adults. First, gay and lesbian people are no longer invisible, but are increasingly acknowledged as an oppressed minority who deserve civil rights. The hate crimes statistic act of 1990 includes sexual orientation, and President Clinton hosted a national summit on hate crimes on 10 November 1997. Kerry Lobel, Executive Director of the National Gay and Lesbian Task Force, attended the summit and shared the stories of gay and lesbian people. The violence perpetuated against gay men and lesbians, and those who are perceived to be gay and lesbian, has become an important part of the national dialogue on hate crimes (Levin, 1997). Gay and lesbian characters are commonly seen on television, and while still controversial in some arenas are no longer presented only as caricatures. On 16 October 1997, Vice-President Al Gore stated that "when the character Ellen came out, millions of Americans were forced to look at sexual orientation in a more open light." Elizabeth Birch, the Human Rights Campaign's executive director, stated: "Television is a mirror of society and, unfortunately, for a very long time, gay people were either invisible or highly distorted. By singling out a positive gay character on a groundbreaking show, the vice president has himself helped to lead Americans to view our community with greater respect" (http://www.hrc.org/feature1/gorellen.html).

Second, along with increased attention being given to gay and lesbian people in the public arena, the professional literature is also challenging its constituents to educate themselves on the unique issues confronting gay men and lesbians. One manifestation of this is the increase in the number of articles and books being written about gay and lesbian issues, which are being published by the mainstream, rather than alternative, press. Almost all professional organizations have included gay, lesbian, and bisexual issues into their annual program meetings, and special task forces, commissions, or allied organizations have been formed to give voice to the special concerns of this group. Recently, the National Institutes of Health and the U.S. Centers for Disease Control and Prevention have formed a Lesbian Health Research Priorities project, which will study lesbian health issues and research methodologies (Johnson, 1997).

Third, political action organizations are now in existence to give voice to the concerns of gay and lesbian people. The oldest organization may be the National Gay and Lesbian Task Force (NGLTF), formed in 1973 to support advocacy and grass roots

organizing in support of civil rights for gay, lesbian, bisexual, and transgendered people. The National Lesbian and Gay Health Association (NLGHA) was formed in 1994 through the merger of the National Alliance of Lesbian and Gay Health Clinics and the National Lesbian and Gay Health Foundation. NLGHA sponsors an annual Lesbian and Gay Health Conference and AIDS/HIV Form. PFLAG (Parents, Families and Friends of Lesbians and Gays) is a national organization that works to create a society that is healthy and that is respectful of human diversity. The National Youth Advocacy Coalition (NYAC) is dedicated to improving the lives of gay, lesbian, bisexual, and transgendered youth through advocacy, education and legislative change.

RESOURCES

A variety of organizations have developed that focus on the issues unique to gay and lesbian people. Most of these organizations are new, having been formed since the Stonewall Riots of 1969. By no means is the following list exhaustive, but each of the following are working on issues related to health and mental health issues for lesbians and gay men.

The Gay and Lesbian Medical Association
459 Fulton Street, Suite 107
San Francisco, California 94102
(http://www.glma.org)

Founded in 1981 as the American Association of Physicians for Human Rights, the mission of the Gay and Lesbian Medical Association (GLMA) is to be "an organization of lesbian, gay, bisexual, and transgendered physicians, medical students, and their supporters. GLMA works to maximize the quality of health and health services for lesbian, gay, bisexual, and transgendered people, to promote full civil rights, and to foster a professional climate in which our diverse members can achieve their full potential." GLMA strives to achieve its goals by:

> educating health care professionals about the unique health care needs of gay, lesbian, bisexual, and transgendered people; helping to develop equitable health care policy; promoting relevant research in health; supporting GLMA members who are challenged by discrimination on the basis of sexual orientation.

The National Lesbian and Gay Health Association
1407 S. St., NW
Washington, D.C. 10009
Phone: 202-939-7880
Fax: 202-234-1467
(http://www.serve.com/nlgha/hewal.htm)

The National Lesbian and Gay Health Association (NLGHA) was formed in 1994 through the merger of the National Alliance of Lesbian and Gay Health Clinics and the National Lesbian and Gay Health Foundation. The mission of NLGHA is to enhance the quality of health for lesbians and gays through education, policy development, advocacy, and the facilitation of health care delivery. NLGHA activities include:

> *Education:* NLGHA serves as a comprehensive resource for lesbian and gay health care providers, existing and

emerging lesbian and gay health care centers nationwide, and the general public.

Technical Assistance: NLGHA provides networking, information sharing, and other support services to existing lesbian and gay health centers and emerging lesbian and gay health projects, clinics, and advocacy groups.

Communication: NLGHA communicates with colleagues in the health professions, in federal agencies, and on Capitol Hill.

Advocacy: NLGHA advocates at the federal level for better care, increased funding, and inclusion of lesbian and gay health issues.

Research: With the formation of its National Research Institute for Lesbian and Gay Health, NLGHA will provide assistance with designing research, identifying funding opportunities, and disseminating research findings for health professional engaged in lesbian and gay health research.

National Health Conference: NLGHA's annual Lesbian and Gay Health Conference and AIDS/HIV Forum provides opportunities to share research data and program expertise, and to educate, learn, and network.

The National Gay and Lesbian Task Force
2320 Seventeenth Street, NW
Washington, D.C. 20009-2702
Phone: 202-332-6483
FAX: 202-332-0207
TTY: 202-332-6219
(http://www.ngltf.org/gi.html)

The National Gay and Lesbian Task Force (NGLTF) is a leading progressive civil rights organization that has supported grassroots organizing and advocacy since 1973. NGLTF is the front line activist organization in the national gay and lesbian movement. As such, it serves as the national resource center for grassroots lesbian, gay, bisexual, and transgender organizations that are facing a variety of battles at the state and local level, such as combating anti-gay violence, battling Radical Right anti-gay legislative and ballot measures, advocating an end to job discrimination, working to repeal sodomy laws, demanding an effective governmental response to HIV, and reform of the health care system, and much more. NGLTF is a progressive organization, committed to building coalition with other communities working for social change. NGLTF's goal is to represent—and work on issues of concern to—the full depth and breadth of diversity in gay and lesbian communities.

Human Rights Campaign
1101 Fourteenth Street NW
Washington, D.C. 20005
Phone: 202-628-4160
FAX: 202-347-5323
E-mail: hrc@hrc.org
(http://www.hrc.org)

Founded in 1980, Human Rights Campaign (HRC) maintains the largest full-time lobbying team in the nation devoted to issues of fairness for lesbian and gay Americans. With a national staff, and volunteers and members throughout the country, HRC:

lobbies the federal government on gay, lesbian and AIDS issues; educates the public; participates in election campaigns; organizes volunteers; provides expertise and training at the state and local level.

HRC has helped pass major legislation, including increased AIDS funding, the Ryan White Comprehensive AIDS Resources Emergency Act, the Americans with Disabilities Act, the Hate Crimes Statistics and Hate Crimes Sentencing Enhancement Acts, and programs for breast and cervical cancer research and screening.

Parents, Families and Friends of Lesbians and Gays
1101 Fourteenth Street, N.W., Suite 1030
Washington, D.C. 20005
Phone: 202-638-0243
FAX: 202-638-0243
E-mail: pflagntl@aol.com
(http://pflag.org)

Parents, Families and Friends of Lesbians and Gays (PFLAG) is a national non-profit organization that provides opportunity for dialogue about sexual orientation and acts to create a society that is healthy and that is respectful of human diversity. The mission of PFLAG is to promote the health and well-being of gay, lesbian, and bisexual persons, their families and friends through:

support, to cope with an adverse society; education, to enlighten an ill-informed public; advocacy, to end discrimination and to secure equal civil rights.

Lesbian and Gay Aging Issues Network
American Society on Aging
833 Market Street, Suite 511
San Francisco, California 94103-1824
Phone: 415-974-9600
FAX: 415-974-00300
E-mail: info@asa.asaging.org
(http://www.healthanswers.com/health_answers/
sponsor_directory/as
a/asa/lgain.html)

The primary goal of the Aging Issues Network is to assist its members in becoming sensitive to the special challenges lesbians and gay men face in aging and the unique barriers this often invisible segment of the aging population encounters in accessing housing, healthcare, long-term care, and social services.

National Youth Advocacy Coalition
1711 Connecticut Avenue, NW, Suite 206
Washington, D.C. 20009-1139
Phone: 202-319-7596
FAX: 202-319-7365
E-Mail: nyouthac@aol.com

National Youth Advocacy Coalition (NYAC) is dedicated to improving the lives of gay, lesbian, bisexual, and transgendered youth through advocacy, education, and legislative change. It is sponsored by the Hetrick-Martin Institute, and was established in 1993 to address the need for a national organization dedicated to improving the lives of young people facing discrimination based on their sexual orientation (NYAC Brochure).

Parents, Families and Friends of Lesbians and Gays contingent at the 1993 March on Washington.

REFERENCES:

Books

Bell, A. P. and M. S. Weinberg. *Homosexualities.* New York: Simon and Schuster, 1978.

Bell, A. P., M. S. Weinberg, and S. K. Hammersmith. *Sexual Preference: Its Development in Men and Women.* Bloomington, Indiana: Indiana University Press, 1981.

Comstock, G. D. *Violence against Lesbians and Gay Men.* New York: Columbia University Press, 1991.

Curry, J. I. *A Legal Guide for Lesbian and Gay Couples.* Berkeley, California: Nolo Press, 1991.

Gilligan, C. *In a Different Voice: Psychological Theory and Women's Development.* Cambridge, Massachusetts: Harvard University Press, 1982.

Humphreys, R. A. L. *Tearoom Trade: A Study of Homosexual Encounters in Public Places.* London: Duckworth, 1970.

Jordan, J. V. *Women's Growth in Diversity: More Writings from the Stone Center.* New York: Guilford Press, 1997.

Jordan, J. V., A. G. Kaplan, J. B. Miller, I. P. Stiver, and J. L. Surrey. *Women's Growth in Connection: Writings from the Stone Center.* New York: Guilford Press, 1991.

Savin-Williams, R. C. *Gay and Lesbian Youth: Expressions of Identity.* Washington, D.C.: Hemisphere, 1990.

Williams, W. L. *The Spirit and the Flesh.* Boston: Beacon Press, 1992.

Winiarski, M. G. *AIDS Related Psychotherapy.* New York: Pergamon Press, 1991.

Chapters in Books

Anderson, S. C. "Substance Abuse and Dependency in Gay Men and Lesbians," in *Health Care for Lesbians and Gay Men: Confronting Homophobia and Heterosexism,* edited by K. J. Peterson. New York: Harrington Park Press, 1996: 59-76.

Bernard, D. "Developing a Positive Self Image in a Homophobic Environment," in *Lesbian and Gay Lifestyles: A Guide for Counseling and Education,* edited by N. J. Woodman. New York: Irvington Publishers, Inc., 1992: 23-32.

Berrill, K. T. "Anti-Gay Violence and Victimization in the United States: An Overview," in *Hates Crimes: Confronting Violence against Lesbians and Gay Men,* edited by G. M. Herek and K. T. Berrill. Newbury Park, California: Sage Publications, 1992: 19-45.

Boxer, A. M., J. A. Cook, and G. Herdt. "Double Jeopardy: Identity Transitions and Parent-Child Relations among Gay and Lesbian Youth," in *Parent-Child Relations through Life*, edited by K. Pillemer and K. McCartney. Hillsdale, New Jersey: Erlbaum, 1991: 59-92.

Brown, L. B. "Women and Men, Not-Men and Not-Women, Lesbians and Gays: American Indian Gender Style Alternatives," in *Two Spirit People: American Indian Lesbian Women and Gay Men,* edited by L. B. Brown. New York: Harrington Park Press, 1997: 5-20.

Callahan, D. "Health and Society: Some Ethical Imperatives," in *Doing Better and Feeling Worse: Health in the United States,* edited by J. H. Knowles. New York: W. W. Norton and Company, 1977: 23-33.

Chan, C. S. "Asian-American Adolescents: Issues in the Expression of Sexuality," in *Sexual Cultures and the Construction of Adolescent Identities,* edited by J. M. Irvine. Philadelphia: Temple University Press, 1994: 88-99.

Dean, L., S. Wu, and J. Marti. "Trends in Violence and Discrimination against Gay Men in New York City: 1984 to 1990," in G. M. Herek, and K. T. Berrill: 46-64.

Espin, O. "Cultural and Historical Influences on Sexuality in His-
panic/Latina Women: Implications for Psychotherapy," in *Plea-
sure and Danger: Exploring Female Sexuality,* edited by C.
Vance. London: Routledge and Kegan Paul, 1984: 149-63.
———. "Issues of Identity in the Psychology of Latina Lesbi-
ans," in *Lesbian Psychologies: Explorations and Challenges,*
edited by the Boston Lesbian Psychologies Collective. Urbana,
Illinois: University of Illinois Press, 1987: 35-51.
Gochros, H. L., and R. Bidwell. "Lesbian and Gay Youth in a
Straight World: Implications for Health Care Workers," in K. J.
Peterson: 1-17.
Golden, C. "What's in a Name? Sexual Self-Identification among
Women," in *The Lives of Lesbians, Gays, and Bisexuals: Chil-
dren to Adults,* edited by R. C. Savin-Williams and K. M. Cohen.
Fort Worth, Texas: Harcourt Brace, 1996: 229-49.
Gonsiorek, J. C., and J. R. Rudolph. "Homosexual Identity: Coming
Out and Other Developmental Events," in *Homosexuality: Re-
search Implications of Public Policy,* edited by J. C. Gonsiorek and
J. D. Weinrich. Newbury Park, California: Sage, 1991: 161-76.
Greene, B., and N. Boyd-Franklin. "African American Lesbians:
Issues in Couples Therapy," in *Lesbians and Gays in Couples
and Families,* edited by J. Laird and R. J. Green. San Francisco:
Jossey-Bass, 1996: 251-71.
Hartman, A. "Social Policy as a Context for Lesbian and Gay Fami-
lies: The Political Is Personal," in J. Laird and R. J. Green: 69-85.
Hidalgo, H. "The Puerto Rican Lesbian in the United States," in
Woman Identified Women, edited by T. Darty and S. Potter. Palo
Alto, California: Mayfield, 1984: 105-50.
Levy, E. F. "Reproductive Issues for Lesbians," in K. J. Peterson:
49-58.
Little Crow, Wright, J. A., and L. B. Brown. "Gender Selection in
Two American Indian Tribes," in L. B. Brown: 21-28.
Liu, P. and C. S. Chan. "Lesbian, Gay, and Bisexual Asian Ameri-
cans and Their Families," in J. Laird and R. J. Green: 137-52.
Mays, V., and S. Cochran. "The Black Women's Relationship
Project: A National Survey of Black Lesbians," in *The
Sourcebook on Lesbian/Gay Health Care,* edited by M. Shernoff
and W. Scott. Washington, D.C.: National Lesbian and Gay
Health Foundation, second edition, 1988: 54-62.
Morales, E. "Gender Roles among Latino Gay and Bisexual Men:
Implications for Family and Couples Relationships," in J. Laird
and R. J. Green: 272-97.
———. "Latino Gays and Latina Lesbians," in *Counseling Gay
Men and Lesbians: Journey to the End of the Rainbow,* edited
by S. Dworkin and F. Gutierrez. Alexandria, Virginia: American
Association for Counseling and Development, 1992: 125-39.
Nicoloff, L. K., and E. A. Stiglitz. "Lesbian Alcoholism: Etiology,
Treatment, and Recovery," in Boston Lesbian Psychologies Col-
lective: 283-93.
O'Neil, M. K. "Affective Disorders," in *Adult Psychopathology:
A Social Work Perspective,* edited by F. J. Turner. New York:
The Free Press, 1984: 148-80.
Peterson, K. J., and M. Bricker-Jenkins. "Lesbians and the Health
Care System," in K. J. Peterson: 33-47.
Savin-Williams, R. C. "Self-Labeling and Disclosure among Gay, Les-
bian, and Bisexual Youth," in J. Laird and R. J. Green: 153-82.
Schwartz, M. "Gay Men and the Health Care System," in K. J.
Peterson: 19-32.
von Schulthess, B. "Violence in the Streets: Anti-Lesbian Assault
and Harassment in San Francisco," in G. M. Herek and K. T.
Berrill: 65-75.

Weathers, B. "Alcoholism and the Lesbian Community," in *Alcoholism in Women,* edited by C. Eddy and J. Fords. Dubuque,
Iowa: Kendall/Hunt, 1980: 142-149.

Periodical Articles

Bailey, J. M. and K. J. Zucker. "Childhood Sex-Typed Behavior
and Sexual Orientation: A Conceptual Analysis and Quantita-
tive Review," in *Developmental Psychology,* vol. 31, 1995: 43-
55.
Berkman, C. S. and G. Zinberg. "Homophobia and
Heterosexism in Social Workers," in *Social Work,* vol. 42,
1997: 319-32.
Berrill, K. T. "Anti-Gay Violence and Victimization in the United
States," in *Journal of Interpersonal Violence,* vol. 5, 1990: 274-
94.
Bradford, J., C. Ryan, and E. D. Rothblum. "National Lesbian
Health Care Survey: Implications for Mental Health Care," in
Journal of Consulting and Clinical Psychology, vol. 62, 1994:
228-42.
Brown, L. S. "New Voices, New Visions: Toward a Lesbian/Gay
Paradigm for Psychology," in *Psychology of Women Quarterly,*
vol. 13, 1989: 445-58.
Brownworth, V. A. "The Other Epidemic: Lesbians and Breast
Cancer," in *Out,* March 1993: 60-63.
Cain, R. "Stigma Management and Gay Identity Development,"
in *Social Work,* vol. 36, 1991: 67-73.
Callender, C. and L. M. Kochems. "Men and Not-Men: Male Gen-
der-Mixing Statuses and Homosexuality," in *Journal of Homo-
sexuality,* vol. 11, 1986: 165-78.
Cass, V. "Homosexual Identity Formation: A Theoretical Model,"
in *Journal of Homosexuality,* vol. 4, 1979: 219-35.
Catalan, J. and K. Pugh. "Suicidal Behavior and HIV Infection—
Is There a Link?" in *AIDS Care,* vol. 7, supplement 2, 1995:
S117-21.
Chaimowitz, G. A. "Homophobia among Psychiatric Residents,
Family Practice Residents and Psychiatric Faculty," in *Cana-
dian Journal of Psychiatry 36* (1991): 206-09.
Chan, C. S. "Issues of Identity Development among Asian-Ameri-
can Lesbians and Gay Men," in *Journal of Counseling and De-
velopment,* vol. 68, 1989: 16-20.
Cole, S. W., M. E. Kemeny, S. E. Taylor, and B. R. Visscher. "El-
evated Physical Health Risk among Gay Men Who Conceal
Their Homosexual Identity," in *Health Psychology,* vol. 15, 1996:
243-251.
Coleman, E. "Developmental Stages of the Coming Out Process,"
in *Journal of Homosexuality,* vol. 7, 1981/1982: 31-43.
Council on Scientific Affairs, American Medical Association Council Report: "Health Care Needs of Gay Men and Lesbians in
the United States," in *Journal of the American Medical Association,* vol. 275, 1996: 1354-59.
Daling, J. R., N. S. Weiss, L. L. Klopfenstein, L. E. Cochran, W.
H. Chow, and R. Daifuku. "Correlates of Homosexual Behav-
ior and the Incidence of Anal Cancer," in *Journal of the Ameri-
can Medical Association,* vol. 247, 1982: 1988-90.
D'Augelli, A. R. "Gay Men in College: Identity Processes and
Adaptations," in *Journal of College Student Development,* vol.
32, 1991: 140-46.
———. "Lesbian and Gay Male Undergraduates' Experiences of
Harassment and Fear on Campus," in *Journal of Interpersonal
Violence,* vol. 7, 1992: 383-95.

Davison, G. C. and S. Friedman. "Sexual Orientation Stereotype in the Distortion of Clinical Judgment," in *Journal of Homosexuality*, vol. 6, 1981: 37-44.

DeCrescenzo, T. "Homophobia: A Study of the Attitudes of Mental Health Professionals toward Homosexuality," in *Homosexuality and Social Work*, vol. 2, 1984: 115-36.

Dennenberg, R. "Invisible Women: Lesbians and Health Care," in *Health/PAC Bulletin*, 1992: 14-21.

Douglas, C. J., C. M. Kalman, and T. P. Kalman. "Homophobia among Physicians and Nurses: An Empirical Study," in *Hospital and Community Psychiatry*, vol. 36, 1985: 1309-11.

Fay, R. E., et al. "Prevalence and Patterns of Same Gender Sexual Contact among Men," in *Science*, vol. 243, 1989: 338-48.

Fitzpatrick, G. "Self-Disclosure of Lesbianism as Related to Self-Actualization and Self-Stigmatization," in *Dissertation Abstracts International*, vol. 43, 1983: 4143B.

Gallagher, J. "The Lesbian Health Crisis," in *The Advocate*, vol. 743, 1997: 20-26.

Garnets, L., G. M. Herek, and B. Levy. "Violence and Victimization of Lesbians and Gay Men: Mental Health Consequences," in *Journal of Interpersonal Violence*, vol. 5, no. 3, 1990: 366-83.

Gentry, S. E. "Caring for Lesbians in a Homophobic Society," in *Health Care for Women International*, vol. 13, 1992: 173-80.

Glaus, K. O. "Alcoholism, Chemical Dependency, and the Lesbian Client," in *Women and Therapy*, vol. 8, 1988: 131-44.

Gonsiorek, J. C. "Mental Health Issues of Gay and Lesbian Adolescents," in *Journal of Adolescent Health Care*, vol. 9, 1988: 114-22.

Greene, B. "Ethnic-Minority Lesbians and Gay Men: Mental Health and Treatment Issues," in *Journal of Consulting and Clinical Psychology*, vol. 62, 1994: 243-51.

Haldeman, D. C. "The Practice and Ethics of Sexual Orientation Conversion Therapy," in *Journal of Consulting and Clinical Psychology*, vol. 62, 1994: 221-27.

Hanson, B. "The Violence We Face as Lesbians and Gay Men: The Landscape Both Outside and Inside Our Communities," in *Journal of Gay and Lesbian Social Services*, vol. 4, no. 2, 1996: 95-113.

Harris, M. B., J. Nightingale, and N. Owen. "Health Care Professionals' Experience, Knowledge, and Attitudes Concerning Homosexuality," in *Journal of Gay and Lesbian Social Services*, vol. 2, 1995: 91-107.

Harrison, A. E. "Primary Care of Lesbian and Gay Patients: Educating Ourselves and Our Students," in *Family Medicine*, vol. 28, no. 1, 1996: 10-23.

Harvey, S. M., C. Carr, and S. Bernheine. "Lesbian Mothers' Health Care Experiences," in *Journal of Nurse Midwifery*, vol. 34, no. 3, 1989: 115-19.

Herek, G. M. "The Context of Anti-Gay Violence: Notes on Cultural and Psychological Heterosexism," in *Journal of Interpersonal Violence*, vol. 5, no. 3, 1990: 316-33.

———. "Documenting Prejudice against Lesbians and Gay Men on Campus: The Yale Sexual Orientation Survey," in *Journal of Homosexuality*, vol. 25, no. 4, 1993: 15-30.

———. "Hate Crimes against Lesbians and Gay Men: Issues for Research and Policy," in *American Psychologist*, vol. 44, no. 6, 1989: 948-955.

Hughes, T. L. and S. C. Wilsnack. "Use of Alcohol among Lesbians: Research and Clinical Implications," in *American Journal of Orthopsychiatry*, vol. 67, 1997: 20-36.

Johnson, S. R., E. M. Smith, and S. M. Guenther. "Comparison of Gynecologic Health Care Problems between Lesbians and Bisexual Women," in *Journal of Reproductive Medicine*, vol. 32, 1987: 805-11.

Kus, R. J. "Alcoholism and Non-Acceptance of Gay Self: The Critical Link," in *Journal of Homosexuality*, vol. 15, 1988: 25-41.

Levin, S. F. "Kansas Hosts Hate Crimes Town Meeting Featuring National Gay and Lesbian Task Force Director Kerry Lobel," in *The Liberty Press: The Official Lesbian and Gay Newsmagazine of Kansas*, vol. 4, 1997: 27.

Lucas, V. A. "An Investigation of the Health Care Preferences of the Lesbian Population," in *Health Care for Women International*, vol. 13, 1992: 221-28.

Martin, A. D. and E. S. Hetrick. "The Stigmatization of the Gay and Lesbian Adolescent," in *Journal of Homosexuality*, vol. 15, 1988: 163-83.

Mathews, W. C., M. W. Booth, J. D. Turner, and L. Kessler. "Physicians' Attitudes toward Homosexuality—Survey of a California County Medical Society," in *The Western Journal of Medicine*, vol. 144, 1986: 106-09.

Mays, V., S. Cochran, and S. Rhue. "The Impact of Perceived Discrimination on the Intimate Relationships of Black Lesbians," in *Journal of Homosexuality*, vol. 25, 1993: 1-14.

McDonald, G. J. "Individual Differences in the Coming Out Process of Gay Men: Implications for Theoretical Models," in *Journal of Homosexuality*, vol. 8, 1982: 47-60.

McGuire, J., D. Nieri, D. Abbott, K. Sheridan, and R. Fisher. "Do *Tarasoff* Principles Apply in AIDS-Related Psychotherapy? Ethical Decision Making and the Role of Therapist Homophobia and Perceived Client Dangerousness," in *Professional Psychology: Research and Practice*, vol. 26, 1995: 608-11.

McKirnan, D. J. and P. L. Peterson. "Alcohol and Drug Use among Homosexual Men and Women: Epidemiology and Population Characteristics," in *Addictive Behavior*, vol. 14, 1989a: 545-54.

———. "Psychosocial and Cultural Factors in Alcohol and Drug Abuse: An Analysis of a Homosexual Community," in *Addictive Behaviors*, vol. 14, no. 5, 1989b: 555-63.

Melbye, M., T. R. Cote, L. Kessler, M. Gail, and R. J. Biggar. "High Incidence of Anal Cancer among AIDS Patients," in *Lancet*, vol. 343, 1994: 636-39.

Moran, N. "Lesbian Health Care Needs," in *Canadian Family Physician*, vol. 42, 1996: 879-84.

Morgan, K. S. "Caucasian Lesbians' Use of Psychotherapy: A Matter of Attitude?" in *Psychology of Women Quarterly*, vol. 16, 1992: 127-30.

Morgan, K. S. and M. J. Eliason. "The Role of Psychotherapy in Caucasian Lesbians' Lives," in *Women and Therapy*, vol. 13, 1992: 27-52.

O'Neill, J. F. and P. Shalit. "Health Care of the Gay Male Patient," in *Primary Care*, vol. 19, no. 1, 1992: 191-201.

Otis, M. D. and W. F. Skinner. "The Prevalence of Victimization and Its Effect on Mental Well-Being among Lesbian and Gay People," in *Journal of Homosexuality*, vol. 30, 1996: 93-121.

Pillard, R. C. "Sexual Orientation and Mental Disorder," in *Psychiatry Annals*, vol. 18, no. 1, 1988: 52-56.

Pitts, F. N., B. Schuller, C. L. Rich, and A. F. Pitts. "Suicide among U.S. Women Physicians, 1967-1972," in *American Journal of Psychiatry*, vol. 136, 1979: 694-96.

Rankow, E. J. "Lesbian Health Issues for the Primary Care Provider," in *The Journal of Family Practice*, vol. 40, no. 5, 1995: 486-92.

Raymond, C. A. "Lesbians Call for Greater Physician Awareness, Sensitivity to Improve Patient Care," in *Journal of the American Medical Association,* vol. 259, 1988: 18.

Remafedi, B. "Male Homosexuality: The Adolescent's Perspective," in *Pediatrics,* vol. 79, 1987: 326-30.

Robertson, M. M. "Lesbians as an Invisible Minority in the Health Services Arena," in *Health Care for Women International,* vol. 13, 1992: 155-63.

Robertson, P. and J. Schachter. "Failure to Identify Venereal Disease in a Lesbian Population," in *Sexually Transmitted Diseases,* vol. 9, no. 2, 1981: 75-76.

Rothblum, E. D. "'I Only Read about Myself on Bathroom Walls': The Need for Research on the Mental Health of Lesbians and Gay Men," in *Journal of Consulting and Clinical Psychology,* vol. 62, no. 2, 1994: 213-20.

Savin-Williams, R. C. "Verbal and Physical Abuse as Stressors in the Lives of Lesbian, Gay Male, and Bisexual Youths: Associations with School Problems, Running Away, Substance Abuse Prostitution, and Suicide," in *Journal of Consulting and Clinical Psychology,* vol. 62, no. 2, 1994: 261-69.

Simkin, R. J. "Lesbians Face Unique Health Care Problems," in *Canadian Medical Association Journal,* vol. 145, no. 12, 1993: 1620-23.

Smith, E. M., S. R. Johnson, and S. M. Guenther. "Health Care Attitudes and Experiences during Gynecologic Care among Lesbians and Bisexuals," in *American Journal of Public Health,* vol. 75, no. 9, 1985: 1085-87.

Smith, M., C. Heaton, and D. Seiver. "Health Concerns of Lesbian Women," in *Female Patient,* vol. 14, 1989: 43.

Stein, T. S. "Homosexuality and Homophobia in Men," in *Psychiatric Annals,* vol. 26, no. 1, 1996: 37-40.

Stevens, P. D. and J. M. Hall. "Stigma, Health Beliefs and Experiences with Health Care in Lesbian Women," in *Images,* vol. 20, no. 2, 1988: 69-73.

Stevens, P. E. "Lesbian Health Care Research: A Review of the Literature from 1970 to 1990," in *Health Care for Women International,* vol. 13, 1992: 91-120.

Taravella, S. "Healthcare Recognizing Gay and Lesbian Needs," in *Modern Healthcare,* 1992: 33-35.

Tash, D. T. and J. W. Kenney. "The Lesbian Childbearing Couple: A Case Report," in *Birth,* vol. 20, no. 1, 1993: 36-40.

Trippet, S. E. "Lesbians' Mental Health Concerns," in *Health Care for Women International,* vol. 15, 1994: 317-23.

Trippet, S. E. and J. Bain. "Reasons American Lesbians Fail to Seek Traditional Health Care," in *Health Care for Women International,* vol. 13, 1992: 145-53.

Troiden, R. R. "The Formation of Homosexual Identities," in *Journal of Homosexuality,* vol. 17, 1979: 43-73.

Vincke, J. and R. Bolton. "Social Support, Depression, and Self-Acceptance among Gay Men," in *Human Relations,* vol. 47, 1994: 1049-62.

White, J. C. and W. Levinson. "Lesbian Health Care: What a Primary Care Physician Needs to Know," in *The Western Journal of Medicine,* vol. 162, no. 5, 1995: 463-66.

Wisniewski, J. J. and B. G. Toomey. "Are Social Workers Homophobic?" in *Social Work,* vol. 32, 1987: 454-55.

Zeidenstein, L. "Gynecological and Childbearing Needs of Lesbians," in *Journal of Nurse-Midwifery,* vol. 35, no. 1, 1990: 10-16.

Other

Johnson, W. "NIH Commissions Panel on Lesbian Health Priorities," 8 August 1997: http://www.washblade.com/.

—K. Jean Peterson

7

AIDS

Seldom has a single disease reverberated through any one community so dramatically—and catastrophically—as HIV has gays and lesbians in the United States. Miracles and heroism, defeats and denials mark the history of the AIDS epidemic, both within and outside the gay and lesbian population. Moreover, HIV infection has fostered a level of visibility for gays and lesbians previously unknown; yet, that forced visibility has contributed to a sadly limited social perception of the community and forever linked HIV/AIDS to homosexuality. In short, both the acquired immune deficiency syndrome (AIDS) itself and the responses to it may best be described as littered with dichotomies.

Infection with the human immunodeficiency virus (HIV) is not immediately apparent. In fact, an individual may be infected for years without developing the signs and symptoms that constitute an AIDS diagnosis. In keeping with this natural history, HIV is classified as a lentivirus, or "slow" virus, as opposed to a "hot" virus, such as influenza, Ebola, or Marburg, that progresses within days from exposure to illness, to either death or recovery. HIV infection began silently spreading in the gay community in the wake of its greatest celebration—the liberated years of the 1970s following the Stonewall Riots of 1969. Not until 1981 did physicians in Los Angeles, San Francisco, and New York raise alarms about strangely devastating symptoms appearing among some of their gay patients (CDC, 3 July 1981, p. 305; Gottlieb, p. 111).

Though a "slow" virus, HIV initially spread exponentially among gay men in the United States. It appeared first in "hot spots"—New York, Los Angeles, San Francisco—and then in other coastal areas—Miami, Houston, Seattle. Gradually it encroached upon areas of the United States that may have thought themselves immune—small towns and rural communities throughout the entire country. The rate of infection increased relentlessly. It took from 1981 to 1989 for the first 100,000 cases of AIDS to be reported in the United States; however, the second 100,000 cases were reported within only the next two years (Stine, 1993, p. 174). While gay men continue to constitute the largest HIV-in-

fected population in the United States, new infections are appearing increasingly among urban women of color, adolescents, injection drug users, and their sexual partners (CDC, 1996, p. 12).

From the beginning, some members of the gay community voiced concerns about sexual behavior in bathhouses and even in private relationships contributing to the number of healthy young men suddenly falling ill. Mostly, however, these warnings were either ignored or labeled as "internal homophobia." And so, another dichotomy, one that echoes through many layers of the epidemic, became evident: acceptance and denial, unity and division. Particularly in New York and San Francisco, efforts by some members of the gay community and public health officials to close bathhouses led to demonstrations that fell little short of riots. HIV rapidly became the most politicized disease in history. The prevention of HIV became entangled with still another contradiction, the politics of the body versus the body politic, a body that was—and to some extent remains—decidedly divided.

Dichotomy endures as the overwhelming, pervasive theme of the epidemic and of responses to it—governmental, community, individual. This dichotomy defines the face of the epidemic among gays and lesbians, as well as some aspects of society at large as reflected through the gay and lesbian community.

Socio-scientific responses to the HIV/AIDS epidemic and events surrounding it reflect characteristics present within the gay and lesbian community as well as attitudes directed toward homosexuals in the United States. The organization of this chapter mirrors some of these responses and characteristics. A brief chronology, with divisions created commensurate with significant medical advances in the treatment of HIV disease and AIDS begins the chapter. Following it are sections on social implications, media response to the epidemic, the battles for treatments, collective grieving, and artistic response to the epidemic. A theme of dichotomy of response, mirrored by dichotomies within the epidemic and the community itself, is the organizing factor for these divisions.

A NOTE ON THE NUMBERS

All numbers of AIDS cases and deaths included in the timelines and in the text are taken from the *HIV/AIDS Surveillance Report*, mid-year edition 1997, Volume 9, No. 1, Table 9. From the beginning, the numbers of individuals infected and numbers whose deaths can be attributed to AIDS-related causes have been in dispute. Virtually the only point of agreement is that the official numbers account for fewer diagnoses and deaths than are actually the case. Typically, reporting to the Centers for Disease Control and Prevention, which produces the surveillance report, lags a year or more behind the report's publication. Consequently, the 1996 and

1997 numbers are almost certainly not representative of the true picture of the epidemic.

BACKGROUND

The human immunodeficiency virus (HIV) is strongly implicated as the causative agent for HIV disease, the end stage of which is acquired immune deficiency syndrome, or AIDS. Two strains of the virus—HIV-1 and HIV-2—have been identified. HIV-1 is the strain commonly found in North America.

Though it is arguably different in many respects from other epidemics, HIV/AIDS has been tracked and measured by epidemiologists in much the same way as other sudden infectious disease occurrences of the twentieth century. Epidemiologists measure disease occurrence by looking at *risk*, *prevalence*, and *incidence*. *Risk* describes the probability of an individual's contracting a given disease. *Prevalence* describes the pervasiveness of a disease in a given population, and *incidence* is the rate at which new cases occur within that population (Greenberg et al., 1996, p. 16). Descriptive epidemiologists use these tools (risk, preva-

lence, and incidence) to characterize the population distribution of a disease by asking Who? Where? and When?, thus identifying persons, places, and times associated with the disease (Greenberg, p. 2). By June 1981, epidemiologists working with the Centers for Disease Control (CDC) had begun documenting the occurrence and distribution of the numbers of cases of what we now call AIDS. Based on data gathered from June 1981 to September 1982, the CDC published its first *Case Definition of AIDS* for national reporting purposes, using a list of pre-defined illnesses and conditions (CDC, 1982). What made AIDS different from all other epidemics was its appearance in overwhelming numbers in primarily a single sub-population: gay men living in coastal urban centers.

The clustering of cases among homosexual men led to the public's initial association of the disease with this population. Not only were the most visible victims of the malady young gay men, even the various names first given to the disease conveyed the association: gay cancer, gay pneumonia, gay bowel syndrome, gay-related immune deficiency (GRID), acquired community immune deficiency syndrome (ACIDS), community

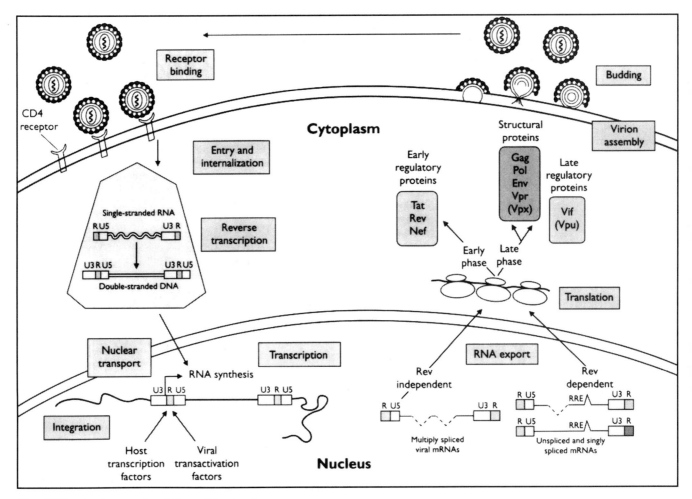

How HIV retrovirus works at the cellular level.

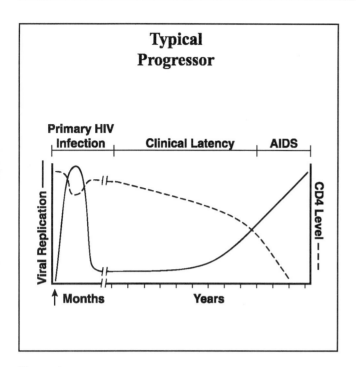

Figure A

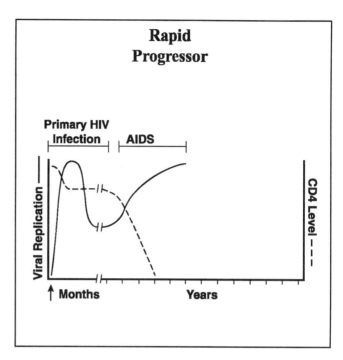

Figure B

acquired immune deficiency syndrome (CAIDS). Not until late 1982 did the Centers for Disease Control (CDC) officially name the mysterious constellation of signs and symptoms appearing primarily among homosexual men "acquired immune deficiency syndrome," or AIDS.

Once physicians in large cities in the United States began reporting cases of AIDS-defining illnesses, epidemiologists were able to identify patterns of occurrence that led to various hypotheses concerning the means of transmission. In classic epidemiology, the attempt to determine how an infectious agent is being transmitted may occur simultaneously with the identification of risk, prevalence, and incidence. Primary modes of disease transmission may be broadly divided into two categories: either *person to person* or *common source exposure*. HIV—like tuberculosis, syphilis, or measles—is transmitted from one individual to another. Most experts agree that transmission of HIV occurs via one of the following means: (1) unprotected sexual practices; (2) receipt of contaminated blood, tissue, or organs; (3) maternal-fetal-infant transmission; (4) shared needles or works among injection drug users; (5) occupational exposure (e.g., needlesticks in clinical settings). The scientific community, over time, has proven how HIV is transmitted; moreover, as early as 1983, a study published in the *New England Journal of Medicine* (Harris, p. 1181) demonstrated heterosexual transmission. Yet even today, nearly two decades into the epidemic, many members of the public ignore the evidence and continue to link the disease solely with homosexuality.

How HIV Works in the Body

A basic understanding of the way the human immunodeficiency virus acts in the body is essential to grasping the enormity of the emergency faced by society in the face of the AIDS epidemic. Scientists have made amazing progress since 1981 in isolating a virus believed to be the cause of the immune suppression that

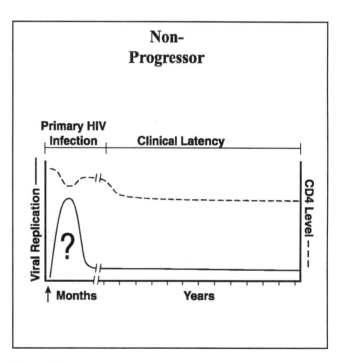

Figure C

Figures A-C: History and progession of HIV. Representative courses of progression to acquired immunodeficiency syndrome (AIDS) in a typical progressor. (Figure A) HIV-infected patients. (Figure B) Rapid progressor. (Figure C) Non-progressor. The question mark in C indicates that few long-term non-progressors to AIDS have been studied during the primary stages of human immunodeficiency (HIV) infection.

leads to AIDS and in understanding both the immune system and retroviral activity within cells.

Viruses are bits of genetic material that substitute themselves for the normal host cell material and "highjack" it for their own use. HIV is a *retrovirus,* so named because of its ability to replicate itself in reverse of the usual process. Retroviruses use an enzyme called *reverse transcriptase* to transfer their genetic information from the ribonucleic acid (RNA) of an infected cell to the deoxyribonucleic acid (DNA) of the host cell (Muma et al., p. 21). Basically, retroviruses use RNA to manufacture genetically altered DNA; they are parasites, lacking DNA, and so must find it within a host. This altered DNA reprograms the cell to produce more HIV.

The primary types of cells infected by HIV, certain white blood cells called T4 or CD4, are also the ones primarily responsible for coordinating the body's immune responses. The proliferation of these genetically altered blood cells eventually leads to the destruction of the body's immune system, rendering it vulnerable to various opportunistic infections. Since HIV is actually integrated into the genetic material of host cells, removing the infected matter is extremely difficult, if not impossible. Current drug therapies use a combination of chemicals that interrupt various stages of the replication process to lower the amount of virus in the body. These therapies, however, have been available only since 1995, and much remains to be learned about their long-term effects and efficacy. In 1981, no one even knew what to call the various symptoms and diseases that were decimating the ranks of gay men in New York and California.

CHRONOLOGICAL ACCOUNT

1981-1987: Confusion and Ignorance

In the early days of the epidemic, members of gay communities in Los Angeles, San Francisco, and New York could hardly imagine what was happening. All too often, men who appeared

---

Before 1981

  93 Documented cases of AIDS
  30 Documented AIDS-related deaths

---

to be perfectly healthy would drop out of sight; then, when (and if) seen again, they would be pounds lighter and appear ravaged with illness. Purplish lesions might be evident on their faces or bodies. Hacking coughs and perpetual fevers plagued some early patients as they attempted to carry on with their lives. Those who survived a bout with pneumonia often returned to their homes only to find that they had no home or job left. Early community responses simply attempted to guarantee that people so sick would have the basic necessities of food, shelter, utility payments,

---

1981

 326 Documented cases of AIDS
 128 Documented AIDS-related deaths

First Centers for Disease Control (CDC) report.

---

and clothing. In the absence of a coordinated response from the government, private charities, the media, or any other source, members of the gay community began forming grass roots organizations. The three earliest—Gay Men's Health Crisis (GMHC), the San Francisco AIDS Foundation (SFAF), and AIDS Project Los Angeles (APLA) were all founded in 1982.

Gay Men's Health Crisis (GMHC): The organization that proudly claims to be the first community-based effort to confront the epidemic is the Gay Men's Health Crisis, based in New York.

1982

1,195 Documented cases of AIDS
  461 Documented AIDS-related deaths

Initial CDC Case Definition of AIDS.

1st case of infection via blood transfusion reported.

AIDS Project Los Angeles (APLA) founded.

Gay Men's Health Crisis (GMHC) founded, New York City.

San Francisco AIDS Foundation (SFAF) founded.

The group's founders, Nathan Fain, Larry Kramer, Larry Mass, Paul Popham, Paul Rapoport, and Edmund White met in Kramer's apartment in January 1982 to discuss ways their community could confront the epidemic. In May, the group started the world's first AIDS hotline, which received 100 calls the first night it was in operation. By July of that same year, the men had produced GMHC's first newsletter. They proudly declared their sexual ori-

---

1983

3,146 Documented cases of AIDS
1,506 Documented AIDS-related deaths

Social Security Administration announces disability benefits for AIDS patients will be expedited.

U.S. Conference of Mayors urges federal government to commit all resources necessary to find cure for AIDS.

Margaret Heckler, Secretary of Health & Human Services, announces that AIDS is not spreading among the "general population."

San Francisco Police Department equips officers with special masks and gloves for handling an AIDS patient.

National Gay Task Force (NGTF) officers meet with a Reagan Administration aide. First ever meeting between representatives of a gay group and a White House official.

---

entation in a bold way that no one could ignore. GMHC has been in the forefront of many civil rights initiatives, outreach efforts, and political movements as the epidemic has evolved. Staffers and volunteers at GMHC organized the first buddy program and pio-

Looking at myself, and realizing how depressed
I look, brings a well known poem into my mind

"The world is such a nice place to live in
and it is such a pity to leave it"

Jef Nicols
FRANKFURT (West Germany)

An end-stage AIDS patient.

neered safer-sex education for lesbians. Today it remains a formidable force in the AIDS arena, well funded and influential.

AIDS Project Los Angeles (APLA): A different coast, a different focus. Declaring a founding ideal of "Unconditional Love,"

1984

6,323   Documented cases of AIDS

3,505   Documented AIDS-related deaths

1st AIDS antibody test release.

LAV, HTLV-3 reported as possible cause for AIDS.

San Francisco bathhouse controversy.

Nancy Cole Sawaya, Matt Redman, Ervin Munro, and Max Drew established a hotline in late 1982. They trained twelve volunteers, prepared a one-page fact sheet, and opened one telephone line in a closet of the Los Angeles Gay and Lesbian Community Services Center. Like every other grass roots organization, fundraising assumed priority. Even before they had a name, they had held their first benefit. Unlike the New York community, they used their name to highlight the fact that AIDS is not just a gay disease. APLA's first brochure appeared in both English and Spanish versions, and since 1985 they have published and regularly revised a book found in the homes of many AIDS patients and their caregivers: *AIDS: A Self-Care Manual.*

San Francisco AIDS Foundation (SFAF): The San Francisco AIDS Foundation began as an emergency response to a health crisis centered in the Castro District of the city. Its first goal was to create and distribute critical information to gay men being stricken with cancer and pneumonia. As the health crisis assumed epidemic proportions and spread to populations beyond the Castro, SFAF expanded its original mission of education to include comprehensive case management services for people with AIDS and publication of a newsletter (*BETA: Bulletin of Experimental Treatments for AIDS*) in three languages.

Dissonant Voices: Given that the gay community, like any other, had never spoken with a single voice, it is not surprising that by 1983 strains were evident in the fledgling populist organizations that had formed in response to emergency. In the intensely political atmosphere of New York, Michael Callen led a group of GMHC clients that demanded to assume positions of authority within the first provider organization. The struggle grew bitter, but from it emerged the first organization founded by HIV-positive people dedicated to taking control of their lives, the People with AIDS Coalition (PWA Coalition). Callen, a self-declared promiscuous gay man, matured suddenly at age 27, when he discovered that his fast-track life had a consequence he did not imagine in the 1970s. Like others who came before and after him, he turned his attention to attacking the disease and death that surrounded the community everywhere. Determined to seize the moment and empower themselves and others who were infected, Callen and several like-minded men from California met in Denver, Colorado, in 1983 and wrote a manifesto of empowerment, which they called the Denver Principles, for all HIV-infected individuals. This group coined the moniker PWA—People with AIDS— in preference to the despised *victim* and *patient.* They formed the PWA Coalition; Callen was the founding editor of their newsletter,

the *PWA Coalition Newsline,* and he edited a volume of advice for the newly diagnosed, which the PWA Coalition published as *Surviving and Thriving with AIDS.* Callen, his physician, Dr. Joseph Sonnabend, and Tom Hannan founded an early buyers' club called the People with AIDS Health Group (Callen, 1990, p. 9).

Other dissonant voices included gay men who strenuously resisted all efforts to regulate their sexual behavior. Very public, bruising battles to close bathhouses in San Francisco and New York led to opposing judicial outcomes that mirrored division within the community itself.

Focus on Treatments—AmFAR and Project Inform: By 1985, with almost 12,000 deaths attributable to HIV disease and no treatment yet in sight, key leaders on the East and West coasts continued to organize. Since various provider agencies were taking

---

1985

11,980   Documented cases of AIDS

6,973   Documented AIDS-related deaths

CDC Revision of the Case Definition of AIDS.

Scientists report that HIV destroys T4 blood cells.

Scientists at University of California, San Francisco (UCSF) announce that condoms can prevent the spread of AIDS.

Routine testing of blood supply in U.S.

American Foundation for AIDS Research (AmFAR) founded.

Project Inform established.

1st International Conference on AIDS, Atlanta.

U.S. insurance industry begins discriminating against AIDS patients and men suspected of being gay.

81% of gay men polled by CDC declare themselves celibate or monogamous.

37% of Americans in Gallup poll declare themselves less tolerant of gays as result of AIDS epidemic.

Los Angeles Times poll finds a majority of respondents favor quarantining AIDS patients and using tattoos as an indication of infection.

New York bathhouse controversy.

Rock Hudson dies.

---

care of food, shelter, and psychosocial support needs of infected gay men, the time had come to focus on therapies. Rock Hudson's death in October 1985 galvanized public attention on the epidemic and led to some public support for committing funds to a search for treatments and a cure for HIV disease.

Mathilde Krim established the AIDS Medical Foundation in 1982. In 1985, the medical foundation originated by Krim merged with the National AIDS Research Foundation, founded by Michael Gottlieb in Los Angeles, to form the American Foundation for AIDS Research, or AmFAR. Actress Elizabeth Taylor committed money to the organization and lent her name and time to its research efforts.

In San Francisco, Martin Delaney reacted to his partner's HIV-positive diagnosis by establishing Project Inform (Kwitny, p. 82). His background in the conservative world of banking and finance served him well as he began working directly with bureaucrats at the Food and Drug Administration (FDA) and, eventually, representatives of pharmaceutical companies. Both AmFAR and Project

---

1986

19,299 Documented cases of AIDS
12,100 Documented AIDS-related deaths

World Health Organization (WHO) announces that AIDS is pandemic.

Scientists name the human immunodeficiency virus (HIV) and implicate it as the probable cause of AIDS.

Scientists determine how HIV works at the cellular level.

AZT goes into clinical trials; halted when most patients receiving it live longer than those not receiving it.

2nd International AIDS Conference, Paris.

Senate gives National Cancer Institute (NCI) additional funds to provide AZT to dying AIDS patients.

Public Health Service (PHS) urges doubling funding to fight AIDS; President Reagan requests that Congress cut funding for AIDS.

Federal government lists AIDS as a dangerous contagious disease that can bar entry to U.S.

U.S. doctors announce they are not reporting all cases of HIV and AIDS for fear of discrimination against their patients.

California Association of Realtors tells members to inform potential buyers if a home had been owned by an AIDS patient.

18% of single Americans and 3% of married ones tell pollsters they have changed their sexual behavior as a result of the AIDS epidemic.

Inform led the effort toward community-based clinical trials.

Additionally, the Centers for Disease Control (CDC) convened the first International Conference on AIDS in Atlanta in 1985. It attracted a small number of basic scientists, clinicians, advocates, and patients from all over the world to assess the current and potential growth of the epidemic and to plot a strategy for controlling it.

The Metropolitan Community Church: In the hysteria that marked the early days of AIDS, Metropolitan Community Churches (MCCs) became part of the effort to offer support to various victims of the epidemic. Since most members of MCCs

are gay men or lesbians, these congregations had ample opportunity to observe the devastation left in the wake of AIDS. The church was founded in 1968 to minister to gay men and lesbians who desired to worship in a Christian fellowship but who often felt unwelcome in mainstream churches. As some members of various Christian denominations throughout the United States trumpeted the message that AIDS was God's punishment for being

---

1987

28,962 Documented cases of AIDS
16,392 Documented AIDS-related deaths

Revision of the CDC Surveillance Case Definition for AIDS.

AZT approved by the Food and Drug Administration (FDA) Aerosolized pentamidine shown to prevent *Pneumocystis carinii* pneumonia (PCP), biggest killer of AIDS patients.

Larry Kramer founds the AIDS Coalition to Unleash Power, or ACT UP.

Cleve Jones and Mike Smith found the NAMES Project.

3rd International AIDS Conference, Washington, D.C.

President Ronald Reagan makes his first speech devoted solely to the AIDS epidemic.

Senator Jesse Helms proposes universal testing for HIV and quarantining all who test positive.

HIV+ male prostitute quarantined in Mississippi.

HIV+, sexually active 14-year-old male quarantined in psychiatric unit in Florida.

Home of 3 HIV+, hemophiliac brothers set afire in Belle Glades, Florida.

U.S. Commission on Civil Rights releases report on stigma felt by AIDS patients; report includes lengthy footnote quoting biblical passages calling homosexuality "an abomination."

1,920 panels of the Quilt are displayed on the Mall in Washington, D.C.

Massachusetts becomes first state to implement comprehensive, statewide AIDS education program.

Dallas Cowboys become first team in national sports to offer voluntary HIV testing.

Government, activist, and civil rights groups shift focus of education for HIV prevention to minorities.

Allstate Insurance Company sponsors a forum, "AIDS: Corporate America Responds."

Peter Duesberg hypothesizes that HIV is not the cause of AIDS. Gallup Poll indicates 52% of Americans favor universal testing for HIV; 60% think that HIV+ individuals should carry an identification card; and one-third favor the right of employers to fire HIV-infected workers.

Art Against AIDS and *Dance for Life* launch efforts to raise funds for community-based AIDS organizations and research.

homosexual, MCC congregations joined forces to care for their sick and dying members and their partners and to provide memorial services for them. The provision of funerals was perhaps their most important role in the beginning. Many mainstream churches and even funeral homes refused to provide services of any kind. In city after city, gay men and women of the Metropolitan Community Church attended to the end of life spiritual matters that eased the transition from life to death for AIDS patients who were part of the fellowship. Even in death, the gay community found that it had to rely on its own resources and institutions, rather

---

1988

35,918   Documented cases of AIDS
21,105   Documented AIDS-related deaths

For the first time in 30 years, numbers of active cases of tuberculosis increases in U.S.; much of increase reported among AIDS patients.

ACT UP demonstrates at FDA; 175 protestors arrested.

New York City allowed to distribute clean needles to injection drug users; first time in U.S. that government provides needles to addicts.

Surgeon General Koop's booklet *Understanding AIDS* is mailed to all U.S. households.

National Center for Health Statistics reports that 26% of Americans surveyed believe they could get AIDS from giving blood, while 36% believe they can get AIDS from a restaurant where the chef is infected.

4th International AIDS Conference, Stockholm

Alyson Publishing coordinates effort with the U.S. publishing industry to distribute free copies of *You Can Do Something About AIDS*.

---

than those of the larger society. In fact, the New York State Funeral Directors Association in 1983 encouraged its members not to embalm the bodies of AIDS patients until the federal government issued guidelines for the safe handling of such cadavers. Governor Mario Cuomo had to intervene and compel morticians to treat the bodies of AIDS patients as they would any others who had succumbed to an infectious disease; eventually, laws had to be passed in several states to enforce the practice. Because of multiple discriminatory practices even after death and the lack of treatments for AIDS patients, the time was ripe for radical activism.

ACT UP: March 1987 marked the formation of "the largest social movement ever created around an epidemic in the medical history of the United States" (Elbaz), the AIDS Coalition to Unleash Power, or ACT UP. A fiery speech given by Larry Kramer at New York City's gay community center spurred the formation of the political action group, organized in response to what Kramer

and his followers perceived as political inaction at every level of United States society where the AIDS epidemic was concerned. ACT UP was immediately successful. On 24 March 1987, members demonstrated against the giant pharmaceutical company Burroughs-Wellcome at the New York Stock Exchange, protesting both the high price of AZT and the FDA's lengthy drug approval process. The FDA announced a two-year reduction in the process the very next day (Levy, p. 1).

The first six years of the AIDS epidemic began with confusion and ignorance, but by the close of the period, anger and determination had replaced the earlier reactions. The first drug shown to prolong the lives of AIDS patients, azidothymidine (AZT), garnered FDA approval. After six years of a mounting AIDS-related death toll, President Ronald Reagan finally delivered his first speech devoted to the epidemic. The AIDS Memorial Quilt was displayed for the first time on the Mall in Washington, D.C. Yet, the threat of quarantine for seropositive individuals was very real. Despite reasoned argument from public health professionals against the idea, Senator Jesse Helms urged universal testing for HIV and the imposition of quarantine on all who tested seropositive. Members of the gay and lesbian community fought both prejudice and apathy in highly visible ways, protesting the deaths, the lack of response from the Reagan administration, dithering bureaucrats, and profit-hungry corporations. Tragedy united the community, unveiled forever its anonymity, and pushed its twin demands for AIDS treatments and civil rights into the national spotlight.

1988-1994: The Search for a Magic Bullet

As the AIDS epidemic spread unchecked across the United States, the first provider organizations (GMHC, APLA, and SFAF) continued to serve as models for the creation of AIDS service organizations (ASOs) in every state and the majority of U.S. cities. ASOs across the United States assured that their clients had food and utility payments; additionally, they mounted regionally available telephone hotlines to assure dissemination of accurate infor-

---

1989

43,095   Documented cases of AIDS
27,775   Documented AIDS-related deaths

AIDS becomes the 5th leading killer of black women.

FDA approves use of pentamidine to prevent PCP.

ddI approved for treatment as an investigational new drug.

Compound Q touted as possible treatment.

FDA considers approving mail-order HIV test kits.

FDA approves expanded access program.

FDA begins including "AIDS Page" in its *FDA Consumer* publication.

5th International AIDS Conference, Montreal.

---

mation about the disease. With basic services in place in most areas, efforts began to consolidate funding and to demand federal assistance for programs such as community-based health care for people infected with HIV, housing, case management, Supplemental Security Income (SSI), education, and prevention. Within the gay community, a sea change occurred in the attitude toward individual testing for HIV.

However, the most visible story of this period was the demand for the wheels of big science to produce effective treatment for HIV disease. When bureaucracies at every level in both the public and the private sectors denied access to drugs deemed promising, buyers' clubs and the AIDS Coalition to Unleash Power (ACT UP) arose in the most profound expression of civil disobedience since the social struggles of the 1960s. Yet, unbeknownst to the activists, the research that ultimately led to the first real anti-HIV therapy had begun in Los Angeles.

1990

48,921   Documented cases of AIDS

31,368   Documented AIDS-related deaths

Deaths of patients taking ddI linked to serious side effect, pancreatitis.

Jonas Salk, developer of the first polio vaccine, announces he will search for an AIDS vaccine.

Kimberly Bergalis announces she is dying of AIDS and was infected via dental treatment.

6th International AIDS Conference, San Francisco.

HIV Conference on Women, Washington, D.C.

1st World AIDS Day.

Ryan White dies.

Passage of Ryan White CARE Act.

Assault on the FDA: The 11 October 1988 demonstration at FDA headquarters in Bethesda, Maryland, concurrent with other gay and lesbian events in Washington, D.C., proved the lengths to which activists would go to shake the federal bureaucracy from its lethargy. Demonstrators, numbering more than one thousand strong, demanded that in light of the emergency, the clinical trial and new drug approval process be short-circuited. Activists insisted that promising treatments be made available immediately to AIDS patients and that individuals with the disease and their advocates participate at the highest levels with all research, education, and prevention efforts. They set off smoke bombs, smashed windows, plastered the building with placards and protest banners, and lay in front of a police bus to prevent its departure. By the end of the nine-hour long demonstration, 176 of the protestors had been arrested.

Eight days later Frank Young, then Commissioner of the FDA, announced that his organization would shorten the time allotted for final testing of drugs. However, Vito Russo, a New York City author and PWA, was unimpressed. "I would rather take my chances with the side effects of an experimental drug. The side effect of AIDS is death" (Harding, p. 12).

1991

59,840   Documented cases of AIDS

36,569   Documented AIDS-related deaths

Breast milk found to be means of HIV transmission.

7th International AIDS Conference, Florence, Italy.

Kimberly Bergalis dies.

Controversy over universal testing of health care workers.

Magic Johnson announces his HIV+ status.

1st *Day Without Art* observed nationwide.

Silence = Death: No institution was sacred to ACT UP. At San Francisco General Hospital, where AIDS patients had been cared for since the beginning of the epidemic, ACT UP held a sit-in to demand wider availability of a drug to halt blindness in cases of advanced AIDS. ACT UP demonstrators blocked traffic on the

---

1992

78,355   Documented cases of AIDS

41,007   Documented AIDS-related deaths

ddI approved for conditional use.

8th International AIDS Conference, Amsterdam.

Mary Fisher (Republican) and Elizabeth Glaser (Democrat), both HIV+ Anglo women, speak at their respective national political conventions about the experience of AIDS.

K-Mart, WalMart, and Walgreens refuse to carry Magic Johnson's book about HIV.

Golden Gate Bridge and disrupted governmental meetings dressed as Grim Reapers. In 1989, they brought trading to a halt on the New York Stock Exchange by chaining themselves to a balcony. Thousands of protesters disrupted Mass at St. Patrick's Cathedral in New York, demanding that the Roman Catholic Church abandon its resistance to the use of condoms and to homosexuality as a legitimate sexual orientation. During the Sixth International AIDS

Conference, held in San Francisco in 1990, ACT UP disrupted sessions at the convention and shouted down a speech by Louis Sullivan, Secretary of Health and Human Services. The group's motto, SILENCE = DEATH, came to symbolize the politics of the AIDS epidemic.

1993

78,452 Documented cases of AIDS
44,291 Documented AIDS-related deaths

Expansion of the CDC Surveillance Case Definition for AIDS.

ddC approved for conditional use.

9th International AIDS Conference, Berlin.

Arthur Ashe dies.

National Gay and Lesbian Task Force: Urvashi Vaid, the executive director of the National Gay and Lesbian Task Force (NGLTF) between 1989 and 1992, assumed a highly visible position in Washington, D.C. A quintessential activist, she integrated AIDS activism with her philosophy about the gay and lesbian movement. In an *Advocate* interview, she stated, "Civil rights is not an end point for the gay community. Social change and transformation is. The goal of the gay and lesbian movement is to achieve a society in which homosexuality is considered as healthy, natural, and normal as heterosexuality" (Simmons, p. 39). Vaid assembled her formidable intellectual, organizational, and media management skills to show the world that AIDS was everyone's issue.

Prevention of Pneumocystis carinii pneumonia: Mounting pressure from voices such as Urvashi Vaid's forced a focus on controlling the most deadly opportunistic infections. From the earliest days of the epidemic, the biggest killer of AIDS patients was a previously rare form of fungal pneumonia, *Pneumocystis carinii pneumonia.* Preventing it was an early goal of AIDS physicians and researchers. In 1987, a report on the use of aerosolized pentamidine as a possible preventative agent in humans appeared in a medical journal (Girard, p. 978), and in 1988 conclusive evidence of its efficacy appeared (Merz, p. 3223). In 1989, the FDA approved aerosolized pentamidine as a prophylaxis for the deadly lung infection. This single act added months, and sometimes years, to the lives of PWAs.

The Testing Controversy: For years gay leaders, staffers of ASOs, and activists had advised gay men not to take the test for HIV antibodies, a simple procedure that became widely available and reasonably accurate by 1987. There were good reasons for advising against the test: (1) activists feared blacklisting of individuals who tested seropositive, since no guarantee of anonymity or confidentiality existed; (2) the test could yield a false positive; (3) no effective treatments or prophylactic therapies existed; (4) even if an individual test yielded a false positive, laws were not yet in effect that would guarantee the continuation of existing insurance coverage; (5) discrimination in employment practices, hous-

ing, and even medical care was rampant; (6) the emotional toll on asymptomatic individuals created an unnecessary psychological burden; and (7) no one knew if the federal government, or individual state governments, might actually quarantine individuals who tested seropositive.

By the late 1980s, most of this had changed. People of reason understood that quarantine was not a viable option. The antibody test became much more accurate, and by the mid-1990s, when viral load testing became possible, the chance of a false positive was slim indeed. AIDS had become a federally defined disability with the passage of the Americans with Disabilities Act of 1990, which meant protection from the more onerous examples of discrimination. Insurance companies could no longer cancel a customer's policy if that person tested positive for HIV antibodies. Most importantly, enough was known about HIV disease progression by the late 1980s that early medical treatment could make a substantial difference in a patient's length and quality of life; furthermore, knowledge of antibody status could protect sexual partners and theoretically reduce transmission of the virus. Consequently, the message changed. The *Advocate* ran repeated reports, written by both Michael Helquist and Martin Delaney, outlining reasons to submit to testing if one had engaged in any of the practices known to put people at risk for contracting HIV. ASOs throughout the United States changed their policies, with certain caveats. First, the testing should be voluntary and all the rules of informed consent should apply; second, testing should be both anonymous and confidential; and finally, counseling both before and after testing should be available to everyone. What

---

1994

70,215 Documented cases of AIDS
47,941 Documented AIDS-related deaths

AZT found to lower risk of maternal-fetal transmission.

d4T approved for conditional use.

10th International Conference on AIDS, Yokohama. Because of lack of progress in treating HIV, organizers decide to meet only every two years.

---

progress had been made against AIDS-related discrimination had come at a price, and the community crafted its messages carefully as a result of past skirmishes with both governmental and medical officials.

By mid-1989, all states had enacted laws regarding testing for HIV. Only ten provided completely anonymous testing centers: California, Kansas, Louisiana, Massachusetts, Nebraska, New Mexico, New York, Ohio, Pennsylvania, and Vermont. Eight other states passed laws at the opposite end of the spectrum, requiring that the names of individuals testing positive be reported to state health officials: Alabama, Alaska, Colorado, Idaho, Minnesota, North Dakota, South Dakota, and South Carolina (Helquist, p. 36).

Dissonant Voices: Peter Duesberg, a faculty member in the Department of Molecular Biology at the University of California,

Berkeley, began questioning the theory that the human immuno-deficiency virus causes the immune system to fail and ultimately leads to AIDS. He published his theory in the journal *Science* (Duesberg, p. 514). He continues to contend that scientists are ignoring critical evidence, but most of the scientific community currently discounts his hypothesis.

Focus on Prevention: Epidemiologists surmised early in the epidemic that the infectious agent that could lead to AIDS was transmissible via blood and semen. As the evidence became overwhelming that unprotected sexual intercourse played a major role in the expanding epidemic, AIDS service organizations (ASOs) established educational programs to encourage the use of condoms and to "eroticize" safe sex. Such an emphasis expanded the role of ASOs to include not only case management but also education for prevention. The ASOs, formed originally by middle class, gay, white men, performed admirably as they blanketed gay enclaves in urban areas with safer sex messages. Particularly during these years of activism, the transmission rate among gay men actually fell significantly in cities such as San Francisco and Los Angeles. Such evidence of unity and the assumption of personal responsibility earned the admiration and respect of many government officials, media representatives, health care workers, and the public. Passage of the Ryan White Comprehensive AIDS Resources Emergency Act of 1990 (CARE) assured funding to pursue prevention programs that were clearly working. Pat Christen, at the time policy director for the San Francisco AIDS Foundation, conceived much of the core of the Ryan White CARE Act and co-wrote the legislation with Senator Edward Kennedy's staff (Gordon, Interview, 1997).

Advances and a Breakthrough: The years from 1988 to 1990 marked several hopeful signs among many despairing ones. Two more drugs were in clinical trials by the end of 1990, and many fewer patients were contracting PCP, thanks to effective prevention. Drugs that to some extent prevented blindness in patients infected with cytomegalovirus retinitis were available. Activists kept the heat on all levels of government, drug companies, and the public, ensuring that the AIDS epidemic was never out of the news. Still, effective antiretroviral treatments seemed only a distant possibility.

From the earliest years of the U. S. epidemic, "treatments *du jour*" had come and gone, but none had been able to halt the wily virus. In 1990, gay publications and treatment newsletters duly reported on a new medical study, one that suggested that HIV never lay dormant in the body, as had been believed, and that perhaps it was better to begin antiretroviral therapy earlier in the disease process as opposed to later (Ho, p. 1621; Helquist, p. 29). Such thinking flew in the face of the current practice, but by 1995, science was poised to earn its first true victory against AIDS.

1995 and Beyond: Guarded Hope

From 1995, when the magic word saquinavir became known among informed individuals in the AIDS arena, patients, caregivers, and health care and service providers have been confronted with issues that had previously been either nonexistent or barely discernible in the background. Saquinavir was the first protease inhibitor, a type of therapy that has prolonged life for many patients, at least in the short term. The protease inhibitors themselves, with all their promise and peril, have since taken center stage. AIDS service organizations (ASOs) and staff within them

that performed brilliantly through the 1980s have risked finding themselves anachronistic in the face of changing patient demographics. As a consequence, the organizations have at times struggled to find a voice outside the gay community, to work with other agencies, and to maintain funding. Whatever the future brings, the epidemic is certainly not over. As Mario Solis-Marich of APLA remarked, "The face of AIDS is not changing; more faces are being added into the picture" (Mirken, p. 42). Also problematic is the schism between seropositive and seronegative gay men and the pressures to engage in unsafe sexual practices.

1995

64,391 Documented cases of AIDS

47,779 Documented AIDS-related deaths

CDC announces that AIDS is now the leading killer of all Americans aged 25 to 44.

AIDS shown to be increasing faster in women than in men.

Saquinavir, the world's first protease inhibitor, approved by FDA.

Greg Louganis announces his HIV+ status.

HIV Conference on Women, Washington, D.C.

HIV and Combination Therapy: Unlocking the mysteries of HIV is a disease detective story worthy of masters of the fictional genre. Once researchers began understanding how HIV replicated itself inside of host cells, the logical therapeutic solution was to interrupt the replication process. What quickly became clear was that no single agent proved effective for long, because the virus would simply reinvent itself and become resistant to the therapy. Combination therapy—mixing potent "drug cocktails" to attack a deadly disease—has long been a standard treatment for many types of cancer; it is also the first seemingly effective defense medical science has been able to mount against the onslaught of HIV. By interrupting replication at more than one point in the process, resistance becomes statistically less and less likely to occur. Today, many patients who expected to die are returning to their lives, hardly daring to believe their good fortune in having survived long enough for the elusive "cure" that might make HIV a serious but still manageable chronic disease. *Wall Street Journal* editor David Sanford wrote poignantly of his experience with the new "drug cocktails":

> One year ago today, I told my colleagues that I was dying of AIDS.... I gave my boss an obituary I had written.... Last week, my doctor ... noticed that I am getting fat and said it wouldn't be a bad idea if I went on a modest diet.... What has happened in the past year, at least for me, is a miracle.... The year 1996 is when everything changed, and very quickly, for people with AIDS.... Thanks to the arrival of the new drugs called protease inhibitors, I am probably

more likely to be hit by a truck than to die of AIDS (Sanford, p. 1).

Across the United States, gay men who were prepared to die secured a reprieve. But, there are caveats. To begin with, the drugs do not work for everyone. No one knows what the long-term effects of such toxic medications will be. Unlike chemotherapy regimens undergone by cancer patients, these drugs can never be withdrawn, according to current knowledge. Not only can they not be withdrawn, but any variation in strict dosing schedules can cause the virus to become resistant and again begin replicating. Although

---

1996

50,176 Documented cases of AIDS
33,883 Documented AIDS-related deaths

Ritonavir and Indinavir approved by FDA.

Combination therapy becomes standard of care.

FDA approves Confide, a home test kit for HIV.

11th International Conference on AIDS, Vancouver.

Quilt is displayed on the Mall, Washington, D.C.

---

activists have fought to reduce the cost of anti-retrovirals, particularly AZT, combination therapy alone costs $15,000 to $20,000 per year. This figure does not include costs for pain and sleep medications, antidepressants, anti-anxiety drugs, appetite stimulants, antibiotics, antidiarrheals, anti-emetics, and other associated costs, such as routine laboratory work and office visits to both primary care physicians and specialists. The financial costs put the therapy out of reach for many of the infected. Finally, the activism that won civil rights, therapeutic agents, and access to drug trials also overhauled the entire drug approval process in the United States; but now that even very toxic, powerful agents such as protease inhibitors and antiretrovirals are approved on a fast-track basis, no one can know what adverse effects may appear down the road.

Like David Sanford, many patients with very few or no T4 cells had prepared themselves to die. Many quit their jobs, spent savings, took the cash from their life insurance policies through viatical settlements, and generally lived from day to day, never knowing when an opportunistic infection of some type would spell the end. But now, for the lucky people who can both afford the medications and tolerate their toxicities, life is suddenly very complicated. Where can they go? Will anyone hire them? Have they even kept up with their former professions so that they can reenter the work force? If they go back to work, their disability payments will end; will they be insurable under a group policy, since their diagnosis is known? Unexpected survival within a community where so many have been traumatized by multiple loss represents yet another cruel irony of AIDS.

Most frustrating of all, some members of both a young generation that has never seen a world without AIDS, and an older, "AIDS-weary" generation of survivors, are testing the possibility of using combination therapy as a "morning after" solution to a night of unsafe sex. The spectre of another round of rampant seroconversion within the community and the concurrent likelihood of yet more suffering and death is a real possibility. Truly, more questions than answers frame the conundrum of the AIDS epidemic at the dawn of a new century.

The De-Gaying of AIDS: Although HIV disease has long been declared a pandemic, cultural response in the United States has been shaped by the fact that men who have sex with men (MSMS) comprise the largest number of HIV-infected individuals and people with AIDS (Huber, 1996, p. 14). That statistic is changing, however. In 1996, only 50 percent of the total of newly reported AIDS cases were in the MSM category (CDC, 1996, p. 11), down from 60 percent just one year earlier (CDC, 1995, p. 11) and from 97 percent in 1981. One of the rallying cries in the gay community from the early 1980s was, "AIDS is not just a gay disease!" Certainly, this is true; diseases rarely confine themselves to a single group, because pathogens are no respecters of gender, income, sexual orientation, or any other such arbitrary factor. At the same time, however, many members of the community adamantly resist the "de-gaying" of the epidemic. Perhaps because of the enor-

---

1997

11,388 Documented cases of AIDS
5,622 Documented AIDS deaths[1]

AIDS deaths fall; now 2nd leading killer of all Americans, 25-44.

50 men volunteer for live HIV vaccine experiment.

Confide home test kit for HIV removed from market for lack of sales.

National Conference on Women and HIV, Pasadena, California.

Miss America, an AIDS volunteer, urges increased attention to education for prevention.

26% of gay men in San Francisco report "less concern" about contracting HIV because of new treatments.

[1]Preliminary numbers, reported mid-year 1997

---

mous effort that has gone into fighting AIDS, survivors feel ownership and a just sense of pride in the bond that has been forged among community members. This dichotomous response joins many other ironies evident late in the second decade of AIDS.

AIDS did first appear in this country primarily among gay men, so the gay community built an infrastructure designed to manage, treat, educate, and prevent HIV disease among the members of this particular group. Most of the major AIDS service organizations are located in gay urban enclaves and are staffed primarily by gay white men. Collectively, they have many years of experience dealing with HIV and the havoc it wreaks wherever it strikes. Culturally, however, interventions and case management modalities that operate very well in a gay setting work far less well among minority communities of color, communities of injection drug users (gay or straight), prisoners, and heterosexual men and women. The largest and oldest ASOs as well as several others around the country that in the beginning served primarily gay men have established outreach programs and offer services and materials in

---

1998

12th International Conference on AIDS, Geneva.

---

languages other than English. The path leading to these programs has sometimes been a difficult one, and certainly it is an effort that cannot cease. These are, after all, the organizations and the people with experience in the epidemic. By working in partnership with communities of color, gay and straight; with lesbians; with straight women; with former prisoners; and with heterosexual couples and children, a great deal of good beyond education and case management can be accomplished. In the words of Rebecca Cole, a New York City activist who played a major role in instituting programs for lesbians at GMHC, "Everyone is going to be better for how awkward this is right now" (Mirken, p. 44).

The Great Divide: Throughout the late 1980s and early 1990s, AIDS was rarely out of the news. The numbers of deaths and new infections, especially among women and people of color, escalated. ACT UP turned up everywhere, refusing to accept anything other than immediate action to gain access to clinical trials and to bring new drugs into the trial process. More money was available for AIDS services than had ever before been the case.

Many of the reforms for which activists agitated were instituted, and by the end of 1996, AIDS had been so mainstreamed that Dr. David Ho, the young scientist whose work laid the foundation for current HIV therapies, was named *Time* magazine's Man of the Year. Many people, gay and straight, breathed a collective sigh of relief and seemed to say, "Well, that's over. Now we can think of something else."

Of course, AIDS is far from over. But much of the society, like gay male survivors of the 1980s, is AIDS-weary. Jamie Schield, Director of Programs at the AIDS Resource Center in Dallas, Texas, says, "The most significant current milestone in the epidemic is the schism in the community between negative and positive issues. HIV-negative gay men and lesbians are now demanding a place at the table, saying that there are health issues other than AIDS that need to be addressed. Unfortunately, the schism has resulted in infections" (Schield, Interview, 1997). Some older men, too, who have been surrounded by death and dying for 15 years and are exhausted from the effort and struggle, are reverting to pre-AIDS sexual behaviors.

This schism results in much that is negative for the community and represents yet another dichotomy. The community united and achieved much, including compassion, recognition, and respect, rather than hatred or bigotry, from everyday Americans. Having achieved so much, leaders now are faced with uniting around a new agenda, one that is broader and more inclusive than a disease, as well as dealing with the challenge of preventing a new round of

infections whenever and wherever possible. The complex questions posed by achieving so much success demand answers from the gay body politic.

SOCIAL IMPLICATIONS

Politics of the Body Versus the Body Politic: Theoretical Foundation of the Socio-Politics of AIDS

Examining the social construct within which HIV and AIDS exist reveals the application of what Michel Foucault and others have termed *politics of the body* or *bio-politics*. This contention is important because it demonstrates societal regulation, both overt and covert, of the HIV-infected individual. In the historical development of civilization, there was an "explosion of numerous and diverse techniques for achieving the subjugation of bodies and the control of populations, marking the beginning of an era of bio-power" (Foucault, p. 140). Bio-power may be thought of in terms of power over bodies by bodies—corporeal and social. Over time however, individuals gained various rights and were no longer subject to absolute sovereign power. Within this context, a "proliferation of political technologies ensued, investing the body, health, modes of subsistence and habitation, living conditions, the whole space of existence" (Foucault, pp. 143-44).

The advent of bio-politics coincided with the emergence of bio-power, both of which continue today. Empowered individuals and institutions in society regulate and control individuals or groups of individuals who are less powerful. For example, formalized religious groups such as the Catholic Church exert power and control over their members; governments administer and regulate the people they govern; the education establishment directs the content, form, nature, and structure of student curricula. Organized religions determine behaviors deemed worthy of an individual's admission to heaven or hell; governments decide what individual practices are legal or illegal; educators select what individuals will or will not be taught. Individuals become political pawns manipulated by the establishment. This factional scheming for power, control, and status has resulted in the struggle between the politics of the body and the body politic. Nowhere perhaps is this clash more obvious within the gay and lesbian community than where HIV and AIDS are concerned.

Social policy and process have been, and continue to be, used to shape the politics of the HIV-affected body—individual and collective. Quarantine, ostracism, and isolation are recurring threats for the HIV-infected. The provision of uniform social support is a constant battle. Incorporating explicit safe-sex information into school curricula continues to be generally prohibited. However, the debate between public health and individual rights is perhaps the most obvious example of strife between bio-power and bio-politics, with regulation of individual sexual practices being the best illustration (Burr, p. 57). Organized religion's stance on the practice of homosexuality, sodomy laws, the judicial view of prostitution, and the lack of inclusion of homosexuality in sex education curricula are but four examples of the establishment's regulating sexual practices.

The existence of bio-politics within the epidemic is not surprising, since sexuality is a focal point for both politics of the body and for issues surrounding HIV/AIDS. Societal normalization of sexuality is an instrument of power. By defining what is normal, the establishment creates a tool that can be applied on various fronts—social, religious, legal, governmental, medical, psy-

A sign at an ACT UP demonstration on Wall Street, 1987.

chological, educational—to control individual sexual behavior. In this way, sexuality becomes a mechanism for reward or punishment. Regarding politics of the body, sexuality is key to the "formation of policies which form the basis of bio-power" (Hewitt, p. 228). Where HIV is concerned, sexuality is directly linked to a primary mode of transmission and is often a major concern for members of the gay and lesbian community. Sexuality unites biopolitics and the epidemic, and for both politics of the body and HIV/AIDS, sex continues to be something that is administered and regulated by the body politic. This theoretical dichotomy translates into pervasive divisions at every level of the epidemic, but particularly within the gay and lesbian community.

Community Unity?

The visibility forced on gay men and lesbians by the AIDS epidemic has transformed the social landscape within the body of the community; moreover, the changes are ongoing as the epidemic itself extends toward ever more individuals and groups within the populace and as gay issues other than AIDS clamor for recognition and resolution. Although the homosexual community shares many of the same concerns as members of its heterosexual counterpart, there are many other issues that are unique to gays and lesbians. While the body politic demands a certain amount of ho-

mogeneity from all its participants, gay culture, as it has evolved, is separate and distinct from mainstream society, though not necessarily unified. "Gays inevitably comprehend straight, because, whatever our sexuality, we all grow up within the straight culture as participators. You can be homosexual from birth, but you can't be gay unless you voluntarily enter the gay world, a culture all its own" (Mordden, p. xii).

Within this unique community, gay men and lesbians have fought HIV together by (1) building on the legacy of Stonewall and strengthening the bond between the two groups; (2) combining activism into mainstream ways of getting things done; and (3) showing the world that the community takes care of its own (Schield, interview, 1997). Although the women's movement was already in full swing, gay liberation sprang into existence only after the Stonewall riots; "Stonewall the event happened very unexpectedly, and Stonewall the culture developed, in response, almost overnight" (Mordden, p. 46). Perhaps only an event of the magnitude of the AIDS pandemic could have so quickly unified a culture so recently emerged from the shadows.

Along the way, gay women and men have not always viewed their issues and concerns as similar, much less identical. Perhaps the biggest social challenge now facing the gay community is identifying other pressing issues besides AIDS and working together to effect a positive outcome, in the process growing together as human beings who share a bond commonly misunderstood by many members of society.

Violence

One of the more urgent issues currently plaguing the community, and demanding a unified response from it, is an upsurge in violence. Increased visibility for gays and lesbians, combined with societal perception of HIV as a gay disease, has contributed to elevated numbers of violent acts committed against members of the homosexual community. Irrational fear of, and terror about, AIDS may be "fueling an increase in anti-gay violence and antihomosexual sentiment in general" ("Homosexuality: Coming Out, or Pushed?", p. 20). Hate crimes committed against gays and lesbians have increased, and people with HIV have not been omitted from the violent onslaught. Indeed, "more than one in five HIV-positive people say they have been the target of assault, harassment, or intimidation because of their infection" ("Report Asks Service Providers to Help Tackle HIV Violence," p. 5). In an epidemic where individuals are so in need of compassion and empathy, some believe that the disease has provided them the moral justification to abuse, beat, and embarrass members of the community most affected (Reyes). Violence certainly includes the right wing picketers whose signs read "Thank God for AIDS" and the Fred Phelps cohort, who are known for picketing the funerals of AIDS victims, forcing their friends and family to run a gauntlet laden with hatred and invective. Unfortunately, many of these hate crimes, whether directed at gays or lesbians, go unreported, since victims are often reluctant to have their identity, sexuality, or HIV status publicized.

Lesbians: One of the Faces of AIDS

Lesbians are sometimes considered the "invisible" members of the gay community. Some gay men perceive that society on the whole is more accepting of lesbians than of themselves. Whether or not this is true, lesbians share the concerns of women throughout U. S. society: typically, they earn less money than their gay male counterparts, traditionally lack political muscle, and are frequently caregivers. Initially, many lesbians began working in the AIDS epidemic not because they thought they were at risk for disease but because they perceived the political nature of AIDS and recognized the impact it could have on the community as a whole. Talk of quarantine, homophobic legislation, and mandatory testing, even if originally aimed at gay men, could easily be turned on other groups in society, including women. Apathy, bigotry, and injustice emanating from government officials, the media, and some members of the medical profession enraged lesbians as well as gay men. Dichotomy, however, has been present in the lesbian response to the epidemic, as it has elsewhere. One woman remarked bitterly, "Gay boys have done shit for lesbians, and now we're rushing to their bedsides. We're acting like nurses, like a bunch of mommies. Like women always do" (Stone, p. 143).

More representative of the response, though, are the many lesbians who have played a significant role in the organization of medical and support services for AIDS patients. Women like Patricia Hawkins, deputy administrator for programs and associate executive director of policy at the Whitman Walker Clinic in Washington, D.C., and Pat Christen, executive director of the San Francisco AIDS Foundation, have lobbied for programs and services at the community level since early on in the epidemic.

Antoinette Young, founder of the National Women and HIV/AIDS Project, sought to give women living with HIV/AIDS a voice in the pandemic. Dr. Joyce Hunter, a long-standing activist and director of the community liaison program at the HIV Center for Clinical and Behavioral Studies at the New York Psychiatric Institute and Columbia University, has fought for community-based research focusing on the dissemination of HIV prevention information for gay, lesbian, and bisexual adolescents. Margaret Johnston, Scientific Director of the International AIDS Vaccine Initiative, was instrumental in planning, implementing, and reviewing HIV/AIDS research programs at the National Institutes of Health as the former Deputy Director of the Division of AIDS. Cindy Patton, author and university professor, has written thoughtful books and articles interpreting the AIDS epidemic in the context of the larger society. Jean Carlomusto has been responsible for ground breaking work in the area of AIDS and film. Many other lesbians labor tirelessly to assure care, service, education, and prevention services throughout the AIDS arena.

Sexual Practices

One of the many terms added to the lexicon as a result of the AIDS epidemic is "safe sex." Sometimes viewed as an oxymoron, and other times as further evidence of discrimination against homosexuals, it is nonetheless generally understood to mean the use of a condom or other latex or polyurethane barrier when engaging in all genital, oral-genital, anal, and oral-anal sexual contacts, whether homosexual or heterosexual. Such barriers are considered essential as protection not only against HIV but also against other sexually transmitted diseases, many of which enhance the possibility of later contracting HIV or developing certain types of cancer.

The civil rights struggles of the 1960s and 1970s, from which emerged a determination to achieve the same rights as other citizens, were heady if dangerous times for gay activists. Along with the heterosexual population, gay men and women participated in the "sexual revolution," reveling in a generally more liberal approach to sexuality. Especially among gay men, this celebration grew in intensity, even though most states in the United States considered consensual homosexual acts a criminal offense, as were consensual heterosexual relations between partners of different races at one time. Regardless of governmental attempts (the body politic) to control behaviors (the politics of the body), such as miscegenation and sodomy, deemed unlawful, some individuals continued to engage in them, as they had since ancient times. One of the great tragedies—and ironies—of the AIDS epidemic has been that the very celebration of gay sexuality that had so recently emerged from the shadows was now collectively asked to submit to scrutiny on the basis of a public health emergency. A question at least as old as Sophocles—What power does the State have to exert control over customs and traditions valued by a segment of society?—emerged in the 1980s and continues today in the wake of a resurgence of sexual freedom among parts of the population, knowledge of the means of HIV transmission, and a generally conservative socio-political climate. Indeed, the HIV Prevention Act of 1997 is a product of this climate. Introduced by Representative Tom Coburn (R-Oklahoma), it would institute nationwide punitive measures that activists of the 1980s thought they had forever quelled. If signed into law, the bill would, among other things, establish a national registry listing all individuals who test positive for HIV and, therefore, force all states to eliminate anonymous testing centers (Bull, 1997, p. 42).

As early as 1982-83, individuals as well as organizations like the American Association of Physicians for Human Rights (AAPHR), the Gay Men's Health Crisis, and the San Francisco Department of Public Health were urging gay men to avoid promiscuity, anonymous sex, and certain behaviors, such as rimming and fisting, already believed, though not proven, to be unsafe (Bayer, p. 28). Many gay men rebelled against such suggestions, leading to a divisiveness within the community that persists today, as some people ignore the guidelines widely considered to be effective against contracting HIV.

The generation of gay men that first confronted AIDS still earns much-deserved praise for the success it had in getting safe-sex messages out into the community and encouraging behavior change to such an extent that the rate of infection in that cohort decreased significantly. Public health experts praised the gay community's "Stop AIDS" campaigns as "one of the most successful examples of behavior modification in the history of public health" (Bull and Gallagher, 1994, p. 37). Many social venues in gay areas, from dance clubs to sex clubs, closed, sometimes when forced by outside authorities, but often at the behest of the community itself. Once lively urban neighborhoods grew silent in the wake of disease, a silence that some thought symbolized death for the community and all the freedom that had been theirs only a few short years before.

Now, nearly two decades into the epidemic, another generation has come of age, one that has never known life without the spectre of AIDS. In 1989, epidemiologists noticed a disturbing trend: the numbers of infections among gay men were once again on the rise. Investigation revealed that the infections were occurring primarily among men in their twenties. The advent of new drugs that tantalize with the possibility of cure only exacerbates the trend, as does advertising that depicts handsome, muscled men discussing increased flexibility in their medication regimens. In Provincetown, Massachusetts, where one in every fifteen residents is HIV-infected, the executive director of the Provincetown AIDS Support Group remarked, "People are exhausted of being careful" (Carton, p. 1). And a local minister said, "You hear talk, this big sigh of relief, 'It's over, things are getting better, let's forget safe sex, let's throw caution to the wind, let's just live'" (Carton, p. 6). Perhaps the community has come full circle; certainly there appears to be a resurgence of all the riskiest aspects of the lifestyle among some segments of the community.

The hype generated by the apparent success of new drug therapies in driving HIV virions to undetectable levels has been shown to affect sexual decision making, at least among gay men. CNN's *Impact* reported on the phenomenon in "Sexual Roulette" (CNN, 1997). A researcher at Florida International University recounted finding that in South Beach, Florida, one in six gay men aged 18-29 is HIV-positive (the count is one in four for all ages) and that 50 percent of all area gay men surveyed had engaged in unprotected sex during the past twelve months. This total includes 75 percent who knew themselves to be HIV-positive.

The situation in South Beach reflects a national trend. An ongoing CDC study reports that in six urban areas of the United States, 40 percent of gay men aged 15 to 22 have engaged in unprotected anal intercourse during the past six months (Shaw, 1997). As the director of programs at Dallas' AIDS Resource Center remarked, "Many young gay men seem to view HIV infection as inevitable, as just part of the lifestyle, almost as a badge of belonging, of full entry into the community. They believe a cure is around the corner, so why not get all the services that accrue to

HIV-positive people and continue the party?" (Schield Interview, 1997). Another perspective on being young and HIV-negative in a gay urban enclave was given by Eric Ruales in Miami. He leads a gay and lesbian youth group, is determined to maintain his negative status, and is also committed to transmitting this determination to other young people. But, he notes, "There's this breath down my neck. It's like, you're next, you're next, you're next, and it's awful. It's awful" (CNN, 1997).

The reality, like the disease itself, is more complex than it first appears. In 1997, a researcher at the University of California—San Francisco surveyed men in three cities. He found that one-fifth of them said they were actually more worried than ever before. However, many are choosing their own version of safe sex, called *seroconcordance*. They engage in unprotected sex, but only with men who share their own HIV status. Unfortunately, such a behavior is far more dangerous than it might appear. Partners may not be candid about their status, or they may not have been tested. Even if both partners are HIV+, unprotected sex is risky. The strains with which the partners are infected may be different; one may suffer from communicable diseases that the other does not have; and it is certainly possible to pass on drug-resistant strains of HIV. "Morning-after" doses of potent drug cocktails are also under discussion; if they become widely available, such an option might encourage risk-taking for the sake of the comfort, emotional intimacy, and sense of freedom that unprotected sex offers (Gallagher, p. 33). Worth remembering in the midst of rising infection rates among young people—gay and straight, male and female—is the belief in invulnerability common to youth in all places and times. Moreover, the notion that adults—gay or straight, male or female—will practice safe sex with every intimate encounter throughout their lives defies reality.

While initially lesbians did not consider themselves personally threatened by AIDS based on sexual behavior, as the means of transmission of the virus became clear, some began to realize that they were indeed at risk for infection. Cheri Pies, author of *Considering Parenthood: A Workbook for Lesbians*, recalls realizing that women who were inseminated with donor sperm from gay men could be infected. By 1983, she was encouraging women who were considering such a step to question potential donors about their past sexual activities (Pies, p. 140).

But this represented only a small part of the total at risk for infection. Some lesbians had sexual relations with bisexual women; others, just in the process of coming out, were still having unprotected sexual relations with boyfriends or husbands; and some were injection drug users. Most frustrating of all, CDC officials refused to acknowledge that female-to-female transmission was possible. Even today, despite some documented cases, no category comparable to "Men Who Have Sex with Men" is included in the *HIV/AIDS Surveillance Report*. Therefore, no one even knows for certain how many cases of female-to-female transmission occur, since the numbers are not reported in this way. The assumption is that if a woman is seropositive, she *must* have been infected by either a male sexual partner or shared works.

Even the large AIDS service organizations have not always thought in terms of lesbians and HIV. A lesbian APLA client reported that when she asked a staff member for an application in 1991, she was handed an employment application (Mirken, p. 42). Today at APLA, as at other ASOs, that would almost certainly not happen, but the fact remains that lesbians have engaged in a struggle on many levels to convince the AIDS establishment that some unprotected female-to-female sexual practices do indeed put them at risk for HIV infection. Speaking at a 1990 meeting in Washington, D.C., concerning HIV and women, Anke Erhardt, a professor of clinical psychology at Columbia University, noted that lesbians had been excluded from all HIV research, clinical care, and prevention efforts. "Our rationale is that transmission from woman to woman is rare. Since we are doing no research on this issue, we will hardly find out how rare it really is" (Corea, p. 282). What little research has been done since 1990 remains inconclusive, but "HIV infection is present among lesbians, and lesbians engage in behaviors that put themselves at risk for HIV infection, in some cases, at higher risk than most others in society" (Stine, 1997, p. 292).

Certainly part of the reluctance to practice safe sex, even though the possible consequences are well-known even to most school children today, stems from the social, familial, and psychological circumscription and isolation that many gay men and lesbians feel. A condom or a dental dam is yet another barrier to full participation in a larger society that is ambivalent at best in its feelings, actions, and pronouncements about homosexuality. Rebellion in the face of known risk defiantly declares, "I am who I am and rejoice in it."

Relationship Issues

Sexual liberation achieved following Stonewall has been characterized, for some, by abandon and excess. While many gays and lesbians have been fighting since pre-Stonewall days to love the person of their choice, others have been battling to have sex when, where, and how they please. Having multiple sexual partners, however, as opposed to being in a monogamous relationship, has been shown to increase the likelihood of becoming HIV-infected. Serial monogamy, or dating monogamously one individual after another for relatively short periods of time, is only slightly less risky. This is not to say, of course, that many gays and lesbians have not enjoyed or do not continue to enjoy monogamous relationships. However, the onslaught of AIDS has made long-term monogamous partnering ever more attractive. The increased incidence of this type of partnering has led to yet another dichotomy, present among both gay and lesbian couples: *serodiscordance.*

With the continued rise in the number of HIV infections, combined with the fact that the HIV-infected are living longer, it seems inevitable that more HIV-positive/HIV-negative, or serodiscordant, couples will exist. Nonetheless, where personal relationships are concerned, HIV-related prejudice and reverse prejudice continue to exist. Many HIV-negative individuals are quite adamant about not getting involved with someone who is HIV-positive, and many HIV-positive people only wish to partner with another infected individual. The number of serodiscordant couples, though, has increased over the duration of the pandemic. Difference in sero status, however, may act as a wedge, ultimately threatening and sometimes ending the relationship. Behavioral and emotional barriers to developing and maintaining lasting partnerships among serodiscordant couples include the ongoing need to practice safe sex, lack of peer support given the questionable nature of the relationship's longevity, perception by the HIV-positive partner that the HIV-negative partner cannot fully comprehend the impact of the disease, and the health status of the HIV-infected partner (Remien, Carballo-Dieguez, and Wagner, pp. 429-38).

Maintaining long-term partnerships has never been without challenge, even before the advent of HIV/AIDS. Gay and lesbian relationships fly in the face of what the body politic has termed "nor-

mal," and they continue to be subject to social ridicule. In addition, a variety of social and sexual practices within the community complicate further the potential for success in the development and maintenance of lasting partnerships. The relative ease in obtaining sex—on the streets, in the clubs, in the bathhouses—is certainly a chief contributor to the demise of many potential relationships as well as a primary facilitator for HIV transmission.

The Battle of the Bathhouses

Nowhere was the dichotomy of response to the AIDS crisis within the gay community played out more clearly than in the 1980s battles to close the bathhouses. These struggles occurred primarily in San Francisco and New York, though other large cities were certainly not immune from their influence.

The two most visible battles over the closing of commercial establishments that provided ample opportunity for the practice of unsafe sexual practices, and therefore facilitated the transmission of HIV, occurred first in San Francisco and then in New York. In both places, members of the gay community, leaders of various gay organizations, AIDS service organizations, gay and straight physicians who treated AIDS patients, public health authorities, politicians, and journalists aligned themselves with one side or the other. Civil libertarians argued that enforced closure or regulation of commercial establishments existing for the purpose of promoting unsafe sexual practices is an unjustified invasion of the privacy rights of individuals, which are constitutionally protected. On the other hand, public health advocates saw the closure or regulation as an acceptable, logical move in response to a growing threat to the common good. Moderate voices drowned in the polarized rhetoric. Eventually, courts in California denied San Francisco's first effort (in 1984) to close public gay sexual venues but mandated the hiring of monitors, the prohibiting of private rooms, cubicles, or other areas in such establishments, and the distributing of safe-sex educational materials and messages. In 1986, Judge Richard W. Wallach upheld the closing of the St. Marks Baths in New York. These two highly visible struggles and their very different judicial outcomes played themselves out across the country, although in major cities other than New York and San Francisco, some bathhouses never closed. By the late 1980s, many of these establishments had succumbed to what moderates had theorized would happen all along: they closed for lack of business. Their dying out in the wake of AIDS was a symbolic death for the community. The resurgence of the bathhouse scene in the mid-to-late 1990s has reopened many of the same controversies of the previous decade.

Pornography, Prostitution, and Drug Use

As the pervasive impact of the epidemic rippled through the community, no facet remained untouched, including the exotic fringes of the sex industry. One educational ploy for advocating safe sex among gay men focused on attempts to eroticize safe sex. One method of doing this was to encourage the use of pornography, alone or with companions, to satisfy sexual needs. While this sometimes worked with the audience, the people who actually starred in the videos were unfortunately sometimes exposed to HIV. With the apparent ravages of the disease growing rapidly, gay pornography's obsession with the heterosexual male reached new heights during the 1980s. The profit-driven industry provided an escape from the daily ordeal of HIV by focusing more and more

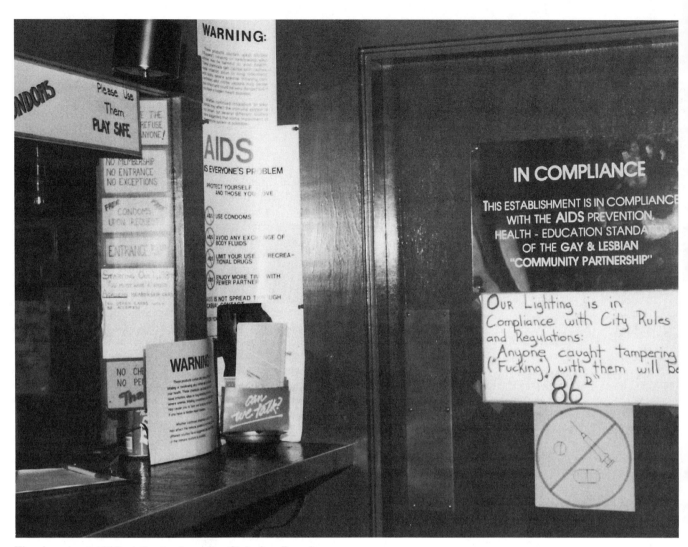

Warning about AIDS at the Academy Sex Club, San Francisco.

on the heterosexual ideal idolized by so many gay men. Depicting the stylized heterosexual male untouched by the disease added fuel to the fires of denial and further vilified the homosexual male, at the same time as it satisfied some sexual needs.

The producers of gay porn missed the opportunity to combine forces with grass-roots organizations and promote eroticizing safe sex. Instead, they sold unsafe sex during an epidemic growth period for the spread of HIV; the use of condoms did not become universal for scenes involving anal intercourse until the late 1980s. Sadly, several stars of gay pornography have been claimed by the disease.

Often intertwined with pornography, the commercial sex industry is as prevalent in the gay community as it is among the heterosexual populace. Male prostitutes are at high risk for HIV infection because of a unique combination of behaviors in which they engage (Eifson, Boles, and Sweat, pp. 79-83). These include simultaneously participating in high risk sex (particularly receptive anal intercourse), having sex with multiple paying and nonpaying partners, and using intravenous drugs. Of course, not all male prostitutes who have sex with men are gay. And condom use is as inconsistent among male prostitutes as it is in the broader

community. All of these high risk behaviors can facilitate transmission of HIV into multiple populations. Given further reduction in condom use with nonpaying partners, risk of transmission is actually higher than with paying partners of prostitutes. If commercial sex work is so risky, then why do some gays turn to prostitution as a way of life? Some hustle out of necessity to survive on the streets; some, for the thrill; some, to support drug habits; and some, because it is seen as easy money.

Recreational or illicit drug use is known to facilitate HIV transmission, either indirectly by affecting the decision-making process or directly through the sharing of needles. While controlled substances are a way of life to using addicts, drugs are once again becoming commonly associated with gay clubs and the party circuit, scenes that typically do not include the average street junkie. Rather, the party set is very often populated with professionals who earn enough disposable income to afford the various recreational outlets associated with the scene, "where gay men are indulging in illicit drugs and wild sex with increasing abandon" (Heitz, 1997, p. 26), reminiscent of the 1970s and early 1980s. At least for some gay men, "in a culture riddled by death, drugs and alcohol are a way of feeling alive" (Heitz, 1997, p. 28). Whether addicted or not, increasing numbers of gay men are accepting drug use as a part of life and are rejecting the mantras of health consciousness that arose in the wake of AIDS.

Theoretical underpinnings regarding the social implications of HIV and AIDS are inextricably tied to the reality of the pandemic. Societal regulation of the HIV-affected body, individual and collective, is quite real. Social policy and processes, both within and without the community, determine the position of HIV within society. And the theoretical dichotomy between politics of the body and the body politic yields division at every level of the epidemic. Nowhere, perhaps, is the struggle between bio-politics and bio-power more clear than in the picture recorded in and by the media.

THE MEDIA: A BATTLE ON MANY FRONTS

The gay community had not only to contend with one of the deadliest, most complex infectious diseases in United States' history but also was forced to do battle on other fronts. First, everyone involved had to deal with the fear and confusion engendered by the disease itself. Gay men who early on saw the possibility that it was sexually transmitted and perhaps promoted by promiscuous lifestyles, and voiced their deepest fears, often endured apathy, denial, or outright derision from other gay men. As if dismissal from their own brothers were not enough, they also struggled against disinterest or hate-filled invective and behavior on the part of some politicians, journalists, and other shapers of public opinion. Partially through the media, they launched a campaign against both the United States government and multinational pharmaceutical companies, first to provide the dollars and priority for research into the causes of the disease and treatments for it, and eventually for access to drugs that showed any promise of halting the virus's relentless assault against the immune system. Eventually, both gay men and lesbians employed alternative media to educate specific groups of people about the prevention of infection.

Background

Cynics maintain that news is reported to sell newspapers. Certainly, sensational stories capture the interest of readers and do encourage sales of newspapers and newsmagazines and coverage by broadcast media. So, what defines a sensational story? In the mainstream press, stories get reported if they contain some aspect of celebrity, innocence compromised, violence, or the possibility that the same thing could happen to someone in middle America. In the early years, AIDS seemed to fit none of these criteria. The epidemic was reported in mainstream publications like the *New York Times*, newsmagazines like *Time*, and the broadcast media only perfunctorily, if at all, but for a handful of instances. Announcements of pediatric AIDS cases and cases resulting from blood transfusions made extensive headlines. The erroneous 1983 contention that HIV can be casually transmitted unleashed a flurry of hysteria, since it led to the conclusion that "everyone" could be at risk of contracting the deadly virus (Oleske, p. 2345). Other inaccurate reports of means of transmission, such as the "mosquitoes carry HIV" scare of 1987, resulted in similar sensational reporting. Regardless, few individuals or organizations seemed to care that gay men and injection drug users were dying by the score. They were considered marginal, disposable human beings, not really legitimate members of the body politic.

Anyone who doubts this assertion need only look at the record. By March 1983, more than two years into the epidemic in the United States, more than 1,100 people were dead of the disease. Yet, the *New York Times,* long revered as America's "journal of record," published only five stories on the epidemic throughout all of 1982. During the same year, the mainstream American magazine press contained a mere nine references to articles published about AIDS. Compare these figures with a similar strange disease outbreak in 1976. The American Legion was holding a national meeting in Philadelphia. One hundred eighty-two individuals fell ill, of whom 29 died. Massive governmental resources were committed to isolating the pathogen that caused the 29 deaths. Comparatively extensive news coverage was also part of the picture, with no fewer than nine articles in the *New York Times* and eight references in the mainstream magazines. The hantavirus outbreak in the Four Corners area, primarily on the Navajo Indian Reservation that occupies much of the 40,000 square miles at the junction of Utah, Colorado, Arizona, and New Mexico, began in May 1993. One month later, 24 cases were confirmed, of which 12 resulted in death. A full-fledged CDC investigation was underway, and by November of that same year, the virus had been isolated and the cause of the outbreak confirmed.

In between these two infectious disease events occurred the first decade of the HIV/AIDS epidemic. Disease outbreaks are complicated events and are sometimes reported extensively, sometimes not. Critical comparative factors in these three outbreaks, and the contrast in news coverage, are worth examining. In two, HIV and hantavirus, the first victims were young, presumably healthy people. The hantavirus outbreak had the great advantage of coming more than a decade after AIDS, so that physicians and public health authorities could apply the lessons learned in the 1980s to a new disease event. In the case of Legionnaires' Disease, the victims in Philadelphia were middle-aged or elderly white males, members of a patriotic organization. Moreover, the initial round of exposures occurred among individuals who had all stayed at the same hotel. What made AIDS victims different? They were young, presumably healthy individuals, primarily male. Their numbers were clustered not in a single building but were found in three specific urban areas, not, at that time, scattered across the country. Their deaths appeared to be caused by either a rare form of pneumonia or a rare cancer and were accompanied by wasting. The appearance of the cancer, Kaposi's sarcoma, was especially problematic, since it had previously been seen almost exclusively among elderly men of Mediterranean lineage. Their story contained all the ingredients of the best disease narrative writing, except that they were gay.

As the means of transmission were gradually identified, the mainstream press still did not report broadly on the epidemic, since the social standards of the time forbade the use of words such as "semen" or "penis," and certainly phrases and concepts such as "anal intercourse." Factored into the equation must also be the false sense of security that lulled most people, including some scientists, into a belief that infectious diseases had been conquered by the arsenal of antibiotics available. If medical science could eradicate a scourge like smallpox from the globe, what had anyone to fear? All of that changed in 1985, driven partly by a growing awareness of the extent of the epidemic. The catalyst, however, was the 1985 appearance of actor Rock Hudson's ravaged face in newspapers and magazines everywhere. Hudson's death, coupled with the recognition that a silver screen idol who typified the handsome, virile, heterosexual male was actually a gay man, so riveted the public's attention that from that point forward, the reporting on the epidemic changed. Certainly not all the battles were yet fought, nor are they still, but critical perceptions and attitudes altered dramatically.

Mainstream Newspapers

Although the *Los Angeles Times* was the first major newspaper to print a front-page story on AIDS (Nelson), two San Francisco newspapers, the *Chronicle* and the *Examiner*, were the first mainstream newspapers in the United States to report extensively and consistently on the epidemic. This was undoubtedly in response to the political clout wielded by the San Francisco gay community, influence unrivaled anywhere else in the world. In fact, Randy Shilts, one of the first openly gay journalists in the United States, worked from 1982 for the *San Francisco Chronicle*. Since San Francisco was hit hard by the epidemic in the early 1980s, the newspaper attention is not surprising. However, due to the sheer volume of cases, New York evolved as the epicenter of the epidemic. The dichotomy of response measured by the newspapers of Los Angeles and San Francisco on the one hand, and New York on the other, mirrors the dichotomies and ironies that appear throughout the history of the epidemic. Bluntly stated, the *New York Times* performed poorly in terms of reporting on the early days of the AIDS epidemic. By the end of 1982, when at least 619 U.S. citizens had died of AIDS and another 1,614 had been diagnosed, the "journal of record" had printed a mere five stories on the epidemic. The first one appeared on 3 July 1981, and it occupied one column on page twenty of the paper's first section. While one segment of New York's population was being jointly stricken with a virulent new disease and abject fear, the newspaper virtually ignored the entire scenario, though its editors were certainly informed of what was happening. Almost from the beginning of the epidemic, Larry Kramer had been writing increasingly vitriolic letters to the editors, demanding newspaper coverage of what he finally began calling a "gay Holocaust."

Finally, when the *Times* failed to report the huge 1983 charity benefit hosted by Gay Men's Health Crisis, a performance of the Ringling Brothers and Barnum & Bailey Circus at Madison Square Garden, a quartet of gay leaders demanded a meeting with the newspaper's publisher. The four were Virginia Apuzzo, executive director of the National Gay Task Force; New York City gay activist David Rothenberg; gay author Andrew Humm; and a local judge, Richard Failla. The four met with the publisher's assistant, Sydney Gruson. Ultimately, all except Humm were invited to meet with the executive editor. They explained that the *Times* didn't just miss the circus; they were missing the entire story. They expressed anger at the newspaper's refusal to report on the gay and lesbian community's positive responses to the horror of the epidemic in their midst, chief among them the establishment of Gay Men's Health Crisis. They also questioned the *Times'* obdurate clinging to the term *homosexual*, in preference to *gay*, when referring to gay men and lesbians (Kinsella, p. 69). The meeting marked a positive change in the *Times'* coverage of the AIDS epidemic. Max Frankel, editor of the editorial page, had already written a number of hard-hitting pieces and continued his effort, particularly noting the paucity of funding allocated to fight the epidemic. What reporters from the *New York Times* have routinely done is provide some of the best follow-up and analysis of major news events available anywhere in North America. Certainly this has

been true of the AIDS story, which by 1988 *New York Times* executives were calling "the story of the decade" (Kinsella, p. 86).

Many other big city newspapers besides those in San Francisco, Los Angeles, and New York eventually contributed valuable information to a wide readership, particularly as the epidemic spread across the United States, reaching even into small communities in the South and Midwest. Even the *Wall Street Journal* began covering AIDS; in fact, the 1996 Pulitzer Prize for national reporting went to the staff of the paper for its coverage of AIDS in both the scientific and business communities.

For people who may not have access to the comprehensive reporting now available in the newspapers of the largest U. S. cities, the National AIDS Clearinghouse (NAC) publishes the *AIDS Daily Summary* (ADS) five days per week, excluding legal holidays. The ADS draws not only on major newspapers like the *Washington Post, New York Times,* and *Wall Street Journal* but also on medical journals and some other periodicals to ensure that interested parties are informed of the most current news. The ADS is available through a variety of World Wide Web pages and is posted daily in AIDS service organizations, gay and lesbian community centers, clinics, and public libraries all over the United States.

Mainstream News Magazines

Newsweek, Time, and *U.S. News and World Report* are widely read magazines that more often reflect than influence what Americans are thinking about current events. Unlike newspapers, they do not rely on wire services to provide clues to breaking news. Rather, they look to major dailies, usually the *New York Times* and the *Washington Post*, to determine a focus. Therefore, it was unusual for a *Newsweek* staffer named Vincent Coppola to attempt to attract editors' attention to a story that had not yet been covered significantly in east coast newspapers. He had a personal reason, though; his younger brother was an early AIDS patient. In his determination to try to find help for his brother and to tell the world how the gay community was coping with the terrifying disease, he pushed *Newsweek* to be the first of the news magazines to run a cover story on the epidemic (Kinsella, p. 89). It appeared in April 1983 and was entitled "The AIDS Epidemic: The Search for a Cure." *Time* printed its first cover story in July 1983, but it was months before either the *New York Times* or the Associated Press prepared major feature stories about AIDS.

Perhaps the greatest contribution made by these news weeklies was in breaking down language barriers that had formerly dictated how far a reporter could go before transgressing the bounds of good taste. Well ahead of newspapers and broadcast media, *Newsweek* and *Time* quoted medical authorities who felt sure that the pathogen that caused AIDS was transmitted through both sexual activity and blood and blood products. Both magazines played important roles in reporting on the gay community and how it was affected by AIDS, on the unfolding scientific story of retrovirology, and on steps people could take to protect themselves from being infected. If at times the stories were inaccurate or even hysterical, at least the epidemic was not ignored.

Other magazines began reporting on AIDS later than *Newsweek, Time,* and *U.S. News and World Report* but today produce thoughtful commentary on the epidemic. From 1984 *Jet* covered AIDS extensively for its largely African-American readership. Its coverage of the death of fashion designer Willi Smith in 1987 proved a wakeup call to the African-American community. The *Nation*, a liberal-leaning magazine that regards itself as a staunch defender of civil rights, began writing about the epidemic in 1983 with a story entitled "AIDS Neglect." The *Atlantic Monthly* and *Harper's* both report frequently on AIDS. During Andrew Sullivan's five-year stint as editor of the *New Republic,* that influential magazine reported not only on HIV/AIDS but also on gay issues, usually from a neoconservative point of view. In April 1996 Sullivan stepped down as editor, announcing his own seropositive status and lending poignancy to the reporting he had championed.

The Gay Press

The trophy for the very first journalist to write about the epidemic belongs to Larry Mass, a physician who on 18 May 1981, authored an article in the *New York Native.* Ironically, he reported that the rumors of virulent disease spreading through New York's gay community had no basis in fact; he reported this assertion after talking with physicians at a New York hospital and the New York City Health Department. Only two weeks later, the *MMWR: Morbidity and Mortality Weekly Report*, a weekly bulletin issued by the Centers for Disease Control and Prevention (CDC) in Atlanta, reported five cases of *Pneumocystis carinii* pneumonia among young gay men in Los Angeles. In July, the *MMWR* reported that a total of 41 cases of either Kaposi's sarcoma (KS) or *Pneumocystis carinii* pneumonia had been diagnosed in young gay men in New York and California; Larry Mass penned "Cancer in the Gay Community" for the *New York Native* two weeks afterward. Once again, Dr. Mass broke new ground by providing the most extensive information yet available to the lay community about the epidemic. It formed the cornerstone of the New York gay community's early education efforts.

As is still true today, however, the hallmark of this early reporting from the gay community was a contradiction of both images and messages. Mass's article was accompanied by photographs of ugly, frightening KS lesions on the hands and arms of patients. But in the same issue of the *New York Native* were advertisements for sex clubs, bathhouses, and other venues that encouraged promiscuous sexual behavior. Suggestive personals were printed beside images of alluring, muscled bodies. From the very beginning of the epidemic, voices in the community argued over the need to preserve the image of gay liberation and the need to abstain from promiscuity. On the one hand, the liberation ideal included the right to engage in unrestrained sexual freedom with little regard for repercussions. Unfortunately, one of the repercussions was a 1970s epidemic of sexually transmitted diseases, including hepatitis B and protozoan infections such as amebiasis. Arguably, these diseases provided a doorway for other pathogens, including deadly ones like HIV. The *New York Native* foreshadowed the newsletters that are still preeminent in delivering news about new treatment directions and clinical trials to a lay public. It was the very first publication of any kind in the United States to list behaviors thought to put one at high risk for infection, to speculate on the possibility that AIDS could be spread via a viral agent, and to provide lists of organizations committed to helping AIDS victims (Kinsella, p. 32). Furthermore, the publication became respected as one that was interpreting what little science knew at the time to the community seemingly most at risk, gay white men living in urban areas.

However, Chuck Ortleb, the owner and publisher of the *New York Native*, suspected the conservative, Reagan-era federal government of deliberately failing to commit the funds and to perform research that would lead to finding the cause and ultimate cure for AIDS. Ortleb became fixated on the possibility that African Swine Fever Virus was the cause of AIDS and that it had been unleashed on the world by the United States government in an effort to cripple the Cuban economy. Ultimately, scientists and journalists outside of the gay community discounted him and his publication, but many gay men continued to rely on it as their most credible source of information about the epidemic. In fact, it typified the dichotomy that marks the community response to the epidemic. Ortleb continued to run stories about treatments and interviews with scientists, even Robert Gallo, whom he skewered editorially because he disagreed with his approaches and pronouncements. He paid Ann Giudici Fettner to write carefully researched, thoughtful articles and even sponsored her travel to Africa to observe and write about AIDS there. But he ranted against the "AIDS establishment" (he coined the term) and printed and championed the "AIDS is syphilis" heresy.

The *New York Native* was the first publication printed by gays, for gays that focused on the epidemic, but it was soon joined by several others. Editors at the *Advocate* assigned Nathan Fain and other well-known, respected journalists to cover AIDS. The magazine's first cover story on the epidemic appeared in 1983, after the *Los Angeles Times* and concurrent with *Time* and *Newsweek*. Galvanized by Larry Kramer's "1,112 and Counting" (see p. 76), Bill Kraus wrote an editorial for San Francisco's *Bay Area Reporter* calling on gays in the city to respond to the crisis and demonstrate their commitment to one another by altering their sexual excesses. Washington D.C.'s *Blade*, long known for its political commentary, provided early coverage of the epidemic. Cindy Patton, an editor at Boston's *Gay Community News* during part of the 1980s, began writing critiques of the way AIDS was seen and how many of those infected were treated by people and institutions across the United States. The gay press consistently broke AIDS stories ahead of their mainstream counterparts, which led to reporters and science editors of wire services and major newspapers and magazines regularly reading one or more of the gay publications. By the mid-1980s, locally produced gay periodicals in major cities across the United States were interpreting the epidemic as it affected gay communities in their regions. In short, "gay journalism grew up, and got noticed" (Kinsella, p. 45). Periodicals that had for the most part begun their lives focusing solely on a gay male readership and some of its prurient interests lost their anonymity as they struggled to report on the disease that was changing both their community and the country forever.

Scientific and Biomedical Journals

Included in the media are scientific and technical journals. Journals are distinguished from other periodicals in that articles that appear in them presumably have undergone a "peer review" process. What this means is that when an author or, more commonly, a group of authors wish to present information of interest to the scientific community, their work is submitted to a panel of senior experts in the field. In theory, this review process ensures that faulty research is identified and kept from publication until deficiencies are corrected. In practice, much needlessly repetitive, poor, or even erroneous research is published every day, while some worthy work may never be made available to the public.

Michael Gottlieb, who in 1980 was a new assistant professor at the University of California-Los Angeles, is credited as being the first physician to sound the alarm of an epidemic, though his name is not affixed to the report. In his effort to alert the medical community to what he was seeing among young gay men in Los Angeles, Gottlieb encountered barriers associated with peer review. By 1981 he knew that he had to let other physicians—his peers—know what he was seeing. Accordingly, he called an associate editor at the *New England Journal of Medicine*. The editor reminded him that it would take at least three months to send an article out for review and that there would be an indeterminate delay between the time the reviewers returned the manuscript with their comments and possible publication. Moreover, any leak of the information to the popular press would mean that it would never be published. Frustrated by the editorial strictures and alarmed by the growing number of strange diseases and deaths he was seeing, Gottlieb and a colleague wrote a brief report for the *MMWR*, "*Pneumocystis* pneumonia in homosexual men—Los Angeles" (Shilts, p. 67). The urgency of the situation short-circuited the traditional process, a pattern that became more the rule than the exception as the epidemic unfolded.

Almost from the beginning of the AIDS epidemic, the slow process of peer-review engendered scorn, derision, and eventually fury among those most affected by the epidemic—patients and their partners, families, and friends. These feelings were only exacerbated by erroneous reports of casual transmission and delayed reports of possible helpful therapies. However, there is another side to the debate. Researchers guard the data they disclose, lest premature and inaccurate information either alarm the public or create false hope. Scientific research only rarely boasts bold breakthroughs in the advance of knowledge; usually, progress is made in painstakingly slow steps. And when mistaken conclusions do find their way into the journal literature, letters and articles generally quickly refute the claims. If fraud is suspected, an agency of the federal government, the Office of Scientific Integrity Review (OSIR), may launch an investigation. The system is far from perfect, but scientists and much of the public feel that it mostly works to the benefit, not the detriment, of the citizenry. As in so many other areas, however, the AIDS epidemic stood the process of scientific publication on its head and altered the means of information distribution.

Perhaps the greatest contribution of the gay and lesbian community to battling the epidemic was its approach to information dissemination. Under the aegis of grass-roots organizations such as GMHC and the San Francisco AIDS Foundation or individual zealots such as Martin Delaney (Project Inform) and John S. James (*AIDS Treatment News*), generally reliable information was passed to the community of those infected with HIV and their caregivers. In many cases, such publications were the only information link to which patients and their caregivers had access. However, not all observers agree that the approach taken has been a sound one (Lauritsen, 1997). Despite the dissent, the combination of an isolated community unwillingly thrust into the spotlight, the youth of those stricken with AIDS, the socially marginal status of many of the ill and dying, and the prejudice and fear engendered by a global plague combined to alter radically the scientific community's approach to clinical trials, scientific publication, and the doctor-patient relationship. As a spokesperson for Agouron Pharmaceuticals explained, "PWAs revolutionized the way medicine is practiced in our country" (Kuller, p. 8).

Radio

National Public Radio (NPR) has consistently been a star in bringing information about HIV/AIDS to the American public.

Reaching as it does into rural as well as urban areas of the United States, NPR has worked since mid-1981 to interpret issues in the epidemic for its listeners. Admiral James D. Watkins, head of the Presidential Commission on the HIV Epidemic and a Reagan appointee, endorsed and affirmed NPR's contributions when he stated, "NPR is singularly responsible for dispelling much misinformation and for building a national base of knowledge about the epidemic" (Kinsella, p. 241).

National Public Radio launched its AIDS coverage on 3 July 1981, when Laurie Garrett, then science reporter for the network, reported on Kaposi's sarcoma among homosexual men. It was the first time the majority of Americans had ever heard of what had been an obscure condition. Reporters other than Garrett, notably Frank Browning, covered social and political angles. Garrett reported from Newark in 1987 in a series called "Third World America"; she interviewed commercial sex workers, injection drug users, and women who took "AIDS babies" that no one else wanted into their homes, bringing love into lives that would almost certainly be cut drastically short. Reporters at National Public Radio early fought the battle of openly discussing anal intercourse.

Despite their groundbreaking start, not everyone at NPR was pleased with the attention being paid to "stories about gays." Frank Browning reports that as late as 1990, a reporter complained to a producer, "You're running far too much about gays" (Browning, p. 10). The combination of Reagan-era cutbacks at NPR and problems with some disgruntled news chiefs and listeners effectively silenced much of the reporting that could have been done. Still, National Public Radio stands as the most effective national radio voice reporting on AIDS.

Television News

In the early 1980s, when the AIDS epidemic was first identified, the evening news broadcasts of the three major networks dominated the market. The disease that gripped gay communities in New York and California was not relevant to the majority of their viewers, at least according to network executives. Robert Bazell, NBC's science reporter, was the first to address AIDS on the evening news, doing so in June 1982. Not until October did ABC broadcast a story on the epidemic, and it was a full six months later that CBS mentioned it. ABC was, however, the first network to mention AIDS; in December 1981, James Curran, who was heading the CDC's investigation into the epidemic, got a 45-second spot on *Good Morning, America*. Ironically, ABC news anchor Max Robinson, at one time the most renowned African-American journalist in the United States, died of AIDS in late 1988. During his lifetime, he never made an official statement about the disease that killed him. Throughout the 1980s, no one in television reported on the alarming and disproportionate infection rate among poor blacks and Hispanics, one gateway to infection of the heterosexual population.

Ted Turner's Cable News Network (CNN), however, did report the story from the beginning. CNN's on-air presence beginning in 1980 corresponded roughly with the dawn of the AIDS epidemic. Perhaps because CNN's headquarters is in Atlanta, also home to the CDC, reporting health news seemed like more of a priority to the young network than to the three majors. Moreover, putting an emphasis on health matters distinguished CNN from the three majors and made sense in terms of the market CNN was after, affluent baby boomers who would shortly be reaching middle age. So perhaps it was only natural that CNN was the first network television outlet to report on AIDS, which it did in July 1981 with a story about Kaposi's sarcoma appearing in young gay men. And just two months later, in September 1981, CNN ran a story reporting that many diseases among homosexuals were transmitted sexually, both orally and anally. In 1983, CNN even went inside a gay bathhouse to report on high-risk sexual encounters taking place there. Unfortunately, only a fraction of U.S. households at the time were wired for cable or, if they were, tuned into the upstart network. The one place on television where the mysteries of AIDS were being unmasked was unavailable to most of the population. Now that most U.S. homes do have cable access, CNN continues its tradition of airing cutting edge reports about HIV.

Newsletters and Electronic Databases

The paucity of response from the mainstream media elicited a deluge of communication, both print and electronic, from within the gay and lesbian community. Begun as underground publications, the AIDS newsletters produced by both ASOs and individuals across the United States quickly became the first line of communication about new treatments, drug toxicities, buyers' clubs, and other issues of importance to HIV/AIDS patients and their caregivers. Paralleling as it has the growth of the Internet and access to it, the AIDS epidemic and the needs of all associated with it has, in part, driven a revolution in biomedical information dissemination, access, and use (Huber and Gillaspy, 1996, p. 293). Angered by botched governmental responses to the ever-escalating numbers of deaths, and determined to prolong the lives of those infected, patients, their caregivers, and medical personnel on the front lines of AIDS communicated with one another through Internet discussion lists, electronic mail, fax, and print in an unprecedented effort to share knowledge about this disease and the devastating infections that accompany it. The newsletter from the People with AIDS Health Group, *Notes from the Underground*, sums it up nicely in its header: "Access to Information Precedes Access to Treatment." As access to the Internet increased, particularly after the development of the World Wide Web, some ASOs and their services and publications became available electronically to the world. Exemplifying their new, mainstream status, nineteen of these newsletters in 1995 attained a legitimacy unimagined in their early days. The National Library of Medicine (NLM), the world's largest medical library, began including them in its database of medical information devoted solely to HIV, *AIDSLINE*.

Like the newsletters that began as underground fact sheets, the *AIDS Education Global Information Service* (AEGIS) started at the grass roots level. A Californian named Jamie Jemison established an online AIDS bulletin board system (BBS), which he called AEGIS, in the mid-1980s. However, the costs, limitations, and related challenges common to networked computers and telecommunications of the time prevented large-scale implementation. In 1990, a Roman Catholic nun living in the Midwest launched the *HIV/AIDS Info BBS* in response to the isolation of AIDS patients she met there. She contacted Jemison, who ceded rights to the name AEGIS to her, and until 1995 the online system was operated by Sister Mary Elizabeth and her order, the Sisters of St. Elizabeth of Hungary. In 1995, AEGIS (http://www.aegis.com/) was reorganized as a nonprofit charitable and educational corporation, but Sister Mary Elizabeth is still the webmaster and consid-

ers the sophisticated system her life's work, a way to put her technical skills to spiritual use. The Centers for Disease Control and Prevention calls AEGIS the best resource of its kind available. The huge database, consisting of almost 350,000 documents online, contains publications from HIV/PWA patient groups, AIDS service organizations, the U.S. government, major newspapers, and international organizations fighting AIDS.

Alternative Media

The politics of AIDS, inextricable from the politics of the gay community, has found part of its voice through the medium of alternative video. Independently produced and generally intended for a narrow audience, such media can deliver messages unhampered by the strictures and prejudices of the broadcast giants. A researcher who has chronicled and analyzed the alternative media of AIDS explains, "Competing visions of reality, or at least what is really important, distinguish the work of alternative and mainstream producers" (Juhasz, p. 142). Creating video productions, a relatively simple process thanks to new technologies, allows for the documentation of activism; the formation of a local response to some aspect of the epidemic; rebuttal of the mainstream media's sometimes erroneous and often over-simplified statements; the transmission of vital information to communities otherwise overlooked; and internal political speech among various factions within the gay community. GMHC has been a leader in this area, hiring Jean Carlomusto as early as 1987 to be its audiovisual specialist. By June of that year she had created the first weekly cable television show devoted to AIDS, *Living with AIDS*, and in 1990 directed *Current Flow*, the first safer-sex video for lesbians. She was also a founder of DIVA TV, ACT UP's activist video collective.

The politics of AIDS, both within and outside the gay community, has particularly impacted media response and reaction to the epidemic. Moreover, the epidemic has emerged concurrent with a revolutionary shift to electronic communication via personal computers, innovations in telecommunications, and cable television, rendering the issues surrounding it a laboratory for modeling like events of the future. For all the potential of the media, it has only occasionally delivered in a way that could help the ordinary American understand the harsh realities of AIDS. Unfortunately, as the reality encompasses an ever wider range of the citizenry, the illumination that could result from thoughtful media attention has grown ever dimmer.

THE BATTLE FOR TREATMENTS AND ACCESS TO THEM

One of the community's finest hours has been the achievement of forcing researchers to look both for treatment for HIV infection itself—and the many opportunistic infections and cancers that appear as the immune system deteriorates—and for access to promising therapies. Not only did patients and their advocates force researchers to turn their attention to the disease ravaging the community, but they also devised effective means of communicating among themselves. In the struggle to find something—anything—that would halt the virus's relentless assault on the immune system, affected individuals communicated through a lightning-fast underground consisting of newsletters, some gay publications, telephone calls, and computer communication. Michael Callen wrote, "I've tried to see AIDS as a challenge to begin living, instead of a sign to begin dying" (Callen, 1990, p. 90). The courage, determination, and activism of Callen and hundreds of others like him transformed not only their personal disease process but parts of the U. S. system of healthcare itself.

As in so many other aspects of the epidemic, the community faced an array of dichotomous barriers. First was the factor of what might be called a "universal yawn." In New York, it certainly appeared to some gay men that neither the federal government nor Mayor Ed Koch's city administration were acting to stem the tide of deaths. Yet, in 1981 the Centers for Disease Control (CDC) had formed a task force, headed by Dr. James Curran, to investigate what appeared to be an epidemic in the making. In July 1982, physicians at New York's Mt. Sinai Medical Center had hosted the first ever international symposium on what many people already recognized as the dawn of a devastating epidemic. Not everyone was ignoring the reality of disease and death haunting the gay community. At the same time, however, too many people both inside and outside the government were all too willing to dismiss the illness and death as some "weird gay epidemic" (Lapierre, p. 120) and therefore of no consequence.

Second was the reluctance among some members of the gay community to admit that lifestyle choices could be playing a part in the disease's spread. Larry Kramer had recognized the reality and threat of sexual promiscuity and written about it in his 1978 novel *Faggots*. Early efforts on the part of some gay men to inform others were met with responses ranging from apathy to accusatory denunciations to outright verbal abuse. Richard Berkowitz and Michael Callen published "We Know Who We Are: Two Gay Men Declare War on Promiscuity" in the *New York Native* in December 1982. They, too, indicted promiscuous lifestyles as contributing to their own and others' illnesses. Not until deaths had reached unimaginable proportions and the major means of transmission were identified, however, did legions of gay men in the first decade of AIDS realize that the exhilarating days of sexual license had to end if the holocaust were to be halted.

Finally, the entire process of scientific inquiry, bolstered by federal bureaucracy and legislation, proved the biggest barrier of all to desperate people with AIDS (PWAs). The relative isolation of the gay community, the lack of trust and interaction with institutions on the part of many gay men, homophobia on the part of many physicians (Gerbert et al., p. 2837), and the sheer lack of knowledge about what was happening in the natural history of this strange, new disease inevitably led to the appearance of some counter-cultural responses to the epidemic. One way these responses took shape externally was in the form of protests against the Food and Drug Administration (FDA), which has been in existence in one form or another since 1927. Various legislative initiatives enacted over the years led to the development of layers of bureaucracy that by 1981 meant, effectively, that it took approximately ten years for new drugs to be made widely available in the marketplace. History may show the most important long-range effect of the HIV epidemic in the United States to have been the revolution in drug-approval processes brought about by AIDS activism and spearheaded by men, women, and organizations of the gay community. The jury is still out on whether these changes will in the long run prove beneficial or harmful, but the story of how the alterations have evolved is inextricable from the AIDS story in the context of the gay and lesbian community.

The Clinical Trials Process

What exactly is the accepted scientific procedure for drug development, and what are its advantages? The standard protocol

for delivering safe, effective prescription drugs to the U.S. marketplace is the *clinical trial*, an experiment performed on humans to evaluate the comparative safety and effectiveness of one or more therapies. The gold standard for such experiments is the randomized, controlled, double-blind trial. *Randomized* means that the subjects of trials are chosen by chance alone, within the guidelines of who may and may not be admitted to the experiment. *Controlled* means that at least two arms of the experiment exist: one group of patients will receive the experimental drug, while a second group (the control group) will receive either a placebo or an established therapy. *Double-blind* means that neither the physician administering the drugs nor the patients receiving them know whether the human subjects are receiving the drug itself or a facsimile of it. The trial runs its course, the data are analyzed, and the FDA makes decisions based on the results.

Controversy, Consensus, and Conundrums

Obvious ethical questions confound the pure science of this approach. They are partially alleviated by a procedure that allows a trial to be halted if the experimental drug yields such overwhelming evidence of efficacy that it would be inhumane to continue to deny the control group the benefits of the therapy. This is exactly what happened in 1987, when the experimental group in the AZT trials proved to have a far lower mortality rate than the members of the control group. The trial was halted, and the FDA approved AZT for use against HIV itself.

As in all other aspects of the epidemic, however, irony compounded by uncertainty clouded the issues. Given the alternatives, the decision to stop the trial and begin marketing AZT was considered both politically and ethically sound at the time. This particular case, however, emphasizes one of the disadvantages of hasty approvals. In the short term, patients who could tolerate the extreme toxicities of the recommended dose of AZT experienced a dramatic increase in the number of their T4 cells. Since the increase in T4 cells translated into an improvement in the functioning of their immune systems, many of these patients flourished. However, the virus found a way to mutate so that AZT no longer worked its magic. Furthermore, some patients' systems reacted violently to the recommended dose of AZT, since one of its side effects is to limit the ability of the bone marrow to replenish the body's supply of red blood cells. For these patients, taking AZT was worse than taking nothing, since it led to severe anemia, which was quickly fatal if not corrected. At the time of the drug's approval, dosage had not been thoroughly tested. Eventually, a lower dose was found to be just as effective as the higher, toxic one, rendering the drug usable by a much larger number of patients.

With the knowledge that a lengthier drug approval process could perhaps have prolonged even more lives if scientists, physicians, and patients had known more about AZT and its toxicities, nationally prominent treatment advocacy groups split over whether to encourage the FDA to grant accelerated approval to a Hoffman-LaRoche product, the first protease inhibitor, saquinavir. For two years, treatment advocates within the community debated how to lobby the FDA with regard to therapies that gave every indication of being the first effective substances available for HIV/AIDS patients.

New York's Treatment Action Group (TAG), itself a splinter of ACT UP, sent a 20 June 1994, letter to David Kessler, then FDA Commissioner. In a radical departure from what had long

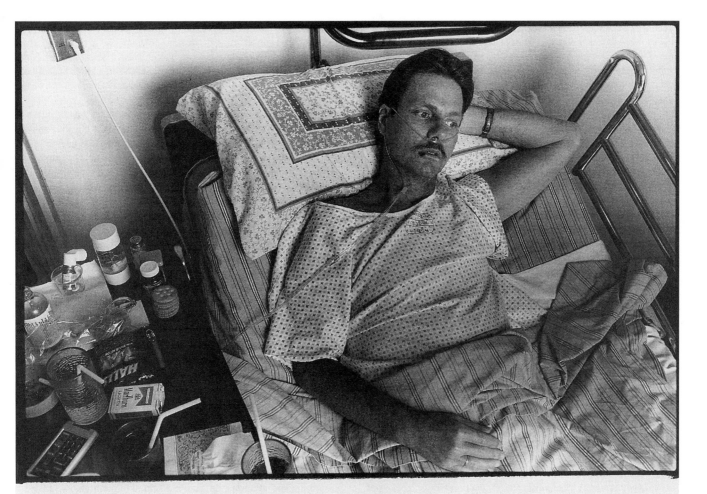

Because of the stage of my illness and the medication for it,
I feel confused and anxious most of the time.
What I want to tell someone is to hang on to what you
have. Time is short and you must not let it slip
away without enjoying every minute.
Also it's a time when you can let people see
who you really are so that you can be healed
and free.

Roger Haynes
June 28, 1988

An AIDS patient.

been activist "policy," TAG argued against accelerated approval for saquinavir. They stated, "We feel that such an approval would penalize people with AIDS/HIV by setting an inappropriately low standard of evidential requirements that would govern the regulation of this entire class of therapies" (Baker, 1994, p. 32). Not only did they oppose granting accelerated approval to Roche, but they also argued that all protease inhibitors, as a new class of therapies, should demonstrate clinical benefits, including either significantly delayed disease progression or increased survival time. To determine clinical efficacy, TAG proposed a traditional clinical trial approach as opposed to a fast-track process.

Other treatment advocacy groups began editorializing and lobbying for a different strategy. Having fought so long and so hard for access to treatments, experimental or not, in an effort to stop the dying, they greatly feared a return to the challenges and frustrations of the first eight years of the epidemic. Their fears were reinforced when *Barron's*, an influential financial magazine, ran a front-page article entitled "Do We Have Too Many Drugs for AIDS?" Writers had picked up on TAG's arguments and were letting their corporate readers know that an AIDS activist group was lobbying the FDA to slow down the drug approval process. If implemented, the return to former policies would negatively impact research costs and eventual profits, possibly meaning that fewer companies would be looking for new AIDS treatments.

More than fifty advocacy organizations and individuals endorsed a consensus statement (Baker, 1994, p. 32). They sent signed copies of the statement to public hearings of the National Task Force on AIDS Drug Development, where comments from all sides concerning the mechanisms in place for early access were heard. Debate and testimony raged for twenty hours over the two days. In what the *Bulletin of Experimental Treatments for AIDS* called "a rare show of unity," nearly everyone from community representatives to research scientists to clinicians favored accelerated approval of the promising new therapies. What was at issue was the timing and evaluation procedures for clinical efficacy (Baker, June 1995, p. 40).

Meetings, position papers, electronic messages, and political turmoil within advocacy agencies continued. TAG and some key supporters within GMHC, the National Minority AIDS Council, the Human Rights Campaign Fund, the AIDS Action Council, and AmFAR continued to support delaying accelerated approval, while ACT UP New York and some West Coast organizations supported a more radical position: "Let research subjects and their doctors determine risks and benefits in early research. Do not suppress and punish potential life-saving experimentation by overprotecting the public" (Baker, June 1995, p. 40). The new class of drugs proved so effective in the short term, and a decade of activism had been so successful, that a fast-track approval process for protease inhibitors was approved in the end.

In short, a lengthy process of testing and eventual approval theoretically means that efficacy against the pathogen has been proven; drug effects including toxicity, side effects, and interactions with other drugs have been thoroughly documented and reported; and the most effective means of administration and lowest effective dosage for all age groups and genders has been established. The tension between demands for therapies, proven or unproven, and the long-term consequences of knowledge gaps about some drugs approved through the fast-track process continues to plague clinicians, ethicists, researchers, and patients. Among the players in the AIDS epidemic, a broad consensus has emerged that basically attempts to strike a balance among the competing forces of scientific rigor, manufacturer profit, and patient need. Whether a conservative or an aggressive approach to drug approval will ultimately prove superior is unknown. What is evident is that while protease inhibitors, in combination with other drugs, have given new life to many patients, case reports of failures are becoming more common in late 1997.

No one pretends that the perfect balance has yet or ever will be found. These new processes attempt to maintain the integrity of the clinical trial process while at the same time providing access to drugs that might benefit patients who do not qualify for specific trials. Certainly, many HIV patients over the years have enjoyed longer lives and greater quality of life as the result of some of these provisions.

Alternatives to the Traditional Clinical Trials Process

Options outside of the standard process are often summarized with the term *expanded access*. Expanded access refers to any mechanism by which experimental drugs can be distributed to patients failing on currently available therapies and unable to participate in existing clinical trials. It is generally understood to include FDA regulations for compassionate use, parallel track (limited to HIV/AIDS patients), and treatment investigational new drugs (IND).

Alternative Medicine and AIDS

In the early days of the epidemic, the numbers of AIDS-related deaths escalated so quickly that many gay men, their partners, and friends began taking treatment and advocacy matters into their own hands. Some tried various herbal remedies, megadoses of vitamins and minerals, and other alternative methods of self-treatment. Once a few clinical trials were established, some patients participated in them, believing that some treatment, even if it was experimental, was surely preferable to doing nothing. The well-established gay grapevine hummed with the promise of various remedies, most of which could not be obtained legally in the United States. Groups of individuals banded together, pooled resources, dealt with foreign pharmacists, and even the U. S. Customs Service to bring promising treatments to desperate patients. Patients who could afford it traveled to Mexico or Canada or to countries in Europe to obtain treatment first-hand. Alternative healing and buyers' clubs were two ways patients assumed control over their lives. Both were forms of activism, and both have affected the way U.S. health care consumers generally approach medicine today.

The U.S. public first became aware of these operations in 1985, when newspapers reported on Rock Hudson's condition. AIDS activists quickly discovered that he was going to Paris for HPA-23, a drug being developed in a laboratory there. Jim Corti, a volunteer with AIDS Project Los Angeles (APLA), and others like him, had already started a de facto buyer's club, driving to Mexico in quest of medicines not approved for use in the United States. Buyers' clubs also became a way for scarce quantities of promising medicines to get to the greatest number of patients needing them. Sometimes approved drugs could not be obtained easily, so the clubs would supplement the U.S. supply with what was available from foreign manufacturers or even what could be made in bootleg laboratories. When patients died, sometimes leaving quantities of pharmaceuticals behind them, the buyers' clubs accepted the remainder and distributed it. Some of the people running these clubs were convinced either that a miracle cure existed or that the advent of AIDS was the result of a genocidal plot, but others simply did not want to wait for the wheels of science or corporations to turn at their usual plodding pace. "Guerrilla clinics" sprang up in some of the most devastated areas, such as Greenwich Village in New York, West Hollywood in Los Angeles, and the Castro District of San Francisco. People operating these clinics stayed in business because their customers wanted to believe that some miraculous potion would halt the relentless conversion of their cells to factories that produced yet more infection. As most individuals and institutions in official channels appeared not to heed the escalating numbers of deaths, desperate people tried anything that offered hope of treatment. As in so many other instances, the focus on alternative therapies among AIDS patients presaged a societal shift in their favor. More people than ever before, especially those suffering from chronic diseases, began extending their treatment options to include herbal remedies, acupuncture, and related nontraditional approaches. Acupressure, acupuncture, and massage therapy have been shown to help AIDS patients and are commonly used by many of them for the abatement of various symptoms. The tremendous popular interest in alternative medicine prompted NIH to establish the Office of Alternative Medicine (OAM) in 1992. OAM funds ten specialty research centers around the country to subject some nontraditional substances to the rigor of the clinical trial process. Bastyr University in Seattle, Washington, is the site where AIDS is studied.

Buyers' Clubs still exist, fulfilling a useful function for many patients and their caregivers. In fact, their numbers are larger than ever, even though at least eleven anti-HIV drugs are now on the market, and many more treatments for various opportunistic infections are available. In mid-1997, ACT UP's World Wide Web page listed fifteen clubs in the United States and two in Canada.

The Current Picture

And what have the protests, the activism, the reforms wrought? As the epidemic has evolved, so have its institutions, including ACT UP. Today, some of the activists who spent much of the past decade shouting in the streets, stopping the New York Stock Exchange, and chaining themselves inside corporate headquarters of multinational drug companies are wearing ties, sitting behind desks, and more often than not being policy wonks. Many of them have a seat at very highly placed tables whenever AIDS issues are discussed. AIDS patients today have more options than ever before in the history of the epidemic. In 1996, for the first time since 1981, deaths from HIV disease actually declined, thanks to the efficacy of sophisticated drug regimens. A combination of people and actions—outrageous acts of civil disobedience, powerful writing, dedicated clinicians, government bureaucrats, and basic scientists—has resulted in the development and approval of eleven anti-HIV drugs, an explosion of knowledge about the immune system, the transformation of the drug approval process, and a host of sociological effects throughout society that have yet to be fully realized. However, the dream of seeing HIV as a chronic, manageable illness remains just that—a dream, regardless of the promise of these new therapies.

The men and women of the gay community have reason, on balance, for cautious optimism and for celebration, for without their efforts, in partnership with policy makers and researchers at every level of government and industry, hundreds of patients who

have returned to nominal good health via combination therapy would probably not still be alive. Most of all, the gay and lesbian community has forged a strength bred by adversity and has demonstrated to the world how to confront crises and make a positive difference. Despite these triumphs, however, the community continues to suffer from the multiple losses inflicted by the epidemic.

COLLECTIVE GRIEVING

Individual and collective HIV-related losses have assaulted members of the community on multiple fronts. Partners, loved ones, friends, and family have succumbed to the ultimate desolation of the disease. Entire friendship networks have been wiped out. Social habits and norms have been altered, eradicated, or replaced. Basic human rights involving politics of the body have been questioned and threatened by the body politic. The veneer of anonymity—whether real or imagined, coveted or despised—has been stripped from many gays and lesbians. Where HIV and AIDS are concerned, grief extends well beyond its common association with death. Like an ominous spectre, the ravages of HIV and AIDS have cloaked the community in a shadowy shroud that has impacted people as seldom before.

The intense emotional and psychological suffering caused by HIV and AIDS has invoked the need for grieving on many levels. Multiple grief processes occurring simultaneously or spread out over time have intensified the feelings of loss. In order to cope, community members have had to recognize losses and engage in individual and collective grieving, mourning, confrontation, and reconciliation.

Progressing through the stages of grief and bereavement as identified by noted researcher Elizabeth Kubler-Ross—denial and isolation, anger, bargaining, depression, and acceptance—has proven to be difficult where HIV and AIDS are concerned, particularly for gays and lesbians. Society's lack of acceptance regarding the homosexual identity and same-sex partnerships has exacerbated further the resolution of grief. Varied, multiple, and repeated losses complicate the process more. In addition, traditional grief and bereavement support networks afforded their heterosexual counterparts historically have not been available to homosexuals. Moreover, existing support networks very often have crumbled due to mass mortality. Grief within the HIV/AIDS arena has been compounded by the social circumscription of the gay and lesbian community.

Society's treatment of homosexuality and homosexuals has left many community members justifiably weary of social interactions and processes. Quarantine and confinement have been recurring dangers proffered in the name of public health where the epidemic is concerned. Balancing the scales between individual rights and the public health remains an ongoing debate, one that has caused much division within and without the community. Although unprotected sex has proven to be an effective mode of HIV transmission, many gay men view any attempt to regulate sexual practices, including the use of condoms, as emasculation. Grief over the loss of the sexual freedom to do as one pleases is hard felt, given that the community had only recently begun fighting for that right—a right that wavers between perception and reality.

The sheer visibility of HIV and AIDS—whether through the physical evidence of a disfiguring disease or the volume of AIDS-related deaths—has removed the veil of anonymity from numerous gays and lesbians. Having the epidemic linked so closely with

I WATCHED MY LOVER DIE, AND REACH HIS ARMS TO HOLD GOD'S LOVE.

    HE WAS SO BRAVE...

      HE IS SO FREE.

ARCHIE STEPPED THROUGH THE LOOKING GLASS ON AUGUST 8, 1988.

          DREW

I am weaker, thinner now than when this photo was taken - it was only several months ago but it seems like years. Well... that's the illusion of time. The Spirit within, my true Self, no longer needs this body. It sounds cliché but soon I'll step "through the looking glass."
    I feel such peace
I wish he could come with me now - but I know, in an instant, we will join again.
       I am Love   Archie

The intense emotional and psychological suffering caused by AIDS has invoked the need for grieving on many levels.

the community has afforded an obvious presence, for better or worse, previously not enjoyed. While many community members have actively fought for increased recognition, others consider this forced visibility or "outing" a true loss. For some, loss of that anonymity is equated with a loss of security and protection.

The body politic historically has regulated—officially and unofficially—homosexuality and the practice of homosexual acts. Sodomy laws, medical management of homosexuality as a disease, and overt or covert discrimination are but three examples. Society in general traditionally has refused to accept the homosexual identity or to acknowledge same-sex partnerships. This lack of recognition directly affects HIV/AIDS-related grief among community members. Partners may or may not be allowed in the emergency room, intensive care unit, or at the hospital bedside as death approaches, since their relationship status is not recognized by law. Gays and lesbians who lose partners to AIDS-related deaths typically are not afforded the same mourning rites as their heterosexual counterparts. Few employers have official policies that extend bereavement leave to gay or lesbian survivors; even fewer organized religions legitimate the loss of a homosexual partner. And sadly, without proper planning and documentation, estates—lifetime properties, financial securities, possessions, and capital built and acquired as a couple—may be claimed by blood relatives or revert to the state.

Owing to the lack of traditional support networks, community members have had to be dependent upon one another in facing grief and bereavement. Unfortunately, many networks of friends and non-traditional family members have been destroyed by the onslaught of AIDS-related deaths. It is not uncommon for whole groups of friends to have been infected with HIV and subsequently died of AIDS-related causes. In addition to having entire social support networks wiped out, these multiple losses easily stand to magnify feelings of acute sorrow and sadness associated with grief and bereavement for individual survivors. In light of limited support, the community has responded with conscientious creativity.

ARTISTIC RESPONSE

HIV and AIDS have dramatically affected both the artistic community and the various creative industries, with the response—literary, performing, and visual—having been to create a noticeable and obvious presence of the illness that could not easily be denied. This highly visible, often visual, representation of the epidemic has helped force the general public to consider the malady in terms of real people rather than faceless strangers. Helping this effort along has been the diverse response from the creative industry, which has ranged in nature from individual artistic expression reflecting rage and remembrance to the formation of organizations such as the *Design Industries Foundation Fighting AIDS* (DIFFA) in 1984 or *Artists Confronting AIDS* in 1985. The artistic response also provided additional means to record the epidemiology of the disease. Although the artistic community has contributed significantly to humanizing HIV and AIDS, the response has received considerable criticism for its representation or misrepresentation of those individuals affected by the pandemic. Critics have argued consistently that the artistic response typically does not represent all affected populations and all too often misrepresents individuals with HIV, thus reinforcing stereotypes such as "HIV is a gay white male disease," or "AIDS equals death." The artistic response to the AIDS pandemic differs little, there-fore, in at least one respect from all other aspects of this disease: Dichotomy pervades the landscape.

The NAMES Project AIDS Memorial Quilt

Perhaps no response to this disease is more visible than the AIDS Memorial Quilt. Based on the American tradition of quilting, the AIDS Quilt is the world's largest continuing community arts project and is growing proportionately to the number of AIDS fatalities (http://www.aidsquilt.org/). This international effort constitutes a patchwork of remembrance, a celebration of lives lost. Each panel, measuring 3 feet by 6 feet or the size of a human grave, was created to honor the memory of someone who has died of AIDS-related causes. In its entirety, the Quilt covers more than 18 acres and weighs in excess of 50 tons. However, the Quilt represents only 21 percent of all U.S. AIDS-related deaths.

It may or may not be surprising that the gay men who initiated the NAMES Project selected a traditionally female art—quilting—to memorialize the dead. Historically, quilting has been viewed as a means for women to record the names of the deceased with cloth and thread. This quintessential American folk art, evoking nineteenth-century nostalgia and a sense of community, is in stark contrast to its masculine counterpart involving stone and steel to commemorate lives lost (Hawkins, 752-79).

Cleve Jones conceived, organized, and implemented the plan for the NAMES Project in the late 1980s, and the Quilt was displayed for the first time at the annual San Francisco Lesbian and Gay Freedom Day Parade on 28 June 1987 (Baker, 1994, p. 131). More than 9 million people have visited this traveling art exhibit that continues to be displayed in sections on a regular basis. Now international in scope, the NAMES Project has chapters in most U.S. states and affiliate offices in countries throughout the world.

In addition to recognizing the many individuals who have been lost to AIDS, the Quilt serves as a mechanism to validate the loss of the loved ones—partners, families, friends—who have been left behind. This validation of grief conceivably is of greatest importance to members of the gay and lesbian community, since more traditional mourning rites and support mechanisms may not be available. And this is the source of one of the Quilt's chief criticisms: that it shifts the attention from the dead to the living; it exists to benefit those who are grieving or mourning rather than those who are mourned. Critics also argue that the Quilt is too political or not political enough, panels are too personal or too impersonal, and the Project fosters passivism rather than activism (Baker, 1994, pp. 131-32). Despite criticisms however, Cleve Jones's goal to create a monument honoring the lives of those individuals lost to AIDS and acknowledging the emotions of those left behind has been achieved.

Visual Arts

Representing the disease and the epidemic in the visual arts—painting, photography, and sculpture—has been controversial for artists and critics alike. There has been little consensus as to whether the focus of the subject should be the HIV-infected individual, the more global perspective of the community surrounding the HIV-positive, the impact of the pandemic on society, or the societal circumscription of the HIV-infected individual. Also at issue has been the degree to which victimization, mortality, sexuality, and scorn for the body politic have been portrayed.

Perhaps the greatest, or at least the most visible, contribution of the visual arts community has been the recognition of HIV/AIDS in the form of the annual Day without Art. Begun 1 December 1989, primarily in New York by a group called *Visual AIDS*, this symbolic acknowledgment of the toll the epidemic has exacted is now carried out worldwide. As Jane Alexander, former chair of the National Endowment for the Arts, explained, "Day without Art is a powerful symbol of the devastating effect of AIDS on the arts community. This day reinforces the vitality and power art brings to our daily lives by showing how the absence of art leaves a void of spirit" (Alexander). How much art has been, and will continue to be, lost to AIDS? One need think only of the whimsical cartoon characters of Keith Haring or the photography of Robert Mapplethorpe and literally hundreds of other talents to begin fathoming the enormity of the loss.

Photodocumentaries

Photodocumentaries concerning this chronic illness typically have been produced for two stated reasons: (1) to validate the existence of those individuals living with HIV, recording the reality and gravity of the epidemic; and (2) to serve as a means by which to raise funds for AIDS service organizations. The emergence of these collections as a genre is fairly recent. They have been both a direct and indirect byproduct of the pandemic, and vary in structure and content. Women, children, and infants, when included at all, are typically under represented. Some photodocumentaries are interspersed with text; part include inscriptions; and others allow the photographs to speak for themselves. The unifying factor is that in some way, whether through subject matter or purpose, they are all concerned with HIV and AIDS and the individuals directly or indirectly affected.

Early photographic collections often were seen as a necessary means by which to put a face with the disease, a way to humanize the illness. These images typically were viewed as a vehicle to present the epidemic in a manner that could not be censored or ignored by society. Sadly, though, the people with AIDS in these photographs were generally depicted alone, often bearing the visible lesions of Kaposi's sarcoma, tied to life support systems, struggling in the extreme stage of illness. This continues to be a common—although not necessarily representational—image of the person with HIV. While these portraits brought the reality of AIDS home to mainstream America, they also perpetuated the societal perception that AIDS equals death. This image nurtured the belief that public health was threatened by the HIV- infected individual's roaming freely throughout society, thus strengthening the argument for quarantine and isolation. The potential benefit derived from these photographs often was overshadowed by the fatal message they delivered, one that could be twisted to cement the social construct framing the disease.

At the opposite end of the spectrum are those photographs displaying the splendor of the human body. These images of healthy, muscled bodies harken to the pre-AIDS era devoid of the manifestations of HIV infection and its various legal, medical, psychological, religious, and social complexities. Portraits of this nature commemorate life and the human form. They appear to possess an air of innocence. This genre typically has been produced with the intent to raise funds for community-based AIDS service organizations. These images, created to capture the spirit of the living, reminisce about humanity and the beauty of the body. As with their counterparts though, these photographs have failed to

strike the balance necessary to avoid societal influence and the continued regulation of HIV by the body politic. The images were completely removed from the cultural context of HIV and AIDS. In order to provide financial support, humanity was depicted as being free from the very illness for which the work was generated. In addition, they lack the complexities associated with the social construct of the pandemic. The unaffectedness of the subject almost suggests that disease transmission implies guilt or blame, unintentionally bolstering the contention for ostracism or confinement.

Music

Music has the power to provoke thought or emotion or to soothe and comfort the soul. It has been called the purest form of poetry, intrinsically lyrical in nature. Music contains messages that people tap into, identify with, and relate to at a personal level. And the music of AIDS is littered with the same dichotomies that pervade much of the epidemic, those of rage and remembrance (Baker, 1994, p. 116).

The music establishment, like other artistic communities, has been criticized for its response to the epidemic. While the music world has been quick to host grand AIDS-related fundraisers, the profession has been equally quick to turn its collective back on its HIV-infected own. It is, after all, a commercial industry. A notable exception, however, is the Red Hot organization. In addition to creating and producing a series of AIDS-related musical benefit projects, the organization has used its broadcast forum for educational purposes relative to HIV. The Red Hot organization's fifth special in the series, *Stolen Moments: Red Hot + Cool*, tackles difficult issues resulting from the rise in incidence of HIV among communities of color.

Another notable contribution from the music world is that of singer William Parker. An internationally known concert and opera baritone, he discovered he was HIV-positive in 1988. Rather than retiring, Parker's response to his diagnosis was to gather some of the nation's foremost composers to assist him in creating *The AIDS Quilt Songbook 1992*, a song cycle that memorializes those claimed by the epidemic. *Songbook* premiered in New York's Alice Tully Hall in Lincoln Center on 4 June 1992. The collective work is a musical rendition of the AIDS Memorial Quilt and consists of diverse musical scores backing lyrics derived from poems about AIDS.

Dance

Dance, the most transitory of art forms, depends primarily on the substance and fluidity of human flesh. It exists, for the most part, in the present. "No other art form—even theater—is quite so dependent on being experienced live. Theater, after all, can be written down, transcribed, filmed, or videotaped, with much of its immediacy preserved intact. Dance never 'lives' on a screen or a page in anything other than two-dimensional moving pictures (in the case of film and video) or frozen moments (still photography)" (Baker, 1994, p. 104). Because of its dependence on human form and necessity to be experienced live, AIDS-related devastation to the dance world is tremendous. In the wake of this disease, countless dancers, choreographers, corps dancers and chorus boys, costumers, designers, dressers, and other behind-the-scenes support people have been lost to the world of dance forever. In dance, more so than in other art forms, the loss cannot be duplicated or replaced. "And in an art so dependent on form, grace, and bodily beauty, AIDS has been especially brutal, attacking, as it does, the very tools of the dancer's trade: the face, the body, even agility itself" (Baker, 1994, p. 104).

Given the extreme and highly visible impact of the pathological on this ephemeral art form, a mixed community response is not unexpected. The struggle relative to HIV within the dance world has been two-fold. At one level, individuals have grappled with striking a balance between "outing" the HIV positive and total denial as to the existence of the disease among members of the dance enclave. On another level, the battle between individual privacy and community denial has been pitted against the desire to craft professional response to the disease in the form of original choreography and performance. The transitory nature of the art form and the utter devastation wreaked by AIDS seem to have been matched by the need to create a live, vocational presence—dance.

Television

Television is one of the most public communication forums in modern society, reaching literally millions of people everyday. The potential for television as an educational and entertainment medium is tremendous, as is its ability to influence individual attitudes and beliefs. However, television is big business, driven by profit, and the profit-driven nature of the industry directly affects what is actually broadcast for public consumption. This influence is apparent where the stigma of HIV and AIDS is concerned.

Both commercially broadcast and cable television could have been used to allay unwarranted fears by educating people as to how HIV is and is not transmitted, realistically depicting individuals affected by the disease, and fostering empathy toward those individuals. However, programming involving HIV/AIDS and individuals affected by the disease has all too often proven controversial enough to prevent this from being the case. CNN, of course, is a notable exception, as it has provided excellent news coverage of the epidemic since the early 1980s. And there are other exceptions as well, including the various specials and made-for-television movies produced in response to the pandemic.

Regular television programming involving HIV/AIDS has evolved in parallel with the disease. Today, HIV-infected characters appear on many daytime soap operas and nighttime dramas. Mode of HIV transmission may not always be evident and character portrayal of the HIV-positive may not always be realistic, but at least the disease has become visible in this very public forum. Mainstream television shows such as *ER* have incorporated HIV-infected characters into the regular storylines. And the evolution has even come so far as to include an evening show, *413 Hope Street*, whose main plot revolves around HIV-positive characters.

Film

At best, Hollywood and the film industry have been slow to respond to the epidemic, despite the fact that this artistic community has been hard hit. Initial response came from independent film producers, not the major motion picture moguls. As a profit-driven industry, Hollywood shied away from the stigmatized disease. Even though New York playwright Craig Lucas's *Longtime Companion* was the closest Hollywood came to dealing with AIDS in a major motion picture prior to *Philadelphia*, it was rejected by

every major studio and finally financed by PBS' *American Playhouse* in 1990 (Baker, 1994, pp. 35-36).

Hollywood's long-lived battle with homophobia and hypocrisy overshadowed the toll HIV was beginning to take on the community. Although the ravages of AIDS were becoming apparent among the individuals who feed the Hollywood illusion—actors, directors, producers, screen writers, makeup artists, costumers, designers, hairdressers, etc.—those known to be HIV-infected were deemed no more than industry pariah. A prime example of this was documented in the words of actor Brad Davis just prior to his AIDS-related death in September 1991: "I make my money in an industry that professes to care very much about the fight against AIDS—that gives umpteen benefits and charity affairs with proceeds going to research and care. But in actual fact, if an actor is even rumored to have HIV he gets no support on an individual basis. He does not work" (McFarlane, p. 91).

The meager professional contributions Hollywood has made have been widely criticized. Criticism, as with other genres, has tended to focus on the representation or misrepresentation of the individuals affected by the disease. Some argue that films like *Longtime Companion* and *Philadelphia* strengthen the misperception that HIV is a gay, white, upper-middle class disease. Others contend that gay relationships are "candy coated" and emasculated so as to be more palatable to the masses. Another criticism is that gays are stereotyped and that those stereotypes perpetuate misperceptions of the community. And in a similar vein, some complain of the heterosexual actor's over-dramatization of his interpretation of the gay male (such as Eric Roberts portraying the lead character, Nick, in *It's My Party*), comparable to the overt gesticulations of a drag queen's impersonating a female. For all of the criticisms and complaints however, it should not be overlooked that these films have provided a vehicle for delivering messages about AIDS to mainstream society.

Theater

"Theater has traditionally been an art form that challenges its audience" (Baker, 1994, p. 176). More intimate than screen or television, the theater allows actors to deliver their lines and give life to the playwright's message with a physical presence that often confronts the audience. The theater has been far from immune to the ravages of AIDS. And in the theater, the connection of HIV with the gay community is painfully apparent, for "what other profession is as gay-identified as theatre?" (Mordden, p. 39).

Given the atmosphere of intimate confrontation and close association with gays, it is not surprising that the theater became home to strong statements about the epidemic early on. Key contributions from playwrights began as early as 1984 and have continued ever since. Many of these plays have been produced Off-Broadway or Off-Off-Broadway in New York City or on smaller, perhaps lesser known, regional stages around the country. Not all have been well received or enjoyed long runs. Some have been criticized for depicting HIV/AIDS through a comedic eye; others for delving into the darker sides of the epidemic. Despite criticisms and waxing and waning support, however, the theater continues to raise its voice in artistic response to the HIV/AIDS pandemic.

Literature

The tremendous literary outpouring in response to HIV/AIDS began early on in the epidemic. Literature may be read

The AIDS Memorial Quilt being shown in Washington, D.C.

as a socio-historical record of the spread and impact of the epidemic. Today, virtually every literary genre is represented, ranging in nature from drama or poetry to fiction and nonfiction. AIDS-related histories, survival guides, biographies, and personal narratives have now given way to what may be termed AIDS studies—detailed literary analyses of various facets of the epidemic.

Literature has been perhaps the least criticized of the artistic responses to HIV/AIDS and probably the most honest in its portrayal of the realities of the disease. In addition to major publishing houses producing works concerning the pandemic, smaller publishers catering to gays and lesbians have been particularly attentive to the community's need to respond to the death surrounding it. Although gay and lesbian literature may be seen as an emerging literary genre, it is established well enough to have afforded authors a mechanism to react to the devastating toll of the epidemic. Within this pubescent body of literature, writers, for the most part, do not have to conform to the standards set by mainstream society. Since the majority of the target audience is the homosexual community, gays and lesbians can be depicted realistically. However, the criticism that does exist concerning the literary response has arisen, for the most part, from the brutal honesty authors have employed in describing the community.

Heavily influenced by the epidemic, the artistic and creative communities ultimately have responded with a level of visibility befitting their respective professions. Whether the response is visual or aural, one dimensional or three, live or recorded, the overall result is the same—the humanization of HIV/AIDS. Although societal influence affects the commercial viability of art, individuals supported by the creative industries have managed to generate an artistic response to the disease that is searing in its portrayal of loss.

CONCLUSION

Miracles and heroism, defeats and denials continue to define the rhetoric, events, and responses of and to the HIV/AIDS pandemic. Wherever the disease reaches in the United States, and whomever it affects, the gay and lesbian community—historically a faintly visible yet openly scorned minority by society at large—remains central to both the ravages and the solutions to the terrible tolls of AIDS. Dichotomy retains its central position in the social stratum bound by the epidemic.

Since 1981, HIV/AIDS patients have elicited compassion from at least some individuals. Often this compassion has taken the form of financial support for various AIDS-related charities. Evidence suggests, however, that compassion has evolved into compassion fatigue. In 1987, *Newsweek* published a story about AIDS fundraising entitled "The Fashionable Charity." Ten years later, the *Wall Street Journal* concluded one of its HIV-related stories, "AIDS is no longer the disease *du jour*" (Burkstrand, p. B7). Compassion fatigue is inflicting great damage on charitable giving. A long-time donor, explaining why she would no longer contribute, said, "My heart doesn't break for them anymore" (Heitz, p. 27), and she spoke of the rising rate in new infections among gay men, particularly young gay men. A greater threat looming over the community, even more than loss of funding, is the loss of what good will, understanding, and respect has rightfully accrued to it. A rising body count may erase forever the small gains achieved at so great a price.

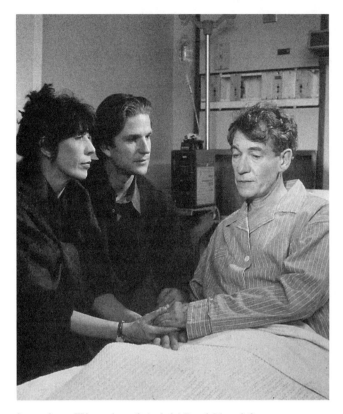

Scene from TV version of *And the Band Played On*.

Ironically, improved treatments mean that AIDS service organizations (ASOs) are facing perhaps the greatest crisis in their short history. The drug cocktails have had the effect of straining agency resources at the very time the organizations are trying to begin serving populations beyond the middle-class, gay, white males who formed such a huge share of the original caseload. Moreover, the cost of these treatments that spell at least some hope for life speaks in cruelly ironic tones to the majority of patients, who can by no means afford them.

Frustration and denial continue to permeate some portions of the AIDS arena. The hedonism evident in the lifestyle choices and sexual behavior of some members of the gay community are in part a denial of the existence of disease; frustration in the face of such attitudes marks the reaction of all those fighting against the epidemic. Yet, while the upsurge in infections may be grabbing the headlines, heroic acts, large and small, exist everywhere. Jose Zuniga (deputy director of the International Association of Physicians in AIDS Care), appearing on CNN's *Headline News* to announce that 50 individuals have volunteered to test a weakened, live vaccine for HIV, explained the motivation behind the act: "I am volunteering for the live attenuated HIV vaccine trial out of a sense of hope in the promise that a live attenuated HIV vaccine may curb the further spread of this disease, and out of a sense of rage that 16 years into the epidemic, we continue to see 8,500 new infections a day worldwide, among them 1,000 children born with HIV."

The increased visibility that AIDS has brought to the gay and lesbian community offers a great opportunity. Speaking at a town meeting in Dallas on 1 May 1997, Elizabeth Birch, executive director of the Human Rights Campaign, posed a challenge: "When

AIDS is all over and done, the gay and lesbian community will not be judged on how well they took care of their own, but on how they took care of everybody with HIV/AIDS" (Schield Interview, 1997). Certainly the major ASOs are making promising strides in this direction. Working toward achieving such a goal can take the lesbian and gay community outside of itself to unite with a global coalition against a common foe currently claiming thousands of lives world-wide. Through such an effort, the political goal shared by Urvashi Vaid, Mathilde Krim, and thousands of others can be achieved: full acceptance of homosexuality as a legitimate sexual orientation. It could result in the greatest irony of the whole epidemic: that millions of future lives are incomparably enriched owing to the loss of thousands of lives in the past and present.

While the ideal achievement would be to have homosexuality generally accepted and gays and lesbians credited with caring for all who are HIV-affected, the impact that such a physically disfiguring disease has had on a community where appearance is such a major focus cannot be underestimated. In a culture where health and beauty are so important, HIV has devastated individuals long before the disease has exacted its ultimate toll. Moreover, HIV transgresses the boundaries of life and death themselves, littering the community of survivors with often unresolved trauma and grief. Far beyond the massive numbers claimed by the pathological repercussions, the epidemic has affected the community in ways seldom, if ever, seen before.

REFERENCES:

Books

AIDS Project Los Angeles. *AIDS: A Self-Care Manual*. Santa Monica, California: IBS Press, 1987.

Baker, Rob. *The Art of AIDS*. New York: Continuum, 1994.

Bayer, Ronald. *Private Acts, Social Consequences: AIDS and the Politics of Public Health*. New York: Free Press, 1989.

Browning, Frank. *The Culture of Desire: Paradox and Perversity in Gay Lives Today*. New York: Crown, 1993.

Burkett, Elinor. *The Gravest Show on Earth: America in the Age of AIDS*. Boston: Houghton Mifflin Company, 1995.

Callen, Michael. *Surviving AIDS*. New York: HarperCollins, 1990.

———. *Surviving and Thriving with AIDS: Collected Wisdom*. New York: People With AIDS Coalition, 1988.

Corea, Gena. *The Invisible Epidemic: The Story of Women and AIDS*. New York: HarperCollins, 1992.

Foucault, Michel. *The History of Sexuality. Volume I: An Introduction*, translated from the French by Robert Hurley. New York: Random House, 1978.

Greenberg, Raymond S., et al. *Medical Epidemiology*. Norwalk, CT: Appleton & Lange, 1996.

Hewitt, M. *Bio-Politics and Social Policy: Foucault's Account on Welfare*, in *The Body: Social Process and Cultural Theory*, edited by Mike Featherstone, Mike Hepworth, and Bryan S. Turner. London: Sage Publications, 1991: 225-55.

Huber, Jeffrey T. *HIV/AIDS Community Information Services: Experiences in Serving Both At-Risk and HIV-Infected Populations*. New York: Haworth Press, 1996.

Juhasz, Alexandra. *AIDS TV: Identity, Community, and Alternative Video*. Videography by Catherine Saalfield. Durham, North Carolina: Duke University Press, 1995.

Kinsella, James. *Covering the Plague: AIDS and the American Media*. New Brunswick New Jersey: Rutgers University Press, 1989.

Klein, Michael, ed. *Poets for Life: Seventy-Six Poets Respond to AIDS*, essays by Paul Moore, Jr., Joseph Papp, and Carol Muske. New York: Crown Publishers, 1989.

Kramer, Larry. *The Normal Heart*. New York: New American Library, 1985.

Kubler-Ross, E. *On Death and Dying*. New York: Macmillan, 1969.

Kwitny, Jonathan. *Acceptable Risks*. New York: Poseidon Press, 1992.

Lapierre, Dominique. *Beyond Love*, translated from the French by Kathryn Spink. New York: Warner Books, 1990.

Monette, Paul. *Borrowed Time: An AIDS Memoir*. San Diego, California: Harcourt Brace Jovanovich, 1988.

Mordden, Ethan. *Buddies*. New York: St. Martin's Press, 1982.

Muma, Richard D., et al. *HIV Manual for Health Care Professionals*. Norwalk, Connecticut: Appleton & Lange, 1994.

Murphy, Timothy F. and Suzanne Poirier, eds. *Writing AIDS: Gay Literature, Language, and Analysis*. New York: Columbia University Press, 1993.

Nassaney, Louie. *I Am Not a Victim: One Man's Triumph over Fear & AIDS*. Santa Monica, California: Hay House, 1990.

Nussbaum, Bruce. *Good Intentions: How Big Business and the Medical Establishment are Corrupting the Fight Against AIDS*. New York: Atlantic Monthly Press, 1990.

Osborn, M. Elizabeth, ed. *The Way We Live Now: American Plays & the AIDS Crisis*, introduction by Michael Feingold. New York: Theatre Communications Group, 1990.

Peabody, Barbara. *The Screaming Room: A Mother's Journal of Her Son's Struggle with AIDS: A True Story of Love, Dedication, and Courage*. San Diego, California: Oak Tree Publishers, 1986.

Pies, Cheri. "Insemination: Something More to Consider," in *AIDS: The Women*, edited by Ines Rieder and Patricia Ruppelt. San Francisco: Cleis Press, 1988.

Ruskin, Cindy. *The Quilt: Stories from the NAMES Project*, photographs by Matt Herron, design by Deborah Zemke, introduction by Elizabeth Taylor. New York: Pocket Books, 1988.

Shilts, Randy. *And the Band Played On: Politics, People, and the AIDS Epidemic*. New York: Penguin, 1988.

Stine, Gerald S. *AIDS Update 1993*. Englewood Cliffs, New Jersey: Prentice-Hall, 1993.

———. *AIDS Update 1997*. Englewood Cliffs, New Jersey: Prentice-Hall, 1997.

Stone, Deborah. "A Selfish Kind of Giving." In Rieder and Ruppelt, 1988: p. 143.

Watney, Simon. *Policing Desire: Pornography, AIDS, and the Media*. Minneapolis: University of Minnesota Press, 1996.

Watney, Simon. *Practices of Freedom: Selected Writings on HIV/AIDS*. Durham, North Carolina: Duke University Press, 1994.

Periodical Articles

Altman, Lawrence. "Rare Cancer Seen in 41 Homosexuals," in *New York Times*, 3 July 1981: A/20.

Baker, Ronald. "Accelerated Approval for New AIDS Drugs Faces Uncertain Future," in *BETA: Bulletin on Experimental Treatments for AIDS*, September 1994.

———. "Reform at FDA: Faster Access to Promising Drugs?" in *BETA: Bulletin on Experimental Treatments for AIDS*, June 1995.

———. "Summit Meeting on Protease Inhibitor Drugs," in *BETA: Bulletin on Experimental Treatments for AIDS*, March 1995: 31-36.

Bull, Chris. "Compassion Fatigue," in *The Advocate*, 27 May 1997: 42.

Bull, Chris and Gallagher, John. "The Lost Generation," in *The Advocate*, 31 May 1994: 36-40.

Burkstrand, Beth. "AIDS Charities Suffer as Treatments Improve," in *Wall Street Journal*, 6 June 1997: B/1, 7.

Burr, Chandler. "The AIDS Exception: Privacy vs. Public Health," in *Atlantic Monthly*, June 1997: 57-67.

Carton, Barbara. "New AIDS Drug Brings Hope to Provincetown, but Unexpected Woes," in *Wall Street Journal*, 3 October 1996: A/1, 6.

CDC. *HIV/AIDS Surveillance Report*, vol. 7, no. 2, 1995.

———. *HIV/AIDS Surveillance Report*, vol. 8, no. 2, 1996.

———. *HIV/AIDS Surveillance Report*, vol. 9, no. 1, 1997.

———. "Kaposi's Sarcoma and Pneumocystis Pneumonia Among Homosexual Men—New York City and California," in *MMWR Morbidity and Mortality Weekly Report*, 3 July 1981: 305-08.

———. "Update on Acquired Immune Deficiency Syndrome (AIDS)—United States," *MMWR—Morbidity and Mortality Weekly Report*, 24 September 1982: 507-08, 513-14.

Duesberg, Peter. "HIV Is Not the Cause of AIDS," in *Science*, 29 July 1988: 514, 517.

Elifson, K.W., Boles, J., and Sweat, M. "Risk Factors Associated with HIV Infection Among Male Prostitutes," in *American Journal of Public Health*, vol. 83, vol. 1, 1993: 79-83.

Gallagher, John. "Slipping Up: The Return of Our Bad Habits," in *The Advocate*, 8 July 1997: 33-34.

Gerbert, B., et al. "Primary Care Physicians and AIDS: Attitudinal and Structural Barriers to Care," in *JAMA*, 27 November 1991: 2837-42.

Girard, P. M. "Pentamidine Aerosol in Prophylaxis and Treatment of Murine Pneumocystis Carinii Pneumonia," in *Antimicrobial Agents and Chemotherapy*, vol. 31, 1987: 978-81.

Gottlieb, G.J., et al. "A Preliminary Communication on Extensively Disseminated Kaposi's Sarcoma in Young Homosexual Men," in *American Journal of Dermatopathology*, 1981: 111-14.

Guly, Christopher. "The Invisible Lesbian Face of AIDS," in *The Advocate*, 6 September 1994: 45.

Harding, Rick. "Gay Direct Action Comes of Age," in *The Advocate*, 21 November 1988: 10-13.

Harris, C., et al. "Immunodeficiency in Female Sexual Partners of Men with the Acquired Immunodeficiency Syndrome," in *New England Journal of Medicine*, 19 May 1983: 1181-84.

Hawkins P.S. "Naming Names: The Art of Memory and the NAMES Project AIDS Quilt," in *Critical Inquiry*, vol. 19, no. 4, Summer 1993: 752-79.

Heitz, David. "HIV Dormancy Theory Challenged," in *The Advocate*, 16 January 1990: 29.

———. "Men Behaving Badly," in *The Advocate*, 8 July 1997: 26-28.

Helquist, Michael. "Update on Getting Tested," in *The Advocate*, 6 June 1989: 36.

Ho, David, Moudgil, T., and Alam, M. "Quantitation of Human Immunodeficiency Virus Type 1 in the Blood of Infected Persons," in *New England Journal of Medicine*, 14 December 1989: 1621-25.

"Homosexuality: Coming Out, or Pushed?" in *The Economist*, 4 August 1990: 20.

James, John S. "AIDS/ARC Guerrilla Clinics Spread," in *AIDS Treatment News #019*, 7 December 1986.

Kuller, Karen. "Happiness Reigns in the Drug Marketplace," in *GMHC Treatment Issues*, April/May 1997: 6-8.

Levy, Dan. "A Decade of AIDS Activism Changed America—and ACT UP," in *San Francisco Chronicle*, 22 March 1997: A/1.

McFarlane, Rodger. "Taking a Hit: Reeling from Crucial Losses to AIDS, Hollywood Still Struggles with Issues of HIV Discrimination," in *The Advocate*, 20 August 1996: 91-93.

Merz, B. "Aerosolized Pentamidine Promising in Pneumocystis Therapy, Prophylaxis," in *JAMA*, no. 259, 1988: 3223-24.

Mirken, Bruce. "AIDS Agencies Struggle to Change: Shifting AIDS Demographics Demand New Programs," in *The Advocate*, 25 February 1992: 42-44.

Nelson, Harry. "Mysterious Fever Now an Epidemic: Started with Gays," in *Los Angeles Times*, 31 May 1982: A/1, 3, 20.

Oleske, J., et al. "Immune Deficiency in Children," in *JAMA*, 6 May 1983: 2345-49.

Remien, R.H., Carballo-Dieguez, A., and Wagner, G. "Intimacy and Sexual Risk Behaviour in Serodiscordant Male Couples," in *AIDS Care*, 1995: 429-38.

"Report Asks Service Providers to Help Tackle HIV Violence," in *AIDS Policy Law*, 3 May 1996: 5.

Reyes, David. "Project to Target Hate Crimes Against Gays—Civil Rights: The Objective Is to Increase Awareness of Such Attacks and to Spur Vigorous Police and Public Response to Them," in *Los Angeles Times*, Orange County Edition, 5 May 1991.

Sanford, David. "One Man's AIDS Tale Shows How Quickly Epidemic Has Turned," in *Wall Street Journal*, 8 November 1996: A/1, 10.

Simmons, Todd. "Comeback Kid," in *The Advocate*, 3 October 1995: 36-43.

Internet Sites

AIDS Education Global Information Service (AEGIS). http://www.aegis.com/. Perhaps the most comprehensive site available.

AIDS Treatment Data Network. http://www.aidsnyc.org/network/index.html. Contains one-page fact sheets about opportunistic infections and treatments, as well as other information.

Bastyr University AIDS Research Center. http://www.bastyr.edu/research/research.html. Contains information about the use of alternative and complementary therapies to treat HIV and HIV-related infections and conditions.

The Body: A Multimedia HIV/AIDS Resource. http://www.thebody.com/cgi-bin/body.cgi. "Insight from Experts," a question and answer forum, is particularly well developed.

HIV/AIDS Prevention. http://www.dcd.gov/nchstp/hiv_aids/chap.thm. Contains key governmental prevention information and links to prevention sites.

HIV/AIDS Project, Vanderbilt University Medical School. http://www.mc.vanderbilt.edu/adl/aids_project/internet.html. Encyclopedic listing of the huge variety of Internet sites.

HIV InSite. http://hivinsite.ucsf.edu/. Contains the full text of *The AIDS Knowledge Base* in a fully searchable format. Also includes population-specific summaries from the Center for AIDS Prevention Studies. Some bilingual areas.

JAMA HIV/AIDS Information Center. http://www.ama-assn.org/ special/hiv/hivhome.htm. Contains full-text of many HIV-related articles from the *Journal of the American Medical Association*, as well as a link to a database of United States physicians specializing in HIV/AIDS care.

National AIDS Clearinghouse. http://cdcnac.aspensys.com/. The *AIDS Daily Summary* originates here. Email reference service, hotline numbers, and order form for AIDS-related publications included.

National Library of Medicine, free medical databases. http://www.nlm.nih.gov/. Currently offers *AIDSLINE, AIDSDRUGS,* and *AIDSTRIALS*, as well as several other medical databases, available free via Internet Grateful Med. Instructions for use appear online.

National Library of Medicine, HIV/AIDS-Related Internet Resources. http://sis.nlm.nih.gov/aidir1.htm. Contains links to all the community-produced newsletters indexed by NLM and available via the Internet.

New York Online Access to Health. http://www.noah.cuny.edu/. Completely bilingual, English and Spanish. AIDS resources include links to New York City area organizations and services.

Organizations

AIDS Project Los Angeles. http://www.apla.org/apla/

American Foundation for AIDS Research. http://www.amfar.org/

Critical Path AIDS Project. http://www.critpath.org/

Gay Men's Health Crisis. http://www.gmhc.org/

International Association of Physicians in AIDS Care. http://www.iapac.org/

The NAMES Project AIDS Memorial Quilt. http://www.aidsquilt.org/

People with AIDS Health Group. http://www.aidsnyc.org/pwahg/index.html

Project Inform. http://www.projinf.org/

San Francisco AIDS Foundation. http://www.sfaf.org/

Other

Alexander, Jane. Media release from *Visual AIDS*, 22 November 1993.

CNN. "Sexual Roulette," on *Impact*, 9 March 1996 and 18 August 1996.

Elbaz, G. "ACT UP as a Social Movement." Paper presented at the Ninth International Conference on AIDS, Berlin, Germany, 16-21 June 1991.

Gordon, Derek. Telephone interview by Mary L. Gillaspy. 11 September 1997.

Huber, Jeffrey T., and Gillaspy, Mary L. "Controlled Vocabulary for HIV/AIDS: An Evolving Nosological Record of a Diseased Body of Knowledge," in *Knowledge Organization and Change*. Proceedings of the Fourth Biannual Conference of the International Society for Knowledge Organization, Washington, D.C., 15-18 July 1996: 293-301.

Lauritsen, John. "Review: *Impure Science*, by Steven Epstein." sci.med.aids, 20 July 1997.

Schield, Jamie. Interview by Mary Gillaspy. 2 May 1997. AIDS Resource Center, Dallas, Texas.

Shaw, W. Fred. "Sexual Roulette: The Protease Inhibitor Sweepstakes." sci.med.aids. 6 September 1997. Commentary and notes from CNN broadcast.

Zuniga, Jose. CNN Headline News. 21 September 1997.

—Mary Gillaspy and Jeffrey T. Huber

8

Education and Scholarship

- University Rights and Privileges
- Academics
- Campus Life
- Academic Production and Scholarship
- Prominent People
- Programs in Gender and Lesbian, Gay, Bisexual, and Transgender Studies at Universities in the United States and Canada

---

Many universities now offer several kinds of services and programs for their queer students. One researcher reported that "thirty institutions have full-time administrators whose sole responsibility is coordinating gay and lesbian activities," a number twice that found in 1992 (Gose, 1996). These services are now beginning to assume some standard forms: undergraduate and graduate courses with significant LGBT content, undergraduate programs in LGBT studies (certificate- or degree-granting), LGBT student centers, and financial aid for LGBT students or for students doing research in queer studies. In addition, university queer communities have usually organized themselves into an assortment of associations; on most university campuses there is a student group, usually recognized by the student governing body, while alumni and alumnae of many universities have also organized; less commonly, there is a LGBT faculty and staff group.

Historically, it is clear that the first to come were the LGBT courses, while financial aid for queer students is the most recent phenomenon; over the past five to ten years programs and centers have been cropping up at universities more or less simultaneously, sometimes the one or the other, occasionally both. Nonetheless, within the last ten years and dramatically within the last five years, LGBT programs, centers, and courses have become noticeably numerous, resulting in a snowballing of resources and services, especially alumni organizations, on-campus legal rights or privileges for LGBT students and employees, and financial aid.

There are many reasons for the recent burst of academic attention given to queer studies and to LGBT students and staff and their campus life. In terms of politics, rights, and privileges, the progress of the liberation movement, broadly conceived, has induced a climate for change in the country over the past generation: gay liberation and the women's movement, including the drive for the Equal Rights Amendment (ERA) and the continuous discourse over the place of lesbians, may themselves be considered to be movements grounded in and parallel to the Civil Rights Move-

ment. In terms of curriculum, the solid and legitimate place that women's studies have secured in the academic world has paved the way for the appearance of queer studies. (For a list of women's studies programs, see http://www.users.interport.net/~kater.) In addition, the current national debates over sex-discrimination, sexual harassment, homosexuals in the military, family values, and, recently, the right for homosexuals to marry, have all highlighted the peripheral place lesbians and gay men occupy in the legal system. It is not surprising, therefore, to see such tensions also played out on campus.

One recent development, however, is part of a national academic revolution: the Internet and the university community's access to it. Although e-mail is now more than 25 years old, it has only been since the early 1990s that the humanities have exploited the Internet to provide a type of communication that approximates direct conversation. On the national level, dialogues on queer issues and the exchange of information once took place mostly at annual national conventions where hundreds participated; they now take place daily and involve thousands of people. If the various intellectual and action movements have set the stage for what now seems like a queer revolution, e-mail and the World Wide Web have turned on the spotlight.

The sections that follow will examine the various forms LGBT life and study have assumed on campus. While these forms are always interconnected, I find that some, like a university's inclusion of sexual orientation in its antidiscrimination clause or a university's decision to support courses in queer studies, provide the incentive for the development of other privileges, such as spousal benefits and umbrella programs, respectively; similarly, out of courses arise eventually an academic program that provides them context. For these reasons I will discuss the major developments of LGBT life, resources, and scholarship on campus in thematic groups. Finally, sketches of seven people active in the area of queer academics close this contribution.

Terminology and Focus

Because of the disparate nature of the material I am describing here, and the different kinds of audiences it targets, I shall use a terminology that includes lesbians, gay men, bisexuals, transgendered people and transsexuals (LGBT) within the more inclusive term "queer"; I shall avoid using the word "gay" as the umbrella term, except when it forms part of a title.

In describing academic developments in queer studies, I shall focus on the undergraduate curriculum and experience at more than 130 universities and colleges (see "Programs in Gender and Lesbian, Gay, Bisexual, and Transgender Studies" section below); information about them comes from a variety of sources, including their published bulletins, their own World Wide Web homepages, and personal communications from students, faculty, and staff. I shall also focus on developments in LGBT resources, not on the repressive and homophobic environments (although see below, "Campus Life") that still can be found at most state-supported and private universities and colleges; there are environments that can become noticeably hostile from time to time, but that are becoming more accepting as the subject itself has become more acceptable. I do not, however, include religious-affiliated institutions: the conservative nature of their supporting regimes has only infrequently allowed these institutions to explore an environment that accepts queer people or academic discussions of LGBT issues.

The undergraduate LGBT experience is relatively rich when compared to high school and graduate environments. High school students seem to be coming out more and more (within the past couple of years, "out" first-year college students have increased dramatically); and many secondary schools try to provide sympathetic environments, with some diversity course-work, LGBT faculty representatives and counselors, and other resources, especially in the face of an alarming suicide rate for queer teens (L. Lane, 1995, p. 23). Nonetheless, only private high schools can afford many of these resources, both financially and in terms of parental and community support. Studies of their environments have been few (Newton and Risch, 1981; Unks, 1993-1994; Woog, 1995; reviewed by L. Lane, 1995).

For post-graduate work, there are no specific LGBT programs. Many university departments do offer graduate courses in queer studies and allow graduate students to do research on and to write on queer topics, but there is at present no graduate program, and no Ph.D. diploma, specifically in the area of "Lesbian and Gay" or "Queer Studies" or the like, although the Center for Lesbian and Gay Studies (CLAGS) at the City University of New York has been proposing one for some time. There are several centers for post-graduate research in LGBT studies, notably CLAGS at CUNY and the Center for Scholars in Residence in Gay, Lesbian, Bisexual and Transgender Studies affiliated with ONE Institute's Center for Advanced Studies and the University of Southern California; no doubt one can do similar work at other senior research centers such as the National Humanities Center in the Research Triangle Park in North Carolina. Again, since there is little formal institutionalization of queer studies at the graduate level, I shall not be discussing many developments in this area (but see below, Programs, Financial Aid, and Centers).

In historical terms, I shall be focusing on the more or less recent period, especially since 1985, and even more especially on the period since 1990 when Lesbian and Gay Studies courses and curricular programs, LGBT Student Centers, and queer theory began emerging with increasing frequency.

For earlier assessments, I give here some brief references. Dynes, 1987 contains sections on libraries and archives (pp. 31-33), women's studies (pp. 52-70), and education (pp. 393-400). This last presents several interesting documents. For the 1970s, five reports concern campus environments (nos. 2658, 2664, 2665, 2675, 2678); three more reflect on gay teachers, including (no. 2701) one by Marc Rubin, the founder of the Gay Teachers Association (New York City) in 1974, and two assessments of attitudes towards gay teachers (nos. 2695 and 2696); finally, two teachers, Rictor Norton and Ron Schreiber, discuss the problems of giving courses in gay studies (nos. 2711 and 2712). For the 1980s, there are fewer references, but one (no. 2679), written by Robert

Martin in 1983, looks back to the first gay student group, the Student Homophile League of Columbia University, that he founded in April 1967.

UNIVERSITY RIGHTS AND PRIVILEGES

Antidiscrimination Clauses

Most institutions of higher learning, and even many secondary schools, now have some sort of antidiscrimination clause that includes the phrases "sexual orientation," "affectional orientation," or the like. This situation seems relatively recent; 10 years ago the number of institutions with such inclusive clauses was dramatically lower, although this has not been documented. When Duke University included "sexual orientation" in its anti-discrimination clause in December 1988, it joined a moderately long list of similar institutions. The Web site list of such universities (http://www.uic.edu/orgs/lgbt/Stratton.html, maintained by LGBT Campus Directors), however, has not been updated since November 1995, possibly because it seems to include almost every university and college in the United States and Canada (plus Australia and a few other English-speaking countries), and their growth no longer seems worthwhile charting. It would be useful if this list were not only updated, but also augmented with the dates these institutions first published their antidiscrimination statement and first included the "sexual orientation" clause.

Not all universities have such a sexual-orientation phrase in their antidiscrimination statement, however (e.g., Southwestern University in Texas); and the inclusion of this phrase is not always a reliable source of ultimate protection on campus. Semi-independent schools within a university may choose to ignore the antidiscrimination phrase: Mooney, 1994 documents how the dean of Yale's Divinity School published a letter denouncing gay students; at Duke, a member of the Divinity School published a letter in 1994 denouncing a colleague's involvement in LGBT studies, in 1996 the Duke Chapel refused to bless or marry same-sex couples (annually, however, it does bless animals), and in the fall 1997 the Law School accepted military recruitment in its building. Similarly, the presence of the military's Reserve Officer Training Corps programs (ROTC) on many campuses seems to fly in the face of the intention of their antidiscrimination clauses. The tolerated military presence on campus is linked, of course, to the financial support they offer students and programs; the tolerated homophobia of religious institutions on campus is linked to the institutionalized religiosity of American life in general.

Institutional Equity

Another type of administrative oversight of LGBT concerns consists of a university's equity or diversity compliance office within the central administration (e.g., a President's Commission at Maryland, College Park; the Office of Educational Equity at Pennsylvania State; the Office of Affirmative Action and Multicultural Programs at Delaware; or the Diversity Education Program under Multicultural Affairs at Idaho). At the University of Hawaii, however, Student Affairs manages the Student Equity, Excellence and Diversity program, and a Task Force on Sexual Orientation oversees LGBT services.

The history of these equity and compliance agencies is interesting and relevant. The Fourteenth Amendment establishes "suspect classes" based on race (including American Indians), sex, age, and unique physical characteristics (e.g., disabilities), and may include other classes organized according to wealth (e.g., the homeless), illegitimacy, and alien status. Subsequent federal statutory laws (e.g., the American Disabilities Act, and Title VI of the Civil Rights Act of 1964), Supreme Court decisions (e.g., that on the *University of California v. Bakke,* 1978), and especially Title IX of the Education Amendments of 1972, not only have refined the implications of the Fourteenth Amendment but have also prohibited state agencies and those that receive federal funding (spent or unspent) from discriminating against the four major suspect classes. To ensure compliance with Title VI, Congress established the Office for Civil Rights (OCR) of the U.S. Department of Health, Education and Welfare in 1964 and 1965 as the regulatory and enforcement agency, and, under the subsequent statutes such as Title IX, Section 504 of the Rehabilitation Act of 1973, and the Age Discrimination Act of 1975, this agency has assumed regulatory responsibility over the general areas of gender, disability, and age.

The OCR conducted its first large-scale surveys of compliance in 1968 and 1969 beginning with public colleges and universities in 10 states with a history of *de jure* segregation. From the late 1960s to the early 1970s institutions across the country began to respond to vigorous regulatory activities by the federal agencies in the areas of race, gender, age, and disability discrimination. These enforcement efforts became largely moribund from 1980 to 1992 under Republican administrations but were resumed under Bill Clinton.

Though lesbians and gay men and other queer persons do not yet constitute a suspect class, and therefore are not now included in federal antidiscrimination policies, they are often included by a university as a class protected in education, employment, access to facilities, and other aspects of campus life under its antidiscrimination policies "for purposes of the campus," i.e., for purposes of convenience, of fairness, or of general inclusivity, a doctrine that also may require religion, free speech, and other basic freedoms to be also specifically cited. Some 8 to 10 states have also included lesbian and gay men in their antidiscrimination statutes for the same general purposes of inclusivity. Even the OCR has shown itself to be sensitive to the concerns of queer persons in a general sense (e.g., its promulgation of peer-on-peer sexual harassment guidelines, March 1997).

Of the universities and colleges that receive federal funds, most have chosen, in addition, to establish an in-house compliance agency to ensure that they are abiding by the various and complicated federal statutes and constitutional and civil codes, especially those that mandate affirmative action in some situations and permit it in others (Conte, 1997). It is in this situation, then, where a university has chosen to include queer persons in its antidiscrimination policies and to establish a compliance agency on campus, that queer students, faculty, and staff may find themselves legitimized and protected, and their needs met.

Spousal Benefits (Domestic Partnerships)

The main issue that affects the LGBT faculty and staff at a university is the availability of same-sex spousal equivalency benefits (SSSE or "domestic partnerships"). A recent list, supplemented with information gleaned from university LGBT homepages, shows that many private universities and some state university systems (e.g. California, Iowa, Michigan, Minnesota, Pennsylvania, and Wisconsin) now offer some kind of spousal benefits, but many other universities, for example private univer-

sities such as Emory and Purdue, and most of the other state universities, do not (http://www.cs.cmu.edu/afs/cs/user/dtw/www/companies.html, updated 8 September 1997). Implementing spousal benefits is usually a slow process at most universities, simply because resistance against it is strong. The two most cited objections concern the eventual cost of the program, which typically is minimal since few employees actually register for spousal benefits, and any broadening of the concept "family." Many institutions that include "sexual orientation" in their antidiscrimination clauses have taken the stance that not to offer spousal benefits is a type of sex discrimination. The great amount of time consumed in gathering information, debating, and voting may instead cost much more than the actual benefits (see http://www.cs.cmu.edu/afs/cs.cmu.edu/user/scotts/domestic-partners/mainpage.html).

ACADEMICS

LGBT campus life operates along two distinctive paths, one that focuses on curricular issues and the other on programming (speakers, events, social life), much like other programs that treat minority studies and students. As is discussed below under Courses, Programs, and Centers, the usual arrangement at the larger universities is to have a faculty committee manage LGBT courses until it can establish an academic program, and to have Student Affairs establish a Student Center to handle the LGBT programming; smaller universities and colleges have either a faculty committee or a dean's office manage both programs. It seems logical, therefore, that the typical development would proceed from a single committee managing both courses and programming to, eventually, separate bodies for each: an academic program for courses and a student center for programming.

In reality, however, universities with student centers do not have university committees for the LGBT curriculum; only Colorado at Boulder, and perhaps the University of Pennsylvania, have both bodies. It is possible, therefore, that the two processes of institutionalizing LGBT programming and courses run along two separate and more or less independent tracks. At Duke, for instance, faculty were meeting to develop the academic Program in the Study of Sexualities at the same time that the University Task Force for LGBT Matters was coordinating student demands for a LGBT center, but the two movements were entirely independent, and few individuals participated in both.

The impetus for both movements was also different at Duke: in 1993, a homophobic campus environment fueled the student demand for a center at the same time that faculty, concerned about the lack of undergraduate opportunities for queer studies, were team-teaching an introductory course to the subject. From what I can glean from the data available from other institutions, Duke's experience seems not to be unusual; for instance, homophobic events in 1994 and 1995 led to the first LGB Studies course at Notre Dame, taught by Professor Carlos Jerez-Faran of the Department of Romance Languages (see *LGSN* 22.2, Summer 1995, pp. 4-6).

When devising new directions for LGBT students and queer studies, it may be worthwhile to keep in mind that LGBT courses and LGBT programming may be satisfying two fundamentally different, though superficially similar, needs.

Courses

"Lesbian and Gay Studies" seems to have acquired legitimacy as a valid academic field in the United States in the mid-1980s, along with the impact of AIDS and Michel Foucault's *History of Sexuality* (Heller, 1990). Scot Bravmann, 1987, summarizes the situation, the lack of lesbian and gay student centers leads to an "extreme isolation of students focusing on lesbian/gay research," a field where "lesbians and gay men are a conceptual category of rather recent generation and are to be found only among certain cultures"; moreover, it is "unrealistic to ignore the political reality of our often marginalized, separate, and hidden sub-cultural experiences.... In light of the variously subtle to extreme rightward shift in political and social attitudes in the United States, exacerbated but hardly caused by the AIDS crisis, the growth of aware, active and multifaceted lesbian and gay studies programs is rapidly becoming, quite literally, central to our political existence."

Courses with significant LGBT content have, however, been taught at universities for some time. It may not be possible to identify the "first" such course in the United States (W. Lane, 1995); early literature courses that treated Oscar Wilde and Walt Whitman, aesthetics courses that concerned Walter Pater and John Ruskin, and courses in Greek literature, philosophy, and art, all conceivably could have included discussions that touched on male homoeroticism. In a somewhat parallel fashion, courses that discussed the homosocial world of women Suffragettes and Temperance Fighters, the plays of Lillian Hellman, or even the career of Eleanor Roosevelt could also have served to channel interest in female homoeroticism and lesbian politics.

As far as I am aware, however, early courses to include specific references to homosexuality, at least in their titles, date from at least the early 1970s (Brogan, 1978; W. Lane, 1995; Cage, 1994); these may have reflected the interest in homosexual rights that followed the Stonewall Rebellion on 27-28 June 1969 (Adam, 1995, pp. 81-96) and the immediate formation of Liberation Fronts both in the United States and in Europe. At the beginning of the 1990s a spate of courses appeared titled "Sexual Orientation and the Law" or "Sexuality and the Law" (e.g. at Loyola Marymount, Harvard, Northeastern, Columbia, New York University, and Georgetown), and these could have reflected interest generated by the Supreme Court decision in *Bowers v. Hardwick* (June 1986) and by the contemporary movements for human rights legislation (Adam, 1995, pp. 131-36).

Most courses in queer studies, however, concern lesbianism and queer literature (W. Lane, 1995). The courses in lesbianism mainly originate in women's studies programs, and these have steadily increased since the early 1980s. Literature courses originate mostly in English and literature departments, and these may include some of the earliest academic courses offered in queer studies.

The recent interest in cultural studies has also encouraged the development of courses that focus on specific themes. Duke University's English department, for instance, has been hosting its spring series of introductory seminars in cultural studies since 1987. Taught by graduate students, these seminars regularly include queer topics. In addition, a steady number of courses in queer film has been growing since the late 1980s. Other academic trends in queer studies can also be detected: since the mid-1980s lesbian and gay history courses have occurred with noticeable frequency, and most universities regularly offer at least one course on AIDS as either a health issue, a political issue, or both.

When gender, homosexuality, and sexuality are considered separately (see below), then the history of gender and queer politics may be taught along with that of other minority politics. Florida Atlantic University offers a graduate course on the relationships between the historical development of black identity and LGBT

identity; the University of California, Berkeley offers "The Rise of Heterosexuality and the Invention of the Modern Jew" (see *LGSN* 22.2, Summer 1995, pp. 14-16); and the University of Oklahoma offers a course that looks at homophobia and misogyny.

To bolster the field of teaching LGBT courses, sample syllabi are available in a variety of media; in published form CLAGS has assembled a three-volume set of syllabi, the *LGSN* has been publishing syllabi on a regular basis since 1991, Barbara Smith, 1982, has produced syllabi for courses on lesbianism, and the American Sociological Association, Teaching Resources Center publishes "The Sociology of Sexuality and Homosexuality: Syllabi and Teaching Materials"; and many Web sites maintain syllabi on-line.

Many teachers have encountered difficulties in teaching queer courses; administrations have been wary and students have occasionally been hostile. Several teachers have published their experiences in both areas: Gonshak, 1994 reminds us that administrations may be sensitive only over the titles of courses that appear on transcripts; Pottie, 1997 and Waxman and Byington, 1997 present creative strategies to prepare students to be receptive to the challenges of queer theory and literature. And Mohr, 1992; Halberstam, 1996; Leonard, 1997; and Meyers, 1997 all discuss the teaching of LGBT Studies as vital components of a general education, in addition to community service.

Some topics that could be queered are only occasionally treated as such: gay men's issues, ethics, psychology, economics, and science. It is often argued that gay men's issues are assumed in most queer studies courses, but it might be interesting to specifically address these issues as part of a dialectical approach to gender, especially if lesbianism is taught separately in women's studies programs. Given the recent interest in professional ethics and the adoption of gay rights by many corporations (sexual orientation in the antidiscrimination clauses, spousal benefits, etc.), there should be separate courses in queer ethics that incorporate discussions of these private challenges to state law. The avoidance of an academic discussion of homosexuality in psychology courses may, of course, reflect the American Psychiatric Association's decision in 1973 (Adam 1995, p. 87) to depathologize homosexuality as a mental illness, but the effects of our society's stigmatizing homosexuality in general still has enormous repercussions on the psychological stability of lesbians and gay men. Even more inexplicable is the relative scarcity of an academic discourse in queer economics (Gluckman and Reed, 1997; Cornwall, 1997). I have found only few courses in the subject and only a few economists (e.g. Richard Cornwall at Middlebury and Marieka Klawitter at the University of Washington) who broach the subject in publication. Since a "gay" lifestyle, and, therefore, spending habits, are generally recognized, and since America still operates according to a capitalist system, it seems to me that a larger discussion of queer economics is needed before the full effects of queer politics can be realized (Cohen, 1997). Finally, the persistent hold that masculinism and heterosexual patriarchy have over western thought is, I think, amply demonstrated by the virtually monolithic construction of science; whenever "science" is invoked we find few women practicing it and little room for queer thought. As far as I know, there have been extremely few attempts to queer science (Risch, 1978).

Programs

Since most universities offer some courses that focus on queer studies, the next logical step is to organize them coherently, if only to give the faculty a sense of direction and ownership and the administration a convenient funding code. The types of programs that have emerged have followed a typical process: on an individual basis faculty offers courses that reflect their own interests and those of their departments; when enough courses have been developed across several departments and when student interest in queer studies has grown administrations then tend first to set up coordinating committees and eventually to approve certificate-granting and minor programs. By the mid-1990s "Lesbian and Gay Studies" had become a noticeable feature of several curricula (D'Erasmo, 1991; Gonshak, 1994).

Faculty-run coordinating committees now manage LGBT Studies courses at several universities, such as Arizona, Southern California (the Gender Studies Program), Colorado at Boulder, Princeton (the Lesbian, Gay and Bisexual Concerns Task Force), and Wesleyan; sometimes a dean provides oversight (e.g., at Wisconsin at Madison, and at Brown).

Certificate-granting programs and the slightly more formalized minor programs are now common, and they originate from a variety of coordinating programs and departments. Independent lesbian, gay, and bisexual studies programs manage their own certificates and minors at several California universities, including the state university branches at Berkeley and Riverside and at San Francisco State University, the University of Wisconsin at Milwaukee, and at Allegheny College in Pennsylvania. Similar programs are titled or managed differently elsewhere: at Stanford, the Feminist Studies Department offers a LGB Studies minor, and Duke offers a certificate from the Program in the Study of Sexualities. Similar programs are being planned by most of the rest of the California state university system, Colorado, Brandeis, and George Mason.

So far, only San Francisco City College has taken the final step; its department of Gay and Lesbian Studies offers a B.A. The University of Chicago, however, allows students to design their own major with a general studies program in the humanities, and a few students have used this option to declare a LGB studies major. Related to this process, Wesleyan offers a LGB concentration in its American Studies major, and other universities are planning similar programs.

Building upon the pioneering work of their women's studies programs, a couple of universities have developed gender concentrations: Rice's Program for the Study of Women and Gender offers its own major, women's studies at Indiana at Bloomington grants a B.A. in Gender Studies, and women's studies at Barnard-Columbia makes a LGB Studies concentration available; similarly, women's studies at the University of Washington offers a graduate certificate program in lesbian studies.

Financial Aid

Like major programs in LGBT studies, financial aid for queer students or for students engaging in LGBT studies is a late development.

There are a few national programs for financial assistance (for complete information see http://www.finaid.org and http://www.duke.edu/web/jyounger/lgbfinaid.html). One offers fellowships only to undergraduate students; for the potential undergraduate, the Minnesota GLBT Educational Fund offers educational grants to LGBT Minnesota residents planning to attend a postsecondary educational institution in Minnesota during the next academic year. And the Gay, Lesbian and Straight Education Net-

work, founded in 1990, offers paid internships in its work to end homophobia in the lower schools.

Three organizations grant money to either undergraduate or graduate students. The Fund for Lesbian and Gay Scholarships (FLAGS) provides financial assistance to lesbian, gay, and bisexual students who are involved in the community. GLOBE (Gays and Lesbians Organized for Better Education; formerly known as ALSO, Alternative Lifestyle Scholarship Organization) is a national non-profit organization that awards academic scholarships to LGBT students who demonstrate financial need, academic excellence, and leadership potential. And the Uncommon Legacy Foundation, Inc., provides $1,000 awards to support projects that address lesbian social, cultural, and educational needs as well as civil rights and well-being; candidates must be lesbian students, and in the three years since the legacy's inception in 1994 50 lesbians have received awards (see http://www.uncommonlegacy.org).

For graduate students only, there are several national scholarships. The American Psychological Association's Division 44 (the Society for the Psychological Study of Lesbian and Gay Issues) provides the Malyon-Smith Scholarship Award of $500 to support graduate students in psychology programs doing research in psychological issues of importance to LGBT individuals, groups, or communities. The National Women's Studies Association provides $500 scholarships to graduate students writing a thesis or dissertation in lesbian studies. And the Martin P. Levine Memorial Dissertation Fellowship awards approximately $3000 to advanced graduate students currently writing dissertations in the field of human sexuality, AIDS, or the sociology of homosexuality. The City University of New York's Center for Lesbian and Gay Studies (CLAGS), founded by Martin Duberman in 1991, offers scholarships and awards to students at the CUNY Graduate School.

Finally, two research centers offer financial assistance to senior scholars in LGBT studies. Through the Rockefeller Foundation, CLAGS funds two fellowships each year, and offers the Martin Duberman Endowed Fellowship in Lesbian and Gay Studies every other year for research not focused on the United States or Western Europe. At the University of Southern California both the Law School and the Center for Scholars in Residence in Gay, Lesbian, Bisexual and Transgender Studies offer residential fellowships.

A new area that is still developing, partly parallel with the growth of LGBT alumni/ae organizations, is financial aid that is specific to students at individual universities. At Brown University, for instance, the alumni association provides a prize in LGB scholarship; the University of Kansas has announced a yearly scholarship for LGBT students; and Barnard-Columbia offer Queer Studies Awards to undergraduates.

CAMPUS LIFE

Homophobia is constantly present on university campuses, since it is constantly fueled by homophobia in the outside communities (Sears and Williams, 1997). Another source of homophobia are the campus newspapers that are supported by the Madison Center for Educational Affairs. These newspapers report on various progressive events at their local campuses in a similar format and negative style that includes insults, sneering, and pillorying of individuals; on the bright side, repeatedly targeted individuals and offices can be readily identified as the liberal activists on campus. The Madison Center Brochure, September 1996, lists the newspapers it supports at 56 campuses.

A student at George Mason University protests against homophobia on campus.

The university, however, may be the location for one's first encounter with diversity, with students and staff from different areas of the country, with different cultural backgrounds, and with different thoughts, aspirations, and orientations (Tierney, 1992). It is to be expected, therefore, that the various manifestations of queer academics on campus will set an annual stage for repeating dialogues about diversity as well as about the challenges to it.

Against this constant and performative dialectic, it is often difficult to judge national swings in opinion, including how liberal the progress (Tierney, 1993) or how conservative the backlash (Mooney, 1992). Though different campus reports contain virtually the same first-person accounts of harassment and raise the same alarms about hostile environments (Nelson and Baker, 1990, Santa Cruz; Duke's LGBTF Rationale 1993), the former wisdom—that teachers should leave their sexuality out of the classroom, at least until they are tenured (Crew, 1978)—has changed. With more students themselves out and needing affirmation (Van Dyne, 1973; Lehman, 1978), and with more academic interest on gender and sexuality, it has often become necessary for teachers to come out to their students in order to demonstrate how one's whole person, including their sexuality, informs their understanding of society and history, their interpretations, and their research (Parmeter, 1988; McNaron, 1996; Bowen, 1996). Personal relationships between students and teachers can be rewarding as well as dangerous; they need to be conducted with considerable care (Gurko, 1996).

Faculty

Lesbian and gay male teachers have always experienced difficulties finding and keeping their jobs. Discrimination at all levels of the employment process, from the telling resume through the tenure process, has been well and steadily documented. Such professional difficulties flourish within state and national environments of homophobia, which often take the form of legislative proposals for legalized discrimination. Except for general sodomy laws, most such proposals have not succeeded.

In the late McCarthy era of the early 1950s, the Florida state university system operated under a "Board of Control Issues Directive on Communism, Homosexuality in Colleges" (reported in *The Tampa Tribune*, 22 October 1962, and reprinted in *LGSN* 8.2, November 1981, pp. 8-9); this directive required fingerprinting of all university personnel and "a confidential quarterly report on action taken with regard to the elimination of sex deviates on the campuses." In the mid-1970s, Anita Bryant and her "Save the Children" campaign, originating from Florida, and, in California, the Briggs Initiative (1978) both attempted to bar homosexual teachers from employment, and both eventually went down to defeat (*LGSN* 4.2, November 1977, p. 1; Ward and Freeman, 1979, pp. 11-26). In 1982, there were two similar movements: the Helms statute to "disqualif[y] from employment in Oklahoma school systems all homosexual teachers, as well as non-gay teachers who advocate gay rights," and the Bush-Trask Amendment (Florida) to prohibit state funding to any public or private college that "charters or gives assistance to ... any group or organization that recommends or advocates sexual relations between persons not married to each other." Neither of these proposals survived court challenges (*LGSN* 9.1, March 1982, pp. 1, 7; *LGSN* 11.3, November 1984, p. 1). In addition, while the modern women's movement was gaining ground, there surfaced numerous allegations of lesbianism lodged against women teachers (*LGSN* 10.3, November 1983, p. 3, reporting on an article in *The Chronicle of Higher Education,* 26 October 1983). Colorado's Amendment 2 is only the latest in this series of legal challenges to the basic rights of marginalized people.

There have been bright spots, however, in the history of queer academe. Over Thanksgiving weekend, 23-24 November 1973, the Gay Academic Union was founded in New York City (Van Dyne, 1973; Gay Academic Union, 1974). A month later, at the end of the national conventional of the Modern Language Association (MLA), the Gay Caucus, now the Lesbian and Gay Caucus, was formed. It held six sessions at the next convention (*LGSN* 2.1, April 1975, pp. 1-5; Zimmerman, 1996, p. 269). Giving structure to the emerging field of "Gay Studies," these powerful academic institutions were instrumental in turning opinion on campus. For instance, in 1976 at Arizona State University, the head librarian was forced to rescind an order to cancel *The Advocate* and other LGBT publications under pressure from professors requesting them for their classes. The MLA passed a Gay Rights Resolution on 29 December 1977 (*LGSN* 5.1, March 1978, p. 1, and 5.2, December 1978, p. 8), and in 1984-85 the MLA's Committee on Academic Freedom successfully challenged the Helms Statute before the Supreme Court. In 1986, the first Gay and Lesbian Studies position was advertised in women's studies at the University of Massachusetts, Amherst; Michele Barale took the post, and it became tenure track in 1989.

The most recent large-scale study of the faculty environment has been sympathetically drawn by Toni McNaron (*Poisoned Ivy,*

1996), herself a long-time reporter of the often hostile campus life ("That Was Then and This Is Now," 1996).

Student Groups

Almost every campus has an undergraduate LGBT student group, and may have a separate one for graduate students as well. Such groups go back to well before Stonewall. I know of no history of these groups, though several have published short accounts in their Web home pages. Duke University's undergraduate group may be typical; once called "Duke Gay and Lesbian Alliance" (DGLA), "Duke Gay, Bisexual, and Lesbian Alliance" (DGBLA), and now "Gothic Queers" (GQ), its goals often swing between social and political, its leadership rotates rapidly, and members use it for a variety of purposes: to socialize, to attend and sponsor events such as films and speakers, and especially to facilitate coming out.

Student Centers and LGBT Programming

In addition to curriculum, many universities provide some LGBT programming, usually managed either by a student center or by some kind of office within the administration, usually the Student Affairs Office. This programming may take various names; most universities use a benign nomenclature that, if combined, would read something like "Office Center for LGBT Resources and Programming." One of the earliest student centers was the Lesbian-Gay Male Programs Office (now the Office of LGBT Affairs) at the University of Michigan, founded in 1971 (Zemsky, 1996, p. 208), two years after the Stonewall Rebellion; in fact, two student centers are even termed "Stonewall Center," the one at the University of Massachusetts, Amherst (founded soon after 1984), and the other at Grinnell College (1986). In 1996, it was somewhat conservatively estimated that "thirty institutions have full-time administrators whose sole responsibility is coordinating gay and lesbian activities," twice the number in 1992 (Gose, 1996). The "Programs in Gender and Lesbian, Gay, Bisexual, and Transgender Studies" section later in this chapter lists 19 LGBT Centers, 9 Programming Offices or task forces, 7 Student Support Services, and 3 Diversity/Equity/Social Justice Offices; for a total of 38 administrative units providing programming for LGBT students. This section also lists 11 student unions, many of which are undergraduate student groups, but some of which seem to be university programming offices.

Beth Zemsky (1996) has published an extensive account of the LGBT Center at the University of Minnesota, founded in 1992 after incidents of homophobic harassment had led to five recommendations: 1) the establishment of a LGBT center; 2) same-sex spousal equivalency benefits (SSSE); 3) educational training; 4) updating all publications to reflect the university's policy on diversity and the inclusion of "sexual orientation" in its antidiscrimination statement; 5) the establishment of a LGBT program—the only recommendation not yet implemented. The purpose of the center is to assist faculty, staff, and students "in fostering a supportive community," to educate and to provide resources, and to support the development of a curriculum by housing a library, course materials, and sample syllabi. Minnesota's Center is conscious of its role as an umbrella to many concerns; one special concern is the place of lesbians in a program that also includes gay men. Zemsky reports that many women identify themselves as marginalized first as women, then as lesbians, and to a much-

smaller extent with the GBT components, though they recognize that politically the "Gs" are necessary; women may also identify with a sexual radicalism that seems apart from feminism (Zimmerman, 1996). Such concerns pull in different directions.

Other sites for administrative oversight of LGBT concerns include the university's equity or diversity compliance office within the central administration, student support services, and student unions. Almost all universities, therefore, oversee the LGBT curriculum via an administrative unit, either the rare program that grants a certificate or degree, or the more common faculty or university coordinating committee; student centers, housed in student Affairs, conduct the LGBT programming. In almost all cases, the university that has no academic program will have either a student center or a faculty/administrative committee; as mentioned above, only Colorado at Boulder, and perhaps Pennsylvania, have both.

One special programming event deserves mention: the Lavender Graduation, first started at the University of Michigan in 1995; it has not yet spread widely to other campuses, but it seems an excellent way to celebrate students who have survived the special vicissitudes of college.

The recent establishment at many universities of some kind of Office of Institutional Equity is long overdue, but the primary intent of such an office is to redress inequities along Black/White lines. Only a few advertise their wider concern with the LGBT community: the universities of Kansas and Wisconsin, and Brown University advertise liaisons; the campus compliance officer, Laura Keohane, at the University of Maryland at College Park is open about her commitment to LGBT issues; so too is the Office of Educational Equity at Pennsylvania State University. Such offices reflect a top-down, governmental approach to the LGBT community, and as such their most important dealings may be in the area of personnel and harassment. Student Centers, however, constitute an extension of the LGBT community, and as such they are authoritative; with queer directors, queer programming, and queer students, speakers, events, politics, and counseling, they guarantee the most important service they can provide: the creation of a safe space. Beyond the university, the national group Campus Directors provides a network of support services: an e-mail discussion list, web homepage, its own national conventions, a caucus at the mid-November "Creating Change" meetings of the National Gay and Lesbian Task Force (NGLTF), and a caucus with the LGBT Network of the National Association of Student Personnel Administrators (NASPA) in mid-March (http://www.uic.edu/orgs/lgbt).

Two major centers have been established for graduate students and senior scholars. Perhaps the most honored research facility is CLAGS, which sponsors two major queer-related conferences a year, plus numerous colloquia and lectures. The second research facility is relatively new. Affiliated with the University of Southern California, the Center for Scholars in Residence in Gay, Lesbian, Bisexual and Transgender Studies began operation in 1994 (Williams, 1996), and cooperates with the International Gay and Lesbian Archives, the ONE Institute's Center for Advanced Studies, the June Mazer Lesbian Collection, and the Homosexual Information Center. The Center offers research space, facilities, and fellowships for dissertations and post-doctorate research.

In addition, the Institute of Gay and Lesbian Education was founded by noted neurologist Dr. Simon LeVay in 1992 to educate the public; it offers non-accredited adult education classes in a variety of areas, lectures, and other events.

Library Resources

Many libraries now have substantial holdings in the area of Lesbian and Gay Studies (Gittings, 1978; Broidy, 1996), following are only a few. The city libraries in San Francisco and New York and the New York University library all specialize in local histories; the New York University library also houses the Fales collection of lesbian and gay literature and queer videos; the University of Massachusetts at Amherst has published a bibliography of its queer collection; Northern Illinois University maintains the Midwest LGB Press Collection; the Schlesinger Library of Radcliffe has placed its holdings on the history of women in America on Harvard's on-line computer system, HOLLIS; the Cornell Library houses the Human Sexuality Collection, a collection of primary documents pertaining to lives, politics, pornography, and changes in social controversies about sexuality and sexual identity; the Davidson Library at the University of California at Santa Barbara (http://www.library.ucsb.edu/subj/gay.html) boasts a collection of more than 2500 volumes. The National Gay Archives in Toronto and the University of Saskatchewan libraries in conjunction with the Saskatchewan Archives Board amply document queer life in Canada.

There are important support services for the library staffs of queer collections as well. The American Library Association's Gay, Lesbian and Bisexual Task Force represents the profession, while the e-mail discussion list "Gay-Libn" keeps its members connected and informed.

Alumni/ae Associations

Bisexual, Gay, and Lesbian Alumni Associations (BiGALAs) have recently begun cropping up at a many universities (http://www.qrd.org/qrd/www/orgs/netgala and http://members.aol.com/sagalamain/sagala.htm). As the various LGBT student and curricular programs continue to grow, development offices will realize the opportunities that LGBT alums offer for special giving (e.g. Northwestern's LGBT alums have given to the library: http://pubweb.acns.nwu.edu/~vmccoy/gift.html), and no doubt more BiGALA associations will form.

The Internet

It may be no coincidence that the virtual surge in LGBT services and offerings on campus within the last decade and especially within the last five years coincides with the burst of resources on the Internet. Search engines make it easy to locate not only material that once was almost impossible to find in a library, but also sympathetic people.

It is impossible to do justice to all the Internet resources now available (http://www.duke.edu/web/jyounger/lgbwww.html), especially since they change almost daily, but a few do need mentioning for their long-standing contributions.

Ron Buckmire placed Queer Resources Directory (QRD; http://www.qrd.org/qrd) on-line in 1991; the listings have become invaluable, and imitation QRDs have appeared in other countries. Linking to the sites listed one can find a myriad of maintained web sites that will serve as guides for teachers of LGBT studies, for LGBT centers, and for the politically minded.

For the production of queer scholarship, Louie Crew (see People section below) has maintained a list of queer scholars and their research interests since 1991 (http://newark.rutgers.edu/~lcrew/

lbg_edir.html and http://newark.rutgers.edu/~lcrew/lbgslinks.html); his list is the only Who's Who in the field.

E-mail discussion lists serve not only to link active scholars and the interested public but also to showcase contemporary developments in thought; there are many LGBT discussion lists (http://www.duke.edu/web/jyounger/lgblists.html), but QSTUDY-L, reorganized in 1994 by Ellen Greenblatt (see People section below), stands out for the high intellectual content of its postings and for its contributors, many of whom number among the forefront of scholarly producers of queer studies and queer theory (http://www.uky.edu/StudentOrgs/QueerInfo/qstudy.htm). Finally, I have mentioned "Campus Directors" several times above; in the still turbulent atmosphere of campus life, it provides a necessary forum for the various LGBT campus services and their often-beleaguered staff.

Conferences

In addition to the many one-time conferences for both faculty and graduate students (http://www.qrd.org/qrd/events), there are important conferences held annually in the field of Lesbian and Gay Studies and the broader area of queer academics. Perhaps the most important is the series of "Creating Change" conferences hosted by the National Gay and Lesbian Task Force in November of each year (http://www.ngltf.org/main.html); 1997 saw the tenth such conference in San Diego. CLAGS organizes an Annual Queer Graduate Studies Conference; its seventh, "Forms of Desire," ran 3-6 April 1997. Similarly, Campus Directors conducts sessions at two conferences, at the NGLTF in mid-November and with the LGBT Network at the National Association of Student Personnel Administrators (NASPA) in mid-March. The Lavender Languages and Literature Conferences are organized by William Leap at American University; in 1997 the fifth such conference took place over three days with more than 100 people from many countries participating in panels and giving papers about queer language, literature, film, photography, and other forms of expressive communication. The last major North American Lesbian, Gay, and Bisexual Studies conference, "Inqueery, Intheory, Indeed," was held in Iowa City 17-20 November 1994, and concentrated on queer theory. The annual Berkshire Conferences on women and gender take place in the summer; the eleventh Berkshire Conference on the History of Women, "Breaking Boundaries," was held 4-6 June 1998 at the University of Rochester, with some sessions devoted to lesbianism. (The delivered papers are collected and preserved at the Arthur and Elizabeth Schlesinger Library on the History of Women in America at Radcliffe: http://www.radcliffe.edu/schles.)

ACADEMIC PRODUCTION AND SCHOLARSHIP

Since the mid-1980s scholars have concentrated on two main areas within Lesbian and Gay Studies: queer history and queer theory (Duberman, 1997; Beemyn and Eliason, 1996; Morton, 1996; Abelove, Barale, and Halperin, 1993). This essay cannot treat these subdisciplines in depth, but I shall try to point out some major accomplishments.

The concept of a history of homosexuality (Padgug, 1990; Abelove, Barale, and Halperin, 1993; Dynes, 1990) takes its impetus from Michel Foucault's *The History of Sexuality*. In his *Introduction* (1978, p. 43) Foucault identifies the year 1870 as the watershed when the "nineteenth-century homosexual became a personage, a past, a case history, and a childhood, in addition to being a type of life, a life form, and a morphology, with an indiscreet anatomy and possibly a mysterious physiology." This characterization of the late-nineteenth century invention of the homosexual with a past induced scholars to begin investigating the ancient Greek "paiderasteia" (Symonds, 1883; Greenberg, 1988; Halperin, 1989; Halperin et al., 1990; Skinner, 1996); this scholarship, when based on Symonds' general outline (1883) and Kenneth J. Dover's detailed description (1978), came to the conclusion that the Greek practice was profoundly different from the modern (Symonds, 1883; Marrou, 1956, pp. 26-35; Houser, 1990; Percy, 1996). This seemed to confirm anthropological observations that expressions of sexuality are not the same ("essentialistic") in all cultures and at all times, but rather are "socially constructed," that is, greatly influenced or even fixed by social and historical moments (Halperin, 1990). Since classical Greece is popularly regarded as the font of western civilization and since a type of homosexuality was not only permitted there but even praised, scholars have examined Greek "paiderasteia," looking for ways in which it is similar to or different from American homosexuality; it therefore has been used in various political agendas, including the controversies of "cultural studies" and "political correctness" (Nussbaum, 1992).

Other major studies have brought western gay history into the modern period: John Boswell (1980) documents homosexuality in the early and medieval catholic church; Lillian Faderman discloses the rich history of modern lesbianism (1991) and the variety of female friendships (1981); d'Emilio and Freedman (1988) give a general account of sexuality in America; and B. Adam (1995) traces the history of contemporary gay rights movements. One of the latest developments is the National Education Association's recognition of October as Lesbian and Gay History Month (*The Washington Blade*, 21 July 1995).

The contemporary AIDS crisis has also received much scholarly attention, with textbooks (Fee and Fox, 1988; and Crimp, 1993) and major studies on living with AIDS both when HIV positive and negative (Barry, 1993 and 1996; and Odets, 1995), and on changing attitudes on sexuality and the practice of sex (Rotello, 1997; Duggan, 1997 and 1995; Bersani, 1987; Meyer, 1991; Dowsett, 1996; Düttmann, 1996; Haver, 1996). The field of gay history has also broadened to include anthropological studies within western culture (e.g., expressions of homosexuality in Asian, Black, Hispanic, and Native American subcultures; Alonso and Koreck, Harper, Almaguer, Lorde, Mercer, Hull, Yarbro-Bejarano, and McDowell in Abelove, Barale, 1993; Bowen, 1996; Halperin, 1993; Hekma, 1989; Roscoe, 1991) and outside the western tradition (e.g. Schmitt and Sofer, 1992; Kimball, 1993).

Queer theory seems to have arisen in the early 1990s and now takes many forms that are difficult to define succinctly (de Lauretis, 1991; Goode and Innerst, 1995; Butler, "Critically Queer," 1993; Malinowitz, 1996; Jagose, 1996; Tierney, 1997). Most queer theories, rather than taking the viewpoint of central society or of the dominant culture, take the viewpoint originating from a socially marginalized periphery and employ feminist principles to examine central society, especially those subjects that heretofore had seemed "natural," "essentialist," and immune to social criticism (Sedgwick, 1990, pp. 75-83). Queer theory, from its eccentric position, can bring fresh social insight and questions to almost any previously aloof subject, from classical music (Leppert and McClary, 1987; McClary, 1991; Kopelson, 1996) to even itself. Interrogating the place of lesbians and lesbianism within the various women's movements has had a long history

(Stanley, 1978); recent studies have used queer theory to examine their place within Lesbian and Gay Studies itself (Halberstam, 1996; Zimmerman, 1996), or to interrogate the very nature of lesbianism (Butler 1990, *Gender Trouble,* and "Imitation and Gender Insubordination," 1990). Recently, the editors of *The Lesbian and Gay Studies Reader* (Abelove et al., 1993) proposed that queer theory even interrogate the connection between sexuality and gender (Freccero, 1995; Butler, 1994; Martin, 1994; Butler, *Bodies That Matter,* 1993).

PROMINENT PEOPLE

Barry Adam

Barry Adam is professor and chair of the Department of Sociology and Anthropology at the University of Windsor, Ontario. His 1987 book, *The Rise of a Gay and Lesbian Movement*, is now into its second edition (1995). His previous work concerns cultural studies on same-sex relationships in Canada, Nicaragua, and elsewhere, but his most recent studies concern homosexuality and AIDS. *Experiencing HIV* (with Alan Sears, 1996) develops his earlier *People with HIV/AIDS Talk about Life, Love, Work, and Family, a Handbook for People Living with HIV Disease*, also written with Alan Sears (1993).

On campus, Professor Adam sees his work as a way of integrating "myself with my research and professional life; by carving out a space for myself and for us in universities" we turn them into "a workplace where cultural representations are transmitted and produced." In his published work, and in his courses on so-

Barry Adam

cial movements, Adam concentrates on mixing the personal and the academic as a "way of addressing concerns and problems of people I care about. I have always seen my work as turning the tools of scholarship toward addressing the concerns and interests of LGBT people rather than exploiting LGBT topics for the interests and concerns of academe. A concern I have around (at least some of) the current wave of queer theory is a strong tendency to do the latter, and thus become disconnected from the collective and everyday lives of LGBT people. A lot of queer theory is exciting; it's great to see so much happening on queer topics; but I'm not always sure why it's being done, or if the very real continuing problems that we face in a homophobic society are getting the attention they deserve." His website (http://www.cs.uwindsor.ca/users/a/adam) links to his bibliography and courses.

Louie Crew

Louie Crew, alias "Queen Lutibelle," is associate professor of English at Rutgers University, Newark. His range of accomplishments and publications is astonishing. He received his B.A. from Baylor in 1958, M.A. from Auburn the next year, and his Ph.D. from the University of Alabama in 1971, all in English literature. Before he came to Rutgers in 1989, he taught at various colleges, including stints in Beijing, China, and Hong Kong. He now teaches literature, including Gay and Lesbian Literature and the Hebrew Scriptures, writes poetry (he's listed in *Who's Who in Poetry*), serves as chair of the Rutgers University senate and on its Board of Governors, writes computer

Louie Crew

programs, and is secretary for the Standing Commission on Human Affairs of the Episcopal Church.

Crew is well known for a string of "firsts": co-editor (along with Rictor Norton) of the first mainstream journal ever to devote a full issue to "lesbigay" issues, *College English* 36.3 (1974); founder the same year of "Integrity," the LGBT justice ministry of the Anglican church; served as one of the first officers of the newly formed GL Caucus of the MLA (1975-76); and editor of the first full volume on queer studies, *The Gay Academic,* with essays by 27 academics (1978).

Of his writing he says: "Much of my prose has been directed to demystify sexual issues, the better to negotiate the bonds of prejudice shaped by vast ignorance about all erotic matters in our culture. I write poetry primarily to re-mystify the discussion for myself, to stay in touch with the *mystery qua mystery* inherent in much that is best about sexuality."

Crew confesses to being "a scholar with a small 's'—and an indefatigable one" (about 1200 publications!). "I have been a journalist, political writer, activist, and preacher. I am enormously grateful for the opportunity to pursue these callings all over the world, in the rural black South, in my native white South, in rural Wisconsin, in Beijing and Hong Kong, and now huddled near Ms. Liberty on the banks of the Passaic in Newark. I have been much nourished by my marriage for the past 24 years, in a partnership across the racial and cultural boundaries that fiercely segregated Alabama when I grew up in the 1930s and 40s.

"The work I am most pleased with is not my own, but my service for the work of others. The *College English* issue, *The Gay Academic*, my special issue of *Margins* on gay male writing, my collection of biographies of lesbigay Episcopalians in *A Book of Revelations*, and other such collections helped to generate still more markets for lesbigay ideas. I have great respect for the theoreticians; early on, most lesbigay theory seemed terribly burdened by the theoretical baggage already promoted in the academy." Since 1991, Crew has been compiling the E-Directory of Lesbigay Scholars that keeps over 700 scholars informed and in touch (http://newark.rutgers.edu/~lcrew/lbg_edir.html). His homepage is at http://newark.rutgers.edu/~lcrew.

R. Ellen Greenblatt

R. Ellen Greenblatt was born in Leiden, the Netherlands. She received her bachelor's from the University of New Mexico in religious studies and philosophy, and an M.A. in librarianship and information science and in history from the University of Denver; since then she has worked as archivist at the Rocky Mountain Jewish Historical Society, leader of the Romance Languages Cataloging Team at Princeton, and catalog editor at State University of New York at Buffalo. Currently, Ellen serves as the assistant library director for Technical Services at the Auraria Library, University of Colorado at Denver, and associate professor of library science.

Ellen worked with and then succeeded Barbara Gittings as chair and co-chair (1986-88) of the American Library Association's Social Responsibilities Roundtable, Gay and Lesbian Task Force (now the Gay, Lesbian, and Bisexual Task Force), which launched her "involvement with queer librarianship.... My entire career as a librarian has focused on improving access to information on queer topics. When I first came out in the mid-1970s, I found it impossible to locate positive queer information. And I was not alone—decades worth of coming-out literature talks about the unavailability of queer-positive information in libraries." Ellen has also served as chair of the ALA's Gay, Lesbian, and Bisexual Book Awards Committee (1993-95).

Apart from her many publications (e.g., Greenblatt & Gough, 1990), Ellen is also well known for her work on the Internet. She is the creator and maintainer of several Web sites, including "Library Q: the Virtual Queer Library" (1995; http://www.cudenver.edu/public/library/libq) and "WSSLinks," the Association of College and Research Libraries Women's Studies Section (1996; http://www.library.yale.edu/wss); and she has founded several important queer discussion lists, notably LEZBRIAN, the Lesbian and Bisexual Women Library Workers List (1996; lezbrian@listserv.acsu.buffalo.edu), and reorganized the influential QSTUDY-L (1994; qstudy-l@listserv.acsu.buffalo.edu). In 1997, Ellen turned the latter list over to be owned and managed by Andy McIntire, who is at the University of Kentucky.

"The Internet has provided us an incredible opportunity to realize our goals; it is such a powerful force for getting the word out, and its dynamic nature makes for quick and easy revision. Electronic discussion lists such as lezbrian and gay-libn (the LGBT librarians network) have created space where queer librarians can network and share information and resources in an international forum. Before this, large-scale networking happened only at conferences once or twice a year. I often wonder how we accomplished things before the Internet!"

Marieka M. Klawitter

Marieka M. Klawitter is assistant professor of public affairs at the University of Washington, Seattle, with an adjunct appointment in women's studies; she received her A.B. in economics from the University of Michigan (1983), and both a MS (1986) and a Ph.D. (1991) in economics from the University of Wisconsin, Madison. Her research includes studies of the effects of child support policies, welfare policies, and antidiscrimination policies for sexual orientation. She teaches courses on women and work and on sexual orientation and public policy, and in 1995 she won the School of Public Affairs Teaching Excellence Award. Klawitter has published several articles on gendered economics (e.g., "Why Aren't More Economists Doing Research on Sexual Orientation?" and "The Effects of Sexual Orientation on the Determinants of Earnings for Women") and on child support.

Klawitter feels that the University of Washington "has been very supportive of my teaching and research" in the area of labor economics. "Elsewhere on campus most people are supportive, but I have also seen expressions of skepticism regarding this work. I'm very proud to have integrated the work and issues I value with my job. I also love that my visibility gives a new generation of queers support for living their lives with dignity." As a university activist, she founded and organized a network for teachers and researchers interested in sexual orientation, has organized panels on sexual orientation and feminist issues in the welfare system, given talks on coming out in the workplace, served on various committees, including the diversity committee, the committee on faculty women, and the steering committee of lesbian and gay employees; she has also been active with local health services and their work in AIDS, domestic violence, and child abuse.

"I think that the diversification of queer studies beyond critical studies has been very important. Most people can't read postmodernist writings (including myself) and don't really find that it speaks to our real lives. I think that queer studies is a great place for interdisciplinary work and that that is critical to understanding the issues."

Marieka M. Klawitter

William Leap

William Leap received his Ph.D. from Southern Methodist University, and is now professor of anthropology at American University in Washington, D.C., where he also teaches in Women's Gender Studies; he organized the fifth annual Lavender Language Conferences in 1997. His recent book, *Word's Out. Gay Men's English* (1996), is into its second printing.

Leap's early research concerned American Indians and language renewal projects, but he "became worried about studying 'them,' and not paying attention to where I was as a gay man, a part of gay culture. Then came AIDS, and a need to pay close attention to how gay men really communicate in real-life settings. Everyone said that AIDS was an epidemic of signification, but very few people were looking at how this played out in face-to-face interaction, the very stuff the AIDS educators need for effective intervention. So I started studying the language of AIDS, and then got asked if I was studying how people talk about AIDS, or how gay men talk about AIDS—or how gay men talk, period."

Leap's interest in "real" language takes "gay language out of abstract, philosophical, semiotic, detached theorizing and locates it back where it has always been, as part of daily life, real experience, and stuff." Like many scholars, he is concerned that "established queer theory seems disinterested in real life experience in all forms. I think this is why so much of queer theory is so inaccessible to readers." Making queer studies accessible has become central to his Lavender Language Conferences.

215

Ronni L. Sanlo

Ronni L. Sanlo is now director of the LGBT Campus Resource Center at UCLA. She received her B.A. in music from the University of Florida. In 1978, she became an AIDS epidemiologist for northeast Florida and "the highest ranking, 'out' lesbian employed by the State." The benefits of the job included being paid to go back to school to get her advanced degrees, a M.A. in education and Ph.D. in education leadership from the University of North Florida Jacksonville, both emphasizing sexual orientation issues in education. After graduation she became the executive director of and lobbyist for the Florida Task Force, Florida's civil rights group. Students of history may remember her task force as the one that "collected thousands of flea collars with pink triangles attached" and presented them to Florida Representative Tom Bush, co-author of a homophobic 1981 amendment; Bush had said of critics of his amendment, "If you lie around with dogs [i.e., lesbians and gay men] long enough, you're gonna get fleas" ([*Lesbian and*] *Gay Studies Newsletter* 9.1, March 1982, p. 7).

In 1994, she became director of the LGBT Student Resource Center at the University of Michigan in Ann Arbor, before moving to UCLA in 1997. Ronni confesses that her passion is education and the young: "I do this work for my children, for other young people like them, and for the families of our LGBT kids. I spend lots of time on children who fear rejection from their families. I love them, hug them, and teach them to be strong leaders. I do this work so that I leave this world in a little bit better shape than when I entered it, so that no one ever has to fear rejection or pain or discrimination because of their sexual orientation."

Ronni L. Sanlo

Ronni has been central to the formation of Campus Directors, the lobbying group that represents the many campus LGBT student resource centers, and she also serves as chair of the LGBT Network of the National Association of Student Personnel Administrators (NASPA). As she sees new centers slowly but steadily emerging across the country, she says she would also like to see the academic side include practical course work alongside queer theory, work in student services, and leadership. At Michigan, for instance, she initiated the first Lavender Graduation, "where we honor our LGBT graduates for no reason other than their making it through college!"

Walter L. Williams

Walter L. Williams is professor of anthropology and gender studies at the University of Southern California, director of ONE Institute's Center for Advanced Studies, and editor of the *International Gay and Lesbian Review*. First involved with museum development, he received his Ph.D. in history and anthropology from the University of North Carolina, Chapel Hill, and taught first at the University of Cincinnati; in 1979 he founded and edited southern Ohio's first gay newspaper, and a year later he co-founded and chaired the Committee on Lesbian and Gay History for the American Historical Association, and served as an officer of the Society of Lesbian and Gay Anthropologists. In 1981, he moved to Los Angeles, teaching American Indian Studies first at UCLA and later at the University of Southern California.

His studies of homosexuality in Native American, southeast Asian, and Polynesian cultures were used by the attorneys for the recent Hawaii same-sex marriage Supreme Court case, and Williams himself is often called as an expert witness in disputes and trials. He has published many articles and books, including the prize-winning *The Spirit and the Flesh: Sexual Diversity in American Indian Culture* and, with James Sears, the recent *Overcoming Heterosexism and Homophobia: Strategies That Work* (see http://www.jtsears.com/overcomi.htm).

As a young man, "growing up in the South, I got involved in the African-American civil rights movement in the 1960s, and later the American Indian movement and the feminist movement. During the Anita Bryant protests of the late 1970s I decided that I had to come out and publicly challenge discrimination against my own group. My strong feeling is that we need to promote stronger alliances between all stigmatized groups. It is my determination to change society so that youth today and in the future do not have to go through the isolation, torment, self-loathing, and ignorance that I and others of my generation had to overcome."

Williams feels that "there is a tendency for each generation to think it is the first, and to discount the lessons from the past. This condemns each generation of scholars to repeat some of the same mistakes, and to spend their time in never-ending theoretical battles whose absolutist positions will never be resolved. More research needs to be done on how best to reduce heterosexism and to improve the socio-economic-political situation of sexual minorities. Theory is important, but right now too many scholars are spending too much time arguing theory based on the same old data, rather than doing research to discover new data that will add to our knowledge base and transform theory in the future. I am especially pleased about new research on transgender issues, bisexuality, pansexuality, studies of people of color and other cultures beyond European/Euro-American perspectives, youth and elderly issues."

ACKNOWLEDGMENTS

In research and writing this chapter I have relied on the work and advice of several people: L. Michael G. Santos Silva and Rosalind Kaplan conducted much needed basic research; Laura Keohane provided much of the information concerning issues of equity; and Chris Shepard submitted an early version of the list of LGBT programs and courses. At various places I have used Duke University as a kind of check; it is a campus rich in its queer resources with student and faculty/staff groups, a student center, a curricular program, and queer faculty doing queer studies. Nonetheless, Duke has experienced episodes of homophobia, and these along with those described by Beth Armitage at George Mason University should keep us aware that much still needs to be done.

PROGRAMS IN GENDER AND LESBIAN, GAY, BISEXUAL, AND TRANSGENDER STUDIES AT UNIVERSITIES IN THE UNITED STATES AND CANADA

The following information is based on a variety of sources (the list first appeared in *LGSN* 22.1, March 1995, pp. 14-15); it is not a complete list of LGBT resources at universities and colleges, and all is subject to change. I have tried to verify as many of the following citations as possible. For an on-line up-dated version of this list, including names of contact persons: http://www.duke.edu.jyounger/lgbprogs.html.

ALABAMA

University of Alabama, Birmingham
Courses

American Studies: Introduction to Lesbian & Gay Studies; The Politics of the Gay & Lesbian Rights Movement

ARIZONA

Arizona State University
Courses

Sociology: Variant Sexuality; Women's Studies: Readings in Lesbian Literature

University of Arizona
Programs

The LGB Studies Committee sponsors courses in various departments.

Courses

Women's Studies 230: Introduction to Sexuality Studies

Resources & Services

The LGB Studies Committee sponsors a film series and a visiting artists and scholars series.

ARKANSAS

University of Arkansas
Resources & Services

LGB Student Association (formed 1982): http://www.uark.edu/~glbsa (or: http://www.uark.edu/studorg/glbsa)

CALIFORNIA

California State Polytechnic University, Pomona
Courses

Ethnicity & Women's Studies (EWS) 407: Sexual Orientation & Diversity

Resources & Services

Gay, Lesbian, & Bisexual Student Resource Center (founded 1995): http://www.csupomona.edu/pride_center

California State University, San Bernardino
Courses

Psychology: Psychology of Gays & Lesbians, one of the earliest courses taught (1976)

Deep Springs College (all male)
Courses

Introduction to Gay Studies

Institute of Gay and Lesbian Education, West Hollywood
Courses

Non-accredited adult education classes: philosophy, screenwriting, foreign languages, gay psychology and queer studies (Moral Issues in Gay and Lesbian Life)

Resources & Services

Since its opening in 1992, West Hollywood's Institute of Gay and Lesbian Education has offered over 75 courses to over 2000 students, covering topics of queer interest in such areas as screen-writing, gay and lesbian history, art and education.

Contacts

The Institute of Gay and Lesbian Education, 626 N. Robertson Blvd., W. Hollywood, CA 90069, Tel.: 310-652-1786, (igle@aol.com)

Loyola Marymount University, Los Angeles
Courses

Law School: Sexual Orientation & the Law

Pitzer College
Courses

Sociology: Sex & Society: LGB Studies; Women's Studies: Cross-Cultural Lesbian Studies; Gender & Sexual Orientation

San Francisco City College (community college)
Programs & Courses

The Gay/Lesbian Studies Department, in cooperation with other departments offers many courses, including: Anthropology of Homosexualities; Survey of G&L Literature (one of the earliest courses offered, 1972); Evolution of Film Expression-Homosexuality on Film; Maintaining Sexual Well-Being; Gay Male Relationships; Issues in Lesbian Relationships; and GL Issues in the Workplace.

Contacts

Gay and Lesbian Studies, City College of San Francisco, 50 Phelan Ave., San Francisco, CA 94112

San Francisco State University
Programs & Courses

An undergraduate minor in Lesbian & Gay Studies: http://www.sfsu.edu/~bulletin/current/programs/gaylesbi.htm. 8

courses total, 2 of which are required (Introduction to Bisexual, Lesbian and Gay Studies; and Gay, Lesbian, and Bisexual History); other courses include: English 618: Studies in Gay and Bisexual Literature; English 633: Gay Love in Literature; Human Sexuality 326: Work and Leadership Issues of Bisexuals, Lesbians, and Gays; Human Sexuality 436: The Development of Maleness and Femaleness; Human Sexuality 421: Homophobia and Coming Out; Women's Studies 550: Lesbian Literature; Women's Studies 552: Lesbian Lives and Thought

Resources & Services

LGS publishes the prestigious *Journal of Homosexuality*.

San Jose State University

Courses

Sociology: Alternative Lifestyles; Sociology of Homosexuality

Resources & Services

Delta Lambda Phi Fraternity; Gay Lesbian Bisexual Alliance

Santa Monica College (community college)

Courses

Contemporary Moral Conflicts; Sex and Sexuality; Gay/Lesbian Literature

Stanford University

Programs & Courses

The Feminist Studies Dept. has an undergraduate minor in LGB Studies.

Resources & Services

Stanford Queer Resources Server: http://www-leland.stanford.edu/group/QR; The Lesbian, Gay, Bisexual Community Center (founded ca. 1989): http://www-leland.stanford.edu/group/QR or http://www-directory.stanford.edu/virtual/campusinfo/infoguide/gay.html; Stanford's queer history: http://www-leland.stanford.edu/group/QR/History; Stanford Gay and Lesbian Alumni (GALA)

University of California, Berkeley

Programs & Courses

Minor in Lesbian, Gay, Bisexual and Transgender Studies, requiring four courses and two upper-division electives; the four required courses are Alternative Sexual Identities and Communities in Contemporary American Society; Interpreting the Queer Past: Methods and Problems in the History of Sexuality; Cultural Representations of Sexualities; Sexuality, Culture, and Colonialism.

Courses

The Rise of Heterosexuality and the Invention of the Modern Jew; BLG People of Color; Our Bodies, Our Lives: Social Aspects LGB Health; Outcast among the Outcast; Multicultural: Literature & Sexuality

Resources & Services

The Lesbian and Gay Center (bblgc@uclink.berkeley.edu); Gay/Lesbian/Bisexual Mentorship Program (alums - students): http://www.alumni.berkeley.edu/~gaylesbi.

University of California, Davis

Courses

English: Special Topics in Literary Studies

Resources & Services

Lesbian, Gay, Bisexual Resource Center (opened 31 January 1994): http://lgbcenter.ucdavis.edu.

University of California, Irvine

Programs

Undergraduate program being planned; Ph.D. in Intersectional Studies in Genders/Sexualities, Race/Ethnicities, and Cultures

Courses

Women's Studies: Psychology of Women from a Lesbian Perspective

Resources & Services

Lesbian, Gay, Bisexual Resource Center: http://www.uci.edu/~lgbtrc; Lavender Graduations

Contacts

Women's Studies and Interdisciplinary Program, 419 Social Science Tower, Irvine, CA 92697-6600, Tel.: 714-824-8582

University of California, Los Angeles

Programs

Lesbian-Gay-Bisexual interdepartmental program

Resources & Services

Lesbian, Bisexual, Gay, and Transgendered Resources Office: http://www.saonet.ucla.edu/lgbt/lgbt.htm; Lavender Graduations

University of California, Riverside

Programs

Interdisciplinary undergraduate minor in Lesbian, Gay & Bisexual Studies (6 courses)

Courses

Courses on gender and sexuality in Art History, English, Ethnic Studies, Dance, History, Psychology, Sociology and Women Studies

Resources & Services

English publishes *Unnatural Acts*; The undergraduate and graduate multiethnic Union of Lesbians, Gays, and Bisexuals; A Chancellor's Advisory Committee on the Status of Lesbians, Gays and Bisexuals monitors campus environment; The Lesbian, Gay and Bisexual Resource Center publishes a quarterly newsletter called "Dish."

University of California, San Diego

Programs

A program is developing in LGB Studies.

University of California, Santa Barbara

Resources & Services

The Davidson Library, Ethnic and Gender Studies Library, Andelson Collection, holds more than 2500 volumes: http://www.library.ucsb.edu/subj/gay.html.

University of California, Santa Cruz

Courses

Several LGB Studies courses.

Resources & Services

Undergraduate Stonewall Alliance

University of Southern California, Los Angeles

Programs

The Gender Studies Program coordinates many LGB Studies courses and a cooperating faculty of 36.

Resources & Services

Gay, Lesbian, Bi Student Support: http://www.usc.edu/dept/GLBSS; Undergraduate and graduate LGB student groups; The Cinema School offers the "Out for Reel" program; Lambda Alumni Association: http://www.usc.edu/go/lambda; The Center for Scholars in Residence in Gay, Lesbian, Bisexual and Transgender Studies began operation in December 1994, in cooperation with the International Gay and Lesbian Archives, the ONE Institute of Homophile Studies, the June Mazer Lesbian Collection, and the Homosexual Information Center. The Center for Scholars in Residence offer research space, facilities, and fellowships for dissertations and post-docs; The Law School offers the nation's first scholarship for LGB Studies in the area of sexual orientation and the law.

COLORADO

Colorado College

Courses

English: Gay Literature & Film

Metropolitan State College of Denver

Resources & Services

Gay Lesbian Bisexual Student Services: http://www.mscd.edu/%7eglbss/Welcome.html.

University of Colorado, Boulder

Programs

The Planning Committee for LGB Studies is also considering proposing a program in LGB Studies.

Courses

Several including: Arts & Sciences 2080, Introduction to Lesbian, Bisexual and Gay Studies; English 3792, Queer Theory

Resources & Services

Lesbian & Gay Alliance; Gay & Lesbian Staff Association; Bisexual Women's Voice

Contacts

The GLBT Resource Center: http://www.colorado.edu/sacs/stu-affairs/glb.html), 334 Willard Hall, University of Colorado, Boulder, Tel.: 303-492-1377

CONNECTICUT

University of Connecticut

Resources & Services

Center for Lesbian, Bisexual, Gay, and Transgender Issues (e-mail: bigala@ops.saup.uconn.edu); BiGALA

Quinnipiac College

Resources & Services

Gays, Lesbians and Straight Supporters (GLAS), the college's gay organization

Wesleyan University

Programs

A queer studies concentration within the American Studies major, coordinated by the Gay & Lesbian Sexuality Studies (GLASS) committee.

Resources & Services

GLB Alliance; GLBT Alumni Resources: http://www.alumni.wesleyan.edu/www/info/cpc/glbt.html.

Yale University

Courses

Several courses, at both the undergraduate and graduate levels, in Gay & Lesbian Studies; students have concentrated in this area using History, American Studies and Women's Studies as home departments.

Resources & Services

A LG Studies Center held a conference in October 1987: "LG Studies: Definitions and Explorations"; LGBT Center: http://www.yale.edu/lgb/yale/gsc.html; The Lesbian, Gay, Bisexual, Transgendered Cooperative: http://www.yale.edu/lgb; Bi Choice; Lesbian & Bisexual Women of Color; Lesbian, Gay & Bisexual Law Students' Association; The Research Fund for Lesbian and Gay Studies was established several years ago from gifts from friends of the late Professor John Boswell; Re-FLAGS (tel.: 203-432-4997) invites lecturers and publishes "The Pink Book," a catalogue of GLBT Studies courses.

DELAWARE

University of Delaware

Resources & Services

LGB Student Union; Office for LGB Concerns: http://www.udel.edu/stuhb/97-98/AffAmP/AAMP.html; LGB Information Line (302-831-411)

Contacts

Office of Affirmative Action and Multicultural Programs, 124 and 305 Hullihen Hall, Tel.: 302-831-8735

DISTRICT of COLUMBIA

American University

Programs

A LGB Studies program is slowly developing.

Courses

LGB Studies program has recently begun offering its first courses; Women & Gender Studies: Lesbian/Gay Cultures; Courses in the departments of Anthropology and Justice, Law & Society.

Resources & Services

Gay and Lesbian Union

Gallaudet College

Resources & Services

Lambda Society (founded 1984)

Contacts

Student Affairs Office, Ely Center, Room #102, Tel.: 202-651-5064

George Washington University

Courses

History: The Gay and Lesbian Experience in America; Women's Studies: Lesbian Issues

Georgetown University

Courses

English: History & Theory of Sexuality; Law: Sexual Orientation & the Law

FLORIDA

Florida Atlantic University
Courses

Introductory undergraduate course in LGB Studies. A graduate course on the relationships between the historical development of black identity and lesbian/gay identity. Communication Department is developing another graduate course: Lesbians, Gays and the Media.

Contacts

Communication Dept., Florida Atlantic University, Boca Raton, FL 33431, Tel.: 407-367-3858

GEORGIA

Emory University
Resources & Services

Office of Lesbian/Gay/Bisexual Life: http://www.emory.edu/LGBOFFICE or userwww.service.emory.edu/~emoryglb; E-mail discussion group, EmoryGLB: http://userwww.service.emory.edu/~emoryglb/emoryglb.html; The Gay, Lesbian, & Bisexual Student Union represents a large gay/lesbian/bisexual student population, which is well organized and presents numerous events each year.

Georgia Technical University
Resources & Services

LGBT Alumni Association

University of Georgia, Athens
Courses

Women's Studies (http://www.uga.edu/~curriclm/ucourses/ws.html): Lesbian and Gay Studies.

Resources & Services

The LGB Student Union: http://www.uga.edu/~lgbsu; BiGALA

HAWAII

University of Hawaii
Resources & Services

Student Affairs, Student Equity, Excellence and Diversity Office, Task Force on Sexual Orientation: http://www2.hawaii.edu/seed, Tel.: 808-956-9250

IDAHO

University of Idaho
Resources & Services

Diversity Education Program: http://www.uidaho.edu/oma

Contacts

Director of the Office of Multicultural Affairs, Tel.: 208-885-2958/2959

ILLINOIS

Knox College
Courses

Gay & Lesbian Identities: Advanced Preceptorial 312

Northern Illinois University
Resources & Services

Midwest LGB Press Collection

Contacts

Electronic Information Resources Management, 15E Founders Memorial Library, Northern Illinois University, DeKalb, Illinois 60115-2868, Tel.: 815-753-1367

Northwestern University
Courses

History: Gay & Lesbian History of US

Resources & Services

Gay and Lesbian University Union: http://www.nwu.edu/gluu; BGL Alliance: http://www.studorg.nwu.edu/bgala; LGBT Alumni: http://bgala.norris.nwu.edu

University of Chicago
Programs

Students can also design their own majors within a General Studies in the Humanities program, and through this option students can declare a LGB Studies major.

Courses

Undergraduate courses: Introduction to Gender Studies; Feminist Theory/Feminist Practice; Social & Gay History of American Subcultures. Graduate courses: Gay and Lesbian Studies Workshop; Feminist Theory Workshop; Sensation, Sensibility, and Sexuality; Gender and Sexuality Theory; Nationalism, Sexuality and Gender

Resources & Services

Office of Gay, Lesbian and Bisexual Concerns (opened in 1994): http://www.uic.edu/depts/quic/oglbc; Gay & Lesbian Alum Association

University of Illinois, Chicago
Programs

There are no efforts to get a GLB program started yet; courses need to be developed first.

Courses

Several gay and lesbian courses, including English 117, Issues in Gender, Sexuality and Literature.

University of Illinois, Urbana
Courses

English: Lesbian & Gay Tradition in Literature; History/Humanities: Lesbian & Gay History; Political Science: Politics of AIDS

Resources & Services

Undergraduate "Out on Campus"; Office of Lesbian, Gay, Bisexual, and Transgender Concerns: http://www.odos.uiuc.edu/glbt/

INDIANA

Indiana University, Bloomington
Programs

The Women's Studies Program (http://www.indiana.edu/~iubwost) offers a B.A. in Gender Studies.

Resources & Services

Gay, Lesbian, and Bisexual Student Support Services: http://www.indiana.edu/~glbserv (e-mail: glbserv@indiana.edu); The LGB Alumni Association; The Kinsey Institute,

Morrison Hall 313, Indiana University, Bloomington, IN 47405

Purdue University

Courses

Interdisciplinary Studies in Sexuality 482: Issues in Gay and Lesbian Studies

Resources & Services

Undergraduate Gay Alliance; Lesbigay Network: http://expert.cc.purdue.edu/~triangle; LGBT Alums: http://expert.cc.purdue.edu/~triangle/alumni.html

University of Notre Dame

Courses

Outspoken Readings: Questions of Homosexuality in Literature

Resources & Services

Undergraduate Gay/Lesbian Organization; Gay and Lesbian Alumni

Valparaiso University

Resources & Services

Alliance, a new campus organization that fights discrimination against Lesbian, gay, bisexual, and transgender people.

IOWA

Grinnell College

Courses

American Studies: Lesbian Lives

Resources & Services

Stonewall Resource Center (founded 1986): http://www.grin.edu/~srcenter (e-mail: srcenter@ac.grin.edu); Committee to End Homophobia

Iowa State University

Courses

English/Women's Studies: Women Identified Literature

Resources & Services

Lesbian, Gay, Bisexual Alliance; Lesbian Gay & Bisexual Student Services: http://www.public.iastate.edu:80/~deanstdt_info/lgbss_home.html; e-mail: lgbtss@iastate.edu

University of Iowa, Iowa City

Courses

American Studies: Lesbian Lives; Women's Studies: Lesbian Literature & Theory

Resources & Services

Gay Peoples Union; Bisexual Support Group

University of Northern Iowa

Courses

Interdisciplinary Studies: Introduction to Gay & Lesbian Studies

KANSAS

Kansas State University

Resources & Services

Bisexual, Lesbian, & Gay, Resource Center

University of Kansas

Courses

Courses in American Studies and in English.

Resources & Services

An annual scholarship for LGBT students.

Contacts

Liaison for Gay, Lesbian, Bisexual, and Transgender Concerns, Student Assistance Center, University of Kansas, Tel.: 913-864-2802

KENTUCKY

University of Kentucky, Louisville

Resources & Services

Student Queer Information: http://www.uky.edu/StudentOrgs/QueerInfo/; Common Ground (student organization): http://www.louisville.edu/rso/commonground

LOUISIANA

Louisiana State University

Resources & Services

Gay & Lesbian Student Association

Northeast Louisiana University (Monroe)

Courses

There are occasional courses.

Resources & Services

Unity of Gays, Lesbians and Friends (e-mail: unityglf@hotmail.com)

MAINE

University of Maine

Courses

Women's Studies: LGB courses

Resources & Services

Gay and Lesbian Alliance

MARYLAND

Towson State University

Programs

A minor in LGB Studies.

Resources & Services

LGB Committee: http://www.towson.edu/~tinkler/lgb/homepage.html

University of Maryland, College Park

Courses (the following is a sample)

Comparative Literature: 291 International Perspectives on Lesbian and Gay Studies; 679Q/English 668 Readings in Modern Literary Theory: Gay, Lesbian, and Queer Theory. English: 379 Gay is Very American: Readings in Lesbian, Gay, and Bisexual Literatures; 435 American Sexual Poetics Revisited; 488 Gay Liberation Rhetorics; 729 Sapphism, Patriarchy and Political Enlightenment During the Eighteenth Century; 748B Dickinson and American Sexual Poetics at the Fin de Siecle; 748B Willa Cather: Contesting/Queering "America"; 749 Lesbian/Gay Theory; 769 Theories of Literature: Feminine Homotextualities; 7XX

Sapphists, Spinsters, Friends: Female Economies in the Long Eighteenth Century. Family Studies: 499A Special Counseling Concerns for Lesbians and Gay Men. French: 478 Gay Issues in French Fiction. Honors Program: 139A Sexuality and Literature: Oscar Wilde's Texts and Contexts. Philosophy: 407 Gay and Lesbian Philosophy. Public Affairs: 6XX Sexuality and Public Policy. Women's Studies: 298E Constructing a Field: An Introduction to Lesbian, Gay and Bisexual Studies; 494 Lesbian Communities

Resources & Services

President's Commission on LGB Issues; LGB Committee: http://www.towson.edu/~tinkler/lgb/homepage.html; LGB Staff/Faculty Association: http://www.inform.umd.edu:8080/UMSLGBSFA

MASSACHUSETTS

Amherst College

Programs

Part of the 5-college area (University of Massachusetts at Amherst, Radcliffe, Hampshire, Amherst College). Michele Barale was hired in the first faculty position advertised for LGB Studies.

Courses

English: Lesbian Literature; Paranoia, Homophobia, & Horror Fiction in Literature & Film; Queer Fictions. Political Science: Authority & Sexuality

Resources & Services

Lesbian, Gay, and Bisexual Alliance; A bibliography of the library's holdings in LGB Studies was published in 1994.

Brandeis University

Programs

An interdisciplinary M.A. in LGB Studies has been proposed by the departments of History, Sociology, American Studies, English. The university is also exploring the possibility of a certificate-granting undergraduate program.

Hampshire College

Programs

Part of the 5-college area (University of Massachusetts at Amherst, Radcliffe, Hampshire, Amherst College).

Courses

Social Science: Sexual Politics & Communities

Harvard University

Courses

Law School: Sexual Orientation & the Law

Resources & Services

Bisexual, Gay, & Lesbian Student Alliance; Gay and Lesbian Caucus for Harvard and Radcliffe Alum, Faculty, and Staff: http://www.hglc.org/hglc

Northeastern University

Courses

Law School: Sexual Orientation & the Law

Radcliffe College

Programs

Part of the 5-college area (University of Massachusetts at Amherst, Radcliffe, Hampshire, Amherst College).

Resources & Services

Gay and Lesbian Caucus for Harvard and Radcliffe Alum, Faculty, and Staff: http://www.hglc.org/hglc; The Schlesinger Library has holdings on the History of Women in America, cataloged on HOLLIS, Harvard's online computer catalog; Schlesinger Library on the History of Women in America, Radcliffe College, Cambridge, MA 02138

Tufts University

Programs

English has many graduate students doing dissertations in the field of gay literature, culture, and theory.

Courses

Many courses offered in various departments, notably English, history, drama, and sociology. English offers a number of graduate courses on queer topics.

Resources & Services

The Center for Lesbian, Gay, and Bisexual Students (since 1995), with a half-time administrator; Lesbian, Gay, and Bisexual Student Organization; An organization of LGB staff and faculty; Domestic partnership benefits

Contacts

Lesbian, Gay, Bisexual Resource Center, Coordinator, Tufts University, N. Carmichael Hall, Bsmt., Medford, MA 02155, Tel.: (617) 627-3770, Fax: (617) 627-3579

University of Massachusetts, Amherst

Programs

Part of the 5-college area (University of Massachusetts at Amherst, Radcliffe, Hampshire, Amherst College).

Courses

Currently there are theme courses offered in Anthropology, French, German, Sociology, and Women's & Gender Studies. English: Queer Theory. Psychology: Lesbian Perspectives. African-American Studies: African-American Gay writing

Resources & Services

The Stonewall Center: A Lesbian, Bisexual, Gay & Transgender Educational Resource Center: http://www.umass.edu/stonewall (e-mail: stonewall@stuaf.umass.edu); The Center (Crampton House/SW) is open every day (MTThF 9-5 & W 12-5), and has information on GLBT Events on Campus; Lesbian Bisexual Gay Alliance: http://www.umass.edu/stonewall/lbga.html (e-mail: lgba@stuaff.umass.edu); GLB Graduate Student Organization; Two in Twenty Floor (LGB residence): L/G & supportive straights; GLBT Academic Information; GLBT Speaker's Bureau

Contacts

The Stonewall Center (stonewall@stuaf.umass.edu), Box 3-1799, University of Massachusetts, Amherst, MA 01003, Tel.: 413-545-4824, Fax: 413-545-6667

Wellesley College

Resources & Services

Wellesley Lesbians, Bisexuals and Friends (tel.: 781-283-3500 x8635); Programs and Services for Lesbian/Bisexual Students

MICHIGAN

Central Michigan University
Resources & Services
Office of Gay & Lesbian Programs; LGBT Commission, Michigan Student Assembly

Eastern Michigan University
Resources & Services
Lesbian, Gay, Bisexual, Transgendered Resource Center; Lesbian, Gay, & Bisexual Student Alliance

Michigan State University
Courses
Courses are being developed. Women's Studies: Lesbian & Gay Studies: Sociology, Psychology, & Cultural Issues
Resources & Services
Alliance of LGB Students

University of Michigan
Courses
Women's Studies: Lesbian Studies. Law School: LGB Legal Issues
Resources & Services
Office of Lesbian Gay Bisexual and Transgender Affairs: http://www.umich.edu/~inqueery (e-mail: lgbpo@umich.edu); the office was established in 1971.

University of Michigan, Flint
Resources & Services
Lesbian, Gay and Bisexual Center

Wayne State University
Resources & Services
Lesbian Gay Bisexual Services

MINNESOTA

Mankato State University
Courses
Women's Studies: Female Bonding

University of Minnesota
Courses
Humanities: Gay Men & Homophobia in the Modern West; Sexuality from Perversity to Diversity
Resources & Services
An endowment has been created to establish the Steven J. Schochet Endowed Center for Gay, Lesbian, Bisexual and Transgender Studies and Campus Life; QGPA: Gay, Lesbian, Bisexual, Transgender Graduate & Professional; Student Association; e-mail: qgpa@tc.umn.edu; homepage: http://www.umn.edu/~qgpa; Gay, Lesbian, Bisexual, Transgender Programs Office: http://www.umn.edu/glbt; Campus Information and Referral Database: LGBT resources: gopher://rodent.cis.umn.edu:11132; Lavender Graduations
Contacts
GLBT Programs Office, University of Minnesota, 340 Coffman Memorial Union, 300 Washington Ave. S.E., Minneapolis, MN 55455, Tel.: 612-624-4461 or 612-626-2324, Fax: 612-626-0909

MISSISSIPPI

University of Mississippi
Resources & Services
Gay, Lesbian, & Bisexual Association: http://www.olemiss.edu/orgs/glba/GLBAHomepage.html (or: e-mail: GLBA@sunset.backbone.olemiss.edu

MISSOURI

University of Missouri, Columbia
Resources & Services
The Gay, Lesbian, and Bisexual Resource Center: http://www.missouri.edu/~peacereb/Peace50/3nov.html; The Triangle Coalition: http://www.missouri.edu/~triangle; The Gay, Lesbian, Bisexual Graduate Students Association: http://www.missouri.edu/~c705363/glbgsa.html

Washington University, St Louis
Courses
American Cultural Studies offers some courses that focus on minority issues: http://www.artsci.wustl.edu/acst.
Resources & Services
The Gay, Lesbian, and Bisexual Alliance: http://www.artsci.wustl.edu/~lambda

NEBRASKA

University of Nebraska
Resources & Services
Lesbian, Gay, Bisexual Student Union; An e-mail discussion list for its LGBT community: UNLGALA (to subscribe, mail subscribe UNLGALA to UNLGALA@juno.com).

NEVADA

University of Nevada, Las Vegas
Courses
Medieval History: Outsiders
Resources & Services
Gay Lesbian Student Union

NEW HAMPSHIRE

Dartmouth College
Resources & Services
Gay, Lesbian, and Bisexual Programming; Dartmouth Alum Gay/Lesbian Organization (DAGLO)

NEW JERSEY

Princeton University
Programs
The Lesbian, Gay & Bisexual Concerns Task Force, Subcommittee on Academics, monitors the LGB Studies curriculum; senior theses on LGBT topics go back to 1936. At least a dozen LGB Ph.D. dissertations have been finished since 1982.
Courses
English first offered a LGB course in 1988; others have been added; in 1995: ten LGB-related courses (in eight

academic departments) were offered, and ten more (in nine departments) are listed.

Resources & Services

Non-discrimination policy of LGBs since 1985; Domestic partnership benefits were recently implemented; Undergraduate Lesbian, Gay & Bisexual Alliance (since 1970); Lesbian, Gay & Bisexual Concerns Task Force; Employees' group, PU-Tops ("The Other Persuasions"); LGB Student Group: http://www.princeton.edu/~lgba.

Rutgers University
Courses

The Writing Program offers graduate LGB Studies courses.

NEW MEXICO

University of New Mexico
Resources & Services

Lesbian & Gay Alliance

NEW YORK

Alfred University
Courses

Human Studies: Gay American History

Barnard-Columbia
Programs

Plans for a major in LGB Studies in Women's Studies.

Courses

Selected undergraduate courses: Women's Studies: Introduction to Lesbian & Gay Studies; The Invisible Woman in Literature: the Lesbian Literary Tradition; Colloquium in Queer Theory. English: Topics in Gay Male Representation; Selected graduate courses. Anthropology: Gender, Sexuality & Culture. School for Social Work: Lesbian & Gay Youth. Columbia Law: Sexuality & the Law

Resources & Services

Graduate Lesbian & Gay Studies Group; undergraduate Queer Studies Awards

City University of New York (CUNY)
Resources & Services

CLAGS (The Center for Lesbian and Gay Studies, CUNY) was established in 1991. CLAGS is headed by a multicultural, interdisciplinary board of directors, representing academic, cultural, civic, and community-based concerns throughout the New York metropolitan area. The center sponsors public forums, lectures, a monthly research colloquium, scholarships, and yearly queer related conferences (it hosted its 7th Annual Queer Graduate Studies Conference, "Forms of Desire," 3-6 April 1997). It offers scholarships and awards to students at the CUNY Graduate School, and it funds, through the Rockefeller Foundation, two fellowships each year for scholars pursuing major research in lesbian and gay studies. The Martin Duberman Endowed Fellowship in Lesbian and Gay Studies offers, every other year, a fellowship in Lesbian and Gay Studies not focused on the United States or Western Europe. There are also plans to establish a Ph.D. program in multicultural studies.

Contacts

City University of New York, Center for Lesbian & Gay Studies (CLAGS), 33 West 42nd Street, New York, NY 10036-8099, Tel. & Fax: 212-642 2924, www: http://members.aol.com/FODQUNY; e-mail: clags@broadway.gc.cuny.edu

Cornell University
Programs

An undergraduate concentration in LGB Studies proposed in 1995; Women's Studies offers a graduate minor in LGB Studies.

Courses

Freshman Writing Seminar: Writing Queer Cultures

Resources & Services

Lesbian Gay Bisexual Resource Office: http://LGBRO.cornell.edu or cu-lbgt-www.cornell.edu; e-mail: lgbro@cornell.edu); Lesbian, Gay, & Bisexual Student Union; The Cornell Library (http://rmc-www.library.cornell.edu) houses the Human Sexuality Collection, a growing collection of primary sources devoted to documenting lesbigay politics and lives at a national level, the politics of pornography, and changes in social controversies about sexuality and sexual identity; Cornell alum association (CuGALA): http:lgbro.cornell.edu/staff/alumni/cugala.html

New York University
Courses

Law School: Sexuality & the Law. School of Education: Working with Gay & Lesbian People

Resources & Services

Gay & Lesbian Student Union; Office of Lesbian, Gay, Bisexual & Transgender Student Services; The NYU Library houses the Fales collection of literature, a strong collection of LGB materials designed to support Ph.D. level work in a variety of fields, especially the social sciences and in humanities materials; special collections including queer novels about NYU and especially Greenwich Village; archival holdings in the Tamiment/Wagner Archives including radical gay materials from the early days of the liberation movement; and a strong collection of queer videos, including documentaries, feature films, experimental films and videos, and other cinema. Lesbian and Gay Studies Selector.

Contact

New York University, 70 Washington Square South, New York, NY 10012, Tel.: 212-998-2596

Pace University
Courses

Women's Studies: Understanding Diversity: Culture Control of Lesbians & Gay Men

Sarah Lawrence College
Contacts

Tel.: 914-337-0700

State University of New York (SUNY), Albany
Courses

English: Lesbian Literature; French: Gay French Novel; Sociology: Homosexuality in American Culture

State University of New York (SUNY), Cortland
Courses
Health: AIDS & Society; Interdisciplinary Studies: Society & Sexual Orientation; Philosophy: Prejudice, Discrimination, & Morality

State University of New York (SUNY), New Paltz
Courses
Women's Studies: Women with Women

State University of New York (SUNY), Stony Brook
Courses
English: Lesbian Literature; History: Homosexuality & History; Sociology: Gay Studies; The Graduate School of Social Welfare: Overview of Gay & Lesbian Issues

NORTH CAROLINA

Duke University
Programs
An undergraduate certificate Program in the Study of Sexualities (1 prerequisite and 4 other courses in the area of gender and sexuality): http://www.duke.edu/web/SXL.
Courses
Undergraduate and graduate courses in Classical Studies, Cultural Anthropology, English, Film & Video, History, Literature, Psychology, Sociology, Women's Studies.
Resources & Services
The University Center for Lesbian, Gay, Bisexual, and Transgendered Life (opened Fall 1994): http://www.duke.edu/lgb/lgbcenter.html (e-mail: lgbcenter@acpub.duke.edu); Duke's Queer InfoServer (http://www.duke.edu/lgb); Undergraduate Duke Gothic Queers; Graduate Gay Professional Students (GYPSY); Law School's Student Committee on Gay and Lesbian Legal Issues (COGLLI): http://www.law.duke.edu/student/act/coglli.html; The University Task Force for Lesbian, Gay, and Bisexual Matters (http://www.duke.edu/web/jyounger/LGBTF); Perkins Library has a good collection of LGB and Women's Studies offerings; An e-mail discussion list for its LGB community: DukeLGB (to subscribe, mail "subscribe dukelgb" to majordomo@acpub.duke.edu); Lavender Graduations; Duke's Gay History: http://www.duke.edu/web/jyounger/SXL/DUGayHist.html.

East Carolina University
Courses
A LGB Studies course in gay literature.
Resources & Services
Student B-GLAD association

Western Carolina University
Courses
English: Gay and Lesbian Literature
Resources & Services
Student B-GLAD association

NORTH DAKOTA

University of North Dakota
Courses
Sociology 340: Sociology of Sex and Gender Roles; 450: Deviance

OHIO

Miami University
Courses
English: Literature & Sexuality: Gay & Lesbian Experience; Religion: Homosexual & Lesbian Experience

Ohio State University
Courses
History: Lesbian & Gay History
Resources & Services
Gay, Lesbian, & Bisexual Student Services; Gay and Lesbian Alum Association

Ohio University, Athens
Courses
Political Science: Gay & Lesbian Politics
Resources & Services
Undergraduate student group "Open Doors."

OKLAHOMA

University of Oklahoma
Courses
English: Gay & Lesbian Representation in Literature; Human Relations: Sexism & Homophobia

OREGON

Southern Oregon State University
Courses
Philosophy: Ethics: Lesbian & Gay Issues; Sociology: Gay Studies

University of Oregon
Courses
Women's Studies: History of the Lesbian Movement
Resources & Services
University of Oregon's LGB homepage: http://darkwing.uoregon.edu/~program; Delta Lambda Phi; Lesbian, Gay, Bisexual, Transgendered Alliance; Lesbian Gay Law Student Association; Department of Sociology offers funding for LGB graduate studies; Lavender Graduations since 1995; BiGALA
Contacts
Lesbian, Gay, Bisexual and Transgender Educational and Support Services Program, 364 Oregon Hall, 5216 University of Oregon, Eugene, OR 97403, Tel.: 541-346-1134, Fax: 541-346-5811

PENNSYLVANIA

Allegheny College
Programs & Courses
A minor in Gay and Lesbian Studies is available: an interdisciplinary program with courses housed primarily in the humanities and social sciences. Soon there will be a new course, Constructions of Sexualities, cross-listed with Psychology.

Bryn Mawr College

Resources & Services

BiGALA alum association; BGALA student organization of Bryn Mawr & Haverford Colleges

Bucknell University

Courses

English: Gay & Lesbian Literature

Resources & Services

Lesbian Gay Bisexual Concerns Office

Pennsylvania State University

Courses

History: Lesbian & Gay History; Human Development: Lesbian & Gay Development; Theories of Sexual Orientation

Resources & Services

Office of Educational Equity: http://www.psu.edu/staff/diversity/lgb.html

University of Pennsylvania

Courses

Communications: Communications, Culture and Sexual Minorities (since 1980)

Resources & Services

Lesbian Gay Bisexual Center: http://dolphin.upenn.edu/~center; Non-academic Program for the Lesbian, Gay and Bisexual Community (since 1982); The Philadelphia Lesbian and Gay Academic Union brings 3-4 speakers per semester to the campus (since 1984).

RHODE ISLAND

Brown University

Programs

Sexuality and Society concentration. The University Committee for Lesbian, Gay and Bisexual Concerns coordinates the curriculum.

Courses

Taught through professors' home departments and in addition to their departmental commitments. Several departments participate at both the graduate and undergraduate level: History, American Civilization, Biology, Philosophy, Women's Studies, Modern Culture and Media, and Comparative Literature. English offers an annual graduate seminar in queer theory.

Resources & Services

LGB undergraduate and graduate organizations; The alumni/ae association provides a prize in LGB scholarship.

SOUTH CAROLINA

University of South Carolina

Resources & Services

Bisexual, Gay, & Lesbian Association: http://web.csd.sc.edu/bgla; e-mail: uscbgla@vm.sc.edu, PO Box 80098, Columbia SC 29225, Tel.: 803-777-7716, press option 3, then option 2

SOUTH DAKOTA

University of South Dakota

Resources & Services

Gay Lesbian Bisexual Alliance: http://www.usd.edu/student-life/orgs/glba/; e-mail: glba@sundance.usd

TENNESSEE

University of Tennessee, Knoxville

Resources & Services

Lambda Student Union: http://funnelweb.utcc.utk.edu/~hodge/lambda, e-mail: denton@utkvx.utk.edu

Vanderbilt University

Resources & Services

The Bisexual, Gay and Lesbian Law Students Association (BiGALLSA): http://www.vanderbilt.edu/css/special_.htm#BiGALLSA; Department of Religion's Office of Gay, Bisexual and Lesbian Concerns (GABLE); Vanderbilt Lambda Association: http://www.vanderbilt.edu/lambda/

TEXAS

Rice University

Programs

The Program for the Study of Women and Gender offers a major: http://www.ruf.rice.edu/~swg; e-mail: swg@rice.edu, 6100 Main, MS 38, Houston, TX 77005-1892, Tel.: (713) 737-5784, Fax: (713) 285-5471

Resources & Services

Gay and Lesbian Support Group

Texas A&M University

Resources & Services

Gay, Lesbian, Bisexual, Trangender Services

University of Houston

Courses

Contested Manliness: Shifting Perspectives of Victorian Masculinity 1850-1910

University of Texas, Austin

Resources & Services

Gay & Lesbian Student Alliance; Lesbians and Gays of Color; University Staff Association Committee for GLBT Concerns: http://www.utexas.edu/students/lbgsa/gaystaff.html

UTAH

University of Utah

Courses

A seminar for public-school teachers and undergraduate education majors trains them to deal more sensitively with gay issues (reported in *LGSN*, vol. 23.2, Summer 1996, p. 14, quoting *Chronicle of Higher Education*, 1 March 1996).

Resources & Services

Lesbian & Gay Student Union

VERMONT

University of Vermont
Courses
Sociology 11: Social Problems
Resources & Services
Gay, Lesbian, & Bisexual Alliance

School for International Training
Brattleboro: e-mail: asa_netherlands@micmail.com
Programs
A college semester abroad at the University of Amsterdam in LGB Studies.

VIRGINIA

George Mason University
Programs
A LGB concentration in the Center for the Study of the Americas is being planned, with an eventual undergraduate minor.
Courses
Communication: Queers in the Media; English 338: Gender & Sexualities; Film & Media Studies: Queer Media and Theories; University Course: AIDS 101
Resources & Services
In 1996, the Board of Visitors removed funding from the LGBT Resource Center (established in 1995; www: http://mason.gmu.edu/~barmitag/glbt.htm); The GLBT Studies Project

College of William and Mary
Resources & Services
Gay & Lesbian Student Union: gaystu@mail.wm.edu; GALA alumni association: http://www.wm.edu/alumni/GALA; Lesbian & Gay Law Association

WASHINGTON

University of Washington, Seattle
Programs
Women Studies offers a graduate certificate program in Lesbian Studies.
Courses
English: many courses, both undergraduate and graduate, including: 306: Responding to AIDS; 489: Lesbian and Gay Studies; Women Studies 354: Lesbianism; American Ethnicity Studies: 489: Women, Minorities, Media. Anthropology: Sexualities, Genders, Bodies. Public Affairs: 573: Sex Orientation & Public Policy. Social Work: 532U: Gay & Lesbian Issues in Practice; 532W: Social Work & AIDS.
Resources & Services
Undergraduate Gay, Bisexual, Lesbian Commission (tel.: 206-685-GBLC); Graduate student-faculty Queer Colloquia; Gay and Lesbian University Employees; A cross-disciplinary queer studies faculty research group; The library has an appreciable gay/lesbian studies collection
Contacts
Gay and Lesbian Studies Coordinator (Libraries)/UW, Suzzallo Reference, Box 352900, University of Washington, Seattle, WA 98195-2900

Washington State University, Pullman
Resources & Services
Gay, Lesbian, Bisexuals, and Allies Program: http://www.wsu.edu/glbap

WEST VIRGINIA

University of West Virginia
Courses
English 189: Sexual Diversity in Film & Literature; Medical Studies 60: Human Sexuality; Philosophy 13: Current Moral Problems
Resources & Services
President's Office for Social Justice http://www.wvu.edu/~socjust; Bisexual, Gay, and Lesbian Mountaineers: http://www.wvu.edu/~biglm or: http://www.wvu.edu/~sos/orgs/biglm.htm

WISCONSIN

University of Wisconsin, Madison
Courses
About 100 current courses with at least some LGB content: http://www.sit.wisc.edu/~tps/lgbcourses.html
Resources & Services
A lengthy report issued May 1997 by the Faculty Senate Committee on GLB Issues offers, among other things, a brief history of LGB studies on campus and recommends setting up an LGBT studies program: http://www.sit.wisc.edu/~tps/report.html. LGBT student groups at the UW-Madison and at eight other branch campuses of the U of Wisconsin system: http://www.sit.wisc.edu/~tps/index.html. GLB Alumni Council

University of Wisconsin, Milwaukee
Programs
18 credit Certificate Program in Lesbian and Gay Studies, with a required introductory course, Gay and Lesbian Studies.
Courses
Many departments offer courses, including Women's Studies: Lesbian Culture.
Resources & Services
A statewide Lesbian and Gay Caucus in the university system.

WYOMING

University of Wyoming
Courses
Women's Studies 4190: Politics of Sexuality
Resources & Services
Lesbian, Gay, Bisexual, and Transgender Association: http://www.uwyo.edu/asa/sorg/lgbta/; e-mail: dbranson@uwyo.edu

CANADA

Toronto, Canadian Gay Archives (largest collection of LGBT documents in Canada), PO Box 639, Station A, Toronto, Ontario M5W 1G2 Canada

ALBERTA

University of Alberta
Resources & Services
Lambda Institute: homepage: http://gpu.srv.ualberta.ca/
~cbidwell/cmb/lambda.htm; e-mail: lambda@compusmart.
ab.ca

ONTARIO

York University, Toronto
Resources & Services
Strong manuscript holdings.

University of Windsor
Programs
M.A. programs in Sociology, History, or Psychology, or
a Ph.D. in Psychology have good resources for doing gay
and lesbian studies.
Courses
G&L Studies
Resources & Services
Undergraduate group Out on Campus: http://
www2.uwindsor.ca/~outonuw.

QUEBEC

University of Montreal
Courses
English: five specialists lesbian and gay studies;
Comparative Literature: Homosexualité et identité
culturelle; Ecrire la différence en sexualité

SASKATCHEWAN

University of Saskatchewan
Resources & Services
University Libraries, in conjunction with those of the
Saskatchewan Archives Board and the University of
Saskatchewan Archives [housed in the same building],
probably contain the second strongest collection in Canada.
The Saskatchewan Archives Board (SAB), Saskatoon
office has a number of important gay and lesbian
collections, especially the Richards collection. According
to the SAB Personal Papers Archivist the scope and depth
of the collection permit the detailed study of Canadian gay
and lesbian life and issues since the 1960s. Other
collections include the personal and public papers of
Canadian LGBT activists.
Contacts
Collections Librarian for Women's and Gender Studies,
University of Saskatchewan Libraries, Saskatoon,
Saskatchewan S7N 5A4 Canada, Tel: 306-966-5979

Saskatchewan Archives Board
Contacts
306-933-8321

REFERENCES:

Books

Adam, Barry D. *The Rise of a Gay and Lesbian Movement.* New
York: Twayne, 1995.

Adam, Barry D. with Alan Sears. *Experiencing HIV.* New York:
Columbia University Press, 1996.

Abelove, Henry, Michèle Aina Barale, and David M. Halperin,
eds. *The Lesbian and Gay Studies Reader.* New York: Routledge,
1993.

Alyson, Sasha, ed. *The Alyson Almanac: The Fact Book of the
Lesbian and Gay Community.* Boston: Alyson Publications,
1993.

Beemyn, Brett and Mickey Eliason. *Queer Studies. A Lesbian,
Gay, Bisexual, and Transgender Anthology.* New York/London:
New York University Press, 1996.

Boswell, John. *Christianity, Social Tolerance, and Homosexuality: Gay People in Western Europe from the Beginning of the
Christian Era to the Fourteenth Century.* Chicago/London: University of Chicago Press, 1980.

Bremmer, Jan, ed. *From Sappho to de Sade. Moments in the History of Sexuality.* London/New York: Routledge, 1989.

Butler, Judith. *Bodies That Matter: On The Discursive Limits of
"Sex."* New York: Routledge, 1993.

―――. *Gender Trouble: Feminism and the Subversion of Identity.* New York: Routledge, 1990.

Conte, Alba. *Sexual Orientation and Legal Rights.* New York: John
Wiley and Sons, 1997.

Crew, Louie, ed. *The Gay Academic.* Palm Springs, California: ETC
Publications, 1978.

Crimp, Douglas, *AIDS. Cultural Analysis, Cultural Activism.* Cambridge, Massachusetts: MIT Press, 1993.

D'Emilio, John, *Making Trouble. Essays on Gay History, Politics
and the University.* New York/London: Routledge, 1992.

D'Emilio, John and Estelle B. Freedman. *Intimate Matters: A History of Sexuality in America.* New York: Harper and Row, 1988.

Dover, Kenneth J. *Greek Homosexuality.* Cambridge, Massachusetts: Harvard University Press, 1978.

Dowsett, Gary W. *Practicing Desire. Homosexual Sex in the Era
of AIDS.* Stanford, California: Stanford University Press, 1996.

Duberman, Martin, ed. *A Queer World. The Center for Lesbian
and Gay Studies Reader.* New York: New York University Press,
1997.

Duberman, Martin, Martha Vicinus, and George Chauncey, Jr., eds.
Hidden from History. Reclaiming the Gay and Lesbian Past.
New York: Meridian, 1990.

Duggan, Lisa. *Policing Public Sex.* South End, 1997.

―――. *Sex Wars.* New York: Routledge, 1995.

Düttmann, Alexander García. *At Odds with AIDS. Thinking and
Talking about a Virus.* Stanford, California: Stanford University Press, 1996.

Dynes, Wayne R. *Homosexuality: A Research Guide.* New York:
Garland Publishing, Inc., 1987.

Dynes, Wayne R., ed. *Encyclopedia of Homosexuality.* New York/
London: Garland Publishing, vol. 1-2, 1990.

Faderman, Lillian. *Odd Girls and Twilight Lovers: A History of
Lesbian Life in Twentieth-Century America.* New York: Columbia University Press, 1991.

―――. *Surpassing the Friendship of Men.* New York: William
Morrow, 1981.

Fee, Elizabeth and Daniel M. Fox, eds. *AIDS: The Burdens of
History.* Berkeley: University of California Press, 1988.

Foucault, Michel. *Histoire de la sexualité/The History of Sexuality.* Vol. 1: *La Volenté de savoir.* Paris: L'editions Gallimard, 1976
(trans.: *An Introduction,* New York: Pantheon, 1978). Vol. 2:
L'usage des plaisirs. Paris: L'editions Gallimard, 1984 (trans.:

The Use of Pleasure, New York: Pantheon, 1985). Vol. 3: *Le souci de soi*. Paris: L'editions Gallimard, 1984 (trans.: *The Care of the Self*, New York: Pantheon, 1986).

Gay Academic Union. *The Universites and the Gay Experience: Proceedings of the Conference Sponsored by the Women and Men of the Gay Academic Union, November 23 and 24, 1973*. New York: Gay Academic Union, 1974.

Gluckman, Amy and Betsy Reed. *Homo Economics. Capitalism, Community, and Lesbian and Gay Life*. New York/London: Routledge, 1997.

Gomez, José. *Demystifying Homosexuality: A Teaching Guide*. New York: Irvington, 1984.

Greenberg, David F. *The Construction of Homosexuality*. Chicago: The University of Chicago Press, 1988.

Greenblatt, R. Ellen, and Cal Gough, eds. *Gay and Lesbian Library Service*. Jefferson, North Carolina: McFarland and Company, Inc. 1990.

Halperin, David M. *One Hundred Years of Homosexuality and Other Essays on Greek Love*. New York: Routledge, 1989.

Halperin, David M., John J. Winkler, and From Zeitlin, eds. *Before Sexuality: The Construction of Erotic Experience in the Ancient Greek World*. Princeton: Princeton University Press, 1990.

Haver, William. *The Body of this Death. Historicity and Sociality in the Time of AIDS*. Stanford: Stanford University Press, 1996.

Jagose, Annamarie. *Queer Theory : An Introduction*. New York: New York University Press, 1996.

Katz, Jonathan Ned. *Gay/Lesbian Almanac. A New Documentary*. New York: Harper & Row, 1983.

Kennedy, Elizabeth Lapovsky and Madeline D. Davis. *Boots of Leather, Slippers of Gold. The History of a Lesbian Community*. New York: Penguin, 1993.

Kopelson, Kevin. *Beethoven's Kiss: Pianism, Perversion, and the Mastery of Desire*. Stanford: Stanford University Press, 1996.

Leap, William. *Word's Out. Gay Men's English*. Minneapolis, Minnesota: University of Minnesota Press, 1996.

Leppert, Richard and Susan McClary, eds. *Music and Society: the Politics of Composition, Performance and Reception*. Cambridge: Cambridge University Press, 1987.

Marrou, Henri-Irenée. *A History of Education in Antiquity*. New York: New American Library, 1956.

McClary, Susan. *Feminine Endings. Music, Gender, and Sexuality*. Minneapolis: University of Minnesota Press, 1991.

McNaron, Toni A. H. *Poisoned Ivy*. Philadelphia: Temple University Press, 1996.

Morton, Donald, ed. *The Material Queer. A Lesbigay Cultural Studies Reader*. Boulder, Colorado: Westview Press, 1996.

Nelson, Randy and Harley Baker. *The Educational Climate for Gay, Lesbian and Bisexual Students*. Santa Cruz: University of California-Santa Cruz, 1990.

Odets, Walter. *In the Shadow of the Epidemic. Being HIV-Negative in the Age of AIDS*. Durham, North Carolina: Duke University Press, 1995.

Percy, William Armstrong, III. *Pederasty and Pedagogy in Archaic Greece*. Urbana: University of Illinois Press, 1996.

Ridinger, Robert B.M. *The Homosexual and Society: An Annotated Bibliography*. New York: Greenwood Press, 1990.

Roscoe, Will. *The Zuni Man-Woman*. Albuquerque: University of New Mexico Press, 1991.

Rotello, Gabriel. *Sexual Ecology: Aids and the Destiny of Gay Men*. New York: Dutton, 1997.

Schmitt, Arno, and Jehoeda Sofer, eds., *Sexuality and Eroticism among Males in Moslem Societies*. New York: Haworth Press, 1992.

Sears, James T. and Walter L. Williams. *Overcoming Heterosexism and Homophobia: Strategies That Work*. New York: Columbia University Press, 1997.

Sedgwick, Eve. *Between Men: English Literature and Male Homosocial Desire*. New York: Columbia University Press, 1985.

———. *Epistemology of the Closet*. Berkeley/Los Angeles: University of California Press, 1990.

Symonds, John Addington. *A Problem in Greek Ethics*. Edinburgh: Ballantyne and Hanson, 1883.

———. *A Problem in Modern Ethics*. London: Private, 1891.

Tierney, William G. *Academic Outlaws: Queer Theory and Cultural Studies in the Academy*. Thousand Oaks, California: Sage Publications, 1997.

Weeks, Jeffrey. *Coming Out: Homosexual Politics in Britain, from the Nineteenth Century to the Present*. New York: Quartet Books, 1979.

———. *Sex, Politics and Society: The Regulation of Sexuality since 1800*. London: Longman, 1981.

———. *Sexuality*. London/New York: Tavistock Publications, 1986.

Williams, Walter, L. *The Spirit and the Flesh: Sexual Diversity in American Indian Culture*. Boston: Beacon Press, 1986.

Witt, Lynn, et al. *Out in All Directions: The Almanac of Gay and Lesbian America*. New York: Warner Books, Inc., 1995.

Woog, Dan. *School's Out: A Book for the Queer Activist/Educator in the High Schools*. Boston: Alyson Publications, 1995.

Chapters in Books

Bowen, Angela. "Completing the Kente: Enabling the Presence of Out Black Lesbians in Academia," in *The New Lesbian Studies: Into the Twenty-First Century*, edited by Bonnie Zimmerman and Toni A. H. McNaron. New York: The Feminist Press at the City University of New York, 1996: 223-28.

Brogan, James E. "Teaching Gay Literature in San Francisco," in *The Gay Academic*, edited by Louie Crew. Palm Springs, California: ETC Publications, 1978: 152-63.

Broidy, Ellen. "Cyberdykes, or Lesbian Studies in the Information Age," in Zimmerman and McNaron: 203-07.

Butler, Judith. "Imitation and Gender Insubordination," in *The Lesbian and Gay Studies Reader*, edited by Henry Abelove, Michèle Aina Barale, and David M. Halperin. New York: Routledge, 1993: 307-20.

Crew, Louie. "Before Emancipation: Gay Persons as Viewed by Chairpersons in English," in Crew, ed.: 3-48.

Gittings, Barbara. "Combatting the Lies in the Libraries," in Crew, ed.: 107-18.

Gurko, Jane. "Sexual Energy in the Classroom," in Zimmerman and McNaron: 16-22.

Halberstam, Judith. "Queering Lesbian Studies," in Zimmerman and McNaron: 256-61.

Hekma, Gert. "A History of Sexology: Social and Historical Aspects of Sexuality," in *From Sappho to De Sade*, edited by Jan Bremmer. London/New York: Routledge, 1989: 173-93.

Houser, Ward. "Education," in *Encyclopedia of Homosexuality*, edited by Wayne R. Dynes. New York and London: Garland Publishing, vol. 1, 1990: 342-44.

Lehman, J. Lee. "Gay Students," in Crew, ed.: 57-63.

Malinowitz, Harriet. "Lesbian Studies and Postmodern Queer Theory," in Zimmerman and McNaron: 262-68.

McNaron, Toni A. H. "That Was Then and This Is Now," in Zimmerman and McNaron: 74-78.

Meyer, Richard. "Rock Hudson's Body," in *Inside/Out: Lesbian Theories, Gay Theories,* edited by Diana Fuss. New York: Routledge, 1991: 259-88.

Mohr, Richard D. "Gay Studies as Moral Vision," in *Gay Ideas: Outing and Other Controversies,* edited by Richard D. Mohr. Boston: Beacon Press, 1992: 243-60.

Padgug, Robert. "Sexual Matters: Rethinking Sexuality in History," in Duberman, Vicinus, and Chauncey: 54-64.

Parmeter, Sarah-Hope. "Four Good Reasons Why Every Lesbian Teacher Should be Free to Come Out in the Classroom," in *The Lesbian in Front of the Classroom: Writings by Lesbian Teachers,* edited by Sarah-Hope Paarmeter and Irene Reti. Santa Cruz: HerBooks, 1988: 44-58.

Risch, Stephen J. "Towards a Gay Analysis of Science and Education," in Crew, ed.: 369-83.

Smith, Barbara, ed. "Sample Syllabi for Courses on Lesbianism," in *Lesbian Studies,* edited by Margaret Cruikshank. Old Westbury, New York: Feminist Press, 1982: 217-35.

Stanley, Julia P. "Lesbian Separatism: The Linguistic and Social Sources of Separatist Politics," in Crew, ed.: 121-31.

Zemsky, Beth. "GLBT Program Offices: A Room of Our Own," in Zimmerman and McNaron: 208-14.

Zimmerman, Bonnie. "Placing Lesbians," in Zimmerman and McNaron: 269-75.

Periodical Articles

Altman, Dennis. "Gay Studies and the Quest for Academic Legitimacy," in *Advocate,* vol. 378, 13 October 1983: 32-34.

Bersani, Leo. "Is the Rectum a Grave?," in *October,* vol. 43, Winter 1987: 197-222.

Bravmann, Scott. "Making Lesbian and Gay Studies Work," in *LGSN,* vol. 14, no. 3, November 1987: 7-8.

Butler, Judith. "Against Proper Objects," in *differences: A Journal of Feminist Cultural Studies,* vol. 6, no. 2-3, Summer-Fall 1994: 1-27.

———. "Critically Queer," in *GLQ: A Journal of Lesbian and Gay Studies,* vol. 1, no. 1, 1993: 17-32.

Cage, Mary Crystal. "A Course on Homosexuality," in *The Chronicle of Higher Education,* vol. 41, 14 December 1994: A19-20.

Cohen, Cathy J. "Punks, Bulldaggers, and Welfare Queens: The Radical Potential of Queer Politics?," in *GLQ: A Journal of Lesbian and Gay Studies,* vol. 3, no. 4, February 1997: 437-66.

Cornwall, Richard. "Deconstructing Silence: The Queer Political Economy of the Social Articulation of Desire," in *Review of Radical Political Economics,* vol. 29, no. 1, Winter 1997: 1-131.

D'Augelli, Anthony. "Teaching Lesbian/Gay Development: From Oppression to Exceptionality," in *Journal of Homosexuality,* vol. 22, 1991: 213-27.

de Lauretis, Teresa. "Queer Theory: Lesbian and Gay Sexualities. An Introduction," in *differences: A Journal of Feminist Cultural Studies,* vol. 3, no. 2, 1991: iii-xviii.

D'Erasmo, Stacey. "In Schools Across the Country, Gay Studies is Coming on Strong," in *Rolling Stone,* 3 October 1991: 83-89.

Freccero, Carla. "Bodies and Pleasures: Early Modern Interrogations," in *The Romantic Review,* vol. 86, no. 2, March 1995: 379-91.

Gonshak, Henry. "A Furor over Gay and Lesbian Studies," in *The Chronicle of Higher Education,* vol. 41, 21 September 1994: A56.

Goode, Stephen and Carol Innerst. "College Curriculums Add 'Queer Theory' to PC Lists," in *Insight on the News,* vol. 11, no. 20, 22 May 1995: 12-14.

Gose, Ben. "The Politics and Images of Gay Students," in *Chronicle of Higher Education,* vol. 42, no. 22, 9 February 1996: A33-34.

Heller, Scott. "Gay- and Lesbian-Studies Movement Gains Acceptance in Many Areas of Scholarship and Teaching," in *The Chronicle of Higher Education,* vol. 37, 24 October 1990: A4-6.

Kimball, Geoffrey. "Aztec Homosexuality: The Textual Evidence," in *Journal of Homosexuality,* vol. 26, no. 1, 1993: 7-24.

Lane, Laura. "Gay Male and Lesbian Youth Suicide," in *LGSN,* vol. 22, no. 3, Fall 1995: 23.

Lane, W. Clayton. "Letter to the Editor," in *LGSN,* vol. 22, no. 2, Summer 1995: 2-3.

Leonard, Garry. "Introduction: Pedagogy," in *College Literature,* vol. 24, no. 1, February 1997: "Queer Utilities: Textual Studies, Theory, Pedagogy, Praxis," 152-55.

Martin, Biddy. "Extraordinary Homosexuals and the Fear of Being Ordinary," in *differences: A Journal of Feminist Cultural Studies,* vol. 6, no. 2-3, Summer-Fall 1994: 100-26.

Meyers, Helene. "To Queer or Not to Queer: That's Not the Question," in *College Literature,* vol. 24, no. 1, February 1997: "Queer Utilities: Textual Studies, Theory, Pedagogy, Praxis," 171-82.

Mooney, Carolyn J. "Attack on Homosexuality Angers Divinity Students," in *The Chronicle of Higher Education,* vol. 41, 16 November 1994: A38.

———. "Homosexuals in Academe: Fear of Backlash Clouds Reactions to Increased Tolerance," in *The Chronicle of Higher Education,* vol. 39, 23 September 1992: A17.

Newton, David E. and Stephen J. Risch. "Homosexuality and Education: A Review of the Issue," in *High School Journal,* vol. 64, 1981: 191-202.

Norton, Rictor. "Homosexual Literary Tradition: Course Outline and Objectives," in *College English,* vol. 35, 1974: 674-78 (with criticism by TK Gordon, 503-04).

Nussbaum, Martha C. "The Softness of Reason: A Classical Case for Gay Studies," in *The New Republic,* vol. 207, no. 3-4, 13 July 1992: 26-32.

Pottie, Lisa M. "Cross-Border Shopping and Niche Marketing: Academic Economies and Lesbian and Gay Studies," in *College Literature,* vol. 24, no. 1, February 1997: "Queer Utilities: Textual Studies, Theory, Pedagogy, Praxis," 183-95.

Rich, Adrienne. "Compulsory Heterosexuality and Lesbian Existence," in *Signs: Journal of Women in Culture and Society,* vol. 5, no. 4, Summer 1980: 631-60. Also in Abelove, Barale, and Halperin: 227-54.

Schreiber, Ron. "Giving a Gay Course," in *College English,* vol. 36, 1974: 316-23.

Skinner, Marilyn B. "The Sexuality Wars in Contemporary Classical Scholarship," in *Thamyris,* vol. 3, no. 1, 1996: 103-23. Reproduced at: http://www.uky.edu/ArtSciences/Classics/gender.html.

Tierney, William G. "Academic Freedom and the Parameters of Knowledge," in *Harvard Educational Review,* vol. 63, no. 2, Summer 1993: 143-61.

———. "Building Academic Communities of Difference. Gays, Lesbians, and Bisexuals on Campus," in *Change,* vol. 24, no. 2, March/April 1992: 41-46.

Unks, Gerald, ed. *The Gay Teenager.* Special double volume issue of *The High School Journal,* vol. 77, no. 1-2, October-November 1993 and December-January 1994.

Van Dyne, Larry. "Homosexual Academics Organize, Seek End to Discrimination," in *The Chronicle of Higher Education,* vol. 18, 10 December 1973: 7.

Ward, Michael and Mark Freeman. "Defending Gay Rights: The Campaign against the Briggs Amendment," in *Radical America,* vol. 13, no. 4, 1979: 11-26.

Waxman, Barbara and Eleanor Byington. "Teaching Paul Monette's Memoir/Manifesto to Resistant Readers," in *College Literature,* vol. 24, February 1997: "Queer Utilities: Textual Studies, Theory, Pedagogy, Praxis," 156-70.

Williams, Walter, L. "Center for Scholars in Residence at the University of Southern California," in *Journal of Homosexuality,* vol. 30, no. 3, 1996: 123-28.

Other

The Gay, Lesbian and Straight Education Network (GLSEN; 121 West 27th Street, Suite 804, New York, NY 10001, Tel.: 212-727-0135, www homepage: http://www.glsen.org, e-mail: glsen@glsen.org), founded in 1990, is the only national organization of gay and straight teachers and community members working to end homophobia in K-12 schools. One of its effective methods is to offer student internships.

—John G. Younger

9

Labor and Employment

Until recently, very little has been written about the situation of gay people in the workplace. Despite the wealth of cross-cultural information about male same-gender sexual behavior in a broad range of societies, there is little written about the lives of such men in their places of work; much less is written about lesbian sexual behavior and relationships, and even less about their workplace issues. Even with the dawn of the gay liberation movement, members of the gay press have given far more ink to sex, relationships, and the social scene than to the place where most of us spend the greatest number of our waking hours: the workplace. In the past few years, the situation has changed, and there is now some qualitative and quantitative information available about the situation of lesbians and gay men at work. As lesbians and gay men continue to come out at work, it is to be expected that they and others will increasingly report on their experiences in both the mainstream and gay media.

HISTORICAL DISCRIMINATION

Discrimination against lesbians and gay men in the workplace has historically taken many forms, and definitions of discrimination have changed over the years.

Experts in the field have found it useful to distinguish between impersonal and personal discrimination, although gay employees routinely conflate the two, particularly in politically sponsored surveys designed to measure the prevalence of discrimination in order to pass nondiscrimination legislation.

Impersonal discrimination is anything that creates a hostile or discriminatory work environment, such as the failure to have or disseminate a nondiscrimination policy, management tolerance of or participation in anti-gay jokes and comments, heterosexism (the assumption that everyone is or should be heterosexual), and differences in benefits between married employees and gay male or lesbian employees with partners.

Personal discrimination is discrimination against a specific individual or individuals who are known or thought to be gay men or lesbians. This discrimination can take the form of failure to hire, failure to promote, firing, name calling, hostile comments or jokes, harassment, sexual harassment, sabotage of work, ostracism, blackmail, threats, and violence against those known or suspected of being gay or lesbian.

While all of these forms of discrimination can seem overwhelming to a gay male or lesbian employee, research shows that they can stem from different causes and are best addressed in different ways. Personal discrimination should never be tolerated, yet in the absence of protective legislation or employer policies, little can be done except in the most egregious cases of personal harm. Throughout history, gay people have fled work situations that posed such threats to their safety and well being. Even today, in situations where protective legislation is in place, some feel that a job in which they are being personally discriminated against is not worth fighting about, and that it is easier to move on to a less hostile situation. Others have chosen to stick it out and fight, and by obtaining management support, have emerged victorious. Where that support is not forthcoming, gay and lesbian employees sometimes "win the battle" for their rights, but "lose the war" in terms of their own personal happiness and career success.

Most impersonal discrimination can and should be addressed at the highest corporate levels, although anti-gay jokes and comments are sometimes rooted in ignorance and can be rectified by conversation and the judicious use of humor; such comments need not always been seen as evidence that the work environment is irremediably homophobic. However, as the social consciousness of gay men and lesbians grows, such jokes and comments should not continue to be given such benefit of the doubt indefinitely. Management is well advised to instruct employees that these forms of expression will not be tolerated. Other forms of impersonal discrimination that are a part of corporate policy require attention from top management. This can sometimes be achieved by the request of a few individuals; more commonly, it is the result of a concerted action by a group of gay men, lesbians, and sometimes allies. As the years pass, discrimination in benefits, which were once seen as "just the way things are" by management and gay people alike, will no longer be considered acceptable for a company that claims not to discriminate on the basis of sexual orientation.

Pre-1970s

Until recently, due to the absence of protective policies or legislation, employers were free to discriminate openly against individuals they knew or suspected to be homosexual. Much of the early documentation on such discrimination refers to examples that today would be seen as gender discrimination, focusing as it did on an individual's gender nonconformity in style of dress, walk, and mannerisms.

Homosexual men were thought to be effeminate, lesbians to be masculine. Neither expression was acceptable in business, irrespective of the additional "problem" of someone having a different sexual orientation. Of course, lesbians were in a double bind— they could not be too feminine, or they would not be taken seriously at work and would be subject to sexual harassment, yet they could not be too assertive or sporty in appearance, as they would then be dismissed as unwomanly.

Except in a few fields, such as music, art, and the theater, it was highly unusual for an individual to come out as gay or lesbian until a decade after the Stonewall Riots in 1969, when it became more common for people to claim a modern gay identity. When gay men and lesbians themselves saw homosexuality as being primarily about sexual behavior, they saw no reason to discuss this subject at work.

The 1950s and 1960s saw the formation and growth of the Daughters of Bilitis and the Mattachine Society, organizations dedicated to integrating the homosexual into respectable society. Dressed in suits (male) and dresses (female), they staged demonstrations demanding equal rights for homosexuals, including the right to be free from discrimination in the workplace. Yet it took a wider social movement led by proponents of sexual freedom to effectuate this program. The change in self-identity brought about by the Stonewall Riots of 1969 is what ultimately led gay men and lesbians to have the confidence to come out at work and cause society to accept them as part of the cultural landscape.

The 1970s

Immediately after Stonewall, it was rare for anyone to come out at work, despite the beginning of gay and lesbian visibility in other social contexts. Merle Miller, whose two-part article, "What It Means to Be a Homosexual" caused a stir in the *New York Times Magazine*, was the first gay professional to come out in the mainstream press; he was not followed by many others.

In 1973, Andrew Tobias, writing under the pseudonym John Reid, penned *The Best Little Boy in the World,* a semi-fictionalized account of his experiences coming out to himself and in the world of business. From today's vantage point, these accounts seem little more than tortured self-analysis and justifications for the right of homosexuals to be treated as human beings. Yet at the time, they were radical acts of daring and honesty.

Gay men and lesbians tended to say to themselves and their friends, "they may suspect or even assume I'm gay—what's to be gained by coming out?" In an environment where it was assumed that "there couldn't possibly be anyone 'that way' here,"

Andrew Tobias

few gay men or lesbians were willing to breach the social code of silence. In most cases, this meant that the assumption of heterosexuality prevailed, and few individuals were thought to be gay in the workplace context. A number of lesbians and gay men got married due to workplace, family, or other social pressures, providing the perfect cover. Others maintained an image of disinterest in anything but work, or conversely, as a party animal.

Throughout the 1970s, as the gay liberation and radical lesbian feminist movements began to gain adherents and visibility. Gay men and lesbians found it less easy to hide at work by simply remaining silent, and fewer chose to marry. This created tremendous anxiety for gay people in most workplaces. In environments where anti-gay comments and jokes were rampant, gay men and lesbians felt no other choice but to closet themselves in order to avoid being treated with the disrespect their coworkers gave to those stereotyped as sexual predators (gay men) and man-haters (lesbians).

But hiding was no longer that easy to pull off. In order to maintain their closet, gay men and lesbians had to create a heterosexual persona. Often, this meant dating someone of the opposite gender, inventing a fiancee, or in the case of gay men, talking about one's (hetero)sexual prowess. In many cases, gay men were able to convince a heterosexual woman friend to act the part of a girlfriend; in other cases gay men and lesbians served this role for each other. Lesbians faced double jeopardy in being seen to date men—not enough men and the perception of social incompetence or rumors about man-hating might start; too many men and she might be seen as a slut.

For some gay men and lesbians, creating this heterosexual persona seemed like second nature, or "just the way things were." For others, it took a tremendous, daily, psychological toll. Until the American Psychiatric Association changed its definition of homosexuality as a mental illness in 1973, lesbians and gay men might subject themselves to "conversion therapy," which promised to change them into heterosexuals through a regimen of counseling and electric shock treatment. Some of the most harrowing tales of personal suffering come from those who managed to hold down jobs or pursue professional careers during the course of such "treatment."

Some gay men and lesbians tentatively came out to a few others at work, but this tended to be an individual phenomenon, with few repercussions beyond that individual and his or her associates. Very few articles in the mainstream or gay press or in the newly emerging field of gay book titles spoke to this issue. As a result, few gay people were able to imagine being out at work.

The 1980s

In the 1980s, gay men and lesbians usually had some degree of comfort in their own gay identity, but generally remained reticent about sharing this information with others at work. While one might be out to heterosexual friends and family and leading an active gay social life, this openness was shed at the office door. Many said they relied on "gaydar" to try to find other gay men and lesbians at work, and some also tried to identify sympathetic heterosexuals. The technique of dropping a series of hints over time about things that only someone in the know would pick up on was the most common way that the subject was broached. However, others preferred to remain isolated rather than risk too much familiarity with others, gay or heterosexual, whom they feared might betray their secret.

As a result of this reticence, most heterosexuals were unaware that anyone in their workplace was gay, despite the increasing visibility of gay people in their personal lives and in the cultural milieu. For many heterosexuals, their discomfort with gay people and gay issues led them to make anti-gay comments or jokes in the workplace that they began to regret. Others tried to be supportive but found that in the absence of open communication from gay colleagues, they did not really know how. Corporate sensitivity training occasionally began to include gay issues, but in a packed hour or two covering sexism, sexual harassment, and race relations, gay issues almost always got the short shrift.

One leader in the field of gay-sensitive diversity training was AT&T, which hired consultant and author Brian McNaught. His 1993 book, *Gay Issues in the Workplace,* was based almost entirely on his experiences there in the 1980s and early 1990s and shows a corporation trying to do the right thing in the midst of widespread ignorance among heterosexuals and silence on the part of gay men and lesbians.

Fear and ignorance about AIDS was also a significant component of workplace prejudice against gay men, and by illogical extension, against lesbians. Although surveys showed that Americans were most likely to believe information about how AIDS is transmitted if they received it at work, only a few companies took the lead in providing this kind of education. As a result, the fear that AIDS could be spread by casual contact persisted among some otherwise educated individuals throughout the decade. For most people, gay or heterosexual, AIDS remained the only way they received confirmation that someone was gay; when an unmarried

man suddenly left work due to illness, or died, his code of silence was often shattered.

Due to the fear of both the repercussions of homophobia and AIDS-phobia, most gay people preferred to keep a low profile about being gay at work. And most gay and lesbian rights organizations followed the lead of their members in seeking to enshrine privacy as the most significant right for gay people. This "don't ask, don't tell" ethos was struck a major blow in 1986 when the Supreme Court ruled in *Bowers v. Hardwick* that there is no right of privacy for gay sexual relationships. This blow to privacy in the sexual context made many gay people realize that the personal and the political are indeed the same, and that only by coming out can they achieve the right to be left alone.

Yet throughout the 1980s, some courageous individuals at all levels of the workforce began to take strides that would lead to increasing freedom for themselves and others. The December 1981 *Fortune* magazine cover story, "Gay in Corporate America," was the first in-depth coverage of gay issues in a business magazine. For many gay people in business, it was the first, and for many years, the only time that they knew of anyone willing to be out at work. Most people who were closeted at work had friends who were also closeted, and for the most part there continued to be almost total mainstream and gay media disinterest in gay men and lesbian workplace issues during the 1980s.

A review of the literature shows that even scholarly and trade journals published almost nothing on the subject, perhaps for scholars' own fears about ruining their careers by focusing on gay subjects. What was reported was typically scandalous, such as the revelations by Foster Winans that he and his boyfriend traded in inside information while he was the "Heard on the Street" columnist for the *Wall Street Journal.*

What is perhaps more surprising is that gay and lesbian authors and journalists writing for the gay press also gave almost no ink to workplace issues. Rather, they continued to focus on sex, parties, and the changes brought about in the lives of gay men due to AIDS. Even in the face of evidence to the contrary, the closet and corporate hostility seemed such entrenched facts of life that it took the gay media years to catch up to the changes that were underway.

Most significantly, a number of gay and lesbian employee groups formed during this time. At first, they primarily fulfilled a social function, but as members began to be more comfortable meeting with each other, their trust in each other grew, and some gained the strength to come out to heterosexuals, bring partners to corporate events, and to pursue corporate benefits such as medical insurance coverage for domestic partners.

Additionally, a number of gay and lesbian professional organizations formed during this period. Meant to bring together people in various fields who shared a geographic location, or people in diverse locations who shared a common field, these groups fostered networking and sowed additional seeds of activism for the 1990s.

The 1990s

Within a few short years—the early 1990s—all the rules changed. Polls now show that most Americans know someone gay—a relative, a friend, a neighbor. And the inclusion of gay people—usually from their own point of view—in popular music, movies, television, books, magazines, and newspapers has meant that gay people are far more visible today than they have ever been.

This major shift in the cultural milieu means that most heterosexuals have a degree of comfort talking about gay people and gay issues. Today, Americans share knowledge of a common culture that can be used when testing the waters before coming out to work colleagues. Discussion about a recent film or television special with a gay character is not unusual these days—whether initiated by a gay person or a heterosexual.

Gay people have more role models to inspire acts of bravery, such as coming out and organizing for equal treatment. When one can read about others who came out at work or won domestic partners benefits, it is easier to think about doing the same.

The media in particular deserve credit for assisting the process of normalizing gay lives. From printing obituary notices that include partners as survivors to feature stories on gay relationships, parents, and workplace victories, the media began to show that gay people had lives that were about far more than just sex.

While "outing" was controversial in 1992, Michelangelo Signorile's column about closeted celebrities and entertainment industry business people in *Outweek* began the process of normalizing the personal lives of gay people. Today, even mainstream publications are far less fearful about revealing personal details about gay business executives. Additionally, some of those who were "outed," have now affirmatively chosen to come out as gay.

As more and more municipalities adopted nondiscrimination policies, the question on every gay employee's mind was whether or not they were enforceable. In 1991, Jeffrey Collins won a multi-million dollar lawsuit against Shell Oil in San Francisco for discrimination based on sexual orientation. The parties eventually settled out of court. This case served as a wake-up call to corporations that they needed to take antidiscrimination laws seriously, and led others to adopt their own nondiscrimination policies.

Another important factor in helping to encourage, affirm, and assist gay people in the process of coming out in the professional workplace and seeking equal treatment was the concentration of books on the subject published in the mid-1990s. Mostly issued by major publishing houses, and hence distributed at chain as well as gay and lesbian bookstores, these books ensured that gay people could read about others in situations similar to their own.

While the first books on the subject, Brian McNaught's *Gay Issues in the Workplace* (1993) and James D. Woods and Jay H. Lucas's *The Corporate Closet: The Professional Lives of Gay Men in America* (1993), did little more than outline the problems faced by those in the closet, later books held out hope that those days would soon be over.

Ed Minkens's *100 Best Companies for Gay Men and Lesbians* (1994) and Daniel B. Baker, Sean O'Brien Strub, and William Henning's *Cracking the Corporate Closet* (1995) investigated which companies were the most gay friendly, while Annette Friskopp and Sharon Silverstein's *Straight Jobs* (1995), Liz Winfeld and Susan Spielman's *Straight Talk about Gays in the Workplace* (1995), and Richard Rast and Lourdes Rodriguez-Nogues's *Out in the Workplace* (1995) gave a glimpse into the lives of those who were changing the face of American business by coming out and seeking equality there.

Additionally, Grant Luckenbill's *Untold Millions* (1995) showed how gay consumers could most effectively be reached by major corporations and small businesses—without the hype that plagued some of the self-serving promotional campaigns led by public relations and advertising advisors.

In the last few years, gay people began coming out in almost every industry all over the country. While most gay people in small towns, Texas, the Midwest, and the South, and those in certain industries still do not enjoy the freedom those in the rest of the country have achieved, the tide has decisively turned. Today, one can find openly gay executives, lawyers, doctors, police officers, firefighters, factory workers, secretaries, teachers, and almost every other sort of worker or professional.

In what sometimes seemed like a stampede due to the media focus, but in reality was just the slow realization that life would go on and probably be even better if they came out, corporate employees became some of the most visible openly gay workers. At all levels on the corporate ladder, though most were concentrated somewhere in the middle, gay men and lesbians could be found quietly telling a few, and then more and more trusted colleagues, that they were gay.

For those in lower level jobs, where day-to-day survival was and is an issue, it is not surprising that fewer have risked coming out. The same applied to certain blue-collar professions where physical violence in the workplace is not unknown. But what keeps managers at the highest levels in the closet? One answer is that they feel their skills are so specialized that it would be almost impossible for them to find another position if they lost one due to homophobia. As word would quickly get all around their industry, moving to a new location would not help. Additionally, fear is always relative. Since top executives do not have too many peers who have come out successfully, they are in the position that most middle managers were a few years ago and remain afraid of the consequences. To date, those at the top who have come out have typically been in the entertainment or fashion industries, which have historically been among the most gay friendly.

Similarly, lesbians and gay people of color remain somewhat more closeted than the typical gay white male. Most cite the fear of double or triple jeopardy: "I'm already discriminated against for being a woman/Black/Hispanic. Why let them know I'm gay too?" On the other hand, those who have come out successfully say things like, "I'm already different because I'm a woman/Black/Hispanic. Why not be fabulous?" By capitalizing on the fact of their difference, these individuals have been able to be recognized, remembered, and use their unique abilities and contacts to succeed. While still fewer in number, the increased presence of women and minorities in the workforce means that lesbians and gay people of color will continue to expand the possibilities of making their presence known.

One new phenomenon in recent years is the way older gay people view younger gay people as role models in terms of coming out at work. Unfettered by the mindset of surviving years of discrimination, some gay people in their twenties and thirties have never been closeted at work or any other place. This is perhaps the easiest way to come out—no years of half-truths or lies to be explained away later. Yet inspired by their example, some seasoned employees are doing just that—coming out at work in later life.

Is there a lavender ceiling for gay men and lesbians? We simply do not know yet. But as openly gay people continue to rise through entry levels and middle management, it will not be surprising to find some at the top as well. Today's openly gay partners at consulting firms and managers at large companies typically endured years of hiding before coming out. But the next generation will have been openly gay all the way up to the top.

A major change in the psychology of gay workers is that the lack of equal benefits is now widely seen as discrimination. While some still feel that nothing can be done about it in their particular workplace, the *recognition* of the lack of fairness is the first step to overcoming it, and that did not exist just a few short years ago.

In the 1990s, a number of companies provide formal recognition of their gay and lesbian employee groups, while at other organizations, the groups remain quasiformal or informal. Activists report that there are pros and cons to each approach. With formal recognition comes access to company financial and communication resources, as well as a clear signal from management that gay employees are a valued part of the company. Being formally recognized also means being officially part of the loop that discusses business strategy, such as target marketing to gay men and lesbians.

On the other hand, formal recognition sometimes means that the group has to support the company, at least by silence, even if its members do not necessarily agree with a particular policy decision the company is taking. For example, AT&T employees often privately complained about feeling that their hands were tied during a highly publicized survivor benefits lawsuit in the 1990s—they felt they could not go on the record as critical of the company's decision not to pay out benefits or to discuss domestic partner medical insurance benefits while the lawsuit was still in the courts.

In the 1990s, the term "queer" gained current usage, especially among young people. It often means gay or lesbian, but also means bisexual, transgendered, or anyone with a different sexuality, such as fetishism, sadomasochism, etc. To date this term has not gained currency in the business world. However, to avoid giving offense, business people are advised to avoid such phrases as "don't queer the deal."

THE MOVEMENT TO PROTECT GAY AND LESBIAN EMPLOYEES FROM JOB DISCRIMINATION

In 1974, IBM, the major computer manufacturer headquartered in Armonk, New York, became the first organization to offer protection from discrimination to gay men and lesbians. AT&T and Levi Strauss followed in 1975. These historic steps were not quickly followed by many other large corporations.

Rather, smaller organizations, such as the *Village Voice*, the New York City-based newsweekly, were among those to add protection by 1977. In 1978, the Bank of America, CBS, Coors Brewing Co., and Morrison & Foerster—a law firm with headquarters in San Francisco, and in 1979, ABC, REI—a sports and outdoor wear company—and Seattle Light City Co. joined the small list of companies granting freedom from protection against discrimination based on sexual orientation, which was often called "sexual preference" or "affectional preference" in corporate handbooks. These policies were often enacted due to requests by a few lesbian or gay employees who had the ear of someone in human resources or higher up the corporate chain of command. While some organizations instituted their policies in response to fear of lawsuits (in which they would have prevailed, but at the cost of time, money, and employee happiness), most did so because they became convinced it was the right thing to do to foster employee loyalty.

Increasingly throughout the 1980s and 1990s, typically in response to informal groups of gay and lesbian employees' requests, hundreds of companies, nonprofit organizations, educational institutions, and governmental agencies have instituted policies that pledged freedom from discrimination based on sexual orientation in their workplaces. At the same time, in response to voter pres-

sure, several hundred municipalities, counties, and states have enacted similar workplace protection for all those employed within their geographic boundaries.

Surprisingly, locales particularly known for their openness to gay men and lesbians in their midst faced some of the most difficult battles for workplace protection. For over a decade, a coalition of conservative religious leaders kept a nondiscrimination ordinance from passing in New York City, until success was achieved in 1993. In 1991 in California, Governor Pete Wilson vetoed a statewide nondiscrimination law, prompting riots in West Hollywood. The following year, a watered-down version of the law, one of the weakest on the books, was enacted.

In both liberal and conservative locations, legislators passed nondiscrimination laws, only to be overturned by voters. In the late 1970s, Eugene, Oregon was among the first to pass and then to overturn such a law (as of 1994 it again offered protection against discrimination based on sexual orientation). Also in the late 1970s, Anita Bryant's so-called Save the Children campaign in Florida was responsible for voter reversal of a law there. More recently, in the 1990s, voters have overturned nondiscrimination protection in Alachua, Florida, Cincinnati, Ohio, and the states of Colorado and Maine.

Courts have been both friend and foe to the cause of nondiscrimination based on sexual orientation. In locales where no specific nondiscrimination legislation exists, most courts have been reluctant to find such an idea embedded in other nondiscrimination statutes. However, a few states have constitutions that have allowed the courts to apply the nondiscrimination brush more broadly. Courts have particularly tended to support the legislative enactment of nondiscrimination over voter repeals. In its historic 1996 Supreme Court case *Romer v. Evans*, the justices ruled that Colorado voters did not have the authority to single out gay people from the political process, and restored the nondiscrimination ordinances of Denver, Boulder, Aspen, and other cities.

Nondiscrimination policies continue to tend to be found in the larger companies and the more liberal cities. Yet their scope is far reaching. More than 500 companies, educational institutions, nonprofit organizations, and government employers have policies prohibiting discrimination on the basis of sexual orientation, and many more are covered by city, county, or state law. More than fifty million residents of American cities, counties, and states are covered by laws prohibiting discrimination based on sexual orientation. The actual number employed in these locations is even greater.

Additionally, the Human Rights Campaign maintains a list of congressional representatives, even those who do not typically vote in favor of gay and lesbian rights issues, who have attested that they do not discriminate based on sexual orientation in hiring for their own staff. On the federal level, President Clinton has implemented nondiscrimination policies department-by-department since his election, and these policies now cover almost all civilian employees. In response to a lawsuit brought by Frank Buttino, the Federal Bureau of Investigation now also pledges not to discriminate.

Of course, there is often still a gap between policy and reality. Sometimes an organization has a nondiscrimination policy, but fails to disseminate it. And the enforcement provisions of most legislation and many corporate and organizational policies are quite weak. Yet most gay and lesbian employees feel that having a nondiscrimination policy in place is an important first step in assessing how comfortable they feel working at and coming out in a given employment environment.

Usually, without the presence of this signal from top management, gay and lesbian employees do not feel comfortable forming a gay and lesbian employee support group. And it is the presence of these support organizations that is typically responsible for further strides in an organization, such as diversity training that includes sexual orientation, inclusion of same-gender partners in workplace social functions, the full range of domestic partner benefits, niche marketing to the gay and lesbian communities, philanthropy to gay and lesbian causes, corporate support for gay and lesbian rights legislation, and targeted recruiting of openly gay and lesbian individuals.

Companies and organizations in other parts of the world have also begun to extend nondiscrimination protection to lesbians and gay men in the workplace. Most of Canada, Australia, and New Zealand have such protection, as does South Africa, which included a nondiscrimination provision in its 1994 constitution. While Norway has had such a law since 1981, other Scandinavian and European countries have been slower to follow suit, including those known for their openness. The following countries have such protection: France (since 1986), Denmark (since 1987), Sweden (since 1988), and the Netherlands (since 1994). Since 1992, Israel has also had nondiscrimination protection. Ironically, some countries, such as Great Britain, may extend partnership rights in the workplace before adopting nondiscrimination protection. Despite these countries' reputations for being gay-friendly, many lesbians and gay men in these countries are not out at work, claiming, like their U.S.-counterparts a decade ago, that "it's nobody's business." While there are a few gay employee groups and gay professional groups outside the U.S., it is only those in Britain, Australia, and New Zealand that have a large percentage of their membership who is out at work.

THE BENEFITS QUESTION

The City of Berkeley, California, was the first U.S. government entity to offer domestic partner benefits, doing so in 1985. A number of other municipalities, government agencies, and educational institutions followed, along with a few small private employers including the *Village Voice*, a weekly New York City newspaper.

In 1991, Lotus Computer Company, a software producer that devised the first popularly used computer spreadsheet program, became the first major private employer to offer health insurance coverage to the same-gender domestic partners of its employees. This announcement received wide coverage, and was the first time gay issues had ever been so prominently featured across national and local business news outlets.

When the sky did not fall, other employers began to follow suit. Medical, educational, and nonprofit institutions, small businesses, and governments were among the first to offer benefits: Blue Cross/Blue Shield Massachusetts; Gardener's Supply Co. of Burlington, Vermont; and Montifiore Medical Center (Albert Einstein College) in New York City in 1991; with Beth Israel Medical Center, New York City; Borland International, a Scotts Valley, California, computer software company; Boston Children's Hospital; the Episcopal Diocese of Newark, N.J.; the Minnesota Communications Group (MCG) (subsidiary: Minnesota Public Radio American Public Radio); and Santa Cruz Operations, all following in 1992.

Among the publicly recognized corporations, the first to follow Lotus's lead were Levi Strauss & Co., of San Francisco, the

MCA/Universal entertainment company, and Silicon Graphics, a high tech firm in Silicon Valley, all of which offered benefits in 1992.

Among the best-known companies and organizations that began to offer benefits in 1993 were computer and high tech related firms: Apple Computer, Microsoft, Oracle Corporation, Sun Microsystems, Sybase, Ziff-Davis Publishing, as well as those in the media and entertainment field: the *Boston Globe* newspaper, Home Box Office, National Public Radio (NPR), Viacom, WGBH Public Television of Boston, and Warner Brothers Pictures. Others included Charles Schwab & Co., the San Francisco-based financial services firm, Fannie Mae, Planned Parenthood, and Starbucks, as well as a bevy of law firms: the Chicago-based Schiff, Hardin & Waite, the New York City-based Milbank, Tweed, Hadley & McCloy, the San Francisco-based Howard, Rice, Nemerovski, Canaday, Morrison & Foerster, and the firm of Orrick, Herrington & Sutcliffe. From then on, first a trickle, and then a steady stream of America's largest employers began to offer medical insurance coverage to domestic partners—some to same-gender couples only, others to both gay and unmarried heterosexual couples.

At first, benefits were offered because of the intervention of a few well-placed or gutsy individuals who lobbied corporate chiefs for support. The groundswell of companies offering benefits should be attributed largely to the role of gay and lesbian employee groups, as well as the recognition by upper management that in order to sell effectively to the gay and lesbian market, it is important to show parity in one's own workplace.

Lawsuits, although a good way to focus media and gay and lesbian consumer attention on the pay disparity between gay and heterosexual employees, have not so far been a tremendously successful tool in achieving benefits. At AT&T, which has long been supportive of its gay and lesbian employees group, and which did some early target marketing to the gay community, the company for years resisted even discussing the possibility of implementing domestic partner benefits while battling a lawsuit over survivors' benefits that was brought by the partner and partner's children of a long-term employee. A few years after the plaintiffs won the suit, Lucent Technologies and National Cash Register, two major portions of the reconfigured AT&T, announced that they would offer benefits starting in 1998. Several other lawsuits are underway at state educational institutions; the outcome of these battles is as yet unknown.

The primary barriers to offering benefits have largely been shown to be false assumptions. Foremost to many companies was the cost issue, and secondarily, the difficulty of persuading insurance carriers to underwrite such policies. Some corporations were forced to self-insure, or to pay higher premiums until the true costs could be sorted out.

Experience has shown that the addition of domestic partners to benefit rolls, usually between one and five percent of insurance enrollees, costs far less than was feared and added even less to the cost of coverage. When coverage is limited to same-gender couples only, the costs are one third of those organizations that offer benefits to unmarried heterosexual couples as well, according to studies performed by Liz Winfeld of Common Ground, the National Lesbian & Gay Journalists Association survey of media and entertainment firms, and the Hewlett Consulting Group.

There are several reasons for the low cost of covering gay employees' partners. Some gay and lesbian employees may still be afraid to come out about their relationships, even to the human resources department, solely for the purpose of obtaining coverage. Partners of gay and lesbians employees are more likely than heterosexuals to be employed with benefits of their own. They are also less likely to become pregnant, and hence to suffer childbirth complications, the most common cause of high health care costs among heterosexuals, and far greater than the costs of AIDS treatments among gay men. But most importantly, the federal tax code implications of taking advantage of medical insurance coverage for same gender couples is much higher than it is for married couples. As a result, gay and lesbian couples use these benefits less than unmarried heterosexuals, and far less than married couples.

Another concern mentioned in some quarters is the possibility of fraud. Some companies were afraid that their employees would sign up an HIV-positive friend for coverage, thus driving up corporate costs. Typically, corporations do not require proof of marriage for heterosexual employees; they simply take the employees' word for it. Yet companies developed a series of rigorous requirements for gay and lesbian employees to prove that their relationships exist.

The most common requirements are usually more stringent than those required for marriage, and include that the parties be over 18 years of age; that the parties are not related so closely as to preclude marriage if opposite gender; that an employee wait a certain amount of time—typically 6 months to a year—after notifying the company of the end of a domestic partnership before getting coverage for a new relationship; and that the parties share some level of financial commitment to each other—from a joint bank account to total responsibility for each other's maintenance and debts. Some companies require that if a local domestic partnership registration is available (which typically requires that the parties take on the responsibility for each other's maintenance and support), that the employee and his or her partner register at it. Often, when a municipality passes a domestic partner registration law, the only guaranteed tangible benefit is for its own employees, who are eligible for domestic partner benefits as the result of registration. Some have pointed out that it is unfair to ask gay couples to assume full responsibility for each other's welfare and debts when not being given the full benefits of marriage, but most activists are so happy to get registration and corporate benefits that they do not press further.

Another corporate concern is the fear of a consumer backlash; yet this fear has mostly proved to be a paper tiger. In 1993, after an initial setback in obtaining tax benefits in Williamson, Texas, where taxpayers objected to the presence of Apple Computer due to their domestic partner benefits plan, Apple ultimately got the concessions it wanted—and the sale of its computers did not suffer, at least for that reason. Due to offering domestic partner benefits and the airing of the *Ellen* character's coming out in prime time in 1997, ABC/Capital Cities/Disney has faced the call for a consumer boycott from the Southern Baptist Association, yet the ban has gained few adherents, and those who do care, care mostly about *Ellen*. It turns out that most people do not care much about a company's internal management policies, and that even more visible signs of corporate support for its gay and lesbian employees and customers, such as sponsoring a gay pride booth or advertising in the gay and lesbian media, is mostly visible to gay men and lesbians, while most of consumer America knows and cares little about it.

Until recently, the greatest difficulty in implementing a benefits program has been the problem in finding an insurance company to underwrite it. Large companies have had little problem in this regard, as they are of a size to pressure their carrier, find a new one, or self insure. But until recently, smaller organizations had some difficulties in this area. Now, although an occasional insurer might balk, there are enough firms that will do the underwriting and benefits consultants who can tell firms where to look.

Today, more than 500 companies, educational institutions, nonprofits, and governmental agencies offer what are commonly referred to as domestic partner benefits. While medical insurance is the most common benefit, many other benefits are regularly part of the package. Typically, these include such soft benefits as leave to care for an ill partner, bereavement leave, moving and travel expenses shared with the employee, as well as hard benefits such as health insurance coverage. Sometimes other insurance coverage, such as dental or vision, is also included, as are retirement benefits, to the extent allowable by tax law. Often a partner's children will be included formally or informally in coverage such as day care, insurance, adoption reimbursement and leave, newborn parental leave, sick child leave, and reduced tuition at universities.

A major controversy among activists continues to be whether to press only for benefits for same-gender couples, or to seek benefits for unmarried heterosexual couples as well. In unions, municipalities, and many nonprofit and educational institutions, strategic alliances between gay and heterosexual employees have resulted in the benefits for all employees' partners. In some cases, and at most for-profit corporations, bottom line pragmatism dictates that the organization offer benefits only to gay couples.

One group of New York City activists developed the Stonewall Principles, which it parallels to the Sullivan Principles that were used for many years to judge corporate involvement in apartheid South Africa. These principles are also used by some investment firms that attempt to track corporate gay friendliness as part of investment criteria. Among other things, these principles demand that corporations offer domestic partner benefits to employees without regard for the gender of their partners. Some consider it contradictory that according to this group, a company that offers no benefits to anyone ranks higher than a company that gives benefits only to same-gender couples.

Outside the U.S., the health care system is managed differently, and medical insurance benefits for domestic partners are a somewhat less important issue. Some Scandinavian countries and the Netherlands already mandate that employers offer these benefits to the partners of gay employees. However, most countries do not have these laws, and even U.S.-based companies that offer domestic partner benefits at home do not do so overseas. As the trend grows towards companies offering private plans to employees that are significantly better than those offered by the state, the pressure from gay employees will continue to grow. Canadian and Israeli government employees have already won these rights by court decision, and others may follow. In addition, gay and lesbian government employees in Europe have won "soft" benefits, such as honeymoon leave (France) and travel benefits (England, in a case now before the European High Court).

GAY AND LESBIAN EMPLOYEE AND PROFESSIONAL ORGANIZATIONS

Gay and lesbian employee organizations now exist in more than 100 corporations and hundreds of educational institutions and governmental bodies. Some, like the one at Apple Computer, exist primarily as email lists. Others, like the one at the Kaiser Permanente HMO, are politically active inside and outside their corporations, sponsoring speakers, lobbying for changes in corporate policies, and marching in local gay and lesbian pride parades.

An important 1990s innovation is the rise of umbrella groups uniting all the gay employee groups in a particular geographic area. While internal company battles are usually won due to the steps taken by industry competitors, regional groups provide an important source of support for activists and members who can get burned out looking at the same faces all the time, and who are revitalized by socializing—and networking—with peers across town.

Organizations such as the Northwest Gay & Lesbian Employee Network in Seattle, the Minnesota Workplace Alliance, and A Group of Groups in the Bay Area, have stimulated local progress, contributed to local charities, and in the case of Chicago's Out at Work (or Not) developed extensive resource lists that they have disseminated country-wide and, via the Internet, all over the world.

Additionally, with the support of the Human Rights Campaign and several corporate supporters, a loose coalition of groups has formed under the PROGRESS umbrella and held several conferences. At first limited to California-based companies, the group now plans to expand its reach. The National Gay and Lesbian Task Force has also sponsored several conferences on workplace issues. These conferences have proved tremendously useful in helping corporate groups start, grow, and learn from each other.

Gay and lesbian professional organizations proliferated during the 1990s. More than 100 are now in existence, with at least one in most major cities in the United States. Most meet monthly, and while some are small, others are quite sizable. The New York Advertising and Communications Network in New York City is the largest, with more than 1,000 members. Typical attendance at events, which are held several times a month, is around 200 people. NYACN, like most groups, brings in speakers in addition to holding mixers and other social events for its members. Most groups welcome both women and men, although a few are single gender only. A number of the lesbian groups are named women's groups, rather than lesbian, but they are lesbian-only.

Some groups have a national or international scope, such as the National Lesbian & Gay Journalists Association, which sponsors a well-attended annual conference, a newsletter, and an up-to-date survey of benefits offered by corporations in the media business. Other groups, such as the National Organization of Gay & Lesbian Scientists & Technical Professionals, are less politically active, but serve an important networking and support function for their members.

Gay and lesbian professional associations today are an international phenomenon, with groups formed in Canada, Britain, the Netherlands, Germany, Switzerland, Australia, and New Zealand. Most are co-gendered, although some are male-only. The international scene also has a few workplace-oriented groups, such as those for police officers and employees of the European Commission.

Some gay and lesbian professional organizations have joined umbrella organizations, such as The Network in the New York City area, with more than 25 member groups, or the Association of Western Regional Gay and Lesbian professional groups. These umbrella organizations have been less active, but serve an important communications link for their member groups. Paid staff at the San Francisco Golden Gate Business Association, Greater San Diego Business Association, and Bay Area Career Women have been instrumental in helping their groups thrive.

ATTITUDES TOWARD GAY MEN AND LESBIANS IN DIFFERENT LOCATIONS AND INDUSTRIES

While it is possible to make some generalizations about where it is better for lesbians and gay men to work (Denmark is better than Zimbabwe, for example), is it important not to apply them too broadly. Generally, companies in large cities on the coasts of the U.S. and in Scandinavian countries, and those in high tech or creative industries, tend to be more gay friendly, while those in the South, Texas, the Midwest, other countries, and in industries such as finance and agriculture tend to be more conservative. In addition, most blue-collar professions are more conservative and are less gay friendly than white-collar professions. In the middle are some surprises—banking and insurance in midsize U.S. cities. Yet there are exceptions to every rule.

Different divisions and locations of a company can have very different environments with respect to gay men and lesbians. A change in area management from one year to the next can also have a major impact. Also, the atmosphere might be good for gay men and hostile to lesbians or vice versa.

The pros and cons of a small versus large organization can be more difficult to judge. A large company is more likely to have a public record and a gay and lesbian employee group, or at least a nucleus of gay people. Yet it may also be more entrenched in its ways and less open to change. At a small organization, one person can make a tremendous and rapid difference. This could be that the boss models gay-friendliness or that the boss is a homophobe. It could be that one can get changes just by asking for them, or that one person is standing in the way and there is no way around him or her.

In assessing how gay friendly a particular career path or job offer is likely to be, it is important to do some very specific research. If possible, one should try to talk with gay men and lesbians in that field, company, or division. See if there is a gay and lesbian employee group in that company, or whether that field has a number of companies with such groups. Examine the company or industry's public record on nondiscrimination policies and domestic partner benefits. If applicable, check their advertising and charitable donations record, and whether or not the management has taken a stand on local or national nondiscrimination legislation.

RACE AND GENDER DIFFERENCES

While white men still have much of the power and prestige in the workplace, women and people of color are gaining ground. For those disadvantaged by race or gender, the contacts made by having a common gay identity can be an important contributor to success. While lesbians and gay men can be racist and gay men sexist, it is also the case that a shared gay identity can sometimes overcome these attitudes.

It is perhaps class differences more than those of race or gender that are paramount. For those who are one paycheck away from the street, the possible repercussions of coming out at work can be so overwhelming that openness is inconceivable. On the other hand, those at the top of their professions report tremendous fear as well, pointing out that it is only recently that large numbers of women and people of color have gained access to the better paying jobs. Many fear that as lesbians and gay people of color, they may be more vulnerable at the top, although there is no statistical data to support this.

Rather, the experience of those who are open shows that like white gay men, those lesbians and people of color who try to remain closeted or undeclared are more likely to experience harassment as well as more subtle forms of discrimination. Those who are not open may be thought of as trying to hide something, and thus not to be trusted, while those who are open are respected for being brave. Furthermore, those who are open have the opportunity to allow bosses, co-workers, and subordinates to really get to know them, which often leads to closer workplace relationships and career benefits. And those who are open are more likely to find and to provide mentoring to other lesbians and gay men.

For lesbians in particular, there are additional benefits to coming out. If they are closeted, they are usually seen as single heterosexual women—with all the attendant stereotypes. Single heterosexual women are thought of as unreliable (she's just going to get married, follow her husband's career, or have a baby and leave the workforce), flirtatious (she's sleeping her way to the top), or lacking social skills (why can't she get a man?).

In contrast, open lesbians benefit from the typical stereotypes of lesbian professionals—hardworking, appropriately aggressive, career minded. Their relationships with men at work are improved because there is no longer any innuendo about the possibility of a sexual relationship. And their relationships with women are improved because they can participate in the usual forms of female workplace bonding by talking about relationships or dating.

Another pitfall common to closeted lesbians can also be avoided by being open. Several studies have shown that closeted lesbians or bisexuals are more likely than heterosexual women to become involved in sexual relationships in the workplace—and to engage in sexual harassment. This may be because closeted lesbians see themselves as having few choices in meeting a suitable partner. So when a closeted lesbian meets another lesbian professional in her own workplace, she is highly tempted to try to develop the relationship. Yet closeted relationships have many pitfalls—trying to avoid reporting responsibilities, trying to arrange simultaneous geographic transfers, or avoiding each other if the relationship ends. Lesbians who are open at work tend to be involved in fewer workplace relationships, and secure employer support in avoiding the problems that even an acknowledged relationship may pose.

The closet is a vicious circle—the fewer lesbians and people of color who are out, the more dangerous it seems to come out. But the reverse is also true—as more lesbians and people of color come out, the safer coming out seems, and the more obvious its advantages are. Many lesbians and people of color today are open to some, most, or all of their workplace colleagues and bosses, but until recently, they have not had the opportunity to share their experiences with a wider audience. Thus, while examples of discrimination are well known, success stories have been less widely reported.

In the recent past, white gay men were far more likely to take advantage of networking opportunities than lesbians and people of color. One reason is the disinclination of lesbians and people of color to participate in social functions or organizations predominated by white gay men, or to read media targeted primarily to white gay men. Another issue for women is the tendency towards the ideal of monogamous couplism in lesbian life, versus the more diverse social life sought by gay men and the social practice of cruising (at least with the eyes), which often leads to new friend-

ships among gay men. However, in the last few years, lesbians and people of color have become increasingly interested in availing themselves of the career opportunities provided by participating in lesbian and gay professional associations and employee groups. Additionally, the opportunities for lesbian professionals to meet each other in lesbian-only settings have multiplied and continue to grow, as have informal gatherings for gay people of color in the business world.

INDIVIDUAL SUCCESSES BY GAY MEN AND LESBIANS IN THE WORKPLACE

Some lesbians and gay men have found success in mainstream companies and educational or nonprofit institutions. While not always completely open, gay people have found success in every field, in every city, in every country. The publishing, music, entertainment, and advertising fields have proven most open to gay talent, and include individuals such as Malcolm Forbes, Barry Diller, and David Geffen among their number.

During the 1980s, the macabre joke was that the obituaries were the gay men's sports page: one could find out who had achieved what success and how out they were by scanning the achievements of youngish men who passed away from AIDS or one of its associated diseases. For the first time, many realized that gay men were successful not only in the arts, but also in business. Additionally, as the media began to give greater attention to women in business, those adept at reading between the lines found lesbian "likely suspects."

At first, the media was only willing to out prominent business people after their deaths. New York City's *Outweek* magazine gave one of its last covers to Malcolm Forbes, the multimillionaire publisher of *Forbes* magazine. But the mainstream media shied away, covering the gay lives of neither living nor dead closeted people in business. For many years, the gay magazines also shied away from outing, giving the hands-off treatment to prominent people. *Outweek* magazine was a leader in this area as well, with Michelangelo Signorile calling for successful media and fashion industry leaders to come out. However, he generally stayed away from outing non-celebrities in the business world, however powerful they might be.

One of the few examples of a gay magazine outing a prominent businessperson occurred in the early 1990s, when the *Advocate* published an interview with *Tales of the City* author Armistead Maupin in which he outed Richard Jenrette, head of the investment bank Donaldson, Lufkin and Jenrette, but no other publication followed up on this news or outed any other business leaders.

In the past, most gay people felt they had to hide being gay on the job, particularly in corporate America, even if they worked for themselves. Today, this is less and less the case. It can be difficult for someone to come out after a lifetime of hiding, but not always. Some who have done so have found it a breath of fresh air. In the case of David Geffen, he claimed that close friends and business associates always knew he was gay, but he avoided coming out in the media until he was outed. He has enjoyed nothing but success since then. Interestingly, despite his willingness to be out, the mainstream press routinely "ins" him. For example, when *Forbes* magazine featured him in its list of the 400 richest Americans, the profile mentioned his social association with female celebrities such as Cher and his contributions to AIDS causes, but omitted saying anything about his involvement in a gay social life or charities.

David Geffen

Today, the mainstream press is becoming somewhat more willing to cover the gay angle in the lives of prominent business people. When Jann Wenner, publisher of *Rolling Stone* magazine, left his wife for another man, it received coverage in the *New York Post*'s page six and was reprinted in media across the country.

Many gay people have become successful by starting a business. As most do not have the responsibility of supporting a partner and children, they are in a good position to go into business for themselves. Due to the fear of discrimination, many lesbians and gay men keep in mind an exit strategy that involves working for themselves. Some serve the gay market, while others cater to the mainstream. Most have achieved success in the arts, fashion, and clothing retail industries, but there have been success stories in other, less-visible pursuits as well, such as computer software titan Tim Gill, who has been a member of the *Forbes* list of the 400 richest Americans.

COMMUNITY SUCCESSES IN THE WORKPLACE

One of the first major breakthroughs by corporate America towards gay and lesbian issues was the widespread recognition of the need for the education of its workforce about HIV/AIDS. As a result, most companies have humane policies regarding their employees' needs for sick and bereavement leave, and many also have flexibility regarding the need of employees to care for partners who are ill. Additionally, corporations can be credited with helping minimize the AIDS hysteria that gripped America in the mid-1980s. Today, virtually everyone knows how HIV is and is not

transmitted and how to talk about AIDS without fear or prejudice, and corporate education and sensitivity programs, along with the media, played a significant role in this.

Today, corporate diversity training is likely to include sexual orientation as well as issues of gender, race, age, handicap, management v. nonmanagement, and so on. While these other issues often get more time in the training sessions, the inclusion of sexual orientation sends an important signal to employees that it is part of the package. As a result, in an increasing number of workplaces anti-gay jokes and comments are not tolerated. This creates a more positive environment for gay people who are thinking about coming out at work and marginalizes those who still harbor homophobic feelings, while giving them the opportunity to be educated further.

Perhaps the most significant change effected by gay activists is that most Americans now understand that being gay is not solely about sex. While an earlier generation of sex radicals worked for the freedom to express and discuss gay sex anytime and anywhere, and while sex and sexual attraction remain an important part of the gay social scene, today most gay men and lesbians subscribe to the code that says that work is not an appropriate place to discuss sex.

Instead, gay people are more freely discussing their relationships, homes, children, jobs, and hobbies. As America has been exposed to these aspects of gay lives in the media and, in many cases, in their daily lives, it is no large leap to talk about such things at work. In the workplace, heterosexuals generally understand that it is inappropriate to say, "I don't talk about my sex life, why should you talk about yours?" or, "I don't care who you sleep with" in response to someone coming out to them. If they do not know this ahead of time, most can be educated to the fact that a gay identity includes more than sexual activity.

Increasing numbers of gay men and lesbians have found that coming out is far better than they had feared. In many cases, they receive positive responses from colleagues, bosses, and subordinates. Perhaps most significantly, they have found that when one comes out the rumors stop and they are free to be themselves. Some hit a plateau and do not continue the process of being out at work on a day-to-day basis. Most continue coming out and being out to additional individuals and in casual conversations with those who already know, finding their work experience improving now that they are no longer guarding a secret.

After coming out, many gay people find that others suspected they were gay all along, but did not feel they had permission to say anything about it. Coming out cleared the air and allowed everyone to talk freely. Most people come out after a period of building support by finding likely allies and coming out to them first. However, some have found success by coming out from the beginning—on resumes, in interviews, on the first day of work. Much depends on the individual's personality. Some people are more comfortable testing the waters; others are not comfortable telling lies of omission for any period.

Some gay people bring partners to workplace social functions without coming out, introducing that person as a friend. Today, however, it is becoming more common for companies to specifically include partners in invitations, and for gay people to bring partners with no subterfuge, at least to events attended only by company employees and families.

In the last decade, the number of organizations offering some form of domestic partner benefits has grown from a trickle to a steady stream. At first, most companies only offered "soft" benefits such as travel perks, relocation assistance, and sick and be-reavement leave. Today, an increasing number offer "hard" benefits such as medical, dental, and vision insurance to an employee's domestic partners and partner's children. In large part, these successes have come due to the efforts of gay and lesbian employee groups or umbrella groups. Hollywood Supports, an organization largely funded by a few prominent gay people in the entertainment industry, was so successful in its mission—at first doing HIV/AIDS education, then doing sensitivity training about sexual orientation, and then seeking domestic partners benefits in the media industry—that it has essentially closed up shop, and merged with the Gay and Lesbian Alliance Against Defamation, which will carry on its mission to a wider audience.

NICHE MARKETING TO THE GAY AND LESBIAN COMMUNITIES

At the dawn of the 1990s, the idea of the lucrative potential of the gay market was a glimmer in the eye of a few forward-thinking gay people, but corporations were not yet biting. This changed rapidly in the course of a few years, as mainstream advertising targeting gay men and lesbians became ubiquitous in gay magazines, gay pride parades, and through an occasional direct mail piece.

Led first by "sin" advertisers (such as alcohol and cigarette manufacturers), clothing, automotive, airline, and other categories followed soon thereafter. Absolute Vodka was the first major advertiser to recognize the potential of and reap the benefit of promoting its product in the gay media. They were rewarded with record-breaking sales in gay bars and clubs. In contrast, Coors Beer, which had gained the reputation of discriminating against lesbians and gay men in their hiring practices, lost a tremendous amount of business for many years when gay venues refused to stock their products. The boycott was called off when Coors implemented domestic partner benefits and pledged to donate to gay philanthropic events.

Some ads were nothing more than the companies' regular advertisements placed in the gay media, or campaigns such as AT&T's direct mail piece that did not specifically address its gay market, but incorporated such symbols as the rainbow and utilized androgynous and "gay looking" models. Campaigns which tended to be more successful in attracting notice and building brand loyalty put a particular gay spin in the ads themselves. Several particularly clever 1997 advertisements: Johnnie Walker Red Label's pitch showing three waifish twenty-something men with the tag line "for the last time, it's not a lifestyle, it's a life," and the ad showing a case of beer in a closet entitled "Closet Case" and exhorting the reader to "be yourself and make it a Bud Light." It proved a delicious irony, as beer companies were once happy to go on record as saying that advertising beer to gay people would make the brand unsaleable to others. In a number of cases, gay and lesbian employee organizations were instrumental in helping identify how best to reach gay consumers and to help craft the editorial portion of the pitch. Another first was an ad in the gay magazine *The Advocate* by IBM touting its domestic partner benefits and calling for resumes from readers.

In addition, gay- and lesbian-owned companies have been highly successful in marketing to lesbians and gay men. Vacations have been especially popular, whether to a tourist destination, a cruise, or a resort. Vacation property in meccas such as Provincetown, the Fire Island Pines, Cherry Grove, the Russian River, and Key

West has become tremendously valuable, as the number of lesbian and gay men willing to shell out for gay-friendly accommodations in these locations continues to grow.

In addition, the gay male bacchanalias know as "circuit parties" have tapped into a lucrative market, with long weekend extravaganzas scheduled in one city or another at least monthly, and total spending in the millions of dollars per event. Olivia Cruises (formerly a women's music company), serving the lesbian market, and several gay male cruise lines continue to flourish, and have added several new vacations to their itinerary in recent years. In addition, these companies have added land-based options such as a Club Med-type experience to their list of offerings.

The catalogue business has been somewhat less successful. Those who entered it with expectations raised by the hype over the gay market found that catalogue shoppers were more willing to spring for low-priced doo-dads than for higher priced handcrafted or imported items. On the other hand, booksellers have continued to do well serving those who do not live near a gay or lesbian bookstore.

TRUTH IN ADVERTISING—DO GAY PEOPLE EARN MORE OR LESS THAN HETEROSEXUALS?

A heated issue among activists has been the question of the number of dollars/pounds/francs/etc. under gay control. In the hands of marketers, the size of the "gay market" or the "pink pound" has often been boosted through faulty assumptions, such as the one that gay people represent 10 percent of any given population, and that those individuals can be reached by ads in the gay media or promotions at gay events. Additionally, some have claimed that gay people are better educated and have higher household incomes than the general population. While this might be true of household income among the readers of gay publications, this finding can scarcely be generalized to the entire gay community.

Responsible gay marketing experts point out that those who can be reached through target marketing to the gay community do tend to be younger, better educated, and more brand loyal than the general population. They also tend to have more disposable income (mostly as the result of being more often male and childless than the general population). Yet they also point out that as for the gay market as a whole, self-identified gay people (as well as those with same-gender sexual experience) are very closely matched to the general population except for their age. (Relative to the population, there is a lower percentage of gay people in their 50s and above than there are in their 20s, 30s, and 40s.)

In the hands of economists, the real question is whether lesbians and gay men earn more or less than heterosexuals. While it may be the case that the gay magazine reading segment of the gay population has a higher household income than an age-matched readership of a mainstream men's magazine, this is due to the fact that men usually earn more than women, so two gay men earn more than a married couple, for example. But several studies indicate that each gay man probably earns less than his otherwise demographically matched heterosexual counterpart.

What remains unknown is how tightly this apparent wage discrimination against gay men, and to a lesser extent, lesbians in the workplace, is linked to the closet. Almost all qualitative studies show that those who try to hide being gay are less productive at work, and at least one shows that those who are open about being gay suffer no disadvantage and may even come out ahead. Research in *Straight Jobs, Gay Lives* shows that those who are willing to take the risk of coming out are admired as brave, and intelligent risk taking is a major key to professional success.

PRESENT TRENDS

The struggle for the full range of equal benefits will continue, as gay people continue to seek travel benefits, relocation assistance, medical, dental, and vision insurance, and sick and bereavement leave. Until now, those who were openly gay at work have been younger, but as this generation matures one area that will gain increasing importance is retirement benefits.

Another area that is continuing to gain in importance is benefits for an employee's partner and the partner's children, including day care, insurance, adoption reimbursement and leave, newborn parental leave, sick child leave, and reduced tuition at universities. In the past, many lesbians and gay men had children from a previous heterosexual relationship. But today, increasing numbers are choosing to bear, adopt, or foster care for children after coming out, and corporations will need to reflect this change in order to remain competitive in hiring and retaining their personnel.

Gay people will continue to come out at work, with coming out to customers, vendors, and suppliers emerging as the cutting edge of this issue. Even companies that have a good track record in dealing with gay employees internally have another set of unknowns to face as employees come out to customers and associate businesses in greater numbers.

Corporate support for gay and lesbian rights legislation is another emerging trend. The Human Rights Campaign has had some success in getting top executives to testify in support of the Employment Nondiscrimination Act (ENDA), the national nondiscrimination bill that is brought before Congress every year. Companies can expect to be approached for support of local legislation as well.

Companies are also becoming more active in gearing their philanthropic dollars to gay and lesbian causes. While in the past corporate funds went only to AIDS-related charities, today more are willing to fund gay causes. Companies like Levi Strauss in San Francisco have supported activities such as education regarding gay history and have sponsored gay organizations at fundraising dinners.

From New York City to Australia (http://www.rainbow.net.au/ staffit/), a few companies have begun offering themselves as employment agencies for gay men and lesbians. A Los Angeles-based firm, McCormick & Co., also places gay and lesbian managers, primarily in the nonprofit sector. In the not-too-distant future, such firms will be more and more able to place gay people in a broader range of opportunities.

An as-yet mostly unexplored area is the target recruiting of openly gay and lesbian individuals for mainstream positions. While a few computer or travel-related companies have given the green light for such efforts, it is likely that gay and lesbian employee groups in an increasing number of firms will offer to help identify appropriate gay media for placing help wanted ads.

GAY-FRIENDLY INVESTING

Until recently, gay-friendly investing meant nothing more than finding a broker or investment advisor who was comfortable working with a gay client. Sensing a market need, Christopher Street investment company was set up in the 1980s to cater to a gay clientele. Primarily, they sold tax-exempt municipal bonds in a gay-

friendly environment; today, they offer a broader range of services. American Express has now leapt on the bandwagon with all of its corporate strength, offering financial planning at household prices and offering investment strategies geared for the life and tax situation of gay couples, as well as unmarried heterosexual pairs and family members.

Another area where gay-friendly investing has begun to thrive is in the area of socially responsible investing. Investment advisor Howard Tharsing uses a "lavender screen" to identify investments for his clients with over $100,000 to invest. He uses these criteria: a nondiscrimination policy, domestic partner benefits, recognition of lesbian and gay employee groups, diversity training, and programs related to HIV/AIDS. With just a few thousand dollars, one can also get into the market with Shelly Meyer's mutual fund Meyers Pride Value Fund. Her criterion is simply that a company have a written nondiscrimination policy covering sexual orientation. Both of these funds are relatively new and, by virtue of their criteria, invest heavily in the technology sector.

"Mainstream" socially responsible funds also sometimes claim to include gay-friendliness as a factor in their stock picks, but they have not publicly released a set of criteria. These funds typically look at the big picture—so for example, Coors, which has nondiscrimination protection, domestic partner benefits, and an officially recognized gay and lesbian group, might not be included because it is an alcohol producer and promoter whose largest shareholders, the Coors family, regularly donate significant sums to right wing anti-gay causes.

NEW AREAS OF ACTIVISM

While some unions have long been active on behalf of their lesbian and gay members, others have not addressed their concerns. Transit workers in several California cities were among the first to gain domestic partners benefits; the *New York Times* corporation gave such benefits to union members years before they extended them to management. Yet other unions, particularly at large companies, have been quiescent. Now that there are several umbrella groups for gay union organizations, that situation should begin to change.

While most activism to date has been in the area of gay and lesbian issues at work, bisexual and transgender issues are beginning to come to the forefront. In some cases, these individuals have found common cause with gay and lesbian groups; in others, they have pursued gains on their on. It can be difficult to find receptive ground in organizations dedicated to only their own cause and those with a social agenda. Typically, bisexual and transgender activists are more likely to find success in groups that are set up to include heterosexual allies and causes such as benefits for unmarried heterosexual couples.

To date, most gay workplace activism has taken place in the U.S. But individuals and groups have also made important strides in other countries. Particularly now that the Internet is available to speed communication and English is becoming widely used in international communication, it should be expected that gains made around the world will be more rapidly communicated and emulated.

PROMINENT PEOPLE

Malcolm Forbes (1919-1990)

Born in 1919 to a Catholic mother and Protestant father, Malcolm Forbes was the middle of five brothers in a deeply divided household. Malcolm and oldest brother Bruce were raised Catholic; their other siblings were raised Protestant. After the death of second-oldest brother Duncan in a car accident where 17-year-old Bruce was driving, the family disintegrated. The parents finally obtained a legal separation in 1943, although they never divorced.

After his military service, Malcolm went to work as a journalist for his father, who had become a prosperous investor and publisher of the *Forbes* business magazine. He became a Protestant, married, and had four sons and a daughter. Brother Bruce ran *Forbes* magazine after their father's death in 1954; Malcolm participated on the editorial side, but also devoted time to his political ambitions. In 1964, however, Bruce discovered he had inoperable cancer, and Malcolm inherited 30 percent of a thriving, debt-free company. By enlisting the support of his brothers, he soon had the voting trust under his complete control, and arranged to buy out the 30 percent share owned by Bruce's widow.

After embarking on a high-profile expansion of the magazine, Forbes made the magazine even more successful. Showcasing personal hobbies such as yachting, hot air ballooning, motorcycling, collecting Faberge eggs, and hob-nobbing with celebrities such as Elizabeth Taylor, Malcolm made a name for himself as a high-living jetsetter, while building a fortune worth somewhere around one billion dollars at his death. His oldest son has succeeded him in running *Forbes* magazine and in his political ambitions.

To his credit, he never denied being gay when asked by journalists; however, he was never willingly open either. In his later years, Malcolm became increasingly flamboyant about his preference for the company of younger handsome men, and according to several sources, propositioning men who worked for him, but it was not until his death in February 1990 that he was outed.

Sandy Gallin (1940-)

Born to a middle-class Jewish family in New York, Sandy Gallin went to work in the mail room of General Artists Corporation (GAC, a predecessor of International Creative Management), a major Hollywood talent agency, after graduating from college. After a year, he became a junior agent, booking the Beatles on the *Ed Sullivan Show.* Gallin has gone on the record as saying that in the mid-1960s, he was transferred to his company's West Coast offices, a move he welcomed, he says, because "I was afraid of being gay and living in the same city as my brother and mother." He also reveals that when he was in his mid-twenties, he fell in love with a man, and it scared him so much he got married (to a woman who knew about his gay past). They were divorced a few years later when Gallin realized he would be happier living a gay life.

After seven years of working for GAC, he had risen to the rank of senior vice president and member of the board of directors, but left to form his own company with his cousin in 1970, an agency that lasted 14 years and had many successes. Gallin has previously represented celebrities Joan Rivers, Cher, Barbra Streisand, Richard Pryor, Lily Tomlin, and Patti LaBelle, and he is currently the personal manager of Dolly Parton, Neil Diamond, Whoopi Goldberg, and Michael Jackson. His current company, Gallin/ Morey Associates, reportedly earns him between $3 and $7 million a year.

For years, Gallin was known to be gay among the entertainment and gay communities, and had been outed in the gay press since the early 1990s. For a time, the mainstream press stayed away from outing him, preferring the innuendo such as pictures

of him with friends David Geffen, Barry Diller, and Calvin Klein. He came out in the mainstream press in January 1994 in a front-page story by the *Los Angeles Times* about Gallin's handling of client Michael Jackson against the child-molestation charges brought by the father of a teenage boy.

In November 1994, he gave his first full-length interview to any journalist for a cover story in *Out* magazine because, he said, he wanted "to let young gay people know that sexuality does not necessarily get in the way of a career in Hollywood," and also, to find a boyfriend. After recovering from cancer 10 years ago, Gallin has become more involved in Jewish prayer and ritual practice.

David Geffen (1943-)

Born poor in New York City, David Geffen has become one of the richest and most powerful men in Hollywood. He obtained his first Hollywood position (in the mail room of William Morris) by claiming a college degree he had never completed. He continued to rise as an agent, and made his primary fortune in music, representing Cher (whom he dated early in his career), Linda Ronstadt, Joni Mitchell, Laura Nyro, the Eagles, Guns and Roses, and Nirvana. Movie and stage production successes include *Little Shop of Horrors, Cats,* and *Risky Business* (which made Tom Cruise a star).

He sold Asylum Records to Warner Communications for $7 million in 1972, and later sold Geffen Records to MCA in 1990 for stock, which netted him $710 million when MCA was sold to Matsushita. He has been a member of the *Forbes* list of the 400 richest Americans since 1988.

He now claims never to have hidden being gay from people in the industry after having come out to himself, but he was unwilling to go on public record until after he was outed in 1994 for handling homophobic acts. Later that year, at a Los Angeles fundraiser for a gay cause, he said, "As a gay man, I've come a long way to be here tonight," which gave the mainstream press permission to report what so many people already knew.

Before coming out, he was active in a variety of AIDS causes, but since coming out he has gained prominence for his contributions to a variety of gay causes, including Hollywood Supports and organizations fighting for the right for openly gay people to serve in the military.

His friendships with Sandy Gallin, Barry Diller, Calvin Klein, and others have prompted some to refer to the group as the "pink" or "velvet mafia," a term that the group of friends finds offensive.

Recently, Geffen has made headlines for his movie business partnership with Steven Spielberg and Jeffrey Katzenberg in Dreamworks SKG. On the personal side, Geffen has spoken frequently to the gay press about wanting to end his single status.

Tim Gill (1954-)

Born in 1954, Tim Gill grew up in a Denver suburb, where he lived with his plastic surgeon father, mother, and two sisters. He studied computer technology at the University of Colorado at Boulder and was openly gay on campus. After graduation, he took a job with Hewlett-Packard in Fort Collins, Colorado, but moved to Denver a few years later to work for a start up company and enjoy gay life in a big city. When the company failed, Gill wrote a speculative computer program for the Macintosh computer called Word Juggler, which proved popular. He started Quark in 1981 with a $2,000 loan from his parents.

Today, Quark, Inc., is a Denver-based computer software company that is the publisher of one of the leading desktop publishing/page layout programs for Macintosh. QuarkXPress is used by almost every major newspaper and magazine in the United States. With just a few hundred employees, Gill has become a multi-millionaire, earning a place on the 1996 *Forbes* list of the 400 richest Americans with a fortune of $425 million. Despite repeatedly informing the magazine that he is in a long-term relationship with Davol, a virologist and electronic music producer, the magazine continues to list him as "single."

In addition to his business interests, he heads the Gill Foundation, established in 1994. It focuses its grants on programs for gay men and lesbians, issues related to HIV/AIDS, and other social justice causes. Large grants have gone to provide computer support to organizations such as Digital Queers, the Service Members Legal Defense Network, Parents and Friends of Lesbians and Gays, and the National Gay and Lesbian Task Force. In addition to awarding grants, the foundation operates special programs providing technical assistance and other resources to support the communities it serves. Since its inception, the Gill Foundation, which has offices in Colorado and Washington, D.C., has provided nearly $4 million in grants, often using matching funds grants to achieve its goals.

Gill has also made grants that are intended to increase public awareness of the ways gays and lesbians support the larger community, such as a donation of $100,000 to the American Red Cross for flood relief to victims of devastating floods in Fort Collins, Colorado. This gift, half of it a dollar-for-dollar match for any Coloradan's private donation of $250 or more, was the largest private contribution to help out in this disaster.

Gill has been an avid skier for 25 years. As a financial and vocal supporter of the boycott of Colorado during the Amendment 2 battle, he cancelled his participation in a gay ski week to be held there. He regretted that the company was unable to reschedule a corporate conference slated for his home state. Gill can probably take credit for getting Norwest Bank to add protection from discrimination based on sexual orientation to its corporate policies. Although the bank says the changes were in the works before Gill's call, the fact that he threatened to pull $25 million out of Quark's account there could not have hurt.

John Maynard Keynes (1883-1946)

Born in Cambridge, England, in 1883, John Maynard Keynes grew up in an intellectual family. His father was a teacher and administrator, and his mother, who was also college educated, became part of the city government, eventually becoming the first female mayor of Cambridge in 1932. Keynes was 12 when Oscar Wilde stood trial for sodomy. A few years later, Keynes attended school at Eton, a prestigious private school for boys, which he enjoyed, not the least because it was there that he first had homosexual relationships with classmates, who remained his lifelong friends. He won a mathematics scholarship to Kings College at Cambridge University, where he was immediately invited to join a prestigious social club by Lytton Strachey, who was also homosexual.

Although Keynes was interested in studying economics, he also threw himself into philosophy, in order to develop a rebuttal to the argument that statistical norms (such as heterosexuality) form the basis of social norms. After graduation, he began a career with the civil service, where he was fearful of being discovered to be homosexual, and had several incidents that he refers to in his letters as being "close calls." When he won a fellowship at Cambridge University, he was only too happy to return to life in

academia. He was in a relationship for many years with Duncan Grant, and the pair became part of the famous Bloomsbury Group of intellectuals when Keynes began writing on monetary theory. When his relationship with Grant began to falter, Keynes devoted more of his attention to investments in international currency plays, which he was ultimately very successful in.

Keynes worked feverishly during World War I, and at peacetime was in a position to suggest at the highest levels that the Allies not seek reparation from Germany. When his advice was not taken, he resigned and wrote one of his most influential works, *The Economic Consequences of the Peace.* He also returned to his work on probability. What neither he nor his friends expected was that he would fall in love with a woman, the ballet dancer Lydia Lopokova, whom he married after 25 years of leading an active homosexual life.

While maintaining his homosexual friendships and writing in favor of sexual openness, Keynes spent the rest of his life in the mainstream of economic and political life. He argued against the gold standard, worked in favor of the Liberal party, and developed economic theories to help lift the world out of the depression caused by the American stock market crash of 1929. He is best known for his proposal that government spending could help spur economic growth, but also proposed that attaching wages to pay for government bonds was the best way to pay for the World War II effort. He was instrumental in the 1944 Bretton-Woods talks that led to the development of a new international monetary system: the International Monetary Fund and the World Bank. He died of a heart attack in 1946.

Hilary Rosen (1953-)

Interested in politics since childhood, Hilary Rosen worked as a phone canvasser in her mother's successful bid to become the first woman town council member in West Orange, N.J. She majored in international business at George Washington University. At 29, she took her first lobbying job at the Recording Industry Association of America, where she has been since 1987. Today, she is president and chief executive officer of the association, and earns a salary of $1 million a year promoting the interests of the $12.5 billion recording industry in areas such as First Amendment issues and copyright issues. Regarding the controversial issue of hate lyrics, she has been quoted as saying "the antidote to bad speech is more speech."

She is on the board of Rock the Vote, an organization that encourages young people to register to vote. Rosen is also a founding board member of the Gay and Lesbian Victory Fund, and a regular organizer of fundraisers for other gay and lesbian issues. As board co-chair of the Human Rights Campaign, she got to know Elizabeth Birch, and they have been together as a couple since 1994. Due to a potential conflict of interest, Rosen resigned from the HRC during the selection process that led to Birch being selected as head of the HRC. As a Washington power couple, the pair has been introduced to President Clinton, and they enjoy a quiet home life in the Maryland suburb of Chevy Chase.

Scott Safier (1963-)

Scott Safier was born in 1963 in McKeesport, Pennsylvania, a suburb of Pittsburgh. Like many other gay youths, he fit certain stereotypes that caused other children to label him a "fairy" or "faggot." He endured this torture until his junior year in high school, when he accepted early admission to Carnegie Mellon University. Safier graduated in 1983 with a B.S. in mathematics and psychology. In 1990 at age 27, he finally put all the baggage from his childhood behind him and accepted the fact that he was gay.

In the early 1990s, the fight for recognition of gay and lesbian relationships was beginning to come into the mainstream of the gay rights movement. At Carnegie Mellon, where Safier worked as a senior research programmer, a committee formed to ask the university to provide domestic partner benefits for same-sex couples. Safier began to collect information about domestic partnerships and domestic partnership plans.

At about this same time, Jeff Dauber at Silicon Graphics, Inc., formed the domestic partners mailing list. This list allows people interested in this issue to exchange information by electronic mail. In 1993, after SGI had acquired benefits, Jeff lost interest in maintaining this list and asked Safier if he would take it over. The list thus moved from Silicon Graphics to Carnegie Mellon.

Also in the mid-1990s, a new technology was being developed at CERN in Switzerland and the University of Illinois called MOSAIC. Mosaic was a document browser that allowed researchers to share their research across the Internet using the World Wide Web. Because Carnegie Mellon is a world leader in computer research, this new technology was quickly adopted on that campus. Safier realized that this new technology provided a mechanism for him to share his collection of articles and papers on domestic partnership and other gay-rights-related topics. He began to create Web pages to share his information collection—on domestic partnerships, coming out, gay and lesbian history, the scientific search for the origins of same-sex attraction, and others. His collection of information was one of the first on the newly forming World Wide Web.

Safier is currently active in the struggle for marriage rights for same-sex couples. He was one of the founders of the Western Pennsylvania Freedom to Marry Coalition, and continues to devote his energies to equality for same-sex relationships. He met his partner, Champ Knecht, through the computer newsgroup soc.motss at its 1995 convention in Washington, D.C.

Andrew Tobias (1947-)

After a childhood of being "the best little boy in the world," in an upper-middle-class New York City family, Andrew Tobias found his world shattering as he began to realize that he was gay. As did many gay men of his era, he began compartmentalizing his life—professional success was his public persona, furtive sexual encounters with men was his private secret. The contrast between the two proved very difficult for him, and his writing about this time reveals great personal pain.

During his attendance at Harvard Business School, from which he graduated in 1972, Tobias met several other gay men who were struggling with the same issue of reconciling their desire for professional success with their desire for men. This social circle of support led him to realize that it was possible to have fulfillment in both a gay life and a career.

Tobias chose not to go back directly into corporate life, but to write about it. He is the well-known author of the bestseller *The Only Investment Guide You Will Ever Need* (1978), *My Vast Fortune* (1997), and numerous other books, articles, and money management software programs. His gay-themed work includes *The Best Little Boy in the World*, written under the pseudonym John Reid in 1973, "Three Dollar Bills," a 1992 *Time* magazine piece on the gay and lesbian student association at the Harvard Business School, and his public coming out, in a feature article in the March 1995 issue of *Out* magazine.

Active in various public interest causes, he divides his time between homes in New York and Miami.

Gianni Versace (1946-1997)

Gianni Versace grew up in Italy as part of a close family. His mother was a dressmaker, and he learned his art at her knee. He got his first job from his older sister Donatella, and spent the early 1970s working for various Italian designers. In 1978, he opened his own company with older brother Santo handling the finances as company chairman and Donatella working in various design positions.

Versace gained prominence with his cutting-edge designs favored by rock and other celebrities and aficionados of leather, rubber, metal, and bondage fetishes. He was openly gay in the press after 1994, and in the fashion world and to his family long before that. Maintaining homes in Italy and the U.S., throughout his career he maintained close ties with his parents, siblings, and other relatives, as well as a long-term relationship with Antonio D'Amico, whom Versace referred to as his boyfriend in press interviews.

Versace was shot to death in July 1997 in front of his Miami Beach home by Andrew Cunanan, who was catapulted onto the FBI's Most Wanted List as a serial killer after murdering several people in a cross-country crime spree; he eventually committed suicide in Miami after being cornered by police. When Versace was shot, D'Amico had rushed in horror to the spot where Versace lay dying, then chased the killer down an alley, only to be turned back by the gun that had just murdered his partner. Yet most press

Gianni Versace

coverage of Versace's survivors failed to identify the grieving partner with whom he had shared his life for more than a decade.

Donatella has taken over the main design duties for the company while Santo is continuing to run the business operations. Versace's niece, Allegra (Donatella's daughter), is his chief heir, making her one of the world's wealthiest children. (The Versace Group reported 1996 worldwide sales of $1 billion and profits of $43.5 million.) Her brother will also inherit a portion of the estate. D'Amico received $30,000 a month and will continue to have the right to occupy the Miami home he shared with Versace and Donatella and her husband and children as well as Versace's other residences in Italy and New York.

Liz Winfeld (1957-) and Susan Spielman

Liz Winfeld and Sue Spielman are the principals of Common Ground, an education/consulting firm specializing in workplace sexual orientation education and a leader in the field of domestic partner benefits' implementation.

Winfeld was born in 1957 and raised on Long Island, New York, and graduated from SUNY Stony Brook with a B.A. in English literature in 1979. She also earned a Master's Degree in education with a specialty in language acquisition. Her professional career started as a teacher of English as a Second Language on Long Island and in New York City. This was followed by a two-year assignment as an English teacher on the high school level at John Adams High School in Queens, New York.

Winfeld relocated to Massachusetts in 1987 and spent several years in the high-tech networking field as an educator and marketing writer before starting her own freelance marketing and writing business in 1992. This continued until late 1993, when her personal need for partner benefits induced her and her partner to start Common Ground.

Sue Spielman was also born and raised on Long Island, and also holds her B.S. from SUNY Stony Brook. After graduating from Stony Brook, Spielman relocated to Massachusetts to work for Data General Corporation and then eventually for Banyan Systems. It was here that she and Winfeld first met, although their personal relationship did not begin until several years later, after Winfeld left Banyan.

It was Spielman who led the charge to get Banyan to offer domestic partner benefits in 1993, following the model of the Lotus Corporation which had implemented the benefits in 1992. Due to her research, she convinced Banyan to offer the coverage and then encouraged Winfeld to put the program they developed for its implementation into a more formal style and share it with other organizations. That was the beginning of Common Ground.

Four years later, Common Ground has worked with hundreds of organizations throughout the United States, helping them to implement domestic partner benefits plans and also education programs within their diversity models focused on sexual orientation issues in the workplace. Spielman and Winfeld are co-authors of *Straight Talk about Gays in the Workplace: Creating an Inclusive, Productive Environment for Everyone in Your Organization* (AMACOM, 1995), and are much sought after speakers and writers on their subject. Common Ground can be accessed on the World Wide Web at http://www.world.std.com/~lwinfeld and can be reached via email at lwinfeld@world.std.com.

Winfeld and Spielman live in Natick, Mass., a suburb of Boston. They celebrated five years together in June 1997 and look forward to tying the knot officially. They also look forward to

helping more organizations implement fully inclusive programs and policies for all of their employees.

REFERENCES:

Books

Baker, Daniel B., Sean O'Brien Strub, and William Henning. *Cracking the Corporate Closet: The 200 Best (and Worst) Companies to Work for, Buy from, and Invest in if You're Gay or Lesbian—and Even if You Aren't.* New York: HarperCollins, 1995.

Beer, Chris, et al. *Gay Workers: Trade Unions and the Law.* State Mutual Books, 1983.

Berkery, Peter M. *Personal Financial Planning for Gays & Lesbians: Our Guide to Prudent Decision Making.* Irwin Professional, 1996.

Buhrke, Robin A. *A Matter of Justice: Lesbians and Gay Men in Law Enforcement.* Routledge, 1996.

Burke, Marc. E. *Coming Out of the Blue: British Police Officers Talk about Their Lives in 'the Job' as Lesbians, Gays and Bisexuals.* Cassell, 1993.

Diamant, Louis, ed. *Homosexual Issues in the Workplace,* "series in" *Clinical and Community Psychology.* Washington, D.C.: Taylor & Francis, 1993.

Dunne, Gillian A. *Lesbian Lifestyles: Women's Work and the Politics of Sexuality.* Toronto: University of Toronto Press, 1997.

Elkin, Larry M. *Financial Self-Defense for Unmarried Couples.* New York: Doubleday, 1995. Originally published as *First Comes Love Then Comes Money: How Unmarried Couples Can Use Investments, Tax Planning, Insurance, and Wills to Gain Financial Protection.*

Ellis, Alan L. and Ellen D. B. Riggle, eds. *Sexual Identity on the Job: Issues and Services.* Harrington Park Press, 1996.

Escoffier, Jeffrey. *John Maynard Keynes,* "Lives of Notable Gay Men and Lesbians" series. New York: Chelsea House, 1995.

Friskopp, Annette and Sharon Silverstein. *Straight Jobs, Gay Lives: Gay and Lesbian Professionals, the Harvard Business School, and the American Workplace.* New York: Scribners, 1995.

Gaines, Steven and Sharon Churcher. *Obsession: The Lives and Times of Calvin Klein.* New York: Carol Publishing, 1994.

Gelberg, Susan and Joseph Chojnacki. *Career and Life Planning with Gay, Lesbian, and Bisexual Persons.* American Counseling Association, 1996.

Gluckman, Amy and Betsy Reed, eds. *HomoEconomics: Capitalism, Community and Lesbian and Gay Life.* New York: Routledge Press, 1997.

Harbeck, Karen M., ed. *Coming Out of the Classroom Closet: Gay and Lesbian Students, Teachers, and Curricula.* Harrington Park Press, 1992.

Henry, Fran Worden. *Toughing It Out at Harvard: The Making of a Woman MBA.* New York: McGraw Hill, 1984.

Hughes, Theodore E. *The Gay & Lesbian Guide to Personal Finance.* Boston: Alyson, 1997.

Jennings, Kevin, ed. *One Teacher in 10: Gay & Lesbian Educators.* Boston: Alyson, 1994.

Larson, Per. *Gay Money: Your Personal Guide to Same-Sex Strategies for Financial Security, Strength, and Success.* Dell, 1997.

Lasser, J. K. *Gay Finances in a Straight World: A Comprehensive Planning Handbook.* 1997.

Leinen, Stephen. *Gay Cops.* Rutgers University Press, 1993.

Luckenbill, Grant. *Untold Millions: Positioning Your Business for the Gay and Lesbian Consumer Revolution.* New York: Harper Business, 1995.

Massow, Ivan. *Gay Finance Guide.* London: Fourth Estate, 1994.

McNaught, Brian. *Gay Issues in the Workplace.* New York: St. Martin's Press, 1993.

Miller, Merle. *On Being Different: What It Means to Be a Homosexual.* New York: Popular Library, 1971. Originally published as "What It Means to Be a Homosexual," parts one and two, in *New York Times Magazine,* 17 January 1971 and 10 October 1971.

Minkens, Ed. *100 Best Companies for Gay Men and Lesbians.* New York: Pocket Books, 1994.

Powers, Bob and Alan Ellis. *A Manager's Guide to Sexual Orientation in the Workplace.* Routledge, 1995.

Rast, Richard and Lourdes Rodriguez-Nogues. *Out in the Workplace: The Pleasures and Perils of Coming Out on the Job.* Boston: Alyson Press, 1995.

Reid, John. *The Best Little Boy in the World.* New York: G.P. Putnam & Sons, 1973.

Simons, George and Amy Zuckerman. *Sexual Orientation in the Workplace* [workbook]. Available through George Simon International, the Galleria Office Park, 740 Front St. #335, Santa Cruz, California 95060. Email: GSIINTISCCA.aol.com.

Smith, Tom. *Half Straight: My Secret Bisexual Life.* Buffalo, New York: Prometheus Books, 1992.

Wardlow, Daniel L., ed. *Gays, Lesbians, and Consumer Behavior: Theory, Practice, and Research Issues in Marketing.* New York: Haworth Press, 1996.

Winans, Christopher. *Malcolm Forbes: The Man Who Had Everything.* New York: St. Martin's Press, 1990.

Winans, R. Foster. *Trading Secrets: Seduction and Scandal at The Wall Street Journal.* New York: St. Martin's Press, 1984.

Winfeld, Liz and Susan Spielman. *Straight Talk about Gays in the Workplace: Creating an Inclusive, Productive Environment for Everyone in Your Organization.* New York: American Management Association, 1995.

Woods, James D. with Jay H. Lucas. *The Corporate Closet: The Professional Lives of Gay Men in America.* New York: Free Press, 1993.

Zurlinden, Jeffrey. *Lesbian and Gay Nurses.* Albany, New York: Delmar Publishers, 1997.

Publications That Cover Gay Workplace Issues

The Advocate. In the early 1990s had a Workline column with Q & A and news about gay workplace issues, now has a Money section with short blurbs and statistics.

Clout! Chicago-based publication.

The Family Next Door: For lesbian and gay, parents and their friends. PO Box 21580 Oakland, California 94620 (510) 597-1304. vol. 2 no. 1-3, 1994, on domestic partner benefits, plus other coverage of workplace issues.

The Gay/Lesbian/Bisexual Corporate Letter. Arthur C. Bain, PO Box 602, Murray Hill Station, New York, New York 10156-0601 (not published recently).

Out & About. 8 W 19 St #401 New York, New York 10011 800-929-2268, www.outandabout.com. Occasional information on gay workplace issues, especially those related to the travel industry.

Quotient: The Newsletter of Marketing to Gay Men & Lesbians. Daniel B. Baker, Sean O'Brien Strub, and William Henning, 349 West 12 St. New York, New York 10014.

Victory Magazine. 2261 Market St. #296, San Francisco, California 94114 (510) 215-7780. For gay business owners and entrepreneurs.

Working It Out: The Newsletter for GLB Employment Issues. Ed Minkens, PO Box 2079, New York, New York 10108, (212) 769-2384 (not published recently).

Periodical Articles and Book Excerpts

"Corporate Bullies Squashing Queer Employees," in *The Advocate,* 11 September 1990.

De La O, Maria. "Lesbians in Corporate America," in *Dyke Life,* edited by Karla Jay. New York: Basic Books, 1995: 265-281.

Earnshaw, Jill and Peter Pace. "Homosexuals and Transsexuals at Work: Legal Issues," in *Vulnerable Workers: Psychosocial and Legal Issues,* by Marilyn J. Davison and Jill Wiley. Chicester, England: John Wiley & Sons, 1991.

Elliot, John E. "Career Development with Lesbian and Gay Clients," in *Career Development Quarterly,* vol. 41, March 1993: 3.

Etringer, Bruce D., E. Hillerbrand and C. Hetherington. "The Influence of Sexual Orientation on Career Decision Making," in *Journal of Homosexuality,* 1964: 103-111.

Fefer, Mark D. "Gay in Corporate America: What It's Like and How Business Attitudes Are Changing," in *Fortune,* 16 December 1991.

Folbre, Nancy. "Sexual Orientation Showing Up in Paychecks," in *Working Woman,* January 1995: 15.

"Frits Sonnegard, corporate executive," in *The Homosexuals: The First Book in Which, Homosexuals Speak For and About Themselves,* by Alan Ebert. New York: Macmillan, 1977.

"Gay, Inc.: The Surprising Health of Our Businesses," in *The Advocate,* 3 March 1987.

"Gay Money, Gay Power," in *The Advocate,* 19 April 1994.

Hall, Marny. "The Lesbian Corporate Experience," in *Journal of Homosexuality,* vol. 12, no. 3-4, 1986: 59-75.

Hollingsworth, Gaines. "Corporate Gay Bashing," in *The Advocate,* 11 September 1990: 28-33.

Jacobs, Bruce A. "Homosexuals in Management," in *Industry Week,* 23 July 1979: 52-59.

Jay, Karla, and Allen Young. *The Gay Report: Lesbians and Gay Men Speak Out about Sexual Experiences and Lifestyles.* New York: Summit Books, 1977.

Jefferson, David J. "Gay Employees Win Benefits for Partners at More Companies," in *Wall Street Journal,* 18 March 1994: 1, 6.

Katchadorian, Herant and John Boli. "Gay Partnerships," in *Cream of the Crop: The Impact of an Elite Education in the Decade after College.* New York: Basic Books, 1994: 191-194.

Kitzinger, Celia. "Lesbians and Gay Men in the Workplace: Psychosocial Issues," in Davison and Wiley.

Kronenberger, G.K. "Out of the Closet," in *Personnel Journal,* vol. 70, 1991: 40-41.

Labbs, Jennifer L. "Unmarried ... With Benefits," in *Personnel Journal,* December 1991: 62-70.

"Lesbians and Gay Men in the Workplace," in William B. Rubenstein, ed. *Lesbians, Gay Men and the Law,* "Law in Context Series Reader." New York: New Press, 1993.

Levine, Martin P. "The Status of Gay Men in the Workplace," in *Men's Lives,* edited by Michael S. Kimmel and Michael A. Messner. New York: Macmillan, 1992.

Levine, Martin P. and Robin Leonard. "Discrimination against Lesbians in the Work Force," in *Signs Journal of Women in Culture & Society,* vol. 9, no. 4, 1984: 700-710.

Lynch, Frederick R. "Nonghetto Gays: An Ethnography of Suburban Homosexuals," in *Gay Culture in America: Essays from the Field,* edited by Gilbert Herdt. Boston: Beacon Press, 1992.

Magee, Bryan. "Lesbians at Work," in *One in Twenty: A Study of Homosexuality in Men and Women.* New York: Stein & Day, 1966.

Miller, Neil. *In Search of Gay America: Women and Men in a Time of Change.* Atlantic Monthly Press, 1989.

Morgan, Kris and Laura Brown. "Lesbian Career Development, Work Behavior, and Vocational Counseling," in *Counseling Psychologist,* vol. 19, no. 2, April 1991. Also in *Between Women, Between Men: Lesbian and Gay Studies,* edited by Linda D. Garnets and Douglas C. Kimmel. New York: Columbia University Press, 1993: 227-286.

Noble, Barbara Presley. "A Quiet Liberation for Gay and Lesbian Employees," in *New York Times,* 13 June 1993.

"Occupation," in *Male Homosexuals: Their Problems and Adaptations,* by Martin S. Weinberg and Colin J. Williams. London: Oxford University Press, 1974.

Traub, Marvin and Tom Teicholz. *Like No Other Store: The Bloomingdale's Legend, and the Revolution in American Marketing.* New York: Times Books, 1993.

Masters Theses on Gay Workplace Issues

Banzhaf, Jane. *Role Model Choice of Gay Students: A Study of Gay While Males Attending College during the 1960s, 70s, and 80s.* University of Rochester, 1990. August 1990, 248 pp.

Eldridge, Natalie Suzanne. *Correlates of Relationship Satisfaction and Role conflict in Dual-Career Lesbian Couples.* The University of Texas at Austin, 1987. April 1988, 214 pp.

Fogarty, Elizabeth Lee. *Passing as Straight: A Phenomenological Analysis of the Experience of the Lesbian Who is Professionally Employed.* University of Pittsburgh, 1980. December 1980, 182 pp.

Greer, Ruth Berman. *Predictions of Self-Disclosure of Sexual Orientation in the Workplace Among Gay Males.* Columbia University, 1992. February 1993, 115 pp.

Hall, Marny. *Gays in Corporations: The Invisible Minority.* The Union for Experimenting Colleges and Universities, 1981. March 1982, 161 pp.

Harvey, James Joseph. *A Study of Employment Discrimination and Re-Education of a Selected Group of Homosexuals.* East Texas State University, 1978. May 1979, 185 pp.

Haselkorn, Harry. *The Vocational Interests of a Group of Homosexuals.* New York University, 1953. 1962, 119 pp.

Hodnett, James Hoyce. *Correlates of Relationship Satisfaction in Dual-Career Gay Male Couples.* The University of Texas at Austin, 1991. October 1992, 209 pp.

Jackson, Katrice Jewelean. *The Relationship Between Black Lesbians' Coming Out in the Straight Black Community and Isolation.* California State University, 1993. Summer 1994, 62 pp.

Logiudice, Angelo James. *Effects of Sex, Sexual Preference, and Worksetting Based Upon Administrators' Beliefs Toward Gay People.* Northeastern University, 1990. February 1991, 442 pp.

Miller, Gerald Vincent. *From Disempowerment to Empowerment: The Gay Male's Odyssey in the Corporate World.* The Union for Experimenting Colleges and Universities, 1987. December 1988, 110 pp.

Schneider, Beth Elise. *Sexualization of the Workplace.* University of Massachusetts, 1981. February 1982, 403 pp.

Shallenberger, David Bruce. *The Gay Male Professional Who Has Come Out at Work: A Naturalistic Study of His Experience.* The Fielding Institute, 1987. January 1988, 315 pp.

Woods, James Desmond. *The Corporate Closet: Managing Identity on the Job.* University of Pennsylvania, 1992. November 1992, 379 pp.

Videos about Gay Workplace Issues

Gay Issues in the Workplace: An Educational Video, Brian McNaught, TRB Productions, P.O. Box 2362, Boston, MA 02107 (617) 236-7800.

Homophobia in the Workplace: An Educational Video, Brian McNaught, Motivational Media, 8430 Santa Monica Blvd., Los Angeles, CA 90069, 1993.

Organizations

American Civil Liberties Union (ACLU)
National Gay and Lesbian Rights Project
132 W. 43rd Street
New York, NY 10036
ph (212) 944-9800 (ext. 545)
fax: (212) 869-9061

Lambda Legal Defense & Education Fund
http://www.lambdalegal.org
666 Broadway, 12th Floor
New York, NY 10012
ph (212) 995-8585

17 East Monroe, #212
Chicago, IL 60603
ph (312) 759-8110

6030 Wilshire Blvd., #200
Los Angeles, CA 90036
ph (213) 937-2728
Atlanta ph (404) 897-1880

Lesbian and Gay Labor Network
P.O. Box 1159
Peter Stuyvesant Station
New York, NY 10009
Publication: *Pride at Work: Organizing for Lesbian and Gay Rights in Unions,* Miriam Frank and Desma Holcomb.

National Center for Lesbian Rights (NCLR)
870 Market St., #570
San Francisco, CA 94102
ph (415) 392-6257

Pride at Work
655 14th St.
San Francisco, CA 94114
ph (415) 861-0318
fax (415) 284-7519

E-mail Lists

DOMESTIC: Email majordomo-domestic@cs.cmu.edu with the following one-line message in the body of your post: subscribe domestic. The purpose of this list is to facilitate networking about domestic partner benefits issues.

GLBT-WORKPLACE: www.queernet.org/lists/glbt-workplace.html. Email majordomo@queernet.org with the following one-line message in the body of your post: subscribe glbt-workplace. The purpose of this list is general discussion of issues relating to gay, lesbian, bi-sexual, and transgender people the workplace.

Internet Sites

Association of Gay and Lesbian Psychiatrists: http://members.aol.com/aglpnat/homepage.html.

Chicago's Gay & Lesbian Building & Trade Professionals Directory: http://www.suba.com/~glbtp.

Demian's Partners Task Force: http://www.buddybuddy.com. Now focuses on marriage rights, but did some of the original compiling of information on domestic partner benefits, which are available at its site.

G & L Personal Finance Association: http://glpfa.cnchost.com.

GayCanada.com's Page of Canadian companies, educational institutions, governmental agencies and nonprofits with DP benefits: http://www.cglbrd.com/categories/business.htm.

Gay and Lesbian Alliance against Defamation: http://www.glaad.org. Covers workplace issues relevant to the media and entertainment industries. They host Hollywood Supports' historical list of companies with domestic partner benefits at http://www.glaad.org/hsupports-root/hsupports/employer-listing.html.

Gay and Lesbian Medical Association (previously American Association of Physicians for Human Rights): http://www.glma.org.

Gay, Lesbian, and Straight Education Network (GLSEN) http://www.glstn.org. 121 West 27th St. #804, New York, NY 10001, tel (212) 727-0135, fax (212) 727-0254, glsen@glsen.org.

Harvard Business School Gay and Lesbian Alumni organization: http://www.nyu.edu/pages/sls/sjgl/hbsgala.html.

Harvard Business School Gay and Lesbian Student Association: http://wasat.hbs.edu/glsa.

Human Rights Campaign Workplace Issues and Project: http://www.hrcusa.org/issues/workplac. Has information on ENDA, and listings on congressional nondiscrimination policies, corporate and municipal nondiscrimination, public sector, educational institutions, corporate and nonprofit organizations with domestic partnership benefits, corporate and governmental gay and lesbian employee groups. This site contains additional bibliographical references.

International Association of Lesbian & Gay Judges: http://pages.prodigy.com/ialgj.

Jason Lorber's 1995 Report on the Gay-Friendliness of the Nation's Top Business Schools: http://www-leland.stanford.edu/group/QR/lorber. Includes information about nondiscrimination policies, domestic partner benefits, the existence of a gay and lesbian student organization, openly gay student featured in the admissions materials, and more.

Kellogg Gay & Lesbian Management Association: http://www.kellogg.nwu.edu/student/club/glma/glma_000.htm.

Larry Bradley's EEO/Orientation list of companies, educational institutions, governmental agencies and nonprofit organizations with nondiscrimination policies that include sexual orientation: http://abacus.oxy.edu/QRD/browse/sexual.orientation.nondiscrimination.list.

LEGAL International is a federation of gay and lesbian law enforcement groups: http://members.aol.com/legalint/wrldlist.html.

Lesbian and Gay Law Association of Greater New York publishes the Lesbian and Gay Law Notes: http://www.users.interport.net/~le-gal/lawnote.htm, which is full of information about employment discrimination cases and domestic partner benefits. There is online information about domestic partner benefits in the legal profession at http://www.users.interport.net/~le-gal/dbase.htm.

Lesbian, Gay and Bisexual Health Science Librarians: http://www.uic.edu/~shaffer/mlalgb.

Liz Winfeld's page: http://www.world.std.com/~lwinfeld. Winfeld is the coauthor of *Straight Talk about Gays in the Workplace, op sit.*

MBA-Q: mbaqmail@aol.com. A New York City-based organization for graduates of MBA programs: (212) 545-1299.

National Gay and Lesbian Task Force: http://www.ngltf.org. Has a search engine that one can use to find various articles relating to the workplace. NGLTF also sponsors occasional conferences on workplace issues.

National Institute of Health and Federal GLOBE (gay and lesbian Federal employees): http://www.recgov.org/r%26w/glef.html.

National Lesbian & Gay Journalists Association: http://www.nlgja.org. Sponsors annual conference.

National Lesbian and Gay Law Association: http://www.nlgla.org. Sponsors annual Lavender Law conference.

National Organization of Gay and Lesbian Scientists and Technical Professionals: http://www.noglstp.org.

1998 International Conference on Trade Unions, Homosexuality and Work: http://utopia.knoware.nl/users/modijk. PO Box 732, NL 2700 AL ZOETERMEER, Netherlands fax: +31-30-271 05 12, phone: +31-30-273 26 27, e-mail: modijk@knoware.nl.

Out At Work (Or Not): http://qrd.tcp.com/qrd/www/usa/illinois/oaw. Chicago umbrella group for gay and lesbian employee organizations; it also maintains a well-stocked homepage.

Progress homepage: http://www.bayscenes.com/np/progress/home.htm. Information about this umbrella group for California and other gay and lesbian employee organizations, a listing of companies with domestic partner benefits, and information about their annual conference.

QRD (Queer Resources Directory) Workplace page: http://abacus.oxy.edu/qrd/workplace; the QRDBusiness, Legal & Workplace Issues page: http://abacus.oxy.edu/qrd/www/qlegal.html; and the QRD Business page: http://abacus.oxy.edu/qrd/business/ are a somewhat random collection of documents and links.

Rainbow Query: http://www.glweb.com/RainbowQuery/Categories/#OntheJob. With related categories.

Scott Safier's page on Domestic Partners and Same Sex Marriage: http://www.cs.cmu.edu/afs/cs/user/scotts/domestic-partners/mainpage.html. One of the first sites to deal with domestic partner issues. Safier is the list owner of domestic@cs.cmu.edu, an email list about domestic partner benefits.

Sharon Silverstein's Gaywork pages: http://www.nyu.edu/pages/ sls/gaywork. Includes listings of companies, educational institutions, governmental agencies and nonprofit organizations with nondiscrimination and domestic partner policies, contact information on gay and lesbian employee groups, gay and lesbian professional organizations, and many other subjects.

Stanford Business School's Out For Business Organization: http://www-leland.stanford.edu/group/QR/orgs.html.

Straight Jobs Gay Lives homepage: http://www.nyu.edu/pages/sls/ sjgl. Includes key findings and other information from Friskopp and Silverstein's, *Straight Jobs, Gay Lives: Gay and Lesbian Professionals, the Harvard Business School, and the American Workplace.*

University of Pennsylvania Wharton School's Out for Business club: http://dolphin.upenn.edu/~out4biz.

—Sharon Silverstein

10

Military

The 1993 debate over President Bill Clinton's campaign promise to sign an executive order ending the military's ban on lesbians and gays raised a number of important historical, political, and policy issues pertaining to the right of openly lesbian and gay people to serve in the United States military. This essay will explore many of these issues. Underlying the analysis is the assumption that while the debate has largely focused on lesbians, gays, and homosexuality, it also reflects the attitudes of heterosexuals and the values associated with the U.S. military.

In placing the issue in its proper historical context, this essay will explore the reality that lesbians and gays have served in the United States military for years and the consequences of the persistent hostility directed toward them. Comparisons will be drawn between the debate over military racial integration in the late 1940s and the recent debate over lesbians and gays. In addition, the essay will discuss the broader implications of the "coming out" process during World War II for the larger lesbian and gay movement.

From a more contemporary political and policy perspective, the essay will examine the Clinton administration's failed attempt to overturn the military ban through executive order and the consequences of the "Don't Ask, Don't Tell" policy for lesbians and gays and the military over the first three years of its implementation. It devotes considerable attention to the harassment that women have faced both before and after the implementation of the new policy. In addition, it explores the legal challenges surrounding the ban and the important individuals who have been at the center of the debate. Finally, the essay will outline the central arguments on both sides of the debate over whether open lesbians and gays should be allowed to serve. In doing so, it will attempt to capture the essence of the debate, from the vantage point of lesbian and gay civil rights activists and from the military establishment.

THE EVOLVING NATURE OF A POLICY

World War I and World War II

During World War I, the punishment of homosexual soldiers was codified into law. The 1916 Articles of War specified that assault with the intent to commit sodomy be identified as a felony crime. This law did not identify sodomy itself as a crime, but revisions to the Articles of War three years later did. Sodomy was identified as a specific felony; the crime was the sexual act itself, whether it was consensual or involved assault. Throughout the 1920s and 1930s, many gay soldiers and sailors were imprisoned as homosexuality was regarded as a criminal act (Shilts, p. 15).

World War I also saw acceptance of the idea of "excluding people for having a homosexual orientation, as opposed to punishing only those who committed homosexual acts" (Shilts, p. 15). This notion was widely accepted by practitioners in the growing field of psychiatry. A San Francisco psychiatrist, Dr. Albert Abrams, wrote in September 1918 (after San Francisco police discovered a number of soldiers during a raid on a gay club) that "while 'recruiting the elements which make up our invincible army, we cannot ignore what is obvious and which will militate against the combative prowess of our forces in this war.... From a military viewpoint, the homosexualist is not only dangerous, but an ineffective fighter.... It is imperative that homosexuals be recognized by the military authorities'" (Shilts, p. 15). These arguments would be repeated over the years by many who wished to prohibit openly lesbian and gay people from serving in the United States armed forces.

This period also saw the first attempt to purge an installation of homosexuals. A chief machinist's mate, Ervin Arnold, was assigned to the Naval Training Station in Newport, Rhode Island in 1919. He launched his own personal investigation of gays in the navy there, gained approval of his plan from his superiors, "and then persuaded seven enlisted men to entrap suspected gays, largely at the local YMCA." Arnold soon expanded his investigation to the point where a number of "presumably" gay soldiers had been caught, were court-martialed for sodomy, and sentenced to five-to-six year prison terms (Shilts, p. 16). Civilians associated with the navy were also identified as homosexual as a part of Arnold's investigation.

During World War II, the move to transform homosexuality from a crime to an illness gained currency. Between 1941 and 1945, the United States armed forces mobilized some 16 million soldiers and sailors. The military establishment needed help in devising guidelines for eliminating those who might not be fit to serve; it turned to the psychiatry profession, a relatively new field that was legitimized by the role that it played in assisting the military to evaluate recruits during World War II. In 1942, the military issued its first regulations to military psychiatrists pertaining to new recruits. The regulations came with the following notation: "persons habitually or occasionally engaged in homosexual or other perverse sexual practices [were] unsuitable for military service."

An Armed Services contingent at the 1993 March on Washington.

The new screening directives and procedures were largely ineffective in excluding the vast majority of gay men from military service. But they did introduce to the military establishment the notion that homosexuals were unfit to serve because they were mentally ill. Indeed, the belief that lesbians and gay men comprised a class of people who had to be excluded from the military became an important and lasting part of military policy (Berube, p. 33). Final regulations, which remained unchanged for some 50 years, were issued in 1943; they banned homosexuals from all branches of the military (Shilts, pp. 16-7).

The diverse policies of the different services were replaced by the Uniform Code of Military Justice (UCMJ) at the end of World War II. The Uniform Code provided for the following:

> Article 125 of the UCMJ prohibits sodomy, defined as anal or oral penetration, whether consensual or coerced and whether same-sex or opposite-sex, and does not exempt married couples. Under Article 125, the maximum penalty for sodomy with a consenting adult is five years at hard labor, forfeiture of pay and allowances, and dishonorable discharge. Article 134 of the UCMJ, also known as the "General Article," sanctions assault with the intent to commit sodomy, indecent assault, and indecent acts, and prohibits all conduct 'to the prejudice of good order and discipline in the armed

forces.' The maximum penalty is the same for each of these offenses as for sodomy, except in the case of assault with intent, which has a maximum of ten rather than five years confinement (D'Amico, p. 6).

Research by several scholars has highlighted the importance of World War II in modern gay history. The work of historian Allan Berube, published in *Coming Out Under Fire,* is particularly important for pointing out that the wartime experience offered many young lesbians and gay men the opportunity to recognize that they were not alone. They also learned that certain cities allowed them to meet others of their kind and that they could have meaningful lesbian and gay friendships as well. As Berube points out, "thousands of young lesbians and gay men, many from small towns and rural areas, met large numbers of other homosexuals for the first time on military bases, in nearby bars, or in hotels where service people congregated" (Berube, p. 5). In these ways, the military's mobilization forced soldiers to confront homosexuality in their personal lives.

As the military expanded its anti-homosexual policies, it forced many officers and soldiers to come out against their will. When induction examiners publicly rejected draftees for military service because they were homosexual, draftees were forced out of the closet against their will. Draftees were often forced out, as well, when they "declared themselves" and received undesirable discharges as a means to escape harassment (Berube, p. 7). By the end of the war, as anti-homosexual policies were vigilantly enforced, many gay men and lesbians were involuntarily discharged, and returned to civilian life with a stigma attached, and in some cases, lives destroyed. Berube points out that when veterans identified their struggles with the government in the broader context of justice and equal rights, they helped to provide ideas that later became a cornerstone of the contemporary lesbian, gay, and bisexual movement.

Racial and Gender Integration of the Military

The United States military embraced a pattern of racial segregation and exclusion throughout the first half of the twentieth century, despite plenty of evidence that racially integrated combat units performed admirably in World War II (Herek, p. 4). Indeed, segregation ended as official government policy only when President Harry Truman issued his historic Executive Order 9981 a few months before the 1948 election. It ordered an end to discrimination on the basis of race and eventually led to desegregation of the military. Desegregation proceeded slowly, but it dramatically increased the proportion of African-American servicemembers at the time of the Vietnam War. There was considerable resistance, however, to the desegregation efforts. Racial tensions led to violent confrontations between blacks and whites by the late 1960s, and these confrontations significantly affected morale. The Armed Services branches responded by creating programs that were designed to reduce interracial conflict and address racial inequities. Most people regard the military's attempt to desegregate the armed forces as successful, despite the fact that some problems still remain (Herek, p. 5). Some have suggested that we can learn from the racial integration experience in ways that will alleviate problems in adopting a policy that allows open lesbians and gays to serve.

The military's efforts to integrate women into its ranks have been much less successful than its racial integration efforts. Congressional passage of the Women's Armed Services Integration Act of 1948 created a political and policy context for expanding the role played by women. Over the years, the integration of women has come about as a result of legislation, political pressure, court rulings, and Department of Defense (DoD) initiatives. The Reagan administration slowed the trend in the 1980s by getting some policies—for example, the resegregation of army basic training—reversed. However, the role of women in the military expanded again during the Bush and Clinton presidencies; many women served, for example, during the 1991 Persian Gulf War. The military has endured continued problems with harassment of women, as evidenced by the 1991 scandal surrounding the Tailhook Convention (Herek, p. 5) and the 1997 scandal involving sexual harassment of women by army training supervisors. As we will see later in this essay, the efforts to expand the role of women in the armed services and the subsequent harassment of women have had tremendous repercussions for lesbians in the United States military.

1950-1993

During the anti-communist hysteria of the McCarthy era of the 1950s, concern for "national security" was identified as the central reason for keeping gays out of government service, including the military. By the early 1950s, the virulent anticommunist and

anti-homosexual views associated with McCarthyism pervaded the political and social milieus. Senator Joseph McCarthy and his colleagues claimed that "homosexuals and other sex perverts" threatened to undermine the nation's moral welfare (Benecke and Dodge, p. 73). Throughout the 1950s and 1960s, individuals were barred from military service for acknowledging a homosexual orientation. For the pre-Stonewall lesbian and gay movement, challenging the military policy became an important goal. For example, the founder of the Washington, D.C., Mattachine Society chapter, Franklin Kameny, had three goals to pursue as a political activist: "to end the Civil Service's ban on gays working for the government, to end discrimination against homosexuals seeking security clearances, and to end the exclusion of gays from the military" (Shilts, p. 194).

The 1969 Stonewall Rebellion, generally identified by scholars as the beginning of the modern lesbian and gay movement, ushered in an array of challenges to discriminatory governmental policies. The military policy became a target of the movement, as reflected in the legal challenge to the policy offered by Leonard Matlovich (Herek, p. 6). On 6 March 1975, air force technical sergeant Leonard Matlovich hand-delivered a letter to his superior, Captain Dennis Collins, the officer in charge of race-relations instruction at Langley Air Force Base in Hampton, Virginia. The letter was addressed to the Secretary of the Air Force and began in this way:

> After some years of uncertainty, I have arrived at the conclusion that my sexual preferences are homosexual as opposed to heterosexual. I have also concluded that my sexual preferences will in no way interfere with my Air Force duties, as my preferences are now open. It is therefore requested that those provisions in AFM-39-12 relating to the discharge of homosexuals be waived in my case....

It ended:

> In sum, I consider myself to be a homosexual and fully qualified for military service. My almost twelve years of unblemished service supports this position (Miller, p. 411).

Matlovich's letter signaled the beginning of the contemporary battle to overturn the U.S. military's policy barring lesbians and gays. During the late 1970s, there were a number of challenges to the military ban. Vernon "Copy" Berg III, a naval ensign, challenged the navy's decision to discharge him after the discovery that he was having an affair with a navy civilian instructor. Rudolf "Skip" Keith came out of the closet during a race-relations class at Dover Air Force Base, near Washington. Two members of the Women's Army Corps at Fort Devens, Massachusetts, Private First Class Barbara Randolph and Private Debbie Watson, declared to their commanding office that they would take their military exclusion to the Supreme Court. Another case from this time period was the case of Miriam Ben-Shalom, a single mother and army reserve drill instructor in Milwaukee who mounted a legal challenge to her discharge (Miller, p. 413). These challenges were largely unsuccessful, but they highlighted the discretion afforded to military commanders who were responsible for implementing existing policy and who applied different degrees of rigor and standards in the implementation process (Herek).

Leonard Matlovich on the cover of *Time* magazine in 1975.

Matlovich's case had the highest profile in the media. He appeared on the cover of *Time* magazine in uniform six months after his letter was delivered. The caption on the *Time* cover was "I Am Homosexual." On the inside, there were photos of him recovering from wounds in Danang, South Vietnam and dancing in a gay bar. The prominent coverage that *Time* granted the Matlovich case encouraged Miriam Ben-Shalom to inform her commanding officer that she was a lesbian and inspired Ensign "Copy" Berg to fight his discharge from the navy (Miller, p. 413).

In November 1975, Matlovich was discharged by the air force, and Federal District Court Judge Gerhard Gesell refused to overturn the air force's decision. But there was legal momentum building in Matlovich's favor. The Court of Appeals ruled in December 1978 that the discharges of Matlovich and Ensign Berg were illegal. It did not order the reinstatement of either man. It did, however, force Judge Gesell to reexamine the Matlovich case. Gesell's September 1980 decision ordered Matlovich's reinstatement to the air force by December 5 of that year (Miller, p. 413).

The air force responded by offering Matlovich a cash settlement in a last-ditch effort to avoid having to take him back to its ranks. Most observers thought that Matlovich would not accept such a settlement. And most realized, as well, that the air force would appeal Judge Gesell's decision to the United States Supreme Court. But in the end, within days of his reinstatement, Matlovich agreed to drop his case and accept the tax-free $160,000 offered by the air force (Miller, pp. 413-14).

The military ban remained in place throughout the 1980s, despite occasional sympathetic lower-court decisions. Military regulations were toughened during the Reagan-Bush years. The military revised its policy concerning homosexuality in 1982. A General Accounting Office (GAO) Report suggests that the revision was implemented for three central reasons: "(1) to establish uniform procedures concerning homosexuality across the service branches; (2) to clarify the specific actions for which a person could be separated; and (3) to define the extenuating circumstances under which persons found to have engaged in those actions might nevertheless be retained" (Herek, p. 6). The 1982 policy mandated the following:

> Homosexuality is incompatible with military service. The presence in the military environment of persons who engage in homosexual conduct or who, by their statements, demonstrate a propensity to engage in homosexual conduct, seriously impairs the accomplishment of the military mission.... The presence of such members adversely affects the ability of the Military Services to maintain discipline, good order, and morale; to foster mutual trust and confidence among service members; to ensure the integrity of the system of rank and command; to facilitate assignment and worldwide deployment of service members who frequently must live and work under close conditions affording minimal privacy; to recruit and retain members of the Military Services; to maintain the public acceptability of military service; and to prevent breaches of security (Herek, p. 7).

These are arguments that have been advanced by the military at various points over the years, and they were central components of the opposition to Bill Clinton's 1993 attempt to overturn the military ban.

That the 1980s were a particularly difficult decade for lesbians and gays in the military is reflected in discharge statistics. Between fiscal years 1980 and 1990, 16,919 men and women were discharged under the separate category of homosexuality. White women, in particular, were targeted. They "were discharged at a disproportionately high rate: 20.2 percent of those discharged for homosexuality were white women, although they constituted only 6.4 percent of personnel" (Herek, p. 7). The navy was disproportionately represented, as it accounted for 51 percent of all discharges related to homosexuality, despite the fact that it constituted only 27 percent of the active force during this time period. These figures do not even include those lesbians and gay men processed under other categories and involuntarily separated from the military.

Advocates for lesbian and gay civil rights embraced overturning the military ban as a priority in the 1980s. Legislation to overturn the ban was introduced by Senator Howard Metzenbaum (D-Ohio) and Rep. Patricia Schroeder (D-Colorado) in 1992. At that point, there appeared to be mounting opposition to the military policy on the part of many national organizations, as well as colleges and universities that chose to ban military recruiters and Reserve Officers' Training Corps (ROTC) programs from their campuses.

THE "DON'T ASK, DON'T TELL" DEBATE AND POLICY

It was in this context that presidential candidate Bill Clinton announced that if he were elected president in the 1992 presidential election, one of his first acts would be to overturn the military ban through executive order. In the fall of 1991, then-presidential candidate Bill Clinton was asked by a student at a Harvard University forum whether he would issue an executive order to overturn the ban on lesbians and gays in the military. Clinton responded "Yes," and explained further: "I think people who are gay should be expected to work, and should be given the opportunity to serve the country." He continued to make this pledge as a presidential candidate and then very early in his presidency (Rimmerman, p. xix).

The military ban and Clinton's attempt to rescind it raise an array of important questions. Why did such furious and sustained opposition emerge to Clinton's original promise? What are the sources of this opposition? To what extent was Clinton's promise related to changing cultural factors regarding lesbians and gays in the larger society? Why did Congress toughen Clinton's compromise proposal? What are the broader implications of how this issue was resolved for the lesbian and gay movement? The first major news story in the period between President-elect Clinton's

election and inauguration was his announcement that he planned to adhere to his campaign promise and overturn the ban on lesbians and gays in the military through an executive order. At that precise moment, Clinton had no idea that this promise would be an enduring controversy for the first six months of his presidency. After Clinton's inauguration, the controversy reached its zenith as the issue dominated radio call-in programs and newspaper headlines for a week. Congressional offices were flooded with postcards, telegrams, and telephone calls from irate citizens who violently opposed the President's suggestion that the military ban be overturned. Some argued that the mobilization of the citizenry against overturning the military ban had been carefully orchestrated by the "religious right." These religious conservatives gained considerable support when the Joint Chiefs of Staff, led by Chairman Colin Powell, expressed strong opposition to Clinton's promise, and when Sam Nunn, chairman of the Senate Armed Services Committee, expressed public concern. Nunn held much-publicized hearings on the issue in spring 1993, hearings that those in favor of overturning the ban later characterized as being biased in favor

The gravestone of Leonard Matlovich.

Dorothy Hajdys, mother of Allen Schindler, with a naval escort. Schindler was murdered by a shipmate in 1992.

of the military. The hearings themselves produced several dramatic moments, most notably Colonel Fred Peck's outing of his own son Scott. Peck, who at the time was the U.S. Army spokesman in Somalia, testified in favor of the ban because of antigay prejudice in the ranks. He concluded that if his son were in the military hierarchy, "I would be very fearful his life would be in jeopardy from his own troops." Scott Peck later responded publicly to his father by stating: "I have a little more faith in members of the military" (Rimmerman, p. 116).

The media's role in defining the context and setting the agenda for the debate was significant. For example, it captured Colonel Peck's dramatic congressional testimony live, televised it into millions of homes, and gave it considerable coverage on the evening news. The brutal beating and murder of Seaman Allen Schindler after he had identified himself as a gay man and as he prepared for discharge was given coverage by the media as well. In addition, Sam Nunn and several of his pro-ban colleagues were given a tour of two navy ships so that they could get a better understanding of the close living quarters experienced by military personnel. He identified for the accompanying C-SPAN camera the closeness of the bunks and shower stalls and asked groups of sailors how they felt about the idea of "open homosexuals" in the armed forces. The press reinforced the most-negative stereotypes regarding lesbians and gays by covering this tour extensively. The

role of the press, Sam Nunn's ability to dominate the debate with his hearings, and the mobilization of the religious right at the grassroots level all had the consequence of forcing the President and opponents of the ban on the defensive. Opponents of the ban never really recovered from this defensive posture.

Much attention was focused on Clinton's role in the debate, given that it was his attempt to overturn the ban that inspired the national attention on the issue. Just what role did Clinton play? When Clinton appeared on a live broadcast of "CBS This Morning," on 27 May 1993, a Virginia minister asked him about the issue of gays in the military. Clinton said the following in response:

> Most Americans believe that the gay lifestyle should not be promoted by the military or anybody else in this country.... We are trying to work this out so that our country does not appear to be endorsing a gay lifestyle.... I think most Americans will agree when it works out that people are treated properly if they behave properly without the government appearing to endorse a lifestyle.

With this response, Clinton employed the worst form of language—"lifestyle," "endorse," "approve," "promote"—from the antigay lexicon in his answer. Members of the lesbian and gay community responded quickly. David Mixner, Clinton's long-time friend and a leading openly gay member of the Democratic party, claimed that he was physically sickened by Clinton's response. Of course, Mixner and others supporting overturning the ban had plenty of good reasons to be disturbed. Clinton had begun to backtrack in public on his promise to overturn the ban through an executive order. One explanation for his actions is that he was trying to distance himself from lesbian and gay groups for political reasons. What better way to do this but to embrace elements of the language of the radical right groups who were so feverishly working to uphold the ban (Rimmerman, pp. 116-17)?

But Clinton's comments also indicate that he was signaling to lesbian and gay groups and their supporters that he would likely compromise on his original promise. There was little surprise, then, when Clinton compromised his original position with his July 1993 "Don't Ask, Don't Tell" proposal. This proposal contained the following details:

1) The policy bars military recruiters from asking if prospective enlistees are gay or lesbian.
2) Homosexual conduct is forbidden both on-base and off-base.
3) What constitutes homosexual conduct?
   a) same-sex intercourse
   b) public acknowledgement of homosexuality
   c) attempting a same-sex marriage
   d) same-sex hand-holding or kissing
4) What constitutes permissible activity?
   a) telling a spouse, attorney, or member of the clergy about your homosexuality
   b) associating with openly gay and lesbian people
   c) going to a gay or lesbian bar
   d) marching in a gay pride march in civilian clothes
5) Military personnel found to have engaged in homosexual conduct could be discharged.
6) Military officials could not launch probes merely to discover if an enlistee is gay or lesbian, but if they suspect, based on "articulatable facts," that a person has engaged in prohibited activity, they may investigate to find out if their suspicion is correct.
7) Capricious outing of suspected gays and lesbians by fellow personnel without evidence is forbidden, and any attempt to blackmail a suspected gay or lesbian member of the armed forces would be punishable by a dishonorable discharge, a $2,000 fine, and a one-year jail term (Bull, p. 24).

Clinton's proposal was modified by Sam Nunn, whose goal was to toughen it in ways that would make it more punitive toward lesbians and gays in the military. Nunn's efforts were ultimately codified into law by Congress under the rubric of "Don't Ask, Don't Tell, Don't Pursue," thus making it more difficult for opponents of the ban to offer serious structural reforms in the future. Because the previous ban was enforced through an executive order, which could at least be changed through presidential missive, the codification meant that any future changes to Nunn's congressional policy would require congressional consent. Nunn's tough congressional language enabled the specifics of the Clinton plan to take effect while codifying the law into a broad statement of policy, one that rejects the idea of accepting lesbians and gays into the military. In addition, the congressional version states that lesbians and gays have no constitutional rights for serving in the armed forces (Rimmerman, p. 118). This final element of Nunn's plan is "exactly what President Clinton hoped to challenge in his original determination to overturn the ban through executive order" ("The Legislative Word on Gays," p. 2076).

Why did President Clinton support a compromise on this issue? How could he do so, given the clear promise that he stated as a presidential candidate and as a newly elected President of the United States? A number of explanations have been identified by individuals both inside and outside the administration. Clinton's approach to governance has always been rooted in building consensus. This was true when he was governor of Arkansas, and the first several years of his presidency suggested that he is someone who embraces consensus as a governing methodology rather than adhering to ideology or principle.

In addition, Clinton was obviously motivated by political considerations. His chief advisors—Rahm Emanuel, David Gergen, Bruce Lindsey, Thomas ("Mack") McLarty, and George Stephanopoulos—clearly wanted him to put this divisive "no-win" issue behind the new administration. Clinton and his advisors believed that it was important for him to embrace the center of the political spectrum as a proud "new kind of Democrat." It made sense, then, for purely political reasons that Clinton would want to distance himself from an unpopular special interest—lesbians and gays. For Clinton certainly did not want to associate himself with Democrats such as Michael Dukakis and Walter Mondale, both of whom had reputations as individuals who could be pushed around by liberal special interests.

It is clear, as well, that Clinton realized that without a major fight, he did not have the congressional votes needed to uphold his original desire to rescind the ban. This view was reinforced by Representative Barney Frank, when he publicly proposed a compromise plan, much to the consternation of many lesbian and gay activists (Rimmerman, p. 118). Under Frank's proposal, which he named "don't ask, don't tell, don't investigate," Pentagon officials would have been forbidden to ask recruits about their sexual orientation. In addition, military personnel also would have been "forbidden to disclose their homosexuality while on duty but would be free to do so during off-duty hours." In providing a rationale for his proposal, Frank argued that it was an improved version of the Clinton/Nunn compromise proposal and that he was worried that Congress was about to codify an even more-restrictive proposal into law (Bull, "No Frankness," pp. 25-7). In the end, then, Frank believed that it was better to get something for lesbians and gays in the military rather than nothing at all. President Clinton obviously shared this compromise spirit, and this rationale underlay his entire approach to resolving the broader issue.

By backing away from his original promise, Clinton could also appease and meet the demands of the Joint Chiefs of Staff. Led by Chairman Colin Powell, the Joint Chiefs were firmly opposed to rescinding the ban. As Commander in Chief of the armed forces, President Clinton had the authority and power to order the Joint Chiefs to obey his directives. But in this case, Clinton chose not to do so. Ultimately, he was convinced that the Joint Chiefs' perspective deserved more attention in the final policy resolution of the issue than the concerns of lesbian and gay activists. Clinton could not forget, either, that the 1992 presidential campaign devoted considerable attention to his activities during the Vietnam War. George Bush and the Republicans hammered away at Clinton's opposition to the war and his lack of foreign policy experience. For Clinton, backing off his support for overturning the ban meant that he could win some much-needed support from the military, the group that seemed to be most threatened by his original campaign promise (Rimmerman, p. 119).

Finally, Clinton and his political advisors feared that they were squandering valuable political capital during his honeymoon period over such an emotionally charged issue. From Clinton's vantage point, his first budget plan, health care, and the ratification of North American Free Trade Agreement were far more important policy initiatives than rescinding the ban. As a result, he did not even lobby members of Congress to overturn the ban, because he realized that their support would be needed on policy concerns of much higher priority to his new administration.

How did Clinton defend his own compromise plan? He publicly identified the plan as an "honest compromise" and acknowledged that the plan's specifics were not necessarily identical to his own goals. In the face of intense congressional and military opposition to lifting the ban, Clinton believed that the policy was the closest he could come to fulfilling his campaign promise. One administration official said: "The President believes that it is a solid advance forward in terms of extending rights to gays and lesbians in the military" (Rimmerman, p. 119).

The Response of the Lesbian and Gay Community to Clinton's Compromise

Lesbian and gay activists and their supporters did not share the President's optimism. Tom Stoddard, the Coordinator of the Campaign for Military Service, a Washington, D.C.-based organization that had been established during the debate to help rally support for overturning the ban, said: "The President could have lifted up the conscience of the country. Instead, he acceded without a fight to the stereotypes of prejudices he himself had disparaged." Torrie Osborn, at the time the Executive Director of the National Gay and Lesbian Task Force, argued that the plan is "simply a repackaging of discrimination." And Tim McFeeley, then Head of the Human Rights Campaign Fund (HRCF), called the Clinton proposal a "shattering disappointment" (Rimmerman, p. 119). Conservative author and columnist Bruce Bawer assailed the Nunn proposal and Clinton's support for the proposal: "This compromise ... would essentially write into law the institution of the closet: while heterosexuals would continue to enjoy their right to lead private lives and to discuss those lives freely, gays would be allowed to remain in the armed forces only so long as they didn't mention their homosexuality to anyone or have relationships on or off base" (Bawer, p. 117). But it was a *New Republic* editorial that perhaps best captured the fury of those who expected the President to follow through on his original campaign promise:

> And the most demeaning assumption about the new provisions is that they single out the deepest moment of emotional intimacy—the private sexual act—as that which is most repugnant. Its assumption about the dignity and humanity of gay people, in and out of the military, in public and in private, is sickening (Rimmerman, p. 120).

These statements by prominent gay and lesbian activists reflected the larger community's enormous disappointment and frustration after the President issued his compromise.

How the Clinton Administration Might Have Avoided Compromise

To supporters of rescinding the ban, the Clinton administration made a number of very serious strategic mistakes, mistakes that could have been avoided. Some believe that the President should have introduced the executive order as he had promised and then allowed Congress to do what it wished, even if that meant passing legislation that challenged this executive order. By embracing such a strategy, the President would have been given credit for following through with a policy promise rooted in principle (Rimmerman, p. 120).

In addition, the administration clearly underestimated the opposition of Congress, most notably Sam Nunn, the Joint Chiefs of Staff, the military, and the religious right. The Clinton administration was surprised that Nunn would attempt to embarrass a new president of his own political party, one who generally supported New Democratic principles.

The administration also failed to establish an honest and open line of communication with lesbian and gay groups. Several officials from an array of lesbian and gay organizations charged that they were deliberately misled about Clinton's intentions regarding overturning the ban from the outset. Apparently during the presidential transition and the first weeks of the Clinton presidency, lesbian and gay groups were told by influential presidential advisors not to lift a finger in terms of organizing grassroots support, because the President would do everything necessary to overturn the ban. In a much-publicized April 1993 White House meeting, just before the March on Washington, President Clinton told lesbian and gay activists in attendance that he would persuade Colin Powell and the Joint Chiefs of Staff to support his plan to rescind the ban.

Yet another serious problem was that during the first several months of the Clinton presidency, no one at the White House was assigned the responsibility of overseeing legislative strategy for overturning the ban. This was the case until David Gergen joined the Clinton White House, at which point George Stephanopoulos was given the responsibility for coordinating the Clinton strategy.

The Clinton administration did little lobbying on Capitol Hill. It is possible that the ban might well have received considerable congressional support had the President used the powers of his office to enlist that support.

In retrospect, it is obvious now that the timing of the issue did not work to the President's advantage. His plan to rescind the ban was not a good issue with which to begin his presidency. Some have argued that Clinton would have been much better off in raising the issue after his first year in office. At that point, he would have established the credibility of his administration with concrete legislative accomplishments. This might have given him more clout in dealing with Congress.

Finally, it is clear to critics that President Clinton did not perform his important leadership role in educating the public about why he believed that it was necessary to rescind the ban. Many presidential scholars have identified the importance of the President's potential role as an educator. In the words of Leon Wieseltier, "It is not leadership to tell people what they want to hear. It is leadership to tell people what they do not want to hear, and to give them a reason to listen" (Wieseltier, p. 77).

Weaknesses in the Lesbian and Gay Community's Strategy to Overturn the Ban

It was not only the Clinton presidency that made strategic errors in the debate over lesbians and gays in the military. The lesbian and gay movement also made a number of tactical mistakes, mistakes that undermined their attempt to garner greater public support for overturning the ban.

At the outset, the mainstream lesbian and gay movement put far too much trust in Clinton. Delirious with excitement because a supposed friend had been elected to the White House, the movement largely ignored Clinton's past less-than-stellar record on lesbian and gay issues while governor of Arkansas. There were some notable exceptions. Michael Petrelis, a member of the Washington, D.C., chapters of ACT UP and Queer Nation, distributed "Impeach Clinton" buttons the weekend before the November 1992 presidential election. Unlike many of his counterparts in the mainstream lesbian and gay movement, Petrelis recognized that supposedly having Clinton on his side was simply not enough. From the outset, Petrelis and other more radical members of the movement distrusted Clinton's motives, his sincerity, and his seriousness of purpose in overturning the ban and addressing AIDS meaningfully.

Some members of the lesbian and gay community pointed to the movement's inability to mobilize at the grassroots level. The Campaign for Military Service was largely a Washington, D.C., organizing effort; it failed to generate the kind of grassroots support needed in states whose Congressional representatives were wavering in their decisions on whether to rescind the ban. In addition, gay rights advocates were never able to marshal the volume of calls and letters from constituents to win over legislators, who were being deluged with calls and mails organized largely by the evangelical right, who supported the ban. Representative Barney Frank received considerable criticism from the lesbian and gay community for identifying the problems associated with the gay and lesbian organizing efforts. Frank said:

We did a very bad job of mobilizing—getting people to write to members of the House and Senate. We spent a lot of our time and energy on things that are irrelevant to a short-term fight in Congress. People assumed that the March on Washington or demonstrations were a good thing. Those have no effect on members of Congress (Osborne, p. 53).

Frank's comments reveal that he was particularly critical of the March on Washington's organizers' inability to generate a massive congressional lobbying effort on behalf of rescinding the ban.

For those supporting overturning the ban, there were further complications. Some lesbians and gays simply could not garner excitement about the issue. This lack of excitement was due to several factors. Many people already thought that the fight had been won by having Clinton as President, especially since he was the one who promised to rescind the ban. The movement had no real experience in dealing with a President who seemingly supported lesbian and gay concerns. In addition, the issue did not seem nearly as important for a community that had been and continues to be ravaged by AIDS. Finally, many lesbians and gays cut their political teeth in the antiwar movement of the 1960s and did not want to legitimate participation in the military.

Early Implementation of the New Policy

The initial reports indicated that the first two months of the implementation of the "Don't Ask, Don't Tell" policy "has not made life easier for many gay servicemen and women and in some ways has made it worse" (Schmitt, p. A1). The principal concern in the early stages of implementation is that while the policy may have been designed to enable lesbians and gays "to serve without fear of persecution if they kept their sexual orientation private," it has been carried out by commanders who have misused "the broad new authority granted under the policy to ferret out homosexuals." Eric Schmitt's *New York Times* account also revealed the following:

In addition, while a few gay servicemen and women said they felt the new policy had improved conditions, most of those who were interviewed said it had instead polarized attitudes toward homosexuals and had shifted the burden of proof to the servicemember if accused of engaging in homosexual acts (Schmitt, p. A1).

These problems were to emerge over and over again in both press accounts and studies undertaken by the Servicemembers Legal Defense Network (SLDN), a Washington, D.C.-based organization founded by Michelle Benecke and C. Dixon Osburn that represents lesbian and gay servicemembers. As the sole national legal aid and watchdog organization for those targeted by the military's new policy on homosexuals, it is the only means currently available to document abuses.

The Servicemembers Legal Defense Network's first year implementation study, released in late February 1995, concluded that the Clinton/Nunn policy revealed a pattern of violations that often renders the policy little more than "Ask, Pursue, and Harass" (Osburn and Benecke). It is important to recognize that SLDN's documented cases are a small portion of the servicemembers who are actually affected by the "Don't Ask, Don't Tell" policy. As the authors of the study point out, "many servicemembers are discharged by the Department of Defense for homosexuality without ever having contacted SLDN, and others are removed from service for homosexuality through ulterior means such as denial of reenlistment" (Osburn and Benecke, p. 250). They admit, too, that their organization's outreach is limited by its scarce resources.

SLDN's second annual report, published in March 1996, concluded that there was a continued pattern of military abuse:

[This military abuse] has effectively rendered the current policy as bad as, if not worse than, its predecessors. Many military members clearly continue to ask, pursue and harass suspected gay troops in blatant disregard of the policy's limits. From 1 March 1995-27 February 1996, SLDN documented 363 specific violations of the current policy. The result, in part, is that the Department of Defense (DOD) discharged more servicemembers under its gay policy in fiscal year 1995 than in each of the past four years at a cost exceeding $21 million in 1995 (Osburn and Benecke, p. i).

The report identified four basic types of violations to the existing policy. The violation categories include cases where servicemembers have been forced to respond to questions about their sexual orientation ("don't ask"); cases where servicemembers

Lesbian-Baiting: **The Disproportionate Impact** **of the Gay Policies on Women**						
Fiscal Year	**Total Active Force**	**Total Women in Active Force**	**% Women in Active Force**	**% Women Discharged Under Gay Policies**	**Total Dischargs Under Gay Policies**	**Total Women Discharged Under Gay Policies**
1980	2,036,672	170,238	8.3%	21%	1,754	364
1981	2,068,885	183,594	8.9%	19%	1,817	351
1982	2,096,644	188,545	9.0%	22%	1,998	435
1983	2,112,067	196,094	9.3%	24%	1,815	439
1984	2,123,428	200,827	9.4%	26%	1,822	469
1985	2,137,415	209,370	9.6%	24%	1,660	404
1986	2,156,593	216,823	10.0%	23%	1,644	372
1987	2,163,578	220,957	10.2%	23%	1,380	312
1988	2,123,669	221,649	10.4%	25%	1,100	280
1989	2,115,234	229,311	10.8%	27%	997	272
1990	2,029,300	223,154	11.0%	21%	932	199
1991	1,985,500	216,681	11.0%	23%	949	219
1992	1,807,100	205,571	11.4%	23%	708	160
1993	1,705,000	199,043	11.7%	27%	682	186
1994	1,610,400	195,027	12.1%	27%	597	160
1995	1,523,300	191,399	12.6%	22%	722	160
1996	1,471,722	192,469	13.1%	29%	850	246

Source: Department of Defense

Figure 1

have been punished for making statements about sexual orientation that are permissible ("don't tell"); cases where servicemembers have been subjected to criminal prosecution or witchhunts because of their suspected sexual orientation ("don't pursue"); and cases where harassment is permitted based on perceived sexual orientation ("don't harass"). Women, who comprise up to 13 percent of the military's total force, were disproportionately targeted for discharge (22 percent of the 722 people discharged were women).

The third annual SLDN report, published in March 1997, found that:

> Many military members continue to ask, pursue and harass servicemembers in direct violation of "Don't Ask, Don't Tell, Don't Pursue." The violations result from a lack of leadership, training and recourse to stop illegal investigations. Some commanders, criminal investigators and inquiry officers blatantly disregard the clear limits on investigations. Others simply do not know any better, as the services have failed to implement adequate, ongoing training in the field. Lastly, those accused under "Don't Ask, Don't Tell, Don't Pursue" have no recourse to stop improper investigations before it is too late.

The 722 people discharged in 1996 is the largest number since 1991, when 949 were discharged, and the highest discharge rate since 1987. Once again, SLDN also found a marked disparity in how women and men are treated under the policy. As Figure 1 indicates, women accounted for 29 percent of those discharged for being homosexual or for violating the policy in 1996, despite the fact that they make up only 13.1 percent of the armed forces.

Lesbian and gay activists cite a climate that tolerates widespread sexual harassment as the central reason for the discrepancy. Joe Zuniga, who was discharged after he came out in 1993, offered this description of how women are harassed: "A male soldier approaches a female soldier who may or not be a lesbian and then, if she doesn't respond to the overture, accuses her of being a lesbian to a higher authority" (Moss, p. 24). In sum, all the empirical evidence gathered thus far on the implementation of the Clinton/congressional policy indicates that it has largely been a failure. Ultimately, the question is this: If President Clinton's "Don't Ask, Don't Tell" policy means that the military is forbidden to search for and target lesbians and gays, why has there been a 42 percent increase in discharges for homosexuality since the policy took effect in 1994? (*The Advocate Report*, 1 April 1997, p. 15).

LESBIANS AND THE MILITARY

The participation of women in the Gulf War and the highly publicized court battles challenging the exclusion of women by the Virginia Military Institute and the Citadel have led to renewed attention on the role played by women in the U.S. armed forces (Benecke and Dodge, p. 71). Any discussion of how les-

bians have been treated in the military over time should take into account significant features of sex-based discrimination that have prevailed over the years. The combination of sexual harassment and lesbian accusations have grown much more pronounced throughout the 1980s and 1990s (Shilts, p. 4). Lesbian baiting in the form of calling or threatening to call women lesbians was a central consequence of the pre-Clinton era military policy, and it continues today despite the implementation of the new policy. Lesbian baiting surely gains its power and legitimacy through the Department of Defense (DOD) policy that bans service by known homosexuals, and from the subsequent codification of this policy into law. The policy is employed in ways that justify campaigns of sexual harassment against women. In its application, the policy helps to control and to confine "women's presence and behavior in the military" (Benecke and Dodge, p. 71). Witch-hunts have contin-

Total Discharges and Rate of Discharge Under Gay Polices

Fiscal Year	USAF	USA	USN	USMC	Total	Total Active Force	Discharged as % of Total Active Force
1980	305	409	973	67	1,754	2,036,672	.086
1981	239	414	1,089	75	1,817	2,068,885	.088
1982	310	454	1,111	123	1,998	2,096,644	.095
1983	341	391	937	146	1,815	2,112,067	.086
1984	330	478	888	126	1,822	2,123,428	.086
1985	289	454	799	118	1,660	2,137,415	.078
1986	332	491	735	86	1,644	2,156,593	.076
1987	279	348	656	97	1,380	2,163,578	.064
1988	230	276	498	96	1,100	2,123,669	.051
1989	198	301	440	58	997	2,115,234	.047
1990	141	220	519	61	941	2,043,700	.046
1991	151	206	545	47	949	1,985,500	.048
1992	111	138	401	58	708	1,807,100	.039
1993	152	156	334	40	682	1,705,000	.040
1994	180	136	245	36	597	1,610,400	.037
1995	234	182	260	46	722	1,523,300	.047
1996	282	206	302	60	850	1,471,722	.057

Source: Department of Defense

Figure 2

Violations of "Don't Ask, Don't Tell, Don't Pursue, Don't Harass" for All Services

28 February 1996-26 February 1997

Service	Don't Ask	Don't Tell	Don't Pursue	Don't Harass	Total
Air Force	30	10	77	25	142
Army	22	4	43	48	117
Navy	25	17	58	46	146
Marine Corps	6	0	12	4	22
Coast Guard	6	0	1	9	16
Totals	89	31	191	132	443

1 March 1995-27 February 1996

Service	Don't Ask	Don't Tell	Don't Pursue	Don't Harass	Total
Air Force	24	10	61	19	114
Army	22	4	39	36	101
Navy	25	4	38	59	126
Marine Corps	6	0	3	13	22
Coast Guard	0	0	0	0	0
Totals	77	18	141	127	363

Source: Servicemembers Legal Defense Network (February 1997)

Figure 3

ued in the first three years of the new policy, and women continue to be disproportionately targeted.

The military used investigative tactics in the 1950s that foreshadowed contemporary investigations of women who were suspected of lesbianism. Air force investigators persuaded women "to spy on the other girls and to list girls who [were] friends and who *might* be engaging in homosexual relations." One air force woman under investigation reported that those who were accused of lesbian activities were informed of their rights. But this was done "in such a way that you [were] sure if you [did not answer questions] the consequences [would] be little short of fatal." For those women who refused to sign discharge papers or request military trials to fight charges, they were involuntarily discharged through administrative procedures (Benecke and Dodge, p. 73).

It was in the late 1970s that the military enlisted more women in an effort to make up for a decline in the number of new male recruits. Legislation to eliminate restrictions on women serving in combat jobs was introduced in 1979. With the economy in recession and unemployment rates high in 1980, the military services successfully recruited more men. Not surprisingly, military offi-

cials began to enforce regulations and procedures that discriminated against all women, lesbians, and gay men much more vigorously. Field commanders who had resisted having women in their units challenged women's continued presence in nontraditional military areas as more men became available to fill recruiting quotas. According to researchers Michelle M. Benecke and Kirstin Dodge, "it appears that this combination of factors resulted in women becoming a special target for discharge" (Benecke and Dodge, p. 74). Indeed, there were a wave of discharges and investigations for alleged lesbian activities in the 1980s.

In the early 1990s, navy and air force women witnessed the expansion of available positions. Women's participation in the Gulf War and the increasing acceptance of women in nontraditional occupations inspired Congress to repeal the statute that excluded women from combat aviation. The navy and air force soon repealed their own aviation exclusion policies (Benecke and Dodge, p. 74).

We should not be surprised, however, with how women are singled out in the military. As Benecke and Dodge point out:

> The outcome of the debate over gays in the military and the continued practice of singling out women for investigation should not be surprising given this environment, especially in combination with career insecurities felt by many servicemen because of the drawdown. In this climate, the antigay policy provides a means to circumvent official policies and regulations opening jobs to women and forbidding harassment. Quite simply, it creates a situation where women may be routed out of the services by a mere accusation of lesbianism, regardless of their service record and despite policies and regulatory safeguards intended to encourage fair treatment of women and gays (Benecke and Dodge, p. 75).

The reality is that women are investigated and discharged at far higher rates than their male counterparts. One possible explanation for this disparity is that men are more likely to be investigated on a case-by-case basis in an attempt to force servicemen out of the military as quickly as possible. Women, on the other hand, are much more likely to "be targeted and discharged as the result of mass investigations, aptly referred to as 'witch-hunts'" (Benecke and Dodge, p. 75). Figure 1 provides empirical evidence to support this claim. There is little evidence that this situation will be addressed in a meaningful way by people in positions of power in the foreseeable future.

LEGAL ISSUES

With the codification into law of the "Don't Ask, Don't Tell" compromise, lesbian and gay groups and their supporters have turned to the courts. Their legal challenge will likely rest on one or more of several principles. The first is the right to privacy, where an individual has a right to engage in any private consensual sexual conduct, as articulated in the Supreme Court's earlier decisions allowing contraception, miscegenation, and abortion. A second approach emphasizes the notion that the military's policies against lesbians and gays violates the Fourteenth Amendment's equal protection clause. Finally, the charge is made that even if the federal government could establish homosexual conduct, it would then have to prove why such conduct made an officer unsuitable for the armed forces (Rimmerman, p. 122).

What gay and lesbian advocacy groups found in the short term is that the courts have been somewhat supportive of lesbian and gay efforts despite the Clinton administration's attempts to pursue a more regressive policy. Interestingly, the Clinton administration defended the military's old lesbian and gay policy in court in an effort to establish precedents that would make challenges to the new policy more difficult. On 1 June 1994, a Seattle federal judge ordered the military to reinstate Colonel Margarethe Cammermeyer, who was forced out of the Washington State National Guard after admitting her lesbianism. Judge Thomas Zilly of Federal District Court "ordered Cammermeyer back to the job she held in 1992, ruling that the military's policy on homosexuals at that time was based solely on prejudice and was a clear violation of the Constitution's equal-protection clause." The judge ruled that "there is no rational basis for the Government's underlying contention that homosexual orientation equals 'desire or propensity to engage' in homosexual conduct" (Schmitt, p. A1).

The Clinton and congressional compromise has also been successfully challenged in the courts. On 30 March 1995, Judge Eugene Nickerson of Federal District Court in Brooklyn ruled in *Able v. the United States* that the "Don't Ask, Don't Tell, Don't Pursue" compromise violated the First and Fifth amendments and also catered to the prejudices and fears of heterosexual troops. The case has been before Nickerson three times in the past three years. To Nickerson, the fact that the new policy attempts to distinguish between sexual orientation and the possibility of acting on such an orientation is "nothing less than Orwellian." Nickerson ruled, as well, that the new policy denies lesbians and gays the protection of the Fifth Amendment by unfairly discriminating against them. His most recent decision in the *Able* case, on 2 July 1997, offered his strongest denunciation of the "Don't Ask, Don't Tell" policy. Nickerson wrote, in part:

A court should ask itself what it might be like to be a homosexual. For the United States government to require those self-identifying as homosexuals to hide their orientation and to pretend to be heterosexuals is to ask them to accept a judgment that their orientation is in itself disgraceful and they are unfit to serve. To impose such a degrading and deplorable condition for remaining in the Armed Services cannot in fairness be justified on the ground that the truth might arouse the prejudice of some of their fellow members (Keen, p. 1).

Both the Zilly and Nickerson decisions are encouraging to lesbians and gays who embrace the legal approach in the presence of a President and Congress who are unwilling to rescind the ban.

One of the most important issues to emerge from the recent cases is the contentious "distinction between homosexual status (sexual orientation alone) and homosexual conduct (engaging in homosexual acts)" (Jacobson, p. 53). Except for the *Able* decision, the recent cases considering the military's policy on lesbians and gays have made clear that the military can justify banning homosexual conduct. As scholar Peter Jacobson points out, "the issue, therefore, is whether the military is justified in assuming that homosexual orientation is tantamount to homosexual behavior (that is, being a homosexual predisposes the person toward homosexual conduct)" (Jacobson, p. 54). This important issue will continue to be addressed by the courts.

If the President and Congress have been unreceptive to extending basic civil rights to lesbians and gays in the military and in the

Margarethe Cammermeyer

larger society, perhaps the movement should turn to the judicial system. But scholars have identified several pitfalls faced by activist organizations who rely on the courts to affect political and social change. One important limitation is the inability of the judicial system to construct coherent public policy. In addition, victories in the courts often energize opponents, who then work to block those gains through other venues. We may well see this latter development as the lower courts rule favorably on plaintiffs in individual cases where the military ban has been challenged. Scholar Richard Pacelle recognizes, however, that "the courts can be useful as a triggering mechanism to provide momentum for a nascent social movement or to remove lingering obstacles" (Pacelle, p. 196). This was certainly the case for the National Association for the Advancement of Colored Persons (NAACP) in the *Brown v. Board of Education* decision (1954) and for women's rights groups in *Roe v. Wade* (1973). Indeed, activists for lesbian and gay rights groups have followed similar litigation strategies, but they have been much less successful than the Legal Defense Fund and women's rights groups.

THE MILITARY BAN

The Case for ...

For those who wished to overturn the military ban, they quickly learned during the first several months of the Clinton administration that the opposition to overturning the ban was rooted in a number of deep-seated concerns, concerns that reflect the longstanding hostility towards lesbians and gays in the larger society. Bruce Bawer points out that an individual might be threatened by homosexuality due to several factors. First is utter incomprehension: he/she cannot understand how other human beings could have such feelings and could experience sexual attraction to a member of the same sex. The idea is so foreign as to be threatening, frightening, and repulsive. A second explanation is the issue of identification. The individual has experienced homosexual attraction him/herself, and fears that he/she may be gay. It is this possibility that is frightening, threatening, and repulsive. Male sexual insecurity also helps to explain some men's hostility toward extending gay rights: those who harbor these concerns fear being the object of desire. Men are used to being in control in their relationships with women and are not used to being the "object of affection" of other men. This fear is reflected in a Michigan airman's fear of what would happen if the ban on lesbians and gays in the military was lifted: "I couldn't sleep at night. I'd be worried that some homosexual is going to sneak over and make a pass at me" (Bawer, p. 117).

These concerns underlie some of the more specific arguments offered by those opposed to overturning the ban. It is interesting to note that some of these same arguments were posited by those opposed to Harry Truman's decision to integrate the military racially by executive order in 1948. As scholar David Ari Bianco's extensive analysis of the comparisons of the debates over race and sexuality in the armed forces points out, those in favor of the ban resisted any meaningful comparisons between race and sexual orientation, despite the fact that there were some clear parallels. For example, Colin Powell, then Chairman of the Joint Chiefs of Staff, wrote the following in a letter to Congresswoman Patricia Schroeder:

> I can assure you I need no reminders concerning the history of African Americans in the defense of their Nation and the tribulations they faced. I am a part of that history. Skin color is a benign, nonbehavioral characteristic. Sexual orientation is perhaps the most profound of human behavioral characteristics. Comparison of the two is a convenient but invalid argument (Bianco, p. 47).

Powell's open opposition to rescinding the military ban had tremendous consequences for the ultimate outcome of the debate. Others certainly shared Powell's views. A non-African American scholar wrote that "to lump blacks with homosexuals is an affront to most African Americans" (Bianco, p. 48). As Bianco suggests, however, few participants in the debate based their conclusions on thoughtful comparisons between the integration of African Americans in the late 1940s and the contemporary debate over lesbians and gays. He concludes that "the arguments used to keep African Americans segregated are so similar to those that barred lesbians and gays in the early 1990s that a gay newspaper, the *Washington Blade,* argued that the history of the military's exclusion of African Americans 'seems to be serving as a blueprint for the military on how to dissuade the government from allowing gays to serve openly in the ranks'" (Bianco, p. 49).

Just what are some of the arguments articulated by proponents of the military ban on lesbians and gays that were also used in the debate to prevent racial integration in the late 1940s? Several of the arguments against lesbians and gays in uniform are informed by the notion that lesbians and gays are inferior to heterosexuals, and as a result, would make poor soldiers. One such argument is

the belief that gay men have such relentless sexual appetites that they simply cannot be controlled in a military setting. As Bianco points out, "the defenders of the military's ban on lesbians and gays frequently raised the specter of homosexual rapists and pedophiles endangering young soldiers and sailors." Southern conservatives made a similar argument during the racial integration debate of 1948, when they claimed that the higher rate of rape and other crimes attributed to African Americans would endanger the daily functions of the military (Bianco, p. 50).

Another line of argument used to defend the military ban on lesbians and gays was to highlight the higher prevalence of sexually transmitted diseases, specifically AIDS, associated with gay men. The Family Research Council, a conservative organization, made this argument in one of its publications:

> The AIDS risk is very real, since two-thirds of all current AIDS cases involved transmission through homosexual activity, according to the Centers for Disease Control. Homosexuals also account for a disproportionate number of cases of sexually transmitted diseases, such as syphilis, gonorrhea, genital warts, hepatitis A, hepatitis B and also diseases associated with anal intercourse, such as the parasites collectively referred to as 'gay bowel syndrome.' According to the American Medical Association, homosexual youths are 23 times more likely to contract a sexually-transmitted disease than are heterosexuals (Bianco, p. 51).

A similar argument was offered by Kevin Tebedo, a cofounder of the conservative group Colorado for Family Values: "There is no question that the homosexual community, particularly males, are (sic) very diseased" (Bianco, p. 51). During hearings on the military ban, one colonel testified: "At the very least homosexuals would have to be specially identified to ensure their blood not be used as a protection to other soldiers." Similar arguments were once again raised in the racial integration debate of the late 1940s. As Bianco notes, "during World War II the Red Cross—with no scientific justification—maintained racially segregated blood banks at the demand of the armed forces." And former Senator Richard Russell highlighted disease rates among African Americans in his quest to keep the military segregated (Bianco, p. 51).

In addition, those opposed to Clinton's campaign promise contended that the presence of lesbians and gays in the armed forces would undermine the "good order, discipline, and morale of the fighting forces" (Shilts, p. 17). Norman Schwarzkopf reinforced this point of view in a 1982 sworn deposition where he "characterized homosexuality as being 'incompatible with military service' because it impaired good order, discipline, and morale." The general said that his twenty-six-year military career led him to conclude that "homosexuals are unsuited for military service" (Shilts, p. 426). The conservative legal scholar Bruce Fein echoed Schwarzkopf's argument and raised the important connection between masculinity and the criteria for being a good soldier as a justification for opposing attempts to integrate lesbians and gays:

> The lifeblood of a soldier is masculinity, bravery, and gallantry. The battlefield soldier is inspired to risk all by fighting with comrades whose attributes conform to his view of manhood.... And it is inarguable that the majority of a fighting force would be psychologically and emotionally deflated by the close presence of homosexuals

who evoke effeminate or repugnant but not manly visions (Rimmerman, p. 114).

Like Schwarzkopf and Fein, decorated Vietnam veteran David H. Hackworth worried that openly lesbian and gay soldiers would undermine the military's illusion of masculine invincibility:

To survive in a killing field, a warrior has to believe he's invincible, that he's wearing golden armor; that he can buck 1,000-to-1 odds and live. To think that way, he has to be macho. Fairly or unfairly, gays threaten that macho. When it goes, the warrior starts thinking, 'Maybe I won't make it.' And from that moment, the unit goes to hell (Bianco, p. 53).

The perceived danger of lesbians and gays in the military is so threatening that Hackworth warned: "I cannot think of a better way to destroy fighting spirit and gut U.S. combat effectiveness." Schwarzkopf's, Hackworth's, and Fein's analyses are important ones because they underscore the importance of how manly visions of masculinity underlie the debate over lesbians and gays in the military. Similar arguments were made during the racial integration debate. Writing in 1948, the *New York Times* military editor, Hanson W. Baldwin, wrote that "one of the surest ways to break down the morale of the army and to destroy its efficiency" is to support racial integration of the military (Bianco, p. 53).

Supporters of the military ban on lesbians and gays argued, too, that if lesbians and gays were admitted, they would undermine the ability of the military "to recruit and retain members of the armed forces." Ban supporters worried that the United States would face "the specter of a depleted military force and weakened recruitment efforts if those who join or remain were forced to associate with people known to be lesbian or gay." Schwarzkopf said:

The impact on the army's public image would also endanger recruitment and retention, by causing potential servicemembers to hesitate to enlist, making parents of potential servicemembers reluctant to recommend or approve the enlistment of their sons and daughters in an organization in which they would be forced to live and work with known homosexuals, and causing members of the army to hesitate to reenlist (Bianco, p. 55).

Schwarzkopf's views were supported by others in the military hierarchy. A four-star general reported to the *Washington Times* that "It would be a wrenching change.... We're not ready for it. Good people will leave the military in droves over this." Similarly, the threat of white desertion was invoked during the debate over racial integration in the late 1940s (Bianco, p. 55).

The navy defined a rationale for its gay policies by making several arguments. An individual's daily performance of military duties could be hindered by emotional or sexual relationships with other individuals and would interfere with proper hierarchical and command relationships that characterize the military. There was also the concern that homosexual individuals might force their sexual desires on others, resulting in sexual assaults. In the early 1980s, the Pentagon argued that lesbians and gays must be banned in order to "facilitate assignment and worldwide deployment of servicemembers who frequently must live and work under close conditions affording minimal privacy" (Mohr). Furthermore, an

internal navy memorandum revealed that "an officer or senior enlisted person who exhibits homosexual tendencies will be unable to maintain the necessary respect and trust from the great majority of naval personnel who detest/abhor homosexuality. This lack of respect and trust would most certainly degrade the officer's ability to successfully perform his duties of supervision and command" (Shilts, p. 281).

All of the above arguments rely on bigoted and negative stereotypes of lesbians and gays. As Richard Mohr points out, "none of them is based on the ability of gay soldiers to fulfill the duties of their stations" (Mohr, p. 93). But it is these arguments that served to define the broader context of the debate, arguments that both Clinton and proponents of overturning the ban had difficulty engaging in ways that would shift the grounds of the discussion (Rimmerman, p. 114).

The Case Against ...

Those in favor of lifting the military ban have offered several arguments. Many suggested that the ban itself is rooted in discrimination and prejudice against lesbians and gays, and we should not countenance any discrimination against individuals or groups in our society. In addition, gays, lesbians, and bisexuals have already fought and died on behalf of this country in an array of wars over the years. As a result, they should be afforded the kind of respect and support that their outstanding service to their country has earned. In practice, this means that they should be treated with decency and dignity in their daily lives. By its very nature, the ban is rooted in the most ugly assumptions about the connections between sexuality and military performance—assumptions that are not confirmed by any evidence. Indeed, one study provides evidence for overturning the ban. In spring 1992, the Penta-

Costs of Training Replacements for Servicemembers Discharged Under Gay Policy

Year	# Discharged	Cost
1980-1990	16,919	$498,555,244
1991	949	$27,964,355
1992	708	$20,862,764
1993	682	$20,096,617
1994	597	$17,591,907
1995	722	$21,275,305
1996	850	$25,047,104
Total	20,577	$606,346,192

Sources: General Accounting Office, Department of Defense

Figure 4

267

State Military Personnel Policies on Sexual Orientation

Exclusion	Inclusion	No Policy
Brazil	Australia	Japan
Chile	Belgium	Poland
Colombia	Canada	South Africa
Greece	France	
Hungary	Germany (conscript)	
Italy	Israel	
Peru	Netherlands	
Romania	Portugal	
Turkey	ROKorea	
United Kingdom	Spain	
Venezuela	Sweden	

Source: Adapted from United States General Accounting Office, *Homosexuals in the Military: Policies and Practices of Foreign Countries* (Washington, D.C.: GAO, GAO/NSIAD-93-215, June 1993), Table 1:5.

Figure 5

gon commissioned a RAND Corporation study of the military ban. The RAND study concluded that "the ban could be dropped without damaging the 'order, discipline, and individual behavior necessary to maintain cohesion, and performance.'" The report also stated that "many of the problems that opponents of lifting the ban anticipate are exaggerated through education and discipline" (Gallagher, p. 28). Unfortunately, the Clinton administration chose to delay the timing of the release of the report in a way that diminished its potential impact. News reports circulated that the report was ready for release long before August 1993, when it was finally shared with the public. Indeed, it was released to the press and public at a down time in Washington, when everyone was on vacation (including the President), so that little attention would be focused on it. The release was inspired by a joint congressional letter signed by those in the House and Senate who were committed to overturning the ban, urging the Clinton administration to make the report's findings public (Rimmerman, p. 115).

For opponents of the ban, the financial costs of enforcement are exorbitant. Ultimately, these unnecessary costs are paid by taxpayers. Writing in 1993, Randy Shilts concluded that "the cost of investigations and the dollars spent replacing gay and lesbian personnel easily amount to hundreds of millions of dollars" (Shilts, p. 4). A June 1992 congressional study revealed that "the ban on homosexuals in the armed forces costs the Pentagon at least $27 million a year" (Bawer, p. 58). Figure 4 provides the most recent and comprehensive numbers regarding the costs associated with military discharges.

Opponents of the ban also point out that many democracies allow lesbians and gays to serve with dignity in their militaries. As Figure 5 suggests, all NATO counties except Britain allow lesbians and gays to serve openly in their militaries. Canada's 1992 decision to revoke its military ban caused little or no controversy, and their experience could have been an excellent lesson for the United States. Unfortunately, we appear to have learned little from Canada's successful experience in eliminating the military ban.

Finally, and perhaps most disturbingly, the ban reinforces the horrors of the closet for lesbians and gays in the military. The closet is then sanctioned by the institutional forces of the United States government in ways that prevent human beings from living open and fully developed lives. The philosopher Richard Mohr offers an analysis of the horrors of the closet:

The chief problem of the social institution of the closet is not that it promotes hypocrisy, requires lies, sets snares, blames the victim when snared, and causes unhappiness—though it does have all these results. No, the chief problem with the closet is that it treats gays as less than human, less than animal, less even than vegetable—it treats gays as reeking scum, the breath of death (Mohr, p. 114).

The incalculable human costs of the military ban have taken a number of forms, as lives have been ruined and careers destroyed. Despairing women and men occasionally commit suicide in the face of the pressure associated with a purge, and the accompanying rumors that often precede one. This is certainly not surprising, given that military policies have created an atmosphere where discrimination, harassment, and violence against lesbians and gays is tolerated and often encouraged. Shilts's analysis of the consequences of the ban provides particularly chilling accounts of how lesbians face significant discrimination and harassment in their daily lives. For this and other reasons, opponents of the military ban argue that it must be overturned.

PROMINENT PEOPLE

Miriam Ben-Shalom

A former staff sergeant in the army reserves, Miriam-Ben Shalom was discharged for being lesbian in 1976. In June 1980, the U.S. District Court in Chicago ordered that the army reinstate Sergeant Miriam Ben-Shalom after her dismissal. The army later appealed and won. In February 1987, she won a ten-year battle with the military when she became the first openly gay person to win reinstatement. Ben-Shalom currently works with at-risk youth in Milwaukee public schools and teaches at Milwaukee Area Technical College.

Margarethe Cammermeyer (1943-)

In 1989, Margarethe (Grethe) Cammermeyer, a colonel in the army national guard, acknowledged her sexual orientation as a part of a security clearance interview for the position of chief nurse for the guard. Cammermeyer was discharged in 1992, despite a brilliant military career in which she was awarded a Bronze Star for her service during the Vietnam War, and was selected from a pool of 34,000 to be the army's Nurse of the Year in 1985. Cammermeyer was the subject of a military investigation, and when the investigation was completed in 1991, she was offered two options: she could request a hearing or resign from the military. She chose the hearing, but despite the support of prominent attorneys in the fields of military law and civil rights, her appeal was unsuccessful. She was reinstated by a federal judge in 1992, but the ruling is being appealed by the military. Cammermeyer's book, *Serving in Silence*, details her experiences in the military and served as the basis for an acclaimed television film produced by Barbra Streisand and starring Glenn Close.

Leonard Matlovich (1943-1988)

As an air force sergeant in 1975, Leonard Matlovich identified himself publicly as a gay man, which ultimately led to his dismissal. Matlovich's coming out letter to his air force superior signaled the beginning of the contemporary battle to overturn the U.S. military's policy barring lesbians and gays. He appeared on the cover of *Time* magazine with the caption "I am a homosexual" in September 1975, six months after his dismissal. After a lengthy court battle, he accepted a $160,000 settlement in 1980 and became a gay rights activist. Matlovich died of AIDS at age 44 in 1988. His headstone says: "When I was in the military they gave me a medal for killing two men and a discharge for loving one."

Keith Meinhold

A petty officer first class in the navy, Meinhold came out on ABC's "World News Tonight" in May 1992 and was discharged in August of that year. He filed suit in federal court, won his case when San Francisco Federal District Court Judge Terry Hatter ordered the navy to reinstate him, and was returned to active duty in November 1992. Meinhold served as an openly gay man for almost four years and retired voluntarily in March 1996.

Mary "Dusty" Pruitt

As a major on inactive duty with the army reserves, the Rev. Dusty Pruitt received an honorable discharge in 1986. Her discharge came on the heels of a three-year investigation that was inspired by a *Los Angeles Times* profile of Pruitt's role as a pastor for the predominantly gay Metropolitan Community Church. With the support of the American Civil Liberties Union, Pruitt won reinstatement and full army reserve retirement benefits. She fought many legal battles in an effort to lift the military ban on lesbians and gays. In 1997, Pruitt helped to start a new Metropolitan Community Church congregation in Long Beach, California.

Allen Schindler (d. 1992)

A 22 year-old gay radioman in the navy, Allen Schindler's brutal murder by a shipmate in late October 1992 became a cause celebre and a symbol of hostility to gays and lesbians in the mili-

Keith Meinhold

tary. The navy reported that the murder occurred in the rest room of a public park in Sasebo, Japan, and said that it was the result of a "difference of opinion." Soon thereafter, however, a pair of gay American entertainers who were working in that seaside town wrote a letter to a navy newspaper charging that the navy was covering up the deadly gay-bashing of Schindler. During the first six months of 1993, there was an investigation of the incident followed by a trial. The trial revealed that Apprentice Terry M. Helvey had conspired with at least one other sailor, Airman Apprentice Charles E. Vins, to brutally beat Schindler to death. Ultimately, Helvey was sentenced to life in prison.

Joe Steffan (1965-)

In 1987, then U.S. Naval Academy midshipman Joseph Steffan was at the top of his class and decorated with honors. Despite his many accomplishments, he was discharged six weeks before graduation after being questioned by military officials about his homosexuality. He was not able to graduate and was denied his diploma. At the beginning of 1989, Steffan, with the help of the Lambda Legal Defense and Education Fund, sued the government in response to his discharge. The suit lost, was won on appeal, and then the decision was overturned in 1991. Washington, D.C., District Court Judge Oliver Gasch refused to disqualify himself from Steffan's case, despite the fact that he used the epithet "homo" three times during a hearing. Gasch ultimately ruled against Steffan.

Joe Steffan

Tracy Thorne

A navy fighter pilot, Thorne outed himself on *ABC News Nightline* in 1992, thus challenging the Department of Defense policy. He was discharged, subsequently sued the navy and was returned to active duty, but finally discharged with the implementation of "Don't Ask, Don't Tell" in 1994. Thorne sued once again, but this time the district court upheld the decision. He is currently a third year law student at the University of Richmond, and he is representing himself as he appeals this most recent ruling to the Fourth Circuit Appeals Court.

Perry Watkins (1948-1996)

A sergeant in the army, Perry Watkins was stripped of his army clearance and was discharged for his homosexuality in 1984. He won a lengthy Supreme Court battle in 1990, as the Court pointed out that the army, realizing he was gay, reenlisted him three times. With the Court's decision, Watkins became the only openly gay man in history who has been permitted to serve in the military by the Supreme Court. Watkins declined to reenlist; instead, he took $135,000 in back pay, full retirement benefits, and an honorable discharge. A gay rights activist, Watkins died in 1996.

Joe Zuniga

An army Solider of the Year in 1992, Zuniga served as a medic and journalist in Operation Desert Storm. He came out during the 1993 March on Washington and was discharged one month later. Zuniga decided not to appeal his case; instead he wrote a book, *Soldier of the Year: The Story of a Gay American Patriot.* He has served as a spokesman for the AIDS Action Council in Washington, D.C., and is now the Deputy Director of the International Association of AIDS Care, based in Chicago.

REFERENCES:

Books

Bawer, Bruce. *A Place at the Table: The Individual in American Society.* New York: Poseidon Press, 1993.

Berube, Allan. *Coming Out Under Fire: The History of Gay Men and Women in World War II.* New York: Free Press, 1990.

Boykin, Keith. *One More River to Cross: Black and Gay in America.* New York: Anchor Books, 1996.

Bull, Chris, and John Gallagher. *Perfect Enemies: The Religious Right, The Gay Movement, and the Politics of the 1990s.* New York: Crown, 1996.

Cammermeyer, Margarethe, with Chris Fisher. *Serving in Silence.* New York: Viking, 1994.

Deitcher, David, ed. *The Question of Equality: Lesbian and Gay Politics in America since Stonewall.* New York: Scribner, 1995.

Dyer, Kate, ed. *Gays in Uniform: The Pentagon's Secret Reports.* Boston: Alyson, 1990.

Herek, Gregory M., Jared B. Jobe, and Ralph M. Carney, eds., *Out in Force: Sexual Orientation and the Military.* Chicago: University of Chicago Press, 1996.

Holm, Jeanne. *Women in the Military: An Unfinished Revolution.* 2nd ed. Novato, California: Presidio, 1993.

Holobaugh, Jim, with Keith Hale. *Torn Allegiances: The Story of a Gay Cadet.* Boston: Alyson, 1993.

Perry Watkins

Humphrey, Mary Ann. *My Country, My Right to Serve: Experiences of Gay Men and Women in the Military, World War II to the Present*. New York: HarperCollins, 1990.

Jackson, Donna. *Honorable Discharge—Memoirs of an Army Dyke: The Donna Jackson Story*. N.p.: Christie and Steffin, 1994.

Miller, Neil. *Out of the Past: Gay and Lesbian History from 1869 to the Present*. New York: Vintage Books, 1995.

Mohr, Richard. *A More Perfect Union: Why Straight America Must Stand Up for Gay Rights*. Boston: Beacon Press, 1993.

Rimmerman, Craig A., ed. *Gay Rights, Military Wrongs: Political Perspectives on Lesbians and Gays in the Military*. New York: Garland, 1996.

RAND. *Sexual Orientation and U.S. Military Personnel Policy: Options and Assessment*. Santa Monica, California: RAND/National Defense Research Institute, MR-323-OSD, 1993.

Rubenstein, William B. *Lesbians, Gay Men, and the Law*. New York: New Press/W.W. Norton, 1993.

Scott, Wilbur J., and Sandra Carson Stanley, eds. *Gays and Lesbians in the Military: Issues, Concerns, and Contrasts*. New York: Aldine de Gruyter, 1994.

Shilts, Randy. *Conduct Unbecoming: Gays and Lesbians in the U.S. Military*. New York: St. Martin's Press, 1993.

Steffan, Joseph. *Honor Bound: A Gay American Fights for the Right to Serve His Country*. New York: Villard Books, 1992.

Stiehm, Judith Hicks. *Arms and the Enlisted Woman*. Philadelphia: Temple University Press, 1989.

Thompson, Mark, ed. *Long Road to Freedom: The Advocate History of the Gay and Lesbian Movement*. New York: St. Martin's Press, 1994.

Vaid, Urvashi. *Virtual Equality: The Mainstreaming of Gay and Lesbian Liberation*. New York: Anchor Books, 1995.

Williams, Colin J. and Martin S. Weinberg. *Homosexuals and the Military: A Study of Less Than Honorable Discharge*. New York: Harper and Row, 1971.

Wolinsky, Marc and Kenneth Sherrill, eds. *Gays and the Military: Joseph Steffan versus the United States*. Princeton: Princeton University Press, 1993.

Zeeland, Steven. *Barracks Buddies and Soldier Lovers: Dialogues with Gay Men in the U.S. Military (Army)*. New York: Harrington Park/Haworth, 1993.

———. *Sailors and Sexual Identity: Crossing the Line Between 'Straight' and 'Gay' in the U.S. Navy*. New York: Haworth, 1995.

Zuniga, Jose. *Soldier of the Year*. New York: Pocket, 1994.

Chapters in Books

Benecke, Michelle M., and Kirstin S. Dodge. "Military Women: Casualties of the Armed Forces' War on Lesbians and Gay Men," in *Gay Rights, Military Wrongs: Political Perspectives on Lesbians and Gays in the Military*, edited by Craig A. Rimmerman. New York: Garland Publishing, Inc., 1996.

Bianco, David Ari. "Echoes of Prejudice: The Debates Over Race and Sexuality in the Armed Forces," in *Gay Rights, Military Wrongs: Political Perspectives on Lesbians and Gays in the Military*, edited by Craig A. Rimmerman. New York: Garland, 1996.

D'Amico, Francine. "Race-ing and Gendering the Military Closet," in *Gay Rights, Military Wrongs: Political Perspectives on Lesbians and Gays in the Military*, edited by Craig A. Rimmerman. New York: Garland, 1996.

Herek, Gregory M. "Social Science, Sexual Orientation, and Military Personnel Policy," in *Out in Force: Sexual Orientation and the Military*, edited by Gregory M. Herek, Jared B. Jobe, and Ralph M. Carney. Chicago: The University of Chicago Press, 1996.

Jacobson, Peter D. "Sexual Orientation and the Military: Some Legal Considerations," in *Out in Force: Sexual Orientation and the Military*, edited by Gregory M. Herek, Jared B. Jobe, and Ralph M. Carney. Chicago: The University of Chicago Press, 1996.

Osburn, C. Dixon and Michelle M. Benecke. "Conduct Unbecoming Continues: The First Year Under 'Don't Ask, Don't Tell, Don't Pursue,'" in *Gay Rights, Military Wrongs: Political Perspectives on Lesbians and Gays in the Military*, edited by Craig A. Rimmerman. New York: Garland, 1996.

Pacelle, Richard. "Seeking Another Forum: The Courts and Lesbian and Gay Rights," in *Gay Rights, Military Wrongs: Political Perspectives on Lesbians and Gays in the Military*, edited by Craig A. Rimmerman. New York: Garland, 1996.

Rimmerman, Craig A. "Introduction," in *Gay Rights, Military Wrongs: Political Perspectives on Lesbians and Gays in the Military*, edited by Craig A. Rimmerman. New York: Garland, 1996.

———. "Promise Unfulfilled: Clinton's Failure to Overturn the Military Ban on Lesbians and Gays," in *Gay Rights, Military Wrongs: Political Perspectives on Lesbians and Gays in the Military*, edited by Craig A. Rimmerman. New York: Garland, 1996.

Mel White protesting the ban on gays in the military.

Stiehm, Judith Hicks. "The Military Ban on Homosexuals and the Cyclops Effect," in *Gays and Lesbians in the Military:* *Issues, Concerns and Contrasts*, edited by Wilbur J. Scott and Sandra Carson Stanley. New York: Aldine de Gruyter, 1994.

Periodicals

Bull, Chris. "Broken Promise," in *Advocate*, 27 August 1993: 24.
———. "No Frankness," in *Advocate*, 29 June 1993): 24.
"Could It Be a Witch-Hunt?," in *Advocate Report,* 1 April 1997: 15.
Gallagher, John. "Terrible Timing," in *Advocate*, 5 October 1993: 28.
Keen, Lisa. "Court Calls Military Policy 'Degrading and Deplorable,'" in *Washington Blade*, 4 July 1997: 1, 23.
"The Legislative Word on Gays," *Congressional Quarterly Weekly Report*, 31 July 1993: 2076.
Moss, J. Jennings. "Losing the War," in *Advocate*, 15 April 1997: 22.
Osborne, Duncan. "Military," in *Advocate*, 25 January 1994: 53.
Osburn, C. Dixon and Michelle M. Benecke. "Conduct Unbecoming: Second Annual Report on 'Don't Ask, Don't Tell, Don't Pursue,'" Servicemembers Legal Defense Network, 1996.
Osburn, C. Dixon, Michelle M. Benecke, and Kirk Childress. "Conduct Unbecoming: The Third Annual Report on 'Don't Ask, Don't Tell, Don't Pursue,'" Servicemembers Legal Defense Network, 1997.
Schmalz, Jeffrey. "Gay Politics Goes Mainstream," in the *New York Times Magazine*, 11 October 1992: 18.
Schmitt, Eric. "Gay Troops Say the Revised Policy is Often Misused," in the *New York Times*, 9 May 1994: A1.
———. "Judge Overturns Pentagon Policy on Homosexuals," in the *New York Times*, 31 March 1995: A1.
———. "Pentagon Must Reinstate Nurse Who Declared She is a Lesbian," in the *New York Times*, 2 June 1994: A1.
Wieseltier, Leon. "Covenant and Burling," in *New Republic*, 1 February 1993: 77.

—Craig A. Rimmerman

11

Politics

Gay and lesbian politics is unique in two distinct ways: first, unlike any other political minority, a community of gay and lesbian people that would be affected through political involvement literally had to be created; second, once that gay and lesbian community was constructed, at least for purposes of politics, gays and lesbians and their supporters integrated themselves into the mainstream of American politics in a very rapid way. That experience, explored chronologically and focusing on the major issues that construction and rapid integration of a gay and lesbian political presence elicited, follows.

CREATING A GAY AND LESBIAN IDENTITY

The first 200 years of gay and lesbian political involvement in the United States is easy to describe: it did not exist. Before a gay and lesbian political experience could be developed and described, an identity known as gay or lesbian had to be created, a construction that did not even begin until the late nineteenth and early twentieth centuries. That is not to say that same-sex practices have not existed as long as humans have been in North America, including Native American berdaches, Spanish settlers in Florida, and settlers around Plymouth Rock, but it was not until the embrace of psychiatry at the beginning of the twentieth century that a typology of personality around a sex practice was even theorized, let alone relied upon. The progression toward a

gay and lesbian community that would insist, through politics, first that it be left alone by its government and later that it be treated equally, required a cultural transformation, led by modern psychiatry, from viewing sodomy as an unpardonable sin or pathology to recasting homosexuality itself as a behavioral characteristic that marked a central personality trait of a particular person.

EARLY REGULATION OF SEX

From the early days of the colonies, Native American territories, or foreign-controlled areas that now make up the United States, there is simply no indication of any gay and lesbian identity as we know it today. There are fragments of evidence of the regulation of same-sex activity, but even those scraps must be seen in the context of a much broader, religiously inspired regime of regulation of most aspects of human behavior, not simply sex. That is, the majority of regulation that would affect gays and lesbians as we know them currently were not directed at "gays and lesbians" per se; rather, the laws in place were directed at certain types of social behavior, and punishment could be meted out severely regardless of the gender of the participants. The driving religious impulse was the sustenance of marriage. Sex or social activity outside of that institution was the offense, not necessarily the gender of the participants. For example, some of the colonies even regulated against cohabitation of unmarried persons, regardless of gender. The regulation was not intended to be anti-gay, although it of course had that effect.

This is not to say that same-sex practices went unnoticed. Nor unpunished. The earliest recorded political act—in the sense of a government regulation—against what we might now consider a gay man occurred 30 November 1624, in Virginia, when that colony executed Captain Richard Cornish upon testimony from a 29-year-old boatswain that Cornish turned him "upon his belly, and so did put [him] to pain in the fundament, and did wet him." In the second recorded political act in what later became the United States, Virginia ordered one Edward Nevell to stand on the pillory and there lose both his ears, to serve the colony for a year, and to forever be incapable of becoming a free man. His offense, apart from the bad luck of preceding the First Amendment: saying that Captain Cornish "was hanged for a rascally boy wrongfully." No gay political movement arose protesting Cornish and Nevell's punishment.

Similarly, the New Netherland Colony (now New York) records in its court proceedings for 25 June 1646, that Jan Creoli, a Negro, shall for the second offense of same-sex sodomy be choked to death and then burnt to ashes, finding that "this crime being condemned of God as an abomination" (citing the verse from Leviticus for the punishment's justification).

The first recorded act of what would now be described as "gay or lesbian" political progress occurred when the Quaker laws of the Commonwealth of Pennsylvania were changed in 1700 and revised in 1706 to eliminate the death penalty for sodomy, if the defendants were white. The death penalty remained for Negroes for "buggery," which encompassed both sodomy and bestiality. Seventy years later, in 1776, Thomas Jefferson unsuccessfully proposed that punishment for violating Virginia's sodomy law be changed for men from death to castration, and for women from death to "cutting thro' the cartilage of her nose a hole of one half inch diameter at the least." There is no record of any gay or lesbian persons, or even people professing to engage in sodomy or buggery, seeking these legislative changes, or commenting on them in any way.

The record is more or less the same until well after the First World War. That is, piecemeal. There was no serious regulation, by government at least, of a defined gay or lesbian person, in part because that personality label had not yet been constructed. There was ample and repressive regulation of same-sex activity, which was viewed culturally as a demonic and sordid practice, but its egregiousness was essentially that it, like adultery, masturbation, voluntary singlehood, and other such choices, subverted the forced norm of married heterosexuality.

FROM SEXUAL ACT TO PERSONALITY TRAIT

The end of the nineteenth century and beginning of the twentieth century mark the first evidence of cells of people who organized around their homosexual desires or activities. A common explanation for such development is the rise of industrialization and urbanization, which brought more division of labor and larger concentrations of people able to live independently and pursue leisure activity. There exists evidence of organized networks of what we would now call gays and lesbians, all secretive and underground, largely social in nature, consisting of clubs, baths, restaurants, bars, and music halls, especially in Boston, San Francisco, Chicago, New York, the District of Columbia, and St. Louis. In the sense that politics is not simply the governance of a people, but also refers to the often-internally conflicting interrelationships among people in a society, the very existence of persons willing to acknowledge their desire for homosexual activity in an overwhelmingly repressive culture, however secretive, is a political act. In an era of hegemonic heterosexual (married) coercion, to even appear in a cafe frequented by others who desired same-sex activity was to risk incarceration and the security provided in otherwise acceptable society. Such risk-taking, personally if not organizationally political, was to be the fact of life for the overwhelming majority of gay and lesbian people well into the twentieth century.

Primary evidence of these early congregations is scarce, but exists. For example, an 1899 New York State special legislative body took testimony from numerous New York City police that includes the following: "Q: Now, this Artistic Club, 56 West Thirtieth St., kept by Samuel H. Bickard, did you close that up? A: Yes ... Q: Did you get any convictions? A: Yes. Q: Who did you convict? A: All the nancies and fairies that were there.... Degenerates." Seventeen years later, a survey of "Sexology" by Dr. James G. Kiernan notes incidents of "negro perverts who solicit men in certain ... cafes.... Chicago has not developed a euphemism yet for these

male perverts. In New York they are known as 'fairies' and wear a red necktie (inverts are generally said to prefer green). In Philadelphia they are known as 'brownies.'"

The first recorded national political event that involved homosexual activity was a scandal that erupted in the summer of 1921 over an investigation into perversion at the Naval Training Station in Rhode Island. It was leaked to the press that during the probe investigators may have been permitted to engage in sodomy to entrap the suspected "perverts," and, in a Republican attempt to embarrass Franklin Delano Roosevelt, who before leaving to run for vice president in 1920 was the assistant secretary of the Navy in charge of the affair, hearings were held to probe the matter. Although Roosevelt had stopped the methods when he learned of them, Republican senators wrote that Roosevelt "allowed enlisted men to be placed in a position where such acts ever liable [sic] to occur is ... a most deplorable, disgraceful and unnatural proceeding."

Although there was academic, political, and social activity in Germany in the late nineteenth century organized around the changing attitudes toward the regulation of same-sex relations, the United States was largely free of such academic and political organizing. For example, well into the twentieth century there remained only one piece of evidence of scholarly work published in the United States in defense of homosexuality, carried in *The Modern Thinker* in 1932, and the first recorded affirmative state involvement was not until 1924, when Illinois issued a charter to the nonprofit group Society for Human Rights, organized "to promote and to protect the interests of people who by reasons of mental and physical abnormalities are abused and hindered in the legal pursuit of happiness which is guaranteed them by the Declaration of Independence." Nowhere was homosexuality mentioned, but the founders were influenced by the earlier German emancipation movement and that country's liberalization of its sex laws. The elliptical nature of the organization's articles of incorporation did not prevent the founders from being arrested for depravity, losing their jobs, and causing the organization to disband.

The only other recorded, pre-World War II political event directly related to homosexuality was another scandal, this one in 1942, during which Democratic Senator David Walsh of Massachusetts was linked in the *New York Post* to an all-male brothel near the Brooklyn Navy Yard. His colleagues rushed to his defense on the floor of the Senate, claiming that it was a smear campaign against those senators who had opposed entry into World War II. Senator Walsh lost his re-election bid in 1946.

FROM IDENTITY TO ORGANIZING: CREATING A "HOMOPHILE MOVEMENT"

The enormous social and demographic changes brought on by World War II are credited with both boosting the number of people who began to identify themselves with a personality of gay or lesbian, and the creation of what later became known as the "homophile movement" in the United States. Great numbers of adults were placed in same-sex environments—barracks and work sites—for extended periods of times, and significant numbers of adults were moved from their hometowns to bases or urban areas, many in port areas, with significant transience and anonymity. These demographic shifts are credited with an explosion of bars and social clubs, however secretive, in many urban areas. The surge in recognizable homosexual activity ironically but predictably led to the first serious, pervasive investment of energy by municipalities in regulating and repressing these activities. In turn, anger at what became persistent and hostile crackdowns on organized social same-sex activity led to the creation of groups, albeit small, to fight the growing repression. This cycle—increased social visibility leading to more repressive government treatment that then inspired more political participation from gays and lesbians—would continue for decades, and prove to be a critical component of gay and lesbian political organizing.

Within five years of the end of World War II, a tiny, courageous group of homosexuals, almost all of whom were individually involved in radical, left-wing (frequently Communist) politics, formed organizations centered on resisting the oppression of homosexuals. These living room activists, and not the later riots at the Stonewall Inn in New York City often credited with creating it, are the progenitors of the modern gay rights movement. Most visible among these early activists was Harry Hay of Los Angeles, California. In November 1950, Hay and four other men gathered in a living room in that city to form what they later dubbed the Mattachine Society, a name taken from a traditional French folk dance performed during the Renaissance by fraternities of clerics whose public performances, always wearing masks, satirized the rich, powerful, high, and holy. Hay had wanted to form a "homophile organization" for some time, and his prospectus for Mattachine, entitled "International Bachelors Fraternal Orders for Peace and Social Dignity sometimes referred to as Bachelors Anonymous," was itself a permutation of an earlier wished-for-but-never-created organization, from 1948, which he playfully called "Bachelors for Wallace," referring to Progressive Party candidate Henry Wallace's bid for president that year.

Hay's prospectus stated that "[w]e, the androgynes of the world, have formed this responsible corporate body to demonstrate by our efforts that our physiological and psychological handicaps need be no deterrent in integrating 10% of the world's population towards the constructive social progress of mankind ... with the heroic objective of liberating one of our largest minorities from ... social persecution." The very formation of the group was heroic, politically and otherwise. Given the hostility of the day, simply congregating as a homosexual group was still an enormous social risk. The regulation of same-sex activity, or those who identified themselves as homosexual, could be severe: few in America would employ a known homosexual, electric shock was the dominant treatment for the disease of homosexuality, beatings and blackmail were common, sodomy was routinely prosecuted as a crime, references to homosexuals in movies was barred, gay bars were routinely raided—even same-sex dancing was illegal.

A focus on the political and social climate at the time is crucial to comprehending how courageous any organized political homophile activity was. The invasiveness of regulation could be profoundly intimate, including a New Jersey Court decision upholding denial of a liquor license for a bar because of its gay clientele—police "knew" the clientele was gay because of the way patrons distended their fingers when holding a drink. And, thirty years later, Michael Hardwick, the named plaintiff in the Supreme Court case that permitted the states to continue to criminalize homosexual sex, *Bowers v. Hardwick,* was arrested by a policeman who stood in the doorway of his bedroom, watching Hardwick have oral sex.

Or, regulation could be pervasively national. In February 1950, Republicans began to make national security the centerpiece of their strategy to discredit the administration of President Harry Truman. After State Department Undersecretary John Peurifoy

testified to the Senate Appropriations Committee that most of the 91 employees dismissed for moral turpitude that year were homosexuals, a barrage of anti-homosexual activity ensued. The Republican Party Chairman, Guy Gabrielson, sent out 7,000 letters to Republican party workers alerting them to the new "homosexual angle" in Washington, that "sexual perverts ... have infiltrated our government in recent years" and they were "perhaps as dangerous as the actual Communists." That summer the Senate authorized a full investigation into alleged employment of homosexuals and other moral perverts in government, and Senator Kenneth Wherry (R-NE) argued that homosexuals and Communists were the same threat when he told the *New York Post:* "You can't hardly separate homosexuals from subversives.... I don't say every homosexual is a subversive, and I don't say every subversive is a homosexual. But a man of low morality is a menace in the government, whatever he is, and they are all tied up together."

The completed Senate report, issued in December 1950, put the government's imprimatur on driving homosexuals from federal employment: "In the opinion of this subcommittee homosexuals and other sex perverts are not proper persons to be employed in Government for two reasons: first they are generally unsuitable, and second, they constitute security risks ... perverts lack the emotional stability of normal persons ... the presence of a sex pervert in a government agency tends to have a corrosive influence upon his fellow employees ... one homosexual can pollute a government office ... it should be borne in mind that the public interest cannot be adequately protected unless responsible officials adopt and maintain a realistic and vigilant attitude toward the problem of sex perverts in the government. To pussyfoot or to take half measures will allow some known perverts to remain in Government."

It is against this backdrop that the meeting of five adult men in a living room to plan an organization to fight for prejudice reduction, removal of sodomy and sex offender laws, and an end to random police harassment and violence, is seen as the revolutionary act that it was. It was not the only daring act, political or otherwise, of its time. Three years earlier a secretary at a movie studio, using the pun-intended pseudonym Lisa Ben, ran off 10 carbon copies of "Vice Versa—America's Gayest Magazine," with book and movie reviews and poetry, meant to be passed to other "gay gals" in Los Angeles. Ms. Ben published nine issues before taking a more-demanding job and losing the free time to do her typing. But, living room discussion groups, which the early Mattachine meetings were, mark the beginning of an uninterrupted chain of gay political organizations that exist to this day.

Apart from the act of simply forming, the Mattachines and similar organizations that followed had a novel principle as well: that homosexuals were a persecuted minority. This view required two premises: the existence of a people or community known as homosexuals, and a collective sense that mistreatment of this group because of their homosexuality was wrong. The inventiveness of this approach can only be fully understood against a backdrop of centuries of opprobrium in which same-sex activity was uniformly viewed as deviant behavior, rather than one of a series of traits that form a complete personality type, healthy or not. Harry Hay and his fledgling group proselytized that, as a political if not merely a social fact, people who practice homosexual acts are members of a community whose membership in that community is insufficient grounds for discrimination.

They had their work cut out for them. What came to be labeled McCarthyism—a spewing of Communist and deviate baiting that started in Congress and spread to America's cultural world—was running on all pistons. In 1951, a widely published columnist, Lee Mortimer, wrote in his syndicated column that "10,000 faggots" had escaped detection by the FBI, and the government remained "honeycombed in high places with people you wouldn't let in your garbage-wagons." At least 1,700 job seekers were denied employment because of homosexuality from 1947 to 1950, and by May 1950, discharges of suspected or actual homosexuals from federal employment averaged 60 per month.

In October 1952, ONE, Inc. was founded by Dorr Legg in California. It was formed as a complement to the relatively militant spirit of Mattachine, but also to publish a homophile-positive magazine. Copies of the magazine were seized by federal officials, in part because of an intimation (true) in one issue that J. Edgar Hoover, then director of the FBI, was sleeping with his confidante Clyde Tolson. The Ninth Circuit Court of Appeals declared the magazine obscene, and in a well-publicized decision, the Supreme Court reversed the decision, which opened the gates for more homosexual-oriented publications. Years later, notes of J. Edgar Hoover confirmed *ONE*'s allegations.

Publicity from the Supreme Court case, and another involving the trial of a Mattachine founder for sex solicitation, drove up membership sharply. Ironically, the new members had a markedly different view of how this nascent political and social movement should comport itself. The Communist ties of the original founders were a growing liability, especially after the *Los Angeles Times* ran a story linking the organizations. Some militant members successfully demanded a change in leadership, and at its Los Angeles convention in April 1953, in front of 500 attendees, Harry Hay announced on the second day that the original board was dissolved because of the Communist baiting, but the convention could keep the name of the organization.

By May 1953 Mattachine had 2,000 members, with more than 100 active discussion groups. A typical topic, from one 1952 Los Angeles meeting, was "what do we do with these effeminate queens and these stalking butches who are giving us a bad name?" This theme was destined to recur in gay politics for some time. Hal Call, the new and—compared to Hay—less radical leader, took a more passive approach to mainstreaming, organizing blood drives, clothes collections, and collecting books and magazines for hospitals. Mattachine and the Daughters of Bilitis, a lesbian organization formed in 1955 in San Francisco by Del Martin and Phyllis Lyon, almost immediately wrestled with a central identity question that would challenge gay political organizations since: are homosexuals a discrete minority group comprised of people with sufficient differences from the majority that the differences should be underscored, celebrated and liberated, or are homosexuals "just like everyone else" such that differences, and ideally the discrimination that flows from those differences, are to be minimized?

After the radical founders of Mattachine lost a power struggle, the organization veered toward the latter view. Gay writer and historian John D'Emilio notes: "[t]hey assiduously cultivated an image of middle class respectability and denied that they were organizations of homosexuals, instead claiming that they were concerned with the problem of the 'variant.' They expected social change to come through the good offices of professionals. They saw their task primarily as one of educating professionals who influenced public opinion and only secondarily as one of organizing lesbian and gay men. Moreover, in defining prejudice and misinformation as the problem, both Daughters of Bilitis and Mattachine often found themselves blaming the victim."

A 1953 report of Mattachine, published in *ONE* magazine, underscores this view, "it must be recorded that the [Mattachine] Foundation never conceived of its contribution as more than that of ... modest inspiration and encouragement, and perhaps that of a mirror to reflect the strength and weaknesses of the community social conscience." The New York chapter of Daughters of Bilitis, founded in 1958 by Barbara Gittings, included in its mission statement: "Education of the variant ... to enable her to understand herself and make adjustment to society.... Education of the public ... leading to an eventual breakdown of erroneous taboos and prejudices. Participation on research projects by duly authorized and responsible psychologists, sociologists, and other such experts directed towards further knowledge of the homosexual. Investigation of the penal code as it pertains to the homosexual, proposal of changes ... and promotion of these changes through the due process of law in the state legislatures."

Still, the public existence of homosexuality today should not obscure the revolutionary act it was in 1953 to identify as homosexual or even express support for the homophile movement. In that year the *San Francisco Examiner* still had a policy of printing in bold type on the front page the names of every gay person arrested for various offenses, including as trivial as being present in a place frequented by homosexuals, as well as his or her age, address, marital and employment status. A speech from Senator Everett Dirksen, who later became the Republican Minority Leader of the Senate, to a Republican gathering in Hollywood, California on 22 September 1954, included the call that homosexuals were "destroyers and traitors in government." In the District of Columbia alone, more than 1,000 people each year were arrested for gay or lesbian activity, not necessarily sexual activity but often presence at what was perceived to be gay or lesbian space, cross dressing, same-sex dancing, and so on, all of which were crimes in many parts of the nation. A *Miami Daily News* headline from 1954 read, "How L.A. Handles Its 150,000 Perverts." Such was the climate in the early 1950s.

By 1958, Mattachine's membership had dwindled to only 117 members, in part because its decreasingly aggressive goals proved less compelling to people, given the enormous social risk that public membership in the organization drew. But, an important aspect of that membership number in 1958 was that it was announced on a radio program in Berkeley, California, on which a Mattachine member was a guest, discussing homosexuality, the public nature of which was a decidedly rare event. Similarly, in 1962, the president of the District of Columbia's Mattachine Society, Dr. Franklin Kameny, appeared on local television for 90 seconds to talk about his organization. Such appearance was so rare and daring that the interview was preceded by a five-minute apology from the announcer for having as a guest a confirmed homosexual. While people were treated to that kind of hostility as a matter of course, other, closeted gays and lesbians in the metropolitan Washington, D.C. area were probably seeing for the first time in their lives a publicly open homosexual, and receiving information about how to contact other gays and lesbians.

That incident underscores the role Mattachine and the Daughters of Bilitis played in the gay political movement: neither organization could in the 1950s point to any serious concrete political advancement—no law changed, no officer was elected, no candidate courted their vote. Rather, their achievement, politically and socially, was to bring homosexuals out of living rooms and bars with code words and secret societies into the public consciousness in a serious way for the first time. Through the two decades of work of homophile organizers, criticized by some for their white-glove approach and narrow goals, a generation of thousands of isolated gay men and lesbians throughout America no longer grew up thinking they were the only gay or lesbian person on the planet. As hostile as the press and political environment were to the nascent homophile activists, the publicity about them forged in the consciousness of thousands of people that there were other gays and lesbians out there. By trying to create a politic based on sexual orientation, these small groups helped draw together a community that would grow to become a liberation movement. As Urvashi Vaid, former director of the National Gay and Lesbian Task Force, wrote, the early groups' decision to define gays and lesbians as a sexual minority, similar to ethnic and cultural minorities, "moved homosexuality from the domain of illness and sociopathic deviance and into the public domain of civil rights."

The irony of the benefit that increasingly public attacks on homosexuals had for the nascent gay political movement would continue for decades. For a group of people that, unlike any other numerical minority in this country, could not publicly identify themselves *even to each other* without enormous social and economic risk, the act of being identified by the majority was a significant political aid. Unlike racial, ethnic, cultural, or religious minorities, gay and lesbian individuals frequently, if not almost uniformly, do not know that others like them exist for a significant portion of their formative years, and in the 1950s and 1960s they may not have met well into adulthood. The mere existence of the Mattachines, Daughters of Bilitis, and later the Council on Religion and the Homosexual in San Francisco, the Los Angeles Homosexual Information Center, and New York's Council on Equality for the Homosexual and Homosexual League, provoked for the first time mainstream press coverage, however ignorant or mean-spirited, about homosexuals that was the necessary ingredient for an explosion of gay activity that would occur in the late 1960s.

A case in point, *Time* magazine editorialized on 21 January 1966, that "[homosexuality] is a pathetic little second rate substitute for reality, a pitiable flight from life. As such it deserves fairness, compassion, understanding, and when possible, treatment. But it deserves no encouragement, no glamorization, no rationalization, no fake status as minority martyrdom, no sophistry about simple differences in taste—and above all no pretense that it is anything but a pernicious sickness." Similarly, *Life* magazine worked with Mattachine/San Francisco to print a photo spread on homosexuality in bars in that city. The layout was filled with ominous and brooding negative images, swathed in darkness (by agreement with members of Mattachine). *Life* magazine at the time had a circulation of more than 7,000,000, and it's unlikely that any of that readership had ever seen a group of gay men conducting themselves in any fashion.

POLITICAL ORGANIZING, DIRECT ACTION AND PROTEST TAKE ROOT

The early 1960s witnessed a series of important political firsts for the homophile movement and for gay and lesbian individuals. The first recorded run for political office in this nation occurred in 1961, when Jose Sarria, a famous (at least in the bar culture) drag queen, ran for San Francisco city supervisor. Sarria had developed a reputation as a talented and politically aware performer whose shows, which included a trademark rendition of "God Save Us Nelly Queens," were very popular. He ran, he says, to "prove to my gay audience that I had the right, being as notorious and

gay as I was, to run for public office, because people in those days didn't believe you had rights." He got 6,000 votes. In addition to taking the honor of being the first openly gay person to run for office in the United States, Sarria's candidacy points out another important struggle for gay and lesbian politics: the role of the transgendered, and even more broadly, the role within the community of those who would not conform to a starched version of middle-class America. The role of that group, whether transsexuals, transvestites, drag queens, leather fetishists, sado-masochistic practitioners, or even those who advocate sex with people below the legal age, has always and will continue to torment gay political organizations.

To the extent that people and organizations within the movement adhere to the assimilationist "we are just like you" model, the role of the nonconformists, gender or otherwise, is minimal. To the extent that people and organizations within the movement adhere to the political model that sees gays and lesbians as a distinct cultural minority with a set of shared values different enough from heterosexuals such that those differences should be delineated, promoted, and celebrated, the gender and other nonconformists play a more active role. And, of course, those two models of a gay and lesbian political agenda are not so neatly divided in real life. Shifting forward for a moment, currently the National Gay and Lesbian Task Force advocates very strongly for the rights of transgendered people (and for that matter bisexuals) but has thus far resisted efforts to change its name to the National Gay and Lesbian and Bisexual and Transgendered Task Force, a decision that has more to do with public perception than room on the letterhead of the organization. Another example of the conflict between competing models for gay and lesbian civil rights was brought to light during the nationally televised March on Washington in 1993. With the twin goals of celebrating a growing culture of pride in gayness and furthering a set of political goals, including urging Congress to lift the ban on gays in the military, should there have been, as occurred, a lesbian comedienne serving as emcee who included in her performance a riff on her desire to have sex with the newly installed First Lady, Hillary Rodham Clinton? The mostly gay and lesbian crowd appeared delighted at the irreverence of the routine, but the same routine was guaranteed to alienate a swath of middle America (mostly uninformed about gay issues) crucial to any mainstream civil rights advancement. Such practical and real world conflicts have always tormented gay political leaders and organizations, and will continue to do so as long as the goal of cultural expression of homosexuality as an acceptable and in fact good personality trait is intertwined with a political goal of equal protection under the law.

However, Sarria was a drag queen, and a famous one at that. He campaigned in drag, and did not shy from that persona. But he was also gay, and ran as a gay candidate, and lost. There is no evidence that anybody else in America tried to run as a gay political candidate for another 13 years.

In December 1962, the Mattachine Society/District of Columbia scored a significant political victory, when its president, Dr. Kameny, persuaded the American Civil Liberties Union of the District of Columbia (on whose board Dr. Kameny sat) to write the United States Civil Service Commission to change its rules with respect to excluding gays and lesbians from employment. Two years later the D.C. chapter of the ACLU persuaded the National ACLU to change its policy, which had been that there was no constitutional right to practice homosexual acts, to a new policy that private, consensual sex between adults could not constitutionally be criminalized. In addition to the importance of such early support from a national organization, the event signals another important effort for gay politics that would become crucial later on: the decision to engage in coalition building to advance a particular political and legal agenda. This political choice, made from many options including the obvious one of separatism, would pay off in important political battles to come.

In May of 1963, Representative John Dowdy (D-TX) introduced a bill to revoke Mattachine's permit to raise funds. Subcommittee Number 4 of the Committee on the District of Columbia held hearings, at which Dr. Kameny testified. Dowdy railed against homosexuals as "revolting to normal society ... [and] banned under the laws of God." Members questioned Dr. Kameny about bestiality, incest, and homosexual orgies. In August 1964, a diluted version of Dowdy's legislation, one that no longer mentioned Mattachine by name—passed the House.

That same year saw the advent of a new public tactic for gays and lesbians, modeled on the growing black civil rights and anti-war movements: pro-homophile picket lines. The first recorded picket, organized by the Homophile League of New York and led by Randy Wicker, occurred at the Whitehall Induction Center, consisting of twelve demonstrators protesting violations of draft record confidentiality pertaining to homosexuals. Organizers of follow-up demonstrations in other cities called them "dignified demonstrations," for they, unlike their anti-war, student power, and black power protesters, but more like the middle-class black protests of the South, were not trying to resist mainstream society, but rather be accepted into it.

In the same assimilationist vein, on 4 July 1965, Mattachine and Daughters of Bilitis held the first of what would become four annual demonstrations at Independence Hall in Philadelphia. That same summer those groups held historic marches at the White House, the Pentagon, and the State Department in Washington, D.C. The 29 May 1965 demonstration at the White House included ten men and three women holding signs that included "Governor Wallace Met with Negroes, Our Government Won't Meet with Us." A follow-up demonstration in October grew to 36 protesters. Amid wide media coverage of the protests, Mattachine and Daughters of Bilitis endured significant infighting and criticism from local homosexuals: those closeted did not want to rock the boat of their relatively unknown subculture, notwithstanding the harassment and social insecurity with which they lived daily.

In keeping with Mattachine's desire for a "dignified demonstration," another aspect of the protests provoked great controversy: the dress code, which was strict—suits for men, and dresses for women. Kameny said, "If you want to be employed, look employable." What should arguably be a minor issue took on enormous significance for a relatively unknown, largely persecuted minority operating against hideous stereotypes. How the members presented themselves to the world was critical, and evoked the central dilemma—are we "just like you," or are we different? These protesters, risking their jobs, homes, families, and physical security, opted for "just like you," or at least a middle-class, starched version of "just like you," to avoid being marginalized further.

COALITION BUILDING AND FIGHTING AGAINST "SICKNESS"

Mattachine Society/District of Columbia took upon itself another campaign at that time: to eradicate the pervasive view that homosexuality was a sickness. A February 1965 statement read,

"the Mattachine takes the position that in the absence of valid evidence to the contrary, homosexuality is not a sickness, disturbance, or other pathology in any sense, but is merely a preference, orientation, or propensity, on par with, and not different in kind from, heterosexuality." With that, and continuing its drive for coalition-based politics, Mattachine embarked on what would be a ten-year, successful campaign to get the American Psychiatric Association to remove homosexuality from its list of pathologies/diseases in the all-important *Diagnostic and Statistical Manual.*

Coalition building, and the desire to move the view of homosexuality from pathology or sin to personality and community, and positive at that, saw a major success in November 1967, when, at Project H, a New York conference sponsored by the Episcopalian Diocese of New York, Connecticut, Long Island, and Newark, 90 priests agreed that the church should classify homosexual acts between consenting adults as "morally neutral."

By 1966, there were enough branches of Mattachine and similar organizations for the leadership of these groups to form the North American Conference of Homophile Organizations (NACHO), intended to be a loose federation of organizations bonded together to pursue common projects, as opposed to a centrally managed gay rights organization that itself could mobilize and control a grassroots movement. NACHO established a national legal fund to pursue litigation, including challenges to bar closings, exclusion of homosexuals from immigration, and rights of gay military personnel. It organized protest days—simultaneous demonstrations—against federal employment policies, including exclusion from the military, and it undertook research of homosexuals and the law for publication. There were a series of national meetings convened by NACHO, often with friction between East and West Coast groups, the former more interested in traditional political organizing, with protests, media, and lobbying, the latter still dominated by the more passive Mattachines/Los Angeles. The 1968 NACHO conference in Chicago adopted the then-radical slogan, "Gay is Good," and a bill of rights, which included the demands that private consensual acts between persons over the age of consent shall not be an offense; that solicitation for any sexual act shall not be an offense except upon the filing of a complaint by the aggrieved party, not a police officer or agent; and, that sexual orientation shall not be a factor in granting/receiving security clearances, visas, citizenship, service in the military, or eligibility for employment.

Of course, the unity of the gay federation itself, and the coalition politics some of the groups undertook, was imperfect. Dissension continually waxed and waned within the gay political community, and advanced dramatically in 1967, when an editorial of *The Ladder,* the Daughters of Bilitis publication, proclaimed that lesbians had more in common with heterosexual women than gay men, which sparked a series of letters and debates within the homophile and women's movements. It was representative of a rift between gay men and lesbians that would continue until the AIDS crisis of the early 1980s brought women and men back together, at least organizationally.

And, outside of the community, limited political success also bred significant defeat, sometimes brutal. On the side of progress, Mattachine/New York successfully lobbied Mayor John Lindsay in 1968 to issue an executive order forbidding city police from making arrests for "homosexual solicitation" without a signed citizen complaint, and in May 1969, New York City authorities confirmed that homosexuality would no longer bar placement in civil service jobs. However, on the opposite side, in California, then-

Governor Ronald Reagan in 1967 first issued a statement that included the declaration that homosexuality was a "tragic disease" and another in 1968 proclaiming that homosexuality should be illegal. And, in 1968, every state save Illinois still criminalized homosexual acts.

STONEWALL: THE "HAIRPIN HEARD 'ROUND THE WORLD"

The gay political movement was ignited in 1969. On 28 and 29 June of that year, riots occurring outside of a gay bar in New York City are credited with sparking enormous changes in how gay and lesbians communicated with the rest of society. So profound were the changes that there would be no turning back to the secretive, humble, but courageous small cells of protesters seeking little more than relief from sexual repression. At 53 Christopher Street, in Greenwich Village, New York City, stood the Stonewall Inn, the semi-lit, allegedly mob-controlled gay bar that catered to all types of homosexuals, but known especially for its drag queens. On the evening of

28 June, around 2:00 a.m., plainclothes policemen entered the bar and, with a warrant, proceeded to close the bar for the selling of illegal alcohol. Employees were arrested and customers told to leave. Without more—some say the heat, some say the funeral the day before of actress Judy Garland, a drag heroine—the raid would have been just an unexceptional example of police harassment. During this time in Los Angeles alone the police estimated 3,000 men and women were arrested per year for little more than presence at such establishments.

But this night was different. One witness noted that "[t]he police mistreated the customers, and from the crowd people began to throw pennies, then cans, rocks and then parking meters at the police, who retreated into the bar, which was then set afire by the crowd. A hose from the club was used to put out the fire, more cops were summoned, and soon more than a thousand people were brawling with several hundred cops."

The next day the bar was in disarray, and the owners noted that money from the bar was missing. The owners threw a party, giving out free liquor. The same witness described the scene in

March in New York City in 1994 commemorating the 25th anniversary of the Stonewall Riots.

more detail: "The crowd grew. Chants of 'Gay Power,' 'We Want Freedom Now,' and 'Equality for Homosexuals' were heard. A bus couldn't get through the growing crowd, which then lunged at the bus. The cops' presence grew, and apparently unprovoked, some of the cops grabbed a boy and began to beat him. Fifty or so 'nelly' men rushed the cops and took the boy back. They then formed a solid front and refused to let the cops through. The cops eventually did clear the crowd, by the use of flying wedges and other formations."

The riots drew ample publicity, and proved critical for gay and lesbian movement organizing. The second night of rioting turned the event from a brawl to one with political significance. Lillian Faderman, a lesbian writer, notes "the riots had perhaps an even greater significance for young gays and lesbians who had not been members of homophile organizations, who had no experience of the repressive fifties and the timidity and self doubt that era had created in older gays. Primed by a decade of militant movements, they brought an unprecedented vitality and conviction to the struggle for our rights. With Stonewall as a symbol, young gays and lesbians developed their own rhetoric of revolution and the tools with which to disseminate it."

Practically and organizationally, it signaled a new day in gay politics. Pre-Stonewall, no homophile demonstration attracted more than a few dozen people, as the Washington, D.C. and Philadelphia marches of 1965 demonstrated. Then, a march organized in New York in June 1970 to commemorate the one-year anniversary of the Stonewall Riots, which eventually turned into the Pride Parades and events now pervasive throughout the United States, attracted 5,000 people, a number that compared to the early years of the homophile movement was a tsunami.

In addition, Stonewall meant the organization of new, more direct action, political groups, most notably the Gay Liberation Front (GLF), which formed in New York City. Although that organization quickly developed fault lines after a vote in late 1969 to support the Black Panthers organization, the core relative radicalism of the group created quite a bit of publicity. At a mayoral candidate's forum in October 1969, sponsored at Temple Torah in Queens, New York, by the League of Women Voters, members of GLF heckled the candidates with questions about gay rights. Although the GLFers were escorted out, members of the congregation asked the candidates to answer the questions, and the incident was carried on local television and in the printed press. Again, the publicity itself, however sensationalized, became an organizing tool for the gay groups.

Another new organization, The Homophile Youth Movement, began distributing flyers after the Stonewall incident that called for gay businessmen to open gay bars that would operate legally, with competitive pricing, for a boycott of New York City bars and the Stonewall Inn itself, to get the criminal element out of running bars, and for gays and lesbians to write Mayor Lindsay to demand investigation of this problem. The new, more-radical political groups were still at the time mostly focused on anti-bar and sex harassment issues from local government, the larger goals of employment, housing, immigration, and military restrictions still too ominous to take on.

And some politicians began to respond. In October 1969, Dianne Feinstein, candidate for the San Francisco Board of Supervisors, who at the time was not a leader on gay civil rights issues, told a gay audience she supported getting police out of restrooms and onto the streets, a position that met with great approval from her audience. And, in the first recorded example of a candidate for federal office courting gay votes, Bella Abzug appeared at a Gay Activists Alliance (GAA) meeting in New York, a group formed as a less-radical alternative to the Gay Liberation Front but more progressive than the Mattachine. GAA's constitution read: "we as liberated homosexual activists demand ... right to our own feelings ... right to love ... to our own bodies ... right to be persons.... While the Mattachine works through the courts, the GAA is engaged in nonviolent activism which is meant to equalize the status of the homosexual." It was reported that Abzug, who went on to win her race and become an early leader for gay civil rights in Congress, was greeted with wildly enthusiastic ovations, in part because of her charisma, in part because she had funded the legal defense for two members of GAA who had been arrested earlier on trumped up charges, and in part because of the heartfelt appreciation of a congressional candidate treating gay and lesbian people seriously, and as political allies. (Actually, it was reported that wearing her trademark big hat she came and went with the drama of Dolly Levi at the Harmonium Gardens, to the swells of the appreciative gay male chorus.)

The relative militancy of younger gays began to clash with the assimilationist but experienced original organizers. While Kameny was scolding two lesbians at the fifth annual Independence Hall protest for holding hands during that march, members of GLF joined a war protest in the District of Columbia where they chanted "suck cock, beat the draft" and participated in a "nude-in" at the Lincoln Memorial reflecting pool. As writer and early activist Jim Kepner later wrote: "our polite earlier movement had sought straight authorities to represent us, to define us, defend us, and perhaps cure us. But suddenly, our movement was transformed—no longer cap in hand, no longer suit and tie. Where we had quietly discussed 'the problem' we began to confront the world. Where we'd begged for understanding, we demanded equality. Where we'd sought acceptance by the establishment, we told the establishment to bug off. Where we had dressed to 'look straight' we dressed for the fun of it, or 'to blow people's minds.' We traced persecution of gays to oppression of women, saying that neither could end without reconstituting society, banishing gender roles, capitalism, religion, and the military industrial complex. We hoped to remake the world ... in turn, some older leaders scorned the new militants." At the 1969 (and last) NACHO conference, the factions finally splintered into anarchy, disagreeing over essentially everything, from litigation strategy to whether to bar organizations that "damaged our image."

COALITION POLITICS

In November 1969, the Eastern Regional Conference of Homosexual Organizations was formed, superseding NACHO. Its stated goals—dominion over one's body, sexual freedom without regard to orientation, freedom to use birth control and abortion, and freedom to ingest the drugs of one's choice—reflect the broad protest and liberation movements of the day, from black rights to women's rights. The new organization decided to advance coalition politics, which includes embracing the goals of organizations and movements deemed important to your goals. But, deciding to form coalitions is only the first step; the second important decision is determining with whom you will coalesce. That decision is crucial in formulating a political message to mainstream America, if that is the intended audience. In September 1969, the American Sociological Association adopted a gay rights plank at its annual business meeting, reflecting a paradigmatic mainstream coalition building effort. Eleven months later, at its convention in Philadelphia, Black Panthers leader Huey Newton called on blacks to view the Gay Liberation Front and the Women's Liberation Front as "friends" and "potential allies" and said that gays "might be the most oppressed people in society." That expression of support, from a decidedly left wing and itself marginalized political group, was coalition building of a very different sort.

And, not all coalition-building efforts were successful. At the National Organization for Women's convention in 1969, a resolution supporting lesbian rights was withdrawn because the national committee judged it too controversial, one year after founder Betty Friedan called lesbians a threat to the women's movement, a comment for which she many years later apologized.

Black civil rights support for gay liberation, and vice versa, was conflicted. Bayard Rustin, a not so openly gay man, was one of the organizers of the historic march on Washington for black civil rights at which Dr. Martin Luther King, Jr., and others spoke. When Senator Strom Thurmond denounced Rustin on the floor of the Senate in 1963 in an attempt to discredit the March, calling Rustin a homosexual, draft dodger, and Communist, there was debate among civil rights leaders about whether Rustin should be allowed to continue his public work with the organizing committee. Dr. King and A. Phillip Randolph supported keeping Rustin on board, but the issue of Rustin's homosexuality was frequently used as a weapon against King by not only white opponents but by other black leaders, most notably among them Adam Clayton Powell of New York. Notwithstanding efforts by Senator Thurmond, Congressman Powell, and the closeted FBI director, J. Edgar Hoover, to exploit this inflammatory issue, it went largely unmentioned when the March was discussed in the black community. But it would be many years before any of the national civil rights organizations or recognized black leaders ever issued a statement of the magnitude of the Black Panther's Newton, although Dr. King's widow, Coretta Scott King, would echo her husband's principles to condemn *Bowers v. Hardwick* and the ban on gays in the military, and later to support the Employment Non-Discrimination Act, a measure to ban workplace discrimination based on sexual orientation.

The early 1970s proved an active time of growth and struggle for the developing second generation of gay political organizations. The basic tensions—mainstreaming and its attendant traditional political advocacy and grassroots, coalition building, and assimilationism, as opposed to minority status celebration and direct action—while not of course mutually exclusive, continued to play out in the organizations. Urvashi Vaid, onetime executive director of the National Gay and Lesbian Task Force, notes that the early 1970s marked a shift in gay politics from liberation and social change to what she calls "legitimation": "gay and lesbian legitimation seeks straight tolerance and acceptance for gay people; gay and lesbian liberation seeks nothing less than affirmation, represented in the acknowledgment that queer sexuality is morally equivalent to straight sexuality."

In 1970, in a completely middle-class triumph of assimilationism, the columnist Dear Abby in response to the question "in your opinion, is homosexuality a disease?" wrote "No! It is the inability to love at all which I consider an emotional illness." And, her twin Ann Landers wrote a column one year later advising a distraught gay teenager to seek therapy, not to convert to heterosexuality, but to find self-acceptance, although she later wrote that while she advocated for civil rights for homosexuals, she considered homosexuality unnatural.

Political and cultural mainstreaming coexisted with direct action, as it did in the black and feminist civil rights movements. In 1971, the Gay Liberation Front of D.C. distributed 10,000 flyers in that city identifying the giver of the flyer as a homosexual, and "tired of 2nd class treatment." In a good example of the blurring of direct action and coalition building, activists "zapped" the American Psychiatric Association's (APA) convention in the District of Columbia by seizing the microphone and screaming "you don't own us."

As external coalitions strengthened, some gay political organizations began to fall apart, sometimes over personalities, sometimes over policy disputes. In 1970, Del Martin, co-founder of the Daughters of Bilitis, wrote and published a dramatic farewell letter to the gay movement in the *Advocate* magazine, saying goodbye to concentrate on the women's movement. She castigated the gay male civil rights movement for its male only clubs and its defense of washroom sex, pornography, and white privilege. She was not alone. The Lesbian Liberation Committee of New York's Gay Activists Alliance broke off from the GAA in 1973 to form the Lesbian Feminist Liberation organization. At the same time lesbian separatism took root as a movement. The early 1970s saw the growth of the Michigan Womyn's Festival, a women-only event that featured music and concomitantly hosted many individual members of local gay organizations, and boasting 8,000 attendees. And in 1973, lesbians at the Gay Pride Rally in Washington Park interrupted the agenda by heckling and booing the drag queen performers. Jean O'Leary, who later went on to head the National Gay Task Force, stormed the stage and railed into the microphone that drag queens demean women. Bette Midler and Barry Manilow "saved" the day from chaos by taking the mike, singing "Friends," and trying to calm down the crowd.

The more and more public political and cultural expressions continued to breed limited success, but also set the stage for a wrenching political backlash that would hit after the middle of the decade. In 1971, 3,000 gays and lesbians marched on the New York State Capitol building in Albany to demand civil rights for homosexuals, and Franklin Kameny ran for delegate to Congress from the District of Columbia as an openly gay man, the first person in this nation to do so, a big step forward in terms of visibility and respectability in the public eye. Nevertheless, he got an underwhelming 1.6 percent of the vote.

In the world series of politics—the national conventions of the parties to nominate candidates for president and vice president—gays were noticed publicly for the first time in 1972, at the Democratic National Convention in Miami. There were openly gay delegates on the floor of the convention for the first time ever—five of them—and during the middle of the night of 12 July, Jim Foster, chairman of the political committee of the Society for Individual Rights of San Francisco, and Madeline Davis, of Buffalo's Mattachine Society of the Niagara Frontier, spoke to the delegates from the platform. CBS carried it live, and NBC interviewed Foster for two minutes at 6:00 p.m. Foster told the convention "we do not come to you pleading your understanding or begging your tolerance. We come to you affirming our pride in our lifestyle, affirming the validity to seek and maintain meaningful emotional relationships and affirming our right to participate in the life of this country on an equal basis with every citizen."

During the campaign later that year, Democrats disavowed gay friendly ads late in the campaign, but the then-popular Rep. Shirley Chisolm, a black Congresswoman from New York and onetime presidential candidate herself, spoke positively about gays, although she did end one of her talks with "every time you see one of these people, just say to yourself, 'There but for the grace of God go I.'"

The coalition building, direct action, and newly discovered ability to affect traditional electoral politics built momentum. In the summer of 1971 the National Student Congress endorsed the creation of a "gay desk" to help campus gay groups function effectively. The next year East Lansing, Michigan, became the first community in the nation to include, by a 3-2 vote of the City Council, anti-discrimination provisions based on sexual orientation as part of the city's personnel rules, with San Francisco following one month later. Candidate for Los Angeles District Attorney Vince Bugliosi visited 16 gay bars in one night the summer of 1972, and Jim Owles, former president of GAA, ran unsuccessfully for New York City's Council. That year San Francisco's GAA disbanded, reformed as the Gay Voters League, and promptly endorsed Richard Nixon's reelection.

In the summer of 1973, the American Bar Association adopted a resolution urging states to repeal their anti-gay sex laws, and Jo Daly of San Francisco became the first openly gay person appointed to a city position anywhere in the nation when she took a post on the Cablevision Task Force. Later that summer, Harvey Milk, an openly gay man, ran but was defeated for the Board of Supervisors of San Francisco, but the gay political steam was building.

At the end of 1973, the District of Columbia's mayor signed a human rights law banning discrimination against homosexuals in public accommodations, bank credit, and employment, and, in a concrete victory for Kameny's Mattachine/District of Columbia group, the United States Civil Service Commission proposed new regulations keyed to job performance, replacing the ban on hiring or retaining homosexuals in federal agencies. The American Psychiatric Association, prodded by its gay and lesbian caucus after activists disrupted its 1971 convention, removed homosexuality from its list of psychiatric disorders. The referendum, insisted upon by member Dr. Charles Socarides after trustees had voted to remove homosexuality, was by secret ballot: 4,854 to remove, 3,810 to keep. Ironically, the influential and powerfully anti-gay Dr. Socarides is the father of Richard Socarides, President Bill Clinton's first openly gay outreach coordinator to the gay and lesbian community.

In 1974, Kathy Kozachenko became the first openly gay person to be elected to public office in the United States, taking a seat on the Ann Arbor, Michigan, City Council. That same year, Pennsylvania Governor Milton Shapp issued the first state executive order banning employment discrimination on the basis of sexual preference (and the next year vetoed an antigay bill passed by unanimous vote of the state senate), Members of Congress Bella Abzug and Ed Koch of New York introduced the first federal civil rights bill for gays, AT&T announced a new policy of nondiscrimination against gays for its 1 million employees, lesbian Elaine Noble of Massachusetts became the first openly gay person to win a seat in a state legislature, and Minnesota State Senator Allen Spear came out as a homosexual in *The Minneapolis Star*. The growing achievements, political and otherwise, would precipitate a backlash very soon. In what would become a common and increasingly aggressive counter-offensive from anti-gay political groups, in 1974 voters in Boulder, Colorado, overturned a gay rights ordinance. Further, in a petty political move, supporters of New Hampshire Governor Meldrim Thomson paid $1,075 to prevent gay students from winning an auction bid for a pancake breakfast with the Republican Governor.

A BACKLASH RECASTS
GAY POLITICS NATIONALLY

Florida sent a hurricane into politics in 1977, when persistent but mostly local harassment and repression of gays and lesbians stormed into the nation's consciousness, brought on by an extraordinarily publicized battle over a gay rights ordinance in Dade County (Miami). Until the Florida election loss, the fight for gay political rights was clearly on the upside. California approved a bill in 1975 decriminalizing consensual sex, a gay civil rights measure was reintroduced in the House of Representatives, and the United States Civil Service Commission dropped its ban on hiring gays and lesbians for nonmilitary federal government jobs. Jimmy Carter, later elected president, announced in February 1976 his opposition to discrimination based on sexual orientation, and that position was included in the plank of the Democratic Convention until June of that year, when Carter withdrew his support of the plank, and the platform committee voted for its removal.

And, national gay rights organizations were growing in size and clout. In October 1973, Martin Duberman, Dr. Bruce Voeller, Ronald Gold, Franklin Kameny, and New York City Health Administrator Howard Brown formed the National Gay Task Force, "to bring gay liberation into the mainstream of American civil rights." That same year, the Lambda Legal Defense Fund was formed in New York to fight for gay civil rights through litigation. In May 1976, the Gay Rights National Lobby incorporated in Washington, D.C., and at its first meeting determined its priority would be seeking the enactment of federal legislation to eliminate employment discrimination.

But the Miami battle is the event that permanently nationalized the gay rights movement. The publicity that surrounded the local battle was unprecedented. After Dade County enacted an anti-discrimination ordinance in January 1977, a repeal effort was organized, led by the former beauty queen runner-up Anita Bryant, a successful singer and internationally known pitch-woman for Florida's huge citrus industry. The campaign for repeal was especially nasty, with television ads showing pictures (none of which were fabricated) from San Francisco's gay pride parades, and implying that these participants, semi-dressed, leather clad, or in drag, wanted to recruit children by teaching in the schools. The pro-gay organization, Dade County's Coalition for Human Rights, was out-funded and relatively inexperienced. The referendum to repeal the anti-discrimination ordinance was successful in June 1977, but not without enormous nationwide dialogue and publicity. Asserting that "homosexuals cannot reproduce so they must recruit," Bryant took her campaign nationwide. Where the Mattachine Society's courageous protests generated relatively little attention in the mass media, a pie thrown in the face of Bryant in Des Moines by a gay activist drew nationwide attention. Even if negative, the publicity around the ballot measure galvanized gays and lesbians and their critics. A writer for the *Advocate* magazine wrote:

> The legacy of Anita Bryant is complex: she helped millions of gay and lesbian Americans to recognize that the closet was a prison and that the fight for safe and free lives depended on the battle being waged as something other than a jailhouse riot. Thanks to Anita Bryant the gay movement finally said that as hard as it is to fight for civil rights in a still homophobic America, lesbians and gays are more likely to win their rights if they come out and

Harvey Milk in front of his camera store in 1976. One year later, Milk was elected to the San Francisco Board of Supervisors.

fight on their own side. Should gay people become more forthright and more successful, their opponents would be more hostile as well. Anita Bryant showed gay people what they had always feared: that to be open was to be vulnerable to hatred, abuse, violence and discrimination. What gay and lesbian people showed Anita Bryant, America, and themselves, however, was that they were no longer willing to keep silent and that the gay liberation movement was set in its course.

The nasty battle in Miami, like the later congressional battles over gays in the military and the right to marry, had the paradoxical effect of deeply wounding gays and lesbians personally and under the law. At the same time the fight galvanized many more gays and lesbians nationwide to commit to not only coming out culturally but also pursuing traditional electoral and organized politics to pursue their civil rights. Importantly, it also drove home the point that "coming out," expressing to either a family member or the entire world that one is gay or lesbian, is a political act. While millions of gays and lesbians had long known it from repression by families, in public accommodations, employment, etc., the campaign in Miami helped to show the nation that simply being gay or lesbian elicited disfavored treatment under the law,

and announcing one's status as such was to accept, but presumably fight against, political disenfranchisement.

While the success of anti-gay groups in Miami encouraged imitators—Eugene, Oregon; St. Paul, Minnesota; and Wichita, Kansas, all repealed their anti-discrimination ordinances—it also made gay politics national news, guaranteeing that gay-related events that previously may not have ranked as newsworthy, would almost always now be covered. For example, President Carter's new administration received national attention when his Presidential Liaison to Minority Communities, Midge Costanza, invited 14 gay activists to the White House.

In November 1977, Harvey Milk became the first openly gay man elected to the San Francisco Board of Supervisors. One year later, on the 27 November 1978, he and Mayor George Moscone were assassinated by co-supervisor Dan White, who was the lone dissenter on the gay rights bill passed earlier by the supervisors. The assassination and subsequent trial of the murderer galvanized the San Francisco gay community. White's sentence to seven years and eight months in prison for the murder of two popular pro-gay politicians, one of whom was the only openly gay elected official in California, sparked widespread unrest and rioting in San Francisco, including a protest march where over 5,000 demonstrators descended on City Hall. After the riot, police descended on the gay Castro area of the city and attacked bar patrons and blood-ied people on the street in a two-hour rampage of retaliation. The calamity in San Francisco was one of a burst of gay-related politi-cal events in California that year: the well-publicized Proposition 6, led by California State Senator John Briggs, which would have mandated the firing of teachers and other school employees in Cali-fornia who "advocate homosexuality as a viable lifestyle," was surprisingly defeated, 58 to 42 percent, with a coalition of teach-ers, unions, religious groups, and even soon-to-be President Ronald Reagan opposing it. And several months later Governor Jerry Brown signed an executive order banning anti-gay discrimination in California state hiring.

On the East Coast, the first openly gay elected statewide offi-cial, Representative Elaine Noble of Massachusetts, launched a bid for the Democratic nomination for the United States Senate, but lost to Paul Tsongas. After deciding not to run for re-election to the State House in 1978, speaking for many gay political lead-ers then and now, Noble told the *Advocate*:

> I think the level of self-hate right now among gay people
> is so damn high that if, when you start trying to work in
> the community in a sane manner, you ask, 'what are you
> doing constructively' it has a self-hate backlash. They can't
> hit the straight world, they can't swing at the straight
> world, so they swing at the person who's nearest to
> them.... [W]henever a minority group has taken or achieved
> access to a political process, they assume that the process
> will be used negatively against them whenever they come
> in contact with it. It is like children who've come out of a
> home where they were battered. Those children will
> probably batter their own children, and will probably go
> into relationships with their hands psychologically over
> their face because they expect to be battered, because their
> only experience with close love relationships has been
> damage. I think that if you've been damaged by the
> political process you're going to want to damage back,
> damage others who are involved in it.

Also on the East Coast that year, an experienced Minnesota activist, Steve Endean, was chosen as head of the Gay Rights Na-tional Lobby. Driving home his personal political philosophy of organizing gay rights around coalition politics, Endean announced that the major political goal of the GRNL was to have a gay rights plank inserted in the platforms of the Republican and Democratic Parties. Endean stated: "Possible benefits for the movement in general will be expanded support for gay interests from progres-sive elements within each of the mainstream political parties, dis-cussion of gay civil rights issues in a national forum, and the po-tential for creating new coalitions," including support from reli-gious groups, unions, and the Leadership Conference on Civil Rights, the nation's largest advocacy organization fighting for a broad range of civil and union rights.

The direct action/coalition-building tension persisted, and the national media covered gay related issues, however negatively, more and more frequently. As the New York City community disrupted the filming of the movie *Cruising,* because of its caricatured por-trayal of gay men as sex predators, President Carter was naming the first openly gay person appointed to a federal position—les-bian Jill Schropp of Seattle, Washington, to the National Advi-sory Council on Women. More importantly, the fall of 1979 wit-nessed the First National March on Washington for Lesbian and

Gay Rights, which according to organizers drew more than 125,000 people who, in marching by the White House, the Capitol, and Washington Monument, hoped to dramatize the need for legisla-tion guaranteeing the federal civil rights of gays and lesbians. The march's impetus began in St. Paul, where the repeal of that city's nondiscrimination ordinance the year before stimulated local ac-tivists to call for a demonstration in Washington, preceded by a gay leadership planning meeting held in Philadelphia in February 1979. The march, on the heels of a vote in the House of Repre-sentatives two months earlier putting Congress on record oppos-ing gay rights (the measure died in a Senate committee), was deemed "the birth of a national gay movement" by the National Gay Task Force.

As had happened with many localities, the more gays and les-bians expressed themselves culturally and politically, now on a national scale, the more aggressive became political opposition. In 1979, the Laxalt Family Protection Act was vigorously debated on Capitol Hill. It would have cut off government funds for "groups which present homosexuality as an acceptable alterna-tive lifestyle" and declared that job discrimination against gays could never be ruled to be an "unlawful employment practice." In response to the Laxalt Act, and a precursor to a similar tactic tried 17 years later when the anti-gay Defense of Marriage Act was voted on in the Senate, three Senators—Paul Tsongas of Massa-chusetts, Lowell Weicker of Connecticut, and Patrick Moynihan of New York—introduced the Senate's first gay civil rights bill. In 1980, two months after the House of Representatives voted over-whelmingly to deny federal funding to legal groups that work for equal rights for homosexuals, conservative Republican Robert Bauman of Maryland confessed to the afflictions of "alcoholism and homosexuality" after he was accused of soliciting a 16-year-old boy for sex. Bauman lost his reelection bid the next month.

Limited successes continued to breed harsh political responses, but the broader picture was that gay and lesbian issues were in-exorably becoming part of the national political dialogue. Presi-dential candidate Ronald Reagan said in the spring of 1980 that he would not condone homosexuality, adding that "in the eyes of the Lord, homosexuality is an abomination," and President Carter is-sued a formal statement dashing hopes that his administration would issue an executive order banning anti-gay discrimination in federal employment, or supporting a gay rights plank at the up-coming Democratic convention. But, he quietly had his director of the Office of Personnel Management issue a memorandum in-terpreting the general civil service law as including protections against discrimination based on sexual orientation in the federal workforce. That summer the Democratic Party acted anyway, prod-ded by Senator Edward Kennedy, and adopted a plank that pro-tected "all groups from discrimination," and opposing the ban on homosexual visitors and immigrants in federal law. There were 77 gay and lesbian delegates at the 1980 Democratic National Con-vention, including Melvin Boozer, a black delegate from the Dis-trict of Columbia, who addressed the convention with a paean to coalition building: "would you ask me how I dare to compare the civil rights struggle with the struggle for lesbian and gay rights? I know what it means to be called a nigger and I know what it means to be called a faggot, and I understand the difference, in the mar-row of my bones. And I can sum up that difference in one word: nothing. Bigotry is bigotry." Boozer, a one-time leader in the Gay Activists Alliance of D.C. and the National Gay and Lesbian Task Force, was the first openly gay person to be nominated as a can-didate for the office of vice president. His nomination was offered by New York activists Virginia Apuzzo and Peter Vogel; he received the necessary 334 delegate votes required for the nomination.

It would be more of the same, one step forward, one step back, for gay and lesbian politics, until a dreadful disease, AIDS, surfaced in the early 1980s, and radically transformed gay politics. As Republican Congressman John Hinson of Mississippi was arrested in a Capitol Hill bathroom and charged with "oral sodomy," receiving a 30-day suspended sentence, Senator Tsongas and five colleagues reintroduced the gay civil rights bill in the Senate. In February 1982, Wisconsin became the first state in the nation to pass a gay rights law. That same year the American Nazi Party held an anti-homosexual rally during Gay Pride Day in Chicago, drawing 2,000 people who participated in a salute to the effigy of Harvey Milk's assassin, Dan White.

AIDS RADICALLY TRANSFORMS GAY POLITICAL ORGANIZING

The early 1980s brought a horrific, but galvanizing, problem to the gay political movement: a disease that would eventually be called the Acquired Immune Deficiency Syndrome (AIDS). Originally reported as a "gay cancer," with the tracking of some 100 cases of Kaposi's sarcoma by September 1981, and 202 deaths reported by August 1982, the later-renamed Gay Related Immune Deficiency Syndrome (GRID) and then AIDS rapidly grew to an epidemic within the male homosexual population, first by ambience, and later in actual numbers of persons affected.

Within a few short years, serious panic beset gay men and the broader public, as it became increasingly apparent that a disease that seemed almost exclusively limited to sexually active gay men was, at least at the time, uniformly and rapidly fatal. Incremental political and cultural gains made by gay men in the preceding two decades were immediately threatened, as media, religious, and political figures in the straight world reacted to the growing medical problem. Particularly challenging politically was that the reaction to the disease was intensely focused on gay male sex, the very issue the repression of which led early activists to form the homophile movement. But the second generation of gay political organizations was trying to move away from this issue in order to focus on employment, housing, custody, and service in the military. The cultural and media treatment of AIDS bordered on panic, from the mild, with the Department of Health and Human Services announcing "prudent and temporary measures": recommending voluntary screening of sexually active gay and bisexual men from blood donation programs; to the egregious, with Evangelist Jerry Falwell, then head of the strong Moral Majority political movement, preaching that AIDS was the "judgment of God" and that the Metropolitan Community Church, the nation's largest coalition of gay and lesbian churches, was a "vile and Satanic system that will one day be annihilated ... [causing a] celebration in heaven."

Consistent with the well-established pattern that vociferous, anti-gay political attacks drew more and more supporters to the cause of gay rights, the response to AIDS, emotionally, organizationally, and individually, proved to be a critical boost to gay politics. Organizations, small and large, formed all over the United States to respond to the growing AIDS crisis. Largely without government support at first, these organizations—private medical research groups, food distribution centers, hospices, support groups, and so on—were staffed overwhelmingly by gay men, and

notably given the rift that had grown between them, lesbians. And, importantly, as more and more gay men were stricken with AIDS and had to rely on their families for support, often coming out as gay to their families in the process, straight family members were drawn into the AIDS organizations. The politicization of these organizations was inevitable, and provided the first serious grassroots structure for gay-related issues, after the spotty and episodically effective Mattachines and Daughters of Bilitis, and a competitive challenge to the new national gay organizations. Without the widespread negative publicity about AIDS and gay men, and formation of these grass-roots organizations, it would have been impossible to mobilize the 9,000 people in Manhattan and 10,000 in Los Angeles and similarly large numbers in San Francisco, Chicago, and Houston in May 1983 for marches demanding federal action on AIDS. And, it would have been impossible ten years later to draw up to 1,000,000 people to Washington, D.C., for the historic third March on Washington.

AIDS did not eclipse gay political organizing, but it certainly reshaped it. However, unrelated to AIDS but occurring at a time when AIDS dominated the reporting of gay issues, an important advance for coalition building occurred in 1982, when, after a five-year push, the Leadership Conference on Civil Rights—an umbrella political organization in Washington, D.C., made up of traditional civil rights organizations and labor unions—agreed to accept the membership applications of the Gay Rights National Lobby and the National Gay Task Force. Steve Endean, who fought hard for such coalition politics, noted that of particular import was the support for the applications from the AFL/CIO and the Catholic Conference. The acceptance by civil rights organizations of gay and lesbian political demands, represented by the GRNL and the NGTF, is another milestone in gay politics. It marks the most important statement on record that the early activists' decision to identify gays and lesbians as a cultural and hence political minority would bring success in the broader political environment. The NAACP, the AFL/CIO, women's organizations, and other important, traditional civil rights advocates, embraced gay and lesbian civil rights as a legitimate part of the movement for basic human rights, and gave an important shot in the arm to the structure and goal of the national gay organizations. The embrace would prove relatively symbolic for a number of years, but would grow to reflect substantive support over time.

But the progress did not stop with a symbolic vote of inclusion. After careful courting of civil rights groups by the national organizations, and after gays and lesbians staged a sit-in to protest the exclusion of black, lesbian poet Audre Lorde from the program celebrating the twentieth anniversary of the 1963 March on Washington, black leaders came out for non-discrimination legislation and equal rights for gays. Presidential candidate Jesse Jackson spoke at the New York dinner of the Human Rights Campaign Fund and invited gays and lesbians to engage in "meaningful dialogue" with the civil rights movement. Two years later, Coretta Scott King would publicly proclaim her "solidarity with the gay and lesbian community" and blast the Supreme Court's decision in *Bowers v. Hardwick,* which upheld the criminalization of gay sex.

In 1983, in the fifth such episode in as many years involving a member of Congress, Congressman Gerry Studds, Democrat of Massachusetts, was censured by the House of Representatives for his relationship with a male, 17-year-old page. What differed with Congressman Studds was that, rather than skulking from the fact of homosexuality, he was the first federal elected official to affirm positively his homosexuality, which he did in a dramatic statement on the floor of the House of Representatives. He was re-elected by his constituents for six consecutive terms following this episode, until he retired in 1996.

The 1984 presidential election was not a particularly bright spot for gays and lesbians, with the notable exception of Jesse Jackson's campaign, which courted gay support, including the co-incidental fact that his political organization was called the Rainbow Coalition, a symbol gays and lesbians had begun to adopt as representative of their community. Although the then-front-runner for the Democratic nomination, Gary Hart, met with gay fundraising groups in Los Angeles, Democratic candidate John Glenn questioned the fitness of gays to serve as schoolteachers and soldiers. The Republicans and leaders of the Christian Right sponsored a pro-family rally, entitled "The Threat of Homosexuality," prior to the Democratic Convention in San Francisco, but 100,000 gays and lesbians marched for gay rights in the streets outside of the convention, as well. The Republican Convention that year saw its first openly gay delegates.

AIDS and the politics surrounding it would dominate gay issues for much of the 1980s. Although California's legislature adopted an employment anti-discrimination act only to have it vetoed by Republican Governor George Deukmejian, the United States Conference of Mayors passed a resolution calling for an end to anti-gay bias. Additionally, rancorous debates about closing down gay bathhouses in New York and San Francisco motivated far more gay people, especially men, to consider action. A November 1985 meeting to discuss these closures organized by what would become the Gay and Lesbian Alliance against Defamation drew 700 people in San Francisco, an amount no other gay political issue could draw. And, when the New York City Board of Education announced for the 1985 school year that it would allow children with AIDS to attend school, nearly 10,000 parents in Queens kept their kids home in protest. Still, gays and lesbians were not formally participating in grass-roots or organized politics. By 1986, the major national gay organizations—HRCF, NGLTF, Lambda, and National Gay Rights Advocates—were estimated to have a combined total of only 40,000 members.

The fact that California voters defeated Proposition 64, a 1986 ballot measure to quarantine people with AIDS and bar from certain jobs those suspected of carrying HIV, the virus thought to cause AIDS (voters also rejected two similar propositions in 1988), did little to stem the persistent view that the government was not doing enough to fight the medical, if not cultural, crisis. That view was exacerbated when James Miller, President Reagan's budget director, told a Senate panel that year that care for AIDS patients should be a "state and local concern."

DIRECT ACTION GROWS AS A POLITICAL TOOL

The response from some in the gay and lesbian community to the perceived inaction on AIDS was a commitment to the politics of direct action. To these activists, the politics of symbolic marches and even traditional lobbying were simply inadequate in the face of the growing crisis, and new, more serious direct action was implemented. In March 1987, 250 activists from a new organization called the AIDS Coalition to Unleash Power (ACT UP) blocked morning rush hour traffic on Wall Street in New York City, to protest inaction on AIDS. Three months later, 64 people were arrested at the White House for protesting President Reagan's lack of leadership against AIDS. Very soon, the passionate protests

would escalate. In March 1988, a dozen activists were ejected from the Presidential Commission on AIDS hearing after disrupting the testimony of Congressman William Dannemeyer, Republican of California, who told the panel that AIDS was God's punishment for homosexuals. The next month 30 new and established gay and lesbian groups across the country staged a series of direct actions, rallies, acts of civil disobedience, and a national day of protest on 7 May, to protest inaction on AIDS, and support the candidacy of Jesse Jackson for president. And, on 11 October 1988, 1,000 activists stormed the headquarters of the Food and Drug Administration outside of Washington, demanding the release of experimental AIDS drugs to patients.

The protests would escalate, based in part on the premise that any attention, even negative, was ultimately helpful toward the goal of increasing the nation's commitment to fight AIDS. In March 1989, 3,000 protesters attempted to "take over" the City Hall of New York City, protesting the collapse of the city's hospital system. The next month hecklers taunted President Bush for his inaction on AIDS by interrupting his nationally televised speech in honor of the bicentennial of President Washington's inauguration. In September, five members of ACT UP made their way to the VIP balcony overlooking the floor of the New York Stock Exchange, and at the opening bell unfurled a banner reading "SELL WELLCOME," threw counterfeit $100 bills inscribed with "fuck your profiteering, we're dying while you play business," sounded foghorns, and chained themselves to the balcony, protesting the price of AZT, an expensive drug privately sold by the drug company Burroughs-Wellcome that alleviated some symptoms for people with AIDS.

It was increasingly clear that direct action was a mixed blessing politically. While it generated publicity and attention about AIDS, and often gay issues, the political response to it wasn't uniformly positive. In 1987, Congress passed the Helms Amendment, which forbade federal funding for AIDS education material that "promotes or encourages homosexuality." That same year, Governor John Sununu of New Hampshire signed legislation making that state the first to prohibit gays from becoming foster or adoptive parents. And, even gay-friendly Massachusetts Governor Michael Dukakis ordered the removal of two children from the care of gay foster parents.

However, there were political successes attributed to direct action, aside from the significant impact that ACT UP had on such items as the drug-approval process. Most notably, the increased visibility of gay and lesbian issues generally is credited with fueling the largest gay and lesbian political event the United States had ever witnessed, when in October 1987 more than 500,000 persons (the figure cited by organizers; 200,000 according to the Park Police) converged on the nation's capitol for the Second National March on Washington for Lesbian and Gay Rights, a protest march. Chanting "What do we want? Gay rights. When do we want it? Now," "Money for AIDS, not war," "We are everywhere, we will be free," the marchers sang "America the Beautiful" and "We Shall Overcome." When they marched past the White House they pointed their fingers and shouted "shame, shame, shame" and "increase AIDS funding, Americans are dying." Two days later, 600 people were arrested at the Supreme Court, protesting its decision the year before in *Bowers v. Hardwick.*

Apart from the publicity generated and solidarity created by this second major march, the event is also credited with motivating thousands of participants to return to their local communities and either organize or strengthen existing gay and lesbian political organizations. The march also forced the nascent national gay organizations—National Gay Task Force and the Human Rights Campaign Fund particularly—to publicly come to terms with the tension between direct action and mainstream political organizing. Vic Basile, then executive director of the completely mainstream HRCF—the national gay organization set up initially as a political action committee to raise and distribute election funds to supportive federal candidates, and which had absorbed the financially failing Gay Rights National Lobby—noted after the march and arrests: "civil disobedience is the appropriate tool in the arsenal of weapons that gay people could use to bring about political change. Frankly, if blacks had mainstreamed all their issues, this country would still be trying to pass a civil rights act." If the head of the most mainstream of gay national organizations was speaking supportively of direct action protests, their potential for success as compared to the more tedious and patient forms of organizing—caucus participation, letter writing, get-out-the-vote efforts, coalition building—was not going to be seriously refuted, at least publicly, by the national gay organizations.

In May 1987, Congressman Barney Frank, a Democrat of Massachusetts, became the first member of Congress to come out as gay voluntarily, answering a *Boston Globe* reporter "yes, so what?" when asked the question, which Frank had indicated to the reporter he was ready to be asked. Although Republican Presidential candidate George Bush would go on to endorse a proposed federal law protecting persons with AIDS against discrimination, the Democratic Party was fast becoming known as the national party more open to gay civil rights, a fact publicized when Republican Senator Orrin Hatch at a Republican Party fundraiser referred to the Democratic Party as "the party of homosexuals."

The difference in attitude of the two national parties would only widen. Once elected, President Bush would call ACT UP protests "an excess of free speech" and tell reporters that his administration had tried to "be very sensitive to the question of babies suffering from AIDS, innocent people that are hurt by the disease," a position that perpetuated the widely held and offensive view that gay men deserved AIDS and were guilty victims of the disease. Then, California Republican Governor Pete Wilson would veto another Democratically controlled State legislature's enactment of job protection for gays and lesbians, but this time angry gays and lesbians took to the streets of Los Angeles and San Francisco, and 7,000 strong in the latter city, stormed state buildings, set fires, and instituted minor rioting, and at speeches pelted Governor Wilson with eggs, paper, and oranges.

More and more creative gay political efforts were implemented, in part bolstered by the grassroots model created in response to the AIDS crisis. In October 1988, Jean O'Leary, executive director of a public interest law firm, National Gay Rights Advocates, and Rob Eichberg, organized the First National Coming Out Day, a now-annual event marked on 11 October. They cited the fact that "invisibility is the essence of our oppression. And until we eliminate that invisibility, people are going to be able to perpetuate the lies and myths about gay people and, in essence, force us into a closet not of our own choosing."

National Coming Out Day is meant as an educational and organizing tool based on the premise of voluntary outing. At the same time, a new political tool was taking root—involuntary outing, or what came to be known simply as "outing." Based on the now-undisputed premise that coming out as gay was good for the individual, for the gay community, and for the larger straight community, those who advocated "outing" took that view one step for-

ward to make the choice for those gays and lesbians, and sometimes for those simply thought to be gay or lesbian, unwilling to do it on their own. The tactic was popularized by *OutWeek* magazine, as its feature column, "Peek-a-Boo," claimed 66 names of famous people who could be gay. A later feature had 31 more names. National groups spoke out publicly against outing, with Urvashi Vaid, executive director of the renamed National Gay and Lesbian Task Force, saying "outing is counterproductive because it doesn't tackle homophobia. It relies on it for titillation." Still, the gap between public condemnation of the practice and private glee at the information gained remained quite large. The spokesman for the Bush administration's Pentagon, Pete Williams, was outed as gay, which he confirmed, and later, when President Clinton nominated Donna Shalala, Chancellor of the University of Wisconsin, as Secretary for Health and Human Services, gay activists sent out press releases stating that she is lesbian. The Clinton administration issued a statement saying that sexual orientation was irrelevant, and Shalala herself issued a statement stating that she is not a lesbian.

Several years later, the public threat of outing alone would prove sufficient. After the *Advocate* and other media outlets intimated they would run a story about the homosexuality of Republican Congressman Jim Kolbe of Arizona, he came out as well, in 1996. Another Republican, Steve Gunderson of Wisconsin, who had served in Congress since 1980, also came out under the threat of outing. He was pressured first by gay activists as early as 1993, and later in Congress itself when the homophobic Republican Congressman Robert Dornan of California made reference to Gunderson's homosexuality on the floor of the House, by saying that Gunderson's life was a revolving door, "in the closet, out of the closet." Gunderson ultimately acknowledged his homosexuality and increased what were his behind-the-scenes but now more public work on pro-gay issues. Gunderson retired in 1996, although not without controversy. After announcing his retirement, he vacillated, and considered re-election, but was told by then Speaker of the House Newt Gingrich that Gunderson would face homophobic opposition from within the Republican Party if Gunderson became chairman of the Agriculture Committee, for which he was next in line. Gunderson stuck with his decision to retire.

Speaking of titillation, a widely reported scandal broke in 1989 implicating Congressman Barney Frank in what was inaccurately reported as a prostitution ring conducted from his home. An employee of Frank's was alleged to have run a largely heterosexual prostitution ring, and after widespread publicity about that, the House of Representatives voted in 1990 to reprimand Frank for different but related events—negligence in transmitting a memorandum concealing how Frank had met the employee, said memorandum ending up in the hands of a prosecutor with oversight of the case against the employee. The scandal was widely thought to signal the end of Frank's tenure in the House, and his role as a leader for gay national politics, but both predictions proved untrue.

Although a national, organized political community formed to do traditional lobbying and advocacy in the fight against AIDS, notably the important AIDS Action Council in Washington, D.C., of which many gays and lesbians were an important part, the direct action politics to seek more attention for the AIDS crisis continued unabated, and generated far more media attention. In January 1990, 14 activists halted the Rose Bowl Parade by unfurling a banner reading "Emergency. Stop the Parade. 70,000 dead of AIDS," and, in an action that would cause a major and well publicized showdown with the Catholic Church, nearly 5,000 people demonstrated outside St. Patrick's Cathedral in New York City, screaming "You say don't fuck, we say fuck you." Several dozen people disrupted services inside the church, and 111 people were arrested. The tension between impatient activists turning the screws on direct action, and the methodical coalition building of the national and regional AIDS and/or gay political organizations, was evident. While the Human Rights Campaign Fund and others in Washington were working within the Leadership Conference on Civil Rights for church and union support on gay issues, a small but increasing numbers of gays, fueled by perceived inaction on AIDS, were willing to stick their thumbs back in the eyes of institutions they perceived as oppressive.

The new decade would see a highpoint in this tension. Queer Nation formed early in 1990, intending to be for homophobia what ACT UP was for AIDS, a direct action response to compulsory heterosexuality and the invisibility of gays and lesbians. Queer Nation organized a kiss-in Philadelphia, and a "queer in" at a mall in Los Angeles, at which gays chanting "we're here, we're queer, we're fabulous, get used to it" were met by 80 policemen wearing riot helmets. That summer, chanting "ten years, a billion dollars, one drug [AZT], big deal" more than 1,000 activists stormed the National Institute of Health's headquarters in Bethesda, Maryland.

Notwithstanding the increasingly jarring activities of gays and lesbians through direct action, coalition politics was continuing to pay off. In April, President Bush signed into law a bill that directed the FBI to collect statistics on hate crimes, and included among other categories, sexual orientation. And, in the reauthorization of the National Endowment for the Arts bill, Senator Jesse Helms's amendment prohibiting money to any art containing homoeroticism, sado-masochism, sex with children, or denigration of religion was diluted by a hortatory, less directly anti-gay amendment. Such "victory"—stopping explicitly anti-gay legislation by watering it down with merely insulting, but hortatory rhetoric—was a sign to some of maturity of the gay political movement, that it could accept insult as a substitute for repressive laws, and not punish its generally supportive legislators who made the political decision to vote for insulting language, as a cover against voting for actually punishing language. This voting trick would be repeated over and over again, with national gay organizations learning to work with supportive members of Congress to fend off homophobic legislation, and learning to convey to the organizations' less-informed membership the distinction between their consistent opponents, and their mostly supportive allies who nevertheless couldn't be with them on every single issue.

Former Congressman Steve Gunderson with partner Rob Morris.

Urvashi Vaid confronting President Bush at a 1990 televised forum about his inaction on AIDS.

In a paradigmatic example of the blending of mainstream and direct action politics, or more accurately, a national gay organization adopting the tactics of more radical activists, Urvashi Vaid, executive director of the National Gay and Lesbian Task Force, publicly confronted President Bush during a televised forum, excoriating him for his inaction on AIDS. His anger at that widely publicized confrontation did not prevent him from signing into law later that year a revision of the immigration laws that included, among many other provisions unrelated to gay issues, an explicit repeal of the longstanding "sexual deviants" exclusion, although it did bar Vaid from the White House ceremony for the signing of the Hate Crimes Statistics Act. Congress' enactment of immigration reform was also a credit to the rapid acceptance of Congressman Frank's and Congressman Studds's homosexuality in the Democratic Caucus, which controlled the House and Senate at the time. Frank, from his key role on the House Judiciary committee, in particular pushed hard for the repeal of the anti-gay exclusion, and his success was a growing sign that notwithstanding his and Studds's scandals several years before, the Democratic party was increasingly willing to embrace them and the gay rights issues they promoted as an important part of the party platform.

GAY ISSUES ARE NATIONALIZED

That Democratic party identification and its important statement that gay issues and politics had been irreversibly nationalized, took a giant leap forward with the success of Presidential candidate Bill Clinton in 1992. Candidate Clinton, though not the first Democratic candidate to do so, moved the courting of gay voters to a new level, specifically reaching out to gay and lesbian local and national organizations, raising money from some of the top gay and lesbian contributors, and publicly meeting with gay audiences. In October 1991, helping set the stage for what would later prove to be one of the biggest debacles of his administration, he declared that, if elected, he would drop the ban on gays serving in the Armed Forces.

The 1992 election was a political watershed for gays and lesbians. With Clinton actively courting gay and lesbian votes, Republican candidate Pat Buchanan used portions of a black, gay film—*Tongues Untied*—in an attack ad against President Bush in the Georgia primary, criticizing Bush for permitting the National Endowment for the Arts to help fund the film. After Buchanan won 31 percent of the vote in the New Hampshire Republican pri-

Roberta Achtenberg (l-r), Harry Britt, and Carole Midgen, all of whom served on the San Francisco Board of Supervisors.

mary, Bush fired NEA head John Frohnmayher, who later said that Bush's Chief of Staff Samuel Skinner called Frohnmayher and told him "things are getting too hot. We're going to throw you off the sleigh as a sop to the political right." The right was not saturated. At the Republican Party's national convention in the summer of 1992, Buchanan supporters waived signs reading "FAMILY RIGHTS FOREVER, GAY RIGHTS NEVER." Buchanan's red meat rhetoric—anti-immigrant, anti-gay, etc.—was cited as a public relations problem for the Republicans, and an enormous sign of cultural and political progress as for the first time an anti-gay position might be a liability in national politics. Bush later said during a prime time television interview that he would love a gay grandchild, but he would tell him that homosexuality was not normal, and discourage him from working for gay rights. At the Democratic Convention, there were many delegates on the floor waiving signs reading "LESBIAN/GAY RIGHTS NOW," and openly lesbian San Francisco politician Roberta Achtenberg, and openly gay and openly HIV-positive Democratic operative Bob Hattoy, both addressed the convention in front of a national audience. All of the Democratic candidates and the platform committee that year endorsed federal civil rights protections, and aggressive action in fighting AIDS.

During the same election cycle, candidate Ross Perot, a major third party candidate running on the Reform Party ticket, said

that he wouldn't appoint a known homosexual to a Cabinet-level post. The combination of Buchanan, Bush, and Perot drove huge numbers of gay, lesbian, and gay-supportive voters into the Democratic column, and Clinton scored a resounding win.

STATE BALLOT INITIATIVES: HARD FOUGHT BATTLES BRING MORE GAYS INTO POLITICAL ORGANIZING

The year of 1992 also witnessed the advent of a new aspect of gay political organizing. The relatively rapid shift in twenty years from completely local organizations to a movement with a noticeable national presence and spotty local activism, largely in the major urban centers, left a gaping hole in what proved to be a critical political arena: the states. In 1992, a loose confederation of fundamentalist Protestant organizations commonly known as the Christian Right instituted a new political assault: state initiatives and referenda to ban gay civil rights. Following the successful methods of Anita Bryant's 1977 campaign, and local ones that followed in St. Paul, Eugene, and Wichita, the Right targeted Colorado and Oregon in 1992. Largely out-financed, and without the critical statewide political organizations to match the confederation of churches that the Christian Right could mobilize, the national gay organizations—principally the Human Rights Campaign and the National Gay and Lesbian Task Force—pitched in with sometimes hastily created state organizations, building upon smaller ones already existing in some of the cities, to fight the anti-gay initiatives, but with only mixed results.

Structurally the battles were initiatives or referenda put directly to the people of a state for their direct vote. In Oregon, Measure 9 would have declared homosexuality "abnormal, wrong, unnatural and perverse." Colorado was more legalistic. Its Amendment 2 would have forbidden any part of that State to "enact, adopt or enforce any statute, regulation, ordinance or policy whereby homosexual, lesbian or bisexual orientation, conduct, practices or relationships shall constitute or otherwise be the basis of or entitle any person or class of persons to have or claim any minority status, quota preferences, protected status or claim of discrimination." The Oregon measure was rejected 57 to 43 percent, while the Colorado Amendment was approved by a 54 to 46 margin. The Oregon vote, although successful for gays and lesbians, was followed by an increase in hate crimes, including murder, against gays and lesbians. The Colorado vote brought that increase in violence as well, plus the political loss. That bad result, as other terrible political and other attacks on gays and lesbians would do, had the ironic result of seriously galvanizing gays, lesbians, and their progressive supporters to fight back, especially organizationally. The effect of the fiercely fought ballot initiatives—which would spread to many states in the next five years until the Christian Right began to back off because of the expense—mixed track record, and successful court challenges brought by gays, was the increase in gay and lesbian involvement in basic, grassroots politics, particularly at the state level. Joining organizations, signing petitions, lobbying elected officials, participating in talk-radio programs, and writing letters to newspapers, all enjoyed significantly higher participation rates, a critical change for a community whose previous invisibility was both the source of some of its greatest oppression, and the single largest obstacle to being taken seriously in mainstream, organized politics, local or national. Notwithstanding the significant growth, by 1993 the combined mailing lists of the major gay and lesbian organizations were estimated at only 300,000.

The substantive aspect of the ballot initiatives was also instructive. The Christian Right fine-tuned a new political attack: "no special rights" for gays and lesbian. Turning the argument for protection against job, housing, and public accommodations discrimination on its head, the savvy of the slogan "no special rights" is that it implied that gays and lesbians were already in some way protected from the discrimination they claimed, and, worse, to legislatively protect gays and lesbians would somehow give them a leg up in the fierce fight among minorities for civil rights remedies and attention from the government. A popular video was distributed through churches—*Gay Rights, Special Rights*—with graphic (but again, not fabricated) images of gay political events, and a purposefully disproportionate number of black narrators, saying things like "it was pure logic that the civil rights act should protect black people from discrimination. This [gay] civil rights act would completely neutralize the civil rights act of 1964. Anyone with any type of sexual orientation [would be included] under this law. This is everyone, so there would be no more protection for minorities." Then, as if creating a wedge among those who support civil rights for blacks and gays wasn't enough, the video surveyed how successful gays are financially. The theme was driven home that gays were not worthy of protection in the same way blacks were, and that if they were, they didn't need it, because they were doing just fine. The effect of these arguments

was so strong that they would continue to be used again and again against gays' pleas for basic civil rights protections. The financial statistics cited by anti-gay forces, which show above average incomes, are not necessarily inaccurate, they are simply misleading. That is, it is commonly accepted that the more educated and more affluent a person is, the more likely he or she is to tell others, particularly strangers who call on the phone to ask facts about finances. So, results from such a survey are of dubious quality, at least with respect to representation.

One important outcome of the state initiative battles, some of which—Oregon, Maine (initially), and Idaho—gay activists were beginning to win, was a surprisingly pro-gay Supreme Court decision in 1996, *Romer v. Evans,* holding that Colorado's Amendment 2 was unconstitutional, essentially because it shut gays and lesbians out of the political process in that state. The surprise victory, from a previously hostile Court, had two long-term implications important for gay politics: 1) it greatly slowed the momentum for further hostile initiatives, and 2) it sent a mixed message to gay and lesbian citizens, that the Court could be a protector of gay rights, rendering less necessary the equally important but uninspiring day to day work of political organizing. It remains to be seen whether the positive ruling of *Romer* will in fact create a long-term problem in that gays and lesbians will perceive that political organizing is less important, drawing them even further from organized politics.

RECENT ISSUES

The gay community remains multi-dimensional. The exact same themes that played out on a purely local level—how gays and lesbians presented to the rest of the world, and why that mattered, for one, which used to translate into whether women should wear nylons to a protest in 1965—are now more complex, with national repercussions. The persistent question—should politics organize around a "we are just like you" model or around a "we are different, and have something to contribute" one?—remain the same, but are being fought on a larger scale. The increasing complexity of the national gay political movement, a tribute to its success in bringing people out of the closet and into politics of some form, means that each of these themes could be pursued in some fora, with often schizophrenic results.

The deputy editor of the *New Republic*, the devoutly Catholic and conservative British national Andrew Sullivan, came out as gay, and advocated a conservative line in 1991, "A better strategy to bring about a society more tolerant of gay men and women would involve dropping our alliance with the current Rainbow Coalition lobby and recapture the clarity of the original civil rights movement." Sullivan argued that gays and lesbians were engaged in special interest gay politics, and should re-emphasize demands that make no sacrifice of heterosexuals, specifically "the right to marry and the right to serve our country. Unlike quotas or anti-discrimination laws, these demands ask for no sacrifice of any heterosexual. Both affirm values of social responsibility and patriotism that few Americans can oppose."

As it quickly turned out, most Americans disagreed with him about both marriage and military service. President Clinton's pledge to lift the ban on gays in the military turned into a political frenzy that was a disaster for gays and lesbians, and for Clinton. First prepared as one of a package of executive orders to be issued in the first days of his presidency in 1993, this particular order lifting the longstanding ban on gays serving in the Armed Forces was

Senators Warner (center) and Nunn (right) visiting a submarine during the 1993 debate about gays in the military.

met with a "over my political dead body" by senators, including fellow Democrat Sam Nunn of Georgia, chair of the crucial Armed Services Committee. Specifically, key senators, especially Nunn and then Majority Leader Robert Dole, said they would offer a codification of the ban as an amendment to the popular Family and Medical Leave Act. Sensing defeat, which legally meant a congressionally enacted ban on gays in the military, replacing the more flexible and easier to change personnel policy in place at that point, a compromise was developed, approved by the national gay organizations, in which Clinton agreed to "study" the issue for six months, and Nunn agreed not to try to enact legislation for six months.

During the six months, the debate deteriorated. In a bipartisan spewing of anti-gay sentiment, Nunn convened a relentless series of hearings to study the issue of openly gay people serving in the military, which included a humiliating scene of several Senators crouched in a crowded barracks asking military men how they felt about possibly sharing such close quarters with a gay man. The public opinion polls were overwhelmingly against lifting the ban, at least when the question posed was "Should straight men be required to serve with gay men?" Surprisingly, although lesbian

baiting in the military was proportionally a far bigger problem than anti-gay male behavior, women were almost completely left out of the national dialogue.

The gay political response to the assault in Congress was immediate, but ultimately unsuccessful. As soon as the threat hit, the national gay organizations, with some support from regional groups, formed a coalition to fight for the lifting of the ban called the Campaign for Military Service, which superseded an earlier organization, the Gay and Lesbian Military Freedom Project, itself formed by a coalition of civil rights groups in 1989. Largely funded by the Human Rights Campaign Fund and several individual gay contributors, CMS—headed by long-time lawyer/activist Tom Stoddard and private lobbyist Tom Sheridan—proved to be organizationally very broad, but shallow in financial and, more importantly, constituent support. It featured a letterhead of very impressive supporters, from mainstream religious groups to unions to traditional civil rights organizations, and a tribute to the cautious coalition-building the national gay organizations had cultivated. But, like the gay community itself on this issue, the grassroots support from these organizations was tepid at best. Compared to the extraordinary outpouring of emotional opposition from members of the military, their families, veterans groups, and the Christian Right, which inundated Congress with passionate opposition to lifting the ban on gays in the military, CMS and its supporters were swamped.

Politically, significant mistakes were made. After promising to lift the ban, and then engaging in very public ruminations about various options, including the bizarre idea of gay-only platoons, Clinton offered a compromise in the late summer of 1993. That compromise was swiftly rejected by Congress, which voted in the fall of 1993 to codify the ban on gays in the military. The episode left gays, and Clinton, scarred. For Clinton, it was a no-win situation. He was widely perceived by conservatives as far too gay friendly for them, which compared to any previous president, was true. Paradoxically, he was widely excoriated by gays and lesbians for "caving" on this important issue, with the critics' premise being that had he insisted on lifting the ban in some more forceful way it would have changed votes in Congress, the locus of the battle.

And the gay political community made significant mistakes as well. The coalition approach, evinced by the formation of CMS as the principal advocacy organization to lift the ban, did not work. The assemblage of support from popular, large organizations with massive memberships—unions, mainstream religions, black and fe-male civil rights organizations, proved to be a necessary first step, but not a substitute for the more important grassroots mobilization critical to winning a national political battle. A variety of causes are attributed to the stunning defeat of gays and lesbians who sought to lift the ban on service, but two of the reasons are critical: 1) a sense that the anti-military sentiment among many progressive gays and lesbians who dominated the leadership and more importantly the funding of the national gay organizations, questioning the very fight to get open gays and lesbians into an institution many disapproved of, put a damper on the communities' ardor for the political fight, and 2) gays and lesbians, so long in the closet and hostile to a government that for decades had persecuted them, were generally reluctant to publicly communicate with their elected officials in protest of a repressive anti-gay policy, for fear that to so communicate would brand them as gay.

But, as would now clearly be the pattern, the enactment into law of the explicitly anti-gay legislation had a silver lining for gay and lesbian political organizers. Never had the nation been treated to such an extensive conversation in the media about gay and lesbian issues. Publicly gay and lesbian people were all over the airwaves, consistently discussing basic issues of affection, commitment, discrimination, and love that had never been so thoroughly addressed before. The political organizations—CMS, HRCF,

According to organizers, the 1993 March on Washington brought out nearly one million people.

David Mixner at the Gay and Lesbian Inaugural Celebration in 1993.

NGLTF—made decisions, consciously or otherwise, to highlight well-groomed, often male, consistently white, advocates on television and in the newspaper, who would promote the gay line that the ban was discriminatory, but also send the message to the world that "we are just like you," of course presupposing and relying on the biased view of what the "all American boy" looked like. Blacks and women, disproportionately affected by the ban and the witch hunts going on in the military to root out suspected gays and lesbians, were not a significant part of the public aspect of the political campaign waged by CMS to fight the ban.

The media storm that the debate precipitated was seeded further by two events that year. First, a statement by Congressman Barney Frank to the *Boston Globe* in the spring of 1993, that was quickly (and widely) reported as a compromise, suggested that measures that regulate on-base, on-duty conduct but did not reach the more private aspects of the lives of gays and lesbians would be better than a total ban on gays in the military. The fact of the compromise, and the media storm that surrounded that statement were critical: President Clinton was given his first break in what was becoming an increasingly tense and poorly handled issue, when the most prominent gay politician in America implied that a compromise could be found. The media storm around the compromise—repeated nationwide

in front page news for some time—proved a challenge to the gay political community. Angry at the compromise, unwilling publicly to agree with Frank that his proposal, if adopted, would be better than a total ban, CMS and the gay political organizations tried to distance themselves from the reported opinion of the gay Congressman whose view on this issue would be critical to the battle.

In the midst of the eleven-month battle in Congress over the issue, the Third National March on Washington for Lesbian, Gay, Bisexual Rights and Liberation was convened. According to its organizers this battle brought out almost 1,000,000 marchers in support of gay and lesbian pride and civil rights (park organizers said there were only 300,000). The march was a high point of the cultural expression of pride, with no event before or since drawing so many gays and lesbians into one place to show their support for anything. One feature of the march was that it also represented the high-water mark of the confusion in which gay organizations were mired over what gay activities were cultural expressions, celebrations of being or stating that a group of people were gay, as opposed to political organizing and action. Since expressing one's homosexuality publicly was and continues to be a political act, the notion that groups of people congregating to do so—the post-Stonewall Pride parades and marches—alone constituted the critical political act proved to be a serious mistake for gay and lesbian organized politics.

Marching and celebrating, even in large numbers with good cheer, had an important impact on cultural views of gays and lesbians, but that is not the same as political organizing. To the extent that gay organizations encouraged people to show up at a rally, or support a dance, or repeat a slogan, those same organizations were not sufficiently encouraging gays and lesbians to contact their members of Congress on a particular gay issue—increased funding for AIDS, opposing the ban on gays in the military, opposing attacks on gay art, changing immigration law—to organize politically on the local level, to show up at party caucuses at which members of platform committees would be selected, to write letters to the editor, or participate in talk radio. Anti-gay elements, including the Christian Right and others, were perfecting these pure political organizing tactics, and legislative results, including the codification of the ban on gays in the military, not surprisingly almost always ran in their direction. The efforts, principally by the HRCF, which started a mail/telegram campaign to inform members of Congress of its membership's views, were unsuccessful in part because so many gays and lesbians were unpersuaded of the critical role direct communication with their elected officials could play on legislation.

The very high profile political defeat with respect to the ban on gays in the military should not obscure the major successes that gays secured during the Clinton administration. With the prodding of HRCF, NGLTF, and other organizations that had supported his election; important pressure provided by such respected gay and lesbian Democrats in the private sector as Hilary Rosen in Washington and David Mixner in California; and the work of openly gay Congressmen Frank and Studds, President Clinton's first term ushered in a political acceptance of gays and lesbians that would have been unthinkable to the earlier activists, most still alive, who labored against a federal government that in their words had declared war on them. Clinton not only appointed but bragged about openly gay and lesbian people in his administration, and put them not in stereotypical human resources positions, but gave them posts as the head of the Patent and Trademark Office, deputy general counsels in the Health and Human Resources Department, within the White House, and in over 100 appointed positions government-wide. Midway through his first term, in part stung by criticism over his handling of the administration's position with respect to a legal challenge to the anti-gay referendum in Colorado, Clinton established an official liaison to the gay and lesbian community in the office of the White House.

Indicative of the complicated political posture in which gays and lesbians found themselves, even though the appointment of a high ranking official as outreach coordinator to the lesbian and gay community by the government that had until recently actively rooted out gays from federal employment was an emotional turning point, the official appointed was in fact Marsha Scott, a straight woman, a demographic fact that no other political interest group—women, blacks, Hispanics, Jewish people, and so on—would tolerate of their political liaison. But no organization publicly objected, and the political successes kept coming. Clinton, by executive order lifted the ban on security clearances based on sexual orientation, took positions against the anti-gay referenda appearing in the states, supported a change in the immigration laws to permit gays and lesbians persecuted abroad to be eligible for asylum in this country based on that fact, and greatly increased funding on basic research and social aid to people with AIDS.

SAME-SEX MARRIAGE: A WEDGE POLITICAL ISSUE

And then another shoe dropped. While the national gay organizations, principally HRC (having eliminated "Fund" from its name), tried to focus the legislative agenda on implementing the Employment Non-Discrimination Act to protect against gay bias in the workforce, political events beyond their control swamped them. In response to a Hawaii court determination that same-sex couples could not be denied a right to marry in that state under state law, the Republican-controlled Congress seized upon that issue as what they hoped would be a significant political wedge against Clinton's re-election campaign in 1996. They introduced and rapidly passed legislation—the Defense of Marriage Act—that would prohibit under federal law same-sex marriages, and tell states they needn't recognize another state's same-sex marriage. Since the law was legally unnecessary—Hawaii was still litigating the question, there was in fact no same-sex marriage anywhere in the nation, and there was no need for a federal definition of marriage, since the states had handled the matter themselves for more than 200 years—it was pushed forward in the hope that Clinton would oppose the anti-gay bill, assuaging gay people but putting himself firmly against public opinion, or, as he did, supporting the anti-gay legislation and angering gays. That is why it is called a wedge issue—it is a political effort to divide what has become an important constituency from its general support of a particular party or candidate.

The wedge strategy put gay organizations in a difficult position with respect to Clinton's re-election. Apart from the harsh, mean, and homophobic substance of the legislation, the political right focused on part two of what it wanted—if Clinton was going to support their anti-gay legislation, then maybe gays and lesbians would support the Republican Party that election year, or at least stay home. HRC and NGLTF wanted to criticize Clinton, legitimately so, but the more they did the more attention was diverted from the serious political enemy, the Christian Right and its mostly Republican supporters who promoted the anti-gay legislation. And, the more that gay organizations bashed Clinton, the more they drove gays and lesbians to do precisely what the conservatives hoped: vote Republican or stay home. And, a new political organization, the Log Cabin Republicans, fueled that effort. Formed as a confederation of local Republican gay clubs, the Log Cabin Republicans mocked Clinton for signing the Defense of Marriage Act, and insisted that he was worse than a Republican candidate because he promised gays and lesbians political equality and then broke that promise when faced with opposition. It was a tempting argument, and difficult for the national gay organizations, officially non-partisan, to counter. It ignored the significant number of concrete political improvements that Clinton had brought to gays and lesbians, and disregarded the fact that the Republican candidate for president, Senator Bob Dole, returned a financial contribution made by the Log Cabin Republicans because he did not want to be associated with their "agenda."

What the conservatives got with the Defense of Marriage Act but didn't anticipate was a surprisingly supportive vote on an important gay civil rights issue. In the Senate, where procedural rules regulating votes are less tightly controlled by the majority party, some senators, notably Democrat Edward Kennedy of Massachusetts, decided with gay political organizations—principally Elizabeth Birch and Daniel Zingale of HRC—to counter the Senate vote on the Defense of Marriage Act with a vote on the Employment Non-Discrimination Act, a long-sought-after federal protection against employment discrimination based on sexual orientation. There was no doubt in anyone's mind that the Defense of Marriage Act would pass by overwhelming margins in Congress, especially given the history that a less-comprehensive vote, denying the District of Columbia the right to effectuate its domestic partnership laws, had repeatedly passed Congress by comfortable margins.

After intense lobbying, and the expression of support from Clinton, the job protection measure lost in the Senate by only one vote, 50-49. Literally, this was a loss. In terms of message and organizing, it was a stunning political victory. For almost one half of the Senate to go on record in support of gay civil rights, a somewhat easier thing to do given the context of the vote attached to the anti-gay Defense of Marriage Act, was a level of support that no gay political organization could have predicted even weeks before the vote. The political message sent was that gay political rights had in fact reached the mainstream of civil rights in the United States—in fact, lobbying off the floor of the Senate that day were leaders of black, women's, and union organizations. Although it will be more years before the legislative goals of gays and lesbians are accomplished, after that vote it was clear in the political world that the momentum was on the side of gays and lesbians, and that it was no longer a question of whether the government would continue to persecute homosexuals in this nation, but now a question of how active the government would be in protecting gays and lesbians from such discrimination.

Significantly, despite the wide antipathy expressed against same-sex marriage, not a single senator or member of Congress who refused to support the anti-gay measure and subsequently stood for re-election in 1996 was defeated. That fact is an important one for future gay-related legislation, since one of the formidable aspects of encouraging wavering elected officials to support gay civil rights is convincing them that they will not be punished by an electorate perceived as significantly homophobic. Still, despite the 100 percent return rate for these pro-gay elected officials, as of 1996 not a single openly gay or lesbian person who is not an incumbent has been elected to Congress. The only openly gay or lesbian non-incumbent elected to any federal office in this country remains Sabrina Sojourner, a long-time activist, black and lesbian, who is the District of Columbia's "Shadow Representative," an unpaid, largely symbolic position meant to highlight the district's structurally inferior political representation in Congress (and not to be confused with the district's Delegate to Congress, the official, paid representative in the House of Representatives).

By the middle of the 1990s, gay political organizations, national and regional, had become established components of the civil rights community: formally included in the Leadership Conference on Civil Rights, explicitly part of the outreach efforts of at least the Democratic National Committee, with an official position in the White House, and with the Human Rights Campaign running one of the largest dollar-volume financial contribution apparatuses of any political organization, let alone gay.

The changes in four decades are stunning. They are not complete, but stunning nonetheless. Significant numbers—some say the majority—of gays and lesbians remain closeted and uninvolved with the many political organizations struggling for their civil rights. It is estimated that the combined mailing lists of the major gay national organizations still number fewer than 300,000 persons. And, while culturally great progress has been made toward accepting gays and lesbians in the fabric of American life, only 11

states and the District of Columbia legally protect gays under the law from discrimination. But, the foundation has been laid for continued political success. While there will be setbacks, violence, and discrimination, the progression under the law through political organizing is essentially in one direction, toward equality.

PROMINENT PEOPLE

Virginia Apuzzo (1941-)

At one time the "pre-eminent leader" of the gay rights efforts in America, Virginia Apuzzo is an activist whose tenure in the movement has brought her from the scrappy turf of candidacy for the New York assembly, to, 20 years later, being the highest openly gay appointed official in this nation's history, as special assistant to the President for Administration and Management. After leaving a convent at the age of 29, Apuzzo became involved in New York state activism, including serving as executive director of the Fund for Human Dignity. In the early 1980s, she moved from her role as a state activist to become first co-director, then sole director, of the National Gay Task Force, building on her past political involvement as a member of the National Women's Political Caucus, an open lesbian on the Democratic Platform Committee, and, in 1976, her service as co-chair of the newly formed Gay Rights National Lobby. Her dominance of national gay politics was so complete for a time that in 1984 the *Advocate* ran an article that posed the question, "is it good for the gay community to have just one national leader?" In 1985, she resigned to return to New York state politics, becoming, among other things, deputy director of the New York State Consumer Protection Board. In 1997, President Clinton appointed her to a senior level management position in the White House. Known not only as a persistent and influential leader in gay politics, from its early marginalized days to its current inclusion in the fabric of mainstream politics, Apuzzo is also a strong advocate of coalition politics. In an early address to the Kennedy Institute of Government at Harvard, she criticized the gay political community for its insularity, reminding the audience that gays are wrong to "believe our success will come ... if we have more of what we have already ... organizations ... volunteers ... support from within our own community."

Elizabeth Birch

After a long history of activism, Elizabeth Birch was appointed executive director of the Human Rights Campaign in late 1994, and embarked on a successful drive to grow and "corporatize" that organization. Building on her experience as former co-chair of the National Gay and Lesbian Task Force and as founder of AIDS Legal Services, a model program for people with HIV in northern California, Birch doubled the membership of HRC and increased its budget to $11 million, making it the largest national gay and lesbian political organization in the country. A former director of worldwide litigation and human resources counsel for Apple Computer, Inc., Birch infused HRC with a polished, corporate demeanor and public perception, which has helped to insert that organization more and more into the mainstream of civil rights advocacy in national politics.

Melvin Boozer

Melvin Boozer had consistent and active contributions to early gay political organizations, a public role made all the more rare and significant because Boozer was African American, which for many others meant relegation to the sidelines. He was president

Elizabeth Birch

of the D.C. Gay Activists Alliance in its formative years, and a leader in coalition politics. In 1980, Boozer earned his place in the history books, when, at the Democratic National Convention in New York City, he became the first openly gay candidate for the office of vice president in American history. The gay caucus at that convention secured the 334 votes required for his nomination, and Boozer's address to the convention put the struggle for civil rights for gays and lesbians into the context of both the historical position taken by the Democratic Party against discrimination, and the effort at the time to secure passage of the Equal Rights Amendment. His address called upon the party membership to grant the requests of "twenty million lesbian and gay Americans whose lives are blighted by a veil of ignorance and misunderstanding."

Steven Endean

Steve Endean, brewed in the state and local politics of Minnesota, was one of the few seasoned political veterans able to help nationalize the gay political rights movement, when that national movement began to take root in the late 1970s and early 1980s. As coordinator of the Minnesota Committee for Gay Rights, Endean played a crucial role in securing passage of gay rights ordinances in Minneapolis and St. Paul. Endean also honed coali-

tion politics in Minnesota—it was his work within the state's Democratic-Farm-Labor party that brought about his appointment in 1974 as an openly gay man to the Minneapolis Commission on Human Relations. He moved to the national scene in the mid-1970s, first as co-chair of the National Gay Task Force, and, in 1978, as head of the Gay Rights National Lobby, a rival organization. Endean understood basic grassroots lobbying efforts—organizing the National Lesbian and Gay Constituent Lobby Week in 1981—as well as important coalition building with potentially sympathetic national organizations. Endean led the successful effort in 1982 to secure admission of the Gay Rights National Lobby and the National Gay Task Force to the Leadership Conference on Civil Rights, the nation's umbrella advocacy organization for major civil rights initiatives, including labor unions and religious organizations. In 1980, Endean, with others, formed the Human Rights Campaign Fund. Modeled on the success of conservative political action committees' ability to influence the 1980 elections, HRCF's mission would be to fund pro-gay candidates in the 1982 congressional races. Within 15 years the HRCF would become the most dominant and largest gay political organization the United States had ever seen.

Barney Frank (1940-)

Congressman Barney Frank, Democrat from the Fourth Congressional District of Massachusetts, has established himself as the preeminent gay political leader of our day. With 25 years of experience in elected politics, and many years of political service before that as a key employee to other politicians, he has successfully merged the roles of effective, mainstream political representation with strong advocacy for gay and lesbian civil rights. Frank served eight years in the Massachusetts legislature before being elected to Congress in 1980. Through pragmatism and political shrewdness, he has been able to hold fast to his devoutly-held liberal ideologies. He worked effectively with other members of Congress to implement important legislation, from banking and housing reform, redress for interned Japanese citizens, to immigration. Even before he came out publicly in 1987 and survived a nasty sex-related scandal and reprimand from the House in 1989, he diligently fought for gay civil rights, and since has prodded Congress to repeal anti-gay immigration laws, encouraged the Clinton administration to repeal the ban on security clearances, and helped to lead the fight against the ban on gays in the military and same-sex marriages. Personally, he and his partner, Herb Moses, play an important public role as a visible and well-liked gay couple in the center of power in Washington, D.C.

Franklin Kameny (1925-)

Franklin Kameny calls himself the father (maybe grandfather) of the gay political movement. He may be right. A military veteran, a Ph.D. in astronomy from Harvard, an openly gay Congressional candidate, Kameny is a man of enormous energy and passion, with a rhetorical style notable for its fluidness and skill. After being discharged from his job with the federal government for no more than being a homosexual, he decided to fight against discrimination. He has won more than he has lost. Kameny was involved, often as a leader, in the most significant battles for gay civil rights. He led the fight to dismantle the longstanding ban on employment and security clearances for gays, to repeal the anti-sodomy provisions in the law in his home of the District of Columbia, and to remove homosexuality from the psychiatric community's list of disorders. His run for Congress as an openly gay man in 1971 was heroic, given the rampant discrimination against open gays and lesbians at the time. According to Kameny himself, his favorite accomplishment was coining the phrase "Gay is Good," modeled on the "Black is Beautiful" campaign, and one that in his words "encapsulates, in a way that has been taken up by others, everything that I stand for and have worked for."

Gerry Studds (1937-)

Congressman Gerry Studds was a popular, well-liked representative from southeastern Massachusetts for 24 years, serving as an unabashed liberal Democrat and defender of civil rights, the environment, and personal freedom. In 1983, he became another in a series of congressmen outed as gay. Studds earned his spot in gay political history not simply by continuing to serve as a Congressman, but by dealing publicly with his homosexuality in an affirming way, and neither belittling nor shaming it, as his predecessors had done. Censured by the House in July 1983 for events involving two House pages ten years earlier, Studds chose to assert a positive gay identity. He went on to continue to serve another 13 years in Congress, championing the rights of gay servicemen, being a leader in the fight for adequate funding for research on HIV/AIDS, and supporting protections against discrimination based on sexual orientation, including support of gay civil rights bills as early as 1975.

Urvashi Vaid (1958-)

Born in India, Urvashi Vaid migrated with her writer/teacher parents to America in 1966. As a college student she was active in liberal and feminist politics and organized women's concerts. She came out during law school, and upon graduating became a lawyer for the ACLU's National Prison Project, through which she became more interested in the treatment of HIV/AIDS prisoners. Vaid later went to work at the National Gay and Lesbian Task Force, and was eventually named executive director. Her passion for the rights of the underprivileged throughout the world won her praise for her leadership and rhetorical skills, and criticism for the diffused focus of a major gay organization that found itself taking positions on issues not directly related to gay issues. But, her work reflected a broad vision of social equality regardless of gender, class, and race, and she continued to believe that gay liberation could not come without victories against the broader oppression based on those categories. Despite the criticism of her stands, she won wide support and accolades from legions of gays and lesbians who identified with her passion and political leanings. After a sabbatical to write a book, Vaid returned to NGLTF to direct its public policy/research division.

REFERENCES:

Books

Blasius, Mark. *Gay & Lesbian Politics: Sexuality & the Emergence of a New Ethic.* Temple University Press, 1994.
Blasius, Mark and Shane Phelan, eds. *We Are Everywhere: A Historical Source Book of Gay & Lesbian Politics.* New York: Routledge, 1995.
Bull, Chris and John Gallagher. *Perfect Enemies: The Religious Right, The Gay Movement, and the Politics of the 1990s.* New York: Crown, 1996.
Button, James W., Kenneth D. Wald, and Barbara A. Rienzo, eds. *Private Lives, Public Conflicts: Battles over Gay Rights in American Communities.* Washington, D.C.: CQ Press, 1997.
Corber, Robert J. *In the Name of National Security: Hitchcock, Homophobia, & the Political Construction of Gender in Postwar America.* Durham, NC: Duke University Press, 1993.
———. *Homosexuality in Cold War America: Resistance & the Crisis of Masculinity.* Durham, North Carolina: Duke University Press, 1997.
D'Emilio, John. *Sexual Politics, Sexual Communities: The Making of a Homosexual Minority in the United States, 1940-1970.* Chicago: University of Chicago Press, 1983.
———. *Making Trouble: Essays on Gay History, Politics, and the University.* New York: Routledge, 1992.
Duberman, Martin. *Stonewall.* New York: Plume, 1993.
Duberman, Martin, et al., eds. *Hidden from History: Reclaiming the Gay and Lesbian Past.* New York: Penguin Books, 1989.
Duggan, Lisa and Nan D. Hunter. *Sex Wars: Sexual Dissent and Political Culture.* New York: Routledge, 1995.
Faderman, Lillian. *Odd Girls and Twilight Lovers: A History of Lesbian Life in Twentieth-Century America.* New York: Penguin, 1991.
Frank, Barney. *Speaking Frankly: What's Wrong with the Democrats and How to Fix It.* New York: Times Books/Random House, 1992.
Katz, Jonathan Ned. *Gay/Lesbian Almanac: A New Documentary.* New York: Carroll and Graf Publishers, 1983.
———. *Gay American History: Lesbians and Gay Men in the U.S.A.* New York: Penguin Books, 1992.
Ridinger, Robert B. Marks. *The Gay and Lesbian Movement: References and Resources.* New York: Simon and Schuster, 1996.
Vaid, Urvashi. *Virtual Equality: The Mainstreaming of Gay and Lesbian Liberation.* New York: Anchor, 1995.

Periodical Articles

Fox, Sue. "At 70, Activist Frank Kameny Is Still Fighting," in *Washington Blade,* 19 May 1995.
Romano, Lois. "Barney Frank, Out of the Closet," in *Washington Post,* 2 July 1987.
Sherrill, Kenneth. "The Political Power of Lesbians, Gays, and Bisexuals," in *PS: Political Science and Politics,* vol. 29, no. 3, September 1996: 469-73.

Organizations

Gay and Lesbian Alliance against Defamation. GLAAD is a national organization that promotes fair, accurate, and inclusive representation of individuals and events in all media as a means of combating homophobia and all forms of discrimination based on sexual orientation or identity. 1875 Connecticut Avenue, N.W., Suite 800, Washington, D.C. 20009; (202) 986-1360; www.glaad.org.

Gay and Lesbian Victory Fund. The only national organization solely dedicated to increasing the number of qualified, openly gay and lesbian elected and appointed officials at all levels of government. (202) 842-8679.

Human Rights Campaign. The nation's largest national lesbian and gay political organization, with 200,000 members. HRC lobbies the federal government, educates the public, and participates in electoral politics on gay and lesbian issues. 1101 14th Street, N.W., Washington D.C., 20005; (202) 628-4160; www.hrc.org.

National Black Lesbian and Gay Leadership Forum. NBLGLF exists to empower black lesbians and gays by increasing visibility, advocating for the interests of the community, and developing and supporting strong leaders for the future. 1436 U Street, N.W., Suite 200, Washington, D.C. 20009; (202) 483-6786; nblglf@aol.com/www.nblglf.org.

National Gay and Lesbian Task Force. A 35,000-member, grassroots-based political organization that works to eliminate prejudice, violence, and injustice against gay, lesbian, bisexual, and transgendered people at the local, state, and national level. 2320 17th Street, N.W., Washington, D.C. 20009; (202) 332-6483; ngltf@ngltf.org.

National Latino/a Lesbian, Gay, and Transgendered Organization. LLEGO is a constituency-based organization of more than 100 latino/a affiliates nationwide and in Puerto Rico. Its mission is to strengthen latina lesbian, latino gay, bisexual, and transgender communities by facilitating access to cultural, political, and community development resources. 1612 K Street, N.W., Suite 500, Washington, D.C. 20006; (202) 466-8240; www.llego.org.

Parents, Families and Friends of Lesbians and Gays. PFLAG promotes the health and well-being of gay, lesbian, and bisexual persons, their families, and friends through support, education, and advocacy. Its membership includes 70,000 households in 400 communities. 1101 14th Street, N.W., Suite 1030, Washington, D.C. 20011; (202) 638-4200; www.pflag.org.

Sexual Minority Youth Assistance League. SMYAL is a youth service agency working to meet the needs of young people, ages 13-21, who are lesbian, gay, bisexual, or transgendered as well as those who are struggling with their identities. 410 Seventh Street, S.E., Washington, D.C. 20003; (202) 546-5940; smyal@aol.com.

—Robert Raben

12

Law

Celebrated by lesbians and gay men throughout the United States as the date of the Stonewall Rebellion, 26 June 1969, is generally credited as marking the beginning of the modern lesbian and gay civil rights movement. Stonewall began an era of increasing visibility and more radical demands on the part of the lesbian and gay community.

Legal challenges to the myriad laws subordinating lesbians and gay men have been an integral part of this increased activism. In 1973, a group of gay lawyers in New York formed Lambda Legal Defense and Education Fund as a public interest law firm, the purpose of which was to litigate and educate for the civil rights of lesbians and gay men. The same year, the ACLU started the Sexual Privacy Project to challenge government regulation of sexuality. In 1984, the privacy project evolved into the Gay and Lesbian Rights Project. Together, these two organizations and a small number of practitioners helped shape gay rights litigation in the United States.

Today, lesbian and gay law is on the cutting edge of many constitutional and other legal issues and is the focus of numerous legislative initiatives. No longer is most of the legal work performed by a few lawyers in public interest organizations. Large law firms, small practitioners, and vastly expanded staffs at public interest groups are all involved in the effort. And the legal agenda has expanded and become more ambitious, moving from a focus solely on equality to one that aims to break down the binary categories of heterosexual and homosexual, redefine the meaning of family, and show the ways in which sexuality and gender are inextricably linked. In the process, lesbian and gay constitutional litigation has begun to redefine the line between public versus private, and sexual versus political, speech in First Amendment doctrine. In addition, litigation involving issues of gender and sexuality is reshaping the meaning of the Equal Protection Clause of the Fourteenth Amendment to the Constitution and redefining the meaning of family.

Success in gay rights litigation and the increased visibility of lesbians and gay men have, predictably, led to an increasingly well-organized and vocal backlash. Legal activity to both continue the march towards equality and to beat back new antigay laws has made this an increasingly active and exciting time to be working in the area of lesbian and gay legal rights.

This chapter will provide a brief history of the legal status of lesbians and gay men in the Western world. It will then discuss the present state of the law, broken down by subject matter. I have struggled with the question of the most appropriate terminology to use in describing the community addressed in this chapter. The most inclusive language is clearly lesbian, gay, bisexual, and transgendered persons. The most radical political stance on gender and sexuality would call the chapter "Queer Law." However, I have chosen instead to refer to lesbians and gay men, primarily because it is a more accurate description of the groups addressed in most of the case law and legislation and the decidedly unradical political perspective represented. I do not mean to exclude transgendered persons and bisexuals from the broader civil rights and queer movements, but rather simply to acknowledge that legal treatment of sexual orientation has mostly failed to move beyond the binary categories of heterosexual and homosexual.

HISTORY OF THE LEGAL STATUS OF HOMOSEXUALITY IN THE WESTERN WORLD

Social historians generally agree that the existence of a homosexual identity is a relatively late phenomenon in Western culture (Chauncey; Fuss; Kennedy & Davis). Several suggest that the homosexual person first emerged in the seventeenth century with the appearance in London of male transvestite or "molly clubs" (McIntosh; Trumbach), others in the eighteenth century with the expansion of wage labor and the growth of urban populations (Adam; Fuss, p. 108). The greatest consensus, however, places the beginning of a distinct homosexual identity, that is, a person defined by her/his sexual object choice, in the nineteenth century (Foucault; Kennedy & Davis; Weeks). During the late 1800s, increasing urbanization created more opportunities for independent living outside extended family units, and Freud and others promoted sexual pleasure as distinct from reproduction, claiming erotic interest as central to a person's being (Kennedy & Davis, p. 9). These changes helped create the conditions that allowed lesbians and gay men to forge a distinctive gay culture. At the same time, medical writers and sexologists began to name and discuss homosexuals as distinct kinds of people, defining as a disease what had previously been sin or crime. To the sexologists, homosexuality was signaled by gender inversion. Abnormality was defined not only by same-sex desire but by broader inversion of the male or female gender role. Thus, only effeminate men and mannish women were labeled homosexuals by the early sexologists. This image, while only partial, was nevertheless representative of much of visible gay culture at the time. Medical discourse described, shaped, explained, and named what it saw in popular culture and social practices to construct the homosexual as a distinct personality type (Chauncey, pp. 1-28; Kennedy & Davis, pp. 324-25; Smith-Rosenberg, pp. 268-71). By World War II, a transition had taken place from defining the homosexual on the basis of gender inversion to a broader definition based on object choice (Chauncey, p. 13-14; Kennedy & Davis, p. 325). However, gender inversion has remained central to the culture and representation of lesbians and gay men.

Although the emergence of a lesbian and gay identity, a historically specific act, is relatively recent, homosexual behavior has always existed in Western culture. Persons were not centrally defined, nor did they define themselves, by their sexual object choices. Nevertheless, the preconditions for the meaning of a homosexual identity and for its equation with gender inversion can be found in the historic treatment of the interaction between sex, sexuality, and gender in pre-nineteenth-century Western cultures.

Ancient Greece and Rome

Male homosexuality was common and broadly accepted among the ancient Greeks (Bullough & Bullough, pp. 24-41; Greenberg, pp. 141-51). However, attitudes towards homosexual conduct were highly hierarchical and gendered. The Greeks practiced an asymmetrical homosexuality in which grown men were the active sexual partners of passive adolescent boys, male prostitutes, and slaves. Affairs between two adult men were less common but did occur. The passive partner in such a relationship was stigmatized as a *molles*, a soft or unmasculine man who departed from the cultural norm of manliness and adopted a feminine identity. Some such "feminine" men were said to adopt the dress, gait, and other characteristics of women (Greenberg, p. 147; Halperin, pp. 45-46). While referring only to deviant behavior and not personhood or identity, the Greek construction of gender deviance bears a close relationship to the male homosexual invert of the late-nineteenth-century sexologists.

A similar, although less well-documented, parallelism can be found between female same-sex behavior in ancient Greece and the construction of the lesbian invert of the sexologists. The Romans shared the male-dominated role stereotypes of the Greeks and tolerated a similar asymmetrical homosexuality that condemned passive sexual behavior by adult male citizens (Greenberg, pp. 152-60). John Boswell finds evidence that by the first century AD the prejudice against adult males playing the passive sex role may have declined, and that same-sex marriages were legal (Boswell, p. 82).

In the Greek and Roman worlds, male asymmetrical homosexuality was accepted in the context of the broader acceptance of human sexuality as a positive good. This attitude ended in late antiquity with the slow disintegration of the Roman Empire and the ascendance of Christianity. By the third century AD, war and conquest, famine and economic problems shattered a sense of confidence in the world, leading many to embrace a philosophy of asceticism first articulated by Plato (Greenberg, pp. 219-20). Asceticism preached that the material world was insignificant as compared with the world of ideas and of the spirit. The ideal life could be lived only by withdrawing from the material world into a sexually abstinent life of contemplation and spirituality. Recognizing the need for procreation, ascetics preached that sex must be restricted to potentially procreative acts within marriage. This view of acceptable sex, while directed to all sexual experiences not leading to procreation within marriage, obviously ruled out all forms of homosexuality (Greenberg, pp. 219-25).

Pre-Renaissance Europe

By the beginning of the sixth century, the process of urban decline begun by the disintegration of Roman rule was hastened by barbarian invasions, altering the social structure of Western Europe and ushering in the predominantly rural feudal Middle Ages. By the ninth century, this process was complete. Government control was so ineffective during the early middle ages that the enforcement of oppressive laws or attitudes was difficult. Nevertheless, it is remarkable how little effort was made by either the church or secular governments to enact laws proscribing homosexual conduct. Although it had been a Christian state for over two centuries, it was not until 533 that the Roman Empire outlawed homosexual behavior. That year the Emperor Justinian placed homosexual relations under the same category as adultery and subjected both to the same civil sanction—punishment by death (Boswell, pp. 169-71).

Neither the Christian hierarchy nor secular governments from the seventh through the tenth centuries considered homosexual behavior any more reprehensible than comparable heterosexual behavior. Following the break-up of the Roman Empire, most areas of Europe had adopted some sort of local law code by the ninth century; none explicitly proscribed homosexual conduct. The thirteenth century marked a period of growing intolerance of minority groups, including women, the poor, Jews and other non-Christians, and homosexuals. The growth of both civil and ecclesiastical power and the strengthening of the administrative machinery necessary to enforce laws allowed both the church and state to carry out an agenda of repression. The Crusades, the expulsion of the Jews, and the Inquisition were manifestations of this increased repression. Both homosexual and gender deviant behavior came under increased scrutiny (Boswell, pp. 269-332; Greenberg, pp. 268-98).

Virtually all secular governments passed laws instituting severe penalties, usually death, for homosexual behavior. And, the first secular law to prohibit sexual relations between women was passed in late-thirteenth-century France. The church began to take a stronger stand against same-sex relations. A theological argument that labeled homosexual acts as violative of the law of nature was developed by Albertus Magnus and expanded upon by Thomas Aquinas in his *Summa Theologiae*. Aquinas explicitly included lesbians in the vice of sodomy. His writings established the natural as the touchstone of Catholic sexual ethics and homosexuality as uniquely unnatural (Boswell, pp. 316-21; Greenberg, pp. 274-75).

The philosophy, theology, and literature of the late Middle Ages reflected a loathing of homosexual acts; canon law was antagonistic and secular law repressive. The permanent and official expression these views of homosexuality achieved in the thirteenth century continues to influence Western thought even today. The arguments used to provide official justification for the repression of same-sex sexuality echo and refine Hellenistic, early Christian, and ascetic views and presage modern attitudes towards homosexuality. Once homosexual conduct had been named as the alien "other," all acts most threatening to society were attributed to it. Homosexual acts were linked to heresy, child molestation, hedonism, unnatural acts, and gender deviance. Traditional Christian teachings continued to dominate sexual and gender ideology throughout the early modern era. From the fourteenth century until the nineteenth century, homosexuality was described as a sin and a crime against nature (Greenberg, pp. 301-02). Additionally, homosexual acts remained linked to heresy, child molestation, hedonism, and gender nonconformity.

Most European cities continued to prosecute sodomy under statutes adopted in the thirteenth century, sometimes with minor amendments. These statutes almost uniformly prescribed the death penalty for acts of sodomy and covered same-sex male and female acts as well as heterosexual sodomy. Some of the statutes defined sodomy to require penetration, thereby including lesbian acts only when performed with an instrument capable of penetration or by a woman found to have an enlarged clitoris. Sex acts not involving penetration such as tribadism were punished under statutes with lesser penalties (Crompton, pp. 18-21).

Early Modern England and the American Colonies

Sodomy in early modern England was handled by ecclesiastical courts. It was not until 1533 that authority transferred to the civil courts with the passage of the Buggery Act, which made buggery a capital offense punishable by hanging. Buggery was defined as "carnall knowledge...by mankind with mankind, or with brute beast, or by womankind with brute beast." This definition excluded lesbian sex. The American colonies followed the law in effect in England, so that male homosexual acts were a capital offense in the new colonies, but lesbian sexual acts were not (Greenberg, p. 304).

Although the legislation condemning sodomy was extremely harsh, enforcement was erratic. Popular indifference punctuated by infrequent episodes of repression remained characteristic of the social response to homosexual conduct throughout the period from the Renaissance through the eighteenth century (Greenberg, p. 347). Until the late 1800s, the only law directly addressing homosexual behavior was that relating to sodomy, and legally little distinction was made between same-sex and opposite sex sodomy. Sodomy was seen as a potential for sin in all human beings, voluntarily entered into and severely punished. Additionally, various laws prohibited cross-dressing, often but not exclusively associated with sodomitic conduct (Greenberg).

In the nineteenth century, the expansion of industrialization and explosive urban growth fundamentally altered the family, the concept of sexual identity and the relations of men and women to production, consumption, and each other. Families were no longer integrated units of production. The move to the cities severed extended family ties and created autonomous nuclear families where the men worked for wages and the women were assigned responsibility for home, consumption and reproduction (Law, p. 200).

The rise of science and the advent of social Darwinism provided a biological basis for the new family order. Gender distinctions were firmly rooted in genital difference. This immutable difference dictated that men and women ought not resemble each other. Men were seen as active, strong, and rational; women as passive, weak, and emotional. This sharp separation between the fundamental natures of men and women also dictated a clear delineation of their roles: men operated in the public world and

women were confined to the private world of the home. Sexual desire itself was theorized as fundamentally gendered. Whereas men's sexual passions had to be restrained, women were seen as passionless and asexual, as the passive objects of male sexual desire (Greenberg, pp. 376-77).

Paradoxically, the rise of capitalism and the growth of large cities also made possible the construction of a distinct homosexual identity. Young single men and women flocked to the cities to find jobs. Freed of family ties, they resided in boarding houses, hotels, and apartments. While their time belonged to their employer during the long workday, they were able to maintain their own private social and sex lives. The individual and group identities that defined these newly visible homosexual persons constituted both a self-representation and a constructed image imposed by physicians and sexologists as part of their medicalization of sexuality (Chauncey, p. 27). It is this latter, objectified and demonized image that has and continues to occupy the space of "other" in the contest over the construction of gender roles in society.

From the late 1800s, physicians actively sought to use science and medicine to help shape legal and social policy related to sexuality and gender roles. Male, and later female, homosexual social networks and institutions emerged made up of those whose identity was defined by choice of same-sex sexual partners. Medical discourse and a newly emerging city-based homosexual subculture radically transformed the conceptualization of homosexuality as one of the distinguishing characteristics of a particular type of person, the gender invert.

The Twentieth Century

World War I brought enormous growth in the numbers and visibility of the gay world in urban centers. This led moral reform societies to focus on homosexuality as a discrete social problem for the first time. To the dominant culture, the mannish lesbian and the effeminate gay man became the objectification of the homosexual as deviant, outside the patriarchal social order, and a threat to its stability. It also caused the police force to direct its attention to the antigay cause as well. The number of men convicted in Manhattan for homosexual sodomy leapt from 92 in 1916 to 238 in 1918 and over 750 in 1920, and an average of over 500 for the rest of the decade. Harassment of cross-dressing men and women under the New York State law prohibiting people from appearing in public in disguise or masquerade increased, with, for instance, 30 arrests for wearing drag over the course of two weeks at a single Harlem club in February 1928. However, enforcement remained sporadic and gay culture continued to flourish. It was not until the 1930s that concerted antigay campaigns, which continued in ever increasing intensity through the 1960s, were used to force the gay world into hiding (Chauncey).

Antigay reaction gained force in the early to mid-1930s as part of the general reaction to the cultural immorality and criminality perceived to have flourished during the prohibition years, and the serious threat to gender roles brought about by the Depression. Similar anxieties over threats to the patriarchal family followed World War II. Persecution of homosexuals, which had lessened during the war years, was renewed with increased vigor. The advent of the Cold War era and the McCarthy campaigns of the 1950s painted an even more threatening picture of the homosexual menace as actively spread by Communists to prey upon and recruit the innocent to a life of depravity, mocking the ideals of marriage and motherhood and sapping the masculine vigor necessary to contain the Communist threat. To control the enemy without, it was necessary to control the enemy within.

Commencing in the 1930s, a complex web of laws and regulations were passed or enforced with renewed vigor that aimed at forcing the gay world into the closet. In addition to the criminal laws that prohibited deviant sexual behavior, gay men and lesbians were barred from federal, state, and local government employment, from the military, from teaching positions in public schools, from qualifying for security clearances, from obtaining custody of their children or visitation rights with them, from entry into the country if an alien, from obtaining liquor licenses or working in businesses where liquor was served or even from being present in such an establishment. In 1950, the United States Senate appointed a committee to conduct an investigation into employment by the federal government of homosexuals and other "sex perverts." The committee concluded that homosexuals were unsuitable for employment because of the criminality and immorality of their behavior, and because of the security risk arising out of their vulnerability to blackmail. It was recommended that homosexuals be dismissed from government service (see p. 60). Homosexuals were purged from the government at higher rates than ever before and broader screening techniques were instituted to keep them from being hired. President Eisenhower issued EP 10,450 calling for the dismissal of all government employees who were sex perverts, and purges of homosexuals by the military increased (Cain).

A number of states passed regulations aimed at eliminating the representation of homosexuality in live entertainment venues such as cabarets or the stage. Some prohibited female impersonators from performing. Hollywood passed a code prohibiting reference to homosexuality in movies. Areas of public life that remained outside of government regulation, such as private employment, engaged in similar discrimination against identifiable homosexuals. Informal policing through ostracism, loss of social respect, gossip, and public jeers also occurred.

The sexologists labeled the homosexual and the law played a crucial role in silencing and subordinating the group so defined. The law as a powerful governmental expression of public values acted to both demonize the behavior attributed to homosexuals and to define their subordinated group status. Much of this was accomplished through prohibiting the presence of identifiable lesbians and gay men in the public sphere, where it was feared they could disrupt public order and normal gender and sexual arrangements.

As George Chauncey has noted, the most effective step in the exclusion of the gay world from the public sphere was the pervasive regime of surveillance and control of social life brought about through the licensing of the sale of alcohol (Chauncey). With the repeal of prohibition, every state stepped in to promulgate alcoholic beverage control laws designed not only to control the consumption of liquor but also to regulate morality in the public spaces in which people congregated to drink. State legislatures enacted stringent rules to govern the conduct of bars and restaurants and established powerful regulatory agencies to enforce them. These rules generally required that an establishment not suffer or permit such premises to become disorderly. The enforcement agencies interpreted the statutes to prohibit the serving of items to homosexuals. Violation of the law led to revocation or suspension of an establishment's liquor license. Proprietors thus became the main enforcement agents, so that policing was pervasive. These new regulations reestablished the boundaries of respectable public so-

ciability, excluding and isolating the gay world from the broader social life of the community (Chauncey).

The First Gay Rights Legal Case

The first gay rights case was probably *Stoumen v. Reilly,* which involved a dispute over whether the California Board of Equalization could suspend the liquor license of the Black Cat Restaurant because it catered to known homosexuals (Cain). A provision in California's Alcohol Beverage Control Act prohibited a licensee from running a disorderly house. The California Supreme court held that the suspension of a liquor license solely because an establishment catered to homosexuals was arbitrary and therefore a violation of the state constitution. The mere presence of homosexuals was not a threat to public welfare and morals. However, homosexual conduct could be valid grounds for revocation. At the core of the decision was a distinction that continues to dominate lesbian and gay rights litigation, that between status and conduct. However, courts in California and elsewhere continued to infer status from conduct.

Any dress, appearance, or behavior coded as homosexual could be sufficient evidence of disorderly conduct. Thus, as one New Jersey judge said, "The evidence proved that they had the conspicuous guise, demeanor, carriage, and appearance of such personalities. It is often in the plumage that we identify the bird" (*Paddock Bar, Inc. v. Div. of Alcoholic Beverage Control,* pp. 408-09). He went on to refer to the medical model of inversion when noting that "the psychiatrist constructs his deductive conclusions largely upon the ostensible personality, behavior and unnatural mannerisms of the patient" (*Paddock Bar,* p. 409). The evidence consisted of "congregated males [who] in a noticeably effeminate pitch of voice addressed each other affectionately as dearie, honey, doll, and darling" (Ibid.). They also "manipulated their cigarettes, giggled, rocked and swayed their posteriors in a maidenly fashion" (Ibid.). Other practices by patrons that marked premises as gay and therefore disorderly included men engaging in feminine actions and mannerisms; rolling their eyes at each other; bearing the odor of perfume; acting like man and wife; wearing eyebrow pencil, eyeshadow, or pancake makeup; calling each other such names as honey, doll, mary, or mother; conversing in a lisping tone of voice; using limp-wrist movements; extending their pinkies in a very dainty manner when they drank; and swishing and swaying when walking. Females were described as dressing in mannish attire, referring to companions as cute butches, and appearing to be men by their dress and makeup but actually being women who used the women's restroom.

In 1960, New York State's highest court upheld a ruling by the State Liquor Authority that the owner of the Fulton Bar in Brooklyn had permitted the bar to "be used as a gathering place for homosexuals and degenerates who conducted themselves in an offensive and indecent manner" because "the majority of the patrons were...wearing tight fitting trousers.... 3 male patrons walk[ed] to the rear of the premises with a sway to their hips...[and two of them spoke] in high pitched effeminate tones and...gesture[d] with limp wrists" (*Fulton Bar & Grill v. State Liquor Auth.,* quoted in Chauncey, p. 344). Thus, effeminate male and mannish female cultural practices were regarded as disorderly and sufficiently dangerous to the social order to merit prohibition and the revocation of a liquor license.

In New York State alone, the State Liquor Authority closed hundreds of bars and restaurants between the 1930s and the 1950s that allowed or failed to notice the patronage of lesbians and gay men. It was not until the 1950s that the courts made any effort to limit the power of the liquor licensing authorities, and well into the 1960s some state courts continued to find that the mere presence of persons manifesting the dress, mannerisms, speech and gestures commonly associated with homosexuals was sufficient grounds for license suspension or revocation. Only in 1971 did New York City eliminate the regulations prohibiting homosexuals from frequenting cabarets, dance halls, and catering establishments and from being employed in cabarets (Chauncey).

LESBIANS AND GAY MEN IN
THE CRIMINAL JUSTICE SYSTEM

The laws and regulations subordinating lesbians and gay men continued in force virtually unchallenged until the advent of the modern lesbian and gay civil rights era. An analysis of the present legal status of lesbians and gay men presents a vastly different picture, although many oppressive laws still remain. The rest of this chapter is devoted to a detailed description of the present legal landscape broken down by subject matter. The following sections will cover, in order of presentation, criminal law, lesbian and gay identity and association, employment law, and family law.

Much of lesbian and gay civil rights litigation has involved challenges to the constitutionality of various state and federal laws. Most rely on challenges brought pursuant to the United States Constitution; some have involved state constitutional challenges. A brief description of the primary constitutional legal theories employed in lesbian and gay rights litigation will enhance the lay reader's understanding of the material that follows.

The First and Fourteenth Amendments to the Constitution have been the primary vehicles for constitutional challenges. The First Amendment provides, in part, that "Congress shall make no law...abridging the freedom of speech, or of the press; or the right of the people peaceably to assemble, and to petition the Government for a redress of Grievances." First Amendment jurisprudence is extremely complex. However, at its core, the First Amendment is meant to protect individuals from undue federal, state, and local government intrusion into free expression. Free expression has been interpreted to encompass not only the freedom to speak out and publish, but also the freedom to associate—to form intimate relationships, groups, and communities for socializing, educating, support, or political activities.

In general, the state may not interfere with free expression so long as it is not obscene and there is no incitement to imminent lawless action. However, the state may often regulate conduct, particularly illegal conduct (sodomy in many states). The battleground in lesbian and gay First Amendment cases has often been the line between advocacy and regulation of illegal or "inappropriate" conduct. A second issue that often arises is whether it is the state or a private entity that is attempting to regulate speech or association. Only state action is covered by the First Amendment, and indeed freedom of association protects the right of private groups to restrict membership and speech.

The Fourteenth Amendment contains two distinct clauses that have provided the legal basis to attack homophobic laws. The first part of Section 1 provides, in part, that "...[no] state [shall] deprive any person of life, liberty or property, without due process of law...." The due process clause has been interpreted to protect individuals from arbitrary and capricious federal, state, or local government action that infringes upon a life, liberty, or property

interest. In most cases, the state's burden of justification is minimal; any rational reason for the state action that is not arbitrary will suffice. However, the Supreme Court has held that certain rights are fundamental. Where these rights are intruded on, the state must prove a compelling reason for its action and show that there is no less-restrictive alternative. This theory was used in sodomy law litigation in an effort to get the United States Supreme Court to declare a fundamental liberty interest in sexual privacy. The effort failed, as will be discussed in the next section of this chapter.

Section 1 of the Fourteenth Amendment also provides that "...[no] state [shall] ...deny to any person...the equal protection of the laws." The Equal Protection Clause acts to insure that state laws do not unfairly impact more harshly on some groups of citizens than others. Virtually all laws impact unequally; the question is when the unequal impact is unfair. In most instances, equal protection challenges will fail if the state is able to articulate any plausible and rational basis for the law. However, in certain instances the state will have a far greater burden. The Supreme Court has held that certain groups constitute suspect classes, and laws that impact on these groups unequally must be subjected to strict scrutiny. These groups include race, national origin, and alienage. Additionally, laws that regulate on the basis of gender are subject to an intermediate level of scrutiny. Such laws must be substantially related to an important government purpose. More recently, the Court has begun to apply what has been termed rational basis with a bite in some of its reviews. This means that the Court is requiring that the government actually show that there is a true rational basis for the law, rather than simply assuming that almost any government justification is acceptable.

Lesbian and gay rights litigators have consistently pressed the argument that sexual orientation should be treated as a suspect classification entitled to heightened scrutiny. Several lower courts have so held in various cases, but the Supreme Court has to date refused to apply more than a rational basis standard of review to classifications based on sexual orientation.

Sodomy Laws

The primary means of society's regulation of sexuality has been the criminal law. Various forms of sexual relations remain illegal in various states today, including prostitution, fornication, rape, incest, solicitation, and, first and foremost for its impact on the lives of lesbians and gay men, sodomy. Sodomy statutes are rarely enforced against consenting adults acting in private, but they are at the heart of legal discrimination against lesbians and gay men. Homosexuality is almost always associated with gay sexual conduct, and thus homosexuality is conflated with criminal activity. Most other discrimination against lesbians and gay men has been justified by the presumption that lesbians and gay men engage in conduct that is criminal and immoral. For instance, the city of Dallas, Texas, justified a policy, since abandoned, prohibiting lesbians and gay men from joining the police force on the grounds that persons who engage in conduct—sodomy—that is a crime in Texas are not eligible to be law enforcement officers. Employers and landlords have argued that they should not be forced to hire or rent to criminals, and sodomy laws have been used to deny custody and visitation to lesbian and gay parents. It is no wonder that the repeal of sodomy laws has been a primary goal of lesbian and gay civil rights.

Sodomy laws were in force in all fifty states until the 1960s. They remain in force in 19 states (NGLTF). The wording and practices actually forbidden by sodomy statutes vary. Most prohibit oral-genital and anal-genital contact and some include other specified acts. Many of the statutes are more general, prohibiting simply crimes against nature or deviant sexual intercourse. In 1973, the Supreme Court held that a generally worded sodomy law was not void for vagueness when read in conjunction with opinions by the state's highest court to apply to specific conduct (*Wainright v. Stone*).

In 1961, a report to the British Parliament by England's Commission on Homosexual Offenses and Prostitution, known as the Wolfenden Report, recommended to Parliament that sexual behavior between consenting adults be decriminalized. Influenced by that report, the 1962 revisions of the Model Penal Code, drafted by the American Law Institute to update and unify American criminal law, made a similar recommendation (Rubenstein). In 1961, Illinois became the first state to repeal its sodomy law when it adopted the Model Penal Code. A number of states followed in the 1960s and 1970s. Starting in the mid-1970s and continuing to the present, the emergence of the gay rights movement and of religious fundamentalism led to a backlash and the end of the repeal movement. Indeed, a number of states actually amended their criminal laws to specify that oral and anal sex was prohibited only between persons of the same sex, thus singling out homosexual acts as crimes. At present, five states have such same-sex sodomy laws (NGLTF).

With legislative repeal increasingly unlikely, lesbian and gay rights activists turned to the courts to challenge sodomy laws as violative of the constitutional right to privacy. These cases arose in many contexts: as defenses to criminal charges of violating the sodomy law, as defenses to refusal to hire or termination from employment justified by the existence of sodomy laws, and by civil test cases devised specifically to challenge such laws.

The right to privacy is nowhere explicitly mentioned in the U.S. Constitution. However, the Supreme Court had found such a right as part of the Fourteenth Amendment's guarantee of life, liberty, and the pursuit of happiness. Privacy was seen as part of a liberty right to autonomy and selfhood. The sodomy challenges looked to a line of cases in which the Supreme Court had found a fundamental right to privacy to use and sell contraceptives because of marital intimacy, a right of even single persons to make procreative choices, and a right of persons to view obscene materials (publications, movies, etc.) within the privacy of their homes. This led to a general argument that sexuality was not a matter of government concern when occurring in the private sphere. In 1981, the New York Court of Appeals struck down New York's sodomy law as applied to consensual sodomy as violative of this right to privacy in the case of *People v. Onofre*.

The Supreme Court finally agreed to hear a sodomy challenge in the case of *Bowers v. Hardwick*, which revolved around the constitutionality of the Georgia sodomy statute prohibiting both heterosexual and homosexual sodomy. The case grew out of an incident in August 1982, when Michael Hardwick was arrested by an Atlanta policeman for committing the crime of sodomy with a consenting adult in his own bedroom. The police were at his house to issue an unrelated warrant, although there is evidence to suggest that the warrant had been issued far more quickly than usual and immediately served personally by the arresting officer because of gay animus. The police were let in by a house guest and stood at the partly cracked bedroom door purposely witnessing the "crime" taking place within. Charges were brought against Hardwick, but the district attorney decided not to prosecute.

Hardwick, with the help of the ACLU, nevertheless brought a civil suit in federal court asking for a declaration that the Georgia statute was unconstitutional (Cain). The statute provided in part that "A person commits the offense of sodomy when he performs or submits to any sexual act involving the sex organs of one person and the mouth or anus of another." Conviction is punishable by imprisonment for not less than one nor more than twenty years. (Ga. Code Ann. SS. 16-6-2 [Michie 1984]).

The federal district court dismissed Hardwick's claim, the Eleventh Circuit reversed, and the Supreme Court agreed to hear the case on 4 November 1985. Hardwick argued that intimate sexual conduct between consenting adults is part of a fundamental right to privacy. If it is a fundamental right, Georgia must provide a compelling state interest for the statute and show that the means are narrowly tailored to accomplish the state interest. Even if there is no fundamental right to privacy, due process requires that there be a rational basis for the statute, although most statutes are able to survive this lesser standard. The Supreme Court upheld the sodomy statute, rejecting a fundamental right of privacy in same-sex sexual conduct. The Court also found that public morality provided a sufficient state interest, although there was absolutely no evidence in the record that the public opposed sodomy or that the law had any effect on public morality.

The opinion by Justice White and a concurring opinion by Justice Burger evince extreme homophobia and hostility to homosexuals as human beings. In spite of the fact that the Georgia statute in question prohibited both heterosexual and homosexual sodomy, and that Hardwick framed the question as one of privacy, the Court framed the issue before it as addressing only the fundamental right to commit homosexual sodomy. The Court went on to rewrite history and declare that the proscriptions against homosexual sodomy have ancient roots and that condemnation of "those practices" (quotations added) is firmly rooted in Judeo-Christian moral and ethical standards (see p. 81). In fact, the proscriptions were against heterosexual and homosexual sodomy and all non-marital sex.

Hardwick was a major setback in the fight to end discrimination against lesbians and gay men and substantially changed the course of gay rights litigation. It has meant that in the federal courts it is necessary to avoid privacy arguments and any claims that sexual conduct is constitutionally protected. The conduct/status distinction, first enunciated in the state liquor licensing cases, has become central to constitutional challenges to discrimination against lesbians and gay men. This has especially been true in the military cases. The argument made is that states cannot discriminate against homosexuals as a class in matters unrelated to sexual conduct. These cases are generally brought pursuant to the Equal Protection Clause of the Fourteenth Amendment to the Constitution, which has been interpreted to require heightened judicial scrutiny for legislative classifications based on race, sex, and national origin. Gay rights litigators have urged the courts to find that classifications based on sexual orientation should also be entitled to heightened scrutiny, thereby requiring the state to provide a substantial justification for the classification. The response from the courts to these arguments has been mostly negative. Most say that *Hardwick* is dispositive: if there is no constitutional protection for homosexual conduct, and the category homosexual is defined by those who engage in homosexual conduct, there can be no special protection for persons within that category. Again, status is equated with conduct.

Since *Hardwick*, challenges to the remaining sodomy laws have shifted to state courts and state constitutional grounds, with some success. In 1992, the Kentucky Supreme Court ruled in *Commonwealth v. Wasson* (842 W.W.2d 487 [Ky. 1992]) that its same-sex-only sodomy law violated both the privacy and equal protection guarantees of the state constitution. In Tennessee, Michigan, and Texas, same-sex-only sodomy statutes were also found to violate the state constitution by trial and intermediate level courts. In all three states, further appeals to the highest state courts were either rejected or no appeals were taken by the states. Similar challenges have been ultimately unsuccessful in Georgia, Louisiana, and Missouri. Thus, the Supreme Court's decision in *Hardwick* has made it possible for sodomy statutes to continue to stigmatize lesbians and gay men in half the states in this country.

Solicitation and Loitering Laws

The decision in *Hardwick* has meant that lesbians and gay men continue to risk arrest simply by expressing their love for one another. However, sodomy laws are rarely directly enforced. The primary means of regulating gay sexual activity are laws proscribing solicitation, loitering, lewd and lascivious behavior, and indecent exposure. Gay men, in particular, are arrested for engaging in sex acts in quasi-public places such as parked cars, parks, and restrooms. These statutes have been challenged, usually on the ground that they are discriminatorily enforced against gay men, but courts have not been sympathetic to the constitutional issues raised. Enforcement most often occurs through the use of plainclothes police officers who are dispatched to "known" gay pickup spots. This raises the possibility of an entrapment defense, but the law holds that there is no entrapment where the defendant has the intent and design to commit the crime and the officer merely furnishes the opportunity.

Bias Crimes

Society has become increasingly concerned about crimes committed against individuals targeted on the basis of their race, gender, or sexual orientation. In 1990, Congress passed the Hate Crimes Statistics Act (28 usca ss934 [1990]), which mandates the Justice Department to acquire data on crimes evidencing prejudice based on race, religion, sexual orientation, or ethnicity. Disability has subsequently been added to the list of bias motivated crimes. The Criminal Justice Information Division of the FBI is in charge of collecting the data. Not all jurisdictions are as yet reporting statistics as required, and reports undoubtedly represent only a fraction of the actual number of incidents. Nevertheless, in 1996, the FBI reported 1,016 sexual orientation bias-motivated criminal incidents, representing almost 12 percent of all reported bias incidents. Most of these crimes were committed against gay men.

As a response to increased awareness of what have been termed hate or bias crimes, states and local governments have attempted to use the criminal justice system to both punish perpetrators of hate crimes and deter their commission. Two types of legislation were initially passed: legislation that created a separate crime for hate-motivated misconduct, and legislation that allowed for an enhanced sentence for otherwise criminal conduct motivated by bias. In *R.A.V. v. City of St. Paul* (505us377[1992]), the Supreme Court struck down a St. Paul, Minnesota, ordinance that made it a misdemeanor to engage in certain conduct that one knows or should know arouses anger, resentment, etc., in others on the basis of race, color, creed, religion, or gender. The court held that such an ordinance is a content-based regulation of speech, since it punishes action, in this case the burning of a cross on a black family's lawn, on the basis of the subject the speech addresses. The Court's holding effectively precludes the creation of separate bias crimes.

However, a later Supreme Court case, *Wisconsin v. Todd Mitchell* (508 us476 [1993]), upheld the use of statutes that allow enhanced sentences for another crime, if the victim was intentionally selected because of his or her actual or perceived membership in a protected group. The challenge for lesbians and gay men is fighting for inclusion of crimes committed on the basis of sexual orientation among those denominated bias crimes entitled to enhanced sentencing. At present, 21 states and the District of Columbia have hate crime laws that include sexual orientation. An additional 19 states have laws that do not include crimes based on sexual orientation. The federal government has also passed a law, the Violent Crime Control and Law Enforcement Act of 1994, providing sentencing enhancement of not less than three offense levels for federal crimes determined to be hate crimes. This law includes sexual orientation. However, Congress has refused to include sexual orientation in the list of bias crimes over which the federal government has assumed jurisdiction, allowing the government to prosecute what would otherwise be state crimes.

Even in those states where enhancement legislation is in place, an additional challenge is ensuring that judges are unbiased in the exercise of their sentencing discretion. Some judges actually impose lesser sentences for crimes committed against lesbians and gay men. A particularly glaring example of this form of homophobia occurred in Texas in 1988, when a Dallas County district judge sentenced the murderer of two gay men to 30 years in prison, making him eligible for parole in 7½ years. Judge Hampton stated that he had given the murderer a lighter sentence because the victims were queers who would not have been killed if they were not out cruising the streets and trying to spread AIDS. He also noted that some murder victims were less innocent than others and said he would put prostitutes and gays at about the same level. In spite of calls for his ouster, the Texas Supreme Court concluded that the judge had not violated judicial conduct standards. Judge Hampton remained on the bench until his retirement in 1997.

LESBIAN AND GAY IDENTITY, ASSOCIATION, AND POLITICAL ACTIVITY

Lesbian and gay identity involves more than sexual object choice or a focus on the individual. Identity is developed and expressed through speech, association with others, media coverage and portrayals, and the formation of political and social groups and organizations. All of these are a prerequisite to achieving civil rights, breaking down stereotypes, and redefining the meaning of gender and the binary categories of hetero/homosexuality. None can occur without the ability to come out without fear of retribution. In the past, the government has clearly understood the link between the closet and identity formation. Indeed, the laws passed from the 1930s to the 1950s were designed to silence all public representations or acknowledgment of homosexuality. Thus, ensuring legal protection for public statements and rallies, publications, and organizations has been a primary goal of the lesbian and gay civil rights movement.

The primary legal mechanism used to challenge suppression of gay identity has been the First Amendment, which protects government intrusion into both free speech and free association. The core of First Amendment protection has always been political speech. Speech about sexuality was excluded from such protection until the late 1950s, when the Supreme Court began broadening protection for sexual speech that was not obscene. However, sexual speech is still treated differently and granted less protection than political speech. Challenges to government regulation of the lives of lesbians and gay men has substantially eroded the boundaries between political and sexual speech as the courts have acknowledged that speech and association about one's sexual identity is itself political (Eskridge & Hunter). This section will cover speech and associational rights in the political arena, within the educational setting, and in other social settings.

Association

The introduction of lesbian and gay civil rights protections and the general increasing activism and success of lesbian and gay political activity has increasingly led to an antigay backlash. One of the most prevalent means of expressing this backlash has been the antigay ballot measure. These ballot measures can take a number of forms. An initiative is a measure in which a certain percentage of the electorate may petition to have a proposed statute or constitutional amendment put directly on the ballot for vote by the electorate. A referendum is a method whereby the electorate may approve or disapprove of a law proposed or already enacted by the legislature. Almost half the states have some form of initiative and three fourths have some form of referendum (Eskridge). Initiatives and referenda may also be available at the local level.

Between 1972 and 1996, approximately 75 antigay ballot proposals were put before voters (Eskridge). The first was Anita Bryant's Save the Children campaign in 1977 to revoke Dade County's anti-discrimination measures. The initiative won. The first statewide initiative was the Briggs Amendment in California in 1978, which targeted lesbian and gay teachers by empowering school boards to fire or refuse to hire teachers for soliciting, imposing, encouraging, or promoting homosexual conduct (Eskridge). The amendment was defeated. In 1988, Oregon approved Measure 8, overturning a gubernatorial Executive Order protecting state employees from discrimination on the basis of sexual orientation. This began a new wave of antigay initiatives aimed at nullifying municipal and county gay rights ordinances.

In 1992, both Colorado and Oregon had state-wide ballot initiatives to repeal all gay rights ordinances in the state and to prevent the enactment of any future gay civil rights laws unless passed by a constitutional amendment. Oregon's initiative also affirmatively obligated the government to teach that homosexuality is wrong, unnatural, and perverse. Both initiatives attempted to place a unique political disability on lesbians and gays, providing that they were the only ones among citizen groups barred from seeking civil rights legislation. The Oregon initiative was defeated, but Colorado's Amendment 2 was approved by the voters (see p. 87).

Suit was immediately filed challenging the constitutionality of Amendment 2. In what is perhaps the single most important legal victory in the fight for lesbian and gay civil rights, the Supreme Court in 1996 invalidated Amendment 2 as unconstitutional. The case, *Romer v. Evans*, is important not only for its result, but for its tone. Coming a mere ten years after the virulent homophobia

of *Bowers v. Hardwick*, *Romer* makes clear that lesbians and gay men are entitled to full rights of citizenship. The opinion starts with a quote from the dissent in *Plessy v. Ferguson* (in which the majority upheld segregation through the concept of separate but equal) that the constitution "neither knows nor tolerates classes among citizens" (163 U.S. 537, 559 [1896]). There is a strong suggestion that the Court's legal treatment of lesbians and gays may hark back to the errors made in the legal treatment of blacks exactly one hundred years earlier, perhaps referring to *Hardwick* as the Supreme Court's gay rights *Plessy*. The full impact of *Romer* on *Hardwick* remains to be seen, especially since the *Romer* opinion made no mention whatsoever of *Hardwick*.

The Court struck down Amendment 2 on the grounds that it violated the Equal Protection Clause of the Fourteenth Amendment. It did not find that sexual orientation was a suspect class, but rather that Colorado failed to articulate even a rational basis for the Amendment. In response to the argument that all the Amendment did was deny homosexuals special rights, the Court stated that there was nothing special in the protections Amendment 2 withholds, protections taken for granted by most people. "Homosexuals, by state decree, are put in a solitary class with respect to transactions and relations in both the private and governmental spheres. The amendment withdraws from homosexuals, but no others, specific legal protection from the injuries caused by discrimination, and it forbids reinstatement of these laws and policies" (*Romer*). The Court goes on to note that the sheer breadth of Amendment 2 is so discontinuous with the reason offered for it that it is inexplicable by anything but animus towards homosexuals, an impermissible state interest. The opinion ends: "We must conclude that Amendment 2 classifies homosexuals not to further a proper legislative end but to make them unequal to everyone else. This Colorado cannot do. A State cannot so deem a class of persons a stranger to its laws" (*Romer*; see p. 88 in "Significant Documents" chapter).

Whatever the positive impact of *Romer*, it will not end the antigay initiative and referendum backlash. The most recent proof of this lies in the February 1998 repeal of Maine's sexual orientation anti-discrimination law in a statewide referendum. *Romer* does seem to hold, however, that animosity towards homosexuals does not constitute a legitimate governmental interest justifying discrimination.

EDUCATIONAL ISSUES AND CASES

Student Expression in High School

In recent years, the Supreme Court has greatly restricted student rights. The Court has articulated a theory of public school education focused on preparing pupils for citizenship and inculcating civility and other fundamental values, and education that requires that free speech rights be balanced against the public interest in teaching students the boundaries of socially appropriate behavior. The Court has made clear that the question of what speech in a classroom, school assembly, or school function is inappropriate rests primarily with the school board, which will be given broad deference (Eskridge & Hunter). Thus, for instance, schools may censor school newspapers and have no obligation to teach students about sex. Likewise, few schools permit useful counseling to gay teenagers or the dissemination of accurate information about their sexual orientation. School boards regularly reject books with tolerant or positive views of homosexuality and disallow any reference to homosexuality in the curriculum. Given the broad deference paid to school boards and the limited legal rights afforded students, legal strategies well worth considering in this area include a legislative strategy on the state and/or local level, and political organizing to influence school boards at both election and policy-making levels.

Although states are not obligated to teach sex education, most states do. The question is what are they teaching. State laws governing sex education and AIDS education exist in most states. These laws generally require factual accuracy and that the content not include religious beliefs or training. Concerning information on homosexuality, some statutes require that there be no reference to homosexuality in the curriculum; some require the provision of information from all sides of the issue and encourage tolerance; and others affirmatively include "no promo homo" policies, which require that sex education send a negative message, not "promote" a homosexual lifestyle or portray it as a positive alternative (Eskridge & Hunter).

In spite of the broad deference paid school boards, there have been some successful challenges to restrictions on lesbian and gay students' rights of free expression. The first major triumph for an openly gay high school student came in the case of *Fricke v. Lynch* (491 F. Supp. 381 [D. R.I. 1980]). Aaron Fricke sued his high school for refusing to allow him to bring another male to the senior prom. He sought a preliminary injunction arguing that the school's refusal violated his First Amendment rights. The school's primary justification was fear of disruption and a potential threat of violence at the prom. The court acknowledged that Aaron's desire to attend the prom with another man was entitled to First Amendment protection because of its communicative content. The court recognized that the communicative content was political, not just sexual. The message conveyed is that homosexuals exist, feel repressed, and wish to emerge from isolation. While acknowledging that the school does have an important interest in student safety and the power to regulate student conduct, barring Aaron from the prom was not the least-restrictive alternative. The court refused to allow a hecklers veto, and Aaron Fricke attended his prom without incident. *Fricke* was only a trial court decision, and subsequent Supreme Court cases may have undermined its reasoning, but it has not been overruled.

A second important area in which student expression and association may be protected is in the formation of noncurriculum related lesbian and gay clubs. In 1984, Congress passed the Equal Access Act (20 U.S.C. ss. 4071-4074), which provides that public secondary schools receiving federal financial assistance create a limited public forum when they grant the opportunity for one or more noncurriculum-related student groups to meet on school premises during noninstructional time, and must, therefore, provide equal access to all such student groups or risk losing federal funding. The purpose of the Act was to ensure that student-sponsored religious clubs would be allowed to operate on school premises. An ironic consequence is that the Act also protects the right of lesbian and gay student groups to meet on school premises.

However, the State of Utah provides a cautionary tale on the battles that lie ahead even with the Equal Access Act. During the 1995-96 school year, students at a Salt Lake City High School attempted to form a gay and lesbian student group. The Salt Lake City Board of Education tried to ban the group following a public outcry, but was advised that it could not do so unless it banned all noncurriculum-related clubs. In a close 4-3 vote, the Board then agreed to eliminate all clubs not tied to courses taught at Salt Lake City High Schools,

effective in the Fall of 1996. The state legislature then passed legislation requiring that local school districts ban clubs that encourage criminal or delinquent conduct, involve human sexuality, or promote bigotry; the legislation also stated that school districts may require every student to obtain written permission from a parent or guardian to participate in extracurricular clubs.

On 19 March 1998, Lambda Legal Defense and Education Fund, along with three other civil rights groups, filed suit against Salt Lake City on behalf of the East High Gay/Straight Alliance. The suit alleges a violation of the Equal Access Act because the high school banned some non-curricula clubs and not others by improperly reclassifying some clubs as curricula and allowing others to meet unofficially. The suit also includes First Amendment free speech and association and Fourteenth Amendment Equal Protection claims. Similar battles are being waged or can be anticipated in other school districts.

A major victory in the protection of students who are identified or identify themselves as lesbian or gay came in the case of *Nabozny v. Podlesny* (92 F.3d 466 [Seventh Cir. 1996]). For years, Jamie Nabozny suffered verbal and physical attacks from other students in the Ashland, Wisconsin, school system. Despite repeated requests for assistance by Jamie and his parents, the administrators of his school did nothing. Even after he was hospitalized as a result of being kicked and beaten, his school principal did nothing. Jamie fought back and, represented by Lambda Legal Defense and Education Fund, went to court. The case was dismissed at the trial level, but in a groundbreaking decision, the Seventh Circuit Court of Appeals held that Jamie had stated a claim for discrimination on the basis of both sex and sexual orientation. The court held that if a female student with similar complaints of harassment would have been treated differently, then the school's inaction in the face of Jamie's harassment constituted sex discrimination in violation of the Equal Protection Clause of the Fourteenth Amendment to the U.S. Constitution. In fact, there was evidence that the school had punished male-on-female harassment. The court also found a violation of the Equal Protection Clause based on sexual orientation discrimination because there was no rational basis for allowing harassment and violence against students because of their sexual orientation. The court sent the case back to the lower court for a trial. At this point, the school district settled the case, agreeing to pay Jamie more than $900,000 for his pain and suffering.

Following the *Nabozny* case, several other school harassment cases have been brought. Lawyers are also attempting new legal strategies in this area. Lambda has recently filed a complaint with the Office of Civil Rights at the U.S. Department of Education claiming that a gay high school student's rights under Title IX of the U.S. Civil Rights Act have been violated. Title IX prohibits sex discrimination in schools and has been held to cover sexual harassment.

Student Expression at Colleges and Universities

Historically, many state universities refused to recognize, fund, and give equal facility access to lesbian and gay student organizations. Universities argued that the existence of such organizations would serve to recruit or turn latent homosexuals into active ones; that allowing such groups would have a negative impact on the universities' relations with the public; that the university had an obligation not to support abnormal behavior; and, where sodomy laws were in place, that such organizations promoted criminal conduct. Uniformly, these refusals have been successfully challenged as violations of the First Amendment.

In *NAACP v. Alabama* (357 U.S. 449 [1958]), the Supreme Court recognized that a prerequisite to the right to speak was the right to assemble or associate. Thus, where a state regulates the ability of individuals to associate for a content-based purpose, the state must show that the regulation is narrowly tailored to meet a compelling state interest. Distinguishing between status and conduct, courts have held that universities may regulate homosexual conduct but not the right to advocate and advance ideas. Thus, organizations formed to discuss ideas, educate about homosexuality, or for social purposes must be allowed. Although efforts to ban lesbian and gay student organizations at state universities have all met with failure, the effort persists.

Most recently, several states including Florida and Alabama have passed state-wide legislation forbidding lesbian and gay student groups on college and university campuses. The Alabama law provided that no public funds or facilities may be used to finance any educational institution that sanctions, recognizes, or supports the activities of an organization that fosters or approves of a lifestyle prohibited by the sodomy laws. The statute attempted to circumvent First Amendment objections by stating that the law did not apply if an organization was founded for the sole purpose of advocacy of change to the sodomy law, thus purporting to distinguish between the regulation of speech and conduct (Alabama Code ss16-1-28). In *Gay Lesbian Bisexual Alliance v. Pryor*, the Eleventh Circuit Court of Appeals struck down the Alabama law, holding that it violates the First Amendment, since advocacy to violate a law constitutes protected speech and the state was attempting to ban speech on the basis of its viewpoint. Nevertheless, the Alabama legislation illustrates both the continued determination on the part of conservatives to prevent any views or organizations supportive of lesbians and gays in public educational institutions, and the increasing sophistication of legislative efforts to achieve their goal.

Where students are banned from forming or gaining full access to money and facilities at a private university, there is considerably less recourse. The First Amendment reaches only state action. Thus, actions by private schools are not subject to First Amendment restrictions. If the university is in a jurisdiction, state, or municipality covered by a human rights law that forbids discrimination in public accommodations on the basis of sexual orientation, the human rights law may provide an avenue for suit. The best known attempt to use such a human rights law to challenge a university's attempt to ban a lesbian and gay campus group occurred in a lawsuit against Georgetown University. It pitted the District of Columbia's non-discrimination law against Georgetown's argument that as a religiously affiliated institution it was entitled to free exercise of its religious beliefs. In the end, the D.C. Court of Appeals held that Georgetown did not have to recognize or endorse the group but did have to provide equal benefits to it. Importantly for future cases, the court did find that Georgetown was covered by the Human Rights Law as a place of public accommodation. Thereafter, Congress imposed an amendment to the human rights law exempting Georgetown and other religiously affiliated institutions from the gay rights law. Georgetown has, however, adhered to the decision and has continued to provide equal benefits to lesbian and gay student groups.

Other Youth Organizations

A variety of private national organizations serve the needs of young people outside of educational institutions, chief among them the Boy Scouts, the Girl Scouts, Big Brothers/Big Sisters, the YMCA, and the YWCA. Only the Boy Scouts adheres to a per se ban on gay and lesbian membership and leadership positions. A number of lawsuits are pending challenging this policy. The lawsuits have been brought pursuant to local or state laws prohibiting discrimination on the basis of sexual orientation. In order for the lawsuits to prevail, a court must find that the Boy Scouts organization is a place of public accommodation and that the nondiscrimination law does not infringe on the organization's First Amendment rights of association. These arguments have met with mixed success in California, where one intermediate appellate court has ruled that the Boy Scouts are not a public accommodation covered by the state's Unrah Act and that in any case the nondiscrimination law would infringe on their First Amendment rights. A California superior court judge in San Diego has disagreed and found that the Boy Scouts could not exclude a gay scout leader. Most recently, in *Dale v. Boy Scouts of America*, a New Jersey intermediate appellate court ruled that the Boy Scouts are a place of public accommodation under the New Jersey Law Against Discrimination and that LAD's prohibition against discrimination does not infringe on the Boy Scout's freedom of association. In the New Jersey case, Dale, a former Eagle Scout and assistant Scoutmaster, was dismissed after appearing in a newspaper photograph of a gay youth conference.

In jurisdictions without nondiscrimination laws that include sexual orientation, successful legal challenges to privately run organizations serving youth are difficult. However, non-litigation public pressure may be brought to bear. For instance, local chapters of the United Way in San Francisco; Portland, Maine; and New Haven, Connecticut, have all retracted commitments of financial support to the Boy Scouts because of its ban on gay scouts (Rubenstein, 321).

LESBIAN AND GAY SOCIAL LIFE

State Efforts to Bar Lesbian and Gay Association

An earlier section of this chapter details the historic efforts of federal, state, and local governments to ban the lesbian and gay world from the public sphere, particularly through the denial of liquor licenses to bars and restaurants serving gay persons. While the law is now clear that a liquor license may not be denied or revoked merely because of the presence of lesbian and gay patrons, states continue to retain the power to grant or deny liquor licenses taking into account issues of public welfare, morality and decency. Thus, confrontations between gay bars and liquor licensing authorities over "conduct"-related issues remains an ever-present possibility.

Litigation has occurred in several other areas in which the state has attempted to interfere with lesbian and gay efforts to undertake social and associational activities. For instance, in a particularly ironic act, Lambda Legal Defense and Education Fund's first client was itself, when the New York Secretary of State refused to incorporate it on grounds that it was contrary to public policy to incorporate an avowed homosexual organization. In 1972, the highest court in New York held that the Secretary of State's actions were arbitrary and ordered Lambda's incorporation (In re

Thom). The practice of attempting to deny incorporation for lesbian and gay organizations appears to have ceased, but the difficulty some lesbian and gay nonprofit organizations have experienced in seeking federal tax-exempt status from the Internal Revenue Service appears to be ongoing. In the past year, several such organizations were initially denied tax-exempt status, although the national outcry caused a quick reversal from the IRS.

Efforts by lesbian and gay organizations to advertise in government-sponsored publications has also met resistance, although the law seems clear that where the government itself has sponsored the publication and created a limited public forum, the First Amendment protects the right of lesbian and gay groups to advertise. Where the classified advertising section of a private newspaper or the privately owned Yellow Pages is involved, the courts have found no legal obligation to accept lesbian and gay advertising and listings. Grassroots and legal pressure has, however, persuaded Yellow Pages publishers in most parts of the country to accept lesbian and gay ads (Rubenstein, p. 374).

Efforts by Private Organizations to Bar Lesbians and Gay Men

Private non-governmental organizations have successfully barred lesbian and gay participation in a number of highly visible clashes. Because constitutional protections are not available where there is no governmental action, lesbians and gay men have relied on non-discrimination statutes to challenge exclusions by private organizations. The most recent clashes have occurred over efforts by lesbian and gay groups to march in the Boston and New York Saint Patrick's Day parades. The legal battles culminated in a Supreme Court ruling in *Hurley v. Irish-American Gay, Lesbian and Bisexual Group of Boston (GLIB)*. In 1992, a group of gay, lesbian, and bisexual Irish-Americans petitioned the association sponsoring the Boston parade to march as a group, as a way of expressing pride in their Irish heritage as openly lesbian and gay individuals and to demonstrate the existence of such a group. The council denied GLIB's application, and GLIB filed suit. The Supreme Court held that the parade was not a place of public accommodation, but rather a privately run parade with its own expressive content. To order the inclusion of GLIB would be to violate the parade organizer's First Amendment rights of expression and association.

LESBIANS AND GAY MEN IN THE WORKPLACE

Lesbians and gay men face considerable discrimination in the workplace. Some employers explicitly or implicitly try to terminate or refuse to hire, persons on the basis of their sexual orientation. Often, the discrimination is more subtle, causing individuals to hide their sexual orientation in the workplace, suffering the psychological, emotional, and performance consequences of remaining in the closet. On a more concrete level, same-sex couples are most often denied the considerable employment benefits married persons receive for their spouses, including health insurance, family leave, and spousal pension benefits. This section will focus on the extent to which employment discrimination laws protect lesbians and gay men in the workplace. It is divided into two main sections: private employment and public employment. Within public employment, separate subsections will address the unique issues applying to teachers, those seeking security clearances, and the military.

Private Employment

The traditional legal relationship governing relations between employees and employers in the workplace is that of employment at will. This means that employees may be hired or fired at the will of the employer, for any reason or no reason at all. Over the past 50 years, the employment-at-will doctrine has been altered and eroded considerably by expanded statutory and common-law rights for employees. For purposes of protection of lesbians and gay men in the workplace, statutes prohibiting discrimination in the workplace have been the most important. The laws governing non-discrimination are a complex web of federal, state, and local laws, executive orders, regulations, and case law.

The most important and comprehensive of the employment discrimination laws is Title VII of the Civil Rights Act of 1964 (42 U.S.C. ss2000e-2000e-17 [1988]), a federal law prohibiting discrimination in both private and public employment on the basis of race, color, religion, sex, or national origin. Additional federal legislation prohibits discrimination on the basis of age, and the Americans with Disabilities Act (42 U.S.C.A. ss12101 [West Supp.1992]) prohibits disability discrimination. Most states have laws paralleling the federal statutes, as do many municipalities. There is no federal law prohibiting discrimination on the basis of sexual orientation, although there has been one pending in Congress since 1974. The present version, the Employment Non-Discrimination Act (ENDA), presently has more than 35 signatories in the Senate and more than 156 in the House, and came within one vote of passage in the Senate in 1996. In 1996, hearings were held on ENDA for the first time in the House. Additionally, the Americans with Disabilities Act provides protection from discrimination based on HIV status. Given the lack of protection from discrimination in federal laws, lesbians and gay men have turned to state and local laws for protection. At present, ten states have laws that ban discrimination on the basis of sexual orientation, including California, Connecticut, Hawaii, Massachusetts, Minnesota, New Hampshire, New Jersey, Rhode Island, Vermont, and Wisconsin. More than 100 municipalities also include sexual orientation in their non-discrimination laws. Some municipal non-discrimination laws go beyond sexual orientation and include protection for transgendered persons or on the basis of dress and appearance.

Hiring and Firing on the Basis of Sexual Orientation. Following passage of Title VII, efforts were made to include sexual orientation discrimination as a form of sex discrimination covered by the Civil Rights Act. Two arguments were made. The first was that the refusal to hire a female employee because she has a female lover is an action that would not be taken against a similarly situated male employee with a female lover. Thus, but for the employee's sex (female), she would have been hired. The leading case rejecting that argument is the Ninth Circuit decision in *DeSantis v. Pacific Telephone & Telegraph Co.* All courts that have considered the question have followed this ruling, holding that sexual orientation discrimination is not sex discrimination within the meaning of Title VII. Courts have also held that discrimination against transsexuals is not prohibited sex discrimination under Title VII.

A second argument put forth and rejected in *DeSantis* was that plaintiffs suffered discrimination for being effeminate and not conforming to gender stereotypes. However, in 1989, the U.S. Supreme Court held that Price Waterhouse had engaged in gender discrimination when it refused to admit Ann Hopkins to partnership on the basis of sex stereotyping (*Price Waterhouse v. Hopkins*). Evidence showed that Hopkins was rejected because she did not fit the proper stereotype of a woman; she was aggressive, required a course in charm school, was macho, and, according to her employers, should "walk more femininely, talk more femininely, dress more femininely, wear make-up, have her hair styled, and wear jewelry." While there are still no cases holding that discrimination against effeminate men constitutes gender discrimination under Title VII, *Hopkins* supports the argument that sexual orientation discrimination is directly related with gender role stereotyping and therefore with Title VII sex discrimination.

Although Title VII has yet to prove a useful vehicle in combating sexual orientation discrimination, the Americans with Disabilities Act provides protection in a limited category of cases. The ADA prohibits discrimination against persons with disabilities who are qualified to perform a job with or without reasonable accommodation. It covers discrimination on the basis of having a disability, having a record of disability, being perceived to have a disability, or because of association with someone with a disability. Thus, it covers persons with AIDS and persons who are perceived to have AIDS because of their sexual orientation, or are discriminated against because their partner or other loved one has AIDS. In a major victory for scope of coverage, the Supreme Court ruled in *Abbott v. Bragdon* that HIV infection satisfies the statutory and regulatory definition of a physical impairment during every stage of the disease, even if the person is asymptomatic.

State and local laws provide far better avenues for relief from sexual orientation discrimination where such laws are available. The first statewide protection against sexual orientation discrimination came in California from the California Supreme Court, which held that "coming out" constituted protected political activity under the State Labor Code (*Gay Law Students Association v. Pacific Telephone and Telegraph Company*). The case reflects recognition of the political content of merely announcing one's sexual orientation in the workplace. In 1993, California enacted an explicit prohibition against sexual orientation discrimination in private employment as part of the Labor Code.

Although such policies do not have the same force of law, hundreds of private companies have adopted non-discrimination policies that include sexual orientation, including more than 50 percent of the Fortune 500 companies. Most of these policies do not reach the status of an employment contract between the employee and the company, and therefore failure of the company to follow its own policy may not provide a legal cause of action. However, in some instances such policies will be held to have created an explicit or implicit contract, allowing suit for breach of contract for failure to comply with the policy. Additionally, most companies provide internal grievance procedures and discipline for violation of company policies.

In those states and municipalities without non-discrimination laws, sexual orientation discrimination by private employers is perfectly legal. The 1997 Congressional hearings on the Employment Non-Discrimination Act graphically documented the human cost of this lack of protection. The story of Cracker Barrel Old Country Store restaurant provides a concrete example of homophobia in the workplace, as well as the use of creative alternative strategies to fight back when there is no direct legal recourse. In 1991, Cracker Barrel adopted a policy stating that the restaurant chain would no longer employ people "whose sexual preferences fail to demonstrate normal heterosexual values." As a result, about a dozen employees were fired. The uproar and a gay-led boycott

caused the chain to rescind its policy, although it did not rehire the terminated workers. Shareholders critical of the policy sought to include a resolution in Cracker Barrel's annual proxy vote, calling on the company to ban discrimination on the basis of sexual orientation. The company refused to include the proposal in proxy materials, and in 1992, the Securities and Exchange Commission ruled that the company's employment policies and practices concerning non-executive employees does not have to be put to shareholder votes. In May 1998, the SEC reversed its ruling and held that companies must permit shareholder votes on "significant social policy issues" relating to employment, such as job discrimination (*The Washington Blade*). In addition to the potential to put pressure on private corporations through shareholder resolutions, pressure to get corporations to include sexual orientation in their non-discrimination policies has come from gay employee groups, the perceived consumer clout of gays, publicity, and pressure from a number of organizations focusing on workplace fairness issues.

Harassment in the Workplace. In addition to prohibiting discrimination in hiring and firing, Title VII and virtually all state and local non-discrimination statutes prohibit discrimination in terms and conditions of work, including workplace environment. The Supreme Court has held that Title VII prohibits sexual harassment when the harassment is sufficiently severe or pervasive to alter the conditions of a victim's employment and create an abusive work environment. The Court has delineated two forms of actionable sexual harassment: quid pro quo harassment, in which workplace benefits are offered by a supervisor in exchange for sexual favors, and hostile environment harassment. Courts have uniformly rejected the argument that harassment of an employee because s/he is lesbian or gay constitutes sexual harassment under Title VII. In one case, *Dillon v. Frank*, the Sixth Circuit Court of Appeals found that Ernest Dillon was taunted, ostracized, and physically beaten by his co-workers because of their belief that he was a homosexual. Nevertheless, the court held that the antigay harassment was not based upon Dillon's sex, but was based upon his sexual orientation.

A related question is whether Title VII covers claims of same-sex harassment. These claims arise in several different contexts. Some involve employees allegedly harassed by gay/lesbian supervisors in quid pro quo cases. These cases fit the classic stereotype of the gay sexual predator, and lower courts have generally found that these cases are actionable under Title VII because the employee would not have been harassed by her/his employer but for her/his sex. The second type of case arises where an employee claims to have been subjected to a sexually hostile work environment by supervisors and/or co-workers of the same sex, but not explicitly because of a belief or knowledge that the employee is lesbian or gay. In many of these cases, the facts suggest that the employee has failed to conform to societal expectations of gender role behavior. Most lower courts have held that this type of same-sex harassment does not state a claim under Title VII, although their reasoning was inconsistent with Title VII legal theories.

One such case involved Joseph Oncale, a roustabout on an oil platform in the Gulf of Mexico. Oncale alleged that he was forcibly subjected to sexually humiliating acts by members of his all-male crew, sexually assaulted, and threatened with rape. On 4 March 1998, the Supreme Court held that Title VII prohibits same-sex harassment in *Oncale v. Sundowner Offshore Services, Inc.* While making clear that there is a cause of action for same-sex hostile environment harassment, the Court was less clear as to what is necessary to successfully make out a cause of action.

The Court emphasized that the mere fact that the harassment is sexual does not create a cause of action for sexual harassment. An employee must prove that the harassment was because of her/his gender. Thus, it appears that most quid pro quo claims would create a cause of action, and that mere sexual horsing around would not. What remains unclear is whether harassment of someone because he is not sufficiently masculine or she is not sufficiently feminine will satisfy the "because of gender" requirement. The argument that it should is based on the sex stereotyping argument and the extent to which this type or harassment is meant to police the production of properly masculine men and feminine women.

Public Employment

Most of the federal anti-discrimination laws covering private employees also apply to government employees, including Title VII, the Age Discrimination in Employment Act, and the ADA, which covers state and local government employees; federal employees are protected from disability discrimination by the Rehabilitation Act of 1973. For the most part, these statutes fail to provide protection for discrimination based on sexual orientation. However, public employees are also protected by civil service rules and constitutional law. Prior to the 1960s, neither the constitution nor civil service regulations provided any protection for lesbians and gay men. To the contrary, as discussed earlier in this chapter, homosexuality was considered grounds for discharge and homosexuals were actively sought out for separation from their government jobs.

General Civil Service Standard. It is now a well-established civil service principle that if an individual's sexual orientation does not affect the efficiency of the service, disrupt the workplace, or impact negatively on the government's public reputation, discrimination is prohibited. The federal government has adopted personnel policies codifying this standard, and many local civil service and personnel policies explicitly prohibit discrimination on the basis of sexual orientation. During the Clinton Administration, most federal agencies adopted explicit policies stating that they would not discriminate on the basis of sexual orientation, and in May 1998 President Clinton issued an Executive Order adding sexual orientation to the list of items for which discrimination is prohibited in the government, thus making non-discrimination standard across all federal agencies. The efficiency of the service standard, however, is fairly vague and ill defined. In an examination of the civil service case law, several relevant factors emerge in determining whether a person's employment disrupts the workplace, including the nexus between sexual orientation and effect on job performance, type of workplace at issue, and how open the employee is about her/his sexual orientation.

An examination of some of the case law reveals the troubling aspects of the general civil service standard. The seminal case articulating the need for a nexus between private conduct and workplace performance was the 1969 District of Columbia Circuit Court decision in *Norton v. Macy.* Norton was arrested for a traffic violation after allegedly being observed picking up another man near a public park. The police notified the security chief at the government agency where he worked, and Norton was terminated from his job for "immoral, indecent, and disgraceful conduct" rendering him unsuitable for government employment. In overturning Norton's dismissal, the court held that employee immorality could support a dismissal only if the acts have a deleterious effect on the efficiency of the service. Norton's furtive acts had no such

effect. However, the court pointed out that homosexual conduct might bear on the efficiency of the service if potential blackmail created a security risk, if the employee made offensive overtures while on the job, or if the conduct was sufficiently notorious to cause negative reactions in other employees or the public.

In contrast to *Norton* is the Ninth Circuit Court of Appeals decision in *Singer v. United States Civil Service Com'n.* Singer was discharged from his position as a clerk typist with the federal government because of his alleged immoral and notoriously disgraceful conduct. To wit, Singer did not confine himself to activities conducted in private, but openly and publicly flaunted his homosexuality, thereby discrediting the federal government. Singer was openly gay at work, was active in the Seattle Gay Alliance, and along with another man applied for a marriage license leading to substantial media publicity. The Ninth Circuit upheld the discharge on the grounds that Singer's "flaunting" of his lifestyle did impede the efficiency of the service and that Singer's First Amendment rights had not been violated. Within the context of government employment, a balancing test is applied to otherwise-protected First Amendment activities in which the interest of the government as employer in the efficiency of public service must be weighed against the interest of employees in exercising First Amendment Rights. In Singer's case, the government interest outweighed Singer's interest in the open and public flaunting and advocacy of homosexual conduct.

The Ninth Circuit's decision was subsequently vacated by the Supreme Court at the request of the federal government following a 1975 revision of the civil service rules (Rubenstein, p. 522). The new rule prohibits a federal agency from discriminating against an employee on the basis of conduct not affecting the actual performance of the employee or others. Nevertheless, the use of civil service rules to police the line between status and conduct and between employees' private and public conduct continues to occur in many state and local civil service systems. The recent case of *Shahar v. Bowers*, tragically illustrates this.

Robin Shahar worked in the office of Michael Bowers, the Attorney General of Georgia, following her second year at Emory Law School. Bowers, of *Bowers v. Hardwick* infamy, offered Shahar a permanent job upon her graduation from law school. Prior to commencing employment, Shahar and her female partner celebrated a Jewish wedding ceremony to which they invited several of Shahar's soon-to-be co-workers. Upon learning of the ceremony, Bowers revoked his offer, claiming that employing Shahar would indicate approval of her marriage ceremony and jeopardize the function of his office. Shahar sued, alleging that Bower's actions violated her First Amendment rights to free association and free exercise of religion, as well as the Equal Protection Clause. A three-judge panel of the Eleventh Circuit found that Shahar's relationship with her partner was protected by the right of intimate association and remanded the case to the lower court to determine if the state could demonstrate that Shahar's firing served a compelling state interest. Bowers petitioned to have the case reheard by the entire Eleventh Circuit, which granted the rehearing and vacated the decision. In a major defeat, the full court upheld the right of Bowers to fire Shahar (*Shahar v. Bowers*). Even assuming that Shahar had a constitutionally protected right of intimate association, the court found that Bowers' interest in the efficiency of the service outweighed that right. Bowers, as an elected official, had the right to limit the lawyers on his professional staff to those he trusted, and he had a legitimate basis for distrust because Shahar's actions conflicted with the sodomy law, which his office was charged with enforcing. Thus, by declaring her love for another woman and not leading a closeted, seemingly celibate life, Shahar forfeited her job. In the ultimate of ironies and hypocrisies, Michael Bowers later admitted publicly that he had been having a long-running extra-marital affair with his secretary, also a violation of Georgia's criminal law.

Teachers. There has been substantial litigation and legislation concerning lesbian and gay teachers. The relationship between gay people and children has always triggered discrimination because of the baseless concern that there is a connection between sexual orientation and child molestation and because of concerns about proper role models for children. Lesbian and gay teachers have always felt particularly vulnerable to termination, even with civil service protections, and their fears have not been baseless. Until well into the 1960s, a teaching license would not be granted to an individual found to be homosexual in most jurisdictions, and it remains true today that some jurisdictions would refuse to hire, or would summarily terminate, a lesbian or gay teacher. Several cases help illustrate the limits of civil service and constitutional protections afforded teachers, as well as the double-bind they may find themselves in concerning concealment versus openness.

In the case of *Gaylord v. Tacoma Sch. Dist. No. 10*, plaintiff Gaylord had been a teacher in the Tacoma School District for more than 12 years. During most of that time, his status as a homosexual was unknown. When the vice-principal of his school was notified of Gaylord's homosexuality, he immediately reported the information to his superiors, and Gaylord's sexual orientation became publicly known. The school board fired Gaylord, who then sued. The court found that the public knowledge impaired Gaylord's efficiency as a teacher because of parental, student, and peer concerns. Thus, the school board was justified in discharging Gaylord. In a later case, *Acanfora v. Board of Educ. of Montgomery County,* Acanfora was transferred to a non-teaching position after speaking out about the rights of homosexuals. He sued, claiming a violation of his First Amendment right to speak out on issues of public concern. The Fourth Circuit found that his speaking out was protected speech that did not disrupt his workplace. However, the court upheld his discharge because he had failed to list his involvement with a gay student group on his application for employment. Of course, remaining silent was a prerequisite to his being hired. Although Acanfora was granted First Amendment protection, merely coming out to colleagues, which then leads to public knowledge about a teacher's homosexuality, a public furor, and thus termination has been held not to be protected speech on a matter of public concern in *Rowland v. Mad River Local School District*. Thus, disclosure is both compulsory (*Acanfora*) and forbidden (*Rowland* and *Gaylord*).

Security Clearances and Law Enforcement Agencies. Much of the anti-homosexual witch-hunts of the 1950s were based on the belief that homosexuals were of such low morality as to be equated with subversives. Their general character, promiscuous sexuality, and vulnerability to blackmail made them a security risk. Security risk has continued to be cited as a rationale for denying employment to lesbians and gay men in intelligence fields—because lesbians and gay men are closeted and fear discovery and disclosure of their sexual orientation, they are vulnerable to foreign operatives. Until quite recently, the CIA and FBI refused to hire and terminated employees found to be lesbian or gay. Lesbian and gay employees were also denied high level security clearances both within government and in private companies working on government projects (usually Defense Department contracts) requiring

security clearances. The CIA and FBI's employment practices had been traditionally unreviewable, and Congress had consistently exempted both from the civil service statutory scheme. Commencing in the late 1980s, there has been a sea change in the government's treatment of sexual orientation brought about in part through litigation and in part by new policies promulgated by the Clinton Administration.

The CIA has always argued that its hiring and firing decisions were completely insulated from judicial review, even when based on the Constitution. In *Webster v. Doe*, the Supreme Court rejected that argument and found that the CIA was bound by the Constitution in its employment decisions. Thus, the CIA is open to suit on the grounds that its refusal to hire someone on the basis of their sexual orientation is a denial of equal protection of the law. No court has ever upheld a claim of discrimination against the CIA. However, in 1994, the CIA adopted a policy statement that it does not discriminate on the basis of sexual orientation in its employment decisions, although sexual conduct (heterosexual or homosexual) may be relevant where it reflects on a persons' stability or could result in blackmail pressure.

Litigation has also been brought against the FBI for its policy towards employing homosexuals. In *Padula v. Webster*, Margaret Padula was rejected for employment with the FBI in spite of high rankings on her written examination and interview, after a background check turned up the fact that she was homosexual. Padula confirmed her homosexuality and the fact that it was well known to her family, friends, and co-workers, thus eliminating the usual argument for blackmail. Padula sued, claiming that the FBI's refusal to hire her solely because of her sexual orientation denied her equal protection of the law pursuant to the Fourteenth Amendment. The District of Columbia Court of Appeals refused to find that homosexuality is a suspect class, applying only the rational basis standard to the FBI's actions. It then upheld the FBI's policy articulating the classic arguments for the exclusion of lesbians and gay men from similar employment. The court easily concluded that the FBI, as a national law enforcement agency, would have its credibility undermined if it hired individuals whose conduct is criminalized in half of the states. This argument has been used by police and other law enforcement agencies at the state and local level to justify similar non-employment policies. The court also held that it is not irrational for the Bureau to conclude that criminalization of homosexual conduct along with the public's opprobrium towards homosexuals exposes homosexuals to the risk of blackmail to protect their partners, if not themselves.

As in the case of the CIA, the FBI issued new guidelines in late 1993 based on a general Department of Justice policy prohibiting discrimination on the basis of sexual orientation. The FBI's guidelines cover investigative guidelines, employment guidelines, and security clearance adjudication guidelines (Rubenstein, pp. 568-70).

Employees working for private companies working on defense department contracts often need security clearances as well. Failure to obtain the necessary security clearance quickly can often cost an employee her/his job. Until recently, the Defense Department Industrial Security Clearance Office (DISCO), which makes these security clearance decisions, subjected lesbian, gay, and bisexual employees to heightened security checks, which delayed their applications. A group of gay employees working in the Silicon Valley in California called High Tech Gays filed suit in 1984 against DISCO, challenging its policy. The federal district court declared the agency policy unconstitutional, finding that classifications based on sexual orientation were constitutionally suspect. Unfortunately, the Ninth Circuit Court of Appeals reversed in *High Tech Gays v. Defense Indus. Sec. Clearance Office*, holding the government to a mere rational basis standard and finding that the government's policy was rationally related to justifiable ends because counterintelligence agencies target homosexuals and, therefore, homosexuals must be investigated more thoroughly to determine if they are subject to blackmail. In 1995, President Clinton signed Executive Order 12968, which removes sexual orientation as a factor in security clearance decisions (Rubenstein, pp. 580-82).

The Military. This section will be brief, since there is an entire chapter of the Almanac devoted to the treatment of lesbians and gay men in the military (see p. 254). Since World War I, homosexuals have been restricted from serving in the armed forces through application of the sodomy provisions of military law or through personnel regulations. Unsuccessful challenges to homosexual discharges occurred sporadically. In 1981, the Department of Defense tightened its regulations regarding homosexuals in the military, and each branch of the service adopted regulations mandating the disqualification of all homosexuals from the armed services without regard to the length or quality of their military service. This policy remained in effect at the time Bill Clinton was elected President. Clinton had promised during his campaign to lift the ban on military service by gay people. Following his inauguration, in January 1993, Clinton prepared to lift the ban but retreated in the face of stiff opposition from key members of Congress and from leaders in the military. To buy time, he ordered his administration to study the issue and propose recommendations by July 1993. Throughout the spring of 1993, Congress held hearings on the subject, and, in what was portrayed as a compromise but was really a defeat for Clinton, Congress enacted legislation in late 1993 known as the "Don't Ask, Don't Tell, Don't Pursue" policy (10 U.S.C.A. ss 654 [1995]; also see p. 86 in "Significant Documents" chapter). Unlike in the decades prior to Clinton's election, the ban on gays serving in the military is now a federal law, not just a military policy.

The new "Don't Ask, Don't Tell" policy provides that a member of the armed forces shall be separated from the armed forces if that member has engaged in, attempted to engage in, or solicited another to engage in homosexual acts; or if a member has stated that he or she is homosexual, unless there is a further finding that the member is not a person who engages in or has a propensity to engage in, or intends to engage in, homosexual acts. The policy also bars the military from questioning service members about their sexual orientation or investigating them without credible information that they have engaged in homosexual conduct. The goal of the policy is to allow homosexuals to serve so long as they are closeted, thus preserving morale and unit cohesion. Although the new policy is purported to be a compromise, improving conditions for gays in the military, Pentagon figures indicate that the number of homosexuals discharged has risen 67 percent since "Don't Ask, Don't Tell" went into effect (*New York Times Magazine*, 28 June 1998, p. 28).

The new law was immediately challenged in court. There have been a number of contradictory court decisions, although all three circuit court decisions to date have upheld the new policy. Oral argument was recently heard in a second circuit court case, *Able v. The United States*, in which the district court struck down the policy on equal protection and First Amendment grounds. Ultimately, the constitutionality of the new policy will likely be de-

cided by the Supreme Court. The first court of appeals decision addressing the new policy was the fourth circuit decision in *Thomasson v. Perry*. Shortly after the Navy implemented "Don't Ask, Don't Tell," Paul Thomasson, a Navy lieutenant, wrote a letter to four admirals for whom he had served, informing them that he was gay. A Navy Board of Inquiry found that Thomasson's letter gave rise to a presumption that he had a propensity or intent to engage in homosexual acts, which, if unrebutted, warranted separation. Thomasson was discharged. He challenged the new policy on two grounds. First, he argued that the statute violates the equal protection of the laws. The court found that sexual orientation was not a suspect classification and that the government need only provide a rational basis for the policy. The belief that the presence of openly gay persons in the military would create a threat to unit cohesion was found to satisfy the government's burden. Second, Thomasson argued that the policy violates the First Amendment, since he was discharged from the service simply for declaring he was gay, thus suppressing his speech on the basis of its content and viewpoint. The court rejected this argument, holding that the statute does not target speech but homosexual acts or conduct, and the speech is used simply as evidence of intent to engage in homosexual acts.

In upholding the policy, the court emphasized that the formulation of the "Don't Ask, Don't Tell" policy received considerable national attention and was the product of prolonged debate and extensive consideration by Congress. The court was hesitant to substitute its judgment for political consensus, particularly in the area of military affairs, where the judgments of Congress and the military are given particular deference. This articulates the unique problems facing challenges to military policy and this policy in particular. In fact, there was a vigorous dissent in the *Thomasson* case that would seem to have had the better of the legal arguments but for the special deference given to the military.

The dissent found violations of both the Equal Protection Clause and the First Amendment in Thomasson's discharge. Concerning the Equal Protection Clause, the dissent argued that the statute was motivated by the desire to accommodate the prejudice of others against homosexuals, never a permissible justification. Further, there was no actual proof that the presence of homosexuals would adversely affect unit cohesion. As to the First Amendment, Thomasson engaged solely in speech, not conduct. There is no real difference in being (silently) and saying, except that saying produces a reaction in others. The policy presumes misconduct from a statement of status. Thomasson did not admit anything except that he was gay. And, because it is no more likely that declared homosexuals will break the rules than undeclared, the rule is clearly targeted at suppressing the speech itself.

While the other decisions upholding "Don't Ask, Don't Tell" followed the rationale of *Thomasson*, the district court decision in *Able* that struck down the policy was based on the legal reasoning articulated in the dissent in *Thomasson*.

In addition to challenges to the "Don't Ask, Don't Tell" policy itself, there have been concerns and recent litigation over violations of the provisions requiring that information concerning sexual orientation not be sought and investigations not be initiated without credible evidence of a violation of the policy. Senior Chief Timothy R. McVeigh, a highly decorated 17-year veteran of the Navy, filed a suit against the Navy following its decision to discharge him. The Navy sought to discharge McVeigh after discovering that he identified himself as gay on his member profile with America Online. McVeigh sought to enjoin the Navy from discharging him under the "Don't Ask, Don't Tell" policy. McVeigh also contended that the defendants violated his rights under the Electronic Communications Privacy Act (ECPA; 18 U.S.C. 2701 et seq). Judge Sporkin enjoined the Navy from discharging McVeigh, finding that McVeigh was likely to succeed on the merits in his claims that the Navy violated the "Don't Ask, Don't Tell" policy in obtaining the identity of an e-mail user from America Online. The court stated that McVeigh did not openly express his homosexuality and that an investigation into sexual orientation may be initiated only when a commander has received credible information that there is a basis for discharge. When the Navy took affirmative steps to investigate the identity of the e-mail user, it violated the very essence of the policy by "launching a search and destroy mission (*McVeigh v. Cohen*, 983 F.Supp. 215 [D.D.C. 1998]). Following this ruling, McVeigh was promoted and agreed to retire from the Navy with full pension and payment of his attorneys fees in June 1998.

FAMILY RELATIONS

Many lesbians and gay men form intimate relationships, and more than three million are parents. Until recently, these relationships were treated as nonexistent by the law, and lesbian and gay parents were forced to hide their sexuality for fear of losing their children. This section will explore the fight for legal recognition of same-sex relationships and the law's slowly changing treatment of lesbians and gay men who have or desire to have children.

Legal Recognition of Same-Sex Relationships

The fight to obtain marriage for same-sex couples has, in recent years, dominated the legal battle for recognition of same-sex relationships. However, other methods exist by which same-sex couples have achieved legal recognition, including domestic partnership ordinances and benefits, expanding definitions of family, and privately drafted legal instruments.

Marriage. Marriage is generally regulated by state laws. However, state power is not unlimited. The right to marry has been declared a fundamental liberty right guaranteed by the due process clause of the Fourteenth Amendment to the United States Constitution.

The lack of legal recognition for same-sex relationships denies the legitimacy of intimate relationships by which lesbians and gay men define themselves. However, there is a debate within the lesbian and gay community about whether legalizing same-sex marriage is the best way to achieve this recognition, given the patriarchal and oppressive nature of the institution of marriage. The arguments pro and con were eloquently articulated by Thomas Stoddard (pro) and Paula Ettelbrick (con) in "Gay Marriage: A Must or a Bust?," printed in OUT/LOOK magazine (Fall 1989). These arguments are summarized below.

There are practical and political/philosophical arguments in favor of the right to marry. From a practical standpoint, lesbians and gay men are denied a host of benefits granted to married persons. These may include tax benefits, government benefits such as social security survivors benefits, health insurance, life, disability and pension coverage as a surviving spouse, spousal immunity in legal proceedings, the right to inherit, to make medical decisions for one's partner, to take advantage of family rates, to be governed by divorce laws upon separation, and, if there are children, to be covered by the laws determining the rights and responsibilities of parents.

In addition to the practical arguments in favor of marriage, there are important political arguments. Marriage has been given a special place in law and society; it is the centerpiece of our social structure and notion of family. Denial of entry into this institution sends the message that gay and lesbian relationships are less important and less entitled to respect than heterosexual relationships. Full equality for lesbians and gay men can never be achieved without entry into the institution of marriage. Furthermore, enlarging the concept of marriage to include same-sex couples will itself transform the institution and make it less sexist and more inclusive.

The central argument against same-sex marriage is that the institution of marriage is steeped in a patriarchal system that takes as its basis dominance of men over women and that privileges heterosexual marriage over all other forms of family and intimate association. Obtaining the right to marry will simply force lesbians and gay men to assimilate into the mainstream and to further anoint marriage above all other forms of relationships. Marriage runs counter to the goals of lesbian and gay liberation, including the redefinition of gender roles, sexuality, and family.

Whatever one's position in the debate, the Hawaii Supreme Court's 1993 decision in *Baehr v. Lewin* has thrust the fight for same-sex marriage into the forefront of the national lesbian and gay civil rights movement. Prior to this point, there were three cases in the early 1970s in which same-sex couples challenged the refusal of the state to grant them marriage licenses. All three were unsuccessful, as were several more recent cases prior to *Baehr* (*Baker v. Nelson*; *Jones v. Hallahan*; *Singer v. Hara*). The cases made three similar constitutional and statutory arguments. First, plaintiffs argued that the Supreme Court had declared the right to marry to be a fundamental right and that the refusal to grant them a marriage license violated their fundamental right to marry. The courts uniformly rejected this argument, holding that the term *marriage* by its definition is the union between one man and one woman. Thus, the fundamental right is defined in terms of a heterosexual couple and does not apply to a same-sex union. Second, plaintiffs argued that they were being discriminated against on the basis of sex, since a man could marry a woman but not a man. This argument was rejected on the grounds that the law applied equally to male and female same-sex couples. Finally, in some states, the marriage license law does not explicitly state that marriage must be between a man and a woman. Plaintiffs argued that the statute itself did not preclude the issuance of a marriage license. The courts rejected this argument by again saying that by its terms, marriage means the union of one man and one woman. As the court observed in *Baker v. Nelson*, "The institution of marriage as a union of man and woman, uniquely involving the procreation and rearing of children within a family, is as old as the book of Genesis" (p. 186).

Baehr grew out of a legal action in 1991, when three couples, all citizens of Hawaii, filed a lawsuit for a declaratory judgment that Hawaii's Marriage Law (Hawaii Revised Statutes ss 572-1) unconstitutionally denied same-sex couples the same marriage rights as different-sex couples. Their claims were based on the privacy and equal protection clauses of the Hawaii Constitution. In 1993, the Hawaii Supreme Court issued its decision in *Baehr v. Lewin*. The court rejected the privacy claim, holding that Hawaii's guarantee of privacy has been interpreted to be co-extensive with the U.S. Constitution's right to privacy, in which the right to marry has been linked with the rights of procreation, childbirth, and child rearing, clearly contemplating a union between a man and a woman. However, concerning the equal protection sex discrimination claim, Hawaii's prohibition against sex discrimination is broader than that contained in the U.S. Constitution. The court found that depriving same-sex couples to access to the rights and benefits contingent on the status of marriage is discrimination based on sex. The freedom to marry is a vital personal right, and on its face, the Hawaii statute restricts that right to male/female couples. Having found that the Hawaii marriage statute discriminates on the basis of sex, the court went on to hold that sex-based classifications are suspect and therefore subject to strict scrutiny. In order to justify the statute, the state would be required to show that it has a compelling state interest in restricting marriage to heterosexual couples and that its interest is narrowly drawn. The Supreme Court remanded the case back to the trial court to allow the state to present evidence at trial justifying the marriage statute.

Trial was held during the summer of 1996. The state's primary argument in support of the statute was that the state had a compelling interest in promoting optimal development of children, which occurred in a two-parent heterosexual home. Both sides called expert witnesses to testify concerning the effect on children of being raised in a lesbian or gay home. Plaintiffs' experts cited numerous studies showing that children suffered no adverse effects from being raised by lesbian or gay parents. The trial judge found that the state had failed to prove a compelling interest in denying same-sex couples the right to marry and struck down the Hawaii Marriage Law. The decision was stayed pending appeal. As of mid-1998, the case was still pending before the Hawaii Supreme Court.

The extent to which conferring the right to marry would impose legitimacy on lesbians and gays and their families is clear from the enormous outcry, backlash, and near panic that has greeted the Hawaii case. Shortly after the Supreme Court's 1993 decision, the Hawaii legislature passed legislation opposing same-sex marriage. Following the 1996 decision by the trial judge, the legislature proposed a constitutional amendment to be sent to Hawaii voters for approval. The amendment, which would permit the legislature to restrict marriage to opposite-sex couples, is on the ballot for the November 1998 election. At the same time that the legislature proposed the constitutional amendment, it accorded same-sex couples the broadest package of domestic partner rights and benefits ever provided by a governmental entity. The message: we will give you second-class recognition, but marriage is a sacred heterosexual institution.

Reaction outside Hawaii was equally swift. Of concern is the potential extraterritorial effect of a Hawaii marriage in other states. Generally, the Full Faith and Credit Clause of the U.S. Constitution requires that states recognize valid marriages performed in other states. To circumvent this requirement, as of May 1998, 29 states have passed legislation prohibiting same-sex marriage in their states, thus declaring that they will not recognize such marriages performed in other states. Additionally, the U.S. Congress passed the Defense of Marriage Act (DOMA) in 1996, stating that no state is required to give effect to the public acts of other states respecting a relationship between persons of the same sex that is treated as a marriage under the laws of such other state (28 U.S.C.A. 115 ss. 1738C). President Clinton signed DOMA into law on 21 September 1996.

Recently, a second state, Alaska, has begun a course similar to Hawaii's. An Alaska state superior court judge in Anchorage ruled in February 1998 that the state cannot deny a marriage license to same-sex couples unless it can show a compelling need to do so. The case is on appeal to the Alaska Supreme Court (*Brause v. Alaska*).

Non-Marital Forms of Recognition. There are a variety of ways in which lesbians and gay men have created some of the rights and benefits enjoyed by married couples short of marriage. These include the use of legal documents, domestic partner ordinances, the provision of domestic partner benefits by employers, and court-ordered benefits and protections applied in limited circumstances.

Partners who have the financial resources and choose to take the necessary affirmative steps may draw up legal documents granting some of the benefits and protections automatically conferred on married persons. These include wills that insure that property passes to partners after death, medical powers of attorney that insure partners will make medical decisions for each other in times of incapacitation, financial powers of attorney that insure the same concerning financial decisions, and relationship agreements—contractual agreements determining the parties' rights and obligations to each other both during the relationship and upon its dissolution. There is some question concerning the enforceability of such relationship agreements, although most courts have upheld them. The law refuses to enforce agreements in which the primary consideration of one of the parties is sexual services. However, where other services form part of the consideration, such agreements are usually upheld.

During the past 15 years, more than 62 cities and municipalities and the State of Hawaii have passed some form of domestic partner ordinance, allowing domestic partners to register with the state/city/municipality. The benefits derived from such registration and the requirements for domestic partner recognition differ considerably. In some jurisdictions, registration grants nothing more than recognition of the relationship. In others, it provides various spousal benefits to the partners of employees of the jurisdiction, including medical benefits and medical and bereavement leave. Most such ordinances define domestic partners as persons living together and sharing in their living expenses. The cities of Atlanta and Minneapolis attempted to extend benefits to domestic partners but lost legal challenges on the ground that their home rule charters did not authorize them to do so. In those states, such benefits would have to be extended on a statewide basis.

In addition to the government-sponsored domestic partner ordinances, more than 420 private sector employers and 99 colleges and universities have established domestic partner policies extending benefits to the partners of same-sex couples. Again, the policies vary and must be examined individually to determine who qualifies, what benefits are extended, and the mechanism for triggering receipt of benefits.

Legal Expansion of Definitions of Family. In addition to efforts to obtain same-sex marriage and provide economic benefits through legal documents and domestic partner arrangements, litigation has challenged courts to apply a less rigid and more functional approach to definitions of family. In *Braschi v. Stahl Assocs., Inc.*, New York State's highest court was called upon to interpret the word *family* in a suit concerning the occupancy rights of a rent-controlled apartment. Miguel Braschi had lived with Leslie Blanchard for more than 11 years until Blanchard's death. Stahl Associates began immediate eviction proceedings against Braschi pursuant to the New York rent-control law, which granted protection from eviction for the surviving spouse of a deceased tenant or other member of the family living with the tenant. The court found that Braschi was a family member, construing the term family to comport with the reality of family life: two adult partners in a long-term relationship with an emotional and financial commitment to each other. The court looked to a functional definition of family as those households with familial characteristics, thus encompassing lesbian and gay relationships within the meaning of family. The *Braschi* decision was later extended to cover rent-stabilized apartments as well.

In a legal battle that consumed more than eight years of their lives, Karen Thompson and Sharon Kowalski were finally recognized as a family of affinity by Minnesota's highest court in *In Re Guardianship of Kowalski*. In 1983, Sharon Kowalski suffered severe brain damage in an automobile accident. She was living at the time with her partner, Karen Thompson. Both Thompson and Sharon's father petitioned for guardianship of Sharon. Sharon's father obtained the guardianship and shortly thereafter terminated Thompson's visitation rights because of the lesbian nature of her relationship with Sharon. Karen Thompson continued to fight for the right to visit Sharon and ultimately to obtain guardianship. In 1990, Sharon's father resigned his guardianship, and Thompson petitioned to succeed him. Although no one else filed a petition, the trial court denied Thompson's petition. Finally, in 1991, the Minnesota Court of Appeals overturned the trial court and granted Thompson guardianship of Sharon Kowalski. In the course of the intervening years, Thompson traversed the country speaking out on the importance of obtaining legal protection for lesbian and gay families. While it would not have been dispositive, Thompson's efforts to obtain guardianship would have been greatly helped had the couple had binding medical powers of attorney and other documents naming each other as guardians.

Parenting Issues

It is estimated that well over three million lesbians and gay men have children. Many of these children are the products of previous heterosexual relationships. More and more frequently, however, lesbian and gay families are choosing to have children through alternative insemination, in vitro fertilization, surrogacy, adoption, and foster placement. While most of the case law involves disputes when previously heterosexual families dissolve and one partner is lesbian or gay, legal issues are increasingly arising in families initially formed by lesbian and gay parents.

Custody and Visitation Disputes between a Heterosexual and a Gay Parent. Until relatively recently, disclosure that a parent involved in a custody dispute was gay meant a per se denial of custody and frequently visitation as well. There are few states, if any, that still claim to follow a per se rule in such custody disputes. The present standard applied in most states in determining custody is the best interest of the child. This is a flexible standard, and the extent to which a parent's sexuality influences the decision will differ from state to state and often from judge to judge. In theory, a parent's homosexuality should not be a factor in determining custody except to the extent that it bears a relationship to the best interest of the child. Nevertheless, a variety of myths, prejudices, and stereotypes about lesbian and gay parents permeate custody decisions. Some of the more common arguments used to deny custody to lesbians and gay men include a belief that living with a gay parent will interfere with a child's normal heterosexual development; cause embarrassment to the child in the eyes of her/his peers; cause undue social pressure because

of the disapproval of society; inculcate the child with a homosexual orientation; or cause the child to contract HIV.

Additionally, judges have denied custody to gay parents in sodomy law states on the grounds that they are engaging in illicit sexual activity. For instance, in July 1998 the Alabama Supreme Court ruled that a child should be removed from the care of her lesbian mother in favor of the child's father; the court cited the state's sodomy law and the mother's "lifestyle." "While the evidence shows that the mother loves the child and has provided her with good care, it also shows that she has chosen to expose the child continuously to a lifestyle that is 'neither legal in this state nor moral in the eyes of most of its citizens,'" wrote judge Champ Lyons, quoting a previous court decision in the process. Likewise, open cohabitation in a non-marital relationship has justified the denial of custody.

In spite of the continued existence of discrimination against lesbians and gay men in custody disputes, many are successfully winning such disputes. However, in addition to denying custody to lesbian and gay parents, courts have also put unreasonable restrictions on the visitation rights of non-custodial gay parents. Such restrictions include forbidding overnight stays, not allowing visitation in the presence of the parent's lover or sometimes any other homosexuals, and not taking the children to any homosexual-oriented activities. Again, non-custodial parents have been increasingly successful at challenging such restrictions.

Creating Lesbian and Gay Families. Most lesbian and gay families start out with one legally recognized parent, because one parent actually gives birth to the child or because one parent goes through the initial adoption proceeding. In order for the second parent to obtain legal rights and obligations vis-a-vis the child, it is necessary to go through a second-parent adoption. Second-parent adoptions do not extinguish the legal rights of the biological parents, rather they add a co-parent to the already existing parent. Without such a second-parent adoption, the partner of the legal parent has no legal obligation to support the child, and the child has no rights of inheritance, nor is s/he eligible for employer or government-provided benefits. Should the parties separate, the second parent is unlikely to have rights of visitation, nor will s/he have any support obligation.

There have been conflicting decisions on second-parent adoptions, but the weight of the case law favors their approval. Such adoptions are governed by statute in each state. Although the wording differs from state to state, there are two general problems with the statutes. First, most adoption statutes cut off the parental rights of the biological parent upon the granting of the adoption. Obviously, that is not the desired outcome in second-parent adoption cases. Most courts have simply said that the cut-off provision can be waived, but those courts that choose to read their statute literally can find that second-parent adoptions do not fit within the statutory scheme. Second, some statutes speak in terms of one male and one female adoptive parent. Again, lesbian and gay parents do not fit within this language, but courts have generally looked to the spirit rather than the narrow language of the statutes.

Many lesbians and gay men seek to create families by adopting children. Two states, Florida and New Hampshire, statutorily bar lesbians and gay men from adopting or from becoming foster parents. There have been legal challenges to both laws, but none have succeeded as yet. In all other states, lesbian and gay parents can adopt, although there may be efforts made by the child's relatives or others to ask the court to bar the adoption.

Other lesbians and gay men turn to artificial insemination or surrogacy to start a family. Where artificial insemination occurs with an unknown sperm donor, the legal risks are minimal. Where a known donor or surrogacy are used, there are complicated issues surrounding the legal rights and obligations of sperm donors, birth mothers, and co-parents that go beyond this chapter. Most states have enacted legislation that attempts to sort out some of these issues.

Disputes within Lesbian and Gay Families. As more and more lesbians and gay men create their own families, it is inevitable that some of these families will dissolve, raising the question of custody and visitation rights. Where both parents have legal custody of the children, the same rights, obligations, and legal standards apply as in the case of a heterosexual custody determination. However, in many instances, one parent is the child's biological mother and the co-parent has no legal status as parent. A number of states have ruled on the visitation rights of a lesbian co-parent following dissolution of the relationship. Most have held that a co-parent does not have standing under the applicable statute to petition for custody or visitation, usually because the co-parent does not fit the statutory definition of parent. A few courts have granted standing to the non-biological parent to seek visitation. Many academics have urged courts to adopt a functional definition of parenthood similar to the functional definition of family adopted in the *Braschi* rent-control case. The class of persons eligible to seek custody and visitation would include anyone who maintains a functional parental relationship with the child when the relationship was created by the legal parent with the intent that it be parental in nature. The results in these cases highlight the importance of seeking second-parent adoption to preserve the legal rights of a co-parent.

PROMINENT PEOPLE

Ernest Dillon

Ernest Dillon, a postal worker who left his wife to move in with his male lover, was pervasively and severely taunted, ostracized, and physically beaten by his co-workers during a period of three years. Management allegedly took minimal steps to ameliorate Dillon's position. Instead, Dillon was told "not to waste their time with his complaints and to fight back when taunted." On the advice of his psychiatrist, Dillon resigned. Dillon filed a complaint against the Postal Service. In *Dillon v. Frank*, a leading case involving discrimination against a gay employee, the Sixth Circuit Court rejected this claim. Dillon testified before the Senate hearings on the Employment Non-Discrimination Act, where he described the brutality he was subjected to at the Postal Service.

Michael Hardwick (d. 1991)

Michael Hardwick challenged Georgia's sodomy law in the famous case of *Bowers v. Hardwick*. Hardwick, an Atlanta bartender, was arrested in 1982 for committing sodomy in his home with another man; he was observed by a police officer who came to the home to serve a warrant on an unrelated matter. Prosecutors later dropped the charge, which carries a maximum 20-year prison penalty upon conviction, but Hardwick sued, challenging the constitutionality of the sodomy law. The case reached the Supreme Court, and on 30 June 1986, the Court ruled against Hardwick, rejecting a fundamental right of privacy in same-sex sexual conduct. Hardwick died of an AIDS-related illness in 1991 at 37.

Nan Hunter

Nan Hunter has been an associate professor at Brooklyn Law School since 1990. She served as deputy general counsel of the Department of Health and Human Services and for a decade for the American Civil Liberties Union, where she was staff counsel to the Reproductive Freedom Project and director of the AIDS and Civil Liberties Project and the Lesbian and Gay Rights Project. Prior to that, she was a founding partner in a community law office in Washington, D.C., and an adjunct professor at the George Washington University School of Law. She holds a B.A. from Northwestern University and a J.D. from the Georgetown University Law Center.

Abby R. Rubenfeld

Abby R. Rubenfeld of Nashville is an attorney in a general practice that includes an emphasis on family law, sexual orientation, and AIDS-related issues. In 1996, she succeeded in her four-year effort to overturn the Tennessee law that criminalized private same-sex consensual adult sexual behavior. Because of that victory, she received the 1996 Bill of Rights Award from the American Civil Liberties Union of Tennessee, and in October 1997, the National Lesbian and Gay Law Association gave her its highest honor, the Dan Bradley Award. Rubenfeld was legal director of Lambda Legal Defense and Education Fund from 1983 to 1988 and was the editor of *AIDS Legal Guide*, the first AIDS-related legal publication in the country. She served four years on the board of directors of the National Gay and Lesbian Task Force.

Robin Shahar

Robin Shahar, a lesbian with a stellar law school record, was fired from an entry-level staff attorney position before she had even shown up for her first day of work. The employer was Georgia Attorney General Michael Bowers. He withdrew his employment offer after he found out that Shahar and her female partner were about to celebrate a Jewish wedding ceremony in front of invited family and friends. That, according to Bowers, meant that Shahar would disrupt the "proper functioning" of his office if allowed to work there. Shahar sued, and at first a three-judge panel of the Eleventh Circuit Court ruled in her favor. However, upon Bowers' appeal, the case was reheard by the entire Eleventh Circuit Court, which ruled that Bowers did have the right to fire Shahar. Shahar, after the disruption and trauma caused by her summary dismissal, has gone on to a successful career as a government lawyer in the Atlanta city attorney's office.

Thomas B. Stoddard (d. 1997)

Thomas B. Stoddard was the executive director of Lambda Legal Defense and Education Fund from 1986 to 1992, tackling civil rights work that ranged from fighting AIDS-related discrimination to the military's anti-gay ban. Under his leadership, the New York-based Lambda grew from a staff of 6 to 22 and began its national expansion by creating regional offices to serve lesbians, gay men, and people with HIV and AIDS around the country. Stoddard was one of the earliest proponents of civil marriage rights for lesbian and gay couples, and he co-authored New York City's lesbian and gay civil rights law and pursued his public role on behalf of lesbian and gay civil rights after leaving Lambda. He was also an active advocate for people with AIDS and HIV, and he served as director of the Campaign for Military Service in the effort to force the Clinton Administration to keep its promise to end discrimination against lesbians and gay men in the military. He graduated from Georgetown University and the New York University School of Law, where he was a fellow in the Arthur Garfield Hays Civil Liberties Program and, from 1981, an adjunct professor of law. Before joining Lambda in 1986, Stoddard was legislative director for the New York Civil Liberties Union, after first serving as counsel to that position. Lambda honored Stoddard for his civil rights work with a Liberty Award in 1993. The Tom Stoddard Fellowship was established at New York University in 1996, to be awarded to third-year law students to work on lesbian and gay civil rights with public-interest organizations. Stoddard died of AIDS-related complications in February 1997.

Karen Thompson

Karen Thompson fought for seven years for the right to care for her lesbian lover, Sharon Kowalski, who had been left a quadriplegic by an auto accident. Kowalski, 35, a former physical education teacher, suffered brain damage and was forced to use a wheelchair after the accident in 1983. Over Thompson's objections, Kowalski's father, Donald Kowalski, won guardianship in 1984 and ended Thompson's right to visit. Thompson, a professor at St. Cloud State University, continued her court battle for several years. Eventually, Donald Kowalski resigned as his daughter's guardian, citing medical problems of his own. A judge then appointed Sharon Kowalski's high school track coach, Karen Tomberlin, as the new guardian, despite Thompson's longtime relationship with Kowalski. That decision was finally overturned in 1991 by the Minnesota Court of Appeals, which granted guardianship to Thompson.

REFERENCES:

Books

Boswell, John. *Social Tolerance and Homosexuality.* Chicago: Univ. of Chicago Press, 1980.
Bullough, Vern L. and Bonnie Bullough. *Cross Dressing, Sex, and Gender.* Philadelphia: University of Pennsylvania Press, 1993.
Chauncey, George. *Gay New York: Gender, Urban Culture, and the Making of the Gay Male World, 1890-1949.* New York: Basic Books, 1994.
Eskridge, William N., Jr. and Nan D. Hunter. *Sexuality, Gender, and the Law.* Westbury, New York: Foundation Press, 1997.
Foucault, Michel. *The History of Sexuality, Volume I: An Introduction.* (Translated by Robert Hurley.) New York: Vintage Books, 1978.
Fuss, Diana. *Essentially Speaking: Feminism, Nature & Difference.* London: Routledge Kegan and Paul, 1989.
Rubenstein, William B. *Cases and Materials on Sexual Orientation and the Law.* St. Paul: West Publishing Co., 1997.
Weeks, Jeffrey. *Coming Out: Homosexual Politics in Britain from the Nineteenth Century to the Present.* London: Quartet Books Ltd., 1977.

Periodical Articles

Adam, Barry D. "Structural Foundations of the Gay World," in *Comparative Studies in Society and History,* vol. 27, no. 658, October 1985.

Cain, Patricia A. Symposium on Sexual Orientation and the Law. "Litigating for Lesbian and Gay Rights: A Legal History," in *Virginia Law Review,* vol. 79, no. 1551, October 1993.
Crompton, Louis. "The Myth of Lesbian Impunity: Capital Laws from 1270-1791," in *Journal of Homosexuality,* vol. 6, no. 11, 1980-81.
"Gay Marriage: A Must or a Bust?," in *OUT/LOOK Magazine,* Fall 1989.
Greenberg, Daniel F. and Marcia H. Bystryn. "Christian Intolerance of Homosexuality," in *American Journal of Society,* vol. 88, no. 515, 1992.
Law, Sylvia A. "Homosexuality and the Social Meaning of Gender," in *Wisconsin Law Review,* vol. 187, 1988.
McIntosh, Mary. "The Homosexual Role," in *Social Problems, vol. 16, no. 182, 1968.*
New York Times Magazine, 28 June 1998: 28.
Robson, Ruthann. "Lesbianism in Anglo-European Legal History," in *Wisconsin Women's Law Journal,* vol. 5, no. 1, 1990.

Book Excerpts

Halperin, David M. "Sex before Sexuality: Pederasty, Politics, and Power in Classical Athens." In Duberman, Martin, Martha Vicinus, and George Chauncey, eds., *Hidden from History: Reclaiming the Gay and Lesbian Past.* New York: NAL Books, 1990.
Smith-Rosenberg, Carroll. "Discourses of Sexuality and Subjectivity: The New Woman, 1870-1936." In Duberman.
Trumbach, Randolph. "The Birth of the Queen: Sodomy and the Emergence of Gender Equality in Modern Culture, 1660-1750." In Duberman.

Cases Cited

Abbott v. Bragdon, 912 F.Supp. 580 (D. Me. 1995), *aff'd,* 107 F.3d 934 (First Cir.)*, cert. granted in part,* 118 S.Ct. 554 (1997), *vacated,* No. 97-156 (U.S., 25 June 1998).
Able v. The United States, 968 F.Supp. 850 (E.D.N.Y 1997).
Acanfora v. Board of Educ. Of Montgomery County, 491 F.2d 498 (Fourth Cir.)*, cert. denied,* 419 U.S. 836 (1974).
Baehr v. Lewin, 852 P.2d 44 (Haw.)*, reconsideration granted in part,* 875 P.2d 225 (Haw. 1993), *appeal after remand sub. nom., Baehr v. Miike,* 910 P.2d 112 (Haw.), *remand,* No. Civ. 91-1394, 1996 WL 694235 (Haw. Cir. Ct. 1996), *aff'd,* 950 P.2d 1234 (Haw. 1997).
Baker v. Nelson, 191 N.W.2d 185 (Minn. 1971), *appeal dismissed,* 409 U.S. 810 (1972).
Bowers v. Hardwick, 478 U.S. 186 (1986).
Braschi v. Stahl Assocs. Co., 543 N.E.2d 49 (N.Y. App. 1989).
Brause v. Bureau of Vital Statistics, No. 3AN-95-6562 CI, 1998 WL 88743 (Alaska Super. Feb. 27, 1998).
Commonwealth v. Wasson, 842 S.W.2d 487 (Ky. 1992).
Curran v. Mount Diablo Council of the Boy Scouts of America, 147 Cal. App.3d 712 (Cal. App. 2 Dist. 1983), *appeal dismissed,* 468 U.S. 1205 (1984), *appeal after remand,* 29 Cal. Rptr. 2d 580 (1994), *appeal granted and opinion superseded,* 874 P.2d 901 (Cal. 1994), *aff'd,* 952 P.2d 218 (Cal. 1998).
Dale v. Boy Scouts of America, 706 A.2d 270 (Sup. Ct. App. Div. 1998).
DeSantis v. Pacific Telephone & Telegraph Co., 608 F.2d 327 (Ninth Cir. 1979).

Dillon v. Frank, 952 F.2d 403 (Sixth Cir. 1992).

Employment Non Discrimination Act Hearings, 142 Cong. Rec. § 10100-02, 104th Congress, 2d Session (Tuesday, 10 September 1996).

Fricke v. Lynch, 491 F.Supp. 381 (D. R.I. 1980).

Fulton Bar & Grill v. State Liquor Auth., SLA Hearing Officer's Report, Exhibit "G" Annexed to Answer, papers on Appeal from an Order, (Feb. 16, 1960). In Chauncey.

Gaylord v. Tacoma School Dist. No. 10, 559 P.2d 1340 (Wash.), *cert. denied*, 434 U.S. 879 (1977).

Gay and Lesbian Bisexual Alliance v. Pryor, 110 F.3d 1543 (Eleventh Cir. 1997).

Gay Law Students Assn. v. Pacific Telephone and Telegraph Co., 595 P.2d 592 (Cal. 1979).

High Tech Gays v. Defense Indus. Sec. Clearance Office, 895 F.2d 563, *reh'g denied*, 909 F.2d 375 (Ninth Cir. 1990).

Hurley v. Irish-American Gay, Lesbian and Bisexual Group of Boston, 515 U.S. 557 (1995).

In re Guardianship of Kowalski, 478 N.W.2d 790 (Minn. App. 1991).

In re Thom, 337 N.Y.S.2d 588 (N.Y.A.D. 1 Dept. 1972), *rev'd*, 301 N.E.2d 542 (N.Y. 1), *remand*, 350 N.Y.S.2d 1 (N.Y.A.D. 1 Dept. 1973).

Jones v. Hallahan, 501 S.W.2d 588 (Ky. 1973).

McVeigh v. Cohen, 983 F.Supp. 215 (D.D.C. 1998).

NAACP v. Alabama, 357 U.S. 449 (1958).

Nabozny v. Podlesny, 92 F.3d 446 (Seventh Cir. 1996).

Norton v. Macy, 417 F.2d 1161 (D.C. Cir. 1969).

Oncale v. Sundowner Offshore Services, Inc., 118 S.Ct. 998 (1998).

Paddock Bar, Inc. v. Div. Of Alcoholic Beverage Control, 46 N.J. Super. 404, 134 A.2d 779 (Sup. Ct. App. Div. 1957).

Padula v. Webster, 822 F.2d 97 (D.C. Cir. 1987).

People v. Onofre, 424 N.Y.S.2d 566 (N.Y.A.D. 4 Dept. 1980), *aff'd*, 415 N.E.2d 936 (N.Y. 1980), *reh'g denied*, 420 N.E.2d 412 (N.Y.), *cert. denied*, 451 U.S. 987 (1981).

Plessy v. Ferguson, 163 U.S. 537 (1896).

Price Waterhouse v. Hopkins, 490 U.S. 228, *remand*, 1989 WL 105318 (D.C. Cir. 1989), *remand*, 737 F.Supp. 1202 (D.D.C.), *aff'd*, 920 F.2d 967 (D.C. Cir. 1990).

R.A.V. v. City of St. Paul, 505 U.S. 377 (1992).

Romer v. Evans, 116 S.Ct. 1620 (1996).

Rowland v. Mad River Local School Dist., 730 F.2d 444 (Sixth Cir. 1984), *cert denied*, 470 U.S. 1009, *reh'g denied*, 471 U.S. 1062 (1985).

Shahar v. Bowers, 836 F.Supp. 859 (N.D. Ga. 1993) *aff'd in part, vacated in part*, 70 F.3d 1218 (Eleventh Cir. 1995), *reh'g en banc granted, opinion vacated*, 78 F.3d 499 (Eleventh Cir. 1996), *reh'g en banc*, 114 F.3d 1097 (Eleventh Cir.) *reh'g denied*, 120 F.3d 211 (Eleventh Cir. 1997), *cert. denied*, 118 S.Ct. 693 (1998).

Singer v. Hara, 522 P.2d 1187 (Wash. App. Div. 1), *review denied*, 84 Wash.2d 1008 (1974).

Singer v. United States Civil Service Comm'n., 530 F.2d 247 (Ninth Cir. 1976), *vacated*, 429 U.S. 1034 (1977).

Stoumen v. Reilly, 234 P.2d 969 (Cal. 1951).

Thomasson v. Perry, 80 F.3d 915 (Fourth Cir.), *cert. denied*, 117 S.Ct. 358 (1996).

Wainwright v. Stone, 414 U.S. 21 (1973).

Wisconsin v. Mitchell, 505 U.S. 476 (1993).

Organizations

Gay & Lesbian Advocates & Defenders: GLAD is a nonprofit, public interest legal organization whose mission is to achieve full equality and justice for New England's lesbian, gay, bisexual, and HIV or AIDS affected individuals. GLAD attorneys handle lawsuits involving sexual orientation discrimination as well as cases involving HIV or AIDS discrimination or invasion of privacy and confidentiality. GLAD also has a public education program, which hosts educational forums on the law pertaining to lesbians, gay men, bisexuals, and people with HIV and AIDS. In addition, GLAD operates a toll-free telephone information hotline with a lawyer referral service serving Massachusetts, Maine, New Hampshire, Vermont, Rhode Island, and Connecticut.

The American Civil Liberties Union: The ACLU is the nation's foremost advocate of individual rights, litigating, legislating, and educating the public on a broad array of issues affecting individual freedom in the United States. The ACLU is a nonprofit, nonpartisan, 275,000-member public interest organization devoted exclusively to protecting the basic civil liberties of all Americans and extending them to groups that have traditionally been denied them. In its almost seven decades in existence, the ACLU has become a national institution and is widely recognized as the country's foremost advocate of individual rights. The ACLU has more than a dozen national projects devoted to specific civil liberties issues: AIDS, arts censorship, capital punishment, children's rights, education reform, lesbian and gay rights, immigrants' rights, national security, privacy and technology, prisoners' rights, reproductive freedom, voting rights, women's rights, and workplace rights. The ACLU appears before the U.S. Supreme Court more than any other organization except the U.S. Department of Justice.

Lambda Legal Defense and Education Fund: A national organization committed to achieving full recognition of the civil rights of lesbians, gay men, and people with HIV/AIDS through impact litigation, education, and public policy work. Lambda pursues litigation in all parts of the country, in every area of the law that affects lesbians, gay men, and people with HIV/AIDS, such as discrimination in employment, housing, public accommodations, and the military; HIV/AIDS-related discrimination and public policy issues; parenting and relationship issues; equal marriage rights; equal employment and domestic partnership benefits; sodomy law challenges; immigration issues; anti-gay initiatives; and free speech and equal protection rights.

—Jane Dolkart

13

Film

At the end of the Hollywood musical *Lady in the Dark* (1944), Mischa Auer, one of Hollywood's stock dandies (a term relative to the "sissy"), has the last word. Auer plays a flaming fashion photographer and, in the final scene, fumbles into the office of Ginger Rogers only to discover that Ginger and her former nemesis Ray Milland are engaged in a passionate kiss. "This is the end!" cries Auer, "The ABSOLUTE end!" A close-up on his face captures this decidedly queer moment before "THE END" fades into view. If Auer's exclamation ends the picture and confirms a stereotype, it then becomes, in an era of lesbian/gay cultural criticism, an invitation to begin our work.

The following discussion approaches the subject of lesbians, gays, and film in the United States through three central concerns: (1) the people who make films (writers, directors, producers, costumers, etc.); (2) film content and styles (the way a film looks based upon camera work, editing, and art direction); and, (3) the audiences of films (critics and public alike). The discussion is divided into two broad historical periods and artistic contexts: Hollywood films and filmmakers from 1914-1997 and underground/avant-garde filmmaking from 1947-1997. Part I, "Lesbians, Gays and the Classical Hollywood Cinema: 1917-1960," explores the Hollywood studio system, which barred the representation of homosexuality in its system of self-censorship, the Production Code. Nevertheless, queer creative personnel worked there, queer themes (either derogatorily presented or heavily disguised) managed to sneak through the gatekeepers, and queer audiences developed tastes for Hollywood genres and stars. Part I consists of four sections. Section 1, "Hearts Of Darkness: *Film Noir*'s Queer Menace," observes the ways in which the classic detective-crime genre often constructed implicitly queer criminal characters. Section 2, "Sex, Lies and Masquerade: Comedy, Gender, and Cross-Dressing," traces the queer streaks in Hollywood comedies since the silent slapstick period. Gay director George Cukor's 1936 cross-dressing comedy *Sylvia Scarlett* closes the discussion. Section 3, "Stars, Sisters and Spectators: The 'Woman's Film' and Lesbian Audiences," views the way lesbian audiences of

the 1930s, 1940s and 1950s appreciated the stars (e.g. Dietrich, Garbo, Hepburn) and stories (e.g. *Blonde Venus, Queen Christina, Christopher Strong*) of the Hollywood "woman's film" genre. The section also discusses the work of Dorothy Arzner, a lesbian director of these genre films. Section 4, "Camp, Hollywood Genres and Gay Stars, Directors and Audiences," views the way camp aesthetics informed the creations of gay Hollywood directors (e.g., James Whale, Vincent Minnelli) in particular genres (e.g., the horror film and the musical) and the way gay spectators appreciated these genres and particular stars, such as Judy Garland.

Part II, "Breaking the (Production) Code in Post-Classical Hollywood: 1960-the Present," examines the many changes in Hollywood after the studio system and the Production Code. Section 1, "Post-Classical Hollywood and Lesbian-Gay Film Characters," examines Hollywood's combined permissiveness and conservatism in the representation of homosexuality. Section 2, "Midnight Movies, Camp Sensibility, and John Waters," views a vital innovation in film exhibition and content whose gay cult status affected subsequent gay filmmaking. Section 3, "The Gay Ghetto and AIDS in Post-Classical Hollywood Films," explores the way the gay ghetto becomes the positive prototype for representing gay life in the 1990s. Section 4, "Queers, AIDS and the Revival of *Film Noir*," investigates the ways in which AIDS informs a number of "neo-noirs." Section 5, "Lesbian Camp in Post-Classical Hollywood Films," observes how 1990s lesbian representations employ camp style, usually associated with gay male filmmakers and audiences.

Part III, "A Cinema of Sexperts: The Lesbian and Gay Avant-Gardes and Cinemas of Identity Politics: 1947-1989," explores, in its first section, "Underground and Independent Filmmaking: 1947-1970." The work of Kenneth Anger, Andy Warhol, Jack Smith, and other gay male avant-gardists and gay-themed underground films receive attention. Section 2, "Feminism, Gay Liberation, and Cine-Activism of the 1970s and 1980s," takes up the lesbian and gay non-mainstream filmmaking in its first explicitly political phase following the Stonewall riots (1969). Part IV, "The New Queer Cinema 1989-the Present," takes up lesbian and gay political, non-mainstream filmmaking in its second phase. Section 1, "We're queer! We're here! We're fabulous! Get used to it!," outlines the political influences and cultural strategies in the emergence of the New Queer Cinema. Section 2, "The Boys in the Band," views the most-pervasive themes in queer films, and their tendency to challenge the "positive images" demands of gay assimilation politics. Section 3, "The 'Other' Side of the New Queer Cinema," investigates the debate about who queer cinema represents. In the wake of the New Queer Cinema, some critics observed how the movement was heavily dominated by gay male filmmakers whose radical approaches avoided considerations of gender and ethnicity. The continuation of the New Queer

Cinema into the 1990s is marked by its attention to lesbian stories as well as stories involving queer people of color. Part V lists many brief profiles of queer directors, producers, critics, and actors, as well as other film artists (heterosexual and/or closeted) whose work has profoundly informed the ways that movies represent sexuality in general and homosexuality in particular.

LESBIANS, GAYS AND THE CLASSICAL HOLLYWOOD CINEMA: 1917-1960

As David Bordwell, Janet Staiger, and Kristin Thompson discuss in their definitive study, *The Classical Hollywood Cinema,* between 1917-30 the United States film industry institutionalized the studio system for the production, distribution, and exhibition of movies. From 1930-60, the same eight studios (MGM, Paramount, RKO, 20th Century Fox, Warner Brothers, Columbia, Universal, and United Artists) controlled the film industry in the United States and developed an increasing influence within many international film markets. Control within the studios was rigidly hierarchical, with the chief executive in New York dictating to the studio chief in Hollywood, and in turn, the studio chief giving orders to his producers, who then oversaw the directors and writers and the course of several film projects.

The period in Hollywood from 1917-60 has been variously referred to as the Golden Age, the Studio System Era, and the Classical Hollywood Cinema. One reason for calling it the Classical Hollywood Cinema relates to the well-honed, systematic nature of all aspects of the industry. For instance, writers crafted their screenplays according to specific standards. These included a linear narrative with a clear cause-effect structure, a goal-oriented, individual hero, and a main plot of action that coincides with a sub-plot (usually involving romance). The ending must resolve the hero's conflicts in a plausible manner, and more often than not, establish him/her within a heterosexual romance. The Classical Hollywood Cinema was also a genre cinema, and so screenplays would also have to conform to the particular sets of conventions in a given genre. Finally, Classical Hollywood's self-censorship codes regulated the content of screenplays and the visual style of films.

In the early 1920s, the studios evaded the sticky and expensive intrusion of local and federal censorship laws and improved their own reputation through the establishment of a self-censorship system. Following a series of Hollywood sex scandals, complaints and threatened boycotts by civic and religious groups issued forth, along with the formation of local censorship boards. In 1922, the studio chiefs installed former Harding administration postmaster Will Hays as the head of the Motion Picture Producers and Distributors of America. Despite Hays's blacklisting of over 117 stars and his 1924 "Purity Code" regulating film content, attacks on Hollywood persisted. In 1934, the studios established the Production Code Administration, headed by the respected Catholic layperson Joseph Breen. Breen, with the aid of Father Daniel Lord and publisher Martin Quigley, co-authored the Production Code. No studio wishing to distribute and exhibit its films in the United States could make a film that didn't have the Production Code seal, unless it wanted to pay a $25,000 fine. Adding to the formulaic nature of Hollywood filmmaking, the Production Code presented a number of prohibitions enumerated by film historian David Cook in *A History of Narrative Film*:

> It forbade depicting "scenes of passion" in all but the most puerile terms, and it required that the sanctity of marriage be upheld at all times.... Adultery, illicit sex, seduction, or

rape could never be more than suggested, and then only if they were absolutely essential to the plot and were severely punished at the end.... Also prohibited were the use of profanity ... and racial epithets; any implication of prostitution, miscegenation, sexual aberration, or drug addiction; nudity of all sorts; sexually suggestive dances or costumes; "excessive and lustful kissing"; and excessive drinking. It was forbidden to ridicule or criticize any aspect of any religious faith, to show cruelty to animals or children, or to represent surgical operations, especially childbirth, "in fact or silhouette."

While the Production Code proscribed the representation of any form of sexual activity besides abstinent, heterosexual courtship, several directors attempted to evade these proscriptions through the uses of visual codes and verbal innuendo. Many *auteur* critics (those interested in the common motifs and styles of a particular director's films, as well as how they reflect that director's psychology and social-historical context) have discussed veiled depictions of homosexuality in the films of Alfred Hitchcock. While Hitchcock was apparently heterosexual (although, according to his biographer Donald Sotto, barely sexual at all in practice), homosexuality plays a central role in many of his films, most obviously in *Rebecca* (1940), *Rope* (1948, based upon the Leopold and Loeb murder case), *Strangers on a Train* (1951), and *North by Northwest* (1959). While Hitchcock's homos are always figures of danger and psychosis (e.g. *Rebecca*'s Mrs. Danvers, Bruno in *Strangers, Rope*'s Brandon and Phillip), they remain among the most complex and entertaining of his films' characters. Furthermore, in Hitchcock's films, heterosexuality and the social institutions that enforce it oftentimes appear as the implicit source of a range of perverse sexual orientations, an ideological commentary that feminist and queer critics have expounded upon. From the fetishistic and misogynist idealization of "woman" in *Vertigo* (1958) to the repressiveness (and potential murderousness) of the small town nuclear family in *Shadow of a Doubt* (1943), seemingly "normal" heterosexual desires arguably spawn obsession and murder.

Hearts of Darkness: *Film Noir*'s Queer Menace

The discussion of homosexuality in Hitchcock's suspense thrillers leads smoothly into a look at how classical Hollywood film genres have implicitly constructed homosexuality, and how lesbian and gay audiences have reacted historically to particular Hollywood film genres. Before the inception of the Production Code and even afterwards, some Hollywood genre films used stock characters who, while rarely named as homosexual, exhibited traits either directly or more implicitly associated with homosexuality. For instance, Hitchcock's genre of choice, the detective/crime film—better known as *film noir*—consistently drew villains whose criminal behavior could be attributed to either repressed or expressed homosexual desires.

The 1940s genre *film noir* depicts the city as a community of sexually perverted outlaws who threaten the well being of the isolated "normal" male detective. As Richard Dyer points out in his classic essay "Homosexuality and *Film Noir*," the pervs fall into three categories: the femme fatale or aggressively sexual hetero woman; the effeminate male criminal; and, less frequently, the villainous bull dagger (more common in the cycle of women-in-prison films). If the *noir* city is a disorienting labyrinth of shadowed sidewalks, dead end streets, and omniscient evil, queer stereotypes constitute the majority population.

The manipulative butch dyke Jo in *Walk on the Wild Side* (1962), the foppy aesthete Waldo in *Laura* (1944) who turns out to be the murderer, and the motley crew of fortune hunters in *The Maltese Falcon* (1941) exemplify the genre's broader tendency to envision moral depravity through traits and behaviors associated with non-heterosexual, procreative behavior. In *Laura,* the character Waldo (played by fey Clifton Webb) is not labeled as homosexual, although he embodies queer urban perversity. Waldo is a cynical New York bachelor dandy who hurls acid barbs at everyone, smokes cigarettes while lounging in his bath tub, appreciates his collection of expensive antiques that adorn his immaculate apartment, and attempts to murder a woman, Laura, whom he cannot love. *The Maltese Falcon* (1941) features Peter Lorre's Rick Cairo, first introduced through his perfume-scented calling card, overly coifed appearance, and falsetto snivel. Cairo's accomplices include Mr. Gutman (Sydney Greenstreet) and his boyish hired-gun, "Ganymede" Wilmer (Elisha Cook, Jr.). Together, they form an alternately menacing and comical community of implicitly homosexual outlaws.

As demanded by the Production Code, if a film had to represent unwholesome, non-Code characters or actions, the film had to also properly punish the transgressors. The villains represent amorality, the male hero (often a detective or repentant criminal) represents some pull toward morality (no matter how tenuous or labored that pull might be), and the hero's victory ultimately results in the disciplining of the villains. If these conventional portrayals appeal to homophobic ideas circulating in political discourse, popular psychology, and social commentary of the 1940s, 1950s and 1960s, they nonetheless provide some of the only cinematic depictions of lesbians and gays until the 1970s.

Sex, Lies, and Masquerade: Comedy, Gender, and Cross Dressing

Hollywood genre films not only constructed criminal queers, but also comedic ones. Cross-dressing, mistaken identity, comic humiliation, male neurosis, and male competition comprise only a few stock comic situations that can make momentary—and always intended to be funny—references to homosexuality. Far fewer examples of suggested female homosexuality arise in Hollywood comedies owing to the films' focus on heterosexual romance and male friendship. Television comedy, indicates Alexander Doty, with its reputation as a "domestic" medium and its appeal to female audiences, presents an array of female heroines and their friends, from *I Love Lucy* to *Laverne & Shirley.* The Hollywood genre of the woman's film also stresses female relationships and varying degrees of possibility for reading lesbian desire between the characters. As for Hollywood comedies, they revel in the comic humiliation of their characters, and depending upon when they were made, some films link the humiliation of men with emasculation and homosexuality. In their book *Popular Film and Television Comedy,* Steve Neale and Frank Krutnik discuss one such instance of comic humiliation (among many) for the silent slapstick duo Laurel and Hardy. In the film *Liberty* (1929), the boys accidentally switch their pants so that Laurel wears Hardy's, and vice versa. When they attempt to rectify this error and swap their trousers, policemen continually keep showing up. If a sexual dimension exists in this (and other) intimate exchanges between the boys, the suspicions of the police draw it into even more pronounced relief.

Thirty years later, in the sex comedy *The Seven Year Itch* (1955), the seemingly heterosexual frustrations of a middle-class married man strangely (and hilariously) lead to numerous homosexual innuendoes. To begin with, the film's protagonist, New York pulp publisher Richard Sherman (Tom Ewell), bids his wife and son goodbye for the summer and returns to his apartment house shared with typically Manhattanite figures: a Jewish intellectual couple who collect African art (the Kaufmans) and a nameless gay couple, "those two men upstairs—interior decorators, or something." In the absence of his wife and "tow-headed space cadet" son, Richard catches "the seven year itch" and fears that he will transform into a sex-hungry molester of innocent women. As this bourgeois-heterosexual dilemma arouses Richard's anxieties, he continually makes a fool of himself. Blatant phallic symbols and a recurrent 1950s sex comedy motif arise only to confound Richard's sense of control, composure, and masculinity.

Humorous cues implying castration and homosexuality manifest themselves through Richard's manic comic behavior in the face of uncontrollable and anti-bourgeois desires. While nervously enjoying the company of the Girl from upstairs (Marilyn Monroe), he pops open a bottle of champagne. When it spurts out, he squeezes his finger into the champagne bottle, and then cannot remove it. In the last scene, Richard awakens to discover that the Girl from upstairs spent the night in his apartment. Afraid of being exposed, he nervously cracks open the front door to retrieve the milk, and then squats down to reach for the newspaper. His buttocks literally teeter inches above the milk bottle. Throughout the film Richard carries a cumbersome canoe paddle which he has to send to his vacationing son. The awkwardly long paddle gets stuck in ceiling fans, becomes an Olympian task to wrap for mailing (on parallel with the Olympian task of resisting Monroe), and continues to be an impediment when, at the end, Richard flees his apartment (and, by extension, his sexual angst) to see his wife and son in the country.

Comic humiliation also generates from the recurrence of cross-dressing, a device that stems back to the Greek comedies of Aristophanes. In Hollywood studio films, men more often perform in drag than women. Despite its conventionality, cross dressing has at times angered conservatives, although it is difficult to gauge the extent to which its uses (and the element of humiliation more often attached to it) are progressive (questioning the stability of gender roles) or reactionary (reinforcing gender roles by the comedic chaos caused by overturning them). Neale and Krutnik, along with gay film critic Vito Russo in *The Celluloid Closet,* isolate Charlie Chaplin's silent short *A Woman* (1915) for the way it raised disapproving critical reactions and inspired censorship threats when it originally premiered. In it, the Tramp is disguised as a woman and drives two men—one of them married with a wife and daughter—to compete over her/him. Chaplin's masquerade humiliates the two hypocritical middle-class men. *A Woman* only barely resolves the problems raised by the Tramp's drag, and the specters of androgyny and homosexuality persist when the men chase the Tramp from the house. Victorian morality found fault in this degrading treatment of the bourgeois family patriarch. Protest against the film bolstered the existing threats of censorship and persuaded Hollywood's comedians to temper their playfulness.

While the conservatism of the Hollywood studio system, codified in 1932's Production Code, did not expunge drag from the nation's movie screens, its uses decreased in terms of frequency and functional importance to film plots. *Bringing Up Baby* (1938) provides a typical example of this use of cross-dressing. Screwball millionairess Katharine Hepburn, in love with absentminded archaeologist Cary Grant, secures him in her aunt's country home by stealing his clothes and leaving him with a skimpy negligée. When the heiress's aunt asks the archaeologist why he's wearing these clothes, he leaps in the air and exclaims, "I just went gay all of a sudden!" (According to historian George Chauncey, "gay" here probably referred less to homosexual desire than the flamboyance of a man donning women's clothes.) Immediately, the archaeologist garbs himself in more masculine, but no less improbable, apparel. Sequences such as this one from romantic comedies join similar but differently motivated uses of drag in "comedian comedies," as discussed by Neal and Krutnik. Here, the wackiness of the comedian—be it Bob Hope, Jerry Lewis, or Milton Berle—motivates the recurrent use of drag throughout his movies.

When drag plays an instrumental part in a film's plot line, the narrative carefully aims its use toward reinstating heterosexual masculinity. Drag functions as a temporary solution to a specific problem. This problem, more often than not, relates to obstacles to heterosexual desire and coupling. Drag, then, makes it possible for the heterosexual romance to progress and be consummated. This is what Marjorie Garber refers to in her book *Vested Interests* as the "progress narrative" of drag performance. For instance, *I Was a Male War Bride* (1949) submits a French war hero (Cary Grant) who must disguise as a WAC in order to marry an American woman officer (Ann Sheridan) and emigrate to the U.S. Before and after this, the Grant character's heterosexuality and masculinity are well established, although the woman he loves does prove to be a more competent soldier. After such tortured masquerading and the delay of their marriage consummation, the final embrace between the newlyweds implies that their love can withstand all trials (even compulsory drag) and will last forever.

The use of drag in *Some Like It Hot* (1959, Billy Wilder), made amid the demise of the Hollywood studio system, also reveals the loosening (and eventual demise) of the Production Code. The film proves to be fraught with ambiguities surrounding the assumed perversity (by status quo standards) of its cross-dressing characters. The functionality of drag (as in *I Was a Male War Bride*)—its employment in order to fulfill a higher, "normal" goal—partly transforms into the pleasures of drag in itself. The film flirts with the notion that ostensibly fixed and permanent gender roles can become, through drag, the eroticized *performance* of gender roles.

When two jazz age musicians, Joe (Tony Curtis) and Gerry (Jack Lemmon), cross dress in order to hide from mobsters, they join an all-girl band. Both Josephine/Joe and Daphne/Gerry fall for the band's chanteuse, Sugar (Marilyn Monroe). While Joe temporarily drops his "Josephine" disguise and masquerades as an impotent Oil Tycoon to seduce Sugar, Gerry remains "Daphne," and an elderly millionaire, Osgood (the comic Joe E. Brown), woos "her." The climax involves the return of the mobsters and Joe and Gerry's attempted flight in drag. However, when Josephine kisses Sugar "good-bye," the mobsters recognize Joe and the chase ensues. By virtue of Osgood's desires for Daphne (to say the least of his high speed motorboat), Joe, Gerry, Sugar, and Osgood speed away together. Joe reveals his true identity to Sugar, she forgives him, and they embrace. This resolves the conflicts separating the heterosexual lovers: Joe's real identity and his sleazy scheme for ensnaring Sugar.

In classical Hollywood terms, when the lovers overcome all obstacles and finally unite, the film is over. This is one way that dominant culture represented heterosexual desire as natural and inevitable: the goal of every Hollywood film is to bring the heterosexual lovers together. Once that happens, *all* conflicts are resolved and the film ends. However, *Some Like It Hot* offers an interesting coda. Gerry/Daphne, now engaged to Osgood, offers a list of reasons for why he can't marry (neglecting to say he's a man), and Osgood dismisses all of them. As a last resort, Gerry confesses his gender,

to which Osgood replies, "Nobody's perfect." Given that deviance in comedies is conventional, according to Neale and Krutnik, as an element of surprise, or as an underlying plot mechanism (such as Joe and Gerry's decision to dress as women), Osgood's last words are not exactly transgressive. It's a surprise when he says "Nobody's perfect," but the entire situation and story of the film motivates this generous concession. Not only do the boys dress as women, but, when Gerry/Daphne dates the droolingly lascivious Osgood, s/he starts to believe that he's a girl and plans on marrying Osgood. On the other hand, what might have remained only implied, the androgyny of desire and objects of desire, here, becomes a clearly articulated and relatively believable possibility. Furthermore, Osgood's tone of taken-for-granted permissiveness might also mean, in turn, that everyone engages in cross-dressing of one kind or another. Indeed, Joe's masquerade as both a woman and a millionaire illustrates how social expectations underpin clothing styles: gender norms as well as class norms dictate the proper "costumes." "Nobody's perfect" also validates the pleasures taken by Osgood (and the film audience) in Gerry/Daphne's drag. It is by virtue of the imperfection of his/her performance—the vivid and oftentimes incongruous mix of "masculine" and "feminine"—that Gerry/Daphne inspires laughter and affection.

While the male-to-female drag of *Some Like It Hot* contains sexually subversive implications, the film nevertheless locates the power of gender-play and unleashed sexual desire in the hands of men. Joe represents the anchored heterosexual lothario who will submit to any number of humiliations (including drag) in order to skillfully "get the girl." Even Gerry/Daphne's more pliable identity, prone to influence (Gerry must remind himself that he's a man after a particularly romantic date with Osgood), signals a fairly complex (if not comical) personality. The character of Sugar (in addition to the star persona of Marilyn Monroe, as discussed by Dyer in *Heavenly Bodies*) contrasts the characters of Gerry and Joe with regard to her consistency, predictability, and vulnerability. Whereas Joe and Gerry forward the plot through their production of one comic surprise after another, Sugar reacts to their actions. Likewise, her body, voice, and temperament remain consistent throughout the film, whereas Gerry and Joe remain in a creative state of flux that tests their intelligence as much as their athleticism (e.g. walking in high heels, inventing new names and life stories). By masculinizing (and to a great extent heterosexualizing) the virtues and pleasures of drag, *Some Like It Hot* resuscitates patriarchal gender roles rather than testing them. Questions of gender remain reserved for the men to ponder and experience.

As an example of female-to-male cross-dressing, *Sylvia Scarlett* (1936) locates the creative power of drag in the female title character and eroticizes the homosexual implications arising from her mistaken identity. The film also repeatedly establishes the universal desirability of the cross-dressing title character, Sylvia (Katharine Hepburn). A box office disaster at the time of its release and the bane of gay director George Cukor's career, *Sylvia Scarlett* might have escaped the inspection of the Production Code Administration, but it bewildered audiences and angered some Hollywood insiders. Cukor biographer Patrick McGilligan relates that, while the audiences of the film were probably confused by the non-linear plot, RKO Studio executives and others resented the blatant if not cocky quirkiness of the film. Not only did *Sylvia Scarlett* not conform to the conventional structure of Hollywood comedies, but the film also flirted with allusions to the homosexuality of its director George Cukor and lead actor Cary Grant.

In *Sylvia Scarlett,* young Sylvia Snow cross dresses as a pubescent boy—Sylvester Scarlett—in order to assist in her recently widowed father Henry's escape from the police. (This mass of information arrives in the first scene of *Sylvia Scarlett.* According to an interview with director Cukor in Boze Hadleigh's *Conversations with My Elders,* the Production Code Administration necessitated this prologue in order to make Sylvia's cross dressing a dire necessity rather than a personal choice.) The male and female characters whom Sylvester encounters inevitably express their attraction to him/her. When Sylvester/Sylvia and her father join ranks with a con man, Jimmy Munkley (Cary Grant), Jimmy extols Sylvester's virtues ("He's got humor, imagination") and proclaims that he knew Sylvester was "the right sort" since the first time they met. Here, "the right sort" refers to Sylvester's shared desire to "beat the system" (as Jimmy puts it) in a life of grifting. Given Sylvia's subterfuge as Sylvester, her desire to "beat the system" also involves dressing as a male and usurping male privileges. Better yet, *as a boy,* Sylvester/Sylvia attracts people and influences them. Sylvester compels Jimmy, first to enlist Henry and her into the life of thievery and confidence games, and next to form a traveling band of players, "The Pink Pierrots." In Jimmy and Sylvester's wagon one nippy evening, Jimmy wants to "get curled up" with Sylvester. "You'll make a proper little hot water bottle," says Jimmy. Michael, an artist whom Sylvester charms in one of their performances, informs Sylvester of "a queer feeling when I look at you." Michael's friend, a Russian heiress, comments that Sylvester is "such a pretty boy" and Maudie, the fourth Pierrot, draws a moustache on Sylvester and kisses him.

Clearly, "Sylvester" is more desirable than "Sylvia." This relates to her/his power as a narrative agent, a willing catalyst of comic events. As lesbian film critic and director Andrea Weiss observes in her book *Vampires and Violets, Sylvia Scarlett* exploits the figure of the Trickster, a "creative force" recurrent throughout world culture whose gender tends to be ambiguous and whose purpose consists in challenging taken-for-granted social conventions and taboos. Then again, the Trickster here complicates matters both by her/his own creative forcefulness and her/his desirability as the indeterminately sexed figure. Indeed, talent, androgyny, and desirability appear inextricably bound in the character of Sylvia/Sylvester. While Weiss notes how Sylvia reveals her identification with women by sympathizing with and defending Maudie, "Sylvester" remains an object of erotic desire for Jimmy, Michael, and Maudie. On the other hand, Michael's laughter and disgust upon the revelation of Sylvia's cross-dressing reveals the social assumptions that distinguish between different forms of androgyny. According to certain Victorian and Edwardian ideas about masculinity and sexuality deriving from Greek classicism, the androgyny of pubescent boys is normal and permissibly erotic. While this discourse reveres femininity in boys, it at best ignores, at worst reviles, the consideration of actual women. If Sylvester's indeterminate pubescent masculinity proves a "queer" attraction to Michael, the disclosure of Sylvia's masquerade (and the reversing of her/his ostensible gender) inspires him to call her an "oddity" and "freak of nature." And, while Michael previously appreciated Sylvester's boyish display of anger, he reacts to Sylvia's now unwomanly show of assertiveness by labeling her a "vixen."

As in *A Woman* and *Some Like It Hot,* in *Sylvia Scarlett* the cross-dresser's humiliation of the folk who misrecognize her/him ultimately ricochets back at the trickster, Sylvia/Sylvester. This climactic moment of reverse-comic humiliation finally resolves the gender "conflict" underpinning Sylvia/Sylvester's masquerade. Michael's derisive laughter, combined with Sylvia's affections for him, function to erase "Sylvester" from the movie. However, in contrast to *A Woman* and *Some Like It Hot,* the pleasures of masquerade are clearly exchanged for the pleasures of heterosexual desire and romance.

Stars, Sisters, and Spectators: The "Woman's Film" and Lesbian Audiences

Katharine Hepburn plays a different kind of cross-dressing character in the "woman's film" *Christopher Strong* (1933). Independent aviatrix Cynthia Darrington dresses as a man and usurps male privilege, yet she suffers a melodramatic fate derived from typical story patterns for female "woman's film" characters. Cynthia is the exceptional woman torn between career (New Womanhood) and love (True Womanhood). Cynthia also suffers over split allegiances between her male lover and her female friends. Finally, she dies for her sins of fornication in the manner of the ordinary fallen woman. Cynthia Darrington and the film *Christopher Strong* serve as specific examples of how lesbian cultural codes intersect with those of the classical Hollywood "woman's film" genre and star system. The woman's film continually featured the figure of the New Woman, the formation of female communities (albeit, heterosexual romances ultimately despoil or replace them), and strong female protagonists played by stars whose images evoked similar qualities of strength.

Cynthia Darrington invokes the "New Woman," a female social type of the first three decades of the twentieth century whose most salient characteristics include the pursuit of a career and a tendency to dress in men's clothes. Feminist and lesbian historians and cultural critics such as Esther Newton and Carroll Smith-Rosenberg have analyzed the importance of the "New Woman" image both to all middle-class women desiring a life outside of domesticity, and more specifically to a burgeoning lesbian identity. According to Newton and Smith-Rosenberg as well as Barbara Welter in her article "The Cult of True Womanhood," the "New Woman" derives from a critique of the Victorian lady or "True Woman"—the domesticized mother, daughter, sister, and wife—by women attempting to break into the public spheres of industry, politics, the academy, and the arts. While the New Women of the early 1900s maintained a Victorian attitude toward sexuality, the New Woman of the 1920s rejected this Puritanism, as well as society's equation of strong women and asexuality.

Christine Gledhill's and Maria La Place's studies of the Hollywood "woman's film" genre also note the repeated figure of the New Woman, oftentimes pitted in angst-ridden opposition to her Victorian counterpart, the "True Woman." And, lesbian film criticism has considered the relationships between the New Woman image, images of lesbian identity, and the activity of lesbian audiences of the "woman's film" genre. As a classical Hollywood genre, the "woman's film" derived from such diverse popular culture as theatrical melodrama, nineteenth- and twentieth-century women's fiction, and realist literature and theater, Gledhill relates. The "woman's film" offered many points of access for lesbian viewers. Female points-of-view, communities, and friendships comprise the genre's iconic features, although many critics have noted how the entrance of a male protagonist (and romantic love interest) tends to undermine the authority of female points-of-view and the bonds of the female community. While so many "woman's films" treat the heroine's transition from female community to heterosexual romance as natural and inevitable, lesbian spectators have been capable of *selecting* certain features of a film's story, art direction, and acting that "speak" lesbian desire and identity, despite other features that manifestly "heterosexualize" a film. Weiss argues, along with the critics Edith Becker, Michelle Citron, Julia Lesage, and B. Ruby Rich of the feminist film journal *Jump Cut,* that audience members actively *negotiate* film meanings. This consideration makes it vitally important for lesbian and gay film critics and historians to consider how queer folk watched movies and made meaning out of them, alongside the evaluation of a film's aesthetic form and content.

For instance, in her definitive study of director Dorothy Arzner, Judith Mayne shows how Arzner's *Dance, Girl, Dance* (1940) appears to give more weight to female relationships than heterosexual romantic ones, even though its plot leads linearly toward a resolution with an apparent heterosexual union. Then again, the embrace between ballet impresario Steve Adams (Ralph Bellamy) and aspiring ballerina Judy could just as easily be paternal as romantic. Likewise, Judy's relationship with her first mentor, Madame Basilova, and the Madame's motivations for trying to help Judy succeed as a dancer, could be read as either romantic or maternal. A lesbian spectator might choose to read the film's conclusion as "paternal" and Judy and Madame Basilova's relationship as potentially romantic. The "woman's film" remains one of the only Hollywood genres to lend itself to such subversive readings.

The factor of studio publicity also figures into speculations of how the film might have been understood by lesbian spectators. Mayne explains how various publicity statements and trade papers extolled the director of *Dance, Girl, Dance* and other "woman's films" as an exceptional individual, the sole woman director in classical Hollywood. Consequently, Arzner was often photographed, and her image appears as the embodiment of the New Woman/mannish lesbian. Posing behind cameras and in other postures of authority, wearing suits, ties, and men's hats, the well-publicized Arzner images appeal to lesbian audiences even if Arzner's public image and films were not explicitly lesbian. Gossip and speculation about Arzner by lesbian spectators might also have influenced speculation about the lesbian aspects of her films. (In the area of auteurism, Arzner's sexuality and the history of her relationships with women provide compelling criteria for unpacking the lesbian meanings in them.)

The example of Dorothy Arzner's image and its probable meaningfulness to lesbian film fans from the 1920s, 1930s, and 1940s suggests the importance of analyzing the attraction of lesbian and gay film fans to particular movie stars. Many members of these audiences "appropriated" and "rewrote" mainstream Hollywood cinema through identifications with, and desires for, particular star images and personas. (Surely, Arzner's image was in no way as pervasive as that of the average female star. Directors did not achieve star status comparable to actresses and actors until the late 1960s and 1970s. However, the fact that Arzner's image was periodically available in fan magazines and trade papers occasionally put her into a similar position as the female star.)

During the classical Hollywood era, many stars popular among lesbian audiences "specialized" in the "woman's film." Classical Hollywood genre films routinely featured the same stars in similar roles. Bordwell, Staiger, and Thompson observe how the association of particular stars and genres served as a marketing mechanism and a means of predicting public reactions to films, an integral aspect of the efficiency of the studio system. While the studio heads and their publicity departments constructed stars' images with the intention of appealing to the largest possible audience, lesbian and gay audiences, particularly those traveling in the urban subcultures, developed informal fan communities honoring certain stars who evoked qualities of "queerness." Weiss, Becker, Citron, Lesage, and Rich all posit that gossip, rumor, and fantasy about these stars also fueled their favor. The "woman's film" genre produced a pantheon of lesbian and gay audience favorites, such as Bette Davis, Joan Crawford, Greta Garbo, Marlene Dietrich, and Katharine Hepburn.

B. Ruby Rich

Weiss explains how several studio-era stars' images appealed to the "New Woman" persona. By virtue of the simultaneous rise of the sexological model of female homosexuality—the "mannish lesbian"—and a woman-oriented consumer culture, the 1920s New Woman flaunted both the butch look and the more mainstream and femme "modern" or "flapper" image. Butch-femme couplings materialize in many Hollywood "woman's films." One classic film pairing of a femme flapper and a mannish lesbian, albeit not from Hollywood, remains the German silent film *Pandora's Box* (G.W. Pabst, 1929), an apocalyptic portrayal of Weimar decadence. Louise Brooks sports her famous "Lulu" haircut as Lulu, the flapper par excellence, and Alice Roberts plays the mannish Countess Geschwitz, one of Lulu's many suitors. Toward the beginning of the film, at Lulu's wedding reception, Geschwitz stares down the bride's new husband in order to secure a tango with her. As for Hollywood, temporary couplings of butch and femme women recur, with varying degrees of erotic implication. For instance, Garbo's male-attired *Queen Christina* (Rouben Mamoulian, 1933) kisses the feminine Countess Ebba. In *Morocco* (Joseph Von Sternberg, 1930), Dietrich's Amy Jolly (clad in a tuxedo) kisses a woman during her nightclub act. And, Arzner's *Dance, Girl, Dance* features the potentially erotic gazes between the mannishly dressed, elderly ballerina Madame Basilova and her tutu-wearing, toe-dancing disciple, Judy O'Brien. Mayne's study also illustrates the butch-femme motif in the publicity photos of Arzner, dressed in her customary suits, ties and hats, posing with femme leading ladies Joan Crawford, Rosalind Russell, Billie Burke, and Lucille Ball.

Lesbian audiences especially recognized how Garbo, Dietrich, and Hepburn evoked traits of the "New Woman's" compatriot from the field of sexology, the "mannish lesbian." Weiss and Olson both highlight elements in the Greta Garbo film *Queen Christina* that might have been perceivable as lesbian references. More specifically, all of these instances illustrate the Garbo character's appropriation of male privileges, one of the proposed "threats" of the mannish lesbian. For instance, Garbo dresses (for the most part) in a tunic, pants, and boots, and stands in a number of power poses traditionally accorded to men. If she appears to emulate men, Garbo/Christina jokingly demeans men and heterosexuality: "How is it possible to endure the idea of sleeping with a man in a room?" Later, Garbo/Christina could be distinguishing a space for her lesbian desires when she vows, "I have no intention to [die an old maid] . . . I shall die a bachelor."

The work of lesbian communities and their notice in films of certain iconographic lesbian styles cannot be underestimated. Garbo and *Queen Christina* co-writer Salka Viertel participated actively in the European upper-class lesbian scene of the 1930s, both the source from which gossip about Garbo might have spread as well as the cultural means for spreading the gossip. Mayne suggests that, in *Christopher Strong*, Katharine Hepburn's second movie and first star billing, Hepburn's maturing star image appears to stem in part through lesbian iconography. Mayne comments, "Many of the attributes later considered so central to the Hepburn persona—independence, athleticism, androgyny, butch flirtatiousness—are amply on display in the film." When *Morocco* premiered in 1930, rumors about Dietrich's affairs with women circulated among lesbians. These rumors informed many lesbians' readings of Dietrich's films and motivated their focus upon the drag sequences as a key to understanding the films. Furthermore, Dietrich dons the New Woman/ mannish lesbian" attire specific to New York and Parisian lesbian culture: white tie and tails, cigarette case, top hat. These seeming references to lesbian codes of dress, coupled with rumors about Dietrich's polysexuality, form the basis for lesbian readings of early Dietrich films. Again, these readings select out the *subtextual,* lesbian dimensions of her roles and star persona from all of the explicitly heterosexual and patriarchal meanings in her films and publicity materials.

As suggested above, some of the genre conventions of the "woman's film" also lend themselves to uniquely lesbian readings even though their ostensible purpose consists in reinstating the status quo. Feminist film critic Molly Haskell notes three variations of character types of the "woman's film." First, there is the "exceptional" woman whose individuality inspires rebelliousness and eventually leads to conflict. The "ordinary" woman's conflicts arise from her stereotypical victimization by exploitative or insensitive men. The last genre variant consists of the ordinary woman who becomes exceptional, whose ordinary suffering transforms into exceptional strength and character. Haskell also describes four categories of plot lines: sacrifice, affliction, choice, and competition. The female protagonist *sacrifices* either her maternal authority for the well being of her children, her career for love and family, her love and family for her career, her marriage/family for a lover, or her lover for marriage/family. Sometimes, the heroine is *afflicted* by a physically or mentally debilitating illness. At other times, she must *choose* between at least two suitors, or, *compete* with another woman for her man. Ironically, the exceptionality of female heroines separates them

from other women, while female relationships oftentimes degrade into competition or dissolve altogether. When women love each other, willed sacrifice, illness, and death all function to separate them. While many "woman's films" begin by foregrounding female relationships, they end up marginalizing them in lieu of the heterosexual romance.

The work of later feminist and lesbian critics such as Weiss, Mayne, and Gledhill contest Haskell and other critics' observations about the secured conservatism of the "woman's film." This second generation of critics considers the activity of female spectators in relation to the female relationships in the films. While many "woman's films" depict female communities as the stage for competitive conflict over men and/or career advancement, the consideration of a specific, socially, and historically defined lesbian audience position or point-of-view can complicate that stereotypical motif. From the standpoint of lesbian spectators, it is possible to view some of the conflicts and antagonisms between female characters as extensions of their relationships and mutual desires, rather than as just a few more sexist Hollywood stereotypes of women at odds with each other.

Christopher Strong offers an extensive example of how "woman's films" can materialize "lesbian" motifs through the presence of the New Woman/mannish lesbian figure, the prevalence of star images, and the formation of female communities. Katharine Hepburn plays Cynthia Darrington, an aviatrix who dresses in jodhpurs and vows devotion to her career to the exclusion of romantic relations. While she eventually engages in a love affair with a married man (the title character Christopher Strong), the film continually establishes Cynthia's desirability through her embodiment of historically "masculine" traits, from her clothes to her adventurousness and honorable self-sacrifice.

Film critic Judith Mayne observes how the film splits Cynthia into two irresolvable figures that correspond to her conflicted desires: career versus (heterosexual) romance, and female bonding versus heterosexual romance. Furthermore, the film visually encodes these oppositional figures through modes of dress: first, the New Woman/ mannish lesbian appearance, defined by her independence and mannish dress; and, second, the domesticized woman, defined by her ornamental and spiritual role as wife, and thus in terms of her feminine appearance and bourgeois values. In many scenes, Cynthia closely resembles the dress, temperament, and class position of Radclyffe Hall's "mannish lesbian" heroine Stephen Gordon in *The Well of Loneliness*. Like Stephen, Cynthia's style of dress, sense of adventurous independence, code of honor, and heroic self-sacrifice all appear as "masculine" qualities more natural to her than "feminine" ones. Yet, as the protagonist in a Hollywood film, with "compulsory heterosexuality" as the ultimate narrative goal, Cynthia must ultimately experience the oppositional pulls between being a career-oriented, asexual butch and a domestically identified heterosexual femme.

As Mayne reads the film through this conflicting split and its visual analogue in Cynthia's styles of dress, the character's gradual decline and tragic conclusion correspond with her increasingly "feminine" adornments, from bracelets to gowns. Mayne notes two key sequences in the film where Cynthia's *lack* of mannish dress coincides with her developing romance with Christopher. First, when Christopher initially proclaims his attraction to Cynthia, she prepares to depart for a fancy dress party. Cynthia dresses as a moth in a lamé gown with antennae affixed to her hood, a costume consistent with her love of flight, but in no other way characteristic of Cynthia. This abrupt, if not absurd, sartorial shift is comparable to a subsequent scene. In the wake of Cynthia and Christopher's first sexual experience, the camera reveals only Cynthia's outstretched arm adorned with a bracelet, a gift from Christopher. Amid the dialogue spoken off-screen, Cynthia remarks, "Now I'm shackled." During this scene, Christopher also requests that Cynthia end her aviation career in order to be his devoted mistress. Here, the visual presence of Cynthia's arm, isolated from the rest of her body and adorned with high class feminine "shackles," ironically reinforces the absence of Cynthia's full, confident, and athletic butch body. Likewise, Cynthia's spirit of independence and adventurousness also dissolves in lieu of a new docility and dependence.

However, Cynthia's desires for a career reemerge alongside a growing sense of loyalty to Christopher's daughter Monica (whom she had befriended) and his wife Elaine. Impregnated by Christopher, Cynthia commits suicide while setting an aviation altitude record, a self-sacrifice that pays tribute to her "mannish" career goals (and dress code) as well as to the other women in her life, Monica and Elaine, who suffer upon learning of Cynthia and Christopher's affair. Thus, *Christopher Strong* maintains conventional morality and the status quo by permanently punishing Cynthia for her transgressions. Yet, the romantic nobility and heroism of her act enthrones her. The film simultaneously exalts Cynthia and banishes her at the literal "height" of her ascent toward patriarchal authority. Echoes of this strategy emerge at the end of *Queen Christina,* as well as in a host of maternal melodramas wherein mothers sacrifice themselves for the good of their daughters' welfare, e.g. *Stella Dallas* (1936), *Imitation of Life* (1934 and 1959), and *Mildred Pierce* (1945).

Camp, Hollywood Genres, and
Gay Stars, Directors, and Audiences

A host of commentators in a variety of media have noted the retrospectively camp tension embedded within closeted actor Rock Hudson's star image. Both Armistead Maupin's 1982 novel *Further Tales of the City* and director Mark Rappaport's 1992 new queer cinema film *Rock Hudson's Home Movies* delve into Hudson's ironic combination of two related yet opposing trends of the 1950s: the idealization of the masculine suburban husband, and the demonization of the unrecognizable "enemy within," usually communists but also homosexuals. When, in the mid-1950s, the Hollywood gossip magazine *Confidential* threatened to print a story about Hudson's homosexuality, Universal Studios prevented its publication, saving the Cold War public from having to ponder this tension between "wholesome" star image and "perverted," secreted private life. However, rumors manage to spread, and by the 1970s, camp reclamations of Hudson's movies, partly based upon gossip about his sexuality, proliferated.

The same can be said for the 1930s horror films of then openly gay director James Whale: *Frankenstein* (1931), *The Old Dark House* (1932), *The Invisible Man* (1933), and *The Bride of Frankenstein* (1935). Each of these films wildly and ecstatically exploits the perverse but repressed currents of sexual desire underpinning horror plots and characters, such as Dr. Frankenstein's masturbatory fantasy-turned-science project, or the latent homosexuality motivating his desire to make a man. These films also contain main characters who mock conventional religion and morality, a quality singled out by the Production Code Administration when examining horror scripts for their approval.

In *The Bride of Frankenstein,* Whale also cast the exceptionally queeny (and apparently gay) actor Earnest Thesiger to portray Dr. Septimus Pretorious, Frankenstein's collaborator. The character's homosexuality is implied through both his dandyish mannerisms as well as his strictly male associates, Frankenstein, the Monster, and the grave diggers. Pretorious first appears by forcing his way into Frankenstein's bedroom, sending away Frankenstein's bride Elizabeth, and, in the words of film historian David J. Skal, "tempting him with an alternative way of creating life." Despite the moralistic punishment eventually met by Pretorious, his camp qualities make him the most likable character in the film. Pretorious exemplifies the delightful camp combination of uppercrust pretensions with perverse desires, such as when he sips wine by candlelight inside a crypt as his gravediggers look for fresh corpses.

The Monster also offers itself to gay interpretations on a less campy, more sympathetic level. As his only wish is to be loved, the Monster is initially not confined to heterosexual mandates. The intimate scene between the Monster and the old blind hermit shows the two men, both outcasts, crying because fate brought them together. The intrusion of two hunters foils their relationship and sends the Monster searching again. Finally, Russo points out that the Monster's failed attempt to win his female Bride's affections leads the Monster to kill himself, Pretorious, and the Bride.

If gay Hollywood stars (and directors) contribute to subsequent camp re-readings of their films, gay male audiences have also historically affiliated themselves with particular stars who were not known to be gay and genres without any explicit gay content. For instance, the genre of many of Hudson's movies was the 1950s "woman's film," re-vamped with the hyperbolic spectacles of cinemascope, stereophonic sound, and technicolor (in order to compete with television). These overblown effects also contribute to the camp re-readings of Hudson's films and many other 1950s "woman's films" and "male weepies" (e.g. *Bigger Than Life, Rebel Without a Cause,* and *Imitation of Life*). The heightened stylization of the image, sound, and acting appeal to a camp sensibility because they stand out as obvious "Hollywood effects." The obviousness of these technologies foregrounds the contrived mechanics of Hollywood films and disrupts any films' attempt to construct an illusion of reality. The 1940s "woman's films" of Bette Davis and Joan Crawford also appeal to this camp pleasure in the obviousness of contrivance. As Susan Sontag, Michael Bronski, Mark Booth, Phillip Core, and Andrew Ross all assert in their explanations of gay camp, Davis and Crawford developed stylized and stylish screen personas that, far from disappearing when they acted, shined exquisitely. It's always the glamorous "Bette" and "Joan" in their films, without any of realist acting's pretenses at creating a "pure" character.

No account of gay male camp and Hollywood films would be complete without reference to the musical genre and one of its preeminent, most hard-working (and notorious) stars, Judy Garland. Garland's significance to certain generations of gay audiences—post-WWII, pre-Stonewall—has been numerously documented and evaluated by, among others, Janet Staiger, Jane Feuer, and Richard Dyer. Indeed, the role Garland's death played in inspiring the 1969 Stonewall riots has been widely suggested. In Nigel Finch's 1995 queer fiction film *Stonewall,* one of the eventual leaders of the uprising, the drag queen Bostonia (actor Duane Boutte) sits in her bedroom watching the TV reportage of Garland's death the afternoon before that historic evening.

Garland's star image and many elements of the musical have ranked high in gay male camp culture for a number of social and cultural reasons. As critic Richard Dyer explains, Garland's star image appeals to the pre-Stonewall generation of gay men because of her qualities of contrived ordinariness, actual androgyny, and camp sensibility, qualities that could also be applied to the musical genre as a whole. For instance, the musical genre's insistent attempts at constructing ordinariness, with stories that revolve around the process of heterosexual courtship, romance, and marriage, run head-on with the genre's most fundamental features: people spontaneously breaking into song within production numbers bathed in unmitigated artifice and glitz. As critic Jack Babuscio explains in his classic essay "Camp and the Gay Sensibility," gay camp readings of the Hollywood musical genre have repeatedly located this incongruous combination of ordinariness and abundant artifice, particularly in the works of Busby Berkeley. Dyer's analysis of Garland also locates incongruities that lend themselves to her camp qualities. To begin with, MGM's publicity on Garland, touting the star's wholesome Americanness, was contradicted by the androgyny of her star image and her projected sense of irony and camp. Dyer specifies *The Pirate* (Vincent Minnelli, 1948) as the film in which Garland delivers her most visibly camp performance, injecting irony into her line readings as her character actively lusts after the skimpily clad Gene Kelley. Feuer and Dyer both observe how later revelations of her close relations with homosexual men, such as her father and her first husband, director Vincent Minnelli, to say the least of her conspicuously queeny following, also inform gay men's historical appreciation of Garland as someone actively working with a gay camp sensibility.

BREAKING THE (PRODUCTION) CODE IN POST-CLASSICAL HOLLYWOOD: 1960-THE PRESENT

Post-Classical Hollywood and Lesbian-Gay Film Characters

Openly lesbian and gay characters, along with the subject of homosexuality, began to populate Hollywood films after the gradual disintegration of the Production Code from the mid-1950s and onward into the 1960s. The period in Hollywood after 1960 is often referred to as "new" or "post-classical," insofar as the industry experienced a series of structural changes. First, the studios lost control of the exhibition arm of the industry, causing a decline in studio film production and the opening up of the field to independent and foreign films. As independent theater owners could no longer rely on Hollywood product to fill their screens, they began turning to foreign and domestic independent producers and distributors.

The establishment of an art film market in the United States led to the distribution of a number of foreign-made films that did not follow the regulations of the Production Code or the studios' revamped self-censorship office, the Motion Picture Association of America. As theater owners were now independent of the studios' controls, including the MPAA, they unswervingly screened films that broke a number of taboos.

In the wake of local censorship attempts, explains Kristin Thompson and David Bordwell in *Film History: An Introduction*, the Supreme Court ruled in 1952 that films were protected under the First Amendment. Furthermore, independent Hollywood producer-directors such as Otto Preminger began making films that increasingly transgressed the Code. Despite the denial of certification by the MPAA, the Preminger films won distribution and soared at the box office. The popularity of non-certified films also proved to Hollywood that it had another possible competitive advantage over the heavily self-censored television industry. (Widescreen, technicolor, stereophonic sound, and blockbuster spectacles comprised other strategies for competing with television.)

The fall of the self-censorship system (and the installation of the ratings system) also signaled the opportunity for Hollywood films to explore taboo subjects in greater detail. Furthermore, the critical and financial successes of adult-themed films such as *Who's Afraid of Virginia Woolf?, Bob & Carol & Ted & Alice, Midnight Cowboy,* and *Cabaret* made it evident that audiences for these films existed. If television stinted on risqué or sexual content, it also ignored most of the prevalent new social movements of the late 1960s and early 1970s, such as the anti-war movement, the Black Power movement, the feminist movement, and the lesbian-gay liberation movement. Post-classical Hollywood films often exploited these movements, such as in the independent and low-budget filmmaking of the early 1970s. The Blaxploitation, sexploitation, martial arts, and slasher genres all pay sensationalized attention to what network television would never represent. While these films exploited the radical sheen of various 1960s liberation movements, they often retained the traditional format of classical Hollywood genre films.

The liberation movement philosophies, combined with the art film styles of Fellini, Bergman, Truffaut, Fassbinder, and Bertolucci, compelled some Hollywood directors to forge an "auteur" cinema in post-classical Hollywood. Melvin Van Peebles's *Sweet Sweetback's Baadassss Song* (1971), Robert Altman's *M*A*S*H* (1970), Martin Scorsese's *Alice Doesn't Live Here Anymore* (1975), Francis Ford Coppola's *Apocalypse, Now* (1979), and Paul Mazursky's *Willie and Phil* (1979) all exemplify this tendency. (A subsequent generation of filmmakers such as Spike Lee, Hal Hartley, and Todd Haynes, along with producers such as Dolly Hall and Christine Vachon, have moved the "Hollywood art film" further toward the style of the art film, while the art film has moved further toward mainstream genres and film styles.)

Willie and Phil is a remake of Francois Truffaut's 1962 art cinema classic *Jules and Jim.* The earlier film's story about a menage a trois between two bohemian men and one woman in turn-of-the-century Paris was updated for the 1970s, making references to feminism, the youth movements, and the so-called "sexual revolution." The film continually reminds the viewer of its relation to the earlier Truffaut film through its title, story events, blatant references to *Jules and Jim,* and imitations of its style. Thus, *Willie and Phil* draws from the signature tendency of many 1960s art films—self-conscious stylization—which reminds viewers they're watching a film. References to social movements remain symbolized by the behavior of the characters. For instance, making reference to feminism, the character Jeannette talks back to her lovers Willie and Phil and affirms her own self-determination. Their menage a trois invokes the free love policies of the sexual revolution, along with many of its hypocritical aspects. While the three main characters consistently avow their mutual love, Willie and Phil consistently disavow homosexual desire between each other. They never make love with each other, nor does the film introduce the possibility for Jeanette to sleep with a woman. Furthermore, despite the feminist allusions, the story is still framed through Willie and Phil's friendship and the two men's encounter with and perceptions of Jeannette.

Both Robert Aldrich's *The Killing of Sister George* (1968) and William Friedkin's *The Boys in the Band* (1970) demonstrate a contradiction in post-classical Hollywood depictions of post-Stonewall lesbian and gay identity. For the heroes and heroines of these movies, the signs of queerness define them as individuals and constitute their greatest strengths and their core flaws. Each protagonist's rise and downfall occurs because of their (and others') queerness. *Sister George* centers on a middle-aged London actress nicknamed "George" owing to her soap opera character "Sister George" and because she is a butch dyke. George engages in blatant expressions of guilty sexual desire both publicly (e.g., she goes to lesbian bars, and in one scene she chases a nun) and privately (she and her young lover Childie carry on a fairly intense s/m relationship). As a liberated woman and a queer, George freely consorts with folk from sexual "subcultures" (e.g., her sex-worker confidante and her abundant lesbian acquaintances).

In the end, duplicitous and closeted friends and work mates of George victimize her. At a crowded lesbian club party, the film's most vivid picture of a lesbian community, George meets her nadir. George's employer, the sadistic and closeted Mercy Croft, fires her, and George's lover Childie leaves her. After the party, George discovers Childie entwined with Mercy, the only explicit sex scene of the film (and, according to Jenni Olson's *The Ultimate Guide To Lesbian & Gay Film and Video,* the first explicit lesbian sex scene in any mainstream film). Phenomena such as lesbian identity, sexual experimentation, sexual openness, and lesbian communities appear as George's ultimate undoing. The film closes on an anguished George, newly unemployed and deserted. The disintegration of community and the isolation of the individual is typical for many "serious" gay and lesbian film characters in the late 1960s and 1970s. From *Sister George* and *The Boys in the Band* to *Sunday, Bloody Sunday* (John Schlesinger, 1971) and *Staircase* (Stanley Donen, 1969), the narratives progress from community and identity to isolation, and, oftentimes self-loathing.

Midnight Movies, Camp Sensibility, and John Waters

Another innovation of the post-classical film era consists in the rise of midnight movies and cult or camp film styles. Cult and camp films usually invoke the audience's knowledge of past popular culture, and they oftentimes also play with liberation discourses. For instance, both Richard Dyer and Robin Wood cite George Romero's *Night Of The Living Dead* (1968) for its use of the 1950s sci-fi/ horror genre toward a critique of white supremacy in line with the Black Power movement. The film aligns the colors white with "evil" and black with "good." Ben, the hero of the film, is an intelligent and generous African-American man. The flesh-eating zombies are all white, and they are often indistinguishable from living Anglo characters. The film also associates death and evil with symbols of whiteness, such as the country home with the white picket fence where the gory action takes place, and the sheriff's posse that ironically guns down Ben, the sole survivor of the zombies' onslaught. The film closes with a series of freeze frames picturing members of the posse proudly posing next to dead zombies as if they were trophies. The frames are redolent of lynch mob photos.

The Rocky Horror Picture Show (1975, Jim Sharman), probably the most famous of all midnight movies, calls upon 1950s sci-fi and horror genre films as read through a gay camp sensibility. Gina Marchetti observes that the film's uses of drag and references to the glitter rock of the Rolling Stones and David Bowie/Ziggy Stardust situate it in a number of camp traditions. As far as gay camp is concerned, the film appropriates dominant culture and reads it against the grain, teasing out incongruities and contradictions. For instance, the film critiques the conservative "happy ending" of the traditional horror film, wherein the representatives of the status quo smite the monster, such as in *Dracula* when Dr. Van Helsing executes the title character. In *Rocky Horror,* the deaths of the transvestite-mad scientist-alien Dr. Frank N. Furter and his beloved creation Rocky appear more tragic than anything else. While this might be a critique of Hollywood horror films, it is also yet another tragic end for queers in love, as in most of the lesbian and gay pulp fiction of the 1950s and 1960s.

Gay film director John Waters's cult classic, *Pink Flamingos* (1972), remains one of the "great works" in the canon of depraved midnight movies, alongside *Rocky Horror Picture Show* and David Lynch's *Eraserhead.* As Dyer observes, Waters's work drew from "the off-off-Broadway brew of drag, kitsch and schlock, which flowered in the late sixties and seventies in [Charles Ludlam's] Theatre of the Ridiculous." *Pink Flamingos* provokes the question of how to distinguish art from filth. The film's original theatrical trailer makes this perfectly clear when it quotes contemporary film reviews that compare *Pink Flamingos* to both the Buñuel-Dali avant-garde classic *The Andalusian Dog* and a septic tank explosion. Indeed, filth inspires the strange stream of events that compel the spectators' voyeuristic gazes for some 90 exploitation-enhanced minutes.

In *Pink Flamingos,* filth is a positive measure of one's social standing. First, there is Babs Johnson, a.k.a. Divine, connoisseur of crime and perversion, who has been hailed by tabloids near and far as "the filthiest person alive." She isn't alone, living in a trailer secluded in the woods with her egg-obsessed mother Mama Edie, her girlfriend Cotton, and her chicken-loving (in the Biblical sense) son, Crackers. On the other, more fashionable side of the tracks live Connie and Raymond Marble, who push heroin and forcibly impregnate young women in order to sell their babies to lesbian couples. The snobbish Connie and Raymond want to steal the title of "Filthiest Person Alive" away from Divine, their class inferior. The Marbles even go so far as to hire a spy, Cookie, who will infiltrate Divine's den of depravity and supply the Marbles with the information that could lead to Divine and company's downfall. Dyer likens the thoroughly unashamed and ultimately cleansing celebration of perversity in Waters's films to the radical role of the drag queen in the Gay Liberation Movement. In these terms, *Pink Flamingos* is a queer classic in the broadest definition of the word "queer." (Indeed, its celebration of what dominant culture calls "filth" makes it the fecal-good movie of every year.)

The midnight screenings of *Pink Flamingos* and so many other gay-made films (e.g., Kenneth Anger's *Scorpio Rising* and Andy Warhol's *Lonesome Cowboys*) and gay-themed films (e.g. Fellini's *Satyricon* and Meyer's *Beyond the Valley of the Dolls*) were signs of the suffering film industry's willingness to experiment in order to attract both television audiences as well as patrons of the "high" arts (theater, opera, and ballet) back to movie theaters. The phenomenon of midnight movies also illustrates a major cultural trend of the 1970s and the 1980s: the shrinking distinctions between art films, exploitation films, and mainstream films. Finally, the abundant queerness of 1970s midnight movies signals the extent to which gay camp style was becoming mainstream style, a point made by Andrew Ross in his essay "The Uses of Camp." Again, the career of John Waters proves exemplary. By 1981, Waters would crossover into mainstream filmmaking with *Polyester,* starring Divine, Tab Hunter, and Edith Massy. In 1988, Waters's *Hairspray* proved a great success, followed by *Cry-Baby* (1990), featuring the TV star/ teen idol Johnny Depp, and *Serial Mom* (1994) with Kathleen Turner.

The Gay Ghetto and AIDS in Post-Classical Hollywood Films

Many queers simply take it for granted that when Dorothy Gale desires to go "over the rainbow," she wants to evacuate her repressive small town home in lieu of the liberating urban ghetto. And, many remain in camp disbelief over Dorothy's ultimate preference for gray-hued Kansas over technicolor Oz. Similar to the African-American ideal of identity, autonomy, and community represented

John Waters

by Harlem, queer mythologies utopianize urban ghetto enclaves such as the Castro. The lives of urban gays and lesbians also provide an attraction in several Hollywood movies and Hollywood art films of the 1980s and 1990s. Metropolitan queers stake out the centers of such movies as *Desert Hearts* (1985), *Parting Glances* (1985), *Philadelphia* (1994), *To Wong Foo, Thanks for Everything, Julie Newmar* (1995), *Jeffrey* (1995), *Stonewall* (1995), *Basquiat* (1996), and *Kiss Me, Guido* (1997). It appears that no one is in Kansas anymore, and audiences like it that way. However, this mainstream sentiment reverses the historical tendency to treat small town life as Eden and the city as a virtual Babylon. When *Mr. Deeds Comes To Town* (1936), from rural New Hampshire to Manhattan, he transforms the cynical city with his small town values. The transition from such jaundiced notions of the city and idealized constructions of the country to the current fad for "'united colors' urban chic" might be attributed to the increasingly violent reputations of self-proclaimed crusaders of "traditional values." Today, Mr. Deeds could conceivably come to town in order to bomb an abortion clinic or blow-up a Federal building.

Jonathan Demme's hugely popular *Philadelphia,* in which Tom Hanks plays a lawyer with AIDS who sues his bosses for discrimination, suggests that traditional/small town values no longer suffice. The film refashions the all-American dictum "and justice for all" according to the wisdom of urban diversity. At first, the city of the founding fathers is controlled by the attitudes of the bigoted white male lawyers who persecute the Tom Hanks character for having AIDS and being gay. At last, it requires the collaborative efforts of two classically urban types, the African-American man and the gay man—Denzel Washington and Hanks—to rejuvenate the principles of the Constitution. The Washington and Hanks characters effectively replace the white bigots as founding fathers for the 1990s.

To Wong Foo, Thanks for Everything, Julie Newmar (Beeban Kidron, 1995) unfolds its story by employing this updated formula. When three New York drag queens drive cross-country and bring their bit of Oz to a small Kansas town, their queer urban-ness revivifies the straight small town. *To Wong Foo* negates all of the 1980s' demonizing stereotypes of urban dystopia—queer disease and colored criminality—that pervaded the news and entertainment media. However, by removing the drag queens from the urban, particular qualities and realities of the urban are removed from the drag queens. All three of them are virtually de-sexualized. And, AIDS remains entirely unacknowledged.

Jeffrey (Christopher Ashley, 1995) takes off where the late Bill Sherwood's art house classic *Parting Glances* (1986) left off. Both films make the case that gay identity and gay sensibility have no substance outside of the urban ghetto and the struggle against AIDS and homophobia. *Parting Glances* forwards this idea less explicitly through two opposing characters who symbolize gay liberation as opposed to gay assimilation. Nick, the rock star with AIDS (Steve Buscemi), represents "post-gay liberation nirvana when freedom was seized on the streets of Manhattan," as gay film critic Vito Russo describes. Nick is an unapologetic citizen of the New York gay ghetto, as opposed to Robert, the health-care worker, whose job transfer to Africa will prevent him from seeing Nick in the most advanced stages of AIDS. The movie treats Robert's flight from Nick (as well as his lover Michael) as an understandable but nevertheless cowardly act. In the tradition of many art films, *Parting Glances* overshadows the political and social undertones of Robert and Nick's characters with personalized motivation. This is not the case in *Jeffrey,* wherein the title character lives in New York until his anxiety over AIDS paralyzes him and he decides to move back to home-town Wisconsin. Jeffrey's queeny best friend harshly criticizes his intended escape from New York because it would be an act of renouncing his gay identity and betraying his responsibility as a gay citizen. Returning to Wisconsin is tantamount to booking passage back into the closet.

In *The Brady Bunch Movie* (Betty Thomas, 1994), the Bradys form a sort of inclusive ghetto community. Their 1950s family values and 1970s fashion values appear maddeningly strange to their neighbors. Yet, the Bradys take for granted that their lifestyle is normal and healthy. The film "queers" the Brady bunch by virtue of their excessive suburban normality, rendering them more urban and up-to-date than any of the supposedly contemporary types. At the end of the film, the Brady's 1970s style proves to be the height of retro fashion. And, their seemingly "family values" position about keeping their house and neighborhood intact pertains to them as much as the gay couple that also lives on the block.

While these works might symbolize a mainstream fascination with middle-class gay ghettos, they never explicitly cite their sources of pleasure. The very plot of *To Wong Foo,* on the other hand, involves the vicarious thrill taken by liberal-minded hets when encountering the queer urban ghetto. This thrill eventually leads to an explicit identification with queer urban identity. The three urban drag queens, Noxeema, Vida, and Chi Chi, literally give a voice to the small townspeople. This affects the formation of an ideally collective "ghetto"-type community within the heartland. Noxeema inspires an elderly recluse to speak for the first time in years, whereupon the elderly woman participates in the town social gatherings. Vida inspires a lonely young man who stutters to join in on the social doings of the town. Besides their "therapeutic" effects upon individuals, the drag queens give a voice to the town as a whole by way of bestowing upon the populous their urban sensibility of fashion and pleasure. They transform the General Store into an urban thrift shop when they lead the way in rummaging through the unsold stock of 1960s and 1970s clothing. Outfitted in retro drag, the townspeople receive their "open sesame" and parade out of their drab daily roles and routines and into jubilant celebration.

The conclusion of the film depicts the town's transformation into nothing less than a gay ghetto, in what seems to be a simultaneous homage to the film *Spartacus* (1960) and the Stonewall riots. A racist and homophobic cop interrupts a fancy dress town party where all are decked out in outrageous red costumes. The cop attempts to "out" the three drag queens (who had been passing as women), expecting to unleash the intolerant wrath of the townspeople. The townspeople collectively and joyously respond to the cop, "I'm a drag queen!" (At the end of *Spartacus,* the Roman generals ask the captured slaves to betray their revolutionary leader, whereupon they all say "I am Spartacus." In the Stonewall riots, drag queens and dykes acted as central instigators by spontaneously protesting.) The Kansas heartland and queer New York ghetto seemingly unify as a sexually (and implicitly ethnically) diverse and tolerant space.

The challenge of representing the city consists of representing the often difficult and disturbing realities of urban diversity while also celebrating the utopian realities and further possibilities of diversity. The city simply cannot be summed up by a single group. By its very constitution, the city is a nexus of hybrid communities and cultures. While it is unfair to expect films and TV shows to represent "everything" that defines a city, a group, and a community, two factors consistently juggled and often canceled out are the subjects of ethnic diversity and AIDS. *Jeffrey* and *To Wong Foo* exemplify these two "sticklers" with respect to celebrations of the queer metropolis.

The complete absence of AIDS from the content of *To Wong Foo* reflects the film's strategy of removing gays and gay styles from their urban contexts and transplanting them in more "mainstream" and recognizable locales. When Chi Chi, Noxeema, and Vida relocate their city sensibilities to the wider arena of the U.S. heartland, they capture the affection of the town, and by extension the straight folk in the movie audience. However, the relocation process renders many of the less stylish facets of urban gay life unacknowledged. When Noxeema, Chi Chi, and Vida leave New York, they also leave behind the subject and reality of AIDS. If *To Wong Foo* presumably dissolves the borders separating gay city and straight heartland, the specter of AIDS maintains an invisible border.

Jeffrey addresses some of the deficiencies of *To Wong Foo's* flight from AIDS and the gay urban ghetto. As mentioned earlier, the story of *Jeffrey* disallows the removal of gay identity from the gay ghetto and the contemporary struggle against AIDS. The film couples its plot line about gays with its use of gay urban styles such as camp. These styles must also remain within the historical context of the gay urban ghetto. Camp signifies not simply a timeless gay urban style but a specific mode of humor, commentary, and survival. When Jeffrey imagines how his parents in Wisconsin would advise him about his sexual dilemma, mom (who's busy in the kitchen) and dad (lounging in the den) suggest that he try phone sex. They offer him a lesson in conversational eroticism. This campy fan-

tasy parodies many right-wing homophobic assertions that polarize gay identity and family values. Right-wing homophobic rhetoric continually calls upon the Victorian mythologies of small town values as under attack by urban decadence. Small town family values and urban gay identity unify in this fantasy sequence. In contrast to this imaginary bridging of Wisconsin and Manhattan, Jeffrey's gay friends more closely approximate the roles of parents or teachers. The campy fantasy, then, also serves the purpose of indicating how urban gay culture actually employs "small town values" or "family values" toward sustaining a gay urban community: in reality, Jeffrey's parents do not cheerfully advise him about safer sex, but his friends certainly do.

However, the film's attention to the specific challenges of gay urban ghetto life overlooks any consideration of the ethnicity of gay identity and urban life. The film's assertion that AIDS and homophobia are or should be the major concerns of gay men ignores other seemingly different concerns, such as racism and class exploitation, thus reflecting the protagonists' positions of social privilege. The AIDS crisis has revealed the enduring connections between homophobia, racism, and economic exploitation, particularly in terms of housing and medical care. While no film should bear the burden of addressing "everything," the exclusion of these concerns coincides with the fact that the principal characters of *Jeffrey* are all white middle-class men. Their gay ghetto remains entirely separate from African-American, Hispanic or lesbian enclaves and issues. This obfuscation of ethnicity reinstates the enduring image of the gay urban ghetto and gay identity as white. (Marlon Riggs's 1989 video *Tongues Untied* delves into this problem of gay ghetto social politics.) While we see no visible borders separating Anglo gays from gays of color, or gays as a whole from other urban groups (besides the fag-bashing sequence), the borders are implicit in the film's focus on a sector of urban gays who closely coincide with mainstream dominant culture. Unfortunately, the film's gay ghetto is distinctly segregated and gentrified.

By contrast, *To Wong Foo* plays with the mythologies of the urban that involve ethnic and sexual difference by representing these facets of the urban as unifying and pro-social rather than fragmenting and destructive. The interethnic community of drag queens and their effects on the town continually hint at the connection between sexual perversity and ethnic diversity. Upon the arrival of the drag queens, a straight African-American man and an Anglo woman in the small Kansas town admit their long repressed attraction to each other. Chi Chi, a Latino, attracts the most earnest romantic attentions from a kindly Anglo farm boy, although they are never realized. Ethnic diversity as sexual perversity also arises through shared cultural sensibilities. Noxeema, an African-American, bonds with an elderly Anglo woman over a mutual devotion to the 1950s movie star Dorothy Dandridge. The woman is a recluse who has not spoken to anyone for years. As Noxeema marvels at the elderly woman's collection of record albums and memorabilia, she begins to speak with him and share in Noxeema's pleasure.

Perhaps the strategy of strict realism should be sacrificed in light of a more campy symbolic route. *The Brady Bunch Movie* (1995) suggests the rampant and complicated hybridity of the city by virtue of its campy depiction of Los Angeles. The movie fashions an allegory of urban diversity in terms of both sexuality and ethnicity. While it never centralizes the subject of gay identity or that of people of color, *The Brady Bunch Movie* plays with the meanings of the normal versus the queer and "blackness" versus "whiteness" through the clash between suburban and urban. The polarized concepts of urban versus suburban, them versus us, black versus white, and perverse versus normal blur together within the Brady family and around them. To begin with, the Bradys represent "whiteness" with their classically patriarchal nuclear family structure, Aryan features, Astroturf lawns, surface asexuality, a seeming lack of excretory activity of any kind, and their simplistic view of Los Angeles as one great big Bedford Falls. Yet, their "whiteness" and "normality" reveal traces of otherness from the start. Little Bobbie wears his "Safety Monitor" uniform, featuring an armband with "SM" prominently printed upon it. Mike Brady always wears a thick leather wristband (even in bed) that could either be a 1970s watchband or a cock ring. Alice the maid wears a leather bustier and engages in clandestine sexual antics with Sam. Noreen, Marcia's best friend at high school, is a young butch dyke whose blatant overtures of love and desire remain unnoticed by Marcia. Noreen finally ends up in the arms of another gorgeous blonde high school girl. Self-loathing Jan Brady seeks the advice of high school social worker Mrs. Cummings, none other than popular drag queen RuPaul. After Mrs. Cummings diagnoses Jan as paranoid schizophrenic, she tells Jan pointedly, "You better work." A close-up features RuPaul's warm and knowing grin as her hit single "Supermodel" starts to throb. At the end of the film, when the Bradys rescue their neighborhood from greedy developers, among their married neighbors stands an interracial gay couple. At this moment, the normal-as-queer (the Brady family) and the queer-as-normal become indistinguishable. Urban harmony is achieved through a combination of social differences and shared territory.

Although the initial persecution of the Bradys and the threat to their "ghetto" somewhat imply AIDS and homophobia, *The Brady Bunch Movie* never refers directly to these conditions. While *Brady Bunch* fans could never forget that Robert Reed (Mike Brady) died of AIDS, the element of nostalgia in the film, particularly the cameos by original Brady Bunch cast members, negates this fact. When Florence Henderson appears in a form-fitting mini-skirt as grandma Brady, the absence of grandpa is never indicated. If nostalgia for the pre-AIDS urban ghetto is rampant in such films as *Longtime Companion* (1990) and *Tales of the City* (1994), it is a nostalgia poised on the awareness that the city isn't what it used to be. In *The Brady Bunch Movie,* such knowing nostalgia is ultimately redirected away from the queerness within the original Brady Bunch and many of the show's fans towards the campiness of the show's style, its fabricated normality.

The Brady Bunch Movie sacrifices queer urban struggles for a camp celebration of style. As in *To Wong Foo,* camp is employed as a queer (and implicitly ethnic) style attractive to both mainstream and gay audiences. The relative realism of *Jeffrey* incorporates an identity politics that concretely connects queer urban styles with queer material realities. However, the limitations of realism in *Jeffrey* arise in the film's claims to be speaking to "all" gays while representing only the most mainstream representatives of the gay urban ghetto.

Queers, AIDS, and the Revival of *Film Noir*

In the 1980s and early 1990s, a host of implicitly queer urban criminals are resurrected from the 1940s genre *film noir*, such as in David Lynch's *Blue Velvet* (1986) and *Wild at Heart* (1989), and Paul Verhoeven's *Basic Instinct* (1992). The homosocial community of Ben Singer's *The Usual Suspects* (1995) seems quite homosexual at moments, as in the Kevin Spacey character's apparent deification of the Gabriel Byrne character, and a near-kiss between two of the other thugs aroused by their mutual hostility toward one another.

While *Pulp Fiction* (Quentin Tarantino, 1994) celebrates the ethnic diversity of urban Los Angeles, something usually suppressed in older *noirs* or demonized in more recent ones (e.g., *Wild at Heart*), it codes urban space as distinctly masculine and heterosexual. The exception to this rule emerges when an African-American crime boss and an Anglo boxer depart from their territory and enter another ghetto, whereupon they encounter white supremacist homosexual sado-masochists. Here, the film offers a revised version of the *noir's* queer perverts, insofar as they now threaten urban masculine harmony as well as urban interracial harmony.

While the *noirs* often associate their villains with mental "illnesses" such as criminality and homosexuality (as it was once defined), physical illness and disease have not figured centrally into classical *noirs*. (Victorian narratives, on the other hand, centralize urban pestilence and epidemics such as influenza, tuberculosis, and venereal diseases.) An exception to this rule is the obscure 1950 film *The Killer That Stalked New York,* wherein a jewel smuggler travels about Manhattan with an illegal haul of diamonds and a contagious disease. *Noir*-ish qualities exude from a number of recent representations of disease in the city.

The controversial film *Kids* (Larry Clark, 1995) presents one example of how HIV transmission and *noir*-like narratives of urban decay and despair overlap. Resembling the classic *noir D.O.A.* (and its remake), an HIV-positive sixteen-year-old girl races to find the boy who infected her before he ignorantly engages in unsafe sex with anyone else. Not only does she not find him in time, but another boy rapes her, possibly contracting HIV as well as passing onto her other STDs. Randy Shilts's descriptions of "Patient Zero," Gaetan Dugas, in *And the Band Played On* figure him as a sort of urban sex criminal, a male *femme fatale* who carries on guiltless sexual forays from one gay urban center to another, inhabiting darkened bath house booths and infecting his sexual liaisons. The investigation-oriented plot of the film version of *And the Band Played On* (Roger Spottiswood, 1993) takes the form of an urban detective story. Here, the mystery of AIDS is even more disorienting than the urban inhabitants who appear to host it. The HIV-positive drug dealer in Spike Lee's *Clockers* (1995) also provides an example of how the *noir* elements of the criminal-urban overlap today with the spread of HIV as well as the perpetuation of drug addiction.

12 Monkeys (Terry Gilliam, 1996) provides the most recent cinematic interconnection between criminality, disease, and urban dystopia. Bruce Willis plays a convict in 2023 in the aftermath of a deadly virus that wiped out 90 percent of the world in 1996. The film literalizes the *noir* association between urban settings and underworld figures, insofar as all survivors have taken refuge underground in what appears to be a giant prison-hospital. When doctors send the Willis character back in time to discover the key to the virus, he inevitably gets lost within the above-ground city. As in *Band,* the confusing maze-like city, its strange inhabitants, and the disorientation it all produces coincides with a chaotic, unsolvable virus.

Lesbian Camp in Post-Classical Hollywood Films

The phenomenon of lesbian camp—a style and sensibility historically attributed to gay men—materializes in a host of 1990s mainstream films and cross-over art films. "Lesbian camp" applies to the work of lesbian filmmakers as well as the more general uses of camp style by heterosexual filmmakers to depict lesbian characters in ways that are positive without being sanctimonious or boringly "PC." Lesbian camp, then, consists of an alternately critical and affectionate treatment of past popular cultural forms that would have either entirely denied the existence of lesbians, or demonized them. This process also includes a playful use of lesbian iconography, particularly the "butch-femme aesthetic," as theater scholar Sue-Ellen Case puts it. The "butch-femme aesthetic" negates the simplistic stereotypes of the aggressive butch and bendable (and sometimes dangerous) femme by extolling the power and pleasure of the pairing.

In both *The Brady Bunch Movie* and *A Very Brady Sequel* (Arlene Sanford, 1996), lesbian subtexts and double entendres are accentuated and meant to be noticed. The first *Brady* flick offers a direct and affectionate acknowledgement of lesbian desire in the character of the young butch teen Noreen. She lusts after the femme-est of femmes, Marcia Brady, and even punches a boy in defense of Marcia's honor. While Noreen's flirtation eludes Marcia altogether, most hilariously during their "sleepover" when the two snuggle together in the same single bed, Noreen ends up with another gorgeous blond girl, also someone harassed by the boy whom Noreen slugged on Marcia's behalf. The most spirited example of lesbian camp in *A Very Brady Sequel* occurs at the end of the film when a kidnapper absconds with Carol Brady to Hawaii. When Mike tells Alice that Carol is "tied-up in Hawaii," Alice replies that the kidnapper probably took her there because of the state's "liberal policies." In Hawaii, the wistful Carol remarks to a tourism official, "I wish I could be gay again, with Marcia, Jan, Cindy and Alice," suddenly and unknowingly homosexualizing her familial relations. Later, when the same tourism official warns Mike that his wife wants to be gay again, Mike responds, "Sure she does. We all do."

While *A Very Brady Sequel* is less expressive about lesbian desire than its predecessor, the film develops a decidedly "queer" idea about the meaning of family. Carol and Mike's marriage and the existence of the Bunch are threatened when Carol's assumed-to-be-dead first husband returns after many years to reunite. In an interview included with the film's press materials, the film's director Arlene Sanford comments on the story line about marriage and the meaning of family, combined with the double entendres and the kitsch of the Brady Bunch:

> There is a serious theme to this movie, which is that you make your own family. Even if it's not the one you were born into. . . . [Mike Brady] says something like, 'The family you make is the family you have and is the only family you need.' . . . The basic idea is that this is a family that wasn't born together, but got married and became a family. And it's true for people who've been married a lot. It's true for gay people who make their own families. And, that's really what I think this is about at its core.

While it isn't clear if Sanford is a lesbian, she observes one of the film's themes that might speak to queers through the classically camp strategy of the lesbian-gay subtext, practiced by Hollywood directors and writers of yore.

The slickly produced *film noir Bound* (Larry and Andy Wachowski, 1996) opens on the virile young heroine Corky, a butch dyke ex-con, bound and gagged in a dark closet. The rest of the film explains how she got there. But there's more to the film's title than this image. At the center of the film, Corky remains romantically bound to Violet, a lavender-leaning gangster's moll. Together, Violet and Corky set out to steal two million dollars from Violet's mobster boyfriend, Caesar. With a mix of traditional genre film and camp irony, *Bound* tests the classic boundaries of the *film noir*

genre, which has been revived and re-vamped for the 1990s in such recent hits as *Fargo* (1996), *Pulp Fiction* (1994), and *The Last Seduction* (1995). Here, the Wachowski brothers offer their own stylish take on the *noir* genre formula. As the brothers remark in an interview included with the film's press materials, their inspiration for *Bound* stemmed from the less-than-ideal offerings of women's movie roles along with a desire to tinker with the stereotypically evil femme fatale figure, a staple in the *noir* repertoire.

Film critic B. Ruby Rich points out how "neo-noirs" of recent years have upped the potency of the femme fatale to near mythic proportions of brilliance and evil, but without ever giving the fatale much in the way of a fully drawn character. Jennifer Tilly (from *Bullets over Broadway*) endows Violet with a fuller figure than the usual *noir* vamp. Furthermore, the depth of Violet's character need not remain concealed from the audience, as happens in the majority of classical Hollywood *noirs*. In a scene from the film, Violet explains to Corky exactly why she's willing to risk everything: to escape from her cloistered—if not closeted—life as a gangster's moll. Violet needs a new life and she can't do it alone, inspiring her passion for and plotting the crime with Corky.

These confessions of a femme fatale, coupled with the lesbian romance in which Violet's true desires blossom into clarity, become the film's central metaphor of freedom. Violet is trying to escape the prison of patriarchy in which she must play the role of the sex-pot object. With Corky, however, Violet can both *act* like a girl and be her own woman. In other words, the lesbian camp twist on the *noir* formula does not rob the film of the playfulness and humor of the femme fatale's seductiveness. For instance, in *Gilda* (1946), when Glenn Ford first knocks on Rita Hayworth's bedroom door and asks if she's "decent," Hayworth enters scantily clad with a gown and a sparkling smile, and asks, "Me? Decent?" It's this kind of playful masquerading, this mockery of ultra-feminine stereotypes, that *Bound* excavates from earlier *film noirs*, minus the eventual humiliation and punishment exacted on so many femme fatales for being too big for their britches—or, for wanting to don britches instead of fishnets. The lesbian romance plot, which is never concealed from the audience as in *Basic Instinct* and any number of films, makes the erotically playful parody of femininity explicitly subversive. Here, a butch dyke and a femme dyke act out the range of gender roles for each other's pleasure, not because they have to.

While glamorously and humorously deconstructing elements of the *noir*, *Bound* adds the extra bonus of a compelling romance plot that does not crash with a cynical conclusion. Violet and Corky's affair is both hot and emotionally compelling. Their love and desire does not dissolve into mere subtext for only knowing queer viewers to notice. Amid the drama of the extended robbery sequence in which Violet and Corky steal $2 million in mob money from boyfriend Caesar, Violet calls Corky, who is hiding in a vacant apartment next door with the stolen dough, and they reaffirm their bond.

The Wachowski Brothers also crafted *Bound* with Susie Bright—a.k.a. Susie Sexpert—as their technical consultant. This respectful treatment of lesbian culture shows, particularly in a lesbian bar scene early on in the film where Bright makes an appearance as a femme leather dyke. When Corky tries to seduce Susie Bright, only to discover that Bright's girl friend is a cop, Corky replies: "When you get tired of *Cagney and Lacey,* find me." This camp line is a testament to lesbian fans of the TV show, and a certain public acknowledgement of the lesbian subtext so many fans read into the show.

I Shot Andy Warhol (1996) tests the boundaries of feminist hero narratives and the tradition of the *herstory*-lesson with camp ferocity. The film is simultaneously a "herstory" and a profane parody of one. The lesbian creative team of director Mary Harron, producer Christine Vachon, and cinematographer Ellen Kurras undertake the story of a most marginal figure, lesbian and feminist Valerie Solanas (played by Lili Taylor). The film ambivalently honors Solanas as a comic, perversely heroic revolutionary. Through Solanas's story, the filmmakers conduct their own interpretation of the Warhol Factory, usually the province of gay and straight male Pop-ists, critics, and historians. The conventional depictions of Valerie Solanas tend to be subsumed by the history of Warhol and the factory (e.g. Warhol's decision to stop directing films after Solanas stabbed him). The filmmakers reverse the usual hierarchy by approaching Warhol and the Factory through Solanas's perspective. Warhol and company inhabit Valerie's universe, not the reverse.

The feminist Solanas, whose lost history the film retrieves from virtual obscurity, certainly eludes the usual criteria for herstories. Her impact upon the course of feminist history is, if not negative (as far as the public perception of feminism is concerned), hardly profound. Yet, as a forgotten character within a marginalized movement; as an ardent butch who appears to represent every negative stereotype of the feminist-as-mankiller; and, as an ironist with a sense of humor and a filthy vocabulary, the hitherto untouchable history of Valerie Solanas provides ripe territory for contemporary dyke camp pleasure.

As in dyke punk music, Solanas's radicalism embraces the low and perverse, the margins of the margins, that which so many gay and feminist activists eschew in lieu of positive images. Solanas panhandles and tricks for her meager living, and she revels in using dirty words. Solanas claims a territory of open sexual investigation historically associated with men and masculinity. When she informs Andy Warhol that she has a contract with the publishers of "high class porn" by Henry Miller and Vladimir Nabokov, Solanas states, "I'm in good perverted company." When she offers to sell a dirty word to a passer-by for fifteen cents, Solanas wittily tells the man that the dirty word is "men." Finally, although Solanas asserts her lesbianism and acts the part of butch dyke, the only character she has sex with in the film is a male anarchist. As in the "pro-sex" dyke sensibility of Pat Califia's writing and queer punk bands, Solanas's feminism places her within the margins of both dominant culture and mainstream feminism. She is a messy artifact, a non-hero, a discredit to the movement, an ideal historical figure for dyke camp.

A CINEMA OF SEXPERTS: THE LESBIAN AND GAY AVANT-GARDES AND CINEMAS OF IDENTITY POLITICS; 1947-1989

Underground and Independent Filmmaking: 1947-1970

"Avant-garde," "underground," and "experimental" filmmaking in the United States, as named at various historical moments, has consistently drawn parallels between the "forbidden" pleasures of homosexual desire and the marginalized pleasures and hidden insights of an alternative cinema language. The 1960s proved an unprecedented period for gay male "underground" filmmakers and, at the end of the decade, the movement-inspired work of lesbian-feminist and gay activist filmmakers.

Critic Juan A. Suárez discusses how the cinematic "underground" derived from a number of sources. First, filmmaker Maya Deren, dubbed the "Mother of the Underground," established a certain defi-

nition both through her groundbreaking experimental film work in the 1940s and 1950s and her establishment of the Creative Film Foundation in 1954 for funding experimental filmmakers. The Beat writers' practice of "subterranean" living—against the dictates of the status quo and outside of the gaze of McCarthyist crusaders—also forwarded the idea of a cultural underground (Suárez, pp. 81-86). Postwar leftist intellectuals such as Dwight MacDonald applauded the notion of a cultural underground as a sort of palliative to the ills of "masscult," a critical epithet for mainstream culture in the United States. The gay male "underground" cinema draws from these historically specific influences, as well as an aesthetic and directorial gay cinematic "family tree" tracing back to the European avant-garde cinemas of the 1920s.

The many films of Soviet Sergei Eisenstein in the 1920s and 1930s, Frenchman Jean Cocteau in the 1930s, 1940s, and 1950s, and the single film by writer Jean Genet in 1950, all left their traces on the American gay underground directors of the 1940s, 1950s, and 1960s, namely Kenneth Anger, Jack Smith, George and Michael Kuchar, and Andy Warhol. The development of college film courses, art museum retrospectives, film festivals, and midnight movie screenings exposed later generations of gay male filmmakers to the European avant-garde work of Cocteau and Genet, and the underground classics of Anger, Smith, the Kuchars, Warhol, and others. Many works of the New Queer Cinema of the late 1980s and early 1990s bear traces of Cocteau, Genet, and Anger, such as Derek Jarman's *Edward II* (1991), Isaac Julien's *Looking for Langston* (1989), Todd Haynes's *Poison* (1991), and Tom Kalin's *Swoon* (1991). In *Super 8 1/2* (1994), queer Canadian punk filmmaker Bruce La Bruce references such Warhol screen tests and (anti-)porn films as *Couch* and *The Chelsea Girls,* and in *Hustler White* (1995) La Bruce quotes *Heat, Flesh,* and *Blow-Job.*

The Soviet film director Sergei Eisenstein (1898-1948), famed for his participation in developing the revolutionary montage film style, is lesser known for his gayness. Audiences for his films tend to be film students and academics interested in the Soviet montage film movement, and are rarely aware of (or broach the subject of) Eisenstein's sexuality. Usually, film scholars describe Eisenstein's influences through the montage editing practices developed by him and his contemporaries. Conceiving montage as a "revolutionary" style of editing, Eisenstein elaborated upon the montage theories of his comrades Kuleshov, Pudovkin, and Vertov by asserting the idea of the "kino fist." The "kino (cinema) fist" involves methods of editing wherein one movie image clashes against another, putting the audience members in a dynamic state of intellectual and bodily stimulation. This "montage of attractions" (as Eisenstein put it) shocks audiences by catching them unaware, following one image with a seemingly incongruous counterpart. Yet, taken together, the opposing images can articulate a number of ideas.

If pressed to search for "gay" content in Eisenstein's films (e.g. *The Battleship Potemkin* [1925], *Strike* [1925], *October* [1928], *Ivan the Terrible* parts I and II [1945-46]), one encounters nothing in the manner of explicitly gay or lesbian characters and stories. However, as gay film critic Parker Tyler observes in *Screening the Sexes* (his germinal 1971 book on sexuality in the cinema), numerous possibilities emerge when unpacking Eisenstein's filmmaking style, such as his eroticizing of the Soviet imagery of powerfully bodied male workers. (Soviet art secondarily glorified female workers, although these images are, for the most part, absent in Eisenstein's work.) If Soviet popular culture's idealized male bodies always signified the liberatory future of the USSR and socialism, Eisenstein's homoerotic collectives of male bodies (e.g. *Potemkin* or *October*) might also be invoking the historically less popular (but nonetheless existing) Soviet sentiment that proletarian revolution would also signal sexual liberation. (Simon Karlinsky describes this brief tendency in his essay, "Russia's Gay Literature and Culture: The Impact of the October Revolution.")

As Eisenstein explores the erotics of the male body from the perspective of the revolutionary collective, Cocteau's visual treatment of men's bodies accentuates the individual. Cocteau's work aligns poetry, not revolution, with homosexual desire. This alignment stems from the aestheticist tradition of Walter Pater and Oscar Wilde, where individuality reaches its zenith through beauty. The pleasures of beauty (or, in Cocteau's case, poetry) are, ultimately, narcissistic ones. Richard Dyer describes two poetic sequences from *Le Sang d'un Poét* (*The Blood of a Poet,* 1930) in which the main character, an artist, exalts in his own beauty. To begin with, the film exalts in the artist's classical figure by picturing him shirtless. As the artist paints a self-portrait, the mouth on the picture comes alive. When he wipes the mouth from the painting, it sticks to his hand. He ends up rubbing the hand affixed with his self-portrait's mouth over his torso, and then downward past his waist and out of the shot. Dyer explains, "The caressing hand with his own mouth in it disappearing below the waist, followed by a shot of his head thrown back . . . clearly suggests masturbation." Later, the artist stares at his image in a mirror, and then walks through the mirror into another universe. Both scenes depict the artist enjoying *himself,* expressing his imagination and watching it come alive (as with the mouth of his self-portrait), or literally entering his own image and imaginary nation. In both instances, the artist experiences the full bodily pleasure of being swept away by his imagination. This narcissistic pleasure is, itself, a result of the artist's individuality, his artistic vision.

While Frenchman Jean Genet and American Kenneth Anger draw heavily from Cocteau's homoerotic, poetic style (Cocteau acted as mentor to both filmmakers), Genet and Anger reverse the priorities of Cocteau's films. Cocteau's films first value artistic virtuosity and aestheticism, which serve to spontaneously motivate the homoerotic imagery. Genet and Anger privilege homosexual situations and imagery, which serve to motivate the artistic virtuosity and aestheticism of their films. In Genet's only film, *Un Chant d'Amour* (*A Song of Love,* 1950), tawdry prison scenes involving a guard peeping in on inmates masturbating in their cells give way to more poetic visions. Shot in a chiaroscuro lighting style—which emphasizes the contrast between light and dark—the second section of the film pictures the prisoners making love with each other. The imagery of the prison appeals to its historically homoerotic associations, which the literature of Genet helped to immortalize, along with gay pulp fiction, pornography, and art (e.g. physique magazines, Tom of Finland, and s/m porn videos). The conventional (bourgeois-heterosexual) power dynamic of the prison, involving men policing other men, gives way to the homoerotic desires it usually forbids. The prison becomes a homosocial universe of "rough trade": hyper-masculine, working-class men, whose images and potential relations with each other inspire poetic film language. In *Un Chant d'Amour,* homosexuality is to masculinity what written poetry is to language: a natural component, usually repressed by convention, that, once revealed, seems both obvious and scandalous. Unlike the work of Cocteau, the eroticism of the characters in Genet's film is not a product of an individual poet's gaze, but of each man's gaze at each other; perhaps, of *every* man's gaze at other men.

The visual poetry of Anger's *Fireworks* (1947), *Scorpio Rising* (1963-64), and *Kustom Kar Kommandos* (1965), as analyzed (separately) by Dyer, Suárez, Tyler, and Hoberman, partly derives from homoerotic styles and symbols that circulated in mid-twentieth century gay male culture: sailors, men's urinals, motorcycles, leather, tightly tailored clothes, and crew cuts. The imagery in each of these films also relates to classically homosocial environments, such as the Navy and motorcycle clubs. The use of montage in Anger's work stems from the work of Soviet filmmakers such as Eisenstein as well as the uses of montage by surrealists Luis Buñuel and Salvador Dali in their two collaborative films, *Un Chien Andalou* and *L'Age d'Or.* The montage of *Fireworks* compares an orgy between a group of sailors and a young man to a brutal attack on the young boy by the sailors. Blood streams down the boy's face, and it even appears that the sailors disembowel him. However, a subsequent shot shows a milky liquid, not blood, pouring down the boy's face. The image then cuts to a shot of a door marked "Gents" (clearly a urinal). A sailor steps out from behind the urinal door with a firecracker sticking out of his unzipped fly, which he ignites. Anger's editing creates shocking visual and conceptual comparisons, as in Eisenstein's montage strategy of the "kino fist" and the surrealists' strategy of arbitrarily linking different objects with each other. Sexual pleasure is juxtaposed to savage violence in so many different ways that the film forces the spectator to ponder—and perhaps take pleasure in—this conceptual pairing.

In both of their studies of gay American underground cinema of the 1960s, Dyer and Suárez locate Eisenstein's, Cocteau's, and Genet's impact on a number of filmmakers. These authors also emphasize the way a camp sensibility about mass culture instructs and inspires the most visible filmmakers of the 1960s' gay underground cinema. Camp filters through a number of 1950s' cultural phenomena reflected in the films of Anger, the Kuchar brothers, Smith, and Warhol. A combined disdain and nostalgia for the lost gloss and failed glamour of Old Hollywood appears in Anger's film *Puce Moment* (1950) and his *Hollywood Babylon* books; Smith's film *Flaming Creatures* (1963) and his tributes to failed starlet Maria Montez; and the Kuchars' "wild trash parodies" of genre films. The gratuitous and sexy violence in Anger's *Scorpio Rising* (1965) and the Kuchars' *Born of the Wind* draws from the (eventually banned) horror comics of the early 1950s featuring excessive violence, lurid plots, and rampant sexual suggestion. Another form of quintessential 1950s youth culture, rock and roll music, fills the soundtracks and informs the styles and themes of Smith's *Flaming Creatures,* several of Anger's films (particularly *Scorpio Rising* and *Kustom Kar Kommandos*), and Warhol's films. Suárez also notes how Warhol's mainstream image remained cemented in rock and roll through his affiliation with the Velvet Underground.

The films of Pop artist Andy Warhol and those of his assistant-turned-director Paul Morrissey repeatedly indicate the proximity between popular and perverse tastes. From Warhol's 1962 paintings of Campbell's soup cans and subsequent silk-screen prints of Marilyn Monroe and Elizabeth Taylor to his film work, Warhol ironizes the visual conventions of popular culture and the way they construct stardom by exploiting their reproducibility. Stardom—or the aesthetic elements that connote stardom, such as sex appeal, beauty, and charisma—falls from being the exclusive province of the "naturally" elite to being the possession of the dispossessed, such as sex workers, drag queens, and drug users. The quest for mainstream fame by Candy Darling, Holly Woodlawn, Ondine, Paul America, Joe Dallesandro, Edie Sedgwick, Nico, and other of Warhol's Factory workers was advanced by their paradoxical coupling of show business conventions and "abnormal" proclivities. Dyer asserts that the Warhol troupe understood how to meet the fundamental requirements of the entertainment industry—sensuous pleasure, glamour, and sexiness, yet its collectively perverse image subverted every assumption about whom mainstream mass culture is supposed to represent.

The films vary stylistically and formally, beginning with a cycle of self-consciously voyeuristic, explicitly sexual, documentary-dramas that combine the qualities of the cinema verité documentary with those of the exploitation film and pornography. *Couch* (1964), *Kitchen* (1965), and *The Chelsea Girls* (1966) convey documentary qualities through their static camera and cinema verité "dead time" wherein people appear to be "themselves" doing nothing particularly distinguished. However, the documentary realism associated with this directionless progress soon, paradoxically, lends itself to the bare-bones pragmatism of exploitation and porn films, where the bottom line is the recording of freak behavior and sex acts. When the characters in these films begin to perform sexually, it remains unclear as to whether or not they are just "being themselves" or if they are fulfilling an acting obligation.

The more narrative-driven "Andy Warhol Presents" films directed by Paul Morrissey, starring hustler Joe Dallesandro (*Flesh* [1968], *Trash* [1970], and *Heat* [1972]) and experimental actor Udo Kier (*Andy Warhol's Frankenstein* [1973] and *Andy Warhol's Dracula* [1974]) explicitly foreground themselves as camp remakes of famous Hollywood films. For instance, *Heat* is clearly an historical updating and cultural downgrading of Billy Wilder's *Sunset Boulevard* (1950), in which jobless scriptwriter William Holden supports himself by acting as gigolo to aging star Gloria Swanson. All of the implied kinky sex and sleaze of the original studio film experiences an efflorescence in the 1972 version, in which Dallesandro plays an ambitious actor who beds with an aging actress (Sylvia Miles), the actress's daughter, and his landlord. Whereas Holden's character submits to symbolic castration and literal death as Swanson's hired lover, Dallesandro more often happily serves his clients. At the end, he neither dies nor becomes a star, but remains a hustler. Paul Morrisey's *Heat,* and other films directed and/or produced by Warhol, question the borders between popular culture and the avant-garde, aestheticism and voyeurism, pornographic fantasy and documentary realism.

Aside the gay male underground work discussed above, the 1967 documentary *Portrait of Jason* directed by Shirley Clarke remains an influential (although currently seldom seen) film. Critic B. Ruby Rich (1993) stresses the film's historical value as a document of gay culture, as it "combines the allure of a pre-Stonewall time-capsule with a race critique as compelling as it is contradictory." As a black gay man's personal testimony, *Portrait of Jason* anticipates Marlon Riggs's AIDS-era time-capsule about being black and gay, *Tongues Untied* (1989), as well as Jennie Livingston's 1990 documentary about black gay drag balls, *Paris Is Burning.* Annette Kuhn's *Women and Film: An International Guide* indicates Clarke's notoriety for her 1950s' and 1960s' underground documentaries and fiction films that employ the cinema verité style toward depictions of various "underground" figures and communities. Cinema verité style includes lengthy, hand-held camera shots that follow "real people" around who are just being themselves. These documentaries typically avoid many conventions of the standard, rhetorical documentary, such as the presence of god-like experts who explain the phenomena to the spectator. In *Portrait of Jason,* Clarke focuses on Jason Holliday, an African-American, middle-aged gay hustler. Shot entirely in Clarke's living room at the Chelsea Hotel, Holliday theatrically imparts his sometimes splendid but often rough life story in what is virtually a 105-minute monologue. Tyler extols the virtues of *Jason* as compared to the panoply of 1960s mainstream films cashing in on the lure of homosexual subjects. Tyler

likens Holliday to Oscar Wilde, insofar as he exhibits a dandyish philosophy of expert wit and controlled self-presentation that reveals a generous sense of humanity. Holliday's often appreciative descriptions of gay life in the 1960s, his perceptive critique of racism, and his affirmation of survival in the face of racist and homophobic "bullshit" (as he puts it) reaches into Marlon Riggs's work, in particular his last project, *Black Is, Black Ain't* (1995). There, Riggs briefly incorporates images and words from *Jason* in order to critique the invisibility of black gay men within the history of the Civil Rights movement. Riggs also quite literally speaks to a cinematic predecessor in terms of his documentary video work on black gay identity and his experimentation with autobiography and testimony. An innovative and influential work at the time of its release, *Jason* still remains one of the few films about black gay life and a vivid example of cinema verité documentary.

Feminism, Gay Liberation, and Cine-Activism of the 1970s and 1980s

As feminist film critic Julia Lesage and Chicano film critic Chon A. Noriega both observe, the 1960s and 1970s saw the efflorescence of identity politics movements in the United States and their subsequent creation of film movements. Besides the inspiration of political engagement, African-American independent cinema, Chicano cinema, and North American feminist and gay cinemas all took off by taking advantage of the developments in 16mm film technology and sound recording. These innovations included portable sound and camera equipment coupled with hardware that became relatively inexpensive. The availability and flexibility of camera equipment opened possibilities for these emerging political film movements to intervene on the cultural production of history. In the face of decades of oftentimes phobic and demeaning misrepresentations, these groups eagerly began to "document" themselves. Straddling the borders of the feminist and gay movements, lesbian-feminist filmmakers such as Barbara Hammer, Gretta Schiller, and Jan Oxenberg proved particularly prolific and influential.

Barbara Hammer remains a pioneer of gay and lesbian cinema. Her films have been screened internationally at such prestigious festivals and institutions as the Berlin Film Festival, the George Pompidou Center in Paris, and the Museum of Modern Art in New York. Her 1970s work exemplifies feminist and lesbian avant-garde filmmaking and artistic practices. Hammer's most noteworthy 1970s films include *Dyketactics* (1974), *Superdyke* (1978), *Double Strength* (1978), and *Women I Love* (1979), each presenting a distinct avant-garde stylistic depiction of classic feminist and lesbian imagery and ideas. *Dyketactics* presents a series of sensual tableaus involving women touching and caressing each other. *Superdyke* presents a playful fantasy of lesbian utopia, with a group of women wearing "Superdyke" t-shirts roaming a variety of landscapes in a sensual and comic manner that combines silent slapstick style with that of a home movie made among friends. Both *Double Strength* and *Women I Love* take a slightly more realistic approach, featuring portraits of women and relationships, including Hammer herself. Critic Liz Kotz notes how Hammer's earlier films have been criticized for their stereotypical coupling of natural "female" imagery, such as flowers with female anatomy. Dyer, on the other hand, explains how *Double Strength* departs from this formula as it privileges female athleticism in its tender portrayal of a relationship between two female trapeze performers.

Lesbian and gay movement-oriented filmmaking in the 1970s and 1980s emphasizes the predominant strategy of 1970s gay liberation politics: coming out and consciousness raising. In order to fulfill the educational project of affirming lesbian-gay identity, community, and politics, and asserting the necessity for all gays and lesbians to come out, these films more often dispense with the ambiguity inherent in avant-garde film styles and, instead, employ the straightforward style of talking head documentary. The leading example in this genre remains *Word Is Out: Stories of Some of Our Lives* (1977, USA, Mariposa Film Group). In *Word Is Out,* 26 lesbians and gay men from a variety of backgrounds and generations discuss their lives before and after coming out. Both at the time of its release and today, lesbian and gay critics have praised the film. In his classic of lesbian and gay film criticism, *The Celluloid Closet,* Vito Russo refers to the film as "an electric piece of history." *Facets Gay and Lesbian Film Guide* describes it as "a landmark effort to assess gay identity," and critic and programmer Jenni Olson asserts, "This one is required viewing for everyone."

Greta Schiller's documentary films *Greta's Girls* (1976), *Before Stonewall* (1985, with Robert Rosenberg), and *International Sweethearts Of Rhythm* (1986, with Andrea Weiss) exemplify the felt need to document lesbian and gay history in its many manifestations, both global and local. As *Greta's Girls* takes a "micro" approach by depicting a lesbian relationship, as does *International Sweethearts Of Rhythm* in its record of a predominantly African-American all-woman band from the 1930s and 1940s, *Before Stonewall* opts for a wider view of lesbian and gay politics and history. The film probes into United States lesbian and gay culture and community before the liberation movement.

If Barbara Hammer's 1970s style combines the dual pulls of most political film movements, with an impulse toward avant-gardism as well as documentary realism, her more recent documentaries couple these tendencies more forcefully. *Nitrate Kisses* (1992) reflects some of the insights and critiques of identity politics launched by 1990s queer activists (discussed below), as the film meditates on the very question of what lesbian and gay history—and by extension, identity—is. As Hammer herself asserts, the simple lack of historical representations of, for, by, and about lesbians and gays raises the stakes on documentary work. However, as her later works such as *Nitrate Kisses* contend, many daunting as well as progressive obstacles emerge in the quest to document lesbian and gay history. For instance, the social proscriptions against homosexuality generally delimited virtually any explicit representations. On top of that, it is also problematic to universalize a notion of lesbian-gay identity, insofar as people's histories and desires exceed the rigid boundaries of any singular identity label.

Nitrate Kisses probes the historical fragments that form a shadowy patchwork of lesbian-gay history and identity. In the spirit of author Willa Cather's artistic fascination with "the inexplicable presence of the thing not named" (as quoted in Claude J. Summers' *The Gay and Lesbian Literary Heritage*), Hammer follows one obscured path of lesbian history into the life of Cather, herself. Although Cather, her friends, and her biographers have all carefully avoided questions about her sexuality, this "thing not named" emerges through her style of dress, way of life, and the fact that she lived with the same woman for 40 years. The film asks, What impression have Cather's ambiguous cues of lesbian desire and identity made upon lesbian identity and history, despite the many denials that Cather was lesbian? Hammer explores other queer things not named, such as homosexuality in Classical Hollywood movies. Hammer incorporates clips from the 1930 American avant-garde film *Lot in Sodom* as evidence of the first explicit (and undeniably erotic) representations of male homosexual desire in an American film, even though the film appears to be launching a moral attack against such desires. *Nitrate Kisses* asserts the importance of conducting a search for lesbian-gay history while questioning the concreteness and universality of lesbian and gay identity and desire.

THE NEW QUEER CINEMA: 1989-THE PRESENT

"We're queer! We're here! We're fabulous! Get used to it!"

In her 1992 article, film critic B. Ruby Rich coined the term the "New Queer Cinema." The theatrical releases of the lesbian and gay-themed films *Paris Is Burning* (1990, Jennie Livingston), *Poison* (1991, Todd Haynes), *Salmonberries* (1991, Percy Adlon), *Edward II* (1991, Derek Jarman), and *My Own Private Idaho* (1991, Gus Van Sant), along with the 1991 PBS airing of Marlon Riggs's *Tongues Untied* (1989), all received unprecedented public attention (sometimes celebratory, sometimes condemning). By 1992, the means for producing, distributing, and exhibiting lesbian and gay films had also progressed. Generally, the Sundance Film Festival has helped reinvigorate the independent film market, as well as being the stage for the premiers of such popular lesbian and gay films as *Paris Is Burning, Poison, Swoon* (Tom Kalin, 1992), *Go Fish* (Rose Troche and Guinevere Turner, 1994), *I Shot Andy Warhol* (Mary Harron, 1996), and *Bound* (the Wachowski Brothers, 1996). Producers such as Christine Vachon (*Poison, Go Fish*) and Dolly Hall (*The Wedding Banquet, All Over Me*), distribution companies such as Miramax, Fine Line, Sony Classics, and Frameline, and art theater chains such as Landmark continue to be vital elements in the establishment and "mainstreaming" of a New Queer Cinema.

While many critics praised the artistic achievements of the early 1990s' outpouring of queer films, much of the widespread attention stemmed from political controversies and star publicity. Both *Poison* and *Tongues Untied* became centers of controversy amid the NEA debates. Conservatives cited the film *Poison,* the video *Tongues Untied,* the Mapplethorpe exhibit "The Perfect Moment," and the performance art of Tim Miller and Karen Finley (among others) as examples of publicly funded "homoerotic" art. *Salmonberries* featured popular lesbian singer k.d. lang as a butch Alaskan in love with a femme librarian and in search of her parents. While the film sank into mainstream obscurity, it became an immediate lesbian cult film. Openly gay filmmaker Gus Van Sant's *My Own Private Idaho* sported mainstream screen idols River Phoenix and Keanu Reeves as street hustlers.

On the cultural front, the style and content of the new queer cinema derives most immediately from lesbian and gay video work and queer activist art work of the 1980s and early 1990s. On the political front, the work of activist groups such as the AIDS Coalition To Unleash Power (ACT UP) and Queer Nation informed the films' perspectives on a host of social questions. In the late 1980s, the identity nomination of "queer" arose through a broader frustration felt by both lesbian and gay men regarding the AIDS crisis and the inefficacy of assimilationist identity politics to remedy this disaster. A new version of activism formed partly through a double critique of assimilationist lesbian-gay identity politics as well as the homophobic social climate of the Reagan-Bush 1980s. Queer activist groups such as ACT UP and Queer Nation and magazines and 'zines such as *Outweek, Bimbox,* and *J.D.'s* exemplify this cultural-political development.

As *Village Voice* writer Alisa Solomon describes, the new queer politics is:

A *liberation* movement for changing the world in coalition with other progressive forces.... To call oneself a queer is to shift the emphasis toward liberation by proclaiming and celebrating marginality.

Lisa Dugan has described queer politics' and theory's attempts "to open up possibilities for coalition across barriers of class, race, and gender, and to somehow satisfy the paradoxical necessity of recognizing differences, while producing (provisional) unity." For instance, ACT UP's analysis of the AIDS crisis (as related in Crimp and Rolston's *AIDS DemoGraphics*) addressed the nexus of marginalized identity groups whose demonized social status rationalized the U.S. government's lack of action in the interests of people with AIDS (PWAs). As an example, AIDS activists revealed how the news coverage about AIDS often demonized both Euro-American Anglo gays and heterosexual black Africans, a radical intersection of racism, nationalism, and homophobia. These kinds of analyses, to paraphrase Dugan, produced provisional unity in the fight against AIDS while also "recognizing differences."

The New Queer Cinema takes deliberate risks in its questioning of "gay" and "lesbian" identity, and in its in-your-face visibility policy that deliberately incorporates expressions of hard core sexuality and flirts with so-called "negative" stereotypes. The play with mainstream taboos of behavior and pleasure as a means of asserting vis-

Todd Haynes

ibility occurs in many queer activist strategies. "Queer Nights Out" involved the "invasion" of an assumed-to-be "ordinary" (read: straight) social space by queers who danced together and kissed in order to assert their visibility. A New York Queer Nation poster action also opts for spectacular visibility in everyday life by changing a "GAP" clothing advertisement featuring then-closeted singer k.d. lang to a "GAY" ad by replacing the "P" with a "Y." Other strategies of visibility included the outing of ostensibly queer public figures, kiss-in protests (wherein large numbers of same-sex couples publicly kiss as a means of claiming mainstream space and protesting the heterosexist bias of public space), and theatrical zaps on homophobic businesses and media institutions. The open outrageousness of these queer spectacles rejects the assimilationist fears of being different in lieu of a "get used to it" attitude.

Cecillia Barriga's video *Meeting Two Queens* (Spain, 1992) appeals to these queer strategies of visibility. A lesbian-gay film festival favorite in the United States, *Queens* intercuts scenes from Greta Garbo and Marlene Dietrich star vehicles such that the two stars, who never co-starred in a film together, communicate with and express their desire for each other. As lesbian and gay icons and practitioners, this meeting bears high stakes. Whether or not spectators recall each film reference, *Meeting Two Queens* explicates the "conflict" and thrill of "introducing" the two women stars given the masculine heterosexist imperatives of Classical Hollywood cinema. The film "exploits" Classical Hollywood's fetishization of female bodies in the acts of suffering and the throes of passion, only to redirect this spectacle in a scenario that fulfills the "forbidden" fantasies of queer Garbo and Dietrich fans. It responds to mainstream popular culture's conservatism by making queerness a natural result of pop culture spectatorship.

Haynes's *Poison* presents a pastiche of mainstream culture and canonized gay culture. The film consists of three interwoven but unrelated stories, differentiated by generic characteristics and visual style. "Horror" is a parody of late 1940s and 1950s B-film (i.e. "cheap") visual styles, as well as late Classical Hollywood sci-fi/horror, *film noir*, and male melodramas that expressly dealt with the Cold War anxieties of gender roles, contagion, and invasion (e.g. *Invasion of the Body Snatchers, The Fly, Laura, Bigger Than Life*). Dr. Thomas Graves, whose love of science drives him toward developing theories of the curative properties of the sex drive, accidentally swallows the sex drive (as it exists in milky, misty liquid form). Graves's error occurs when distracted by his desire for his intern, Dr. Nancy Olsen. As a result, Graves experiences a bodily transformation, steadily accruing sores on his face and hands. Graves's illness develops concurrently with a social disease ravaging the city at large, the causal connections between the two left ambiguous. Eventually, the news media dub him "The Leper Sex Killer." After Nancy dies from the illness, the police appear at her apartment. Pursued by a police-led mob, Graves hides in his apartment and eventually jumps to his death after denouncing the hostile crowd for its hypocrisy.

The narrative of "Horror" references the spectacle of AIDS hysteria promulgated by print and broadcast news. The social fears of utter abjection through disease and contagion related in "Horror" also arise through a camp technique of playing with particular popular film genres that reflect historical periods where public anxieties over disease, contagion, and social perversity soared. For instance, feminist film critic Tania Modelski analyzes how sci-fi/horror films such as *The Fly* (1958) and *The Incredible Shrinking Man* (1957) center upon the relation between disfigured male bodies, the expansion of scientific investigation, and the loss of patriarchal roles. *Film noir*'s

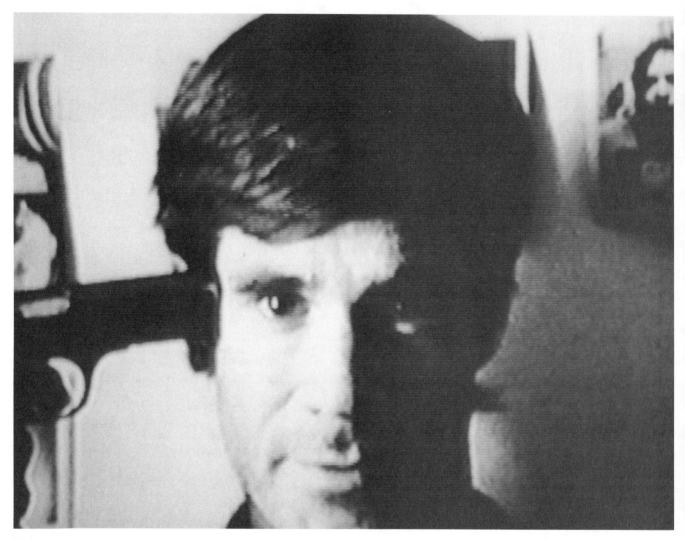

Gus Van Sant

femme fatales and "perverse" men serve as obstacles and "puzzles" for the patriarchal investigator, and these characters were notable for their abject body types. "Male melodramas" illustrate the decay of the bourgeois man's body and spirit, and a film such as *Bigger Than Life* (1956) figures this explicitly through the ailment developed by the protagonist through overwork, and his subsequent hypermasculine, violent hysteria. In *There's Always Tomorrow* (1956), depression and extra-marital desire haunt the protagonist. His body and life are visually likened to the mechanical gestures of a toy robot, and his wife only ever describes his body as healthy (but in need of a bath to avoid "stiffness") after a weekend away from home with his almost-lover.

If Graves begins by killing a woman, an excessive attempt to redeem his masculine privilege, he ends his life as a demonized object whom the public wants to capture. In other words, the tables have turned. Before he jumps to his death, Graves addresses the carnival-like mob that has gathered beneath his window. His speech once again turns the tables, this time on the public who demonize him:

> You think I'm scum.... You think I'm dirt. Don't you? Well,
> I'll tell you something. Every one of you down there is

exactly the same. But, you'll never know it.... Because, you'll never know what pride is. 'Cause pride is the only thing that lets you stand up to misery. And, not this kind of misery [indicating his physical condition]. But, the kind of misery the whole stinking world is made of!

"Hero" is a "documentary" involving the strange disappearance of a little suburban boy, Richie Beacon. According to Felicia Beacon, Richie's mother, Richie shot his father (Fred Beacon) in order to prevent him from killing Felicia (whose affair with the gardener Fred had discovered), and then proceeded to mount the window sill and fly away. The documentary consists of interviews with Felicia, Richie's classmates, neighbors, teachers, and other experts, whose contradictory estimations of Richie's status as victim, saint, or demon elucidate the violence of Richie's school and home life.

This piece's grand guignol spectacle of a bloody murder clashes with the "innocent" familial/suburban scene. This incongruity coincides with the effects and moods achieved by popular films such as *The Bad Seed, Psycho,* or *Amityville Horror,* as well as "reality" programming such as daytime talk shows with their daily parades of the strange-normal. What is more, the questions posed by the narrator—What *really* happened? Who and where is Richie?—

remain ensconced in the individualist terms of most mainstream news/information organs, asking these questions about Richie, his family, and the event of the murder without investigating the social/political reasons behind what happened. It is the menacing aspect of these facades of ordinariness, the family photo and the house, which (posed so perfectly) stare back at the viewer, that the subsequent treatment in the film exploits. They hint at the way repressed desires and meanings creep from the margins of normality and explode into everyday life. Furthermore, the witnesses' accounts of Richie's life tend to undermine the scientific accuracy of the documentary genre by presenting bipolar views of Richie. When they construct "Richie" either as a "bad object" or divine subject, the witnesses end up talking more about their own fears, desires, and anxieties than really explaining *who* Richie Beacon is. For instance, the next-door neighbors are entrenched in the mass culture spectacle of the Beacon family mystery. Felicia Beacon's "extraordinary account of her son's disappearance" (as the omniscient voice-over puts it) trades on religious spectacle. Each of these testimonies invokes figures of suburban camp or kitsch that recall Diane Arbus photos and John Waters films such as *Polyester* (1981), where the cultural trappings of the banal and "normal" exhaust themselves, appearing absurd and nonsensical.

"Homo" derives from the works of Jean Genet, a canonized figure in gay literature. The story involves an imprisoned thief, John Broom, in love with fellow inmate Jack Bolton. While tracking Broom's growing obsession with Bolton, "Homo" also includes Broom's disclosure of thoughts through voice-overs, and Broom's recollections of his and Bolton's experiences together in a boy's reformatory, portrayed in flashbacks. Eventually, Broom somewhat fulfills his passion through a nocturnal encounter with Bolton, although thereafter Bolton remains emotionally distant. During a fight between them, Broom rapes Bolton. Later, Bolton escapes with another prisoner, his lover, only to be shot in the process. "Homo" plays with the poetic codes of gay avant-garde films by Cocteau, Genet, and Anger, the stereotypes of "the homosexual," as well as following in Genet's own form of camp expression. "Homo" also risks homophobic stereotyping in its prison narrative of humiliation, anal rape, and masochism. These follow in queer films' general challenges to the narrowly defined notions of positive and negative gay images, as defined by assimilation-minded identity politics.

The Boys in the Band

The style and tone of *Poison* are similar to many subsequent queer films, such as *The Living End* (Gregg Araki, 1991), *Swoon* (Tom Kalin, 1991), *Postcards from America* (Steve McClean, 1994), and *Frisk* (Todd Verow, 1995). Each of these films deliberately invokes "negative" film images of gay men (and to a lesser extent, lesbians) as hyper-sexed psycho killers. However, the films place stereotypes into social, historical, and cultural contexts, and the presentation of stereotypes defies the aesthetics of realist filmmaking, such as "Actor's Studio" believability and linear, forward-moving, easy-to-follow plot lines. Gregg Araki's *The Living End* (1992) follows two young HIV-positive men who embody two different 1980s gay clone images: the middle-class, new-wave, urban gay man and the beach stud. Together, they go on a crime spree attacking homophobes, stealing, and having lots of sex. They end up in Death Valley, handcuffed to each other, contemplating suicide.

Swoon mixes bio-pic with queer critique in its rendering of the Leopold and Loeb murder trial. Nathan Leopold and Richard Loeb, two college-age, well-to-do Jewish homosexuals from Chicago, mur-

dered and sodomized a little boy in 1922. Their trial attracted national attention. The film employs the real transcripts from the trial along with stylized acting, poetic dialogue, and many anachronistic references to gay culture. Through Leopold and Loeb's relationship and the events of the court case, the film attempts to study how racism and homophobia affected their actions and the state's punishment of them.

Frisk investigates the connections between sex and danger through its protagonist Dennis, a young, gay, middle-class hunk whose life of privilege permits him to develop violent fantasies about sex and death. Dennis records these fantasies of torture and mutilation and sends his accounts to friends and lovers who worry that he's telling the truth. On the one hand, the film can be read as a cautionary tale about sexual decadence. Nevertheless, *Frisk* explores the manner in which commodity culture legitimizes some perversions while demonizing others. By demonizing some kinds of fantasy, dominant culture manages two effects. First, it tries to convince us that those fantasies are no different from really performing those acts. Second, it makes those fantasies all the more alluring. This line of reasoning explains why the gay psycho-killer has remained an enduring stereotype in mainstream popular culture, and why s/m fantasy and sex scenes are so pervasive in urban, middle-class gay male culture.

Postcards from America takes its title from an essay by the late artist and AIDS activist David Wojnarowicz. The title describes the film very well, as the audience receives a series of glimpses from Wojnarowicz's life: his Eisenhower-Kennedy era childhood spent in a working-class home with a cruelly abusive father, his late adolescence in 1970s New York as a prostitute and petty thief, and his adulthood in the 1980s when his lover dies from AIDS. The adult David (played by James Lyons) also wanders throughout the film, hitchhiking on highways out West, stepping through abandoned warehouses, and journeying through cruising areas. The only times we don't see him in transit occur at the end, when the film cuts between David sitting with his dying lover in a hospital and David's recollections of their life together.

When David's gratuitously brutal father kills himself on Christmas, a shot of the lifeless body cuts to an excessively blissful scene: young David opening presents around an ideal Christmas tree with snow sprinkling down upon him and Connie Francis piping a Christmas ballad. The contradictory combination of tragedy and rejoicing wound-up in the father's suicide can only be expressed through such deliberate irony. Another scene simply consists of the late adolescent David sitting in a room with a fellow hustler and listening to a drag queen friend tell a hilarious story about an impotent john who loved to act out his orgasms. Scenes like this illustrate the "postcard" element of the film and resemble a most obvious predecessor, *My Own Private Idaho*. That film was also a series of postcards and portraits, with such stylized testimonies as the porno magazines in the adult bookstore whose front cover models come to life and talk about their experiences.

Even as the film presents us with so many postcards, so many abbreviated and condensed accounts of drama, romance, and reflection, it is neither sensationalistic nor voyeuristic. David is not a tourist on vacation ogling at the landscapes. The people whom he encounters are not reduced to quirky curiosities or mere props to glorify the main character. Everyone speaks, everyone in some way offers an understanding of her/his own life, from the biggest shmucks to the quickest tricks. No one is simplistically explained, and while the characters posit insights, they still remain enigmas. David's travels reveal a sense of risk, curiosity, and vulnerability whose alternately bleak and absurd directions never cancel out a respect for and love of people.

Each of these films—*Poison, The Living End, Swoon, Postcards from America,* and *Frisk*—critique mainstream gay identity politics and its cultural policy of producing "positive" gay images. They also explore the connections between desire, danger, and social norms. However, these and the majority of New Queer Cinema films privilege the perspective of Anglo gay men, circumventing investigations into how queer identity intersects with gendered and ethnic identities.

The "Other" Side of The New Queer Cinema

B. Ruby Rich closes her 1992 evaluation and critique of the new queer cinema with pressing questions centering on the margins *within* this already marginal cinema:

> The Queer New Wave has come full circle: the boys and their movies have arrived. But will lesbians ever get the attention for their work that men got for theirs? Will queers of color ever get equal time? Or video achieve the status reserved for film?

Indeed, it could be argued that the video work of lesbians and documentary film work of gays and lesbians of color were, along with the historical gay avant-garde, preeminent influences on the direction of the New Queer Cinema of the 1990s.

For instance, in the video *Grapefruit* (1989), director Cecilia Dougherty develops her own camp sensibility and critiques lesbian identity politics and filmmaking. As critic Liz Kotz (1993) observes, "The video is not explicitly 'lesbian,' in terms of realist representation or content," a telling comment given that most lesbian-gay filmmaking of the 1970s and 1980s remains realistic both in terms of its content and style (how it expresses the content). *Grapefruit,* a 40-minute bio-pic about John Lennon and Yoko Ono, features Susie "Sexpert" Bright as John and Shelley Cook as Yoko. Dubbed by the San Francisco Lesbian and Gay International Film Festival as "a wry lesbian retake on popular culture," the video quotes and imitates assumed-to-be-straight popular culture in a way that "perverts" its mainstream meanings. Kotz celebrates the video's uses of impersonation and critical parody mixed with affectionate fandom. The effect of such a mixed strategy is, on the one hand, "to reappropriate mass cultural figures and reinvest them with lesbian fantasies and desires." However, Kotz continues, by suggesting that lesbian desire (and culture) arises *within* mainstream (read: heterosexual) culture, the film complicates the usually oversimplified divisions of mainstream culture versus lesbian subculture, and heterosexual desire versus lesbian desire. In *Grapefruit,* John and Yoko become lesbians as well as icons in a gesture that both critiques and paradoxically reaffirms dominant mainstream culture. Subsequent work by Dougherty, along with the work of Su Friedrich, Abigail Child, Julie Zando, Cheryl Dunye, and Shu Lea Cheang, develops these currents of lesbian camp critiques of identity politics.

As "queer" ideally aims to be a plural identity, a "coalition with other progressive forces" in defining itself and its activism, the critique of the implicitly Eurocentric aspects of feminist and lesbian-gay identity politics and culture also characterizes the New Queer Cinema. The New Queer Cinema reflects the eagerness to embrace the plurality and open-endedness of "queerness" as well as the frustrations regarding the limits of pluralism. Two quotations taken from interviews with queer filmmakers, the first by Pratibha Parmar and

the second by Isaac Julien, articulate certain drawbacks of the New Queer Cinema and "queer" as an identity label:

> In queer discourses generally there is a worrying tendency to create an essentialist, so-called authentic, queer gaze. My personal style is determined by diverse aesthetic influences, from Indian cinema and cultural iconography to pop promos and [19]70s avant-garde films. My film, *A Place of Rage,* which explores questions of sexuality but doesn't prioritise these, sold out in the [Los Angeles] and San Francisco lesbian and gay festivals, proving that queer audiences are hungry for queer visions painted on a broader canvas.
>
> *Young Soul Rebels* may sit uncomfortably in a new queer cinema, and I'm glad it does. In the context of black cinema and a straight black audience, *Young Soul Rebels* is a very queer film. Maybe for a gay audience, it's not queer enough. There's a strategic positioning that's to do with how under attack different communities have been and why they revert to essentialist positions around identity. But I still hold an ambivalent position towards new queer cinema in terms of address. For most white queer filmmakers there is no intersection of race.

A cinematic precursor to the New Queer Cinema's attempts to rethink sexual identity along ethnic lines, *La Ofrenda: The Days of the Dead* (1989, USA) never employs the terminology of queer, feminist, or lesbian/gay identity politics, although both of its creators, Lourdes Portillo and Susana Muñoz, are lesbians. However, *La Ofrenda* produces numerous "queer" moments that confound the categories of Eurocentric and patriarchal culture. In this respect, the film exemplifies both Julien's call for a queer cinema that inspects the intersection of race and sexuality, and Parmar's desire for "queer visions painted on a broader canvas."

La Ofrenda: The Days of the Dead is a documentary about "el Día de los Muertos" ("Day of the Dead") festivities, a holiday at the beginning of November that honors the temporary return of the dead to earth. Elaborate altars, food, artwork, fiestas, and theatrical displays all constitute offerings by the living to their dead loved ones. The film traces the celebrations in Mexico City and Oaxaca, then, following one path of the Amerindian Diaspora, travels to San Francisco's Mission district in the second part of the film for Chicana/o interpretations of "el Día de los Muertos."

A recurrent motif renders the identity of the film both Chicana and queer: the labor that produces the holiday is related to the work of women and woman-identified men. The Mexico sequences of the film feature girls and women of all ages cleaning grave sites, preparing elaborate meals, and making the altars. The sequence draws to a close after a scene in which an effeminate man cross-dressing for the festivities explains the meaning of the "ofrenda" (offering). Removing his wig, the celebrant explains the significance of the offering as an unconditional gift, an act of reaching out and exposing oneself. Footage cuts in of two elderly women filling a basket of fruit offerings. When the scene returns to the cross-dressing celebrant, he/she offers an apple to a person behind the camera, beyond the screen. Here, the act of offering transforms into reaching beyond the limits of "reality," in this case, traditional gender roles. If patriarchal cultures associate the act of offering with passivity and femininity, during the Day of the Dead, the sacrificial labor of both women and woman-identified men serves as the basis for all celebration. The desire and pleasure of sacrifice exceeds the tradition of the holiday, the rigidity of gender roles and even the movie screen itself.

The San Francisco scenes seem to extend this reaching beyond both the screen and conventional ideologies of gender, ethnicity, and sexuality. In San Francisco, a city central to both North American queer and Chicano/a mythologies, the woman-centered aspects of "el Día de los Muertos" are no longer buried in the central yet silent female and woman-identified labor for the festival. In the film, San Francisco-based Chicana artist/critic Amalia Mesa-Bains and social worker Concha Saucedo explain the diasporic celebration of the Day of the Dead in San Francisco's Mission District. In an extended sequence, a Chicano man discussing his altar implies the extent to which matriarchal identifications between women as well as men and women arise and intersect through the holiday's signal gesture of sacrifice. The altar features a *calavera* (parodic skull or skeleton iconic of the holiday) with "SIDA" (AIDS) stamped upon it, and is in honor of friends and family who died of AIDS, as well as friends and family who died young. The man also mentions that his grandmother influenced his celebration of "el Día de los Muertos," and her death (along with his grandfather's) the altar also honors. His gestures of identification and affiliation signify the manifest political significance of "el Día de los Muertos" that traverses Chicano/a and queer communities.

The San Francisco section of the film also invokes "camp," such as in the display of one altar honoring Rita Hayworth replete with Hollywood studio photos and a large mirror inscribed by hand with "Rita." However, camp tactics of reception and reinscription do not give adequate substance to the elements of identification and mourning at work here. If "Rita" was a possible gay camp icon, especially with her signature song "Put the Blame on Mame," her Hispanic lineage also makes her a possible icon for Latinos (despite the Hollywood studios' attempts at her "anglicized" make-overs).

Thematically, *La Ofrenda* grapples with many issues that intersect with both contemporary Chicana/o and queer cultures, especially related to AIDS: pleasure, death, popular culture, marginalization, community, kinship, childhood, identity, history, female communities, and woman-identification. Such woman-identified scenes of "authentic" Mexican/Chicana (and queer) popular culture challenge the tendency to equate masculine heterosexuality with authentic *mexicanidad* (Mexicanness) or liberated Chicano identity. These sequences also challenge the ethnocentrism of Euro-American feminist and queer identity politics. While its style eschews the militancy of ACT UP and many queer films, the film's depiction of identity and AIDS very much coincides with the developing "queer" position.

Isaac Julien subtitles his film *Looking for Langston* (GB, 1989) a "meditation on Langston Hughes and the Harlem Renaissance," but the film can also be described more broadly as a critical meditation on the relationships between black gay culture and both African-American (heterosexual) culture and gay (Anglo) culture. While the film partly takes the form of a protest against white gay racism and black homophobia, it nonetheless traces the harmonies in these cultural relationships. Literary critic Henry Louis Gates, Jr. notes that:

> The usual roll call [for the Harlem Renaissance] would invoke figures such as Langston Hughes, Claude McKay, Alain Locke, Countee Cullen, Wallace Thurman, and Bruce Nugent—which is to say that it was surely as gay as it was black, not that it was exclusively either of these.

Furthermore, film critic Kobena Mercer (1993) locates the film's visual homages to several European and Euro-American gay film-

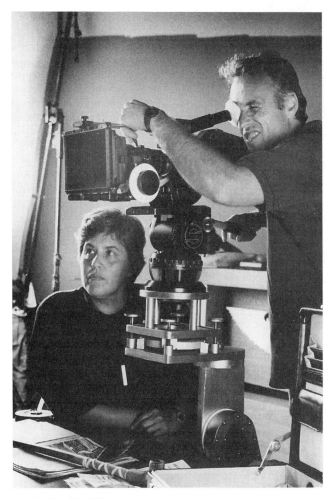

Lourdes Portillo (left)

makers, such as Jean Cocteau, Kenneth Anger, and Jean Genet. Mercer concludes that director Isaac Julien "acknowledges the importance of the Euro-American avant garde as much as the importance of black American literature" toward the creative expression of black British artists.

Then again, the film takes up a critique of African-American and Anglo gay culture. States Gates, "If *Looking for Langston* is a meditation on the Harlem Renaissance, it is equally an impassioned rebuttal to the virulent homophobia associated with the Black Power and black aesthetic movements." Feminist critic Michelle Wallace also analyzes the way the film confronts the critical issue of black visibility, particularly the charged issue of sexualized images of blacks. The history of white supremacy in the United States is largely a visual history, a history of stereotypical images by Anglos depicting African Americans as inferior due to a heightened sexuality (as opposed to intellect). In the post Civil Rights era, it remains difficult for black visual artists (as opposed to musicians and writers) to create images of themselves, sexualized ones in particular, because of the visual terrain's historically racist legacy. *Looking for Langston* addresses that visual inheritance by questioning the "gendered" and "racialized" power relations influencing the ways people look at each other: black at black, black at Anglo, and Anglo at black. Furthermore, Wallace remarks on how the film bravely opts to aestheticize and sexualize black men's bodies despite the historical risk of these projects.

According to Mercer, who expands on Wallace's line of reasoning, the film both critiques and quotes the styles of black literature as well as Robert Mapplethorpe's (ambiguously) racist photographs of men of color. In one scene, the image of a white actor looking at Mapplethorpe's *The Black Book* conjoins with a voice-over reading of an Essex Hemphill poem about white gay racism. However, the film eventually employs visual motifs and styles familiar in Mapplethorpe's photos of black male nudes. These motifs include the visual fragmentation of black male nude bodies into so many individual, stereotypical physical features, such as penises and thick lips. Mapplethorpe's "chiaroscuro" lighting style works to heighten the fetish quality of these body parts. (It's also worth mentioning that the films of Cocteau, Genet, Eisenstein, and especially Anger employ similar visual styles toward rendering *all* male bodies.) With full knowledge of the risks of repeating old stereotypes, Mercer concludes that Julien injects these well-known stereotypes with a vital difference. First, Julien's eroticized black male figures are the objects of *his* own socially defined point-of-view, as a black gay British man. Second, the film most consistently and poetically depicts the eroticized black male figures as the objects of black characters' gazes. Consequently, the black male bodies in *Looking for Langston* emerge as the aesthetic and erotic product of black men looking at, desiring, envying, and identifying with other black men.

Pratibha Parmar's *A Place Of Rage* (GB, 1991), a documentary survey of feminist movements, defines feminism as a differentiated movement involving diverse political and cultural contexts. The film traces the confluence of anti-colonialist, anti-racist, and anti-homophobic movements that, together, formed the basis for the feminist movement. Indeed, the film suggests that there is not one unitary feminism but a number of feminisms. As the film rejects a singular, restricting definition of both "woman" and the feminist movement, it simultaneously calls into question any kind of unitary definition of identity, be it related to race, ethnicity, sexuality, or nationality.

A Place of Rage takes risks with the way it addresses feminist spectators. Rejecting any definitions of sisterhood born in sameness and uniformity, the film encourages the audience to identify with a movement germinating from the differences between women as much as from their shared experiences. The film exemplifies the queer lesbian response to previous generations of lesbian-feminist identity politics and filmmaking. As film critic Liz Kotz explains:

> Once strongly based in, and accountable to, self-defined 'women's communities,' lesbian film today is often made by individuals who may feel deeply ambivalent about their relation to these communities—particularly younger women, women of color, or others whose lives are distant from the lesbian feminist utopias envisioned and made visible during the mid-1970s.

For instance, in *A Place Of Rage,* poet June Jordan connects her involvement in feminism with her participation in African-American and lesbian-gay politics. Jordan also translates her personal experiences into political allegories that exemplify this connectedness, from her witnessing of racist police harassment as a child, to her humorous recollections of the patriarchal dimensions of the Black Power movement. By desegregating the often isolated terms of gender, ethnicity, nation, and sexuality, Parmar's film also brings into question and holds up for possible transformation the very meanings and associations of the terms "queer" and "queer film." In this respect, *A Place of Rage* challenges a variety of labels, such as "black British film" (as Parmar is both black—of South Asian descent—and British), "films by people of color," "independent film," "U.S. queer film," or "British queer film."

Marlon Riggs's documentary video *Tongues Untied* (USA, 1989) received major public attention two years after its premier when PBS aired it on the *P.O.V.* program in 1991. The video draws connections between ethnicity, sexuality, gender, and class. Alternately autobiographical and broadly socio-cultural, *Tongues Untied* speaks from and about black gay life in the United States in the era of AIDS and Reaganism. The video consists of poetry written and performed by Riggs, Essex Hemphill, Steve Langley, and Allan Miller, documentary testimonials from Riggs and several more African-American gay men, and moments of parodic and satiric revelry. The "SNAP! diva" sequence in the video foregrounds a number of these elements, in terms of the varied use of documentary testimonials and a humorous parody of the "ethnographic documentary" genre (notorious for its racism and nationalism). In the sequence, several men recall their experiences of openly gay expression, white gay racism, and instances of spectacular visibility. The SNAP!, as a sign of resistance or jubilation, closes each recollection. The video then cuts to a circle of men, Marlon Riggs included, SNAP!ping. The title "Institute of SNAP!thology" is superimposed over the scene, and, as each man produces a particular configuration of SNAP!s, a new title designating the "genre" of SNAP! appears. Yet another man's testimonial cuts in, demonstrating and explaining a variety of SNAP!s.

In this sequence, *Tongues Untied* both analyzes and expresses the SNAP! effect: conspicuous and resistant interruption that militantly and stylishly pries open another way of looking at an otherwise taken-for-granted situation. The SNAP! shatters the status quo of a specific locale and strengthens the agency of the person whom this status quo threatens to silence or reject. Besides conveying the meanings and varieties of the SNAP!, this sequence combats a range of taken-for-granted notions about race, from the Anglicized meanings of "gay" identity to the ethnographic documentary tradition. One of the testimonials accounts for racism within white gay culture, and the man's SNAP! at the end of his story is exactly that which made it possible for him to speak in the first place. In other words, this testimonial is not just another "victim" narrative, but a story of resistance and appropriation signaled by the SNAP!

The "Institute of SNAP!thology" parodies and critiques the ethnographic documentary film genre which, in film critic Bill Nichols's words, constructs "an 'ethnotopia' of limitless observation. . . . The fascination of the Other is stressed; it avails itself for knowledge. It is a world in which We *know* Them, a world of wisdom triumphant." If Riggs risks the reproduction of an ethnographic model by making a documentary about the familiar-yet-"exotic" moments of everyday black gay life, he incorporates the resistance of the SNAP! into his video form and style. He SNAP!s the ethnographic documentary and its audience that desires a bit of the Other by ironizing the whole project of informing the viewer about the SNAP!. Yet, Riggs never diminishes the social-cultural vitality of SNAP! practices or black gay life in the United States. As Riggs shows how SNAP!ping has a history in black gay culture, his ironic style undermines the authoritative film styles of traditional ethnographic documentaries: the talking heads of "objective" experts sitting in front of impressive bookcases and whose explanatory voice-overs adjoin voyeuristic views of "exotic" cultures or subcultures. At the same time, such parody also encourages thought about the mainstream invisibility of black gay men while so much of their popular culture—such as the SNAP!—has attained broad popularity through stars such as Madonna and RuPaul.

the film [*Young Soul Rebels*] is about a bringing to consciousness of the possibilities of those clubs.

Young Soul Rebels focuses on the soul music scene in London during the summer of 1977, the season of the Queen's Jubilee celebrations, the height of punk, and the resurgence of racist British nationalism. The plot involves Chris and Caz, devoted friends and "soul boys" who produce a pirate radio show, "Soul Patrol." The two young men defy a host of common racial and sexual stereotypes. Caz is a dark skinned, rather masculine gay man and Chris is a light skinned, effeminate straight man. A white, closeted, gay working-class man, Ken, murders their friend T. J. in an after-dark gay cruising area at the neighborhood park. The police wrongly and hastily accuse Chris of committing the crime. Chris endeavors to discover the true murderer in order to absolve himself. The social landscape of the film depicts the steady rise of nationalist racism (including the persecutory behavior of the police), and climaxes with a riot incited by National Front members at an anti-Jubilee party. Ken dies during the riot in an attempt to murder Chris, who has evidence of his guilt. Before the murder investigation, Caz and Chris begin to drift apart over Chris's decision to pursue work in mainstream radio. Chris also develops a romantic relationship with Tracy, an upwardly mobile production assistant at the radio station where Chris seeks employment. At the same time, Caz begins to date an obnoxiously politically correct white punk boy named Billibud.

The film dramatizes a number of social ideas through its generic hybrid of mainstream movie genres: *film noir,* the musical, and the romantic drama. For instance, toward the beginning of the film, Chris and his sister Trish dance to soul music in the park where T. J. was murdered, a brief interlude that incorporates all of the musical's utopian dimensions. However, the park is not only the site of T. J.'s murder but is also crawling with white police who eye Chris suspiciously, attesting to the dystopic underside of the musical, the detective/crime film, or *film noir.* Surveillance for the purpose of committing a crime or solving one constitutes a recurrent motif in *film noir.* As in so many Hitchcock films, the murderous gaze usually coincides with a desirous one. In detective films, the police search for criminals yet often make false accusations. Conventional visual styles of *film noir,* such as chiaroscuro lighting and ominous shadow-effects, emphasize the sense of surveillance and entrapment. There are several moments in *Young Soul Rebels* where the film *noir*'s murderous and policing gazes suggest larger ideas about race relations in Britain. For instance, when Chris and Caz walk through the park and past the scene of T. J.'s murder, the police patrolling the scene eye them suspiciously. The film also depicts the mixture of desire, envy, fear, and murderousness in the racist white gaze when the camera takes Ken's voyeuristic point-of-view watching various black characters. In one scene, Ken peers through a hole in a roof and spies on Chris as Chris masturbates. In another instance, he watches Carlton (Caz's brother) taking a shower. Bars of shadow fragment Carlton's body as the water pours down upon him.

The film employs the utopian elements of the movie musical (despite its conservative history) as a means of relating the main characters' energetic and creative resistance against social oppression. Trish and Chris's dancing strikes as a resistance to the murder and the presence of the police. The gay romance between Caz and Billibud begins with a similar sort of romantic "inevitability" as in MGM musicals such as *Meet Me in St. Louis* (1944) or *Good News* (1947). The young men meet at an underground soul and punk party where Caz and Chris are DJs, lending the romance between

Marlon Riggs

While both camp and SNAP! practices involve strategies of halting the flow of the status quo, they differ on a material level. Camp necessarily involves buying something, if not devoted shopping. In this respect, camp retains an aura of bourgeois privilege, leisure, and conspicuous consumption. Camp can also have the luxury of remaining relatively private, in terms of "private" ownership. The SNAP! articulates through the body, the most elemental symbol of agency and ownership. The SNAP! does not involve an exchange any more pricey than the movement of one finger against another. It renders everyday "reality" as a cultural site, even when most of us do not think of "reality" as a culture, but as "simple" reality. As the arena of the SNAP! is everyday culture, it is essentially public, *out.*

Isaac Julien speaks of his impetus for making the film *Young Soul Rebels* in *Diary of a Young Soul Rebel*: the soul and p-funk club scene in late 1970s London and its "wonderfully hybrid space— black/white, gay/straight." Julien describes these all but forgotten locales as spaces where shared rebellious pleasures in music and dancing redefined a wide range of seemingly separate identities:

> This space opened up a whole variety of simultaneous transactions—the excitement and importance of which one could see on the dance floor but nobody was writing about or recording. For me these clubs really offered a range of experience that gay clubs could not. The gay clubs were important but they were a very white space; there was a sense in which you had to leave parts of yourself outside the door. At one and the same time they excluded part of you and fetishized an-'Other'.... For me, clubs like *Global Village* offered a much more utopian space.... In a sense

Caz and Billibud a sort of boy/subculture-next-door quality. Yet, the utopian dimensions of the dance party and Caz and Billibud's mutual desire arise, in part, from the elements of resistance and transgression that the party and their coupling exemplify. The same can be said of Chris and Caz's pirate radio show, "Soul Patrol." Their enthusiasm for soul music, which is barely played on mainstream radio owing to cultural racism, leads them to produce the radio show. Their ingenuity, passion, and risk become a distinctly politicized variant of the "do-it-ourselves" barn shows that typify Judy Garland-Mickey Rooney musicals like *Babes in Arms* (1939) and *Girl Crazy* (1943) and inspire their utopian feelings of energy, intensity, and community. The film ends with Chris, Caz, Tracy, Billibud, and Jill (Tracy's friend) dancing together after the riot, the community finally unifying through a musical number, albeit tentatively. The larger social problems that the film unearths have not been resolved, as we and the filmmakers know from the ensuing years of Thatcherite conservatism. Thatcher was elected to office in 1978, the year after the Jubilee when the narrative of *Young Soul Rebels* takes place.

Audiences and critics greeted *Young Soul Rebels* in its initial release with a certain amount of ambivalence. For *San Francisco Examiner* movie critic Barry Walters, the character of Ken appeared not as a complex symbol of nationalism and racism, but as the stereotypical gay psycho killer. Walters's condemnation of the stereotype overlooks the ways in which the film traces the intersecting paths of racism and homophobia through other characters. For instance, Caz observes Billibud's unselfconscious liberal racism with a sense of humor: when Billibud plays reggae music to seduce Caz, assuming the cultural equation between black leftism and reggae, Caz responds, "'Ow about quiet?" and turns off the music for their lovemaking. Caz also confronts homophobia from his brother Carlton and from Davis (Carlton's workmate), both black nationalists, and calls them to task for their racist distrust of Chris for being "half-caste."

The video work of Sadie Benning is akin to the projects of Julien, Parmar, and Riggs. As Amy Taubin explains, "To find a cinema that is queer and feminist, one must look even further into the margins, where Sadie Benning is using a toy Pixelvision video camera to monitor and exhibit her adolescent lesbian identity." Sadie Benning, a young dyke from Milwaukee, began making her autobiographical video art at the age of 15, in her bedroom. Benning's method of "sampling" (as Mia Carter puts it) the "trash" of mass culture and her willingness for the spectator to actively read her pastiches parallels performance traditions such as rap, hip-hop, and queer punk music and 'zine subcultures. The videos unravel Benning's stories of coming of age and coming out within a social-political framework. As B. Ruby Rich declares, "With an absolute economy of means, Benning constructed a *Portrait of the Artist as a Young Dyke* such as we've never seen before." The heterogeneity of themes and styles in Benning's work also attests to the versatility of video, with low-scale capital and labor demands that marginalized artists can exploit.

The sequence concluding *A Place Called Lovely* (1991) demonstrates Benning's particular version of "coming-out": proclaiming lesbian desire while resisting the restrictive labels of "lesbian" and "gay," the limitations of coming-out as a political strategy. First, Benning appears holding an old picture-portrait of a young, blond white man. Her lips move next to the picture, telling a story about how, sitting in her father's truck, she witnessed a horrible car accident. The camera travels down the picture, capturing in extreme close-up Benning's hand and then the eye of the man in the pic-

ture. (Carter notes the recurrence of extreme close-ups of eyes in Benning's work.) The image cuts to a white hand on a dark table, performing a dangerous trick with a knife, with Benning's voice-over: "Tragedy ... that can happen to anyone." The image then cuts to a series of picture-portraits of African-American children. Benning's voice-over narrates the events of the murders in Atlanta of African-American children in 1979 and 1980. The voice-over relates the murders, not specifically to currents of racism but to Benning's growing questioning of and disenchantment with the world around her. The following image pictures Benning in Americana drag: wearing a blond wig and a sometimes-visible polka-dot blouse or dress, and standing before an American flag, Benning flutters her eyes, smiles and gushes to the blaring strains and labored lyrics of "America, the Beautiful." After a bit of this, Benning's voice-over explains that her grandmother "always wanted me to be like one of those sweet little white girls who was some people's dream of what was right in the world." The image cuts to another of Benning's poses, an "in-your-face" dyke with close-cropped hair, flipping her head and shirtless shoulders up and into frame. An intertitle appears: "That scared me too," a response to the "white girl" image of her grandmother's fantasy and the "other" dyke image that she embodies and that negates the "sweet-little-white-girl" fantasy. The last shot of the film is an extreme close-up of Benning's eye. A tear wells up and the camera follows its fall down her cheek.

The progression of images and text (both voice-overs and intertitles) provides a vivid critique of patriarchal whiteness and finally calls into question a queer politics, as well as modes of queer history and autobiography, that separates homophobia from racism. The series of portraits of the murdered African-American children follows the portrait of (presumably) Benning's blond, white father, which she holds. The pictures of the children (along with the factual reportage of the voice-over) are a minimalist representation of an unspeakable tragedy, made more ironic by the fact that the children smile in their portraits. The picture of her father stands in stark contrast to the pictures of the Atlanta children, and in conflict to Benning's own self-image. The fragmented close-up of Benning's lips and hands, as connected to the picture of her father—the picture of American normativity—reveals the extent to which she feels implicated by the tragedies around her to which she bears witness. Her father is also an implicit witness to these tragedies (the car wreck and the Atlanta murders), yet he remains frozen in ideality. His race and gender and generation materially distance him from the chaos. Benning, who could also participate in the "picture" of normality (by being in a separate car and of a "separate" race), frustrates the composition.

First, she holds the picture of her father. Such a dominant image is, finally, only an image. It must be placed and framed in order to perpetuate its mythology. Here, not only can we see her hands and lips, but the camera eerily closes-in on the father's eye at the end of the shot, disorienting even more the autonomy and the geography of this dominant image. Then, Benning invokes the Atlanta murders and the pictures of the children that have been burned onto her memory and that incited her "uncertain" sense of "the world I had become a part of." The tableau in front of the flag, another "picture-perfect" scene, a virtual portrait, drives the tragedy of the Atlanta murders even further. What is the difference between Benning's "sweet-little-white-girl" smile and that of the children preceding her (besides the obvious irony and knowingness of her pose)? Such images of "some people's dream of what was right in the world" perpetuate the mainstream (white) public's willful disavowal of racism. Benning implicates herself in that fantasy in terms of her

Anglo upbringing. But, she overdoes the performance of white femininity. The following image of her sensual dyke identity, with short cropped hair and the same waifish look of a young River Phoenix, clearly criticizes the "sweet-little-white-girl" image.

However, even with the increasing critical and sexual consciousness of her contemporary life as a young dyke, her tears finally signify that the personal liberation of coming-out is never enough. As a white dyke in the early 1990s, the strategies of coming-out—appropriating the image of heterosexual masculinity (the picture of her father and her own androgynous appearance) and ironizing the image of heterosexual femininity—must simultaneously involve questions of race. In the formation of dyke and queer communities, coming-out must not be defined in solely sexual or personal terms.

Benning continues her interrogation of white femininity and dyke identity in *It Wasn't Love* (1992), the story of a young girl's erotic adventures with a fugitive dyke (both of whom are "played" by Benning). Benning intercuts a series of scenes from the film *The Bad Seed* (1956), the story of a "perfect" little girl, Rhoda—blond, sweet, smart, and homicidal. The clips, placed within the personal narrative (or fantasy) of erotic and illegal doings, reveal the machinery of some demonizing stereotypes of lesbian subjectivity. Benning shows how Rhoda is a pre-pubescent variant of the killer-lesbian stereotype. The normative "horrors" inspired by the "killer-lesbian" stereotype (especially in a film such as *Basic Instinct*) in part relate to the paradoxically desirable and dangerous image of white femininity. This element of irony—the fact that white femininity can "actually" contain such "deviance"—arises at the very beginning of the clip, when Rhoda's hysterically emphatic admission of murder cuts to a smiling, fatherly white man saying, "Now there's a little ray of sunshine, that one." The same could be said about the "sweet little white girl" standing in front of the flag in *A Place Called Lovely*. And, the same kind of "horror" that Rhoda-the-bad-seed produces (along with her siblings of the "killer-lesbian" stereotype) might be compared to the joyously provocative sequence in *A Place Called Lovely* where the "dyke" image virtually barges in or dethrones the "sweet little white girl." In the earlier work, the "sweet little white girl" and the dyke are separated by an edit but connected by Benning, who straddles both positions. In *The Bad Seed* clips from *It Wasn't Love,* pre-pubescent Rhoda seductively caresses her mother's face and says, "I wanna play the way we used to, mommy. Please play with me." This gesture of nostalgic intimacy cannot conceal Rhoda's "hidden" or latent "evil." In the lesbian stereotype, this becomes a hidden desire that is indistinguishable from "evil." However, Benning's appropriation of the figures of "the sweet little white girl," the horrific girl, and the stereotype of the lesbian killer eroticizes their horrific elements and transforms the affective element of "horror" into an identification with an "in-your-face" posture.

In the context of lesbian and gay culture, Benning's work demystifies the coming-out narrative, as such personal-social acts cannot rely on simply the awareness of the politicized dimensions of sexuality. Coming-out is only one dimension of embattling homophobia and, perhaps, only the tip of the iceberg. What is more, resisting and exposing homophobia inevitably involves a complex of other related phobias of difference, according to the disparate contexts in which homophobia emerges. Thus, for Benning, a resistance to the position of white heterosexual femininity necessitates her attention to the ways white heterosexual femininity functions in relation to racist, sexist, and homophobic ideologies.

Go Fish (1994), produced by Christine Vachon, written by Guinevere Turner, and directed by Rose Troche, confronts the challenge of how to create a lesbian romantic comedy. The conventions of the classical Hollywood romantic comedy genre place limits upon any extended wrangling with serious social questions. Yet, the subject of lesbian desire, both in identity politics and popular fictions, carries an air of gravity. Surely, anything political cannot be (intentionally) funny or romantic. As for popular culture, lesbian desire has historically been the terrain of art films, exploitation books and pics, and the melodrama genre (from 1962's *The Children's Hour* to 1986's *Desert Hearts* to 1992's *Claire of the Moon*). *Go Fish* employs camp to demystify this aura of seriousness without belittling lesbian life and culture. The film's self-conscious sense of levity and its pro-sex attitude underpin its uses of camp. The character of Kia, a thirtyish academic, is instrumental in this strategy. Of all of the characters, Kia's point-of-view guides the film in terms of her comical take on lesbian life and the action (or inaction) of the lesbian romance plot.

The film opens on Kia teaching a lesbian history course. She observes that constructing lesbian histories remains a challenge. After all, lesbian figures remain hidden throughout the dominant histories, which means that formulating lesbian history prompts a change in the larger history. The same might be said about the romantic comedy genre or film history as a whole. In its own way, and given its unprecedented success as a queer film, *Go Fish* redefines the "het" genre of romantic comedy through the lesbian romance, and redefines the use of lesbianism in film by rendering it through the genre of romantic comedy. After the didactic opening, Kia's tone remains jocular and wry. She becomes the primary "Puck" figure in her attempts to hook up two single girl friends, Max and Eli, without them noticing her machinations.

Most importantly, Kia consistently steps out of the film by commenting on the action (or lack of it). Her distanced, humorous observations touch upon the subject of lesbian romance stories and the progress of lesbian culture as a whole. When Kia discusses the seeming dead-end of Eli and Max's romance with her girl friend Evie and their friend Daria, Kia grows impatient: "What is this? The lesbian *Gandhi*? I don't have the time to wait." Kia's restlessness is iconoclastic. She does not desire the great epic lesbian romance film, something sanctified and stereotypically sensitive. When Max rebukes Daria (a twenty-something, sex-loving urban dyke) for sleeping around, Kia's response invokes the entire sex debate within lesbian feminism, as well as the subject of lesbian films as a whole: "Wouldn't you rather our collective lesbian image be hot, passionate, 'say yes to sex' dykes than touchy-feely, soft-focus sisters of the woodlands?"

Go Fish is undeniably a "hot, passionate, 'say yes to sex' dyke" film, whereas previous lesbian dramas like *Claire of the Moon* (1992, USA, Nicole Conn) or *Lianna* (1983, USA, John Sayles) are unquestionably "touchy-feely, *soft-focus* sisters of the woodlands" films. (*Claire* even takes place in a bucolic retreat.) This pro-sex attitude self-consciously confronts some of the historical assumptions about the definition of lesbian identity. When Daria has sex with a man, an "inquisition" scene erupts in which a group of women accuse Daria of inauthentic lesbianness. In turn, Daria challenges regulations against promiscuity that have historically been a facet of "lesbian" identity. Daria refutes several assumptions about HIV: that transmission is causally related to the amount of sexual contact one has, and that only men (gay or straight) and heterosexual women need concern themselves with safer sex. More centrally, she also defies the notion that any heterosexual desire dispels lesbian identity. The scene addresses the lived "risk" of sexual experimentation given normative definitions of lesbian identity and popular misunderstandings about HIV transmission.

Producer Dolly Hall has been behind two of the few films about queer life among teenagers: Maria Maggenti's *The Incredibly True Adventures of Two Girls in Love* (1995) and the Sichel sisters' *All Over Me* (1997). In *Two Girls in Love,* teenage, working-class dyke Randy Dean (Laurel Hollomon) spends her wonder years in what she describes as "just your normal, typical, regular lesbo household." Reared by her Aunt Rebecca (a hardworking mechanic), Rebecca's lover Vickie, and ex-lover Lena (a New Age pugilist), Randy Dean nevertheless experiences the worst of adolescent alienation. Enter Evie Roy (Nicole Parker), an upper-middle-class, peerlessly urbane high school peer of Randy's. Besides the differences in their economic classes, Evie is African American and Randy Anglo. Naturally, the two girls fall in love. *All Over Me* focuses on Claude (Allison Folland), a sixteen-year-old high school girl from Hell's Kitchen who, with her single mother, runs the house and virtually rears herself. Claude spends her summer working at a pizza parlor, hanging with her best friend Ellen, playing her guitar, and negotiating her sexuality. This film bravely explores the shifting and often confusing state of adolescent desires, as Claude and Ellen figure out what form their relationship should take as they transition to adulthood.

Cheryl Dunye's feature film debut *The Watermelon Woman* (1996) plays with film genres, film history, and lesbian identity. Intermingling romantic comedy and documentary, the film focuses on a young, black, lesbian filmmaker reflexively named Cheryl Dunye. Cheryl undertakes a project about a (fictional) African-American actress and nightclub performer, Fay Richards, nicknamed the "Watermelon Woman" for her appearances as a servant in a number of old Hollywood films. As Cheryl explains, Richards also acted in independently made "race movies" made by and for African Americans during the 1920s, 1930s, and 1940s. The search for Fay Richards intermingles some of the recent historical discussions circulating in black and queer cultural studies, such as the history of the Race Movies and investigations into closeted stars and directors in Classical Hollywood. Cheryl's documentary aspirations involve all of the challenges met by women filmmakers, filmmakers of color, and lesbian filmmakers. For all of them, the challenge remains to uncover histories whose artifacts and evidence exist only in the bits and pieces to be found in people's memories and attics, as well as underfunded and disorganized women's history archives.

Questions of gay history also arise in *Stonewall* (1995), produced by Christine Vachon and directed by the late Nigel Finch, a stylish and impassioned film about the historic event that sparked the United States lesbian and gay liberation movement. The film forwards its history lesson through a fictional love story between savvy Hispanic drag queen LaMiranda (Guillermo Diaz) and a hunky Anglo bumpkin-turned-political activist named Matty Dean (Frederick Weller). A subplot involves LaMiranda's grand dame drag queen mentor Bostonia and her affair with Skinny Vinnie, the closeted mobster who runs the Stonewall Inn. Drag acts, expertly choreographed and performed to popular period tunes, interrupt the action as a form of campy commentary.

The problems and strengths of *Stonewall* reside in its representation of differences *within* the Stonewall-era gay community. On the one hand, the film problematically limits the role of lesbians in the creation of the gay liberation movement to an all-but silent presence among the homophile activists and a sprinkling of nameless butch dykes among those who rebelled at the riots. In the film's definition of the birth of contemporary gay identity, lesbians rank second. Despite that imbalance, *Stonewall* cleverly dramatizes many

Cheryl Dunye

issues of lesbian and gay identity politics that continue to be prevalent today: the vanguardist elitism of activists, prejudice within the gay community against drag queens, and the Anglo, middle-class biases of urban gay politics and culture. Despite LaMiranda's street-taught awareness of homophobia and her many gestures of dissent, Matty Dean, a participant in the assimilationist homophile movement, continually assumes that LaMiranda is too feeble-minded and queeny to be a political activist. After dumping LaMiranda, Matty Dean visits Fire Island and encounters complacent, white, "straight-acting" gay men who obsessively police their own behavior. Matty Dean's reconciliation with LaMiranda coincides with his disaffection with the elitist and quietist homophile movement and the eruption of the Stonewall riots.

PROMINENT PEOPLE

Chantal Akerman (1950-)

Akerman is a Belgian lesbian filmmaker whose work is broadly applicable to feminist ideas and exemplifies continual stylistic and conceptual experimentation. Director of the feminist classics *I, You, He, She* (1974) and *Jeanne Dielman* (1975), Akerman has resisted being labeled a "feminist" and "lesbian" filmmaker, although she plays a bisexual woman in the earlier film, which features a brave (for its time) lesbian lovemaking scene.

Pedro Almodóvar (1951-)

Almodóvar is an openly gay Spanish director of post-Franco comedy-melodramas that employ a mixture of Spanish and Mexican mass culture, punk culture, and gay culture, along with U.S. popular culture, particularly Hollywood. Ambiguously feminist and gay liberationist, Almodóvar's films anticipate the radical experiments with identity labels and film genres in the New Queer Cinema of the 1990s. Films include *Pepi, Luci, Bom* (1980), *Dark Habits* (1983), *What Did I Do To Deserve This?* (1984), *Law of Desire* (1987), *Women on the Verge of a Nervous Breakdown* (1988), and *High Heels* (1991).

Kenneth Anger (1929-)

Gay underground filmmaker of the 1940s, '50s, and '60s. He also authored the *Hollywood Babylon* books, chronicles of Hollywood's dirty underbelly of scandals and perversity. Films include: *Fireworks* (1947), *Scorpio Rising* (1964), and *Kustom Kar Kommandos* (1965).

Gregg Araki

One of the directors of the New Queer Cinema, Araki's output includes the apocalyptic road/buddy film *The Living End* (1991) and the "teen angst" trilogy of *Totally F****d-Up* (1994), *The Doom Generation* (1995), and *Nowhere* (1997).

Dorothy Arzner (1900-1979)

The only woman director in Classical Hollywood and a lesbian, Arzner directed "woman's pictures" that featured stars Clara Bow (*The Wild Party*, 1929), Katharine Hepburn (*Christopher Strong,* 1933), Rosalind Russell (*Craig's Wife,* 1936), and Lucille Ball (*Dance, Girl, Dance* 1940).

Sadie Benning

Hailed as a prodigy for her autobiographical videos made as a lesbian teenager in the process of coming out, Benning's work combines a fascinating stylistic and conceptual avant-gardism with the erotic and commodified pleasures of MTV. Works include *Me and Rubyfruit* (1989), *A Place Called Lovely* (1991), *It Wasn't Love* (1992), and *Girl Power (Part 1)* (1993).

Catherine Saalfield

Lizzie Borden (1954-)

Director and writer of the lesbian-feminist classic, *Born in Flames* (1983), a futuristic parable about a complacent, racist, and sexist United States after the social revolutions of the 1960s. A smart, fun, and inspiring film, *Born in Flames* envisions the possibility for a multi-cultural feminist revolution in which gendered, racial, sexual and class hierarchies are overturned.

Gregg Bordowitz, Jean Carlomusto, Ray Navarro, Catherine Saalfield, and Ellen Spiro

AIDS activists, video artists, and filmmakers who worked in conjunction with ACT UP (AIDS Coalition To Unleash Power), the Gay Men's Health Crisis, and other AIDS and queer activist organizations. Bordowitz, who has AIDS, has created other projects that explore gay and Jewish identity. Carlomusto's work includes the video *L Is For the Way You Look* (1991), a witty and tender look at lesbian film fans. Before his death, Navarro revolutionized AIDS awareness videos for Hispanic communities. Saalfield's other work includes films that interrogate the junction of sexuality and ethnicity. Spiro's AIDS videos include the widely acclaimed *Diana's Hair Ego: AIDS Info Upfront* (1990).

Tim Burton (1960-)

Hollywood director of both blockbusters such as *Batman* (1989) and *Mars Attacks!* (1996), as well as more personal films such as *Edward Scissorhands* (1990) and *Ed Wood* (1994). Burton's films consistently represent the pleasantly perverse complications of sexuality and desire, such as the gayness of Pee-wee Herman in *Pee-wee's Big Adventure* (1985), the rampant s/m and fetishism of *Batman* and *Batman Returns,* and the cross dressing protagonist Ed and transgendered-wannabe Bunny in *Ed Wood.*

Jean Cocteau (1889-1963)

Accomplished gay avant-garde artist, playwright, and filmmaker, Cocteau's films are rife with homoeroticism. Many of his films feature his longtime lover, actor Jean Marais. Cocteau mentored the novelist Jean Genet and the American avant-garde filmmaker, Kenneth Anger. Works include *The Blood of a Poet* (1930), *Beauty and the Beast* (1946), *Orpheus* (1950), and *The Testament of Orpheus* (1959).

Quentin Crisp (1908-)

The 1980 movie *The Naked Civil Servant* is based upon his 1968 book of the same name. The 1994 documentary *Resident Alien* surveys Crisp's daily life and cultural significance in the United States. Crisp has published several books and also writes movie reviews for various gay publications.

George Cukor (1899-1983)

Prolific gay Hollywood director whose films include the classic dramas and comedies *Little Women* (1933), *The Women* (1939), and *The Philadelphia Story* (1940), as well as the controversial (at its time) gender-bender *Sylvia Scarlett* (1935).

Terrence Davies (1945-)

Gay British filmmaker whose beautifully stylized portraits of London working-class families in the 1950s combine the Hollywood melodrama and musical genres, gay camp sensibility, and 1950s British "kitchen sink" realism. Davies's films explore the intersection of class, gender, sexuality, and culture. They remain painful, funny and unique works. Films include *The Terrence Davies Trilogy*

(1976, 1980, 1983), *Distant Voices, Still Lives* (1988), *The Long Day Closes* (1992), and *The Neon Bible* (1995).

Donna Deitch (1945-)

Feminist and lesbian filmmaker whose keystone film remains the lesbian cross-over classic, *Desert Hearts* (1985). A lush, 1950s-type romantic melodrama with a touch of camp (redolent of Douglas Sirk's *All That Heaven Allows,* 1956), *Desert Hearts* is set in 1950s Reno and tells the story of a divorced academic from New York, Vivien, who stays at a ranch while her divorce transpires. She falls in love with Kay, the openly lesbian stepdaughter of Frances, the ranch's colorful owner. The film lovingly mingles camp, Hollywood melodramatic conventions, and a conviction to relate the romance and heat between Vivian and Kay.

Jonathan Demme (1944-)

Successful and controversial Hollywood director whose 1991 thriller *Silence of the Lambs* received so much criticism from queer activists for its transvestite serial killer character that he went ahead and made *Philadelphia* (1994), the heroic tale of a gay PWA and lawyer (Tom Hanks) who, with the help of another lawyer (Denzel Washington) successfully sues his law firm for discrimination.

Cheryl Dunye

Lesbian filmmaker whose work employs the romantic comedy genre and explores questions of desire as related to ethnicity. Many critics compare her wry humor and insight into race issues to that of Spike Lee. Dunye's films include the shorts *The Potluck and the Passion* (1993) and *Greetings from Africa* (1995), as well as her debut feature, *The Watermelon Woman* (1996).

Blake Edwards (1922-)

Hollywood filmmaker whose films continually employ gay themes and characters, such as: *The Great Race* (1964), *The Revenge of the Pink Panther* (1978), *Victor/Victoria* (1982), and *Switch* (1991).

Sergei Eisenstein (1898-1948)

Gay Soviet filmmaker and theorist, among those who revolutionized the theory and practice of montage. His influence is visible in a host of popular films, including repeated homages to the "Odessa Steps" sequence from *The Battleship Potemkin* (1925). Gay filmmakers such as Kenneth Anger have also employed Eisenstein's montage style, as well as the director's aesthetic of the male body.

R. W. Fassbinder (1946-1982)

Gay German director and one of the founding members of the New German Cinema of the 1960s and 1970s. As Jane Shattuc explains in her book *Television, Tabloids and Tears,* Fassbinder's movies continually employed camp, Hollywood style, and the visceral avant-garde theatrical styles arising in the 1960s. Fassbinder's films also focused on the intersection of sexuality and class, displaying an array of heterosexual, homosexual, transsexual, and bisexual characters entrapped by commodity culture. Among his thirty-eight films: *The Bitter Tears of Petra Von Kant* (1972), *Fear Eats the Soul* (1974), *Fox and His Friends* (1975), *Despair* (1977), *The Marriage of Maria Braun* (1978), and *Querelle* (1982).

Nigel Finch (d. 1995)

Served for ten years as editor/executive producer of *Arena,* a British television program about the arts that produced many documentaries about queer artists and/or lesbian-gay themes. Finch also directed *The Lost Language of Cranes* (1988) and *Stonewall* (1995). During the post-production stage of *Stonewall,* Finch died from AIDS-related complications.

Stephen Frears (1931-)

British director whose mid-1980s art cinema hits feature main characters and secondary ones who are gay and lesbian. *My Beautiful Laundrette* (1985) involves a young Pakistani man whose attempts to become an entrepreneur coincide with his affair with a London punk lad. *Prick Up Your Ears* (1987) is an adaptation of John Lahr's biography of gay playwright and enfant terrible, Joe Orton. *Sammy and Rosie Get Laid* (1987) critiques Thatcher-era sexual, racial, and class politics, and its large cast of sexual outlaws includes a politically radical lesbian couple.

Su Friedrich (1954-)

Since 1978, this lesbian experimental filmmaker has played with various genres of the avant-garde and commercial cinemas. For many, her 1980s works appear as forerunners of the 1990s New Queer Cinema. Films include: *Gently Down the Stream* (1981), *The Ties That Bind* (1984), *Damned If You Don't* (1987), *First Comes Love* (1991), and *Bedtime Stories* (1996).

Richard Fung

Gay Asian-American filmmaker and critic whose documentary films explore issues of sexuality, AIDS, and racism. Films include *Orientations* (1994), *Chinese Characters* (1986), and *Fighting Chance* (1990).

Donna Deitch

Jill Godmilow (1943-)

Feminist filmmaker whose films *Waiting for the Moon* (1986) and *Roy Cohn/Jack Smith* (1993) have featured lesbian and gay historical figures. *Moon,* winner of the 1987 Sundance Festival's Grand Jury Prize, relates the rich relationship between modernist writer Gertrude Stein and her secretary/lover, Alice B. Toklas. *Cohn/Smith* records Ron Vawter's one-man show of the same name, as well as intermingling moments from Vawter's rehearsals and dressing-room prep before the show and between the acts.

Marlene Gorris (1948-)

Dutch lesbian-feminist filmmaker who got his start with the support of Belgian lesbian filmmaker Chantal Akerman. Gorris's 1981 thriller *A Question of Silence* remains a feminist classic, and although the film does not contain a lesbian character, woman-to-woman desire remains the only viable possibility for the female characters' liberation and community. Gorris's Academy Award-winning 1995 film *Antonia's Line* tells the story of a feminist, sex-positive matron who puts together an extended family with several women (and some men). Antonia's daughter is a lesbian, and her realization of her love for the village school marm (and vice verse) remains one of the most beautiful and funny "coming out" scenes in recent years.

John Greyson (1960-)

Gay Canadian film and video maker whose work develops many critical ideas about homophobia and AIDS hysteria in the late 1980s and early 1990s. Greyson's imagination and humor blooms in his 1993 film *Zero Patience,* a musical about AIDS-era disease hysteria, sexual Puritanism, and homophobia. In *Patience,* the "first" gay PWA, French-Canadian Gaetan Dugas, better known as "Patient Zero," rematerializes on earth in the 1990s, romances a Victorian sexologist, and gets involved in an ACT UP demonstration. Other films include *Urinal* (1988) and *The Making of Monsters* (1990).

Dolly Hall

Independent producer whose work includes several notable lesbian and gay films, along with several Asian films. These focuses combine in director Ang Lee's incredibly successful *The Wedding Banquet* (1993), a story about international and intergenerational relationships between a first generation gay Chinese man living in New York, his Taiwanese parents, his Anglo male lover, and a young Chinese artist whom he marries for the sake of his parents. *Banquet* received an Academy Award nomination for Best Foreign Film in 1993. Hall's other productions include two films about teenage lesbians, *The Incredibly True Adventures of Two Girls In Love* (1995) and *All Over Me* (1997).

Barbara Hammer (1939-)

The germinal lesbian filmmaker whose career spans the period from the second wave of feminism and the gay liberation movement through the New Queer Cinema. Her many films reflect Hammer's political beliefs and certain intellectual strands in feminism and lesbian-gay politics. Films include *Dyketactics* (1974), *Superdyke* (1978), *Double Strength* (1978), *Women I Love* (1979), and *Nitrate Kisses* (1992).

Todd Haynes (1961-)

New Queer Cinema director whose films, all produced by Christine Vachon, include the award-winning *Poison* (1991), *Dottie Gets Spanked* (1993), and *Safe* (1995).

Alfred Hitchcock (1899-1980)

The inimitable (but oft-imitated) Hollywood "master of suspense" whose films are rife with hetero- and homosexual anxiety. A host of homosexual characters appear in Hitchcock's films, although their sexuality is more often linked to criminality: *Murder* (1930), *Rebecca* (1940), *Rope* (1948), *Strangers on a Train* (1951), and *North by Northwest* (1959).

Rock Hudson (1925-1985)

One of the models of masculinity in Eisenhower-era United States, Hollywood star Rock Hudson narrowly avoided being outed in the 1950s by *Confidential* magazine. Maintaining a pristinely heterosexual and masculine image for twenty-five years, Hudson acted in several of Hollywood's finest comedies and melodramas from the 1950s: *Magnificent Obsession* (1954), *All That Heaven Allows* (1955), *Giant* (1956), *Written on the Wind* (1957), and *Pillow Talk* (1959). In 1985, Hudson came out publicly as a person with AIDS, and died a few months later.

James Ivory (1928-) and Ismail Merchant (1936-)

Director and producer team whose many adaptations of gay author E. M. Forester's novels include *Maurice* (1987), a sensitive melodrama about an upper-class Edwardian homosexual. Their adaptation of Henry James's *The Bostonians* (1984) features Vanessa Redgrave as a sympathetic, although hopelessly puritanical, turn-of-the-century feminist and repressed lesbian.

Derek Jarman (1942-1994)

Gay British avant-gardist whose films adapt the style and humor of Kenneth Anger with the addition of radical gay liberationist and socialist-feminist identity politics. While Jarman made his films with extremely low budgets on the fringes of the film industry, he also directed music videos and concerts for the music groups The Smiths and The Pet Shop Boys. One of the highpoints of *Edward II* (1991) consists of Annie Lennox singing (gay composer) Cole Porter's song "Every Time We Say Goodbye" as the gorgeous young King Edward and his soon-to-be-banished male lover Gaveston dance together for the last time. That the same film includes an appearance by members of the British queer activist group Out Rage, along with an aggressive queer critique of the Thatcher years, suggests the variety and complexity of Jarman's films, where intense romance intermingles with radical activism. Jarman's last film, *Blue* (1994), consists of a multi-hued blue screen and poetic voice-over soundtrack, reflecting Jarman's recurrent blindness from AIDS-related illnesses. Other films include: *Sebastiane* (1977), *Caravaggio* (1985), and *Wittgenstein* (1993).

Isaac Julien (1960-)

Black, British, and gay director whose eclectic oeuvre includes fairly traditional documentaries such as *A Darker Side of Black* (1994), a brilliant examination of hip hop and dance hall music, experimental avant-documentaries such as *Looking For Langston* (1989), and the feature thriller *Young Soul Rebels* (1991). Julien helped found Sankofa, a black British film collective.

Tom Kalin

New Queer Cinema director and producer whose *Swoon* (1991) remains one of the film movement's earlier and more salient offerings. Like many of his associates, Kalin made videos in conjunction with AIDS activist work.

Ellen Kurras

Lesbian cinematographer whose work includes several New Queer Cinema films: *Swoon* (1991), *Roy Cohn/Jack Smith* (1993), *Unzipped* (1995), *Postcards from America* (1995), and *I Shot Andy Warhol* (1996).

Bruce LaBruce

Queer punk Canadian filmmaker whose work is a playful combination of classic underground filmmaking (particularly that of Andy Warhol and Paul Morrisey), pornography, and popular genre films. Films include *No Skin Off My Ass* (1990), *Super 8 1/2* (1994), and *Hustler White* (1995).

Jennie Livingston (1960-)

Lesbian filmmaker whose 1990 documentary about black gay drag balls, *Paris Is Burning,* won the Grand Jury Prize at the 1990 Sundance Festival and proved incredibly popular in its original release. Upon its release, the film sparked debate among black and queer critics about its politics. Some, like bell hooks, claimed that *Paris* replicated the most conservative examples of Anglo anthropological films about exotic black peoples. Others, such as Isaac Jackson of the *Gay Community News* and lesbian literary critic Judith Butler, defended the film for its revelations about specifically African-American and Latino queer structures of family and culture.

Paul Morrisey (1939-)

Warhol associate who took over the camera after Valerie Solanas's attempted assassination of Warhol. His Joe Dallesandro films (*Flesh* [1968], *Trash* [1970], *Heat* [1972], *Andy Warhol's Frankenstein* [1973], and *Andy Warhol's Dracula* [1974]) are all masterful examples of camp minimalist takes on Hollywood genre films. Morrisey also crossed over into mainstream filmmaking with *Spike of Bensonhurst* (1988), a comedy about Italian-American life in which the protagonist's mother is a lesbian.

F. W. Murnau (1889-1931)

Gay German director whose Expressionist and *Kammerspiel* films *Nosferatu* (1922), *The Last Laugh* (1924), and *Sunrise* (1927) remain classics.

Ulrike Ottinger (1942-)

One of Germany's leading lesbian-feminist filmmakers, Ottinger's films are fantastic feminist allegories decked out in fabulous gowns, costumes, and color schemes. Works include: *Madame X—An Absolute Ruler* (1977), *Dorian Gray in the Mirror of the Popular Press* (1984), and *Joan of Arc of Mongolia* (1993).

Jan Oxenberg

Lesbian-feminist filmmaker whose work combines autobiography, wry humor and cultural analysis. Films include: *Home Movie* (1975), *Comedy in Six Unnatural Acts* (1975), and *Thank You and Goodnight* (1991).

Pratibha Parmar (1955-)

Black, British, lesbian filmmaker whose diverse documentary, fiction, and experimental films explore the intersections of nation, ethnicity, class, gender, and sexuality. Parmar began by studying at the Center for Contemporary Cultural Studies in Birmingham, developing critiques of capitalism and racist cultural representations. Her films reflect many of the theoretical premises of British Cul-

Jan Oxenberg

tural Studies, in particular its attention to the manner by which identities form through their intersections rather than separations. Thus, social groups are both inevitably connected to each other as well as laced with differences both within themselves and between them. Parmar's many films include: *Emergence* (1986), *Memory Pictures* (1989), *Khush* (1991), *Place of Rage* (1991), and *Warrior Marks* (1995).

Pier Paolo Passolini (1922-1975)

A multi-talented gay novelist, poet, and filmmaker whose movies remain among the most controversial and fascinating of the post-war Italian auteurs and movements. Passolini's early films (1961-64) apply the neo-realist documentary-type film style and Marxist social perspective. He later took forays into the Bible (*The Gospel According to St. Matthew* [1964]), Greek tragedy (*Oedipus Rex* [1967] and *Medea* [1969]), and the Marquis de Sade (the 1975 controversial adaptation of *120 Days of Sodom,* updated to Mussolini-era Italy). Passolini's brutal and mysterious death at the hands of a male sex worker has been the subject of speculation, and the documentaries *Whoever Tells The Truth Shall Die* (1981) and *Passolini, An Italian Crime* (1995) suggest various conspiracy theories behind his murder.

Lourdes Portillo

San Francisco-based Chicana lesbian filmmaker whose work focuses most acutely on questions of Chicano/a identity. Portillo's short film *After the Earthquake* delves into the lives of Nicaraguan political refugees, and the particular bind experienced by a young woman whose life of greater independence in the U.S., as opposed to the domestic path expected of her, inspires friends and family to criticize her. *La Ofrenda: The Days of the Dead* (1989) takes a feminist and pro-gay approach toward an examination of the Mexican and Chicano holiday, the Day of the Dead.

Sally Potter (1949-)

British feminist director of several lesbian-themed films, including *The Gold Diggers* (1983) and *Orlando* (1992). *Diggers* is a feminist musical whose romantic happy ending consists of the two heroines riding away on a horse together. *Orlando* is an adaptation of the novel of the same title penned by the celebrated author Virginia Woolf.

Yvonne Rainer (1934-)

Lesbian-feminist avant-garde filmmaker whose films include *Film about a Woman Who...* (1985) and *Privilege* (1990).

Paul Reubens (1952-)

Actor, writer, and producer whose television show *Pee-wee's Playhouse* and two *Pee-wee* films immortalized a queer figure of the 1980s: the Eisenhower-era sissy Pee-wee Herman, whose slight frame, tight and immaculate suits, and queeny manner remains a figure of camp fun for queer audiences.

Tony Richardson (1928-1991)

Bisexual British director whose prominence as a British New Cinema director was galvanized with his "kitchen sink" dramas, *Look Back in Anger* (1958), *The Entertainer* (1960), and *A Taste of Honey* (1961). *Honey* also distinguishes itself with a sensitive portrayal of a young gay man. Richardson died from AIDS-related complications.

Marlon Riggs (1957-1994)

African-American gay filmmaker whose documentaries span a range of issues pertinent to African-American culture and identity. Works include *Ethnic Notions* (1987), *Tongues Untied* (1989), *Color Adjustment* (1991), *No Regrets* (1992), and *Black Is, Black Ain't* (1995).

Ken Russell (1927-)

British art film director in whose films homosexuality continually arises in distinctly tragic, tormented, and campy ways, such as in his film version of D. H. Lawrence's novel *Women in Love* (1969), adapted for the screen by gay novelist and playwright Larry Kramer. Other homo-themed films include the bio-pics *The Music Lovers* (1970, about Tchaikovsky), *Mahler* (1974), and *Valentino* (1977); the horror film *The Lair of the White Worm* (1988); and *Salome's Last Dance* (1988), an adaptation of Oscar Wilde's play *Salome* as performed by Wilde in drag in a London brothel.

Vito Russo (1946-1990)

Gay film critic who adapted his popular lecture on the history of homosexuality in Hollywood films into a twice published (in 1981 and 1987) book-length study, *The Celluloid Closet*. The book was made into a documentary film by Robert Epstein and Jeffrey Friedman in 1995.

John Sayles (1950-)

Independent filmmaker whose liberal outlook is obvious in his films' attention to social issues involving class (*Baby, It's You*, 1983), race (*The Brother From Another Planet*, 1984), gender, and sexuality (*Lianna*, 1982). *Lianna* is a lesbian-feminist "coming out" story

that relates the title character's journey from housewife to out lesbian.

Greta Schiller (1954-)

Lesbian documentarist whose classic *Greta's Girls* and *Before Stonewall* (1985), among others, endeavor to locate virtually lost figures and events in lesbian and gay history.

John Schlesinger (1926-)

Gay British New Cinema director whose *Midnight Cowboy* (1970) and *Sunday, Bloody Sunday* (1972) provide two early, sensitive portrayals of gay men and homosexual relationships. His television film *An Englishman Abroad* (1983) chronicles the meeting between gay, British ex-patriot spy Guy Burgess and British actress Coral Browne in Moscow in the mid-1950s. Schlesinger also plays a small role as a gay author in Nigel Finch's film adaptation of David Leavitt's novel, *The Lost Language of Cranes* (1991).

Paul Schraeder (1946-)

Director, screenwriter, and critic whose heroes sometimes wrestle with the homoeroticism brimming underneath their hyper-masculinity. Films include *Mishima* (1985) and *The Comfort of Strangers* (1990).

Bill Sherwood (1952-1990)

Sherwood's 1985 art house hit *Parting Glances* remains a witty and poignant look at post-Stonewall gay life in New York as the AIDS crisis accelerates.

Jack Smith

New York experimental theater director, writer, and actor whose only completed film, *Flaming Creatures* (1963), remains a classic of the American underground movement of the 1960s.

Susan Sontag (1933-)

Lesbian cultural critic whose essay "Notes on Camp" (1964), as well as another on filmmaker Jack Smith, remain germinal discussions of urban, North American, gay male style.

Monika Treut (1954-)

German lesbian filmmaker whose films reflect her immersion in the U.S. dyke scene and identification with a sexual underground that undermines the identity categories of gay/straight and feminine/masculine. Treut also has quite a sense of humor and knows how to develop the radical aspect of comedy toward both a social critique and an enthusiastic affirmation of perversity. Films include: *The Virgin Machine* (1988), *My Father Is Coming* (1991), and *Female Misbehavior* (1992).

Rose Troche and Guinevere Turner

Director and writer/star, respectively, of the 1994 art house smash hit, *Go Fish*. Troche subsequently turned down Paramount Studios' offer for her to direct *The Brady Bunch Movie,* and now works in video. Turner has since appeared in Cheryl Dunye's *The Watermelon Woman* (1996). *Go Fish* tells the story of a number of twenty-something lesbians and dykes in Chicago and remains as much a phenomenon for its threadbare budget and gradual production over several years as for its charm as a romantic comedy. *Go Fish* was the first New Queer Cinema feature fiction film directed, written, and produced by lesbians to receive widespread attention and critical acclaim.

Vito Russo

Parker Tyler (1904-1974)

Prolific gay film critic who wrote the first analysis of films and sexual representation, *Screening the Sexes: Homosexuality in the Cinema* (1970). Tyler also wrote *The Magic and Myth of the Movies,* in which he developed his theory of film and, in 1933, penned (with Charles Henri Ford) *The Young and Evil,* a sizzling novel about gay New York in the roaring twenties.

Christine Vachon

Lesbian producer whose work and collaborators include a host of films and filmmakers in the New Queer Cinema. Her films include *The Living End* (1991), *Poison* (1991), *Swoon* (1991), and *Go Fish* (1994). Lately, Vachon has produced queer-themed works with increasing cross-over appeal, such as *I Shot Andy Warhol* (1996) and *Kiss Me Guido* (1997). She also produced Larry Clark's controversial 1995 film *Kids.*

Gus Van Sant (1950-)

Gay independent director whose works often focus on nomadic denizens of the Pacific Northwest, be they straight heroine addicts (*Drugstore Cowboy,* 1989), gay hustlers (*My Own Private Idaho,* 1991), or lesbian cowgirls (*Even Cowgirls Get the Blues,* 1994). The 1986 low-budget *Mala Noche* explores a gay store clerk's undying love for an illegal Mexican immigrant, displaying Van Sant's ability to create complicated gay characters who remain sympathetic

and insightful even as they do not conform to standard gay "positive" images.

Paul Verhoeven (1938-)

Dutch-turned-Hollywood director whose oeuvre on both continents includes controversial lesbian and gay characters. Perhaps exploitative, perhaps insightful, the surreal *The Fourth Man* (1983) traces the machinations of a gay author who becomes involved with a wealthy femme fatale in order to seduce her boyfriend. *Basic Instinct* (1992) raised the ire of queer activists owing to its use of the lesbian psycho-killer stereotype. However, lesbian and gay critics such as B. Ruby Rich and Douglas Crimp championed the film for its campy celebration of lesbian desire and humiliation of heterosexual masculinity.

Gore Vidal (1925-)

Gay writer whose screenplay for the Biblical epic *Ben Hur* (1959) develops a gay subtextual relationship involving its title character. Vidal's camp novel about Hollywood and transsexuals, *Myra Breckinridge,* was adapted into a film in 1970 starring camp queen Mae West and film critic Rex Reed.

Luchino Visconti (1906-1976)

Gay Italian director who worked in the neo-realist period of Italian filmmaking (1945-60) as well as in the auteur cinema of the 1960s and 1970s. In this latter period, Visconti made his most explicitly homosexual and politically controversial films: *The Damned* (1969), which explores the relationship between fascism, homoeroticism, and homophobia, and *Death in Venice* (1970), an adaptation of Thomas Mann's novella about a writer (in the film, a composer) who travels to Venice and falls deeply in love with a beautiful young boy amid a cholera epidemic.

Rosa von Praunheim

German gay filmmaker whose radical gay politics and low-tech "trash" style have become his signature. Von Praunheim's films maintain a confrontational posture matched by a willingness to question lesbian and gay identity politics. Films include: *Army of Lovers* (1979), an examination of the gay movement in the United States; *Silence = Death* (1990), a series of artistic presentations protesting the AIDS crisis; and *Neurosia: Fifty Years of Perversity* (1996), von Praunheim's salute to himself on his fiftieth birthday.

Andy Warhol (1928?-1987)

Pop artist whose abundant creations include several underground films either directed or produced by him. Directorial efforts include *Blow-job* (1964), *My Hustler* (1965), *Chelsea Girls* (1966), and *Bike Boy* (1967).

John Waters (1946-)
and Divine (née Glenn Milstead, 1945-1988)

Trash master of the midnight movie scene of the 1970s and his leading star, respectively. The two made eight films together, including the notorious *Pink Flamingos* (1972), *Female Trouble* (1975), *Polyester* (1981), and *Hairspray* (1988). The last two of these films evidence the height of each artist's creative abilities. *Polyester* relates the melodramatic story of an unhappy housewife, a brilliant trash adaptation of 1950s melodramas such as *Peyton Place*. In *Hairspray*, Divine plays the working mother of a high school girl who becomes a Baltimore television dance show celebrity.

Oscar Wilde (1854-1900)

Gay writer whose witty critiques of the bourgeoisie and eventual imprisonment (owing to his homosexuality) have informed gay culture and gay politics. Three films have been made about him, *The Trial of Oscar Wilde* and *Oscar Wilde* (both 1960), and *Wilde* (1997). His plays, stories, and novels have inspired many film adaptations, including a wonderful version of *The Importance of Being Earnest* (1952) starring gay actor Michael Redgrave (father of Vanessa and Lynn) as Earnest and the esteemed character actress Dame Edith Evans as the campiest of mother-in-laws, Lady Bracknell. Wilde's novel *The Picture of Dorian Gray* has been adapted three times: in 1948 as *The Picture of Dorian Gray*; in 1972 as *Dorian Gray* (and modernized to the swinging seventies); and in 1984 as *Dorian Gray in the Mirror of the Popular Press*, directed by German lesbian director Ulrike Ottinger. In 1922, lesbian actress Natasha Rambova directed an all-gay male cast in an adaptation of Wilde's last play, *Salome*. In 1988, director Ken Russell made *Salome's Last Dance*, an adaptation of *Salome* as performed by Wilde in drag in a London brothel.

Billy Wilder (1906-)

Hollywood director whose grimly comic and humorously abject films and characters play with bourgeois sexual anxieties, oftentimes referring to homosexual desire (or its possibility). In *The Seven Year Itch* (1955), the main character, a near-hysterical heterosexual husband living in Manhattan, refers benignly to his upstairs neighbors, two male interior decorators. In *Some Like It Hot* (1959), the two male protagonists dress in drag throughout much of the film, and one of them actually considers one man's marriage proposal. *Kiss Me, Stupid* (1964) focuses on a husband whose jealousy of his wife drives him to comically—and, sometimes homoerotically—manhandle his supposed rivals. *The Private Life of Sherlock Holmes* (1970) suggests that Holmes is homosexual and Watson is a latent homosexual. While *Sunset Boulevard* (1950) has no gay characters, its heroine, Norma Desmond as played by former silent film star Gloria Swanson, is a camp queen. Her luxurious suffering and refusal to age gracefully strike a camp chord for both gay and mainstream culture.

Tennessee Williams (1911-1983)

Gay playwright and one of the most celebrated theatrical realists of the twentieth century. Many of his plays have received screen treatment: *The Glass Menagerie* (1950 and 1987), *A Streetcar Named Desire* (1951), *The Rose Tattoo* (1956), *Suddenly Last Summer* (1959), and *The Night of the Iguana* (1963). The last two films also contain examples of Williams's secondary gay and lesbian characters.

REFERENCES:

Books

Anzaldúa, Gloria. *Borderlands/La Frontera: The New Mestiza*. San Francisco: Spinsters/Aunt Lute Book Company, 1987.

Bogle, Donald. *Toms, Coons, Mulattoes, Mammies and Bucks: An Interpretive History of Blacks in American Films*. New York: Continuum Publishing, 1991.

Booth, Mark. *Camp*. New York: Quartet, 1983.

Bordwell, David, Janet Staiger, and Kristin Thompson. *The Classical Hollywood Cinema*. New York: Columbia University Press, 1985.

Bronski, Michael. *Culture Clash: The Making of Gay Sensibility*. Boston: South End Press, 1984.

Butler, Judith. *Bodies That Matter: On the Discursive Limits of "Sex."* New York: Routledge, 1993.

Chauncey, George. *Gay New York*. New York: Basic Books, 1994.

Cook, David. *A History of Narrative Film*. New York: W. W. Norton & Co., 1990.

Core, Philip. *Camp: The Lie That Tells The Truth*. New York: Delilah Books, 1984.

Crimp, Douglas and Adam Rolston. *AIDS Demographics*. Seattle: Bay Press, 1990.

de Lauretis, Teresa. *Technologies of Gender: Essays on Theory, Film, and Fiction*. Bloomington: Indiana University Press, 1987.

Doty, Alexander. *Making Things Perfectly Queer: Interpreting Mass Culture*. Minneapolis: University of Minnesota Press, 1993.

Duberman, Martin, Martha Vicinuc, and George Chauncey, Jr., eds. *Hidden from History: Reclaiming the Gay and Lesbian Past*. New York: Meridian, 1989.

Dyer, Richard. *Now You See It: Studies on Lesbian and Gay Film*. New York: Routledge, 1990.

Faderman, Lillian. *Odd Girls and Twilight Lovers*. New York: Penguin, 1992.

Feil, Ken. *From Queer to Hybridity: Questions of Cultural Difference in Contemporary Queer Film and Video*. Ann Arbor, Michigan: University Microfilm, 1995.

Feuer, Jane. *The Hollywood Musical.* Bloomington, Indiana: Indiana University Press, 1993.

Fregoso, Rosa Linda. *The Bronze Screen: Chicana and Chicano Film Culture.* Minneapolis, Minnesota: University of Minnesota Press, 1993.

Garber, Marjorie. *Vested Interests: Cross-dressing and Cultural Anxiety.* New York: Routledge, 1992.

Gever, Martha, John Greyson, and Pratibha Parmar, eds. *Queer Looks: Perspectives on Lesbian and Gay Film and Video.* New York: Routledge, 1993.

Gilroy, Paul. *Small Acts: Thoughts on the Politics of Black Cultures.* London: Serpent's Tail, 1993.

Hadleigh, Boze. *Conversations with My Elders.* New York: St. Martin's Press, 1986.

———. *Hollywood Lesbians.* New York: Barricade Books, 1994.

———. *Hollywood Gays.* New York: Barricade Books, 1996.

Haskell, Molly. *From Reverence to Rape: The Treatment of Women in the Movies.* Chicago, Illinois: The University of Chicago Press, 2nd edition, 1987.

Julian, Isaac, and Colin MacCabe. *Diary of a Young Soul Rebel.* London: BFI Publishing, 1991.

Krutnik, Frank. *In a Lonely Street: Film Noir, Genre, Masculinity.* New York: Routledge, 1991.

Kuhn, Annette. *Women's Pictures.* London: Pandora Press, 1986.

Kuhn, Annette, and Susannah Radstone, eds. *Women in Film: An International Guide.* New York: Fawcett Columbine, 1990.

Marchetti, Gina. *Film and Subculture.* Ann Arbor, Michigan: University Microfilms, 1985.

Mayne, Judith. *Directed by Dorothy Arzner.* Bloomington, Indiana: University of Indiana Press, 1994.

Mercer, Kobena. *Welcome to the Jungle: New Positions in Black Cultural Studies.* New York: Routledge, 1994.

Modleski, Tania. *Feminism without Women: Culture and Criticism in a "Postfeminist" Age.* New York: Routledge, 1991.

Neale, Steve and Frank Krutnik. *Popular Film and Television Comedy.* New York: Routledge, 1990.

Nichols, Bill. *Representing Reality.* Bloomington, Indiana: Indiana University Press, 1991.

Olson, Jenni, ed. *The Ultimate Guide to Lesbian & Gay Film and Video.* New York: Serpent's Tail, 1996.

Russo, Vito. *The Celluloid Closet: Homosexuality in the Movies.* New York: Harper and Row, 1987.

Schatz, Thomas. *Hollywood Genres.* New York: Random House, 1981.

Shattuc, Jane. *Television, Tabloids and Tears: Fassbinder and Popular Culture.* Minneapolis, Minnesota: University of Minnesota Press, 1995.

Skal, David J. *The Monster Show: A Cultural History of Horror.* New York: Penguin Books, 1993.

Staiger, Janet. *Interpreting Films: Studies in the Historical Reception of American Cinema.* Princeton, New Jersey: Princeton University Press, 1992.

Steven, Peter, ed. *Jump Cut: Hollywood, Politics, and Counter Cinema.* New York: Praeger, 1985.

Suárez, Juan A. *Bike Boys, Drag Queens, and Superstars: Avant-Garde, Mass Culture, and Gay Identities in the 1960s Underground Cinema.* Bloomington, Indiana: Indiana University Press, 1996.

Summers, Claude J., ed. *The Gay and Lesbian Literary Heritage.* New York: Henry Holt and Co., 1995.

Thompson, Kristin, and David Bordwell. *Film History: An Introduction.* New York: McGraw-Hill, 1994.

Tyler, Parker. *Screening the Sexes: Homosexuality in the Movies.* New York: Da Capo Press, 1993.

Weiss, Andrea. *Vampires and Violets: Lesbians in Film.* New York: Penguin Books, 1992.

Wood, Robin. *Hollywood from Vietnam to Reagan.* New York: Columbia University Press, 1986.

Chapters in Books

Auguste, Reece, and the Black Audio Film Collective. "Black Independents and Third Cinema: The British Context," in *Questions of Third Cinema,* edited by Jim Pines and Paul Willemen. London: BFI Publishing, 1989: 212-217.

Babuscio, Jack. "Camp and the Gay Sensibility," in *Gays and Film,* edited by Richard Dyer. New York: New York Zoetrope, 1984.

Becker, Edith, Michelle Citron, Julia Lesage, and B. Ruby Rich. "Lesbians and Film," in *Jump Cut: Hollywood, Politics, and Counter Cinema,* edited by Peter Steven. New York: Praeger, 1985.

Bergman, David. "Strategic Camp: The Art of Gay Rhetoric," in *Gaiety Transfigured: Gay Self-Representation in American Literature.* Madison, Wisconsin: University of Wisconsin Press, 1991.

Bordowitz, Gregg. "The AIDS Crisis Is Ridiculous," in *Queer Looks: Perspectives on Lesbian and Gay Film and Video,* edited by Gever et al. New York: Routledge, 1993: 209-224.

Case, Sue-Ellen. "Towards a Butch-Femme Aesthetic," in *The Lesbian and Gay Studies Reader,* edited by Henry Abelove, Michèle Aina Barale, and David M. Halperin. New York: Routledge, 1993.

Chamberlain, Joy, Isaac Julien, Stuart Marshall, and Pratibha Parmar. "Filling the Lack in Everyone Is Quite Hard Work, Really . . . ," in Gever et al.: 41-60.

Dyer, Richard. "Monroe and Sexuality" and "Judy Garland and Gay Men," in *Heavenly Bodies: Film Stars and Society.* New York: St. Martin's Press, 1986.

———. "Homosexuality in *Film Noir*" and "White," in *The Matter of Images: Essays on Representations.* New York: Routledge, 1993.

Elsaesser, Thomas. "Tales of Sound and Fury," in *Film Genre Reader,* edited by Barry Keith Grant. Austin, Texas: University of Texas Press, 1986.

Gates, Jr., Henry Louis. "The Black Man's Burden," in *Black Popular Culture,* edited by Michelle Wallace and Gina Dent. Seattle: Bay Press, 1992.

Gledhill, Christine. "The Melodramatic Field," in *Home Is Where The Heart Is: Studies in Melodrama and the Woman's Film,* edited by Gledhill. London: BFI Press, 1987.

Hall, Stuart. "New Ethnicities," in *ICA Documents 7: Black Film, British Cinema,* edited by Kobena Mercer. London: Institute of Contemporary Arts, 1988: 27-31.

———. "What Is This 'Black' in Black Popular Culture?" in *Black Popular Culture,* edited by Michelle Wallace and Gina Dent. Seattle: Bay Press, 1992.

Hallam, Paul, Isaac Julien, and Derrick Saldaan McClintock. "Young Soul Rebels: Film Script," in *Diary of a Young Soul Rebel,* by Isaac Julian and Colin MacCabe. London: BFI Publishing, 1991.

Hammer, Barbara. "The Politics of Abstraction," in Gever et al.

hooks, bell, and Isaac Julien. "States of Desire," in Julian and MacCabe.

Julien, Isaac. "Black Is, Black Ain't: Notes on De-Essentializing Black Identities," in Wallace and Dent.

Julien, Isaac, and Kobena Mercer. "True Confessions: A Discourse on Images of Black Male Sexuality," in *Brother to Brother: New Writings by Black Gay Men,* conceived by Joseph Beam and edited by Essex Hemphill. Boston, Massachusetts: Alyson Publications, 1991.

Karlinsky, Simon. "Russia's Gay Literature and Culture: The Impact of the October Revolution," in *Hidden from History: Reclaiming the Gay and Lesbian Past,* edited by Duberman et al. New York: Meridian, 1989.

Kotz, Liz. "Anything But Idyllic: Lesbian Filmmaking in the 1980s and 1990s," in *Sisters, Sexperts, Queers: Beyond the Lesbian Nation,* edited by Arlene Stein. New York: Plume, 1993: 67-80.

———. "An Unrequited Desire for the Sublime: Looking at Lesbian Representations Across the Works of Abigail Child, Cecilia Dougherty, and Su Friedrich," in Gever et al.

La Place, Maria. "Producing and Consuming the Woman's Film: Discursive Struggle in *Now, Voyager,*" in Gledhill.

Mayne, Judith. "Lesbian Looks: Dorothy Arzner and Female Authorship," in *How Do I Look?* edited by Bad Object Choices. Seattle: Bay Press, 1991.

Mercer, Kobena. "Dark and Lovely Too: Black Gay Men in Independent Film," in Gever et al.

———. "Looking for Trouble," in Abelove et al.

Mulvey, Laura. "Notes on Sirk and Melodrama," in Gledhill.

Navarro, Ray. "*Eso, me esta pasando,*" in Gever et al.

Nero, Charles I. "Toward a Black Gay Aesthetic," in Hemphill.

Newton, Esther. "The Mythic Mannish Lesbian: Radclyffe Hall and the New Woman," in Duberman et al.

Noriega, Chon A. "Between a Weapon and a Formula: Chicano Cinema and Its Contexts," in *Chicanos and Film: Representation and Resistance,* edited by Chon A. Noriega. Minneapolis, Minnesota: University of Minnesota Press, 1992: 141-167.

Rich, B. Ruby. "In the Name of Feminist Film Criticism," in *Movies and Methods,* edited by Bill Nichols. Berkeley, California: University of California Press, vol. 2, 1985: 340-358.

———. "When Difference Is (More Than) Skin Deep," in Gever et al.

Riggs, Marlon. "Black Macho Revisited: Reflections of a SNAP! Queen," in Hemphill: 253-257.

Ross, Andrew. "The Uses of Camp," in *No Respect: Intellectuals and Popular Culture.* New York: Routledge, 1989.

Saalfield, Catherine. "On the Make: Activist Video Collectives," in Gever et al., 21-37.

Smith, Valerie. "The Documentary Impulse in Contemporary U.S. African-American Film," in Wallace and Dent: 56-64.

Smith-Rosenberg, Carroll. "Discourses of Sexuality and Subjectivity: The New Woman, 1870-1936," in Duberman et al.

Snead, James. "'Black Independent Film': Britain and America," in *ICA Documents 7: Black Film, British Cinema,* edited by Kobena Mercer. London: Institute of Contemporary Arts, 1988: 47-50.

Sontag, Susan. "Notes on Camp," in *Against Interpretation and Other Essays.* New York: Farrar, Straus and Giroux, 1966: 275-292.

Staiger, Janet. "Taboos and Totems: Cultural Meanings of *Silence of the Lambs,*" in *Film Theory Goes to the Movies,* edited by Jim Collins. New York: Routledge, 1993: 142-154.

Viegner, Matias. "Kinky Escapades, Bedroom Techniques, Unbridled Passion, and Secret Sex Codes," in *Camp Grounds: Style and Homosexuality,* edited by David Bergman. Amherst, Virginia: University of Massachusetts Press, 1993: 234-256.

———. "'The Only Haircut that Makes Sense Anymore': Queer Subculture and Gay Resistance," in Gever et al.: 116-133.

Wallace, Michelle. "Modernism, Postmodernism and the Problem of the Visual in Afro-American Culture," in *Out There: Marginalization and Contemporary Cultures,* edited by Ferguson, et al. Cambridge, Massachusetts: The MIT Press, 1990: 39-50.

Williamson, Judith. "Two Kinds of Otherness: Black Film and the Avant-Garde," in Mercer: 33-37.

Articles

Almaguer, Tomás. "Chicano Men: A Cartography of Homosexual Identity and Behavior," in *differences: A Journal of Feminist Cultural Studies,* vol. 3, Winter 1991: 75-100.

Collis, Rose. "So Dish! Rose Collis Meets Christine Vachon, the Hotshot Producer Credited with the Invention of New Queer Cinema," in *Gay Times,* May 1994: 66-67.

Dugan, Lisa. "Making It Perfectly Queer," in *Socialist Review,* vol. 22, January-March 1992: 11-31.

Fusco, Coco. "*Las Madres de la Plaza de Mayo*: An Interview with Susana Munoz (sic) and Lourdes Portillo," in *Cineaste,* vol. 15, 1986: 22-25.

Giannaris, Constantin, Derek Jarman, Isaac Julien, and Pratibha Parmar. "Queer Questions: Is Queer Cinema Possible? Four Film-Makers Living in Britain Respond to the Arguments and Passion of B. Ruby Rich's Article," in *Sight and Sound,* vol. 5, Fall 1992: 34-35.

Gutierrez, Eric. "Spitting Poison: Filmmaker Todd Haynes Talks About Being a Homosexual, a Woman, a Black," in *High Performance,* vol. 54, Summer 1991: 14-17.

Hoberman, J. "Explorations," in *American Film,* March 1981: 16-18, 78.

Jacobowitz, Florence. "The Man's Melodrama: *Woman in the Window* and *Scarlet Street,*" in *CineAction!,* vol. 13, no. 14, Summer 1988: 64-73.

Laskawy, Michael. "Poison at the Box Office: An Interview with Todd Haynes," in *Cineaste,* vol. 18, Summer 1991: 38-39.

Lesage, Julia. "The Political Aesthetics of the Feminist Documentary Film," in *Quarterly Review of Film Studies,* Fall 1978: 507-523.

Medhurst, Andy. "That Special Thrill: *Brief Encounter,* Homosexuality and Authorship," in *Screen,* vol. 32, Summer 1991: 197-208.

Moore, Darrel. "Politics and Pleasures in the Nineties," in *Border/Lines,* vol. 29, no. 30, 1993: 88-92.

Musto, Michael. "Old Camp, New Camp," in *Out,* April/May 1993: 32-39.

Newman, Kathleen. "Steadfast Love and Subversive Acts: The Politics of *La Ofrenda: The Days of the Dead,*" in *Spectator,* vol. 13, Fall 1992: 98-109.

Powers, John. "Toxic Shock Syndrome: *Poison*'s Bold New Angle of Intolerance," in *LA Weekly,* 17-23 May 1991: 29.

Rich, B. Ruby. "Dumb Lugs and Femmes Fatales: Film Noir Is Back with a Vengeance," in *Sight and Sound,* November 1995: 6-10.

———. "New Queer Cinema," in *Sight and Sound,* vol. 5, Fall 1992: 30-34.

———. "Reflections on a Queer Screen," in *GLQ,* vol. 1, no. 1, 1993: 83-91.

Smith, Roberta. "A Video Artist Who Talks Through a Keyhole," in *New York Times,* 28 March 1993: section 2, 33.

Solomon, Alisa. "In Whose Face? A Gay Generation Is Not an Age Group," in *Village Voice,* vol. 36, 2 July 1991: 28-29.

Taubin, Amy. "Beyond the Sons of Scorcese," in *Sight and Sound,* vol. 5, Fall 1992: 37.

Trebay, Guy. "In Your Face!" in *Village Voice,* vol. 35, 14 August 1990: 34-39.

Viegner, Matias. "Decontrolled Boundaries: The Body as Artifact," in *Documents,* 1993: 69-70.

Walters, Barry. "'Young Soul Rebels' With a Cause," in *San Francisco Examiner,* 5 December 1991: D8.

Welter, Barbara. "The Cult of True Womanhood: 1820-1860," in *American Quarterly,* vol. 18, Summer 1966: 151-174.

Wyatt, Justin. "Cinematic/Sexual Transgression: An Interview with Todd Haynes," in *Film Quarterly,* Summer 1993: 2-8.

Other

Carter, Mia. "Trans-Posing the Subject: Technological and Cross-Cultural Autobiographic Performance in the Video Works of Sadie Benning." Duke University Press, forthcoming.

Feil, Ken. "Pee-wee [Morphous] Perverseness: Mainstream (Gay) Camp and *Pee-wee's Playhouse.* Unpublished Paper, 1992.

—Ken Feil

14

Literature

Virtually everyone who has read literature of any sort has read gay and lesbian literature. However, unless they intentionally sought the genre, they were likely unaware that it was gay and/or lesbian. This review serves as an introduction to 20th-century United States gay and lesbian literatures by providing an overview of its evolution.

Four clarifications are in order. First, at times, the use of the phrase "gay and lesbian literatures" is anachronistic. The sexualized definitions that the United State's mainstream and alternative cultures now ascribe to the words "gay" and "lesbian" are 20th-century social constructions which become clearer as one follows the evolution of the literatures. Second, the working definitions and the lists of representative texts provided do not intend to present in full U.S. 20th-century gay and lesbian literatures.

Third, I purposely identify gay and lesbian literatures as separate literatures. While there are many thematic similarities between them, these connections do not justify the conflation of the two subjects. For instance, while some of the lesbian literature, from as early as the turn of century, included gay charters and plot developments, until the 1970s none of the gay literature included lesbian characters and plots. This observation is not accusatory. It does suggest, though, that until the sexual revolution of the 1960s and 1970s, the gay and lesbian literary communities were not connected. Thus, to combine them under the heading "gay and lesbian literature" would be an ill-informed decision, one that could ostensibly silence significant writers and themes of either literature. Finally, this gay and lesbian literature review makes no pretense to original research. While the review collects many gay and lesbian authors' and scholars' perspectives, the research of James Levin and Lillian Faderman proved to be especially useful both in contextualizing definitions of gay and lesbian literature and in identifying authors and texts.

As two bodies of work, gay and lesbian literatures refuse narrow definitions. Instead, the gay and lesbian literary communities insist on creating a community of diversity. Together these literary collectives create both history and vision for gay and lesbian literary futures. To understand how literary scholars situate gay

and lesbian literatures necessitates a working definition of "literature." Definitions of gay and lesbian literatures follow. Then, explanations of each literature's important periods clarify the respective working definitions. One interesting feature of both literatures is that fiction predominates. While there could be several reasons for this, it's possible that fiction serves both as an encoding device and as a way to imagine what gays' and lesbians' real-life futures can be.

GAY AND LESBIAN LITERATURES' RELATIONSHIP TO THE DEFINITION OF LITERATURE

Samuel Taylor Coleridge's *Biographia Literaria* introduced Western culture to literary commentary. Since then, literary scholars have argued about the purpose and definition of literature. For some literary scholars and aficionados, literature simply teaches. Readers who hold tightly to this definition are usually the same ones who work ardently to censor texts that present characters and plots that challenge mainstream mores. For a second group of scholars and readers, literature reflects the cultures from which it comes. For this group of readers, literature represents an archeological find of sorts. It tells people about themselves. Finally, for a third group of scholars and readers, literature is a tool by which cultures can envision change. While some scholars and readers align themselves with one of these distinct definitions, more scholars and readers combine these three perspectives to claim, as critic Stuart Kellogg does, that literature allows cultures to explore the "history of humanity's self-portrait" (Kellogg, p. 1). A combined literary perspective encourages people to use literature to understand better the past and to work towards specific cultural changes. Together these three understandings of literature suggest that literature is all about capturing the human experience. Since both hetero- and homosexuality are part of the human experience, both should be explored in literature. And yet, this has not been the case historically.

Gay literature has been traced to the Greeks and Romans, and lesbian literature to Sappho on the island of Lesbos. Gay and lesbian literatures certainly have histories, but they are histories that scholars are only recently exploring, and ones that will be difficult to tell fully. While some of this literature is extant, much of it was destroyed by the Christian church. The literature has not been limited only by institutions such as religions and wary publishers. Some gay and lesbian authors themselves have kept their texts private to protect themselves, their families, and their lovers.

Writers' decisions to include gay and lesbian characters represent literary riskiness. Therefore, across the decades, the inclusion of significant gay and lesbian characters has experienced ebbs and flows. Whether writers create gay and lesbian characters or discuss issues of particular interest to gays and lesbians, all writers confront the human experience of sexuality in their work. Kellogg claims that, in fact, all writers deal with homosexuality, too. Those who fear it, ignore it, but by including or not including homosexuality in a text, writers deal with the subject. Like the writers who avoid the topic of homosexuality, readers too can displace homosexual characters and plots in texts, usually out of fear. Those who identify with homosexuality will notice the development, or lack thereof, of gay and lesbian characters and plots (Kellogg, p. 7).

Kellogg's research helps to situate homosexual literatures by providing four reasons why an author might address homosexuality:

1) *Safe Zone:* Some writers want to create an Arcadia, a place where people connect to the universal desire to be free but safe; to be free from critics but not lonely. Arcadian literature is a dream—Peter Pan-like. Arcadia does not remind homosexuals of their supposed inferior sexuality. Instead, it fulfills their dream of being accepted, of being safe, of being loved even though the culture that surrounds them reminds these authors often of their inferior sexuality.

2) *Political:* Other writers use their literature to support, question, or challenge social paradigms. For the writer who creates a homosexual text for political reasons, the work may include despicable and revered gay and lesbian characters.

3) *Sociological:* As social outsiders, homosexuals tend to be keen observers of the world. This sociological rationale can explain both the reason gay and lesbian writers publish, and the reason homo- and heterosexual writers may include gay and lesbian characters.

4) *Psychological:* This rationale links well with the sociological reason. The result of gay and lesbian authors' and characters' keen observations is what Kellogg calls forbidden knowledge. They know what cultures are not supposed to know. This new knowledge allows them to be even more skillful observers of themselves and of the society from which they come (Kellogg, p. 7).

These reasons provide possible rationales for the evolution of gay and lesbian literatures provided below.

Defining Gay Literature

It was years before either mainstream or alternative cultures used as a categorical device the phrase "homosexual literature" or "gay literature." In fact, "The term 'homosexuality' (*Homosexualitat*) was actually used for the first time in 1869 by Karl Mariz Kertbeny, a German-Hungarian campaigner for the abolition of Prussia's laws that criminalized sexual relations between men" (Miller, p. 13). Gay literature could not safely be labeled such even by gays until the gay community took ownership of the word "homosexual," taking away the negative associations ascribed to the word. Once the gay community took "homosexual" and then "gay" as positive labels for its community, then its literary community had labels for its literature.

The labels, however, did not define the literature. The perpetual questions remained: What is a gay text? Is a text a gay one if the

author is gay? Is a text gay if a character is gay? What if both situations exist? Critic Gregory Woods answers these questions, questions that apply to both gay and lesbian texts, by quoting lesbian critic Bonnie Zimmerman:

"If a text lends itself to a lesbian reading, then no amount of biographical 'proof' ought to be necessary to establish it as a lesbian text." Exactly. A gay text is one which lends itself to the hypothesis of a gay reading, regardless of where the author's genitals were wont to keep house (Woods, p. 4).

And, argues Woods, a text can be considered gay or lesbian regardless of how many gay or lesbian characters there are (Woods, p. 4). This suggests that for both gay and lesbian texts, there are numerous factors, of which the author's and characters' sexualities are only two, that may invite a gay or lesbian reading.

TWENTIETH-CENTURY U.S. GAY MALE LITERATURE

The review that follows focuses on 20th-century U.S. gay male literature. To appreciate the momentum and corresponding progress made in this century, though, the discussion must begin in the 19th century with Walt Whitman and Oscar Wilde, two writers whose literature represents the "Literature of Romantic Friendships." From there, the review moves to "Literature between the Wars"; "Postwar Permissive Literature"; "Literature of the Freudian Fifties"; "Literature of the Transitional Years"; "Literature of Politics, Power, and Pride"; "Literature of the Paradoxical Eighties"; and finally to "Political, Theoretical, and Experimental Literature." The work of journalist Neil Miller and literary critic James Levin provides these labels and much of the research that follows.

Romantic Friendship Literature: Mid- to Late 19th Century

During the 19th century, "homosexual" represented a neologism more than an established word. As noted above, the first recorded use of the word was in 1869, and in that case, it was used in Prussia in an attempt to criminalize sexual relations between men. The word "gay" was not yet a sexualized word. For all intents and purposes, no language described male homosocial relationships or romantic or erotic love between two men. The best the 19th-century U.S. culture did in terms of language was to call such relationships "romantic friendships," the same phrase used to describe similar relationships between two women. The boundaries between romantic friendship and erotic love were unclear, both for those in the relationships and those who were not. Interestingly, the historical research, literary and otherwise, does not suggest that the culture perceived this unclear labeling as problematic. No one seemed to question the concept or reality of romantic friendships. E. Anthony Rotundo explains the Victorian response to homosexual impulses in his book *American Manhood*:

A man who kissed or embraced an intimate male friend in bed did not worry about homosexual impulses because he did not assume that he had them. In the Victorian language of touch, a kiss or an embrace was a pure gesture of deep affection at least as much as it was a an act of sexual expression (Miller, p. 4).

Whitman and Wilde: A Beginning to Gay Male Literature

Literary critics claim that Walt Whitman, in his life and work, arguably exemplified premodern attitudes toward homosexuality. As a writer, Whitman is recognized both as the spokesman for the 19th century renaissance and as the gay man who promoted homosexual self-consciousness in the U.S. and abroad. Whitman earned this recognition because of the public response to his homoerotic "Calamus" poems. He included these poems in the 1860 edition of *Leaves of Grass*, a collection that is said to be his song of himself, his country, his century. It was not only his poetry that earned him this title, however. It is also critics' understandings of the letters he wrote.

Whitman served as a "wound dresser" during the Civil War. According to historians Justin Kaplan and Jonathan Ned Katz, Whitman's friends recognized, during the war, his genuine attachment to wounded soldiers. As Katz's research reveals, it is from Whitman's letters that we know of these male attachments. Whitman wrote of deep affection for his comrades, and, in some cases, indicated when and with whom he slept. However, Katz cautions 20th century readers from applying contemporary definitions to "slept with." Alternatively, Katz does note that if we are interested in understanding the history of homosexual relations, this 19th century reality is important.

Historian Peter Gray claims:

> Whitman himself tried to give the subject a name—the 'love of comrades' or 'adhesiveness'—but these terms were deliberately vague and ambiguous and imprecise. In his old age, Whitman was to deny that he had any intention of advocating sexual love between men. It was finally left to the sexologists to do the labeling and the cataloguing and eventually to pronounce homosexuality as deviant and perverse (Miller, p. 4).

More-contemporary historians and literary scholars try to explain Whitman and his work in relation to his sexuality. The truth is, as Gray explains, "Whitman was the product of the age in which homosexuality wasn't labeled or understood, the age that 'chose the spurious safety of ignorance over the risky benefits of knowledge'" (Miller, p. 4).

No real language existed to express the relationships and desires Whitman articulated in his poetry and in his letters, which in turn encouraged the denial of such feelings, if they existed. In his prose and poetry, Whitman consistently stopped short of professing the reality of sexual love between men. There were some, such as Oscar Wilde in England, "who viewed Whitman's celebrations of 'the need of comrades' and of 'athletic' and 'manly friend-

Walt Whitman

ship' as constituting a kind of early homosexual manifesto. [And apparently,] Whitman did nothing to disabuse them of such ideas" (Miller, pp. 10-11). It is fair to say then that Whitman was a lover of men. The most that critics and contemporaries could claim, however, was that Whitman's life and work revealed romantic friendships.

Poet and playwright Oscar Wilde visited Whitman in Camden, New Jersey, where Whitman spent the final years of his life with family. On his second visit to Whitman, only four months after the first visit, Wilde claimed: "Whitman talked freely about his attractions to other men. The 'kiss of Walt Whitman,' Wilde would say later, 'is still on my lips'" (Miller, p. 12).

Wilde is important to an understanding of 20th-century U.S. gay literature, not only because of his admiration for Whitman, but also because of his gay writing, most notably his novel *The Picture of Dorian Gray* (1890, 1891), a story filled with decadence and self-indulgence. "Perhaps more responsible than any other single text in establishing the stereotypical link between art, decadence, and homosexuality," critic Claude J. Summers argues, "the work deserves credit as a pioneering depiction of a particular gay ambiance, yet it is divided against itself" (Miller, p. 21). However, Wilde is best known within the circles of gay literary scholarship because of the now-infamous Wilde trials.

When Wilde visited Whitman, Wilde was nearing the height of his fame. Critics and audiences spoke with great enthusiasm about his comic plays *Lady Windermere's Fan* (1892) and *A Woman of No Importance* (1894). His most famous work, *The Importance of Being Earnest* (1895), was forthcoming. Not only is this play a significant literary text, it is also credited with making public male homosexuality, specifically Wilde's homosexuality, particularly his relationship with Lord Alfred Douglas, nicknamed "Bosie." When the two became lovers, Wilde was 36 and Douglas 21.

The problem in this relationship was not Wilde and Bosie. The problem was Bosie's father, Queensberry, a controlling and sometimes violent man who despised Wilde. Bosie's father plotted to disrupt the opening-night performance of *The Importance of Being Earnest*. Later, Queensberry left an inappropriate note for Wilde. Wilde then sued for libel, a move that turned out to be disastrous. Lawyer Sir Edward Carson read a passage from *The Picture of Dorian Gray* during his cross-examination of Wilde. This examination was Carson's attempt to use Wilde's novel to force him to admit to homosexual intimacy. Carson did not accomplish that goal, but the result favored Queensberry, for the judge threw out the case. Within hours Wilde was arrested and charged with sodomy and indecent behavior. At Wilde's second trial, he publicly defended homosexuality in England. This second trial, which resulted in Wilde's two-year prison sentence, invited a public response to homosexuality. A public connection between homosocial and -sexual relations had been made, a connection to which 20th-century English and American gay writers felt compelled to respond for decades.

Wilde responded in writing to his imprisonment. According to Summers, Wilde's most important fiction, *De Profundis* (1897), represents Wilde's prison novel. He used his imagination to free himself from gay oppression. Summers explains that Wilde's work established themes that gay authors, especially U.S. authors, would explore in the decades ahead: the desire to avoid or dismantle moralistic prohibitions, the desire to recover and to celebrate an Arcadian past in which homosexuality is valued and respected, and the depiction of divided selves (Miller, p. 20).

Taken together, Wilde's novels and plays and Whitman's poetry established two themes, now perceived as central to gay literature: the relationship of the individual and society and the validation of the emerging homosexual consciousness. Their literature and their life-experiences encouraged the culture that followed to name "romantic friendships" homosexual relationships.

U.S. Gay Male Literature between the Wars: 1920-1943

Around the world, the gay literary community created four bohemias on both sides of the Atlantic. One, the Bloomsbury group of approximately 20 British men and women intellectuals who regularly met to think and talk together, came into existence before World War I. The second notable group congregated in Paris in the 1920s. By the end of the decade, Paris was the irrefutable art center of the Western world. The other two bohemias were in the United States: New York's Greenwich Village, an area whose inexpensive accommodations attracted intellectuals and activists, and New York's Harlem. Together these bohemias created havens for intellectual and artistic hetero- and homosexuals. Ideas about the human experience that evinced themselves in these communities contributed to the post-World War I attitude that challenged the established order represented by the Victorian era. Social timidity defined pre-World War I U.S. culture, while social boldness was the hallmark of the post-World War I era. The bohemias reify this boldness. The irony is that this time of social change existed during a time of conservative politics.

The literature of the 1920s received much critical attention, due in large part to this interesting mix of social progressiveness and political conservatism. While this literary decade introduced changes in social mores, the progressives were not fully capable of introducing a new value system to sustain people. This reality led to the legendary labels "The Lost Generation" and "The Roaring Twenties" (Levin, p. 22). While the writers of this era may not have been completely successful in providing a new set of social values, Levin argues that as a group writers such as Ernest Hemingway, John Dos Passos, F. Scott Fitzgerald, and Sherwood Anderson sought new values regarding sexual morality. These writers and others, like many of their non-writing contemporaries, encouraged sexual experimentation. Sexual freedom in literature had yet to be granted, however.

Carl Van Vechten mixed fantasy and reality. This is especially true of his first two novels, *Peter Whiffle* (1922) and *The Blind Bow Boy* (1923); his characters behave in a campy way—witty conversation with intentionally silly behavior. In Van Vechten's novel *Parties* (1930), Roy Fern is passionate for David, who never returns the passion, but Roy's sexuality is not evident in the story (Levin, p. 23). In Sherwood Anderson's story "Adolescence," set in *Winesburg, Ohio* (1919), the character of Carl explains that he enjoys his friend, Philip; Philip attends a costume party dressed as a woman. A young boy is attracted to the "woman" Philip, and the youth never figures out that Philip is another boy. Philip ends up kicking the boy away—not a typical homosexual response (Levin, p. 24). While these stories hint at homosexuality and some characters respond to it, none of these novels make homosexuality an overt issue. Levin argues that it is the minor novelists who address homosexuality more directly, writers such as Waldo Frank in *Dark Mother* (1920); Clarkson Crane in *The Western Shore* (1925), arguably the most positive portrayal of homosexual characters of the decade; and J.A. Norcross in *The Strange Confession of Monsieur* (1928). The 1920s may have been a decade of sexual freedom, but it was only a heterosexual freedom. Homosexuals remained closeted in life and literature.

Levin describes the 1930s as one big cultural lag. This was the first decade to provide a substantial number of gay novels, however, the character development in the literature is not especially strong as most of the characters are rather wooden. But readers are introduced through literature to homosexual men and their world. Some of the texts include Blair Niles's *Strange Brother* (1931), a text written by a woman, which introduced 1930s readers to homosexual literature; George Davis's *The Opening of a Door* (1931); Myron Brinnig's *This Man Is My Brother* (1932), which is more direct than Davis's book but provides a limited picture of homosexuality; Bradford Rope's *42nd Street* (1932), which established the basis for the film and Broadway play that followed (in both cases the entire gay element is deleted); F. Scott Fitzgerald's *Tender Is the Night* (1934), which has two minor homosexual characters; and Jerry Cole's *The Secrets of a Society Doctor* (1935), an unusual text that is perceived as a nearly pornographic novel that provides more insight into the human experience than many of the other works of the period.

In the second part of the decade, significantly fewer works about homosexuality were published. The six below capture the contemporary tone of homosexual literature. Djuna Barnes's *Nightwood* (1937), critically acclaimed as a gay and lesbian classic, focuses on a tortured lesbian triangle that includes a male transvestite. In John Evan's *Flying* (1936) and Murrell Edmund's *Sojourn among the Shadows* (1936), homosexuality is arguably hidden. Daphne Greenwood's *Apollo Sleeps* (1937) focuses "on women who are 'victimized' by gay men" (Levin, p. 47). Raymond Chandler's *The Big Sleep* (1939) suggests, as the sexologists claimed, that gay men experience gender confusion.

Levin explains that while a handful of gay novels were published, only one novel between 1939 and 1945 had homosexuality as its central theme: Harlan C. McIntosh's *This Finer Shadow* (1941). The author became so frustrated by numerous manuscript rejections that he committed suicide. Critic John Cowper Powys finally secured the novel's publication after McIntosh's death (Levin, pp. 49-56).

Postwar Permissive Literature: 1946-1950

Following World War I, the U.S. mainstream felt compelled to reconsider the sexual mores established in the 19th century and still proscribed in the early 20th. One might think that this focus on sexuality provided solid support for the emerging gay community. As the "Literature between the Wars" suggests, more writers began to refer to homosexuality, but many did this covertly. World War II made a substantial difference for gay men than did World War I. Although homosexuality was not necessarily discussed anymore than it had been before World War II, the second war created a larger audience for homosexual literature.

The increase in homosexual publications may be the result of two particular publications, namely the Kinsey reports of 1948 and 1953. These reports may have piqued writers' interest in creating homosexual characters and plots and mainstream culture's interest in homosexuality. Alfred C. Kinsey's reports challenged the prevailing claim that to be gay was to be ill. Kinsey, a University of Indiana researcher, interviewed more than 10,000 white American men and women about their sexual habits. He published the research results in two best-sellers, *Sexual Behavior in the Human Male* (1948) and *Sexual Behavior in the Human Female*

(1953). In designing the studies, Kinsey worked to keep prevailing sexual mores out of his study. He worked diligently to create a purely scientific study. His results startled the U.S. culture, especially his findings about homosexuality.

Kinsey's research claimed that significant numbers of heterosexual men and women engaged not only in premarital and extramarital sex, but also in autoerotic sex. He also maintained that approximately 10 percent of the population was homosexual. The public expressed shock at these findings; writers published more homosexual texts.

In 1945, according to Levin, two books situated homosexuality as very important: Richard Brooks's *The Brick Foxhole* (1945), a novel about the anxiety of soldiers in camp before being sent to the battle lines, takes limited steps toward accepting homosexuality by suggesting that the oppression experienced by blacks, Jews, and gays may be similar; and William Maxwell's *The Folded Leaf* (1945), a story of adolescent homoerotic feelings.

Nineteen forty-eight resulted in three gay classics. The first text to examine homosexuality seriously, Gore Vidal's *The City and the Pillar,* was published. Vidal's novel was the landmark text of 1948 and his third in three years. His ability to produce a succession of quality literature and, in particular, his naturalistic treatment of homosexuality in *The City*, firmly established Vidal as a key 20th century U.S. writer. However, Norman Mailer's *The Naked and the Dead* was the year's best seller. The third significant author of 1948, Truman Capote, published *Other Voices, Other Rooms*, a story about an adolescent boy raised by his mother in New York who goes to live on his father's estate in rural Mississippi.

Nineteen fifty produced another gay classic, James Barr's *Quatrefoil*, a story like many of the decade that combines positive and negatives depictions of homosexuality, and highlights the hallmark of this era's fiction most succinctly. Novels of this period are marked by confusion. Writers and characters alike are unsure about whether to depict gayness as healthy or not. The tone of this era's gay literature and the increase in gay publications suggest that the culture intended to discuss gayness seriously.

This five-year period was the first time in which all gay men were not characterized as wanting to be women, and all gay men were not described as effeminate. The literature introduced masculine gay men and homophobia as significant social issues. It is through literature, then, the gay community crafted an appeal for sexual tolerance.

Literature in the Freudian Fifties: 1951-1959

The five years following the war were marked by more open discussions about homosexuality and a greater number of gay literary publications. While these discussions did not end suddenly in 1951, intellectual conservatism marked the 1950s. It is difficult to prove, but critics argue that the conservatism of the era likely influenced people's responses to homosexuality. Perceived cultural norms included stay-at-home moms, particular fashions for men and women, and regular church attendance. With each of these expectations came a certain degree of thought patrol. The result was a culture shocked by slight deviations. Specific social norms were prescribed, and homosexuality was clearly proscribed.

Freud rejected sexologists' claims that homosexuality was the result of degeneracy or that homosexuals represented a third sex. Freud claimed that homosexuality resulted from an "arrested development." In maintaining this position, Freud intended to support homosexuals. However, Freud's followers eschewed his claim (Miller, p. 24). The U.S. culture became more intrigued by the dogmatic claim that homosexuals were emotionally damaged. Thus, Freud's followers rejected the Kinsey reports and promoted the gay-is-ill claim.

Levin explains that increasingly in 1951 and 1952, novels embraced psychoanalytic ideas about homosexual behavior as manifested illness. Between 1952 and 1953, no fewer than 20 novels presented gayness as neurosis. Some of these texts include Mary MacLaren's *The Twisted Heart* (1952); Russell Thacher's *The Tender Ages* (1952); Chandler Brossard's *The Bold Saboteurs* (1952); Wilma Prezzi's *Dark Desires* (1953); and Oakley Hall's *The Corpus of Joe Bailey* (1953). Gore Vidal's *Death in the Fifth Position* represents the only 1952-53 novel that escapes general adverse attitudes regarding homosexuality (Levin, pp. 123-28).

The neurosis claims only gained support between 1954 and 1955. Jean Evan's *Three Men* makes the neurosis-focus most succinct. By 1955, the gay-is-ill position was so firmly established that only four novels even mentioned homosexuality. While these

James Baldwin

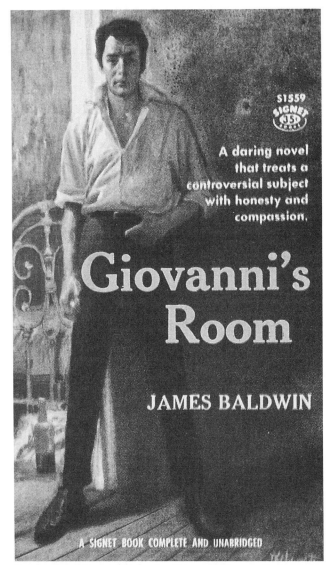

Cover of the first paperback edition of *Giovanni's Room* by James Baldwin.

negative claims mark most texts, some writers tried to search for positive elements in homosexuality. Christopher Isherwood's *The World in the Evening* (1954) provides the most cogent exception to the negative books. While homosexuality plays second to the heterosexual events in the story, gayness is significant. With the book's gay bourgeois couple, Charles and Bob, Isherwood connects gayness to the middle class (Levin, p. 138).

Poetry of the time captured the same perspective. Thom Gunn's first collection of poetry, *Fighting Terms* (1954), introduces the continued focus of his later work. He explores both love and sexuality and public and private expressions of affection. Like his later poetry, his poetic technique remains tight and focused. However, unlike his later publications, his first publication, similar to contemporaneous novels, represents controlled sexuality.

According to Levin, 1956 produced more texts that focused on homosexuality than in 1955, but the attitude towards homosexuality remained highly negative. James Baldwin published the most important book of the year, *Giovanni's Room,* the story of David, who realizes his homosexual desires when he is suddenly attracted to Giovanni, another gay man. However, when David's girlfriend returns to marry David, he leaves Giovanni. Neither man is happy; the novel tells another bleak story (Levin, p. 143).

Vidal, in his acceptance of homosexuality, represents an aberrant 1950s author. In his 1956 novel, *The Judgment of Paris*, the protagonist, Philip, spends a year in Europe after completing his ivy league education (Levin, p. 148). While he is not homosexual, and never accepts advances from homosexuals, he is an important character since he befriends homosexuals with ease.

By the mid-1950s, Allen Ginsberg's poetry began to challenge social expectations, something most novels had difficulty doing. Ginsberg did not hide sexuality in his poems. Following the war, his personal code challenged orthodox sex and politics, for instance, like his mother, he supported Communism. These ethics informed his philosophy of language and his poetry. His most celebrated piece, "Howl" (1956), speaks for the downtrodden and the oppressed, including gays, while attacking American systems. "Howl" uses words that challenge the 1950s normalcy by speaking for the "Others" and by celebrating the love between men.

Finally, by 1958, the new response to homosexuality that Ginsberg inaugurated began to appear in novels. Fifteen books with central homosexual themes were published. Unlike in earlier eras, in 1958 the least-literate books, by authors such as Eve Linkletter, Deborah Deutsch, Herbert Kastle, and Dennis Murphy, perpetuated homosexual intolerance.

Cultural tolerance gained momentum, argues Levin. Representative novels include Walter Ross's *The Immortal*, a story that mirrors James Dean's life; Jack Kerouac's *On the Road*, a precursor to the Beat Generation; Vance Gourjaily's *The Violated*; Wilfred Motley's *Let No Man Write My Epitaph*; Ramsey Ullman's *Day on Fire*; William Talsman's *The Gaudy Image*; William Goldman's *Your Turn to Curtsy, My Turn to Bow*; and Robert Phelps's *Heroes and Orators* (Levin, pp. 158-62).

By 1959, it was clear that the literary focus was moving away from novels that necessarily connected homosexuality and psychoanalysis. William Burroughs's *Naked Lunch* creates homo- and heterosexual fantasies. Reginald Harvey's *Park Beat* directly challenges the psychoanalytic point of view, while Lonnie Coleman's *Sam* also makes clear that there is room in society for homosexuals (Levin, pp. 162-64).

To read gay literature of the 1950s is to read of neurosis and social rejection. By 1952, the culture maintained that homosexuality was an illness caused by domineering mothers and complacent or absent fathers. Homosexuals supposedly needed therapy. Homosexuality meant a life of unhappiness and certain premature death. By the mid-1950s, the psychoanalytic claim that homosexuals were ill and in need of therapy permeated the social and literary culture to the extent that few challenged the position, even indirectly. It was not until 1958 that writers began to question the psychoanalytic view point, but not even established writers such as Vidal and Isherwood dared to challenge the position very loudly. The quiet conformity of the 1950s was so powerful that the mainstream and alternative cultures internalized gayness as illness. Even the gay community believed the psychoanalytic dogma.

The Transitional Literature: The 1960s

The 1960s endorsed tolerance, questioning, and change. This cultural reality invited writers to use words to dismantle the psychoanalytic responses to homosexuality found in the 1950s. Cultural and literary critics suggest that two realities encouraged the slow change that began at the close of the 1950s. First, groups of minority people began to challenge the internalized oppression that resulted in their subculture-inferiority status. Second, people questioned the middle-class definition of success. This meant that 1950s public attitudes towards family, home, and sex were challenged and, in most cases, dismantled. The questioning attitude of the 1960s meant social experimentation. Together heterosexual rebels and gay men challenged the supposed "bourgeois paradise" of the 1950s.

While change defines the novels of the 1960s, the change was not immediate. Taken as a group, though, the novels published in the 1960s do represent a marked shift in attitudes towards homosexuality. The psychoanalytic perspective of the 1950s evinces itself as literary residue in novels published in 1960, such as Roy Dolliner's *Young Man Willing* and Alexander Federoff's *The Side of the Angels*. Federoff's work is especially intriguing not only for its many homosexual characters but also for the fact that the main characters are from distinct geographical regions around the United States (Levin, p. 179).

The 1961 novels did not present much change. However, significant changes began to appear in a few 1962 novels. Christopher Isherwood's *Down There on a Visit* represents what Levin calls the clearest positive changes. This novel appears to be semi-autobiographical. In it, as in most of Isherwood's work, he suggests that he values hetero- and homosexuality equally. James Baldwin's *Another Country* surprised the critics in that it represented a significant shift in Baldwin's attitudes towards homosexuality within a decade. In this novel, homosexuality is legitimate, not an illness as it was in *Giovanni's Room* (Levin, pp. 186-89).

The range of novels continued in 1963. Susan Sontag's *The Benefactor* and Paul Goodman's *Making Do* display positive pictures of homosexuality. Other novels show subtle changes. These include Jack Richardson's *The Prison Life of Harris Filmore*, Thomas Baird's *The Old Masters*, Richard Sale's *The Oscar*, Basil Burwell's *A Fool in the Forest*, Edward Wallant's *The Tenants of Moonbloom*, and Charles Wright's *The Messenger*. Finally, two best sellers, John Rechy's *City of Night* and Gavin Lambert's *Inside Daisy Clover*, represent psychoanalytic novels (Levin, pp. 193-99).

In Christopher Isherwood's 1964 novel, *A Single Man*, the author offers no justification for homosexuality, making it the most significant book of the year. He simply allows homosexuality to exist. Gore Vidal's *Julian*, his first work of historical fiction (the story is set in Rome), also positively presents homosexuality. Two other positive texts include George Cuomo's *Bright Day, Dark Runner* and Buck Tone's *The Devil's Profession*. Less-positive views of homosexuality are evident in R. V. Cassils's *The President* and Maud Hutchins's *Honey on the Moon*. Alternatively, Bert Blechman's *Stations*, Dariel Telfer's *The Corrupters*, and Roderick Thorp's *The Detective* present highly negative views of homosexuality. At this time, paperback "pulp" fictions and gay pornography became increasingly more popular, too.

The novels of 1965 included even greater numbers of texts with significant homosexual characters and plots. Donald Windham's *Two People* provides the most positive view of the year, while Eli Weber's *David* represents the sophisticated discussion of how negative views of homosexuality can prevent social progress. Other novels of the year included Edmund Schiddel's *The Good and the Bad Weather*, Sanford Friedman's *Totempole*, William Gingerich's *The Gay American*, May Sarton's *Mrs. Stevens Hears the Mermaids Sing*, R. McCoy's *Entrapment*. James Herlihy's *Midnight Cowboy* (also adapted into a major motion picture), was a best seller but with a negative view towards homosexuality (Levin, pp. 206-12). Also published were several pulp novels that provided negative views of homosexuality.

The novels of 1966 represented the public's range of responses to homosexuality. The cultural attitude is clearly in flux, as indicated by the following novels: Richard Armory's *The Song of the Loon*, George Baxt's *A Queer Kind of Death*, Don Carpenter's

Christopher Isherwood (left) with Don Bachardy

Hard Rain Falling, Charles Wright's *The Wig,* and Peter Boynton's *Games in the Darkening Air* are all positive towards homosexuality; however, in Tom Lockwood's *The Ugly Club* and *Destination Nowhere* the ambivalent attitude evinces itself (Levin, pp. 214-17).

A range of views continued in 1967. Christopher Isherwood produced his third novel of the decade, *A Meeting by the River,* a novel that provided a positive view of homosexuality. Others with positive views included Robert Somerlott's *The Flamingos,* James Purdy's *Eustace Chisholm and the Works,* and Irving Rosenthal's *Sheeper.* The other novels of the year presented more indifferent attitudes, including Norman Mailer's *Why Are We in Vietnam* and Floyd Salas's *Tattoo the Wicked Cross.* In both novels, the authors discuss the relationship between sexuality and power (Levin, pp. 219-23).

Gore Vidal's *Myra Breckinridge* (1968) led the quick shift away from power and sex. His novel makes it clear that homosexual novels need not be serious. His campy novel engages questions about the relationship between gender identity and, as Levin describes, "sexual object choice" (Levin, p. 227). Other novels of the year included Nathaniel Burt's *Leopards in the Garden* and John Coriolan's *A Sand Fortress.* Finally, it was William Carney's *The Real Thing* that connected the gay culture with sado-masochistic love and sex, a connection many gays despised (Levin, pp. 226-30).

The Stonewall Rebellion of 1969, "a riot that occurred after patrons of a bar in New York were arrested by the police," marked a significant change in the gay culture (Levin, pp. 234-35). At the Stonewall Inn Riots, the gay community represented a force against the New York City police. Only the power of the special police riot squads suppressed the protesters. However, the rebellion that united gay culture did not result in an immediate change in the gay culture's literature. Levin claims that the only important novel of the year was Edmund Schiddel's *Good Time Coming.* What is significant in this novel is that the gay characters are presented in a non-judgmental way (Levin, p. 236).

The older claims that homosexuality was evil still surfaced in novels such as James Dickey's best seller, *Deliverance,* and Ellery Queen's *The Last Woman in His Life.* But even though novels with throwback attitudes continued to exist, the contention that homosexuality needed no justification became stronger. Certainly the Stonewall Rebellion along with the growing counter-culture contributed to the increasing acceptance of homosexuality without justification. Most important, literature changed in the 1960s, eventually supporting the portrayal of homosexuality as positive. This was the first decade that produced gay literature of acceptance. Interestingly, though, no connections were yet made in fiction that united sexism and heterosexism. Furthermore, although university campuses led social change, no plots were set on college campuses (Levin, p. 238). With the advent of literature that accepted gay men, the political action of the 1970s became possible.

Literature of Politics, Power, and Pride: 1970s

Significant change marked gay fiction of the 1970s. The literature revealed the drastic cultural changes that began in the mid-1960s. Civil unrest and anti-war demonstrations distinguished the late 1960s and early-to-mid-1970s. Arguably, the shifting economic reality decelerated the momentum for social change. Although the pace slowed, the progress of the 1960s resulted in real legislative and social changes in the 1970s. More and more cities passed laws to protect gays' and lesbians' rights. Some states decriminalized sodomy. The major psychiatric associations retracted their definition of homosexuality as a mental illness. Although activists of the early 1970s generated great change, the social changes did not fully manifest themselves in the gay literature until the mid-1970s. This lag was due in part to the deceleration of social change after the late 1960s, but it was also due to the built-in delay in getting works published. Furthermore, there was a significant shift away from fiction to nonfiction. Increasingly, writers expressed greater commitment to political advocacy through words. Many writers believed this was best accomplished through nonfiction.

Gay writing became prolific. In fact after the late 1960s, it is difficult to provide finite lists of gay publications. The concerns that dominated the first six decades of the century almost vanished. Gay male characters were finally shown to be healthy more often than not.

In the early 1970s, gay literature was easily accessible to most readers. However, most of the fiction did not yet reflect the social change. Leo Skir's *Boychick* appears to have been written before Stonewall, and the protagonist in Daniel Curzon's *Something You Do in the Dark* is filled with the kind of internal doubt that defines characters a decade earlier. Other novels included Frank Hilare's prison novel *Thanatos;* Dirk Vanden's *All is Well,* an indictment of homosexual repression; Gore Vidal's *Two Sisters;* and John Rechy's *The Vampires* (Levin, pp. 250, 256-260). Thom

Gunn's poetry represented one exception to the literary lag. In his 1971 publications *Moly* and *My Sad Captain*, unlike his 1954 poetry collection, Gunn speaks candidly about his homosexuality.

In the mid-1970s, nonfiction marked the literature, for the time-intensive nature of book publishing kept fiction from leading the era's social movements. However, newspapers immediately made public gay voices and ideas. By the mid-1970s, most major U.S. cities had gay newspapers and other gay publications—the *Washington Blade*, the *Philadelphia Gay News*, San Francisco's *Bay Area Reporter* and *Gay Sunshine*, Chicago's *Gay Life*, Cleveland's *High Gear*, New York's *Come Out*, and Boston's *Fag Rag*. The most successful newspaper press was the West Coast-based *Advocate*, founded in 1967. These post-Stonewall presses were significant in that they were marked by an activist tone, not an apologetic one.

The shift for which the 1970s is recognized became noticeable in fiction in 1974. Finally, the novel presented liberation ideas. Instantly popular, Patricia Nell Warren's *The Front Runner* fictionalized political ideas evident in the newspapers, and Terry Andrews focused successfully on gay liberation in *The Story of Harold* (Levin, pp. 265-269).

The activism of the mid-1960s to early 1970s was tempered by 1975. Anita Bryant's campaign against homosexuality in 1976 jolted strong activism against the gay and lesbian communities. She intended to use her national crusade to retract the legislative and social progress gays and lesbians had made. While gay and lesbian activists were busy responding to Bryant, their literature did not reflect this mid-decade event.

None of the novels published in 1977 were especially noteworthy. Levin notes that by 1978, gay literature responded to the Anita Bryant backlash with Andrew Holleran's *Dancer from the Dance* and Larry Kramer's *Faggots*. Both novels responded with a critical tone to the reality of recreational sex within the gay community. Also in response were Patricia Nell Warren's *The Beauty Queen* and N.A. Diaman's *Ed Dean Is Queer*. Not all of the literature of the year was political; including Armistead Maupin's *Tales of the City* and Edmund White's *Nocturnes for the King of Naples*, the latter being the most successful book of the year (Levin, pp. 284, 286-289).

The last year of the decade represented well the progress of the mid-1960s to 1970s. Gay newspapers thrived, and not one novel portrayed homosexuality as a sign of mental illness. Similarly, writers no longer made direct appeals for gay rights, for this had largely been accomplished. To appreciate the progress through literature, one can note the following novels: Wallace Hamilton's *David at Olivet*, Ensan Case's *Wing Men*, Marion Zimmer Bradley's *Catchtrap*, Peter Fisher and Marc Rubin's *Special Teachers, Special Boys*, John Rechy's *Rushes*, and James Baldwin's *Just above My Head*. Many of these novels share the gay characters' struggles in coming out (a significant trend among gays in the 1970s) and of being accepted by their nuclear families.

Gay fiction and nonfiction in the early 1970s was strident. However, as the decade of social change progressed, the literature increasingly reflected a variety of gay lifestyles. Homosexuality appeared less exotic and more real. By the end of the decade, writers were no longer stigmatized for including homosexual characters and plots. Homosexuality was finally an accepted part of U.S. literature.

Literature of the Paradoxical 1980s

The 1980s represented the paradoxical decade. While membership in gay organizations grew enormously, under the leadership of President Reagan, the national politics of the decade grew increasingly more conservative. The simultaneous growth of the gay community and of conservative politics is difficult to explain. Furthermore, this paradox did not present itself in the literature of the decade.

The political activism of the 1970s resulted in certain rights for gays. They were no longer perceived as ill or confused about gender identity. However, such progress should not suggest that gays were fully welcome in the mainstream, for the mainstream questioned the gay sexual revolution of the 1970s. The 1980s represented the decade of AIDS, a discovery that allowed the mainstream to question the gay community. The result was a cultural backlash against gays.

While much gay literature was published in the 1980s, critics argued that it was generally weak. Arguably the most successful novel of the decade, Charles Nelson's epistolary novel, *The Boy who Picked the Bullets Up* (1981), tells the story of a gay man in Vietnam. The protagonist, Kurt, represents many living gays' lives. He accepts his homosexuality. However, he is not out to his family or to heterosexual friends. Interestingly, Nelson develops his character fully, so that through Kurt's letters, his heterosexual friends and family know him well; they just do not know of his homosexuality (Levin, p. 322).

A range of novels continued in 1982; novels that focused on politics, history, humor, adventure, and mystery. Some of the authors included Anthony Costello, Robert Reinhart, Edmund White,

Gore Vidal

Thom Gunn

Richard Senett, Edmund Schiddel, Vincent Verga, John Caffey, Gordon Merrick, Victoria Silver, Virginia Rich, Susan Braudy, Owen Levy, Nathan Aldyne, and Bob Heron.

The work of two poets, Thom Gunn and James Merrill, is especially noteworthy. Gunn's *The Passages of Joy* (1982) reveals his open homoeroticism, and the sexual frankness of these poems invites a comparative analysis of his earlier work. In the same year, James Merrill, a poet whose first collection appeared in 1942, published his epic work, *The Changing Light at Sandover*, his most popular collection. In it, he argues that art shapes thought. Critics such as Charles Molesworth comment that Merrill's work might be compared to Yeats and Blake.

In 1983 and 1984, gay novels focused less on the past. Still, few of the stories were influential pieces of literature. Writers included Paul Rogers, Andrew Holleran, Nathan Heard, and Joseph Torcia. The most significant novel of the year, Judith Rossner's *August,* shares the story of a young woman who was raised by two lesbian women and a gay man but whose biological mother is heterosexual. The protagonist's most-significant struggles are with her birth mother. In 1984, a novel finally mentioned AIDS: Daniel Curzon's *The World Can Break Your Heart*. Admittedly, though, Curzon does not devote the story to AIDS. It is only mentioned in the last ten pages (Levin, pp. 338, 340).

The literature between 1985 and 1987 was especially weak. What was increasingly clear, however, is that literature of this decade often avoided contemporary issues. David Leavitt's *The Lost Language of Cranes* (1986) represented an exception. This story focuses on the simultaneous coming out of Philip, a 25-year-old New Yorker, and his 52-year-old father. Other authors included

Paul Reddinger, Robert McCartney Moore, Krandall Kraus, Robert Reinhart, Michael Nava, Larry Duplechan, Richard Stevenson, Freddie Gershon, and Steven Simmons.

The later half of the decade brought better-quality literature. In 1988, Edmund White published *The Beautiful Room Is Empty*, the second in his autobiographical series, in which he shares the experience of being a gay college student in the 1950s at the University of Michigan. The disturbingly refreshing surprise of the year was Robert Ferro's *Second Son*, the story about a gay man with AIDS—probably the first novel devoted to the subject. Another novel about AIDS followed in 1989: David Feinberg's *Eighty Sixed* which showed how gay men's lives changed between 1980 and 1986, the year in which the AIDS virus, HIV, was finally identified and named (Levin, pp. 353-54).

Taken as a whole, the 1980s produced seemingly weak literature. It is difficult to determine what contributed to this: the conservative politics or the gay community's struggle to live with AIDS. The 1980s' literature, like that in the 1970s, did not appear to keep pace with the cultural changes. However, by the decade's close, literature connected more directly to the gay community's social reality.

Political, Experimental, Theoretical Literature: 1990s

In the 1980s, the gay community learned to live with AIDS and began to write about the disease. In the late 1980s, some tried to write fiction about it, namely the aforementioned Robert Ferro novel, *Second Son* (1988). However, the gay community's attempt to fictionalize the epidemic was not especially successful. Later, Andrew Holleran explained that possibly the difficulty in writing AIDS fiction was because AIDS is too horrific to fictionalize. In fact, in the 1990s the growing gay literary theory on AIDS, in books such as Judith Laurence Pastore's *Confronting AIDS through Literature* (1993), suggests that gay literary essays may represent a more appropriate genre for AIDS discussions.

Nevertheless, AIDS was treated in several genre. Collections of short stories such as Jameson Currier's *Dancing on the Moon: Short Stories about AIDS* gave fiction another role to play. Currier introduces his anthology of stories by explaining, "These stories deal with the impact of AIDS. They are not intended to be a comprehensive examination of the epidemic" (Currier, p. ix). The focus on the impact of AIDS indicated a significant turn from the informational, nonfiction essays.

The AIDS epidemic called for writing that connected the personal and political, an approach to writing and thinking that lesbian-feminists inaugurated and that Paul Monette fully realized. Before the AIDS crisis, he wrote *Taking Care of Mrs. Carroll* (1978), a novel that explores the 1960s-70s gay scene. Then he wrote two novels that explore the relationship between gay men and straight women: *The Gold Diggers* (1979) and *The Long Shot* (1981). While he published novels, he also published collections of poetry such as *The Carpenter at the Asylum* (1978) and *No Witnesses* (1981). Then the AIDS crisis emerged, and it brought Monette's poetry to a halt. As Monette explained to critic Malcolm Boyd, a culture's best literature comes out of crisis, and for Monette, poetry's audience—small and elitist—was not the community on which he intended to focus his energy. He wrote one publisher-forced novel, *Lightfall* (1982) (Malinowski, pp. 272-74). Then his work changed.

The writing that emerged from Monette following the discovery of AIDS connects words to his life, connects words to AIDS.

Paul Monette

His next novel, *Afterlife* (1990), tells the story of a broad group of people living with AIDS, an experience that was very real, as Monette's lover was diagnosed with AIDS in 1985. *Halfway Home* (1991) is the gay love story Monette always wanted to write. *Borrowed Time: An AIDS Memoir* (1988) tells the story of his lover's diagnosis with AIDS and eventual death. Later, Monette wrote his own autobiography, *Becoming a Man: Half a Life Story* (1992), nonfiction that brought him great praise and critical respect. Monette's novels, poetry, and nonfiction capture life's health and illness.

Increasingly, gay male writers brought words to AIDS using poetry. Poets such as Mark Doty (*My Alexandria* [1993] and *Atlantis* [1995]) and Gunn (*The Man with Night Sweats* [1992]) recognized that poetry allows for the expression of outrage, despair, love, and hope in ways that novels and essays do not. More memoirs were written, including Doty's *Heaven's Coast* (1996), which centers on the death from AIDS of his lover, Wally. In other words, then, the literature of the early 1990s represented AIDS and politics.

The literature that has followed has continued to offer new writers and narrative voices. Ken Siman's *Pizza Face, or, The Hero of Suburbia* (1991) represents, early in the decade, the goals of mid- and late-1990s gay literature, which is evidenced in Dale Peck's novels *Martin and John* (1993) and *The Law of Enclosures* (1996). Stories such as Michael Scalisi's "Three," a story that plays with format, voice, and subject matter; Brad Gooch's "Satan"; and Richard Davis's "Marty" represent the changing literature of the 1990s. John Weir's "Homo in Heteroland," according to critic Ethan Mordden, may epitomize 1990s literature: it tricks you. Weir's story at first reads like fiction but later reveals itself as journalism. This twist suggests that gay literature creates fiction and nonfiction that plays with postmodernism. Mordden claims that 1990s fiction is of its gay fathers but different—"more playful (read [Scott] Heim), more appetitive (read [John Edward] Harris), alienated by hypocritical conventions (read [Abraham] Verghese and

[Robert] Trent), and kinkier (read [Brad] Gooch)" (Mordden 1994). Brian Bouldrey's *Best American Gay Fiction 1996* represents a collection of stories published in mainstream and alternative magazines and of novel excerpts. The anthology makes clear the focus of 1990s gay literature: it takes risks. Authors who published in this period included Edmund White, Scott Heim, Michael Cunningham, Christopher Bram, R. S. Jones, Jason K. Friedman, Joe Westmoreland, and Michael Lowenthal.

In addition to the experimental texts, gay writers continue to further establish gay literature by theorizing the gay experience. Leading theorists include Henry Abelove, Joseph Boone, David M. Halperin, and Eve Kosofsky Sedgwick.

The politics and experimentation of the 1990s gay literature reveals the evolving definition of the subject. Gay male literature is all about telling what it is to be gay without apology. It recognizes the role of fantasy in the lives of real gay men who spent much of their youth fantasizing about who they are while they pretended to fit into the heterosexist world. Gay literature of the 1990s finally celebrates gayness fully.

DEFINING LESBIAN LITERATURE

"Lesbian" is a 20th-century social construction. The evolution, then, of lesbian literature corresponds directly to the definition of "lesbian." "Lesbianism" as a sexual term did not enter English until the 19th century, and its entrance was quiet. Ideas of late 19th- and early 20th-century professionals such as German physician Karl Westphal, German lawyer Karl Heinrich Ulrichs, and professor of psychiatry Richard von Krafft-Ebing helped sexologists such as Havelock Ellis name both gayness and lesbianism. In other words, writers did not finally name homosexuality; the sexologists did. Sexologists in particular were the first to describe and name lesbians as abnormal or sick, "men trapped in women's bodies." Sexologists used this definition of abnormality to construct for the public lesbianism as a phenomenal sexual perversion.

The lesbian literature of the 20th century responded to this sociological definition of "lesbianism" by first accepting the homophobic definition. Over the course of the century though, lesbian literature has dismantled the sexual inversion definition and constructed a sequence of definitions. Lesbian literature thus represents evolving definitions of both "lesbianism" and lesbian literature. Women's real experiences of loving other women and the cultural responses to it contribute significantly to lesbianism and to lesbian literature in particular. The review of lesbian literature that follows shows this evolution by identifying the six larger lesbian literary movements and corresponding significant writers as identified by scholar Lillian Faderman. Together the six defining movements create a lesbian aesthetic.

TWENTIETH-CENTURY U.S. LESBIAN LITERATURE

To contextualize the U.S. lesbian literary movements of the 20th century, the review begins by explaining "Romantic Friendship" literature of the mid- to late-19th century. From the classical period until the 20th century, affectionate relationships between women were not perceived of as sexual relationships. However, by the early 20th century, sexologists defined affectionate friendships between women as lesbian relationships and identified the women as sexual perverts. According to Faderman, with the 20th-century sexualization of lesbianism, women who found themselves passionately attached to other females had only four options:

1) She could see her own same-sex attachment as having nothing to do with attachments between 'real lesbians,' since the sexologists who first identified lesbianism and brought the phenomenon to public attention said that lesbians were abnormal or sick 'men trapped in women's bodies,' and she knew that she was not.

2) She could become so fearful of her feelings toward other women, which were not seen as natural, that she would force herself to repress them all together, to deny even to herself that she was capable of passionate attachment to another female.

3) She could become so fearful, not of her own emotions but of her community's reaction to them, that she would spend her whole life in hiding . . . leading a double life, pretending to the world—to everyone but her female friend . . . .

4) She could accept the definitions of love between women that had been formulated by the sexologists and define herself as a lesbian . . . acceptance would mean that she could live her attachment to women for the rest of her life, without having to acknowledge that a heterosexual relationship had precedence over her same-sex love; it would mean that she could—in fact, *must*—seek ways to become an economically and socially independent human being, since she could not rely on a male to support and defend her; and it would mean that she was free to seek out other women who also accepted such an identity and to form a lesbian subculture, such as could not have existed before love between women was defined as abnormal and unusual (Faderman, *Odd Girls,* pp. 3-4).

Twentieth-century lesbian literature reflects these options and shows how, as the century progressed, lesbians felt increasingly free to alter the sexologists' definitions of lesbians. To show this literary reality, the following review uses Faderman's literary labels and begins with the 19th-century "Romantic Friendship Literature." The review then moves to the "Literature of Sexual Inversion"; "Literature of Exotic and Evil Lesbians"; "Literature of Lesbian Encoding"; "Lesbian-Feminist Literature"; and finally to "Post-Lesbian-Feminist Literature."

Romantic Friendship Literature: Mid-19th Century to Early 20th Century

"Lesbian" was not a recognizable word in the 19th-century United States. Although the sexualized word "lesbian" did not exist, intimate relationships between women certainly did. In fact, Sappho's partially extant lyric poetry from the island of Lesbos suggests that lesbianism dates back at least as far as the classical period. Before First Wave feminism in the United States, which occurred in the mid-1800s, women from the middle and upper classes were socialized in what 19th-century observers aptly labeled "separate spheres." Men were trained to lead public lives with other men away from home, while women were trained to lead domestic lives, lives that kept them at home. Women were permitted to socialize with other women. However, interactions for men and women to socialize together were usually arranged. The middle and upper class valued female chastity. Women who lost their virginity outside of marriage also lost their

social value. Ostensibly to preserve female chastity, then, male and female interactions outside of marriage were culturally perceived as dangerous. To prevent such danger meant that during the 19th century, most middle- and upper-class men and women led homosocial lives. However, the culture did not acknowledge that some girls and women were sexually attracted to each other. For those who did acknowledge homosexual attractions, the attractions were perceived as inconsequential episodes in girls' or women's lives. Women and girls certainly were not to write about such attractions.

Early Greeks and Romans maintained that "most intimate, important, and even passionate friendships were between men rather than men and women" (Faderman, *Chloe,* p. 3). This belief pervaded Western literature for the next 300 years. Faderman suggests that possible male-male friendship and intimacy was believed to be so important that men chose not to interfere with women and their passionate, same-sex friendships. In fact, allowing women to also experience intense same-sex relationships allowed men to maintain their homosocial and -sexual relationships. Male homosexuality did not necessarily limit heterosexual institutions, however. Men recognized that middle- and upper-class women needed to be supported financially. Heterosexual marriage continued to be the only institution that allowed these women to maintain certain standards of living and to produce legitimate children.

Faderman also suggests that female same-sex relationships stimulated male voyeurism, which arguably resulted in pornographic sexual entertainment for hetero- or bisexual men. Furthermore, affectionate relationships between women could be perceived by men as especially practical during eras of war when women far outnumbered men. These same-sex relationships prevented women from being lonely. Finally, until the 20th century, intimate relationships between women were not perceived of as a threat to heterosexual institutions because most people maintained that female intimacy was not sexual, for supposedly "without penetration by a penis nothing 'sexual' could take place" (Faderman, *Chloe,* p. 4).

Before the 20th century, then, what were termed "female friendships" or "romantic friendships" were universally encouraged. In *Odd Girls and Twilight Lovers,* Faderman shares American writer William Cullen Bryant's 1843 *Evening Post* essay to show what the culture accepted. Bryant had observed a loving relationship between two maidens and wanted to share their history:

> In their youthful days, they took each other as companions for life, and this union, no less sacred to them than the tie of marriage, has subsisted, in an uninterrupted harmony, for 40 years, during which they have shared each others' occupations and pleasures and works of charity while in health, and watched over each other tenderly in sickness . . . . They slept on the same pillow and had a common purse, and adopted each others' relations, and . . . I would tell you of their dwelling, encircled with roses, . . . and I would speak of the friendly attentions which their neighbors, people of kind hearts and simple manners, seem to take pleasure in bestowing upon them (Faderman, *Odd Girls,* p. 1).

Before the 20th century, U. S. culture accepted loving female relationship, but romantic female friends could not write of their intimacy. In fact, although the relationships were culturally permitted, a social institution surrounded romantic friendships. Faderman explains,

1) If an eligible man came along, the women were not to feel that they could send him on his way in favor of their romantic friendship.

2) They were not to hope that they could find gainful employment to support a same-sex relationship permanently or that they could usurp any other male privileges in support of that relationship.

3) They were not to intimate in any way that an erotic element might possibly exist in their love for each other (Faderman, *Odd Girls,* pp. 1-2).

Romantic friendship literature suggests that these same-sex friendships were in fact the most important relationships in women's lives. Marriage was economic. Upper- and middle-class women married estates, not lovers (Faderman, *Chloe,* p. 5).

Women of the 17th, 18th, and 19th centuries who identified themselves as serious intellectuals often turned to each other for conversation, support, and affection. These women, also called bluestockings, created romantic friendships. In fact, much mid-19th century literature captures these relationships, what women of the time refereed to as "raves," "spoons," "smashes," or "crushes." At the same time, a growing number of women committed themselves to professional lives. Faderman argues that a "Boston Marriage," a relationship in which two romantic women shared a life and home together, became increasingly more common among serious career women (Faderman, *Chloe,* p. 6). Our literary history does not indicate whether working-class women enjoyed Boston marriages. It is likely that such relationships were not exclusive to the middle and upper class. However, working-class women did not have the leisure to record their history.

Significant U.S. "Romantic Friendship" authors included poet Emily Dickinson, Mary E. Wilkins Freeman, Sarah Orne Jewett, Katharine Lee Bates, and Helen Rose Hull. Dickinson's voluminous works are included in *The Letters of Emily Dickinson,* in three volumes, and *The Poems of Emily Dickinson,* also in three volumes. Throughout much of this decade, scholars have worked ardently to identify the reclusive Emily's male lover, a muse that has yet to be found. In fact, the research seems to make a more convincing case for Dickinson's passionate love for other women. Most of her poems represent lyric poetry directed towards a female. The majority of her 128 extant letters and 276 poems are directed to Sue Gilbert, a woman with whom Dickinson arguably fell in love in 1851. Sue married Emily's brother seven years later. Sue's marriage to Austin Dickinson troubled Emily. However, Emily found that she could still share her writing with Sue. Through words then, they remained connected as loving women.

Mary E. Wilkins Freeman, a New England spinster who chose to remain single or live in a Boston marriage, wrote two collections of short stories, namely *A New England Nun and Other Stories* (1891) and *A Humble Romance and Other Stories* (1887). Some of these stories, such as "Two Friends," focus on two women's relationship together. Freeman's Boston marriage with Mary Wale afforded her the time and money to spend her life writing. Freeman's later literature contributions are listed further down, under "Literature of Exotic and Evil Lesbians."

Sarah Orne Jewett's poetry and novels and the fact that she had several romantic friendships define her as a contributor to "Romantic Friendship" literature. In her story "Tom's Husband," she suggests that heterosexual marriage can destroy women be-

cause of the way the institution takes away women's identities. In her 1884 novel, *A Country Doctor,* Faderman explains, Jewett "argued that as a society 'becomes more intelligent' it will recognize the unfitness of some women for marriage and will promote their pursuit of occupations that are more appropriate for them" (Faderman, *Chloe,* p. 97). "Romantic Friendship" writer Katharine Lee Bates is best remembered as the author of the anthem "America the Beautiful." She also wrote numerous poems to her lover, Katharine Coman. Many of these poems are collected in *Yellow Clover: A Book of Remembrances* (1922).

Finally, Helen Rose Hull, a prolific writer of approximately five dozen short stories and 20 novels, spent most of her adult life in a Boston marriage with Mabel Robinson. While she lived in a romantic friendship for most of her life, only her early works deal with love between women. Hull wrote a five-story sequence about a young feminist, Cynthia, who rejects conventions. Her 1922 novel *Quest* incorporates much from the five-story Cynthia sequence. In the novel, the protagonist, Jean, falls in love with an older woman. In her 1923 novel, *Labyrinth,* Hull contrasts an unhappy heterosexual couple with a successful Boston marriage. After *Labyrinth,* Hull no longer wrote about love between women. She maintained her feminist perspective but felt social proscriptions about same-sex love meant literature prevented her from exploring such relationships any further. By the mid-1920s, romantic friends were perceived as corrupt and neurotic.

"Romantic Friendship" literature from both the 19th and 20th centuries makes it clear that often the authors' personal relationships coupled with the intended audience for the literature define this literary period. If these women authors wrote passionately to women or if they lived in Boston marriages, their literature contributed to Romantic Friendship literature. The disappearance of romantic friendships as a social institution and the decline of their resultant literature began in the 1920s. Romantic friendships became linked with feminism. Then, more women became self-supporting, the "companionate marriage"—a belief that husbands and wives could be friends—became popular, and sexologists defined love between women as abnormal (Faderman, *Chloe,* p. 7).

The Literature of Sexual Inversion: Early 1900s-1920s

Twentieth-century sexologists' sexualized definition of lesbianism and their claim that a lesbian was "a man trapped in a woman's body" led to the dissipation of the romantic friendship institution. Until the early 1900s, romantic friendships were not questioned, for they allowed the patriarchy to continue. Furthermore, during the class-conscious and patriarchal years of romantic friendships, most men had great difficulty imagining women's sexual agency. In other words, most men could not imagine women acting on their own sexual desires.

"Sexual Inversion" literature suggests the growing power of the scientific community. It also points to the way the medical community combined its claims with religion-defined social mores to construct lesbianism as sexual inversion. Increasingly, some women's desires to act sexually outside of heterosexual relationships were labeled inappropriate gender behavior and were said to result from a weak moral code. As Faderman explains, "What their Judeo-Christian background had taught the medical men to consider *immoral* now often became, in their writings, *abnormal*" (*Chloe,* pp. 136-37). Heterosexual women who dressed as transvestites in order that they might travel with their male lovers, women who dressed as transvestites in order that they might travel alone or acquire higher paying jobs, women who demanded educations, women who dressed in tailored clothes in order that they might fulfill their professional jobs with greater ease, or women caught with dildos—all of these women led sexologists to link feminism to lesbianism and lesbianism to sexual inversion. Such a conclusion suggests that lesbianism is all about performance.

The sexologists' linking of feminism, lesbianism, and sexual inversion changed lesbian literature profoundly. "Sexual Inversion" literature fictionalizes the sexologists' claims: 1) The lesbian as "a man trapped in a woman's body," 2) as a woman struggling with penis envy, and 3) as an ill woman (Faderman, *Chloe*, pp. 139-141). The pulp fiction of the 1950s and 1960s represents the greatest collection of this literature (see the pulp fiction of Ann Bannon and Paula Christian). However, it should be noted that "Sexual Inversion" literature dates back to the 18th century with authors such as Henry Fielding, Richard von Krafft-Ebing, Charlotte Cibber Charke, Maria Edgeworth, and Anne Lister.

Willa Cather represents the most significant U.S. female author whose literature is identified with sexual inversion. Biographies of Cather consistently describe her as a woman with a masculine presentation. She is remembered for hair shorter than that of most men and tailored, mannish clothes. Although none of her literature deals specifically with lesbian relationships, critics argue that her short stories and many of her novels such as *My Antonia* (1918) and *One of Ours* (1922) represent encoded lesbian stories: stories that hide lesbian sexual inversion by creating male characters who are women in drag. Cather minimizes the attention drawn to gender-switching by creating stories that include the women in drag. The assumption is that Cather intentionally allows for both a lesbian and heterosexual interpretation of the story so as not to draw attention to lesbianism, especially not her own.

The Literature of Exotic and Evil Lesbians: Early-to-Mid-20th Century

Before the 19th century, male authors produced a significant body of literature that depicted sexual relations between women. Around the world, male writers created the exotic literary lesbian as both destructive and evil (Faderman, *Chloe*, p. 294). The lesbian archetype so intrigued artists and writers that the growing disapproval of lesbianism became blurred by male eroticized and voyeuristic interests. With French writer Charles Baudelaire, exotic lesbians become "beasts that mark their victims with their teeth and then gloat at leisure on their hapless prize. They are wild-eyed sadists and pallid prey" (Faderman, *Chloe*, p. 295). The result is the image of lesbian as vampire, an image 1990s post-lesbian-feminists reclaimed.

Well into the mid-20th century, if lesbian characters were not constructed as sexual inverts, they were exotic and evil vampires. Interestingly, although men usually created the image of the lesbian as exotic and evil, lesbian writers adopted the image. "Exotic and Evil Lesbian" literature includes works by Mary E. Wilkins Freeman, Rose O'Neill, Djuna Barnes, Anais Nin, and even Jewelle Gomez toward the end of the century. Although Wilkins's first stories, published in 1887, represented "Romantic Friendship" literature, by 1895 some of her stories presented the lesbian evil. In "The Long Arm," for example, one woman works to possess another woman by violently trying to interfere with her heterosexuality. Wilkens's relatively quick move from "Romantic Friendship" literature to "Evil Lesbian/Vampire" literature hints at the rapidity with which cultural attitudes towards lesbianism changed.

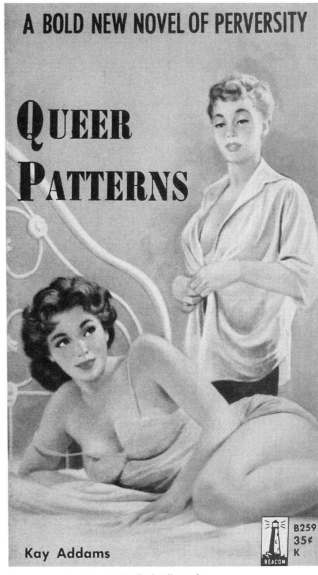

A BOLD NEW NOVEL OF PERVERSITY

QUEER PATTERNS

Kay Addams

B259 35¢ K BEACON

Cover of a lesbian "pulp fiction" work.

Rose O'Neill, the creator of Kewpie dolls, wrote Gothic romances such as *Garda* (1929) and *The Goblin Woman* (1930). Unlike her novels, several poems in her poetry collection, *The Master-Mistress* (1922), deal with lesbianism. Repeatedly, the lesbians in her poems are constructed as exotic, strange, and potentially dangerous.

The decadence of the 19th century and the evil and exotic depictions of lesbians intrigued Djuna Barnes, a leading women modernist writer of the first half of the 20th century. She spent her early years in Greenwich Village as an art student. In 1920, she left for Europe. She became a member of the Natalie Barney circle of expatriate lesbians in Paris. Barnes's interest in the lesbian as potentially exotic and evil likely informed her 1923 poem, "Six Songs of Khalidine," a poem that speaks of her first lover's flaming red hair that creeps and crawls. Her 1929 story, "A Little Girl Tells a Story to a Lady," creates an erotic and what Faderman calls an "exotically charged setting," reminiscent of French and English 19th-century Decadent novels. Critics suggest that the setting Barnes created for her lesbian characters reflects her interest in lesbian perversity.

In Paris, Barnes fell in love with sculptor Thelma Wood, a relationship that ended in 1931. Immediately following this relationship, Barnes wrote the semi-autobiographical novel for which is best known, *Nightwood* (1936). The life that the two women characters, Nora and Robin, live is one of despair and destruction.

Jewelle Gomez, the African American author of two poetry collections, *The Lipstick Papers* (1980) and *Flamingoes and Bears* (1983); *The Gilda Stories* (1991); and many essays, transforms the horrific images of the lesbian vampire. By defusing the mystery and supposed evil surrounding the supernatural, she attributes what Alice Walker defines as womanist values—positive, woman-centered values—to the lesbian vampire. By the 1980s then, the lesbian vampire is no longer frightening.

The Literature of Lesbian Encoding: Early 1900s-50s

"Literature of Lesbian Encoding" is the fourth lesbian literary model presented. However, its position in this review of lesbian literary models should not imply that encoded literature necessarily follows the "Literature of the Exotic and Evil Lesbian." To encode, to hide, to conceal that which is not culturally accepted represents a rhetorical strategy used by gay and lesbian writers for centuries. Encoding is evident in the literatures of "Romantic Friendship," of "Sexual Inversion," and of "Exotic and Evil Lesbi-

Jewelle Gomez

ans." Already mentioned are the lively debates which persist about the sexuality of "Romantic Friendship" writer Emily Dickinson.

The historical culture that surrounds what this review anachronistically labels lesbian literature reveals that much of literature has been obfuscated. In fact, critic Elaine Marks quotes French lesbian author Monique Wittig to explain the reality: "Male homosexual literature has a past and a present. Lesbians, in contrast, are silent—just as all women, at all levels, are silent" (Faderman, *Chloe,* p. 441).

Faderman provides three reasons to explain why the literature of love between women is difficult to trace. First, 20th-century culture has socialized itself to be oblivious to the literature. Second, literary critics have confounded this reality by working ardently to deny the existence of such literature. Third, the literary "New Critics" have argued that a given text contains all that a reader needs to understand it fully, ostensibly negating writers' autobiographies and biographies.

Arguably until the 1970s and Second Wave feminism, lesbian literature was veiled or simply not written. Until the 1970s, many lesbian writers assumed that to write clearly about lesbianism was to stigmatize themselves. Faderman claims, though, "[D]espite many lesbian authors' attempts at subterfuge, even in their writings that are ostensibly heterosexual or without sexual subject matter, a lesbian sensibility often reveals itself" (Faderman, *Chloe,* p. 444). This reality speaks to the rhetorical ingenuity of lesbian writers. Their literary maneuvers can be categorized as either passive or active means of concealing lesbianism. The most marked passive approach is simply not to write or to limit writing considerably. For instance, critics claim that American lesbian writer Angelina Grimkè produced brilliant work but did not write as much as she could have.

The other option, active concealment, is accomplished by encoding literature. Writers have devised several strategic options:

1) Bearded pronouns—replacing the gender specific pronouns "he" or "she" with the awkward referents "some" or "one."

2) The double entendre—using words whose second meanings were recognizable [only] to the lesbian subculture.

3) The veil of antiquity—directing love poetry to the long-dead mother of Lesbos, Sappho . . . . The mainstream culture accepted such reverent literature (Faderman, *Chloe,* p. 445).

The process now of decoding lesbian literature enlivens and gives literary historical foundation to literature that celebrates women loving women.

Gertrude Stein, a renowned Modernist poet, is also the queen of lesbian encoding. As a famous poet among literary and artistic expatriates in Paris, Stein made public her marriage-like relationship with Alice B. Toklas. Stein's wealthy brother supported them financially while Toklas acted as Stein's protective wife. While the Stein and Toklas relationship was public knowledge in Paris and in the States, Stein encoded lesbianism in her writing. She was particularly fond of referents such as "some" or "one" in place of gender-specific referents such as "he" or "she." She also withheld works such as her novel *QED*, a story that presents lesbian characters as complex rather than as diseased or congenitally defective. To have published the book in 1903 when it was written would have meant stigmatization. To change the story by making the lesbians African American allowed audiences to focus on racial "Otherness" instead of sexuality. Stein worked consciously to make her lesbian points without offending censors.

Like Stein, Modernist poet Amy Lowell encoded lesbianism in her poetry. Many of her poems are collected in *Pictures of the Floating World* (1919) and in her posthumous volume, *What's O'Clock* (1925), the volume for which she received a Pulitzer Prize. Lowell made known her bisexuality and later her lesbianism in her diaries, but her poetry conceals it well. After her death, critics attacked her work for her homosexuality, and the negative criticism generated a bandwagon effect. Those who had not stigmatized Lowell while she lived agreed in her death that as an unattractive, overweight woman, she produced poetry that could not reach real people. Katherine Mansfield's stories help critics willing to decode works such as "Bliss" (1918) to understand her love-hate reaction to lesbianism. She was in fact married twice (to encode her lesbianism) but maintained lesbian relationships throughout both marriages. However, in "Bains Tur" from *In a German Pension* (1911), Mansfield expresses the fulfillment love between women brings. The struggles her lesbian characters present suggest the social challenge of being lesbian in a heterosexist world.

African American playwright and poet Angelina Weld Grimkè's published writing focuses on racial injustice, while much of her unpublished poetry focuses on love between women. However, this Harlem Renaissance writer was well aware of the stigma attached to lesbian literature. For that reason, she became her own censor. In fact, by 1930 she appears to have stopped writing both on race and women's love, for literature on race was then "out of fashion" and lesbian literature had yet to be accepted. Critic Gloria Hull claims that Grimkè's unpublished writing is voluminous. What we could know, had she published, remains her secret.

This review focuses almost exclusively on U.S. writers. However, in order to appreciate more fully both gay and lesbian literature, it is important that particular non-American writers be acknowledged. One such writer is English fiction and nonfiction writer Virginia Woolf. Woolf came from an established English family of great intelligence. While knowledgeable people and resources filled her family's home, her diaries and letters reveal her fierce frustration at not having access to a formal education. Although Woolf was a significant contributor to the Bloomsbury group, a literary group that prided itself on honesty, including discussions of sexuality, Woolf hid her sexuality. In fact, she married Leonard Woolf in 1912. Ten years later, she met Vita Sackville-West, whom she loved and who acted as a muse for much of Woolf's work.

Woolf coded her ambivalent lesbian thoughts in much of her literature. For instance, her novel *Mrs. Dalloway* (1925) arguably presents Woolf's feelings for Vita and for her childhood crush Madge Vaughan. Woolf continues her exploration of lesbianism in *Orlando* (1927), a novel that represents "the longest and most charming love letter in literature" (Faderman, *Chloe*, p. 491). In it Orlando (who represents Vita) lives through four centuries, changing gender within and across time. This novel, like *Mrs. Dalloway*, requires significant decoding. Finally, Woolf felt she took her greatest risk with incorporating sexuality in literature in *A Room of One's Own* (1929). She feared the statement "Chloe liked Olivia" might be too revealing. As her literary career developed, Woolf worked to understand and expose lesbianism. Arguably, her intellectual and emotional struggles and her bouts of severe depression led to her suicide at 59.

For Imagist poet Hilda Doolittle (1886-1961), or H. D. as she preferred, only some of her works hint at lesbianism. When she addressed it, she usually shrouded it in the antiquity of Sappho.

Carson McCullers

In one of the few semi-autobiographical novels she published, *Palimpsest* (1926), she veils lesbianism by setting the novel in the ancient world and by assigning a masculine gender to those characterizations that our culture has appropriated as male. She also minimizes the lesbian relationships in the text. The publishing histories of *Paint It To-day*, written in 1921 and only recently published; *Asphodel* (1922), an unpublished novel; and *HERmione* (1926-27), published in 1981, point to H. D.'s repeated strategy for encoding and not publishing.

The literature of Carson McCullers offers yet another means of encoding lesbianism. She provided few heterosexual relationships in her novels, but she also did not include lesbian protagonists in relationships. Instead, relying on her girlhood friendships with a group of gay boys, most of her novels including *The Heart Is a Lonely Hunter* (1940), *Reflections in a Golden Eye* (1941), *The Ballad of the Sad Cafe* (1943), and *Clock Without Hands* (1961) focus on male-male relationships.

Jane Bowles married a gay composer, Paul Bowles, in 1937 as a way for both of them to conceal their homosexuality. While both Jane and Paul were open with each other about their numerous homosexual relationships, Paul's success first as a composer and then as a novelist perpetuated Jane's insecurities as a writer. These were exacerbated by her family's contention that her only completed novel, *Two Serious Ladies* (1943), was too obviously lesbian. As her novella "Andrew" (1971) suggests, like McCullers,

Jane felt more comfortable constructing gay male characters. Critics claim that her most-intriguing lesbian novel, *Going to Massachusetts*, was never finished, another act of self-censorship.

Like many of her contemporaries, including lesbian poet Elizabeth Bishop, Muriel Rukeyser believed that homosexuality was and should remain "the love that dare not speak its name." Rukeyser was a prolific poet. Her 1935 collection of poetry, *Theory of Flight,* won the Yale Younger Poets Award. It is her 1968 collection, *Speed of Darkness,* that lesbian critics identify as a celebration of "coming out." Those same critics explain that her lesbian encoding is so subtle that only those in the lesbian literary culture understand it. Her 1973 collection, *Breaking Open,* does just what the title suggests. This volume reveals her transformation from a writer of encoded literature. With the support of Second Wave feminists, she "came out" in her writing in 1973.

May Swenson, born and raised as Mormon in Utah, began publishing her poetry during the homophobic 1950s. In order to write and be published, she had to hide herself and her lesbianism. To lesbian writer Lee Hudson, Swenson explained that she encoded lesbianism by creating poetry without people but with animals instead. She also created androgynous people. The intentional confusion encouraged readers to think.

Rita Mae Brown

The Literature of Lesbian-Feminism: 1960s and 1970s

"Lesbian-Feminist" literature is rooted in the late 1960s in the United States. The literature suggests that together feminists and lesbian-feminists led America's Second Wave of feminism. Arguably the first lesbian-feminists were Americans. This group of women created a culture that not only celebrated women, but celebrated lesbian-feminist women in particular. The goal was a womanist culture. The lesbian-feminist motto became "Feminism is the theory; lesbianism is the practice" (Faderman, *Chloe,* p. 548). This newly evolving women-centered culture encouraged all women to work together to imagine and define the lesbian continuum, a continuum that represented women who worked against male tyranny and supported women.

"Lesbian-Feminist" literature made known its values. This literature rejected literature that treated lesbians as "men trapped in women's bodies." It celebrated lesbianism. In doing so, it rejected encoded literature. Lesbian-feminist writers used humor to challenge the patriarchy and homophobia. Furthermore, this literature celebrated women's sexual autonomy and presented sex as mutually satisfying. The literature honestly and openly celebrates women loving women. Lesbian-feminist science fiction imagined a world with more lesbian couples' mothering via artificial insemination. For many older lesbians, "Lesbian-Feminist" literature finally spoke the principles that lesbians followed in their lives throughout the century.

"Lesbian-Feminist" literature has not been void of criticism, though. For many global and multicultural lesbians, the culture lesbian-feminists created represented separatism, a luxurious space afforded only to middle- and upper-middle class white women. Furthermore, although the lesbian continuum supposedly created space for all women, many women felt the separatism generated stringent rules that ultimately limited the lesbian-feminist culture. Significant lesbian-feminist writers have included Rita Mae Brown, Audre Lorde, Adrienne Rich, Judy Grahn, Joanna Russ, Jane Rule, and Pat Parker.

In the late 1960s, Rita Mae Brown committed her life to challenging the male power system and supporting women. She became a significant civil- and gay-rights activist. In the early 1970s, Brown was one of the most charismatic and effective lesbian-feminist spokeswomen. She declared lesbianism as a social and political choice. Her most famous novel, *Rubyfruit Jungle* (1973), is a comic novel that laughs at heterosexuality. Her later novels continue to use humor but are much less political than her first.

Caribbean-American poet Audre Lorde celebrated black lesbian-feminism. This self-identified warrior poet used her poetry and prose to confront racism, sexism, and homophobia. Her works include *From a Land Where Other People Live* (1973), a finalist for the National Book Award; *Chosen Poems: Old and New* (1982); biomythography *Zami: A New Spelling of My Name* (1982); and *Sister Outsider: Essays and Speeches* (1984).

Among feminists, lesbian and nonlesbian, Adrienne Rich is a prominent poet and writer of prose. Her first book, *A Change of World* (1951), earned her the Yale Younger Poets Award. This meant the male establishment recognized her talent as a writer. Her feminist values begin to appear in published writing in her 1963 collection *Snapshots of a Daughter-in Law*. In her 1976 essay, "It Is the Lesbian in Us," Rich defines lesbian-feminism for herself. Her published work during the 1970s certainly celebrates the strength of female energy: *Sister Wisdom*, a lesbian-feminist

Audre Lorde

journal edited with her partner Michelle Cliff, a Caribbean lesbian-feminist; *Diving Into the Wreck* (1974); *Norton Critical Edition of Adrienne Rich's Poetry* (1975); *Of Woman Born* (1976); *The Dream of a Common Language* (1978); *On Lies, Secrets, and Silence* (1979); and "Compulsory Heterosexuality and Lesbian Existence" (1980). Her post-1970s writing does not focus exclusively on lesbian-feminist thought. It engages other personal and political issues. This work includes *A Wild Patience Has Taken Me This Far* (1981); *Your Native Land, Your Life* (1986); *An Atlas of a Difficult World* (1991); and an edited collection, *Bridges: A Journal for Jewish Feminists and Our Friends*.

Lesbian-feminist poet Judy Grahn writes from her perspective as a working-class white woman. Two collections of poetry, *A Woman Is Talking to Death* (1974) and *The Work of a Common Woman* (1978), celebrate the common voice while revealing the working class's powerlessness in the middle- and upper-middle-class power structure.

Joanna Russ, a recognized lesbian-feminist science fiction writer, believed that science fiction provided a way to encode lesbian-feminism. By the late 1960s, she identified fully as a radical lesbian-feminist. Her science fiction includes "When It Changes," (1972), *The Female Man* (1975), *The Adventures of Alyx* (1976), and *The Two of Them* (1978). Her feminist criticism includes *How to Suppress Women's Writing* (1983) and *Magic Mamas, Trembling Sisters, Puritans & Perverts* (1985).

Writer Jane Rule's first novel, *Desert of the Heart* (1964), preempted the lesbian-feminist movement of the 1970s. Unlike most literature of the time, her protagonists are not murdered, do not commit suicide, and do not struggle with depression. Instead, the novel presents a successful lesbian relationship, one filled with happiness. This novel was made into a 1980 film, *Desert Hearts*. Her other work includes *Against the Season* (1971), *Theme for Diverse Instruments* (1975), *The Young in One Another's Arms* (1977), *Lesbian Images* (1975), and *A Hot-Eyed Moderate* (1985).

The work of Greek-American writer Olga Broumans is unabashedly lesbian. Her first volume of poetry, *Beginning With O*, won the 1977 Yale Younger Poets Award. Her work displays high style and musical form—which the mainstream admires. For some, the way she tells the truth is too strident. It is this truth-telling, though, that lesbian-feminists most celebrate. Other works include *Soie Sauvage* (1980) and *Pastoral Jazz* (1983).

Jewish-American Irena Klepfisz views her Jewishness and her lesbian-feminism as connected. In fact, her 1982 poetry collection *Keeper of Accounts* explores this connection. Klepfisz is a founding editor of *Conditions* (1977); contributing editor to *Sinister Wisdom*; co-editor of *The Tribe of Dina: A Jewish Woman's Anthology* (1986); and author of *Different Enclosures: The Poetry and Prose of Irena Klepfisz* (1985); *A Few Words in the Mother Tongue: Poems Selected and New, 1971-1990*; and *Dreams of an Insomniac: Jewish Feminist Essays, Speeches and Diatribes* (1990).

Finally, Pat Parker's early poetry responded to the civil-rights and black-liberation movements. In the 1970s, she expanded her civil-rights commitment to include gay- and feminist-rights. As a feminist, she identified herself as a Third-World lesbian-feminist. She represented a minority position within lesbian-feminism, a perspective that challenged the white, separatist agenda of most lesbian feminists. Lesbian feminists credited her with being one of the most-successful "identity politics" poets. Her work includes *Child of Myself* (1972); *Pit Stop* (1973); and *Womanslaughter* (1978).

Post-Lesbian-Feminist Literature: 1980s and 1990s

The values and strength of lesbian-feminism continued into the early 1980s, although its strongest presence was felt in the early 1970s. In the mid-1980s, "Lesbian-Feminist" literature was more accurately labeled "Post-Lesbian-Feminist" literature. This literature assumes lesbian-feminist principles, so writers were less likely to foreground intentionally their texts in lesbian-feminism. This shift is marked by a lighter lesbian-feminist tone, a tone that often relies on satire. Both as a literature movement and as a lived culture, post-lesbian-feminists' proscriptions for behavior are looser than those identified by lesbian feminists. "Lesbian-Feminist" literature challenged heterosexist sexual mores. This challenge afforded post-lesbian-feminist writers the opportunity to explore the sexually forbidden with a lessened sense of danger (Faderman, *Chloe,* p. 690). The work of lesbian-feminist writers has helped to remove the stigma traditionally attached to writers' explorations of sexuality through literature. The result of this literary sexual freedom is a body of lesbian literature that targets lesbian pleasure for lesbians, not straight men.

This literature of sexual freedom encourages a new consideration of the lesbian continuum with a focus particularly on sexuality. Post-Lesbian-Feminist literature argues that, as critic Eve Sedgwick explains in *Tendencies* (1993), we need to become more aware of sexual ecology. She explains that the epistemology of the closet reveals that

> contemporary homo- and heterosexual definitions have become so exacerbated a cultural site because of an enduring incoherence about whether it is to be thought of as an issue only for a minority of (distinctly lesbian or gay) individuals, or instead as an issue that cuts across every locus of agency and subjectivity in the culture (Sedgwick, *Tendencies,* p. xii).

Post-lesbian-feminist (and contemporary gay) writers thus present queerness, what Sedgwick identifies as "the open mesh of possibilities, gaps, overlaps, dissonances and resonances, lapses and excesses of meaning when the constituent elements of anyone's gender, of anyone's sexuality aren't made (or can't be made) to signify monolithically" (Sedgwick, *Tendencies,* p. 8). Queerness refigures the lesbian continuum by suggesting that just as cultures cross and mix, so do gender and sexuality. Queerness explores what it means to be a sexual outlaw. The queer aesthetic intends to outrage the conventional. It will not tolerate the oversight of people of color or of the working class as gay liberation and lesbian-feminism did. The queer aesthetic in life and literature is inclusive and forward-thinking. To put it succinctly, "'queer' means to fuck with gender" (Faderman, *Chloe,* pp. 691-92). While promoting the freedom to explore sexuality without the moralizations of earlier decades, Post-Lesbian-Feminist literature does not explore only sexuality. It also celebrates multiculturalism.

The body of post-lesbian-feminists, queer theorists, and writers continues to grow. The queer aesthetic is evident in popular post-lesbian-feminist pornography such as *Serious Pleasures* (1990), *More Serious Pleasures* (1991), *Erotica* (1992), *Bushfire* (1991), and *An Intimate Wilderness* (1991). Significant post-lesbian-feminist writers include Beth Brant Degonwadonti, Kitty Tsui, Cherrie Lawrence Moraga, Emma Pèrez, Rebecca Brown, Sarah Schulman, Marilyn Hacker, Pat Califia, Cheryl Clarke, Frankie Hucklenbroich, Dorothy Allison, Minnie Bruce Pratt, and Jackie Kay.

Beth Brant Degonwadonti, a Bay of Quinte Mohawk lesbian, includes her Native-American perspective in her writing: *A Gathering of Spirits* (1983) and *Mohawk Trail* (1985). Asian-American writer Kitty Tsui (1953) explores the challenges of the Chinese-American lesbian experience in her works: *The Words of a Woman Who Breathes Fire* (1983), the collective *Unbound Feet*, and *New Phoenix Rising: The Asian/Pacific Lesbian Newsletter*. Lesbian Cherrie Moraga, born to an Anglo father and a Chicana mother, is hugely responsible for the acknowledgement of and evolution of the Latina literary tradition. For her, loving women is concomitant with reclaiming her mother's race. Her works celebrate women's sexual independence: her poetry, *Loving in the War Years* (1983); her play, *Giving Up the Ghost* (1986); her co-edited anthologies, *This Bridge Called My Back* (1981) and *Cuentos: Stories by Latinas* (1983).

Rebecca Brown uses postmodernist techniques such as mixing fantasy and fact and using the surreal, the allegorical, and the fantastic to argue ideas. For Brown, the family provides a perpetual battleground for working through ideas and realities. Her works include *The Evolution of Darkness* (1984), *The Haunted House* (1986), *The Children's Crusade* (1991), *The Terrible Girls* (1992), *Annie Oakley's Girl* (1993), and *The Gifts of the Body* (1994).

Sarah Schulman's postmodernist, post-lesbian-feminist work consistently offers the unexpected. As a postfeminist, much of

Cherrie Moraga

her work challenges and, at times, betrays feminist values. Her works include *The Sophie Horowitz Story* (1984); *Girls, Visions, and Everything* (1986); *After Delores* (1988); *People in Trouble* (1990); and *Empathy* (1992). Marilyn Hacker is recognized by many lesbians as arguably the most polished contemporary lesbian poet. Her poetry includes *Presentation Piece* (1975), for which she won the National Book Award; *Taking Notice* (1981); and *Love, Death and the Changing of the Seasons* (1986).

The work of Pat Califia, the leader of lesbian sexual radicals, purports politically incorrect images of lesbian sexuality such as maternal incest, group sex, sado-masochism, and lesbian-gay male sex (Faderman, *Chloe,* p. 746). Her works include a lesbian sex manual, *Sapphistry* (1981), and a collection of lesbian sex stories, *Macho Sluts* (1988).

For Cheryl Clarke, writing poetry in the tradition of black women celebrates their voices. This focus allows her to explore black lesbian sensuality and sexuality. In her poetry, Clarke does not dissect racial difference; she assumes it. Her poetry includes *Narratives: poems in the tradition of black women* (1983), *Living as a Lesbian* (1986), and *Humid Pitch* (1989).

Dorothy Allison describes her work as "hard assed." This poet and prose writer, born out of wedlock to a working-class teenager, challenges lesbian-feminist proscriptions, especially regarding sexuality. Allison strongly defends lesbian sado-masochism. Her "in your face" tone is evident in *The Women Who Hate Me*

Dorothy Allison

(1983); *Trash* (1988); *Bastard Out of Carolina* (1992), which resulted in a 1996 film directed by Angelica Huston; and *Skin: Talking about Sex, Class, and Literature* (1994). Finally, most of Minnie Bruce Pratt's work continues the lesbian-feminist tradition, namely her poetry collections *The Sound of One Fork* (1981) and *We Say We Love Each Other* (1985). Her 1990 publication of *Crime against Nature* moves beyond "Lesbian-Feminist" literature to focus on the struggles lesbian mothers confront. For her, lesbian motherhood meant lossing her two boys to her ex-husband once he learned she was gay. This book about lesbian motherhood received the Lamount Prize.

PROMINENT PEOPLE

Dorothy Allison (1949-)

Allison's work is brutally honest and filled with simple emotional realism. Her fiction is tied to her poor southern roots. In her attempt to define lesbian sexuality honestly, she writes of desire, lust, past history, violence, need, class, politics, and love.

Bastard Out of Carolina (1992), her first novel, moved Allison from the gay/lesbian literary margin to the mainstream. This semi-autobiographical story about Bone, a young girl who is deeply loved by her mother Anney and who is physically and sexually abused by her step-father, speaks frankly about the relationship between family life and violence. While the novel does not center on lesbianism, the story is told from a lesbian-feminist perspective. Actress Angelica Huston made her directing debut in the 1996 made-for-television movie based on the novel.

In "Her Body, Mine, and His" (1991), Allison describes an exhausting and powerful sexual encounter in graphic detail, as explained by critic Michael Bronski (Malinowski, pp. 7-9). Much of her writing works to understand and accept the ways in which violence constructs our lives.

Allison's honest look at violence troubles many anti-pornography feminists. In fact, some feminists critical of Allison's sadomasochistic perspective and desires picketed her at a Barnard College symposium in 1983. Even with this response, Allison explains in *Trash* (1988), "I write stories. I write fiction. I put on the page a third look at what I've seen in life—the condensed and reinvented experience of a cross-eyed working class lesbian, addicted to violence, language and hope, who has made the decision to live, is determined to live, on the page and on the street, for me and mine" (*Trash*, p. 12). Allison collected approximately 12 years of nonfiction essays in *Skin: Talking about Sex, Class, and Literature* (1994), and in 1995, she published *Two or Three Things I Know for Sure*, a memoir that was originally written as a performance piece. Allison's second novel, *Cavedweller*, was published in early 1998.

James Baldwin (1924-1987)

An ardent civil rights activist, Baldwin in his plays, novels, and essays articulates the effects of racial strife in the United States. Many of his novels, such as *Go Tell It on the Mountain* (1954), *Giovanni's Room* (1956), and *Another Country* (1962), centrally address black and white issues. But they move beyond that to include issues regarding identity politics. Many critics claim that Baldwin's most significant contribution to American literature, however, is not his fiction but his nonfiction work, now collected in *The Price of the Ticket: Collected Non-fiction, 1948-1985* (1985). Critics argue that by extending his literary discussions of race to include identity politics, he contributed significantly to the beginning of the gay liberation movement of the 1960s.

Jane Bowles (1917-1973)

As Bowles crossed the Atlantic by ship, a stranger found her reading Louis-Ferdinand Cèline's novel *Voyage to the End of the Night*. He asked her about the book, to which she replied, "He is the greatest writer in the whole world" (Robert E. Lougy). The stranger, explains biographer Thomas Wiloch, was Cèline. After her conversation with Cèline, she vowed to become a writer.

While Bowles's characters usually include two women who struggle to free themselves from bourgeois sexual expectations, none of her characters appears to be as openly lesbian as Bowles herself. The work for which she is best known, *Two Serious Ladies* (1943), tells the story of two female friends' attempts to break away from bourgeois sexuality. Bowles neither portrays physically healthy lesbians nor was she one herself. By the age of 40, she was disabled for life by a stroke.

Her list of publications is not long. In addition to *Two Serious Ladies,* Bowles wrote three additional stories: "Plain Pleasures" (1942, 1966), "Andrew" (1971), and "Emmy Moore's Journal" (1971); the first of these was published initially in *Harper's* and then in 1966 in book form, while the latter two were published in *Antaeus.* She also wrote a play, *In the Summer House* (1954). Wiloch claims that Bowles's legend rests both on her work and on the years she spent in Tangier, Morocco. During the 1950s, no gay writer or artist's visit to Tangier was complete without a visit to the home Bowles shared with her husband, Paul.

Rita Mae Brown (1944-)

The lesbian and straight communities read Rita Mae Brown's words. In fact, she is likely the most widely read lesbian writer in the 1980s and 1990s. She received recognition with her first two novels, *Rubyfruit Jungle* (1973) and *In Her Day* (1976). Brown began writing in the political environment of Second Wave feminism in the 1970s. As a visible member of the women's liberation movement and the radical lesbian movement that followed, Brown worked with other feminists to lay the ground work for Second Wave feminist-lesbian theory. Brown makes real the gender, sex, and class politics of the United States in her first novel. She combined graphic lesbian sex and progressive politics and still reached the lesbian and straight communities. In *Six of One* (1978), Brown continued to use the novel genre to explore oppressive politics. However, this novel reached a straight audience more immediately than did the first two by focusing on eccentrics in a Pennsylvania-Maryland border town, a setting she returns to in *Bingo* (1988). The oppression of lesbians is still evident in both books but less explicitly. In a sequence of three novels, *Southern Discomfort* (1982), *Sudden Death* (1983), and *High Hearts* (1986), Brown moved the settings to the deep south. Critics such as Michael

Bronski explain that her recent work combines wonderful storytelling and plotting with her famous raucous humor, a humor connected to her progressive politics (Malinowski, pp. 54-56). In addition to her successful novels, Brown is a recognized mystery writer, poet, screenplay and television film writer, and essayist.

Lillian Faderman (1940-)

Faderman's work as an educator and writer contributed significantly to Second Wave feminism, especially lesbian feminism. *Surpassing the Love of Men: Romantic Friendship and Love between Women from the Renaissance to the Present* presents the shifts in societal views towards lesbianism from the 16th century to the 20th century. In her second book, *Odd Girls and Twilight Lovers: A History of Lesbian Life in Twentieth Century America*, she focuses on the changes in societal attitudes towards lesbianism in the 20th century. Her most recent publication, *Chloe Plus Olivia: An Anthology of Lesbian Literature from the Seventeenth Century to the Present*, Faderman collects a range of lesbian texts from the 17th century to the 20th century. Together her books provide important information about how lesbianism has been defined over the years, with particular emphasis on 20th-century Austrian psychoanalyst Sigmund Freud's influence in labeling lesbianism as "morbid" and lesbians as "diseased." Institutions accepted these

Lillian Faderman

Allen Ginsberg

labels, using the supposed knowledge to repress lesbians in the 1910s, 1930s, and 1950s. Faderman's research empowers lesbians to define themselves and provides strong evidence for labeling mainstream culture's 20th-century response to gays and lesbians as evidence of cultural homophobia.

Allen Ginsberg (1926-1997)

Ginsberg, a World War II veteran and a literary leader of the Beat Generation, lived a sexually permissive, bohemian life after the war. Following the war, his personal code challenged orthodox sex and politics. Like his mother, he supported Communism. These ethics informed his philosophy of language and his poetry. His most celebrated piece, "Howl" (1956), speaks for the downtrodden while attacking American systems. Ginsberg was a prolific post-World War II poet who used words both to speak for the "Others" in our culture and to celebrate the love between men.

Jewelle Gomez (1948-)

Jewelle Gomez, the African American author of two poetry collections, *The Lipstick Papers* (1980) and *Flamingoes and Bears* (1983); *The Gilda Stories* (1991); and many essays transforms the horrific images of the lesbian vampire. By defusing the mystery and supposed evil surrounding the supernatural, she attributes what Alice Walker defines as womanist values—positive, woman-centered values—to the lesbian vampire.

Thom Gunn (1929-)

Born and raised in England, Gunn completed his education at Cambridge before following his lover, American Mike Kitay, to San Francisco. Gunn's first collection of poetry, *Fighting Terms* (1954), explores both love and sexuality, and public and private expressions of affection, and it introduces the focus of his future publications. Over the years, his poetic technique has remained tight and focused. What has changed is the degree to which he expresses his own sexuality. A review of *Moly* and *My Sad Captain* (1971) and *The Passages of Joy* (1982) reveal his open homoeroticism. He did not publish again until 1992, at which time he published *The Man with Night Sweats*. Notably, the decade of silence occurred during the outbreak and height of the AIDS epidemic. The poems in *The Man with Night Sweats* do not focus on his sexuality but instead are laments to his friends who have suffered with and died from AIDS.

Andrew Holleran (1943?-)

Andrew Holleran's first novel, *Dancer from the Dance* (1978), captured the attention of gay and mainstream reviewers and readers. This represented a first for the post-Stonewall generation of writers. Earlier books by Gore Vidal, James Baldwin, and John Rechy attracted popular attention from the mainstream. The difference with Holleran's novel is that this was the first time that both book and author were fully recognized as part of the gay literature genre. Holleran's first novel focuses on the gay male nightlife in Manhattan's disco world. The success and popularity marked a significant accomplishment, especially since the novel moved beyond the common post-Stonewall writing act of declaring "gay as good." Holleran shows the gay dark side, too. Doing so clearly represents risky writing.

Nights in Aruba (1983), Holleran's second novel, also attracted attention from the gay and straight community. This book focused on a gay man's struggle to care for his aging parents and to live life freely as a gay man. While the book did not receive the attention of the first (something which may be attributed to the cultural focus on AIDS rather than literature in the 1980s), it is important to note Holleran's success at reaching the gay and straight cultures without encoding the gay experience. Holleran's contributions as an essayist are noteworthy, especially *Ground Zero* (1988), a collection that represents some of the most-thoughtful published essays about AIDS. Finally, his most recent publication, *The Beauty of Men* (1996), continues the AIDS theme in fiction. Lark, a gay man in his forties, feels guilty because his friends continue to die of AIDS, but he remains HIV-negative. This novel of despair makes real what it is to live today as a healthy gay man.

Christopher Isherwood (1904-1986)

Born in England, Isherwood published seven of his 11 novels there. The gay literary community credits Isherwood with presenting homosexuality honestly and naturally, even when it was not culturally safe to do so. His early works include *All the Conspirators* (1928), *The Memorial: Portrait of a Family* (1932), *The Last of Mr. Norris* (1935), *Sally Bowles* (1937), *Goodbye to Berlin* (1939), *Prater Violet* (1945), and *The Berlin Stories* (1946).

Gay Americans embraced him as a writer when he became a U.S. citizen in 1946. Increasingly, his novels focused specifically on the plight of gay men in a homophobic society. In doing so, his novels voiced the experiences and feelings of many gay men. His American novels include *The World in the Evening* (1954), *Down There on a Visit* (1964), *A Single Man* (1964), and *A Meet-*

ing by the River (1967). Critic Claude Summers explains that Isherwood's novels capture homosexuals' personalities and their common humanity.

David Leavitt (1961-)

David Leavitt is a prominent post-Stonewall novelist, author of short stories and of nonfiction. His stories, which include collections such as *Family Dancing* (1984) and *A Place I've Never Been* (1990), focus on family constructions and relations, a thematic focus of 1980s and 1990s fiction. His first novel, *The Lost Language of Cranes* (1986), extends the challenge of the coming-out story by creating the character of Rose, whose son and husband admit to being gay. To create Rose's story is significant. Most gay literature does not include women, a point of significant criticism for feminists. However, Leavitt not only includes women in his literature, his female characters are fully developed. His second novel, *Equal Affections* (1989), includes another mother, a reluctant one. While Leavitt is critiqued for maintaining his family focus, his work certainly marks the movement of gay literature into the early 1990s.

Audre Lorde (1934-1992)

Audre Lorde, a self-described "black lesbian feminist warrior poet," crafted intensely personal poems, essays, and speeches. While her words may have appeared self-absorbed at times, most critics agree that her poetry transforms private pains and joys into universal and timeless concerns.

Her early collections of poems, *The First Cities* (1968) and *Cables to Rage* (1970), express her own political disillusionment as represented by the failure of freedom and equality for all Americans. The themes and tone of these collections make clear her "unladylike" rage. In both *From a Land Where Other People Live* (1973) and *Between Our Selves* (1976), Lorde creates a tone that tells about the reality of white racism upon African Americans. These collections of poems convinced Lorde that she must work ardently to use personal reality to transform thoughts into action.

Lorde began to accomplish these goals with a sequence of poetry collections, namely *Coal* (1976), *The Black Unicorn* (1978), and *Our Dead Behind Us* (1986), in which she represents vignettes of her relationships with people. Other poem collections include *New York Head Shop and Museum* (1974); *Chosen Poems, Old and New* (1982); *Undersong: Chosen Poems, Old and New* (1992); and *The Marvelous Arithmetic of Distance: Poems, 1987-1992* (1993).

Lorde used other genres, in addition to poetry, as language-tools for fighting racism, sexism, classism, and heterosexism. As she relied on the personal to write *The Cancer Journals* (1980), Lorde's account of her breast cancer diagnosis, and *Zami: A New Spelling of My Name* (1982), what she called her biomythography, she spoke loudly against the oppressive "-isms." For Lorde, racism, sexism, classism, heterosexism, and her personal life were not separate. Therefore, they had to be addressed together in texts. For Lorde, to separate them was to be blind to their interconnectedness. Finally, Lorde's critical theory is foundational to lesbian-feminist criticism. Works such as "The Master's Tools Will Never Dismantle the Master's House" and "The Uses of the Erotic: The Erotic as Power" speak to women's power and ability to feel. By understanding our own individual power, developing our abilities to feel, and being honest with ourselves, Lorde's works contend we can come together as social, caring people. It is then that we can effect positive change for each other.

Carson McCullers (1917-1967)

The Heart Is a Lonely Hunter (1940), McCullers first novel, established her as an important American writer. The works that followed, namely *Reflections in a Golden Eye* (1941), *The Member of the Wedding* (1946), and *Clock without Hands* (1961), confirmed her position as a significant writer.

Throughout her writing, McCullers skillfully set her stories in the comfort of America's small towns. At the same time, she created characters and plots that challenge cultural mores, especially those assumptions about racial inequality and the supposed unnaturalness of homosexuality. In other words, her stories project American social prejudices. McCullers's stories do not offer magical solutions to bigotry and sexism. Her characters experience real life, which sometimes means their own deaths. As biographer Pamela Bigelow explains, in McCullers's work, "[U]ltimately, love and life are richer, if instead of being blind to differences such as color and gender, differences are accepted as enhancements of our species."

Paul Monette (1945-1995)

Monette's first novel, *Taking Care of Mrs. Carroll* (1978), represents a fun opportunity to explore the 1960s-70s gay scene. In the two novels that follow, *The Gold Diggers* (1979) and *The Long Shot* (1981), he explores the relationship between gay men and straight women. While he published novels, he also published collections of poetry such as *The Carpenter at the Asylum* (1978) and *No Witnesses* (1981). Then the AIDS crisis emerged.

The AIDS crisis brought Monette's poetry to a halt. As Monette explained to Boyd, a culture's best literature comes out of crisis, and for Monette, poetry's audience addresses a very small, elitist community, not the community on which Monette intended to focus his energy. He wrote one publisher-forced novel, *Lightfall* (1982). Then his work changed.

The writing that emerged from Monette following the discovery of AIDS connected words to his life and to AIDS. His next novel, *Afterlife* (1990), tells the story of a broad group of people living with AIDS, an experience that was very real, as Monette's lover was diagnosed with AIDS in 1985. *Halfway Home* (1991) is the gay love story Monette always wanted to write. *Borrowed Time: An AIDS Memoir* (1988) tells his lover's story of AIDS diagnosis and dying. Then Monette wrote his own autobiography, *Becoming a Man: Half a Life Story* (1992), nonfiction that brought him great praise and respect. Monette's novels, poetry, and nonfiction capture life's health and illness.

Cherrie Moraga (1952-)

Cherrie Moraga, born to an Anglo father and a Chicana mother, is hugely responsible for the acknowledgement of and evolution of the Latina literary tradition. For her, loving women is concomitant with reclaiming her mother's race. Her works celebrate women's sexual independence: her poetry, *Loving in the War Years* (1983); her play, *Giving Up the Ghost* (1986); and her co-edited anthologies, *This Bridge Called My Back* (1981) and *Cuentos: Stories by Latinas* (1983).

Adrienne Rich (1929-)

Among feminists, lesbian and nonlesbian, Adrienne Rich is a prominent poet and writer of prose. Her first book, *A Change of World* (1951), earned her the Yale Younger Poets Award. This meant the male establishment recognized her talent as a writer. Her feminist values begin to appear in published writing in her

Adrienne Rich

1963 collection *Snapshots of a Daughter-in Law*. In her 1976 essay, "It Is the Lesbian in Us," Rich defines lesbian-feminism for herself. Her published work during the 1970s certainly celebrated the strength of female energy: *Sister Wisdom*, a lesbian-feminist journal edited with her partner Michelle Cliff, a Caribbean lesbian-feminist; *Diving into the Wreck* (1974); *Norton Critical Edition of Adrienne Rich's Poetry* (1975); *Of Woman Born* (1976); *The Dream of a Common Language* (1978); *On Lies, Secrets, and Silence* (1979); and "Compulsory Heterosexuality and Lesbian Existence" (1980). Her post-1970s writing does not focus exclusively on lesbian-feminist thought but rather engages other personal and political issues. This work includes *A Wild Patience Has Taken Me This Far* (1981); *Your Native Land, Your Life* (1986); *An Atlas of a Difficult World* (1991); and an edited collection, *Bridges: A Journal for Jewish Feminists and Our Friends*.

Gore Vidal (1925-)

Considered by many gay critics to be the most significant post-World War II gay male writer, Gore Vidal has written no fewer than 28 novels along with collections of short stories, plays, screen-

plays, and television plays. His first novel, *Williwaw* (1946), does not address homosexuality. In his second novel, *In a Yellow Wood* (1947), homosexuality is in fact a thematic device used to allow protagonist Robert Holton to reconcile his desire to add unconventionality to his highly ordered life. The novel with which most associate Vidal and homosexuality is his full-text study of a gay man, Jim Willard, in *The City and the Pillar* (1948). The novels that immediately followed were commercial failures: *The Season of Comfort* (1949), *A Search for the King: A Twelfth-Century Legend* (1950), *Dark Green, Bright Red* (1950), *The Judgment of Paris* (1953), *Messiah* (1954), and *Three: Williwaw; A Thirsty Evil: Seven Short Stories; Julian, the Apostate* (1962). Critic James Levin argues that Vidal's lower-quality writing is due to his emphasis in the 1950s on establishing himself financially. Vidal turned his focus from honing his writing skills to making money in Hollywood by writing television plays.

Financially stable by 1964, Vidal regained literary success with his novel *Julian*. What followed were more-controversial books such as *Myra Breckinridge* (1968) and *Live from Golgotha* (1992), books that continued to focus on homosexuality. While each of

Vidal's books has not been a commercial or critical success, critics applaud him both for his strength to contribute so consistently to the body of gay literature with books that do not encode homosexuality and for his willingness to be defined as a gay author who takes stylistic risks. The risks do not always work, but they certainly allow gay literature to prosper.

Edmund White (1940-)

As a significant post-Stonewall novelist, White diligently uses words to explore homosexuality in a culture that really only has surface-level democracy, a system that is not fully available to the gay culture. He explores the gay experience in *Forgetting Elena* (1973) and *Nocturnes for the King of Naples* (1978). However, his skill as a novelist and his willingness to identify himself publicly as a gay writer successfully launched his third novel, *A Boy's Own Story* (1982). The post-Stonewall culture identified White as a transforming writer of gay literature and publishing. His nonfiction, which includes *The Joy of Gay Sex: An Intimate Guide for Gay Men to the Pleasures of a Gay Lifestyle* (1977), *States of Desire: Travels in Gay America* (1980), and *Genet: A Biography* (1993), continues to earn praise from the gay community.

Walt Whitman (1819-1892)

Whitman is recognized as the poet of our land, for his verse envisions equality, national purpose, and international brotherhood. In fact, Whitman was the first U.S. poet to gain international stature. With each revision of Whitman's collection of poems, *Leaves of Grass*, he further propelled his democratic message. His third

Bonnie Zimmerman

edition, published in 1860, included his "sex poems," which the Victoria culture described as evil. Two groups of poems comprised the sex poems: the "Children of Adam" poems, which focused on heterosexual love, and the "Calamus" poems, which focused on homosexual romantic friendships. Whitman's prose provides literary insight to his democratic perspectives, texts such as the preface to *As a Strong Bird* (1872), *Democratic Vistas* (1870), and *Specimen Days and Collect* (1882). His letters continue to provide critical support for literary scholars' critiques of his "Romantic Friendship" verse and for biographers reconstructing his life as our country's most renowned gay poet.

Bonnie Zimmerman (1947-)

As one of the first openly lesbian professors in academe, Zimmerman established the first Women's Studies Program in the country at San Diego State University. She has been a pioneer in lesbian studies and literary criticism, and has written extensively as a lesbian literary critic. The work for which she is best known and for which she received the Lambda Literary Award, *The Safe Sea of Women: Lesbian Fiction, 1969-1989*, reviews contemporary lesbian fiction. As a frequent speaker at national conferences, Zimmerman encourages lesbian-feminists to embrace the multicultural perspective that post-lesbian-feminists embrace.

GAY AND LESBIAN PRESSES

Clearly gays and lesbians publish. However, securing publishers has not been easy. The history of gays' and lesbians' encoded languages makes that evident.

Since Stonewall and the Second Wave feminist liberation movement, gay and lesbian literatures have increased significantly in quantity; this steady increase in gay and lesbian publications certainly reflects American's shifting social mores. However, the increase in presses' willingness to publish gay and lesbian texts does not suggest the social acceptance of gays and lesbians or their literature or literature about them. Commercial publishers meet the needs of mainstream readers first. As critic Valerie Miner explains, "[T]he American publishing industry, monopolized by media conglomerates, is not in the business of triggering earthquakes" (Miner, pp. 16-17). Commercial publishers ignored the gay and lesbian communities even after both communities created their own social earthquakes with Stonewall and Second Wave feminism. The gay and lesbian communities knew that they had to publish their voices in order to establish themselves as part of the U.S. social culture.

Gay and lesbian publishing became a burgeoning field in the 1970s not because of the mainstream but because of the gay and lesbian communities' commitments to printing their words, to publishing their voices. Their newspapers, magazine, and journals likely captured the range of their voices most clearly. The post-Stonewall era is marked by the establishment of the gay and lesbian presses. By the mid-1970s, most major U.S. cities had a gay newspapers and other gay publications—the *Washington Blade*, the *Philadelphia Gay News*, San Francisco's *Bay Area Reporter* and *Gay Sunshine*, Chicago's *Gay Life*, Cleveland's *High Gear*, New York's *Come Out*, and Boston's *Fag Rag*. The most-successful newspaper press was the West Coast-based *Advocate*, founded in 1967. These post-Stonewall presses are significant in that they are marked by an activist tone, while an apologetic tone distinguishes pre-Stonewall presses such as *One*, *The Ladder*, and *Mattachine Review*.

While the post-Stonewall presses claimed to provide coverage of gays and lesbians, with the exception of Boston's collectively run *Gay Community News*, the focus was clearly on gay men. The result was a lesbian community that did not fully support the gay presses. Instead, many lesbians read feminist newspapers such as *Off Our Backs*.

Newspaper presses inaugurated the gay and lesbian publishing boom, for the newspaper venue encouraged the truth-telling that the pre-Stonewall and -Second Wave feminist eras discouraged and, in some cases, forbade. The newspaper presses continued to serve as a vital publishing tool that both gave the gay and lesbian communities voice and convinced these communities to keep publishing. The result was a multitude of small gay and lesbian presses, some of which include: Alamo Square Press; Alicejamesbooks; Alyson Publications; Amethyst Press, Inc.; Banned Books, An Imprint of Edward-William Austin Publishing Company; Barricade Books, Inc.; Bay Press; Beacon Press; Blackwell Publishers; Brick House Books, Inc.; Calamus Books; Cassell Academic; Celestial Arts; Chelsea House Publishers; Circlet Press, Inc.; City Lights Books; Cleis Press; Crossing Press; Daughter; Diane Publishing Company; the Feminist Press; Firebrand Books; Gay Presses of America; The Groundwater Press; Kitchen Sink Press; Kitchen Table/Women of Color Press; Knights Press; Lavender Press; Los Hombres; Naiad Press; New Press; New Directions Publishing; Pride Publications; Rising Tide Publishers; Seal Press; Soho Press, Inc.; South End Press; Spinsters/Aunte Lute; Woman in the Moon Publications; and Women's Press Collective. Beginning in the early 1980s, mainstream publishers began to recognize the potential gay and lesbian market. Since then, academic and major commercial companies such as Columbia University Press, Cornell University Press, State University of New York Press, University of Illinois Press, University of Minnesota Press, Weleyan University Press, Dutton, Harper, Penguin, Plume, Routledge, St. James Press, and St. Martin's Press have published gay and lesbian titles.

With the success of the gay and lesbian liberation movement, gays and lesbians have made permanent space on bookshelves for their words. Their words will be published, be it by conglomerates or by independent publishing houses.

REFERENCES:

Archive

Gay and Lesbian Literary Archive. University of Southern California, Los Angeles.

Books and Articles

Abelove, Henry, Michèle Aina Barale, and David M. Halperin, eds. *The Lesbian and Gay Studies Reader.* New York: Routledge, 1993.

Anzaldúa, Gloria. *Borderlands/La Frontera: The New Mestiz.* San Francisco: Spinsters, 1987.

Auerbach, Nina. "Engorging the Patriarchy," in *Feminist Issues in Literary Scholarship,* edited by Shari Benstock. Bloomington: Indiana University Press, 1987: 150-60.

Bergman, David. *Gaiety Transfigured.* Madison: The University of Wisconsin Press, 1991.

Boone, Joseph A. and Michael Cadden. *Engendering Men: The Question of Male Feminist Criticism.* New York: Routledge, 1990.

Bouldrey, Brian. *Best American Gay Fiction 1996.* New York: Little, Brown & Company, 1996.

Bulkin, Elly and Joan Larkin. *Lesbian Poetry.* Watertown, Massachusetts: Persephone Press, 1981.

Califia, Pat. *Macho Sluts.* Boston: Alyson, 1988.

Coleridge, Samuel Taylor. *Biographia Literaria: or, Biographical Sketches of My Literary Life and Opinions.* London, 1817.

Cruikshank, Margaret. *Lesbian Studies: Present and Future.* New York: The Feminist Press, 1982.

Currier, Jameson. *Dancing on the Moon.* New York: Viking, 1993.

de Beauvoir, Simone. *The Second Sex* (1949). New York: Knopf, 1953.

de Lauretis, Teresa, ed. *Feminist Studies/Critical Studies.* Bloomington: Indiana University Press, 1986.

de Lauretis, Teresa. "Upping the Anti (sic) in Feminist Theory," in *Conflicts in Feminism,* edited by Marianne Hirsch and Evelyn Fox Keller. New York: Routledge, 1990.

———. *The Practice of Love: Lesbian Sexuality and Perverse Desire.* Bloomington: Indiana University Press, 1994.

Faderman, Lillian. *Chloe Plus Olivia: An Anthology of Lesbian Literature from the Seventeenth Century to the Present.* New York: Penguin Books, 1994.

———. *Odd Girls and Twilight Lovers.* New York: Penguin, 1991.

———. *Surpassing the Love of Men: Romantic Friendship and Love between Women from the Renaissance to the Present.* New York: William Morrow, 1981.

Foster, Jeannette H. *Sex Variant Women in Literature.* 1956. Tallahassee, Florida: Naiad, 1985.

Freud, Sigmund and Josef Breuer. *Studies on Hysteria.* New York: Penguin, 1991.

Gibson, Paul. "Gay Male and Lesbian Youth Suicide," in *Report of the Secretary's Task Force on Youth Suicide,* by the U.S. Department of Health and Human Services: Washington, D.C., 1989: 110-142.

Jay, Karla and Joanne Glasgow. *Lesbian Texts and Contexts: Radical Revisions.* New York: New York University Press, 1990.

Kaplan, Justin. *Walt Whitman.* New York: Simon and Schuster, 1980.

Katz, Jonathan. *Gay American History: Lesbians and Gay Men in the USA.* New York: Avon, 1978.

Kellogg, Stuart, ed. *Essays on Gay Literature.* New York: Harrington Park Press, 1985.

Levin, James. *The Gay Novel in America.* New York: Garland, 1991.

Malinowski, Sharon. *Gay and Lesbian Literature.* Detroit: St. James Press, 1994.

Malinowski, Sharon and Christa Brelin. *The Gay & Lesbian Literary Companion.* Detroit: Visible Ink Press, 1995.

Mann, William J. "The Gay and Lesbian Publishing Boom," in *Harvard Gay & Lesbian Review,* vol. 2, no. 2, 1995: 24-27.

Marcus, Jane. *Art and Anger: Reading Like a Woman.* Columbus: Ohio State Press, 1988.

Marks, Elaine. "Lesbian Intertexuality," in *Homosexualities and French Literature: Cultural Contexts/Critical Texts,* edited by George Stambolian and Elaine Marks. Ithaca, New York: Cornell University Press, 1979.

Martin, Del and Phyllis Lyon. *Lesbian/Woman.* San Francisco: Glide Publications, 1972.

Martin, Robert. *The Homosexual Tradition in American Poetry.* Austin: University of Texas Press, 1979.

Martindale, Kathleen. *Un/Popular Culture: Lesbian Writing after the Sex Wars.* New York: State University of New York Press, 1997.

Miller, Neil. *Out of the Past: Gay and Lesbian History from 1869 to the Present*. New York: Vantage Books, 1995.

Miner, Valerie. "An Imaginative Collectivity of Writers and Readers," in Jay and Glasgow: 13-27.

Moraga, Cherrie and Gloria Anzaldúa, eds. *This Bridge Called My Back: Writings by Radical Women of Color*. Watertown, Massachusetts: Persephone, 1981.

Mordden, Ethan. *Waves: An Anthology of New Gay Fiction*. Vintage Books: New York, 1994.

Morse, Carl and Joan Larkin. *Gay and Lesbian Poetry in Our Time: An Anthology*. New York, St. Martin's Press, 1988.

Murphy, Timothy F. and Suzanne Poirier, eds. *Writing AIDS: Gay Literature, Language, and Analysis*. Columbia University Press: New York, 1993.

Nelson, Emmanuel S., ed. *Contemporary Gay American Novelists: A Bio-Bibliographical Critical Sourcebook*. Westport Connecticut, Greenwood Press, 1993.

Pastore, Judith Laurence, ed. *Confronting AIDS through Literature*. University of Illinois Press: Chicago, 1993.

Rich, Adrienne. "Compulsory Heterosexuality and Lesbian Existence," in Abelove, Barale, and Halperin.

Rotundo, E. Anthony. *American Manhood*. New York: Basic Books, 1993.

Sedgwick, Eve Kosofsky. *Epistemology of the Closet*. Berkeley: University of California Press, 1990.

———. *Tendencies*. Durham: Duke University Press, 1993.

Smith-Rosenberg, Carroll. "The Female World of Love and Ritual," in *Signs*, vol. 1, Autumn 1975: 1-29.

Stambolian, George, ed. *Men-On-Men*. New York: Dutton, 1992.

Stimpson, Catharine R. "Afterword: Lesbian Studies in the 1990s," in Jay and Glasgow: 377-382.

———. "Zero Degree Deviancy: The Lesbian Novel in English," in *Writing and Sexual Difference*, edited by Elizabeth Abel. Chicago: University of Chicago Press, 1982: 243-59.

Summers, Claude J. *Gay Fictions: Wilde to Stonewall*. New York: Continuum, 1990.

Wilhelm, James J. *Gay and Lesbian Poetry: An Anthology from Sappho to Michelangelo*. New York: Garland, 1995.

Wittig, Monique. *The Lesbian Body*. New York: Bard, 1976.

———. "The Straight Mind," in *Feminist Issues*, vol. 1, no. 1, Summer 1980: 102-10.

Woods, Gregory. *Articulate Flesh: Male Homo-Eroticism and Modern Poetry*. New Haven: Yale University Press, 1987.

Young, Ian and Graham Jackson. *The Male Homosexual in Literature: A Bibliography*. 2nd ed. Metuchen, New Jersey: The Scarecrow Press, 1982.

Zimmerman, Bonnie. "What Has Never Been: An Overview of Lesbian Feminist Literary Criticism," in *The New Feminist Criticism: Women, Literature and Theory*, edited by Elaine Showalter. New York: Pantheon, 1985: 200-24.

———. *The Safe Sea of Women: Lesbian Fiction 1969-1989*. Boston: Beacon Press, 1990.

Internet References

www.Amazon.com
www.bookwire.com
www.fatso.com
www.gaymart.com
www.geocities.com/Athens/Parthenon
www.geocities.com/WestHollywood
www.igc.apc.org/Womansnet
www.sappho.com
www.thewomens-press.com
www.well.com

—Dawn M. Formo

15

Media

U.S. media have been far from unbiased in their choice of both fictional and non-fictional stories. In both news and entertainment programs, they have a long history of ignoring or marginalizing blacks, women, the poor, the disabled, and the aged while privileging the world of the white, professional, straight, youthful, and economically advantaged male. Perhaps no group has been closed out more systematically than homosexuals have been.

Historically, this pattern of exclusion has hardly been limited to mass media. And because industry practitioners are shaped by the culture just as surely as they help shape it, they no doubt have taken their cues from the larger context of 20th-century American culture in which homosexuality typically has been vilified. Religious organizations have called it immoral. The field of psychiatry until 1973 considered it pathological. State statutes as well as court rulings, some of which still stand, have made it a crime. In that setting, the marginalization of and bias toward homosexuality in all mass media is not surprising.

While Hollywood explicitly banned the portrayal of homosexuality in American cinema, neither broadcast television and radio nor print media faced legal or direct regulatory prohibitions against homosexual depictions, but instead relied on their own codes to determine story selection. Those codes, however, are not autonomous but "derive from and interact with larger cultural discourses" (Kozol, 1989, p. 167) and typically reflect the attitudes and the socioeconomic hierarchies in society at large (Hartley, 1982; Fiske and Hartley, 1978). This is what Hartley calls the absent-present paradigm (Hartley, 1982, p. 42), in which some subordinate groups and unacceptable topics are marginalized out of existence.

Historically, this was the case with regard to representations of lesbians and gays (*Talk Back,* 1982; Marotta, 1981), but in the 1990s, that picture changed dramatically in virtually every medium. This essay will attempt to examine the complex and varied reasons that created the pressures for those changes to occur. The focus of this chapter will be on mainstream media, particularly entertainment television and radio, and journalism on television, radio, and in print. Material on film and theater is dealt with in other chapters.

Terminology

For the purposes of this paper the term homosexual may be used to refer to both men and women homosexuals. As is common in writing by homosexuals, the term lesbian will be used to refer to homosexual women and the term gay will be used to refer to homosexual men. Thus the typical construction, "gay and lesbian," will be used throughout this text interchangeably with the word homosexual.

MASS MEDIA AND SOCIETY

While traditional society defined itself through its rituals, modern society does so through its arts, which "offer a metalanguage, a way of understanding who and what we are, how values and attitudes are adjusted, how meaning shifts" (Carey, p. 61). Among the arts, today's mass media clearly are the most pervasive and powerful creators of "public thought" (Carey, p. 60). Far from being solely communication technologies, modern mass media are social institutions that have to a significant degree replaced school, church, and family (Williams, 1975, p. 22). The media have thus become the site of struggle for the very creation of culture (Fiske, 1989, p. 22).

In the mid-1970s, communications scholars advanced the concept of "symbolic annihilation" as a way of explaining the mechanism through which mass media have excluded a host of racial, ethnic, and other minority groups, (Gerbner and Gross, 1976, pp. 173-99) and women (Tuchman, 1978, pp. 3-38). The significance of "symbolic annihilation" centers on the notion that representation in mass media itself constitutes a kind of cultural power. For gays and lesbians specifically, their symbolic annihilation by mainstream American media—newspapers, magazines, radio, and television—was pervasive well into the post-World War II period.

When media representations did begin to appear, they were considered particularly potent because in an era of gay invisibility many audience members had no way of independently or critically judging their validity. And, to the extent that mass media rely on and reinforce stereotypes, their depictions could be especially problematic for gay and lesbian activists who typically were excluded from established power structures and could not easily or effectively counteract their messages. In an increasingly fragmented society, the mass media, and particularly television, are increasingly responsible for "providing the basis on which groups and classes construct an 'image' of the lives, meanings, practices and values of other groups and classes" (Hall, 1977, p. 340). Social sub-groups are keenly aware of this process and its impact.

> As the media world becomes virtually everyone's second-hand world of reference, any group sensitive to its social standing makes claims on this national registry of symbols. The aggrieved party may not credit the image, but believes that other people do, which spurs him or her to take it seriously indeed (Gitlin, 1983, p. 248).

When mass media devalue and marginalize a group, as they have done with gays and lesbians, the social consequences can be damaging to public perceptions of those groups. The relative invisibility of gays in the media—a phenomenon that lasted into the 1990s—helped to keep them from acquiring political power. An examination of television's treatment of gays and lesbians makes that conclusion virtually inescapable.

TELEVISION AND CULTURAL VALUES

Television has replaced other mass media as the country's single most dominant medium, its "national medium" (Newcomb and Hirsch, p. 60). The public discourse of television virtually defines the public discourse of American society. Television's power

> to shape the public outlook on the world is believed to lie in its symbolic representation of sociocultural norms and values, which through regular and cumulative exposure become absorbed into the psyches of viewers (Gunter, 1988, p. 46).

The way television represents lesbians and gays is a direct reflection of their status in the society. Hence, to understand the move from invisibility to center stage, one must understand television's treatment of gays and lesbians. "How a group is spoken for, or speaks for itself (and the distinction can be crucial), is how it is constituted politically, that is, in relation to power in society" (Dyer, 1981, p. 6).

In viewing television as a cultural forum where norms and values are negotiated, it is also crucial to note that the debates that take place within the forum will not leave every audience member to draw the same conclusion, i.e., the meanings produced from the discourse of television will be varied. Rather than delivering messages with monolithic meaning that exert a complex sort of political control (Newcomb and Hirsch, p. 62), the television text delivers audiences with a multiplicity of meanings (Fiske and Hartley, 1978, p. 126). In this cultural forum, "almost any version of the television text functions as a forum in which important cultural topics may be considered" (Newcomb and Hirsch, p. 62). Even in such an early and predictable program as *Father Knows Best*, the text was often an arena for the negotiation of important social and cultural changes. For example, in one episode, older daughter Betty says she wants to be an engineer, thus

foregrounding the idea of gender stereotyping. Ultimately, the narrative is resolved along very traditional lines. However, the fact that the text opened up the issue of sex discrimination is as significant as its predictable conclusion.

> It would be startling to think that mainstream texts in mass society would overtly challenge dominant ideas. But this hardly prevents the oppositional ideas from appearing. Put another way, we argue that television does not present firm ideological conclusions—despite its *formal* conclusions—so much as it *comments on* ideological problems. The conflicts we see in television drama, embedded in familiar and non-threatening frames, are conflicts ongoing in American social experience and cultural history. In a few cases we might see strong perspectives that argue for the absolute correctness of one point of view or another, but for the most part, the rhetoric of television is the rhetoric of discussion (Newcomb and Hirsch, pp. 63-64.).

It is through this "rhetoric of discussion" that television since its inception has taken up the contested topic of gays and lesbians.

EARLY LESBIAN AND GAY DEPICTIONS

U.S. television never explicitly prohibited the portrayal of lesbians and gays in either fictional programming or in news. Nonetheless, in the early days of television such portrayals were rarely explicit. Comedy routines that relied on effeminate male behavior were popularized in the 1950s and early 1960s by some of the most well-known performers of the day. The *Jack Benny Show*, for example, has been cited for numerous references to unmanly men, a veiled and stereotyped way of referring to homosexuality. In one such episode, a limp-wristed, swishy ballet teacher named Gay Finski is introduced and shown prancing around his studio, attempting to train cast member Don Wilson in the finer points of dance.

Wally Cox, who starred in the popular comedy series *Mr. Peepers*, was the quintessential sissy. While he never made any direct mention of being homosexual, his character regularly extolled the virtues of men with the muscles and the macho that so completely eluded this quiet, reticent, and comic character.

Billy DeWolfe, Paul Lynde, Richard Deacon appeared as unmistakably gay types (although their homosexuality was never actually named) on *The Pruitts of Southampton*, which starred Phyllis Diller. Frank Nelson, whose effeminate character Freddie Filmore appeared on both *I Love Lucy* and *The Jack Benny Show*, became a familiar television figure, "portraying everything from dress salesmen to a waiter, but always responding with a wild-eyed 'Yee-e-es'" (Fejes and Petrich, 1993, p. 400).

Milton Berle similarly played with gender boundaries by appearing in drag as a regular part of his 1950s prime time television program, the *Show of Shows*.

Early dramatic portrayals of gays and lesbians were more overt and more hostile in their approach and also more infrequent. The detective show *N.Y.P.D.* was one of television's first dramas to take up a gay theme, doing so in 1969. The script described homosexuality as "an area of human activity feared and detested everywhere." That portrait and the few that followed were typically negative in the extreme (Russo, 1981, p. 224). But starting in the 1970s, programming started to become less restrictive and more daring.

ADVANCES AND RETREATS

In the 1970s, on the heals of the civil rights movement and in the midst of the antiwar and women's liberation movements, television programs and policies changed in significant ways. Several examples of gay and lesbian characters emerged in prime time and on talk shows, although here too the evidence suggests that in the face of audience objections the networks were quick to retreat.

By the early 1970s, the gay rights movement was becoming politically organized and active. One of the top priorities of the newly created National Gay Task Force was to lobby the television networks to avoid stereotypes and socially repugnant behaviors in their portrayals of homosexual characters (Montgomery, 1989). It was only in 1973 that American television offered its first sympathetic portrayal of homosexuality with the made-for-TV movie *That Certain Summer*, starring Hal Holbrook as a gay father coming out to his son (Henry, 1987, p. 43). A few other shows with homosexual themes followed in the late 1970s, but that abruptly changed in 1980 when a more conservative national mood gave rise to the Moral Majority's campaign against television shows with too much sex and violence. ABC and CBS canceled their plans for four separate productions with gay themes, and NBC revamped its *Love, Sydney* sitcom to virtually eliminate any explicit reference to the main character's homosexuality (Levine, 1984, pp. 225-26).

By the second half of the 1980s, network attitudes appeared to be shifting once again, this time toward a more liberal approach to both language and story themes. Lesbian characters, always a rarity in the past, were no longer invisible. Starting in the mid-1980s, lesbian characters and story lines began their fictional coming out, the result at least in part of a changing institutional context in which what was once taboo became potentially viable and sellable. *Golden Girls, Kate and Allie, LA Law, Hill Street Blues, Moonlighting, Hunter* and *Hotel*—some of the most popular shows of the 1980s—all had episodes with lesbian characters. *My Two Loves*, an ABC Monday Night Movie, explored in uncommonly explicit visual detail two women involved in a love affair. In addition, ABC introduced *HeartBeat* in the spring of 1988. The hour-long dramatic series about a women's medical group featured actress Gail Strickland as Marilyn McGrath. Her role as an older woman, a nurse-practitioner, a mother, and a lesbian no doubt gave her considerable demographic appeal. After its initial six-episode spring run, ABC renewed the show and put it on its fall 1988 schedule. Because of lackluster ratings, the show was canceled in 1989 and subsequently appeared in reruns on the Lifetime cable channel.

At the same time, however, New Right religious groups began organizing once again to clean up American entertainment television. One of their chief targets was the positive television portrayal of homosexuality, something they regard as an insult to family values (Moritz, 1990). And indeed when the popular drama *thirtysomething* showed a gay character talking in bed with another man, thus implying that the men had spent the night together ("the first time homosexuals have been seen in bed together on a prime time TV series"), advertisers pulled $1.5 million in commercials, and ABC reportedly received 400 phone calls from viewers, most of which were critical (Ross, 1989, p. C9).

Just how do shows with gay and lesbian characters and story lines get created and aired? The answer lies in the complex interplay of producers, network executives, and advocacy group members—all key players in the production process.

IDENTIFYING THE KEY PLAYERS

The creation of any prime time television show for an American commercial network typically begins on the so-called creative side. Producers and writers are central to the process of script creation, even if the idea for a show originates among network programmers or business executives. It is estimated that more than 1,000 ideas for new shows are considered each season by each network. Of those, about 125 become serious contenders for production, with only 25 actually produced as pilots (CBS video, *Making Television*).

Once a show is in production, it is the team of producers and writers that develops story lines and ultimately produces scripts. Their power over the show's content and direction is such that they have been referred to as "the princes of television ... little gods." Writer-producer Alan Burns, who with James Brooks created and developed *The Mary Tyler Moore Show*, is one of many insiders who has described television as a producer's medium. Some shows, including past examples such as *The Mary Tyler Moore Show, Dear John* and *The Golden Girls*, will have one or more person at the helm who functions both as a writer and a producer, and this writer-producer is the most potent person on a television set.

The authority and control of writers, producers, and writer-producers has its limits. Each network has a department of "Standards and Practices" or "License and Standards" that also claims at least a degree of authority and control over any show's visual and written content, with the exception of material emanating from news departments. In theory, the standards representatives have ultimate veto power over scripts. In practice, however, their power is often successfully challenged by the creative team, particularly by those individuals who have impressive track records in the industry. In reality, then, the process often is one of negotiation between standards and program creators.

While standards representatives may have some impact on any given production, it is important to recognize that standards people do not create shows, write scripts, or submit ideas for development. They do not generate material. Instead, they respond to material that is generated elsewhere, typically from the writer and producer teams. Nonetheless, they are also important cultural interpreters. Gitlin calls standards departments "political brokerages, antennae always thrust into the wind for trends" (Gitlin, 1983, p. 248). As Newcomb and Hirsch point out:

> Perhaps as much as any individual or group they present us with a source of rich material for analysis. They are actively engaged in gauging cultural values. . . . In determining who is doing what, with whom, at what times, they are interpreting social behavior in America and assigning it meaning. They are using television as a cultural litmus that can be applied in defining such problematic concepts as "childhood," "family," "maturity," and "appropriate" (Newcomb and Hirsch, p. 70).

In addition to negotiating with producers and writers, one of the chief responsibilities of executives in the standards offices is to negotiate with special interest groups that Newcomb and Hirsch also cite as significant in the creation of the television text. "We see these groups as metaphoric 'fault lines' in American society. Television is the terrain in which the faults are expressed and worked out" (Newcomb and Hirsch, p. 69).

Gitlin concluded that as early as the 1970s television had become a "contested zone" where various groups fought over ideological representations (Gitlin, p. 248). Montgomery's study of advocacy groups reported that while all mass media have been targeted by special interests, no medium had been more heavily bombarded with demands than television.

> Motion pictures, comic books, plays, newspapers, and textbooks have been subjected to pressure. But prime time television has far surpassed all of these as a focus of protest. No other medium has experienced as much pressure from as many organized groups for as long a period of time. . . . By the early eighties more than 250 advocacy groups had been involved in efforts to change network television (Montgomery, 1989, p. 6).

GAY ADVOCACY GROUPS

The creation of television advocacy or pressure groups began with a landmark challenge mounted in 1964 by black civil rights activists to the license of station MLTB in Jackson, Mississippi. The groups accused the station of discriminating against blacks in both hiring and programming policies. After the groups engaged in a lengthy battle with the Federal Communications Commission, the matter went to court.

> In 1966, the U.S. Court of Appeals for the District of Columbia ruled that the FCC had to grant these groups a hearing. This historic decision meant that the petition to deny could now be used as a weapon against station licensee. . . . Out of this landmark case emerged a movement committed to reforming television. Media watchdog groups began to spring up around the country. Many of them represented those disenfranchised segments of American society that had begun to mobilize in the wake of the civil rights movement: Hispanics, women, homosexuals (Montgomery, 1989, pp. 23-24).

The gay rights movement in the United\States drew wide attention with the Stonewall Riots in1969, when New York City police raided a Greenwich Village bar frequented by homosexuals. Angered by long-standing police harassment, patrons responded with a full-scale revolt, and the uprising marked a turning point in the effort to organize gays to work for political and social change (Barron, 1989, p. 1, 19). After Stonewall,

> gay voices publicly entered the ideological struggle for social acceptance and legitimation within the mainstream discourse. Using their newfound activism, gay liberationists attacked outright negative representations of gay men and lesbians, including those found in fictional television programming (Buxton, pp. 2-3).

Formed in 1974, the National Gay Task Force (NGTF), for example, was created in part to lobby the television networks to avoid stereotypes and socially repugnant behaviors in their portrayals of homosexual characters (Montgomery, pp. 75-100). Activists had already succeeded in getting the American Psychiatric Association to remove homosexuality from its list of mental illnesses. But television show creators, when willing to portray homosexuals at all, had not gotten the message (Montgomery, p. 82).

The popular medical drama *Marcus Welby, M.D.,* took up the topic of homosexuality in 1973 with an episode entitled "The Other Martin Loring." In that program, a gay character goes to Dr. Welby for advice on dealing with his homosexual tendencies and is assured that "as long as he suppressed his homosexual desires, he would not fail as a husband and father" (Montgomery, p. 79). The following year, another *Welby* episode, "The Outrage,'' focused on a gay teacher who molests a teenage boy. ABC showed a copy of that script to members of NGTF, asking for comments on language choices.

> a story line that appeared negotiable to the executives proved to be unacceptable to the activists. The very premise of the episode—tying homosexuality to child molestation—was a prime example of what gay activists wanted to eliminate from the mass media (Montgomery, p. 80).

When ABC refused to cancel the production, NGTF mounted a massive campaign against the network and its affiliates. Ultimately, five local stations refused to carry the program, seven advertisers withdrew their commercial support, and the program lost money for ABC. The APA came out publicly against the show, as did the National Education Association. Although ABC refused to cancel the show, it re-shot several scenes and later agreed that it would not rerun the episode (Montgomery, pp. 80-85).

The incident demonstrated to the gay lobby how to influence all the networks most effectively. NGTF, for example, developed a list of the negative television images it wanted eliminated from networks. These included depictions of gay men as effeminate and lesbians as masculine and the linking of homosexuality with a variety of criminal and pathological behaviors including child molesting, sexual promiscuity, and mental illness (Montgomery, p. 89; Buxton, p. 6).

In a number of dramatic depictions, critics had found that gays and lesbians often were characterized as "developmentally retarded," thus opening the way for their "cure" or movement toward maturity, meaning becoming heterosexual, as the story line progresses. *Soap Opera Weekly*'s recapitulation of a lesbian plot line in *The Young and the Restless* illustrates the point.

> Bible-thumping Brock Reynolds (Beau Kayzer) stopped the women's vacation to Hawaii, saying it was "unnatural," among other choice language. Then Brock told Joann's estranged husband Jack about the situation and Jack took Joann to bed and "cured" her.
> Call it the Big Bang theory (Wolf and Kielwasser, 1991, p. 8).

Early television depictions of homosexuality repeatedly were "linked to promiscuity, immorality, and 'all sorts of sleazy subjects,' even 'bloody violence'" (Wolf and Kielwasser, p. 9). Such linkage provided a technique for building dramatic appeal. The so-called spider woman approach is one example of how the process worked in the early 1970s to create texts that relied on negative stereotypes for impact:

> One of the worst of these shows, an episode of *Police Woman* called "Flowers of Evil," about three lesbians who murdered patients in their old age home ("I know what a love like yours can do to someone," Angie Dickinson told

the trio when she busted them), prompted one of the first organized gay "zaps" at the networks. A group of lesbians, one a mother with her children, held a sit-in at the offices of the NBC top brass, during which the little tykes expressed their sentiments by parading through the executive washroom. (Coincidentally or not, after that, gay groups generally found NBC more receptive than the other networks to their image-improving suggestions) (Levine, 1984, p. 226).

Nonetheless, more than a decade later, similar techniques were still in use. A 1986 episode of *Hunter* in which two lesbians play man-hating murderers offered a similarly negative portrayal and engendered another protest at NBC. Activists reported network executives claimed to have few script submissions that showed lesbians in a positive light, a claim the activists strongly rejected (Bryant, personal interview, 20 July 1987).

> I've seen good scripts submitted where the executives say, 'Change the two dykes into a man and a woman and we'll do the story.'. . . The networks say they don't think people will accept these shows. They say they get far more negative mail on them. But I think they themselves just are not comfortable with the whole topic (Deiter, personal interview, 25 October 1987).

Eventually, the gay lobby became institutionalized in network television, and protests were often replaced by the use of so-called "agents in place."

> According to gay activists, there were a substantial number of gay people working in the television industry who were not open about their life-style. Some held high level positions. While unable to promote the gay cause on the inside, they could be very helpful to gay advocates on the outside, especially by leaking information (Montgomery, p. 78).

At the start of the 1980s, industry executives themselves reported that pressure groups had become a fully established part of the industry landscape (Montgomery, pp. 6, 95). While early dramatic portrayals were objectionable because they focused on homosexuality as deviant behavior, later depictions—no doubt at least in part in response to lobbying efforts by gay and lesbian right groups—moved toward a more "balanced" approach. Yet critical battles still lay ahead.

EPISODIC VS. REGULAR CHARACTERS

One of the strongest and most persistent objections to early network depictions of lesbians and gays was their transient status in terms of episodic or serial prime time television. Unlike most of television's fictional characters, lesbian and gay characters who were being presented more frequently as the 1970s wore on rarely lasted beyond a single episode. They were, with only a few exceptions, episodic; the gay or lesbian character would appear one time only as contrasted to regular cast members who appear on every episode and to recurring characters who appear occasionally over the course of a series or who appear regularly for several episodes as part of an arcing storyline (Buxton, p. 12). In their roles as episodic characters, television's fictional lesbians

and gays typically functioned to explain sexual otherness to the straight characters (Wolf and Kielwasser, p. 30; Montgomery, p. 74; Buxton, p. 9).

In the majority of these instances, gay characters are the episodic "problem" which upsets narrative stability and instigates conflict among a show's regular cast. Series such as *All in the Family, The Mary Tyler Moore Show, Alice, Medical Center* and *The Rockford Files* used gay characters. External to the constellation of regular characters populating these series, episodic characters are [an] outside phenomenon to which the regulars react and readjust in order to reinstate narrative stability. In their earliest incarnations as episodic plot devices, gay characters provided motivation for heterosexual characters to discuss sexual "otherness."

Because they were used as problems to initiate narrative conflict, gay characters were often presented at best as self-destructive and at worst as evil (Buxton, pp. 5-6).

In fact, NGTF, the Gay Media Task Force, and other pressure groups all had longstanding requests before the networks for the initiation of gay and lesbian characters as regular cast members. The rationale being that in this way, fictional gays and lesbians would no longer be the outside problem, but rather they would provide a position from which to examine both homosexuality and heterosexuality.

> In many ways, the regular gay character functions to naturalize sexual "otherness" within the domain of mainstream television narratives and allows that "otherness" to speak for itself. With gay characters incorporated into the ensemble, sexual differences (which diverge from gender differences) form an ongoing subtext of that television series which continue to threaten both narrative and ideological stability (Buxton, p. 14).

A few serial programs, including *Soap, The Nancy Walker Show*, and *Love, Sidney* attempted to incorporate continuing gay characters into the regular cast. In all three cases, the characters drew strong objections from both pro-gay and anti-gay pressure groups. The Jodie Dallas character in *Soap*, for example,

> offended both gay activists and moral conservatives. After the airing of the first few episodes, the stereotypical elements of the character were modified suiting gay activists and overt outrageous sexual behavior (at least on the part of Jodie Dallas) was toned down. To a great degree this stifled conservative objections as well. Other early sit-coms with regular gay characters were short lived. *Love, Sidney* originally centered upon an overtly gay character, but due to pressure from conservative forces, his gayness became less than incidental— it disappeared completely. . . . Even if the *Nancy Walker* show had been successful, gay activists found the (gay) representation too stereotypical: limp-wristed and swishy (Buxton, pp. 12-13).

Following those early efforts, *Dynasty, Hooperman, HeartBeat*, and the daytime soap opera *As The World Turns* all incorporated gay characters into their ensemble casts, *HeartBeat* being the first to do so with a lesbian character. With the exception of the Steven Carrington character in *Dynasty*, all of them were "comfortably reconciled with their sexuality . . . [which] is no longer a problem for the gay character." Even in the *Dynasty* case,

> the gay subplots perform a pivotal role in critiquing the power of a heterosexual patriarchy. When Blake Carrington stood trial for the death of his son's gay lover, Steven Carrington's homosexuality fueled much of the melodramatic conflict. The courtroom melodrama became important because it provided the ideological space for Steven to critique his father's homophobia, patriarchal dominance and sense of socially constructed gender roles—not from one out of a variety of heterosexual positions, but from that of a gay man (Buxton, pp. 13-14).

In the 1980s, recurring gay characters appeared in *Barney Miller, thirtysomething, Hill St. Blues*, and *The Tracey Ullman Show,* and these characters, far more so than episodic ones, allowed for an expanded discussion of sexuality. The regular gay character in *Hooperman* and the regular lesbian character in *HeartBeat* even went beyond these other characters in their attempts to "naturalize gay lifestyles." In *Hooperman*, Officer Silardi was not only gay, he was the "bastion of sexual normalcy" while his straight counterparts were

> defined as deviant through incidents of sexual discipline, voyeurism, and harassment. At times gay oppression does surface as the narrative focal point. This happens especially when Silardi's narrative function shifts from a subtextual position to the surface narrative. When this occurs, it is the homophobic heterosexual male disrupting the aura of sexual tolerance and acceptance who is defined as the "problem" and not the gay character (Buxton, pp. 14-15).

While *Hooperman* naturalized gayness in the professional sphere, *HeartBeat* naturalized lesbianism in both the professional and the domestic realm. Here the lesbian character was seen as facing the same kinds of problems as her straight colleagues, and this opened up a discussion of alternative sexual behavior.

Yet some aspects of alternative sexual behavior were still clearly problematic:

> Representation of gays and lesbians on television is still marked by the absence of any overt signs of homosexual affection. . . . [C]haracters are still routinely denied expression of such minimal acts of affection and love (as kissing) (Wolf and Kielwasser, p. 30).

If that standard is breached, as it was in the episode of *thirtysomething*, typically there has then followed public reaction from producers, censors, actors, network executives and audience members involved with the particular show. This was the case with an episode of *Roseanne* in which the show's star visits a gay bar and is kissed by Mariel Hemingway, who is playing a lesbian character. After the show was taped, ABC initially refused to give it an air date. Roseanne responded with a talk show blitz in which she threatened to pull the entire series—a consistent top ten ratings draw at the time—off the network unless "The Kiss" was run. The network backed down and the show aired in markets across the country, but not without considerable debate on

talk shows, in newspapers and news magazines, by columnists, by consumers, by the pro-gay lobby and the anti-gay lobby.

RECUPERATION AND GAY CHARACTERS

Media critics use the term recuperation to describe a narrative strategy in which characters who have violated long-standing social norms are dealt with in the story's conclusion. Fictional portrayals of women in 1970s film and television routinely followed this formula. Female characters who deviated from their roles as wives and mothers typically would be recuperated into a more acceptable space. "Often narrative closure itself seems to necessitate the resolution of problems and ambiguities brought up by the desire of women characters to go to work, to be sexual beings, or both. The end of the story becomes the solution of that story when the woman is returned to her 'proper' place, i.e., with her husband, at home" (Walker, 1982, p. 167).

While other narrative closures for these kinds of liberation stories did exist, they ran a narrow range. Feminist film critic Annette Kuhn suggested that recuperation is inevitable and is accomplished "thematically in a limited number of ways: a woman character may be restored to the family by falling in love, by 'getting her man,' by getting married, or otherwise accepting a 'normative' female role. If not, she may be directly punished for her narrative and social transgression by exclusion, outlawing or even death" (Kuhn, 1982, p. 34).

This strategy has been routinely applied to gay characters since they began appearing on television. An episode of the 1980s detective series, *Hunter,* offers an example of recuperation to bring about narrative closure. In "From San Francisco with Love," the macho Los Angeles cop for whom the series is named unravels the murders of a millionaire and his son. As the story unfolds, Hunter realizes that a fellow cop, Sgt. Valerie Foster, is the lesbian lover of the millionaire's very young and sexy widow. Together, the women plan on getting away with murder and an $80 million fortune. Eventually, Hunter uncovers the sordid scheme and both women are caught and brought to justice.

The recuperation in this story ending is both unambiguous and complete. The characters have transgressed by being lesbians and murderers. They obviously are beyond restoration to a "normative" female role. For these actions, they must and will be removed from society and properly punished.

This episode of *Hunter* was considered to portray lesbians so negatively that it drew a protest at the time it aired from the Alliance of Gay and Lesbian Artists (AGLA), an activist group based in Los Angeles. "The network realized why (we protested) and afterwards came to us and asked us to submit scripts (that would be acceptable to the group)," according to AGLA member Jill Blacher (Moritz, 1988, p. 11).

An episode of the prime-time dramatic series *Hotel* took a far different approach to its narrative closure, but the recuperation of its lesbian subjects was no less complete. Here the sexual involvement of hotel co-workers Carol Bowman and Joanne Lambert comes out only after Joanne tragically dies in a car crash. Carol is left not only to grieve her lost mate but also to deal with Joanne's father, who comes from the East Coast to take home his daughter's body and her personal effects. The father has no idea that his daughter has been living with a female lover, but he finds out when a hotel attendant brings him a package from his daughter's employee locker that is addressed to him. The package contains a videotape that he watches from his suite.

Joanne *(on videotape):* Happy birthday, Dad. My gift to you this year is a heart to heart talk, at least my half of it. I know it's never been easy between us. . . . I know you never meant to be so stern, so unapproachable. . . . (Carol and I have) been together for six years now, Dad. Like they say, I guess it must be love.

Enraged, the father now storms into the office of the hotel's top executive, Mr. McDermott, and accuses Carol Bowman of corrupting his daughter.

Lambert to McDermott: My daughter was always a good girl. Unfortunately, she and I were not very close. At home, she was rather shy, quiet. I always felt she was too easily led, influenced by others. One of her friends, a member of your staff, took advantage of Joanne, corrupted her. . . . Whatever our problems might have been at home, my daughter was not abnormal. She dated a great deal. She was not interested in other women.

McDermott: Why are you telling me this?

Lambert: Good Lord, man, isn't it obvious. This Bowman woman works with the public every single day representing you and your hotel.

McDermott: What do you want me to do? Fire her?

Lambert: You certainly aren't going to leave her in a position of being able to prey on other unsuspecting young women.

Given Mr. Lambert's distinct disapproval, Carol Bowman decides that he can have everything and that she will be satisfied with her memories. In the final scene, we see Carol and Mr. Lambert packing up Joanne's things. When Mr. Lambert finds a doll that he gave his daughter at age five, he begins to cry, and Carol comes to his side to comfort him.

Mr. Lambert: Maybe you're right. Maybe memories are the most important things. I was always a better talker than a listener. . . . Maybe it's time I started listening a little.

Carol: What do you mean?

Mr. Lambert: You're the only one who can help me fill in all the blanks. Keep what's important to you. . . . Just do me a favor. Just take me through them, tell me what they meant . . . and maybe I can understand who Joanne grew up to be while I wasn't looking.

They embrace and the camera begins a long, slow pullout from above, suggesting the heavenly presence of the deceased daughter. This narrative closure is ambiguous in that it does offer a degree of hope and acceptance for the lesbian lover. The irate father does after all admit that he wants and needs to know about his daughter's life, and that he will rely on her lover to give him that very personal information. Even though the daughter and her lover both are granted a measure of acceptance, that happens only after their relationship has been irrevocably terminated. The daughter

is recuperated by virtue of her ultimate exclusion (death), and her lover is restored only now that she no longer is in the illicit relationship. In other words, the terms of their acceptance are based on their separation by death.

A DECADE OF CHANGE

Soap operas routinely present heterosexual acts of intimacy on a daily basis, and dramas do much the same in prime time, yet the limits of physical expression for gay characters on all television remains a contested issue. Nonetheless, it is clear that gay characters and story lines have attained a prominence on contemporary television. Several factors that coalesced in the 1980s help explain this growing visibility. The emergence of AIDS, regulatory and ratings changes, the increasing popularity of cable television and home VCRs and its negative implications for network audience share, the demonstrated commercial viability of gay-themed material in other mass media, and the appeal of emerging social issues in general as a backdrop for broadcast productions all have contributed to the creation of a climate in which homosexuality emerged on American television.

The Impact of AIDS

When asked about future programming decisions designed to keep his network in first place, Brandon Tartikoff, then president of NBC Entertainment, cited "lack of predictability" and "contemporariness" as two "essential" ingredients for success in new prime time programs. "The audience now has 35 years of television-watching behind them. TV shows no longer go away. They're just on earlier or later, but they're still on. That audience has seen those story lines over and over again. We have to avoid the predictable; we have to find new wrinkles to the old tales" (Tartikoff, 1987, p. 57).

In fact, the emergence of AIDS in the early 1980s offered the television networks an issue that was topical, socially relevant, and never before explored. Yet precisely because homosexual relations had only rarely been explored by either the news or the entertainment industries, and because homosexuals were linked to the disease from its inception, AIDS proved highly problematic for fictional television. Despite their own insistence that networks were striving to be socially relevant and contemporary, no network took up the topic of AIDS in a prime time drama until NBC offered the made-for-TV movie *An Early Frost* in late 1985.

The problem clearly was not lack of social relevance or of topicality. AIDS was a social issue of the greatest import. But here we see an instance in which the description of network executives about what they were looking for in television programming ran counter to their actions. The networks indeed very often take on topical, socially relevant issues. The problem in the instance of AIDS was that relevance and topicality ran counter to what Sylvia Law, a legal scholar who has studied the civil rights of homosexuals, calls a "cultural contempt for homosexuals. Seventy percent of the population believes homosexuality is wrong. Sex education either ignores homosexuality or presents inaccurate information. The media offers no gay Cosby" (Law, 1989).

The script for *An Early Frost*, for example, reportedly went through 12 re-writes and several production postponements while NBC executives pondered the wisdom of doing the show at all. By the summer of 1985, the show was given a January 1986 air date. But that same summer, Rock Hudson died of AIDS, and

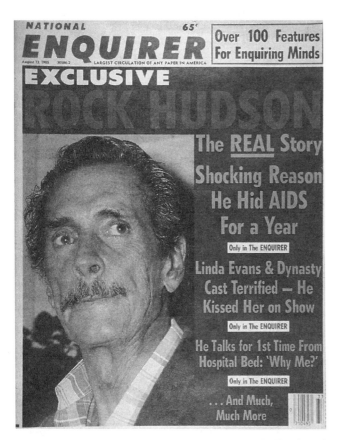

Rock Hudson's death from AIDS in 1985 dramatically altered media coverage of the disease.

the treatment of these topics, however, as Russo and others have argued, is oriented toward the implications of these issues for white, middle-class America (Russo, 1985). In dramatic presentations particularly, scripts often rely on ambiguous endings in an effort to avoid alienating audiences.

Constructed in this way, television shows can tap into dramatic subjects and capitalize on their currency, getting ratings without risking audience retribution. By the mid-1980s, when AIDS began to appear in television programs, audiences had already come to expect TV to cover controversial and sensitive social issues. A 1984 Epcot Poll for *TV Guide,* for example, asked 47,000 respondents if topics such as rape and incest should be covered on TV. Close to 80 percent said yes, 7 percent said they would place no restrictions on TV fare, and 46 percent said such shows should carry warnings to parents (Lipton, 1984, p. 6).

And audiences were backing up those views with their viewership. *The Burning Bed*, starring Farrah Fawcett as a battered wife, was the fourth highest rated TV movie on record when it aired. TV movies with homosexual themes including *An Early Frost* and *Consenting Adult* also did well in the ratings. Both advertisers and network programmers responded accordingly.

> Advertisers who once shied away from controversial or downbeat programs (like ABC's nuclear-war movie *The Day After*) are increasingly willing, even eager, to sponsor them. Moreover, in the face of growing competition from cable, social-issue dramas take on a new programming significance. Explains Perry Lafferty, a senior vice president at NBC: "How do the networks fight back against cable? We can't do it by putting on more sex and violence, but we can probe the social issues that haven't been explored" (Zoglin, 1985, p. 65).

Certainly gay lifestyles fell into the "haven't been explored" category when it came to prime time TV. While this began to change, it is important to note that the pace and shape of that change was determined by a system that reinforces mainstream cultural values. According to Hall, the picture of social reality created by television is not designed to accurately reflect subcultures as much as to incorporate them into the cultural framework so that they no longer constitute a challenge. The effect is to mask the contradictions in the system, to fragment the subgroups and keep them from forming a unified force, and to present the illusion of unity within the system (Hall, p. 337). In short, following the death of Rock Hudson, gay portrayals began showing up more frequently, but the portrayals themselves were designed by industry image-makers for mainstream audiences.

Gay activists are unanimous in saying that AIDS resulted in far more television coverage of homosexual men than would have been the case had the disease never existed. This increased visibility, not only in television but in all mass media, resulted in increased public awareness of gays and gay issues.

Yet the AIDS coverage had its negative side, particularly for lesbians. Portrayals of homosexual men became almost routinely linked to an AIDS story line. The tendency was "to equate stories about AIDS with stories on gay life generally" (Bryant interview). The networks then argued that they were meeting their responsibility to the entire gay community when in fact their coverage was heavily weighted toward gay men and largely focused on AIDS.

Meantime, the gay community itself was becoming less involved in media portrayals, precisely because of AIDS. The Gay Media

NBC's "hot potato was a hot item with hit potential. NBC sped up the production schedule and gave the film a new air date in one of the November 'sweeps' weeks, when vital ratings data are gathered" (Russo, 1985, p. 6). It was not until the death of Hudson, the quintessential Hollywood romantic lead and a cultural symbol of masculinity, thrust the AIDS story onto the front pages of magazines and newspapers around the world that network television showed heightened interest in treating the topic. Now the subject of AIDS was not only topical and relevant, but the attention it got in other media made it socially acceptable for the public discourse of television. Since then, dozens of dramatic presentations, news reports, talk shows, and documentaries have been done by both network and local stations, all on the topic of AIDS.

Gay activists have gone on record saying that most of television's AIDS portrayals have been sympathetic. Comments such as "very well handled," "extremely well done," "to be commended for its support of the gay relationship," are typical of those in the AGLA Media Watch notations that accompany listings of shows about homosexuals suffering from AIDS. In the case of *An Early Frost*, AGLA members actually passed out leaflets urging people to watch the program after NBC showed them an advance screening. Following the regular broadcast, more than 7,000 letters of support were sent to the network.

The networks can, when the circumstances are ripe, cash in on new, topical, and sometimes controversial themes, including homosexual ones. The viewing public is apparently quite willing to be both entertained by and informed about controversial issues;

Task Force says activism focusing on TV images dropped off just when progress was being made.

> the networks were listening. We got more and more ability to give them input. Always our concern was for television portrayals. Today . . . people (in the gay community) are more concerned with AIDS. Image isn't as high a priority. It's gone far beyond that (Deiter interview).

The negative implications for lesbian portrayals on television are fairly obvious. First, intense focus on AIDS effectively captured center stage and took the spotlight away from other issues that might relate more directly to lesbians' lives. In addition, the consequent linking of AIDS to homosexuality in general created a negative social climate for lesbians perhaps just as much as for gay men. Ironically, lesbians are among the lowest risk groups for the disease, yet this distinction is frequently ignored: the vast majority of information about AIDS links it to "homosexuals" in general. As a result, lesbians may have been inaccurately represented as transmitters of a disease that rarely afflicts them.

Regulations, Ratings, Technologies

As the television industry evolved, a wide array of change involving regulations, ratings, and emerging technologies also contributed to an increase in gay visibility. Imposition of the Prime Time Access Rule is a case in point. In effect, this move required the networks to relinquish the actual production of prime time programs. Media historians have argued that the emergence of independent production companies ultimately worked to create a more "hospitable production environment" for shows with gay and lesbian themes.

> the networks turned to independent producers such as Norman Lear's Tandem Productions and MTM Enterprises, Inc. for programming. As it turned out, these program producers were willing to address subject material, including homosexuality, that had previously been ignored by programming in which the networks had a direct financial interest (Buxton, 1989, pp. 1-2).

At the same time, increasingly sophisticated analyses of ratings data proved an additional reason for the emergence of lesbian and gay themes along with other controversial topics. Specifically, for the first time in the mid-1970s,

> undifferentiated mass numbers as the basis for advertising rates gave way to the first wave of demographic marketing towards an urban rather than a rural audience. In conjunction with the moxie of independent program producers, explicit gay characters began to surface in fictional broadcasting programming because urban viewers, at least in the perception of the networks, were less inclined to take offense over the inclusion of controversial topics (Buxton)."

By the 1980s, network programming executives were under intense competitive pressure for audience share. The swift and deep penetration of both cable television and home VCR systems were shrinking network viewership. At the end of the 1989 spring viewing season, the three networks claimed 67.4 percent of the prime time viewing audience, marking the first time the combined network audience share fell below 70 percent, a downward trend that has continued into the 1990s ("Three-Network Viewing Falls Below 70%," *Broadcasting*, 1989, p. 29).

As the audience for network programs was declining, the audience for advertiser-supported cable television was growing rapidly throughout the 1980s. "The Cabletelevision Advertising Bureau said average weekly viewing to basic cable networks rose 17 percent in the fourth quarter of 1988 ... for a total share of 26" ("Fourth Quarter Viewing Patterns," *Broadcasting*, 1989, p. 50). One of the reasons for the growth of cable may be found in audience perceptions of cable programming. The 16th biennial study of Americans' attitudes toward television, conducted by the Roper Organization for the Television Information Office (TIO), showed that Americans were ranking cable as superior to network television in terms of quality and variety of programming.

> Forty-seven percent of respondents to the latest poll said that cable TV had better entertainment programs than "regular TV" (defined in the poll as networks and independent stations). Twenty-six percent said that regular television had better entertainment programs, while 16 percent rated both media as equally good. By similar majorities, respondents associated cable television with a greater amount of educational, sports and cultural programming. By a greater margin, respondents also said cable TV programming had more sex, violence and profanity (Cable Comes on Strong in Last TIO Roper Poll," *Broadcasting*, 1989, p. 1).

A similar pattern with advertising revenue migrating from the networks to cable outlets was also evident. In the first quarter of 1989, advertising sales for national cable networks were up 40 percent over 1988 first quarter figures, according to Arbitron Ratings Company's Broadcast Advertiser Reports. At the same time, Arbitron reported a cumulative loss of advertising sales by the three commercial networks. Total sales at ABC, CBS, and NBC in the first quarter of 1989 were down 7.7 percent compared to the year earlier figure. Robert Alter, president of CAB, attributed the impressive cable sales increases to "increased penetration, larger audience share and the medium's general acceptance by agency planners as part of the overall media mix" (Terranova, 1989, p. 6).

Broadcasting, meantime, was reporting that industry experts predicted similar growth trends in the years to come, saying that they expected advertising revenues at the networks to run from zero to 2 percent ahead of 1988 figures. Given their projected inflation rate of 4.5 percent to 5.5 percent, the networks would actually be losing financial ground. Cable advertising, however, was expected to be among "the fastest growing segments in the industry" ("Cable, Syndication Advertising Expected to Be Fastest Growing Segments of TV Industry in '89," *Broadcasting*, 1989, p. 50).

With other alternative forms of entertainment, such as home VCRs, becoming increasingly appealing and available to audiences, network television found itself in a relatively marginalized position. Under those circumstances, industry executives were keenly aware of other programming successes.

Cable television and cinema both were demonstrating that gay themes could be money in the bank. *Variety*, for example, offered this full page headline in April 1986: "Gay-Themed Features Hot B. O. Stuff." The report said that four films, including the lesbian love story *Desert Hearts,* were doing "brisk business in the New York market and elsewhere among arthouse audiences." (The others were *My Beautiful Launderette, Parting Glances,* and *Dona Herlinda and Her Son,* all films featuring male homosexual relations.) The report went on to say that the movies all appealed to straight as well as gay audiences.

> Distributors, exhibitors and filmmakers say the turnout for these films reflects mainstream acceptance of homosexual lifestyles and a willingness among audiences to recognize 'universal' elements in gay love stories. The gay-themed pics also demonstrate the ability of filmmakers and distributors to decisively address cinematic subject matter that's avoided or handled cautiously by the Hollywood majors (Gold, 1986, p. 5).

An editor of the gay-oriented *New York Advocate* wrote at the time that widespread support for the films demonstrated a growing awareness of homosexuals and a merging of their concerns with those of the larger community. The director of *Desert Hearts,* Donna Deitch, said her film's initial robust reception demonstrated that audiences "are open to and interested in this sort of relationship and find it interesting to see" (Gold).

Cable television provided a similar example of success with Showtime's *Brothers,* a sitcom about three brothers, two straight and one gay, and their efforts to understand each other. The cable company reported that the show was a hit, one of the most popular programs offered on the service. In May 1986, Showtime expressed its faith in the long-term success of *Brothers* by ordering 50 new episodes, something *TV Guide* called "a rare move in an industry that counts a 22-episode order a huge vote of confidence" (Newton, 1986, p. 26). In addition, the show was sold to stations in Australia, England, Italy, and Canada. When it began playing in Toronto in February 1986, CITY-TV called the viewer response "phenomenal," generating 100 letters and 200 phone calls with "only about five negative" reactions (Newton, p. 28). This kind of viewer support and accompanying commercial success was not missed in the offices of network executives who were seeing topical, relevant, and previously untreated social issues as a way of competing for the cable audience.

While network television may not have been willing to take the lead in pushing boundaries, it could not afford to ignore the cultural shifts that inevitably take place in society and the way those shifts are represented by other mass media outlets. "[N]on-network popular talk shows such as *Donahue* and the *Oprah Winfrey Show* have presented programs on gay and lesbian topics that have allowed gays and lesbians to speak out on their own behalf. In addition, the Public Broadcasting System (PBS), National Public Radio (NPR), cable networks such as HBO, and public access cable have provided more exposure to gay and lesbian issues and concerns" (Fejes and Petrich). Newspapers and news magazines began to increase their coverage significantly as well. Thus, when gay rights became an important news and talk show topic, as it did during the 1992 election campaigns in Oregon and Colorado, and as it has during the ongoing debates over gays in the military, entertainment television could not help but sit up and take notice. In this sense, there is a continual interaction between fictionalized gays and lesbians and what might be called real ones. The important

point, however, is that both fictional and factual accounts are constructed in accordance with prevailing professional practices and embedded in an industry that is always impacted by social and cultural change, new technologies, and overriding economic imperatives.

THE 1990s: "A SEA CHANGE"

In April 1997, television history was made when the television sitcom *Ellen* had its central character declare that she was gay. At the same time, star Ellen DeGeneres announced in print and on televised accounts that she was not just playing a gay character but that she herself was gay as well. The combination of events turned into one of the biggest news stories of that year.

One poll that examines major television newsmagazines placed the DeGeneres coming out story third in importance in 1997, behind only the coverage of the death of Princess Diana and the murder of JonBenet Ramsey. A similar survey done by the *Philadelphia Daily News* showed readers evenly split between DeGeneres and Princess Diana in their opinions on "TV that rocked our world." Meantime, *TV Guide* placed DeGeneres third in its "Best of '97" selections, while *Time* called her coming out episode the second best television event of 1997. *People* magazine placed DeGeneres among its "25 Most Intriguing People of the Year," and Barbara Walters included her in ABC's annual special focusing on the ten most fascinating individuals of the year.

Ellen DeGeneres made headlines with her television character's—and her own—coming out in 1997.

Indeed, *Ellen* was groundbreaking, a major milestone for gay visibility in mass media. In a cover story about the *Ellen* phenomenon, *Time* explained the significance of the event this way:

Like Mary Richards before her, Ellen Morgan functions as her show's center, around whom the rest of the cast revolves—structurally, Ellen Morgan *is* Mary Richards, except she likes girls. She provides the window into the show's comedic world; she is the character we are asked to identify with, the person to whom we are asked to give tacit approval. That's why, in a country that still has a lot of conflicts about homosexuality, this formerly innocuous, intermittently funny series is now pushing buttons in a way that other shows with gay characters haven't (*Time*, 14 April 1997, p. 80-81).

The *Ellen* story was certainly the biggest gay media event of that year, one of the most noteworthy media events in a long list of cultural, social, legal, and economic developments that collectively helped propel gays and lesbian from virtual media invisibility to center stage. Indeed, the 1997 fall television schedule included a record-setting 30 lesbian, gay, and bisexual characters, up 23 percent from the 1996 number, which itself had set a record. The year 1997 also saw eight prime-time television shows with gay, lesbian, or bisexual characters nominated for the prestigious Golden Globe awards. As the 1990s, the so-called "Gay '90s," drew to a close, gays and lesbians had become a media presence in every television genre—talk shows, news, drama, sitcom, and soaps.

The 1990s saw the emergence of several recurring and regular characters in prime time. ABC's hit sitcom *Roseanne* introduced actor Martin Mull as Roseanne's gay boss, and later Sandra Bernhard joined the cast in the role of a bisexual. NBC's *Friends* included a lesbian couple and eventually a lesbian wedding. *Beverly Hills 90210* and *Melrose Place*, both created for Fox TV, regularly dealt with lesbian, gay, and AIDS themes. *One Life to Live* and *All My Children* broke new ground for soap operas by including ongoing gay characters.

Many of the shows that appeared in the 1990s worked toward redefining the family to include gay and lesbian parents. The lesbian couple on *Friends* had a baby, as did the character Norma on *Sisters*; on *Party of Five*, a gay male character adopted a child. And on *Courthouse*, audiences were introduced to television's first African-American lesbian couple, who are raising a family together.

What can we conclude about this new-found media visibility in the last decade of the 20th century? For one thing, the days of gay invisibility seem to be a thing of the past. Not only are there record numbers of gay characters on television, they are now in regular and recurring roles. In the case of *Ellen*, the long-hoped-for central character became a reality.

Yet, for the all positives associated with greater representation, there are ongoing concerns on the part of media critics and gay advocacy groups. In situation comedies, gratuitous gay jokes are now standard fare, often used to mark acceptable gender boundaries. Homosexuals, it has been argued, "'have become the new stock character, like the African-American pal at the workplace'" ("Roll Over, Ward Cleaver," 1997, p. 80). On talk shows, gays became a predictable presence, but in many cases, gay life is highly sensationalized in the talk format, and the central point of the discussion frequently is to have the presumably straight audience debate whether gayness itself is acceptable.

In fictional programming, narrative strategies are often predictable. One standard approach might be called mainstreaming. Here,

the gay characters are designed to be just the same as everyone else, which permits an erasure of gay difference. Recuperation is another narrative strategy that still has currency. The popular police drama *NYPD Blue* had a lesbian character in its ensemble cast. Over several episodes, viewers saw her at home with her lesbian lover and learned that the couple was going to have a baby. But before the happy event, the lesbian lover was murdered by a former lover, a lesbian who was a psychotic killer. When challenged about a script that seemed to repeat a reactionary pattern, the show's producers responded by saying that in the 1990s, there are sufficient positive depictions of gays to serve as balance.

In the 1990s as in the past, gay and lesbian characters on prime time network television for the most part are white and middle class. Interracial friendships are virtually nonexistent. One notable exception is the sitcom *Spin City*, which features a gay man who is also African American. Perhaps just as much as in the past, the visual remains the hot button issue for many viewers. It is far more problematic to have gay characters show up in the same bed, kiss, or even hold hands than it is for straight characters. One recent example is the made-for-TV movie about the life of Olympic diving champion Greg Louganis. Before *Breaking the Surface* aired on USA Network (19 March 1997), a number of media critics who had seen the film in previews "lamented the omission of any real same-sex intimacy" in the film. Typical was this comment by reviewer Renee Graham in the *Boston Globe*: "The same old tired rules apply when it comes to portraying a same-sex relationship—you won't see Greg and Tom exchange a kiss. But the network doesn't hesitate to show the violent aspects of their relationship. It's as if there's an unwritten 'You can kill him but you can't kiss him' policy when it comes to homosexual relationships. When is television going to finally grow up?" (*GLAADAlert*, 21 March 1997).

It still takes a powerful producer or star (Roseanne, Barbra Streisand) to push the TV envelope. In serial television, audiences still must be "prepared" for the shock of finding out that an important character is gay or lesbian. It wasn't until the third season of *Ellen* that ABC even considered a lesbian identity for the main character. And even then, the network continued to run disclaimers as subsequent episodes aired. Networks still rely on audience polls, many of which are now conducted on the Internet rather than carried out by researchers, to justify their timidity and to determine appropriate story content.

On public television, many stations in the PBS network have been highly supportive of gay issues. PBS itself has run critically acclaimed television movies with gay themes, including *The Lost Language of Cranes, Oranges Are Not the Only Fruit*, and the mini-series *Portrait of a Marriage* and *Tales of the City*. Nonetheless, its overall track record has been termed "an embarrassment." PBS executives, for example, insisted on cutting what it considered controversial lesbian scenes from *Portrait of a Marriage*, on electronically blocking out sexual images from *Tales of the City* and on withdrawing funding for the sequel. In addition, PBS refused to fund the documentary *Celluloid Closet* (based on the Vito Russo book about gays in Hollywood films) and refused to air the critically acclaimed documentary *Tongues Untied* by Marlon Riggs because of its sexual content and theme: it explored the lives of black, HIV-positive men in Harlem.

On radio, NPR (National Public Radio) has been in the forefront of covering gay and lesbian issues. News departments at commercial radio stations around the country have to a large extent also supported what the Gay & Lesbian Alliance Against

Defamation (GLAAD) has called "legitimate debate on lesbian and gay issues by holding panel discussions and roundtables on the air." But radio entertainment programming is still the source of intense criticism. Much of talk radio is designed "to shock and their verbal gay-bashing is clearly intended to arouse hatred." Such an approach is, according to GLAAD, "a common feature of programming on thousands of radio stations nationwide. . . . Truly remarkable is the lack of openly gay or lesbian disc jockeys on all radio stations. Instead, anti-gay speech has flourished on rock music programs, and lesbian and gay stereotypes are still standard fodder for radio DJs" (GLAAD, *Lesbian and Gay Images*, 1995, p. 25).

NEWS DEPICTIONS: THE STRAIGHT PRESS

News organizations, print and broadcast, never have been prohibited from writing and reporting on gays and lesbians. But unwritten news codes—those generally accepted definitions of what constitutes a story—for decades provided a powerful barrier to coverage of many minority groups, including gays and lesbians. Far from being independent, news codes flow out of the larger culture and reflect the attitudes and socioeconomic hierarchies in society at large. Despite journalistic claims that they don't make the news, they just report it, news organizations have a well-documented history of being selective, and biased, in their choice of

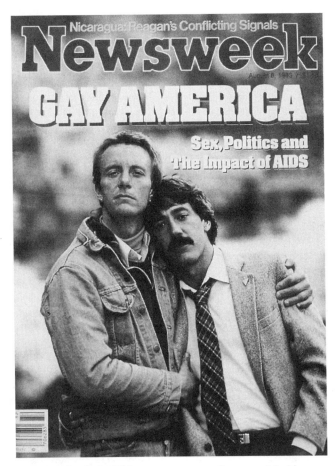

An example of straight press coverage of gays and lesbians.

news topics. "The works of Epstein, Gans, Tuchman and others have made it axiomatic that what mainstream journalism offers as 'news' is a highly selective text and that what it portrays as reality is highly constructed" (Moritz, 1992, p. 157).

Given that system, it is hardly surprising that gays and lesbians were not considered worthy of coverage well into the 1980s (Colby and Cook, 1989). In 1987, to cite one notorious case, both *Time* and *Newsweek* ignored the gay rights march in Washington, D.C., the largest civil rights demonstration in the capital since 1969 (Freiberg, 1993).

What coverage the incipient gay rights movement did get was often problematic. Before 1973, when the American Psychiatric Association removed homosexuality from its list of mental illnesses, the occasional news accounts that did exist often framed gayness as psychological sickness. Stories on gays and lesbians have a long history of being cast as "morality tales, with the homosexual being the negative reference point in a discourse that reaffirmed society's sense of what is normal" (Fejes and Petrich, p. 402). In the 1980s, news media attention focused on the emergence of AIDS and re-framed gays around their "'promiscuous and abnormal' sexual behavior and lifestyle. . . . A common news frame was to distinguish between the 'innocent' victim of AIDS, those who did not acquire the virus from gay sexual contact, and, implicitly, the 'guilty' victims of AIDS, those who did" (Fejes and Petrich, pp. 403-04).

As AIDS became *the* gay story of the 1980s, gayness became equated with deadly disease. Yet at the same time, the news organizations could point to their coverage of AIDS as satisfying gay advocates' demands for visibility; even in this instance, the coverage of the emerging epidemic was limited until the story of Rock Hudson's death from AIDS in 1985 sparked the first significant media response to the disease.

Ironically, the subtext of the Rock Hudson story was that AIDS might be infiltrating the straight world. "Now fears are growing that the AIDS epidemic may spread beyond gays and other high risk groups to threaten the population at large," *Newsweek* reported ("AIDS: Special Report," 1985). *Time* offered a similar narrative: "For years it has been dismissed as the 'gay plague,' somebody else's problem. Now, as the number of cases in the U.S. surpasses 12,000 and the fatal disease begins to strike the famous and the familiar, concern is growing that AIDS is a threat to everyone" ("The Frightening AIDS Epidemic Comes Out of the Closet," 1985).

While coverage of AIDS no doubt has had its negative implications, in some real ways, the epidemic also gave gays and (by implication and association) lesbians increased public visibility. "[I]t was not until the AIDS crisis that stories about individual gay men and lesbians—and the issues that concerned them—began to appear with regularity" (Freiberg, p. 55). In the 1990s, that trend has accelerated into what the gay and lesbian newspaper *Washington Blade* has described as an explosion of interest, a "radical departure" from news practices of even the late 1980s, a "sea change," like being on "a different planet" (Freiberg, p. 55). Even the formerly distant *New York Times* did an about-face, increasing its coverage of the gay and lesbian community by "65% from 1990 to 1991 and the paper began using the word 'gay' instead of 'homosexual'" (Fejes and Petrich, p. 405). Because of its impact as the national paper of record, this change has created "what many activists and media watchdogs assert is a 'ripple effect' on other media." In addition, as of 1993, the newly organized National Lesbian and Gay Journalists Association has attracted more than 1,000

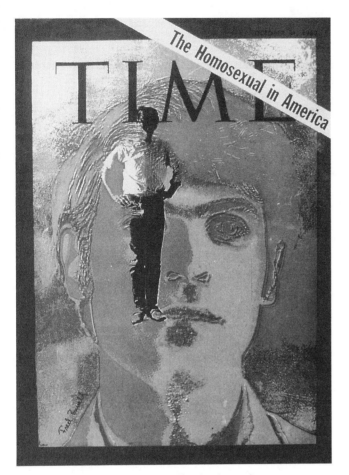

Further coverage of homosexuality in the mainstream press.

members in more than a dozen chapters around the country. Among its goals is increased visibility in newsrooms and in news content.

Despite vast improvements in news coverage of gay and lesbian issues, heterosexism remains a prevailing norm. In 1990, the American Society of Newspaper Editors (ASNE) decided for the first time to examine the coverage of gays and lesbians as well as the working conditions for gay and lesbian newsroom personnel. Its national survey gave the nation's newspapers "a grade of mediocre" on the issue of coverage and said that anti-gay attitudes remain "the last acceptable basis for discrimination among so-called acceptable Americans, including editors." While the study found newsrooms "largely hospitable" to gay and lesbian employees, it also noted "a palpable undercurrent of bias" (Aarons, 1990, p. 40).

In news coverage, that bias surfaces in a number of different ways. For example, contemporary news accounts increasingly are focused on issues of gay rights. But even as demands for equal protection are viewed as legitimate news, "the legitimacy" of those demands is still viewed as "questionable" (Fejes and Petrich). The ongoing media debate over the appropriateness of outing offers another example. Outing, after all, rests on the homophobic assumption that being identified as gay or lesbian is still a stigma. If it were not, then it would not be problematic to reveal any person's sexual orientation (Fejes and Petrich). News headlines in local papers still refer to "openly gay" individuals (Knopper, 1993, p. B4).

As recently as July 1993, well after the media flurry around gays in the military, the *Chicago Sun-Times,* a major metropolitan paper, felt the need to define "coming out" in an article about a gay newscaster (Williams, 1993, p. 2-1). And, while many newspapers have editorialized about lifting the ban on gays in the military, "they are often quick to point out that such support does not mean they 'endorse the gay lifestyle'" (Fejes and Petrich, p. 405).

The creation and selection of images to represent gays and lesbians represents another level of concern. In terms of mass media images, gay men have been limited to a few very stereotyped portrayals: hair dressers, floral designers, houseboys, men in black leather, men in baths, men in bars—often faceless, shown from the back or from an angle designed to obscure their faces—men in doctors' offices, in hospital beds, men with AIDS.

Lesbian images are far more rare on television and in print—just as images of women in general are far more rare than images of men in the media. The few lesbian images that have been featured over the years have relied on stereotypes that have included sadistic prison wardens, blood-sucking vampires, murderers, or, at the other extreme, asexual spinsters. Even today, our collective imagery does not include visual vocabulary that defines gay or lesbian.

In news, both still photos in print and moving images in television have been a point of contention. In their early attempts to depict gays and lesbians, journalists often utilized the bizarre to illustrate the homosexual look. News editors showing gay pride parades, for example, typically selected 20 seconds of footage that featured whips, chains, and bare breasts. Gay watchdog groups in cities around the country pressured television newsrooms to change. GLAAD still instructs media personnel on the issue. "Do not show or describe only the most unconventional members of our community. There is nothing wrong with unconventionality—many in our community quite properly celebrate it—but it is nevertheless unfair to reinforce misperceptions that all lesbians and gay men are into, say, leather or drag" (*Media Guide to the Lesbian and Gay Community,* 1993, p. 31).

Television news practices did begin to change, and images that reflected a more mainstream look became more common. But that technique led conservative critics to complain that the liberal media was sanitizing the gay issue in an effort to be politically correct. In essence, they argued for a re-framing of gay images not only to illustrate perversion but also danger. These critics were particularly upset with news coverage of the massive 1993 March on Washington, arguing that front page images prominently featured khaki pants and polo shirts but excluded almost entirely the far more prevalent bizarre images at the event.

Overall, the straight press has made efforts at inclusiveness and diversity. The *New York Times*, CAP Cities/ABC, and other major media corporations have adopted domestic partner benefits. *USA Today* has a diversity committee that deals with gender, ethnic, and racial issues. Editors report that diversity in the workplace and in the newspaper is more broadly defined today and does include gay issues.

THE GAY PRESS

As the decades-long quest to win acceptance in the mainstream media played out, many gays and lesbians produced their own publications as a way of providing an alternative voice that would represent the gay community more fully and accurately. Go to any major magazine stand in any major American city today and you will see the results of that vision: an impressive assortment of gay publications including national glossies, specialty publications, and community newspapers—in all, more than 850 gay and lesbian publications with a combined circulation of two million readers. *The Advocate*, perhaps the most well known of today's glossies, has been joined by *Out* (1992, New York), *Square Peg* (1992, Los Angeles), *OUT/LOOK*, now defunct (1988, San Francisco), and *10 Percent* (1992, San Francisco), all targeted to both sexes. *Genre* (1991, Los Angeles) is targeted exclusively to men, while *Deneuve*, now renamed *Curve* (1991, San Francisco), *Frontiers* (1982, Los Angeles), the older *Lesbian News*, *Girlfriends* (San Francisco), and *Circles* (1998, Boulder) are for women. *BLK* (1988, Los Angeles) is aimed at an African-American audience, *Victory!* (1993, Sacramento) at entrepreneurs, and *POZ* (1994, New York) at people who are HIV positive.

In *Unspeakable: The Rise of the Gay and Lesbian Press in America,* author Rodger Streitmatter says the 1990s brought "the emergence of a bumper crop of slick, upscale magazines brimming with the same full-page ads appearing in tony mainstream magazines. . . . Most of the editorial content wrapped around the ads was decidedly moderate in tone, reading like the inoffensive articles some advertisers demand that magazines publish if they expect to secure long-term contracts" (Streitmatter, p. 309). The "spectacular growth" of the glossies coupled with the continued success of urban-based newspapers such as the *Windy City Times*, the *Washington Blade,* and the *Philadelphia Gay News* meant that more gay readers are subscribing to the alternative gay press than ever before.

Given the humble origins of the gay press, today's successes are even more notable. With the rise of gay studies in universities around the country, a number of researchers have begun to document various aspects of gay history and culture, including gay media. One of the earliest and best-known stories involves the production of *Vice Versa*, which, according to historian Streitmatter, marked the birth of the country's lesbian and gay press.

In the summer of 1947, a secretary at RKO Studios in Southern California single-handedly started *Vice Versa*, writing under the pseudonym Lisa Ben, a transmogrification of lesbian. Its nine monthly issues, each with 12 typewritten copies, "contained no bylines, no photographs, no advertisements, no masthead, and neither the name nor the address of its editor" (Streitmatter, p. 1). Nevertheless, it inaugurated a new journalistic genre, establishing the basic format for the general gay magazine—"with editorials, with short stories, with poetry, with book and film reviews, and with a letters column" (Streitmatter, p. 2; author's interview with Jim Kepner, founder and curator of the International Gay and Lesbian Archives, 26 April 1993, in Washington, D.C.). Ben distributed *Vice Versa* personally in Los Angeles bars and through the mail (Streitmatter, p. 5; Marcus, 1992, p. 9).

Not long after that, America's first widely distributed gay and lesbian publications began to appear. Like *Vice Versa*, the monthly publications of the 1950s were based on the West Coast: two magazines by and for gay men—*ONE*, founded in Los Angeles in 1953, followed by *Mattachine Review* in San Francisco in 1955—and one by and for lesbians—the *Ladder*, founded in San Francisco in 1956. "These magazines advanced beyond *Vice Versa* in several crucial respects. They were distributed nationally. They withstood attacks by the U.S. Senate, postal officials, and the FBI to win [in a 1958 U.S. Supreme Court decision (Streitmatter, pp. 34-36)]

the legal right for gay-oriented materials to be sent through the mail. They also achieved longevity: each of the three published for more than a dozen years" (Streitmatter, p. 18). "The first issue of *ONE* carried three ads, but all three—for a bookstore and design service—had been placed by staff members at no charge to the businesses" (Streitmatter, p.29). By the end of the 1950s, the three magazines' aggregate circulation totaled 7,000 (Streitmatter, p. 28).

The early and mid-1960s witnessed the advent of a generation of more militant publications. According to Barbara Gittings, the leading editor of the era, during the 1950s, "homosexuals had looked inward, focusing on themselves and their problems, begging society for tolerance. In the 1960s, we looked outside ourselves for the roots of the problem. We came to the position that the 'problem' of homosexuality isn't a problem at all. The problem is society. Society had to accommodate us, not try to change us" (Streitmatter, p. 51; author's telephone interview with Barbara Gittings, 10 September 1993). A renewed version of the *Ladder* joined *Homosexual Citizen* (1966, Washington, D.C.) and *Drum* (1964, Philadelphia) as the most-representative publications of that kind. Still, advertisers were difficult to find, and the magazines continually grappled with their precarious fiscal status.

Other new publications in the 1960s (*Vector* [1964], *Citizens News* [1961], and *Cruise News & World Report* [1965], all in San Francisco) were precursors of the entertainment-oriented publications that would play a major role in the future. (Streitmatter, pp. 53-54).

The turbulent times of the late 1960s brought the struggle for gay and lesbian liberation closer to the counterculture movement and its call for sexual liberation. In the three epicenters of the "youthquake"—New York, Los Angeles, and San Francisco—"gay male journalists seized the moment to escalate their discussion of topics such as promiscuity and anonymous sex, while gay male as well as lesbian journalists broke new boundaries in the publication of homoerotic images." In New York, gay press veterans Jack Nichols's and Lige Clarke's "Homosexual Citizen" column in *Screw* (1968), a smutty sex tabloid, reflected the values of bohemian Greenwich Village—the site of the Stonewall Rebellion. In Los Angeles, the *Los Angeles Advocate* (1967) "became the genre's first true newspaper, destined to evolve into the largest publication in the history of the gay press." In San Francisco, *Town Talk* (1964) "focused very specifically on capturing the essence—and the advertising potential—of the bar scene in the country's gay mecca" (Streitmatter, p. 83).

The 1969 Stonewall Riots served as a further catalyst for the gay press. Among the many publications that emerged following the riots, there were radical, extremist, anarchistic, and/or separatist newspapers including *GAY* and *Come Out!* (1969) and *Gay Times* and *Gay Flames* (1970), all in New York; *Gay Sunshine* and the *San Francisco Gay Free Press* (1970) in the San Francisco area; and also *Lavender Vision* (1970) in Boston, *Gay Liberator* (1970) in Detroit, and *Killer Dyke* (1971) in Chicago. By 1972, there were approximately 150 publications being produced. "Many were internal newsletters of the professional organizations gay people created after Stonewall. The aggregate circulation figure surpassed 100,000. If the circulation of *Screw*, which continued to publish the 'Homosexual Citizen' column, were added, the total was upward of 250,000" (Streitmatter, p. 117). In addition, the radio show *New Symposium* debuted on WBAI, the New York station in the nonprofit Pacifica radio network. It was the first time gay and lesbian

America had a spot of its own in the electronic media (Streitmatter, p. 84; Armstrong, 1981, p. 249).

By the mid-1970s, lesbians and gay men were moving to a new stage of their history. After the winds of Stonewall "had swept women and men out of the closet in unprecedented numbers, that newly empowered generation set out to define exactly what being gay meant." Gay journalism played a singular role in leading this change: newspapers, magazines, and journals "ultimately created a tangible record of the activities, fantasies, and ideologies gay people valued and cherished as their very own." Yet this era also "witnessed a split into two distinct presses—one for lesbians, one for gay men" (Streitmatter, pp. 154-55).

The lesbian press was led by two sharply different publications: *The Furies* (1972, Washington, D.C.), a radical newspaper that circulated for a year and became known by its political and personal essays; and *Lesbian Tide* (1971, Los Angeles), a magazine whose "news stories and editorials combined to set a journalistic standard that to this day remains unparalleled in the annals of the lesbian press" (Streitmatter, p. 155). At this same time, David B. Goodstein, a Wall Street investment banker, bought the *Los Angeles Advocate*—America's largest gay publication—for $1 million (Streitmatter, p. 183; author's interview with Mark Thompson, 8 July 1993). He transformed it from a hard-hitting news-paper into a magazine about gay culture and lifestyles. In 1976, with a circulation of 60,000, the *Advocate* was "being recognized by the publishing industry as one of the dozen fastest-growing magazines in the country, gay or straight" (Streitmatter, p. 185). "By 1975, there were 300 gay male publications, six times the number aimed at lesbians. Perhaps more significantly, by the mid-1970s, the gay male press was becoming a financially lucrative institution; while the lesbian press remained a labor of love—and impoverishment" (Streitmatter, p. 185; Smith, 1976, p. D-1).

The rise of the New Right and the subsequent election of Ronald Reagan in 1980 intensified the difficulties for lesbians and gays. Fighting back conservatism not only brought men and women together again, but also prompted the emergence of several publications leading the mobilization effort for gay civil rights. The *Gay Community News* (1973, Boston), *The Body Politic* (1971, based in Toronto), the *Bay Area Reporter* (1971, San Francisco), the *San Francisco Sentinel* (1974), *Gaysweek* (1977, New York), *Big Apple Dyke News* (1981, New York), the *Washington Blade* (1969, Washington, D.C.), *Lesbian News* (1975, Los Angeles), *Leaping Lesbian* (1977, Ann Arbor, Michigan), the *Philadelphia Gay News* (1976), and the *Seattle Gay News* (1974) all spoke with strength and power for their activist communities. In 1980, there were 600 publications, a large number of them the internal newsletters of

Gay periodicals have exploded in number and in popularity since Stonewall.

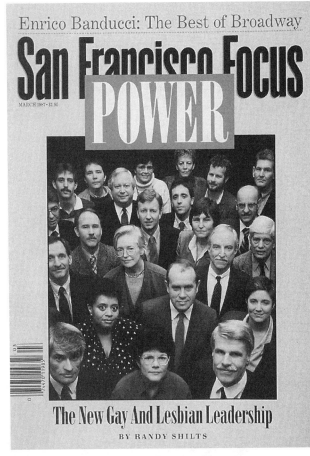

Enrico Banducci: The Best of Broadway

San Francisco Focus

POWER

MARCH 1987 • $1.95

The New Gay And Lesbian Leadership

BY RANDY SHILTS

The cover of an issue of *San Francisco Focus.*

the local social clubs and political organizations. "The *Advocate* remained the giant, with a biweekly circulation of 80,000. And total circulation of the lesbian and gay press surpassed 500,000—two and a half times that of a mere decade earlier" (Streitmatter, p. 214).

In the early 1980s, some important gay publications focused their attention on the growing AIDS epidemic, which was significantly underreported by the mainstream news media and virtually ignored by the Reagan White House. The *New York Native* (1980) and the *Washington Blade* were in the forefront of the crusade. "Such papers acted with courage because the message they carried was one their readers did not want to hear, one that seemed to deny gay men the very foundation of the sexual liberation they had finally begun to enjoy. To close the bath houses and sex emporiums, many activists argued, would be to take a huge step backward" (Streitmatter, p. 244). But many other gay publications shied away from the topic, perhaps fearing the loss of advertising support from bath houses (Streitmatter, p. 245).

Despite the AIDS crisis, or perhaps because of it, gay publications proliferated. By the mid-1980s, some 700 different magazines and newsletters were being produced, many of them tied to social, political, professional, and spiritual organizations gay people had created en masse. While the *Advocate* had the largest circulation, its circulation stayed "flat at 80,000. The combined circulation of all lesbian and gay publications had, by 1985, risen to 800,000—again, double that of a decade earlier" (Streitmatter, p. 247).

In 1985, with the death of Rock Hudson, the AIDS story was suddenly major news, with widespread reporting on the epidemic carried in daily newspapers and news magazines around the country. Much of the reporting suggested that AIDS was now spreading beyond the gay community and into mainstream society. What followed was a "virulent antigay backlash that AIDS and AIDS hysteria had spawned" (Streitmatter, p. 276). The lesbian and gay press reacted with "rage against the status quo" and with a more radical approach to gay civil rights. *Outweek* (1989, New York) burst onto the scene with a bold strategy: reveal in print the identities of powerful, closeted gays and lesbians who were not supportive of gay rights (Streitmatter, p. 277). That period also marked the emergence of notable lesbian magazines celebrating explicit sexual content—*On Our Backs* (1984, San Francisco), *Yoni* (1986, Oakland), and *Bad Attitude* (1984, Boston)—besides the more characteristically political *Lesbian Contradiction* (1983, San Francisco and Seattle), *Hag Rag* (1986, Milwaukee), and *Lesbian Ethics* (1984, Los Angeles). The *Advocate* "had become a gay *People* magazine, and making profits remained its driving mission. *Gay Community News*, at the forefront of radicalizing the gay and lesbian press, jumped to a national circulation of 60,000." By then, the total circulation of all gay publications had reached more than 1 million (Streitmatter, pp. 278-79).

The 1990s saw not only an explosion of glossy magazines but also the successful entry of gay and lesbian journalism into other arenas as well. "'Zines are cutting another wide swath across the Gay Nineties landscape because all it takes is one or two creative minds and a computer to make a single original that is then photocopied and sent on its way. Punk rhetoric and explicit sex dominate the dozens of 'zines that range from *Up Our Butts* and *Taste of Latex*, to *Meandyke, teen fag* and *Dragnett: The Feminist Militant Drag Queen Superhero Comic with a Mission*. The biggest explosions of all will happen along the information superhighway" (Streitmatter, p. 341).

While their efforts have been far more extensive in print and Internet publishing, gays have also made an impressive entry into broadcasting on radio and television. In its six-year history, the New York-based television series *In the Life* has won critical acclaim as well as a loyal audience. When it was launched in 1992, only six PBS stations chose to carry the hour-long, bi-monthly newsmagazine show. But five years later, it was regularly featured on more than 100 PBS outlets, including 19 of the 20 largest markets in the country. To date, it is the only nationally broadcast news program focusing on gay issues.

While the series is carried on public television stations, PBS itself has never endorsed the series nor has it helped with its funding. *In the Life* is offered free of charge to public television, and its $130,000 per-episode cost is financed by donations and grants. It is estimated that the program has 1.5 million viewers.

Other efforts have been noteworthy as well.

In 1992, KGAY became, for one frenetic year, the first twenty-four-hour gay and lesbian radio station, using satellites to broadcast its signal throughout the United States. The syndicated radio magazine show *This Way Out* broadcasts interviews to 80 stations in 6 countries.

Our World Television brings gay public affairs and cultural programming to 300,000 cable subscribers in Southern California. Gay Entertainment Television uses satellites to beam programming, including the talk show *Inside/Out*, from New York to 7 million homes nationwide. Network

Q subscribers receive a two-hour video in their mailboxes each month, keeping them informed about gay cultural events (Streitmatter, p. 341; Yarbrough, 1994).

Gay-owned and -operated media outlets still face tremendous financial challenges. Nonetheless, gays and lesbians today constitute a significant market, and advertisers are spending more money to reach them than ever before, a subject taken up in the next segment.

GAY MARKETING AND ADVERTISING

For decades, about the only businesses that targeted gay consumers were small ones: gay magazine and newspaper publishers, gay bars, and bath houses. But the growing visibility of gays in society and in mass media has gradually changed that. Today, the gay and lesbian market is big business, and advertisers are spending millions of dollars every year to be part of it. In 1997, major advertisers spent approximately $95 million attempting to reach the gay market, up almost 30 percent from the year earlier figure, according to a report from the New York marketing firm Mulryan/Nash (Wilke, 1997, p. 1).

Seagram America's Absolut vodka and fashion designers such as Gucci and Yves St. Laurent, all pioneers in the gay and lesbian market, have been joined by IBM Corp., America Online, Aetna Life & Casualty, Chase Manhattan Corp., Johnson & Johnson, Lotus Development Corp., Merrill Lynch & Co., Samsung Electronics America, Subaru of America, United Airlines, US West, Benneton, Banana Republic, Calvin Klein, Kenneth Cole, Philips, Apple Computer, Miller Beer, Ikea, and The Gap. Other famous trademarks are expected to join in with ads specifically designed for gay audiences in product categories yet untapped: soft drinks, beauty care, juice, and pet foods. "The frontier has moved," according to Stephanie Blackwood, principal at the gay marketing agency Spare Parts in Westport, Conn. "The standard has been raised as to what constitutes gay marketing. It's no longer enough to work sponsorships [of events] and never place an ad in gay media or just run a mainstream ad in gay media" (Wilke).

If gay marketing has been difficult to define, so has the gay market. Questions as to whether gays and lesbians have more disposable income are still the subject of debate. In 1993, however, the research company Yankelovich Partners Inc. included a question about sexual identity in its annual survey, which has tracked consumer values and attitudes since 1971. The survey produced what is considered the first nationally representative and projectable research on the subject and provided a detailed portrait of gays and lesbians as consumers.

Among 2,503 participants in the 1993 Yankelovich Monitor survey, the 143 interviewees who defined themselves as "gay/homosexual/lesbian" (5.7 percent of the sample) presented the following demographic characteristics:

* They are twice as likely as heterosexuals to have graduate education

* They are highly concentrated in the top 25 metropolitan markets

* They are more concerned about physical fitness, well-being, and self-enhancement, which manifests itself in everything from keen interest in new shopping outlets to greater use of cosmetics and fragrances

* They report more stress in their lives than heterosexuals do, which could make them likely prospects for everything from escape-style vacations to home security systems

* They are self-employed at a rate almost two-thirds higher than that of heterosexuals, which could make them prospects for technological products such as cellular telephones and fax machines

Furthermore, the findings contradicted often-reported figures that gays are more affluent than the general population. In this regard, the Yankelovich data indicated little noticeable difference between the homosexual and heterosexual respondents. Among the gay men, the mean household income was $37,400, compared with $39,300 among the heterosexual men. Among the lesbians, it was $34,800, compared with $34,400 among the heterosexual women (Elliott, 1994, p. C-1).

While the gay market is proving increasingly attractive to many advertisers, many others consider it risky business, often citing organized product boycotts of the past. The coming out episode of *Ellen* offers an illustration of the range of corporate responses to gay-themed material. Chrysler Corporation opted to stay away from the show, while Volkswagen of America Inc. chose to run a humorous commercial depicting "two young men with nothing to do but drive a Volkswagen." Explained Chrysler spokesperson Megan Giles: "We don't think it is a smart business decision to be advertising in an environment that is so polarized." Volkswagen counter-argued: "Volkswagen respects the differing opinions people have about the subject matter. . . . [T]he Volkswagen ad on this episode is not really about sexuality, nor does it endorse a particular lifestyle . . . it's about advertising our products to a target audience of drivers, which matches the viewers of 'Ellen' and which would include many different lifestyles" (Canedy, 1997, p. D-8).

In addition, there is contention that commercials featuring lesbians are easier to sell to the general audience than are ads featuring gay men. The widely publicized rise of "lesbian chic" is a distinct counterpoint to the longtime persistence of stereotypically derisive images of gay men, despite their relatively higher purchasing power in the gay and lesbian market. "Lesbianism has marketing legs," as reporter Mike Antonucci describes it. "It taps into the erotic fantasies of heterosexual males. It's politically and psychologically friendly to some women fed up with sexism, boys' clubs or men in general. It has the better list of icons who have come out publicly. And it looks safe and almost delicate compared to the more physical, AIDS-threatened images of male gay life."

Howard Buford, president of Prime Access, a New York ad agency specializing in gay and lesbian, Latino, and African-American markets, sees a similar reluctance to accept depictions of gay male relationships: "Most of the social struggles in this country are centered around groups whose presence makes straight white males uncomfortable. Gay men make straight white males almost more uncomfortable than anything else, and that makes same-sex affection a really hot issue" (Antonucci, 1997, p. 5-F).

PROMINENT PEOPLE

Leroy F. Aarons

Leroy F. Aarons is founder of the National Lesbian and Gay Journalists Association (NLGJA). He coordinated the first national survey of gay and lesbian journalists for the American Society of

Newspaper Editors. *Alternatives: Gays and Lesbians in the Newsroom* (1990) was the first comprehensive survey of gay journalists, a group that was for decades largely invisible. It also marked the first time news editors had information about how their gay and lesbian employees were treated and how they rated their own paper for coverage of gay issues. The survey proved to be a watershed, documenting "a palpable undercurrent of bias" despite a largely hospitable atmosphere. The study rated U.S. newspapers mediocre at covering gay issues and reported that many, perhaps most, gay journalists are closeted on the job.

Under Aarons's leadership, the NLGJA grew into a major professional organization, with more than 1,000 members in 17 different chapter cities. NLGJA-Canada became an affiliate in 1995.

Aarons was a national correspondent and editor for the *Washington Post* for 14 years. He became Executive Editor of the *Oakland Tribune* in 1985, and three years later he was named Vice President for News. In 1994, Aarons became a syndicated columnist for the New York Times Syndicate, writing on a variety of gay issues. His book, *Prayers for Bobby*, traces a family's struggle with the suicide of a gay son. It was published in 1995 by Harper Collins and is now in its third printing.

Deb Price (1958-)

On 8 May 1992, Deb Price of the *Detroit News* began the first nationally syndicated column on gay issues in mainstream newspapers. The pioneering column, instantly recognized as a landmark in journalism, for the first time brought a gay voice regularly into newspaper households. While news organizations had increased coverage of gay and lesbian issues in recent years, Price promised to offer readers something different: life from a gay perspective. Her first column, for example, described how awkward it was for Price to try to introduce the woman she loves to her boss, because no universal language exists to describe gay couples. "So tell me, America, how do I introduce Joyce?"

The Deb Price column was immediately picked up by other newspapers in the Gannett chain and has been published in scores of diverse communities, including Des Moines; El Paso; Niagara Falls; Springfield, Missouri; Nashville; Muskogee, Oklahoma; Honolulu; and Guam. Media attention swiftly followed: in addition to radio and television programs such as *Oprah, Donahue*, CNN's *Sonya Live*, and the BBC television special *Out in America*, Price has discussed her endeavor in countless articles, including ones in *Newsweek, U.S. News & World Report*, the *New York Times*, the *Wall Street Journal, Editor & Publisher*, the *Chicago Tribune*, and *People* magazine. The *Washington Post* called her "one of the most high-profile lesbians in the news business."

The column has won numerous awards, including first place in the annual Best of Gannett contest for columns, first place in the Michigan AP Editorial Association contest, and the 1996 top prize from the National Lesbian and Gay Journalists Association.

In August 1995, her disclosure that front-runner Robert Dole was the first Republican candidate in history to accept $1,000 from a gay group prompted the campaign to return the contribution, a reversal that made front pages nationwide.

Price, 40, is the former deputy Washington bureau chief for the *Detroit News*. Before arriving at the *News* in 1989, Price worked for the *Washington Post*. She has a B.A. and M.A. in literature from Stanford and lives in the Washington, D.C., area with writer Joyce Murdoch. Together, they authored *And Say Hi to Joyce* (Doubleday), which won the Gay and Lesbian Alliance Against Defamation's Outstanding Achievement in Publishing award and

was a 1995 LAMBDA Literary Award finalist. *Kirkus Reviews* dubbed them "the Anna Quindlens of gay America: personal, committed and engaging." They are working on a second book.

Randy Shilts (1951-1994)

A pioneering journalists and best-selling author, Randy Shilts perhaps more than any other single individual put the issues of AIDS and of civil rights for gays and lesbians on the national agenda. A longtime reporter for the *San Francisco Chronicle*, Shilts was the first openly gay journalist to work at a major newspaper. *And the Band Played On: Politics, People and the AIDS Epidemic*, was widely credited with raising national consciousness about the political as well as the personal aspects of the disease. When Shilts died of AIDS in 1994, the *Chronicle* said he "played an extraordinarily influential and positive part in the great, wrenching crisis of our times. . . . (He) opened the eyes of this community, the nation and the world to the reality—tragic and complex—of AIDS." His other works include *The Mayor of Castro Street: The Life and Times of Harvey Milk* and *Conduct Unbecoming: Lesbians and Gays in the U.S. Military*.

REFERENCES:

Books

Dyer, Richard, et. al. *Coronation Street.* London: British Film Institute, 1981.

Fiske, John and John Hartley. *Reading Television.* New York: Methuen, 1978.

Gitlin, Todd. *Inside Prime Time.* New York: Pantheon Books, 1983.

Hartley, John. *Understanding News.* New York: Methuen, 1982.

Innes, Charlotte, ed. *Lesbian and Gay Images: An Entertainment Media Resource.* New York: Gay and Lesbian Alliance Against Defamation, 1995.

Marotta, Toby. *The Politics of Homosexuality.* Boston: Houghton Mifflin Company, 1981.

Media Guide to the Lesbian and Gay Community. New York: Gay and Lesbian Alliance Against Defamation, 1993.

Montgomery, Kathryn C. *Target Prime Time.* New York: Oxford University Press, 1989.

Russo, Vito. *The Celluloid Closet: Homosexuality in the Movies.* New York: Harper & Row, 1981.

Streitmatter, Rodger. *Unspeakable: The Rise of the Gay and Lesbian Press in America.* Boston: Faber and Faber, 1995.

Talk Back: A Gay Person's Guide to Media Action. Boston: Alyson Publications, 1982.

Williams, Raymond. *Television: Technology and Cultural Form.* New York: Schocken Books, 1975.

Periodical Articles and Book Excerpts

Aarons, L. F. "Alternatives: Gays and Lesbians in the Newsroom," in *Newspaper Research Journal*, Vol. 11, Summer 1990: 38-43.

"AIDS: Special Report," in *Newsweek*, 12 August 1985: 20-29.

Antonucci, Mike. "The Culture Still Is Wary of Gay Men," in *The Buffalo News*, 6 July 1997: 5-F.

Barron, James. "Homosexuals See 2 Decades of Gains, but Fear Setbacks," in *New York Times*, 25 June 1989: 1, 19.

"Cable Comes on Strong in Last TIO Roper Poll," in *Broadcasting*, 3 April 1989: 1.

"Cable, Syndication Advertising Expected To Be Fastest Growing Segments of TV Industry in '89," in *Broadcasting*, 6 February 1989: 50.

Canedy, Dana. "The Media Business: Advertising," in *The New York Times*, 30 April 1997: D-8.

Carey, James. "A Cultural Approach to Communications," in *Communication Research*, Vol. 2, No. 1, 1975.

Elliott, Stuart. "A Sharper View of Gay Consumers," in *The New York Times*, 9 June 1994: C-1.

Fejes, Fred and Kevin Petrich. "Invisibility, Homophobia and Heterosexism: Lesbians, Gays and the Media," in *Critical Studies in Mass Communication*, Vol. 10, No. 4, June 1993: 396-422.

Fiske, John. "Popular Television and Commercial Culture: Beyond Political Economy," in *Television Studies: Textual Analysis*, edited by Gary Burns and Robert J. Thompson. New York: Praeger, 1989: 22.

"Fourth Quarter Viewing Patterns," in *Broadcasting*, 6 February 1989: 50.

Freiberg, P. "Gays and the Media," in *Washington Blade*, Vol. 24, 23 April 1993: 53-57.

"The Frightening AIDS Epidemic Comes Out of the Closet," in *Time*, 12 August 1985: 40-47.

Gerbner, George and Larry Gross. "Living with Television: The Violence Profile," in *Journal of Communication*, Vol. 26, No. 2, 1976: 173-199.

Gold, Richard. "Gay Themed Features Hot B.O. Stuff," in *Variety*, 9 April 1986: 5.

Gunter, Barrie. "The Perceptive Audience," in *Communication Yearbook/11*, edited by James A. Anderson. Newbury Park: Sage, 1988: 46.

Hall, Stuart. "Culture, The Media, and the Ideological 'Effect,'" in *Mass Communication and Society*, edited by James Curran, Michael Gurevitch, and Janet Woollacott. London: Sage, 1977: 340.

Henry, William. "That Certain Subject," in *Channels*, April 1987: 43.

Knopper, S. "Openly Gay Flirtations Mix Goofy Fun with Stirring Solemnity," in *Boulder Sunday Camera*, 21 November 1993: B4.

Kozol, Wendy. "Representations of Race in Network News Coverage of South Africa," in Burns and Thompson: 167.

Levine, Richard M. "Family Affair," in *Esquire*, March 1984: 225-226.

Lipton, Michael A. "Is TV Getting Better—or Worse?" in *TV Guide*, 10 November 1984: 6.

Moritz, Marguerite. "How US News Media Represent Sexual Minorities," in *Journalism and Popular Culture*, edited by Peter Dahlgren and Colin Spakrs. London: Sage, 1992: 157.

Newcomb, Horace A. and Paul M. Hirsch. "Television as a Cultural Forum," in *Interpreting Television: Current Research Perspectives*, edited by Willard D. Rowland, Jr., and Bruce Watkins. Beverly Hills, California: Sage, 1984.

Newton, Helen. "'Brothers' Is Coming Out of the Closet," in *TV Guide*, 10 May 1986: 26.

"Roll Over, Ward Cleaver," in *Time*, 14 April 1997: 80.

Ross, Chuck. "Gay Stays on 'thirtysomething,'" in *San Francisco Chronicle*, 18 November 1989: C9.

Russo, Vito. "AIDS in 'Sweeps' Time," in *Channels*, September/October 1985: 6.

Smith, Dave. "Gay Community's Advocate: Glass Door at Maze's End," in *Los Angeles Times*, 11 November 1976: D-1.

Tartikoff, Brandon. "Viewpoints," in *Television/Radio Age*, 23 November 1987: 57.

Terranova, Joe. "Variety of Factors Cited for Cable's Ad Growth," in *Multichannel News*, 5 June 1989: 6.

"Three-Network Viewing Falls Below 70%," in *Broadcasting*, 17 April 1989: 29.

Tuchman, Gaye. "Introduction: The Symbolic Annihilation of Women By the Mass Media," in *Hearth and Home: Images of Women in the Mass Media*, edited by G. Tuchman, A. K. Daniels, and J. Benet. New York: Oxford University Press, 1978: 3-38.

Wilke, Michael. "Big Advertisers Join Move to Embrace Gay Market," in *Advertising Age*, 4 August 1997: 1.

Williams, S. "Going Out in Public," in *Chicago Sun-Times*, 27 July 1993: section 2, p. 1.

Zoglin, Richard. "Troubles on the Home Front," in *Time*, 28 January 1985: 65.

Other

Bryant, Steve, AGLA board member, interviewed by telephone from Los Angeles, California, 20 July 1987.

Buxton, Rodney A. "From Stereotype to Social Type: Continuing Gay and Lesbian Characters in Fictional Television Programming." Paper presented at the International Communication Association, San Francisco, California, May 1989, pp. 1, 2.

CBS video, *Making Television*, 1985.

Colby, David C. and Timothy Cook. "The Mass Mediated Epidemic: AIDS and Television News, 1981-1985." Paper presented at the International Communication Association, San Francisco, May 1989.

Deiter, Newton, Executive Director, Gay Media Task Force, interviewed by telephone from Los Angeles, California, 25 October 1987.

Law, Sylvia A. "Homosexuality and the Social Construction of Gender." Lecture presented at Lindsley Memorial Courtroom, Fleming Law Building, University of Colorado, School of Law, 23 February 1989.

Moritz, Marguerite J. "The Fall of Our Discontent: The American Networks, The New Conservatism, and the Disenfranchising of Sexual Minorities." Paper presented at the annual conference of the International Communication Association, Dublin, June 1990.

Wolf, Michelle A. and Alfred P. Kielwasser. "The Sound (And Sight) of Silence: Notes on Television and the Communication Ecology of Adolescent Homosexuality." Paper presented at Western States Communication Association, Tucson, Arizona, February 1991, p. 8.

Yarbrough, Jeff. "Gays in the Glossies." Panel discussion, National Lesbian and Gay Journalists Association convention, 24 September 1994, Minneapolis.

—Marguerite Moritz

16

Music

- **Pop/Rock Music**
- **Prominent People in Pop/Rock Music**
- **Classical Music and Opera**
- **Prominent People in Classical Music and Opera**

This chapter discusses the achievements of gay men and lesbians in the field of music. The chapter covers three chief areas: pop/rock, classical, and opera; pop/rock music is discussed first, followed by a combined discussion of classical music and opera. Please note that biographies of notable artists are not grouped together in a single section but are presented within each section. Thus, readers will find biographies of pop/rock artists at the end of the pop/rock section and biographies of artists in classical music and opera at the end of the classical music and opera section. However, the bibliographic references for the various sections are all found in the "References" section at the close of the chapter; this final section is subdivided by discipline and further divided by type of resource (e.g. "Books," "Periodical Articles," etc.).

POP/ROCK MUSIC

Overview

The term "popular" in reference to music is a concept that only makes sense as a comparative. Defined against "classical music" ("high art" growing out of the European tradition, such as symphony, ballet, and opera) and traditional kinds of "folk music" (non-commercial, often anonymously sung tunes), popular music is then a music produced for "the people" (in other words, a body of consumers) that makes use of the mechanical means of reproduction of both music and text. To expand briefly upon the idea of "the people" as possibly more than a mere sector of the market, it is important to consider this social body as a group (or a collection of groups) that are formed *by* and *through* the cultural practices in which they engage. As a set of cultural practices (including dress, dance, and speech acts) based around the production and the consumption of non-elitist, non-folk, commercial music, popular music must also be seen as form of expression that *produces* a particular form of collective identity, a particular set of attitudes and values, a particular sort of recognition, and a particular sense of belonging.

This essay will analyze the ways in which popular music both forms and informs gay and lesbian identity (and vice-versa) in twentieth-century British and American cultures. Focusing spe-

cifically on commercial popular music since the 1950s (yet giving some due to early-twentieth-century songbirds and blues/jazz performers), this essay will first sketch a historical/generic timeline of popular music forms in which lesbians and gay men have not merely participated but have carved out a space for the exploration of queer sexualities, subjectivities, and politics. Next, the essay will offer brief biographical and cultural analyses of ten queer performers who changed the pop music world.

Introduction

For centuries, music has occupied a privileged yet problematic place in Western culture. As far back as Plato's sketch of the ideal city in *The Republic,* music has appeared at the center of sociocultural life as a foundational practice necessary to any "civilized" society. Viewed as essential for the cultivation of youth, the education of the soul, and the building of both moral and social character, music has time and again been granted an exalted status ("the ultimate symbol of man's conquest for life, the utmost unity man can achieve," according to Paul Henry Lang [Lang, 1941, p. xix]), historically playing a crucial role in humanity's myriad attempts to envision the "considered" life. Yet alongside its ever-important cultural duties, its glorified role as the "ultimate symbol" of human expression and achievement, music has been simultaneously constructed as a threat to the very cultural foundations it supposedly fortifies. Popular music in particular—the non-elitist, oft-denounced "other" of Western music—pockmarks the historical record as a most troublesome musical form. A so-called low art designed for commercial consumption, and one for decades virtually ignored by academic musicology, popular music has nonetheless proven to be an aesthetic practice capable of re-imagining social relations, including norms of gender and sexuality. From Plato's proscriptions against "the sovereignty of the audience" in ancient Greece to the diatribes by the late philosopher Alan Bloom and Tipper Gore, wife of U.S. vice president Al Gore, against rock-n-roll as seductive and corruptive to the youth of America in the 1980s and 1990s, popular music has historically been deemed resistant to authority, emasculating, effeminizing, capable of instilling a thirst for liberty, and ultimately "unsettling of the most fundamental political and social conventions" (Plato, as quoted in Weiss and Taruskin, 1984, p. 7). In a culture so rigidly structured in terms of a mind-body split, a culture that has set the rational above and in opposition to the sensual, popular music has historically been most unpopular with those music and governmental authorities committed to upholding the schism between the material and the judicious, those most invested in sustaining music's status strictly as a site of intellectual and cultural prestige, and, ultimately, those authorities most intent upon maintaining the (heteronormative) social order.

But how and why is popular music so threatening? What might popular music *do* to and for the populace that other art forms do not? For starters, popular music is in many ways linked to the formation of identity. Especially since the birth (i.e., the initial commercial success) of rock-n-roll in the 1950s, popular music and its associated cultural practices including dress, dance, and speech has become a clear marker of identity, speaking to and about an individual's subjectivity (selfhood) and social status. To identify strongly with a particular genre or style of popular music is to forge a social position, to stake out and claim a specific cultural terrain, to identify with a particular way of seeing (or hearing) the world. In short, popular music since the 1950s arguably speaks *to* and *about* more individuals than any other cultural practice within modern Anglo-American cultures. While all music engages the human body in some way—be it the liberation of the body on the dance floor or the stiffening of the body in an orchestra hall chair—popular music is, historically, an art form designed to *maximize* physical engagement, an art form that often speaks directly to the body. Thus, the diatribes against popular music's seduction and effeminization are clearly based upon the ways in which this music construes and, more importantly, *moves* the body. John Calvin, recognized music's power to "bend the morals of men this way or that," and his influence led his followers to restrict the use of music in early American colonies for fear of "emasculating ourselves with immoderate pleasure" (Ross and Rose, 1994, p. 31). Centuries later in the 1980s, Alan Bloom argued similarly that the new form of openness engendered by rock music appeals only to "a sexual desire undeveloped and untutored" (Grossberg, 1992, p. 197). Interestingly, and important for the purposes of this essay, the innumerable warnings against the corrosive effects of popular music that recur as constants throughout the history of Western music reveal not only a blatant sex-and-body-phobia, but also a (sometimes unspeakable yet clearly related) homophobia—"emasculation" and the "bending" and "opening" of men's bodies "this way and that" are undoubtedly connected to *sexual* bending/emasculating and thus the disruption of heteronormal cultural practices. In a culture that connects masculinity—and by extension the patriarchal authority of church, state, and so on—with the hermetically sealed, impenetrable male body, "effeminate" (or rather "effeminizing") popular music harbors the potential of being nothing less than a threat to the social order itself, a cultural force capable of altering the way people experience their bodies in relation to music and, effectively, in relation to other bodies.

Not surprisingly then, gay, lesbian, bisexual, and transgendered bodies have flocked to popular music in droves over the past 50 years, succeeding in numbers disproportionate to the ten percent of the population that they supposedly comprise. From Little Richard's patented orgasma-shrieks to Wayne (later Jane) County's gender-bending noise rock to Ani DiFranco's outspokenly bisexual folk-punk, GLBT individuals have played a major role in creating and queering mainstream popular culture through their participation in commercial music. For gay and lesbian audiences, popular music has historically functioned not only as mere entertainment, but has often played a fundamental role in establishing gay self-identity and maintaining community solidarity. Just as the history of popular music must not be separated from its relation to the body, the history of post-Stonewall American GLBT leisure and politics must be viewed in relation to the ways in which popular music has moved and motivated the *queer* body. Gay and lesbian discos, bars, and music festivals—spaces that come to life to the soundtracks of popular musics—have been important meeting grounds for lovers and activists alike, bringing lesbian and gays together in the name of fun yet simultaneously collecting and uniting an otherwise autochthonous and indigenous community. Further, the gay liberationist notion of making the private public, a political mantra from the early days of gay rights activism, has thus occurred to an extent over the past 30 years due in part to the emergence of out pop superstars such as Elton John, k. d. lang, and Melissa Etheridge. Overcoming the once commercially doomed and marginalizing labels of "gay artist" and "lesbian artist," these three figures in particular have achieved international success before and after coming out to the world, paving the road to fame for future queer musicians while setting a place at the pop culture table for gay and lesbian issues. Prompting important questions regarding the liberatory potential of mass-consumed media as well as making visible the double bind of gay and lesbian mainstream success (in Corey Creekmur's words: "'selling out,' the pop fan's worst condemnation, and 'staying in,' the queer fan's worst nightmare" [Creekmur and Doty, 1995, p. 404]), discussions resulting from the success of out pop epitomize in some ways the contentious debates within the queer community over assimilation within versus resistance to regimes of the normal.

And what better medium to flesh out queer debates and/or make the private public than music? Because of its non-representationality, music itself is arguably *the* art form that most closely resembles the structure of human desire. Fluid, malleable, and intangible, music may be most suited to speak desires that might otherwise remain unspeakable. Particularly, twentieth-century popular music—the most readily available, most widely accessible, and most globally distributed music of modern Western culture—in many ways reveals an alternative history of desire, a history that until recently has been closeted, erased, ignored, or denigrated. Over the last decade, however, music's closet door has been swung open by a new school of gay and lesbian musicologists intent upon revealing the secret histories of silenced desires. Labeled "shrill marauders" on an "ideological crusade" by the conservative academic priesthoods of musicology (historically bent on maintaining music's autonomy from society and culture, let alone from sexuality), the progressive practitioners of the new lesbian and gay musicology are out to diversify and, in some ways, rescue a discipline that has operated under unrecognized and unarticulated classist, racist, masculinist, and heternormative premises for too long. The invasion of popular musicology and sexuality studies into the once seemingly impenetrable academic redoubts has resulted in valuable analyses of disenfranchised and marginalized discourses, giving voice to the silenced and reconnecting cultural practices to the bodies that produce and consume them. Books such as *Queering the Pitch: The New Gay and Lesbian Musicology, Feminine Endings: Music, Gender, and Sexuality, Queer Noises, Running with the Devil,* and *Out in Culture* have provoked new questions regarding what it is that makes music pleasurable and how music is shaped by notions of gender, sexuality, and sexual identity. From Handel to Heavy Metal, these volumes cover a wide range of popular and elite music practices and forms, providing a foundation to this essay's (admittedly subjective and impossibly incomplete) sketch of the intersection of GLBT bodies and popular musics of twentieth-century British and American cultures.

Popular Music through the Twentieth Century

As noted earlier, popular music, broadly defined, characterizes a music defined against both art and folk music; in short, a commercial music literally for the people. The genealogy of popular music as we think of it today—as a mechanically reproduced, commodified, commercialized form—can be traced to the Renaissance and the appearance of printed song books and sheet music. But, of course, popular music flourished long before the advent of the printing press, and though our knowledge of homosexual thematics in the music of all earlier periods is scant—little research has been done and detailed histories remain to be written—we do know, for example, that as early as the fourteenth century "sodomitical songs" were being banned in Florence (Dynes, 1990, p. 857). While the lyrics and music to these songs are lost, the very existence of such an ordinance reveals the presence and possibility of an explicit homosexual discourse circulated through song as early as the Middle Ages. In this section, I wish to trace the emergence of this "homosexual discourse" within popular music beginning with early-twentieth-century popular song and concluding with present-day rock cultures and pop musicians. Because any historical sketch is by definition exclusionary, I am limiting my analysis here to nine genres within British and American popular music in which out gay men and women have emerged. My aim is to highlight and contextualize the importance and influence of these musicians within their respective genres. Suggestions for further reading are provided at the conclusion to this chapter.

Songbirds: Early Commercial Music. With the emergence of the mass commercialization of popular music in the early twentieth century through radio and phonograph recordings, the English-speaking world embraced a new form of mass-marketed popular song. Taken out of the context of the music hall and the vaudeville stage, venues that, in the nineteenth century, saw a vogue for drag performances, the new standardized recordings of popular songs often threw a gender-bending twist into seemingly straight love themes. Without the visual display of female impersonation, early recordings such as John Terrell's "He Certainly Was Good to Me" (1898) and Billy Murray's "Honey Boy" (1907) took on a notably queer valence outside their original performance sites. Marlene Dietrich's celebrated renditions of "I've Grown Accustomed to Her Face," Bing Crosby's gender-neutral and lilting "Gay Love" (1929), Ewen Hall's 1930s "Delicate Cowboy" (originally entitled "Lavender Cowboy," but changed because of the color's linkage to homosexuality), along with countless "buddy" tunes about "gay times" in the military (precursors to the Village People's "In the Navy") all introduced queer types of love to mainstream music audiences of the time. No two songwriters stand out of the closet more noticeably in the early days of pop music than Noel Coward (1899-1973) and Cole Porter (1893-1964). A British playwright, songwriter and entertainer, Coward barely masked his queerness in such sexually scandalous plays as *Easy Virtue* and *Fallen Angels* (1925), while his Wildean wit and cynically parodic style mocked the rigid sexual and aesthetic conventions of the era. In songs such as "Why Must the Show Go On?" and "There Are Bad Times Just around the Corner," Coward imbued the popular music of the twenties and thirties with a camp sensibility that would later influence countless other gay and lesbian pop musicians from Morrissey to k. d. lang. Cole Porter's sexually provocative tunes likewise loosened up the pop music world. Born in Peru, Indiana, and later expatriating to Britain, Porter composed such controversial hits as the matter-of-fact "Let's Do It," the

bisexual manifesto "I'm a Gigolo," and the kept-boy classic "My Heart Belongs to Daddy." Most often recognized for raising the "lowly" medium of commercial music to a "respectable" art form, Porter must also be remembered for his sly yet sophisticated queering of a generation of music listeners—a queering that set precedents for generations to come.

All That Blues (and Jazz). The 1920s and 1930s saw the rise of a number of African-American blues and jazz musicians whose brazen voices spoke volumes about the marginalization of racial and sexual "others" in the inter-war years. Though the much-renowned blues singer Bessie Smith claimed she could not understand "a mannish-acting woman and a skipping, twisting woman-acting man" in 1927's "Foolish Man's Blues," her many collaborations with gay-identified pianist Porter Grainger and her numerous lesbian relationships reveal otherwise. Countless other blues songs and biographies further suggest that male and female homosexuality had a place in American black culture early in the twentieth century. Smith's mentor, Gertrude "Ma" Rainey, openly sang about her lesbianism in 1928's unapologetic "Prove It to Me Blues" ("Went out last night/ With a crowd of my friends/ They must be womens/ Cause I don't like mens"), while the often-performed yet anonymously penned "Sissy Man's Blues" described a male narrator's willingness to participate in same-sex relations as an alternative to both "his woman" and his hand.

Further, though too-often-homophobic jazz historians might recount otherwise, the early American jazz scene also became a site where black queers congregated and composed. From the unabashedly out yet largely ignored Ellington-songwriter Billy Strayhorn to jazz giant Cecil Taylor (who, according to certain critics, couldn't properly play the piano because he was queer), to orchestra leader and spaced-out jazz noise-monger Sun Ra, to the disputably bisexual Miles Davis, queer jazz musicians stand out as some of the most important and influential innovators of American popular music. Originally giving voice and sound to marginalized groups, often shunning mainstream music conventions for free-form improv structures, and continuously pushing the boundaries of what might be called music, jazz is an art form practically born queer.

Let There Be Rock: The 1950s and 1960s. From its inception in the United States in the early 1950s, rock-n-roll was a music specifically about sex and the body. A fusion of black rhythm-n-blues, gospel, doo-wop harmonic singing, and white rockabilly (among other pop music forms), rock-n-roll was not only a site of convergence between black and white music, but also a medium that bridged the age-old Western cultural schism between the mind and the body. With roots in Afro-Caribbean voudoun (a "voodoo" religion that practiced spirituality through dynamic, polyrhythmic music and unrestrained, some might say crazed, dance), rock became a sound in which the body and emotion took precedence over rationality, a music imbued with an ideology of desire, liberation, and freedom from the puritanical, anti-sexual norms of post-World War II America. The term "rock-n-roll" itself, borrowed from the juke joints in the American South, meant, quite simply, engage in sex, an act often slyly alluded to yet most often unspoken in earlier forms of popular music.

With the rise of rock-n-roll came also the creation of consumer-ready youth cultures. Like never before in Western cultural history, popular music, in the form of rock-n-roll, became an arch-commodity—a commodity as reliant upon marketing, promotion, publicity, and image-making as it was on music itself. Thus, the *personalities* of rock musicians—their looks, private lives, backgrounds, sexualities—featured prominently in selling a sound, inventing a gimmick, and making a star. Because of the importance of personality in marketing rock musicians, then, it is of little surprise that the subject matter and overall image of rock-n-roll was resolutely heterosexual. Though gay and lesbian rock musicians of course existed, their sexualities were rigorously hidden, kept in the closet for fear of losing target audiences. Little Richard, whose (hetero)sexually charged "Good Golly Miss Molly" is arguably the most important, if not the first, rock-n-roll tune, eventually denounced his homosexuality (for which he was kicked out of his home at the age of thirteen), first for marketing reasons and later for religion. Cry-er extraordinaire Johnny Ray, whose weeping, sobbing, and falling-to-pieces stage shows induced some of the earliest cases of fan hysteria, was fairly open about his homosexuality (and was in fact arrested on a sexual indecency charge in the 1960s), and, no doubt due in part to his openness, was critically panned for being "over-emotional" and "effeminate." Janis Joplin, whose bisexuality in the free-loving sixties is so often ignored by rock historians, pursued lesbian relationships passionately and unapologetically, setting an in-your-face, proto-femi-

Elton John

nist precedent for future women in rock. Finally, Brian Epstein, sometimes called "the fifth Beatle," revolutionized the look and sound of rock-n-roll, managing the Beatles to international fame and legendary status, all the while identifying as a gay man. Though this short list most assuredly has not mentioned *all* of the important and influential—other notable gay and lesbian early rockers include British bluesman Long John Baldry, pop superstar Elton John, once-bisexual Who guitarist Pete Townshend, and Who manager Kit Lambert, to name a few—the rock-n-roll explosion in some ways left the presumed inevitability or "naturalness" of heterosexuality in its rubble. Though the rock industry did its best to ignore (if not eradicate) the dreaded presence of homosexuality, both the music's direct relation to sex and the body and its historical memory of liberation and rebellion opened the pop music closet a bit farther.

All That Glitters: Glam Rock. In the early 1970s, the once-heteronormative marketing of rock-n-roll took a turn towards the sexually ambiguous. Led by David Bowie, the "glam rock" phenomenon questioned the strictly straight, overwhelmingly masculine image heretofore put in place by such rock musicians as Elvis Presley and the Beach Boys. Espousing a philosophy of camp and escape (Bowie's drug-addled world of modern-day dandyism, for example), glam opened up questions of sexual identity and practice, bringing androgyny, bisexuality, and transvestitism into the spotlight. Almost like the Kinks' 1971 hit "Lola" come to life (a song that seems to have foreseen the future of rock with the line: "Girls will be boys and boys will be girls..."), sexual ambiguity became the key to glam rock success. Artists such as Lou Reed (Velvet Underground, solo), Marc Bolan (T-Rex), Iggy Pop (Stooges, solo), the New York Dolls, and Jobriath (the only out gay man of the glam bunch, and, not surprisingly, the least well-known) all donned the make-up, the dress, and the glitter that was glam, setting aesthetic and fashion trends for the youth cultures of Britain and America. Whereas the hippies questioned gender norms and puritanical sexual politics, glam fans lived the messiness of a more queer aesthetic, often risking gay-bashing (whether they were gay or not) for dressing like their favorite pop star. Though resolutely anti-political (an anti-hippie philosophy later adopted by punk), glam inadvertently politicized the cross-dressed fan's body and in many ways "queered" rock-n-roll. While glam has been condemned by gay critics as a "straight" marketing ploy of gay identity, the music, the image, and the attitude that were glam created a safe space in which youth could act out and experiment with both sexual and transgendered difference.

Enjoying Being Girls: Womyn's Music and the "New Breed." With the mass emergence of feminist theory and practice in the 1970s, lesbian songwriters and performers (a heretofore viable, yet silenced, presence throughout the history of popular music) found a means to incorporate their sexual identities into a new musical genre. Rooted in the folk tradition of protest songs and defined against the masculinist "cockiness" of other rock cultures, women's music (or, in certain circles, *womyn's* music) sought to create a cultural space that would positively value feminist/lesbian experiences and accomplishments. Olivia Records, a pioneering women's music label founded in 1973, sought not only to make accessible non-mainstream female talent but also to revolutionize the process of record making itself. Looking to erase the distinctions between industry, performer, and audience while at the same time making visible and audible the gendered and sexualized inequities of the pop music industry, Olivia Records gave voice and gainful employment to a number of immeasurably influential lesbian singer/songwriters such as Cris Williamson (whose 1975 album *The Changer and the Changed* has sold over a quarter of a million copies). Other independent lesbian artists and womyn's labels of the 1970s include Holly Near (who started her own Redwood Records out of the front room of her home), Alix Dobkin (whose 1973 Wax Records album *Lavender Jane Loves Women* is said to be the first out lesbian record), Meg Christian, Janis Ian, Mathilde Santing, and Ferron, among many, many others.

As Arlene Stein notes in her essay "Crossover Dreams" (*Out in Culture,* 1995), the 1980s found womyn's music in the grip of an identity crisis. Between the Second-Wave feminist questioning of the previously assumed universality of womanhood, the popular backlash against lesbian separatism, and the undercapitalization of the music itself, womyn's music as a viable anti-establishment phenomenon languished. In addition, the co-opting of womyn's music by major record companies made superstars out of a select few lesbian performers (mainly those who were initially willing to water down their sexual personae), while other, more blatantly out lesbian performers remained in relative obscurity. A "new breed of women" had emerged, or so the rock journalists wrote, and fame was visited upon such ambiguously lesbian artists as Tracy Chapman, k. d. lang, Michelle Shocked, the Indigo Girls, Melissa Etheridge, Phranc, and Two Nice Girls, all recognized for "defying conventions of femininity in popular music and moving 'back to basics' from artifice and role-playing into authenticity" (Stein in Creekmur & Doty, 1995, p. 419). Signed, according to record executives, because they were "just so *real,*" these women became household names, due in part, to their marketability. In a music industry famous for recuperating subcultural styles and sounds (disco, after all, had its origins in the black gay dance floors of New York), Melissa, k. d., and Tracy, among others, became commercially viable and mainstreamed as somewhat tamer representatives of the historically radical-feminist and lesbian-separatist movements. Marketable only in muted sexuality (gender-nonspecific lyrics) and androgyny (playing with lesbian signifiers within the boundaries of a heteronormative consumer base), lesbian pop superstars in the 1980s relied upon increasingly identity-conscious lesbian audiences to correctly read their somewhat ambiguous words and images. Until k. d. lang and Melissa Etheridge came out in the 1990s, the categories "out lesbian" and "pop star" seemed mutually exclusive. Clearly, however, if 1970s womyn's music had not existed, the pop cultural landscape would be a much straighter place today. Were it not for such lesbian renegades as Near, Dobkin, and the performers and producers at Olivia Records, the out lesbian superstars of today just might still be hiding in the closet.

Glad to Be Gay: Punk and Queercore. While the origins of punk music are endlessly contested (did it begin with the Ramones and the New York Dolls in the mid-1970s at New York's CBGBs or were England's Sex Pistols the first "true" punk band?), the influence of gays and lesbians on the formation of punk subcultures is beyond question. Not only did early punk and gay fashions overlap (leather, fetish wear, piercings, and so on), but punk, as a descendant of glam, also re-imagined gender and sexual identities in a manner similar to some of the post-Stonewall liberation movements, producing some of the most defiantly queer music in the history of rock-n-roll. Bisexual, punk-poet Patti Smith's 1976 album *Horses* featured a cover photograph of a mannish-dressed, lesbian-coded Patti as well as a queer love dirge, "Redondo Beach." Tom Robinson's "Glad to Be Gay," ironically, an angry, punk-inspired tune raging against queer-bashing and police brutality, be-

Melissa Etheridge

came a surprise underground hit in Britain in 1978. The Buzzcocks' Pete Shelley sang about bisexual orgasm addicts and "falling in love with someone you shouldn't fall in love with," later coming out and hitting it big in gay dance clubs with the laughably suggestive "Homo-sapien" ("I'm a cruiser/You're a loser/Me and you, sir/Homo-sapiens, too"). Finally, Wayne County introduced popular music to transgenderism, changing his name to Jane and undergoing a sex-change operation in the late 1970s. All in all, early punk provided GLBT-identified individuals with an alternative to an alternative—rather than living an increasingly ghettoized post-Stonewall gay existence, punk provided a musical space outside of the disco club and the Womyn's Music Festival for gays and lesbians to experiment, rebel, and create.

Near the turn of the decade, punk underwent a transformation not unlike the womyn's music's "identity crisis" in the 1980s. The emergence of American-based hardcore punk (faster, louder, less melody) brought with it some of the dreaded trappings of traditional homophobia. Bad Brains frontman H.R. (whose name, ironically and hypocritically, stands for "Human Rights") spoke out publicly against the "unnaturalness" of homosexuality, while neo-fascist skinheads bashed queers in the name of America. This recidivistic aggression was countered by the queer and queer-friendly likes of California's MDC (a band that changed its name every album: "Millions of Dead Cops," Millions of Damn Christians," etc.) and a new emotional (i.e., "emo") hardcore centered around Dischord Records in Washington, D.C. Subsequently, a thriving "queercore" scene emerged transglobally in the 1980s and early 1990s, complete with a punk do-it-yourself ("DIY") ethos, and a fistful of fanzines, shows and record labels to boot. San Francisco became home to both the highly influential *Homocore* fanzine and *Outpunk* label/magazine (the latter recording the confrontative God Is My Co-Pilot and the self-described "neanderthal dykes" of Tribe 8), and also fostered arena-rockers Pansy Division. Olympia, Washington, was put on the rock map by Riot Grrrls Bikini Kill, Bratmobile, Heavens to Betsy, and (a little farther south in Portland) Team Dresch, which directed their neo-feminist, often lesbian-inflected songs against the patriarchal heterosexism of the scene. Toronto housed the outrageous "Renaissance Man" of queer, Bruce La Bruce, whose magazine (*JD's*), films, (*Super 8 1/2, Hustler White*), and academic writings ("Pee Wee Herman: The Homosexual Subtext") made queercore multimedia. And finally, Britain bred one of the first waves of queercore with post-Riot Grrls, Sister George and the anti-gay (yet ahead-of-his-time queer) Spud Jones of Tongue Man.

Thus, as a response to both the ghettoizing of gay cultural life and the increasing homophobia in the punk scene, queercore emerged not so much as a musical revolution, but ultimately as a revolution in *attitude*. Adopting the countercultural, sometimes nihilistic aesthetics of early punk, queercore fans and performers today practice an attitude unprecedented in pop music, bashing back against the heteronormativity of rock and mainstream cultures as well as critiquing the claustrophobia of gay culture. In the words of Matt Wobensmith, editor of the now-defunct *Outpunk*:

> gay people are already on the outside. To be accepted (our greatest desire—how sad), we learn to follow the rules and perfectly imitate in order to assimilate.... Gay culture is disgusting, boring, pathetic, self-hating, and middle-of-the-road. So, "queercore," for me, must always remain on the edge (*Outpunk*, Issue 7, p. 3).

Feelin' Mighty Real: Disco and House. If ever there was a specifically "gay male" music, disco is most assuredly it. Peaking in the late 1970s, disco provided the soundtrack, the social space, and the means to move the queer body throughout the liberationist decade following Stonewall. With its insistent, disciplined beat and non-teleological structure, the mechanical music of disco (i.e., music made for "discs" as opposed to live performance) was a music produced specifically for dancing, a music that could be re-mixed, mutated, and reappropriated by and for an audience that could use it in ways unintended by its creators. Thus, while the majority of disco musicians were not openly gay, the majority of disco audiences were. Gay men in particular, potentially liberated from the shackles of a hetero-socialized masculinity following Stonewall, often constructed their identities by and through their dancing, socializing, and cruising within the disco scene. As the beat penetrated their bodies, possibly dissolving their heteronormativized selves, gay men were arguably transformed into a new type of man. Ecstatically turned on by the music, intensely eroticized by the masses of moving bodies, and blissfully enraptured by the lights, the sound and—(let's not forget)—the drugs, gay men in many ways *became* gay (i.e., forged a modern aesthetic, social, and personal identity) through the disco scene. The early 1980s "Death to Disco" movement (bolstered by radio, tele-

vision, and various other mainstream media) can be read in some respects then as a homophobic reinstatement of heteronormativity and masculinism within popular music.

Most often erased in historical discussions of disco is the influence and importance of African-American gay men in pioneering the genre. Though heterosexualized in films like *Saturday Night Fever* and white-washed by the Village People, disco began in small gay black clubs in New York City, where as early as 1969 DJs were manipulating Temptations tunes into non-stop dance tracks. Sylvester, the most successful out gay black disco musician, epitomized the sound of the 1970s black gay underground, blending gospel and soul-influenced vocals with complex patterns of polyrhythmic percussion. His late-1970s Top 40 hits, "You Make Me Feel (Mighty Real)" and "Dance (Disco Heat)" are club standards today, often re-mixed by DJs in honor of the late performer. Sylvester and the 1970s black gay club scene are also influential precursors of modern-day "House" music. Deriving its name from a Chicago club, the Warehouse (opened in 1977), House took disco to the next level, further cutting up, speeding up, and re-mixing standard disco tracks. Reversing the Western impulse to give primacy to harmony and melody, House stressed rhythm and percussion even more than previous club music, taking the disco beat to extreme levels and leaving behind pop structures altogether. Further, House fostered a new form of gay dance called voguing (a dance style co-opted by Madonna in the early 1990s) and revamped the cult of diva worship (mainstreamed in the media-friendly RuPaul). As disco was in the 1970s, House music today is central to gay aesthetics and sociality. From the frequency with which the music fills the rooms of present-day gay clubs to the historical linkage of dance and divas with gay culture, any sketch of modern gay identity is incomplete without a discussion of the importance and influence of both disco and House.

Boys with Thorns in their Sides: New Wave and 1980s Britpop. In the early 1980s, disco and punk (though enemies at heart) had a baby and named it "New Wave." Combining the ever-synthetic instrumentation of dance music with the rebellious attitude and gender-bending aesthetic of glam and punk, New Wave quickly became the commodified rage. With standard verse/chorus pop structures and a more domesticated (though not necessarily class-based) punk angst, New Wave was radio-friendly and marketable: hip but safe. Emerging from the aftermath of this short-lived trend, near-queer performers such as Depeche Mode, the Smiths, Soft Cell, Culture Club, and the Pet Shop Boys gained lasting popularity. Following the tried-and-true formula of hiding behind the masks of celibacy, sexual ambiguity, and asexuality in order to gain commercial success, these Brit-poppers came out of their respective closets years after their stars had risen. Three male groups, however, broke the "only-gay-after-we're-famous" mold in the 1980s and presented themselves both in public and in their lyrics as out gay men. Bronski Beat, a jeans-n-sneakers trio with a leftist political agenda, had a near-Top 40 hit with "Smalltown Boy," a song about a gay adolescent's struggle to come out. Frankie Goes to Hollywood told the world to "Relax" in 1984, using S&M iconography, a gay pornographic music video, and an orgasmic chorus exclaiming "I'm cummin', I'm cummin'!" to cement its status as a very queer one-hit wonder. And last but certainly not least, techno-poppers Erasure camped their way from the gay clubs to the British charts, covering ABBA tunes like "Gimme Gimme Gimme (A Man after Midnight)" and preaching the gospel of gay rights in interviews and concerts. Though none of these bands achieved superstar status, all three helped make queer visibility commonplace and increasingly acceptable within the pop music world.

Random Acts of Queerness, or So What Do We Do Now That We're Everywhere? In the 1990s, out gay and lesbian pop performers seemed to be everywhere. Whereas earlier uses of veiled queer allusions and barely disguised gay-references by rockers such as Queen and Judas Priest (Queen frontman Freddie Mercury's drag performances and constant references to his or another's "gun" or Judas Priest vocalist Rob Halford's very obvious leather fetish) once titillated gay audiences while going right over the heads of most straights, in today's pop cultural climate everything and everyone is sexually suspect. Though historically a certified road to ruin, today "gay," when used to describe a pop star most often signifies either an "interesting" (if not easily exploitable) angle for the rock journalist or, worse, a "new market" for the rock businessmen. The 1990s ascension of the "Big Gay Three," the more-popular-after-he's-out Elton John, *20/20* star Melissa Etheridge, and make-up model k. d. lang, while of course a testament to their talents, might also be attributed in part to homo-chic, a commodity-driven, MTV-generated alternative culture, and ultimately a heteronormative public's pressing need to have everyone wear his/her sexuality on his/her sleeve. But what can one expect? In a late-capitalist consumer culture, even identities are commodities. Sexually evasive artists such as Ani DiFranco, Bob Mould (formerly of punk revolutionaries Husker Du), and R.E.M.'s Michael Stipe, who understandably (yet still inexcusably) avoid the hungry public's plea to speak their sexualities, lose devoted queer fans on "moral" grounds (in other words, for political identity reasons). Way-out acapellans the Flirtations and wacky jokesters Romanovsky and Phillips, whose (homo)sexualities are the very foundations of their groups, remain relatively unknown in the mainstream pop music world due in part to the fact that their music is accessible only to a strictly gay-cultured audience. And out indie rockers, Kitchens of Distinctions, Extra Fancy, and Lotion, all of whom take fairly middle-of-the-road stances on gay identity politics, often speak volumes to gay fans, yet their gayness is sometimes unrecognizable, if not easily avoidable for straights (not unlike, Queen and Judas Priest). The point here is not, of course, to rate a rock performer for levels of outness, nor to denigrate and desert them for not being "out enough." Indeed, what needs to be critiqued (and altered) is the impoverished pigeon-holing that the commodification of identity engenders. In a pop music industry that is increasingly friendly to out lesbians and gays, an industry that capitalizes on queerness, nothing is more ironic than a world in which queer sells, while actual, living queers are still discriminated against.

PROMINENT PEOPLE IN POP/ROCK MUSIC

The following are short biographies and analyses of ten pop music performers who effectively brought GLBT issues to the mainstream. While this list is by no means complete, the goal here is to offer more in-depth sketches of ten musicians from various backgrounds, musical genres, and sexual orientations who have contributed to the increasing visibility (and audibility) of GLBT concerns worldwide.

David Bowie (1947-)

The man who fell to Earth and sold the world bisexuality. As androgyne-extraordinaire in the early 1970s (cultivating a genderless aesthetic comprised of full-length frocks, dandy-esque floppy hats, heavy pancake make-up, and a flaming red, spikey coif), Bowie literally changed the face and look of rock-n-roll by declaring open season on gender roles and traditional (hetero)sexuality through "glam" style and image. A consummate self-publicist and controversy hound, Bowie was one of the first rock celebrities to conduct an interview with the British gay press (the January 1970 issue of *Jeremy*), and later to come out as gay in a popular rock magazine ("Yes, of course I'm gay and always have been," Bowie told *Melody Maker* in 1972). Though Bowie's outness has been criticized as a mere marketing ploy (tapping into a gay audience starved of contemporary queer culture), as an exploitative use and promotion of homosexuality as freakery, and as a sensationalistic stepping stone in the ever-evolving career of one (now consummately heterosexual) David Jones (the birth-name of Bowie), the self-created myth of Queer David *simultaneously* opened up a breathing space both for queers and for those who were not sure about their sexuality (or the sexuality of others). As out rock journalist John Gill writes: "it is hard to totally hate David Bowie.... I belong to a generation that probably has to thank Queer David for the comparative ease with which we came out" (Gill, 1995, p. 110).

Image aside, Bowie's music and lyrics further open up fields of ambiguity in which queers might locate themselves. The majestic campiness of 1971's *Hunky Dory* (the cover of which features Bowie doing his best Garbo impersonation) exemplifies Bowie's uniquely androgynous musical style ("macho" distorted guitars laced with limp-wristed piano, standard rock/blues riffs accompanied by "effeminate" swelling strings) and Oscar Wildean wit (gloriously insincere sentiment, cleverly phrased gender non-specific lyrics), and easily lends itself towards queer readings. For example, the chorus of the raucous "Queen Bitch" focuses on a "she" (biological female or a male queen?) described as "so swishy in her satin and tat/In her frockcoat and bipperty bopperty hat," ending with a jealous, catty Bowie snapping "Oh God, I could do better than that." Matched with other songs such as "John, I'm Only Dancing" (a queer retort to a jealous lover?) off of *ChangesOneBowie* and concert performances in which Queer David would "fellate" lead-guitarist Mick Ronson's "instrument," Bowie brought the ever-present yet "unspeakable" queerness of rock-n-roll into a visible/audible and, most importantly, *accessible* space for gays and straights alike to occupy and, most importantly for Bowie, to consume.

Ani DiFranco (1970-)

For starters, Ani DiFranco is not a dyke. Nor is she straight. In fact, she won't even claim bisexuality. When asked to define her sexuality, she doesn't.

> I'm attracted to different things that may or may not have to do with gender. The person that I'm in love with now— the Goat Boy—the thing that makes our relationship so perfect is that it's so dubiously gendered. We take turns. It's supposed to be, "Oh, big righteous babe falling for a man. Boo, hiss, taboo, betrayal." And it's like, You should see him! He's more of a girl than I am! (*Addicted to Noise*, on-line web site).

But this isn't the usual "my sexuality is my personal business," or "my music is what matters" rock-star routine; DiFranco wants to change the way the world thinks about sexual identity. An in-your-face dyke at the outset of her career (that is, *before* she be-

Ani DiFranco

came famous), DiFranco doesn't shrink from terms such as "lesbianism" and "bisexuality" for fear that it will threaten her fame; she simply wants out of binary logic altogether. In an identity-politicked world, however, a world that insists that one's sexuality speaks an all-important, essentialized truth about the individual, DiFranco's refusal to label her sexuality is noble, if not blissfully utopian. Her insistence on fluidity, on working beyond/between/around socially prescribed roles and definitions, is indeed what DiFranco's music and public image have been about from the beginning. Emerging from the coffee-houses, bars, and streets of Buffalo, N.Y., DiFranco released her first album, *Ani DiFranco*, on her own independent label, Righteous Babe Records, in 1990. At that time, the 20-year-old DiFranco was a woman-identified folk singer (in the tradition of Alix Dobkin and the Olivia Records gang back in the 1970s), and her fan base was largely comprised of feminists and lesbians. By 1996, however, DiFranco was dating men, her music had evolved into something like folk-punk, and though her records were selling hundreds of thousands of copies, she refused to go the road of "major-label-rock-star," continuing to release her albums on the same small label run out of her Buffalo home. But this fierce independence, this refusal to play music industry games and refusal to occupy traditional identity roles, has gotten DiFranco into a lot of trouble with her fans. Not dyke enough for the dykes, not pretty girl enough for the straight men, not "accessible" enough for the radio stations, DiFranco remains an anomaly on the pop cultural landscape. In a post-gender, post-genre, post-identity politicked world, DiFranco would be a queen in her *Little Plastic Castle* (1998). As things are, however, Ani

DiFranco is crossing borders, blurring boundaries, and destabilizing fixed categories en route to becoming one of the most important pop musicians of the 1990s.

Melissa Etheridge (1961-)
    Born in Leavenworth, Kansas, schooled in Boston, and discovered in Los Angeles, Melissa Etheridge experienced an American Dream-like ascension to superstar status that seems almost a clichéd rags-to-riches rock-n-roll-rebel story. Rejected by the ever-important womyn's music label, Olivia Records, in the early 1980s, Etheridge's music, blending Springsteen-like roots rock, jealous rage-ridden lyrics, and emotionally drenched Joplin-esque vocals, categorically clashed with the non-aggressive, neo-folk sound popular within women's music circles of the time. Etheridge, rather, drew her early fan-base from a scene somewhat removed from the popular Womyn's Music Festivals, most notably a bar called the "Que Sera Sera" in Long Beach, California, home to a group of lesbians known as "wilders" (of which Etheridge considered herself a member). Named for their mischievous, late-night, hootin'-n'-hollerin' escapades on the streets of L.A., the "wilders" represented, in Etheridge's words, "a new generation of lesbians coming out who learned to rock and dance,...weren't into folk music, [and]...wore silly metallic clothing and stayed out all night" (Luck, 1997, p. 65). Etheridge's "wilder" days in Long Beach ended, however, when Chris Blackwell (founder of Island records) strolled into the Que Sera one night in late 1986 with a record contract in hand. The Etheridge/Blackwell partnership resulted in five albums, *Melissa Etheridge* (1988), *Brave and Crazy* (1989), *Never Enough* (1992), *Yes I Am* (1993), and *Your Little Secret* (1995), and transported Etheridge from a renowned bar rocker to an international pop musician.
    Viewing Etheridge's rags-to-riches success story in its proper socio-historical context, it becomes clear that many factors were at work in making Etheridge the so-called "First Lady of Rock-n-Roll." While a die-hard fan might argue that "Melissa" (as fans refer to her—intimately, on a first name basis) rose to fame solely because of her talent as a songwriter and her very sincere and real presence, the construction of Etheridge-as-star coincides with a late 1980s music journalist trend of pronouncing a "new breed of women" in rock music. Marketable, surprisingly enough, for defying traditional conventions of femininity and for presenting an image of authenticity financially viable within rock cultures, Etheridge achieved overnight success as part of a larger trend in which a specifically female rock audience market was discovered. However, because this womyn rocker's roots lie in the "wilder" (lesbian) side of Los Angeles, the classic double bind of homovisibility became a reality for Etheridge. Moving into the spotlight, all the while teetering between the commercially doomed label of "lesbian artist" and the dreaded moniker "sell-out," Etheridge played out her sexually ambiguous image until January 1993. Flanked by k. d. lang and several thousand screaming GLBT party-goers, Etheridge came out publicly at the Triangle Ball in Washington, D.C., celebrating President Clinton's inauguration. From there, the *Advocate, People, Rolling Stone*, and even TV news show *20/20* publicized the event, conducting interviews with Etheridge and partner Julie Cypher, all of which seemingly bolstered Etheridge's career (*Yes I Am*, released in 1993 after Etheridge's coming out, sold more than five million copies). Be it "lesbian chic" (yet another media recuperation of a potentially threatening identity), a change in public consciousness regarding gay and lesbian issues (doubtful, considering the necessity of com-

ing out only *after* one achieves fame), or a testament to Etheridge's talent, the success of Melissa from Kansas speaks to the simultaneous marginality and membership lesbian pop musicians experience in dominant culture.

Elton John (1947-)

Born Reginald Dwight in Middlesex, England, pop superstar Elton John has changed not only his birth-name, but also his image, appearance, and, most importantly for this essay, his sexual identity throughout his 30-year musical career. From 4-foot Mozart pompadours to hair transplants, from the profane "The Bitch Is Back" to the sacred "Candle in the Wind 1997" (John's tribute to the deceased Diana, Princess of Wales), and from outspokenly bisexual to married heterosexual to partnered homosexual, John has transformed his public image arguably more than any other performer in the history of rock-n-roll. These transformations, however, possibly speak more about the ebbs and flows of the societal acceptance of homosexuality in British and American cultures since the 1960s (and John's cunning to market himself accordingly) than they do about the sexual identity of one Reginald Dwight.

Labeled "rock's token queen" by David Bowie in the mid-1970s, John initially came out of the closet to controversy in 1976. Seemingly less a publicity stunt than Bowie's contrived marketing ploy (though Queer David's post-out popularity and skyrocketing sales assuredly influenced John's coming out), John's queer confessionals read a bit more sincere, a bit more believable than Bowie's blasé "of-course-I'm-gay." In a 1979 issue of *Creem* magazine, John commented on his previous *Rolling Stone* coming out interview:

> The only reason I made that statement about being gay was because nobody had actually asked me before. I don't think it was some startling revelation—a lot of people already knew. I felt I'd rather be totally honest about it than try to cover it up... get married for the sake of appearances and lash it to a toothbrush" (Hadleigh, 1991, p. 171).

That said, John married in 1984. A speculated "marriage of convenience" ("He preferred the company of men. She preferred the company of women," wrote the *Sun* in 1987 [Hadleigh, 1991, p. 171]), John's heterosexual phase might also be read in relation to the queer scare and the virulent anti-gay backlash in the early days of the AIDS pandemic. Facing a break-up with longtime songwriting partner Bernie Taupin, a significant dip in popularity, and ongoing drug problems, John may have "gone straight" (both narcotically and sexually) to salvage his career by dissociating his image from the once-hip drug-induced bisexuality of his earlier days. His 1980s tunes such as "I'm Still Standing" and "Wrap Her Up" seem to support this hypothesis—the first describes a declaration of survival, the second, a heterotypical "I love women" proclamation. But whatever the 1980s might have told us about "who Elton John is," the 1990s promised to obfuscate.

Coming back out with a string of hits, a new (this time, male) lover and a revised "I-was-gay-all-along" attitude, John transformed his career yet again in the 1990s, this time boasting Top 10 albums, huge stadium tours, and the largest-selling single of all time (the devotional "Candle in the Wind 1997"). Now as spokesperson of sorts for the increasingly visible, increasingly acceptable GLBT community/market, John contributes millions of dollars to AIDS charities and composes Top 40 music (widely accessible music for the masses) about the sometimes hidden truth of sexuality and the horrors of AIDS ("The Last Song," 1992). Without contest, then, John is the most

recognized and possibly the most important out gay man to emerge in pop music, bringing contemporary gay issues to an enormous, unprecedented amount of people. Yet, again, reading his career in relation to historical shifts in the societal acceptance of homosexuality, John's willingness to jump in and out of the closet seems more a response to the public attitude towards homosexuality at a given historical moment and more a quite understandable career-saving tactic, than any essentialized identity-truth about Reginald Dwight. Like David Bowie, Elton John played the queer market—won big in the 1970s, suffered in the 1980s, and came out on top in the 1990s. The future of Elton John's career will certainly be influenced by this market, as well as by the success or failure of gay and lesbian politics in general.

k. d. lang (1961-)

Out of the closet and into fame, fortune, and queer-icon status, k. d. lang released her platinum-selling fifth record, *Ingenue,* in 1992 with a near-simultaneous *Advocate* interview revealing her lesbianism. Elevating the issue of coming out to a new level of public awareness (and selling a ton of records to boot), lang's career is arguably the most unlikely lesbian success story in pop music history. Rising out of the overwhelmingly conservative and straight-laced American country music scene, lang, an uncharacteristically mannish crooner and a native of Consort, Alberta, cross-

k.d. lang

dressed and camped her way to stardom, eschewing traditional notions of femininity and birthright. With minimal radio airplay and outspoken left-wing politics (numerous radio stations boycotted lang for her appearance in a People for the Ethical Treatment of Animals commercial), lang nonetheless skyrocketed in popularity the early 1990s. Though country music purists took lang's playful attitude toward tradition as disrespectful, her early gender-bending aesthetic (looking like a cute teenage boy in a tailored suit) and controversial image (for instance, orchestrating, in mock-homage to Norman Rockwell Americana, a *Vanity Fair* cover shoot featuring a scantily clad Cindy Crawford "shaving" k. d. in a barber-shop setting) transgressed gender and sexual identity boundaries that once seemed ossified.

Lang's self-described "torch and twang" style of music (a hybrid of ballad jazz and country) encodes a sexually transgressive aesthetic as well. Blending passion and mischief in her singing, lang takes full advantage of the vocal and lyrical conventions of country music while simultaneously critiquing the politics and meanings of those very conventions. For example, in her cover of Wynn Stewart's 1962 "Big Big Love" (on *Absolute Torch and Twang*), lang sings (in an ironic, tongue-in-cheek manner): "Can't you see my love a-growin'/Can't you see it, ain't it showin'/Oh you must be knowin'/I got a big big love." As Martha Mockus

notes (Brett, Wood, and Thomas, 1994, pp. 261-63), lang's adoption of what was once a male subject position (Stewart's phallic, lusty first-person) and her emphasis on the double entendre of the lyrics (calling attention to that mysterious thing "a-growin'") invites a queer reading of this once-straight text—toying with the notion of a lesbian erection, while critiquing the societal insistence on constructing sexual desire in terms of the male anatomy. Further, taking into account the entirety of lang's ever-mutating career, the act of queering seems again to be lang's forte. Moving from "torch and twang" to what she calls "post-nuclear cabaret" (*Ingenune*) to an ethereal, mostly instrumental soundtrack (*Even Cowgirls Get the Blues*), and lately to adult-contempo-pop (*All You Can Eat, Drag*), lang continues to blend, bend, and send many an established musical genre into states of flux and uncertainty. Ever critiquing the social and stylistic norms of popular music, lang resists the pigeon-hole that was once "lesbian artist" while opening up an unprecedented space for gay and lesbian issues (and bodies) amidst the pop cultural landscape.

Pansy Division

Bored with disco? Tired of two-steppin'? Heard one too many Streisand songs? Pansy Division might be for you. Formed in 1991 by San Franciscans Jon Ginoli (vocals/guitar) and Chris Freeman

Pansy Division

(bass/vocals), the Pansies make music that is a cross between a queer Ramones and a potty-mouthed Partridge Family. Easily the most mainstream group to emerge from the do-it-yourself Queercore movement, Pansy Division gained national recognition in 1994 as the opening act for arena-rocking, MTV darlings Green Day. In doing so, as Cynthia Fuchs has pointed out (Swiss, Sloop, and Herman, 1998, pp. 108-10), the band raised important questions regarding the possibilities and problematics of queer activism and visibility in a meta-media universe. Is it possible to remain "queer" (i.e., resistant to heteronormativization) in the spotlight of dominant culture? Is it possible to be out and "sell out" at the same time? What determines these categories and who decides? In the pop music world, answers to these questions are always connected to that ever elusive category, "authenticity." But the connection between authenticity and punk music is a tenuous one—one might say a performative one. In Angela McRobbie's words, "it became clear, especially after punk, that the romanticism of authenticity became a false and idealized view" (as quoted in Swiss, Sloop, and Herman, p. 108). Using punk as a vehicle to demystify populist conceptions of the gay lifestyle, Pansy Division plays with the notion of authenticity, destabilizing and questioning the usefulness of the category in both identity politics and musicality. The Pansies live show, for instance, is chockfull of campy, tongue-in-cheek "rock-star" moves (bassist Freeman makes it all too clear that, yes, the guitar *is* a replacement phallus) that mock the clichéd conventions of a rock performer's supposed sincerity and intensity. Further, the Pansies' lyrics parody oft-reified social stereotypes of gay men (hyper-sexuality, body fascism, bitchiness, and so on) so as to debunk them. Though the Pansies are thoroughly sex-positive, part of their mission is to spread safe-sex information in an age in which "condom" is still a dirty word. On each of their albums (*Undressed, Deflowered, Pile Up,* and *Wish I'd Taken Pictures*), the Pansies sing the praises of safe-sex sluttiness, celebrating the pleasure of gay sex while cautioning the kids to play safe. All in all, the importance and influence of the Pansies on both pop music and GLBT history has yet to be ascertained. Whether novelty act or subversive gay activists, Pansy Division has undoubtedly queered the very masculinist culture of rock, bringing the often-silenced secret of homosexuality to arena-rock mentalities.

RuPaul (1960-)

The argument can be made that drag queen-extraordinaire RuPaul would not be the pop personality she is today without the earlier, marginal successes of Sylvester and Boy George, among others. Sylvester, with his gay-themed, overtly effeminate, falsetto disco hits, and George, who made drag Top 40 in the 1980s, both carved out niches in an increasingly conservative Britain and America. RuPaul, it might be said, then, simply took the (drag) ball and ran with it. Emerging in 1993 with the hit "Supermodel (You Better Work)" (released on the album *Supermodel of the World*), the former RuPaul André Charles transported drag from the houses of urban queens and made it a heterological *household* word. Not unlike the controversial *Paris Is Burning* (Jennie Livingston's 1991 documentary about drag families and drag balls in New York City), RuPaul took what was once relegated to gay cultures (not merely cross-dressing, but the spectrum of socio-cultural practices associated with drag, including the language [e.g., "she" to describe a male-gendered body], diva-worship, lip-synching, glamour, "fabulousness," and so on) and transported it into the

dominant cultural spotlight. Five years have passed since "Supermodel" hit the airwaves, and, for better or for worse, drag is now everywhere. Patrick Swayze, Dennis Rodman, and Howard Stern don dresses and make-up to boost their careers. Businessmen across America "do" drag for comic relief and stress-reduction at tense board meetings. RuPaul has her own talk show (VH-1 aired *RuPaul Show*), a radio show (mornings on New York's WKTU), a best-selling autobiography (*Lettin' It All Hang Out*), and a new album (*Foxy Lady,* 1998). What the Village People did for/to gay male culture (i.e., made both gay men and the constructedness of masculinity visible), RuPaul has done for/to drag culture, and in a sense for/to all drag queens. Be it the recuperation of a non-normative gender practice, the co-optation of a potentially hip look, or a watered-down, domesticated version of the real thing, RuPaul's drag has effectively blurred the boundaries of a binary-logicked gender and sexuality.

Billy Strayhorn (1915-1967)

For a man who didn't live to see or reap the benefits from the 1969 Stonewall Riots, Billy Strayhorn was fiercely, unabashedly queer. Commenting on Strayhorn's ahead-of-his-times outness, an Ellington Orchestra clarinetist notes: "There wasn't a lot of guys who was homosexual and acted like that, like there it was and you have to accept it—and if you don't that's your problem" (Hadju, 1996, p. 70). Born in 1915 in Dayton, Ohio, Strayhorn moved into Duke Ellington's New York City family home in 1939, where he became songwriter and arranger for Ellington's orchestra for nearly three decades. Composing such jazz standards as "Take the 'A' Train" and "Satin Doll," Strayhorn was in many ways the driving force behind the music now thought of as "classic Ellington." Overshadowed by Ellington's giant presence, Strayhorn's influence and importance to jazz history have been too often ignored, if not erased, and this erasure is undoubtedly connected with Strayhorn's unapologetic identity politics. Dressing like a dandy, arm-in-arm in public with his lover(s), Strayhorn lived his life as a visibly out gay man, refusing the suffocating world of the closet. Before the days of the civil rights movements, before the days of being "here, queer, and fabulous," Strayhorn, in a sense, *chose* to live his life as a triple minority: black, gay, and *open* about his homosexuality in a (literally) fascistic, heteronormative era. As an anonymous friend of Strayhorn's proclaims in *Lush Life: A Biography of Billy Strayhorn*:

> The most amazing thing about Billy Strayhorn to me was that he had the strength to make an extraordinary decision—that is, the decision not to hide the fact that he was homosexual. And he did this in the 1940s, when nobody, but nobody did that. We all hid, every one of us, except Billy. He wasn't afraid (Hadju, 1996, p. 79).

Strayhorn recorded a handful of critically acclaimed solo albums—*Lush Life, Billy Strayhorn Live!,* and *The Peaceful Side,* to name a few—as well as numerous collaborations with the Ellington Orchestra, Louis Armstrong, and Lena Horne, yet he died in relative obscurity in 1967. After a passionate, vivacious life, Strayhorn went out like so many other jazz greats, with one extraordinary exception. At the age of 51, his body wracked by esophageal cancer and alcohol abuse, Billy Strayhorn died by the side of his then-lover, Bill Grove.

Tribe 8

Known for dildo-castrating stage antics, a pro-anger philosophy, and a loud, aggressive punk/heavy metal sound, Tribe 8 represents a new school of lesbian-feminist politics articulated through a music labeled Queercore. Taking its name from the term "tribadism," an antiquated word describing lesbian sex, the group released their first song on a 1991 Outpunk compilation entitled "There's a Dyke in the Pit." From there this all-dyke, 5-piece went on to record a number of 7-inch singles, EPs, and CDs (1991's *Pig Bitch*, 1993's *By the Time We Get to Colorado*, and 1995's *Fist City*, to name just a few) and have toured with fellow queerpunks Pansy Division and Team Dresch.

In many ways, Tribe 8 encapsulates the historical tensions within the lesbian-feminist movements since the 1960s. Traversing the line between "woman-identification" (founded upon a model of "sisterly love") and "dyke" (a more in-your-face, queer resistance strategy) the Tribe has caused controversy within traditional feminist and lesbian circles. For example, when the band played the 1994 Michigan Womyn's Music Festival, protesters picketed the stage claiming that "Tribe 8 promotes violence against women" and "Tribe 8 hate women." Because its songs deal explicitly with such topics as rough S/M sex, raping and looting, and "using" women for sex, Tribe 8 has been critiqued for championing a queerness that comes into being only through a masculinist denigration of feminism. The Tribe, however, claims it is representing a new generation of dykes—dykes who are as scary, pathological, and "hysterical" as psychiatric discourses have historically made them out to be; dykes who perform the supposed emasculating fears that lesbians inspire in men (e.g., castration anxiety, loss of power), and who make visible (almost through imitation) the strategies by which women-oppression has been enacted (objectification, abuse, and so on). Whichever way one reads Tribe 8, however—anti-feminist woman-haters or leaders of a dyke revolution—its presence within the pop music world cannot be ignored.

Village People

Thanks to the Village People, America can no longer look at masculine icons as anything but a campy joke. The brainchild of disco producer/composer Jacques Morali, the Village People formed (or rather, were chosen) in post-Stonewall Greenwich Village in the mid-1970s. With the intention of selling gay music to the masses, Morali "assembled a group of male dancers and singers, dressed them in hypermasculine-iconographic-fetishistic regalia (biker, cop, cowboy, American Indian, soldier, construction worker), and had them record a batch of songs" (Studer, 1994, p. 250). These songs led to instant fame and success (their first three records, 1977's *The Village People*, 1978's *Cruisin'*, and 1979's *Go West* all went platinum), and by 1984, the Village People had become the best-selling disco act of all time with total record sales somewhere in the neighborhood of 20 million singles and 28 million records worldwide. But how and why did the (straight) world let this happen? How did five screaming queens dressed in the sacred drag of manhood camp their way to stardom? How did songs paying homage to San Francisco, Fire Island, and the Y.M.C.A.—sites synonymous with gay liberation, gay vacationing, and gay locker-room sex—become Top 10 hits? What was the U.S. Armed Forces thinking when it considered "In the Navy"—a song that fetishizes men in uniform and ironizes gay recruiting strategies—as a possible theme song for conscription campaigns? The answers to these questions relate to both

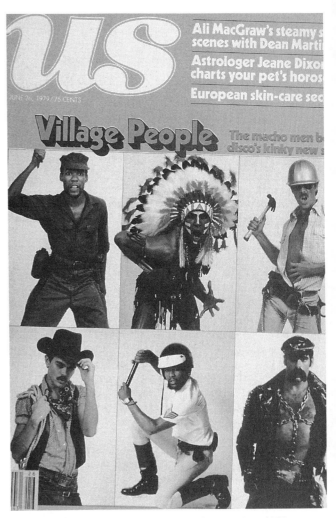

The **Village People** on the cover of *US* magazine, 1979.

America's general ignorance of gay liberationist discourse in the 1970s and to the process whereby marginalized cultures get co-opted and exoticized within the mainstream. Once the Village People's inside joke (that they were eroticizing masculinity, not merely reinscribing it) was discovered, America's naiveté regarding homosexuality ended. The "Disco Sucks" backlash of the early 1980s, not coincidentally at the height of the Village People's career, can and must then be read as a homophobic response to the overwhelming gayness of disco, a response intended to reinstate traditional (hetero)sexuality and masculinity as the norm. Though initially popularized as a harmless if not ridiculous group of mere entertainers, the queer joke that was the Village people went on just a little too long and was just a little too successful, ultimately leaving a bad taste in America's mouth—a bad taste, however, that brought gay liberation to the unsuspecting masses.

CLASSICAL MUSIC AND OPERA

Gay and lesbian identities, influences, and presence in classical music and opera can scarcely be overestimated. Indeed classical music is and has long been a field, as the queer musicologist Philip Brett notes, to which a "large number of homosexuals . . . flock"

(Brett, 1997, p. 152), and undoubtedly the art of music has been significantly shaped and constituted by gay and lesbian lives and sensibilities. Of course, the full extent to which music and homosexuality intersect and reflect one another can never be known, especially given the longstanding and pervasive effects of the closet—whose own contours are variously inscribed upon and determinative of Western art music, as any student of Britten's operas, or Thomson's criticism, might well know.

But a recuperative and generative project (in which the present essay takes part) of exposing and overtly enacting musical queerness and queer musicality is now underway in every significant arena of American musical creation, performance, and discourse. The outlines of this project are narrated and (to some extent) mirrored in the "Production and Performance" and "Reception and Criticism" sections below. The former section considers lesbian-gay involvements in music's cultural production and performance, distinguishing here four loci of practice: (1) The professional activities of gay and lesbian creative and performing musicians, contemporary and historical—their traditional (closeted) presence in classical music and opera, and recent and ongoing amplifications in visibility and voice. (2) The post-Stonewall birth and growth of amateur lesbian and gay choruses, bands, and orchestras, functioning as musical and sociopolitical bodies. (3) The recent appearance and increasing use of overt gay and lesbian themes (including musical responses to the AIDS crisis and other subjects) in art-musical and operatic composition. (4) New marketing strategies in the music industry that target lesbian and gay audiences with specially packaged recordings and concerts.

The "Reception and Criticism" section presents a concise history and overview of the new queer music studies, and distinguishes two primary modes of discourse being cultivated there: (1) Discourse that frankly and integratively reads queerness in the musical objects of its (biographical and critical) contemplation. (2) Discourse that frankly and integratively reads queerness in its own subject position and critical gaze vis-à-vis musical objects that may or may not themselves be assumed queer. The latter mode, entailing fundamental reconceptions of music, listener, composer, performer, and the relations among these, appears particularly significant in its potential to reshape and redefine music-critical perspectives and practices.

The "Prominent People" section identifies 70 prominent and noteworthy figures in classical music and opera who are openly, or are known to have been, gay or lesbian. The primary focus here is on twentieth-century American musicians, and the work and lives of 20 of these (virtually all composers) are treated individually in a series of brief entries. The remaining 50 musicians are presented in two alphabetical lists (of Americans, and others) giving names and musical specializations, and identifying further relevant homo-explicit readings.

The four prose sections below frequently refer the reader (by parenthetical author-date citations) to the final section, "References," which lists bibliographic resources under five subsections: "Books," "Essays in Edited Collections," "Periodicals," "Internet Sites," and "Recordings and Other." Given the ample availability of standard musical and music-critical texts that ignore or deny gay and lesbian issues, and the scarcity of texts that acknowledge and integrate these, the present reference list is devoted exclusively to materials of the latter, homo-explicit sort. The "References" section thus assembled represents probably the most comprehensive selective compilation to date of resources on gay and lesbian issues in American classical music and opera. It will undoubtedly

be most useful when used in conjunction with the prose discussions that precede it, which identify, contextualize, and suggest connections among topics treated in the cited texts (whose titles are usually insufficient as indicators of their contents). For references beyond the date of this publication consult the ongoing bibliography in *GLSG Newsletter: For the Gay and Lesbian Study Group of the American Musicological Society* (see AMS entry under "Internet Sites" in "References").

Production and Performance

The number of openly gay and lesbian composers and performers in American classical music has risen dramatically in recent years, mirroring similar shifts in many other fields and society at large. But even in past times ruled by the closet and the open secret, the classical music and opera worlds have been known within gay and lesbian circles as highly queer domains, and to some extent (in certain musical and instrumental specializations particularly) as predominantly queer-determined ones. We can now observe, for example, some 15 years after the event, that when Virgil Thomson received Kennedy Center Honors in 1983 for lifetime achievement in the arts, he was not only (as has been remarked) the third classical composer-musician thus honored since the awards' 1978 inception, but the third *queer* classical composer-musician thus honored: Aaron Copland and Leonard Bernstein had preceded him in 1979 and 1980, respectively. The gay unanimity in this trio of artists, formally recognized as America's most outstanding living contributors to classical music, went scrupulously unacknowledged by all involved; but today all three, now deceased, are discussed rather uncontroversially in relation to the facts of their gay lives and identities. If this instance suggests a central role and formidable, even saturating, presence of queer persons in the twentieth-century American (and broader) culture of classical music, it also points to the potent and often impenetrable forces of silence and invisibility that marginalize, appropriate (under compulsory heterosexuality), and efface the lives and contributions of gays and lesbians in art music—and hence the problems and difficulties of assembling any fair and representative picture in this realm.

Recent postmodern discourses on music challenge received constructions of Western art music as abstract, eternal, transcendent, and hence removed from bodily and sexual—particularly homosexual—concerns. But mainstream culture has long regarded as taboo any suggestion of connections between abject queerness and exalted classical music—even while betraying suspicions of these very connections, suspicions evinced in the sometimes clamorous homophobia that has often attached to classical music and its culture (see Brett, 1994a for an extended comparison of "musicality" with "homosexuality," and Tick, 1993 for examination of gyno- and homophobia as vividly expressed by the composer Charles Ives). The inextricable coupling of such homophobia with misogyny and gynophobia (within conventional conceptions of male homosexuality as effeminacy) hints at the traditional male dominance of the musical art and profession—perhaps most importantly and tenaciously in positions of power and authority such as composer and conductor. All of this can further suggest the marginalized position of lesbian women within music in general, and by comparison with gay men in music. Lesbians are found among classical musicians and music scholars of every stripe, from pioneering women composers and conductors to opera divas. But while the presence and contributions of lesbians in art music are significant, they are far less visible and readily documented than those of gay men; the present essay in its focuses and emphases reflects these facts of asymmetrically gendered musical life.

Although serious music has long involved homosexuals in large numbers and important positions, it has not, until very recently, overtly reflected gay and lesbian presence or experience. Closeted queer composers wrote, and performers presented, works on themes of heterosexual lives and loves, or else created and performed abstract instrumental works to be appropriated under the mantle of the putatively "universal" themes of mainstream culture. A strict separation of musicality and homosexuality (in light of their apparent dangerous affinities) was enforced by means both unofficial and official. One illustration of this can be found in accounts, given by the composer David Diamond and others, of Director Howard Hanson's purges of homosexual faculty and students from the prestigious Eastman School of Music in the 1930s (Schwarz, 1994, p. 24). Similarly, in the 1940s, a close-knit group of important composers including Diamond, Aaron Copland, Virgil Thomson, Marc Blitzstein, and Leonard Bernstein moved powerfully on the New York scene, but while their homosexuality was an open secret in the music world, publicly it was unacknowledged, disguised, denied from all sides—in the 1940s, certainly in the 1950s (when Copland was called to testify before the House Un-American Activities Committee), and well beyond.

Of course, public denials do not deter private gossip, and gay composers' success in 1940s New York inspired conspiracy theories among resentful straight colleagues, as in other times and places speculations have flourished on the existence of a gay cabal controlling the serious music world (see Secrest, 1994, pp. 256-57 for some uncritically cited examples; and Tippett, 1991, p. 214 for critical mention of similar scuttlebutt in 1940s Britain, centering on Britten and Pears). In fact, certain gay composers including Henry Cowell and Lou Harrison were among the earliest and most vocal champions of the music of straight modernist colleagues such as Ruggles, Varèse, and Ives; that the recipients of these efforts, meanwhile, were themselves generative of gay-conspiracy theories (see Schwarz, 1994, p. 24 on the Varèse-Ruggles correspondence) and in the case of Ives virulent homophobic fulminations suggests an ironic tale warranting further illumination.

But musical culture post-Stonewall shows ever expanding queer effects and openness on several fronts of musical performance and production. One resonant development has been the growth of amateur lesbian and gay performing ensembles, which now exist in large cities and smaller towns across the country (and internationally as well). Beginning from the formation of the San Francisco Gay Men's Chorus in 1978 and of choruses in Los Angeles, Chicago, and Seattle over the following year, by 1993 the Gay & Lesbian Association of Choruses (GALA) claimed 188 member choruses throughout North America (Attinello, 1994). Amateur orchestras and bands have also sprung up; the Lesbian & Gay Bands of America umbrella organization held its first meeting in 1982, and by 1992 claimed 23 member bands, including marching, concert, and big bands. All such groups, by their fundamental organizing principle of lesbian/gay membership and focus, and from a grassroots level, defy and erode the traditional enforced separation of musicality and homosexuality in the music world.

By comparison with the amateur-ensemble sphere, queer inroads have been forged somewhat less readily at professional and institutional levels of musical performance. And the significant lesbian-gay developments here are found in other performance-pro-

John Corigliano (left) and William Hoffman

duction dimensions, including those of individual creative and performing artists who are openly gay or lesbian (see "Prominent People" below), and of gay and lesbian themes treated in musical works. Probably the most celebrated example in the latter regard is John Corigliano's Symphony No. 1 (1989), a tribute to persons with AIDS. Other responses to the AIDS crisis have come from gay and straight composers and performers both and include Robert Moran's requiem *Chant du Cygne* (see Schwarz, 1996c), and the *AIDS Quilt Songbook* project conceived and organized by the late baritone William Parker (Parker, 1994). The year 1995 saw the premiere of the first major opera to feature an openly gay central character, composer Stewart Wallace and gay librettist Michael Korie's *Harvey Milk*, treating the rise and 1978 assassination of San Francisco's gay supervisor (see Peraino, 1997). Recent works on lesbian themes include two featured on CRI's *Lesbian American Composers* disc (Dalton, 1998): Linda Montano's piece "Portrait of Sappho" (1997), and Paula M. Kimper's opera *Patience and Sarah* (1997), with a libretto by Wende Persons based on Isabel Miller's classic lesbian novel. Premiered at New York's 1998 Lincoln Center Festival, *Patience and Sarah* is the first opera ever to focus on a romantic love between two women (see Hilferty, 1998b).

Most recently, gay and lesbian sexuality has figured as a theme not only of musical works, but one around which to organize concert programs and recordings (e.g., the *AIDS Quilt Songbook*), and as a basis for marketing strategy. In 1995, Atlantic Records became the first major record company to create a department exclusively devoted to understanding and targeting gay and lesbian markets (see Wyman, 1995; Miller, 1996). By 1996, several classical music labels had released CDs specifically addressed to lesbian and gay audiences (see Hannaham, 1996; NPR, 1996; Ulrich, 1996). In addition to purported gay-lesbian demographic factors of educated tastes and disposable income, the plausibility and proven profitability of such marketing strategies seems linked to a particularly queer engagement with classical music and opera—to an extent no longer extant in the larger culture, and involving a kind of fetishism-of-the-abandoned registered rhapsodically by Wayne Koestenbaum: "just at the moment that opera became a museum piece . . . it invited gay appropriation" (Koestenbaum, 1993, p. 47). Indeed, the classical music marketed to gay and lesbian audiences has mostly comprised compilation CDs of reissued and remastered classical tracks, well-known "chestnuts" of the repertory recombined and (usually) homoerotically repackaged. Examples include Teldec's gay-targeted *Sensual Classics* and *Sensual Classics, Too;* BMG Classics' *Ultimate Opera Queen;* and RCA's *Out Classics* and (cosexually targeted) *Out Classics II;* lesbian-targeted offerings include Rising Star Records' *Classical Erotica* and *Classical Erotica II: Dreams of Desire.* Somewhat by contrast, the nonprofit CRI label has issued gay- and lesbian-focused CDs featuring lesser-known works and newly issued tracks: releases include *Gay American Composers,* vols. 1 and 2 (Dalton, 1996, 1997), and the above-mentioned *Lesbian American Composers* (Dalton, 1998).

Reception and Criticism

Recent interfacings with gay-lesbian and gender studies have significantly transformed the reception and criticism of art music; this has been important news for queer-interested music studies and for music scholarship generally, as such linkages have engendered some of the most vital and stimulating recent work in the field. Fundamental changes in reception have developed hand-in-hand with postmodern theory's displacement of universalist discourses in favor of diverse and clearly specified "positionalities"—of objectivity by subjectivity. Thus age-old questions—Does homosexuality make any difference in one's experience, creation, or performance of music? What might such difference(s) be?—are being asked and answered, fleshed out, and complicated by a broad array of affirmative responses. A body of recent discourses acknowledge the existence of gay and lesbian musicians and consider possible connections between their sexual identities and music; examples include Philip Brett's work on Benjamin Britten, Elizabeth Wood's work on Ethyl Smyth, work on Schubert and Handel, and more. Other recent discourses focus on queer receptions of music (itself presumed queer or not); examples include Koestenbaum's (1989, 1993) and Mitchell Morris's (1993) opera queens' readings of various operatic performances, Suzanne Cusick's (1994) and Judith Peraino's (1995) lesbian readings of classical music and opera, and a growing number of further writings (see list at the end of this section).

The history of gay and lesbian music scholarship is a very recent one that might conveniently be dated from 1989 (see Brett, 1994c). In that year, the prestigious journal *19th Century Music*

published Maynard Solomon's essay "Franz Schubert and the Peacocks of Benvenuto Cellini," which proposed that the revered nineteenth-century composer had engaged in erotic activities with other men. Also in 1989, after some years of informal gatherings and organizing led by Philip Brett, the American Musicological Society (AMS) officially sponsored on the program of its annual meeting in Austin, Texas, the first Gay and Lesbian Study Group. In 1990 at University of California-Berkeley, Brett led a groundbreaking "Music and Sexualities" seminar, and later that year in Oakland, the AMS meeting included the Society's first session on gay and lesbian issues, "Composers and Sexuality." The Minneapolis Feminist Theory and Music Conference in June 1991 proved a signal event: several seminal papers on music and sexuality were first presented here, and the biennial conference has continued to be an important forum for queer, as well as feminist, music scholarship. All of these developments took place in relative quiet, unknown to many music scholars and surely to the wider public.

In February 1992, Susan McClary gave a lecture in New York that sparked a public furor. Under the auspices of the Ninety-Second Street Y's annual Schubertiade, McClary presented a paper entitled "Schubert's Sexuality and His Music." The reaction that ensued was fueled not only by McClary's lecture, but also by Solomon's earlier Schubert essay, McClary's recently published book *Feminine Endings* (1991), and by the advent of a new movement in music scholarship dubbed "the New Musicology." A charter text of the New Musicology was McClary's book, controversial for its readings of Chaikovsky's music in relation to his homosexuality, and in general for its linkage of classical music, putatively abstract and transcendent, with such material and such embodied issues as gender, politics, and sexuality. These trends would continue in a trio of books appearing in 1993 and 1994, all landmarks for lesbian and gay musical discourse: *The Queen's Throat* presented the highly imaginative, idiosyncratic, and queer takes on opera of the poet, writer, and (soon-to-be) librettist Wayne Koestenbaum (1993) and was reviewed widely and importantly; and two edited collections of scholarly essays were crucially catalyzing within the academic music community: *Musicology and Difference* (Solie, 1993), and *Queering the Pitch* (Brett, Wood, and Thomas, 1994).

McClary's 1992 Schubertiade paper was immediately answered by a series of critical and even parodic responses in the *New York Times.* The *Times*'s publication of these critiques of a lecture completely unavailable in print (see McClary, 1992 and 1994), and its neglect to print any letters rebutting its own critics' columns (see McClary, Brett, and Wood, 1992), simultaneously attested to and further fueled the fierce intensity of this polemic. The Schubert debate raged on in a special issue of *19th Century Music* (Kramer, 1993) comprising pro and con responses to Solomon's 1989 essay from nine scholars. (That none of the participants in this debate were openly gay or lesbian has been noted by Peraino [1994, p. 12] and, in an essay that at last rectified this absence, by Brett [1997, p. 150].) The responses of Solomon's opponents boiled down mainly to two: those protesting the doubts cast on Schubert's presumed heterosexuality, and those questioning the relevance of the composer's sexuality to his music. The latter more tenacious question is addressed in relation to Schubert and a number of other composers in a recent body of musical discourse that deals openly and integratively with composers' queer sexuality and their work—as indeed orthodox music history, denials and "relevance" questions notwithstanding, has always made heterosexuality a part of its narratives about composers and their work. The recent work includes writings on Leonard Bernstein (Peyser, 1987; Burton, 1994; Secrest, 1994), Marc Blitzstein (Gordon, 1989; Metzer, 1995), Paul Bowles (Schwarz, 1995b, 1996b), Benjamin Britten (Brett, 1992, 1993a, 1993b, 1994a, 1994b; Hodgson, 1996; McClatchie, 1996), P. I. Chaikovsky (Poznansky, 1991, 1996), Aaron Copland (Moor, 1991), Henry Cowell (Hicks, 1991), G. F. Handel (Thomas, 1994), Lou Harrison (Levine, 1996; Schwarz, 1997b), Laura Karpman (Isherwood, 1995; Schwarz, 1995c), Pauline Oliveros (Schwarz, 1996a), Harry Partch (Blackburn, 1997), Ned Rorem (Rorem, 1994), Franz Schubert (Solomon, 1989; Kramer, 1993; McClary, 1991, 1992, 1994; Muxfeldt, 1996; McKay, 1997), Ethel Smyth (Wood, 1993, 1994, 1995, 1996; Collis, 1994), Virgil Thomson (Tommasini, 1997), and Michael Tippett (Tippett, 1991).

Perhaps it is not surprising that increased attention to the relevance question—the question of whether and how a composer's sexuality has relevance for her/his music—has elicited both further elucidation and problematization. Many queer-positive composers and commentators have by now reached agreement that a composer's sexuality is indeed relevant to his/her music. But still there is widespread resistance to assuming any simple or universal correspondence between an artist's sexual identity and creative work and to essentializing, reductive, or ghettoizing formulations such as some generalized "gay/lesbian musical aesthetic." Even among openly queer contemporary composers, one finds a diverse range of positions toward the existence and nature of connections between sexuality and creativity, as is illustrated by the composer-contributors' liner notes for the recent disc *Gay American Composers* (Dalton, 1996) and by other writings in which these questions are targeted (Rycenga, 1994; Wood, 1994; Levine, 1996).

Meanwhile, a growing body of music scholarship has begun to answer the relevance question in a way that bypasses the sexuality-creativity issue and suggests a broader and more radical importance for queer music studies. Philip Brett describes this project: "What queer musicology can do for music in general is to stop fetishizing the composer and turn the attention onto the listener. There are many pieces of music that have special gay meanings, and there is no reason that shouldn't be the basis of a new kind of analysis. . . . [I]f I hear [a musical gesture in Corigliano] as gay, then it *is* gay, whether or not others care to sympathize" (Schwarz, 1994, p. 24). Frankly subjective and/or reception-oriented queer-informed critical perspectives are taken up in Abel (1996), Brett (1997), Castle (1995), Cusick (1994), Hutcheon and Hutcheon (1996), Koestenbaum (1989, 1993), Kopelson (1996), Mass (1994a), Morris (1992, 1993, 1995), Peraino (1994, 1995), Robinson (1994), Steele (1983), and Wood (1993, 1995, 1996).

PROMINENT PEOPLE IN CLASSICAL MUSIC AND OPERA

This section focuses on the work and lives of prominent and noteworthy persons in classical music and opera who are openly, or are known to have been, gay or lesbian. Given below in alphabetical order are entries discussing 20 twentieth-century American musicians. Whereas exhaustive catalogs, discographies, and similar "standard" facts of these artists' careers and lives are readily available from other reference sources, the present text particularly emphasizes gay-lesbian issues relevant to each figure: issues of his/her lesbian or gay identity and professional and personal

gay-lesbian affiliations, and identification of further homo-explicit information sources.

The lists at the end of this section give names and relevant homo-explicit readings to suggest further inquiries into gay and lesbian lives in classical music and opera. Needless to say, there are many more gay and lesbian classical musicians than those mentioned here. In all cases their exclusion points to one or more of three reasons: they do not fit with the present emphases on prominent twentieth-century American figures, they are not out publicly as queer persons, or their out-queer status was not confirmed by the present author. General sources for further identification and discussion of gay and lesbian musicians and their contributions include: Bernstein and Severson, 1986; Collis, 1994; Dynes and Donaldson, 1992; Gill, 1995; Hadleigh, 1991; Howitt, 1995; Mass, 1996; Pela, 1996; Outmusic Online; and the ongoing bibliography in *GLSG Newsletter: For the Gay and Lesbian Study Group of the American Musicological Society.*

Samuel Barber (1910-1981)

Samuel Barber is known for his ravishingly beautiful music in a distinctive romantic neotonal idiom. Among his best-known works are *Knoxville: Summer of 1915* (1947) for voice and orchestra, and *Adagio for Strings* (1936), one of the most popular works in all of American art music. Barber's first opera, *Vanessa* (1957), earned him a Pulitzer Prize in music, and he won a second Pulitzer for his *Piano Concerto* (1962). His other prizes and recognitions included the American Prix de Rome (1935), three Guggenheim fellowships (1945, 1947, 1949), and an honorary doctorate from Harvard (1959). Barber was notably open in his lifelong relationship with Gian Carlo Menotti, an Italian-born American composer of operas including *The Medium* (1946), and Barber's librettist for *Vanessa* and other projects. See Ardoin, 1989; also Schwarz, 1996e; Dalton, 1997.

Leonard Bernstein (1918-1990)

Conductor, composer, and pianist Leonard Bernstein was the first American-born conductor to achieve international fame; the fame he achieved may well eclipse that of any other conductor in history. For several decades in his lifetime, he was the most renowned of all American musicians, and by his prodigious talent, intelligence, and charisma he eventually became a superstar on the world stage. Best known as a conductor, his primary post was with the New York Philharmonic, as its first American-born music director (1958-69), and then as its laureate conductor. Bernstein conducted major orchestras all over the world and cultivated extensive relationships with several, especially the Israel Philharmonic and the Vienna Philharmonic. Bernstein also achieved great success as a composer in the American musical theater, especially with *On the Town* (1944) and *West Side Story* (1957). In the classical arena, his compositions include three symphonies; the materially, stylistically, and religiously ecumenical *Mass* (1971); and a number of other works in chamber, vocal, and symphonic media. Bernstein was also an outstanding pianist, a brilliant lecturer and author of several successful books, and the recipient of innumerable international awards and honors, including election to membership in the American Academy of Arts and Letters (1981).

Bernstein's gay liaisons (he was married, with children) were legend in (especially queer) music circles for many years. Nevertheless, Joan Peyser created something of a stir in her 1987 Bernstein biography by pronouncing in relation to such a figure the love that dare not speak its name. Humphrey Burton's biography (1994), published after Bernstein's death, gives frank treatment to Bernstein's relationships, including his relationships with men. See also Secrest, 1994.

Marc Blitzstein (1905-1964)

Marc Blitzstein was a composer primarily of songs and stage works—operas and musicals. He is best known for one of his Broadway scores, the depression-era musical *The Cradle Will Rock* (1937), which reflects a social consciousness that features in much of his work. Also well known about Blitzstein are the circumstances of his death: in 1964, he was robbed, beaten, and left for dead by three sailors he met in a waterfront bar on the island of Martinique. Eric Gordon's biography of Blitzstein, *Mark the Music* (1989), is one of the first studies of a classical music figure in which the subject's homosexuality is frankly and fully integrated. See also Metzer, 1995; Dalton, 1997.

Paul Bowles (1910-)

Paul Bowles is distinguished both as a writer (poet, novelist, critic) and composer. Within a 1930s apprenticeship that included studies with Aaron Copland (and a few lessons with Nadia Boulanger) and participation in the Stein-Toklas Paris circle, Bowles's travels took him to North Africa, which became his adopted home and an inspiration for much of his work, musical and literary. As a composer, Bowles worked in various media, excelled in dramatic settings—film scores, incidental music for plays, and operas—and often used North African, American, and Mexican elements. One landmark in Bowles's compositional career (which flourished between 1930 and 1955) was *The Wind Remains* (1943), an opera after Spanish poet Federico Garcia Lorca written under auspices of a Guggenheim fellowship (1941). The first of Bowles's many novels, *The Sheltering Sky,* was published in 1949, and an autobiography, *Without Stopping,* appeared in 1972. He was married to the lesbian novelist and playwright Jane Auer Bowles (d. 1973). See also Weinrich and Warnow, 1993; Miller, 1994; Schwarz, 1995b and 1996b.

John Cage (1912-1992)

John Cage achieved singular renown as an innovative, avant-garde, "ultramodernist" composer, performer, writer, philosopher, and visual artist. From within an immense oeuvre broaching these varied creative realms (often within a single work), several items are regarded as his cardinal contributions: the establishment of compositional indeterminacy (in works determined by chance methods using the Chinese *I Ching*); and the cultivation within Western "high" art of an aesthetic and attitude of play, resonating with both his musical adaptations of Zen Buddhism (as in the *I Ching* works) and his lifelong engagement with the music and anti-art notions of Erik Satie. One of Cage's earlier and more concrete contributions, following studies with Henry Cowell and Arnold Schoenberg, was his invention of the "prepared piano": developing Cowell's technique of playing directly on the strings of the instrument, Cage's idea was to place various objects (erasers, metal washers, paper clips) on particular strings; his first composition for prepared piano was *Bacchanale* (1938), and other works ensued, from Cage and a number of composers.

An interesting and curious phenomenon, given his 54-year artistic and personal partnership with dancer and choreographer Merce Cunningham, his vitality well into the post-Stonewall era, and his celebrated iconoclastic tendencies, is Cage's lifelong silence on matters of sexuality. An intriguing parallel can be found in Cage's

work and its manifest preoccupation with silence (Katz, 1998), conspicuous examples of which include his best-known (and silent) composition *4' 33"* (1952), and writings such as "Lecture on Nothing" in *Silence: Lectures and Writings* (1961). A fascinating pair of essays appearing since Cage's death view his silence as a thundering void, a creative, complexly meaningful, and active gesture of resistance to hegemonic artistic and cultural forces—those of the hypermacho Abstract Expressionist community (Jones, 1993), or of homophobic Cold War culture and its coercive binarisms (Katz, 1998). Such readings suggest promising avenues for future, queer-informed inquiries.

Cage's awards and recognitions include election to membership in the American Academy and Institute of Arts and Letters (1968) and the American Academy of Arts and Sciences (1978), being named Commander of the Order of Arts and Letters by the French Minister of Culture (1982), Japan's Kyoto Prize (1989), and induction into the American Academy of Arts and Letters (1989). See also Revill, 1992; Hines, 1994; Dalton, 1997.

Aaron Copland (1900-1990)

For many years in the first half of the American century, Aaron Copland reigned as the "Dean of American Music." In a spate of enormously popular works including *El Salón Mexico* (1936), *Quiet City* (1938), the ballets *Billy the Kid* (1938) and *Appalachian Spring* (1944), *Lincoln Portrait* (1942), *Fanfare for the Common Man* (1942), and film music for *The Red Pony* (1948), Copland defined for the world an "American style" and thus realized for American serious music a long-awaited goal. His compositional language combined folk elements with modernist dissonances in an ultimately tonal framework, and became so ubiquitous throughout concert, television, and film music that it can be difficult now not to hear his original scores in terms of musical clichés.

Copland set out for Paris in 1920 and thence early exemplified a program of training and aesthetic orientation that would be revisited by a number of other gay composers, even into mid-century: arriving in Paris, he became a student of Nadia Boulanger and developed a distinctive quasitonal idiom displaying (as he often emphasized) French, as opposed to German, aesthetic allegiances. (Indeed, a fascinating study could be made of the coded resonances between Teutonic-Gallic and hetero-homo binarisms within modernist music's closet.) Following great successes in the 1930s and 1940s, Copland fell onto difficult times in the 1950s: he came under extended scrutiny from, and testified before, the House Un-American Activities Committee, and was consequently rendered something of an untouchable. As a composer, he would never again see the heights of popularity he had enjoyed in previous years; in the mid-1950s, Copland began a successful career as a conductor, however, and this would last into the 1980s.

A founder of the Yaddo Festivals (1932) and of the American Composers Alliance (1937), Copland received a Guggenheim fellowship (1925-27), a Pulitzer Prize in music for *Appalachian Spring* (1945), an Academy Award for his film score for *The Heiress* (1950), a Gold Medal for Music from the American Academy for Arts and Letters (1956), the Presidential Medal of Freedom (1964), the National Medal of Arts (1986), and numerous honorary doctorate degrees. Though his homosexuality and friendships with many other gay musicians are well known, little as yet has been written on Copland from a queer-informed perspective. See also Moor, 1991; Dalton, 1997.

John Corigliano (1938-)

John Corigliano is among the most highly regarded of living American composers and one of the most visible openly gay figures on the classical music scene. He served as the first composer-in-residence of the Chicago Symphony Orchestra (1987-90), which gave the premiere of his Symphony No. 1 (1989). A deeply moving AIDS tribute, the Symphony won international acclaim in widespread performance and by its very successful recording; it also earned Corigliano the Louisville Grawemeyer Award (1991), the largest award of its kind in music ($150,000). Corigliano's opera *The Ghosts of Versailles,* a collaboration with his life partner, playwright William Hoffman, debuted at the Metropolitan Opera in 1991 (see Mass, 1991).

Henry Cowell (1897-1965)

Henry Cowell was a pioneer in the exploration and invention of new sound resources, using traditional and electronic instruments. As early as 1912 he was writing hand and forearm clusters for the piano, and he documented his investigations into clusters, new notations, and contrapuntal and rhythmic innovations in a book entitled *New Musical Resources.* Probably his best-known compositions today are *Aeolian Harp* (1923) and *The Banshee* (1925), in which harmonics, plucking, and scraping the piano strings are used to striking, often beautiful and haunting musical effect. By the mid-1920s, Cowell had undertaken serious studies of non-European music, which led him toward new sounds and principles of musical organization: his idea of "elastic form" allows the performer to determine the order in which composed segments are played, and thus to participate in the compositional process. This early conception of indeterminacy is exemplified in the "Mosaic" String Quartet (1934), which predates by 17 years the *Music of Changes* of Cowell's pupil John Cage. For 25 years, beginning in 1927, Cowell published his *New Musical Edition,* largely devoted to music of the Americas, and by the early 1930s, he was something of an international celebrity in the music world. In 1936, Cowell was arrested on sodomy charges and sent to San Quentin Prison; while there he taught music to more than 1500 inmates, composed 50 pieces, and wrote a book and several journal articles. He was released in 1940 and granted a full pardon in 1942, but his career and person never fully recovered (Hicks, 1991). See also Dalton, 1997.

David Del Tredici (1937-)

David Del Tredici received the 1980 Pulitzer Prize for "In Memory of a Summer Day," from *Child Alice,* one of his numerous large-scale settings of texts from Lewis Carroll's *Alice in Wonderland.* Del Tredici first gained prominence in the 1960s as a composer of atonal music, but his pursuit since the 1970s of a tonal idiom recalling Strauss and Wagner has established him as a leader in the neoromantic revival. See also Dalton, 1996.

David Diamond (1915-)

Like many serious composers of his era, David Diamond ventured to Europe as a young man to pursue advanced studies and cultural credentials. And like so many gay composers around this time, he chose Paris as his destination (arriving in 1936), sought out studies with Nadia Boulanger, and cultivated a distinctive quasitonal idiom. On the strength of such works as *Psalm* for Orchestra (1936) and *Rounds* for Strings (1944), Diamond ascended to the first rank of American composers, and over the course of his career created an important body of work in orchestral, cham-

ber, and vocal media. Among his many awards and honors, Diamond has received three Guggenheim fellowships (1938, 1941, 1958), the Prix de Rome (1941), the New York Music Critics' Circle Award (1944, for *Rounds*), election to membership in the National Institute of Arts and Letters (1966), the William Schuman Lifetime Achievement Award (1985), the Edward MacDowell Gold Medal (1991), and the Medal of Arts from President Bill Clinton (1995). See also Sigman, 1992; Schwarz, 1994; Dalton, 1997.

Charles Griffes (1884-1920)

During and following studies in Berlin (1903-07), Charles Tomlinson Griffes wrote music in a German romantic style. Around 1911, Griffes (sometimes called "the American impressionist") began to cultivate an impressionist idiom, and later pursued orientalism and some atonal writing. Within a career that lasted only 13 years, Griffes managed to create a significant output; among his most popular compositions are the piano piece *White Peacock* (1915) from *Roman Sketches,* and the orchestral work *The Pleasure Dome of Kubla Khan* (1917). See Anderson, 1993.

Lou Harrison (1917-)

Lou Harrison is a composer and occasional performer and critic whose large body of work reflects a broad variety of musical interests. Like Harry Partch, Harrison has explored the possibilities of nontempered tuning systems (particularly just intonation) and invented instruments. Perhaps most predominantly and persistently, Harrison's music, like that of his former teacher Henry Cowell, evinces strong interests and engagements with non-Western music and new sound sources. His oeuvre includes operas, ballets, orchestral, chamber, choral, and solo works, as well as some 30 compositions (written since 1972) for the Indonesian gamelan, sometimes in combination with other (often Western) instruments or voices. Harrison has held several academic posts and received Guggenheim fellowships in 1952 and 1954. In recent years, he

Lou Harrison

has been the subject of frequent interviews, which usually include reference to his relationship and collaboration with longtime partner William Colvig. See also Dalton, 1996; Levine, 1996; Schwarz, 1997b.

Jennifer Higdon (1963-)

Jennifer Higdon is a composer who also performs and records as a flutist and conductor. She has received numerous commissions and awards including a Guggenheim fellowship (1997-98), awards from the American Academy of Arts and Letters, and the "Best New Piece of 1996" designation from *USA Today*. A former student of Ned Rorem, among others, Higdon currently serves on the faculty of the Curtis Institute of Music in Philadelphia. See also Dalton, 1998.

Laura Karpman (1959-)

Laura Karpman has composed instrumental works in various media and scores for a number of film and television projects. Karpman discussed her work and came out as a lesbian in a 1995 interview in *The Advocate* (Isherwood, 1995). See also Schwarz, 1995c.

Dimitri Mitropoulos (1896-1960)

One of the most brilliant and original interpreters of the twentieth century, the Greek-born American conductor, pianist, and composer Dimitri Mitropoulos is credited with definitive readings in late romantic and modernist repertories. He served as music director of the Minneapolis Symphony from 1938 to 1949 and of the New York Philharmonic from 1950 to 1956. As a conductor, Mitropoulos was known for his remarkable memory and dynamic (batonless) physicality and, in an age of conductor-tyrants, for his extraordinary humility. He was a mentor to the young Leonard Bernstein, who became his successor in the Philharmonic post. A recent biography deals with Mitropoulos's life and work, including his sexuality (Trotter, 1995).

Pauline Oliveros (1932-)

Pauline Oliveros is a composer, performer, writer, and philosopher whose work centrally involves an integrated spirituality. She abandoned musical notation early in her compositional career, claiming to locate value in the transmission of method rather than (any particular) music. In 1981, she left the music academy (a tenured professorship at University of California-San Diego), convinced that it was not structured to support her spiritual and artistic mission. Oliveros has defined her mission in terms of seeking out good sounds to appeal to listeners' humanity, and of loosening, through music, the "boundaries that oppress the human spirit." In 1985, she founded the Pauline Oliveros Foundation, Inc., which sponsors and distributes information, recordings, and publications of her work. Oliveros's music characteristically involves improvisation, and often theater; in some work, she has collaborated with her partner Ione. Oliveros's awards include a Guggenheim fellowship (1973), many consecutive ASCAP awards (1982-94), three NEA composer's fellowships (1984, 1988, 1990), and a Foundation for Contemporary Performance Arts Grant (1994). See also Schwarz, 1996a; Dalton, 1998.

Harry Partch (1901-1974)

Harry Partch was one of the most highly individual figures in the history of American music: a self-educated musician who reinvented the art form according to his own principles, and a "Hobo Composer" who spent years riding the rails as a member of the homosocial, and significantly homosexual, hobo subculture. Partch was vehemently opposed to many of the fundamental assumptions and materials of classical Western music, including its perceived suppression of corporealism and valorization of abstraction; its vocal technique (which for Partch manifested the tendencies just mentioned); and most emphatically, its tempered tuning. He professed a concern not with the liberation of dissonance (Schoenberg's credo) but rather with true, pure consonances, which he defined as those intervals characterized by simple frequency ratios (and contrasted with equal temperament's intervallic compromises and hence complex ratios). Partch set forth his aesthetics and methods in a book, *Genesis of a Music* (1949). To execute his musical vision, he created original instruments and established a performing group, the Gate 5 Ensemble; his greatest success came with a late work, *Delusion of the Fury* (1969). A recent book treats Partch's music and life, including his sexuality (Blackburn 1997). See also Dalton, 1997; Gilmore, 1998.

Ned Rorem (1923-)

Ned Rorem, as one commentator notes, "was one of the first and remains the best-known of openly homosexual figures in the world of music" (Mass, 1994b, p. 85). Rorem has written chamber and orchestral music, including his 1976 Pulitzer Prize-winning orchestral suite *Air Music,* but he is especially known as a composer of art songs—over 300. Rorem has also distinguished himself as a writer of eloquent and engaging prose. His 13 books include a series of journals and memoirs documenting

Ned Rorem

his life in the music and art worlds of Paris and New York, particularly, and offering his intelligent and frankly personal commentaries on music and culture, past and present. Though Rorem has always written and spoken openly about his gayness, he also long contended that an artist's homosexuality had no relevance to his or her work and was not worthy of comment (see Mass, 1994b). Rorem's liner notes in the recent CD *Gay Composers* (1996) imply some shift in his position, however; he states that he is "willing to fight" on behalf of the new queer political presence. He has lived since 1967 with his partner, organist James Holmes. See Mass, 1990; Parker, 1994; Rorem, 1994; Dalton, 1996.

Virgil Thomson (1896-1989)

Composer and music critic Virgil Thomson was an important voice in American music and culture for the greater part of the twentieth century. A central figure among American expatriates in the art and literary scene of Paris between the wars, Thomson returned to the U.S. in 1940 and took over as chief critic of the *New York Herald Tribune.* Serving in this post until 1954, he established himself as the preeminent American music critic of his time. Thomson's prose is distinguished by a straightforwardness, at once plain and elegant, that also characterizes his music, and in his lifetime these qualities undoubtedly served him better in the former sphere than in the latter. Indeed, as his biographer notes, Thomson's music "in comparison with composers of equal name recognition . . . has been ignored" (Tommasini, 1997, p. 6). That Thomson met with considerable frustration in seeking performances and recognition of his tonal, tuneful, repetitive, and self-consciously simple music is often linked to an ascendance of complexity and academic rigor in the postwar contemporary music scene.

Thomson nevertheless managed to produce a sizeable musical output in a variety of vocal and instrumental genres. His vocal music is universally praised for its masterful prosody—its musically and dramatically effective setting of the English language. Thomson's operas, if infrequently performed, are considered among the finest and most original American operas of the century; their importance and influence is cited by such musicians as the minimalist and experimental opera composer Philip Glass. A sympathetic marriage of Thomson's musical language with Gertrude Stein's singular textual style yielded two celebrated operatic collaborations: *Four Saints in Three Acts* (1928), on a libretto concerning real and imaginary saints and eschewing plot, narrative, and any indicated action; and *The Mother of Us All* (1947), loosely treating the life of Susan B. Anthony. Thomson collaborated with the gay poet-playwright Jack Larson on a final opera, *Lord Byron* (1972). His output also includes more than 150 musical portraits (comparable to Stein's well-known verbal ones) depicting nearly all his colleagues, friends, and lovers, as well as other subjects captured in many decades' "sittings." Among Thomson's film scores was *Louisiana Story,* which earned him the 1949 Pulitzer Prize in music (the only one ever awarded for film music).

On the topic of sexuality, Virgil Thomson was fiercely guarded and secretive, even by standards of his oppressively homophobic era. His longtime friendship with composer Ned Rorem suffered a serious rupture in 1966 upon publication of Rorem's *Paris Diary,* which scandalized with its candid accounts of Rorem's gay life; Thomson hastened to disassociate himself publicly from Rorem (Tommasini, 1997, p. 475). Anthony Tommasini's excel-

lent recent biography nevertheless treats Thomson's gayness frankly and integratively and suggests that the composer granted him implicit permission thus to "tell the whole story" after his death (1997, p. xii). This claim finds corroboration in Susan McClary's statement that Thomson had once invited her to be his official biographer "because he knew [she] would not shy away from [gay] issues" (McClary, Brett, and Wood, 1992, p. 14). See also Dalton, 1997.

Ben Weber (1916-1979)

From 1938 onward, Ben Weber worked as a 12-tone (or serial) composer and was the only queer composer among significant serialists of his generation. Among his honors and awards were two Guggenheim fellowships (1950 and 1953), election to the presidency of the American Composers Alliance (1959), and election to membership in the National Institute of Arts and Letters (1971). Weber's oeuvre included a variety of orchestral, chamber, and piano works and songs, and a memoir entitled *How I Took 63 Years to Commit Suicide* (1979). See also Rorem, 1981; Dalton, 1997.

Further American Lesbian and Gay Musicians

Christopher Alden, opera director: see Schwarz, 1996-97.
Ruth Anderson, composer: see Dalton, 1998.
Brian Asawa, countertenor: see Hilferty, 1998.
Eve Beglarian, composer: see Dalton, 1998.
Chester Biscardi, composer: see Dalton, 1996.
Madelyn Byrne, composer: see Dalton, 1998.
Conrad Cummings, composer: see Dalton, 1996.
Chris DeBlasio, composer: see Dalton, 1996; Parker, 1994.
Lori Freedman, composer: see Dalton, 1998.
Robert Helps, composer: see Dalton, 1996.
William Hibbard, composer: see Dalton, 1996.
Lee Hoiby, composer: see Dalton, 1996; Parker, 1994.
Vladimir Horowitz, pianist: see Schonberg, 1992.
Jerry Hunt, composer: see Dalton, 1996.
Sharon Isbin, classical guitarist: see Schwarz, 1995a.
Paula M. Kimper, composer: see Dalton, 1998.
Marilyn Lerner, composer: see Dalton, 1998.
Annea Lockwood, composer: see Dalton, 1998; Parker, 1994.
Robert Maggio, composer: see Dalton, 1996.
Colin McPhee, ethnomusicologist and composer
Gian Carlo Menotti, composer: see Ardoin, 1989; Schwarz, 1996e;
    Samuel Barber entry.
Linda Montano, composer: see Dalton, 1998.
Robert Moran, composer: see Schwarz, 1992, 1996c.
Alwin Nikolais, composer: see Dalton, 1997.
Kurt Ollman, baritone: see Heymont, 1991; Parker, 1994.
William Parker, baritone: see Parker, 1994.
David Sabella, countertenor: see Velez, 1996.
Sanford Sylvan, baritone: see Parker, 1994; Schwarz, 1996f.
Jeffrey Tate, conductor.
Nurit Tilles, composer: see Dalton, 1998.
Stephen Wadsworth, opera director and librettist: see Heymont,
    1991.

Other Musicians Known or Purported to Be Lesbian or Gay (those marked * are proposed to have been homosexual in the sources given)

Ludwig van Beethoven,* composer: see Kupper, 1967.

Sanford Sylvan

Benjamin Britten, composer: see Brett, 1992, 1993a, 1993b, 1994a, 1994b; Hodgson, 1996; McClatchie, 1996.

Pyotr I. Chaikovsky,* composer: see Poznansky, 1991, 1996.

Glenn Gould, pianist.

Percy Grainger, composer: see Bird, 1976.

Reynaldo Hahn, composer.

George Frederic Handel,* composer: see Thomas, 1994.

Hildegard of Bingen,* composer: see Holsinger, 1993.

Modest Musorgsky,* composer: see Turner, 1986-87; Taruskin, 1993.

Peter Pears, tenor.

Francis Poulenc, composer: see Poulenc, 1991.

Camille Saint-Saëns, composer.

Franz Schubert,* composer: see Solomon, 1989; Kramer, 1993; McClary, 1991, 1992, & 1994; Muxfeldt, 1996; McKay, 1997; Brett, 1997.

Kunsu Shim, composer.

Ethel Smyth, composer: see Wood, 1993, 1994, 1995, 1996; Collis, 1994.

Gerhard Stäbler, organist and composer.

Jean-Yves Thibaudet, pianist: see Foster-Bayliss, 1995; Schwarz, 1996d, 1997a.

Michael Tippett, composer: see Tippett, 1991.

Claude Vivier, composer.

REFERENCES:

Pop/Rock Music: Books

Attali, Jacques. *Noise: The Political Economy of Music.* Minnesota: University of Minnesota Press, 1985.

Bennett, Tony, L. Grossberg, J. Shepherd, and G. Turner, eds. *Rock and Popular Music: Politics, Policies, Institutions.* New York and London: Routledge, 1993.

Berger, M., B. Wallis, and S. Watson, eds. *Constructing Masculinity.* New York and London: Routledge, 1995. (See "Gosh Boy George, You Must Be Awfully Secure in Your Masculinity!," by Sedgwick, Eve K.)

Brett, Philip, Elizabeth Wood, and Gary C. Thomas, eds. *Queering the Pitch: The New Gay and Lesbian Musicology.* New York and London: Routledge, 1994.

Bronski, Michael. *Culture Clash: The Making of Gay Sensibility.* Boston: South End Press, 1984.

Bryson, V. *Feminist Political Theory: An Introduction.* Basingstoke: Macmillan, 1992.

Case, Sue-Ellen, Philip Brett, and Susan Leigh Foster, eds. *Cruising the Performative: Interventions into the Representation of Ethnicity, Nationality, and Sexuality.* Bloomington and Indianapolis: University of Indiana Press, 1995.

Champagne, J. *The Ethics of Marginality: A New Approach to Gay Studies.* Minneapolis: University of Minnesota Press, 1995.

Chesebro, James W. ed. *GaySpeak: Gay Male and Lesbian Communication.* New York: Pilgrim Press, 1981. (See "Gay Masculinity in Gay Disco," by James W. Chesebro and Kenneth L. Kleuk, pp. 175-188.)

Creekmur, Corey and Alexander Doty, eds. *Out in Culture: Gay, Lesbian, and Queer Essays on Popular Culture.* Durham, North Carolina, and London: Duke University Press, 1995.

Dynes, Wayne R., ed. *Encyclopedia of Homosexuality Vols. 1 & 2.* New York and London: Garland Publishing, 1990.

Easthope, A. *What a Man's Gotta Do: The Masculine Myth in Popular Culture.* New York and London: Routledge, 1992.

Edwards, T. *Erotics and Politics: Gay Male Sexuality, Masculinity, and Feminism.* London and New York: Routledge, 1993.

Fiske, John. *Understanding Popular Culture.* London and New York: Routledge, 1989.

Fleming, Lee, ed. *Hot Licks: Lesbian Musicians of Note.* Charlottetown, P.E.I.: Gynergy Books, 1996.

Frith, Simon and Andrew Goodwin, eds. *On Record: Rock, Pop, and the Written Word.* London and New York: Routledge, 1990.

Gaar, Gillian G. *She's a Rebel: The History of Women in Rock-n-Roll.* Seattle: Seal Press, 1992.

Gamman, L. and M. Marshment, eds. *The Female Gaze: Women as Viewers of Popular Culture.* London: Women's Press, 1988.

Garofalo, Reebee. *Rockin' Out: Popular Music in the USA.* Boston: Allyn and Bacon, 1997.

Gelder, K. and S. Thornton, eds. *The Subcultures Reader.* London and New York: Routledge, 1997.

Gill, John. *Queer Noises.* Minneapolis: University of Minnesota Press, 1995.

Grega, Will. *Will Grega's Gay Music Guide.* New York: Pop Front Press, 1994.

Griffin, G. *Popular/Rising Lesbian Texts.* London: Pluto Press, 1993.

Grossberg, Lawrence. *We Gotta Get Out of This Place: Popular Conservatism and Postmodern Culture.* New York: Routledge, 1992.

Grosz, E. and E. Probyn, eds. *Sexy Bodies: The Strange Carnalities of Feminism.* London and New York: Routledge, 1995.

Hadju, David. *Lush Life: A Biography of Billy Strayhorn.* New York: Farrar, Strauss, and Giroux, 1996.

Hadleigh, Boze. *The Vinyl Closet: Gays in the Music World.* San Diego: Los Hombres Press, 1991.

Hall, Stuart and T. Jefferson, eds. *Resistance through Rituals.* London: Routledge, 1989.

Hebdige, Dick. *Cut 'n' Mix: Culture, Identity, and Caribbean Music.* London and New York: Routledge, 1987.

———. *Subculture: The Meaning of Style.* New York and London: Routledge, 1979.

hooks, bell. *Black Looks: Race and Representation.* London: South End Press, 1992.

Juno, Andrea, ed. *Angry Women in Rock: Volume 1.* New York: Juno Books, 1996.

Lang, Paul Henry. *Music in Western Civilization.* New York: W.W. Norton and Company, 1941.

Lewis, L.A. *The Adoring Audience: Fan Culture and Popular Media.* London: Routledge, 1992.

Lipsitz, George. *Dangerous Crossroads: Popular Music, Postmodernism, and the Poetics of Place.* London and New York: Verso, 1994.

———. *Time Passages: Collective Memory and American Popular Culture.* Minneapolis: University of Minnesota Press, 1990.

Luck, Joyce. *Melissa Etheridge: Our Little Secret.* Toronto: ECW Press, 1997.

Mass, Lawrence. *Homosexuality as Behavior and Identity: Dialogues of the Sexual Revolution, Vol. II.* New York and London: Hayworth Press, 1990.

Marcus, Greil. *Lipstick Traces: A Secret History of the Twentieth Century.* Cambridge: Harvard University Press, 1989.

———. *Mystery Train: Images of America in Rock-n-Roll Music, 4th Edition.* London: Penguin, 1991.

McClary, Susan. *Feminine Endings: Music, Gender, and Sexuality.* Minneapolis: University of Minnesota Press, 1991.

McRobbie, Angela. *Postmodernism and Popular Culture.* New York and London: Routledge, 1994.

Middleton, R. *Studying Popular Music.* Milton Keynes, United Kingdom: Open University Press, 1992.

Moore, A.F. *Rock: The Primary Text.* Buckingham, United Kingdom: Open University Press, 1992.

O'Brien, Lucy. *She Bop: The Definitive History of Women in Rock, Pop and Soul.* New York: Penguin Books, 1995.

Oliver, P., ed. *Black Music in Britain: Essays on the Afro-Asian Contribution to Popular Music.* Milton Keynes, United Kingdom: Open University Press, 1990.

Reynolds, Simon and Joy Press, eds. *The Sex Revolts: Gender, Rebellion, and Rock-n-Roll.* Cambridge: Harvard University Press, 1995.

Rorem, Ned. *Settling the Score: Essays on Music.* San Diego: Harcourt Brace, 1988.

Rose, Tricia. *Black Noise: Rap Music and Black Culture in Contemporary America.* Hanover, New Hampshire: Wesleyan University Press, 1994.

Ross, Andrew and Tricia Rose, eds. *Microphone Fiends: Youth Music and Youth Culture.* New York and London: Routledge, 1994.

Sakolsky, R. and F. Wei-Han Ho, eds. *Sounding Off: Music as Subversion/Resistance/Revolution.* New York: Autonomedia, 1995.

Savage, John. *England's Dreaming: Anarchy, Sex Pistols, Punk Rock and Beyond.* New York: St. Martin's Press, 1992.

Schwichtenberg, C., ed. *The Madonna Connection.* Boulder, Colorado: Westview Press, 1993.

Shepard, S. and M. Wallis, eds. *Coming On Strong: Gay Politics and Culture.* London: Unwin Hyman, 1989.

Shuker, R., *Understanding Popular Music.* London and New York: Routledge, 1994.

Smith, P., ed. *Boys: Masculinities in Contemporary Culture.* New York: Westview Press, 1996.

Solie, Ruth A., ed. *Musicology and Difference.* Berkeley: University of California Press, 1993.

Stokes, M., ed. *Ethnicity, Identity, and Music: The Musical Construction of Place.* Oxford: Berg, 1994.

Studer, Wayne. *Rock on the Wild Side: Gay Male Images in Popular Music of the Rock Era.* San Francisco: Leyland Publications, 1994.

Swiss, Thomas, John Sloop, and Andrew Herman, eds. *Mapping the Beat: Popular Music and Contemporary Theory.* Oxford: Blackwell Publishers, 1998.

Ventura, Michael. "Hear That Long Snake Moan." In *Shadow Dancin' in the USA.* Los Angeles: J.P. Tarcher, 1985.

Walser, Rob. *Running with the Devil: Power, Gender, and Madness in Heavy Metal Music.* Hanover, New Hampshire: Wesleyan University Press, 1993.

Weil, K. *Androgyny and the Denial of Difference.* Charlottesville and London: University Press of Virginia, 1992.

Weis, Piero and Richard Taruskin, eds. *Music in the Western World: A History in Documents.* New York: Schirmer Books, 1984.

Werthem, Frederic. *The World of Fanzines: A Special Form of Communication.* Carbondale: University of Illinois Press, 1973.

Whitely, Sheila. *The Space between the Notes: Rock and the Counter-Culture.* London and New York: Routledge, 1992.

———, ed. *Sexing the Groove: Popular Music and Gender.* London and New York: Routledge, 1997.

Wicke, P. *Rock Music.* Cambridge: Cambridge University Press, 1990.

Pop/Rock Music: Periodicals Articles

Balfour, Ian. "Revolutions Per Minute on the Pet Shop Boys Forever," in *Surfaces,* vol. 1, no. 2, 1991: folio 1.

Block, Adam. "Cracks in the Closet," in *Advocate,* 23 December 1982: 43-47.

———. "Rebel, Rebel: Confessions of a Gay Rocker," in *Advocate,* 15 April 1982: 43-47.

Closs, Larry. "Pet Shop Boys, Frankly," in *Out,* December 1993.

Coleman, Ray. "Power in the Darkness: Tom Robinson's Greatest Hit," in *Melody Maker,* 22 October 1977: 30-32.

DeMoss, Virginia. "Disco: From High Camp to High Tech—Gay Got It All Together," in *Advocate,* 25 January 1979: 17-19.

Emerson, Ken. "The Village People: America's Male Ideal?" in *Rolling Stone,* 5 October 1978: 44-46.

Faber, Nancy. "Never in the Closet or on the Charts; Holly Near Sings Uncompromisingly of Gay Love," in *People Weekly,* 13 July 1981: 103-4.

Gaar, Gillian G. "Women in Rock '92," in *Advocate,* January 1993: 77.

Garber, Eric. "T'aint Nobody's Business," in *Advocate,* 13 May 1982: 12-13, 15.

Gore, Lesley. "Lesley Gore on k. d. lang...and Vice Versa," in *Ms.*, July/August 1990: 30.

Grillo, Rudy. "Gay Moments in Straight Music," in *Gay Books Bulletin*, vol. 8, 1982: 22-26.

Herman, J.P. "Orgasm Addicts," in *Village Voice*, 10 January 1995: 57-58.

Klein, Howard. "They're Playing Our Song: Rock Grooves on Gay," in *Advocate*, 19 April 1978: 25-26.

Kopkind, Andrew. "The Dialectic of Disco: Gay Music Goes Straight," in *Village Voice*, 12 February 1979.

Phillips, Gretchen. "I Moshed At Mich," in *Village Voice*, 6 September 1994.

Phoenix, Val C. "From Womyn to Grrrls: Finding Sisterhood in Girl Style Revolution," in *Deneuve*, January/February 1994: 40-43.

Rice, Jerry. "Village People," in *In Touch for Men*, August 1978: 69-71.

Shilts, Randy. "Pop Music: Strictly Between the Lines," in *Advocate*, 29 June 1977: 10-11.

Stein, Arlene. "Androgyny Goes Pop: But Is It Lesbian Music?" in *Out/Look 12*, Spring 1991: 26-33.

Thomas, T. "Music for the Tribe: Interview with Tribe 8," in *Girlfriends*, July/August 1995: 20-22, 46.

Pop/Rock Music: Internet Sites

http://www.addict.com/ —*Addicted to Noise* Rock music magazine on-line.

http://www.advocate.com/ —*The Advocate* on-line. Often features articles on GLBT pop musicians.

http://www.gayweb.com/ —Look for "The Best in Gay Music" section.

http://www.glama.com/ —The Gay and Lesbian American Music Awards web site. Great links to other queer pop music sites.

http://www.io.com/larrybob/ —*Holy Titclamps*. Great section entitled "Queer Music Explosion."

http://www.neo.com/Monk/SanFrancisco/ —*Monk* magazine on-line. A fun, queer spin on pop music/culture.

http://www.ourworld.compuserve.com/ —"Sappho Central" web page. Women's/Lesbian Music and Links to other Gay/Lesbian Music sites.

http://www.powerup.com/ —The "Queensland Queers" guide to the gay music scene. Features different out gay artists periodically.

http://www.sirius.com/~corps —Outpunk on-line. Where to go for Queercore.

http://xpress.comm.utulsa.edu/iaspm —The International Association for the Study of Popular Music web page.

Pop/Rock Music: Journals

Hot Wire: The Journal of Women's Music and Culture
Empty Closet
5210 N. Wayne
Chicago, Illinois 60640

Journal of Popular Culture
Popular Press
Bowling Green State University
Bowling Green, Ohio 43402

Media, Culture, and Society
Sage
6 Bonhill Street
London EC24A 4PU

Popular Music
Richard Middleton
The Open University, Northern Region
Eldon House, Regent Centre
Gosforth, Newcastle upon Tyne NE3 3PW, England

Textual Practice
Routledge
11 New Fetter Lane
London EC4P 4EE

Theory, Culture, and Society
Sage
6 Bonhill Street
London EC2A 4PU

Pop/Rock Music: 'Zines

Androzine [French homopunk zine]
BP 192, 7523
Paris Cedex 13, France

Bitchfield [Catering to "teenage indie pop queer punk riot grrrls"]
Courtney Bennett
120 NE State #1206
Olympia, Washington 98501

The Burning Times [Australia's answer to *Homocore*]
PO Box 425
Clifton Hill VIC 3068
Australia

Gay Black Female [Long-running black lesbian zine]
6312 North Hollywood Blvd. #23
Hollywood, California 90028

Inside Out [Queer youth zine]
PO Box 460268
San Francisco, California 94146-0268

Noise Queen [Canadian queercore zine]
Tim Murphy
238 Glen Castle Road
Kingston, Ontario, Canada K7M 4N8

Outpunk [Now defunct, but worth the back issues]
PO Box 17051
San Francisco, California 94117

Picklejar [Long-running queercore zine]
PO Box 9785
Friendship Station
Washington, D.C. 20016

Queer Zine Explosion [The source for underground queer zines]
PO Box 590448
San Francisco, California 94159-0488

SBC [Black Gay Male Magazine]
1155 4th Avenue
Los Angeles, California 90019

Teen Fag [Caters to adolescent queer youth]
Chow Chow Productions
PO Box 20204
Seattle, Washington 98102

Trikone [South Asian Lesbian and Gay Male Magazine]
PO Box 21354
San Jose, California 95151

The V Files [Queer Indie Rock Zine]
PO Box 7984
London, United Kingdom SE13 7XR

Violin Outbreak [Long-running queerpunk zine]
321 West 16th Street Apt 2W
New York, New York 10011

Classical Music and Opera: Books

Abel, Sam. *Opera in the Flesh: Sexuality in Operatic Performance.* Boulder: Westview Press, 1996.

Anderson, Donna K. *Charles T. Griffes: A Life in Music.* Washington: Smithsonian Institution, 1993.

Bernstein, Harry and William Severson, eds. *A Catalogue of Musical Works by SGLC [Society of Gay and Lesbian Composers] Members: July 1986.* San Francisco: Micro Pro Litera Press, 1986.

Bird, John. *Percy Grainger.* London: Elek, 1976.

Blackburn, Philip, ed. *Enclosure Three: Harry Partch.* Saint Paul, Minnesota: American Composers Forum, 1997.

Blackmer, Corinne E. and Patricia J. Smith, eds. *En Travesti: Women, Gender, Subversion, Opera.* New York: Columbia University Press, 1995.

Brett, Philip, Elizabeth Wood, and Gary C. Thomas, eds. *Queering the Pitch: The New Gay and Lesbian Musicology.* New York: Routledge, 1994.

Burton, Humphrey. *Leonard Bernstein.* Boston: Faber & Faber, 1994.

Burton, William Westbrook, ed. *Conversations about Bernstein.* New York: Oxford University Press, 1995.

Collis, Rose. *Portraits to the Wall: Historic Lesbian Lives Unveiled.* New York: Cassell, 1994.

Dynes, Wayne R., and Stephen Donaldson, eds. *Homosexuality and Homosexuals in the Arts.* "Studies in Homosexuality," vol. 4. New York: Garland Publishing, 1992.

Gill, John. *Queer Noises: Male and Female Homosexuality in Twentieth-Century Music.* Minneapolis: University of Minnesota Press, 1995.

Gilmore, Bob. *Harry Partch: A Biography.* New Haven: Yale University Press, 1998.

Gordon, Eric. *Mark the Music: The Life and Work of Marc Blitzstein.* New York: St. Martin's Press, 1989.

Hadleigh, Boze. *The Vinyl Closet: Gays in the Music Industry.* San Diego: Los Hombres Press, 1991.

Hodgson, Peter J. *Benjamin Britten: A Guide to Research.* New York: Garland Publishing, 1996.

Howitt, Basil. *Love Lives of the Great Composers: From Gesualdo to Wagner.* Toronto: Sound and Vision, 1995.

Hutcheon, Linda, and Michael Hutcheon. *Opera: Desire, Disease, Death.* Lincoln: University of Nebraska Press, 1996.

Koestenbaum, Wayne. *The Queen's Throat: Opera, Homosexuality, and the Mystery of Desire.* New York: Poseidon Press, 1993.

Kopelson, Kevin. *Beethoven's Kiss: Pianism, Perversion, and the Mastery of Desire.* Stanford, California: Stanford University Press, 1996.

Mass, Lawrence D. *Confessions of a Jewish Wagnerite: Being Gay and Jewish in America.* New York: Cassell, 1994a.

McClary, Susan. *Feminine Endings: Music, Gender, and Sexuality.* Minneapolis: University of Minnesota Press, 1991.

McKay, Elizabeth Norman. *Franz Schubert: A Biography.* Oxford: Clarendon Press, 1997.

Miller, Jeffrey, ed. *In Touch: The Letters of Paul Bowles.* New York: Farrar, Straus, & Giroux, 1994.

Peyser, Joan. *Bernstein: A Biography.* New York: William Morrow & Co., 1987.

Poulenc, Francis. *"Echo and Source": Selected Correspondence, 1915-1963.* Translated and edited by Sidney Buckland. London: Gollancz, 1991.

Poznansky, Alexander. *Tchaikovsky's Last Days: A Documentary Study.* New York: Oxford University Press, 1996.

———. *Tchaikovsky: The Quest for the Inner Man.* New York: Schirmer Books, 1991.

Revill, David. *The Roaring Silence. John Cage: A Life.* New York: Arcade, 1992.

Rorem, Ned. *Knowing When to Stop: A Memoir.* New York: Simon & Schuster, 1994.

Schonberg, Harold. *Horowitz: His Life and Music.* New York: Simon & Schuster, 1992.

Secrest, Meryle. *Leonard Bernstein: A Life.* New York: A. A. Knopf, 1994.

Solie, Ruth A., ed. *Musicology and Difference: Gender and Sexuality in Music Scholarship.* Berkeley: University of California Press, 1993.

Taruskin, Richard. *Musorgsky: Eight Essays and an Epilogue.* Princeton: Princeton University Press, 1993.

Tippett, Michael. *Those Twentieth-Century Blues: An Autobiography.* London: Hutchinson, 1991.

Tommasini. Anthony. *Virgil Thomson: Composer on the Aisle.* New York: W. W. Norton, 1997.

Trotter, William R. *Priest of Music: The Life of Dimitri Mitropoulos.* Portland, Oregon: Amadeus Press, 1995.

Classical Music and Opera: Essays in Edited Collections

Attinello, Paul. "Authority and Freedom: Toward a Sociology of the Gay Choruses," in *Queering the Pitch: The New Gay and Lesbian Musicology,* edited by Philip Brett, Elizabeth Wood, and Gary C. Thomas, 1994: 315-46.

Brett, Philip. "Britten's Dream," in *Musicology and Difference: Gender and Sexuality in Music Scholarship,* edited by Ruth A. Solie. Berkeley: University of California Press, 1993a: 259-280.

———. "Eros and Orientalism in Britten's Operas," in Brett, Wood, and Thomas, 1994b.

———. "Musicality, Essentialism, and the Closet," in Brett, Wood, and Thomas, 1994a.

Castle, Terry. "In Praise of Brigitte Fassbaender: Reflections on Diva Worship," in *En Travesti: Women, Gender, Subversion, Opera,* edited by Corinne E. Blackmer and Patricia J. Smith. New York: Columbia University Press, 1995: 20-49.

Cusick, Suzanne. "On a Lesbian Relationship with Music: A Serious Effort Not to Think Straight," in Brett, Wood, and Thomas: 67-84.

Hines, Thomas S. "Then Not Yet 'Cage': The Los Angeles Years, 1912-1938," in *John Cage: Composer in America,* edited by Marjorie Perloff and Charles Junkerman. Chicago: University of Chicago Press, 1994: 65-99.

Katz, Jonathan. "John Cage's Queer Silence, Or How to Avoid Making Matters Worse," in *"Here Comes Everybody": John Cage,* edited by David Bernstein. Chicago: University of Chicago Press, 1998.

McClary, Susan. "Constructions of Subjectivity in Schubert's Music," in Brett, Wood, and Thomas, 1994: 205-34.

Mass, Lawrence D. "A Conversation with Ned Rorem," in Brett, Wood, and Thomas, 1994b: 85-114.

———. "Musical Closets: A Personal and Selective Documentary History of Outing and Coming Out in the Music World," in *Taking Liberties: Gay Men's Essays on Politics, Culture, and Sex,* edited by Michael Bronski. New York: Masquerade Books, 1996: 387-440.

Morris, Mitchell. "Admiring the Countess Geschwitz," in Blackmer and Smith: 348-70.

———. "Reading as an Opera Queen," in Solie: 184-200.

Peraino, Judith A. "I Am an Opera: Identifying with Henry Purcell's *Dido and Aeneas,"* in Blackmer and Smith: 99-131.

Rycenga, Jennifer. "Lesbian Compositional Process: One Lover-Composer's Perspective," in Brett, Wood, and Thomas: 275-96.

Thomas, Gary C. "'Was George Frideric Handel Gay?': On Closet Questions and Cultural Politics," in Brett, Wood, and Thomas, 1994: 155-204.

Tick, Judith. "Charles Ives and Gender Ideology," in Solie: 83-106.

Wood, Elizabeth. "Lesbian Fugue: Ethel Smyth's Contrapuntal Arts," in Solie, 1993: 164-83.

———. "The Lesbian in the Opera: Desire Unmasked in Smyth's *Fantasio* and *Fête Galante,"* in Blackmer and Smith, 1995: 285-305.

———. "Sapphonics," in Brett, Wood, and Thomas, 1994: 27-66.

Classical Music and Opera: Periodical Articles

Ardoin, John. "Gian Carlo Menotti: Dialogue V," in *Opera Quarterly,* vol. 6, no. 3, Spring 1989: 39-47.

Brett, Philip. "Are You Musical? Is It Queer to Be Queer?" in *Musical Times,* vol. 135, June 1994c: 370-76.

———. "The Authority of Difference," in *Musical Times,* vol. 134, November 1993b: 27-28.

———. "Britten's Bad Boys: Male Relations in *The Turn of the Screw,"* in *representations,* vol. 1, no. 2, Fall 1992: 5-25.

———. "Piano Four-Hands: Schubert and the Performance of Gay Male Desire," in *19th Century Music,* vol. 21, no. 2, 1997: 149-76.

Foster-Bayliss, David. "Jean-Yves Thibaudet," in *focusPoint,* vol. 2, no. 18, 20-26 September 1995: 20.

Hannaham, James. "Feeding the Gay Market," in *Out,* vol. 38, November 1996: 117-18; 162.

Heymont, George. "A Grand Passion: Kurt Ollman and Stephen Wadsworth Share a Life on and off the Operatic Stage," in *Advocate,* vol. 568, 15 January 1991: 59.

Hicks, Michael. "The Imprisonment of Henry Cowell," in *Journal of the American Musicological Society,* vol. 44, no. 1, Spring 1991: 92-119.

Hilferty, Robert. "Hitting the High Notes," in *Advocate,* vol. 759, 12 May 1998a: 75.

———. "Women in Love: Paula Kimper and Wende Persons' *Patience and Sarah,"* in *Opera News,* vol. 62, no. 17, June 1998b: 26.

Holsinger, Bruce Wood. "The Flesh of the Voice: Embodiment and Homoerotics in the Music of Hildegard of Bingen (1098-1179)," in *Signs,* vol. 19, no. 1, 1993: 92-125.

Isherwood, Charles. "Laura Karpman: A TV Composer's Life is an Open Sound Track," in *Advocate,* vol. 680, 2 May 1995: 54-55.

Jones, Caroline A. "Finishing School: John Cage and the Abstract Expressionist Ego," in *Critical Inquiry,* vol. 19, Summer 1993: 628-65.

Koestenbaum, Wayne. "Callas and Her Fans," in *Yale Review,* vol. 79, 1989: 1-20.

Kramer, Lawrence, ed. *Schubert: Music, Sexuality, Culture,* in Special issue of *19th Century Music,* vol. 17, no. 1, Summer 1993.

Kupper, William. "Immortal Beethoven: A Repressed Homosexual?" in *One Magazine,* vol. 15, no. 2, February 1967: 4-6.

Levine, Mark. "Annals of Composing the Outsider," in *New Yorker,* vol. 72, no. 25, 26 August 1996: 150.

McClary, Susan. "Schubert's Sexuality and his Music," in *GLSG Newsletter: For the Gay and Lesbian Study Group of the American Musicological Society,* vol. 2, no. 1, 1992: 8-14.

McClary, Susan, Philip Brett, and Elizabeth Wood. "Letters: McClary and the *New York Times,"* in *GLSG Newsletter: For the Gay and Lesbian Study Group of the American Musicological Society,* vol. 2, no. 1, 1992: 14-16.

McClatchie, Stephen. "Benjamin Britten, *Owen Wingrave,* and the Politics of the Closet; or, 'He Shall Be Straightened Out at Paramore'," in *Cambridge Opera Journal,* vol. 8, no. 1, March 1996: 59-75.

Mass, Lawrence D. "Cover Story: Ned Rorem," in *Opera Monthly,* vol. 2, no. 10, February 1990: 5-13.

———. "John Corigliano and William M. Hoffman," in *Opera Monthly,* vol. 4, no. 7, November 1991: 5-12.

Metzer, David. "Reclaiming Walt: Marc Blitzstein's Whitman Settings," in *Journal of the American Musicological Society,* vol. 48, no. 2, Summer 1995: 240-71.

Miller, Cyndee. "Record Label Puts New Spin on How It Markets to Gays," in *Marketing News,* 12 August 1996: 17, 19.

Moor, Paul. "Fanfare for an Uncommon Man: The Real Score on Composer Aaron Copland," in *Advocate,* vol. 568, 15 January 1991: 54-55.

Morris, Mitchell. "On Gaily Reading Music," in *repercussions,* vol. 1, no. 1, Spring 1992: 48-64.

Muxfeldt, Kristina. "Schubert, Platen, and the Myth of Narcissus," in *Journal of the American Musicological Society,* vol. 49, no. 3, Fall 1996: 480-527.

Pela, Robert L. "Out Variations," in *Advocate,* vol. 721, 26 November 1996: 44-50.

Peraino, Judith A. "Condensed Milk: A Review of the Opera *Harvey Milk* (San Francisco Opera, Orpheum Theatre, 9-30 November 1996)," in *GLSG Newsletter: For the Gay and Lesbian Study Group of the American Musicological Society,* vol. 7, no. 1, March 1997: 11-14.

———. "Queer Ears in Musicology: A Survey," in *GLSG Newsletter: For the Gay and Lesbian Study Group of the American Musicological Society,* vol. 4, no. 1, March 1994: 10-12.

Robinson, Paul. "The Opera Queen: A Voice from the Closet," in *Cambridge Opera Journal,* vol. 6, 1994: 283-91.

Rorem, Ned. "A Composer's Diary: Thinking of Ben," in *Christopher Street,* vol. 5, no. 4, February 1981: 49-52.

Schwarz, K. Robert. "Arias of Expertise: Christopher Alden Makes Opera More Direct," in *Out,* vol. 39, December/January 1996-97: 54-55.

———. "A Beastly Opera: Composer Robert Moran Gets Beneath the Skin of *Beauty and the Beast,*" in *Advocate,* vol. 597, 25 February 1992: 75.

———. "Bringing Bowles Back," in *Out,* vol. 26, October 1995b.

———. "Composers' Closets Open for All to See," in *New York Times,* 19 June 1994: sec. 2, pp. 1, 24.

———. "Claude Debussy, *The Complete Works for Solo Piano, Vol. 1,*" in *Out,* vol. 40, February 1997a: 54.

———. "88 Keys to Style," in *Out,* vol. 33, June 1996d: 52.

———. "Oliveros' Twist," in *Out,* vol. 30, March 1996a: 20-21.

———. "O Pioneers! Iconoclastic Composer Lou Harrison Celebrates 80 Years of Breaking the Rules," in *Out,* vol. 43, May 1997b: 42-43.

———. "Outside It's America," in *Classical Pulse!,* vol. 18, October/November 1996g: 10-13.

———. "Paul Bowles: *Migrations,*" in *Out,* vol. 32, May 1996b: 44.

———. "Robert Moran: *Rocky Road to Kansas,*" in *Out,* vol. 32, May 1996c: 44.

———. "Samuel Barber: *Capricorn,*" in *Out,* vol. 33, June 1996e: 58-59.

———. "Sanford Sylvan: *L'horizon chimérique,*" in *Out,* vol. 36, September 1996f: 65.

———. "Six-String Virtuoso," in *Out,* vol. 23, June 1995a: 54.

———. "A Woman of Independent Themes," in *Out,* vol. 27, November 1995c: 72.

Sigman, Matthew. "The Facets of David Diamond," in *Symphony,* vol. 43, no. 1, January/February 1992: 32-35.

Solomon, Maynard. "Franz Schubert and the Peacocks of Benvenuto Cellini," in *19th Century Music,* vol. 12, no. 3, Spring 1989: 193-206.

Steele, Thomas E., ed. *Christopher Street,* vol. 6, no. 9, [Opera Queen Issue], 1983: 18-59.

Turner, Jane. "Musorgsky," in *Music Review,* vol. 47, 1986-87: 153-75.

Ulrich, Allan. "Back to Brunhilde [*sic*]," in *Advocate,* vol. 720, 12 November 1996: 83-84.

Velez, Andrew. "Dressed to Trill," in *Out,* vol. 32, May 1996: 35.

Wood, Elizabeth. "Performing Rights: A Sonography of Women's Suffrage," in *Musical Quarterly,* vol. 79, no. 4, 19 March 1996: 606-43.

Wyman, Bill. "Selling Out: Atlantic Records' New Target Market: Gay Music Fans," in *Rolling Stone,* vol. 721, 16 November 1995: 40.

Classical Music and Opera: Internet Sites

American Musicological Society: http://musdra.ucdavis.edu/Documents/AMS/AMS.html. Of particular interest is the Gay and Lesbian Study Group of the AMS and its *GLSG Newsletter,* which includes articles, reviews, and in each issue an invaluable listing of current bibliographic resources pertaining to lesbian and gay issues in classical and popular music.

Classical Music Department of the World-Wide Web Virtual Library: http://www.gprep.org/classical/.

Outmusic Online: http://www.outmusic.com/. "[N]ational organization dedicated to creating opportunities for and increasing awareness of lesbian and gay composers, lyricists, performers, and their supporters."

Classical Music and Opera: Recordings and Other

Dalton, Joseph R., producer. *Gay American Composers,* vol. 1. CRI CD 721, 1996. Billed as "[t]he first disc to survey the work of living gay composers" by Composers Recordings, Inc. (CRI), a nonprofit enterprise dedicated to the advancement of American contemporary music. The volume features music by Chester Biscardi, Conrad Cummings, Chris DeBlasio, David Del Tredici, Lou Harrison, Robert Helps, William Hibbard, Lee Hoiby, Jerry Hunt, Robert Maggio, and Ned Rorem; and includes liner notes mostly by the composers, with statements about sexuality and creativity.

———, producer and annotator. *Gay American Composers,* vol. 2. CRI CD 750, 1997. Features the work of twentieth-century composers identified in the liner notes as known homosexuals: Samuel Barber, Marc Blitzstein, John Cage, Aaron Copland, Henry Cowell, Alwin Nikolais, Harry Partch, Virgil Thomson, and Ben Weber.

———, producer. *Lesbian American Composers.* CRI CD 780, 1998. Features the work of eleven living composers: Pauline Oliveros, Nurit Tilles, Linda Montano, Lori Freedman and Marilyn Lerner, Paula M. Kimper, Eve Beglarian, Jennifer Higdon, Annea Lockwood, Madelyn Byrne, and Ruth Anderson.

NPR. "Gay Composers Marketed as Such Debate Musical Aesthetic." *All Things Considered* (National Public Radio), 26 June 1996.

Parker, William, creator and executive coproducer. *The AIDS Quilt Songbook.* Harmonia Mundi 907602, 1994. Features 15 songs from *The AIDS Quilt Songbook,* a cycle comprising songs by 18 composers on texts by or about persons living with AIDS. The project was conceived and organized by the late William Parker, who performed the cycle in relay fashion with fellow baritones Kurt Ollman, William Sharp, and Sanford Sylvan for its June 1992 New York premiere, and for this recording two days later. All poets, composers, performers, and other participants in the project donated their talents and waived all fees and royalties, and all proceeds go to assist persons with AIDS.

Weinrich, Regina, and Warnow, Catherine, producers. *Paul Bowles: The Complete Outsider.* New York: First Run/Icarus Films, 1993.

—Pop/Rock Music by Thomas J. Roach
—Classical Music and Opera by Nadine Hubbs

17

Performing Arts

- **Theater**
- **Dance**
- **Performance Art**
- **Prominent People**

This chapter covers the achievements by gays and lesbians in the following three fields of the performing arts (and in the following order): theater, dance, and performance art. Within each field, the discussion is divided by gender, with gay male issues covered first and lesbian issues covered second; the performance art section follows this structure but begins with a general overview section. Please note that all biographies are integrated and collected in the "Prominent People" section, regardless of the field in which the person worked; this section follows the discussion of lesbian performance art. Also, there is a single "References" section that brings together citations for all three fields; this section is the final one in the chapter and follows immediately after the "Prominent People" section.

THEATER

Gay Male Theater

While there are records of theatrical performance in North America dating back to 1538, the beginning of professional theatrical activity in America is generally ascribed to 1752, when the Company of Comedians from London, led by Lewis Hallam, Sr., began performing in Williamsburg, Virginia. Given the proliferation of gay theater written and performed in the United States at the end of the twentieth century, it might seen prophetic that the Hallam troupe chose to make their debut in the American colonies with a performance of Shakespeare's *The Merchant of Venice.* It is unclear what seventeenth-century colonial audiences made of Antonio's willingness to be killed for his love of Bassanio, but what is not contested is the quality and quantity of plays containing gay male characters written by American playwrights two centuries later.

We do not know the extent to which homoerotics were featured in plays performed in the United States in the eighteenth and nineteenth centuries. Nevertheless, the first play produced in America that contained a homosexual character did not occur until 1927 with the arrival of Mae West's *The Drag.* Queer theory asserts that until rigid definitions of sexuality were formed in the late nineteenth century, there was no such designation as "homosexual" or

"heterosexual"; rather, sexual tastes could fluctuate across a broad continuum without exclusivity. Until the homosexual was viewed as a distinct personality type, there was little need for the presence on stage of gay characters, and since Victorian views of sexuality were shaped by homophobia, when such a character did appear on stage, it was not a flattering portrait.

While there is no consensus on terminology, this entry will follow William H. Hoffman's definitions as he set them down in *Gay Plays: The First Collection* (1979): "A 'gay play' is one in which principal character or characters are homosexual or one in which the major theme or focus of the play is homosexuality. A gay play is *not* necessarily written by a homosexual or for homosexuals" (Hoffman's emphasis). It is important to note that "gay play" as a literary genre is distinct from "gay theater," which is defined by its method(s) of performance. "Gay theater" is predicated on the notion that the work is being interpreted by homosexuals, and that homosexuals in the audience will be the ones to better appreciate and read this performance. "Gay theater" invariably employs "camp" in some capacity, a sensibility that embraces the coded, the marginal, the artificial, the exaggerated, and/or emphasizes style over content. Some form of gender blurring or transvestitism may occur in gay theater, but not necessarily any more so than cross-dressing is used as a heterosexual theatrical device. Any play can be performed with a gay aesthetic because it is a matter of style or subtext, not subject.

Whether the world of the theater attracts a higher percentage of homosexuals in its audiences than exist in the general population, or whether more homosexuals pursue a vocation or avocation in the theater, is impossible to ascertain. What is quantifiable is the perception that the theater does attract homosexuals and offers them a sympathetic environment. In 1956, a gossip magazine, *Tip-Off,* warned readers that "Broadway [was] the 'GAY' White Way." And not only did homosexuals have a "stranglehold over the theatre," even the circus was "strongly infested with the limp wrist set." Alarmed by what he perceived to be a shaping of popular culture by homosexuals, Howard Taubman published "Not What It Seems: Homosexual Motif Gets Heterosexual Guise" in *The New York Times* (1961). Taubman focused on three unnamed gay playwrights (Tennessee Williams, Edward Albee, and William Inge) whom he considered anti-marriage and anti-women. These sentiments were echoed several years later by theater critics Stanley Kaufman and William Goldman. Goldman warned his readers in 1969 that one-third to one-half of the producing/directing talents involved with Broadway productions were homosexual. While Goldman conceded that many of the best plays of the 1950s and 1960s were written by homosexuals, he nevertheless found their work troubling; when the gay male playwright writes a boy-girl relationship, argued Goldman, "he really means a boy-boy relationship," so he is forced to alter it in order to be produced. According to Goldman, this subterfuge causes anger that is manifest in the mean-spirited and vicious heterosexual characters created by the gay playwright. Goldman concluded by noting that Tennessee Williams, Edward Albee, and William Inge were all "bachelors," and that they should avoid writing about heterosexual relationships.

Goldman's homophobia was echoed by the *New Republic* critic Robert Brustein. Despairing of the "squishy allegories" written by Tennessee Williams, Arthur Laurents, and Edward Albee, Brustein often attacked Albee for his choice of subject matter: "the malevolence of women, the psychological impact of Mom, [and] the evolution of the invert."

Early Stage Roles for Homosexual Characters

Mae West (1893-1980) not only wrote some of the first roles for homosexual characters on the American stage, she also was one of the first Caucasian performers to write African-American characters and insist that African-American actors play them— no black-face in a Mae West play. While the plot constructions of her plays are weak, the dialogue is often witty and hilarious.

Under the pseudonym Jane Mast, West wrote *Sex* (1926), a play that concerns itself with a prostitute who gives up her love for a young man when his wealthy family opposes the match. Undeterred, she takes up with a navy lieutenant, but there is no apology, renunciation, or reformation of the former prostitute. While West was still performing in *Sex* on Broadway, her next play, *The Drag* (1927), opened in Patterson, New Jersey, then moved to Bridgeport, Connecticut, and Bayonne, New Jersey, where it was closed after a campaign by the Society for the Suppression of Vice. *The Drag* is a landmark in American gay drama as the homosexual characters are drawn with a sympathetic hand, even though same-sex desire was regarded as a perversion at the time. One scene features a party where 30 men, half dressed as women, dance and sing. West later wrote that "It was the oddest party ever produced on an American stage during a serious play." Billed as "a homosexual comedy in three acts" and "The Male Version of *The Captive,*" the play is in fact a serious work that contains extensive discussions of the current scientific research of the day concerning sexuality as explored by Ulrichs, Krafft-Ebing, and Freud. New York City Police Commissioner Joseph B. McKee could not censor *The Drag* because it was not yet playing in New York, but he could hurt West by closing *Sex*. So after running for 339 performances on Broadway to sold-out houses, *Sex* was shuttered, and West arrested and convicted when a jury declared that the play was immoral; West served eight days in jail and was fined $500.

Undeterred by the adverse reaction to *Sex* and *The Drag,* West wrote and starred in *Diamond Lil,* which opened at the Royale Theatre (9 April 1928) and played for 22 weeks. Bolstered by this success, in October 1928 she opened another play she had written. *The Pleasure Man*'s main character is a sexually promiscuous heterosexual who savagely abuses a former lover and is then castrated by the girl's brother. The cast of characters also includes eight homosexual female impersonators. The cast and crew were arrested opening night, released, and arrested again after the play's second performance. The case went to trial 13 March 1930, and West was accused of purveying obscene material, but a jury acquitted her. (In 1975, West published a novel, *The Pleasure Man,*

based on her 1928 play, though much of the gay male material was removed and replaced by a lesbian villain.) Curiously, just as West tried to broaden the discussion of sex on the stage, her plays and Edouard Bourdet's *The Captive* inspired legislators to add the Wales Padlock Act to the New York Penal Code. Outlawing plays "depicting or dealing with, the subject of sex degeneracy, or sex perversion," a theater presenting such work could be padlocked for a year, and even lose its operating license. Now joining the same restrictive atmosphere that had existed in England since the Lord Chamberlain's office was created in 1737, American plays could only hint that homosexuals existed. Such inference led to the codification of stock gay male caricatures: effeminate, sensitive, artistic, pederast, fop, misogynist, and the homosexual's ultimate fate of isolation, either social isolation or the ultimate isolation, death.

Since homosexuality was rarely discussed rationally in a play between 1930 and 1961, and homosexuals do not have visual characteristics, stereotypes were an efficient short-hand to make the homosexual visible and recognizable. But as John Clum points out, "there is no 'truth' to the stereotypes themselves nor the assumption underlying them: gay people are as different from each other as heterosexuals are." For many playwrights, it was not enough to use the stage homosexual to confirm the standard of heterosexuality; the homosexual was seen to threaten the lifestyle of other characters (and the audience) and must be eliminated to restore order.

One of the first plays to celebrate the dead homosexual was J. B. Priestly's *Dangerous Corner* (1932). Directed by Tyrone Guthrie, the play ran for 151 performances in London and 26 weeks in New York. Kaier Curtin notes that the play contains the first gay character in a public theater production in London since the Matchmaker in Sir John Vanbrugh's *The Relapse* (1697). Martin, an off-stage character, is assumed to have committed suicide, but he is revealed to have been a bisexual drug addict who was accidentally killed by a woman as he attempted to rape her. On stage, Gordon Whitehouse declares his love for the deceased Martin, even as Gordon's wife confirms that there is no sexual activity in their marriage.

After a six-month run in London, Mordaunt Shairp's *The Green Bay Tree* arrived in New York in 1933, where it played for five months. While one homosexual is killed in the play, by his own jeweled revolver in the hands of a minister, another is allowed to live, albeit isolated from the rest of society. Nicholas de Jongh calls it "the most dishonest and morally disreputable play about homosexuality" between the wars. Chronicling the failed attempt of a spoiled young man to leave his middle-aged benefactor for a heterosexual marriage, the play's message is clear that homosexuality is dangerous, corroding, and evil. While coded language avoids any direct mention of homosexuality, it is obvious that Mr. Dulcimer is gay and that his relationship with his young ward Julian is decidedly homoerotic. Laurence Olivier presented a very epicene Julian in the original West End and Broadway productions, and the play was successfully revived in New York in 1945 and 1951, no doubt titillating audiences with its foray into "forbidden" territory.

Noel Coward did not attempt to secure the Lord Chamberlain's approval for *Design for Living* (1933), knowing that the material was far too explicit for the West End, so he premiered this vehicle for himself, Alfred Lunt, and Lynn Fontanne in New York. Written by the most popular playwright in the English-speaking world at the time, *Design for Living* is a sophisticated sex comedy in which two men and one woman convince themselves that their class entitles them to live out a *ménage à trois*. The play makes clear that this "erotic hotch-potch" is an equilateral triangle; in fact, Leo and Otto were romantically involved before they knew Gilda. For audience members who were privy to the sexual interests of the playwright and his two stars, the full extent of the on-stage liaisons was very clear. After the play enjoyed a 17-week run on Broadway, Coward actually secured a license from the Lord Chamberlain in 1939 for a West End production of *Design for Living.* No doubt moved by Coward's popularity and the veiled bisexuality of Leo and Otto, permission was granted, and Rex Harrison led the cast into a 25-week run.

The next gay play to be produced on Broadway was also written by a British playwright. J. R. Ackerley's *The Prisoners of War,* which also escaped the Lord Chamberlain's ban because its stage homosexual is an anti-hero, was presented in London in 1935. Among a set of British officers who are interned in Switzerland during World War I, a captain longs romantically for a second lieutenant. When they are separated, Capt. Conrad loses his mind, manifested by him embracing a pot of azaleas. While Ackerley later contended that the play contained only one homosexual, the homoerotic banter between Lieut. Terford and Capt. Rickman seems to connote that these two men are more than merely pals. Conrad's sense that he would never find homosexual love is parallel to Ackerley's life as presented in his posthumously published autobiography, *My Father and Myself.* Praised by influential critic (and homosexual) James Agate, the West End engagement of *Prisoners* ran for 26 performances; its New York debut lasted only a week.

A banner year arrived in 1938, when three plays featuring homosexual characters opened on Broadway. Leslie and Sewell Stokes's *Oscar Wilde,* based on Frank Harris's biography, sensationalizes Wilde's homosexual tendencies and acquaintances, yet the author is sympathetically drawn as a genius who suffers a tragic downfall due to the fatal flaw of being reckless. Galvanized by the Broadway debut of the gifted actor Robert Morley, the play ran for 247 performances, winning its place as the first play of the twentieth century to present a frank discussion of homosexuality on the stage. *Oscar Wilde* was followed by two plays that focused on homosexual youth, advocating that they should be encouraged to be themselves and accepted for who they are. After running 827 performances in London, Mazo de la Roche's adaptation of her novel, *Whiteoaks of Jalna,* came to Broadway for 14 weeks with Ethel Barrymore. Eighteen-year-old Fitch is a talented pianist, although he is disgusted by his homoerotic feelings. Not only is the young man not punished for being gay, he is rewarded in the world of the play when he becomes the sole beneficiary of his grandmother's will. Like Fitch, Howard in Chester Erskine's *The Good* is described as "slender," "sensitive," and "emotional," but this 16-year-old is involved in a sexual relationship with a choirmaster in his thirties. Remarkably, the play finds no depravity in this relationship, although the family doctor views Howard's homosexuality as a family catastrophe. *The Good* lasted only a few performances on Broadway, possibly because Howard is presented as a well-adjusted young man who lives in a society that does not wish to grant him such self-esteem.

Williams and Inge

The combined effect of the British dramas that were performed in New York in the 1930s (*Dangerous Corner, The Green Bay Tree, Design for Living, The Prisoners of War, Oscar Wilde,*

Whiteoaks, and *The Good*) was that for American audiences the caricature of the stage homosexual was now fixed: wealthy, effete, and British. As New York theater moved into the 1940s and the country was forced into another world war, the stage homosexual changed from an object of humor or pity to one fashioned with a renewed sense of evil; *Newsweek* warned in 1949 that "scores of inverts" had infected the armed services in America. Senator Joe McCarthy added to the hysteria by insinuating that homosexuals were also potential traitors and spies.

In this repressive climate, the plays of Tennessee Williams are nothing short of remarkable for their inclusion of gay male characters who are individuals, not the caricatures of the 1920s and 1930s. While the relationship between Brick and Skipper in *Cat on a Hot Tin Roof* (1955) is oblique, Big Daddy makes it clear that he respected a gay couple (Peter Ochello and Jack Straw)—the previous owners of the plantation—and that he loves his son regardless of his sexual orientation. (It is important to note that Peter Ochello and Jack Straw, like many of Williams's homosexual characters, never appear on stage.) For all of his groundbreaking work enlarging the scope of the homosexual stage character, Williams wrote only one gay play—one in which the lead character or primary focus of the play is homosexual—*Confessional* (1968).

Cat and *Streetcar Named Desire* (1947) are significant for introducing to the American stage the male character as sexual object. Marlon Brando's muscles clearly visible through his clinging T-shirt, and Ben Gazzara's Brick dressed in a pair of silk pajamas, made these two plays unquestionably the work of a gay male playwright. The display of their bodies was not necessarily prurient, but their sexual energy was a vital part of their characterization. With the training these actors received from the Actors Studio and the lines of Tennessee Williams, a new male character type had been realized, a man who knew how to be firm and soft, able to access muscular strength and heartbreaking vulnerability with equal facility. (Not insignificantly, many of the male heartthrobs of the 1950s and 1960s were gay or bisexual: Montgomery Clift, Rock Hudson, James Dean, Tab Hunter, Johnny Mathis, and so on.)

Labeled America's "Closet Gothic" by John M. Clum, playwright William Inge (1913-1973) dramatized the sexual tensions of "respectable" lower-middle-class Midwesterners. He rarely wrote about homosexual characters, but like Williams—his mentor, friend, one-time lover, and professional rival—Inge created dynamic male characters who were crafted to be the object of the audience's gaze: Turk in *Come Back, Little Sheba* (1950), Hal in *Picnic* (1953, Pulitzer Prize, New York Drama Critics Circle Award), and Bo in *Bus Stop* (1955). During the peak of his popularity, the 1950s, Inge wrote two one-act plays about homosexuals. *The Tiny Closet* and *The Boy in the Basement* (both published 1962) present lonely, weak homosexual men whose protective "closets" and illusions are destroyed. Mr. Newbold (*The Tiny Closet*) has no sexual life but finds pleasure in wearing women's hats he has constructed for himself, until his landlady discovers his secret: "I'd rather he was a Communist.... But a man who makes hats? What can you tell about such a creature?" In *The Boy in the Basement,* Spencer frequents gay bars in a neighboring town, but his homosexuality is indicated more by his arrested social development and his domineering mother. In these plays, and in *Where's Daddy* (1966), Inge takes the Freudian position that homosexuality is a case of arrested development, therefore his gay men have no possibility of happiness.

Inge has been acclaimed by some critics as one of America's finest and most perceptive dramatists and attacked by others for purveying a trite surface realism that offers love as a universal panacea. Unable to find an audience for his plays in the 1960s, Inge turned to writing novels (*Good Luck, Miss Wyckoff,* 1970, and *My Son Is a Splendid Driver,* 1971), and teaching at the University of California at Irvine. On 10 June 1973, William Inge committed suicide at the age of 60.

With the arrival of Tennessee Williams, homosexuality became more of a topic of discussion on Broadway, but this did not mean that old stereotypes disappeared. Robert Anderson's *Tea and Sympathy* (1953) and Arthur Miller's *A View from the Bridge* (1955) both use homosexuality as the worse accusation that could be leveled at a man. While *Tea and Sympathy* does not validate homosexuality, it does challenge the standard macho mentality that masculine equals heterosexual / feminine equals homosexual. The work is certainly not a gay play, since it denies the existence of homosexuality, suggesting that a woman can prove a man is a heterosexual by making love to him: "Years from now . . . when you speak of this . . . and you will . . . be kind." But as every gay man in the audience knows, if Tom Lee is a homosexual, having sex with Laura Reynolds is not going to change his identity. Even as stereotypes continued to appear on Broadway in Wolcott Gibb's *Season in the Sun* (screaming queens; 1950), Maxwell Anderson's *The Bad Seed* (a "larvated homosexual"; 1954), Michael Gozzo's *Hatful of Rain* (psychotic; 1955), and Meyer Levin's *Compulsion* (murderers; 1957), a small coffee house opened in 1958 in Greenwich Village at 31 Cornelia Street, which would support and produce gay drama and gay theater.

Caffe Cino

Caffe Cino [pronounced "CHEE-no"] is generally acknowledged to be the first Off-Off-Broadway theater, even though the term itself was not coined until 1960 by critic Jerry Tallmer of the *Village Voice.* Actually, Joe Cino (1931-1967) originally intended it to be just a coffeehouse, but soon poetry readings, art exhibitions, folk singing, and dramatic presentations filled the tiny space, generally overflowing its postage-stamp-sized acting space (eight-by-eight feet). Producing the work of Soren Agenoux, Edward Albee, Haal Borske, Josef Bush, George Birmisa, Daniel Haben Clark, Diane DePrima, Tom Eyen, Paul Foster, John Guare, Oliver Hailey, Robert Heide, William H. Hoffman, Allen James, H. M. Koutoukas, Claris Nelson, Tom O'Horgan, Robert Patrick, Sam Shepard, Charles Stanley, David Starkweather, Ronald Tavel, Jean-Claude van Itallie, Jeff Weiss, Doric Wilson, and Lanford Wilson, Caffe Cino provided a venue for many important playwrights early in their careers.

Since the theater was unlicensed, police busts were not uncommon. But this was a safe space for queer artists and audiences, presided over by the benevolent spirit of Joe Cino. Variously described as a Santa Claus or Big Papa, Cino regularly fed starving playwrights and actors. According to Robert Patrick, Caffe Cino ran on a "non-economic level"; there was no admission charge for theatrical events, the only money changing hands was the charge for food and drink, and the actors would pass a hat at the end of each performance. Both gay theater and gay plays were a fixture at the Caffe Cino, but neither was the sole goal of its owner. Joe was gay and so were many of his customers, but according to critic Michael Smith, Joe "had no aesthetic theories, no pretensions, no impulse toward selfless service, nothing to prove."

Robert Patrick

Rather, he would admonish artists to "Do what *you* have to do…. This is my room…. Make magic!" Cino was not interested in making money but in creating an environment where "The best things happen when the entire company works together with concern for the entire production … when the entire company is completely involved with the production, onstage and off." When the spirit moved him, Joe would drop his trousers, moon the crowd, and bellow, "On with the show!"

Since budgets at Caffe Cino were small or nonexistent, the emphasis was on language rather than production values or physical movement. While most productions ran for one or two weeks, Lanford Wilson's *The Madness of Lady Bright* ran for 168 performances. The longest run at Caffe Cino was the musical *Dames at Sea*—music by Jim Wise, with book and lyrics by George Haimsohn and Robin Miller—which later moved to the Bouwerie Lane Theatre (20 December 1968) and the Theatre DeLys for a commercial run Off-Broadway, making a star of Bernadette Peters.

Born in Texas, Robert Patrick (1937-) arrived at the Caffe Cino in 1961 after attending Eastern New Mexico University. Arriving in New York to visit a friend, Patrick wandered into the Cino during the rehearsal of an all-male cast production of *The Importance of Being Earnest* and became a nightly attendee for the next three years. Patrick's first play, *The Haunted Host* (1964), is representative of many of the gay plays produced at the Cino. About a gay man who refuses to conform to a heterosexual's idea of him, the play presents a gay character and a portrait of gay life that renounces the negative and disparaging terms that had been the standard in pre-1960s drama. A prolific playwright of more than 100 produced plays, Patrick has peopled over half of them with gay male characters, essaying a larger range of personality types than any other playwright. Curiously, Patrick's most famous play, *Kennedy's Children* (1975), is not representative of his style. Constructed as a series of interlacing monologues delivered by five different characters, even though the play contains one gay male character, the focus is activism and optimism of the 1960s being replaced by the apathy of the 1970s. More typically, Patrick tackles serious subjects in his plays with an intelligent comic sensibility, played out with a fast pace and witty one-liners. In 1988, Patrick published *Untold Decades: Seven Comedies of Gay Romance,* a collection of one-act plays that chronicle gay male love in America from the 1920s to the 1980s. Never one to minimize the importance of the Caffe Cino in his development as a gay man and a playwright, Patrick not only included various tributes to the Cino in his plays, but also wrote a fictionalized account of its history in his novel *Temple Slave* (1994).

After working in advertising in Chicago, Lanford Wilson (1937-) joined the forces at Caffe Cino in 1962 as director, actor, and designer. Early in his long and prolific career, Wilson peopled several plays with many homosexual characters. *The Madness of Lady Bright* (1964) is primarily a monologue delivered by a transvestite who decides to renounce the world that has already rejected him. Other important plays from his days at the Cino include *Home Free!* (1964) and *Balm in Gilead* (1965), the latter a sympathetic look at 29 societal "outsiders," including gay and lesbian hustlers, who gather in an Upper West Side coffee shop on Hal-

loween night. Wilson rarely wrote about homosexual characters after his days at the Cino, and while his pre-Stonewall homosexual characters are treated as individuals, they share a self-hatred and denigration that is absent from characters in his later plays. In *Fifth of July* (1978), the gay relationship between two men is the healthiest marriage in the play, and their union is seen as the center of the Talley family; Wilson was awarded the 1980 Pulitzer Prize for *Talley's Folly.* Along with Rob Thirkield, Tanya Berezin, and director Marshall W. Mason, Lanford Wilson helped found the Circle Repertory Company, where he was also a playwright-in-residence and director beginning in 1969.

Other Gay Voices: 1960s to the Present

Caffe Cino was by no means the only producer of gay drama in the 1960s. First presenting his performances out of his loft on 36 Greene Street, Jack Smith reveled, as Stefan Brecht points out, in "the sheer beauty of junk." In works such as *Withdrawal from Orchid Lagoon* (1970), *Claptailism of Palmola Christmas Spectacle* (1971), and *Gas Stations of the Cross Religious Spectacle* (1971), Smith wrote and starred in "happenings" that often involved the audience in the performance. While the presentation and/or investigation of homosexuality was not the primary focus of his work, Smith nevertheless can be seen as one of the early practitioners of "queer theater." Extensive use of performative transvestitism, drag queens, double entendre, and camp kept the aesthetic of his productions decidedly gay. While his theater work privileged presentation over content, films such as *Scotch Tape* (1961) and *Flaming Creature of 1962/3* contain gay characters and transvestites. Richard Foreman told the *Village Voice* in 1978 that the "so-called leaders" of the American experimental theater owed "volumes" to Jack Smith.

Playwright/screenwriter Ronald Tavel and actor/producer John Vaccaro, veterans of Jack Smith productions, established The Play-house of the Ridiculous in 1966, declaring, "We have passed beyond the absurd. Our position is absolutely preposterous." Soon joined by playwright and actor Charles Ludlam, tensions developed in the company, so when Ludlam was fired, seven other members left in protest and formed the Ridiculous Theatrical Company in 1967. Opening with two of Ludlam's plays running in repertory, *When Queens Collide* and *Big Hotel,* this debut engagement ran for six months, establishing what would become a powerful presence Off-Off-Broadway and in gay theater.

The Ridiculous Theatrical Company was the first American troupe to articulate an openly gay theater aesthetic. Ludlam's famous "Manifesto: Ridiculous Theatre, Scourge of Human Folly," includes such maxims as "Treat the material in a madly farcical manner without losing the seriousness of the theme," and "Scare yourself a bit along the way." As playwright, producer, actor, and director, Ludlam proved he was a master of satire, burlesque, and travesty with a keen eye for the absurdities of life. While the Ridiculous Theatrical Company did not have a permanent home until 1978, when Ludlam acquired the Sheridan Square Theatre, from its inception the company was supported by a loyal following in New York, and by national tours of works such as *Bluebeard* (1970) and *The Ventriloquist's Wife* (1978). Ludlam also inspired the loyalty of several of Off-Off-Broadway's leading performers, many of whom were with him for 20 years: John Brockmeyer (1940-1990), Lola Pashalinski (1936-), Georg Osterman (1953-1995), Black Eyed Susan, and Eureka.

Charles Ludlam

Even though Ludlam is considered one of the most influential gay theater artists of the twentieth century, only a few of his 33 plays contain homosexual characters; two examples are *Caprice, or Fashion Bound* (1976) and *How to Write a Play* (1984). On the other hand, the gay aesthetic of his plays in production is crystal clear, when Camille (played by Ludlam) calls out, "I'm cold. Nanine, throw another faggot on the fire!" Nanine responds, "There are no more faggots in the house." The stage directions inform that Camille is "Plaintively looking out at the audience" as she questions, "No faggots in the house? Open the window, Nanine. See if there are any in the street." In the 144-seat basement Sheridan Theatre, high camp theatricality on a shoe-string budget was the hallmark of the Ludlam aesthetic.

Upon Charles Ludlam's untimely death from AIDS-related pneumonia in 1987 at the age of 44, the artistic directorship of the theater company passed on to his lover and long-time company member, Everett Quinton. In addition to revivals of Ludlam's plays, Quinton produced new work (by himself and other playwrights), all staged with Ludlam's signature blend of lunacy, paradox, and wit. After calling One Sheridan Square home for 17 years, the company lost a long protracted dispute with its landlord and was forced to give up its lease in 1995. Now without a permanent home, the Ridiculous Theatrical Company is forced to lease theaters on an individual basis.

In addition to Caffe Cino and the Ridiculous Theatrical Company, other Off-Off-Broadway theaters that often produced gay drama and gay theater included La MaMa and the Judson Poets Theater. Established in 1961 and run with a firm if idiosyncratic hand by Ellen Stewart, La MaMa has produced works by such gay playwrights as Harvey Fierstein, Charles Ludlam, Lanford Wilson, Tom Eyen, Robert Patrick, William Hoffman, and Jean-Claude van Itallie. In 1971, Candy Darling, Holly Woodlawn, Ondine, and Taylor Mead appeared in *Vain Victory,* with a score by Peter Allen. Charles Ludlam and the Ridiculous Theatrical Company presented *Bluebird* here in 1970, Larry Ree performed as a ballerina with the all-male Trockadero Gloxinia Ballet Company in 1972, and groups such as the Open Theatre and Mabou Mines began at La MaMa. By 1983, Stewart had produced more than 1,100 plays, more than any other Off-Off-Broadway organization. Harvey Fierstein has remarked that "eighty percent of what is now considered the American theater originated at La MaMa."

Like the Playhouse of the Ridiculous and Ludlam's Ridiculous Theatrical Company, Judson Poets Theater was more interested in a gay theatrical style than in presenting plays with homosexual characters. Al Carmines established the new theater south of Washington Square in 1961 and installed Gertrude Stein as patron saint. Dedicated to producing small-scale musicals—many by Carmines and Maria Irene Fornés—Judson was also home to post-modern dance pioneers (Trisha Brown, Lucinda Childs, David Gordon, Yvonne Rainer, Twyla Tharp) and theater experimenters (Rosalyn Drexler, Ronald Tavel).

Joe Cino attempted suicide on 31 March 1967, and died three days later at the age of 36. Caffe Cino actor and playwright Charles Stanley kept the theater going at first, before *Village Voice* writer Michael Smith and harpsichord manufacturer Wolfgang Zuckerman took over its management. Still, Caffe Cino closed its doors in 1968. After giving birth to the Off-Off-Broadway movement, supporting scores of playwrights, and presenting the most experimental, most honest, most realistic portrayals of gay life New York had ever seen, it was nevertheless impossible to continue without the presence of its founder. Significantly, 1968 is also the

Joe Cino, founder of the groundbreaking Caffe Cino.

year that the first gay play, in William Hoffman's words, that "publicized homosexuals as a minority group" was presented in New York City.

Like Tennessee Williams, Mart Crowley (1935-) was fired from his Hollywood screenwriting job, so he returned to New York determined to become a professional playwright. This Mississippi native's first produced play was a turning point in gay drama. *The Boys in the Band* (1968) played Off-Broadway for 1,001 performances. Produced by Richard Barr for $10,500, this groundbreaking play about nine gay men was the first commercially successful play set in a homosexual household. Crowley followed this success by writing the screenplay and producing the motion picture of *The Boys in the Band* (1970), directed by William Friedkin. The eight gay men in the play represent stereotypes and negative images, which while comforting to a heterosexual audience—confirming that time-honored caricatures were still alive and well—seemed to offer little pride to homosexuals in the audience. While many see in the play only self-loathing and self-destructive behavior, a 1996 revival, directed by Kenneth Elliott, prompted many critics to recognize the courage it took Crowley to write a play (a year before Stonewall) in which a diverse group of gay men were presented, not as the heroine's best friend or the psychopath next door, but as complicated human beings. In Crowley's play, it is clear that the men in this play are homosexual because they have sex with men. This honesty, and Hank and Larry's vow of love to one another in front of the heterosexual Alan, are at the very core of the play. Veteran playwright Neil Simon remarked that "*The Boys in the Band* did for plays what *Oklahoma!* did for musicals." The play flung open a door and the gay theatrical closet hasn't been shut since.

After *The Boys in the Band,* Crowley wrote primarily for film and television, with subsequent plays—*A Breeze from the Gulf* (1973), *For Reasons That Remain Unclear* (1993)—failing to find approval with audiences or critics.

While it is customary to point to the police raid of the New Year's Day 1965 Mardi Gras Ball in San Francisco and the June 1969 Stonewall Riots in New York City as galvanizing events in the modern gay rights movement, it is important to recognize that gay drama and gay theater were being presented previous to these events. Small organizations established to present gay drama/theater to gay audiences date back to 1958 with the Caffe Cino, and plays presented on Broadway that contain gay characters to 1927 with Mae West's *The Drag*. But by inspiring thousands to add their voices to the growing gay liberation movements, these events collectively ushered in a new era of gay drama/theater. No small factor in this growth was the fact that New York's ban on plays dealing with homosexuality had been repealed in 1967.

The first wave of post-Stonewall drama did not explore complex, diverse, and complicated gay male characters, but instead trafficked down well-worn roads peopled with gay stereotypes and clichés. Bruce Jay Friedman's *Steambath* (1970) and the Betty Comden/Adolph Green/Lee Adams/Charles Strouse musical *Applause* (1970) contain cardboard gays, homosexuals who are exotic appendages to the play. A favorite with regional and community theaters, Ron Clark and Sam Bobrick's *Norman, Is That You?* (1970) is a patronizing look at an interracial homosexual relationship.

Helping to usher in a new decade and a new perspective, the second wave of post-Stonewall drama ran the gamut from box office successes (*Boys in the Band*), to sub-culture plays written for a gay audience, to the work of gay playwrights being interpreted as "gay" even though the subject matter concerned heterosexual relations.

David Gaard's gay romantic comedy *And Puppy Dog Tails* (1969) enjoyed a run of 141 performances Off-Off-Broadway at the Bouwerie Lane Theatre. Martin Sherman's *Bent*, first performed in London at the Royal Court in 1979, created an equal stir in New York when it opened on Broadway later the same year, running for 240 performances. Nominated for two Tony Awards, *Bent* is the first play to depict the Nazi's persecution and incarceration of homosexuals during World War II. Sherman included homosexual characters in some of his other plays, including *Passing By* (1974), which chronicles the disintegration of a gay male relationship, and *A Madhouse in Goa* (1989), in which a man living with AIDS recognizes that the pre-AIDS homosexual world will never return. After years of delays, Sherman's screenplay for *Bent* was finally filmed in 1997.

Born in Brooklyn on 6 June 1954, Harvey Fierstein began his performing career in New York City in 1971 as a female impersonator and an actor in Andy Warhol's play, *Pork*. La MaMa produced three of his one-act plays: *The International Stud* (1976), *Fugue in a Nursery* (1979), and *Widows and Children First!* (1979). The plays were performed together as a trilogy, first at the Glines Theatre, then on Broadway, where the combined piece—*Torch Song Trilogy*—ran 1,222 performances and won the 1983 Tony Awards for Best Play and Best Actor (Fierstein). (In 1988, Fierstein wrote the screenplay and starred in the film of *Torch Song Trilogy*.) Sans suicide and alcohol or drug addiction, the play follows drag queen performer Arnold Beckoff in his quest for love, first with bi-sexual Ed, later through experiments with anonymous backroom sex, and at last finding a soul-mate in Alan. After Alan is murdered by gay bashers, Arnold adopts a young gay boy to raise. Just as *Torch Song Trilogy* is the first gay play to mirror the commercial success of *Boys in the Band* (1968), it is also radically different. In Fierstein's world, gay life is not isolated, but is

in constant negotiation with society at large. One year after the Broadway opening of *Torch Song Trilogy*, Fierstein again penned a blockbuster. The musical *La Cage aux Folles*, with a book by Fierstein and score by Jerry Herman, played the Palace Theatre for 1,762 performances, winning six Tony Awards in 1984, including Best Musical and Best Book. This musical, which also enjoyed lengthy national tours, celebrates a relationship between two men who are neither young nor beautiful, and acknowledges that they have been good parents to their heterosexual son.

Hounded throughout his career by critics who insist that *Who's Afraid of Virginia Woolf?* (1962) is really a play about two gay couples, and directors who wanted to stage it that way, Edward Albee had a clause put into the contract that a producer must sign with Dramatists Play Service before presenting the work that "All of the roles must be played by actors of the same sex as the characters." Angered by the gay relationship interpretation, Albee fumed, "I don't know of any gay relationship where one of the characters had an hysterical pregnancy."

Albee, unquestionably one of the most-significant American playwrights of the twentieth century and a three-time Pulitzer Prize-winning author, rarely mentions homosexuality in his plays. Jerry in *The Zoo Story* (1959) tells a story of a homosexual experience he had when he was a teenager, and the Young Man in *Three Tall Women* (1994) "loves his boys." Albee told *American Theatre*'s Don Shewey (April 1992) that "Butler in *Tiny Alice* is probably gay. Certainly Jack in *Everything in the Garden* (1967) is gay." But when Albee told gay and lesbian writers at the Out Write '91 conference in San Francisco that homosexual writers should aspire to the mainstream and avoid ghettoizing themselves, he was booed. *Finding the Sun* (1983) is his only play that contains a gay male relationship, but the lovers eventually break it off and marry women. Not a champion of gay drama, Albee finds Crowley's *Boys in the Band* "loathsome" and Harvey Fierstein's work equally bothersome because they "contribute to the heterosexual attitude about what it is to be gay."

With the royalties from *Who's Afraid of Virginia Woolf?*, Albee and Richard Barr set up the Playwrights Unit, which produced 1,500 new plays over the next 15 years. Unit writers included Mart Crowley, John Guare, LeRoi Jones, Adrienne Kennedy, Terrence McNally, Sam Shepard, Lanford Wilson, and Doric Wilson.

Theatrical Works by and for Gays

One immediate outgrowth of the "gay pride" movement was the creation of theater companies specifically organized to present the work of gay playwrights to a gay audience. The proliferation of these organizations is evidenced in the establishment of the Gay Men's Theater Collective (1977) and the Gay Theatre Alliance (1983), which soon counted 40 theaters in its membership. Some were intended primarily for gay men, while other organizations focused on lesbians, and still others presented Lesbian/Gay/Bisexual/Transgender material, embracing diversity in the non-heterosexual world. Unquestionably, the "flagship" organizations of American gay theater are Chicago's At the Drama Shelter (est. 1972), the Glines in New York City (est. 1976), Theatre Rhinoceros in San Francisco (est. 1977), Janus in Phoenix (est. 1981), and Alice B. Theatre in Seattle (est. 1983 to be "a gay and lesbian theatre for all people"). Alice B. Theatre was host of the first National Gay and Lesbian Theater Festival in the United States, held in 1990 in conjunction with the Goodwill Games.

With the proliferation of homosexual characters that began to appear in American drama after the Stonewall Riots, it is helpful to organize these plays by category. It is important to note that these groupings were never distinct movements or devised by articulated theory; rather, these groupings organize plays according to a common theme, subject, or point of view. These categories include: biographical plays about famous queers; gay plays that contain male nudity; plays that include a major character who is off-stage, dead, and homosexual; plays about bisexuals; plays about transsexuals; plays about transvestites; plays that use drag as a performative device; and AIDS plays. Since art does not follow strict thematic configurations, many gay plays do not fit neatly into this matrix. For example, Tony Kushner's *Angels in America* is about a famous queer (Roy Cohn), contains male nudity, transvestitism, drag as a performative device, and AIDS. So for the purpose of this study, plays are categorized under their primary attribute.

Plays about Famous Queers

Beginning with Christopher Marlowe's *Edward II* (1591), the genre of gay biographical play is rich with dramatic material that gives a physical stage presence to a homosexual character. While the motivation to write about homosexuals previous to Stonewall was most likely to capitalize on the sensationalism of the subject, plays written in the modern gay liberation era celebrate the diversity and achievements of its fathers and grandfathers.

Without question the most dramatized queer is Oscar Wilde. First brought to the stage by Leslie and Sewell Stokes in *Oscar Wilde* (1936), this celebrated wit is featured in Eric Bentley's *Lord Alfred's Lover* (1978), John Gay's *Oscar Wilde—Diversions and Delights,* and Moisés Kaufman's *Gross Indecency: The Three Trials of Oscar Wilde* (1997), and David Hare's *The Judas Kiss* (1998). Wilde and (closet homosexual) A. E. Houseman are the focus of Tom Stoppard's *The Invention of Love* (1998), and Wilde is one of many historical characters in Noel Greig and Drew Griffiths' *As Time Goes By* (1977). Moving from Victorian England to Nazi Germany to Cole Porter, the play makes the point that the gay rights movement began long before the Stonewall Riots. Other "journey" gay plays include Robert Patrick's *Un-tied States* (1990) and Peter Parnell's *Romance Language* (1985), in which Walt Whitman floats through American culture and meets Charlotte Cushman and Emily Dickinson's lesbian lover. In addi-

Flyer advertising a performance by the Gay Men's Theater Collective.

tion to *Bent,* other significant historical plays set during World War II include Oliver H. P. Garrett's *Waltz in Goose Step* (1938), which focuses on Nazi captain Ernst Röhm. Hugh Whitmore's *Breaking the Code* (1986) explores the life and death of Alan Turing, the Englishman who broke the "enigma" code.

Not specifically about a single historical homosexual, plays about Stonewall range from Doric Wilson's *Street Theatre* (1982) to a musical created by Tina Landau for En Garde Arts, *Stonewall: Night Variations* (1994).

Famous gay artists are the subject of many plays, including: Paul Verlaine and Arthur Rimbaud in Christopher Hampton's *Total Eclipse* (1968); Jack Kerouac in Martin Duberman's *Visions of Kerouac* (1977); Lord Byron in Romulus Linney's *Childe Byron* (1981); Tennessee Williams in Joe Besecker's *Tennessee in the Summer* (1985); the famous castrato La Zambinella in Neil Bartlett's *Sarrasine* (1991); Jack Smith in Gary Indiana and Ron Vawter's *Roy Cohn/Jack Smith* (1992); and Noel Coward in Craig Archibald's *Private Life* (1998). Robert Patrick deserves his own mention as the author of *Ludwig and Wagner* (1980), *Diaghilev and Nijinsky* (1980), *Michelangelo's Models* (1981), and *The Trial of Socrates* (1988).

Jonathan Katz's *Coming Out* (1972) includes portraits of little-known figures from gay American history, and *Crimes against Nature* (1977) created by the Gay Men's Theater Collective of San Francisco, consists of nine personal accounts of various survival techniques of gay men. Other historical gay men brought to the stage include New York's transvestite Governor, Viscount Cornburg, in William H. Hoffman and Anthony Holland's *Cornburg: The Queen's Governor* (1979). Playwright David Henry Hwang changed the names of French diplomat Bernard Boursicot and Beijing Opera performer Shi Peipu to create *M. Butterfly* (1987), while Harvey Milk is the subject of both Emily Mann's *Execution of Justice* (1986) and the opera *Harvey Milk,* music by Stewart Wallace and libretto by Michael Korie (1995). Finally, murderers Richard Loeb and Nathan Leopold are the subject of John Logan's *Never the Sinner* (1997).

Gay Plays that Contain Male Nudity

Riding on the crest of the gay pride movement, male nudity became almost as much a convention on Broadway as female nudity was for the motion picture industry. The dressed, sexually powerful male characters created by Tennessee Williams and William Inge were replaced by a proliferation of gay men who reminded heterosexual audiences that homosexuals are so named because they are sexually attracted to one another. In the heady years following Stonewall, gay men were free to admit that looking at naked men on stage was pleasurable. Terrence McNally's *The Ritz* (1975) and Martin Sherman's *Bent* (1979) provide audiences with naked male flesh. While Robert Patrick's work contains many male characters who remove their clothes, *T-Shirts* (1978) criticizes the narcissism and exploitation of the New York gay scene. With the discovery of AIDS, the gay male body became a complicated site of often conflicting messages. Robert Chesley sought to reclaim the joy of gay sex, at the same time acknowledging the responsibilities of physical love; *Night Sweat* (1984) and *Jerker, or The Helping Hand* (1986) reaffirm sexual celebration despite the specter of AIDS. Chesley's *Hold* offers another image, that of a naked man covered in Kaposi's sarcoma lesions, a powerful image of the character's deceased lover.

As the AIDS epidemic wore on, many gay men understandably longed for the "good old days" when desire led to sex rather than sex leading to death. Another wave of plays featured lots of nudity, and often little else: Anthony Bruno's *Soul Survivor* (1989); David Dillon's *Party* (1993); James Edwin Parker's *2 Boys in a Bed on a Cold Winter's Night* (1995); and Ronnie Larsen's *Making Porn* (1996), which starred at one point or another porn stars Rex Chandler, Kurt Young, and Ryan Idol. Many gay-oriented theaters learned that these plays were popular with audiences despite their lack of artistic content; Los Angeles' Celebration Theatre saved itself from bankruptcy in 1988 with a production matching its stark title: *Naked Boys Singing.*

Plays that Include a Major Character Who Is Off-Stage, Dead, and Homosexual

A favorite convention in the closeted days of the twentieth century, the off-stage, dead homosexual was much easier for audiences to accept than a homosexual character on stage. Not to mention the legal restrictions against such a personage, the off-stage homosexual was dramatically often more powerful than his own stage presence might have been. As a cipher on which the audience could project their worst fears or fantasies, the off-stage homosexual often was the central character in a play. Despite his importance to the play, the off-stage homosexual also reflected the invisibility of the homosexual in pre-Stonewall America: rumored to exist, but without a public face or body. Examples include: Arthur Hornblow, Jr.'s *The Captive* (1926); J. B. Priestly's *Dangerous Corner* (1932); and Tennessee Williams's *Streetcar Named Desire* (1947), *Cat on a Hot Tin Roof* (1955), and *Suddenly Last Summer* (1958). Curiously, after Stonewall, playwrights still found the convention of the off-stage, dead homosexual to be powerful, despite the growing visibility in life and on stage of gay men: Terrence McNally's *Lips Together Teeth Apart* (1991); A. R. Gurney's *The Old Boy* (1991); Horton Foote's *The Young Man from Atlanta* (1995); and Kevin Elyot's *My Night with Reg* (1997).

Plays about Bisexuals

Despite Tennessee Williams's theory, "I don't think there is such a thing as a precise sexual orientation. I think we're all ambiguous sexually," and the findings of the Kinsey report that only 50 percent of American men are exclusively heterosexual, there is a paucity of plays containing bisexual characters. Pre-Stonewall plays—Noel Coward's *Design for Living* (1933) and *Present Laughter* (1942); J. B. Priestly's *Dangerous Corner* (1932); Augustus and Ruth Goetz's *The Immoralist* (1954); and Joe Orton's *Entertaining Mr. Sloane* (1964)—usually presented bisexuals as morally dangerous, since they did not play by the "rules" and required multiple sex partners, thus upsetting any kind of monogamous relationship. After 1968, with the exception of Ira Levin's *Deathtrap* (1978), stage bisexuals were rarely depicted as criminals, but their position as transgressive agents had not diminished. Examples can be found in Richard O'Brien's *The Rocky Horror Show* (1973); Neil Simon's *California Suite* (1976) and *London Suite* (1995); Bill Davis's *Mass Appeal* (1980); Christopher Durang's *Beyond Therapy* (1983) and *Laughing Wild* (1987); and Wendy Wasserstein's *The Sisters Rosensweig* (1992). Indicative of the uneasy status of bisexuals in American society—embraced by neither the heterosexual community nor the gay community—stage bisexuals are usually found in a comedy, as opposed to being the subject of a serious play in which a discussion of bisexuality might transpire.

With a book by Joe Masteroff, lyrics by Frank Ebb, and music by John Kander, the musical *Cabaret* (1966) was a successful adaptation of Christopher Isherwood's *Berlin Stories* and John van Druten's play, *I Am a Camera* (1952). In the 1966 Broadway version, the young American writer is ostensibly heterosexual, since it is presented that he only has sex with Sally Bowles, but in the 1972 film (screenplay by Jay Presson Allen and Hugh Wheeler) it is clear that he is bisexual. When Harold Prince directed the 1987 Broadway revival of *Cabaret,* the writer's sexual orientation followed the course as laid out in the film, yet as licensed by Tams-Whitmark, only the 1966 libretto is available, thus returning Cliff Bradshaw to heterosexuality.

Plays about Transsexuals

Like the subject of bisexuality, the presence of transsexuals is similarly scarce in spoken drama. A staple topic on the television talk-show circuit, male-to-female or female-to-male sexual reassignment surgery has not captured the imagination of many playwrights. Notable exceptions include Ed Graczyk's *Come Back to the 5 & Dime, Jimmy Dean, Jimmy Dean* (1976), Nick Bicat/David Hare/Tim Rose Price's musical, *The Knife* (1987); Kate Bornstein's *Hidden: A Gender* (1989); Brad Fraser's *Poor Superman—A Play with Captions* (1994); and John Cameron Mitchell's *Hedwig and the Angry Inch* (1997).

Plays about Transvestites

Plays about transvestites, individuals who dress in the clothing of the opposite sex, comprise a particularly complicated realm of analysis in gay drama, since the intent that motivates the character to cross-dress may not inform the audience's interpretation of that activity. Tellingly, the most commercially popular gay plays of the 1980s—Harvey Fierstein's *Torch Song Trilogy* (1981), Jerry Herman/Harvey Fierstein's *La Cage aux Folles* (1983), and David Henry Hwang's *M. Butterfly* (1987)—seemingly reinforce the stereotype that homosexuality equals effeminacy, and that male-male relationships are a parody of male-female relationships. On the other hand, it is possible in all three plays to hear the thesis that gender is a cultural construction that has no relationship to genital equipment.

While some plays that contain transvestite characters, like Mae West's *Drag* (1927) and *The Pleasure Man* (1928), do so basically for the shock value of having drag queens on display, other plays investigate the lives of transvestite performers (Martin Sherman's *Bent,* 1979; Peter Nichols's *Privates on Parade,* 1983). Some playwrights have seen the transvestite as a possible shaman of society, one whose fluidity with gender gives him special powers: Richard O'Brien's *The Rocky Horror Show* (1973) and George C. Wolfe's *The Colored Museum* (1986). In Jonathan Larson's *Rent* (1996), Angel's transvestitism is taken seriously, and his transcendence of traditional gender roles makes him a better human being. David Ives's *The Red Address* (1997) explores the world of a male heterosexual cross-dresser.

Plays that Use Drag as a Performative Device

Distinct from plays that contain a transvestite or characters that cross-dress for a particular reason are plays that employ performative transvestitism that has nothing to do with the identity of the character. Instead, the theatrical use of cross-dressing underscores the fluidity of gender and deconstructs sex roles in their own right. In addition to these metatheatrical resonances, the use of drag is also frequently utilized to provide a showcase for the virtuosity of the performer.

The work of actor/playwright Charles Busch, combining cross-dressing and camp, is a direct link with the work of Ronald Tavel and Charles Ludlam. After playing 2,024 performances, Busch's *Vampire Lesbians of Sodom* (1984) secured its place as the longest-running non-musical show in Off-Broadway history. That same, year long-time associate Kenneth Elliott and Busch co-founded Theatre-in-Limbo, a small ensemble of approximately eight performers for whom Busch writes material. Busch's early work was very broad comedy, like *Psycho Beach Party* (1988), which satirizes Annette Funicello beach movies. Later works—*The Lady in Question* (1989) and *Red Scare on Sunset* (1991)—employ drag as secondary to content.

Marketed as "the show Ziegfeld would have produced had he been gay," actor/designer/playwright Howard Crabtree's *Whoop-Dee-Doo!* (1993) was a feast of outlandish costumes, brilliant camp, and snappy tunes. With the nine male cast members required to be everything from Nancy Reagan to a large beefsteak, the operating aesthetic was decidedly nutty and very gay. Crabtree (1955-1996) followed this success with *When Pigs Fly* (1996). Together with Bill Russell, Frank Kelly, and Albert Evans's *Pageant* (1992), Marvin Laird and Joel Paley's *Ruthless* (1992), and John Epperson's shows as Lypsinka, these small-scale musical entertainments made camp, caricature, and drag popular with Off-Broadway audiences in the 1990s.

Other uses of performative gender illusion that proved popular with audiences include: the Jewel Box Revue (1939-75), the longest-running touring drag show in America; Les Ballets Trockadero de Monte Carlo (est. 1974), an all-male dance company that spoofs classical and modern dance; and La Gran Scena Opera (est. 1981), which lampoons the world of opera.

Plays Responding to the AIDS Epidemic

Both produced in 1985, William H. Hoffman's *As Is* and Larry Kramer's *The Normal Heart* paved the way for the use of the theater as a forum for AIDS education and a cathartic outlet for the anxiety, anger, and grief caused by the proliferation of the virus. Part autobiography and part angry polemic, Kramer's play is an impassioned call for political action. Rejecting Kramer's despondency, Hoffman embraces hope in *As Is* without denying the terrifying aspects of a disease with no known cure.

As Robert Chesley explored sexuality in defiance of "sex equals death" (*Night Sweat,* 1984; *Jerker,* 1990), other playwrights explored the effects of an AIDS-related illness and death on the victim's loved ones: Michael Cristofer's *The Shadow Box* (1977), Lanford Wilson's *Poster of the Cosmos* (1988), Terrence McNally's *Andre's Mother* (1990), William Finn's *Falsettoland* (1990), and McNally's *Love! Valour! Compassion!* (1995). As AIDS became a reality to be accommodated, second-generation AIDS plays focused on the living. The People with AIDS Theater Workshop (PWATW) was established in 1987 by Nick Pippin and Sylvia Stein. Comprised of performers with AIDS or ARC, their first two plays were *People Living with AIDS* and Lanie Robertson's *AIDS Alive.* While Larry Kramer continued his attack on the government's response to AIDS treatment in *The Des-*

tiny of Me (1992), lighthearted approaches to the epidemic arrived with Robert Patrick's dark comedy *Pouf Positive* (1988), Robert Berg, David Stanley, and Wendell Jones's *AIDS, The Musical!* (1993), and Paul Rudnick's comedy *Jeffrey* (1993). A life-affirming force is present in Tony Kushner's *Angels in America* (1992) and in Steve Schalchlin and Jim Brochu's musical *The Last Session* (1997).

"The Gay '90s"

The last decade of the twentieth century easily earned the moniker "The Gay '90s" with the proliferation of gay plays produced on Broadway and around the country. This era started with a bang with the premiere of John Guare's *Six Degrees of Separation* (1991 Tony Award for Best Play) and Tony Kushner's *Angels in America: The Millennium Approaches* at the Mark Taper Forum in 1990. Joined by Part Two, *Angels in America: Perestroika,* which had its premiere at the Mark Taper Forum in 1992, Kushner's "Gay Fantasia on National Themes" was complete. As directed by George C. Wolfe, the Broadway production of *Millennium Approaches* won the Pulitzer Prize for Drama and the 1993 Tony Award and Drama Desk Award for Best Play, while *Perestroika* followed with the 1994 Tony Award for Best Play. Joining the accolades showered on this production, Jack Kroll of *Newsweek* proclaimed, "The entire work is the broadest, deepest, most searching American play of our time." Moving from reality to dreams, from heaven to earth, the various threads of *Angels* weave together the lives of a gay couple, a Mormon couple, historical figures Roy Cohn and Ethel Rosenberg, and several angels. Although Larry Kramer and *New Republic* editor Andrew Sullivan criticized *Angels* for flouting a lifestyle of homosexual complaisance and for being "a West Village version of Neil Simon," most critics and audiences applauded the complexity and diversity of the gay men in the play. WASP Prior Walter struggles with living with AIDS and the possibility of being a prophet. Jewish Louis Ironson fights his own sense of justice as he leaves Prior and takes up with Joe, a right-wing Republican judicial clerk who has left his wife. Roy Cohn denies his homosexuality and the AIDS virus in his body with the logic that he is a heterosexual man who sleeps with other men, and just happens to have liver cancer. African-American Belize dabbles in drag and is faced with being one of the hospital nurses assigned to Cohn. Informed by an epic sensibility, Kushner paints a world where there are no degrees of separation, and ends with a poignant note of hope by the final curtain, despite portraying America as perilously dysfunctional.

Not only were the number of plays featuring gay male characters abundant on the Great White Way, the genre had matured to the point that gay drama was now attracting large audiences and critical acclaim. Two parts of "The Marvin Trilogy" were joined together for the Broadway production of *Falsettos* (*March of the Falsettos* score by William Finn, 1981, and James Lapine and Finn's *Falsettoland,* 1990), which won the 1992 Tony Awards for Best Score and Book of a Musical. The Metropolitan Opera House presented its first world premiere in 25 years with *The Ghost of Versailles.* With a libretto by William Hoffman and music by John Corigliano, the opera is neither gay drama nor gay theater, but rather this grand-opera-buffa, written by two openly gay artists, was labeled "subversive" by Bernard Holland of the *New York Times* for turning the conventions of opera on its head.

In 1993, not only was Kushner's *Millennium Approaches* honored, but *Kiss of the Spider Woman* garnered seven 1993 Tony

A scene from Tony Kushner's Pulitzer Prize-winning drama, *Angels in America.*

Awards, including Best Musical, Best Book of a Musical (Terrence McNally), and Best Musical Score (John Kander and Fred Ebb). Kushner's *Perestroika* was awarded three 1994 Tony Awards, while Terrence McNally returned to the winner's box with *Love! Valour! Compassion!* (1995 Tony Award for Best Play) and *Master Class* (1996 Tony Award for Best Play). Fifty-four years after he made his New York playwriting debut, Horton Foote won the 1995 Pulitzer Prize for *The Young Man from Atlanta,* a drama about a Texas couple who grapple with the reality that their son was a homosexual and had committed suicide. Receiving both the Pulitzer Prize and the 1996 Tony Award for Best Musical, Jonathan Larson's *Rent,* with its lesbians, gay men, and drag queens living in the East Village, was heralded as *Hair* for the 1990s.

Rent was not the first play to contain gay male characters of color, and indeed it joined a small but growing number of gay dramas that were produced in the 1990s that explored the various experiences of non-Caucasian homosexuals. Singapore-American playwright Chay Yew is the author of *Porcelain* (1993) and *A Language of Their Own* (1995), while Nicky Parasio's *Asian Boys* (1994) examines the life of a Filipino-American man from Queens. Homosexuality and slavery in the 1831 South is the subject of Robert O'Hara's *Insurrection: Holding History* (1996). Examples of gay Hispanic drama include Edwin Sánchez' *Clean* (1995) and

Pomo Afro Homos

Trafficking in Broken Hearts (1994), and Guillermo Reyes' *Men on the Verge of a His-Panic Breakdown* (winner in 1997 of the Third Annual National Hispanic Playwriting contest).

While the African-American homosexual is often presented as a criminal or amoral character—David Rabe's *Streamers* (1976), John Guare's *Six Degrees of Separation* (1991)—the character of Miss Roj in George C. Wolfe's *Colored Museum* (1986) is in possession of unique perception, if not paranormal power. Of the losers and users of Pearl Cleage's *Blues for an Alabama Sky* (1996), the flamboyant, homosexual costume designer Guy Jacobs is the only winner. This more positive voice was echoed by Pomo Afro Homos (Postmodern African American Homosexuals), a trio of writer/performers—Brian Freeman, Djola Bernard Branner, and Marvin K. White—whose work was a blend of satire, drama, and rage exploring the joy, pain, and contradictions of black gay life. In existence from 1990 to 1995, the group toured such works as *Fierce Love* and *Dark Fruit,* collections of sketches and monologues that addressed living in the margins of two cultures, gay and African American.

Conclusion: Gay Male Theater

From the appearance of homosexual characters in drama previous to Stonewall to the overt gay drama and gay theater that evolved during the gay liberation movement, the growing maturity of this work is evident in the evolution from the "only happy homosexual is a dead homosexual" in Crowley's *Boys in the Band* (1968) to Prior Walter's proclamation in Kushner's *Angels in America*: "We won't die secret deaths anymore. . . . We will be citizens." Moving beyond the stock characters that held the stage in the early part of the twentieth century, playwrights began to explore the range and depth of what it meant to be a gay man in America. Finding popular and critical acceptance in the 1990s, gay drama has earned a place not only as a vital genre on its own, but also within the canon of great American dramatic literature.

Lesbian Theater on Broadway, 1896-1974

The first play in the United States to present two women actors on stage passionately hugging and kissing each other was *A Florida Enchantment* by A. C. Gunter. It premiered in April 1896 at the Park Theatre in New York, and apparently the love scenes were so shocking to audiences that the theater management felt it was necessary to have ushers circulating in the house with ice water for patrons in danger of fainting.

The play, however, was not about lesbians. According to the *New York Dramatic Mirror*, "A young girl becomes possessed of a few magical seeds that confer a change of sex upon any individual who swallows one of them. The maiden courageously swallows a seed, and finds herself [to be] a young man." The male lead also swallows a seed, but whereas the woman finds her transformation liberating, the man is mortified by his sex change. The reviewer concluded that the playwright's goal was "to show that in a measure men have a better time than women."

The first play with a lesbian character ever produced on an English-language stage in New York was *The God of Vengeance*, which premiered at the Provincetown Theatre in Greenwich Village in December 1922, and then moved to Broadway on 19 February 1923. *The God of Vengeance* was the English translation of Sholom Asch's Yiddish play *Gott fun Nekoma*, written in 1905 and produced on and off in various Yiddish theaters in New York for 17 years. By 1922, it had been translated into a dozen languages and produced in Russia, Austria, Poland, Holland, Norway, Sweden, and Germany. In spite of this long and successful production history, the English-language production in New York caused a scandal.

The play is set in a Jewish house of prostitution in a small town in Poland. The proprietor, played by the Viennese stage star Rudolph Schildkraut, lives one floor above the brothel, using the prostituted women below him to finance his social ambitions. He buys a Torah in order to bless his home as well as his hopes to make a propitious marriage for his daughter Rivkele. To ensure her virtue, he has kept her a virtual prisoner in the house. Rivkele, however, falls in love with one of the prostituted women downstairs, and the play depicts the seduction of the young woman in a tender and explicitly erotic scene. The two women, played by Dorothee Nolan and Virginia MacFayden, enter soaking wet from a frolic in the rain, and then the older woman, referring to Rivkele as her bride, takes the young woman in her arms and begins to kiss and fondle her. Rivkele responds enthusiastically to her touch and agrees to sleep with her. Later, the father discovers his daughter's affair, and, dragging her by the hair, banishes her to work in the brothel. He blames the newly acquired Torah for failing to protect his home.

Although produced more than 70 years ago, *The God of Vengeance* remains unique in the canon of Broadway plays depicting lesbianism. The lovemaking scene has never been rivaled for frankness and sensuality, and the lesbianism was portrayed as an act of resistance to the patriarchal prostitution of women, in marriage as well as in brothels. Asch's play suggests that female-to-female physical intimacy could be a survival strategy as well as a substitute for the maternal nurturing absent from the patriarchal home. Subsequent representations have sensationalized lesbianism as a perversion, pathologized it as a sickness, or neutralized its subversive content in a male-dominant culture by reducing it to an alternative lifestyle or a sexual practice.

Although the critics expressed their distaste for certain scenes, it was not until the play moved to Broadway that it attracted the ire of certain middle-class citizens. Charges of anti-Semitism as well as indecency resounded, and Asch was compelled to defend his play as one that was originally intended for all-Jewish audiences. Later, during the Nazi era, however, Asch himself would ban productions of the play.

On 6 March 1923, detectives appeared backstage at the Apollo to inform the theater owner, producer, and the actors that they had been indicted by a grand jury for presenting an "obscene, indecent, immoral, and impure theatrical production." Interestingly, none of the papers covering the trial made mention of lesbianism.

The show moved from Broadway to the Bronx, and then reopened in one of the smaller theaters where it had originally been presented. All in all, it ran for 133 performances, an impressive run, especially in light of the fact that most newspapers refused to carry advertisements for the play.

Four years later, on 29 September 1926, *The Captive* premiered on Broadway at the Empire Theatre. *The Captive* was a translation of the French play *La Prisonnière* by Edouard Bourdet. In *The Captive*, Irene de Montcel, played by Helen Menken, is a woman who has fallen in love with a certain Madame d'Aiguines—a lesbian who never appears on stage. Irene, terrified of her lesbianism, attempts to cure herself with a heterosexual marriage, but in the end she returns to Madame d'Aiguines, and her husband goes back to his former mistress.

The Captive opened to positive reviews and was the hottest ticket of the season, with weekly box office receipts totaling between $21,000 and $23,000. In spite of its success, press baron William Randolph Hearst decided to make *The Captive* the centerpiece of his campaign for legislation supporting stage censorship in New York. (Laws for motion picture censorship were already on the books.) The Hearst papers began running editorials attacking the show, and prestigious drama critic George Jean Nathan added fuel to the fire by labeling it a "documentary in favor of sex degeneracy."

The play was raided during a performance on 9 February 1927, more than four months after it had opened, and on the same night, police also raided Mae West's star vehicle *Sex*. West's show, which had been running for eleven months, was probably raided in what proved to be a successful attempt to discourage West from bringing to Broadway her gay male show *Drag*, then in out-of-town tryouts.

Two months after the raid, legislation was passed in New York prohibiting plays "depicting, or dealing with, the subject of sex degeneracy or sex perversion." It was not until a Supreme Court ruling 48 years later that theater in the United States would receive the same protection from advance censorship and prohibition that books and newspapers have always enjoyed.

The first lesbian play by a U.S. playwright opened in Atlantic City one month after *The Captive*'s Broadway debut. *Hymn to Venus* by William Hurlbut was given the more lurid title *Sin of Sins* during its race to open in Chicago before the touring production of *The Captive*. The show, like *The Captive*, focused on a triangle, but in the more-sensational *Sin of Sins*, the lesbian seductress not only appeared on stage, but was revealed as the murderer of her girlfriend's male suitor. The show was panned by two of Chicago's three drama critics, and it closed after three weeks.

Because of the show's poor reception, the touring company of *The Captive* decided to avoid Chicago. Well-received in Cleveland and Baltimore, *The Captive* was raided in San Francisco, Los Angeles, and Detroit. Twenty-four years later, the play was revived in San Francisco, but by this time audiences were frankly disinterested.

In December 1929, the first play with a "bull dyke" character opened Off-Broadway at the Garrick Theatre. This was *Winter Bound* by Thomas H. Dickinson, and although it drew fair-sized audiences, the stock market crashed during the run, causing the producers, the Provincetown Players, to lose the backing that might have kept the show running for more than 39 performances.

Winter Bound is about two women who have moved to the country as an experiment to escape male oppression. Tony Ambler, played by Aline MacMahon, dresses and swears like a man, and prefers to spend her days in outdoor activities with the stable boy for a companion. When her partner Emily reminds her that she, Tony, is a woman, too, Tony protests, "I'll be damned if I am. Not your kind anyway."

Tony, however, is not in a sexual relationship with Emily, nor does she want one, although in other respects they are living like a heterosexual couple. Tony identifies sexual love as a desire to own another person, and she claims she would like to abolish it: "Sex. Sex. Sex. And the women are the worst. . . . And everywhere women with their naked bodies showing. As if she didn't have anything but a body." Her partner, who does not share her views, eventually leaves to marry the boy next door.

The critics, ignorant of the lesbian tradition of the asexual "Boston Marriage," were confused by the play and accused the author of fear of censorship. Dickinson maintained that Tony was "trying to work through the sex miasma to rational thinking." In today's climate of awareness about survivors of sexual abuse, Tony's character might be more sympathetically received.

The tomboy lesbian would appear again on Broadway three years later, in the play *Girls in Uniform*, an English translation of Christa Winsloe's *Gestern und Heute*. Unfortunately for producer Sydney Phillips, the German-language film version, *Madchen in Uniform*, had opened 15 weeks earlier and one block away from the theater. The day after the Broadway opening, the New York film critics named *Madchen* the best picture of the year, and the advertisements for the film ran on the theater page with the words "At Prices Everyone Can Afford," a powerful incentive for audiences at the height of the Depression. The play closed after only 12 performances.

There was another reason audiences preferred the movie to the stage version: the movie had a happy ending. The protagonist of both the film and the play is Manuela, a sensitive, motherless 14-year-old girl. New to the Prussian boarding school, she develops a crush on one of the teachers, Fraulein von Bernberg, and in an inebriated state, she declares her passion in front of the entire school. Manuela is removed from the dormitory, and her beloved teacher renounces their friendship. In the play, Manuela kills herself, but in the film, she survives.

Girls in Uniform has been reviewed as a fable of anti-fascism, with the affection between Bernberg and Manuela valorized as a humanizing force in an otherwise totalitarian regime. Contemporary critics, however, have pointed out the exploitative nature of the inappropriate gestures the teacher makes toward Manuela, including supplying her with her own undergarments. Whether a victim of a social system or a personal betrayal, or both, Winsloe's protagonist was the first lesbian stage character to take her own life as a result of her lesbianism. Two years later, another lesbian character would follow suit.

The Children's Hour by Lillian Hellman was based on an actual suit for slander filed by two school mistresses in Scotland in 1810. The two women had been accused of lesbianism by one of their students, and the girls' grandmother had spread the story. Technically vindicated, the lives and reputations of the women were ruined. Hellman, however, chose a more dramatic ending for the teachers. As a result of the scandal, one of the teachers loses her fiancé, and the other shoots herself after confessing her "guilt" at having experienced a lesbian attraction for her friend.

The play was produced by Herman Shumlin, and to avoid pre-opening publicity, he refused to allow visitors at rehearsals and did not hold out-of-town tryouts. The show opened November 20, 1934, and ran for 691 performances in New York before embarking on a successful tour. (It was banned only in Boston.) It was rumored, however, that *The Children's Hour* was passed over for the 1934-35 Pulitzer Prize because of the lesbian subject matter.

Ann Revere, who played the role of the suicidal Martha, insisted, "I never thought that Martha was a lesbian. . . . Under stress she cracks and thinks she is." This is, however, inconsistent with the script, in which Martha is described as having a "fit" every time a man comes into her house. When the playwright herself had the chance to direct the 1952 revival, she had Patricia Neal light the other woman's cigarette in a traditionally butch gesture.

Two other plays with blatantly lesbian themes opened in 1937. Both were written by British playwrights and both had been hits in London. New York audiences, however, were not impressed. *Wise Tomorrow* by Mrs. Guy Bolton closed after three performances, and *Love of Women* by Aimee and Philip Stuart lasted only five days.

Wise Tomorrow reprised the theme of *The Captive*, in which an innocent heroine is seduced away from a heterosexual fiancee by a sophisticated, vampiric older woman. In this case, the lesbian is an aging film star who leaves her estate and her butch secretary to her girlfriend. In *Love of Women*, the two women in the triangle have collaborated successfully on a stage play, and the arrival of the man signifies not only the renunciation of a lesbian liaison, but also the loss of a career.

The only lesbian role on Broadway during World War II was that of butch army nurse Steve, played by Carol Channing, in *Cry Havoc* by Allan R. Kenwood—later retitled *Proof through the Night*. Like Martha in *The Children's Hour*, Steve is accused of lesbianism, but before she can resolve her identity crisis, she is shot by a spy. Opening on 25 December 1942, it ran for 11 performances.

In 1945, Dorothy and Howard Baker's *Trio* became the first lesbian play since *The Captive* to be found in violation of New York's penal code. After two months of running, the show was closed by the Commissioner of Licenses, setting off a huge outcry from actors, stagehands, producers, playwrights, and the American Civil Liberties Union. Both the Commissioner and the Mayor were ridiculed by the press, and there were no further attempts to close Broadway productions because of lesbian or gay roles. The censorship law, however, stayed on the books until 1967.

Trio combined a number of conventions: the obvious triangle, the seduction of an innocent young woman by an older lesbian teacher, and the suicide of the lesbian. A mediocre play, *Trio*'s greatest claim to fame was that it became a *cause célèbre* in the fight against censorship.

Two seasons later *No Exit*, the English translation of Jean-Paul Sartre's play, opened on Broadway. Although it had run for two years in Paris, it closed after a month in New York. The failure was partially attributed to the fact that the lesbian role of Inez had been played with more restraint than in the London or Paris productions.

Carson McCullers had two adaptations of her work produced in 1948 on Broadway: *Member of the Wedding*, which she had dramatized, and *Ballad of the Sad Cafe*, adapted by Edward Albee in 1963. The lead character in *Member of the Wedding* is a 12-year-old tomboy named Frankie, neither child nor adult, who is violently resisting socialization to both white supremacy and to heterosexualism. Although not explicitly lesbian, Frankie fits the image of the "baby dyke." The protagonist of *Sad Cafe* is a butch woman with a violent antipathy for sex, a latter-day Tony Ambler.

The McCarthy era threw a chill over playwrights, and when, in 1953, Tennessee Williams premiered the gay-themed *Suddenly Last Summer* with a very closeted lesbian one-act *Something Unspoken*, he chose to open the plays off-Broadway, where audiences tended to be more tolerant.

The 1950s were an era of virulent homophobia and witch-hunting of gay male playwrights. In 1966, *The Killing of Sister George* by Frank Marcus was imported from London. *The Village Voice* noted that lesbianism, treated as a disease in *The Children's Hour*, was now being subjected to "nasty and uncompassionate treatment . . . as a joke." Sister George was a soap opera character played by a sado-masochistic butch lesbian who reveled in degrading and humiliating her slavish and infantilized lover, Childie. Her character on the soap opera is killed, symbolizing the deterioration of the lesbian's life.

In February 1980, Jane Chambers's play *Last Summer at Bluefish Cove* opened at the Shandol Theatre and became the first play written for and about lesbians to enjoy a successful Off-Broadway run. The repressive Wales Padlock Act that had prohibited the portrayal of gays and lesbians on stage had finally, after more than four decades, been repealed, and Mart Crowley's *The Boys in the Band*, produced in 1968, had officially ushered in the era of openly gay theater.

Contemporary Lesbian Theater

According to lesbian theater editor and historian Rosemary O'Keefe Curb, "Theatre and drama which calls itself 'lesbian' emerged as a collective movement throughout the western world in the 1970s as part of the feminist and gay/lesbian theatre movements from roots in Black, pacifist, socialist, and other leftist theaters. Like other protest or agit-prop performance art, it rose on the crest of a rainbow coalition of progressive liberation movements which built in force throughout the 1970s, reached a crescendo of visibility and power in the mid 1980s, and waned in the 1990s."

Toward the end of the 1990s, lesbian culture began to receive mainstream attention, lesbian studies became an accepted academic discipline, and, for the first time, regional mainstream theaters implementing policies of multi-culturalism began to present lesbian drama.

Some of the early theaters that focused primarily or exclusively on lesbian productions included the Red Dyke Theatre in Atlanta, the Lavender Cellar Theatre in Minneapolis, the Portland Women's Theatre Company in Portland, Oregon, Front Room Theatre in Seattle, the WOW Cafe in New York City, and It's Just a Stage in San Francisco. Medusa's Revenge, one of the first lesbian theaters in the world, was founded in New York City in the early 1970s by Ana Maria Simo, a Cuban lesbian playwright. Medusa's Revenge was in existence for eight years, producing plays during a period when even the avant-garde performance spaces in New York were closed to lesbian work.

The history of early lesbian theater is impossible to separate from the history of feminist theaters, and many of the early women's theaters were founded by lesbians, incorporated lesbian themes into their work, or placed lesbian plays in their seasons. These theaters included Lilith in San Francisco, At the Foot of the Mountain Theater in Minneapolis, the Women's Experimental Theatre in New York City, and Brava! For Women in the Arts in San Francisco.

During the 1980s, gay and lesbian theaters, including Celebration Theatre in Los Angeles, Theatre Rhinoceros in San Francisco, and the Alice B. Theatre in Seattle, produced lesbian plays, although these productions were sometimes token offerings in seasons dominated by gay male plays.

Several organizations arose in the 1990s to promote lesbian theater. Sisters on Stage (SOS), founded in 1994 in New York City by Barbara Kahn, Janis Astor del Valle, and Beverly Thompson, is an organization of professional playwrights, actors, and directors from the lesbian community. SOS sponsors an annual lesbian theater conference where its Nancy Dean Distinguished Playwriting Award is given each year to a different lesbian playwright. The Lesbian Exchange of New Drama (LEND), founded in New York in 1993 by Anne Harris and Vanessa Agnew, originally served as a clearinghouse for lesbian plays. In 1997, LEND changed its name to the Lesbian-Identified Performance Project (LIPP) and expanded its mission to support the development of lesbian theater artists of all disciplines. LIPP presents a series of readings of lesbian work; the LOLA's, a biennial award program named after lesbian performer Lola Pashalinski; and an international lesbian playwright exchange.

The Purple Circuit, founded by Bill Kaiser and based in Los Angeles, is a national association of gay and lesbian theaters. The Purple Circuit newsletter provides networking opportunities for gay and lesbian playwrights, performers, and producers. Dialogus Play Service in Dallas, Texas, a press founded in the mid-1990s, specializes in publishing the work of gay and lesbian playwrights.

Prior to the mid-1990s, lesbian plays in the U.S. were published by the smaller women's presses or by the playwrights themselves. In 1985, *Places, Please! The First Anthology of Lesbian Plays*, edited by Kate McDermott, was published by Aunt Lute Books. The anthology included works by Terry Baum, Carolyn Myers, Sarah Dreher, Ellen Gruber Garvey, and Julia Willis.

During the next decade, three collections of works by single playwrights were published. In 1988, New Victoria Press published a collection of plays by lesbian mystery writer Sarah Dreher titled *Lesbian Stages: Plays*. A collection of Chicago playwright Claudia Allen's work, *She's Always Liked the Girls Best*, was published in 1993 by Third Side Press. In 1994, the first collection of radical lesbian-feminist plays, *The Second Coming of Joan of Arc*

A scene from *Dress Suits for Hire* by Holly Hughes, performed at the WOW Cafe.

and Other Plays, by Carolyn Gage, was published by HerBooks, Inc.

In 1996, Applause Books became the first mainstream press in the United States to publish a collection of lesbian drama. *Amazon All Stars: 13 Lesbian Plays* was edited by Rosemary O'Keefe Curb and included the work of Jane Chambers, Janis Astor del Valle, Gloria Joyce Dickler, María Irene Fornés, Shirlene Holmes, Joan Lipkin, Susan Miller, Patricia Montley, Canyon Sam, Joan Schenkar, Carolyn Gage, Sue Carney, Megan Terry, and Paula Vogel. Each play was accompanied by an introductory essay by a lesbian scholar.

Also in 1996, *Clit Notes: A Sapphic Sampler,* by lesbian playwright and performance artist Holly Hughes, was published by Grove Press, and Routledge published *Split Britches: Lesbian Practice/Feminist Performances*, which included performance art pieces by Peggy Shaw, Lois Weaver, and Deb Margolin, with commentary by Sue-Ellen Case.

In 1997, *Intimate Acts* was published by Brito Lair. Edited by Nancy Dean and Manuel Soares, the collection included works by Terry Baum, Nancy Dean, Janis Astor del Valle, Harriet Malinowitz, Rosemary McLaughlin, Renee, Sarah Schulman, and Beverly Thompson.

The Playwrights

Angelina Weld Grimké wrote the first recorded play written and performed by an African American in this century. *Rachel* was produced in 1916 by the Drama Committee of the District of Columbia NAACP. Grimké, an African-American lesbian, did not treat lesbianism explicitly in her play, but the plot centers around a young African-American woman's refusal to marry and have children in a racist world that treats black children so viciously. In the play, the protagonist also confronts the male dominance of her boyfriend and defies the indifference of a male deity.

Lorraine Hansberry, the first African-American playwright to break the color line of Broadway theater, was also a lesbian. Although lesbianism is implied in her play *Toussaint*, she, like Grimké, did not treat it directly. It was not until the 1980s that African-American women playwrights began to incorporate lesbian themes into their work as an integral part of the black woman's experience. Alix DeVeaux's plays *No* and *A Season to Unravel* both deal with love between two women. P. J. Gibson's award-winning 1985 play, *Long Time Since Yesterday,* features a lesbian relationship as the main story line.

Angelina Grimké

African-American playwright Shirlene Holmes has produced 14 mainly African-American lesbian plays in Atlanta. Her 1995 play *A Lady and a Warrior*, set in the 1890s, blends Southern folklore with a tender love story about an itinerant lesbian butcher and a woman who runs a boarding house. Shay Youngblood's widely produced play *Shakin' the Mess Outta Misery* follows a young girl's journey into womanhood, guided by memories of the women who raised her. Ira Jeffries, an African-American playwright and journalist, has had her work produced Off-Off-Broadway and in Harlem-based community theater. Excerpts from *The Bag Lady and Ole Becky* were read at the 1994 SOS Lesbian Theatre Conference.

Jane Chambers was the first lesbian playwright to produce and publish plays based on lesbian experience. In 1980, *Last Summer at Bluefish Cove* became the first lesbian play to enjoy a successful Off-Broadway run. Sarah Dreher, like Jane Chambers, writes in the tradition of American realism. Her play *Alumnae News* told the story of homophobia at a women's college in the 1950s, and *Hollandia '45* exposed the lesbian witch-hunting of the Army Nurse Corps in World War II.

Terry Baum was one of the founders of the feminist theater Lilith in San Francisco in 1974. A pioneering lesbian playwright and author of 12 plays, Baum has also toured extensively in her plays *One Fool*, about the confusion between true love and good sex, and *Immediate Family,* in which a lesbian confronts the legal barriers that separate her from her hospitalized and comatose lover. With Carolyn Myers, Baum wrote *Dos Lesbos*, an extremely popular, cabaret-style comedy with music in which a newly out lesbian and her longtime lesbian partner explore through various theatrical genres ways of "coming out" to one's family.

Carolyn Gage, a radical lesbian-feminist playwright, toured nationally in her one-woman show *The Second Coming of Joan of Arc*, a play in which the legendary martyr is portrayed as a teen-aged butch lesbian runaway. Gage also co-wrote with Sue Carney *The Amazon All-Stars*, the first lesbian full-book musical to be published by a mainstream press. Her book *Take Stage! How to Direct and Produce a Lesbian Play* is the first book on lesbian community theater, and she also wrote the first collection of scenes and monologues for lesbian actors.

Janis Astor del Valle, a co-founder of Sisters on Stage, is a Bronx-born, Puerto Rican lesbian playwright and performer. Her work has been presented at Mabou Mines and the Women Playwrights' Collective in New York. In *I'll Be Home Para Navidad*, del Valle explores the interface of lesbian and Latino culture when a Latina lesbian brings her lover home for Christmas. Barbara Kahn, also a co-founder of Sisters on Stage, is a director, performer, and playwright. She has written several plays integrating Jewish history with lesbian culture. Her play *Whither Thou Goest* is set in a home for immigrant girls in 1922 and presents a painful relationship between a Russian-Jewish lesbian immigrant and an American Jewish lesbian, who cannot stand up to her homophobic father.

Nancy Dean began writing plays in 1983 and became a playwright-in-residence for Actors Alliance in New York. She specializes in writing comedies from a lesbian perspective. Sarah Schulman, author of ten books, including *My American History: Lesbian and Gay Life during the Reagan/Bush Years*, has had her lesbian plays performed at La MaMa, the Performing Garage, PS 122, and other venues in New York. Susan Miller, winner of two Obies, two NEA grants, and a Rockefeller grant, features lesbian characters in *Nasty Rumors and Final Remarks, Confessions of a Female Disorder* and *It's Our Town, Too.*

Cherríe Moraga, co-editor of the groundbreaking anthology *This Bridge Called My Back: Writings by Radical Women of Color*, has a national reputation as a Chicana feminist, poet, thinker, and cultural activist. Her plays *Giving Up the Ghost* and *Shadow of a Man* both feature lesbian characters.

Playwrights Megan Terry and María Irene Fornés, major award-winning avant-garde artists whose works span three decades, have both produced impressive bodies of work that helped lay the foundation for contemporary U.S. experimental theater. Terry's play *Willa Willie Bill's Dope Garden* celebrates the lesbianism of author Willa Cather, and her *Babes in the Bighouse* focuses on lesbians' survival skills in a prison environment. Fornés' plays *Fefu and Her Friends* and *Springtime* feature lesbian characters.

Joan Schenkar, winner of seven NEA grants, has written macabre and chilling comedies that demonstrate women's anger and desire for vengeance. In *Signs of Life*, scenes of ritual violence against women are interspersed with scenes between Alice James and her partner. Paula Vogel, winner of an Obie award for *The Baltimore Waltz* and a Pulitzer Prize for *How I Learned to Drive*, includes lesbian scenes in her play *Desdemona*, a look at the behind-the-scene lives of Shakespeare's characters from *Othello*. Playwright Joan Lipkin founded a feminist and lesbian/gay-inclusive company, That Uppity Theatre, in St. Louis. In *Small Domestic Acts*, the friendship between a heterosexual couple and a lesbian couple becomes complicated by shifting sexual alliances. Claire Chafee's play *Why We Have a Body*, a postmodern exploration of lesbian relationships, has been successfully produced in theaters across the country. Martha Boesing, a co-founder of feminist theater At the Foot of the Mountain in Minneapolis, wrote *Love Song for an Amazon*, in addition to producing many works about woman-identified passion and resistance. Clare Coss, from the Women's Experimental Theatre in New York, wrote the lesbian play *The Blessing,* and Muriel Miguel, one of the Kuna-Rappahannock sisters who make up New York's Spiderwoman Theatre, wrote and performs a one-woman lesbian show called *Hot'n'Soft*.

Adele Prandini co-founded one of the first lesbian theaters, It's Just a Stage, in 1974 in San Francisco, and many of her plays have been produced at Theatre Rhinoceros. Red Jordan Arobateau, a self-described butch dyke of mixed-race heritage, writes "street-dyke" lesbian plays about lesbians in San Francisco struggling against urban poverty and violence. Canyon Sam, a Chinese American writer, performance artist, and activist for Tibetan rights based in San Francisco, has written and toured in The *Dissident*, a play about a Tibetan nun.

Lesbian theater has traditionally embraced marginalities and diversities far more than mainstream drama, and it has never adopted a monolithic political stance. Lesbian theater has a history of celebrating diversity in age, race, social and economic class, ethnicity, physical ability, religious and spiritual practices, political positions, and modes of presentation. Although much contemporary lesbian dramatic work is defined as performance art, the distinction is not always clear, and many playwrights and performers incorporate a range of styles in their work.

DANCE

Gay Male Dance

Martha Graham once said that "movement never lies." If we accept this maxim, then the work of a gay choreographer or the dance performed by a gay performer will physically manifest a

Lorraine Hansberry

gay sensibility. For choreographer Mark Morris, however, "My concern is whether it's a good dance. You can do anything you want, it just has to be good. That's all I care about."

Downplaying a gay sensibility or presence of homosocial/homoerotic subtext in his dances, Morris claims "I have a high visibility [as a gay artist], and so that's nice. I can do that, and I chose to do that. I didn't have to do that, but that's what I'm like. Not everybody is. It's not my business if [choreographer] Paul Taylor doesn't do the same thing I do. He's a lot older than I am. So what if a gay choreographer only makes up breeder dances? That's fine, that's a prerogative. If Paul Taylor wants to make all his dances in a heterosexual context, that's his right and his preference, and it tells more about him than anything else. It's his work. I don't think he's lying. You can't lie and do good work. It's impossible."

Years before Morris's interview in the *Advocate,* Paul Taylor told *Dance Magazine* (in 1991) that "I think it's possible to *read* anything, and it doesn't bother me, but I just don't think of my work as an autobiographical form" [Taylor's emphasis].

The dancing body is outside of the narrative conventions that govern spoken theater and literature—the body in motion is a body in motion regardless how that body finds sexual excitement. Utilizing the components of space, weight, time, and flow, a dancer creates physical structures and sometimes projects a persona; sometimes this persona is more detailed and specific, resulting in a character. Yet regardless of whether the dancer is performing in a plotless dance or is creating a defined character in a narrative work, the performer is generally engaged in representation, not autobiography. To view the creative act of choreography or the performance of dance as a mirror of the artist's sexual orientation is to reduce this activity to pathology, not art. Needless to say, if the choreographer/dancer presents autobiographical material, then the above strictures do not apply. So to err on the side of consensus—since there is no current agreement as to a theory of gay sensibility—this essay will discuss only those American gay male choreographers who create autobiographical work, and/or create gay characters and/or explore gay themes in their dances. Included in this overview of gay choreographers are two queer producers who had an enormous influence on creating the shape of American dance: Lincoln Kirstein and Oliver Smith.

While various genres of dance were popular in vaudeville and burlesque, concert dance was virtually nonexistent in America in the early part of the twentieth century. Even Anna Pavlova, the most popular of touring ballerinas, avoided the United States during the last seven years of her career, making her final tour of America in 1924. Sol Hurok imported the Ballet Russe de Monte Carlo in 1933, only to watch his underwriters lose money. Despite this initial setback, the company persevered, making the United States its unofficial home until it folded in 1963.

This Russian ballet invasion was viewed with alarm and contempt by Lincoln Kirstein (1907-1996). Convinced that ballet was moribund in Europe, he reasoned it would be easier to resuscitate in America, a country with no stultifying dance traditions of its own. After seeing several ballets by George Balanchine, Kirstein met him in London and promptly invited the 29-year-old choreographer to come to New York, where they would build an American ballet tradition. Balanchine's famous response, "But, first a school." The School of American Ballet opened in 1934, with Lincoln Kirstein as President, a position he would hold until his retirement in 1989.

Balanchine and Kirstein would establish four different companies before New York City Ballet was formed in 1948: American Ballet Company (1934-35), Ballet Caravan (1936-40), American Ballet Caravan (1941), and Ballet Society (1946-48). Invited to become the resident company at City Center, New York City Ballet was established with Lincoln Kirstein as general director, a post he held until 1989. In 1964, NYCB moved to the Lincoln Center for the Performing Arts, created through the political and financial largesse of Kirstein's longtime patron Nelson Rockefeller, and given a permanent home in the State Theatre, which had been designed for the company by Kirstein's Harvard friend Philip Johnson.

One of the most astonishing and influential figures in twentieth-century American culture, Lincoln Kirstein was full of contradictions and at the same time a visionary who shaped modernism in the twentieth century. The author of more than 30 books and hundreds of articles on painting, sculpture, photography, film, architecture, and dance, Kirstein also wrote the librettos to several ballets, including Lew Christensen's *Filling Station* (1938) and Eugene Loring's *Billy the Kid* (1938). A Jew who converted to Catholicism, a homosexual who married, this Renaissance man's primary passion was ballet. With his stewardship, money, and behind-the-scenes maneuvering, Kirstein literally made New York the dance capital of the Western world. George Balanchine could have created choreographic masterpieces for any ballet company, but without Lincoln Kirstein there would not have been the New York City Ballet.

America's other premier ballet company was also formed in response to the annual tours of the Ballet Russe de Monte Carlo.

With members of the floundering Mordkin Ballet (1937-40), Ballet Theatre was formed in 1940 to provide a venue for original American classical ballet; the company became American Ballet Theatre in 1957. The personality of the company was molded by dancer Lucia Chase and designer/producer Oliver Smith, who served as co-artistic directors from 1945 to 1980. Widowed in 1933, the modestly talented but financially wealthy Chase supported the Mordkin Ballet and was a major underwriter of Ballet Theatre, thus insuring her dream of being a professional ballet dancer. The concept of Ballet Theatre was unique: the first major ballet company to include the works of a diverse group of choreographers, free of the pressure and interference from a supervising choreographer. Founding choreographers included Agnes de Mille, Antony Tudor, Michel Fokine, Anton Dolin, Eugene Loring, and Bronislava Nijinska. Devoted to the grandeur and glamour of ballet, the company promoted its own stars and featured scores of guest artists.

Oliver Smith (1918-1994) returned to ABT as co-director (this time with administrator Jane Hermann) upon the 1989 departure of artistic director Mikhail Baryshnikov. With the termination of Hermann's three-year contract, former ABT principal dancer Kevin McKenzie was named the troupe's new artistic director, while Smith stepped aside as director emerita; Lucia Chase remained as trustee emeriti. In addition to serving as co-director for ABT for 38 years, Smith had a parallel career as a designer and producer. Jack Anderson of the *New York Times* considers Smith "one of the most prolific and imaginative designers in the history of the American theatre." Smith's work includes Broadway (seven Tony awards for Best Scenic Design): *On the Town* (also co-producer, 1944), *Brigadoon* (1947), *Gentlemen Prefer Blondes* (also co-producer, 1949), *Pal Joey* (1952), *My Fair Lady* (1956), *Candide* (1956), *Flower Drum Song* (1958), *The Sound of Music* (1959), *Camelot* (1960), *Hello, Dolly!* (1964), *Plaza Suite* (1968), *Indians* (1969), and *Gigi* (1973); ballets designs include *Rodeo* (1942), *Fancy Free* (1944), *Fall River Legend* (1948), *Swan Lake* (1965), *Giselle* (1970), and *Sleeping Beauty* (1974); opera designs include *La Traviata* (Metropolitan Opera), *Naughty Marietta* (New York City Opera), and Gian Carlo Menotti's *The Most Important Man* (New York City Opera); designs for motion pictures include *Oklahoma!* (1955), *Guys and Dolls* (1955), *The Unsinkable Molly Brown* (1964), and *The Sound of Music* (1965).

Smith's home in Brooklyn Heights served as a veritable boarding house for talented homosexuals. At one point or another Benjamin Britten, W. H. Auden, Carson McCullers, and Truman Capote lived with Smith.

One of the highlights of Smith's career was *West Side Story* (1957), a work created by four gay Jewish artists (Jerome Robbins, Leonard Bernstein, Stephen Sondheim, and Arthur Laurents) and designed by three more homosexuals: Smith (sets), Jean Rosenthal (lights), and Irene Scharaff (costumes). None of the collaborators of this heterosexual love story interpreted anything queer in the work; rather, Laurents felt that "*West Side* can be said to be informed by our political and sociological viewpoint; our Jewishness as a source of passion against prejudice; our theatrical vision, our aspiration, but not, I think, by our sexual orientation." Nevertheless, Charles Kaiser in *The Gay Metropolis* asserts that "to many gay adults coming of age in the sixties, the romance, violence, danger, and mystery so audible on the original cast album all felt like integral parts of the gay life they had embraced."

What is not in question is the choreographic and directorial genius Jerome Robbins brought to *West Side Story*. While George Balanchine (*On Your Toes*, 1936; *The Boys from Syracuse*, 1938;

Cabin in the Sky, 1940) and Agnes de Mille (*Oklahoma!,* 1943; *Carousel,* 1945; *Brigadoon,* 1947) raised musical theater choreography to the artistic level of concert dance, it was Robbins who expanded the use of dance beyond the musical theater dream ballet to create a world where it looked perfectly natural for his gangs of Sharks and Jets to fight, love, and develop their characters via the medium of dance. When *West Side Story* opened on Broadway 26 September 1957, the *Herald Tribune*'s Walter Kerr praised "the most savage, restless, electrifying dance patterns we've been exposed to in a dozen seasons." Richard Watts, Jr., of the *New York Post* found that the "choreography has been fused with the story so effectively that the ugliness and horror of the war to the death between the boys is never lost." (Robbins received an Oscar for co-directing the 1961 motion picture version, as well as a special Academy Award for recreating his choreography.)

As one of the few choreographers of musical theater equally adept at direction, Robbins followed his *West Side Story* triumph with serving as the director/choreographer of the Broadway premieres of *Gypsy* (1959), *A Funny Thing Happened on the Way to the Forum* (1962), *Funny Girl* (1964), and *Fiddler on the Roof* (1964). Robbins's spiritual heirs can easily be seen in the director/choreographers who dominated Broadway in the 1970s and 1980s: heterosexual Bob Fosse (1927-1987) with *Sweet Charity* (1966), *Pippin* (1972), *Chicago* (1975), and *Dancin'* (1978); and bisexual Michael Bennett (1943-1987) with *A Chorus Line* (1975), *Ballroom* (1978), and *Dreamgirls* (1981); and Tommy Tune (1949-) with *Best Little Whorehouse in Texas,* (1978), *Nine* (1982), *Grand Hotel* (1989), and *Will Rogers' Follies* (1991).

Lesbian Dance

The history of lesbians in professional dance begins in Europe in the eighteenth century, where classical ballet was popular among the aristocratic classes; however, archival and historical sources reveal that the beginning and end of the twentieth century are two prominent periods for lesbians in professional dance, particularly in modern and postmodern dance.

Lesbians were responsible for many of the groundbreaking changes in twentieth-century dance. As dancers and choreographers questioned the gender bias of classical ballet technique and the lack of women choreographers, women began to use dance as a way to promote a revolutionary change in the way that women relate to their bodies. Historian and dance theorist Judith Lynne Hanna has documented how early modern dancers helped to free women from tightly laced corsets and how this change encouraged not only freedom of movement but also a more open view towards women's sexuality.

Writings on the contributions of lesbians in dance are relatively scarce in comparison to that of male homosexual dancers. Some current cultural theorists of dance propose that this is because lesbians rarely faced prosecution for their sexuality as men did and that therefore they were less vocal in periods before the 1960s. However, it is evident from the variety of lawsuits involving lesbian dancers and choreographers that they, as well as gay men, have experienced censorship and public defamation either because of their sexuality or because of their portrayal of sexual minorities on the stage. The two prolific periods for lesbian dancers are 1900 through 1930 and 1970 to the present; these two periods differ considerably in their aesthetic concerns. Whereas the earlier period was centered in Europe and often treated orientalist themes and portrayed women as mythical figures, the later period has

focused on community building, social justice, political action, and individual experiences.

Early Ballet

Little is known about pre-twentieth century instances of lesbian dancers. However, Marie Sallé (1707-1756), rumored to be a lesbian, danced and choreographed primarily in France. She was popular for her character performances and satirical ballets; her unique style may be the result of her early experiences with popular theater and street fairs.

When the cult of the ballerina was at its height in the 1830s, Paris Opéra dancers Caroline Forster and Elina Roland, who lived together, were accused of being lesbians by a journalist against whom they later brought a lawsuit for defamation of character.

Early Modern Dance

Several early modern dancers were lesbian or bisexual and made contributions to the representation of lesbians in dance. The majority of these dancers and choreographers worked and performed in Europe because French and British audiences were more open to early modern dance and because there was an active artistic lesbian community in Paris during the early part of the twentieth century.

One of the most innovative early modern dancers, Loie Fuller (1862-1928), was born in Illinois and began performing as a young child. She worked as an actress in New York but went to Paris to establish her career as a dancer. There, she made a smashing debut at the Folies-Bergère in 1892. She is known for her voluminous costumes made of china silk that surrounded and covered her entire body. Fuller was a pioneer in the use of electric light on the stage and illuminated her costume with lights projected from various positions including from below. Fuller was her own choreographer, dancer, lighting designer, and technician. In 1899, Fuller met Gab Sorère, who would be her lover and collaborator for the rest of her career, which lasted well into the 1920s. Fuller founded an all-women dance company in 1907, and late in her career she experimented in film. Due to her use of technology, Fuller's work is particularly modern for her period.

Like many early modern dancers, Fuller developed orientalist themes and performed a version of *Salome* in which the young temptress was portrayed as a victim of Herod's patriarchal power structure rather than as the bloodthirsty femme-fatale that other dancers, including lesbians, performed. Fuller was not part of the fashionable Paris lesbian scene termed "Paris Lesbos" or "Sapphic Paris" (a reference to Sappho, the ancient Greek poet who wrote about her love for women). This community was led by actress Sarah Bernhardt and included Colette (a writer who danced early in her career), Réné Vivian (writer), and Ida Rubenstien (dancer and choreographer); they cultivated diva-like images of femininity that were in general very sexualized and also included fashionable cross-dressing. Oscar Wilde's play, *Salome,* was popular with the Paris Lesbos group.

Popular as an exotic dancer, Maud Allan (1883-1956) was born in Canada and grew up in San Francisco; she later moved to England, where she performed as a music-hall dancer. Her best known solo, *The Vision of Salomé,* established her reputation as an erotic dancer. She was cast to star in a private production of Oscar Wilde's *Salome.* Due to the anti-homosexual movement in England and paranoia about the exploitation of "sexual degeneracy" being used as a war strategy by the Germans against England, journalist Noel Pemberton-Biling wrote that the production would be a meeting of the "Cult of the Clitoris." This was no doubt a reference to Allen's sexual orientation and to that of the producers of the play; Allen and the would-be producer of the play brought a libel suit against the journalist in 1918. This case is an important example of the ways that attacks on sexual identity and the portrayal of alternative sexualities have been tied to conservative political agendas.

Russian-born Ida Rubenstein (1885-1960) worked with Nijinsky and the Ballets Russes and danced the roles of Cleopatra and Salome (her version of Wilde's play was not allowed to play on the Parisian stage). She arrived in Paris in 1909 and stayed until the beginning of World War II as part of the "Paris Lesbos" group. From 1928 to 1935, she sponsored a ballet company for Bronislava Nijinska (1891-1979), who choreographed for the Ballets Russes in Paris. Nijinska's *Les Biches* ("The Deer," 1924) portrayed a lesbian relationship. She worked with Diaghelev, Folkine, and Nijinsky and was the only woman choreographer for the Ballets Russes.

Lesbian Dance: Mid-Century in the United States

Not surprisingly, there are few known examples of lesbians in dance during the mid-century in the United States. The experi-

ence of Ruth Page provides an example of why lesbian dancers were not particularly open about their sexuality during this period. In 1944, Ruth Page (born in 1905) choreographed *Triov*, which dealt with a lesbian relationship. Reporters and religious groups protested the performance for its portrayal of "sexual deviation"; it was banned in Boston but did play in New York with some last-minute changes. Her production of *Frankie and Johnny* (1938) portrayed a lesbian relationship as well.

Despite the lack of information on lesbian dancers from the 1950s, it is relevant that choreographers such as Alwin Nikolai eschewed traditional gender roles often portrayed in classical ballet and emphasized androgyny. This trend has continued in the work of many postmodern dancers.

Recent and Current Lesbian Dance in the United States

Since the 1970s, lesbian dancers and choreographers have become active in modern and postmodern dance, often combining personal experiences and political statements in their work. Many current lesbian dance performances employ a mixture of voice-overs, film, and dialogues or monologues as well as pieces about important women in history. Community involvement and collective choreography seem to be important for many lesbian dancers

A performance by Axis Dance Theatre Company.

and choreographers. Dance historian Jack Anderson has proposed that modern dance has focused on individual accomplishments; however, many recent lesbian dancers have emphasized the importance of community experiences as well as individual ones as a basis for the creative process. For choreographers working since 1990, it is important to note that artists receiving funds from the National Endowment for the Arts (NEA) have been subject to considerations of "general standards of decency." This conservative movement to legislate the "morality" of artistic production is led by Senator Jesse Helms.

Aesthetically, recent choreographers have emphasized athleticism and the martial arts in their dance. Important dancers and choreographers who are lesbian or treat themes of lesbianism in their work include: Krissy Keefer of the Wallflower Order and Dance Brigade, Johanna Boyce of the Dance Theatre Workshop, Judith Smith of Axis, Amy Pivar of Amy Pivar Dances, and Jill Towaga of the Purple Moon Dance Project.

The Wallflower Dance Order, including collective members Nina Fichter, Pamela Gray, Krissy Keefer (lesbian dancer and choreographer), Laurel Mear, and Lyn Neeley, was founded in 1975 as a dance collective concerned with political and social issues. The Wallflower Order's witty choreography, mime, and spoken words focused on issues of social injustice, oppression, and revolution. They performed in conjunction with various activist groups and in prisons; in order to aid in the accessibility of their work, dances and dialogues were often accompanied by sign language for hearing-impaired spectators. Krissy Keefer has also been involved in the Berkeley-based dance collective Dance Brigade with Nina Fichter and Kim Epifano. Notable works by the Dance Brigade include *The Revolutionary Nutcracker Sweetie* (1988), which offered political and popular culture figures playing the Nutcracker roles and a satirical dance about a parade of American "glamour girls."

Choreographer Johanna Boyce has worked in New York since 1978. Her company, Dance Theatre Workshop, often uses untrained dancers and everyday movement. *Ties That Bind* (1984), performed by lovers Jennifer Miller and Susan Seizer, combines movement with the telling of childhood stories that culminate in verbal and movement interpretations of their lesbian relationship. At one point in the performance, as they are rolling together, bodies intertwined, they mention to the audience that people often wonder what two women do in bed. Boyce's work often includes the personal histories of her dancers and emphasizes individuality as well as community experiences.

Dancer and choreographer Judith Smith of Axis, founded in 1987, is lesbian and is also confined to a wheelchair. Axis includes dancers with and without disabilities and performs for community organizations, schools, universities, conferences, and festivals. Smith has worked extensively with wheelchair movement through postmodern dance, martial arts, and improvisation. *Ellipsis* consists of a series of love duets, starting with one between a man and a woman, and ending with another between two women.

Amy Pivar founded Amy Pivar Dances in 1990 with partner and psychotherapist Freda Rosen. Themes of their dances and dialogues/monologues include sexual violence, racial relations, stereotypes of women, the death of Communism, historical inquiries into the loves and works of Gertrude Stein and Alice B. Toklas, and finally, contemporary feminism. Pivar and Rosen seek to move beyond postmodern aesthetics in order to address human concerns over political issues. Amy Pivar Dances mixes jazz, Afro-Brazilian dance, modern funk, athleticism, and ballet in its movement.

Amy Pivar performing *These Women.*

Pivar sees the experience of being a lesbian as parallel to that of being an artist.

Jill Towaga of the Purple Moon Dance Project, founded in 1992, is a Japanese-American lesbian born in Hawaii. Her very personal work seeks to explore the voices of lesbians and women of color through collaborative work between dancers and with artists from other disciplines. Towaga and her colleagues teach workshops for women without formal dance training.

PERFORMANCE ART

Overview

Artists from many disciplines have chosen live performance as a means of expression for the better part of a century. Performance art as a distinct genre, however, can be traced to the 1970s (Goldberg, 1988, p. 7). As with all coherent artistic movements or styles, performance art came into being through the influence of previous movements. For example, feminist political actions are related to Happenings (performance events that crystallized in the late 1950s), which, in turn, related to Action Art in North America and the Gutai Group in Japan in the 1950s. All of these movements and styles of expression can then be traced to the work of the Futurists, the Constructivists, and the Dadaists from the turn of the century (Goldberg, 1988, pp. 7-9; Kistenberg 1995, p. 91). Performance art history is rich and inextricably linked to the development of modern and postmodern art, providing a fluid means of creative expression when the demarcations of a single movement or style have proven to be too limiting for the articulation of certain ideas. Performers in dance, theater, and music as well as poets, novelists, historians, and scientists have found performance art a valuable resource in light of their own discipline's limitations or hardened conventions. Gay men and lesbians have always sought ways to break free of convention, and for many performance art was, and is, the perfect vehicle.

Performance and the Body

Performance art, due to its dependence on the body in performance space or within a performance context, is less reliant on formalistic concerns. In other words, art as object-making is not of great consequence in this genre. As such, the human body, along with issues surrounding the body and its functions, often becomes both the material and the means of production in a given performative work. For this reason, performance art is often subsumed in the critical and art historical analyses of Body Art, and just as often they are understood to be one and the same. Performance art, however, cannot be categorized so simply, for any attempt to do so inevitably excludes other important artists and artists' works.

Even though it is imprudent to exaggerate the importance of the body and bodily functions and issues in the performance art genre, to dismiss it is equally foolhardy. After all, the body is most often the tool by which the artistic idea is expressed in performative situations; therefore, the body must be factored into the content of the message. The honesty and immediacy of performance art requires nothing less than a full and gracious bow to the material and its processes.

Many performance artists have found that the body and body issues provide the necessary content in a given piece. For decades, these artists have created commentary aimed at social, political, cultural, religious, and institutional spheres in order to undermine or question their power. In North American society, as in many Western societies, the body is highly politicized. Artists have been compelled to express their concerns about body image and ideals of beauty as they have changed over time; they have reacted to, and fashioned debate about, the eroticized and sexualized body and sexual identity; they have questioned the ethics of gendered movement and gendered spaces as well as the hierarchies of power that result from such constructions; they have fought for and criticized health care availability as well as medical and mental care practices; and they have challenged the ages-old Cartesian dichotomy of the mind/body and spirit/body split by creating ritual and mytho-poetic performance pieces that seek to combine the three.

Process

Because performance art is less aligned with the formalistic concerns of most art practice, it is often characterized as conceptual art. Very simply, conceptual art favors the process by which a work of art is made rather than the product. As such, conceptual art is able to avoid as well as ridicule the system by which art is commodified (Stiles, 1996, p. 679). When performance art, as we now understand it, developed into its own distinct genre of art in the 1970s, it was, among other things, a reaction to the exclusivity, cronyism, and misogyny of the art gallery. Moreover, since the turn of the century, work seen in art galleries was increasingly dependent upon the marketability and prestige of the artist or art-

work shown. Clearly, artists were in need of alternative venues in order to show their work. Conceptual art, according to Kristine Stiles in *Theories and Documents of Contemporary Art: A Sourcebook of Artist's Writings,*

> referred generally to the ideational content and conceptual perception conveyed by an object. The result, initially, was that the term became a convenient category for exhibiting almost any form of art except traditional painting and sculpture (Stiles and Selz, 1996, p. 806).

Conceptual art could include object-making, but formalistic concerns were subservient to the concept that initiated its production; furthermore, concept, as it was rationalized, was driven by theory and contingent upon language (Stiles, 1996, 804). Language shapes meaning, and this art form, like Dadaist art in the early 1900s, centered on the notion that reshaping meaning would precipitate reshaping the world. In this regard, conceptual art was highly subversive though subliminally political. Perhaps, conceptual art sought to reshape less the world than the art world. Nevertheless, because of its obvious standing outside the realm of painting and sculpture, and since its intentions were most often subversive as well, performance art was often tucked neatly into this category. Performance art, however, has never rested comfortably in any category other than its own, despite the efforts of art historians, dramaturgists, musicologists, and literary critics to minimalize its impact.

Conflation with Theater

More than any other genre or discipline, performance art has been confused with theater. This is understandable but terribly inaccurate. While it is true that some performance artists and their works utilize theatrical traditions, they just as often disparage or critique them. Actors and some performance artists work in performance spaces, both typically use the body to communicate, both may use scripts, and both may establish a performer/spectator relationship. All other comparisons, however, ring false. Theatrical conventions, history, and modes of production diverge sharply with that of performance art. Perhaps the origins of theater are most accurately comparable to performance art practice in that its initial purpose was "sacred storytelling" (Miller and Roman, 1995, p. 178), and the engagement of ritual space for consciousness transforming opportunities. In this regard, temples, cathedrals, stages, and performance spaces are all places with a common root and a common purpose, to offer the viewer the chance to reflect or enter into another state of being. Performance art, however, seeks to bypass the conventionalized aspects of theater and religious space by making its purposes more overt, more connected physically, mentally, and psychically to the spectator.

Time

With the exception of Brechtian or Dadaist theater, performance art seldom employs the *fourth wall* that separates spectator and performer, and it often avoids the strictures of unilinear narrative flow. Performance art works generally seek to bridge the gap between performer and spectator, establishing a link in real time, and performance art performers are more apt to present *themselves* to their audiences rather than characters created by another author. The conventions most frequently practiced in theater arts preclude the actor's own experience, for the most part, in favor of the playwright's voice; whereas, in performance art, the performer is most likely the author, director, and producer of the material presented. This allows the performance artist enormous freedom of expression and the contingency for relating personal experience. Since theater until very recently excluded or ignored the voices of queer people, performance art provided a means by which such stories could be told. Not dependent upon the marketability of the material presented, performance artists could, and continue to, explore the performative potential of autobiography and identity formation, maintenance, and fluidity. In a performance art context, theatrical time may be rejected, and the creative expression given whatever temporal structure is deemed necessary. Many artists employ stream-of-consciousness monologues, improvisational movement and vocalization, and direct conversation, confrontation, or deliberation with the audience or other performers. In addition, performances may last mere seconds, hours, days, or years depending upon the concept of the piece. The incredible flexibility of time in performance art has allowed the artist the possibility for performing the most profound or the most mundane of experiences. Queer artists have not been bashful about embracing these alternative modes of expression.

Illusion

Traditional theater persistently creates illusion through dialogue, costuming, settings, lighting, audio, proscenium, or other stage boundaries (sometimes in historical context), as well as directed action that occurs on the stage alone. The audience is typically engaged via two of the five senses, sight and sound. We are invited to participate in the unfolding story only so far as these senses allow. Involvement in the reality onstage is tempered by the knowledge that what is witnessed is a sublime or heightened representation separate from the cozy reality of the audiences' domain. Except for Dadaist, Absurdist, or avant-garde experimental theater, such divisions are the norm. The theater audience is generally a safe place, but the performance art audience is more likely to be challenged to participate more sensorially, to join the discourse that the performer initiates, to question or even search for signs of illusion. The purpose of much of postmodern performance art is to disorient the audience, which is most probably pre-conditioned to a theatrical setting, so that such expectations can be banished right away. For this reason, performance art, artists, and spaces are the object of some level of scrutiny. The performance art scenario can be an intimidating experience when devoid of theatrical illusion. Audiences unwilling to let go of their performance expectations risk estrangement from the artist's communication, and they unwittingly miss the transformative potential of the event by looking for escapist entertainment. Performance art dispenses with the comfortable sphere of theatrical illusion "to both articulate resistance and generate necessary social change" (Reinelt and Roach, 1992, p. 218). Performance art is necessarily, or problematically (depending on your position), associated with social issues and social change. Its power lies in its insistence on addressing these problems face-to-face with the audience member. In this regard, performance art, unlike conceptual art, can be a means for enacting change outside the realm of the art world.

The Political Manifesto

One of the Futurist manifestos, at the turn of the century, proclaimed that artists should take their art and ideas to the streets (Goldberg, 1988, p. 16; Kistenberg, 1995, p. 27), thus placing the art content clearly in the political sphere. For this reason, artists were often in danger of arrest (Kistenberg, 1995, p. 27) or even violence. Performance as protest continues to this day, most recently with the actions of ACT UP and Queer Nation, and, of course, yearly "Pride" parades in a great number of U.S. cities. The history of protest performance, as stated earlier, extends to the early 1900s and stretches to the present including, along the way, labor charades and dancing pickets in the 1930s (Fuoss, 1997) as well as actions presented by the Gay Liberation Front and the Lavender Menace in the late 1960s and early 1970s.

Generally, protest performance is not understood to be performance art because the performers are not necessarily, or even usually, artists. The idea that only artists, indoctrinated artists for that matter, can be certified practitioners of performance is woefully short-sighted. Joseph Roach, author of *The Player's Passion*, has said,

> Performance ... though it frequently makes reference to theatricality as the most fecund metaphor for the social dimensions of cultural production, embraces a much wider range of human behaviors. Such behaviors may include what Michel de Certeau calls "the practice of everyday life," in which the role of spectator expands into that of participant (Parker and Sedgwick, 1993, p. 46).

Into political performance space steps artist and non-artist alike. If we are to understand performance art as a genre of art that includes political and social change among its many manifestos, then we must surely include protest performance and its many practitioners.

Similarly, camp or drag performance may be seen as precipitating change, but, in this case, through social critique, however veiled in burlesque or masked in humor they may be. Camp is by no means apolitical, for it has, over the course of time, served as substitute voice for a historically silent group. Moe Meyer, eminent art critic, defines camp "as the total body of performative practices and strategies used to enact queer identity, with enactment defined as the production of social visibility" (Meyer, 1994, p. 5). Camp was, and is, a socially accepted, albeit coded, way for queer people to express identity. At the same time, these practices and strategies allow(ed) for open parody of the social norms of the day without the same risks and repercussions that flagrant opposition might invite. The reason for enacting queer identity is, of course, linked to the assumption that visibility breeds tolerance and/or acceptance, thus social controls and conventions can be challenged and reconstructed in the dominant culture.

The Ephemeral Nature of Performance Art

Performance art may occur in public or in private, in mental or conceptual space; it may involve the solo performer, groups of individuals, whole communities, or geographically removed locations; and it may appear in any number of narrative or non-narrative forms with witnesses or without (Stiles, 1996, p. 680). As indicated, this genre is extremely diverse in terms of content, presentation, time, location, audience, transmission, and mode of communication. Notwithstanding, *documentation* is, by most accounts, the most contentious of issues among scholars, critics, and artists themselves. Based on the idea that no one performance can ever be the same as the original, or that which is deemed superior out of all performances given, these groups privilege the ephemeral nature of the art form. In other words, if one has not experienced "X" performance, one has not experienced the performance at all. Performances may be repeated but they are always utterly and inherently dissimilar. According to Gérard Genette, a French social science scholar, performance is a process that "can be experienced only once, because a process is by definition irreversible and, in the strict sense, unrepeatable" (Genette, 1997, p. 63). Genette's view is held by the vast majority of art scholars and critics. Nevertheless, it may be argued that *any* experience of *any* work of art is ephemeral because the viewer him/herself comes to a work of art differently each time said work is experienced. At this point, however, Genette's view is the standard by which performance art is judged and intellectualized. For this reason, documentation is understood as problematic: documentation would, in essence, make the performance repeatable. Moreover, documentation of a performance experienced by an audience excludes the necessary *liveness* by which performance art is defined (Goldberg, 1988, p. 7). Without the physical, mental, psychical interaction between performer and spectator, the performance becomes something else (Phelan, 1993, p. 31). For example, the performance becomes simply a video, a film, a photograph, etc. Yet, if we posit that the content of a given artwork may be conveyed by other means, then is the impact any less effective? Both arguments seem to contain specific fallacies and assumptions, and the debate is likely to continue.

Performance art, a distinct genre in the history of Western art, has stimulated, agitated, and reshaped art politics and the sociopolitical systems of this country for nearly four decades. Other performance movements and genres have been key to its development, but its concerns are unique, insisting on a wide palette for creative production, expression, and diffusion. For queer artists in many disciplines and many fields, it has become an invaluable medium, an open forum for the articulation of ideas and the validation of identity.

Gay Male Performance Art: Early Movements

The precursors to the performance art medium are those movements at the onset of the twentieth century: Futurism, Constructivism, Dadaism, Surrealism, and the Bauhaus. Next came innovators such as John Cage and Merce Cunningham, whose astoundingly original and provocative work influenced a new generation of artists by mid-century (Goldberg, 1988, p. 123). At this point, very distinct movements began to appear again in the performance art timeline. The Gutai Group from Japan emerged just prior to the advent of Happenings in the United States. Happenings, performance events that crystallized in the late 1950s, sought to move traditional painting and sculpture into "actual space and time" (Haskell, 1984, p. 33). Another classification of performance developed within the same time frame and immediately caught the attention of the art world and the public. Fluxus was characterized by single-action performance or *The Monomorphic Event* (Stiles, 1996, p. 685). Both Happenings and Fluxus Group events featured intermedia works, or works involving the blending and juxtaposition of many and diverse media, Fluxus actions much less so. Coinciding with these performative movements

was the work of New York dancers and choreographers now known as The New American Dance. Chief among these innovators were Paul Taylor, and, again, Merce Cunningham who, like John Cage, laid the foundation upon which much of postmodern performance art is built. By the early 1970s, a united gay movement was making it possible for queer artists to express their aesthetic sensibilities in ways never before practicable. Over the course of four decades, declarations of queer identity as well as explorations of queer issues in performative works have become more conspicuous and more celebratory than ever before.

While it is true that same-sex attraction and same-sex sex have been recognized and practiced since time immemorial, sexual identities have not. Lesbian, gay, straight, bisexual, and transgendered (or homosexual and heterosexual) are terms and concepts with a more recent and anxious history (Katz, 1995, p. 189). To lay claim to queer ancestors thus becomes a rather dicey business. At the turn of the century, a negligible number of people would or could identify by any of these monikers save homosexual, which carried a burden of meaning associated with pathology and deviation. Some still adhere to this belief, but at that time the notion was widespread and modeled into every social construction imaginable. It has taken the better part of a century to begin to dismantle such rampant and insidious misinformation. Because of mainstream fear and loathing of this perceived pathology, records of queer Futurist, Constructivist, Dadaist, Surrealist, Bauhaus, or other avant-garde artists cannot be verified. Even those purported to be homosexual in this period of history are beyond any dependable measure of such a designation. What is true is that people attracted to members of their own gender have always existed; therefore, most assuredly, they practiced and performed, experimented and provoked within these movements.

Though these movements never attempted to question or protest public, private, or institutionalized perceptions about homosexuality or homosexual behavior per se, they did succeed in provoking the literary and fine arts academies through propaganda and publicity (Goldberg, 1988, p. 11). The artists who worked within the avant-garde at the beginning of the 1900s were just as rebellious and revisionist as any twentieth-century performer; however, few if any attempted to agitate for a new paradigm of sexuality. Instead, these artists were interested in deconstructing the conventions of art in western society and in establishing new forms of expression. The Futurists went so far as to call for violence and revolution (Goldberg, 1988, p. 11), while many of the Dadaists employed the most aggressive tactic of any heretofore—humor.

What ultimately connects these movements, aside from their rather anarchistic approach to artmaking and social change, is performance, which served as a means "of breaking down categories and indicating new directions" (Goldberg, 1988, p. 7). Each of these movements, now best known for the objects they produced or appropriated and then displayed for public consumption, commenced with works designed for performative settings. Fascinated with scientific advances in the understanding of movement and time (De La Croix, Horst, Tansey 1991, p. 965), the Futurists then took a logical next step in the direction of live performance with its natural inclination for defining the body in space and its mandate for temporality. True to their manifesto for insurgency, the Futurists

> instructed painters to "go out into the street, launch
> assaults from theatres and introduce the fisticuff into the

artistic battle"... missiles of potatoes, oranges, and whatever else the enthusiastic public could lays their hands on from nearby markets, flew at the performers.... Arrests, convictions, a day or two in jail and free publicity in the next days followed many evenings. But this was precisely the effect they aimed for (Goldberg, 1988, p. 16).

An intellectually based movement possessed by the idea that only complete cultural, political, and artistic transformation would do, the Futurists took their battle to the public arena (Arnason, 1986, p. 181). The immediacy of the performance situation helped establish this movement; furthermore, shortly thereafter it became an international phenomenon. Of course, by this time artists had begun producing objects (i.e., paintings and sculptures), and the initial performative stage had passed. Subsequent art movements, most of them European in origin but highly influential in the United States as well, followed a similar pattern. Artists used performance for its prompt and direct results, as it became a way to advertise a movement's ideology. Moreover, artists came to understand that it was a unique and effective medium for experimental thought and boundless expression.

No artists from these early movements have been identified as homosexual, and to do so would have been dangerous at any rate. Man Ray and Marcel Duchamp of the Dadaist movement engaged in gender play for performances and photographs (Goldberg, 1988, p. 93), alternating dressing as women for portraits or balletic parody. Surrealist artist Salvador Dalí is said to have experimented with homosexuality quite briefly in obeisance to his mentor, yet claimed heterosexuality throughout his lifetime. Few artists actually utilized performance art, or even object art, as a means for validating or representing sexuality of any kind with the exception of some notable Dadaists and Surrealists. Benjamin Franklin ("Frank") Wedekind was "[n]otorious as a man determined to provoke.... He would even urinate and masturbate on stage" (Goldberg, 1988, p. 50). But such exploits were really less about sexuality than they were about displaying an anti-bourgeois sentiment. These ordinarily private actions were performed primarily for political ends rather than gratification and certainly not for affirmation of physical or sexual autonomy. Nevertheless, Dadaists and Surrealists who advocated "free sexuality as a means to liberate experience" (Stiles and Selz, p. 638) became exemplars for the erotic Happenings that developed in the 1960s.

Cage and Cunningham

The value of performance as a medium for unlocking creativity, intuition, and emotion, or as a mechanism for propaganda and public discourse, was felt much less significantly in the United States until the 1930s. Here, the antecedent to postmodern performance art emerged under the canopy of North Carolina trees at Black Mountain College. European exiles from Europe, Bauhaus artists flushed from their German art institution by the Nazis, assembled and produced a curriculum that featured performance as a means for engaging and presenting the predominant theories and concepts of other disciplines (Goldberg, 1988, p. 122). But it was the innovative work of musician/composer John Cage and dancer/choreographer Merce Cunningham that prepared the way for the vast majority of late-twentieth-century performance art works. Cage and Cunningham are key figures in the development of the postmodern performance aesthetic in a number of disciplines.

Next to Marcel Duchamp, John Cage is most often cited as a central influence in the early careers of many noted artists and art innovators. Though trained as a musician, Cage's designation as conceptual artist is much more apt since his interest lay in process and change rather than product and determinacy. Paving the way for the artists of the last four decades, Cage sought to bridge the gap between art and life. He did so by working with ambient sound and improvisational rhythm, unconventional materials to be sure.

In short, as Cage brought the chancy and noisy world into the concert hall (following Duchamp, who did the same in the art gallery), a next step was simply to move right out into that uncertain world and forget the framing devices of the concert hall, gallery, stage, and so forth. This was the theoretical foundation of the Happening, and for some years Bodyworks, Earthworks, Information pieces, and Conceptualism variously extended that idea (Kaprow, 1993, p. 225).

At Black Mountain College in 1952, Cage, collaborating with Cunningham and a host of prospering young artists, presented a multimedia performance piece that scholar Kristine Stiles contends anticipated the Happenings movement of the early 1960s (Stiles, 1996, p. 681). On the strength of that performance as well as Cage's thriving reputation as a teacher and intellectual, young artists began to flock to his Experimental Composition class at the New School for Social Research in New York City (Henri, 1974, p. 89). Among those students were many of the innovators and leading proponents for new art forms in the coming years.

Cage's sexuality was seldom the subject of discussion and has only recently been addressed in any significant way as a factor in his personality and charm. That Cage was homosexual is certain (Kepner, 1995, p. 37); that this fact encouraged other homosexual artists and performers is not. Having lived his young adult years in a time when sexuality was a personal matter and when visibility for the queer community was all but nonexistent, Cage, like most people of his time, remained a very private man concerning this aspect of his identity. What was indisputable about Cage was his accessibility as a teacher, his renown as a theorist and intellectual, his cross-disciplinary methodology, and his groundbreaking approach to artmaking and its connection to living in the world. A proponent of the works of Buckminster Fuller, Henri David Thoreau, and Mao Tsetung as well as the Chinese system of chance operations, the *I-ching* (Henri, 1974, p. 89), Cage was able to integrate the supposed chaos of life and nature with the human penchant for order and ideology.

Cage's longtime associate Merce Cunningham is best known as a choreographer, but his career began with an emphatic performance art practice very much based on the principles of chance and indeterminacy. Like Cage, Cunningham set out to find new forms of expression in what is generally understood to be the mundane. "Cunningham proposed that walking, standing, leaping and the full range of natural movement possibilities could be considered as dance" (Goldberg, 1988, p. 124). Such movements in a performative situation, and also quite removed from the conventional dance canon, were quickly designated as abstract. By the time Cunningham, Cage, and the other artists and intellectuals had performed their *proto-happening* at Black Mountain College in 1952, the two had already been working together for more than a decade, planning and collaborating on numerous projects and performative works (Goldberg, 1988, p. 127). Soon, both artists moved to New York. Cage began teaching at the New School, and Cunningham founded his own dance company, in which he continued his experiments with the nature of human movement. He began forming new alliances with other artists for collaborative works, all the while insisting that no single element (i.e., music, meter, décor, or traditional dance technique) overwhelm the innate and individual physical articulations of his dancers. Cunningham's technique became widely venerated, and by the 1960s he was "acknowledged as the major influence in American contemporary dance. He [was] the spearhead of the avant-garde movement" (Rogosin, 1980, p. 64).

New Dance

One of Cunningham's students, Paul Taylor, began his career doing abstract or nonliteral choreography as well (Turner, 1971, p. 18). Taylor's work had changed by the 1960s, however, when he began to modify his aesthetic sensibility in the direction of the traditional dance canon. Nevertheless, the impact of his early work in performance was felt strongly among avant-garde artists. Taylor, like many dancers of his time, was disenchanted with traditional dance. Unlike Taylor, though, many of these dancers went on to establish a new dance form in part based on the work of Cage and Cunningham. They "quickly found in the art world a more responsive and understanding audience" (Goldberg, 1988, p. 138). These dancers, in turn, demonstrated new ways for artists to utilize the body and motion in performative practice. By the 1970s, such practices had developed into techniques and formulas that strengthened and expanded the possibilities of the performance artist in the performance space.

"Contact improvisation," which "explores the body's relations to gravity and to other bodies" (Foster, 1997, p. 250), not only offered an artistic outlet for the performer, it offered association with a burgeoning social movement whose aims were epitomized by spontaneity, group intuition, and the inclinations of the individual body in its particular space and time. In this regard, contact improvisation followed the precepts espoused by Cage and Cunningham: art and life are inseparable. Task-oriented performance, though, with its ties to the new and hugely successful Minimalist movement in art, moved the austerity of Cunningham's dance concept in a different direction. Artists began to explore the psychological and social implications of directed movement in space, movement that was still connected to the mundane, thus to the ordinary and to the everyday business of living. Like contact improvisation, task-oriented performance involved moving objects and/or bodies in space toward a specific goal or result, and like many of the major art movements since the turn of the century, it sought to emphasize process rather than product, psychological inquiry rather than representation or ideology.

Happenings and the Fluxus Group

Not until the start of the gay liberation movement in 1969 did artists really begin to identify themselves as gay or lesbian or any other designation for that matter. So it is that we have so few names to associate with large art movements until that time. Perhaps we might attribute to this paucity a certain narrowness in art historical vision as well. Literary and academic works about pre-1970s art and artists have a general tendency to showcase *art stars*, giving short shrift to the players who both supplemented

and enriched their respective movements. We know much about the key players in Happenings and the Fluxus Group but precious little about ancillary participants and their lives. Moreover, absent the force of a dramatic social movement to unite a marginalized group and the organization to address its particularized concerns, modes of expression, determination, or confrontation tend to be limited. So it was with gays, lesbians, bisexuals, and transgendered people prior to the Stonewall Riots.

Happenings and Fluxus Group works are fascinating and provocative movements in the history of art, distantly related to the manifestos of the Dadaists but more accurately the offspring of John Cage's experimentation with ambient sound as "found art" as well as his radical redefinition of art and art production (Haskell, 1984, p. 31). Stressing an engagement with the audience on a participatory level and an abandonment of logic and associative actions, Happenings tapped into the very principles of indeterminacy. Some art historians have attempted to connect the aims of the Happenings with the philosophy of the Action painters who often performed the painting process for an audience (Stiles, 1996, p. 680). Yet these performances concluded with a product that was then mounted and displayed, entering the public arena as well as the art market. Happenings, of course, did no such thing. "Happenings—impermanent and not replicable—were inherently uncommercial" (Haskell, p. 46). Fluxus events, also driven by chance operations and indeterminacy, were, nonetheless, quite distinct from Happenings in that costumes and elaborate sets were absent, and the action performed was usually a single "unitary gesture, such as a light going on and off, or a line of performers shuffling across the floor" (Haskell, p. 49). Of note is the fact that Fluxus performers came directly from Cage's course at the New School for Social Research in New York City. Oddly enough, art historians have been much quicker to link Happenings to Cage's influence than they have to Fluxus events. Nevertheless, the Fluxus Group and Happenings participants shared a common principle, to blur the line between performer and audience (Haskell, p. 49). Once achieved, this tactic could shake the very foundations of art aesthetics and art consumption.

Gay Male Performance Art: 1970s

The late 1960s to the 1970s and onward saw the proliferation of performance art in every imaginable venue for every imaginable exposition of thought, emotion, or action. Political and social upheaval, economic uncertainty, and the development of new and accessible media provided artists with rich sources for experimentation and interpretation throughout the 1970s. Also, many artists continued to work with the concepts and strategies advanced by John Cage, attacking, satirizing, or questioning the prevailing conventions in the world of the fine arts. Perhaps the largest single issue concerning artists at the close of the 1960s and the beginning of the 1970s was a general belligerence associated with the old political, social, and class order in the United States. Artists in Europe were affected as well, and their work often crossed national borders thanks to advancing technologies and the presence of an ever-expanding global community. Women's art and feminism infused the dominant culture, and artists were quick to respond to its call for equity and social reformation. For queer artists, though, the birth of the gay rights movement suddenly made possible an open forum for specific issues that had been, until that time, private or too stigmatized to be made public. In this broiling social and political climate, queer concerns were simply conjoined with the myriad concerns of women, people of color, and a host of other marginalized and disenfranchised groups.

Indicative of North American performance art was the use of the body as the art material (Taylor, 1995, p. 26). Gilbert and George, a British performance art team later known for their large photodocument panels, were international artists by the late 1960s and quickly charmed the New York avant-garde audience. Best known for their 1971 performance art piece, *The Singing Sculpture*, which was in fact first performed in London in 1969 and called *Underneath the Arches* (Goldberg, 1988, p. 167), this duo transformed their bodies into the art objects for a public viewing at the Sonnabend Gallery. Skin covered in metallic paint and dressed as proper English gentlemen, the two men mouthed the words to an audio recording of a British pre-war song while standing on a table in the gallery (Arnason, 1986, p. 570). The effect was reported to be rather surreal but not without a certain mockery of the British art scene. Later works were less audience-oriented and eventually moved toward a great deal of homoerotic content.

John Giorno, whose work has spanned four decades, is a true exemplar of intermedia, combining language and technology, autobiography, and "overheard material" (McAdams, 1981-82, p. 40). Giorno's principal medium is poetry, performed for compact disc, video, theater, movies, radio, and performance art audiences. In 1968, the artist created *Dial-a-Poem*, a worldwide telephone service, and from 1965 to 1970 he created Electronic Sensory Poetry Environments or ESPE, another wedding of language and science (Dery, 1985, p. 49). Giorno is indeed a prolific artist, and the bulk of his material has never shied from controversial or overt sexual content. In fact, the artist's work in performance is quite frankly best described as one long, taut-bodied rant against the self, urban decay, and loneliness. Like the work of his friend and fellow writer/performer William Burroughs, Giorno's poetry is punctuated with biting wit and social commentary but never strays far from personal accountability. Another performance artist to adopt the intermedia possibilities of performance is Robert Wilson, whose works, unlike others up until this time, were most often staged as large-scale spectacles. Wilson's collaboration with Philip Glass called *Einstein on the Beach* was produced in 1976, and it is perhaps the artist's best-known piece. Wilson's works typically involve artists, performers, and technicians from many disciplines who are mobilized to produce huge multimedia events. Not so unlike opera or theatrical fare (Goldberg, 1988, p. 199), these presentations, however, favored avant-garde elements in staging, sound, narrative, and time. Repetition, slow movement, and an absence of dialogue or traditional theatrical plot devices are hallmarks of Wilson's work (Tomkins, 1976, p. 228). A conflation of performance art practice and theatrical practice could be said to be the outcome from such collaborations, but Wilson's work always retains the unique integrity of what has been termed *The Theatre of Images* or the performance art fringe (Goldberg, 1988, p. 185).

Artists of the 1970s still interested in the fusion of art and life were Jerry Dreva and Paul Best. These two artists were featured prominently in the early years of *High Performance* magazine. As testament to the increasing range of performance art content, space, and spectatorship, these artists helped expand the critical view of performative function and presentation. Dreva was an early participant in Mail Art, an appropriator of printed media for collage and political satire, the founder of his own fan club, a journalist, and vandal among other things. Dreva, like Paul Best, took

his life/art to the streets. Best, a San Diego-based performance artist from the mid-1970s, explored issues of gender in street performances that he termed *city work*, as well as issues of body image in gay culture long before scholars began examining the phenomenon. His androgynous alter-ego, Octavia, was the subject of much work during this time, venturing into public spaces for chance encounters with shopworkers and passersby. Best's work is important for its precocious attention to gay male matters, while other artists were still toying with performance art form and abstract concepts.

Of interest at the close of the 1970s was Ron Vawter, whose performance work continued into the mid-1990s, when he died due to AIDS complications. Alternately working as an actor, Vawter chose subject matter with a decidedly gay bent (i.e., solo performance works about Roy Cohn, real-life New York lawyer and antagonist in Tony Kushner's *Angels in America* as well as gay filmmaker Jack Smith). A member of the Wooster Group, an experimental theater ensemble, Vawter, along with Dreva and Best, anticipated the veritable explosion of queer performance artists in the 1980s (Russell, 1994, p. 17).

Gay Male Performance Art: 1980s

The queer voice rang strong and clear in the 1980s, nowhere more so than in the arts. Thanks to the groundbreaking work of feminists and their utilization of autobiography (Miller and Román, 1995, p. 180) to counter the prevailing standpoint on gender, sexuality, and race in the dominant culture, queer men had a model with which to analyze and accommodate their own stories. With the introduction of AIDS and all of its political, social, and religious implications as well as the reintroduction of shame, dependency, loss, and grief, queer artists were faced with new dilemmas in regards to autobiography and identity maintenance. This new threat to the community and the subsequent backlash from religious and political organizations and frightened individuals produced a defensive posture in the queer community. Unified in anguish and rage, the "Artist as Activist" was born. Besides the dominant performance art themes of the 1980s, autobiography and activism, some time-tested themes prevailed: work associated with the body and its processes; a fascination with science and new media; a continued interest in Dadaist nonsense, contradiction, and anti-culture sentiment; and, of course, the Cageian legacy. Also, with an ongoing history all its own, gay culture was becoming the subject of celebration as well as a bit of good-natured scrutiny.

Arguably the most influential and successful solo performance artist of the last two decades, Tim Miller rose to prominence in New York City in the early 1980s. There he also founded *P.S. 122*, the city's preeminent performance art space. A succession of consciously queer performance pieces followed, among them *Postwar* (1981), *Buddy Systems* (1985), and *Some Golden States* (1987). All Miller performance pieces are autobiographical, relating his personal and artistic development to the prevailing queer culture, and the vast majority of these works in some way respond to the AIDS crisis in this country. In addition, most pieces are designed with an activist's propensity for social reformation and individual or spiritual transformation. Such calls to action infuse Miller's performances with an urgency that penetrates the customary separation of performer and audience. Miller cofounded *Highways* performance space with Linda Frye Burnham in 1989, thus beginning a long period of work and artistic sponsorship on the West Coast. There he developed his quintessential performance artwork, *My Queer Body*, as well as a series of performance art sermons with Episcopal priest Malcolm Boyd (Miller and Román, 1995, p. 179). In 1990, Miller became one of the notorious NEA Four when his fellowship award was overturned by pressure from the religious right and the political machinations in Congress and the art world. Miller and three other artists successfully sued the federal government for these monies (Mendoza, 1993, p. 51), and he quickly returned to the performance space to tell the tale. Miller's work has continued into the 1990s, more charged with purpose than ever before, his enthusiasm for storytelling opening doors in Europe and Australia as well as those in leading performance spaces in North America.

A number of bold and angry artists had broached the troubled topic of HIV and AIDS by the middle to late 1980s, including Richard Elovich, Carlos Gutierrez-Solana, and the founder of eXperimental Art Research Terminal (XART), Billy Curmano. Also, by the mid-1980s the art world had lost a number of artists to the disease, among them Ethyl Eichelberger and the highly gifted Philip-Dimitri Galas. Expressing the great fear and despondency felt by the queer community, artist Hudson performed a collection of low-tech but richly textured pieces in performance spaces in Chicago, St. Paul, Cincinnati, and New York. *Deep Kissing*, a 1986 work by Hudson, was indicative of not only the 1980s' most

critical concern but a Dadaist tendency for randomness and disjointed narrative (Hudson, 1986, p. 40). David Wojnarowicz, one of the most fascinating artists of the late 1980s and early 1990s, worked in many mediums including collage, painting, writing, installation, video, and performance. Wojnarowicz, also lost to AIDS, was "[a] self-described outsider" (Stiles and Selz, p. 294), and his works attempted to express the alienation and degradation associated with discrimination. The artist's works were often characterized as dangerous due to the use of pornographic images, depictions of the excesses of hate and rage, and other taboo subject matter. Nevertheless, Wojnarowicz's contribution to performance art, and all the other media he produced, has left a lasting impression in the world of art.

Essex Hemphill was one of the most powerful artists to have challenged societal assumptions about the intersection of race, ethnicity, and sexual orientation. With poetry as his medium, the artist entered into a variety of performative situations from his collaboration in Voicescapes: An Urbanmouthpiece in the mid-1980s to his work with Marlon Riggs in the controversial and exquisitely beautiful *Tongues Untied,* part performance-for-film project and part anti-dominant-culture diatribe. Ishmael Houston-Jones's performance art work might be described as politicized "talk dance" (Lippard, 1984, p. 43). Speaking often of the clash

Tim Miller

of races or the contrariness of cultures, Houston-Jones engages the performance space in a seeming effort to make connections yet demonstrating that such efforts are not really possible. Always embedded in the structure of the artist's monologues is a deep mistrust of government and a fascination with Western interventions in third world cultures.

Standout artists from the 1980s include the Abject art of Mike Kelley; the performance and video art of activist John Greyson; the experimental theater and performance art work of David Schweizer; the regional and historical portraits of Mel Andringa; the choreographic team Bill T. Jones and Arnie Zane; and New York performance art partners Keegan and Lloyd. As is apparent, by the 1980s performance art content had diversified greatly, and the suffusion of queer people in the genre indicates that audiences were more than prepared to absorb the material presented: they were eager. As was true from the start, artists from any number of disciplines were coming to performance art when full expression in others was either too difficult or impossible to achieve. Like Tim Miller, John Kelly began his creative life as a dancer but abandoned it at age 21 for fashion illustration at Parson's School of Design in New York (Gruen, 1992, p. 62). Kelly then went on to explore other creative outlets only to find that performance art was the medium that allowed him "to balance [his] private and public impulses" (Morrissey, 1992, p. 97). The winner of numerous performance awards as well as critical acclaim, Kelly has found the instrument for conveying his thoughts on movement, historical characterization, sexuality, and humor.

Finally, the 1980s saw the introduction of the comic monologue as a performance art technique, exemplified in the work of David Cale as well as the campy send-up of popular culture and gender attribution found in the work of John Fleck. Cale's work also incorporated popular song, an entertainment device that, most likely, would not have been considered by artists of the 1970s. Fleck's performances strip the media culture bare, exposing its repressive stereotypes, its rigidity about the body and sexuality, and its hollow assurances about the depths of intellect and spirituality. According to Matias Viegener, professor at CalArts,

> Fleck's full-length pieces offer us a pathetic rendition of this culture of the self.... The overall effect is that of a sentimental education against a backdrop of scandal, banality, and neon with John Fleck as the trisexual schoolmarm at the head of his own Gothic classroom (Viegener, 1991, p. 39).

Fleck's subject matter and the sometime use of his naked body in performance made him the target of anti-gay politics, and he, like Tim Miller, was singled out in 1990, becoming one of the NEA Four. The subsequent climate for performative work in the United States was anxious and petulant, and performance artists were forced to find new ways to respond to politics, media, the public, and even performance subject matter.

Gay Male Performance Art: 1990s

Quickly adjusting to the scarcity of federal grants and fellowships, more artists than ever before applied to local and state arts organizations. Seemingly undaunted by the political and economic roadblock constructed by performance art naysayers—the most

John Kelly as Egon Schiele

potent of its kind until this point—these artists continued their work without missing a beat. Of course, many artists were nonplussed by the attention, and many consciously adjusted their performative content. Nevertheless, performance artists largely kept to their mission, determined to deliver their messages with or without federal or civic endorsement.

Artists emerging in the 1990s included Ron Athey, John Goss, David Mura, Scott Timm, Jon Weaver, Lawrence Steger, Hung Nguyen, Leo García, Curtis York, and Frank Maya, who successfully crossed over into stand-up comedy. Group acts High Risk Group and Pomo Afro Homos, while very different in performance methodology and substance, found enthusiastic audiences in this decade. In the tradition of the eminent body art performers of the past, Keith Hennessy uses the performance space to express the body's functions. Hennessy is best known for his spittle pieces executed with great physicality and elegant form. Similarly, Tim Miller has continued working with issues of the body and autobiography, performing older as well as new pieces involving nudity and the locating of spirituality in sexual identity and intimacy. Marcus Kuiland-Nazario, activist and artist in the Latino community, is most often identifiable in the performance setting as the indefatigable Carmen. Using drag performance to educate her audience about gender, sex, race, and class, Kuiland-Nazario's philosophy is one of service to the community and sensitivity to the unique concerns of Latinos. Luis Alfaro, the current director of the Mark Taper Forum Latino Theatre Initiative, also uses the performance setting to educate about his environment, Los Angeles, and the common stereotypes about the city. Alfaro's work in the early 1990s was thus an extension of the 1980s' concern for autobiography as a tool for deconstructing the normalized view of Latinos and the customary assumptions about regional zones in North America. Alfaro's most recent work also addresses the AIDS epidemic as well as the persistent notion of binary gender. That said, transgender performance artist Kate Bornstein should be mentioned as one of the driving forces in gender and sexual studies and performance. Fitting neither the category male nor female, nor gay or straight, Bornstein defies the cultural order and embodies a new standard of human integration.

Gay Male Performance Art: Conclusion

Performance art has accommodated the queer community like no other art form, providing a space for any practitioner to test or enact ideas and emotions. For nearly 30 years, this genre of art has been nurturer to creative expressions involving sexual identity, spiritual transformation, political allegiance, and scientific as well as philosophical experimentation. Ever expanding, ever inclusive, ever challenging, performance art moves into the next millennium.

John Fleck

Lesbian Performance Art

Lesbian performance art is a unique hybrid of feminist and gay modes of theatrical practice. Owing both to a dedication to identity politics and to "camp" aesthetics, lesbian performance art has celebrated, interrogated, and defined lesbian lives and sexuality in diverse ways. It has injected feminist performance art with humor and sexiness and it has impacted America's cultural identity.

Autobiography and storytelling have been important factors in the creation of lesbian performance art. Solo performance artists have mined personal history to create characters and interrogate social and political circumstances. Companies such as Spiderwoman Theater, Split Britches, and the Five Lesbian Brothers have broken down social stereotypes, using improvisation to create transformative worlds. Whether solo or as a group, lesbian performance artists have used the feminist principle "the personal is political" to create theater and transform personal histories. Borrowing from burlesque and drag performance, lesbian performance art has also challenged feminist notions of gender and sexual identity.

It is difficult to pinpoint a beginning to the history of lesbian performance art. Lesbians have been actors in art-performance movements throughout history, though they have sometimes avoided defining themselves as lesbian for personal or political reasons. Lesbian performers have also made performance art that was not overtly about sexuality. In the 1980s, performance art gained popularity and notoriety, however, precisely as a venue for self-expression and cultural critique by lesbians, people of color, sexual minorities, and women. Lesbian performance artists were among the vanguard of performance artists who defined the possibilities of performance art.

A decisive moment in the history of lesbian performance art was the formation of the WOW Cafe. A New York performance space, WOW (Women's One World) started in 1980 as an international women's theater festival. (It found its first permanent home in 1982 and is still going strong.) Many prominent lesbian performance artists were part of WOW's origin, and hundreds more lesbian artists have claimed it as their home base. The creation of performance-community spaces for women (lesbian and non-lesbian) was critical to the proliferation, depth, and range of contemporary lesbian performance art. The allure of an empty stage that one could own for a limited time, regardless of the content of one's work, nurtured a genre that defied the boundaries of traditional theater and the visual arts. And the collective spirit of working with and for other women nurtured creative experimentation.

Lesbian Performance Art in the 1970s

Performance art came about in the 1970s as an outgrowth of conceptual art. Conceptual artists, wanting to question the status of the art "object," used their bodies as artistic media. Performance was a means of liberating the plastic arts, of posing questions about the meaning of art and experience itself.

For women, people of color, and sexual minorities in the 1970s, questions about objectification, equal rights, and institutional access also needed addressing. Women in the art world engaged in feminist politics challenged the status of "woman" as object and muse for male artists. They created works that addressed political issues and spoke to their individual experiences as part of an oppressed class. During the 1970s—dubbed the "Amazing Decade" of performance art by women in the United States (Roth, 1983)—artists challenged their publics in the streets as well as in galleries; creating large-scale public performances, as well as indi-

Luis Alfaro

vidualized and collective rituals, they protested stereotypes and spoke out against violence against women. For many women artists, using their bodies was the most direct, effective, and meaningful way to get their messages across.

Despite the breadth and collective energy of much women's performance art, explicit lesbian themes were conspicuously absent from the majority of women's performance art in the 1970s. There was, in fact, a great deal of tension and controversy over lesbianism in the feminist movement of the 1970s. By and large, sexual issues were conceived in terms of women's oppression at the hands of men, or as celebrations of women's biological and spiritual connection to nature. And while we can assume that lesbian performance artists participated in these "womanist" works—as lesbians have participated in every aspect of the feminist movement—identifiably lesbian sexual practices such as butch/femme coupling were viewed as "heteropatriarchal" in many cases. Yet it is from butch/femme performance and gay male theater that explicitly lesbian performance art got its force and material.

The 1980s: Creating a Lesbian Performance Art Scene

Lesbian performance art blossomed in an environment of drag and burlesque theater, consciousness-raising meetings, and potlucks. Lois Weaver and Peggy Shaw, who with Deb Margolin made up the popular Split Britches troupe, created a venue where sexually explicit and humorous material could be put onstage without censure.

WOW was an idea hatched by Weaver and Shaw while they were traveling in Europe with Spiderwoman Theater and Hot Peaches (a gay theater company) in the 1970s. After meeting other women's companies who wanted to perform in the United States, Weaver and Shaw decided to host the first international women's theater festival in the United States. It took place in October 1980 at the Allcraft Center on St. Mark's Place, in New York City.

With no capital or institutional support, and little time to raise money, Weaver and Shaw formed "Allied Farces" with Jordi Mark and Pamela Camhe. They amassed a crew of volunteers who produced benefits—usually wild costume parties—to raise money for the festival. The fundraisers not only spread excitement about the festival, but they also provided practical technical training for the WOW volunteers. The festival ran for two weeks with two or three performances a night, and occasional afternoon shows.

When the festival ended, the theater management offered the organizers the space to continue producing performances. So for months, WOW volunteers produced dance, theater, and poetry every Wednesday night, and sometimes on Thursdays, splitting the receipts between the performers and the house. WOW continued to grow in popularity but lost its space after the Flamboyant Ladies, a black lesbian group, performed a "very, very hot, very sensual" show (Weaver, quoted in Solomon, 1996, p. 43). The Allcraft Center, afraid of losing its funding from the city, padlocked the door to the theater. Although WOW would produce anything by women, regardless of sexual identity, they had acquired a reputation for doing lesbian work, and this opened them to attack.

When WOW planned to organize a second festival, in 1981, they decided they wanted a cafe where performers and spectators could hang out together. This was the beginning of the WOW Cafe. At the conclusion of the second festival, artists decided that they did not want to stop creating work in a collective atmosphere, so WOW began searching for ways to create a permanent cafe. WOW began hosting benefits—like the Freudian slip party, in which guests came in lingerie, a Debutante ball, and "X-rated Xmas"—that brought enough financial success for them to rent a space, 330 East 11th Street, in March 1982.

The WOW Cafe is still a performance collective in New York City's East Village (in 1997 located at 59 East 4th Street). Its mission is straightforward: "WOW is a non-profit performance space run by and for women. WOW is a loose anarchy of women striving to create our own theater, by our own experiences and definitions. There are no oaths taken, no dues collected, rarely any rules applied to the group. Any woman is welcome to join this chaos." Staff meetings are held weekly and volunteers work in a variety of capacities, from acting, directing, and running the lightboard to managing the box office and concessions. Many prominent lesbian performance artists have graced its stage, working collectively with other performers, writers, designers, and technicians.

The WOW Cafe was not the only venue for lesbian performance arts. The East Village supported an amazing number of galleries and clubs for alternative performance works in the 1980s, the heyday of performance art in the United States. Carmelita Tropicana, a fully realized persona in modified Carmen Miranda drag, hosted informal "cheet chat seis" at Club Chandalier, dancing, singing, cooking sushi chicken, and conversing with guests on hot lesbian topics of the day. At the same time, Holly Hughes's play *The Lady Dick* was playing around the neighborhood after first being produced at WOW in 1985. Tropicana (Alina Troyano) and Hughes were both creating a kind of lesbian performance that celebrated lesbian marginality with raunchy wit and intelligent humor.

Lesbian Performance Art in the 1990s

Although many of New York's East Village clubs closed in the 1980s—victims of market glut, restrictive city ordinances, and changing audiences—lesbian performance art has continued to flourish at WOW and other places in New York, San Francisco, and elsewhere. In 1989, the National Endowment for the Arts withdrew grants from four performance artists, including Holly Hughes, touching off a national debate about government support for the arts, censorship, and artistic freedom that still rages on many fronts. But the need to make art in the age of AIDS and to speak out about racism, homophobia, and violence against women had prompted artists to create performance in a wide variety of styles and voices. Lesbian performance artists continue to address their audiences with rage, wit, and sexual outspokenness.

PROMINENT PEOPLE

Alvin Ailey (1931-1989)

When Alvin Ailey died of an AIDS-related rare blood disease at the age of 58, he was nine months into a collaboration with writer A. Peter Bailey on *Revelations: The Autobiography of Alvin Ailey.* Unfinished at the time of his death, in this book Ailey comes across as a self-contradictory artist on many subjects who nevertheless is candid about his homosexuality and struggle with cocaine addiction in the 1980s. (The autobiography was eventually published in 1995.) Speaking frankly about the misery of his romantic liaisons, Ailey bemoans his proclivity for falling in love with "young men who take things."

Ailey was born in Rogers, Texas, a poor, rural, segregated town 50 miles south of Waco. Alvin Ailey, Sr., abandoned his family when his son was six months old; later in life Ailey became variously obsessed with finding his father and terrified at the idea of meeting him. (Several of his ballets explore this specter of a father: *Fix Me, Jesus,* a section of *Revelations,* and the offstage figure of vengeance in *Masekela Language.*) Lula Elizabeth Cooper Ailey moved with her six-year-old son to Navasota, Texas, where the gospel music of the True Vine Baptist Church and the blues and jazz of the Dew Drop Inn were to make deep impressions on young Ailey, as seen later in his three signature works, *Blues Suite* (1958), *Revelations* (1960), and *Cry* (1971).

While studying languages at the University of California at Los Angels, Ailey began to take technique classes with Lester Horton, and he made his debut as a dancer with the company the following year. With the unexpected death of Horton in 1953, Ailey took over the company; his first three choreographic works were performed by the troupe in 1954. But that same year, Ailey and Carmen de Lavallade moved to New York to be the featured dancers in the Broadway musical *House of Flowers.* Subsequently, Ailey appeared on Broadway in several musicals and non-musical plays. When Ailey assembled a troupe of dancers to present a concert of his choreography in 1958, critic John Martin noted that while "As a performer he [Ailey] has a rich, animal quality of

movement and an innate sense of theatrical projection," Ailey's choreography was "impressive," containing "inherently substantial stuff," "beautifully staged," and "superbly danced." Ailey's choreography has been performed by the American Ballet Theatre, Joffrey Ballet, Paris Opera Ballet, London Festival Ballet, Royal Danish Ballet, and companies in Italy, Venezuela, and Israel. Ailey choreographed the dances for the premiere of Leonard Bernstein's *Mass* at the Kennedy Center for the Performing Arts in 1971. Also in 1971, the Alvin Ailey American Dance Center was established as the official school of the company and a junior company was also established, the Alvin Ailey Repertory Ensemble.

Inspired by Lester Horton's vision, when Ailey formed his own company in 1958 he produced works by black and white choreographers, and presented these dances with a multiracial cast. A spellbinding raconteur off-stage and on, he called his company the Alvin Ailey American Dance Theatre to emphasize the fact that the bulk of the repertory were dances with stories, not abstract pieces. Unimpressed by esthetic categories, Ailey combined elements from jazz and Caribbean and ballet idioms and set the resulting work with equal panache to Duke Ellington or Bartók or Andreas Vollenweider. Taking the rich vocabularies of modern dance and his black heritage, Ailey welded them together, thus honoring both. Unworried by convention, he elicited from his male dancers an unprecedented sensuality and raw muscularity. The striking theatricality and exuberant energy of his entire company was in direct contrast to the tormented and austere work of most other modern dance troupes.

From its inception, the Ailey troupe was to be a repertory company, not a showcase for one choreographer's work. Soon the most popular dance company on the international touring circuit, Ailey's vibrant dancers performed works by Katherine Dunham, Pearl Primus, Ted Shawn, Talley Beatty, Donald McKayle, George Faison, Bill T. Jones and Arnie Zane, Elisa Monte, Ulysses Dove, and others. In a 1989 interview, Ailey remarked that he wanted to be remembered not primarily as a dancer or as a choreographer but as man who had created both a company and a home. Alvin Ailey American Dance Theater celebrates its fortieth anniversary in 1999; the enduring legacy of the company easily qualifies Ailey as the most influential black artist in American modern dance. Upon Ailey's death, former star of the company Judith Jamison was appointed artistic director of the company. *BC*

Luis Alfaro

Luis Alfaro is a native of Los Angeles, a city that has figured prominently in his performance work. Eager to dispel the myths about this region of the country as well as stereotypes about the Latino community, Alfaro unfolds a narrative both autobiographical and profoundly political. His most recent work is about loss and grief associated with AIDS. Alfaro's work includes the following: the play *Bitter Homes and Gardens*; the performance art pieces *Pico-Union* and *Downtown*; and a solo spoken word CD entitled *Downtown.* Alfaro is currently the director of the Mark Taper Forum's Latino Theatre Initiative. *DT*

Les Ballets Trockadero de Monte Carlo (est. 1974)

While men have probably been dancing on their toes ever since the pointe shoe was developed in the 1830s, the first company of men performing as ballerinas *en pointe* occurred on 31 August 1972, at the tiny Jean Cocteau Theatre in New York City's East Village. Led by Larry Ree (Madame Ekathrina Sobechanskaya),

Bill T. Jones

the five men in the Trockadero Gloxinia Ballet Company sought to evoke the glamour of late-nineteenth-century Russian ballet. Armed with more attitude than dance technique, the Gloxinia nevertheless attracted a following. In 1974, three members of the troupe, chafing under the restricted aesthetic of the Gloxinia (their ballets never contained male characters), decided to form their own troupe. Established by Peter Anastos (1948-), Antony Bassae (1943-1985), and Natch Taylor (1948-), Les Ballets Trockadero de Monte Carlo made its debut at the Westside Discussion Group, a "homophile" organization on West Fourteenth Street in New York City.

The new company was more interested in parody and satire than in the glorification of the drag ballerina. Within the company's first month, Arlene Croce wrote a glowing review in the *New Yorker,* and soon the Trocks—as they were affectionately known—were playing larger Off-Off Broadway theaters. In 1976, the company signed with a management firm, began to tour, and qualified for the National Endowment for the Arts Dance Touring Program.

The majority of the ballets the Trockadero perform are the traditional "work horses" in the classical ballet repertory: *Swan Lake* Act II, *Giselle* Act II, *Les Sylphides, Pas de Quatre.* Sticking faithfully to the original choreography, humor arises in how the choreography is performed and who performs it. The Trock preparation for a step might be exaggerated, or the movement may begin with the wrong point of initiation, or a muscled preparation may lead up to nothing more than a single *pirouette.* Sanson Candelaria's (1941-1986) incomparable Tamara Boumdiyeva, although possessing solid dance technique, nevertheless always appeared a little rattled. Keith Glancy's (1955-1995) Natalia Zlotmachinskaya was an Edward Gorey-type ballerina, one with osteoporosis. Mike Gonzales's (1954-1996) muscled Natasha Notgoudenoff did not glow like a ballerina but sweated like a race horse.

Original choreography performed by the Trocks pinpoints specific choreographers: Anastos's *Go for Barocco* is a deconstruction of George Balanchine; Anastos's *Yes, Virginia, Another Piano Ballet* targets Jerome Robbins; Shawn Avrea's *Phaedra Monotonous #1148* skewers Martha Graham, and Roy Fialkow's *I Wanted to Dance with You at the Cafe of Experience* dissects Pina Bausch.

The Trocks have performed in 41 of the 50 states and in Washington, D.C., in addition to international tours that have taken them to more than 100 cities in 11 countries, on 6 continents. Not only is the Trockadero the only comedic dance company that has been financially successfully, it is the oldest all-male dance ensemble in America. The Trocks are a non-profit organization, yet they have never applied for private or government grants, and exist without a guild of well-heeled patrons. That they have been able to survive financially, completely dependent on box office income alone, makes them unique. The success of the company is also not linked to one performer, choreographer, or artistic director: Bassae left the Trocks in 1976 to form his own company, Les Ballets Trockadero De La Karpova (1976-1983); Anastos left in 1978 to pursue a career as a free-lance choreographer; and Taylor was voted out by the board in 1990. Tory Dobrin, a dancer who joined the company in 1980, assumed responsibility for artistic matters when he was appointed associate director in 1991. Two links of continuity are general director Eugene McDougle and company archivist Anne Dore Davids, who began working with the Trocks in the second month of their existence.

The world of Les Ballets Trockadero de Monte Carlo is total artifice: they are based in New York, not Monte Carlo; most of the dancers are Americans, despite their faux-Russian names; men assume the roles of ballerinas; and *Swan Lake* is done with a cast of ten instead of a hundred. But their knowledge of dance history, various styles of dance, and comedic timing have made them an international success. *BC*

Paul Best

Paul Best, a pioneer performance artist from the 1970s who boldly addressed issues of gender in his *city work* pieces featuring the androgynous character Octavia, presented a series of works at alternative performance space Sushi, and wrote about his docu-

Robert Chesley

mented outings in downtown San Diego in the earliest issues of *High Performance* magazine. In the early 1980s, the artist presented *A Gender Show* in New York at Group Material, a conceptual artist collective concerned with the ever-present commodification of art. Best studied with Eleanor Antin, Allan Kaprow, Barbara Smith, and Suzanne Lacy at the University of California at San Diego beginning in 1977. In the early 1980s, Best began performance work, conceived as a two-year "life" piece, dealing with bodybuilding, and this work helped initiate a serious examination of ideal beauty standards in gay male culture. *DT*

Marie Cartier

Marie Cartier is a poet, instructor, and incest survivor who uses solo performance art to publicly heal the wounds of incest. Her plays include *Come Out Come Out Wherever You Are, Stumbling into Light, Leave a Light On When You Go Out, Freeze Count, Closer to Home, This Is My Body, This Is My Home, Blessed Virgin,* and *Ballistic Femme.* Cartier's mission has been to transform therapy through drama, poetry, and movement. In workshops designed especially for incest survivors, Cartier leads women through creative exercises that allow them to shape their memories of abuse into positive, shameless expressions of survival.

Blessed Virgin (1994), Cartier's first one-woman show, explores Cartier's belief in Roman Catholicism. The play is structured around a Catholic mass; Cartier portrays a priest who steps outside the altar to tell her story. Her second one-woman show, *Ballistic Femme* (1997), asks persistent questions about butch/femme relationships. She is based in California. *JR*

Jane Chambers (1937-1983)

Jane Chambers was the first lesbian playwright to produce and publish plays based on lesbian experience in the tradition of American realism. She began her career by writing for radio and for television. She founded Corpswoman Theatre, which performed for mainly African-American audiences, and then in 1973 she founded, with Margot Lewiton, the Women's Interart Theatre. Her first lesbian-centered play, *Eye of the Gull*, was written in 1971, and it was one of the first lesbian plays to define homophobia, not lesbianism, as a sickness. *A Late Snow* was optioned for Off-Broadway in 1974, but because of the subject matter, the producer was unable to find backers. In 1980, *Last Summer at Bluefish Cove* opened at Shandol Theatre for a very successful run. *Bluefish Cove*, set in a lesbian summer resort, centers on the romance between a woman just coming out and her lover, who is dying of cancer. Unlike Mart Crowley's *Boys in the Band*, the play that in 1968 ushered in the era of queer theater, *Bluefish Cove*'s characters demonstrate courage and loyalty, barely referring to the homophobia of the outside world. Chambers died of a brain tumor in 1983. *CG*

Robert Chesley (1943–1990)

The author of more than 20 one-act and seven full-length plays, Robert Chesley was "the most intensely physical of gay playwrights," in the words of John Clum. For Chesley, the naked male body is not just a site for desire, but an erotic locus that should embrace sensuality in defiance of AIDS. His debut work, *Hell, I Love You*, premiered at Theatre Rhinoceros in 1981. Chesley's *Night Sweat* (1984), the first full-length AIDS play to be produced in New York, predates Larry Kramer's *The Normal Heart* and William Hoffman's *As Is*. Chesley's best known work is *Jerker, or The Helping Hand: A Pornographic Elegy with Redeem-*

ing Social Value and a Hymn to the Queer Men of San Francisco in Twenty Phone Calls, Many of Them Dirty (1986). In 1996, The Robert Chesley Foundation Award for Lifetime Achievement in Playwriting was established; winners include Doric Wilson and Robert Patrick. *BC*

Cheryl Crawford (1902-1986)

Cheryl Crawford was a highly successful independent producer on Broadway whose successes included *One Touch of Venus* (1943), *The Tempest* (1944), *Brigadoon* (1947), *The Rose Tattoo* (1951), *Paint Your Wagon* (1951), and *Sweet Bird of Youth* (1959). She helped found the Group Theatre, the Actor's Studio, and also (with Margaret Webster and Eva Le Gallienne) the American Repertory Theatre. *CG*

Creach/Koester (est. 1982)

From 1982 to 1996, Terry Creach and Stephen Koester were co-directors of Creach/Koester, an all-male company based in New York City. After 11 years of presenting duet work, in 1993 Creach/Koester expanded their choreography and company to a troupe of ten men to present *Rough House*. In 1995, they choreographed a work for five men, *I Witness—The Noir Studies*. The company was dedicated to exploring men dancing, the art of partnering, and the collaborative process.

In 1997, Creach joined the dance faculty at Bennington College and Koester became the owner and innkeeper of the Yellowstone Riverview Lodge Bed & Breakfast in Paradise Valley, Montana. *BC*

Merce Cunningham (1919-)

A native of Centralia, Washington, Merce Cunningham began dance lessons at the age of eight, learning the popular vaudeville dances of the day. Later studying with a former member of Martha Graham's dance company, Cunningham met the legend herself at Mills College in Oakland, California. Subsequently, Cunningham moved to New York City and began to perform with Graham's company (1939-45), creating such important roles as the Revivalist in *Appalachian Spring*. A remarkable performer, Cunningham was heralded for his acute concentration and soft, springing jump. Although slowed down by painful arthritis, Cunningham continued to perform into his seventies.

Avant-garde composer John Cage's (1912-1992) first meeting with Cunningham in 1938 was to have a profound effect on both their private and professional lives; by 1944, Cunningham and Cage were presenting their own collaborative programs. Cage divorced his wife in 1945 in order to make Cunningham his personal as well as artistic partner. Even though the couple did not share an apartment until 1971, their relationship spanned 54 years. Reticent about discussing their private life, Cage once offered this insight: "I do the cooking and he does the dishes."

Cage's discovery of the *I Ching*, the Chinese *Book of Changes*, in 1951, had a major effect on the composer and his partner. Cage and Cunningham began to explore the use of chance in determining decisions in the creation of their respective art works. Rejecting the traditional hierarchy that put decor and music at the service of the choreography, the pair made all three elements equal in their work, and often the three elements were not united until opening night, thus preserving their autonomy. (Attracted to this equality of the components, prominent visual artists such as Robert Rauschenberg, Jasper Johns, Frank Stella, and Andy Warhol collaborated with the troupe.) Similarly rejecting narrative, character, and theme, Cunningham sought to create dances that were

solely about movement. Cunningham and Cage put these theories to test on a large scale when they created the Merce Cunningham Dance Company in 1953. Their resultant work was the beginning of a movement often labeled the postmodern aesthetic, where an interest in the creative process is valid for its own sake.

The clean, hard lines of Cunningham's 70-plus dances are coupled with rapid shifts in weight, direction, and rhythm; he generally rehearsed the works without music, thus freeing the dancers from any emotional connection to a sound score. His plotless works have been labeled "refreshingly pure, cool, and astringent" by Tobi Tobias of *New York*, but "pallid and pastel, flat-footed classroom classicism" by Clive Barnes of *Dance Magazine*. Constantly intrigued by new technologies, Cunningham has been a pioneer in the field of dance on video (working with filmmakers Charles Atlas and Elliot Caplan), and was instrumental in developing computer softwares Life Forms and Compose, which can be used as choreographic tools.

Cunningham's work is in the repertoire of Rambert Dance Company (*Septet*, 1953), New York City Ballet (*Summerspace*, 1958), Paris Opéra (*Un Jour ou deux*, 1973), and American Ballet Theater (*Duets*, 1980). Ex-company members who have established their own careers include Viola Farber, Paul Taylor, Remy Charlip, Steve Paxton, Douglas Dunn, and Karole Armitage. *BC*

Charlotte Cushman (1816-1876)

Charlotte Cushman was the first great tragedienne of the American stage. Born in Boston to a working-class family, Cushman trained to become an opera singer, but it was as a dramatic actress

Charlotte Cushman

in the role of Lady Macbeth that she achieved her first success. In 1837, she signed with the Park Theatre in New York, where she performed 120 roles in three years, including Emilia (*Othello*) and Nancy Sykes (*Oliver Twist*). Moving to Philadelphia to manage the Walnut Street Theatre, Cushman fell in love with Rosalie Sully, who became her first lover. In 1845, Cushman crossed the ocean, becoming the first American actor to score a critical success with London audiences. Cushman specialized in "breeches parts," cross-dressing to perform the male roles of Romeo (which she played to her sister's Juliet), Cardinal Wolsey (*Henry VIII*), Hamlet, Oberon (*Midsummer Night's Dream*), and Claude Melnotte (*The Lady of Lyons*). During one of her many periods of retirement, Cushman moved to Rome, where she became the center of a circle of expatriate lesbian artists (the "Jolly Female Bachelors") that included sculptors Harriet Hosmer and Emma Stebbins, who later became her "wife." Diagnosed with breast cancer, Cushman underwent one of the first mastectomies and spent her final years touring the United States with a successful series of readings. *CG*

Mark Dendy (1962-)

A former dancer with Martha Graham's junior company, Mark Dendy formed his own troupe in 1993, Dendy Dance and Performance. The name of the company reflects the repertoire of the company: pure dance works and full-scripted narratives with dialogue. A celebrated female impersonator on the drag club circuit, Dendy often performs female characters in his work. In *Fire* (1993), he plays an alcoholic southern mother who rejects then accepts the fact that her daughter is lesbian. In *Dream Analysis* (1998), Dendy appears as one of the two Martha Grahams in this dance play that also features two Vaslav Nijinksys and Judy Garland. Dendy has choreographed 46 works in 15 years. *BC*

The Five Lesbian Brothers

The Five Lesbian Brothers—Moe Angelos, Babs Davy, Dominique Dibbell, Peg Healy, and Lisa Kron—have been a performance group since they met at the WOW Cafe in 1989. Their four full-scale productions are *Voyage to Lesbos*, *Brave Smiles: Another Lesbian Tragedy*, *The Secretaries*, and *Brides of the Moon*. *JR*

The Five Lesbian Brothers

John Fleck

Media parodist John Fleck is an acclaimed solo performance artist whose work is both surreal and substantive, using disjointed imagery and narrative to skewer our consumer culture. Fleck's work also examines gender and gender attribution as well as sexuality, AIDS, and the body. Because of his use of homoerotic content, he, like Tim Miller, Holly Hughes, and Karen Finley, was singled out by the religious right in 1990, and their NEA fellowships were withdrawn. The four artists successfully sued the federal government for reinstatement of the funds, and a settlement was awarded in 1993. Fleck's performance works include *Psycho Opera*, *I Got the He-Be-She-Be's*, *Blessed Are the Little Fishes*, and *A Snowball's Chance in Hell. DT*

María Irene Fornés (1930-)

María Irene Fornés has been called the "dean of Hispanic playwrights in New York," having won eight Obies (Off-Broadway theater awards) as well as a Guggenheim Fellowship and grants from the Rockefeller Foundation and the National Endowment for the Arts. Born in Cuba, she immigrated to the U.S. in 1945 and became a citizen in 1951. Trained as a painter, she did not begin writing plays until 1960. A prolific playwright, Fornés has written in both Spanish and English, and she has successfully adapted plays by García Lorca, Chekhov, and Calderón de la Barca. Her plays are notable for their unusual and exciting forms and their strong characterizations. In 1972, Fornés founded the New York Theatre Strategy to create opportunities for playwrights whose works would not otherwise be produced. In 1977, this organization produced one of Fornés' most successful plays, *Fefu and Her Friends*, which featured a lost lesbian affair. Fornés' work has been widely produced and published in several collections. *CG*

Loie Fuller (1862-1928)

Born in 1862 in Illinois, Loie Fuller is arguably the first modern dancer. After working as an actress in New York and finding it impossible to succeed as a dancer, Fuller went to Paris, where she made her debut in 1892. Her *Serpentine*, *Butterfly*, and *Lily* dances, which she performed in venues such as the Folies-Bergère, made the music-hall popular with a new audience of women and children as well as the traditional male spectators. In her dances, she used a voluminous costume of white or patterned fabric that more or less covered all but her head; by dancing underneath the fabric, she created images of flowers, butterflies, or serpents that were lit with electric light. Aesthetically, Fuller's dances avoided narrative and focused instead on an image or a theme. As one of the first performers to make use of electric light on stage and as her own lighting designer and technician, Fuller revolutionized theater technology as well as dance.

For most of her career, Fuller lived openly with her partner and collaborator Gab Sorère. Their relationship was intimately intertwined with Fuller's art, and Sorère worked on several dances with Fuller. In 1908, Fuller founded a company of all women and girls. They performed full-length ballets that were based on otherworldly themes often including witches, fairies, and baccantes. Late in her career, Fuller became interested in film. She often used projected images in her ballets, and in 1923 she made a film entitled *Le Lys de la vie* ("The Lily of Life"), based on a tale by Queen Marie of Romania. The young René Clair (then René Chomette), gay avant-garde filmmaker, played a part in Fuller's film.

Fuller has been marginalized in dance history, and several dance historians have proposed that this may be in part because of her sexuality. However, the important effect that Fuller had in the Paris art world can be seen in the writing of the Symbolist Poets, the aesthetics of Art Nouveau, and in the work of several sculptors of the period. *JT*

John Giorno (1936-)

John Giorno is the premier poet/performance artist in the United States. With a body of work spanning three decades, the artist has covered nearly the whole of postmodern performance art. The New York City poet is the creator of *Spoken Word* and *Performance Poetry* as well as *Dial-A-Poem* and *Giorno Poetry Systems*. He is the author of numerous books of poetry, including *The American Book of the Dead*, *Balling Buddha*, *Cancer in My Left Ball*, and *You Got to Burn to Shine*. In addition, Giorno has produced upwards of 40 compact discs, LPs, cassettes, and videos, each of which chronicles the artist's unique vision of life, death, sexuality, and the rhythm of language. A Tibetan Buddhist for over 30 years, he has hosted Tibetan lamas in his New York loft. He has appeared in countless performances, events, benefits, and tours, and was the star of *Sleep* (1963), Andy Warhol's first film. Giorno's associates have included William Burroughs, Keith Haring, Laurie Anderson, and Allen Ginsberg, among others, and he continues to create alliances with the great talent of our age. In 1984, he started the AIDS Treatment Project, which extends emergency money to people with AIDS. *DT*

John Glines

Briefly associated with Doric Wilson's TOSOS (The Other Side of Silence), John Glines formed his own theater, the Glines, at the Gay Art Center in TriBeCa in 1976. The first show was *The Soft-*

John Glines

Core Kid, a comedy-farce by Frank Hogan and Walter Kubran; posters featured a titillating photo of star Dennis Walsh opening his pants. In 1976, the company presented 199 performances of 30 plays; in 1977, it produced 45 plays for 230 performances. Despite the popularity of the company, money was always tight. In 1982, the Glines opened three plays by Harvey Fierstein for an eight-week run in a 99-seat Off-Off Broadway house. Previously produced individually at La MaMa, the three were joined to form *Torch Song Trilogy.* After two weeks, unable to find an audience, Glines and Fierstein agreed to cut the run short, when a rave review in the *New York Times* changed everything. The production moved to Actors Playhouse, then to Broadway, where it played for three years. Glines created quite a stir when he thanked his lover on the air during his acceptance speech for winning the 1983 Tony Award for Best Play. Glines's most-produced play, *In Her Own Words* (1989), is a biography of the lesbian playwright Jane Chambers. *BC*

Marga Gomez

Marga Gomez is a Harlem-born, San Francisco-based performer who has earned a living in theater and comedy since 1980. She has performed with the Tony Award-winning San Francisco Mime Troupe, Lilith Feminist Theatre, and the ground-breaking Latino Ensemble Culture Clash. Gomez's solo performance works include *Memory Tricks, Marga Gomez Is Pretty, Witty & Gay,* and *A Line around the Block. Memory Tricks* was first produced as a work in progress in 1990; it premiered as a one-act at the New York Shakespeare Festival in 1993. *Marga Gomez Is Pretty, Witty &*

Marga Gomez

Gay premiered at Josie's Cabaret, San Francisco, in 1991, and has been produced at numerous venues, including P.S.122, New York City; the Whitney Museum's Biennial Performance Series, New York City; Highways Performance Space, Santa Monica, California; the New WORLD Theater; the International Theatre Festival of Chicago; the Wellington Theatre; and the Edinburgh Fringe Festival. *A Line around the Block* was read at the Mark Taper Forum, Music Center, Los Angeles, in May 1994, and was workshopped at Josie's Cabaret, San Francisco, and the New WORLD Theater in 1994.

Gomez, the only child of a Cuban comedian and Puerto Rican dancer, draws on her experience as a child of the New York Latino theater circuit for her solo performance pieces. *Memory Tricks* confronts Gomez's fears of becoming her mother; *A Line around the Block* looks at her father's legacy as a performer; *Marga Gomez Is Pretty, Witty & Gay* "flaunts" Gomez's sexuality and wit. Excerpts of her monologues are included in the anthology *Contemporary Plays by Women of Color* (Perkins and Uno, 1996). *JR*

Angelina Weld Grimké (1880-1958)

Angelina Weld Grimké wrote and staged one of the first African-American plays ever professionally produced in the U.S. Originally titled *The Pervert,* and then *Blessed Are the Barren,* Grimké's play finally opened 3 March 1916, under the sponsorship of the Drama Committee of the District of Columbia, with the title *Rachel.* The heroine renounces marriage and motherhood as a protest against a god who permits the racist attacks on black children. Rachel's position is also an act of resistance against her domineering suitor, and the play can be read as a defense of lesbianism. Grimké's poetry, much of it addressed to women, reflects lesbian romantic themes, as well as themes of rejection and loneliness. Grimké lived alone with her father until his death, and toward the latter half of her life, she retreated into isolation and stopped writing. *CG*

Lorraine Hansberry (1930-1965)

Lorraine Hansberry, author of *A Raisin in the Sun,* was the first African-American female playwright to have her work produced on Broadway. The play won the New York Drama Critics Circle award for Best Play of the Year for the 1958-59 season. Secretly separated from her husband in 1957, Hansberry remained publicly closeted about her lesbianism, although she was a member of the Daughters of Bilitis, one of the first lesbian organizations in the U.S. At the age of 26, she was writing anonymous letters to the *Ladder,* an early lesbian publication, defending lesbianism as a political choice. A Pan-Africanist, she had a long history of radical activism. Hansberry wrote for Paul Robeson's radical paper *Freedom,* lobbied for the Student Nonviolent Coordinating Committee (SNCC), publicly criticized the House Un-American Activities Committee, and led a walk-out at a meeting of prominent blacks with Attorney General Robert Kennedy. Her second play, *The Sign in Sidney Brustein's Window,* confronted black homophobia and gay sexism. Four years after her early death from cancer, excerpts of her work were staged as a play titled *To Be Young, Gifted, and Black: Lorraine Hansberry in Her Own Words.* The work was expanded and published as a book the same year. *CG*

Lester Horton (1906-1953)

Lester Horton choreographed theater, film musicals, and night club acts, using this work to subsidize his little studio-theater (133 seats) on Melrose Avenue in Hollywood, most likely the first American theater dedicated solely to the presentation of modern dance. Horton devised his own unique dance vocabulary influenced

Ishmael Houston-Jones

by Japanese theater and Native American dance, combining with this synthesis of dance forms one of the first racially integrated dance companies in America. Horton's vividly dramatic choreographic work was often accompanied by sets, costumes, and music that he devised. Concert works include *Orozco, Liberian Suite, The Beloved* (repertory of Dance Theatre of Harlem), and a *Rite of Spring* staged in the Hollywood Bowl. When a sudden heart attack killed Lester Horton at the age of 47, he was survived by his companion and associate, Frank Eng. At the time of Horton's death, *New York Times* critic John Martin called him "a tower of strength to the modern dance for the last twenty years."

The Horton Dance Theater (est. 1931) included such luminaries of American modern dance as Bella Lewitzky, Carmen de Lavallade, James Truitte, Joyce Trisler, Rudi Gernreich, and Alvin Ailey. "Lester was a great artist," according to Ailey, "a great teacher and a great, great human being" who had "the vision and the courage to transcend the racism that plagued and too often still plagues decision making in the dance world." *BC*

Ishmael Houston-Jones

Political "talk dance" artist Ishmael Houston-Jones is one of the most distinctive and significant figures in performance art. Utilizing political narratives, improvisation, and dance in order to manifest his views, the artist fills the performance space with great energy and urgency. Houston-Jones's work extends back to the early 1980s, all the while reflecting his particular sensibilities about the government, culture, and sexuality. The artist's works include the following: *DEAD, Relatives, f/i/s/s/i/o/n/i/n/g, Lace, Babble: First Impressions of the White Man, Without Hope,* and *The End of Everything.* In 1987, he toured extensively with sponsorship provided by the National Performance Network. Houston-Jones has performed at the leading performance spaces in this country, including Sushi in San Diego and P.S. 122 in New York. *DT*

Hudson

Artist Hudson was one of the first performers to do work associated with HIV/AIDS, then known as HTLV. The artist ran Feature Gallery in Chicago as well as touring extensively with *Deep Kissing, Buzz Tone Outlet, Sexpot,* and *Sophisticated Boom Boom.* Performances by Hudson were intermedia affairs, utilizing music, projections, costumes, movement, and nonlinear narrative, and all addressed issues peculiar to gay men. The artist received numerous state art grants as well a National Endowment for the Arts Fellowship in 1984. *DT*

Holly Hughes

Holly Hughes gained a national audience as one of the "NEA Four," one of four performance artists whose grants were revoked

473

by the National Endowment for the Arts in 1989 when her work was labelled as obscene due to its sexual content. As a central figure in the political debate about governmental support of the arts, Hughes used the controversy to speak nationally about feminism, lesbian and gay rights, and censorship.

Hughes began her performance career at WOW in 1983. Her plays, including *The Well of Horniness, The Lady Dick, Dress Suits to Hire, World without End,* and *Clit Notes* are collected in *Clit Notes: A Sapphic Sampler* (Grove Press, 1996). *JR*

Joffrey Ballet (est. 1956)

Born Abdulla Jaffa Anver Bey Khan in Seattle, Robert Joffrey (1928-1988) was the son of an Afghan father and an Italian mother. As a teenager, Joffrey had an affair with Gerald Arpino, then a pharmacist in the Coast Guard. Joffrey convinced his new love to study ballet, and Arpino eventually became a dancer and resident choreographer of the Joffrey Ballet. Even when sexual relations ceased between the two men, they remained loyal to each other, living together until Joffrey's death in 1988. In 1973, Joffrey met A. Aladar Marberger, an art gallery director who became the great love of his life. When Marberger learned he had AIDS, he made it public. Joffrey remained silent about his own HIV-positive status, and spokespersons for the company announced he was suffering from complications from asthma. When he died in 1988 at the age of 57, the cause of death was listed as liver, renal, and respiratory failure.

In 1953, Joffrey established his own school, American Ballet Center (now the Joffrey Ballet School), and in 1956 Joffrey and Arpino established the Joffrey Ballet with six dancers and a borrowed station wagon for touring. With the 1966 transfer of New York City Ballet to Lincoln Center, the Joffrey was invited to become the resident company of City Center.

Joffrey set out to create a commercially successful company, one aimed at a broad audience, but with a repertory unlike any other company. Rarely seen twentieth-century masterpieces choreographed by Kurt Joos, Léonide Massine, Sir Frederick Ashton, and Vaslav Nijinsky were on the same bill with rock ballets by Arpino and Joffrey and "crossover" ballets by modern dance choreographers, including Twyla Tharp, Laura Dean, Bill T. Jones, Mark Morris, and Moses Pendleton. The troupe showcases young dancers in an eclectic mix of dance styles that juxtaposes a sexy, pop-culture aesthetic and the experimentation of downtown dance with the more formal sensibility of classical ballet. Unusual also is the company's practice to list its 40 dancers alphabetically, with no hierarchy of principals, soloists, and corp members. And long before multiculturalism became a buzz word, the troupe was interracial.

Joffrey choreographed few ballets for his company; instead, he was proud that in the first 25 years of the company he commissioned 103 new ballets. Joffrey's multimedia rock ballet *Astarte* (1967) created a media sensation, ending up on the cover of *Time* and *Life.* Among Joffrey's 15 complete works is *Pas des Déesses* (1954), one of the most popular ballets in the repertory of London's Ballet Rambert.

As resident choreographer—responsible for one third of the company's repertoire—Arpino gave the Joffrey its reputation for pop ballet and youthfulness with his fast, hard-dancing, and high-spirited works. Arpino's ballets are flashy and glitzy, but he often needed an assistant to help him fit steps to the music. But as popular as Arpino's works were with the public, they were often dismissed by critics as lightweight. Arpino's *The Clowns* (1968)

dealt with nuclear disaster, while the rock-music-driven *Trinity* (1970) was often called the balletic equivalent of the musical *Hair.*

In addition to major revivals such as *The Green Table, Petrushka, Parade, L'Après-midi d'un faune,* and *Le Sacre du primtemps,* one of the company's most popular works was *Billboards* (1993), a full-length ballet set to 14 songs by Prince, choreographed by Laura Dean, Charles Moulton, Margo Sappington, and Peter Pucci.

Although based in New York, the Joffrey became the first major dance troupe to have two home bases when it became the resident dance company of the Music Center of Los Angeles County (1983-90). Two years after Joffrey's death, faced with a deficit of $2 million, the company's board of directors established a nine-member committee to effectively supplant Arpino's power as artistic director. He responded by resigning on 1 May 1990, taking with him his ballets and those of Robert Joffrey. Three weeks later Arpino re-established contact with the company and resumed the responsibilities of artistic director. Fleeing rising costs, the company left New York in 1995 to become the Joffrey Ballet of Chicago, but the Joffrey-affiliated school remained in Manhattan. *BC*

Bill T. Jones (1951-) and Arnie Zane (1947-1988)

Strikingly opposite, Bill T. Jones (tall and black) and Arnie Zane (small and white) nevertheless intertwined their lives and careers in a choreographic partnership unique in American modern dance. There is a good case to be made that they were the most celebrated, if not the most notorious, out gay couple in America.

William Tass Jones enrolled in the State University of New York at Binghamton on a sports scholarship (as a runner) with the intention of becoming an actor, but after seeing Martha Graham's company in performance and meeting Arnie Zane (a Jewish-Italian photography major), Jones's life changed. For the next 17 years, Jones and Zane shared their personal and creative lives.

From 1972 to 1980, Jones and Zane danced and choreographed with American Dance Asylum, a collective formed by Lois Welk. *Blauvelt Mountain* (1980) was a tour de force indicative of their unique choreographic vision, containing (among other things) a capella singing, talking, pedestrian movement, and highly complex physical work based on contact improvisation. Similarly, their next major work, *Social Intercourse: Pilgrim's Progress* (1981), contained another characteristic of work by Jones/Zane: anger. Jones's solo contained a monologue that could be interpreted as misogynist and racist. The American Dance Festival reacted by not inviting the troupe back for ten years, and the *New Yorker*'s Arlene Croce announced that "Bill T. Jones has marched the New Narcissism right into the fever swamp." When Jones created a commission for Alvin Ailey American Dance Theater, he retaliated by calling it *Fever Swamp* (1983). But the pair's other work has a hip downtown flavor, like *Secret Pastures* (1984) with settings by graffiti artist Keith Haring, score by Peter Gordon, and costumes by fashion designer Willi Smith. Equally evident in the choreography is a sensuality and homoerotic tension; indeed, until 1988, Jones never choreographed a heterosexual duet of any length or seriousness.

By the time they had formalized their own company, Bill T. Jones/Arnie Zane & Company in 1982, the two had together choreographed 11 dances. Independently, Jones had made almost 30 and Zane had completed a dozen. But in 1986, Zane was diagnosed with HIV. Jones spent the next two years helping his partner through various medical regimes and two major operations. Jones also was diagnosed HIV-positive, but remains asymptomatic. Following Zane's death, Jones poured his rage and grief into a flood of choreographic output, creating more than 20 works in the next 10 years, including *Absence* (1989) and *D-Man in the Waters* (1989), both of which revolve around rescue, death, and survival.

Zane and Jones assembled a company unlike any other. Averaging around ten dancers, the troupe featured an amazing range of body types and included white, black, Hispanic, and Asian performers. The composition of dancers was as eclectic as the repertoire. Touching on politics, matters of race, sexual preference, and history, the three-hour *Last Supper at Uncle Tom's Cabin/Promised Land* (1990) utilizes Jones's mother singing gospel, parts of the historic play, and a real-life clergyman. For *Still/Here* (1994), Jones conducted a series of workshops around the country with terminally-ill people of all races, ages, and occupations searching for "the resourcefulness and courage necessary to perform the act of living." Croce launched a national debate when she refused to review its New York premiere, stating that "victim art" was outside of the purview of criticism. Despite the arguments fueled by this act (mainly between individuals who had not seen the work), *Still/Here* is considered one of the landmarks of twentieth-century dance. In 1995, Jones collaborated with Nobel Prize-winning author Toni Morrison and legendary drummer Max Roach for *Degga*. As resident choreographer of the Lyons Opera Ballet, Jones created *24 Frames per Second* (1995) to mark the one-hundredth anniversary of the invention of motion pictures.

Jones received a MacArthur "genius" fellowship in 1994. In addition to his concert dance work, Jones also directed and choreographed the opera *The Mother of Three Sons* for New York City Opera (1991) and directed Derek Walcott's *Dream on Monkey Mountain* (1994) for the Guthrie Theatre. *BC*

Krissy Keefer

Krissy Keefer, lesbian dancer and choreographer, has been a member in two collective dance companies: The Wallflower Order and Dance Brigade. The Wallflower Dance Order, including collective members Nina Fichter, Pamela Gray, Laurel Mear, and Lyn Neeley, was founded in 1975 as a dance collective concerned with political and social issues. The Wallflower Order's witty choreography, mime, and spoken words focused on issues of social injustice, oppression, and revolution. Some critics noted the importance of ideas over technique in the Wallflower Order's dances; however, dance critic and historian Deborah Jowitt writes that the wide range of different styles embodied by this collective led to a distinctive and personal style. Jowitt does note that the collective seemed to "soft-pedal" the subject of lesbianism in its work. They performed in conjunction with various activist groups and in prisons; in order to aid in the accessibility of their work, dances and dialogue were often combined with sign language for hearing-impaired spectators.

Keefer has also danced in the Berkeley-based dance collective Dance Brigade with Nina Fichter and Kim Epifano. Notable works include *The Revolutionary Nutcracker Sweetie* (1988), which used the traditional Nutcracker story as the basis for a social commentary. The characters include Clara as a Latin American refugee, the Nutcracker as an African warrior woman, and the battle between the mice and the toy soldiers as a conflict between CIA agents and women guerrillas. Popular culture figures such as Madonna and Prince are guests at the party scene. According to Janice Ross of *Dance* magazine, the Dance Brigade's performance, as opposed to many other postmodern dance companies, attaches dance

to the realities of late-twentieth-century life by addressing social injustice and human suffering: "In an age overrun with art as a cold slick commodity, the Dance Brigade's work remains the real thing." *JT*

John Kelly (1954-)

Performance and multimedia artist John Kelly began his creative career as a dancer, picking up some design experience along the way from Parsons School of Design in New York. Since that time, Kelly has established himself as one of the leaders in postmodern performance art in this century and has acquired a number of awards along the way (Bessie Awards in 1986 and 1988, an Obie Award and an American Choreographer Award in 1987, and a 1989 Guggenheim Fellowship). His works include *Troubadour, Go West Junger Mann, Long Live the Knife, Diary of a Somnambulist, Find My Way Home*, and his signature work, *Pass the Blutwurst, Bitte* in which he portrays Egon Schiele, the Viennese Expressionist painter. Kelly's work is characterized by music and movement; spoken narrative is only expressed when sung—Kelly is also an accomplished counter-tenor. His pieces are nostalgic in content but performed with an expressivity and purpose not usually associated with such romanticism. Kelly's work is often referred to as "collage events" because so many disciplines intermingle in the performative setting. Additionally, the artist plays with gender by switching male and female characterizations onstage as well as by constructing works based on historically feminized individuals such as Narcissus and Saint Sebastian. *DT*

Larry Kramer (1935-)

Described by Susan Sontag as "one of America's most valuable troublemakers," this screenwriter, novelist, playwright, and AIDS activist was born in Bridgeport, Connecticut. After working in London during the early 1960s as a production executive for Columbia Pictures, he moved to Hollywood and United Artists, where he worked on such films as *Here We Go Round the Mulberry Bush* (associate producer, 1967) and *Women in Love* (screenwriter and producer, 1969), for which he received an Oscar nomination. Kramer was fired from his next film, whereupon he moved to New York City and began to write plays. After *Four Friends* (1973) and *Sissies' Scrapbook* (1974) failed to find public or critical acceptance, he turned to completing a novel, *Faggots* (1978). In part fueled by his own inability to sustain a lasting relationship with either a man or a woman, the novel chronicles one gay man's quest for love in a culture obsessed with sex. Vilified by the gay press for its criticism of promiscuity, the novel nevertheless found an audience (selling over 400,000 copies) and is now considered a watershed moment in gay literature. (At the age of 58, Kramer fell in love with architect David Webster, and joyously exclaimed to the *New York Times*: "After 20 years, I am finally getting everything I wanted.")

Merging two of his talents (AIDS activist and writer), Kramer wrote a milestone in AIDS drama, *The Normal Heart*. This thinly veiled autobiography charts the course of Ned Weeks, who is kicked out of an AIDS organization he founds, rails against promiscuity, and loses a lover to the virus. While the play volleys caustic attacks against the *New York Times* and Ronald Reagan and "outs" New York City Mayor Ed Koch, it is balanced by a passionate belief that positive change can occur. *The Normal Heart* holds the record for the longest run at the New York Shakespeare Festival's Public Theatre and has enjoyed more than 600 productions worldwide. Having previously cofounded the Gay Men's

Larry Kramer

Health Crisis, in 1987 Kramer returned to activism and established ACT UP (AIDS Coalition to Unleash Power). "The whole idea," reported Kramer, "was to get drugs into bodies." Taking the theater of AIDS into the streets, ACT UP often staged elaborate demonstrations to call public attention to the high cost of AIDS treatment drugs and government inaction. At its height, ACT UP had 60 chapters across America and Canada. In 1988, Kramer tested positive for HIV. While his farce *Just Say No* (1988) was a critical failure, his next foray into playwriting produced the heralded *The Destiny of Me* (1992), directed by Marshall W. Mason. A sequel to *The Normal Heart*, *Destiny* features Ned Weeks discovering that he is HIV-positive. He becomes a participant in an experimental drug trial, which prompts him to recall his childhood relationship with his parents and awareness of his homosexuality. In 1997, Kramer offered Yale University, his alma mater, several million dollars to endow a permanent, tenured professorship in gay and lesbian studies. Yale declined the offer; "gay and lesbian studies is too narrow a specialty to lock in a professorship for life," explained Provost Dr. Alison Richard. *BC*

Eva Le Gallienne (1899-1991)

Eva Le Gallienne, actress and director, founded the Civic Repertory Theatre (1925-1932), renowned for its outstanding interpretations of the classics and adventurous stagings of new plays at popular prices. Born in London and raised in Paris, Le Gallienne made her Broadway debut in 1915. In 1921, she scored her first major success as Julie Jordan in *Liliom*. Raped backstage during the run by an actor, Le Gallienne later left Broadway at the height of her fame to found a theater in Greenwich Village. The roster of lesbians who worked at the Civic include author May Sarton, designer Gladys Cathrop, actress Alla Nazimova, author Clemance Dane, and director Margaret Webster. Le Gallienne lived upstairs with her lover, actress Josephine Hutchinson. Le Gallienne specialized in playing Ibsen heroines, and her translations of his plays are still in print. The Civic closed after five seasons as a result of the Depression, but in 1946 Le Gallienne joined with Webster and lesbian producer Cheryl Crawford to found the short-lived American Repertory Theatre. In 1975, she returned to Broadway in *The Royal Family*, and in 1980 she made her film debut with Ellen Burstyn in *Resurrection*. Le Gallienne wrote two books of memoirs and a study of Eleanora Duse. *CG*

Lar Lubovitch (1943-)

Anna Kisselgoff considers "the most famous male duet in the international dance world" to be in Lar Lubovitch's *Concerto Six Twenty-Two* (1985). Commissioned by the National Center for Contemporary Dance in France and set to Mozart's Concerto for Clarinet and Orchestra (K.622), the work has been included in the

1987 "Dancing for Life" AIDS benefit, and is in the repertory of Lubovitch's company, American Ballet Theater, and the White Oak Dance Project. Since founding the Lubovitch Dance Company in 1968, Lubovitch has choreographed on Broadway—*Into the Woods* (1987), *The Red Shoes* (1993), *The King and I* (1996 Broadway revival)—and has also worked for other companies, including a full-length *Othello* (1997) for American Ballet Theater. An intensely private man, Lubovitch in his work nevertheless is unabashedly romantic in tone, staging it with a lyricism, freedom, and passion that are rare in modern dance. Lubovitch declines to talk publicly about his background or personal life—even to explain what his first name is diminutive of—yet, as Jennifer Dunning of the *New York Times* exclaimed, he has "created dances so warm and sensuous and pretty, he seems to have created a new category—dances to bask in." *BC*

Charles Ludlam (1943-1987)

The winner of four Obie Awards, fellowships from the Guggenheim, Rockefeller, and Ford Foundations, and grants from the National Endowment for the Arts and the New York State Council on the arts, Charles Ludlam and his work were a crucial bridge between the insular world of much gay drama produced Off-Off-Broadway in the 1960s and 1970s, and the Broadway success of Harvey Fierstein's *Torch Song Trilogy* (1982) and the Jerry Herman/Harvey Fierstein musical *La Cage aux Folles* (1983). Ludlam's two-actor tour de force, *The Mystery of Irma Vep,* was not only a hit for the company and its two actors (Ludlam and Everett Quinton), but was for many years the most-produced play in American regional theater.

Born and raised in Northport, Long Island, Ludlam graduated with a degree in drama from Hofstra University in 1965. A life-long student of theater history, Ludlam produced an oeuvre that contains a dizzying variety of genres and dramaturgical styles: *Anti-Galaxie Nebulae* (1978), a sci-fi puppet play; *Corn* (1972), a country-western musical; *Camille* (1973), an adaptation of a classic nineteenth-century melodrama; *The Mystery of Irma Vep* (1974), a penny dreadful, "low" melodrama; *Jack and the Beanstalk* (1975), a play for children; and his own adaptation of Charles Dickens's *Christmas Carol* (1979). Acknowledged as a master teacher, Ludlam taught or staged productions at New York University, Connecticut College for Women, Yale University, and Carnegie Mellon University. In 1967 he founded the Ridiculous Theatrical Company.

Ludlam met his longtime lover Everett Quinton in 1975, and a year later Quinton joined the company, even though his previous acting experience had been limited to *Rip Van Winkle* in the Cub Scouts. Nevertheless, within a few years he was an acknowledged star performer in the company. When Ludlam died in 1987, Quinton shared the management of the Ridiculous Theatrical Company with Steven Samuels, taking over completely in 1989. Quinton also supervised the publication of *The Complete Plays of Charles Ludlam* (1989). After 17 years at 1 Sheridan Square, the Ridiculous Theatrical Company lost a court case with its landlord and thereafter rented theater space.

Although Ludlam's plays and productions featured a liberal dose of cross-dressing, double-entendre, and comic exaggeration, he rejected the labels of camp or gay theater, noting that these artistic ghettos imply that "you have no real interaction with the culture, and whatever impact you may have had on that culture is nullified. If people take the time to come here . . . they see I don't have an ax to grind even though I do have a mission. That mission

is to have a theater that can offer possibilities that aren't being explored elsewhere."

Towards the end of his life, having appeared as an actor in the title role in the American Ibsen Theatre production of *Hedda Gabler* in Pittsburgh (1984), and in roles on television and in major motion pictures such as *The Big Easy* (1987), Ludlam was entering the world of "mainstream" American culture. At the time of his death, he was scheduled to direct Shakespeare's *Titus Andronicus* at Joseph Papp's New York Shakespeare Festival and was finishing the text to *A Piece of Pure Escapism,* a stage play about the magician Harry Houdini. *BC*

Terrence McNally (1939-)

Educated at Columbia University, Terrence McNally was born in St. Petersburg, Florida, but grew up in Corpus Christi, Texas. Since 1971, with his wacky gay couples in *Bad Habits,* McNally has consistently created plays with homosexual characters. Most of these plays express the friction and tension that results when homosexuals and heterosexuals come into contact with one another. The two heterosexual couples in *Lips Together, Teeth Apart* (1991) confront their homophobia and the reality of AIDS when Sally's brother dies of complications from the virus. Similarly, the one-act *Andre's Mother* (1988) focuses on an offstage gay male character who has died of AIDS; his family, which is overwhelmed with grief over his death; the incomprehensibility of the capriciousness of AIDS; and the character's sexual orientation. McNally later expanded *Andre's Mother* into a screenplay for American Playhouse (1990). *The Lisbon Traviata* (1989) is a prime example of McNally's gift of combining raucous black humor with tragedy. The play starts with two hysterically funny gay opera fanatics who are revealed to be socially dysfunctional. When Stephen learns his lover is leaving him, he turns their farewell into an opera, complete with an obligatory death. McNally won Tony Awards for Best Play two years in a row for *Love! Valour! Compassion!* (1994) and *Master Class* (1995). Many critics saw *Love! Valour! Compassion!* as McNally's response to Crowley's *Boys in the Band,* as it explores the relationships between eight gay male friends who meet over three holiday weekends. *Master Class* is a return to the world of opera and diva worship, and while there are no gay characters in the play, the work is a fictionalized account of gay cult figure Maria Callas's workshops at Julliard. McNally has also written the librettos to several musicals, including *The Rink* (1984), *Kiss of the Spider Woman* (winner of seven Tony Awards in 1993, including Best Musical and Best Book), and *Ragtime* (1997, winner of four 1998 Tony Awards, including Best Book). In 1998, McNally was at the center of a major controversy over his new play *Corpus Christi,* which features a gay character who resembles Jesus. The Manhattan Theatre Club planned to present the play but canceled its plans after receiving threats of violence directed toward McNally and others involved in the production. Following an outcry from many prominent members of New York's theatrical community, several of whom charged the theater with censorship for caving in to the play's opponents, the Manhattan Theatre Club reversed its decision and decided to go ahead with the production. *BC*

Tim Miller (1958-)

Tim Miller is perhaps the most distinguished queer performance artist of the 1980s and the 1990s. Born and raised in suburban Los Angeles, the artist has a particular sensitivity to the crossings of culture and race, identity formation and middle-class values, as well as politics and spirituality. The artist's work is auto-biographical in nature, devoted to queer culture issues, and committed to articulating a response to AIDS in every aspect of life. His performance works include *Postwar, Buddy Systems, Some Golden States, Stretch Marks, Sex/Love/Stories, Naked Breath, Fruit Cocktail*, and the quintessential Miller performance art piece, *My Queer Body*. The artist has performed in Europe, Australia, and the United States in addition to leading performance workshops for gay men worldwide. The founder of Performance Space 122 in New York and the co-founder of Highways in Santa Monica, Miller has provided celebrated venues for the presentation of exciting and controversial performance art. Miller is also the recipient of numerous grants and fellowships including several NEA fellowships, one of which was rescinded in 1989 due to political pressure from the religious right. Miller and the three other performance artists successfully sued the federal government for these funds, receiving a settlement in 1993. *DT*

Cherríe Moraga (1952-)

Cherríe Moraga, a Chicana feminist playwright, poet, thinker, and cultural activist, has won the PEN West Literary Award for Drama, the Critics' Circle Award for Best Original Script, and a grant from the National Endowment for the Arts. Co-editor of the ground-breaking anthology *This Bridge Called My Back: Writings by Radical Women of Color*, Moraga also co-founded Kitchen Table, Women of Color Press, which published the work. Her plays include *Giving Up the Ghost, Shadow of a Man, Heroes and Saints*, and *Watsonville*. Moraga was a playwright-in-residence at INTAR, studying under María Irene Fornés, whom she credits for initiating her into the world of theater without compromising her poet's voice. In 1990, Moraga began a long-term relationship with Brava Theatre in San Francisco, a theater committed to producing work by women of color and lesbians. Moraga has taught Chicano Studies, Feminist Studies, and Theatre and Creative Writing at UC Berkeley, Stanford, and San Francisco State University. *CG*

Mark Morris (1956-)

A former dancer with Lubovitch Dance Company, Mark Morris also performed with Eliot Feld, Hannah Kahn, and Laura Dean before he established the Mark Morris Dance Group in 1980. Within four years, *Time* called him "the hottest young choreographer in the country," and *Newsweek* heralded "the crown prince and long-awaited savior of the dance world." This openly gay dancer/choreographer, variously the darling of many critics and audiences, is seen by others as erratic, self-indulgent, campy and over-literal in his treatment of music and narrative. Adding fuel to the fire that Morris is overrated, Joan Acocella published a biography in 1994 of this "big hairy guy" from Seattle, then only 37 years old. A true postmodernist who freely combines elements from classical ballet; modern, international dance forms; and jazz, he has choreographed to everything from Bach and Vivaldi, country and western, gospel, Indian movie music, traditional Tahitian, Liberace, and Yoko Ono. No one has ever accused him of repeating himself, remarkable considering Morris choreographed 50 dances between 1980 and 1990. While *One Charming Night* contains fantasies of rape and *Tamil Film Songs in Stereo* contains campy drag, other works explore romantic love, and still other pieces are infused with an infecting sense of humor. Morris is drawn to breaking down traditional gender roles by choreographing the same movement on his male and female dancers. One of

Mark Morris

his most controversial pieces was casting himself as Dido and The Sorceress in Henry Purcell's *Dido and Aeneas* (1989). While critics often use the term "outrageous" when discussing Morris's work, the most radical element about this innovator is his knowledge and use of traditional forms. In Morris's own words: "I'm a structure queen."

Morris has been alternately praised and criticized for his slavish adherence to the architecture of the music he uses, a criticism he embraces, happy to be placed in the same category with other choreographers obsessed with music visualization, such as George Balanchine. While most of Morris's inspiration for dances comes from music, other influences include essays by Roland Barthes that resulted in *Mythologies* (1986). Drawn to vocal music more than most choreographers, Morris has choreographed concert dances to Handel (*L'Allegro, il Penseroso ed il Moderato*, 1988), Brahms (*Love Song Waltzes*, 1982; *New Love Song Waltzes*, 1989), and Stephen Foster (*Somebody's Coming to See Me Tonight*, 1996). Morris has also choreographed two operas by John Adams—*Nixon in China* and *The Death of Klinghoffer* (both directed by Peter Sellars)—Seattle Opera's production of *Orpheus and Eurydice* (1988), and the ill-fated Broadway musical, Paul Simon's *Capeman* (1998).

Mark Morris was engaged to follow Maurice Béjart as director of dance at the state-supported Théâtre Royal de la Monnaie in Brussels from 1988 to 1991. Cumbersomely renamed Monnaie Dance Group/Mark Morris, the eclectic creations of Morris were mostly abrasively received by the Belgium press. But Morris's last work for the company has become his most financially lucrative: a cartoon-like staging of Tchaikovsky's *The Nutcracker,* now called *The Hard Nut,* reflecting Morris's interpretation of the original libretto by E.T.A. Hoffman (1813). Transported to the 1960s, Act One's party is fueled by numerous cocktails and wayward hormones. Act Two does not take Marie to the Land of Sweets but rather into a dark subplot of Hoffman's tale; after a fierce Rat Queen bites the baby princess and turns her into an ugly freak, Drosselmeyer goes in search of the magical Hard Nut that will break the spell. All ends happily with Marie dancing with the Nutcracker (transformed into a young Drosselmeyer). Part of the whimsy of the piece is reversed gender casting, including Mrs. Stahlbaum and her maid performed by men in drag, Marie's brother Fritz performed by a woman *en travesti*; and a mixed chorus of men and women (the assignment of pointe shoes not determined by gender) who perform "Waltz of the Flowers" and "Snowflakes." PBS broadcast *The Hard Nut* in 1992.

Even before leaving Brussels, Morris began choreographing works for the White Oak Project (est. 1990), produced by philanthropist Howard Gilman and dance superstar Mikhail Baryshnikov. Once his contract was up with Théâtre Royal de la Monnaie, he brought his dancers to New York and reformed the Mark Morris Dance Group. Morris was one of the recipients of the 1991 MacArthur Foundation fellowships. *BC*

Nance O'Neill (1874-1965)

Nance O'Neill, born Gertrude Lamson, established her reputation at the turn of the century as a major touring star specializing in strong roles for women, such as Rosalind, Queen Elizabeth, Magda, and Lady Macbeth. Having grown up in San Francisco during the Gold Rush, she made her stage debut at the age of 19 under the direction of McKee Rankin. In 1896, she arrived in New York in the smash hit *True to Life,* where she played several seasons before going on national tour in the title role of Hedda Gabler. Three years later, she embarked on a tour of Australia, New Zealand, South Africa, Egypt, and England. By 1903, she was back in the States, appearing as Lady Macbeth at Boston's Colonial Theatre, where her unusual interpretation attracted the attention of acquitted axe murderess Lizzie Borden, who happened to be attending a performance. Borden and O'Neill later became lovers. In 1909, O'Neill was "discovered" by David Belasco and cast as Odette in *The Lily.* Even as Hollywood began to make inroads into the world of theater, O'Neill managed to continue working, performing often-important supporting roles on both stage and screen well into the 1940s. *CG*

Stephen Petronio (1956-)

The first male dancer in Trisha Brown's dance company, Petronio grew up in Nutley, New Jersey, the child of a middle-class Italian-American family. Even though he did not begin dancing until relatively late (age 18), by the time he was 23 his unique fusion of speed and liquid movement made him a natural for Brown's fluent work. In 1984, he established the Stephen Petronio Company. While he was groomed on formalists like Brown and Cunningham, most of Petronio's work seeks to convey specific dramatic images through movement. Petronio described *The King Is Dead (Part I)* (1993) as "the symbolic death of the male figure, an exploration of the strength of a woman within the male, the redirection of aggression and the power discovered in retreat." Trademarks of Petronio's style are angular, harsh, and athletic movements.

The eclectic nature of his choreography is in many ways a mirror of his personal life. In 1990, his daughter Bella was born. He reported matter of factly, "She's half-Italian and half-Jewish. Her mother was one of my first friends in New York. It was very carefully thought out. It's a very lovely thing in my life—incredibly lovely." the *New York Times* reported in 1992 that Petronio was "truly, madly, deeply in love with Michael Clark, the 29-year old 'bad boy' of British Ballet; they have been together for three years." Sporting their signature shaved heads, the two appeared in Petronio's 1991 *Middlesex Gorge; Dance Magazine* reported that watching the two perform in corsets in this dance was "something else."

Petronio's choreography is high-speed, rhythmically complex, sensual, and often delivered with a witty edge. The *San Francisco Examiner* calls him "the most audaciously virtuosic dance choreographer of his generation." His work has been performed by the Frankfurt Ballet (*Simulacrum Court,* 1987). *BC*

Amy Pivar

Amy Pivar founded Amy Pivar Dances in 1990 with partner and psychotherapist Freda Rosen. Pivar's previous experience includes dancing with Bill T. Jones/Arnie Zane Dance Company, the Urban Bush Women, and Loremil Machado's Afro-Brazilian Dance Company. Freda Rosen practices as a psychotherapist, has written and edited for various journals, has performed as a dancer,

Nance O'Neill

and has collaborated on many works with Amy Pivar. Themes of their dances and spoken texts include sexual violence, racial relations, stereotypes of women, the death of Communism, historical inquiries into the loves and works of Gertrude Stein and Alice B. Toklas, and finally, contemporary feminism. Pivar and Rosen seek to move beyond postmodern aesthetics in order to address human concerns over political issues.

Pivar and Rosen mix jazz, Afro-Brazilian dance, modern funk, athleticism, and ballet in their movement. In conjunction with their performances, they offer on-site performatory workshops that investigate on a more personal level issues raised in the work and offer positive direction towards empowerment. Pivar sees the experience of being a lesbian as parallel to that of being an artist; of her choreography, she says, "My work is very out, in your face." *JT*

Peter Pucci (1958-)

A nine-year veteran of Pilobolus, Peter Pucci is director and sole choreographer of Peter Pucci Plus Dancers, which he established in 1986. As a choreographer, Pucci is comfortable using a large movement vocabulary—everything from pedestrian to abstract to dramatic narratives—in addition to retaining some of the love of sculptural shapes and sense of slapstick that pervades the work of Pilobolus. Yet Pucci's repertoire also includes pieces with a darker, more formal side. Performed in silence, *Love Duets* (1992) brings together three couples—two women, two men, and a man and a woman—who repeat the same simple dance. Pucci explains that "There's a lot of inequality in how we perceive people who are of the same sex and who have a loving and caring relationship. The stereotypes and prejudices are there in terms of sexuality in men and women. I felt strongly that it was something that was equal." Outside of his own company, Pucci choreographed "Willing and Able" for Joffrey's *Billboards* (1993) and the movement for the Off-Broadway production of Sam Shepard's *Eyes for Consuela* (1998). *BC*

Yvonne Rainer (1934-)

Yvonne Rainer's career has spanned from modern dance to avant-garde film. A founder of the groundbreaking Judson Dance Group, New York, in 1962, Rainer experimented relentlessly with the formal elements of performance, incorporating rehearsal, metanarrative commentary, and film in her dance and performance works. Her performance, *This is a story of a woman who...*, eventually became *Film about a Woman Who...* (1974*)*, mining the romantic and political conflicts between men and women. Her more recent work, *MURDER and murder* (1997), deals explicitly with lesbian romance, queer theory, and breast cancer. Rainer, a breast cancer survivor, appears in the film as a tuxedoed narrator. *JR*

Jerome Robbins (1918-)

Born Jerome Rabinowitz in New York City, Robbins he made his debut as a dancer with the Sandor-Sorel Dance Center in 1937. Subsequently, he danced in several Broadway musicals and revues before joining Ballet Theatre in 1940. His first piece of choreography, *Fancy Free* (1944), catapulted him into instant fame. Just eight months later, Robbins made his Broadway debut as a choreographer with *On the Town,* a musical theater version of his ballet, with music by Leonard Bernstein and lyrics by Betty Comden and Adolph Green. For the next 20 years, Robbins not only continued to work in both musical theater and concert dance, he created masterworks in both genres. Of the 14 Broadway musicals choreographed by Robbins, the list includes such classics as *The King and I* (1951), *West Side Story* (also directed, 1957), *Gypsy* (also directed, 1959), and *Fiddler on the Roof* (also directed, 1964). Robbins returned to The Great White Way in 1989 with *Jerome Robbins' Broadway,* a revue containing excerpts from 11 of his Broadway musicals.

Jerome Robbins left ABT in to join New York City Ballet in 1949 as a dancer and choreographer; Balanchine named Robbins associate artistic director in 1950. Robbins choreographed more than 60 ballets for NYCB, including masterpieces such as *The Cage* (1951), *The Concert* (1956), *Dances at a Gathering* (1969), and *Glass Pieces* (1983). Robbins's style is an amalgamation of social dance with classical ballet vocabulary, which gives most of his work a frankness and casual easiness and makes him one of the most accessible of modern dance choreographers. Following Balanchine's death in 1983, Robbins and Peter Martins were appointed joint ballet masters of the company. A Festival of Jerome Robbins' Ballets was produced by NYCB in June 1990 and included 28 Robbins ballets. As part of the celebration of Robbins's 50-year association with NYCB, his version of *Les Noces* (1965) was revived by the company in 1998.

Murray Gitlin, cast member in the original run of *The King and I,* remembers a very difficult Robbins who "was always weird.... He does this to people. He turns people off. Something snaps." Indeed, by the time *West Side Story* opened in New York, none of the other collaborators were talking to Robbins due to his acerbic personality. In 1953, Robbins testified before the House Committee on Un-American Activities, admitting his own three-year membership in the Communist party and naming eight other former party members. Some felt that he agreed to testify because he felt committee members would expose him as a homosexual. Arthur Laurents disagreed with this theory, claiming Robbins wanted a movie career and did not want to be blacklisted. *BC*

Ted Shawn (1891-1972)

Known as "The Father of American Modern Dance," Ted Shawn created a remarkable body of pioneering achievements: first internationally known American male dancer; choreographer of the first all-dance moving picture (*The Dance of the Ages*, 1913); first male dancer to be listed in *Who's Who in America*; first American dancer to be awarded an honorary degree by an American college (Springfield College, 1936); first to form an all-male dance company; and the first to build a theater designed and used only for dance.

Born Edwin Myers Shawn in Kansas City, Missouri, Shawn was paralyzed when he was 18 years old after an attack of diphtheria. Determined to walk again, he enrolled in a ballet class while studying for the Methodist ministry at the University of Denver. Shawn not only regained the use of his legs, he developed quickly into a riveting performer, blessed with a he-man physique. In 1914, Shawn met the great dancer Ruth St. Denis (1877-1968) and was immediately attracted to her personally and to her choreographic style. Five months after they met, the 22-year-old Shawn married 36-year-old Ruth St. Denis at New York City's City Hall.

The two began the Denishawn school in Los Angeles in 1915, the first dance academy in America to produce a professional company. A second studio, the Denishawn House in New York City, opened in 1927. Denishawn Dancers, with a repertoire of works by choreographed by Shawn and St. Denis, toured the United States, Europe, and Asia until 1931. Famous students of Denishawn include Jack Cole, Martha Graham, Doris Humphrey, Pauline Lawrence, and Charles Weidman.

The Denishawn aesthetic featured various "primitive" dance forms, ballet, several Asian dance traditions, and eventually included modern German dance. Shawn felt that "the art of dance is too big to be encompassed by any one system, school or style. On the contrary, the Dance includes every way that men of all races, in every period of the world's history, have moved rhythmically to express themselves." While Denishawn has been criticized for appropriating ethnic materials for their "exotic" appeal, Shawn defended his synthesis of various styles: "I have always gloried in the word 'eclectic,' for it means choosing of the best, and using everything that is good, regardless of the source from which it comes—and also not being classifiable as belonging to any one 'school.'"

Over 6 feet tall and weighing 175 pounds, Shawn often exhibited his striking physique clad only in the briefest of costumes. While he did not posses the ideal dancer's body—he was big and husky—and though his personal style owed more to raw power than finesse, Shawn was a commanding presence on the stage. Distressed by St. Denis's constant infidelities and her refusal to bear him children, Shawn also grew weary of being treated as her inferior. The final rift in the marriage came when the two fell in love with the same man; their marriage and Denishawn ceased in 1931.

In the 1932-33 academic year, Shawn taught some 500 men who were training to be physical education teachers and/or coaches at Springfield College (MA). Shawn realized that his personal success in modern dance had not yet created opportunities for other men in dance, so he came to the conviction that something must be done to restore masculine dancing to what he considered to be its rightful prestige and legitimate dignity. In the summer of 1933, Shawn invited eight men to live and train at Jacob's Pillow—a 100-year-old farm in the Berkshire Hills of Massachusetts he had bought—to prepare for a tour he had booked for the fall. In the middle of the Depression, promoting any kind of dance was a risky venture, but to market an all-male modern dance company looked impossible.

Traveling by car, the first tour (1933-34) racked up 23,000 miles and 111 performances. For the next six years, the company (Ted Shawn and His Men Dancers) lived, trained, and presented work each summer at Jacob's Pillow, before embarking on national tours, which also included Canada, Cuba, and England. Using the raw material of sports movement, a great deal of Shawn's choreography was aggressively "masculine," showcasing his dancers as laborers, athletes, and warriors. When the armed services called for his dancers, Shawn dissolved the company in 1940; they had performed 1250 times in 750 cities before more than a million people.

Besides Shawn, the other star of the company was his lover, Barton Mumaw (c. 1912-). After Barton finished his tour of duty in the U.S. Army, Shawn began to groom his partner into a solo artist. Even though various critics hailed Mumaw as the "American Nijinsky," he did not posses the presence to command an entire evening by himself. After the two went their separate ways, Mumaw danced in Broadway shows (*Annie Get Your Gun, My Fair Lady*), then worked in business, although he continued to dance and teach occasionally.

Shawn started the Dance Festival at Jacob's Pillow in 1933, with the summer performances by his Men Dancers. In 1940, Shawn sold Jacob's Pillow to a non-profit corporation so that he could operate a summer dance school and festival. When the Ted Shawn Theatre was completed in 1942, Shawn launched his "University of Dance," dedicated to broadening the dance education of dancers and audiences alike. This 500-seat venue was the first theater in America to be designed exclusively for dance. As impresario, Shawn introduced American audiences to the Royal Danish Ballet, the National Ballet of Canada, Scotland's Celtic Ballet, Ballet Rambert, and other international artists.

Tirelessly active as a choreographer, lecturer, author, and producer, Shawn continued to dance until he was in his seventies. "Papa" Shawn has been called the father of American modern dance, even though very little of his choreography (more than 200 pieces) has been performed since his death in 1972. Rather, his significant contributions include his popularizing of the male dancer in American modern dance, establishing a successful international dance festival, justifying a place for dance at the university level, and his extensive writings on dance history and pedagogy. According to critic Clive Barnes, "Shawn did not merely enrich American dance—he was one of the people who created it." *BC*

Anna Deveare Smith (1950-)

Anna Deveare Smith is a performer and playwright who uses interview and mimicry to document and transform complex social problems. Her one-woman shows, *Twilight: Los Angeles, 1992* and *Fires in the Mirror: Crown Heights, Brooklyn and Other Identities*, are part of a series called *On the Road: A Search for American Character*. Smith's technique is based on reproducing an interviewee's speech as faithfully as possible, finding a character's depth through this surface linguistic mimicry, and transforming a political-cultural event by representing diverse and dissenting voices honestly. Her recent play, *House Arrest* (1997), interrogates the relationship between the presidency and the press. Smith believes her work restores character in an age where media, especially in politics, tears character down. *CG*

Spiderwoman Theater

Spiderwoman Theater, a Native American performing arts group, is named for the Hopi goddess Spiderwoman, who taught the people to weave and said, "you must make a mistake in every tapestry so that my spirit may come and go at will." Spiderwoman Theater uses the technique of "storyweaving" words and movement to create comic and fantastical theater. Spiderwoman Theater's principal performers are Lisa Mayo, a founding member of Spiderwoman Theater and Off the Beaten Path; Gloria Miguel, a founding member; and Muriel Miguel, founding member and artistic director of Spiderwoman Theater. Together they have created more than 20 shows. *JR*

Split Britches

Split Britches is a three-woman company consisting of Deborah Margolin, Peggy Shaw, and Lois Weaver. The trio has written and directed five productions together: *Split Britches* (1981), *Beauty and the Beast* (1982), *Upwardly Mobile Home* (1984), *Little Women* (1985), and *Anniversary Waltz* (1989). They adapted Isabel Miller's lesbian novel *Patience and Sarah* in 1984; and with the members of the group Bloolips, Shaw and Weaver collaborated on the production *Belle Reprieve* (1991), a piece loosely based on Tennessee Williams's *Streetcar Named Desire*. Weaver and Shaw have also performed Margolin's script entitled *Lesbians Who Kill* (1993).

Peggy Shaw and Lois Weaver formed the idea for the play *Split Britches* while performing with Spiderwoman Theater's *Evening of Disgusting Songs & Pukey Images*. *Split Britches* captures Weaver's West Virginia family of aunts and great aunts, and was developed during 1980 and 1981. When Deborah Margolin joined the troupe in 1981, she added additional monologues and materials to the play, including reminiscences of her elderly aunt. Split Britches has successfully taken personal materials and everyday occurrences and turned them into vaudevillian and burlesque hilarities of monologue, song, dance, and narrative. While Split Britches is no longer a company, each performer continues to write and perform solo work. *JR*

Paul Taylor (1930-)

Having performed with both Merce Cunningham (1953-54) and Martha Graham (1958-62), Paul Taylor devised his own unique choreographic style notable for its lyricism and sunny joy of movement. A large man (6 feet 3 inches) who attended college on a swimming scholarship, Taylor tends to hire male dancers who are larger than the ballet norm. A constant refrain in criticism of the Taylor company is praise of "Paul's Men"—dynamic performers such as Elie Chaib, Christopher Gillis, and David Parsons—who are often featured in pieces like the athletic *Arden Court* (1981).

In his autobiography *Private Domain* (1987), Taylor leaves his own sexual identity teasingly unresolved, but in some of his choreographic work a homosocial world is present. In the pedestrian-movement-based *Esplanade* (1975), one woman appears dressed like the men in the piece. She expresses her feeling for another woman, is rebuffed, and then disappears. The mother and father figures in *Kith and Kin* (1987) seem to be presiding over an extended family that includes same-sex as well as mixed couples. Set during World War II, *Company B* (1991) includes a section where two male soldiers appear to be yearning for each other while a recording of the Andrew Sisters' "I Can Dream Can't I?" plays.

Taylor established his own company in 1955, gaining notoriety in 1957 with a concert so anti-dance that one critic summarized the proceedings with a review consisting entirely of blank space. Mind boggling in the range of works he has created (100 dances in 45 years), Taylor excels in everything from witty, joyous works such as *Funny Papers* (1994) and *Offenbach Overtures* (1995) to dark dance dramas such as *Speaking in Tongues* (1989). In 1987, a Paul Taylor Dance Company concert included work by other choreographers for the first time, and in 1992, he established a junior company, Taylor 2.

Considering how many former members of the Paul Taylor Dance Company (Twyla Tharp, Dan Wagoner, David Parsons, Laura Dean, and Pina Bausch) have gone on to establish their own companies, and the fact that his dances have been performed by more than 50 companies world-side, Taylor is one of the most influential of modern dance choreographers. *BC*

Carmelita Tropicana

Carmelita Tropicana (Alina Troyano), "Beauty Queen of the Lower East Side," defines solo performance art "as a survivalist strain of self-production." Using the persona of Carmelita Tropicana, Troyano explores the multiple strains of her identity as an American Latina, as an exile from her native Cuba, and as a lesbian. She has performed at the WOW Cafe, nationally, and internationally since 1984.

Troyano has written plays with Uzi Parnes and Ela Troyano, and coauthored with Ela Troyano the award-winning film *Carmelita Tropicana: Your Kunst Is Your Waffen* (1993). Her full-length play *Milk of Amnesia/Leche de Amnesia* (1995), was published in the theater anthology, *Latinas on Stage: Criticism and Practice* (Third Woman Press). *JR*

Margaret Webster (1905-1972)

Margaret Webster specialized in directing Shakespeare's plays, and one of her greatest successes was her 1943 production of *Othello* with Paul Robeson in the title role, Jose Ferrer as Iago, Uta Hagen as Desdemona, and herself as Emilia. In 1946, she would join with lesbians Eva Le Gallienne, her lover for several years, and Cheryl Crawford to found the American Repertory Theatre. After this theater closed, Webster toured the U.S. in her own Shakespeare company. *CG*

Tennessee Williams (1911-1983)

Born Thomas Lanier Williams in Columbus, Mississippi, this second of three children was nicknamed "Tennessee." The shy, emotionally awkward Tennessee was a failure at the University of Missouri, so he returned home to work in a St. Louis shoe factory. The emptiness of his loveless home, his sister Rose's mental deterioration, and his own lack of sense of purpose led to a nervous breakdown in 1935. While recuperating, 24-year-old Williams enrolled in Washington University, determined to be a writer.

In 1937, at the age of 27, Rose was confined to a mental hospital; when insulin shock therapy was deemed ineffective treatment, she received a lobotomy in 1943. Rose served as a model for many of Williams's characters who are not able to protect themselves from the rest of the world. Fascinated by the lost souls and mis-

Carmelita Tropicana

fits of society, Williams spent the next 40 years writing about their inability to be "normal." Williams is always clear that these sensitive, intelligent creatures are morally preferable to the compromised mediocrity around them, yet these protagonists are usually forced to choose some route of escape—alcoholism, insanity, violence, or suicide.

In 1939, the first work to appear under the name Tennessee Williams, a short story titled "The Field of Blue Children," was published. That same year, he signed with literary agent Audrey Wood, who not only secured grants, scholarships, performance dates, and publication for his work, but also became a lifelong friend. While his first full-length play to receive a professional production, *Battle of Angels* (1940), closed in Boston, and he was fired from a screenwriting job at MGM, Williams did not give up. *The Glass Menagerie* (1945) ran two years on Broadway, earning him his first (of four) New York Drama Critics Circle Awards, and critical acclaim for actors Laurette Taylor, Eddie Dowling, and Julie Haydon.

Two years after *Glass Menagerie, A Streetcar Named Desire* (1947) garnered Williams his second New York Drama Critics Circle Award and his first Pulitzer Prize. The plot of this revolutionary play could have been rendered as a classic melodrama in the hands of Boucicault or Belasco, but Williams instead spun a work of poetic realism, neither a social problem play with a message nor an expressionistic work concerned with the mind of one character. *Streetcar* explores the struggle between Puritanism and sensuality, a subject he was to return to again and again, as in *Cat on a Hot Tin Roof* (1955), which won Williams his third New York Drama Critics Circle Award and his second Pulitzer Prize.

While some critics chafe at the ambiguity that surrounds many of the gay characters or homoerotic tension in his plays, *Los Angeles Times* critic Dan Sullivan suggests that Williams the poet knew the power of something unspoken. This interpretation is consistent with a common motif in the plays, that the mystery in people's lives should be protected, not solved or "corrected." While there is perhaps reticence in his plays, Williams lived his life openly and wrote frankly about homosexuality in two collections of short stories, *One Arm, and Other Stories* (1948) and *Hard Candy, and other Stories* (1954); two collections of poems, *In the Winter of Cities: Poems* (1956) and *Androgyne: Mon Amour* (1977); a novel, *Moise and the World of Reason* (1975); and his autobiography, *Memoirs* (1975). Two significant relationships of his life were with Frank Merlo, to whom he dedicated *The Rose Tattoo* (1951), and Donald Windham, who chronicled their relationship in *Tennessee Williams' Letters to Donald Windham 1940-1965*. Although their relationship was not monogamous, Williams and Merlo lived together from 1948 until Merlo's death from lung cancer in 1963. Williams' voice as a writer did not change with Stonewall, although as an individual he became more politicized and often contributed his energy to gay rights causes. Tennessee Williams left behind a canon of masterpieces in American drama, forever altering how we view the sexual impulse in men and women. *BC*

Doric Wilson (1939-)

A native of Los Angeles, Doric Wilson worked in several theaters in Washington State before attending the University of Washington. Arriving in New York City with two unproduced plays and the intent of studying scenic design, Wilson had one of his plays produced by Caffe Cino in 1961. Wilson's Off-Off-Broadway work continued until he was approached by the Richard Barr/ Edward Albee/Clinton Wilder Playwrights Unit to join them as a

Doric Wilson

founding member and playwright-in-residence. After two years with the Playwright's Unit, Wilson became artistic director of the Ensemble project (1965-1968), and then helped found the Circle Repertory Company, where he was also playwright-in-residence (1969-1971). Wilson returned to a more gay-oriented work in 1969, when he established TOSOS (The Other Side of Silence), the first openly gay professional theater company, run by and for gays. Structured as a cooperative and existing primarily off Wilson's job as a bartender, TOSOS produced work for five years, ending with the premiere of Wilson's *The West Street Gang* (1977). As a playwright of gay drama, Wilson is best known for *A Perfect Relationship* (1979) and *Street Theatre* (1981). First performed at the Mineshaft (a leather and sex bar in Greenwich Village), *Street Theatre* can, in many ways, be considered true gay theater, since it is a play that contains homosexual characters and whose audience is comprised of gay men. A celebration of the Stonewall Riots, *Street Theatre* is also a parody of a classic by a closeted homosexual (Thornton Wilder's *Our Town*) and the self-loathing characters in *The Boys in the Band*. *BC*

David Wojnarowicz (1954-1992)

A prolific artist and participant in many kinds of media, including performance art, David Wojnarowicz contributed to the artistic discourse on taboo subject matter and discrimination against homosexuals. His writings include *The Waterfront Journals, Being Queer in America, Living Close to the Knives*, and *Post Cards from America: X-Rays from Hell*. Wojnarowicz's work has been exhibited extensively and not without some controversy. In 1989, the artist exhibited at Artists Space in the Soho district of New York in a show entitled *Witnesses: Against Our Vanishing*. His catalogue entry for the show was an angry assault on Cardinal O'Connor, Senator Jesse Helms, and Representative William Dannemayer, and the three promptly scuttled for a repeal of the show's NEA grant. Wojnarowicz's performance pieces were powerful political statements that influenced a great many artists who identified with his rage, his anarchistic leanings, and his outsider status. *DT*

REFERENCES:

Theater: Books

Brecht, Stefan. *Queer Theatre*. Frankfurt am Main, Germany: Suhrkamp Verlag, 1978.

Brustein, Robert. *The Third Theatre*. New York: Knopf, 1969.

Case, Sue-Ellen. *Split Britches: Lesbian Practice/Feminist Performance*. New York: Routledge, 1996.

Chambers, Jane. *Last Summer at Bluefish Cove*. New York: JH Press, 1984.

Clum, John M. *Acting Gay: Male Homosexuality in Modern Drama*. New York: Columbia University Press, 1994.

Curb, Rosemary, ed. *Amazon All Stars: Thirteen Lesbian Plays*. New York: Applause Books, 1996.

Curtin, Kaier. *"We Can Always Call Them Bulgarians."* Boston, Massachusetts: Alyson Publications, Inc., 1987.

Dean, Nancy and Manuel Soares, eds. *Intimate Acts*. New York: Brito Lair, 1997.

Dreher, Sarah. *Lesbian Stages*. Norwich, VT: New Victoria Publications, 1988.

Fornés, Maria Irene. *Fefu and Her Friends*. New York: Performing Arts Journal, 1990.

Furtado, Ken and Nancy Hellner. *Gay and Lesbian American Plays: An Annotated Bibliography*. Metuchen, New Jersey: Scarecrow Press, 1993.

Gage, Carolyn. *The Second Coming of Joan of Arc and Other Plays*. Santa Cruz, California: HerBooks, Inc., 1994.

————. *Take Stage! How to Direct and Produce a Lesbian Play*. Lantham, Maryland: Scarecrow Press, 1997.

Goldman, William. *The Season*. New York: Harcourt, Brace, and World, 1969.

Hansberry, Lorraine, adapted by Robert Nemiroff. *To Be Young, Gifted, and Black: Lorraine Hansberry in Her Own Words*. New York: Samuel French, 1971; New York: Vintage Books, 1995.

Hart, Lynda and Peggy Phelan, eds. *Acting Out: Feminist Performances*. Ann Arbor: University of Michigan Press, 1993.

Helbing, Terry. *Gay Theatre Alliance Directory of Gay Plays*. New York: JH Press, 1980.

Hoffman, William H., ed. *Gay Plays: The First Collection*. New York: Avon Books, 1979.

Hughes, Holly. *Clit Notes: A Sapphic Sampler*. New York: Grove/Atlantic, 1996.

Hull, Gloria T. *Color, Sex, and Poetry: Three Women Writers of the Harlem Renaissance*. Bloomington: Indiana University Press, 1987.

Jongh, Nicholas de. *Not in Front of the Audience: Homosexuality on Stage*. London: Routledge, 1992.

Kavanagh, Julie. *Secret Muses: The Life of Frederick Ashton*. New York: Pantheon, 1997.

Leach, Joseph. *Bright Particular Star: The Life and Times of Charlotte Cushman*. New Haven: Yale University Press, 1970.

McDermott, Kate, ed. *Places, Please! The First Anthology of Lesbian Plays*. Iowa City, Iowa: Aunt Lute Book Company, 1985.

Miller, Carl. *Stages of Desire: Gay Theatre's Hidden History*. London: Cassell, 1996.

Moraga, Cherríe. *Heroes and Saints and Other Plays: Giving Up the Ghost, Shadow of a Man, Heroes and Saints*. Albuquerque, New Mexico: University of New Mexico Press, 1994.

Patrick, John, ed. *The Best of the Superstars 1998: The Year in Sex*. Sarasota, Florida: STARbooks Press, 1997.

Patrick, Robert. *Temple Slave*. New York: Masquerade Books, Inc., 1994.

Phelan, Peggy. *Unmarked: The Politics of Performance*. New York: Routledge, 1993.

Sheehy, Helen. *Eva Le Gallienne: A Biography*. New York: Knopf, 1996.

West, Mae. *Three Plays by Mae West*. Lillian Schlissel, ed. New York: Routledge, 1997.

Wilcox, Michael, ed. *Gay Plays*. London: Methuen, 1985.

————, ed. *Gay Plays: Volume Two*. London: Methuen, 1986.

Dance: Books

Anderson, Jack. *Ballet and Modern Dance: A Concise History*. Princeton, New Jersey: Princeton Book Company Publishers, 1992.

Fuller, Loie. *Fifteen Years of a Dancer's Life*. Boston: Small, Maynard & Company Publishers, 1908.

Hanna, Judith Lynne. *Dance, Sex and Gender: Signs of Identity, Dominance, Defiance, and Desire*. Chicago: University of Chicago Press, 1988.

Kettle, Michael. *Salome's Last Veil: The Libel Case of the Century*. London: Granada Publishing, 1977.

Lista, Giovanni. *Loïe Fuller: Danseuse de la Belle Époque*. Paris: Stock-Éditions d'Art Somogy, 1994.

Dance: Periodical Articles

Hanna, Judith Lynne. "Men, Women, and Homosexuality in Dance," in *Drama Review*, vol. 31, no. 1, Spring 1987.

————. "Shock Troupes: Helms, Kitty Kat, and So What?" in *Ballet Review*, vol. 20, no. 3, Fall 1992: 85.

Performance Art: Books

Arnason, H. H., *History of Modern Art: Painting, Sculpture, Architecture, Photography*, 3rd ed. New York: Harry N. Abrams, 1986.

Baker, Rob. *The Art of AIDS*. New York: Continuum Publishing, 1994.

Battcock, Gregory. *Why Art: Casual Notes on the Aesthetics of the Immediate Past*. New York: E. P. Dutton, 1977.

Battcock, Gregory and Robert Nickas. *The Art of Performance: A Critical Anthology*. New York: E. P. Dutton, 1984

Bornstein, Kate. *Gender Outlaw: On Men, Women, and the Rest of Us*. New York: Routledge, 1994.

Bouldrey, Brian, ed., *Best American Gay Fiction 2*. Boston: Little, Brown, 1997.

Brelin, Christa, ed., *Strength in Numbers: A Lesbian, Gay and Bisexual Resource*. Detroit: Visible Ink Press, 1996.

Cage, John. *Silence*. Cambridge: M.I.T. Press, 1961.

Carr, Cynthia. *On Edge: Performance at the End of the Twentieth Century*. Hanover, New Hampshire: University Press of New England, 1993.

Champagne, Lenora, ed. *Out from Under: Texts by Women Performance Artists*. New York: Theatre Communications Group, 1990.

Clarke, Mary and Clement Crisp. *The History of Dance*. New York: Crown, 1981.

De La Croix, Horst, Richard G. Tansey, and Diane Kirkpatrick. *Gardner's Art through the Ages*, 9th ed. San Diego: Harcourt, Brace, Jovanovich, 1991.

Felshin, Nina, ed., *But Is It Art?: The Spirit of Art As Activism*. Seattle: Bay Press, 1995.

Frueh, Joanna. *Erotic Faculties*. Berkeley: University of California Press, 1996.

Fuoss, Kirk W. *Striking Performances/Performing Strikes*. Jackson: University Press of Mississippi, 1997.

Garber, Frederick. *Repositionings: Readings of Contemporary Poetry, Photography, and Performance Art*. University Park: Pennsylvania State University Press, 1995.

Genette, Gérard. *The Work of Art: Immanence and Transcendence*. Translated by G. M. Goshgarian. Ithaca, New York: Cornell University Press, 1997.

Giorno, John. *Balling Buddha*. New York: Kulchur Foundation, 1970.

Goldberg, RoseLee. *Performance Art: From Futurism to the Present*, 2nd ed. New York: Harry N. Abrams, 1988.

———. *Performance Art: Live Art 1909 to the Present*. New York: Harry N. Abrams, 1979.

Hart, Lynda and Peggy Phelan, eds. *Acting Out: Feminist Performances*. Ann Arbor: University of Michigan Press, 1993.

Haskell, Barbara. *Blam!: The Explosion of Pop, Minimalism, and Performance 1958-1964*. New York: Whitney Museum of American Art, 1984.

Henri, Adrian. *Total Art: Environments, Happenings, and Performance*. New York: Praeger, 1974.

Herbert, Frank John. "American Nervousness." Ph.D. diss., University of Iowa, 1990.

Hughes, Holly. *Clit Notes: A Sapphic Sampler*. New York: Grove, 1996.

Jones, Therese, ed. *Sharing the Delirium: Second Generation AIDS Plays and Performances*. Portsmouth: Heinemann, 1994.

Juno, Andrea and V. Vale, ed. *Angry Women*. San Francisco: RE/Search Publications, 1991.

Kaprow, Allan. *Essays on the Blurring of Art and Life*, edited by Jeff Kelley. Berkeley: University of California Press, 1993.

Katz, Jonathan Ned. *The Invention of Heterosexuality*, with a foreword by Gore Vidal. New York: Plume/Penguin, 1995.

Kistenberg, Cindy J. *AIDS, Social Change, and Theatre: Performance As Protest*, Garland Studies in American Popular History and Culture. New York: Garland, 1995.

Kostelanetz, Richard. *On Innovative Performance(s): Three Decades of Recollections on Alternative Theater*. Jefferson: McFarland & Company, 1994.

Lacy, Suzanne, ed. *Mapping the Terrain: New Genre Public Art*. Seattle: Bay Press, 1995.

Lippard, Lucy R. *Overlay: Contemporary Art and the Art of Prehistory*. New York: Pantheon Books, 1983.

Lucie-Smith, Edward. *Art in the Seventies*. Ithaca, New York: Cornell University Press, 1980.

Martin, Carol, ed. *A Sourcebook of Feminist Theatre and Performance*. New York: Routledge, 1996.

McAdams, Donna Ann. *Caught in the Act: A Look at Contemporary Multimedia Performance*. New York: Aperture, 1996.

Meyer, Moe, ed. *The Politics and Poetics of Camp*. London: Routledge, 1994.

Miller, Carl. *Stages of Desire: Gay Theatre's Hidden History*. London: Cassell, 1996.

Miller, Tim. *Shirts and Skin*. Los Angeles: Alyson Books, 1997.

Morrissey, Lee, ed. *The Kitchen Turns Twenty: A Retrospective Anthology*. New York: Phillip Morris Companies, 1992.

Museum of Contemporary Art, Chicago. *Performance Anxiety*. New York: Distributed Art Publishers, 1997.

Parker, Andrew and Eve Kosofsky Sedgwick, eds. *Performativity and Performance*. New York: Routledge, 1995.

Perkins, Kathy A. and Roberta Una, eds. *Contemporary Plays by Women of Color: An Anthology*. New York: Routledge, 1996.

Phelan, Peggy. *Unmarked: The Politics of Performance*. London: Routledge, 1993.

Reinelt, Janelle G. and Joseph R. Roach, eds. *Critical Theory and Performance*. Ann Arbor: University of Michigan Press, 1992.

Rogosin, Elinor. *The Dance Makers: Conversations with American Choreographers*. New York: Walker and Company, 1980.

Roth, Moira, ed. *The Amazing Decade: Women and Performance Art in America, 1970-1980*. Los Angeles: Astro Artz, 1983.

Russell, Mark, ed. *Out of Character: Rants, Raves, and Monologues from Today's Top Performance Artists*. New York: Bantam Books, 1997.

Sandford, Mariellen R., ed. *Happenings and Other Acts*. London: Routledge, 1995.

Sayre, Henry M. *The Object of Performance: The American Avant-Garde Since 1970*. Chicago: University of Chicago Press, 1989.

Schulman, Sarah. *My American History: Lesbian and Gay Life during the Reagan/Bush Years*. New York: Routledge, 1994.

Steinman, Louise. *The Knowing Body: The Artist as Storyteller in Contemporary Performance*. Berkeley: North Atlantic Books, 1995.

Stiles, Kristine and Peter Selz, eds. *Theories and Documents of Contemporary Art: A Sourcebook of Artists' Writings*. Berkeley: University of California Press, 1996.

Strathern, Andrew J. *Body Thoughts*. Ann Arbor: University of Michigan Press, 1996.

Sussman, Elisabeth. *Mike Kelly: Catholic Tastes*. New York: Harry N. Abrams, 1993.

Taylor, Brandon. *Avant-Garde and After: Rethinking Art Now*. New York: Harry N. Abrams, 1995.

Thompson, Philip, John Williams, and Gerald Woods, eds. *Art without Boundaries*. New York: Praeger Publishers, 1972.

Tomkins, Calvin. *The Scene: Reports on Post-Modern Art*. New York: Viking Press, 1976.

Turner, Margery J. *New Dance: Approaches to Nonliteral Choreography*. Pittsburgh: University of Pittsburgh Press, 1971.

Ugwu, Catherine, ed. *Let's Get It On: The Politics of Black Performance*. Seattle: Bay Press, 1995.

White, Robin, ed. *Music, Sound, Language, Theatre*. Oakland, N.p.: Point Publications, 1980.

Witt, Lynn, Sherry Thomas, and Eric Marcus, ed. *Out in All Directions: The Almanac of Gay and Lesbian America*. New York: Warner Books, 1995.

Performance Art: Periodical Articles and Book Excerpts

Alfaro, Luis. "Luis Alfaro," in *High Performance*, vol. 15, Winter 1992: 34-5.

Apple, Jacki. "John Fleck: *Psycho-Opera*," in *High Performance*, vol. 10, 1987: 64-5.

Best, Paul. "Octavia Goes Out for a Beer," in *High Performance*, vol. 2, September 1979: 42-3.

———. "Octavia Goes Shopping in Her New Hair Color," in *High Performance*, vol. 2, March 1979: 50-1.

———. "Paul Best: The Gay Pursuit of Muscle," in *High Performance*, vol. 5, Spring-Summer 1982: 62, 179.

———. "Transformation," in *High Performance*, vol. 3, Summer 1980: 56.

Breslauer, Jan. "Tim Miller: *Some Golden States*," in *High Performance*, vol. 11, Fall 1988: 63-4.

Burnham, Linda. "An Unclassified Number: An Interview with John Fleck," in *Drama Review*, vol. 35, Fall 1991: 192-7.

———. "Ishmael Houston-Jones: *Lace*," in *High Performance*, vol. 10, 1987: 78.

———. "Running Commentary," in *High Performance*, vol. 13, Fall 1990: 10-11.

Burnham, Linda and Steven Durland. "An Interview with David Schweizer," in *High Performance*, vol. 9, 1986: 25-7.

Carlson, Lance. "John Goss: *Forbidden Planet*," in *High Performance*, vol. 13, Summer 1990: 61.

Champagne, Lenora. "Richard Elovich: *If Men Could Talk, The Stories They Could Tell*," in *High Performance*, vol. 13, Summer 1990: 70.

Conner, Lynne. "Scott Timm: *The Age of Innocence*," in *High Performance*, vol. 13, Fall 1990: 70.

Cooper, Dennis. "Who Will Save Us Now?: Dennis Miller on Tim Miller," in *High Performance*, vol. 5, Fall 1982: 78-9, 101-2.

David, Martin A. "On the Boulevard of Mattresses: *Buddy Systems*," in *High Performance*, vol. 8, 1985: 92.

Dery, Mark. "John Giorno: Where There's Smoke There's Poetry," in *High Performance*, vol. 8, 1985: 46-50.

Durland, Steven. "An Anarchic, Subversive, Erotic Soul: An Interview with Tim Miller," in *Drama Review*, vol. 35, Fall 1991: 171-7.

Evenden, Michael. "Inter-mediate Stages: Reconsidering the Body in 'Closet Drama,'" in *Reading the Social Body*, edited by Catherine B. Burroughs and Jeffrey David Ehrenreich. Iowa City: University of Iowa Press, 1993: 244-69.

Forte, Jeanie. "Women's Performance Art: Feminism and Postmodernism," in *Performing Feminisms: Feminist Critical Theory and Theatre*, edited by Sue-Ellen Case. Baltimore: Johns Hopkins University Press, 1990: 251-69.

Foster, Susan Leigh. "Dancing Bodies," in *Meaning in Motion: New Cultural Studies of Dance*, edited by Jane C. Desmond. Durham: Duke University Press, 1997.

Fuller, Cal. "David Cale: *Deep in the Dream of You*," in *High Performance*, vol. 14, Summer 1991: 56.

Gautier, Roberto. "Benefit of the Future," in *High Performance*, vol. 8, 1985: 67-8.

Giorno, John. "On Playing Samuel Beckett's *Eh Joe*," in *Art & Design*, vol. 10, November-December 1995: 64-7.

Goodman, Lizbeth. "Bodies and Stages: An Interview with Tim Miller," in *Critical Quarterly*, vol. 36, Spring 1994: 63-72.

Grover, Jan. "The Convergence of Art and Crisis," in *High Performance*, vol. 9, 1986: 28-31.

Gruen, John. "John Kelly: Notes from the Underground," in *Dance Magazine*, February 1992: 60-3.

Haile, Mark. "Pomo Afro Homos: *Fierce Love*," in *High Performance*, vol. 14, Winter 1991: 42.

Howell, John. "David Cale, *Smooch Music*," in *Artforum International*, vol. 25, Summer 1987: 122-3.

Hudson. "*Deep Kissing* a Performance by Hudson," in *High Performance*, vol. 9, 1986: 40-1.

———. "Hudson/Buzz Tone Outlet: Living the Life," in *High Performance*, vol. 5, Spring-Summer 1982: 93, 181-2.

Jarrell, Joe. "God Is in the Details: Wojnarowicz Is in the Courts," in *High Performance*, vol. 13, Fall 1990: 20-1.

Kaplan, Rachel. "High Risk Group: *A Bitter Pill to Swallow: or AZT Why Can't I Love You?*" in *High Performance*, vol. 13, Winter 1990: 50.

———. "High Risk Group: *Falling*," in *High Performance*, vol. 15, Spring 1992: 47.

———. "Jon Weaver: *Beauties, With*," in *High Performance*, vol. 14, Spring 1991: 46.

Kelly, Patrick and Otis Stuart. "Dancing the Difference," in *Dance Magazine*, January 1989: 34-8.

Kuhn, Laura and Richard Kostelanetz. "John Cage," in *High Performance*, vol. 10, 1987: 20-9.

Lacher, Roger Flandrin. "Billy Curmano: *Performance with Dancing Flames*," in *High Performance*, vol. 14, Summer 1991: 61.

Licata, Elizabeth. "Ways in Being Gay," in *High Performance*, vol. 14, Spring 1991: 54-5.

Lippard, Lucy. "Art and Politics: Questions on a Politicized Performance Art," in *Art in America*, vol. 72, October 1984: 39-45.

———. "Silence Still = Death," in *High Performance*, vol. 14, Fall 1991: 28-31.

Martínez, Rubén. "Carmen, a.k.a. Marcus Kuiland-Nazario: The Stage Is Politics," in *High Performance*, vol. 17, Spring 1994: 36-7.

McAdams, Lewis. "Nightclubbing with William Burroughs, John Giorno, and Laurie Anderson," in *High Performance*, vol. 4, Winter 1981-82: 38-43.

McDonald, Robert. "Philip-Dimitri Galas 1954-1986," in *High Performance*, vol. 9, 1986: 21.

Mendoza, David. "Marlon Riggs," in *High Performance*, vol. 17, Summer 1994: 16-7.

———. "*NEA Four* Win Settlement....," in *New Art Examiner*, vol. 21, September 1993: 51-2.

Miller, Tim and David Román. "Preaching to the Converted," in *Theatre Journal*, vol. 47, 1995: 169-88.

Mizrahi, Isaac. "Shall We Dance?" in *Out*, October 1997: 108-10, 152.

Muñoz, José Esteban. "No es fácil: Notes on the Negotiation of Cubanidad and Exilic Memory in Carmelita Tropicana's *Milk of Amnesia*," in *TDR*, vol. 39, no. 3, Fall 1995: 76-82.

Navarre, Max. "Art in the AIDies: An Act of Faith," in *High Performance*, vol. 9, 1986: 32-6.

Nickard, Gary. "Carlos Gutierrez-Solana: *Shattered Dreams*," in *High Performance*, vol. 12, Summer 1989: 65.

Riddle, Mason. "David Mura: *Relocations, Images from a Japanese-American*," in *High Performance*, vol. 14, Fall 1991: 66.

Robertson, Clive. "John Greyson: Colliding Atoms of a Gay Culture," in *High Performance,* vol. 9, 1986: 55-8.

Rubin, Edward. "John Kelly," in *The New Art Examiner,* April 1995: 48-9.

Russell, Mark. "Ron Vawter," in *High Performance,* Summer 1994: 17.

Sayre, Henry M. "A New Person(a): Feminism and the Art of the Seventies," in *The Object of Performance: The American Avant-Garde since 1970.* Chicago: University of Chicago Press, 1989: 66-100.

Schwendenwien, Jude. "Frank Maya: *Unauthorized Autobiography,*" in *High Performance,* vol. 14, Winter 1991: 52.

Scott, D. Travers. "Lawrence Steger: *Worn Grooves,*" in *High Performance,* vol. 14, Spring 1991: 58.

Solomon, Alisa. "The WOW Cafe," in *A Sourcebook of Feminist Theatre and Performance,* edited by Carol Martin. New York: Routledge, 1996: 42-51.

Steinberg, Janice. "Neofest," in *High Performance,* vol. 13, Fall 1990: 48-9.

Toepfer, Karl. "Nudity and Textuality in Postmodern Performance," in *Performing Arts Journal,* vol. 54, September 1996: 76-91.

Tropicana, Carmelita. "Milk of Amnesia/Leche de Amnesia," in *TDR,* vol. 39, no. 3, Fall 1995: 94-111.

Viegener, Matias. "Curtis York: The Boys in Curtis York," in *High Performance,* vol. 14, Summer 1991: 45.

———. "John Fleck," in *High Performance,* vol. 15, Fall 1992: 38-9.

———. "Luis Alfaro: *Downtown,*" in *High Performance,* vol. 14, Spring 1991: 41.

Williams, Kimmika. "Michelle Parkerson, Essex Hemphill, and Wayson Jones: *Voicescapes: An Urbanmouthpiece,*" in *High Performance,* vol. 9, 1986: 79-80.

Yarbro-Bejarano. "The Lesbian Body in Latina Cultural Production," in *Entiendes? Queer Readings, Hispanic Writings,* edited by Emilie L. Bergmann and Paul Julian Smith. Durham: Duke University Press, 1995: 181-200.

Gay Male Theater and Dance—Bud Coleman
Gay Male Performance Art and Overview—Darrell Taylor
Lesbian Theater—Carolyn Gage
Lesbian Dance—Julie Townsend
Lesbian Performance Art—June Reich

18

Visual Arts

This chapter will explore gay and lesbian achievement and influence in the fields of art, photography, and architecture. The fields of art and photography are discussed in comingled fashion, while the field of architecture is discussed separately. The "Prominent People" section, however, combines people from all three fields; immediately following each individual biography, the author is indicated by italicized initials. The "References" section likewise incorporates all three fields, although subheads help to delineate sources by the appropriate field.

IRRECONCILABLE DIFFERENCES: LESBIAN AND GAY ARTISTS IN THE 20TH CENTURY

This section of the Visual Arts chapter seeks to present a broad overview of the work of a number of lesbian, gay, bisexual, and transgendered artists, as well as to locate that work within a broader historical context. This essay is by no means intended as a definitive queer history, and it ultimately seeks to problematize a number of expectations with regard to just what constitutes lesbian and gay art. For instance, not all lesbian, gay, bisexual, and transgendered artists produce work about sexual identity. Thus, in acknowledging the desire for a queer art history, one must also recognize that individual creativity and aesthetic concerns are mediated through any number of social, cultural, historical, and ideological positionings and affiliations.

While there have been a number of books addressing lesbian and gay art, the general focus of such publications has been solely to address work with overt lesbian and gay themes, usually communicated through overtly erotic imagery, symbolism, and accompanied with a hearty dose of biographical conjecture. This essay

will include a wide range of artists, some of whom work with familiar lesbian and gay imagery, others of whom locate themselves firmly within modern and postmodern artistic practices; not surprisingly, many incorporate elements from both worlds. It is this schism between the various incarnations of the avant-garde and popular forms of queer culture that shall be the indirect focus of this essay; the schism becomes particularly interesting when such seemingly disparate worlds as high art and queer Pop overlap, as they did in the many controversies surrounding the photography of Robert Mapplethorpe. Mapplethorpe became the subject of numerous debates over the National Endowment for the Arts' (NEA) use of public funds, and these controversies were fueled by the larger question of determining artist merit. In spite of the slow dismantling of the NEA, queer artists continue to make inroads into museums and galleries, and in recent years the work of gay erotic artists such as Tom of Finland and Bruce of Los Angeles have moved from the pages of erotic publications to the walls of museums. Such transformations skew the traditional boundaries between high art and popular culture and begin to pose a number of questions for artists on both sides of the spectrum. Queer popular culture can of course be seen in everything from Calvin Klein ads to gay charge cards, but queer art has always been seen as a subcategory or footnote to the official pages of art history. Clearly, there have always been artists who were same-sex oriented, but their sexual practices may have merited little attention in the official history books. Today, as readers search out such categories, and as artists are increasingly willing to self-identify, it is up to publications such as this to draw links back into those official histories. Those links may expand such histories, or they may eventually lead to what Henry Louis Gates, Jr., in *Hybridity Happens* has suggested: the move away from essential notions of identity, informed by cultural theory that such categorizations may eventually become unnecessary. For the moment, such a time remains unforeseen.

In defining the fine arts as a field of knowledge, one must recognize the distinct roles played by museums, academic and arts institutions, galleries, not-for-profit spaces, critics, collectors, audiences, theorists, and artists. This is not to suggest that such institutions are the sole purveyors of taste but rather to acknowledge the role played by this non-conventional industry in shaping the official histories of individual artists. With that in mind, one must recognize that while a number of the artists are nationally and internationally recognized within museums and history books, others function primarily within the queer community. This essay attempts to acknowledge such disparities and has included a wide range of artists, each contributing to a particular set of issues or ideas within both the fine arts and queer communities.

Many of the most adamant art enthusiasts continue to position aesthetic pleasure oppositionally to culturally or politically informed work. Such arguments inevitably reinscribe the status quo notion of the art object as a transcendental communicator of a universal sublime, and tend to look skeptically upon the notion of the artist as provocateur, social commentator, and/or political advocate, and is part of what many see as an ongoing crisis within the arts that pits the so called "identity artist" against claims for a Modernist universalism.

The dilemma for many queer artists is that much of their work foregrounds the search for represen†ation and internalizes the necessity for a certain legibility in the production of queer objects. Frequently, such work references specific histories or images that then function as discernible clues for the viewer. However, when aesthetic pleasure is characterized primarily in relationship to physiological pleasure, then one must recognize that such an interpretation assumes that the viewer always already embodies the full range of themes, topics, and strategic interventions that they will then encounter, and value as good or bad. Clearly, experience and individual subjectivity play an important part in determining artistic value, but most will also recognize that artistic innovations frequently pose challenges for the viewer; after all, the Impressionists were considered quite outrageous in their day. If learning can be thought of as labor, then the conception of pleasure as an effortless and instantaneous recognition of the already known, the recognizable, becomes highly problematic in that the unknown, or unrecognizable, is reduced to some degree of displeasure or ambivalence. If ambivalence hovers within the middle ground, then displeasure demands an evaluation, which whether accepted or rejected must be seen as an interruption to unbounded pleasure. Some degree of displeasure may ultimately contribute to the expansion of aesthetic boundaries.

In "Helmut and Brooks, N.Y.C.," 1978, from Robert Mapplethorpe's *The X Portfolio,* the viewer is presented with an image of a man being fisted. The image has been defended on aesthetic and erotic grounds but finally is left straddling the fine line between high and low, between art and eroticism. Composition, tonal range, titillation, fascination, disbelief, and documentary truth may all have their appeal and yet may remain inconclusive. Clearly, the image functions both as art and eroticism simultaneously for different viewers, but its status speaks to the transformative power of displeasure in that it recognizes some level of social determinism.

In "Man in Polyester Suit," 1980, Mapplethorpe presents a black man in a three-piece suit, his penis protruding from his fly. The rather unimpressive suit is set against a rather impressive penis and has been highly criticized for its racist undertones: a headless black person reduced down to one appendage and a few stray fingers. In other works, Mapplethorpe literally puts an African American man on a pedestal, such objectifications suggesting something of a racial fetishization. Cultural theorist Kebena Mercer has written about Mapplethorpe's work in two seminal essays. The first of these problematizes Mapplethorpe in terms of the racial discourse cited above, and the second counters such a critique through the observation that as the product of a gay man taking photographs of other gay men, such work can be seen to transform such racial dynamics into an articulation of gay male desire. Crudely oversimplified, such arguments speak to the mutability of the aesthetic experience. While seemingly obvious, such shifts are significant because they foreground the social and contextual legibility of a given work of art, an aspect that becomes particu-

larly clear with regard to Mapplethorpe's work, which has been interpreted in such drastically different ways. This is not to critique Mercer, nor to suggest that either interpretation is incorrect, but rather to highlight the difficulties of establishing a queer aesthetic.

As we near the close of this century, it seems only appropriate to take a focused look back upon the 20th century and trace out a number of elements that might at least help to articulate some of the implications and benefits of exploring such categorical boundaries.

Trapped in the schism between officially recognized art practices and emerging queer scholarship, and fearful of the general marginalization of identity-based work, several artists refused to be included in this essay. One very well known lesbian photographer refused to reply to any correspondence. Several other artists are well known for their dismissal of any emphasis upon sexual orientation with regard to their artistic practice. One must hope that publications like this may one day be able to include their work, so that we might all selfishly take pride in their achievements.

PHOTOGRAPHIC ORIGINS: FROM THE PICTORIALISTS TO FASHION

The origins of modern-day gay culture are to be found in the work of the Pictorialists, a small number of photographers working within the period that loosely dates from 1880 to 1920. Indistinguishably linked with the excitement surrounding the development of readily available photographic technology, the Pictorialists were caught in the battle between classical idealism and the documentary power of the photographic medium that so characterized this period. Prior to this period, straight artists such as Edgar Degas and Thomas Eakins were busily, if secretly, photographing their studio models in order to enhance the realism of their paintings, but it was the Pictorialists who began to present the photographic medium as an end in itself. For painters, the photographic medium was invaluable in capturing increasingly naturalistic poses, poses that their models would have previously been unable to sustain for the long periods necessary to be depicted in oils. In addition, the medium offered a great deal more information than a traditional figure study done in charcoal. The increased naturalism provided by the photographic document suggested a refreshing and occasionally shocking level of realism to audiences trained to recognize a limited pantheon of idealized poses. Such new and seemingly mid-action poses provided a revitalizing breath of fresh air to realist painting and quickly led to the development of numerous photographic studios whose primary function was to supply a wide range of figure studies to well-established painters. Alongside such uses, a second market quickly emerged for photography that concerned itself with the overtly erotic image, and dates back to the emergence of the photographic medium itself, as early images of both male and female nudes attest.

A small number of photographers began to see the photograph as an artistic medium in and of itself. Of this group, the New England publisher F. Holland Day must be seen as one of the most important contributors. Known to and among the homophile circles of Oscar Wilde, Day mastered Victorian soft-focus techniques, creating painterly photographs that veiled their homoerotic imagery in a wide range of Christian themes, as his well-known and highly scandalous self-portrait as the crucified Christ testifies. Day was at the center of the controversy over photography's blasphemous power of illusion, its literal or realistic content frequently overpowering its metaphoric intentions. His "St. Sebastian," 1906, depicts the bare chest of youthful St. Sebastian bound and wounded, with head and arm drawn back and lips parting in ecstatic if sacrilegious devotion. Both Stephen Parrish and Thomas Waugh have noted that letters to Day from Oscar Wilde and Aubrey Beardsley confirm what many a gay historian had previously only suspected, that Day was indeed homosexual (Waugh, 1996, p. 78).

Also known by Oscar Wilde was the work of Baron von Gloeden. Von Gloeden's work rarely indulged in the soft-focus technique employed by Day; moreover, von Gloeden made his living by producing both conventional and erotic tourist cards. Many of von Gloeden's nudes take on classical themes, the objectifying gaze of the camera preferring highly detailed depictions of each dark-skinned boy. Rich in voyeuristic titillation, and existing beyond the stylized haze so popular among the Victorian avant-garde, von Gloeden's boys appear in secluded courtyards, or amidst Minimalist props intended to evoke the Arcadian bliss of a world in which serpentine youths stretch and twist before an unseen lens, their faces and genitals skillfully caught in perfect focus for an unseen but ever-present collector/consumer. With a little retouching, many of his images were able to cater to a booming post card trade interested in the classical nude. Photographers such as von Gloeden, Vincenzo Galdi, and Wilhelm von Plüschow frequently offered second- and third-tier portfolios whose eroticism might even include erections, bondage, or a fond embrace with sidelong glances for those men willing to pay the price, both financially and legally, since possession of overtly homosexual images could lead to legal complication and imprisonment. It should be kept in mind that in Victorian society, and even in the United States prior to the civil rights movement, southern Italians were frequently seen by many Anglo-Europeans as racially and culturally different. Thus, for von Gloeden the dark-skinned Italian signaled not only cultural difference but the idealized relations between men and boys in the classical age. By positing the ephebe as Other, von Gloeden embraced a particular Victorian Orientalism that was enhanced through serpentine elongations and an abundant clutter of patterns, portals, and props through which such overtly stylized and stereotypical differences become the indirect measure of an erotic charge rooted in the scientific racism of the 19th century.

By 1930, a new breed of photographer had begun to emerge in both Europe and America. Associated with *Vogue* and *Harper's Bazaar,* these artists symbolized a clear break with the Pictorialist aspirations to painting, instead responding to the changes within popular culture. Jazz, cinema, the infamous Weimar Period, and the Great Depression had reshaped the world, and the emergence of mass-produced periodicals was changing the role of photography. Fashion magazines, cinema, and this new society of the spectacle were redrawing the lines of culture itself. A new breed of transatlantic photographers began to emerge, and among their members something of a gay avant-garde began to take shape. This movement was headed by George Hoyningen-Hene (1900-68), a Baltic baron whose family had fled from the Russian Revolution. Hoyningen-Hene brought the clean lines of constructivist composition to his photographic works, skillfully blending boldly graphic elements into sensuously lit fashion shots. These seemingly larger than life images could be summarized in one word: glamorous. Hoyningen-Hene became the presiding fashion photographer at *Vogue* from 1926 to 1935 (Waugh, p. 105). His German protégé

Piece from the *Youths in Grotto* series by Baron von Gloeden.

and lover Horst P. Horst (b. 1906) also found a place in the annals of *Vogue,* which, it turned out, provided a number of young photographers with commercial success and name recognition (Waugh, p. 105). Transatlantic fashion and avant-garde circles intermingled within an emergent clique of openly gay men who could be found amidst the empty cocktail glasses that lined the sitting parlors of those visionary Modernists: Jean Cocteau, Gertrude Stein, and Coco Chanel. Likewise, in New York in the 1930s a new generation was already on the way. A young American, George Platt Lynes, was to be initiated within this collusion between the art world and the fashion industry. Writing to Gertrude Stein while still in his late teens, Lynes visited Stein and Alice B. Toklas in Bilignin, France, in 1925 (Crump, 1993, p. 137). This ambitious young photographer clearly recognized Stein and Toklas as the symbolic fusion of the avant-garde with emerging notions of sexual freedom. Once back in New York, Lynes established himself as both a fine art and fashion photographer. In 1936, Lynes was included in the Museum of Modern Art's exhibition "Fantastic Art, Dada, Surrealism," which then established him as a Surrealist photographer. In 1950, Lynes produced a series of prints for the New York City Ballet's production of Balanchine's *Orpheus,* but unfortunately the images were deemed too controversial by ballet administrators and went largely unpublished. While Lynes struggled to keep his studio going on commercial work, he embarked on his photographic portraiture of New York's gay intelligentsia along with his more overt erotic work. Ultimately, the recurrent homoerotic content of his images proved problematic to both his commercial and fine art careers. Toward the end of his career, he turned against the restraints of commercial photography, and after a failed attempt at Hollywood, returned to New York, where he stepped-up his radical investigation of the male figure. Lynes's work documents a considerable slice of the gay intelligentsia, photographing friends, professional models, and hustlers. Lynes created a vast archive of finely crafted images, some in the best of portraiture traditions while others clearly centered upon an overtly erotic, if illegal, content. But it was noted sex researcher Dr. Alfred Kinsey who is perhaps most responsible for establishing a legacy for Lynes's work. Kinsey's interest in the relationship played by erotic photography within the homosexual male led him to begin collecting Lynes's work in the 1950s. Today the Kinsey Institute has more than 600 vintage prints.

Together Hoyningen-Hene, Horst, and Lynes represent a vision of gay life that seems surprisingly open to contemporary readers, and it is perhaps for this reason that their work has drawn the attention of a number of queer historians.

PICTURING WOMEN:
FROM THE *HAUTE MONDE* TO THE AVANT-GARDE

In 1908, an American expatriate took up residence in a fashionable quarter of Paris on the Avenue Trocadéro. Her name was Romaine Brooks, and she had just inherited a great deal of wealth, all of which only solidified her position as a part of the *haute monde.* Her status was reaffirmed when she created a stir by decorating her apartment with black mohair-covered furniture, gray walls, and abundant vases of white flowers, all of which reflected and enhanced the muted palette of her paintings (Breeskin, 1986, p. 23). Recognized for this bold style, Brooks acquired some renown as an interior decorator for the elite, a position that ultimately facilitated her new role as a society portraitist. Best known for her portraits of the French elite of the arts and letters, Brooks had her first solo exhibition in 1910 at the Galeries Durand-Ruel in Paris. In 1912, Brooks painted Gabriele d'Annunzio, the Italian poet in exile, and in 1914 she painted a little-known Jean Cocteau. By the fall of 1914, the flow of Americans to Paris began to wane and much of the European art community was drawn into the Great War, serving either in military or medical capacities. Romaine Brooks received some critical attention for her portrayal of a battlefield nurse in "La France Croix," 1914, which depicts a young woman on the front lines after the battle, a cathedral discernible in the smoky distance. To her audiences the piece spoke to the gravity of the war, as well as to changing social conditions, particularly as many young women took an active part in the war. Stylistically, Brooks's work was linked more closely to the painting of an earlier American expatriate in Paris, James Abbott McNeil Whistler, than to her contemporaries over at 27 Rue de Fleurs. It was of course during this period that Gertrude and Leo Stein had been filling up their studio with the work of Picasso, Cezanne, and Matisse, among others. Whistler represented an earlier aesthetic and had participated in the Salon des Refusées, and his well-known "Arrangement in Gray and Black No. 1: Portrait of the Artist's Mother," 1871, better known as "Whistler's Mother,"

had already found its way into the Musée du Luxembourg. Independently wealthy, Brooks traveled in slightly different circles from the emergent avant-garde, preferring the likes of Gabriele d'Annunzio, Ida Rubinstein of Diaghilev's Russian Ballet, and Natalie Barney, otherwise known as "L'Amazone," whose salons were frequented by a small literary group that counted Marcel Proust, André Gide, and Colette among its numbers. In 1925, Brooks had solo exhibitions in London, Paris, and the Widenstein Galleries in New York. For historians of queer culture, Brooks provides a small glimpse into lesbian portraiture of the 1920s. Historical accounts clearly recognize that several of Brooks's sitters self-identified as lesbians and lived openly as such. Lady Troubridge would eventually write of her life with Radclyffe Hall, and Hall modeled the characters from *The Well of Loneliness* after Lady Troubridge and even Brooks herself (Breeskin, p. 35). In "Peter (A Young English Girl)," 1923-24, Brooks depicts an angular young woman sporting a coat, vest, and tie, her short hair and erect posture signaling the independence usually associated with 19th-century depictions of males. For the early Modernists, women were frequently depicted as working-class laborers, laundresses, and of course prostitutes, but rarely with the self-assurance of Brooks's sitters. Closely linking their work with literary realism, artists such as Henri de Toulouse-Lautrec and Edgar Degas depicted women as burlesque and ballet dancers, washerwomen, and in the pursuit of numerous activities. In fact, in his essay "The Painter of Modern Life," originally published in *Figaro* in 1863, Charles Baudelaire commented on the artist's necessity to look for inspiration in the mark of modernity, which he proposed could be found "across the great human desert" that he saw reflected in the new social order of the streets (Baudelaire, 1982, p. 23). Clearly, working women would play a key role in this new vision of modernity. Brooks, in rejecting such gender conservative imagery, inadvertently managed to suggest an under-theorized relationship between constructions of gender and modernity.

Hannah Höch was born 15 years after Brooks, and into a far different world. In Germany, the Great War, the Kaiser's abdication of the throne, the establishment of a republic, the influence of German Expressionism, Höch's own involvement with the writer/artist Raoul Hausmann after 1915, and the fact that women's suffrage was guaranteed in the 1919 constitution all contributed to the transgressive promise of the avant-garde. Working as a graphic designer within the decorative arts industry, Höch, like most Germans, must have been struck by the explosion of photographic illustrations within the popular press. Although Höch worked in a variety of media, it is her photomontages that have continued to draw critical attention. Largely ignored in official accounts of the Dada movement, Höch and her work were not critically reconsidered until the late 1950s. Höch participated in the first Berlin Dada Exhibition in 1919, and in 1920 her work was included in the First International Dada Fair. Höch began making photomontages sometime in 1918, and the majority, if not all, of her Weimar period works challenge a wide array of conventionally held beliefs. Acting as Hausmann's unofficial secretary, Höch was exposed to a great deal of Dadaist material. This, combined with her use of photomontage and her application of it to a work entitled "Schnitt Mit Dem Küchenmesser Dada...," 1919-20, would link Höch with Berlin Dada in the minds of many. After the breakup of the Dada group and her relations with Hausmann, she began what would be a nine-year relationship with a woman, Dutch writer Til Brugman. It was during Höch's years with Brugman that her photomontages began to include numerous same-sex couples along with a slew of androgynous figures.

Höch's bisexuality is also suggested within a number of photomontage works from the "New Woman" and "From an Ethnographic Museum" series, many of which suggest a strangely precarious fusion of ethnographic imagery with the female form. The montage of ethnographic and popular press materials clearly drew from the Dadaist rejection of the status quo that Höch applied specifically to popular conceptions of the "New Woman" and German nationalism.

"Fredme Schönheit" (Strange Beauty), 1929, from the series "Aus Einem Ethnographischen Museum" (From an Ethnographic Museum), depicts a reclining female nude with a rather brutish face. Taken from an unknown source, its darkly rendered face is completed with bifocals and two squinting eyes. Disturbing in its use of what appears to be an ethnographic sculpture, one must recognize that Höch is attempting to draw the viewer's attention to the historical objectification of the female form by transforming it into a Dadaist fetish object that problematizes the nude through the growing European fascination with the ethnographic subject. Such cross-cultural comparisons were clearly provocative in the Weimar period, and may still be so today, but must be historically located within the Modernist struggle for new forms. In Weimar Germany and even later, popular manifestations of "comparative science" continued to suggest an evolutionary privileging of Western culture. Social Darwinism and Fascist politics eventually led to the idealization of the Aryan culture as the culmination of indigenous and nationalistic interests. In an earlier piece entitled "Mischling (Half-Caste)," 1924, Höch depicts the face of a black or West Indian woman with the rosebud mouth of a white woman. While the piece is disconcerting to contemporary viewers, exhibition biographers have elucidated such juxtapositions by explaining that Höch was specifically responding to the racist hysteria in Germany concerning the post-war presence of back and mixed-race Africans (Makela, 1996, p. 70).

By the same token, "Die Ewigen Schuhplattler" (The Eternal Folk Dancers), 1933, depicts two buffoon-like figures who can be seen dancing the "Schuhplattler," a traditional Bavarian folk dance in which the thighs, knees, and heels are slapped. Done in the same year the Nazis took power, its critique is embodied in the montage techniques also found in her earlier Dada work. Specifically, Höch deploys a disjuncture in scale, where large heads and small limbs serve to construct caricatures of a nationalism gone wild. In "Fluct" (Flight), 1931, one sees a winged head chasing a figure whose face is composed from the joined fragments of a white woman and a chimpanzee. Clearly referencing mixed-race persecution, the question remains as to whether its sardonic humor and that of the "Schuhplattler" function in similar ways, or if there are fundamental differences. Obviously, one may never know how these images would have been received by mixed-race viewers, or even by the white populace for that matter, but one must remember that any critique of Höch's deployment of such ethnographic material is not intended to undermine the appreciation of her artistic contribution but to open discussions of material that has frequently been undervalued within the development of such avant-garde movements. Unlike an explicitly erotic, scientific, or politically charged photograph in which the exchange between author, audience, and model is predicated on certain dynamics related to the colonialist and imperialist exchange of labor and capital, Höch's appropriated images defy such essentialist arguments with regard

to their redeployment. Höch's images, which sought pleasure in their revolutionary promise, were clearly intended to provoke the viewer. In "Bäuerliches Brautpaar" (Peasant Wedding Couple), 1931, Höch depicts a rural Aryan couple, the husband with the head of a black man, and the wife with the head of an ape capped in blond pigtails. Despite its overt critique of German nationalism and racism, one must acknowledge that such an image inadvertently denigrates people of color through its underlying assumptions with regard to an unspoken construction of the primitive, which locates apes and blacks as symbolically and perhaps even metaphorically primitive, a strategy that can be seen in the engagement of Otherness throughout the work as a whole. Clearly, the image is no less problematic even if one denies its symbolic level, but most significantly, Höch's work provides a surprisingly resonant model for both social critique and proto-feminist applications inexorably linked with aesthetic pleasure.

BETWEEN THE WARS: MEN IN UNIFORMS

Paul Cadmus painted the world of the 1930s in the United States, touching on everything from soldiers on leave to the beaches of Fire Island. Cadmus was at the center of the circle of gay men who were prominent within the arts world in New York City. His brother-in-law was Lincoln Kirstein, founder of the American School of Ballet and a key player in the career of the photographer George Platt Lynes. For a time, Lynes lived with both Monroe Wheeler, a director of exhibitions at the Museum of Modern Art, and writer Glenway Scott, and their cocktail parties corresponded with the development of an openly gay presence within New York. Cadmus, Bernard Perlin, Jared French, and George Tooker would later come to be known as the Magic Realists, and their depictions of youthful male nudes represented a freedom that would be short lived, not reemerging again until after World War II. Cadmus's "The Fleet's In!," 1933, which is ostensibly heterosexual in its narrative depiction of sailors flirting with young ladies, nevertheless manages to suggest a rather intimate exchange between a well-dressed civilian and a sailor to whom he offers a cigarette. The civilian sports a red tie, a widely accepted signal of homosexuality from at least as early as the turn of the century to the 1930s. For many, this exchange suggests an openly homosexual subtext, and Jonathan Weinberg in *Speaking for Vice* has gone so far as to suggest that this subtext led to the painting's removal from a 1934 exhibition at the Corcoran Gallery (Weinberg, 1993, pp. 33-34). In Cadmus's 1933 painting, "YMCA Locker Room," Cadmus leaves even less room for speculation in what appears as an overt homoerotic pretext for allowing him to paint young men in various states of disrobement, a strategy continued in works such as "Horseplay" and "Gilding the Acrobats," both from 1935.

In 1937, Cadmus along with Jared and Margaret French began to experiment with photography during their trips to Fire Island and Provincetown. Known as the PAJAMA (Paul-Jared-Margaret) Group, they photographed each other along with their friends and visitors over a 20-year period. Together the images provide insight into a period of great creativity and freedom. Both Cadmus and Jared French, his lover, painted WPA murals that included an abundance of slender waists and well-toned abdomens. Cadmus's "The Bath," 1951, depicts Jack Fontan and Jensen Yow in a domestic bathroom (Leddick, 1997, p. 104). Three pairs of socks can be seen hanging from the towel bars, a forth pair being worn by the standing figure. While circumstantial, the abundance of socks at least begins to suggest a shared domestic life. The stand-

The Fleet's In (1934) by Paul Cadmus

ing man combs his hair before a wash basin while the other proceeds to wash himself. Clearly, this is a domestic scene that might pass for social-realist depiction of working-class brotherhood were it not for the suggestive positioning of the bathing figure. Each figure looks away from the viewer, constructing a conventionally voyeurististic scenario in which the viewer is inescapably located within this most private of domestic spaces. This transgression is further heightened by the rather awkward pose of the bathing figure, who kneels within the tub, his left hand guiding a bar of soap over his lower posterior. In case the presumed viewer were to miss the scarcely veiled eroticism, Cadmus has positioned the soap in such a way as to conceal its front-most corner behind the right buttock, hinting at penetration. Stylistically, the picture draws from age-old conventions in which the traditionally nude female would cover her genital area with a clasped hand, her curving fingers somehow never quite fully visible. Cadmus appropriates a typically heterosexual device in order to construct his overtly homoerotic scene.

Charles Demuth, perhaps best known for his "Figure 5 in Gold," 1928, which represented a certain achievement in Modernist Abstraction, also created a second body of work that had a far more private life, although much of it was never exhibited during his lifetime. Mostly done in watercolor and pencil on paper, these works spoke of an emerging gay culture. One such work, "Eight O'Clock (Morning # 2)," 1917, depicts three men in various stages of disrobement, their scattered clothes suggesting an impromptu soirée. Identifiable within the scene are a top hat and cane on one side, and a bowler on the other, suggesting an exchange between an upper-class gentleman and a street youth. This association is only furthered by its companion piece, "Eight O'Clock (Evening)," 1917, which seems to suggest that the merriments began the night before.

In it, one man can be seen disrobing while another seems to be finishing a cup of tea. The casualness of their attitudes has been read as a matter-of-fact exchange of services, which were probably commanded by the wealthy gentleman (Weinberg, pp. 25-27). Such a reading is of course based on speculation, but in looking to another work, "Turkish Bath Scene with Self-Portrait," 1918, one again sees three male figures, one draped in a towel and engaged in an exchange with the image of Demuth, whose towel is already lying on the floor, while a third man stands before the first, his legs spread, his carefully rendered penis clearly presented for inspection. In the background two figures can be seen, one holding his hands to his genital area while a second man appears to crouch, his angled head facing an unseen specter. In the middle ground a man appears to be surveying the seated figure of a nude male. Historical accounts of gay bathhouses cite many such locales within New York City during this period, and while such interpretations may be based on conjecture, it seems a reasonable assumption that such a bathhouse was the source of the painting, because of the intimate positioning of the figures, the abundance of male flesh, and the stylistic curvature of the figures themselves, which like the serpentine lines of a female Odalisque provide an erotic subtext to the work. Art history has long since recognized the erotic value of the female nude, but today one should be able to suggest such an analysis for the homoerotic nude male as well.

Should any such analysis prove unconvincing, Demuth has left us with a number of far-less obtuse works. His "Three Sailors on the Beach," 1930, depicts a sailor dressed only in a tank top and boots, his spread legs revealing an erect penis, his gaze turned to the man standing behind him. Dressed only in his boxers, this second man holds his penis in one hand while his other directs the first man's head toward it in what clearly suggests fellatio. In the background, a third man seems to be undressing. Demuth's initials can be seen on the second figure's arm, located in the center of a heart-shaped tattoo.

Another American painter, and a close friend of Demuth, was Marsden Hartley. Like Demuth, Hartley had also made his pilgrimage to Paris, and in 1912 Hartley introduced himself to Gertrude Stein. It has been widely cited that Stein championed Hartley for his use of color and the emotive value of his abstractions. Hartley first visited Germany in 1912 and preferred it to the Parisian art world. In Germany, Hartley had become acquainted with the *Blaue Reiter* group. Even after the start of World War I in August 1914, Hartley continued to live in Germany, and it was only after the death of his lover, a young German soldier named Karl von Freyburg, that he returned to the States (Weinberg, p. 3). Hartley's "Portrait of a German Officer," 1914, includes von Freyburg's initials along with his own. Hartley's painting of the German military machine were obviously received with a grain of salt, and his interest in and persistent use of military themes seems to have reached beyond any specific relationship and spoke to a particular eroticization of homosocial militarism that led him to write admiringly of Germany as "essentially masculine with ruggedness and vitality" (Weinberg, p. 147). Hartley continued to return to his particular notion of masculinity painting, although he applied it in a slightly different direction. In "Christ Held by Half-Naked Men," 1940-41, one sees an all-male pieta but recast with Nova Scotia fishermen, their robust forms speaking to a devotion beyond piety. Stylistically removed from his earlier abstractions, this work takes on a strangely brutish realism in order to communicate its particular conception of a masculine world.

BEEFCAKE: THE FINE LINE BETWEEN HIGH AND LOW

By the 1940s, a wide variety of homoerotic imagery had entered the public domain through male fitness or "physique" magazines such as *Strength and Health, Muscle Power,* and *Tomorrow's Man,* which were in increasing circulation, and by 1969 (and the Stonewall Riots) such publications abounded. Produced for a variety of audiences, these magazines primarily catered to fitness

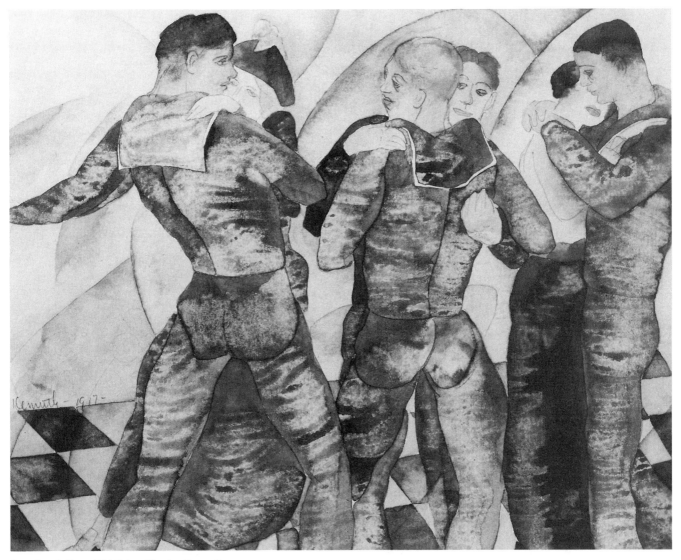

Dancing Sailors (1917) by Charles Demuth

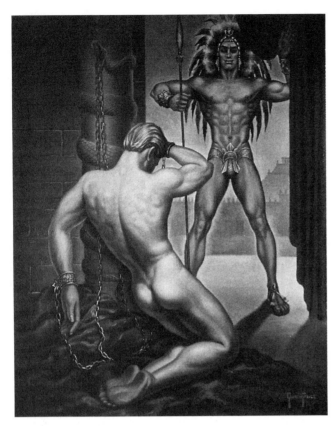

White Captive (1951) by George Quaintance

buffs and a growing gay subculture. As this subculture grew, so did the variety of magazines available. Likewise, the photographic images moved from strict representations of weight-lifters and barbells to images of naked young men in campy interior shots or wrestling in the great outdoors.

Such magazines frequently included brief stories on the life of the bachelor and handy wrestling hints for you and your partner, and one unsigned/undated article from *Manhattan Man* even expounded on the benefits of drinking fruit juice over milk. Others gave detailed exercise instructions by bodybuilders explaining everything from knee-bends to push-ups, and were accompanied by a variety of scantily clad men flexing and posing. Many such magazines also presented idealistic, if not fantastic, illustrations of muscled young men in varied surroundings. Perhaps one of the best known of these artists was George Quaintance, whose highly rendered paintings of bulging male muscles frequently depicted semi-clad or nude men, their muscles glistening as they lay lounging about in barns, battling lions on steep mountain cliffs, or just generally prancing though waterfalls. Quaintance's work appeared on the covers of such magazines as *Physique Pictorial* and *Fizeek Art Quarterly,* and although Quaintance never depicted complete frontal nudity, he managed to lay out an array of sexual scenarios. In "Havasu Creek," 1948, he depicts four Latino ranch hands taking a break under a waterfall. The piece is stylistically similar to his earlier work, but here Quaintance has replaced his earlier blond heroes with equally idealized Latino men. In "White Captive," 1951, Quaintance takes on a Mezo-American theme in depicting a chained blond muscle boy being approached by a smiling chief-

tain; the image is completed with a stepped pyramid in the background. "Manolo," 1952, shows a smiling Mexicano, muscles and pants bulging as he takes his eager horse out for a ride. "The Bandit," 1953, takes a moody interior as its locale, depicting two Mexicanos and one Anglo under guard, the candelabra and violet and purple linen suggesting a sultry evening. Together these images present a humorous theatricality and an overall illustrative quality that marks their functionality as gay erotica. The difficulty of considering such work within the context of the previous two sections is that regardless of its merits, such work exists outside of modernist art practices. Quaintance's status as an erotic artist positions him somewhat outside of modernist narratives, and yet his increased popularity, and the overall interest in queer cultural studies, demand that we address such difficulties between high and low cultural models. Some have argued that such subculturally specific work functions as would a craft object, a quilt, or a toll painting, and exists independent from high art criticism and scholarship. Others argue that such distinctions simply mask class privilege and academic elitism and might give the now highly collected works of von Gloeden, F. Holland Day, and perhaps even Mapplethorpe's "X Portfolio" as examples of art historical reevaluation. Without reducing the arguments to some relativist stance, one must recognize that modernism, or postmodernism for that matter, has not yet adequately theorized such work. In recognizing that historical revisions frequently reconsider individuals, periods, and entire bodies of work as a matter of due course, it seems conceivable to imagine a day when the history of specifically queer work might appear far differently than it does today. In defense of modernist and postmodern artistic practices, one must remember that they represent an equally significant historical progression of ideas and investigations and that aesthetic strategies must be recognized within the history of ideas, beliefs, and desires. Art, it has been argued, simply gives form to thought. Suffice it to say that this essay seeks to provide an array of officially recognized artists along with a number of image-makers whose work may ultimately contribute to our understanding of queer scholarship and perhaps even end the marginalizing discourse typically associated with culturally specific work.

In the 1950s, as photographic reproductions slowly replaced hand-drawn illustrations in a wide variety of print media, it should come as no surprise to find a similar phenomenon within the lesbian and gay community. Numerous photo studios such as the Athletic Model Guild, the Western Photography Guild, and Spartan of Hollywood began to emerge, and by the 1950s Bruce Harry Bellas, better known as Bruce of Los Angeles, was the most recognized photographer within a booming gay subculture. Like Quaintance, Bruce explored a wide range of motifs, and it was not unusual to see a model dressed as a cowboy, a construction worker, a buccaneer, a Spartan wrestler, or simply relaxing in the great outdoors. Among some thousands of photographs, primarily of Anglo men, one does find a number of somewhat iconic representations of masculinity. In one, an African American male poses as a construction worker. In another, a white man is painted like an Indian from a Hollywood set. Such stereotypical representations are familiar, and one need only think of the popular music group the Village People to be reminded of how deeply ingrained such imagery is within popular culture. One interesting side note is that these photographs allow us to examine the overall whiteness of the early gay movement while at the same time suggesting an attempt to reformulate masculinity within a specifically gay context. Countering the many negative representations that treated

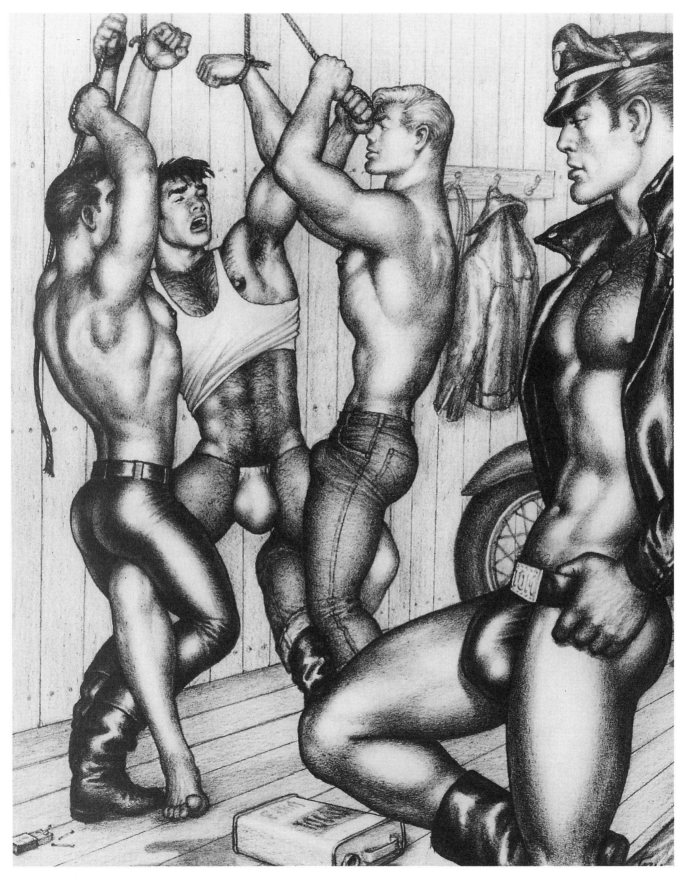

A work by Tom of Finland

lesbians and gays as psychologically ill, such camp and homo-erotic narratives provided affirming images of gay life.

No discussion of 1950s Beefcake would be complete without a discussion of the drawings of Tom of Finland. Like the work of Bruce of Los Angeles, Finland's work appeared on the pages of gay male erotica and is credited by many Finland fans as being a predominant force in transforming gay male identity. Finland rejected the fine arts practice of signaling a queer subtext through the presence of slender and somewhat dandyish men, as seen in Cadmus's "The Fleet's In," choosing instead to recast the gay male within a new hyper-masculinity of bulging biceps, V-shaped shoulders, and the rippled abdomens so admired today. In addition, Finland replaced the sensitive and somewhat effete artist/poet symbolized by writers such as Oscar Wilde with the aggressive machismo of policemen, lumberjacks, and leather-clad bikers. Their sideburns, mustaches, tattoos, and uniforms acknowledged a growing subculture and suggested a rejection of discreet invisibility. Their visible erections became an unapologetic symbol of gay liberation. Citing his rage against social and legal injustice, John Rechy in his 1977 book, *The Sexual Outlaw: A Documentary,* articulates this new attitude when he writes, "The Promiscuous homosexual is a sexual revolutionary. Each moment of his outlaw existence he confronts repressive laws, repressive 'morality.' Parks, alleys, subway tunnels, garages, streets—these are the battlefields" (Rechy, 1977, p. 28). Unlike Quaintance, who seemed content to depict gay men within some idyllic utopia or within the confines of an enclosed space, Finland constructed a vision of the streets, parks, and meeting places of his new man. Furthermore, in giving form to this eroticized world, Finland also constructed/reflected sexual scenarios emphasizing role-play. Perhaps recognizing the mutability of masculinity itself, Finland queered masculine authority, transforming the cop into an unbridled lover of men, the hoodlum into a sex radical. He went on to construct an infinite array of erotic combinations that explored the erotic boundaries of dominance and submission, meticulously unraveling the pleasures of each. Even his prison scenes, populated with prisoners of purportedly equal standing, are cast into an elaborate web of precisely defined roles. While seemingly obvious, such explicit depictions gave form to something inconceivable in its specificity to previous artists who could only hint at their desire and longing subtextually. Quaintance, Cadmus, and Lynes all depicted their male subjects as passively coded objects onto which the viewer was to construct his own subtext. Clearly, narrative clues were given or implied, but it was Finland who would sweep away such pretexts by forcing the viewer into an inescapably gay context. Throughout the more than four decades of his career, Finland was able to articulate a vast amount of fact and fiction, S/M, B/D, fellatio, mutual masturbation, and anal intercourse, all of which managed to find their way onto the page, forming a codex whose mass-produced existence served to initiate many a novice into the elaborate world of sexual role play. Finland's work, which evolved hand in hand with the evolution of a gay male subculture, has recently found its way within high art venues, triggering new rounds of debate over high and low cultural forms. In engaging discussions of class privilege and the marginalization of the Other, this work can be located among the many debates over the inclusion of subcultural work within the historical legacy of modernism, postmodernism, and its relationship to avant-garde practices. For those unfamiliar with the term "Other," it need simply be thought of as a place holder for those marginalized discussions or race, class, and gender.

Pushing the line between this notion of high and low is contemporary artist G. B. Jones, popularly referred to as the female Tom of Finland. Her drawings depict a new lesbian fantastic, which like Finland's has resulted from the collision of leather, punk, S/M, and a dose of queer cultural history, all manifested in an assault against dominant cultural objectification. Unlike Tom of Finland's drawings, with their smooth and sometimes bulging forms, Jones's work is drawn with a slightly sharp hand, its scratchy and stiff figures suggesting a raw subversiveness that in the 1990s may have stronger links to the *Riot Grrrls* (and high art for that matter) than 1950s pornography, with its emphasis on an erotic utilitarianism. One must be clear, however, that Jones's work does not simply mimic some idyllic gay male past, nor do her characters don gay cultural paraphernalia as a narrowly defined *lesbian chic.* Rather, it is her undeniable concern with lesbian visibility, and those emergent cultural practices that are developing, changing, and being challenged in a number of lesbian communities, that is the subject of her work. Her interest in constructing a specifically lesbian erotic is apparent in the series of drawings titled "I Am a Fascist Pig." This series recalls scenes from a dyke fantasy. In it one sees a female motorcycle cop being seduced by two punk girls, who tie her up and steal her bike. In the final image one sees the cop tied to a tree, her posterior exposed while the aggressors make a fast getaway. Like Tom of Finland, Jones is laying out an explicit scene whose aggressive subtext defines a scenario of bondage and dominance in which the aggressor or Top determines and supplies the erotic pleasure of both the Top and the submissive Bottom. Like Finland, Jones anticipates the viewer's implicit voyeurism and uses it to heighten the erotic tension of the scene.

POP CULTURE, POP ART: A REJECTION OF ABSTRACT EXPRESSIONISM

This represents perhaps the most difficult section in this essay, because Jasper Johns, Robert Rauschenberg, and even Andy Warhol have never spoken extensively about their sexual orientations, but recently a number of published works have positioned them as gay or bisexual men. While problematic with respect to their inclusion, and difficult with regard to the volume and importance of their work, this section nevertheless seeks to recognize their rejection of Abstract Expressionism as the linchpin for a renaissance of representational imagery that would culminate in Pop art.

Rauschenberg's reintroduction of representational subject matter within the art world was a direct reaction to the dominance of Abstract Expressionism. Rauschenberg was firmly established among the New York Abstract Expressionists and had already been included in a number of significant exhibitions before meeting Johns. Jonathan Katz, in his essay "The Art of Code: Jasper Johns & Robert Rauschenberg," has convincingly argued that Rauschenberg's "White Paintings" and "Erased de Kooning," 1953, already expressed something of an ambivalence towards Abstract Expressionism. Shortly after meeting Johns, Rauschenberg began creating hybrid works that incorporated elements from both painting and sculpture and were termed "Combines." Rauschenberg continued to create Combines during the six years he and Johns were lovers (Katz, 1994, p. 189). Perhaps the most revealing comment from Rauschenberg came when he said, "I'm not frightened of the affection that Jasper and I had, both personally and as working artists. I don't see any sin or conflict in those days when each of us was the most important person in the other's life" (Johnson, 1996, p. 127). Using the canvas as a support, Rauschenberg was

Triple Elvis (1964) by Andy Warhol

able to employ an additive process in which each element could be seen as an addition within a signifying chain and which inherently recognized that artistic meaning must be constructed. That is to say that the artistic gesture of combining elements could no longer be seen as a transparent window into the artist's soul, but rather could project outward onto the world around him. Rauschenberg's "Bed," 1955, creates a mock bed from an old quilt and pillow, which is then covered with highly gestural brush strokes.

After Rauschenberg and Johns's falling out, Rauschenberg began to experiment with silk-screen printing, eventually incorporating it into his paintings. This technique can also be found in the work of Andy Warhol.

Like Rauschenberg, Johns also incorporated a variety of media into his works. His "Target with Plaster Casts," 1955, combines a painting of concentric circles typifying a target, above which one finds a series of small niches, each containing a different body part, and a hinged door. Again, the work makes clear references to formalist abstraction, but in choosing the target shape Johns has taken a popular cultural icon and made it into a play of signification. The enclosed body parts clearly suggest the author, or an individual, who becomes both a metaphoric and literal target. This

kind of tongue-in-cheek manipulation was also found in his "Flag" paintings, in which he re-presented the American flag as a neutral or abstract configuration; this could be seen as a primal moment for Pop art, which would rely heavily on appropriated popular cultural icons. Warhol picked up on this innovation and took it a step further, employing a wide range of images from popular culture, including everything from Coca-Cola and Pepsi bottles to Del Monte and Campbell's soup cans.

Warhol took the problem of representation and turned it upside down, as much of his early work drew its imagery directly from newspapers, ads, comics, and advertisements. Known as the father of Pop art, Warhol looked to popular culture for his subject matter. Two themes quickly grew out of this: his "Disaster" and "Celebrity Icon" series. For many, Warhol's depictions of Marilyn Monroe, Elvis Presley, Natalie Wood, and Elizabeth Taylor have come to exemplify Pop art, but in many ways the "Disaster" pictures were necessarily linked with the celebrity work. The "Disaster" images covered a broad range of topics, perhaps the best known of which were the automobile crashes; though his "Electric Chair" pieces were not technically disasters, they nevertheless contain the same properties as any highly charged topic. It was around this time that Warhol began employing a photo-silkscreen technique as a way of completely removing the artist's hand and further enhancing the pieces' Pop immediacy. Embracing the mass-media's, and the public's, fascination with such highly charged subjects as disasters and celebrityhood, Warhol chose subjects that represented extremes of the human condition, preferring those that suggested something of the heroic and the tragic, preferably in the same breath. This strategy is nowhere more apparent than in "Jackie (The Week that Was)," which evoked a series of film stills from the Kennedy assassination. Its appearance suggested a television screen, and its title was clearly intended to play off the name of the well-known television show. It was at this point that Warhol began his fascination with Jackie Kennedy, and she became a recurrent theme in his work precisely because of the extreme conditions of her public life.

Contemporary artist Deborah Kass takes Warhol as her subject in her "My Andy" series, in which she brilliantly updates and even appropriates some of the Warhol hype by poking holes in Warhol's seemingly seamless Pop vision. In her "Jewish Jackie Series," Kass clearly stakes a claim in the play of signification. If Warhol acknowledged society's obsession with popular culture, then Kass takes this theme a step further and comments upon Warhol's own obsession with pop culture. Mimicking Warhol's "Double Elvis," Kass created her striking parody, "Triple Silver Yentl (My Elvis)," 1992. The movie *Yentl* was, of course, Barbra Streisand's foray into drag when she portrayed a young woman pretending to be a male Talmudic scholar in order to get her education. In selecting Streisand, Kass mercilessly exposes Warhol's narrow idealism to the broader socio-cultural spectrum of the 1990s. If commodity culture and excess were the underlying themes of Warhol's work, then Kass reconstructs the Pop canon around her own feminist, lesbian, Jewish perspective. Warhol was clearly fascinated with the glamorous starlet, but Kass introduces a new set of women into the canon, as Gertrude Stein and Barbra Streisand stand in for Elizabeth Taylor and Marilyn Monroe. As a project, Kass's work exemplifies the postmodern critique of a unified subject position for the author/artist. By rejecting any claims to authenticity, claims that fundamentally position the artist as author, Kass displaces her own authorship within the artificiality of Warhol's persona, capturing both the brilliance of his strategies

Triple Silver Yentl (My Elvis) **(1993) by Deborah Kass**

while defining her own. In "Altered Image # 1," 1994, based on Christopher Makos's 1981 photograph of Warhol in drag, Kass becomes a lesbian woman impersonating a gay man impersonating a woman. Since Warhol's own sexuality, though well known, was rarely stated, it further confounds the situation by suggesting that he was in fact a gay man impersonating a straight man impersonating a straight woman. Such questions foreground the humor inherent in much of Kass's work.

Imploding Pop art's legacy of slick recontextualizations, contemporary artist Lari Pittman willfully embraces the tenets of Pattern and Decoration, while blatantly rejecting Clement Greenberg's warnings surrounding the collapse of high art into commodity culture (Jones, 1995, p. 41). If Greenberg can be seen as the chronicler and spokesman for the merits of Abstract Expressionism, then Pittman's work must be seen as a renewed rejection of such formalist strategies. Densely patterned canvases are filled with cartoon-like vignettes of pointy shoes, stylized undergarments, and bodily excretions, all bound within a tangle of patterns, textures, and shapes. Graphically aligned with certain Pop stylizations, Pittman maneuvers through suffocating layers of stenciled, brilliantly crafted images, which both delight and unsettle the viewer. In "Untitled #1," 1992, Pittman presents a true cacophony of fetishistic imagery that, among other images, wills forth a brief-clad, Pinocchio-nosed, cartoon-like character who appears upside down,

bound in electric cords, and floating in a playful mire of light bulbs, feces, and "S.O.S." signs, each painted in the neutral hand of a stylist, but which cumulatively suggest far more than any single part, offering up their darker inner workings only to the patient viewer.

BEYOND THE FLESH:
TRANSGENDER AND PERFORMANCE

After having traveled through this short history, some readers might be surprised to find themselves back in the early days of this century. In considering the notion of gender, however, it is necessary to trace out a new path. Claude Cahun (1894-1954) was educated at Oxford and the Sorbonne. Born Lucy Renée Matilde Schwob, she began making photographic self-portraits sometime around 1912, and by 1917 had adopted her pseudonym Claude Cahun. In 1922, she moved to Paris with her stepsister and lifelong partner, Suzanne Malherbe, also known as Marcel Moore (Greene, 1997, p. 206). Cahun's self-portraits were never exhibited and remained largely unknown until their inclusion in a number of Surrealist photography exhibitions in the mid-1980s. Among her various personae, one finds a giant doll-like figure, one resembling a Bavarian folk dancer, another sternly draped in black and appearing with a rather masculine hairline, and still another depicting her with a shaved head and a dark suit, seemingly imitating a young man. Many of the photographs served as source images for her collages, but regardless of their various manifestations Cahun seems to have anticipated the contemporary fascination with gender play. Her images clearly go the first step towards destabilizing the notion of gender as fixed, positing gender as little more than a masquerade.

Working in the 1960s and 1970s, Pierre Molinier created a particularly curious body of work. Using himself and others, Molinier created an army of femme automatons whose strangely photomontaged and retouched bodies can be found knotted and arranged into various tangles of limbs. But what its rampant misogynistic fetishism lacks in theoretical complexity it makes up for in undermining monolithic interpretations of gender performativity and speaking of a psychologically disembodied subject whose absolute self-effacement has yet to be fully considered. Peter Gorsen in "The Artist's Desiring Gaze on Objects of Fetishism" explains that while "Molinier lived a male transvestite's bisexual life," such over-determined categories provide little insight into the highly individualistic and unquestionably transgressive practices of this artist (Gorsen, 1997, p. 21). Seamlessly crafted through the overlaying and rephotographing of retouched or manipulated photographs, Molinier's work positions itself uncomfortably between transvestitism and a self-guided exploration of auto-eroticism and gender performativity.

Contemporary artist Hanh Thi Pham has been engaged in an exploration of Asian transgendered and transsexual representation, and frequently invokes elements from both traditional Vietnamese culture and Western culture. Her piece "Lesbian Precepts," 1992-94, was inspired by accounts of the Buddha taking on the form of a woman in order to instruct the people. Pham's 1996 piece, "The Living Buddha Is a Transsexual," takes a more subtle stance, articulating her own challenge to the male authority of organized religion in both Asia and the West. In "No Man/No Woman," 1995, Pham can be seen standing before a full-length mirror, her arms outstretched with a meat cleaver in one hand and a knife or poker in the other, and wearing a black strap-on dildo. One text panel reads, "I have little to hide. My lips are drawn back, I grin, I breath the Silence, So don't you dare define me." Clearly challenging gender conformity by literalizing the performative utterance, Pham struggles to capture the performative instant in a static form, and her use of multiple images, text, and installation techniques is certainly a beginning.

Contemporary photographer Loren Cameron approaches the problem from a slightly different vantage point, employing documentary strategies in his project "Body Alchemy," which documents the struggles and triumphs of his own female-to-male transition. In doing so, he also employs conventional environmental portrait and documentary reportage imagery in order to provide a normative view of the FTM community. In "Erik," (n.d.), we see a young man with long hair, a faint mustache, and a goatee, wearing a heavy-metal T-shirt and riding a dirt bike, his cut-off jeans revealing his tattoos and high tops. Surprisingly, it is with this simple, rather deadpan documentary style that Cameron's environmental portraits do the most to undermine conventional gender play precisely through their seamless emulation of it. Moving beyond the notion of masquerade, which presumes an underlying true, if hidden, gender, Cameron goes one step further and confounds the entire notion of gender as fixed and yet undeniably asserts its physicality, suggesting something of an endlessly recurring instant that is just about to begin or end.

TRESPASSING: EXCAVATING LITERARY, HISTORICAL, AND MUSEOLOGICAL REPRESENTATION

This section is rather playfully entitled "trespassing" because it looks at the way a number of artists excavate the official histories of Western culture, frequently extracting or including objects that refute dominant cultural representations of the Other. Critically engaging literary, historical, and museological representations, these artists draw from familiar avant-garde devices, employ text, appropriate images, mount installations, and work in a wide range of media in order to facilitate their practice.

Clearly, artists have always borrowed from a wide range of sources, but unlike artists from earlier periods, artists in the 1980s began to re-present objects in an unaltered state. These appropriated images sought to relocate the artistic gesture at the conceptual level and not within the authorship of the object itself. In 1917, when Marcel Duchamp placed a signed urinal in a New York exhibition, he cast the first stone against the idea of the artist as craftsman. In signing "Fountain," Duchamp also foregrounded his recognition that no institutional or gallery space is ideologically neutral. In order to clarify the impact of ideologically coded space, one need only consider Duchamp's role in this essay. Duchamp is included for his contributions to art, yet given the context of this essay some readers may mistakenly presume he was also gay.

If postmodernism can be understood as a critical break with the Enlightenment notion of the autonomous self, then this section seeks to acknowledge Michel Foucault's disruptive hypothesis that if to know is to represent, to represent is to wield power. Foucault recognizes that not all representations are equal and cites the importance of their relationship to power, hegemonic power. Foucault destabilizes the Western self and conceptually begins to open spaces from which to critically examine the many troubled categories of the center, of dominant culture. If we begin by considering the generic museum as a kind of cultural machine that orders, interprets, and distributes dominant culture, then one can also imagine it as a site rich in deconstructive potential.

Perhaps no artist has better understood this potential than Fred Wilson in his "Mining the Museum," which was presented by the Contemporary and the Maryland Historical Society in Baltimore, Maryland, in 1992-93. In a project initiated by the Contemporary, Fred Wilson was invited to choose a museum within the Baltimore area. Wilson chose the Maryland Historical Society and worked closely with its administrators and staff in developing his project. Unlike with other museum exhibitions, for his installation Wilson asked that none of the usual museum-authored explanations be appended to the exhibition. Instead, after polling staff members, a simple photocopied handout was developed addressing a number of frequently asked questions. Wilson created a series of installations that juxtaposed objects from the collection in order to undermine its presumed neutrality. By focusing the viewer's attention on the larger institutional narrative suggested by the museum's collecting practices, Wilson was able to clarify how truth claims mask ideology. In "Truth Trophy and Pedestals," Wilson presents a globe-shaped trophy with the word "truth" written across it and surrounded by six pedestals, three on each side. To the right one sees the busts of Napoleon Bonaparte, Henry Clay, and Andrew Jackson, and to the left one sees three empty pedestals with the names Harriet Tubman, Benjamin Banneker, and Frederick Douglass. The three absent Maryland residents clearly stand as a critique of the racial and cultural inequities at play within the museum collection and foreground the ghostly absence of historical representation.

In another instance, Wilson presents a vitrine labeled "Metalwork 1793-1880," in which he includes a number of silver vessels done in the Baltimore repoussé style along with a set of slave shackles from the same period. In this example, we can see how Wilson uses the text or label to signal his intervention, which was intended to emphasize the underlying economic conditions that allowed the luxurious decadence symbolized by the repoussé style to exist in the first place. The shackles are a stark reminder of slave labor and racial inequality, and yet they signal a pedagogical shift that actually transforms the museum space from a depository of the status quo into a site of historical analysis and discovery.

In the 1970s, responding to the presumed "transparence" of the social documentary traditions left by the Photo League and the Farm Security Administration, a generation of photographers such as Martha Rosler, Connie Hatch, Alan Sekula, and Deborah Bright began to apply Structuralist and Poststructuralist critical practices to the history of photography. As a lesbian artist and scholar, Bright is of particular interest within the context of this

White Girl (1995) by Millie Wilson

essay. Throughout her career, Bright has been engaged in projects that expose those histories concealed within the presumed neutrality of the American landscape. Her "Battlefield Panorama" series, 1981-84, took an ironic look at battlegrounds-turned-subdivisions, while her "How the West Was Won (Caution-Do Not Dig)," 1985, focused on a rather unobtrusive granite marker that was located over a radioactive waste site in suburban Chicago. Both projects employ a straightforward documentation of objects or sites that can then be discursively unpacked. In a 1997 project created for the arts journal *Frame-Work,* Bright created a four-page spread critiquing formalist photography's aesthetic idealization of the industrial landscape. Then, in focusing on the commercial appropriation of such high art imagery, Bright showed how even queer identity is co-opted for commercial gain, ultimately reducing a social/political movement to a niche market. The project begins with a grid of contemporary photographs documenting a number of industrial and commercial spaces that have been closed and are now available, and under which one sees the word "disinvestment." This image is paired with an appropriated image dating from the 1920s and 1930s by the well-known photographer Charles Sheeler and labeled as "art." The image itself depicts a monumental landscape photograph documenting Ford Motor Company's River Rouge automotive plant in Detroit. Sheeler's formalist interest in line, composition, and tonality ostensibly fail to include any reference to the working conditions of the factory, which it turns out was the site of heated labor struggles that were suppressed by Ford's private security forces. On the third page one sees the appropriated image of a well-known photograph by Lewis Hine of a man tightening a bolt on a large cog, which suggests an idealized union between man and machine, synchronized for the betterment of mankind in the glory of the industrial age, a premise refuted by the previous "disinvestment" page. This cog image is set against the fourth page, which re-presents an advertisement for the "Rainbow Card," a Visa credit card whose ad features lesbian tennis star Martina Navratilova pulling a giant cog, a commercial image that clearly draws from a fine art image. If art idealizes industrialism, and industrialism employs art, then clearly one must rethink art's disruptive promise. The "Rainbow Card," one learns, "lets us express our pride and strengthen our support of the lesbian and gay community," and Bright has captioned this image as "marketing." While somewhat didactic, this work is not intended to criticize Navratilova or the lesbian and gay communities but rather to draw the viewer's attention to the way that commodity culture erases social struggles in order to redeploy those communities in the service of capital. This is not to suggest a conspiracy theory but to acknowledge the play of ideology within commodity culture. Just as the formalist pleasure of Sheeler's towering smokestacks masked the labor conditions contained within, so to the "Rainbow Card" replaces the ongoing political struggle for lesbian and gay rights with consumerism. Constructing her piece largely from appropriated images, Bright seeks to foreground Marx's premise that commodity culture disassociates objects from their means of production, replacing social relations with object relations. Like those strategies employed by Fred Wilson, Bright's work recognizes that a single object, artifact, or concept may be metaphorically unpacked, in turn revealing at least some of the material and social conditions surrounding its given historical moment.

Contemporary artist Millie Wilson approaches history from a slightly different vantage point, creating objects whose discrete charms are culled from literature, early modernism, minimalism, and popular culture. In 1989, Wilson presented an installation entitled "Fauve Semblant: Peter (A Young English Girl)," at Los Angeles Contemporary Exhibitions. The work suggested the retrospective exhibition of a little-known early modernist. The work's title was clearly intended to invoke the Romaine Brooks painting by the same name, and depicted something of a gender radical. Unfortunately, Brooks's silent images tell us little of the struggles or strengths of this furtive moment within lesbian history, let alone modernist art history. Wilson, sporting short hair and a bow tie, presents her own version of Brooks's portrait and uses her own image to problematize any normative presumptions of authenticity. The exhibition hinted at the life and work of this now-fictionalized character whom Wilson has positioned among the Fauves, and hence the exhibition title, "Fauve Semblant." The title suggests that just as Höch's work had been excluded from the historical canon of Berlin Dada, so too Peter's work has inevitably been distanced from its cultural moment, and has since been historically reconstructed, but in the dim pallor of resemblance. Wilson thus forcefully argues that not even the most avant-garde of practices would disrupt the historical marginalization of women. One text panel told viewers that Peter was a woman, who dressed like a man, "sought fame and fortune, and eventually had to sacrifice everything for . . . a desire like hers." Lesbian desire is constructed as a dark consuming cloud that causes the end of her artistic production and seems to suggest the end of Peter's public life as well. This notion of a secretive love is closely linked with discussions of lesbian invisibility and serves as both a narrative and metaphoric device for the work. One piece in the exhibition consisted of a single unused palette. This palette suggests not only the absent paint, but the unnamed desire as well. Further into the exhibition viewers were presented with a series of photographs depicting Peter's smoking jacket, shoes, hat, and other effects, all of which appeared next to a text panel suggesting that these items signaled more than the sexual orientation of the wearer and began to allude to a certain level of "privileging." The precise boundaries of this "privilege" remain unclear, but one could assume it referred to the privileges of the white heterosexual male. Clearly, this installation employed the rhetoric of museum display in order to counter the absence of such histories, and yet the specificity of its title, its art historical references and aspirations, all locate Wilson's work as a kind of historical metaphor that ultimately seeks to question her own historical legacy. By standing in for Peter, Wilson signals the absence of lesbian representation within dominant cultural history. Conversely, "Peter" stands in for Wilson by opening a conceptual space between the project's dual illusion of representing either Wilson or Peter. That is to say that by destabilizing Wilson's own subject position as an artist, a lesbian, and a white woman, Wilson attempts to use Peter to address modernism's inability to recognize its own sexual, cultural, racial, and economic privileging. One should remember that Wilson is not concerned with a strictly factual or literal reconstruction of lost histories, but rather seeks to deconstruct the false promise of modernity itself.

Significant Lesbian and Gay (and/or Queer) Exhibitions

1973-76: "Annual Exhibition," Gay Academic Union, New York, New York.

1982: "Extended Sensibilities: The Homosexual Presence in Contemporary Art," curated by Daniel J. Cameron, The New Museum for Contemporary Art, New York, New York.

1990: "A Survey of Lesbian and Gay Artists," curated by Lewis Holman, Penine Hart Gallery, New York, New York; "Queer: Out in Art," curated by John Wessel and Bill O'Conner, Wessel O'Conner Gallery, New York, New York.

1991: "Outrageous Desire: The Politics and Aesthetics of Representation in Recent Work by Lesbian and Gay Artists," Rutgers University, Mason Gross School of the Arts, New Brunswick, New Jersey; "Situation: Perspectives on Work by Lesbian and Gay Artists," curated by Nayland Blake and Pam Gregg, New Langton Arts, San Francisco, California.

1992: "On a Queer Day You Can See Forever," Eye Gallery, San Francisco, California.

1993: "2 Much: The Gay and Lesbian Experience," curated by Lucy R. Lippard, UMC Fine Arts Gallery, The University of Colorado at Boulder.

1994: "Stonewall: Breakthroughs," 494 Gallery, New York, New York; "Stonewall 25: Imaginings of the Gay Past, Celebrating the Gay Present," curated by Bill Arning, White Columns, New York, New York; and many other exhibitions nationwide.

1995: "A Family Affair: Gay and Lesbian Issues of Domestic Life," curated by Deborah Bright, Atlanta College of Art Gallery, Georgia; "In a Different Light," curated by Nayland Blake and Lawrence Rinder, University Art Museum and Pacific Film Archive, University of California, Berkeley; "Pervert," curated by Catherine Lord, Fine Arts Gallery, University of California, Irvine; "Fag-o-sites," Gallery 400, University of Illinois at Chicago.

1997: "Queer in the Year 2000: The Millennium Understood," Parsons School of Design, New York, New York.

There are many additional exhibitions that could not be listed, and each year Stonewall celebrations nationwide contribute to this growing history.

Significant Exhibitions Addressing AIDS

1987: "Art against AIDS," Gracie Mansion Gallery, New York, New York; "Art about AIDS," Freedman Gallery, Albright College, Reading, New York.

1989: "Whitnesses: Against Our Vanishing," curated by Nan Golden, Artists Space, New York, New York; "Against Nature," Los Angeles Contemporary Exhibitions (LACE), California.

1990: "The Indomitable Spirit," International Center of Photography, New York, New York; "AIDS = AIDS", The BAUhouse, Baltimore, Maryland.

1991: "From Media to Metaphor: Art about AIDS," curated by Robert Atkins and Thomas Sokolowski of Independent Curators, Inc., New York, New York (traveled); "Art Fights AIDS," WORKS, San Jose, California.

1993: "Art against AIDS," Peggy Guggenheim Museum, Venice, Italy; Guggenheim Museum, SoHo, New York, New York; "In the Face of AIDS," Adam's Art Center, Dunkirk, New York.

1994: "Creating in Crisis: Making Art in the Age of AIDS," curated by Jeffrey Grove, Michael Milligan, and Dan Postotnik, SPACES, Cleveland, Ohio.

Significant Lesbian Exhibitions

1978: "A Lesbian Show," curated by Harmony Hammond, 112 Greene Street Workshop, New York, New York.

1980: "The Great American Lesbian Art Show" (GALAS), curated by Bia Lowe, Louise Moore, Jody Palmer, Barbara Stopha, Tyaga, and Terry Wolverton, at The Woman's Building, Los Angeles, California (plus over 50 exhibits nationwide).

1990: "All But the Obvious," curated by Pam Gregg, Los Angeles Contemporary Exhibitions (LACE), California.

1992: "The Lesbian Museum: 10,000 Years of Penis Envy," Franklin Furnace, New York, New York.

1994: "Lesbian Voices in the Arts," Cork Gallery, Lincoln Center, New York, New York.

1996: "Gender, Fucked," curated by Harmony Hammond and Catherine Lord, Center on Contemporary Art (CoCA), Seattle, Washington.

ARCHITECTURE: OVERVIEW

This section on American architects attempts to do three things. The first is to retrieve gay/lesbian architects from history and identify current architects (including those who prefer the contemporary term of queer) working in the field. I will look at specific designers and their careers to describe the contributions they made to architecture. While I will not cover anyone in too much detail, I hope to provide an overview of the field as well as an introduction to the people and their major works.

By identifying architects as gay/lesbian, I uncover what are often unknown truths about people's lives. Since sexuality is a prominent aspect in our lives, it influences our work as well. This identifying process does not reduce the final design project nor does it necessarily provide links between one gay/lesbian architect and another. Instead, my "naming" is an attempt to give these architects fuller lives and expand their visibility. While some of those discussed kept their private lives hidden and wished to be judged by their work alone, I include their sexuality as a fact of life, as part of the influences that go into the design process and its completion.

My second intent is to discuss how non-architects occupy space and thereby, influence architecture. As gays/lesbians claim and define space, their presence affects personal, communal, and urban issues. The creation of gay/lesbian "ghettos," often in neglected areas, or the sometimes-controversial gentrification of ethnic neighborhoods is a rather visible achievement of gay/lesbian communities. In contrast, some public parks and bathrooms have been used as spaces for sexual relations by gay, straight, and bisexual men. The "threat" of homosexual visibility has meant the removal of plantings, the closing of restrooms, and the surveillance of private space in public territories.

The third area of discussion is the growing interest in what is called Queer Space. Queer Space combines the conscious occupation of space with an activist agenda. Most of the spaces we know were developed to support majority positions, to make heterosexuals feel comfortable. This is sometimes achieved by excluding homosexuals and other marginalized groups. The prominent public action group in the early 1990s, Queer Nation, with its slogan "We're Here, We're Queer, Get Used To It," staged kiss-ins at shopping malls and weddings near conservative churches in order to infiltrate the public spaces that tried to quiet their lives. They understood that space is a social construction. As individuals in this society, queer people attempt to break down or at least point to the spatial hierarchies that surround them in order to change them.

Gay and Lesbian Architects from the 19th and 20th Centuries

Architecture is the design, planning, and construction of residential, public, and commercial spaces and buildings and their grouping into neighborhoods and cities. The arrangement of space, material, and light shelters and protects inhabitants from a sometimes-unpredictable environment. The architect is the person who designs, organizes, and draws out the plans for these places and then sees that these plans are followed by the contractors and workers who construct the buildings. He/she tries to balance efficiency and comfort, use and beauty, proportion and scale. What we regard as architectural style can vary widely depending on personal, regional, and national concerns. Sexuality is but one factor in the mix.

Gay men and the occasional lesbian have always held positions of influence in the design professions. (The field has been extremely slow to accept and promote woman architects.) For a while, it was rumored that all interior designers were gay men. Today we have a better sense of the mix of gays/lesbians in the profession. However, a lot of research still needs to be done to recover the past. Recent research on architects alone has claimed the homosexual orientation of Louis H. Sullivan (1856-1924), Ralph Adams Cram (1863-1942), Julia Morgan (1872-1957), and Eleanor Raymond (1887-1989). Since buildings survive their creators' lives, material on the final product, the actual artifact, is prevalent but material on the personal lives that created them is harder to come by.

For those architects (of the ones who follow, all are male) whose careers can be traced to the pre- as well as post-Stonewall periods, I have found a varying degree of openness about sexuality. While often an open secret within the profession, it is hard to detect how clients and the general public viewed these men. Philip Johnson (1906-) is one of the people responsible for bringing the International Style to the United States. He has had a long, if often critically lambasted, career. While never completely hiding his long-term relationship with curator David Whitney, Johnson did not officially come out until 1993, when his biography by Franz Schulze was released.

Bruce Goff (1904-82), Paul Rudolph (1918-97), and Charles Moore (1925-93) came to prominence by rejecting the International Style. The modern glass boxes that were constructed in cities across the country had become neutral containers; they were often characterless and repetitious. The group of architects who rebelled against modernism developed new styles of architecture such as Brutalism, Postmodernism, and more recently, Deconstruction. They manipulated shape and form to achieve their desired effects. Varied building forms and different structural solutions helped bring the architects to fame.

While sexuality may have adversely affected the careers of some architects, it did not hold back others. Paul Rudolph and Charles Moore, both highly respected, each chaired the department of architecture at Yale University. Bruce Goff chaired the program at the University of Oklahoma. Jorge Silvetti (1941-) is currently head of the architecture program at the Graduate School of Design at Harvard University. Robert Stern (1939-) has sat on the board of the Walt Disney Company and has taught for many years at Columbia University. Alan Buchsbaum (1935-87), considered

Model for the Cathedral of Hope, Dallas, Texas, designed by Philip Johnson.

one of the creators of the High Tech Style, designed apartments for a healthy list of celebrities including Bette Midler, Diane Keaton, and Christie Brinkley.

A number of gay architects have headed up the architectural departments at major museums: Philip Johnson at the Museum of Modern Art in New York, Mark Robbins (1956-) at the Wexner Center of Art in Columbus Ohio, and Aaron Betsky at the Museum of Modern Art in San Francisco. Many have also written about architecture and space. Herbert Muschamp is the architecture critic of the *New York Times*. Stanley Abercrombie, Jonathan Boorstein, Arthur Drexler, Meyer Rus, Jim Russell, Joel Sanders, Henry Urbach, and Wayne Attoe are responsible for numerous articles, magazines, and books. Ralph Adams Cram (in 1928) and Philip Johnson (in 1979) are among the very few architects who have appeared on the cover of *Time* magazine.

Regionally, gay/lesbian architects have come from and lived around the country, although the list (like most prominent architects) is concentrated on the East and West coasts. Philip Johnson, Robert Stern, Alan Buchsbaum, and Roger Ferri (1949-91) all came to prominence in New York. Charles Moore, Julia Morgan, and Frank Israel (1945-96) all lived and worked in California. Judging from the playful and some would say anarchic quality of the work, the rules that apply to many architects around the county do not really exist in California.

While the sexuality of architects has received little analysis, changes are occurring. In June 1994, coinciding with the 25th anniversary of the Stonewall Riots, New York's OLGAD, the Organization of Lesbian and Gay Architects and Designers, sponsored Design Pride '94, the first international conference for queer practitioners. With the theme, "Reclaiming Our Past/Mapping Our Future," speakers brought up the sexuality of architects from the past, addressed issues of professional invisibility and workplace discrimination, and explored the relations between cultural identity, place-making, and design sensibility.

At the same time, an exhibit entitled "Design Legacies" served as a tribute to architects and designers who had died of AIDS. The exhibit, sponsored by OLGAD, DIFFA (founded in 1984, the Design Industries Foundation Fighting AIDS funds service and education programs in the U.S.), and the Elsie de Wolfe Foundation (Elsie de Wolfe, 1865-1950, was a lesbian who is considered to be the first professional interior designer. She helped remove the dark woods and heavy curtains of Victorian-era tastes, and in their place brought light colors and casual settings.), included such architects as Alan Buchsbaum, Roger Ferri, Mel Hamilton, and Mark Kaminski. Since that exhibit, many other gay architects have died of AIDS, including Frank Israel.

The American Institute of Architects (AIA), a national organization, began sponsoring an annual diversity conference in 1994.

The conference focuses on the links between the design professions, genders, sexualities, cultures, and experiences. Annually, at least one of the sessions or workshops focuses on gay/lesbian/queer issues. Out of these conferences, an AIA gay and lesbian caucus has developed. The conference has also brought about changes in other architectural organizations. The Association of Collegiate Schools of Architecture, the National Trust for Historic Preservation, and the Society of Architectural Historians have all featured papers on queer subjects at their conferences.

In 1996, there seemed no greater sign of the changes taking place in the architectural profession than the appearance of Philip Johnson, perhaps the most famous architect in the United States, on the cover of *Out*, a gay and lesbian magazine. Asked to design a new sanctuary for the Dallas branch of the Universal Fellowship of Metropolitan Community Churches (MCC), the nation's largest gay and lesbian religious denomination, Johnson made public his design for the Cathedral of Hope. The 2500-seat sanctuary, larger than two football fields, rises at the altar to the height of an eleven-story building. Johnson describes the project as "my big chance to make a civic statement," one that will be a symbol of strength, hope, and unity.

Monumental in scale, startling in appearance, this unconventional design has been called a concrete iceberg. This house of worship includes traditional elements such as stained glass, choir loft, baptistery, organ, center aisle, and pews as well as non-traditional elements such as walls that tilt, lean, bulge, twist, curve, and fold. The Reverend Michael Piazza, senior pastor at the Cathedral, says that the building design, with "no parallel lines and no straight surfaces," is "intentional. It symbolizes strength, steadfastness and continuity for people of faith who have long since been disenfranchised by religious intolerance."

Herbert Muschamp in the *New York Times* wrote: "The formal mutability of Johnson's cathedral takes on a particular meaning from the congregation it will house. As a congregation of lesbians and gay men, the Metropolitan Community Church has a social and psychological as well as a spiritual mission. It ministers not only, or even primarily, to the needs of gay people for self-acceptance. It ministers to society's need for self-acceptance; for the wisdom to perceive that gay men and lesbians are integral to society, not alien from it" (Muschamp, p. 29).

Gays, Lesbians, and Urban Space

People create their physical, social, and political environments in order to have a space for physical survival, personal expression, and cultural liberation. Gays/lesbians have too often been silenced in their daily routines, following the dominant social relations and sometimes passively absorbing the negative messages about gay/lesbian life that surround them.

With the emergence of the modern gay/lesbian movement in the 1960s and 1970s, gays/lesbians have taken a more active role in the shape, meaning, and direction of space. Their places validate the reality of their lives as social and sexual beings. These spaces tell the world that they have the same right to be here as anyone else. The territories of the bar, disco, community center, church, public park, and public street create the personal and social networks that help form communities. A visible territory, a place where people work, live, and socialize that is both identifiable and defensible, plays a significant role in one's way of being and helps accelerate the shifts in society's attitudes.

Historically, gays/lesbians have often moved to large urban areas to escape the sometimes-provincial attitudes of their birthplaces and to find larger groups of men/women "like them." It used to be easy to recognize gay/lesbian spaces within the city. They hid their entrances and darkened their windows, closing themselves off from their surroundings. They camouflaged their insides with solid doors and, if they had a sign at all, it was discreet and quiet. One came to know the bars through word-of-mouth or intuition. Gays/lesbians developed what is sometimes referred to as "gaydar," the ability to read a building for what goes on behind the facade.

That learned skill may no longer be necessary. Today, the glass is clear, the signs are neon, and gay/lesbian spaces jut out onto the sidewalk demanding a presence for themselves. These spaces are no different from other spaces: they are all commercial ventures trying to succeed in competitive economic times. Today, gay/lesbian communities can be active and visible environments providing legal protection from anti-gay discrimination; community centers where a large array of organizations meet; health care facilities focusing on needs; publications and bookstores for news and information; clubs, theaters, and coffee houses for entertainment; and a multitude of other services that are relevant and necessary to gay/lesbian lives.

Urban areas where there are a large congregations of gay/lesbian residents and visitors include: the Castro and Mission in San Francisco, California; Greenwich Village and now Chelsea in New York City; Park Slope in Brooklyn, New York; West Hollywood, California (the first town in the country to have gays/lesbians control the government); Silverlake, California; Hillcrest in San Diego, California; Midtown in Atlanta, Georgia; East Lakeview in Chicago, Illinois; Capitol Hill in Seattle, Washington; Miami Beach, Florida; Boston's South End, Northhampton, and Jamaica Plain in Massachusetts; Dupont Circle in Washington, D.C.; Montrose in Houston, Texas; Oak Lawn in Dallas, Texas; and the Upper French Quarter and Faubourg Marigny in New Orleans, Louisiana. Resort towns that cater to a large gay/lesbian clientele include: Provincetown, Massachusetts; Palm Springs, Russian River, and Laguna Beach, California; Key West, Florida; Rehoboth Beach, Delaware; Fire Island, New York; New Hope, New Jersey; Saugatuck, Michigan; Eureka Springs, Arkansas; and Ogunquit, Maine.

While architectural space may not paint a gay history, the appropriation of space with users and uses not intended by the original architects and builders has led to the creation of original environments. Often, when gays and lesbians grow up and realize their difference from the dominant iconography that surrounds them and exclusion from the accepted activities that everyone else seems to participate in, they experience profound rejection. Some distance themselves from the people around them. Some find or create satisfying communities. Some stress their difference while others construct lives in which they can hide or "fit in."

One means to define oneself is through collection; by appropriating a history one can begin to create an identity. Some gay men collect artifacts in order to construct a place for themselves and a place in history. (It may be because society has not, until recently, begun to sanction a homosexual history.) The rehabilitation of existing buildings, the development of "gay ghettos," constructs a stable environment for self-expression. This concentration of gay/lesbian residents results in an architectural exuberance coupled with practicality. Houses are remade to fit the lifestyles of their inhabitants. Rooms are reorganized, amenities are added, rainbow flags are hung in order to mark the lives who reside there.

Queer Space

For anyone who has grown up outside the standards of "normality" and "conformity," those standards are oppressive, economically, politically, and physically. In order to deform and reform the accepted discourses, models, and stereotypes, queer people have begun to create their own categories through their work. Being queer alters perspective; one looks at the world differently. Queer Space, then, is the conscious recognition of sexual difference in architectural projects. It defies and resists existing structures of power by shaping space through the relationship of sexuality, identity, and place-making.

The queer use of space offers fluctuating positions; queer people assert their flexible identities rather than take on the identities imposed by others. Imagine a culture where the institutions of heterosexuality do not determine human relationships and order society. The presence of same-sex or transgendered partners on the streets, kissing or holding hands, and the discomfort and social anxiety it can cause, helps one understand how straight the city is.

Queer space is a place where identity is affirmed, not questioned, where spiritual, cultural, and emotional attachments can form, where ideas can be proposed and developed. By bringing issues of queer experience into the public realm, queer space helps locate and position minority communities and socially distinct groups against oppressive environs.

As examples, we can look to "House Rules," an exhibit from 1994 organized by Mark Robbins that brought together 10 teams of architects, social critics, and theorists to propose alternatives to the single-family home. A few of the projects had a queer bias.

"Queers in a Single Family Space," a project by theorists Michael Moon and Eve Kosofsky Sedgwick, with architects Benjamin Gianni and Scott Weir, inserted a hidden stairway to the garage between bedroom closets in a typical suburban house. The stair makes it possible for children or adults to sneak out of the house unnoticed. The project also acknowledges the mutual closet raids by parents and teens seeking knowledge of each other's sexual materials.

Architectural theorist Henry Urbach and the Interim Office of Architecture looked at the ambiguous threshold of the closet. At this potent and highly charged boundary, a world of "normality" confronts its hidden desires; individuals find out things they did not know or did not want to know.

The proposal by art historian Jonathan Crary with architect Joel Sanders places two back-to-back houses on a single lot in which strategic apertures in the bedrooms and kitchens allow the occupants to peer into the unit next door. A lap pool connecting both houses below grade allows neighbors to swim over for a visit instead of knocking at the back door. The project questions the stability and cohesion of suburban attitudes and separations.

Theorist Allucquere Roseanne Stone with architects Steven Fong and Suzan Selcuk also took on the spatial arrangement of suburbia by orienting a house so that front and back yards merge into a single outdoor space exposed to the street. The project explores how designed spaces enable or inhibit self-presentation. This new design, in which they place a person in the process of changing gender, alters the hidden, private spaces of traditional yards. By

transitioning a divided yard into one side-yard, a new kind of community can emerge.

"Queer Space," an exhibition at the Storefront for Art and Architecture, showed how gays and lesbians establish their own territory in an ostensibly straight environment. Some works were site-specific, such as nine New York places marked with pink triangles installed by REPOhistory, an artists' collective. There were other installations mapping the ways gays and lesbians carry out their day-to-day rituals next to their straight neighbors, the internal workings of one's mental space, the recollection of places where one came out of the closet, and the site-specific pleasures of looking, innuendo, and fantasy.

Steven Harris has designed a project involving locker rooms with translucent shower stalls on which the occupants' shadow profiles appear. There are also partitions that are cut to reveal rather than hide people. Kennedy Violich Architecture created new bathrooms for the Boston Center for the Arts. Hinting at issues of gender instability, the present women's room exists in the former men's room. It has the remains of urinals now cut down to the ground, their bowls filled with clear resin. In the men's room (now housed in the former women's room), the holes for the piping from removed toilets have been filled in with white epoxy, vivid marks on a dark floor. The stalls in the men's room have steel walls that have been gouged and filled in. The walls remind one of the peep and glory holes that used to be prevalent in public bathrooms.

Architecture grows out of the social and political issues important to the architect, the needs of the end users, the material available, and the building techniques that are developed. Queer Space explores the relationship of the body to space and investigates what places become when inhabited by sexual minorities. Each of us perceives and uses space in a subjective manner; interpretation varies from person to person. If architecture can be described as a series of constructed relationships, then one's status in society, one's cultural identity, one's differences affect the creative process. Queer Space is a design sensibility based not just on sexuality, but also on the possibility of disrupting and expanding the occupation of space in our society.

PROMINENT PEOPLE

Laura Aguilar (1959-)

Laura Aguilar was born in San Gabriel, California, in 1959. Aguilar attended East Los Angeles Community College and went on to participate in numerous photography workshops, including the Friends of Photography's workshops in 1989, and the Santa Fe Photographic Workshops in 1991. Aguilar's "Latina Lesbian Series," mostly dating from 1987-88, were shot in a straight documentary format that included handwritten narratives beneath each image. Employing this familiar form, this work sought to give representation to an underserved portion of the lesbian community. Without tackling the various positions around lesbian invisibility, one can still address questions surrounding the presence or absence of representations within dominant culture, which are closely linked with questions surrounding a community's ability to be represented and to self-represent, and to identify with those representations. Documentary photography as a medium has had to respond to the unequal power dynamic at work within any subject/object relationship. It has been argued that this dynamic shifts within collaborative or community-supported projects. Aguilar's early work can be seen as a part of the documentary projects that came out of the women's art movement in the 1970s. To a large extent, such work has been positioned outside of avant-garde practices and has yet to be adequately theorized. Aguilar lives in Rosemead, California.

Selected Solo Exhibitions: 1986: "The Black & White of It All: Portraits by Laura Aguilar," Los Angeles Photography Center, California. 1989: "The World Around Me, Black & White Photography of Laura Aguilar," Los Angeles City Hall, Bridge Gallery, California; "The Photography of Laura Aguilar," Los Angeles Contemporary Exhibitions (bookstore), California.

Selected Group Exhibitions: 1987: "Women Photographers in America 1987," Municipal Art Gallery, Barnsdall Art Park, Los Angeles, California. 1990: "Laura Aguilar & Joe Smoke," Highways Performance Space Gallery, Los Angeles, California; "All But the Obvious," Los Angeles Contemporary Exhibitions (LACE), California. 1991: "Laura Aguilar & Ester Hernandez, Tangible Realities," Women's Center Gallery, University of California, Santa Barbara; "Situation: Perspectives on Work by Lesbian and Gay Artists," New Langton Arts, San Francisco, California. 1992: "Breaking Barriers: Revisualizing the Urban Landscape," Santa Monica Museum of Art, California. 1993: "Aperto 93," at "Biennale di Venezia," Venice, Italy. 1994: "Fire Without Gold," Center for Photography at Woodstock, New York; "Bad Girls," The New Museum of Contemporary Art, New York, New York; "Bad Girls West," Wight Gallery, University of California, Los Angeles. 1995: "Vital Signs," Municipal Art Gallery, Barnsdall Art Park, Los Angeles, California; "P.L.A.N. – Photography Los Angeles County," Los Angeles County Museum of Art, California; "In A Different Light," University Art Museum, University of California, Berkeley; "Pervert," Fine Arts Gallery, University of California, Irvine; "Pride and Prejudice," 494 Gallery, New York, New York; "The Portrait Now," Elga Wimmer Gallery, New York, New York; "Deterritorialization," Center Cultural De La Raza, San Diego, California; "James D. Phelan Art Award in Photography Exhibition," San Francisco Camerawork, California. 1996: "American Voices: Latin American Photographers in the United States," Smithsonian Institute's International Gallery, Washington, D.C., organized by Photo Fest Inc., Houston, Texas; "Sexual Politics: Judy Chicago's *Dinner Party* in Feminist Art History," UCLA at the Armand Hammer Museum of Art and Cultural Center, Los Angeles, California; 1997: "Shifting Terrains: Laura Aguilar + Maxine Walker," Zone Gallery, Newcastle-upon-Tyne, England; "Sunshine & Noir: Art in Los Angeles 1960-97," Louisiana Museum of Modern Art, Humlebaek, Denmark (traveled). *KGD*

Judie Bamber (1961-)

Judie Bamber was born in Detroit, Michigan, in 1961 and received a B.F.A. from the California Institute of the Arts, Valencia. In 1994, Bamber completed a series of meticulously rendered paintings, most measuring just over six inches tall and less than two inches wide, depicting the genitalia of a single woman. Indescribably well-crafted, these images confront the viewer in what might be seen as the ultimate feminist gesture. Rendered in micro-photographic detail, each image is quickly distinguished from the next, and at least for the novice, each configuration of the clitoris and lips are surprisingly diverse. The intimate scale of these works requires the viewer to approach rather closely in a somewhat embarrassing examination, only to reveal the technical virtuosity of each brush stroke. Experientially, it is the material presence of these *objet* that so absolutely deconstructs any associations between this work and commercially produced erotic/pornographic

images. Formally, much erotic or pornographic imagery relies on some degree of spatial posturing in order to suggest an implied narrative or scenario. Conventionally, it is important for the majority of viewers to be able to recognize an erotic potential in relationship to the narrative of the scene. In eliminating all perspectival space, Bamber also eliminates all social space, leaving the viewer little room for conventional narrative projection. Historically in art, one need only think of Corbet's "L'Origin du monde," 1866, in the Musée d'Orsay, to recognize the significance played by the perspectival distortions of the flesh with regard to the intended eroticism of the image. In Bamber's work we find the exposed vagina, even more isolated and fetishized, and preserved upon a rectilinear visual plain that excludes nearly all but the genitalia itself. At first glance such disembodied forms are unsettling and unclear in their implications, but a closer investigation reveals that the images are composed of a vast web of brush stokes whose near invisible traces speak of a sustained concentration that pushes the work past the immediacy of the pornographic into the extended contemplation of their material creation. Bamber currently lives in New York City.

Selected Solo Exhibitions: 1989: Larie Rubin Gallery, New York, New York. 1990, 1991: Roy Boyd Gallery, Santa Monica, California. 1992: Rubin/Spangle Gallery, New York, New York. 1994, 1996: Richard Telles Fine Art, Los Angeles, California.

Selected Group Exhibitions: 1987: "LA Hot & Cool," MIT List Visual Art Center, Cambridge, Massachusetts; Jeffrey Linden Gallery, Los Angeles, California. 1988: "LA Hot & Cool: Selections," Stux Gallery, New York, New York; "Contention," New Langton Arts, San Francisco, California; "LACE Annuale," Los Angeles Contemporary Exhibitions (LACE), California. 1989: "Thick and Thin," Fahey/Klein Gallery, Los Angeles, California; "Climate 89," Laurie Rubin Gallery, New York, New York; "300 Years of Still Life," Michael Kohn Gallery, Los Angeles, California. 1990: "Faces," Marc Richards Gallery, Los Angeles, California. 1991: "Uprooted," N.A.M.E., Chicago, Illinois. 1992: "In Pursuit of a Devoted Repulsion," Roy Boyd Gallery, Santa Monica, California. 1993: "Regarding Masculinity," Arthur Roger Gallery, New Orleans, Louisiana; "Contemporary Identities: 23 Artists, The Phoenix Triennial," Phoenix Art Museum, Arizona. 1994: "Bad Girls West," Wright Art Gallery, University of California, Los Angeles. 1995: "In a Different Light," University Art Museum, University of California, Berkeley; "Pervert," Fine Arts Gallery, University of California, Irvine; "The Moderns," Feature, New York, New York. 1996: "Sexual Politics: Judy Chicago's *Dinner Party* in Feminist Art History," UCLA at the Armand Hammer Museum of Art and Cultural Center, Los Angeles, California; "Drawing from L.A.," The Armory Center for the Arts, Pasadena, California. *KGD*

Nayland Blake (1960-)

Nayland Blake was born in New York City in 1960. Blake received a B.F.A. from Bard College in 1982, and an M.F.A. from the California Institute of the Arts, Valencia, in 1984. His "Restraint" and "Table" pieces frequently combine the medicinal coolness of stainless steel with the highly suggestive qualities of leather restraints, eye rings, knives, and other objects that imply a number of semi-fetishistic applications to the viewer. These scenarios are veiled beneath the minimalist trappings of the objects themselves. It is the strategic deployment of artistic conventions that signals the viewer that he/she should be prepared to read not only the material object itself, but to recognize its context within the institutional space of the museum or gallery. In turn, such work challenges the lingering ideal of artistic "aura," that is to say the notion of the art object as either transcendental or ahistorical: either of which might emphasize the mastery of a technical skill or embody an expectation of complete self-evidence, neither of which problematizes the visual experience within historical and cultural meta-narratives. This is nowhere more clear than in his recent work, which manipulates cartoon-like rabbits in order to engage the viewer in a range of discussions around archetypal male behavior like sex and violence. As a gay male of African and European descent, his use of the "bunny" has also been seen as a modern twist of the Uncle Remus tales. Blake lives in San Francisco.

Selected Solo Exhibitions: 1989: "The Schreber Suite," MATRIX Gallery, University Art Museum, Berkeley, California; Richard Kuhlenschmidt Gallery, Santa Monica, California; "The Ellision of Failed Effect," Mincher/Wilcox Gallery, San Francisco, California. 1990: Mincher/Wilcox Gallery, San Francisco, California; "Punch Agonistes," Richard Kuhlenschmidt Gallery, Santa Monica, California. 1992: Residency and Exhibition, Milch Foundation, London; Galerie Xavier Hufkens, Brussels, Belgium; Mincher/Wilcox Gallery, San Francisco, California. 1993: "The Philosophers Suite," San Francisco Artspace, California; "Stoney End," Matthew Marks Gallery, New York, New York; Jack Hanley Gallery, San Francisco, California. 1994: "The Philosopher's Suite," Thread Waxing Space, New York, New York; "El Dorado," Christopher Grimes Gallery, Santa Monica, California. 1995: "Video," Matthew Marks Gallery, New York, New York; Jack Hanley Gallery, San Francisco, California. 1996: "Hare Attitudes," Contemporary Arts Museum, Houston, Texas; "Hare Hole," Christopher Grimes Gallery, Santa Monica, California. 1997: "The Black/White Album," Matthew Marks Gallery, New York, New York.

Selected Group Exhibitions: 1993: "Mr. Serling's Neighborhood," Christopher Grimes Gallery, Santa Monica, California; "Building a Collection: The Department of Contemporary Art," Museum of Fine Arts, Boston, Massachusetts; "I am the Enunciator," Thread Waxing Space, New York, New York; "The Uncanny," Sonsbeek, Arnhem; "I Love You More Than My Own Death," Biennale de Venizia, Venice, Italy. 1994: "Body and Soul," The Baltimore Museum of Art, Maryland; "Outside the Frame: Performance and the Object," Cleveland Center for Contemporary Art, Ohio; "Don't Leave Me This Way: Art in the Age of AIDS," National Gallery of Australia, Canberra; "Black Male," Whitney Museum of American Art, New York, New York. 1995: "In a Different Light," (co-curator) University Art Museum and Pacific Film Archive, University of California, Berkeley; "Into a New Museum—Recent Gifts and Acquisitions of Contemporary Art," San Francisco Museum of Modern Art, California. 1996: "Intermission," Basilico Fine Art, New York, New York; "a/drift," Center for Curatorial Studies Museum, Bard College, Annandale-On-Hudson, New York. 1997: "New Work: Drawings Today," San Francisco Museum of Modern Art, California.

Books: Richard Armstrong, *Mind Over Matter,* New York, Whitney Museum of American Art, 1990; Nayland Blake, Lawrence Rinder, Amy Scholder, eds. *In A Different Light: Visual Culture, Sexual Identity, Queer Practice.* San Francisco, City Light Books, 1995. *KGD*

Ross Bleckner (1949-)

Born in New York, Ross Bleckner was raised in Hewlett Harbor on Long Island. He received a B.A. from New York Univer-

sity in 1971 and an M.F.A. from the California Institute of the Arts, Valencia, in 1973. At New York University Bleckner studied with internationally recognized artists such as Sol Lewitt and Chuck Close, but it was at CalArts that Bleckner became close friends with his contemporaries David Salle and Julian Schnabel. Together they were to shape much of the New York Gallery scene in the late 1980s. In fact, it was Bleckner who introduced Salle and Schnabel to his dealer, Mary Boone. Bleckner's well-known vessel and urn paintings seem to rise out of their dark under painting, their ghostly shapes appearing within what at first glance might appear to be a modernist color field painting. These works are incredibly luminous in their use of color, and for many these images have become haunting tributes for those lost to AIDS. In the 1970s, color field paintings had been typically minimalist in their use of form, usually including little more than simple lines or grids, and so Bleckner's insertion of such recognizable forms, particularly in light of their social references, absolutely recontextualized these earlier modernist painting traditions. Whether it is a hummingbird or a viral cell, Bleckner has repeatedly culled radiant images from the simplest of forms, forms that bridge the gap between Modernist abstraction and the changing world around us by reinscribing the figurative somewhere between the heroic and the sublime. Bleckner currently lives in New York.

Selected Solo Exhibitions: 1979, 1980, 1981,1983: Mary Boone Gallery, New York, New York. 1984: Nature Morte Gallery New York, New York. 1985: Boston Museum School, Massachusetts. 1986,1987: Mary Boone Gallery, New York, New York. 1988: San Francisco Museum of Modern Art, California; Mary Boone Gallery, New York, New York. 1989: Milwaukee Art Museum, Wisconsin; Carnegie Museum of Art, Pittsburgh, Pennsylvania. 1991: Mary Boone Gallery, New York, New York; Fred Hoffman Fine Art, Santa Monica, California. 1994: Mary Boone Gallery, New York, New York. 1995: Solomon R. Guggenheim Museum, New York, New York. 1996: Mary Boone Gallery, New York, New York.

Selected Group Exhibitions: 1975: "Whitney Biennial," Whitney Museum of American Art, New York, New York; Paula Cooper Gallery, New York, New York. 1979: "New Paintings/New York," Hayward Gallery, London. 1983: "Drawing it Out," Baskerville and Watson Gallery, New York, New York; John Weber Gallery, New York, New York. 1984: "Modern Expressionists," Sidney Janis Gallery, New York, New York; "Still Life with Transaction: Former Objects, New Moral Arrangements, and the History of Surfaces," International With Monument Gallery, New York, New York. 1985: "Paravision," Postmasters Gallery, New York, New York; "Currents," Institute of Contemporary Art, Boston, Massachusetts. 1986: "End Game: Reference and Simulation in Recent American Painting and Sculpture," Institute of Contemporary Art, Boston, Massachusetts. 1987: "Whitney Biennial," Whitney Museum of American Art, New York, New York. 1988: "Biennale of Sydney," Sydney; "Carnegie International," Carnegie Museum of Art, Pittsburgh, Pennsylvania. 1989: "Pre-Pop Post-Appropriation," Stux Gallery, New York, New York; "Whitney Biennial," Whitney Museum of American Art, New York, New York, "Prospect 89," Frankfurt Kunstverein and Schirn Kunsthalle, Frankfurt; "10+10: Contemporary Soviet and American Painters," Modern Arts Museum of Fort Worth, Texas (traveled). 1991: "Nayland Blake, Ross Bleckner, Donald Moffett," Simon Watson Gallery, New York, New York; "From Media to Metaphor: Art about AIDS," Independent Curators, Inc., New York, New York (traveled). 1993: "I Am the Enunciator," Thread Waxing Space, New York, New York. 1995: "Painting-Singular Object," The National Museum of Modern Art, Tokyo. *KGD*

Deborah Bright (1950-)

Deborah Bright was born in Washington, D.C., in 1950. She received a B.A. from Wheaton College in Wheaton, Illinois, in 1972 and an M.F.A. in painting from the University of Chicago in 1975. She is currently an associate professor of art history and photography, as well as the graduate program coordinator, for the photography department at the Rhode Island School of Design. It has been argued that Bright's work begins where photography's social documentary tradition ended. If Lewis Hine and projects like those encouraged by the Farm Security Administration laid the groundwork for Bright and a generation of younger artists such as Connie Hatch and Allan Sekula, then critical theory was to provide these and other artists with the means to examine the presumed "transparence," or truth, of the photographic document. In Bright's own work, one recognizes that a single object, artifact, or concept may be metaphorically unpacked, in turn revealing at least some of the material and social conditions of its given historical moment. Her pivotal essay, "Of Mother Nature and Marlboro Men: An Inquiry into the Cultural Meaning of Landscape Photography," excavates the historical documentation surrounding the development of the National Parks and other landscape spaces. Such documents are then read as texts, as artifacts that can be seen as material repositories of the social and historical conditions that produced them.

Selected Solo Exhibitions: 1982: "Battlefield Panoramas," Chicago Public Library Cultural Center, Illinois; "Photomural Installations," San Francisco Camerawork, California. 1983: Battlefield Panoramas," WPA Gallery, Chicago, Illinois. 1992: "Monumental Fictions/Lost Histories: Chicago Stories," University Art Gallery, University of California, Irvine, and Mason Gross School of the Arts, Rutgers University, New Brunswick, New Jersey. 1996: "Being and Riding," the Maurine and Robert Rothschild Gallery, The Bunting Institute, Cambridge, Massachusetts. 1997: "All that is Solid," Atlanta College of Art Gallery, Georgia, and Wheeler Gallery, Providence, Rhode Island.

Selected Group Exhibitions: 1981: "Chicago Photographers," WPA Gallery, Chicago, Illinois. 1984: "Tenth Anniversary Show," San Francisco Camerawork, California. 1985: "Wide Perspectives," and "Chicago Photographers Project," Museum of Contemporary Photography, Chicago, Illinois. 1986: "Images of War," Hallwalls, Buffalo, New York. 1987: "Boston Now: Projects," Institute of Contemporary Art, Boston, Massachusetts. 1988: "That's What It's All About," Erector Square Gallery, New Haven, Connecticut. 1989: "Landscape at Risk," Houston Center for Photography, Texas. 1990: "Polemical Landscapes," The California Museum of Photography, Riverside; "Sexuality and the Politics of Obscurity," Hera Gallery, Wakefield, Illinois; "Looking at Labor," Randolph Street Gallery, Chicago, Illinois. 1991: "Working: Six Media Installations," Artists Space, New York, New York; "Stolen Glances: Lesbians Take Photographs," Stills Gallery, Edinburgh, Scotland; "Lost Illusions: Recent Landscape Art," The Vancouver Art Gallery, British Colombia, Canada. 1992: "Between Home and Heaven: Contemporary Landscape Photography in America," National Museum of Art, Smithsonian Institute, Washington, D.C.; "On a Queer Day You Can See Forever," Eye Gallery, San Francisco, California. 1993: "2 Much: The Gay and Lesbian Experience," UMC Fine Arts Gallery, The University of Colorado at Boulder. 1994: "Diagnosis: Breast Cancer," Denise Bibro Fine Arts, New York, New York, and Peter Madero Gallery, New York, New York; "Telling . . . Stories," Randolph Street Gallery, Chicago, Illinois. 1995: "No Place to Hide," Jan Kesner Gallery, Los Angeles, California; "Global Sweatshop," Art In General, New York, New York; "Warworks: Women, Photography and the Iconography of War," The Victoria and Albert Museum, London (traveled). 1996: "Gender, fucked," Center on Contemporary Art (CoCA), Seattle, Washington.

Books: Deborah Bright, *The Passionate Camera,* London, Routledge, 1998; Grant Kester, *All that Is Solid: An Installation by Deborah Bright,* Atlanta, Atlanta College of Art, 1997. *KGD*

Romaine Brooks (1874-1970)

Romaine Brooks was born Beatrice Romaine Goddard in Rome in 1874 but spent much of her early childhood in and around New York. From 1880 to 1881, Brooks lived with her mother's washerwoman, selling papers in the street, before being rescued by an aunt and moving to Chestnut Hill, Pennsylvania. Brooks received her early education from an Episcopal school in New Jersey, eventually attending schools and traveling throughout England, Italy, and France. In 1898 and 1899, Brooks concentrated her studies on art, studying at the Circolo Artistico and the Scuola Nazionale in Rome, before briefly going on to study at the Académie Colarossi in Paris. In 1902, after the deaths of her mother and brother, Brooks became financially independent and eventually established residence in Paris as an American expatriate with sojourns in Italy during each of the World Wars. Today she is best known for her portraits of the French elite from the arts and letters. Painted in a muted palette, Brook's portrait "Una, Lady Troubridge," 1924, depicts a young lady with a monocle, short hair, and a tuxedo-like costume; in short, all the trappings of a gender radical from the 1920s. The sitter was actually a close friend of the author Radclyffe Hall, whose novel *The Well of Loneliness* has remained a cornerstone of early lesbian literature. Lady Troubridge would eventually write of her life with Radclyffe Hall. Brooks died in Nice, France, on 7 December 1970.

Selected Solo Exhibitions: 1910: Galeries Durand-Ruel, Paris. 1925: "L'Exposition de Romaine Brooks," L'Alpine Club Gallery, London; Galerie J. Charpentier, Paris; Wildenstein Galleries, New York, New York. 1931: "L'Exposition de dessins de Romaine Brooks," Galerie Th. Briant, Paris. 1935: Arts Club of Chicago, Illinois. 1971: "Romaine Brooks, 'Thief of Souls,'" National Collection of Fine Arts, Smithsonian Institution, Washington, D.C.; "Romaine Brooks, 'Thief of Souls,'" Whitney Museum of American Art, New York, New York. 1976: "Romaine Brooks, 'Thief of Souls'," organized by the Smithsonian Institution Traveling Exhibitions Service, Washington, D.C.(traveled). 1980: "Romaine Brooks, 1874-1970," organized for the Ramapo Consortium of Colleges by the National Collection of Fine Arts, Smithsonian Institution, Washington, D.C.

Selected Group Exhibitions: 1911: Goupil Gallery, London. 1913: "Prima Esposizione internazionale d'arte della 'Secessione'," Rome. 1920, 1922: Salon de la Société Nationale des Beaux-Arts, Paris. 1926: Galerie Jean Charpentier, Paris. 1972: "Old Mistresses: Women Artists of the Past," Walters Art Gallery, Baltimore, Maryland. 1973: "Diaghilev and His Collaborators," Cordier & Ekstrom Gallery, New York, New York. 1974: "American Self

Portraits," International Exhibitions Foundation, Smithsonian Institute, Washington, D.C. 1984: "The Feminist Gaze: Women Depicted by Women, 1900-30," Whitney Museum of American Art, New York, New York.

Books: Adelyn D. Breeskin, *Romaine Brooks,* Second Edition, Washington D.C., Smithsonian Institute Press, 1986. *KGD*

Bruce of Los Angeles (1909-1974)

Bruce of Los Angeles was born Bruce Harry Bellas in Alliance, Nebraska, on 7 July 1909. While in Nebraska he embarked on a career in chemistry and actually went on to teach before moving to California in the early 1940s. Always a dabbler in the photographic medium, Bruce began his photographic career by working as a freelance photographer, documenting bodybuilding competitions for a rapidly growing market of consumers interested in bodybuilding culture. By the late 1940s, Bruce had become a staff photographer for Joe Weider publications and spent much of his time traveling to bodybuilding contests in several states. His photographs appeared in such magazines as *Strength and Health, Muscle Power,* and *Tomorrow's Man.* Initially intended for bodybuilding enthusiasts, these magazines also caught the attention of an emerging gay subculture, and by the 1960s Bruce was able to publish his own magazine entitled *The Male Figure.* Postal regulations forbade the posting of frontal male nudity until 1968, and as a result many of his nudes were sold out of the hotel rooms he occupied on his travels across the country. His work can still be found in both the seediest of bookstores and the best of auction houses, and reminds one of the difficulties of historically relocating such work on a scale somewhere between nostalgia and the most radical revisionist notion of a queer avantgarde. Bruce Harry Bellas died in 1974.

Selected Exhibitions: Only in recent years has Bruce of Los Angeles's work been included within a fine arts context, but it has been included in numerous group exhibitions and at least one solo exhibition at Wessel O'Conner Gallery in N.Y.

Books: Jim Dolinsky, editor, *Bruce of Los Angeles,* Bruno Gmünder, Berlin, 1990. *KGD*

Alan J. Buchsbaum (1935-1987)

Alan J. Buchsbaum, an originator of the High Tech style, was born in Savannah, Georgia. He received his B.S. from Georgia Institute of Technology and his Bachelor of Architecture Degree from MIT. After working for several New York offices, he established his own firm in 1967. He died in 1987 of complications from AIDS.

In the houses, stores, apartments, and lofts he designed, Buchsbaum created informal and adventurous spaces. Through his original use of off-the-shelf, industrial materials, he helped discover and create high tech settings. By transforming raw loft spaces into witty, polished, high-style yet unpretentious interiors, he became an influential designer among movie stars, accommodating the freer, moneyed lifestyles of the late 1960s and 1970s. He also designed the places where these people shopped including the New York stores for Charivari and Ecco shoes, and socialized, including Film Forum, an alternative movie theater.

His fresh approach included symbols of pop culture such as inflatable plastic hassocks to the more serious Bank of England swiveling chairs. He worked with extravagant colors and textures while remaining nonchalant so that furniture could be moved around and interiors could be personalized. He designed the framework in which people became what they wanted to be.

"The older I get, the more impatient I become with polite conversation," he said. "I always find myself wanting to open with some insulting question, like 'How much did that cost?' or 'Is the rumor I hear about you true?' The last thing I'm interested in is a living room that is going to promote polite banality" (Bethany, Section 4, p. 100). *IT*

Loren Cameron (1959-)

Loren Cameron was born in Pasadena, California, in 1959 but spent his adolescence in rural Arkansas. He moved to San Francisco in 1979 and began the transition from female to male in 1987. Largely self-taught as a photographer, Cameron is known for his documentary images, although these have not yet been widely exhibited. His project "Body Alchemy" documents the struggles and triumphs of the FTM community, most of which take place within the framework of daily survival. For many, it is the images of genital reconstruction that are most striking, because they make clear the complexity of such choices. For others, it is the simple, rather deadpan documentary style of Cameron's environmental portraits that most undermines conventional gender play precisely by emulating it. Cameron's project seeks to enlighten a broad-based audience about the conditions, histories, and practices of the FTM community, and in this respect it does so with the candor and earnestness found in the best of documentary work. Cameron currently lives in San Francisco, California.

Selected Exhibitions: 848 Community Art Space, San Francisco, California; Highways Gallery, Santa Monica, California; San Jose Institute of Contemporary Art, California; Richmond Art Center, California; "Strange Fruits," Los Angeles Center for Photographic Study (LACPS), California.

Books: Loren Cameron, *Body Alchemy,* Pittsburgh, Cleis Press, 1996. *KGD*

Mark I. Chester (1950-)

Mark I. Chester was born in Milwaukee in 1950. He received a B.S. from the University of Wisconsin in Madison in 1972, and then an M.S. in educational psychology in 1973. Chester is a self-described gay radical sex photographer, as well as a curator, performer, and writer, and was admittedly disowned by his own biological family. Chester's photography is the result of interactions with friends, lovers, and his chosen family, in an attempt to articulate the complexity of emergent or underrecognized communities. Chester claims to have had his work destroyed, removed, and severely criticized by the San Francisco police department, fire department, newspapers, and other media. For many unsympathetic viewers or those marginally tolerant of the queer community, Chester's work has been seen as obscene. Discussions around the emergence or recognition of a radical sex community can lead to heated debates and comparisons with historically established racial, national, and cultural constructions of community. Nevertheless, the existence of gay radical practices must be recognized on some level. Once accepted, Chester's project can most readily be understood within the context of documentary traditions established by artists such as Diane Arbus and Robert Mapplethorpe, whose environmental portraits continue to spark debates around the line between affinity and exploitation, along with a gamut of questions surrounding individual expression versus community representation. Like Mapplethorpe's, Chester's work has also been criticized as obscene or pornographic, a criticism that Chester rejects, citing instead a history of oppression that stretches back to the destruction of D. H. Lawrence's erotic paintings, the scandalous furor that accompanied F. Holland Day's self-portrait as the crucified Christ, the critical denouncement of Allen Ginsberg's *Howl* as obscene, and of course the obscenity trial of the Cincinnati Museum for showing Robert Mapplethorpe's photographs.

Selected Solo Exhibitions: 1993: "Mark I. Chester-Sexual Photography: 1980-92," Leslie-Lohman Gay Art Foundation, New York, New York.

Selected Group Exhibitions: 1986: "Naked Eyes-A Celebration of Gay Men's Visual Arts," International Gay and Lesbian Archives, Los Angeles, California. 1987: "Chain Reaction 3," San Francisco Arts Commission Gallery, California. 1990: "Against the Tide: The Homoerotic Image in the Age of Censorship and AIDS conservatism, repression and American culture," Nexus/SAME, Atlanta, Georgia; "69 Hours," a trans-oceanic, multi-media event, part of an international conference on AIDS, various locales, including San Francisco, California. 1991: "Art Fights AIDS," WORKS, San Jose, California; "Art and the Forbidden: Exploring the Sacred Magnifying Cultural and Sexual Taboos," Student Union Art Gallery, San Francisco State University, California. 1992: "Seeing Red, White or Blue: Censorship in America," Visual Arts Center of Alaska, Anchorage. 1993: "Rated X," Neikrug Photographica, New York, New York; "Gay Photo Annual," Leslie-Lohman Gay Art Foundation, New York, New York.

Books: Mark I. Chester, afterword by Pat Califia, *Diary of a Thought Criminal,* San Francisco, RFD Press, 1996. *KGD*

Tee A. Corinne (1943-)

Corinne was born in St. Petersburg, Florida, in 1943. She grew up in places as varied as North Carolina and the Bahamas. She received a B.A. from the University of South Florida in 1965, and an M.F.A. from Pratt Institute, Brooklyn, in 1968. Portfolios of her work have been published in *Feminist Studies, Gallerie: Women's Art, The Advocate, The Inciter,* and *Femalia.* Corinne was a co-facilitator of the Feminist Photography Ovulars, 1979-81, and a co-founder of *The Blatant Image: A Magazine of Feminist Photography,* 1981-83. She is also a founding board member and past co-chair of the Gay and Lesbian Caucus (an affiliated society of the College Art Association), and a past national board member of the Women's Caucus for Art. Corinne's interest in how women's bodies age has resulted in a recent photographic series entitled "Goddesses for the New Millennium," which documents the torsos of 20 women from ages 23 to 84. Photographically manipulating her images, Corinne seeks to challenge the cultural obsessions with the young, thin, female form by creating beautifully rendered images of the mature form, envisioning it as a symbol of strength and fertility, and with a photographer's eye to the play of light and dark against the robust curvature of her subjects. In her artist's statement Corinne explains that, "When I started the series I thought I was going to make pictures of my lumpy middle-aged body and those of my friends. Instead, I found echoes of ancient figures of power, the voluptuous Venus of Willendorf, the bas-relief Venus of Laussel, Clycadic figures, and sculptures from Moravia, Malta, India, and Mexico . . . . [F]igures traditionally labeled as fertility goddesses are more likely celebrations of menopausal women's bodies, images with raging, changing, flowing lines." Corinne lives in San Francisco.

Selected Solo Exhibitions: 1996: Maude Kerns Art Center, Eugene, Oregon; Artworks Gallery, Grants Pass, Oregon.

Selected Group Exhibitions: 1980: Womanart Gallery, New York, New York; "The Great American Lesbian Art Show (GALAS)," Women's Building, Los Angeles, California. 1981: "Heresies Show," Hibbs Gallery, New York, New York. 1982: Ollie's Gallery, Oak-

land, California. 1984: "Erotica," University of Wisconsin, Milwaukee. 1987: Central Washington University, Ellensburg; Coos Art Museum, Coos Bay, Oregon. 1988: Grants Pass Museum of Art, Oregon. 1991: "Visible for a Change," Harvard University, Boston, Massachusetts. 1994: "Unity '94," The Cork Gallery, Lincoln Center, New York, New York. 1995: "In a Different Light," University Art Museum, University of California, Berkeley. 1996: "Sexual Politics: Judy Chicago's *Dinner Party* in Feminist Art History," UCLA at the Armand Hammer Museum of Art and Cultural Center, Los Angeles, California. *KGD*

Ralph Adams Cram (1863-1942)

Ralph Adams Cram was born in Hampton Falls, New Hampshire, went to Exeter High School, and moved to Boston in 1881. At the age of 17, he helped to create a close-knit network of architects, artists, writers, and intellectuals that has been documented in the book *Boston Bohemia.* After a trip to Europe and conversion to Anglo-Catholicism, Cram started his own firm in 1889. His creative and personal collaboration with Bertram Grosvenor Goodhue began in 1892 and lasted until the early 1900s. The Cadet Chapel for the Military Academy at West Point brought them both national fame.

A leading practitioner of the Gothic style, Cram is best known for his American Gothic churches, including: All Saints' in Ashmont, Boston, St. Thomas's and Cathedral of St. John the Divine in New York City, and University Chapel at Princeton. The influence of his work can be found in many suburban parish churches nationwide.

The evidence collected in *Boston Bohemia* implies that Cram and many of his male friends were homosexual at a time when the term homosexual was just being recognized. They were dandies, breaking the barriers of convention and provoking the conservatism and reserve of Boston residents. Throughout his life, Cram focused on the relationship of art and religion, and struggled with the contradiction between sexuality and religion. His energy and anxiety went into his work; his churches became the communicator of beliefs, convictions, emotions, and drives. "Anglo-Catholicism became for Cram the principal expression or carrier of his sexual orientation—and in a most characteristically Platonic way" (Shand-Tucci, p. 198). *IT*

Patricia Cronin (1963-)

Patricia Cronin was born in Beverly, Massachusetts, in 1963. She received a B.F.A. from Rhode Island College in Providence in 1986, and an M.F.A. from Brooklyn College in New York in 1988. In 1991, she attended the Skowhegan School of Painting and Sculpture in Skowhegan, Maine. Cronin first became known for her watercolor series based on Polaroids she took of herself and her lover, Deborah Kass. Their nude and semi-clothed bodies were taken from a rather intimate range and resulted in strangely explicit documents of female-to-female sexuality, their interlocking limbs and folds of flesh at times becoming distorted to the point of abstraction. Cronin's recent work has gone in a slightly different direction but is still concerned with female sexuality, or perhaps more appropriately, pre-sexuality, and her "Pony Tales" project suggests a somewhat tongue-in-cheek exploration of horses. Cronin culls photographs submitted by teens to magazines such as *Young Rider* and *Horse Illustrated* for her portraits, and with names such as "Parfait Prince" and "Palatial Summer," Cronin seeks to draw our attention to the subversive play between bubble gum cuteness and a fetishism implicit in such pre-sexual obsessions.

Selected Solo Exhibitions: 1997: "Pony Tales," Wooster Gardens, New York, New York. 1998: "Unbridled," Wooster Gardens, New York, New York; "Pony Tales," Arthur Roger Gallery, New Orleans, Louisiana.

Selected Group Exhibitions: 1993: "Coming to Power: 25 Years of Sexually Xplicit Art by Women," David Zwirner Gallery, New York, New York, and Real Art Ways, Hartford, Connecticut; "The Return of the Cadavre Exquis," The Drawing Center, New York, New York. (traveled); "Songs of Retribution," Richard Anderson Gallery, New York, New York; "Women's Art, Women's Lives, Women's Issues," Tweed Gallery, New York, New York. 1994: "The Long Weekend," Trial Balloon, New York, New York; "Stonewall 25: Imaginings of the Gay Past, Celebrating the Gay Present," White Columns, New York, New York. 1995: "Pervert," Fine Arts Gallery, University of California, Irvine; "Way Cool," Exit Art/First World, New York, New York. 1996: "The Strange Power of Cheap Sentiment (Or A Bientot To Irony), White Columns, New York, New York; "Gender, fucked," Center on Contemporary Art (CoCA), Seattle, Washington; Richard Anderson Gallery, New York, New York; Arthur Roger Gallery, New Orleans, Louisiana. 1997: "The Name of the Place," Casey Kaplan Gallery, New York, New York; "Queer in the Year 2000: The Millenium Understood," Parsons School of Design, New York, New York. *KGD*

Nicole Eisenman (1965-)

Nicole Eisenman was born in Verdun, France, in 1965. She received an M.F.A. from the Rhode Island School of Design in Providence in 1987. Her drawing style is reminiscent of many WPA works, particularly those employing sweeping compositions, and are particularly reminiscent of those done by painters such as Thomas Hart Benton and Paul Cadmus. Eisenman creates fantastic compositions that at times sprawl across entire walls, their rings of interwoven female figures forming fantastic tangles whose anxious interrelations become the subject. In "Logger House," Eisenman depicts a male figure tied to a tree, his body about to be cut in two by a large circular saw. Throughout the scene, women can be seen socializing, embracing, and cheering. Eisenman's sense of the fantastic and the humorous sets her apart from many of her contemporaries, and while her drawing style is as accessible as a *Saturday Evening Post* illustration, it is the sardonic wit of each piece that holds one's attention. In her "Self-Portrait with Exploded Whitney," included in the 1995 Biennial exhibition at the Whitney Museum of American Art in New York, Eisenman applies her biting wit to the museum itself, depicting it as a shamble of ruins. Originally cited as a reaction to her assigned location on the basement level of the museum, her critique nevertheless touched a nerve among many reviewers who saw it as a scathing critique of museums per se. Eisenman's work has taken the shape of painting, drawing, collage, assemblage, found objects, murals, and of course installations. Eisenman currently lives in New York City.

Selected Solo Exhibitions: 1992: Shoshana Wayne Gallery, Santa Monica, California. 1993: Shoshana Wayne Gallery, Santa Monica, California; Trial Balloon, New York, New York. 1994: Jack Tilton Gallery, New York, New York. 1995: Centraal Museum Utrecht, Utrecht. 1996: Jack Tilton Gallery, New York, New York; Galerie Cokkie Snoei, Rotterdam (w/Jason Fox). 1998: Shoshana Wayne Gallery, Santa Monica, California.

Selected Group Exhibitions: 1993: "Bad Girls," Institute of Contemporary Art, London; "Coming to Power: 25 Years of Sexually Xplicit Art by Women," David Zwirner Gallery, New York, New York; "1920," Exit Art/The First World, New York, New York;

Elizabeth Koury Gallery, New York, New York. 1994: Kunstverein Munich, Germany; Sonnabend Gallery, New York, New York; White Columns, New York, New York; "The Seventh Wave," Museum of Contemporary Art, Los Angeles, California; "Bad Girls," Wright Art Gallery, University of California, Los Angeles. 1995: "Pervert," Fine Arts Gallery, University of California, Irvine; "Picassoid," Whitney Museum of American Art, New York, New York; "Inside Out: Psychological Self Portraits," Aldrich Museum of Art, Ridgefield, Connecticut; "Way Cool," Exit Art, New York, New York; "Whitney Biennial," Whitney Museum of American Art, New York, New York; "Selection and Betrayal," Galerie Krinzinger, Vienna. 1996: "Identity Crisis: Selections from the Whitney Museum of American Art," Alexandros Soutzos Museum, Athens, Greece, (traveled); "a/drift," Bard College Center for Curatorial Studies, Annandale-on-Hudson, New York; "Be Specific," Rosamund Felsen Gallery, Santa Monica, California; "Gender, fucked," Center on Contemporary Art (CoCA), Seattle, Washington; "The Comic Depiction of Sex in American Art: Nicole Eisenman, Erika Rothenberg, Jimmy Shaw, Benjamin Weissman, Sue Williams," Galerie in Haus 19, Munich; "Sexual Politics: Judy Chicago's *Dinner Party* in Feminist Art History," UCLA at the Armand Hammer Museum of Art and Cultural Center, Los Angeles, California; "Defining the Nineties: Consensus-Making In New York, Miami and Los Angeles," Museum of Contemporary Art, Miami, Florida; "Screen," Friedrich Petzel Gallery, New York. 1997: "The Gaze," Momenta Art, New York, New York; "The Road Show," Bronwyn Keenan Gallery, New York, New York; "Sex/Industry," Stephan Stux Gallery, New York, New York; "The Name of the Place," Casey Kaplan, New York, New York. *KGD*

Roger Ferri (1949-1991)

Roger Ferri grew up in Wantagh, Long Island, and studied architecture at Pratt Institute in Brooklyn and figure drawing, anatomy, and painting at the Art Students League of New York. Ferri opened his own firm in 1987 and built a variety of houses based on a harmony between landscape and architecture. He designed the building and its surroundings as well as the furniture and decorative objects inside, hoping to revive American craftsmanship. The house he built on Fire Island acts as a balcony overlooking the ocean. During his too-brief life, he was a visiting design critic at the University of Miami and taught freehand drawing for architects at Columbia University. After his death of AIDS, his drawings and archives were given to the Avery Library at Columbia.

Using drawing as a conveyor of ideas about architecture, Ferri produced in 1979 "A Proposal for an American Architecture and Urbanism in the Post Petroleum Age" for an exhibit at New York's Museum of Modern Art. He proposed that architects should return to nature as the source of their inspiration. His drawings show a pedestrian city centered on a great domed hall. Around the dome are groups of columns that burst into bloom. The curves of lily-like petals form a vaulted roof. His other influential theoretical projects integrating nature and structure include a 44-story glass skyscraper in Manhattan imagined as a mountain of trees, goats, rocky landscapes, and running streams. While the core of the project was a rather orthodox modern tower, it was surrounded by terraces and hanging gardens. *IT*

Robert Flynt

Robert Flynt has spent the last decade making surreal and sensual photo-montages of the male nude. His figures exist in an ethereal, weightless environment. Using an underwater camera, Flynt captures the improvised movements of his swimming collaborators. In each photograph, one also finds images drawn from a variety of sources such as anatomy charts, first aid textbooks, astronomical maps, 19th-century etchings, menswear catalogues, and even classic Roman sculptures. Such juxtapositions allow Flynt to create collage-like images addressing a broad range of themes, each concerned with issues of design, composition, and strangely reminiscent of alternative process work from the 1960s and 1970s, but replacing darkroom manipulations with digital ones.

Selected Exhibitions: 1990: "AIDS=AIDS" and "BEAMS," The BAUhouse, Baltimore, Maryland; Witkin Gallery, New York, New York. 1991: "The Body in Question," Burden Gallery, New York, New York; Southern Light Gallery, Amarillo, Texas; Photographic Resource Center, Boston, Massachusetts. 1992: "New Photography 8," Museum of Modern Art, New York, New York; "Medicine Body", Illinois State University, Normal; Witkin Gallery, New York, New York; "De Man," Brouwersgracht Twee Drie Acht, Amsterdam; "Figure," Pyramid Arts Center, Rochester, New York; Anderes Ufer, Berlin. 1993: "Proof Positive," Maryland Art Place, Baltimore; "Queering Family Values," Maryland Art Place, Baltimore; Nye Gomez Gallery, Baltimore, Maryland. 1994: "Sea Change," Josh Baer Gallery, New York, New York. 1995: "Camera Invisible," Temple Abroad Gallery, Rome; "The Body Photographic," Contemporary Art Center, New Orleans, Louisiana; Craig Krull Gallery, Santa Monica, California; G. Gibson Gallery, Seattle, Washington. 1996: "Blind Trust," Donna Beam Fine Art Gallery, University of Nevada, Las Vegas; Craig Krull Gallery, Santa Monica, California; "Masculine Measures," Kohler Arts Center, Sheboygan, Wisconsin.

Books: Berman/Groff, *Whitman's Men,* Universe/Rizzoli, New York, 1996; E. Cooper, *Fully Exposed,* Routledge, New York, 1995; Sappington/Stallings, *Uncontrollable Bodies,* Bay Press, Seattle, 1994. *KGD*

Gilbert (1943-) & George (1942-)

Gilbert was born in Dolomites, Italy, in 1943. George was born in Devon, England, in 1942. Gilbert studied at the Wolkenstein School of Art, the Hallein School of Art, and the Munich Academy of Art. George studied at the Dartington Adult Education Center, the Dartington Hall College of Art, and the Oxford School of Art. They met and studied at the St. Martins School of Art in London, 1967. Pushing the boundaries of art-making beyond the conventional limits of the gallery space, Gilbert & George are perhaps best known for their piece "The Singing Sculpture," in which they appeared suit- clad, standing on a table, with their faces and hands covered in metallic paint, holding a hat and cane (one each, and exchanged between verses), and singing a pop tuned entitled "Underneath the Arches." From 1969 to 1973, they appeared not only in museums but at pop concerts and night clubs, performing as much as eight hours a day for as long as a fortnight. In doing so, Gilbert & George sought to challenge conventional notions of artistic value and the material privileging of the object over the artistic gesture. In foregrounding action, time, and space, Gilbert & George's performances posited individuals as indistinguishable, and focused attention away from the artist as virtuoso, in an attempt to assert the merits of experiential truth, while playfully suggesting the transformative power of such conceptually driven work.

Selected Solo Exhibitions: 1968: "Shit and Cunt," Robert Fraser Gallery, London. "Frozen into the Nature for You Art," Françoise Lambert Gallery, Milan. 1970: "Frozen into the Nature for You

Art," Heiner Friedrich Gallery, Cologne. 1971: "The Paintings," Whitechapel Art Gallery, London; "The Paintings," Stedelijk Museum, Amsterdam; "The Paintings," Kunstverein, Düsseldorf. 1973: "The Shrubberies & Singing Sculpture," National Gallery of New South Wales, John Kaldor Project, Sydney; "The Shrubberies & Singing Sculpture," National Gallery of Victoria, John Kaldor Project, Melbourne. 1975: "Bloody Life," Sonnabend Gallery, Paris; "Bloody Life," Sonnabend Gallery, Geneva; "Post-Card Sculptures," Sperone Westwater Fischer, New York, New York; "Dead Boards," Sonnabend Gallery, New York, New York. 1976: "The General Jungle," Albright-Knox Art Gallery, Buffalo, New York. 1977: "Red Morning," Sperone Fischer Gallery, Basle. 1978: "New Photo-Pieces," Sonnabend Gallery, New York, New York. 1980: "New Photo-Pieces," Sonnabend Gallery, New York, New York; "Modern Fears," Anthony d'Offay Gallery, London. 1981: "Photo-Pieces 1971-80," Kunsthalle, Düsseldorf; "Photo-Pieces 1971-80," Kunsthalle, Berlin; "Photo-Pieces 1971-80," Centre national d'Art et de Culture Georges Pompidou, Paris; "Photo-Pieces 1971-80," Whitechapel Art Gallery, London. 1982: "New Photo-Pieces," Gewad, Ghent. 1983: "Modern Faith," Sonnabend Gallery, New York, New York; "Photo-Pieces 1980-82," David Bellman Gallery, Toronto, Ontario, Canada; "New Works," Crousel-Hussenot Gallery, Paris. 1984: "The Believing World," Anthony d'Offay Gallery, London; "Hands Up," Gallery Schellman & Klüser, Munich. "Gilbert & George," The Baltimore Museum of Art, Maryland; "Gilbert & George," The Solomon R. Guggenheim Museum, New York, New York. 1985: "New Moral Works," Sonnabend Gallery, New York, New York. 1986: "Pictures 1982-85," Kunsthall, Basle; "Pictures 1982-85," CAPC Musée d'Art contemporain, Bordeaux. 1987: "The 1986 Pictures," Sonnabend Gallery, New York, New York; "New Pictures," Anthony d'Offay Gallery, London; "Gilbert & George Pictures," Aldrich Museum of Contemporary Art, Connecticut; "Pictures 1982-86," Palais des Beaux-Arts, Brussels; "Pictures 1982-86," Hayward Gallery, London. 1988: "The 1988 Pictures," Ascan Crone Gallery, Hamburg. 1989: "The 1988 Pictures," Christian Stein Gallery, Milan; "For AIDS Exhibition," Anthony d'Offay Gallery, London.

Selected Group Exhibitions: have been omitted in order to allow more room for entries above.

Books, Wolf Jahn, trans. by David Britt, *The Art of Gilbert & George or an Aesthetic of Existence,* New York, Thames and Hudson, 1989. *KGD*

Robert Gober (1954-)

Robert Gober was born in Wallingford, Connecticut, in 1954. He studied at the Tyler School of Art, Temple University in Rome, from 1973 to 1974, and received a B.F.A. from Middlebury College in 1976. When Marcel Duchamp placed his Readymade artwork entitled "Fountain" (a signed urinal), 1917, within a gallery space he forever transformed our understanding of the artistic gesture. Duchamp's Readymades transformed the artist's role from that of craftsman to that of author. Gober, on the other hand, inverts the Readymade by painstakingly recreating everyday objects such as a sink, a closet, a bag of donuts, and a piece of plywood. Even in those surreal instances where a limb protrudes from a gallery wall, it is the realism that signals the rupture of expectations and provides the viewer with the first measure of the artistic intervention. Gober currently lives and works in New York.

Solo Exhibitions: 1984: Paula Cooper Gallery, New York, New York. 1985: Paula Cooper Gallery, New York, New York; Daniel

Weinberg Gallery, Los Angeles, California. 1987: Paula Cooper Gallery, New York, New York. 1988: The Art Institute of Chicago, Illinois; Galerie Gisela Capitain, Cologne; Galerie Max Hetzler, Cologne. 1989: Paula Cooper Gallery, New York, New York. 1991: Galerie Nationale de Jea de Paume, Paris (traveled). 1992: "Robert Gober," Dia Center for the Arts, New York, New York.

Selected Group Exhibitions: 1988: "Utopia Post Utopia: Configurations of Nature and Culture in Recent Sculpture and Photography," The Institute of Contemporary Art, Boston, Massachusetts; "XLIII Biennale di Venezia," Venice, Italy. 1989: "Whitney Biennial," Whitney Museum of American Art, New York, New York; "Horn of Plenty: Sixteen Artist from N.Y.C," Stedelijk Museum. 1990: "Culture and Commentary: An Eighties Perspective," Hirshhorn Museum and Sculpture Garden, Smithsonian Institution, Washington, D.C.; "Objectives: The New Sculpture," Newport Harbor Art Museum, Newport, California. 1991: "Whitney Biennial," Whitney Museum of American Art, New York, New York. 1992: "Documenta 9," Kassel. 1993: "Whitney Biennial," Whitney Museum of American Art, New York, New York.

Books: Dave Hickey, *Robert Gober: In the Dancehall of the Dead,* New York, Dia Center for the Arts, 1993. *KGD*

Bruce Goff (1904-1982)

Bruce Alonzo Goff was born in Alton, Kansas. While never university-educated in architecture (he had no formal education beyond high school), he began an apprenticeship at age 12 and completed his first major commission at age 22. Goff then opened his own small office where, although he completed some churches, his best known projects are residential. From 1947 to 1955, Goff was chairman of the School of Architecture at the University of Oklahoma. His influence is still strong at the school and each semester, a Goff Professor is appointed for a period of two to eight weeks.

Goff practiced what might be called organic architecture. He fully appreciated nature and the human spirit and tried to express his passions through his designs. His imaginative houses follow a intricate geometry; they grow in three dimensions according to the needs of the clients and site. His creative problem-solving and the potential for human involvement led to highly individual and poetic solutions. Goff is quoted as saying that "my work is not 'in the Main Stream.' I am thankful for that. I live for what I can accomplish, not in the shadows of those before or now" (Cook, 1978, Foreword).

His strange and wonderful buildings include Seabee Chapel (San Lorenzo, California) which he designed from Quonset Huts; Ledbetter House (Norman, Oklahoma) built with a cable suspension system; Ford House (Aurora, Illinois) where he used amorphous, curvilinear forms; Bavinger House (Norman), which is shaped with the curves of a seashell; and Price House (Bartlesville, Oklahoma), which has a richly jeweled interior. He is also responsible for the Shin'enkan Pavilion for Japanese Art, an addition to the Los Angeles County Museum of Art that opened in 1988, a few years after his death. *IT*

Felix Gonzalez-Torres (1958-1996)

Felix Gonzalez-Torres was born in Güaimaro, Cuba, in 1958. He was sent to Spain in 1971 by his family and eventually made his way to Puerto Rico where he lived with an uncle. In 1983, Gonzalez-Torres received a B.F.A. from Pratt Institute in Brooklyn. In 1981 and 1983, he attended the Whitney Museum's Independent Study Program. In 1987, he received an M.F.A. from the International Center of Photography and New York University. In the same year, he joined the artists' collective "Group Material." In 1990, Gonzales-Torres moved to Los Angeles, taught at CalArts, and had his first solo show at Andrea Rosen Gallery in New York. He returned to New York in 1992. Drawing from a minimalist aesthetic, Gonzalez-Torres created his stack pieces, which at first appeared as Minimalist cubes, only to reveal upon a closer inspection that each stack was in fact made of single sheets of paper that visitors were welcome to take. The stack pieces challenged the viewer to locate the art object not in the single sheet, or even in the stack for that matter, but within the concept itself. As a form, such conceptually driven work tends to frustrate the more traditional art enthusiast, but Gonzalez-Torres' work allows for a refreshing level of conceptual and physical interaction that seduces viewers with its clarity of form and function. Felix Gonzalez-Torres died of an AIDS-related illness in Miami in 1996.

Selected Solo Exhibitions: 1988: "The Workspace," New Museum of Contemporary Art, New York, New York. 1989: Sheridan Square Billboard, sponsored by the Public Art Fund, New York, New York; Brooklyn Museum, New York. 1990: "Billboard Project," in cooperation with INTAR Gallery, New York, New York; "Strange Ways, Here We Come," University of British Colombia, Vancouver, Canada; Andrea Rosen Gallery, New York, New York. 1991: Luhring Augustine Hetzler, Los Angeles, California; Massimo de Carlo, Milan; "Every Week There Is Something Different," Andrea Rosen Gallery, New York, New York. 1992: Galerie Peter Pakesch, Vienna; Andrea Rosen Gallery, New York, New York; "Billboard Project," organized by the Museum of Modern Art, New York, New York. 1993: "Travel #1," Galerie Jennifer Flay, Paris; "Travel #2," Galerie Ghislaine Hussenot, Paris; "Migrateurs: Felix Gonzales-Torres," Musée d'Art Moderne de la Ville de Paris, France; "Currents 22: Felix Gonzales-Torres," Teweles Gallery, Milwaukee Art Museum, Wisconsin; Andrea Rosen Gallery, New York, New York. 1994: "Details from Twenty Sculptures," Printed Matter, New York, New York; "Travelling," The Museum of Contemporary Art, Los Angeles, California (traveled); Matrix Gallery, University of California, Berkeley. 1995: Andrea Rosen Gallery, New York, New York; The Solomon R. Guggenheim Museum, New York, New York. 1996: "Felix Gonzalez-Torres (Girlfriend in a Coma)," Musée d'Art Moderne de La Ville de Paris, France. 1997: "Untitled (Beginning)," Andrea Rosen Gallery, New York, New York.

Selected Group Exhibitions: are far too numerous to list, with over 27 in 1997 alone.

Books: Dietmar Elger, ed. *Felix Gonzalez-Torres: Catalogue Raisonne,* Hannover, Sprengel Museum, 1997. *KGD*

Group Material

Group Material was an artists' collaborative founded in New York in 1979 to organize exhibitions and public projects on social themes. Its "AIDS Timeline" fostered an interdisciplinary approach to history that sought to counteract the isolationist AIDS policies of the Reagan, Bush, and the media, which primarily focused on "risk groups" such as gay men and intravenous drug users and ignored the larger issue of prevention. While not all of the group's members were gay or lesbian, the "AIDS Timeline" was significant, not only in bringing discussions of AIDS within museum or gallery walls, but also for its challenge to those resilient and resistant boundaries that usually separate art from advocacy. Members included: Doug Ashford, who was born in Rabat, Morocco, in 1958, received a B.F.A. from Cooper Union, New York, in 1981, and currently lives in New York; Julie Ault, who was born in Boston in 1957, studied at the University of Maine from 1973 to 1975, and currently lives in New York; Felix Gonzalez-Torres (see separate bio); and Karen Ramspacher, who was born in Pennsylvania in 1965, received a B.A. from Wellesley College in 1978, and currently lives in New York. Many other artists were invited to participate, assist, or contribute to Group Material projects.

Selected Solo Exhibitions and Projects: 1982: "Primer (for Raymond Williams)," Artists Space, New York, New York. 1984: "Timeline: The Chronicle of US Intervention in Central and Latin America," P.S. 1, Institute for Art and Urban Resources Long Island City, New York, New York. 1988: "Democracy," Dia Art Foundation, New York, New York. 1989: "AIDS Timeline," Matrix Gallery, University Art Museum, University of California, Berkeley. 1990: "AIDS Timeline (Hartford, 1990)," Wadsworth Atheneum, Hartford, Connecticut.

Selected Group Exhibitions: 1985: "Whitney Biennial," Whitney Museum of American Art, New York, New York. 1987: "Documenta 8," Kassel. 1991: "Whitney Biennial," Whitney Museum of American Art, New York, New York.

Books: Brian Wallis, ed. Democracy: A Project by Group Material, New York, Dia Art Foundation, 1990. KGD

Keith Haring (1958-1990)

Keith Haring was born in Kutztown, Pennsylvania, in 1958. He embarked on one his first adventures in 1977 when he traveled through Montana and Oregon on his way to the West Coast. His journal recounts everything from hitchhiking and camping in the Rocky Mountains to taking a bus to Disneyland. While at the School of Visual Arts in New York City in 1978 and 1979, he experimented with a calligraphy-like brush stroke, and already the playful lines of his cartoonish style could be found on the pages of his notebook. In 1980, Haring began drawing on the blank advertising panels that were such an elemental part of the New York City subways. Few would have imagined that such temporary and unnoticed spaces could be the launching pads for an international art career, not to mention Swatch watches. By 1982, Haring had his first solo exhibition at Tony Shafrazi Gallery. Characterized by maze-like intricacies, his drawings and paintings employed an all-over patterning whose Pop appeal allowed Haring to enter into popular culture and suggested an art that could live in the streets as much as in the museums. With hindsight it must be recognized that such a populist stance, while widely accepted in Europe, met with a mixed response from the art press and museum professionals in this country. Keith Haring died of an AIDS-related illness on 16 February 1990, in New York.

Selected Solo Exhibitions: 1983: Fun Gallery, New York, New York; Wadsworth Atheneum, Hartford, Connecticut. 1985: Leo Castelli Gallery, New York, New York. 1986: Galerie Daniel Templon, Paris. 1988: Hans Mayer Gallery, Dusseldorf. 1989: Gallery 121, Antwerp; Fay Gold Gallery, Atlanta, Georgia; Galerie Hete Hünermann, Dusseldorf; Commissioned by the city of Pisa to paint permanent mural on Sant'Antonio Church, Pisa; Keith Haring Foundation founded. 1990: Charles Lucien Gallery, New York, New York; Tony Shafrazi Gallery, New York, New York; Galerie Nikolaus Sonne, Berlin; Gallery 56, Geneva. 1991: Museum of Modern Art, Ostend; Ericka Meyerovich Gallery, San Francisco, California; Steffanoni Gallery, Milan. 1992: Tony Shafrazi Gallery, New York, New York. 1993: Queens Museum,

New York (traveled); "Keith Haring: A Retrospective," Mitsukoshi Museum of Art, Tokyo; "Complete Editions on Paper: 1982-90," Galerie Littmann, Basel (traveled). 1994: Tony Shafrazi Gallery, New York, New York; Retrospectives in Italy, Germany, Israel. 1995: Andre Emmerich Gallery, New York, New York; Retrospectives in Spain, and Austria.

Selected Group Exhibitions: 1982: "Documenta 7," Kassel. 1983: Biennial Exhibition, Whitney Museum of American Art, New York, New York. 1984: "XLI Biennale di Venezia," Venice. 1986: "Sacred Images in Secular Art," Whitney Museum of American Art, New York, New York. 1987: "Comic Iconoclasm," Institute of Contemporary Arts, London. 1991: "Whitney Biennial, Whitney Museum of American Art, New York, New York; 1992: "Allegories of Modernism," Museum of Modern Art, New York, New York; "From Media to Metaphor: Art about AIDS," Independent Curators, Inc., New York, New York (traveled). 1993: "American Art in the Twentieth Century: Painting and Sculpture," Martin Gropius Bau, Berlin; Royal Academy, London. 1994: "2 X Immortal: Elvis + Marilyn," McDaris Exhibition Group, Memphis, Tennessee (traveled). 1995: "In a Different Light," University Art Museum and Pacific Film Archive, University of California, Berkeley; "Male Desire: Homoerotic Images in Twentieth-Century American Art," Mary Ryan Gallery, New York, New York.

Books: John Gruen, Keith Haring: The Authorized Biography. New York, Simon & Schuster, 1991; Werner Jehle and Klaus Littmann, Keith Haring, complete Editions on Paper, 1982-1990. Stuttgart, Cantz Publishing, 1993; Germano Celant, Keith Haring, Milan, Charta Publishing, 1994; Keith Haring, Intro. by Robert Farris Thompson, Preface by David Hockney, Keith Haring Journals, New York, Penguin Books, 1996. KGD

Richard Hawkins (1961-)

Richard Hawkins was born in Mexia, Texas, in 1961. He received a B.F.A. from the University of Texas in 1984 and an M.F.A. from the California Institute of the Arts, Valencia, in 1988. Hawkins first received critical attention for his pieces composed largely from images of male models, celebrities, and bits of porno, all paper-clipped to strands of shredded felt or Naugahyde, and hanging flaccidly down the wall. Such pieces suggest a fantastically subversive level of identification and projection at play within the work. In selecting wholesome images of celebrities such as Jason Priestly and Kirk Cameron, Hawkins confronts the commodification of youthful male beauty by citing his own alienated pleasure, which is inexorably bound within this abundance of images. By employing the simplest of assemblage techniques, Hawkins relocates such pop images within a specifically queer context. This is as undeniably subversive as it is titillating, precisely because in such a context it exposes the precision with which male beauty is commodified. Hawkins's pieces at times suggest everything from self-admonishment to unrequited love. If today our desire is imagined for us in pop magazines, and experience has been replaced with the sheen of a four-color spread, then Hawkins seeks to create objects that push the viewer to the place where consumer anxiety and over-identification stand in for the pleasure of looking.

Selected Solo Exhibitions: 1992: Roy Boyd Gallery, Santa Monica, California; Mincher/Wilcox Gallery, San Francisco, California. 1993: Feature, New York, New York; Richard Telles Fine Arts, Los Angeles, California. 1995: Ynglingagatan 1, Stockholm; Richard Telles Fine Art, Los Angeles, California. 1996: Richard

Telles Fine Art, Los Angeles, California; Feature, New York, New York.

Selected Group Exhibitions: 1990: "Que Overdose!," Micher/ Wilcox Gallery, San Francisco, California. 1991: "Stussy," Feature, New York, New York; "Presenting Rearwards," Rosamund Felsen Gallery, Los Angeles, California; "Situation: Perspectives on Work by Lesbian and Gay Artists," New Langton Arts, San Francisco, California; "Examples: Cool and Lonely," Roy Boyd Gallery, Santa Monica, California. 1992: "Trouble Over So Much Skin," Feature, New York, New York; "Man Alive," Dooley Le Cappelaine, New York, New York; "In Pursuit of a Devoted Repulsion," Roy Boyd Gallery, Santa Monica, California. 1993: "Caca," Kiki, San Francisco, California; "Trisexual," TRI, Los Angeles, California; "Stoned (HighLow)," Ruth Blum Gallery, Santa Monica, California; "Commodity Image," International Center of Photography, New York, New York (traveled); "This Can't Be Love," Clay Doyle Gallery, Los Angeles, California. 1994: "Pure Beauty: Some Recent Work From Los Angeles," American Center, Paris (traveled); "Mechanical Reproduction," Galerie van Gelder, Amsterdam; "The Use of Pleasure," Terrain, San Francisco, California; "Tiny Shoes," New Langton Arts, San Francisco, California. 1995: "Its Only Rock & Roll: Currents in Contemporary Arts," The Contemporary Art Center, Cincinnati, Ohio (Traveled); "Crystal Blue Persuasion," Feature, New York, New York; "Smells Like Vinyl," Roger Merians Gallery, New York, New York; "Narcissistic Disturbances," Otis Gallery, Otis College of Art & Design, Los Angeles, California; "In a Different Light," University Art Museum and Pacific Film Archive, University of California, Berkeley. 1996: "Nirvana: Capitalism and the Consumed Image," Center on Contemporary Art (CoCA), Seattle, Washington; "How will we behave," Robert Prime, London; "Ginny Bishton, Richard Hawkins, Pae White," Richard Telles Fine Arts, Los Angeles, California. *KGD*

Hannah Höch (1889-1979)

Hannah Höch was born Anna Therese Johanne Höch in the Thuringian city of Gotha in 1889. In 1912, Höch entered the School of Applied Arts in Charlottenburg. From 1915 through 1920, she studied at the School of the Royal Museum of Applied Arts in Berlin. In 1919, Höch participated in the first Berlin Dada Exhibition, and in 1920 she was also included in the First International Dada Fair, which contained over 170 works by more than 25 artists. After the break up of the Dada group and her relations with Raoul Hausmann, she began what would be a nine-year relationship with a woman, Til Brugman, a Dutch writer. It is during this period that her photomontages begin to include numerous same-sex couples along with a slew of androgynous figures. In 1935, after her break up with Brugman, Höch met Heinz Kurt Matthier, a businessman 21 years her junior. The pair divorced after a brief marriage. Höch is recognized as bisexual, and her "New Woman" and "Ethnographic Museum" series of photomontages suggest a strangely precarious fusion of ethnographic imagery with the female form. No doubt the incongruous inclusion of the ethnographic material was intended to add a level of shock and transform the passivity historically associated with the female nude and provide a critique of the historical objectification of women. Höch died in Berlin in 1979.

Selected Solo Exhibitions: 1929: "Hannah Höch," Kunstzaal De Bron, The Hague (traveled);"Hannah Höch," Kunstzaal D'Audretsch, The Hague. 1934: "Hannah Höch," Kunstzaal D'Audretsch, The Hague. 1935: "Aquarelle en Fotomontages door

Hannah Höch," Kunstzaal D'Audretsch, The Hague. 1949: "Hannah Höch und Dada," Galerie Franz, Berlin. 1955: "Hannah Höch zeigt Aquarelle und Zeichnungen," Galerie Spitta und Leutz, Berlin. 1957: "Hannah Höch: Collagen," Galerie Gerd Rosen, Berlin. 1959: "Hannah Höch: Collagen 1959," Galerie Gerd Rosen, Berlin. 1961: "Hannah Höch: Bilder, Collagen, Aquarelle 1918-61," Galerie Nierendorf, Berlin. 1963: "Dada-Hannah Höch-Dada," Galleria del Levante, Milan (traveled). 1964: "Hannah Höch zum 75. Geburtstag," Galerie Nierendorf, Berlin. 1966: "Hannah Höch," Marlborough Gallery, London. 1968: "Hannah Höch: Aquerelle, Zeichnungen, Linolschnitte aus den Jahren 1915-65," Galerie im Schinkelsall, Berlin-Tegel. 1969: "Hannah Höch: Ölbilder, Aquerelle, Collagen, Gouachen," Kunstverein, Kassel. 1971: "Hannah Höch: Collagen aus den Jahren 1916-71," Akademie der Künste, Berlin (traveled). 1973: "Hannah Höch: Fotomontagen und Gemälde," Kunsthalle, Bielefeld; "Hannah Höch: Aquerelle, Zeichnungen, Städtische Sammlungen, Rheinhausen. 1974: "Hannah Höch: National Museum of Modern Art, Kyoto; "Hannah Höch: Collagen + Zeichnungen," Galerie Elke Dröscher, Hamburg. 1975: "Hannah Höch: Noch nicht gezeigte Blätter: Aquerelle, Collagen, Zeichnungen," Galerie Nierendorf, Berlin. 1976: "Hannah Höch: Collages, Peintures, Aquarelles, Gouaches, Dessins/Collagen, Gemälde, Aquarellen, Gouachen, Zeichnungen," Musée d'Art Moderne de la Ville de Paris (traveled); "Hannah Höch," Muzeum Sztuki, Lodz, Poland. 1977: "Hannah Höch: Collages and Photomontages," Goethe House, New York, New York; "Hannah Höch," Carrus Gallery, New York, New York. 1978: "Hannah Höch," Graphothek, Berlin; "Hannah Höch: Ein Leben mit der Pflänze," Städtisches Museum, Gelsenkirchen.

Books: Peter Boswel & Maria Makela, *The Photomontages of Hannah Höch,* essays by Peter Boswel, Carolyn Lanchner, Maria Makela, chronology by Kristin Makholm. Minneapolis, Walker Art Center, 1996. *KGD*

David Hockney (1937-)

David Hockney was born in Bradford, England in 1937. He attended Bradford Grammar School and at the age of 16 went on to study at the School of Art in Bradford. After leaving art school in 1957, Hockney completed his national service, for which he worked in a hospital in Bradford. Eventually, he studied at the Royal College of Art, where, among others he met the artist Ron Kitaj. Hockney began his career as a painter who rebelliously worked in a highly figurative manner. Hockney employed the solid color fields usually associated with modernist abstraction. In doing so, he created images that are striking in their deployment of a brightly hued palette, and his juxtaposition of solidly rendered figures and objects against flat, abstracted forms would become the hallmark of his early success. There is a playfulness in much of Hockney's work, and this is nowhere more apparent than in the quirky and somewhat scratchy lines of his many drawings. Even his highly popular Polaroid and snapshot assemblage pieces suggest a certain playfulness with regard to the medium that few traditionally trained photographers would have embraced. Hockney's set designs and recent paintings speak to his continued interest and indulgence in color, along with a greater liberation of form. The exhibitions listed below constitute about half of the total number of shows Hockney has taken part in between 1976 and the present. In addition, due to the great number of group exhibitions, only his solo exhibitions have been listed here in an attempt to give some representation to his early career. Hockney's work has spanned more than three decades and continues to af-

Drager House, Los Angeles, designed by Franklin D. Israel.

fect several areas of the arts world. Hockney lives in England and Los Angeles.

Selected Solo Exhibitions: 1963: Bear Lane Gallery, Oxford, England; "David Hockney: A Rake's Progress and Other Etchings," Editions Alecto, The Print Center, London; "David Hockney: Pictures with People In," Kasmin Limited, London. 1964: "David Hockney: A Rake's Progress and Other Etchings," Lane Gallery, Bradford, England; "Exhibition of Original Contemporary Lithographs, Including the Suite A Rake's Progress by David Hockney,"

Heffer Gallery, Cambridge, England; "David Hockney: A Rake's Progress," Prestons Art Gallery, Bolton, England; "David Hockney," Alan Gallery, New York, New York. 1965: "David Hockney: Pictures with Frames and Still Life Pictures," Kasmin Limited, London. 1966: Palais des Beaux-Arts, Brussels; Studio Marconi, Milan; "David Hockney," Galleria dell'Ariete, Milan; "David Hockney: Tekeningen en Etsen," Stedelijk Museum, Prentenkabinet, Amsterdam; "David Hockney: Preparatory Drawings of the Set for the Production of Ubu Roi by Alfred Jarry . . .

Twelve Etchings Inspired by the Poems of C.P. Cavafy," Kasmin Limited, London. 1967: Norwich School of Art, England; "David Hockney: New Paintings and Drawings," Landau-Alan Gallery, New York, New York; "David Hockney," Mala Galerija, Ljubljana. 1968: Museum of Modern Art, New York, New York; "David Hockney Exhibition," Alecto Gallery, London; "David Hockney: A Splash, a Lawn, Two Rooms, Two Stains, Some Neat Cushions and a Table," Kasmin Limited, London; "David Hockney: Oeuvrekatalog-Graphik," Galerie Mikro, Berlin. 1969: André Emmerich Gallery, New York, New York; "Exhibition of Paintings and Prints by David Hockney," Whitworth Art Gallery, Manchester, England; "David Hockney Etchings," Kasmin Limited, London. 1970: Galerie Springer, Berlin; "David Hockney," Lane Gallery, Bradford, England; "David Hockney: Paintings, Prints and Drawings, 1960-70," Whitechapel Gallery, London (traveled); "David Hockney: Six Fairy Tales from the Brothers Grimm and other New Etchings." André Emmerich Gallery, New York, New York. 1972: Renée Ziegler, Geneva; Kinsman Morrison Gallery, London; D.M. Gallery, London; Fieldborne Gallery, London; "David Hockney: New Paintings and Drawings," Kasmin Limited, London. 1973: Holdurne Museum, Bath, England; André Emmerich Gallery, New York, New York; Jordan Gallery, London; "David Hockney," Galerie Herbert Meyer-Ellinger, Franfurt; "David Hockney: Print Retrospective," M. Knoedler & Co., New York, New York. 1974: "David Hockney," Gallery 21, London; Kinsman Morrison Gallery, London; "David Hockney: Print Retrospective," D.M. Gallery, London; "David Hockney: Drawings," Dayton's Gallery 12, Minneapolis, Minnesota; "David Hockney: Tableaux et Dessins: Paintings and Drawings," Musée des Arts Décoratifs, Paris; Michael Walls, New York. 1975: Margo Leavin Gallery, Los Angeles, California; Dorothy Rosenthal Gallery, Chicago, Illinois; "David Hockney: Dessins et Gravures," Galerie Claude Bernard, Paris; Elaine Ganz European Gallery, San Francisco, California; Gallery 21, London; "David Hockney: Designs for The Rake's Progress," Manchester City Art Gallery, Manchester, England.

Books: Nikos Stangos, ed. *Pictures by David Hockney: My Early Years,* New York, Harry A. Abrams, 1979; David Hockney, Introduction by Henry Geldzahler, *David Hockney by David Hockney,* New York, Harry N. Abrams, Inc., 1976; Maurice Tuchman and Stephanie Barron, *David Hockney: A Retrospective,* Los Angeles, Los Angeles County Museum of Art, 1988. *KGD*

Frank Israel (1945-1996)

Franklin D. Israel was born in Brooklyn and grew up in Elizabeth, New Jersey. He studied architecture with Louis Kahn at the University of Pennsylvania, did post-graduate study at Yale University, and received a Master in Architecture from Columbia University. In 1973, he received the Rome Prize in Architecture for two years of study at the American Academy in Italy. After a few more years on the East Coast, Israel found his true home in the free-form traditions of Southern California. In Los Angeles, his architecture commented on and contributed to the culture of the city. Upon learning of his HIV-status, Israel was determined to continue working; he claimed his illness encouraged him to take greater risks.

Israel designed private homes for Hollywood figures such as director Robert Altman, actor Joel Grey and his partner, and agent Howard Goldberg and his partner Jim Bean. His offices for production companies include the headquarters for Propaganda Films

(Hollywood), Limelight Productions (Los Angeles), and Virgin Records (Beverly Hills). He also created sets for Paramount Studios and such films as "Star Trek: The Motion Picture" and "Night Games." "Film and architecture share the same wonderful mix of the mythical and commonplace," Israel said (Oliver, p. B8).

His buildings are beautiful, innovative, challenging, and livable. They test one's perceptions of equilibrium and order by addressing the promises and limitations of Los Angeles, a cityscape of fragmented texture with a shifting, unstable ground. Israel believed that the juxtaposition of new and old structures symbolized the heterogeneity of the contemporary city and designed his bold interiors to capture the variety, surprise, and unexpected visual experience of a sometimes schizophrenic urbanism.

For his retrospective at Los Angeles's Museum of Contemporary Art (1996), Israel designed a dynamic, sculptural environment within the museum's windowless galleries. His tilting, folding, white plaster planes, blurring lines between vertical walls and horizontal ceilings, looked to some like crumpled pieces of paper. Defying gravity and disrupting expectations, Israel created ambiguities between function, space, and scale that were wildly imaginative and entertaining.

Richard Weinstein, from the UCLA Department of Architecture and Urban Design where Israel taught, has said, "It was not necessary to explain his architecture because it gave so much delight to the eye—even though it carried many wry, edgy and even angry meanings. In this way the work faced the anxieties of the contemporary moment we all experience, and overcame them—as he did himself—with inspiring humor and strength" (Koshalek, p. F1). *IT*

Philip Johnson (1906-)

Philip Cortelyou Johnson was born in Cleveland. After graduating from Harvard, he became the founding director of the department of architecture at the Museum of Modern Art in New York. He first came to fame at the age of 26 when he curated the "International Style: Architecture since 1922" exhibit at the museum and wrote a book about the subject in collaboration with Henry-Russell Hitchcock. The book and exhibit introduced modernist European architecture to America.

Johnson became an architect at the age of 37 after attending Harvard's Graduate School of Design, and he is now among the world's most famous. His prominence rose with his much-publicized glass house in New Canaan, Connecticut, in 1949. With John Burgee, his business partner for over 20 years, Johnson designed some of the nation's most visible structures. His corporate skyscrapers designed as either stripped down International Style or flamboyant postmodernism (the postmodern movement resurrected themes from the past in a spirited if artificial way) can be seen in cities such as Boston, Denver, San Francisco, Dallas, New York, Minneapolis, and Houston. He is now part of the firm Philip Johnson, Ritchie & Fiore, with a new style sometimes referred to as Deconstruction, and working on smaller, more personal projects.

Johnson is known for his intelligence, grace, versatility, and enthusiasm. His body of work includes a variety of provocative shapes, eclectic styles, and striking visual forms. He is also known as a dilettante. Restless and unpredictable, he has had a chameleon-like career, not following any particular style. "Whoever commissions buildings buys me. I'm for sale. I'm a whore. I'm an artist" (Cook and Klotz, p. 37). This lack of conviction has often been described as a lack of artistic integrity. He borrows from numerous sources and claims to be uninterested in originality or innovation; he is more interested in aesthetics than social content or

The AT&T Building in New York City, designed by Philip Johnson.

ideology. His greatest asset may be his ability to create and re-create himself.

The various structures at Johnson's home and grounds present a career in architecture. He began with his glass house, a simple, modern rectangle, made with 8 black steel columns as a framework, transparent walls, and a brick cylinder that holds the bathroom and fireplace. He has added such stylistic experiments as a solid-walled private guest house, a concrete arched pavilion on an island in the lake, an underground painting gallery, a brick sculpture gallery with trussed skylight, a climbable tower, and a new disorienting, angle-walled entrance hall. The estate has been donated to the National Trust for Historic Preservation and will be open to the public after Johnson's death. *IT*

G. B. Jones (1965-)

Jones was born in Bowmanville, Ontario, Canada, in 1965. He is an openly queer artist, filmmaker, rock musician, writer, and magazine publisher. Popularly referred to as the female Tom of Finland, Jones has created drawings that depict a new lesbian fantastic, which is the result of the collision of leather, punk, S/M, and queer cultural history manifested in an all-out assault against dominant culture. One must be clear, however, that Jones's work does not simply mimic some idyllic gay male past, nor do her characters don gay cultural paraphernalia as a narrowly defined *lesbian chic.* Rather, its her undeniable concern with lesbian visibility, and those emergent cultural practices that are developing, changing, and being challenged within a number of lesbian communities, which is the subject of her work. Jones currently lives in Toronto, Ontario, Canada.

Selected Solo Exhibitions: 1991: Feature, New York. 1994: "Girrly Pictures: G.B. Jones," Mercer Union, Toronto.

Selected Group Exhibitions: 1990: "All But the Obvious," Los Angeles Contemporary Exhibitions, California. 1991: "Situation: Perspectives on Lesbian and Gay Artists," New Langton Arts, San Francisco, California; "Outrageous Desire: The Politics and Aesthetics of Representation in Recent Works by Gay and Lesbian Artists," Mason Gross School of the Arts at Rutgers University, New Brunswick, New Jersey. 1992: "Trouble Over So Much Skin," Feature, New York, New York; "Part Fantasy," Trial Balloon 2, New York, New York; "Drawings," Stuart Regen Gallery, Los Angeles, California. 1993: "Up With People," Feature, New York, New York; "Tom of Finland, G.B. Jones," Daniel Buchholz, Cologne; "Eau de Cologne 1983-93," Monika Sprüth Galerie, Köln; "Coming to Power: 25 Years of Sexually X-Plicit Art by Women," David Zwirner Gallery, New York, New York. 1994: Stonewall 25: Imaginings of the Gay Past, Celebrating the Gay Present," White Columns, New York, New York; "Coming to Power: 25 Years of Sexually X-Plicit Art by Women," Real Art Ways, Hartford, Connecticut; "(Tiny) SHOES," New Langton Arts, San Francisco, California; "Truth Be Told: It's All About Love," Lennon, Weinberg, Inc., New York, New York; "Oh boy, it's a girl!," Kunstverein München, Munich; Kunstraum Wien, Vienna, Austria; "Part Fantasy," Jack Hanley Gallery, San Francisco, California. 1995: "Beauty #2," The Power Plant, Toronto, Ontario; "Representational Drawings," Feature, New York, New York; "Fag-o-sites," Gallery 400, University of Illinois at Chicago, Illinois. 1997: "Flying Buttress Please," Torch, Amsterdam. *KGD*

Deborah Kass (1952-)

Deborah Kass was born in San Antonio, Texas, in 1952. Kass received a B.F.A. from the Carnegie-Mellon University in Pitts-

burgh in 1974. She studied at the Whitney Independent Study Program in 1972 and at the Art Students League in New York City from 1968 to 1970. Through her appropriation of Andy Warhol's graphic Pop style, Deborah Kass is able to insert images such as Barbra Streisand's Yentl within a tongue-in-cheek examination of identity, ethnicity, and the idea of celebrityhood. Her project "Let Us Now Praise Famous Women" examines not only famous women, but famous lesbian women, and her use of Gertrude Stein can be taken as a critique of the heterosexual desire inherent to the construction of the celebrity within Warhol's work. Kass currently lives in New York.

Selected Solo Exhibitions: 1982: Zolla/Lieberman Gallery, Chicago, Illinois. 1984, 1986: Baskerville and Watson Gallery, New York, New York. 1988: Scott Hansen Gallery, New York, New York. 1990: Simon Watson Gallery, New York, New York. 1992: "The Jewish Jackie Series and My Elvis," fiction/nonfiction, New York, New York; "The Jewish Jackie Series," Simon Waton, New York, New York. 1993: Arthur Roger Gallery, New Orleans, Louisiana; "Chairman Ma," Jose Freire Fine Art, New York, New York. 1994: Barbara Krakow Gallery, Boston, Massachusetts. 1995: Arthur Roger Gallery, New Orleans, Louisiana; "My Andy: A Retrospective," Jose Freire Fine Art, New York, New York.

Selected Group Exhibitions: 1996: "Too Jewish?: Challenging Traditional Identities," The Jewish Museum, New York, New York (traveled); "Gender, fucked," Center on Contemporary Art (CoCA), Seattle, Washington. 1995: "In a Different Light," University Art Museum and Pacific Film Archive, University of California, Berkeley; "Pervert," University of California, Irvine; "Semblances," Museum of Modern Art, New York, New York. 1994: "2 X Immortal: Elvis + Marilyn," McDaris Exhibition Group, Memphis, Tennessee (traveled). "Absence, Activism and The Body Politic," Fischback Gallery, New York, New York; "Bad Girls West," Wright Art Gallery, University of California, Los Angeles. 1993: "Ciphers of Identity," University of Maryland, Baltimore, (traveled); "I Love You More Than My Own Death, A Melodrama In Parts By Pedro Almodovar," Zitelle Guidecca, Biennale di Venezia, Venice; "Cutting Bait," Randolph Street Gallery, Chicago, Illinois. 1992: "Fear of Painting," Arthur Roger Gallery, New Orleans, Louisiana. 1990: "The Last Laugh: Irony Humor, Self-Mockery and Derision," Massimo Audiello Gallery, New York, New York; "Fragments, Parts and Wholes: The Body in Culture," White Columns, New York, New York. 1988: "Meaningful Geometry," Postmasters Gallery, New York, New York. *KGD*

Zoe Leonard (1961-)

Zoe Leonard was born in Liberty, New York, in 1961. Working in collaboration with film/video maker Cheryl Dunye and film/video scholar Alex Juhasz, Leonard has created 82 photographs for Dunye's feature film *The Watermelon Woman.* Dunye is the writer/director/star of *The Watermelon Woman,* and Juhasz is the film's producer. The photographs depict the characters from the film in range of activities and make up the "evidence" for the film's narrative about the complexities of lesbian relationships, both historically and in contemporary culture. This work also addresses interracial issues, which are all complicated by the narrative authority of the medium itself. Leonard is best known for her photographs. She currently lives in New York.

Selected Solo Exhibitions: 1990: Galerie Gisela Capitain, Cologne. 1991: Galerie Gisela Capitain, Cologne. 1992: Paula Cooper Gallery, New York. 1995: Galerie Jennifer Flay, Paris. 1997:

Philip Johnson's Glass House, Canaan, Connecticut.

"Zoe Leonard," Museum of Contemporary Art, Miami, Florida (traveled).

Selected Group Exhibitions: 1990: Andrea Rosen Gallery, New York. 1992: "Documenta 9," Kassel. 1995: "In a Different Light," University Art Museum and Pacific Film Archive, University of California, Berkeley; "Photographs and Objects," Paula Cooper Gallery, New York. *KGD*

Glenn Ligon (1960-)

Glenn Ligon was born in New York in 1960. He studied at the Rhode Island School of Design and Wesleyan University. In 1985, he attended the Whitney Museum of American Art's Independent Study Program in New York. Ligon is best known for his large canvases that at first glance resemble modernist color-field paintings, but in this case the fields of color are made from the repetitive overlay of text. Conceptually, these paintings speak to the play between "text" as both form and content. Ligon's recent work includes painting and mixed-media installations along with some rather provocative photo albums in which family-style photos are interspersed with early porn style images of black men. Such images challenge the illusion of wholesome family values usually embodied within the family album while at the same time suggesting the

hidden presence of gay family members. The images also begin to suggest a history of desire between black men, a desire rarely seen within early gay publications. Ligon lives in New York.

Selected Solo Exhibitions: 1990: BACA Downtown, Brooklyn, New York; P.S. 1 Museum, The Institute for Contemporary Art, Long Island City, New York. 1991: Jack Tilton Gallery, New York, New York; White Columns, New York, New York. 1992: Max Protetch Gallery, New York, New York; "Glen Ligon/Matrix 120," Wadsworth Atheneum, Hartford, Connecticut.

Selected Group Exhibitions: 1989: "Selections 46," The Drawing Center, New York. 1990: "Spent: Currency, Security, and Art on Deposit," The New Museum of Contemporary Art at Marine Midland Bank, New York, New York. 1991: "Whitney Biennial," Whitney Museum of American Art, New York. 1992: "Double Take: Collective Memory and Current Art," Hayward Gallery, London; "Allegories of Modernism," Museum of Modern Art, New York, New York; "Slow Art: Painting in New York," P.S. 1 Museum, The Institute for Contemporary Art, Long Island City, New York; "Knowledge: Aspects of Conceptual Art," University Art Museum, University of California, Santa Barbara. 1993: "Whitney Biennial," Whitney Museum of American Art, New

York, New York. 1996: "Prospect 96" Frankfurt Kunstverein, Frankfurt. 1997: "Biennale di Venezia," Venice.

Books: Thelma. Golden, *What's White...?*. New York, Whitney Museum of American Art, 1993; D. A. Bailey, Kobena Mercer, *Mirage, Enigmas of Race, Difference and Desire.* London, ICA, 1995. *KGD*

George Platt Lynes (1907-1955)

George Platt Lynes was born in 1907, in an era when erotic photography of the male nude was not only taboo but illegal. Loosely veiled within a surrealist aesthetic, Lynes's early work found a certain acclaim within high art circles, while his later work focused more overtly upon his particular fascination with the male form. Today, Lynes's photographs for Balanchine's *Orpheus* are perhaps his most widely recognized works and provide an interesting point of departure into the more overtly erotic portraits that make up the bulk of his *oeuvre*. There is little doubt that Lynes was well established within literary and avant-garde circles as his portraits of Gertrude Stein, Jean Cocteau, and Max Ernst testify. But it was sex researcher Alfred Kinsey who is perhaps most responsible for establishing a legacy for Lynes's work. Kinsey's interest in the relationship played by erotic photography within the homosexual male led him to begin collecting Lynes's work in the 1950s. Today the Kinsey Institute has more than 600 vintage prints along with a large collection of Lynes's negatives. Lynes died of cancer on 6 December 1955.

Selected Solo Exhibitions: 1932: Leggett Gallery, New York. 1941: Pierre Matisse Gallery, New York. 1960: "George Platt Lynes: Portraits 1931-52," Art Institute of Chicago, Illinois.

Selected Group Exhibitions: 1932: Julian Levy, New York; "International Photographers," Brooklyn Museum, New York. 1936: "Fantastic Art, Dada, Surrealism," Museum of Modern Art, New York, New York. 1942: "Twentieth Century Portraits," Museum of Modern Art, New York, New York.

Books: James Crump, Intro. by Bruce Weber, *George Platt Lynes: Photographs from the Kinsey Institute,* Bullfinch Press Book: Little, Brown and Company, New York, 1993. Jack Woody, *George Platt Lynes: Photographs 1931-55,* Twelve Trees Press, Pasadena, 1981. *KGD*

Rodolfo Machado (1942-) and Jorge Silvetti (1941-)

Rodolfo Machado and Jorge Silvetti have known each other since 1974; they are partners in life and practice. The work their firm, incorporated in 1985, produces does not follow any one architectural style. Instead, they are uniquely concerned with beauty, both in their drawn representations and in the finished artifacts. While originally known for their highly regarded though often unbuilt

Robert F. Wagner Park, New York City, designed by Rodolfo Machado and Jorge Silvetti.

competition entries, their more recent projects have been completed and are diverse in size and scope, including both urban planning and building design.

In 1991, the firm was given the first Award in Architecture by the American Academy and Institute of Arts and Letters for twenty years of "boldly conceived and brilliantly executed urban projects," and their design investigations were commended for being "uncompromisingly dedicated to envisioning a meaningful architecture of the public realm." All of their projects are characterized by a creative intelligence, theatrical flair, and strong material vocabulary.

One of their most visible projects is Robert F. Wagner, Jr. Park on the southern tip of Battery Park City. Overlooking New York Harbor and the Statue of Liberty, their design, in collaboration with landscape architect Laurie Olin and garden designer Lynden Miller, brings people into contact with the iconic features located off the site. The central element of the project is an elevated terrace that aligns with Liberty Island. Two solid masonry pavilions are joined by a metal bridge that frames the harbor; two sets of flowing steps lead down from the pavilions.

Machado and Silvetti's better known projects in the United States include the Princeton University Comprehensive Master Plan, Engineering Quadrangle Parking Structure and Fields Dormitory, the renovation and addition to the J. Paul Getty Villa, the University of Cincinnati Dormitory and Sigma Sigma Commons Tower, Seaside Commercial/Residential building in Florida, Cranbrook Academy Entrance Gate, and the master plan and redesign of Dewy Square in Boston. *IT*

Monica Majoli (1963-)

Monica Majoli was born in 1963. She received a B.A. from the University of California, Los Angeles, in 1989, and an M.F.A. in 1992. Majoli paints small, meticulous works, depicting S/M scenes, self-portraits, and isolated body parts. In one untitled work dated 1990, the viewer sees a man in a bathtub being urinated on from several sides. Majoli paints scenes that would more readily appear across the pages of a hard-core gay male publication than on a museum wall, but these intimate paintings are not taken from printed material; rather, they draw upon actual experiences for their inspiration. Acknowledging minor alteration, Majoli insists that the work functions as documentary, memorializing events and relationships. The male sex scenes began when a close friend of the artist became increasingly involved with the S/M scene. The images are highly erotic and speak to the play of gender and the complexity of pleasure, identification, and a movement by a number of lesbian artists to appropriate and subvert gay male imagery in the service of an emergent aesthetic reflecting the diversity of the lesbian and gay community. In Majoli's work, her subversive appropriation of gay male erotica is visible not only in her subject matter but in her treatment of the forms themselves, which frequently allow firm muscles and broad shoulders to give way to soft curves and an interchangeability of genders that is surprisingly applicable to much of the human form. Majoli currently lives in Los Angeles.

Selected Solo Exhibitions: 1995: Galerie Air de Paris, Paris.

Selected Group Exhibitions: 1990: "All but the Obvious," Los Angeles Contemporary Exhibitions (LACE), California. 1991: "Someone or Somebody," Meyers/Bloom Gallery, Santa Monica, California; "Situation," New Langton Arts, San Francisco, California. 1992: "Trouble Over So Much Skin," Feature, New York, New York. 1993: "Regarding Masculinity," Arthur Roger Gallery,

New Orleans, Louisiana; "Coming to Power," David Zwirner Gallery, New York, New York (traveled). 1994: "The Sacred and the Profane," Jan Baum Gallery, Los Angeles, California. 1995: "In a Different Light," University Art Museum and Pacific Film Archive, University of California, Berkeley; "Vital Signs," Municipal Art Gallery, Barnsdall Art Park, Los Angeles, California. 1996: "First Person," Marc Foxx Gallery, Santa Monica, California. 1997: "Scene of the Crime," UCLA at Armand Hammer Museum of Art and Cultural Center, Los Angeles, California; "Smooth," Air de Paris, Paris. *KGD*

Robert Mapplethorpe (1946-1989)

Robert Mapplethorpe was born in 1946 in Floral Park, Queens, New York. He attended the Pratt Institute from 1963, apparently ending his studies in 1969 when he moved to the Chelsea Hotel with the singer and poet Patti Smith. In 1971, he was given a Polaroid camera by John McKendry, curator of prints and photography at the Metropolitan Museum of Art in New York. In 1972, Sam Wagstaff bought a studio loft for Mapplethorpe at 24 Bond Street. Mapplethorpe is perhaps best known for his X and Y portfolios, which were composed of S/M and flower images, respectively. His work spanned a range of media and subject matter, from self-portraiture to portraiture, still life, and assemblage, but it was his documentation of certain S/M practices that pushed his portraiture beyond the conventional limits of studio work and thrust his work into the center of the controversies over censorship in the arts, First Amendment rights, obscenity, and the use and purpose of National Endowment for the Arts (NEA) funding. In Cincinnati, the Contemporary Arts Center and the museum's curator, Dennis Barrie, were actually indicted on counts of obscenity and child pornography. They were acquitted. Ultimately, the NEA ended all grants to individual artists and greatly decreased institutional support for museums and a wide range of arts organizations, directly causing many to close, raise admissions costs, and reduce security, staff, and service hours. In 1988, Mapplethorpe established the Robert Mapplethorpe Foundation to manage his estate, assist medical research, and to encourage institutional photography programs. He died on 9 March 1989, of an AIDS-related illness.

Selected Solo Exhibitions: 1973: "Polaroids," The Light Gallery, New York, New York. 1977: "Erotic Pictures," The Kitchen, New York, New York; Holly Solomon Gallery, New York, New York; 1978, 1979: Robert Miller Gallery, New York, New York, 1981: "Robert Mapplethorpe," Kunstverein, Frankfurt (traveled); Robert Miller Gallery, New York, New York. 1982: Contemporary Art Center, New Orleans, Louisiana; Larry Gagosian Gallery, Los Angeles, California. 1983: Institute of Contemporary Art, London; Centre National d'Art et de Culture Georges Pompidou, Paris; Robert Miller Gallery, New York, New York. 1984: "Lady," Hara Museum of Contemporary Art, Tokyo. 1985,1987: Robert Miller Gallery, New York, New York. 1988: Robert Miller Gallery, New York, New York; Retrospective at Whitney Museum of American Art, New York, New York; "Robert Mapplethorpe: The Perfect Moment," Institute of Contemporary Art, Philadelphia, Pennsylvania (traveled). 1991: Robert Miller Gallery, New York, New York.

Selected Group Exhibitions: 1977: "Documenta VI," Museum Fridericianum, Kassel. 1978: "Mirrors and Windows: American Photography since 1960," Museum of Modern Art, New York, New York (traveled). 1979: "People Watching," Museum of Modern Art, New York, New York. 1981: "Whitney Biennial,"

Whitney Museum of American Art, New York, New York. 1982: "Documenta VII," Museum Fridericianum, Kassel. 1983: "New Art," Tate Gallery, London; "Drawings and Photographs," Leo Castelli Gallery, New York, New York. 1985: "Message from 1985," Light Gallery, New York, New York; "Entertainment," Josh Bayer Galley, New York, New York; "Homework," Holly Solomon Gallery, New York, New York. 1986: "The Nude in Photography," San Francisco Museum of Modern Art, California. 1987: "Legacy of Light," International Center of Photography, New York, New York. 1988: "Identity: Representations of the Self," Whitney Museum of American Art, New York, New York. 1989: "Photography Now," Victoria and Albert Museum, London; "150 Years of Photography," National Gallery of Art, Washington, D.C. (traveled). 1990: "The Indomitable Spirit," International Center of Photography, New York, New York (traveled); "The Last Decade: American Artists of the 80's," Tony Shafrazi Gallery, New York, New York.

Books: John Cheim, ed. *Robert Mapplethorpe, Early Works,* New York, Robert Miller Gallery, 1991; Arthur Danto, *Mapplethorpe,* New York, Random House, 1992. *KGD*

Pierre Molinier (1900-1976)

Pierre Molinier was born in Agen, France, in 1900. He attended a local art school and attended evening classes at the l'Ecole des Beaux-Arts. After a brief period in Paris, he moved to Bordeaux, where he lived for much of the rest of his life. Molinier began his career as a painter, and it was not until around 1950 that he began to produce the self-portraiture for which he has since become known. In 1955, Molinier approached the well-known Surrealist André Breton, who consequently gave him a solo exhibition at his Paris gallery. Molinier's photomontage work depicted sexually charged scenarios in which he and other models wore numerous fetish garments such as stiletto heels and corsets, and frequently donned a peculiarly stylized mask of a woman's face. Molinier then positioned his strangely gendered figures into fantastic compositions that ranged from clearly auto-erotic images to entangled groups. Molinier's work positions itself somewhere between transvestitism and a highly personal exploration of auto-erotic fetishism. Molinier committed suicide in 1976.

Selected Exhibitions: 1955: l'Etoile Scellée, Paris. 1973: "Korpersparche-Body Language," Graz, Vienna; "Transformer," Luzern, Graz, Bochum. 1979: Retrospective, Musée d'Art

The rotunda of the Williams College Museum of Art, renovation designed by Charles Moore.

Moderne, Center Georges Pompidou, Paris (traveled). 1988: "La Femme et le Surréalisme," Lausanne. 1988-89: "Fotovision," Hannover, Vienna, Zurich. 1989: "Pierre Molinier-Die Fetische der Travestie. Fotografische Arbeiten 1965-75," Galerie Faber, Vienna. 1990: Brent Sikkema Fine Arts, New York, New York. 1991: Gallerie Bouqueret & Lebon, Paris. 1993: "L'images dans le tapis, Cercle de l'Arsenal, Biennale di Venezia," Venice; Galerie Bougueret; "Pierre Molinier," organized by Plug In Gallery at Floating Gallery, Winnipeg, Canada; University of British Columbia, Fine Arts Gallery, Vancouver; "Les Cent jours d'art," CIAC, Montreal; Cabinet Gallery, London. 1994: "Pierre Molinier," Australian Center of Photography, Sydney; Toronto Photographers Workshop, Toronto; NGBK, Berlin; "Biennale di Venezia," Venice. 1995: Galerie Lumiere, Winnipeg; "FOTOFO," Bratislava. 1996: Wooster Gardens, New York, New York; Ubu Gallery, New York, New York; Casa Triangulo, Sao Paulo. 1997: Santa Monica Museum of Art, Santa Monica, California.

Books: Pierre Molinier, *Pierre Molinier,* essays by Wayne Baerwaldt, Peter Gorsen, Scott Watson. Plug In Editions, Winnipeg/Smart Art Press, Santa Monica. *KGD*

Charles Moore (1925-1993)

Charles Willard Moore was born in Michigan and spent many years living in California. He attended the University of Michigan and graduated from Princeton University's Architecture School. He devoted his life to teaching, working, and living. He maintained four architectural offices, and over the years taught at Princeton, University of Utah, University of California at Berkeley, and University of Houston. He was chair of Yale Architecture School in the 1960s, chair of the architecture department at UCLA in the late 1970s and early 1980s, and helped found the Architecture School at University of Texas, Austin.

Early in his career, Moore rejected the repression found in the normative boxes of modernism and became one of the creators of postmodernism, which used classical elements, incorporated playful, cultural symbolism, and contained an honest concern for urban context. He made a conscious effort to design distinct individual buildings and bring a human scale to public space. "To make a place is to make a domain that helps people know where they are, and by extension, know who they are" (Whiteson, Part 5, p. 1).

Moore and his partners in Moore, Lyndon, Turnbull, Whitaker achieved fame with one of their first commissions, Sea Ranch, a condominium complex on the Sonoma County coast. The wooden structures with sloped roofs fit into the heavily timbered landscape rather than overpower it. As his work developed, Moore brought pop vernacular and lively colors to his buildings. He often used cheap, ordinary materials in new ways and designed with a sophisticated sense of humor. By juxtaposing thin, free-standing walls against solid forms, he enveloped the user in three dimensional, easily identified space. The theatricality and exuberance of his designs came close to but never quite descended into kitsch. His ideas challenged and enriched the architectural landscape of the 1950s, 1960s, and 1970s.

His work includes civic centers in Beverly Hills and Oceanside, the faculty club at University of California, Santa Barbara, the Piazza D'Italia in New Orleans (a mock classical composition with columns capped with neon, stainless steel arches, and abundant fountains), St. Matthew's Episcopal Church in Pacific Palisades, a rainbow colored, corrugated sheet metal Wonderwall for the 1984 New Orleans World Exposition, a housing project for West Berlin, and museums at Williams College and Dartmouth College. *IT*

Julia Morgan (1872-1957)

Julia Morgan was born in San Francisco, earned an engineering degree from the University of California, Berkeley, was the first woman admitted to the architecture program at L'Ecole des Beaux Arts in Paris, and was the first woman architect to be registered in California. With a healthy practice in San Francisco, Morgan designed many homes, schools (Mills College in Oakland), and churches (St. John's Presbyterian Church in Berkeley). She also designed a large number of buildings for women including clubs (Berkeley Women's City Club), sorority houses (Kappa Alpha Theta and Delta Zeta in Berkeley), and YWCAs (Asilomar Conference Center in Pacific Grove). She is best known, however, for her architectural relationship with William Randolph Hearst. She completed a number of Hearst projects over a 36-year period including the most famous: San Simeon, a theatrical, fanciful castle compound north of Los Angeles on a hilltop.

Classically trained, Morgan worked within the objectives of her clients and site while drawing from her diverse interests in historical precedent, Arts and Crafts principles, Mission style architecture, and International Style simplicity. She produced both the first house built of reinforced concrete in Berkeley as well as the Hearst Estate, where she oversaw the work of hundreds of artisans who carved, cast, weaved, plastered, and painted the highly ornamented surfaces.

With numerous YWCA commissions in Oakland, San Jose, Vallejo, Salt Lake City, Pasadena, Fresno, Long Beach, Hollywood, Honolulu, and San Francisco, Morgan became an expert with pools employing skylights, courtyards, and decorative highlights. "Morgan had a special knack for swimming pools, using color, light, and shape to create sumptuous designs that flaunted a hedonism startling for so modest an architect" (Boutelle, p. 7).

Work-oriented, she led a private, anonymous life and had all her files and drawings destroyed at the time of her death. While there has been some debate about the issue, it is believed that Morgan was a lesbian. *IT*

Catherine Opie (1961-)

Catherine Opie was born in Sandusky, Ohio, in 1961. She received a B.F.A. from the San Francisco Art Institute in 1985, and an M.F.A. from the California Institute of the Arts, Valencia, in 1988. Best known for her portraits, striking images of her friends seated before brightly colored backdrops, Opie explores large format photography in her work. As a result, her images have vast amounts of information, often capturing the models' features in somewhat shocking detail, offering everything from tattoos and piercings to the occasional clogged pore. Set against the anonymous and traditionally ahistorical space of the backdrop, her work has been both glorified and occasionally vilified for the objectification of its subjects. Supporters of her work have argued that it is significant for its documentation of the contemporary lesbian, gay, and transgendered community, and that on a somewhat theoretical level her images of FTM's and queer-identified gender benders speaks to the ambiguity of gender and refreshingly destabilizes the age-old myth of the photographic document as objective and neutral. Her critics have argued that however much the artist may identify with the individuals or community members represented, the work nevertheless objectifies and dehumanizes the individuals depicted, regardless of any specific relationship to their depictor. If one acknowledges that her portraits attempt to give representation and dignity to her sitters, then her more re-

The Hearst compound at San Simeon, designed by Julia Morgan.

cent photographs of houses must be seen to invert this strategy. Each image catalogues the fussy, incongruous, outdated, and occasionally kitsch demeanor of houses in Los Angeles's flashiest neighborhoods, forever debunking their illusions of class superiority.

Selected Solo Exhibitions: 1991: "Being and Having," 494, New York, New York. 1994: "Portraits," Regen Projects, Los Angeles, California; "Portraits," Kiki Gallery, San Francisco, California; "L.A. Freeways," Jack Hanley Gallery, San Francisco, California. 1995: "Portraits," enterprise, New York, New York; "Portraits," Parco, Tokyo, Japan; "Portraits," Gallerie Massimo De Carlo, Milan, Italy; "Portraits and Freeways," Richard Foncke Gallery, Gent. 1996: "Houses and Landscapes," Regen Projects, Los Angeles, California; "Houses and Freeways," Jay Gorney Modern Art, New York, New York; "Freeways," Feigan Gallery, Chicago, Illinois. 1997: "Houses and Landscapes," Ginza Art Space, Shiseido, Tokyo.

Selected Group Exhibitions: 1985: Camerawork Gallery, San Francisco, California. 1987: "Five Women Artists," Los Angeles Contemporary Exhibitions (LACE), California. 1990: "All But the Obvious," Los Angeles Contemporary Exhibitions (LACE), California. 1991: "Situation: Perspectives on Work by Lesbian and Gay Artists," New Langton Arts, San Francisco, California; "Someone or Somebody," Meyers/Bloom Gallery, Los Angeles, California. 1992: "Breaking Barriers," Santa Monica Museum of Art, California. 1993: "Regarding Masculinity," Arthur Roger Gallery, New Orleans, Louisiana; "Queerly Defined," Eye Gallery, San Francisco, California; "Dress Codes," Institute of Contemporary Art, Boston, Massachusetts; "I am the Enunciator," Thread Waxing Space, New York, New York. 1994: "In the Field: Landscape in Recent Photography," Margo Leavin Gallery, Los Angeles, California; "Little House on the Prairie," Marc Jancou Gallery, London; "Out West and Back East: New Work in Los Angeles and New York," Santa Monica Museum of Art, California. 1995: "Transformers: The Art of Multiphrena," Decker Galleries, Maryland Institute College of Art, Baltimore, (traveled); "Images of Masculinity," Victoria Miro Gallery, London; "Portraits," Jancie Guy, New York; "Feminine-Masculine: the Sex of Art," Museé National d'Art Modern, Centre Georges Pompidou, Paris; "P.L.A.N.: Photography Los Angeles Now," Los Angeles County Museum of Art, California; "Pervert," curated by Catherine Lord, Fine Arts Gallery, University of California, Irvine; "In a Different Light," University Art Museum and Pacific Film Archive, University of California, Berkeley; "Whitney Biennial," Whitney Museum of American Art, New York, New York. 1996: "Evident," The Photographers Gallery, London; "a/drift: Scenes From the Penetrable Culture," Center for Curatorial Studies Museum, Bard College, Annandale-on-Hudson, New York; "Nirvana: Capitalism and the Consumed Image," Center on Contemporary Art (CoCA), Seattle, Washington; "Gender, fucked," Center on Contemporary Art (CoCA), Seattle, Washington. "Sexual Politics: Judy Chicago's *Dinner Party* in Feminist Art History," UCLA at the Armand Hammer Museum of Art and Cultural Center, Los Angeles, California. 1997: "Sunshine & Noir: Art in Los Angeles 1960-97," Louisiana Museum of Modern Art, Humlebaek, Denmark (traveled); "Identity Crisis: Self Portraiture at the End of the Century," Milwaukee Art Museum, Wisconsin; "Spheres of Influence," Museum of Modern Art, Los Angeles, California; "Rrose is a Rrose is a Rhose: Gender Performance in Photography," Guggenheim Museum, New York, New York. *KGD*

Hanh Thi Pham (1954-)

Born in Saigon (presently Ho Chi Minh City), South Vietnam, in 1954, Pham left Vietnam in 1975 and settled in California. She received a B.A. and an M.F.A. from California State University at Fullerton in 1982 and 1986, respectively. Pham was a special faculty/visiting artist at the California Institute of the Arts from 1989 to 1992. Her work includes photography and mixed-media installations. As an artist, she has engaged in an a highly personal vision of the self, acted out in the public sphere. Many of her pieces include photographs of solitary acts that become emblematic documents addressing themes such as Asian immigration, Asian-American feminist issues, and Asian transgendered and transsexual representation. Until recently, Pham resided in Glendora, California.

Solo exhibitions: 1995: "Hanh Thi Pham A Retrospective: Get the Duck on the River Rage," Mesa Art Gallery, San Diego, California. 1997: "The Fukuoka Annual X," Fukuoka Art Museum, Fukuoka.

Selected group exhibitions: 1992: "Here and Now, Now and Then," Longwood Arts Gallery, Bronx, New York (traveled). 1994-96: "Asia/America: Identities in Contemporary Asian American Art," Asia Society, New York, New York. 1995: "(dis)Oriented: Shifting Identities of Asian Women in America," Henry Street Settlement, New York, New York; "Strange Fruits," Los Angeles Center for Photographic Studies (LACPS), Re:Solution gallery, Los Angeles, California; "Picturing Asian America: Communities, Culture, Difference," Silver Eye Center for Photography, Pittsburgh, Pennsylvania, and Arlington Museum of Art, Texas. 1996: "Gender, Fucked: An Exhibition Made by Lesbians about Gender," Center on Contemporary Art, Seattle, Washington.

Books: Margo Machida, Kuroda Raiji, *Hahn Thi Pham, A Vietnamese: Her Body in Revolt,* Asian Artists Today-Fukuoka Annual X, Fukuoka, Fukuoka Art Museum, 1997. *KGD*

Lari Pittman (1952-)

Lari Pittman was born in Los Angeles in 1952, studied at University of California, Los Angeles, from 1970 to 1973, and received a B.F.A. from the California Institute of the Arts, Valencia, in 1974, followed by an M.F.A. in 1976. Working out of the principles established by Pop art, Pittman subverts the modernist neutrality suggested by Pop's quotations and recontextualizations of popular culture. Recognized for a lyrical painting style, Pittman's images are layered, stenciled, brilliantly crafted works that delight the viewer with a cacophony

of highly stylized images interspersed with fantastic vignettes that cumulatively suggest more than any single element, rewarding the patient viewer with their often-dark inner workings. Pittman currently lives in Los Angeles.

Selected Solo Exhibitions: 1983: Rosamund Felsen Gallery, Los Angeles, California; Newport Harbor Museum, California. 1984, 1985, 1987, 1988, 1989, 1990, 1991: Rosamund Felsen Gallery, Los Angeles, California. 1992, 1994: Jay Gorney Modern Art, New York, New York. 1995: "Like You," Regen Projects, Los Angeles, California. 1996: "Lari Pittman," Los Angeles County Museum of Art, California (traveled); "Lari Pittman: Drawings," University Art Museum, University of California, Santa Barbara (traveled); White Cube, London.

Selected Group Exhibitions: 1989: "Prospect 89," Frankfurter Kunstverein, Frankfurt; "Whitney Biennial," Whitney Museum of American Art, New York, New York. 1990: "Just Pathetic," Rosamund Felsen Gallery, Los Angeles, California; "The Museum of Contemporary Art, Los Angeles, California. 1991: "42nd Biennial Exhibition of Contemporary American Painting," The Corcoran Gallery of Art, Washington, D.C. 1992: "Helter Skelter: L.A. Art in the 90's," The Museum of Contemporary Art, Los Angeles, California; "Fear of Painting," Arthur Roger Gallery, New York, New York; "Masquerade (Body Double)," Postmasters Gallery, New York, New York; "In Pursuit of Devoted Repulsion," Roy Boyd Gallery, Los Angeles, California. 1993: "Legend in My Living Room," Rhona Hoffman Gallery, Chicago, Illinois; "Drawing the Line Against AIDS," Guggenheim Museum, Venice, Italy; The Return of the Cadavre Exquis," The Drawing Center, New York, New York. 1994: "Love in Ruins," Long Beach Museum of Art, California; "Animal Farm," James Corcoran Gallery, Santa Monica, California; "Don't Look Now," Thread Waxing Space, New York, New York. 1995: "In a Different Light," University Art Museum and Pacific Film Archive, University of California, Berkeley; "Love Flight of Pink Candy Hearts," Holly Solomon Gallery, New York, New York; "Dutch Wives, Phone Sex, and Other Cheap Thrills," Apex Art, New York, New York; "Whitney Biennial," Whitney Museum of American Art, New York, New York. 1996: "Mutate/Loving the New Flesh." Lauren Wittels Gallery, New York, New York; "The Legacy of American Modernism," Kohn Turner Gallery, Los Angeles, California; "Social Frictions: Lari Pittman/Andrea Zittel," The Grossman Gallery of the School of the Museum of Fine Arts, Boston, Massachusetts; "Paintings on television, television on painting," Friedrich Petzel Gallery. 1997: "Documenta X," Kassel; "Sunshine & Noir: Art in Los Angeles 1960-97," Louisiana Museum of Modern Art, Humlebaek, Denmark (traveled); "Whitney Biennial," Whitney Museum of American Art, New York, New York. *KGD*

George Quaintance (1910-1957)

George Quaintance was born in 1910 in Stanley, Virginia. He seems to have acquired some fine art training as a youngster, and by his early twenties Quaintance had moved to New York, where he worked primarily as an illustrator for advertising firms. By the 1940s, Quaintance had relocated to Los Angeles and began creating those images for which he is best known. His painting style resembles the stylized realism of 1950s advertisements in which a smiling poodle-skirted housewife might be gently pointing to some new appliance. Quaintance looked to mythology and ancient civilizations for much of his imagery, and later, after his move to Phoenix, concentrated on southwestern images of cowboys and Latino ranch hands. In Phoenix, Quaintance ran a ranch and worked on his painting commissions and his mail-order business, which marketed reproductions of his work and sculpture. His images were frequently included in gay erotic magazines and appeared on the cover of *Physique Pictorial* more than once. In recent years, there has been a great deal of interest in such early publications and, of course, his work in particular, because it focuses on a vision of a gay male fantastic located in a heroic past, when semi-nude men frolicked in wholesome virility. From today's perspective, Quantance's interest in ancient civilizations may position him as one of the first queer revisionists. His fascination with the Southwest, and particularly the numerous images of Latino men, provide an interesting window into the past, suggesting a Latino presence not usually found within the gay male world of the 1950s and raising more than few questions about how race functioned within an emergent queer culture. Quaintance died in Los Angeles of a heart-attack on 9 November 1957.

Books: F. Valentine Hooven III, *Beefcake*, Benedikt Taschen Verlag, Germany, 1995. Biographical material taken from unpublished manuscript by Richard Hawkins, who is a leading scholar on Quaintance and generously supplied the information for this entry. *KGD*

John Rand (1956-)

John Rand was born in Oakland, California, in 1956. He has lived in California for most of his life. He received a B.F.A. from California State University, Fullerton, in 1982, and an M.F.A. from the University of California, Irvine, in 1987. His photographs have been included in a variety of publications, including *Artweek, Bear, American Bear,* and *International Drummer.* Working mostly in black-and-white photography, Rand in his work offers a curious blend of documentary and erotic photography traditions. Unlike George Platt Lynes or Bruce of Los Angeles, Rand is engaged in documenting what he refers to as a subculture of the gay community: "bear culture." Rand's work is driven by a personal engagement/admiration for this community, and as such his project suggests a social re-evaluation of the idealized male form. In introducing a hairy, heavyset form within the gay male canon, Rand's construction of the "natural man" has yet to be fully incorporated within the ongoing debates surrounding masculinity. His work has received little attention within the art world, perhaps due to its precarious use of the erotic; nevertheless, Rand offers an interesting counterpoint to dominant photographic representations of the male form and raises interesting questions with regard to the commercialization of queer identity within dominant culture. Rand currently lives in Los Angeles.

Selected Solo Exhibitions: 1996: "John Rand," Rupert Goldsworthy Gallery, Berlin.

Selected Group Exhibitions: 1995: "Strange Fruits." Los Angeles Center for Photographic Studies (LACPS) Re:Solution Gallery, Los Angeles, California. 1994: "Annual Erotic Show," Leslie Lohman Gallery, New York, New York. 1994: "Underexposed," Los Angeles Municipal Art Gallery, Barnsdall Art Park, Los Angeles, California. 1993: "Queerly Defined," Eye Gallery, San Francisco, California. 1988: "Concept and Reality," Los Angeles County Museum of Art, California.

Books: Les Wright, *The Bear Book,* Binghamton, The Haworth Press, 1997. *KGD*

Eleanor Raymond (1887-1989)

Eleanor Raymond graduated from Wellesley College in 1909 and from the Cambridge School of Architecture and Landscape Architecture, a school for women founded by two professors at Harvard, in 1919. (The Harvard Graduate School of Design [GSD] did not admit women until the early 1940s.) While she designed a number of churches and the Tau Zeta Epsilon Sorority House at Wellesley College, Raymond, who as a woman was kept out of the mainstream of male practice, focused on small New England houses that fit into the landscape. These projects included a modern house for her sister in Belmont, Massachusetts (one of the first to introduce the International Style to New England), a colonial complex on the North Shore, an urban garden residence at the foot of Beacon Hill, and a prefabricated plywood dwelling. She also wrote the book *Early Domestic Architecture of Pennsylvania.*

"Houses were the things I liked," she said. "I like the personal contact with whoever is going to use what I design. Also, I think houses are so important in the background of children that I feel important in doing their houses" (Taylor, p. 18).

Raymond was an innovator, an architect who explored technology, structure, form, solar benefits, and materials while designing simple buildings that met the daily needs of her clients. For sculptor Amelia Peabody, Raymond designed the Sun House (the first solar-powered house in New England) in Dover, Massachusetts, in 1948. Raymond, with Dr. Maria Telkes of MIT's Solar Laboratories, believed that the use of solar power for heat would one day become necessary even though the energy supply at that time seemed endless. They continued their research and by 1957 had perfected solar heating, although they received little recognition for their efforts.

Raymond was still living in Cambridge when she died at the age of 102. Her papers and architectural drawings are held at the Harvard Graduate School of Design. She also established a fund at the school to help other women pay for their architectural education. *IT*

Herb Ritts (1952-)

Herb Ritts was born in Los Angeles in 1952. He left for Bard College in 1970 to study economics. He later returned to West Hollywood and worked as a sales representative for the family business. This job allowed Ritts to travel and to pursue one of his interests, photography. His first success as a photographer came in 1978, when a movie industry friend allowed Ritts a brief moment on the set of *The Champ*. Ritts quickly posed actors Jon Voigt and Ricky Schroeder and snapped a shot that *Newsweek* was to publish on its "Newsmakers" page. But it would be the sensuously charged image of a young Richard Gere that would launch Ritts's career as a commercial photographer. Throughout the late 1970s and early 1980s, he continued working in the entertainment industry in Los Angeles, building on his rapidly growing reputation as a celebrity portraitist. While working for *Interview* magazine in 1985, Ritts exhibited his photographs in a gallery setting for the first time. Since then his career has escalated, moving from fashion photography for the top national and international fashion magazines such as *Harper's Bazaar, Vogue,* and *Elle,* to publishing collections of his work. In the past decade, Ritts has published several books, the first of which was entitled *Men/Women* and dates from 1989. In it, Ritts employs both male and female forms in a sensuous and graphically charged manner, blending both fine art and commercial traditions. In *Duo*, 1991, Ritts presents the viewer with a series of nude studies of gay couples. Clearly sexualized by their nudity, these images nevertheless draw from documentary strategies in which the subject is positioned in such a way as to encourage viewers to identify with the sitters on a humanist level that strategically diminishes such culturally charged terms as gay and straight, and as strategy can be found at the center of much documentary work. In 1992, Ritts's success as a celebrity portraitist was showcased in *Notorious,* one of his most successful books to date. His 1994 book, *Africa,* presents a photographic study of the Masai people within a stark African landscape. Drawing from such cross-over photographic traditions as those employed by fashion photographer Irving Penn in his numerous studies of non-western peoples, Ritts's own work displays a striking command of the photographic medium but may suggest a number of problems with regard to the representation of non-Western cultures, particularly when approached from a formalist perspective in which attention to composition and tonality occasionally serve to romanticize racial and cultural differences. "Herb Ritts: Work," at the Museum of Fine Arts in Boston, represents the first time his photographs have been exhibited in a major museum.

Selected Solo Exhibitions: 1996: "Herb Ritts: Work," Museum of Fine Arts, Boston, Massachusetts.

Books: see above. *KGD*

Mark Robbins (1956-)

Mark Robbins is an architect as well as curator of architecture at the Wexner Center for the Arts in Columbus, Ohio. As architect, he constructs one-of-a-kind furniture with metaphorical references to sexuality as well as museum installations that trace the ways specific populations, often gay, appropriate places for themselves in American cities. As curator, his exhibits sometimes address the relationship of gay/lesbian/queer individuals to spatial design. Whether avoiding, hiding, passing, or accepting their place in the public sphere, gay/lesbian/queers use their unique perspectives to establish a presence in the public realm. Commenting or participating in this can become part of one's architectural practice.

In *Angles of Incidence*, P. A. Morton writes that Robbins "investigates the body in the city as the point at which the politics of the body's sexual formation (by the city) becomes explicit. . . . By making the male body the object of the gaze, Robbins causes a disruption of the 'normal' sexual economy of the gaze. . . . The male nude body, as Robbins uses it, is not just the neutral 'scale figure' or classical human referent for the building, but the sexually coded body as it is constructed in the city" (Robbins, p. 18).

In "American Fiction," a collaborative installation with Benjamin Gianni, two walls are set parallel to one another. One wall, like a porch, is made of screen doors that, when opened, create small enclosures which can be read as the rooms in a bathhouse or toilet stalls. The other wall contains framed openings, one at eye level and the other at the level of the genitals. The walls juxtapose the bodies of the users, challenge the perceived order of space, and encourage the possibility of affiliation. When photographed, these projects often include male (and sometimes female) "dancers"—clothed, semi-clothed, and nude. These bodies make visible the interplay of occupant and observer within these open volumes.

Many of these ideas are also visible in "Framing American Cities," which focuses on New York and San Francisco (two meccas for queers) and Columbus (Robbins's home). *IT*

Paul Rudolph (1918-1997)

Paul Rudolph was a gifted draftsman and versatile form-maker. He was also a somewhat controversial figure; he helped create what came to be known as the Brutalist style, a bold, expressive, and some would say highly masculine form of architecture. While sometimes fortress-like, the results of Brutalism are often lively and exuberantly three dimensional; massiveness is used to create memorable forms. Many, however, now see these often adventurous and imaginative buildings as arrogant and unfriendly.

One of the best known examples is the Art & Architecture Building at Yale University. Rudolph, former chair of the department at Yale, designed this brutal concrete building with vertical towers, textural surfaces, and overlapping spaces. Some argue that the building is more concerned with statement than use, complexity rather than good looks. Over the years the building has come under attack by both students and administrators, been divided to enclose spaces, and suffered the wear and tear of daily use. It cannot live up to its innovative potential.

Rudolph completed numerous campus buildings at such universities as Colgate, Dartmouth, Emory, Southeastern Massachusetts, and Wellesley. He designed such inventive structures as the Christian Science Student Center in Urbana-Champaign, Illinois, the Tuskegee Chapel at the Tuskegee Institute, Alabama, and the incomplete State Service Center in Boston. He has also been responsible for large-scale government, commercial, and residential buildings around the world.

One of Rudolph's trademarks is rough, striated, and molded concrete block. (With exposed aggregate concrete, interior surfaces often echo the exterior finishes.) These units create plastic, rounded, sinuous forms. Soaring towers with contrasting horizontal beams, long circuitous ramps, and clerestory windows or skylights often combine to make unusually arranged buildings; they play with light and shadow, texture and form to engage the user. Many are dramatic, dynamic, and ultimately enjoyable studies of abstraction and raw materiality. As Rudolph sometimes said, "You overdo it in order to make it visible" (Cook and Klotz, p. 121). *IT*

Connie Samaras

Samaras received a B.F.A. from the University of New Mexico in 1972 and an M.F.A. from Eastern Michigan University in 1980. Samaras's various projects and installations have focused on the relationship between dominant cultural representations and their inevitable misrepresentation of culture per se. In her ongoing project entitled "Excerpts from a Partial Correction to the Representation of Earth Culture Sent Out to Extraterrestrials on the 1977 U.S. Voyager Interstellar Space Probes," Samaras confronts the heterosexist predisposition of NASA's representation of earth culture as conveyed by the signs and symbols included on the two Voyager spacecrafts launched in 1977, which among other things chose to depict human inter-relations as exclusively heterosexual. For Samaras, "Excerpt from a Partial Correction..." proposes a progressive feminist and lesbian correction to such misrepresentations and seeks to acknowledge the broad range of social issues then at work in the U.S., and yet clearly not included. Civil rights, feminism, and gay and lesbian liberation are nowhere present; instead, depictions of women as reproductive "vessels" and of non-Western cultures as primitively beyond technology have been inalterably sent out into space. In her work, Samaras takes on the role of corrector, and by citing the date of the correction, Samaras seeks to acknowledge the mutability of any representation in that its meaning is always constructed within a specific historical moment. Additionally, Samaras incorporates bio-

The Art and Architecture Building at Yale University, designed by Paul Rudolph.

graphical material into her corrections, foregrounding their own subjectivity while effectively drawing attention to the presumed neutrality of what was originally a highly subjective process. For Samaras, the Voyager messages proved incapable of acknowledging their own white male heterosexual subjectivity, even in light of what must be seen as unprecedented levels of social reform. Samaras lives in Los Angeles.

Selected Solo Exhibitions: 1996: "Excerpt from a Partial Correction to the Representation of Earth Culture Sent Out to Extraterrestrials on the 1977 U.S. Voyager Interstellar Space Probes," Los Angeles Contemporary Exhibitions (LACE), California. 1994: "Excerpt from a Partial Correction . . . ," New Langton Arts, San Francisco, California.

Selected Group Exhibitions: 1997: "2nd International Installation & Environmental Art Symposium, Taechong Lake, and Chongju Museum," Nine Dragon Heads Kunst House, Taechong Lake, South Korea. 1996: "Diorama," Walter Phillips Gallery, Banff Center for the Arts, Canada; "The Incident," ICA, London. 1995: "In a Different Light," University Art Museum and Pacific Film Archive, University of California, Berkeley.

Books: Melanie Calvert and Jennifer Terry, eds. Connie Samaras, "Is It Tomorrow or Just The End of Time?," *Processed Lives: Gender & Technology in Everyday Life,* Routledge, London, 1997. *KGD*

Robert A. M. Stern (1939-)

Robert A. M. Stern was born in New York City. He received degrees from Columbia University and Yale University, and established his own firm in 1977. While best known for residences built for affluent clientele, he has also designed hotels, showrooms, museums (in 1992, he completed the Norman Rockwell Museum at Stockbridge, Massachusetts), and large, mixed-used retail/office buildings for urban centers. As a planner, Stern created a Times Square Feasibility Study that encouraged the reuse of theaters in disrepair. His efforts on the plan and in convincing Disney to restore one of the theaters are partly responsible for Times Square's rebirth and redevelopment. Stern is also a writer, co-authoring both *New York 1900* and *New York 1930.* In 1986, he created *Pride of Place: Building the American Dream,* a television documentary on American Architecture for the Public Broadcasting System. His growing name recognition has led to the design of tableware, furniture, bed linens, and textiles.

Formerly on the board of the Walt Disney Co., Stern has produced many projects for Disney including the Casting Center and Yacht & Beach Club at Walt Disney World and the Newport Bay Club Hotel at Euro Disney. He also designed the Feature Animation Building in Burbank. His imagery is borrowed from movies and theme parks relying on turrets, colorful surfaces and the Mickey Mouse silhouette. Celebration, Florida, Disney's new Florida town, is the result of a master plan by Stern in collaboration with Cooper, Robertson & Partners. (They also designed most of the retail, office, and apartment buildings in and around the downtown area.) The instant town incorporates some of the best features from historic town plans, celebrating architecture, public space, and community spirit. Public buildings in Market Square were designed by Philip Johnson and Charles Moore, among other well-known architects.

Stern's suburban developments and residential communities rely on architectural coherence to attract their customers. Stern provides design guidelines to create an overall order in which diversity can happen. His modern classicism with arches, mold-

ing, and columns relies on classical forms and massing, as well as generously proportioned vernacular elements. His residences borrow heavily from both seaside architecture and shingle-style homes with hip roofs, dormers, bay windows, and deep porches. Stern has said, "An artist cannot choose his themes; they become his by virtue of what he knows and feels" (Rueda, p. 6). *IT*

Louis Sullivan (1856-1924)

Born in Boston, Louis Sullivan studied at MIT and L'Ecole des Beaux-Arts in Paris. He became full partners with Dankmar Adler (a renowned engineer) in 1883. When their partnership dissolved in 1895, Sullivan worked on his own. During his life, he built landmark multi-use structures in Chicago (including the Auditorium Building and Carson Pirie Scott Department Store), legendary skyscrapers in Chicago, St. Louis (Wainwright Building), New York City (Bayard Building), and Buffalo (The Guaranty Trust or Prudential Building), and handsome, jewel-like banks in small towns throughout the Midwest (including National Farmers Bank, Owatonna, Minnesota, and People's Savings Bank, Sidney, Ohio). He also wrote numerous articles and books (including *Kindergarten Chats*), was teacher to Frank Lloyd Wright (Wright worked in his office between 1888 and 1893), and was responsible for the infamous phrase, "form follows function." Unfortunately, this intense, individualistic, early modern master died in poverty as an alcoholic and was not fully recognized until after his death.

As a critic of imitation historic styles, Sullivan helped develop a modern architectural style that expressed the technical and structural innovations of the time period. (He dealt with electricity, elevators, and the cladding of steel multi-storied structures.) Also a master of decorative art, he invented his own style of ornamentation based on nature, Art Nouveau decoration, and rational thinking. He used the "organic" to soften and humanize his structures. Through his often-poetic artistry, he expressed the social content of architecture. The messages he tried to convey regarding democracy, business, education, culture, criticism, the physical world, and creation were clearly issues larger than mere construction.

While no one can confirm that Sullivan was interested in men or that he ever had sexual relations with a man, Robert Twombly, in his highly regarded bibliography of Sullivan, wrote, "There is a good deal of evidence—some personal, some architectural—to suggest that Louis Sullivan may have been homosexual" (Twombly, p. 399). *IT*

Tom of Finland (1920-1991)

Touko Laaksonen, better known as Tom of Finland, was born in Kaarina, Finland, in 1920. Working at the forefront of the gay liberation movement from the 1950s on, he created drawings that could be seen on the pages of dozens of erotic magazines catering to gay audiences. Finland's drawings depict scenes such as buffed leather cops having their way with young, Levis-clad hoodlums, muscles and pants bulging. Stylistically, Finland's work can be seen as establishing a whole canon of gay male erotica, and its depictions of sailors, bikers, cops, and convicts have articulated combinations of submission and dominance and sexual promiscuity, and have even defined the physical typology of the beefcake for nearly half a century. Such images may be responsible for sending a generation of gay men diligently to the gym, forever removing the stigma of the homosexual as

National Farmers Bank in Owatonna, Minnesota, designed by Louis H. Sullivan.

a scrawny, horn-rimmed nerd. Known mostly for its erotic content, it has only been in recent years that Finland's work has been allowed *entré* into "high art" venues such as museum and galleries. This is not to suggest that such distinctions are arbitrary but speaks to a number of pressures effecting Modernism's hold over the fine arts at this *fin de siècle*. The Museum of Modern Art in San Francisco and the Los Angeles County Art Museum have been the first American institutions to acquire Tom of Finland's work. Tom died in Helsinki in 1991, and has recently been recognized as the National Artist of Finland.

Selected Solo Exhibitions: 1978: Eons Gallery, Los Angeles, California; Fenway Gallery, San Francisco, California; Rob Gallery, Amsterdam. 1980: Robert Samuel Gallery, New York, New York; Rob Gallery, Amsterdam. 1981, 1983, 1985: Rob Gallery, Amsterdam. 1988: Feature, New York, New York. 1993: Daniel Bucholz Gallery, Cologne. 1994: Schwules Museum, Berlin. 1995: Emmanuel Perrotin Gallery, Paris. 1997: Mark Moore Gallery, Santa Monica, California.

Selected Group Exhibitions: 1986: Los Angeles Contemporary Exhibitions (LACE), California. 1989: The New Museum of Con-

temporary Art, New York, New York. 1990: Mincher/Wilcox Gallery, San Francisco, California; Wessel O'Conner Gallery, New York, New York. 1991: Matrix Gallery, University of California, Berkeley; Whitney Museum of American Art, New York, New York; Rosamund Felsen Gallery, Los Angeles, California. 1992: Stuart Regen Gallery, Los Angeles, California.

Books: "Tom of Finland Retrospectives" I, II, and III; "Tom of Finland, His Life and Times" by F. Valentine Hooven, III; The Tom of Finland Company in Los Angeles is publishing many of Tom's erotic comic books, including: "Kake in the Wild West," "Raunchy Truckers," and "Highway Patrol." *KGD*

Andy Warhol (1928?-1987)

Andy Warhol was born Andy Warhola in Pittsburgh, Pennsylvania, in approximately 1928. In 1949, Warhol received a B.F.A. from the Carnegie Institute of Technology, and he moved to New York that same year. It is also at this time that he began using "Warhol." Warhol began his career as commercial illustrator working for magazines such as *Vogue, Harper's Bazaar,* and the *New Yorker* but quickly became one of the leading figures of the Pop art movement, along with artists such as Roy Lichtenstein, Jasper Johns, and Robert Rauschenberg. More than any of his contemporaries, Andy Warhol exploited the boundaries between high and low culture. His now-familiar Pop artworks employed commercial silk-screening techniques to mechanically reproduce consumer images such as Brillo boxes and Campbell's soup cans. Warhol's art also involved a general contemplation of consumerism and media culture, as could be seen in his use of popular icons such as Elvis Presley and Marilyn Monroe. His many film works are addressed in the chapter on film. From 1978 to his death in 1987, Warhol was featured in as many as 100 exhibitions, and many more took place posthumously. Due to the great number of group exhibitions, only listed a selected collection of his solo exhibitions are listed in an attempt to at least give some representation of the evolution and scope of Warhol's artistic career. Warhol died during routine surgery in 1987.

Selected Solo Exhibitions: 1952: "Andy Warhol: Fifteen Drawings Based on the Writings of Truman Capote," Hugo Gallery, New York, New York. 1954: "Warhol," Loft Gallery, New York, New York. 1956: "Drawings for a Boy-Book by Andy Warhol," Bodley Gallery, New York; "Andy Warhol: The Golden Slipper Show or Shoes Shoe in America," Bodley Gallery, New York, New York. 1957: "A Show of Golden Pictures by Andy Warhol," Bodley Gallery, New York, New York. 1959: "Wild Raspberries," Bodley Gallery, New York, New York. 1962: "Campbell's Soup Cans," Ferus Gallery, Los Angeles, California; "Andy Warhol," Stable Gallery, New York, New York. 1963: "Andy Warhol," Ferus Gallery, Los Angeles, California. 1964: "Warhol," Galerie Ileana Sonnabend, Paris; "Warhol," Stable Gallery, New York, New York; "Andy Warhol," Leo Castelli Gallery, New York, New York. 1965: "Andy Warhol," Galerie Ileana Sonnabend, Paris; "Andy Warhol," Galeria Rubbers, Buenos Aires; "Andy Warhol," Institute of Contemporary Art of the University of Pennsylvania, Philadelphia; "Warhol," Gian Enzo Sperone, Turin. 1966: "Andy Warhol," Leo Castelli, New York, New York; "Andy Warhol Holy Cow! Silver Clouds!! Holy Cow!," Contemporary Arts Center, Cincinnati, Ohio; "Andy Warhol," Institute of Contemporary Art, Boston, Massachusetts. 1967: "Kühe und Schwebende Kissen von Andy Warhol," Galerie Rudolf Zwirner, Cologne; "Andy Warhol Most Wanted," Galerie Rudolf Zwirner, Cologne; "Andy Warhol—The Thirteen Most Wanted Men," Galerie Illeana Sonnabend, Paris. 1968: "Andy Warhol," Moderna Museet, Stockholm (traveled); "Andy Warhol," Rowan Gallery, London. 1970: "Andy Warhol," Pasadena Art Museum, California (traveled). 1971: "Andy Warhol," Musée d'Art Moderne de la Ville de Paris, France. 1973: John Berggruen Gallery, San Francisco, California; New Gallery, Cleveland, Ohio; Irving Blum Gallery, Los Angeles, California. 1974: "Andy Warhol," Musée Galliera, Paris; "Warhol," Milwaukee Art Museum, Wisconsin; "Andy Warhol: Old Paintings, New Prints," Max Protetch Gallery, Washington, D.C.; Galerie Ileana Sonnabend, Paris; Jared Sable Gallery, Toronto, Ontario, Canada; Mayor Gallery, London. 1975: "Andy Warhol," Margo Leavin Gallery, Los Angeles, California; "Andy Warhol: Paintings 1962-75," The Baltimore Museum of Art, Maryland; "Andy Warhol," Max Protetch Gallery, Washington, D.C. 1977: "Retrospective Exhibition of Paintings by Andy Warhol from 1962-76," Pyramid Galleries, Washington, D.C.; "Andy Warhol Hammer and Sickle," Galerie Daniel Templon, Paris; "Athletes by Andy Warhol," Coe Kerr Gallery, New York, New York; Heiner Friedrich Gallery, Cologne; Leo Castelli, New York, New York.

Books: Kynaston McShine ed., *Andy Warhol: A Retrospective,* New York, Museum of Modern Art, 1989; Jennifer Doyle, Jonathan Flatley, & José Estaban Muñoz, eds. *Pop Out, Queer Warhol,* Durham and London, Duke, 1996. *KGD*

Bruce Weber (1946-)

Bruce Weber was born in Greenberg, Pennsylvania, in 1946. He studied at the New School for Social Research as well as at New York University's art and film schools in New York City. Additionally, he attended the Humm School in Princeton, New Jersey, and Denison University in Ohio. Working as a commercial photographer, Weber has also produced commercials, videos, and a number of films, including *Broken Noses*, 1987. Weber's 1990 publication, *Bear Pond,* unquestioningly seeks to imbue New England wilderness environments with a masculinity that is at once homosocial and homoerotic. Like the photographs of Thomas Eakins taken nearly a century earlier, Weber's images project a world filled with well-defined youths rough-housing, swimming, sleeping, and reclining, all in a presumably unself-conscious naturalism. Interestingly enough, *Bear Pond*'s final image is that of a single canoe banked on a shore. Painted to represent a highly stylized Indian canoe, and given its prominence as the final image, it is clearly intended to foreground associations of an idyllic balance between man and nature, an image associated with Native American culture. This is a conception frequently employed within 17th- and 18th-century representations of the New World in which the natural man or "noble savage" lived in idyllic bliss. The toy-like quality of the canoe is meant to distance the cultural specificity usually associated with such objects in order to function metaphorically and suggests a curious relationship between gay male culture and an eroticism associated with the racial Other, even when that Other is absent.

Selected Solo Exhibitions: 1984: "Athletes," Robert Miller Gallery, New York, New York; "Athletes," Gallerie Texbraun, Paris. 1986: "New Work," Kunsthalle, Basel; "O Rio de Janeiro," Robert Miller Gallery, New York, New York; "O Rio de Janeiro," Fay Gold Gallery, Atlanta, Georgia. 1987: "O Rio de Janeiro," PPS Galerie, Hamburg; "O Rio de Janeiro," Parco Galleries, Tokyo. 1988: "Bruce Weber," Arthur Roger Gallery, New Orleans, Louisiana; "Figure Studies," Robert Miller Gallery, New York, New York. 1989: "Figure Studies," Karsten Schubert Ltd., London; Frankfurter Kunstrereins Gallery, Frankfurt. 1990: "Figure Studies," Xavier Hufkens, Brussels, Belgium; "Bruce Weber, Photoworks 1982-90," Mai 36 Galerie, Lucerne, Switzerland. 1991: Fahey/Klein Gallery, Los Angeles, California; Fay Gold Gallery, Atlanta, Georgia; Parco Exposure Gallery, Tokyo, Japan (traveled). 1994: "Gentle Giants," Robert Miller Gallery, New York, New York; "Never Never Land," Galeria Photology, Milan, Italy.

Selected Group Exhibitions: 1985: "Messages from 1985," Light Gallery, New York, New York; "Shots of Style," Victoria and Albert Museum, London. 1987: "Whitney Biennial," Whitney Museum of American Art, New York, New York. 1988: "Return of the Hero," Burden Gallery, New York, New York. 1989: "Images of Desire: Portrayals in Recent Advertising," Goldie Paley Gallery, Moore College of Art, Philadelphia, Pennsylvania; "Photography Now," Victoria and Albert Museum, London; "Fragments of History," Albany Museum of Art, Georgia; "Recent Portraits," Tatistcheff Gallery, Santa Monica, California; "Images of Illusion," The Forum Gallery, St. Louis, Missouri. 1990: "The Indomitable Spirit," International Center of Photography, New York, New York (traveled); Kunstforum Vienna, Austria; "Photographie: de la

Réclame á la Publicité," Centres Georges Pompidou, Paris; "Borofsky," Paula Cooper Gallery, New York, New York. 1991: "La Revanche de l'Image," Galerie Pierre Huber, Geneva; "Portraits on Paper," Robert Miller Gallery, New York, New York. 1992: "Summer Pleasures," Staley/Wise Gallery, New York, New York; "American Pictures: Traditional Themes by Contemporary Photographers," James Danziger Gallery, New York, New York. 1993: "I Am the Enunciator," Thread Waxing Space, New York, New York; "Supreme Shots-Fashion," Galeria Photology, Milan; "The Image of the Body," Frankfurter Kunstverein, Frankfurt; "Short Stories," Danziger Gallery, New York, New York. 1994: "Short Stories," Fahey/Klein Gallery, Los Angeles, California. 1995: "Fashion is a Verb," F.I.T., New York, New York; "The Portrait/The Nude," Fahey/Klein Gallery, Los Angeles, California. 1996: "FE:MALE—The Beauty of Human Form," Galerie im Haus 19, Munich.

Books: John Cheim, ed. *Bruce Weber,* New York, Alfred A. Knopf, 1989; Bruce Weber, *Bear Pond,* Bulfinch Press, Little, Brown and Company, 1990. *KGD*

Fred Wilson (1954-)

Fred Wilson was born in the Bronx, New York, in 1954. He studied at S.U.N.Y. at Purchase, and received a B.F.A. in 1976. In 1987, he was appointed the curator of the Longwood Gallery of the Bronx Council of the Arts, and his exhibition entitled "Rooms with a View: The Struggle between Culture, Content, and the Context of Art" was to lay the groundwork for much of his later work. In it he created three exhibition spaces, one salon style, one as the modern gallery space or "white cube," and the third as an ethnographic museum. This display recontextualized the artist's works in such a way as to foreground the authority of museum space itself, an intervention that has since propelled Wilson into a series of site-specific installations that might best be thought of as an odyssey into the relationships between objects, institutions, and the viewers who visit them. Wilson lives in New York.

Solo Exhibitions: 1988: "Portrait of Audubon," outdoor project of The Public Art Fund, New York, New York. 1990: "The Other Museum," White Columns, New York, New York. 1991: "Primitivism: High & Low," Metro Pictures, New York, New York; "The Other Museum," Washington Project for the Arts, Washington, D.C.; Gracie Mansion Gallery, New York, New York. 1992: "Panta Rhei: A Gallery of Ancient Classical Art," Metro Pictures, New York, New York; "Mining the Museum," The Contemporary and The Maryland Historical Society, Baltimore, Maryland. 1993: "The Museum: Mixed Metaphors," Seattle Art Museum, Washington; "The Spiral of Art History," Indianapolis Museum of Art, Indiana; "An Invisible Life: A View Into the World of a One Hundred and Twenty Year Old Man," an off site project of Capp Street Projects, San Francisco, California. 1994: "OpEd: Fred Wilson," Museum of Contemporary Art, Chicago, Illinois; "'Insight: In Site: Incite-Memory,' Artist and the Community: Fred Wilson," South Eastern Center for Contemporary Art, Winston-Salem, North Carolina. 1995: "Collectibles," Metro Pictures, New York, New York. 1997: "Collectibles," Rena Bransten Gallery, San Francisco, California; "Reshuffling the Deck: Selections from the U.C. Davis Collections," Richard L. Nelsen Gallery & the Fine Arts Collection, University of California, Davis.

Selected Group Exhibitions: 1990: "Public Mirror: Artists Against Racial Prejudice," The Clocktower Gallery, New York, New York; "Notes on the Margin," Gracie Mansion Gallery, New York, New York. 1992: "Past Imperfect: A Museum Looks at Itself," Parrish Art Museum, Southhampton, New York; "Rosamund Felsen Clinic," Rosamund Felsen Gallery, Los Angeles, California; "Putt Modernism," Artists Space, New York, New York; "Inheritance," Los Angeles Contemporary Exhibitions (LACE), California; "The Order of Things: Toward a Politic of Still Life," New Art Ways, Hartford, Connecticut; "The Big Nothing, or le Presque Rien," The New Museum of Contemporary Art, New York, New York. 1993: "Whitney Biennial," Whitney Museum of American Art, New York, New York; "Readymade Identities," Museum of Modern Art, New York, New York; "The Theater of Refusal: Black Art and Mainstream Criticism," Fine Arts Gallery, University of California, Irvine; "Artists Respond: The New World Question," The Studio Museum in Harlem, New York, New York; "Ciphers of Identity," Fine Arts Gallery, University of Maryland, Baltimore. 1994: "Don't Look Now," Thread Waxing Space, New York, New York; "Crash: Nostalgia for the Absence of Cyberspace," Thread Waxing Space, New York, New York; "Western Artists/African Art," Museum of African Art, New York, New York; "Notational Photographs," Metro Pictures, New York, New York; "Transformers: The Art of Multiphrenia," organized by ICI (traveled); "Black Male: Representations of Masculinity in Contemporary American Art," The Whitney Museum of American Art, New York, New York. 1996: "Cultural Economies: Histories from the Alternative," The Drawing Center, New York, New York; "New Histories," The Institute of Contemporary Art, Boston, Massachusetts; "Burning Issues: Contemporary African-American Art," Museum of Art, Fort Lauderdale, Florida. 1997: "Irredeemable Skeletons (the ones that got away)," Shillam and Smith 3, London; "Collected," The Photographer's Gallery and British Museum, London; "Collectibles," The Light Factory, Charlotte, North Carolina; "Museum Studies: Eleven Photographer's Views," High Museum of Art, Atlanta, Georgia.

Books: Lisa A. Gorman, *Mining the Museum: An Installation by Fred Wilson,* Baltimore, The New Press/The Contemporary, 1994; Patterson Sims, *The Museum: Mixed Metaphors,* Seattle, Seattle Art Museum, 1993. *KGD*

Millie Wilson (1948-)

Millie Wilson was born in Hot Springs, Arkansas, in 1948. She attended the Yale Summer School of Art and Music in New Haven in 1970. Wilson received a B.F.A. from the University of Texas at Austin in 1971 and an M.F.A. from the University of Houston in 1983. Wilson's "Museum of Lesbian Dreams," portions of which have been exhibited between 1989 and 1991, explores the dilemmas of lesbian identity within postmodernism's construction of the Other. Discussions around Otherness have become an integral part of post-colonial and postmodern cultural criticism, particularly when addressing the historical construction of such categories as race, class, and gender. Wilson's work frequently takes the form of installations, Readymades, and mixed media works. In "Fauve Semblant: Peter (A Young English Girl)," Wilson constructs an elaborate trope around a little-known early modernist. In referencing the title of a work originally done by Romaine Brooks, Wilson conceptually repositions the original work along with its marginalized link to modernist art practices, practices that have largely disregarded the full play of gender within the development of modernism. Wilson lives in Los Angeles.

Selected Solo Exhibitions: 1989: "Fauve Semblant: Peter (A Young English Girl)," Los Angeles Contemporary Exhibitions (LACE), California. 1990: "Fauve Semblant: Peter (A Young

English Girl)," San Francisco Camerawork, California. 1991: "Sweet Thursday," Meyers/Bloom Gallery, Santa Monica, California. 1992: "A Disturbing Emotional Coloring," White Columns, New York, New York; "Living in Someone Else's Paradise," New Langton Arts, San Francisco, California. 1993: "Wolf in the Garden." Ruth Bloom Gallery, Santa Monica, California. 1994: "Not a Serial Killer," Jose Freire Fine Art, New York, New York. 1995: "Monster Girls," Ruth Bloom Gallery, Santa Monica, California.

Selected Group Exhibitions: 1989: "Thick and Thin: Photographically Inspired Paintings," Fahey/Klein Gallery, Los Angeles, California; "The Body You Want," Southern Exposure, San Francisco, California; "Self/Evidence," Los Angeles Contemporary Exhibitions (LACE), California. 1990: "All But The Obvious," Los Angeles Contemporary Exhibitions (LACE), California; "Post-Boys and Girls," Artists Space, New York, New York; "Queer," Wessel O'Connor, New York, New York. 1991: "Situation: Perspectives on Work by Lesbian and Gay Artists," New Langton Arts, San Francisco, California; "Someone or Somebody," Meyers Bloom Gallery, Santa Monica, California; (Dis)Member," Simon Watson Gallery, New York, New York. 1992: "Clinic and Recovery Center," Rosamund Felsen Gallery, Los Angeles, California; "Re-Visions," Randolph Street Gallery, Chicago, Illinois; "The Politics of Difference: Artists Explore Issues of Identity," Riverside Art Museum, University of California, Riverside; "Facing the Finish," San Francisco Museum of Modern Art, California (traveled). 1993: "I am the Enunciator," Thread Waxing Space, New York, New York; "Empty Dress: Clothing as Surrogate in Recent Art," Independent Curators, Inc., Neuberger Museum, State University of New York, Purchase (traveled); "Kink," Mark Moore Gallery, Santa Monica, California; "Regarding Masculinity," Arthur Roger Gallery, New Orleans, Louisiana. 1994: "Duchamp's Leg," Walker Art Center, Minneapolis, Minnesota (traveled). 1995: "Pervert," Fine Arts Gallery, University of California, Irvine; "Threshold/Recent American Sculpture," Serralbes Foundation, Oporto, Portugal; "Something Borrowed," collaboration with Catherine Lord, Site Santa Fe, Museum of Fine Arts, Sante Fe, New Mexico; "In a Different Light," University Art Museum and Pacific Film Archive, Berkeley, California.

Books: Karen Moss and Scott Boberg, eds. *Altered Egos,* Santa Monica, Santa Monica Museum of Art, 1994. *KGD*

David Wojnarowicz (1954-1992)

David Wojnarowicz was born in Redbank, New Jersey, in 1954. Accounts of his early childhood can be found throughout his artworks and writings, in which he tells of a troubled home life, of living in boarding homes, and even being kidnapped by his father. Wojnarowicz dropped out of school in 1970, and from 1972 to 1978 he hopped freight trains and hitchhiked his way across the country several times, at one point even working as a farmer on the Canadian boarder. In 1979, he began both his photographic series "Arthur Rimbaud in New York" and his stenciled street paintings. With Rimbaud, Wojnarowicz marked his affinity with, and subversion of, the romantic model of the artist. Rimbaud is pictured in everyday activities, riding a subway, eating in a diner, and masturbating; together, these images suggest a portrait of alienation and difference, themes that would continue throughout his *oeuvre*. In 1980, working with Julie Hair, Wojnarowicz began doing "action installations," one of which included stenciling an empty plate, knife, and fork

on the wall of Leo Castelli's staircase. Wojnarowicz is perhaps best known for the photo-based work that was at the center of the NEA censorship controversy because of its overt gay content. Wojnarowicz worked in a wide range of media throughout his career. Even his paintings usually employed text, photography, and a graphic painting style in which diverse images were culled from popular culture and juxtaposed within a highly personal iconography, which in the mid-1980s was termed "Neo-Expressionist," largely for its passionate idiosyncrasies. Wojnarowicz died of an AIDS-related illness in 1992.

Selected Solo Exhibitions: 1982: Milliken Gallery, New York, New York. 1983: Hal Bromm Gallery, New York, New York; Civilian Warfare, New York, New York. 1984: Gracie Mansion Gallery, New York, New York; Anna Friebe Galerie, Cologne. 1985: "Messages to the Public," Public Art Fund, New York, New York. 1986: Gracie Mansion Gallery, New York, New York; Anna Friebe Galerie, Cologne. 1987: Gracie Mansion Gallery, New York, New York; Ground Zero Gallery, New York, New York. 1989: P.P.O.W., New York, New York. 1990: "David Wojnarowicz: Tongues of Flame," University Galleries, Illinois State University, Normal (traveled).

Selected Group Exhibitions: 1984: "Studio Program Exhibition," The Clocktower, New York, New York. 1985: "Whitney Biennial," Whitney Museum of American Art, New York, New York. 1987: "Art Against AIDS," Gracie Mansion Gallery, New York, New York. 1988: Vollbild-AIDS, N.G.B.K., Berlin. 1989: "Whitnesses: Against Our Vanishing," Artists Space, New York, New York.

Books: David Wojnarowicz, foreword by William S. Burroughs, *Sounds in the Distance,* London, Aloes Books, 1982. Barry Blinderman, ed. *David Wojnarowicz, Tongues of Flame,* Normal, University Galleries of Illinois State University, 1990. *KGD*

REFERENCES:

Books and Articles: Art and Photography

Baudelaire, Charles. "The Painter of Modern Life," in *Modern Art and Modernism: A Critical Anthology,* edited by Francis Frascina and Charles Harrison. London: Harper & Row, 1982.

Blessing, Jennifer. "Introduction," in *Rrose is a Rrose is a Rhose: Gender Performance in Photography.* New York: The Solomon R. Guggenheim Foundation, 1997.

Breeskin, Adelyn D. *Romaine Brooks in the National Museum of Art.* Washington D.C.: Smithsonian Institution Press, 1986.

Butler, Judith. *Bodies That Matter: On the Discursive Limits of "Sex."* New York and London: Routledge, 1993.

———. "Decking Out: Performing Identities," in *Inside/Out,* edited by Diana Fuss. New York and London: Routledge, 1991.

Crump, James. *George Platt Lynes: Photographs from the Kinsey Institute.* New York: Bulfinch Press Book, 1993.

Gorsen, Peter. "The Artist's Desiring Gaze on Objects of Fetishism," in *Pierre Molinier.* Santa Monica: Plug In Editions, Winnipeg/Art Press, 1997.

Greenberg, Clement. "Avant-Garde and Kitsch," in *Art and Culture: Critical Essays.* Boston: Beacon Press, 1961.

Greene, Vivien. "Artist Biographies: Claude Cahun," in *Rrose is a Rrose is a Rhose: Gender Performance in Photography,* by Jennifer Blessing. New York: The Solomon R. Guggenheim Foundation, 1997.

Johnson, Jill. *Jasper Johns: Privileged Information.* London: Thames & Hudson, 1996.

Jones, Amelia. "Lari Pittman's Queer Feminism," in *Art & Text,* vol. 50, 1995: 41.

Katz, Jonathan. "The Art of Code: Jasper Johns & Robert Rauschenberg," in *Significant Others,* edited by Whitney Chadwick & Isabelle de Courtivron. London: Thames and Hudson, 1994.

Leddick, David. *Naked Men: Pioneering Male Nudes 1935-1955.* New York: Universe Publishing, 1997.

Makela, Maria. "From an Ethnographic Museum: Race and Ethnicity in 1920s' Germany," in *The Photomontages of Hanna Höch,* edited by Peter Boswell and Maria Makela. Minneapolis: Walker Art Center Press, 1996.

Rechy, John. *The Sexual Outlaw: A Documentary.* New York: Grove Weidenfeld, 1977.

Riviere, Joan. "Womanliness as a Masquerade," in *The International Journal of Psychoanalysis 10,* 1929: 303-13. Reprinted in *Formations of Fantasy,* edited by Victor Burgin, James Donald, and Cora Kaplan. New York: Routledge, 1986.

Tomkins, Calvin. *Off the Wall: Robert Rauschenberg and the Art World of Our Times.* New York: Penguin, 1980.

Waugh, Thomas. *Hard to Imagine: Gay Male Eroticism in Photography and Film from Their Beginnings to Stonewall.* New York: Columbia University Press, 1996.

Weinberg, Jonathan. *Speaking for Vice.* New Haven and London: Yale University Press, 1993.

Books: Architecture

Boutelle, Sara Holmes. *Julia Morgan Architect.* New York: Abbeville Press Publishers, 1988.

Cook, Jeffrey. *The Architecture of Bruce Goff.* New York: Harper & Row Publishers, 1978.

Cook, John W. and Heinrich Klotz. *Conversations with Architects.* New York: Praeger Publishers, 1973.

Raymond, Eleanor. *Early Domestic Architecture of Pennsylvania.* N.p.

Robbins, Mark. *Angles of Incidence.* New York: Princeton Architectural Press, 1992.

Rueda, Louis F., ed. *Robert A. M. Stern: Buildings and Projects 1981-1986.* New York: Rizzoli, 1986.

Shand-Tucci, Douglass. *Boston Bohemia 1881-1900, Ralph Adams Cram: Life and Architecture.* Amherst: University of Massachusetts Press, 1995.

Schulze, Franz. *Philip Johnson: Life & Work.* New York: Alfred A. Knopf, 1994.

Stern, Robert A. M. with others. *New York 1900: Metropolitan Architecture and Urbanism, 1890-1915.* New York: Rizzoli, 1983.

Stern, Robert A. M. with others, ed. *New York 1930: Architecture and Urbanism between the Two World Wars.* New York: Rizzoli, 1987.

Twombly, Robert. *Louis Sullivan: His Life and Work.* New York: Elisabeth Sifton Books—Viking, 1986.

Periodical Articles: Architecture

Bethany, Marilyn. "When Enough Is Enough," in the *New York Times,* 19 December 1982: Sec. 4, p. 98.

Hightower, Susan. "A Populist Architect Puts His Personal Stamp on Texas," in *Los Angeles Times,* 25 July 1995: D10.

"House Rules." Exhibition catalogue. *Assemblage.* 24.

Koshalek, Richard. "Appreciation," in *Los Angeles Times,* 14 June 1996: F1.

Muschamp, Herbert. "A Building That Echoes A Protean Journey," in the *New York Times,* 7 July 1996: Sec. 2, p. 29.

Oliver, Myrna. "Obituary: Franklin D. Israel," in *Los Angeles Times,* 11 June 1996: B8.

Taylor, Jerry. "Obituary: Eleanor Raymond," in the *Boston Globe,* 28 July 1989: 18.

Whiteson, Leon. "Architecture: A Search for Sanctuary," in *Los Angeles Times,* 20 March 1989: Part 5, p. 1.

Wright, Chapin. "House Fantasies Fulfilled," in the *Washington Post,* 6 January 1979: E1.

Other: Architecture

http://www.AIA.org. This web site covers the American Institute of Architects.

http://www.machado-silvetti.com. This web site covers the firm of Machado and Silvetti.

Stern, Robert A. M. *Price of Place: Building the American Dream, A Personal View.* Princeton, New Jersey: Films for the Humanities, 1986.

—Art and Photography by Ken Gonzalez-Day
—Architecture by Ira Tattelman

19

Religion and Spirituality

There are many snapshots as one peruses the viewbook of homosexuality and religion, images that portray reverence to condemnation, tolerance to rejection. This chapter presents the various viewpoints of major world religions as well as other spiritual teachings toward homosexuality. Contemporary views and groups are listed under each religion/spirituality. Common biblical arguments for and against homosexuality are also presented.

The chapter first gives a historical background of the ancient world that informs the study regarding the roots of cultural, philosophical, and biblical beliefs. Christianity is divided into two sections: 1) "Early and Premodern History"; and 2) "Recent American History." These sections serve as bookends to the chapter so that the early historical material can inform the "Homosexuality and the Bible" section, which in turn feeds into a discussion of other major world religions, beginning with the "Homosexuality and Judaism" section. This flow also allows the comparison and contrast of various cultures historically. The final section then wraps up the contemporary context with "American Christianity."

The "Prominent People" section offers a quick review of key leaders in history. The "References" section provides the reader with information for a more in-depth study of homosexuality and religion.

HOMOSEXUALITY IN EARLY AND PREMODERN CHRISTIANITY

In the late twentieth century, as the Southern Baptist Convention boycotts the Walt Disney Corporation for providing domestic partnership benefits for the partners of its gay and lesbian employees, Christianity and homosexuality seem to be incompatible partners. However, this is only one snapshot in the long history of lesbian and gay people and Christianity. For ammunition, the Southern Baptists quote ancient Biblical texts—passages written

in a particular historical and cultural context. In that world, homosexuality was not understood as it is today—as a sexual orientation. Interestingly, though, the practice of homosexuality was a widely known and accepted—sometimes honored—practice.

In order to set the stage for a study of contemporary homosexuality and Christianity, it is important to return to early history to understand the context out of which came sacred texts such as the Bible. It is equally important to acknowledge homosexuality as a long-standing, historical practice. Furthermore, we must recognize that though religion has shaped culture, so culture and its taboos have shaped religion. The varying views of homosexuality throughout history testify to the dynamic between religion and culture.

Historical Context of Premodern Europe

For many Christians espousing anti-gay rhetoric today, the notion that homosexuality has been present—even tolerated—in the church throughout history is foreign. "Contrary to a presumptive claim often rhetorically asserted, the church has not consistently condemned, much less persecuted, homosexual persons throughout its history. There have been periods of silence, indifference, toleration, and even tacit acceptance of homosexuality" (Swidler, *Homosexuality and World Religions*). The following section shows how we know homosexuality was present in the ancient world and through premodern European history. It will also show that tolerance certainly varied throughout the centuries. Some of the key influences shaping that tolerance are noted as well.

As we move into this study, remember that the importance of sexuality in general and sexual orientation in particular was relatively low. Especially in the early church, the primary focus of Christians was not on sexuality but on the imminent return of Christ. In fact, there was even a devaluation of heterosexual marriage. "To Christian converts expecting the imminent conclusion of the world, and dramatically transforming their lives in preparation for it, marriage—along with all other human pleasures and satisfactions—seemed trivial, or—worse—a dangerous distraction" (Boswell, *Same-Sex Unions in Premodern Europe*).

Another relevant piece of the historical context was the ancient world's identification of sexuality in general. Whereas modern Westerners view sexuality on more personal terms as one's identity, the ancients viewed it as sex acts that were social in nature. In this way, sexual acts simply portrayed social power relations. "If there is a lesson that historians should draw from this picture of ancient sexual attitudes and behaviors, it is that we need to de-center sexuality from the focus of the interpretation of sexual experience.... [W]e ought not therefore to conclude that everyone has always considered sexuality a basic and irreducible element in, or a central feature of, human life" (Duberman et al., *Hidden from History*). It is important to keep in mind this ancient perspective about sexual practices as we move on to a closer examination of the presence of homosexuality in the ancient world.

In his books *Christianity, Social Tolerance, and Homosexuality* and *Same-Sex Unions in Premodern Europe*, John Boswell provides a thorough study of gay life from the beginning of the Christian era to the fourteenth century. His research reveals art, literature, and liturgies that reflect the practice of homosexuality. The Greek and Roman cultures, which shaped both eastern and western Christianity, tolerated homosexuality. Love between two men was at times idealized as the noblest love. While this idealization reflects the second class view of women, it does show that male homosexuality was indeed common and known not simply as an act of sexual gratification but as an emotional and romantic bond. "Plato and the Roman Emperor Hadrian could be claimed as advocates of homosexual love" (Swidler).

Many writings reveal not only the presence but the acceptance of homosexual life. "Influences supporting gay love throughout the Middle Ages included such classical (pre-Christian) stories as the abduction of Ganymede by Zeus and the valor of Greek lovers such as Harmodius and Aristogiton, both of which influenced the medieval courtly love and romance that spread from Provencal toward the end of the first millennium. Medieval monks and nuns also provided sometimes unwitting support by writing of spiritual friendship in passionate, sometimes apparently homosexual tones" (Swidler).

Other writings of church leaders throughout the first 13 centuries make evident the presence of homosexual behavior among both Christian laity and clergy. Though mainly condemning homosexual acts, the fact that church leaders wrote about such acts meant that they were widely practiced. Two church leaders known for their written attacks were Bishop John Chrysostom in the fourth century and Saint Peter Damian in the eleventh century. Another indication of homosexual practice was the instruction by monastic authorities for avoiding homosexual attractions among monks. There are basically mild canonical penalties for homosexual behavior in general, although in many periods strict theologians tried unsuccessfully to get church authorities to sanction heavier penalties for homosexual clergy. Some of these clergy were well-known bishops.

With the presence of homosexual practice established, we turn to the evidence of tolerance for homosexuality. The tolerance level decreased and increased in relation to the ebb and flow of urban life. Up to the late twelfth century, tolerance for homosexuality was greatest in urban settings. "The urban culture that predominated until the fall of Rome in 430 was a force for tolerance of gay Christians" (Swidler).

From roughly the third through the sixth centuries, hostility against homosexual persons became visible in church and civil legislation. However, in the eleventh and twelfth centuries, "with the reemergence of urban centers and more stable social and economic conditions, there appeared a flourishing and publicly visible homosexual subculture that exercised considerable cultural influence, experienced little animosity, and, in fact, was widely tolerated by both religious and civil leaders" (Swidler).

In the latter half of the twelfth century and increasingly in the following two centuries, a distinctively deadly hostility toward homosexual persons began to surface. "Boswell has argued that although 'the causes of this change cannot be adequately

explained...they were probably closely related to the general increase in intolerance of minority groups,' especially Jews, to the crusades against non-Christians and heretics, and to the rise of the Inquisition and the persecution of witchcraft" (Swidler). This intolerance—towards those who visibly deviated from the norm— is readily apparent in the theological and ethical writings of the late Middle Ages. By the end of the sixteenth century, all of Christian Europe had legislation against homosexual practices.

Influences Shaping Christian Ethos

Other influences that have shaped the dominant Christian ethos about homosexuality include a negative view—theologically and morally—of human sexuality in general. The split between spirituality and sexuality that separates spirituality from the body and creates a dichotomy of good and evil has served to make any discussion of sexuality difficult and fraught with bias. "Rather than embracing sexuality as a dimension of sacred passion, Augustine targeted it as its opposite: the source of sin, setting in theological motion a violent antagonism, which christians (and others) have suffered to this day. Split in his passion, disintegrated at the root, the converted Augustine (followed by christian men for 1,600 years) made the connections wrong—between sex and God" (Heyward, *Touching Our Strength*).

Scholar Marvin M. Ellison notes two particularly significant motifs of the negative legacy toward human sexuality. "The first, dating from the early church writers, is a pervasive negativity toward the body and deep moral suspicion about sexual passion in particular. A second motif is the strongly procreative ethic shaping attitudes and practices" (Ellison, "Homosexuality and Protestantism"). According to this norm, all homosexual acts would be judged wrong, as they did not serve a procreative function and therefore were against nature.

The Roman Catholic teaching on human sexuality continued to promote the primacy of procreation and therefore to dismiss homosexuality as unnatural. With the Protestant Reformation, there was a shift away from the view that sex should occur solely for the purpose of procreation. For example, in John Calvin's writings, marriage is meant not only to contain lustful desires nor to channel those passions for procreation but as a "provision for companionship and the mutual care and love between husband and wife" (Ellison). This view still held heterosexuality as the norm but left open the possibility of nonprocreative sexual activity such as homosexuality. In general, though, the Protestant reformers did not challenge the prevailing judgment against homosexuality.

The prevailing attitudes about gender, the power of males over females, the ownership of property, and subsequent behavioral expectations were other factors influencing views about homosexuality in this period. To be a male homosexual that is acted upon was to be like a woman. "(I)t seems that many ancients conceived of 'sexuality' in nonsexual terms: What was fundamental to their experience of sex was not anything *we* would regard as essentially sexual; rather, it was something essentially social—namely, the modality of power relations that informed and structured the sexual act" (Duberman et al.).

Boswell enumerates other claims about gay people—the threats homosexuals pose—that influenced the general level of intolerance. One is the ancient claim that societies that tolerated homosexual behavior were thought to do so to their own detriment. "(I)f all their members engaged in such behavior, these societies would die out. This argument assumes—curiously—that all humans would become exclusively homosexual if given the chance" (Boswell, *Christianity, Social Tolerance and Homosexuality*). It also assumes that erotic and reproductive desires are mutually exclusive, for many persons who had homosexual relations were also in heterosexual relationships and had children.

Boswell goes on to describe a second purposed threat that could explain intolerance towards gays relating to "naturalness." He describes two uses of the word "nature," both of which are crucial to understanding ancient texts as well as modern rhetoric about homosexuality. It is important to distinguish which meaning is in use. The first judges homosexual behavior by whether or not it is ordinary in the physical world. The other definition judges by what is culturally believed to be ideal (and thus "natural") behavior.

The first view of "nature," which he calls "realistic," is defined by its relation to the physical world and observations of it. This would include the thought that unnatural would be uncharacteristic. The "realistic" view questions homosexuality in that it does not serve the "natural" procreative process. "[T]he idea that behavior which is inherently nonreproductive is 'unnatural' in an evolutionary sense, is probably applied to gay people inaccurately. Nonreproductivity can in any case hardly be imagined to have induced intolerance of gay people in ancient societies which idealized celibacy or in modern ones which consider masturbation perfectly 'natural,' since both of these practices have reproductive consequences identical with those of homosexual activity" (Boswell, *Christianity, Social Tolerance and Homosexuality*).

Proponents of "realistic nature" would also claim that homosexuality is not present in nature among animals other than humans. This is of course demonstrably false. Several studies of homosexual behavior and animal life show same-gender pair-bonding (Boswell, *Christianity, Social Tolerance and Homosexuality*).

The second category of "natural/unnatural" opposition relies on what could be called "ideal nature." In this vein, "nature" is always believed to be good; it is idealized. Anything outside of this ideal is "unnatural." Adherents to this concept could label homosexual behavior "unnatural" if they objected to it for religious or personal reasons.

Boswell writes, "Concepts of 'ideal nature' are strongly conditioned by observations of the real world, but they are ultimately determined by cultural values. This is particularly notable in the case of 'unnatural,' which becomes in such a system a vehement circumlocution for 'bad' or 'unacceptable.' Behavior which is ideologically so alien or personally so disgusting to those affected by 'ideal nature' that it appears to have no redeeming qualities whatever will be labeled 'unnatural,' regardless of whether it occurs in ('real') nature never or often, or among humans or lower animals, because it will be assumed that a 'good' nature could not under any circumstances have produced it" (Boswell, *Christianity, Social Tolerance and Homosexuality*).

Scholar and theologian Daniel Helminiak examines the apostle Paul's term "natural" to help unlock key biblical passages about homosexuality. Paul seems to refer to "naturalness" through Boswell's "realistic" category. "For Paul something is 'natural' when it responds according to its own kind, when it is as it is expected to be. For Paul, the word 'natural' does not mean 'in accord with universal laws.' Rather, 'natural' refers to what is characteristic, consistent, ordinary, standard, expected and regular. When people acted as was expected and showed a certain consistency, they were acting 'naturally.' When people did something surprising, something unusual, something beyond routine, some-

thing out of character, they were acting 'unnaturally.' That was the sense of the word 'nature' in Paul's usage" (Helminiak, *What the Bible Really Says About Homosexuality*).

Many who are opposed to homosexuality today often claim that it is "unnatural," using the "ideal nature" tradition while quoting from Paul. However, as previously stated, Paul's use of the word "unnatural" is not meant as an ethical condemnation. An indepth study of Paul's writings clearly shows that this is not his intent. As Helminiak points out, Paul refers to God as "unnatural." "In Romans 11:24, Paul uses those very same words to talk about God. Paul describes how God grafted the Gentiles into the olive tree that is the Jews. Now Jew and Gentile are one in Christ. But to graft a wild tree into a cultivated tree is not the ordinary thing to do; it is something unusual. Still, that is what God did through Christ. In Paul's understanding of the words, God himself acted *para physin*. God did what was 'unnatural.' God behaved 'in an unusual way.' If to act *para physin* is immoral, then God must be immoral—and that is patently absurd. Therefore, there can be no moral meaning in those Greek words for Paul" (Helminiak).

Ancient schools of philosophy that held to the "ideal nature" concept and taught that nonprocreative sex was "unnatural" greatly influenced Western thought. Boswell explains their impact: "The scientific, philosophical, and even moral considerations which underlay this approach have since been almost wholly discredited and are consciously rejected by most educated persons, but the emotional impact of terms like 'unnatural' and 'against nature' persists. Although the idea that gay people are 'violating nature' predates as much as two millennia the rise of modern science and is based on concepts wholly alien to it, many people unthinkingly transfer the ancient prejudice to an imagined scientific frame of reference, without recognizing the extreme contradictions involved, and conclude that homosexual behavior violates the 'nature' described by modern scientists rather than the 'nature' idealized by ancient philosophers" (Boswell, *Christianity, Social Tolerance and Homosexuality*).

OVERVIEW OF KEY PASSAGES ABOUT HOMOSEXUALITY IN THE BIBLE

With this general overview of the historical context of the ancient world and some of its philosophical viewpoints, we now move to a study of Hebrew and Christian scriptural texts often cited in discussions on homosexuality. What Christians refer to as the Old Testament, Jews refer to as the Hebrew Bible. The first two citations from scripture are shared by these religions; the other two refer to Christian scripture alone. In the section "Homosexuality and Judaism," there are additional comments on the Genesis, Judges, and Leviticus texts.

Key arguments for and against homosexuality in the Bible generally stem from varying approaches to biblical interpretation. Two common ways to read the Bible are the literal approach and the historical-critical approach. The literal approach takes the text simply as it reads. The historical-critical approach factors in the historical context and the original reader/audience in order to interpret what it says for today. Without knowing historical and cultural nuances, a literal reading of the Bible allows for as many interpretations as there are readers. Every reader takes her or his own cultural norms and background into the reading. It is helpful to have guidelines to study the Bible so that one can approach that study as objectively as possible, without bringing one's own prejudices and projecting them onto the text. The historical-critical method is not without flaw, but it does foster an in-depth study that is designed to take the text back to its original composition, learn what the intended message was in that context, and then reflect on what it means for us today.

The following brief overview of the biblical passages thought to pertain to homosexuality are presented here by way of a historical-critical interpretation. When these texts are read with a literal interpretation, they are often cited as being judgmental of homosexuality.

From a Christian viewpoint, no matter which approach a reader takes to biblical interpretation, it is important to note that these texts are by far very few in relation to the entire Bible. The Christian scripture simply is not preoccupied with homosexuality.

Finally, it is crucial to note that the word homosexual was not in use in the English language until 1897 and did not appear in a Christian biblical translation until 1952 with the publication of the Revised Standard Version. The original languages in which the Christian Bible was written, Hebrew and Greek, have no word for homosexuality. Furthermore, the ancient world had no specific vocabulary to "connote any particular understanding of sexuality, gender identity, or sexual orientation" (Alexander and Preston, *We Were Baptized Too*).

The two angels came to Sodom in the evening; and Lot was sitting in the gateway of Sodom. When Lot saw them, he rose to meet them, and bowed down with his face to the ground. He said, "Please, my lords, turn aside to your servant's house and spend the night, and wash your feet; then you can rise early and go on your way." They said, "No; we will spend the night in the square." But he urged them strongly; so they turned aside to him and entered his house; and he made them a feast, and baked unleavened bread, and they ate. But before they lay down, the men of the city, the men of Sodom, both young and old, all the people to the last man, surrounded the house; and they called to Lot, "Where are the men who came to you tonight? Bring them out to us, so that we may know them." Lot went out of the door to the men, shut the door after him, and said, "I beg you, my brothers, do not act so wickedly. Look I have two daughters who have not known a man; let me bring them out to you, and do to them as you please; only do nothing to these men, for they have come under the shelter of my roof." But they replied, "Stand back!" And they said, "This fellow came here as an alien, and he would play the judge! Now we will deal worse with you than with them." Then they pressed hard against the man Lot, and came near the door to break it down. But the men inside reached out their hands and brought Lot into the house with them, and shut the door. And they struck with blindness the men who were at the door of the house, both small and great, so that they were unable to find the door (Genesis 19:1-11 New Revised Standard Version [NRSV]).

Both Genesis 19 and Judges 19 are stories of gang rape and protection of male visitors. In both stories a mob of men comes to the door demanding that the visitors of the city be thrown out to them so that they can do with the visitors as they please. The host in each home does not give the visitors to the mob. The practice of showing hospitality to strangers was a grave teaching, so

for the men of the city to do harm to a visitor is what is remarkable. The harm is male gang rape.

The stories address violence toward and subjugation of men. They are not about men loving men; they are about men forcing other men into humiliated submission (the same low status as women). "In the Biblical world of male values, the humiliation of a male was best achieved by making the males act like women in the sex act. To act like women, to be the passive participant in coitus, was thought to be insulting to the dignity of the male. This, far more than homosexuality, was the underlying theme of the Sodom story. The hero of this tale was Lot, a citizen of Sodom, who offered the sanctuary of his home to the angelic messengers and who protected them from the sexual abuse of the men of Sodom. Few preachers go on to tell you that Lot protected these messengers by offering to the mob for their sexual sport his two virgin daughters. You may 'do to them as you please'" (Spong, *Rescuing the Bible from Fundamentalism*).

Biblical scholars Danna Nolan Fewell and David M. Gunn comment on the Judges 19 story: "Finally, an old man, himself a native of Ephraim, takes the tired troop in. While they are relaxing in the old man's house, the men of the city, a worthless lot, surround the house insisting that the Levite be brought out that they might 'know' him. Hardly a welcoming committee, their intent is torture and humiliation, 'sport' at the expense of the Levite. The old man protests, offering him his daughter and the Levite's wife instead. The men, however, are adamant and the Levite, in desperation and no doubt blaming his wife for the situation he is in, seizes her and throws her out to the mob" (Fewell and Gunn, *Gender, Power and Promise*). The very real tragedy is that anyone gets thrown out to the mob, but in both stories women—as men's property—are either offered or are sent out in the visitors' place. Only men and visitors are protected.

You shall not lie with a male as with a woman; it is an abomination (Leviticus 18:22 NRSV).

If a man lies with a male as with a woman, both of them have committed an abomination; they shall be put to death; their blood is upon them (Leviticus 20:13 NRSV).

Leviticus 18:22 and 20:13 are verses that focus on men and their role within a patriarchal society. They are not about lesbian/gay love. In fact, women are not mentioned. "For readers bent on culling from the Bible a blanket condemnation of 'homosexuality' this omission (lesbian sex) is an embarrassment. It is, however, eminently understandable. The text does not construct an essential category of 'homosexuality' but rather it defines sexual boundaries which are part of the construction of patriarchy through the privileging of male control of seed" (Fewell and Gunn).

This segment of the Holiness Code in Leviticus was part of an overall effort to maintain the identity of a minority culture and religion. Male homosexual acts seemed to be a waste of "seed." "There is also the real possibility that male homosexuality (lesbianism is not mentioned in the Hebrew Bible) was abhorred in ancient Israel because it seemed to involve a prodigal waste of 'male seed,' which according to ancient misunderstanding was thought to be limited in quantity or potency. In that event, to be a homosexual was to be derelict in fathering the large families that were the cultural norm for agricultural Israelites" (Gottwald, *The Hebrew Bible*).

However, in contrast to the above, the fear of underpopulation that necessitated protection of the "male seed" was in fact alleviated by the common practice of homosexuality by married men. Some scholars argue that the issue in this passage was not in fact the destruction of the seed but was one of cultic origins (Horner, *Jonathan Loved David*).

Helminiak writes, "Among the early Israelites, as Leviticus sees it, to engage in homogenital sex meant to be like the Gentiles, to identify with the non-Jews. That is to say, to engage in homogenital acts was to betray the Jewish religion." These verses are part of a list in what is called "The Holiness Code," which is a set of instructions on how the Israelites were to remain holy and set apart as God's chosen people. Therefore it was important that the Israelite identity was clearly separate from that of the Gentiles—in particular the Canaanites whom they had conquered to take over the Israelites' Promised Land. "The point is that The Holiness Code prohibits male same-sex acts because of religious considerations, not because of sexual ones.... Homogenital sex is forbidden because it is associated with pagan activities, with idolatry, with Gentile identity" (Helminiak).

The word "abomination" is used in this text and refers to what is unclean. "An abomination is a violation of the purity rules that governed Israelite society and kept the Israelites different from the other peoples" (Helminiak). In a closer examination of the Hebrew and Greek words used for abomination, it becomes clear that the intended meaning is uncleanness and not sin. "The very Hebrew term used in Leviticus conveys the meaning just explained. 'Abomination' is a translation of the word *toevah*. This term could also be translated 'uncleanness' or 'impurity' or 'dirtiness.'... [A]nother Hebrew term, *zimah*, could have been used—if that was what the authors intended. *Zimah* means, not what is objectionable for religious or cultural reasons, but what is wrong in itself...an injustice, a sin" (Helminiak). As the Greek translation followed, similar words were chosen, maintaining the idea of uncleanness rather than sin.

> Do you not know that wrongdoers will not inherit the kingdom of God? Do not be deceived! Fornicators, idolaters, adulterers, male prostitutes, sodomites, thieves, the greedy, drunkards, revilers, robbers—none of these will inherit the kingdom of God. And this is what some of you used to be. But you were washed, you were sanctified, you were justified in the name of the Lord Jesus Christ and in the Spirit of our God (I Corinthians 6:9-11 NRSV).

> "...fornicators, sodomites, slave traders, liars, perjurers, and whatever else in contrary to the sound teaching..." (I Timothy 1:10 NRSV).

First Corinthians 6:9-11 and I Timothy 1:10 deal with idolatrous activity, not with homosexuality as known in its modern sense. "We must acknowledge that 'homosexuality' is not the topic in this passage, and that the two words which, taken together, constitute a reference to it, are part of a traditional list of miscellaneous vices commonly attributed by Jews to Gentiles. Paul uses the list as a reminder to his readers that as Christians, they should have put their old ways behind them. There is no indication that he is aware of or has been asked about any particular problem of homosexual practice in Corinth. In fact, the sexual immorality with which he is specifically concerned in this context is heterosexual in nature" (I Cor. 5:1-5; 6:12-20; Furnish, *Moral Teachings of Paul*).

The key issues in these passages center around the ambiguity of the translations of the words *malakos* and *arsenokoites*. The

first word's meaning is "soft" or "weak," by extension "effeminate." This word was often used for boys who offered their bodies for pay. The second word's literal meaning would be "those who go to bed with males" and has been used to refer to the man who is the active sexual partner. "Although I Corinthians 6:9 is the first documented use of the word, because it is associated here with the term *malakoi* it probably refers to males who engage in sexual activity with other males.... Since *malakoi* would refer to the 'effeminate' or passive partner in such a relationship ... *arsenokoitai* doubtless refers to the male who assumes the more active role" (Furnish). These passages focus on male prostitution and pederasty (adult men having sex with boys), not with what we know of homosexuality today—especially mutual, loving relationships between two adult men.

> For this reason God gave them up to degrading passions. Their women exchanged natural intercourse for unnatural, and in the same way also the men, giving up natural intercourse with women, were consumed with passion for one another. Men committed shameless acts with men and received in their own persons the due penalty for their error (Romans 1:26-27 NRSV).

Romans 1:26-27 is the only verse in the Bible that refers to lesbian sex and is the one that is most specific about same-gender sex. Again, it is important to remember that Paul had no understanding about modern sexual identity or sexual orientation. He is also influenced by the Hellenistic culture that judged homosexual acts because they were nonprocreative as well as because they relinquished traditional gender roles. In this passage he borrows a standard Hellenistic list of moral failings.

Scholars also see that Paul is using a rhetorical argument to get both the Jews' and Gentiles' attention. "To summarize, in the two specific references to same-sex acts in the letters of Paul, they are united with a root cause, idolatry and fornication or adultery. These three components are found in Hellenistic Judaism, especially in the Wisdom of Solomon...also attested in the Deuteronomic history. Paul, therefore, is utilizing a tradition...characterized by Judaism's perspective on gentile depravity. The critical question is, How does Paul regard this threefold tradition? Is it taken up at face value, uncritically, or does Paul use it rhetorically in order to gain the assent of the Jewish boaster whose judgment against gentiles becomes his own condemnation in Romans 2? In this final section the view is maintained that Romans 1:26-27 stands in rhetorical context wherein Paul uses a traditional Jewish pattern of ideas directed against gentile depravity in order to turn the accusation against the accuser" (Edwards, *Gay-Lesbian Liberation*).

Paul is writing to both Jewish Christians and Gentile Christians in Rome. He uses their prejudices against each other to make a point to each of them. Thus he uses rhetorical flair. Interestingly, since homosexuality was an accepted practice, Paul chooses homosexuality as a topic because it is non-threatening. Today, he would likely stay away from the topics of homosexuality or abortion because they are so divisive, instead choosing something more benign. Helminiak explains: "Paul could not talk about clean and unclean foods because debate over foods was still splitting the Christian communities. Likewise, circumcision was still too sensitive an issue. But evidently homogenitality was not. It was an obvious point of difference, and apparently there was no argument over it." The Jews knew the Levitical code denying male-

male sex as unclean; they would not call the Gentiles sinners because of homosexual practices. This mention would only allow the Jewish Christians to feel superior. Simultaneously, the Gentiles were aware of the Jewish attitude towards homosexual acts. Helminiak continues: "The Gentiles just chuckled and shrugged the whole thing off. They would not be offended if Paul raised that issue in his letter. Besides, they knew that Paul was the 'apostle to the Gentiles' (Romans 11:13). Surely, if anything, he was on their side.... The letter to the Romans certainly does not consider homogenital acts to be sinful. Indeed, the success of Paul's letter to the Romans depends on this being so."

HOMOSEXUALITY AND JUDAISM

Historical View

Historically in Judaism as in other religions of the times, sexuality was not understood in terms of a sexual orientation but was thought about in terms of sexual acts. This outlook permeated Jewish history and consequently its traditions. In contemporary Jewish religion, there are diverging views of homosexuality depending on the acceptance of a modern view of sexuality in general. "Sexual acts, not sexuality, provide the foundation for traditional Jewish understandings of the role of sex in human life. People perform sexual acts. Marriage is seen as the proper relationship in which sexual intimacy is to occur" (Eron, "Homosexuality and Judaism").

In the context of marriage, procreation was primary: "Be fruitful and multiply." Sexual pleasure, however, was also part of the picture. In the twelfth century, Rabbi Abraham ben David of Posquieres (Rabad) identified four proper motivations for sexual activity in marriage. "They are (1)procreation and the prescribed times for *onah*, the conjugal rights due to a wife, (2)improving the health of a fetus, (3)satisfying the sexual desires of the woman beyond the prescribed frequency, and (4)restraining the man's sexual desire" (Eron). An ambivalence about sexual activity can be seen within Jewish sources: affirming sexual expression yet encouraging followers to refrain from what was thought of as sexual excess. Regardless of this ambivalence, marriage was viewed as the proper context for sexual activity.

Biblical Roots

A full account of various arguments for or against homosexuality is presented in the Bible section of this chapter. Here are a few more interpretations to add to the Jewish perspective. The Hebrew Bible tells the account of Sodom in Genesis 19. Sodom then is referred to throughout the sacred text as a reference for evil. "The Hebrew Bible...does not focus on the sexual wickedness of the Sodomites but pictures Sodom as the archetype of the sinful nation. The prophets charge the Sodomites with a variety of crimes, including lack of justice (Isa. 1:10; 3:9), disregard of moral and ethical values (Jer. 23:14), and ignoring the impoverished (Ezek. 16:48-49).... On the whole, the rabbis of the Talmud do not interpret the Sodomites' sin as that of homosexuality. Rather, they describe the Sodomites as mean, inhospitable, uncharitable, and unjust" (Eron).

The Holiness Code, also discussed in the Bible section, is often cited by those arguing against toleration of homosexuality. The Code is an ancient group of Israelite legal material within the Book of Leviticus (Leviticus 17-26) that charges the foreign cults of the

Canaanites and Egyptians with a variety sexual sins. "The motivating factor behind the legislation in the Holiness Code is the aspiration that the people of Israel emulate their God in holiness.... [O]bedience to these decrees will distinguish the Israelites from other nations" (Eron). Sexual sinfulness then is seen as idolatrous rebellion against God.

As seen in other religions, the idea that homosexuality goes against the natural order is present in Judaism. "According to rabbis of the Talmud,... male homosexual relations, incest, adultery, and bestiality are...seen as perversions of the natural order" (Eron). This thought ties into the traditional reasons for sexual activity, especially sex for procreation. Even though sex is also for pleasure, it was held that homosexual sex did not provide the same pleasure as heterosexual sex as there was no possibility of offspring. It was also said that male homosexual acts did not provide for the wife's rights or desires and was solely for the purpose of indulging one's own desire. Again we see the uneasiness about gratifying one's sexual desire for pleasure.

Punishment for two Jewish men who have homosexual intercourse is two fold: (1) to be cut off from the people of Israel; and (2) death. "It is doubtful whether this penalty was ever enforced in postbiblical Judaism. First, the Jewish community rarely had the authority to impose the death penalty. Second, even if it did have such authority, in rabbinic literature there is a clear aversion to capital punishment" (Eron). There is clearly not as much information about sex between women (as between men) and the penalty for it. Even then, the prohibitions were rooted in rabbinic teachings rather than biblical law. The prescribed punishment was flogging.

Interestingly, later in the Hebrew Bible, there is evidence of powerful same-gender friendships—what some would even label homoerotic relationships—in the tales of David and Jonathan and Ruth and Naomi. "It would appear that despite the severe commandments of Leviticus and Deuteronomy, attitudes toward same-sex love and gender variance may have relaxed somewhat as struggles with Canaanites lessened. At the very least, it appears as if passionate friendships between members of the same sex were tolerated and even celebrated" (Conner et al. *Cassell's Encyclopedia of Queer Myth, Symbol, and Spirit*).

Contemporary Views

Today, there are varying views of homosexuality in Judaism, from acceptance to judgment. The ranges of acceptance are somewhat related to an openness to contemporary views of sexuality in general and homosexuality specifically.

In conservative circles, the starting point in contemporary Judaism is still the assumption that heterosexuality is the norm and that homosexuality is an aberration. It is discussed as willful sin or mental illness. In addition, many prejudiced perceptions abound, such as the view of homosexuals as pederasts and rapists. Homosexuality is also thought to endanger marriage and family.

Acceptance of gay and lesbian Jews is present in non-Orthodox Judaism. "In 1977, the Central Conference of American Rabbis (C.C.A.R.—Reform) adopted a resolution supporting civil rights for gay people. Similar resolutions were passed by the congregational branch of the Reform movement, the Union of American Hebrew Congregations (U.A.H.C.) in 1975, 1985, 1987, 1989. Gay Jews have formed congregations, and several are now members of the Union of American Hebrew Congregations (Reform)" (Eron). There is also a trend in rabbinical schools toward not considering applicants' sexual orientations in evaluating their admission to the school. Furthermore, within Reform and Reconstructionist Judaism, there has been an increasing acceptance of gay and lesbian rabbis as well as the rights of gay and lesbians in general.

The Conservative movement has kept a more traditional approach, although the rabbinic and congregational branches have adopted similar resolutions on gay and lesbian Jews as the Reform and Reconstructionist movements. While prescribing heterosexuality, the Conservative movement still expressed concern for lesbian and gay Jews as individuals. However, in 1992, the Conservative movement further defined its position. Although the welcoming of gay and lesbian Jews was affirmed, openly gay Jews were not allowed into the movement's rabbinical and cantorial schools or into its Rabbinical Assembly and Cantors Assembly. The Conservative movement also prohibited same-sex commitment ceremonies.

In the 1970s, several gay and lesbian Jewish organizations were formed around the world. In 1972, members founded the gay synagogue Beth Chayim Chadism in Los Angeles and applied for membership in the Union of American Hebrew Congregations. In 1980 in San Francisco, the World Congress of Gay and Lesbian Jewish Organizations was founded to serve as a coordinating body for the many gay Jewish groups. Currently, Congregation Beth Simchat Torah in New York City, with more than 1,000 members, is the largest gay and lesbian synagogue in the world. In the 1990s, smaller groups such as San Francisco's Dyke Shabbos, where lesbians and other women come together to celebrate Shabbat, are also prospering. Several excellent resources for the study of contemporary lesbian and gay Jewish life and thought abound, including Christie Balka and Andy Rose's anthology *Twice Blessed: On Being Lesbian, Gay, and Jewish* and Lev Raphael's book *Journeys and Arrivals: On Being Gay and Jewish*.

HOMOSEXUALITY AND ISLAM

Historical and Scriptural Overview

Although the Koran—Islam's revealed scripture—is explicit in its judgment of homosexuality, in practice what one does in private is of little public concern. In addition, homosexuality is referred to only five times in the Koran, which to some would mean that it was not a matter of primary importance. "In spite of what one might think, the Koran mentions homosexuality only five times...[and] four are references to Lot... Only once is there any mention of homosexuality by Prophet Mohammed, and he says, 'If two men commit indecency, punish them both. If they repent and mend their ways, let them be. God is forgiving and merciful.' There is no mention of the type of punishment nor is there a strongly negative attitude portrayed against it" (Comstock and Henking, *Que(e)rying Religion*).

In fact, several prominent Muslims throughout history were known to have been gay or bisexual. Two examples are Sultan Mehmet Fatih, the Ottoman conqueror of Constantinople (Istanbul), and Sultan Mahmud Ghaznawi, who invaded India from Afghanistan (Duran, "Homosexuality and Islam"). The key here is that these men did not publicly profess their sexuality but instead kept the facade of a heterosexual life, thus avoiding public offense.

The traditional Islamic view holds that the Koran explicitly condemns homosexuality. This is seen in the context of Lot, the Hebrew Bible prophet, also esteemed by the Holy Book of Islam. In fact, in Islamic terminology, homosexuals are known as "Lot's people." In addition, the Koran takes a familiar view of the purpose of sexual activity as that of procreation, although sex for sexual pleasure is also permitted. "Homosexuality is condemned as a transgression against the will of God. It is seen as threatening the human race with extinction. God created humanity not in a playful mood, but to worship God. Homosexuality goes against this very purpose of creation" (Duran). As in Judaism and Christianity, similar refrains about homosexuality being a violation of nature also appear in Islam. Heterosexual activity was made a sacred act; celibacy was abhorred; homosexuality had no place. However, the homosexual act had to be made publicly offensive for it to be punishable.

Cultural Influence

With the traditional view of the Koran alongside the private practice of homosexuality, the cultural climate in Muslim countries adds another layer to understanding Islamic views of homosexuality. There is an impression that homosexuality is a Western notion and thus to be abhorred; the idea of gay rights is vehemently rejected. As Khalid Duran writes in "Homosexuality and Islam," "the situation will probably continue to remain conflictive in the Muslim world more than elsewhere, because a movement for gay rights will not be viewed as indigenous. Rather, it would be considered objectionable as yet another symptom of 'Westernization' or what Khomeinists have come to label as 'Westoxication' (gharbzadegi, literally, 'to be smitten by admiration of things Western')" (Duran).

Also working against the idea of gay rights is the image of gays not as victims but as aggressors. "In order to understand this, one must be aware of the role of homosexual assault in traditional societies with frozen codes of honor. Homosexual rape is regarded as a tool of humiliation surpassed only by the rape of the enemy's female relatives" (Duran). The roots of gay intolerance would then seem to be greatly steeped in cultural ideologies.

Contemporary Outlook

Duran concludes that there is some hope for gays in the reformation of Islamic thought brought about by Ustadh Mahmud M. Taha in Sudan, or possibly in antinomian sufism (mysticism). Clearly, change will occur only as Islamic thought is probed and studied in light of contemporary experience and knowledge. As one gay Muslim writes, "The only way out of this predicament is to realize that Islam is not an absolute religion, with all facets of its belief structure having equal value, but rather it is relative and some aspects of Islam were temporary, some meant for a certain community, some for a certain time, some for the present level of social and cultural evolution of humankind" (Comstock and Henking).

In the United States, the growing Islamic presence is expected to uphold traditional disapproval of homosexuality, although there are a few places of refuge for gay Muslims. "The Islamic Information and News Network, for example, urges Muslims to condemn homosexuality and deny homosexuals human rights; but a few gay Muslims have found tolerance within particular mosques.... In Los Angeles, a Muslim man looked forward to the formation of Salaam, a new group in Los Angeles, because 'it will offer me a safe place to begin my own interpretation of Islam on the issue of homosexuality'" (Comstock).

HOMOSEXUALITY AND HINDUISM

The difficulty of the study of homosexuality and Hinduism is in the lack of information available. There is evidence that homosexuality was known, especially as seen in the punishments listed for it in Hindu canonical and secular law. Otherwise, some scholars say that there is not much that shows that it was widely practiced. Other scholars think that the evidence was actually destroyed in India by direction of Mohandas Gandhi (known as Mahatma in the West) and later under Prime Minister Jawaharlal Nehru. First in the 1920s to 1940s and then in the mid-1940s to mid-1960s, respectively, these leaders demanded that all positive references to same-sex eroticism be erased. These included carvings in Hindu temples dating from the eleventh century (Conner et al.).

Hindu Conceptual Framework

Even with the difficulties described, Arvind Sharma suggests a framework by which one can look at homosexuality through the Hindu lens. He proceeds to use Hindu axiology to view homosexuality through the four classical Hindu legitimate ends of life described in the Purusarthas. They are called *dharma*, which considers righteousness, duty, and virtue; *kama*, which considers material gain; *artha*, which considers love or pleasure; and *moksa*, which considers renunciation of other activities for devotion to religious or spiritual activities in order to liberate oneself from worldly life (Sharma, "Homosexuality and Hinduism"). These concepts underlay the Hindu attitude toward life and daily conduct.

Sharma provides a lengthy presentation of homosexuality as viewed through the concepts of each of the four ends of life. He concludes: "It appears from the foregoing account that, *save for the emphasis on renunciation*, Hinduism is a sex-positive religion in relation to all three ends of human life—*dharma, artha, kama*—and even in relation to *moksa* in the context of the Tantra. This should not be taken to mean, however, that it also views homosexuality within the general field of sex in a positive light" (Sharma). In Sharma's estimation, Dharma and Artha literature somewhat oppose homosexuality, Kama is neither opposed nor supportive, and Moksa would in general downplay sex altogether.

Historical and Cultural Influences

Hinduism is more tolerant of homosexuality as a religion than as a culture. The historical roots for this lie with encounters with non-Hindu cultures such as the Greek, the Islamic, and the British. The practice of homosexuality has thus become associated with these other cultures. In fact, some scholars believed that Gandhi and Nehru's actions to wipe away homosexual references were to erase their connection to Hinduism and to leave the impression that the presence of homosexuality was due only to foreign influences (Conner et al.).

Though the Hindu religion shows some tolerance toward homosexuality, the modern Indian culture still does not. "It seems that in Neo-Hinduism, with the strong element within it of Hindu nationalism as a cultural reaction to foreign domination, homosexuality has come to be identified increasingly as characteristic of the dominant minorities—the Muslims and the British—and therefore reprehensible by association" (Sharma). Though there have been Hindu cultures in history that reflected homoeroticism in their religious carvings and others that were indifferent to ho-

mosexuality, the nationalism in present-day India now reflects great hostility toward homosexuals.

Recent Organizing

In recent years, gay and lesbian persons of South Asian heritage and/or of Hindu background have started to organize socially, politically, and spiritually. "Such groups have also begun publishing journals including *Anamika* (US commencing 1985), *Trikon* (US), *Khush Khayal* (Canada), *Shakti Khabar* (UK), and *Freedom* (India).... Hindu-based groups involving both Indian- and non-Indian individuals, such as the Sadhana Brothers in San Francisco, have also been founded in recent years. Although not limited to Hinduism, the finest book to date on the interrelationship of queer-identified persons and the spiritual traditions of South Asia is Rakesh Ratti's anthology *A Lotus of Another Color: An Unfolding of the South Asian Gay and Lesbian Experience* (1993)" (Conner et al.).

HOMOSEXUALITY AND BUDDHISM

There is great diversity within Buddhist tradition, especially considering various locales such as India, China, Japan, Tibet, and North America as well as different historical periods. Therefore, one cannot distinguish a single Buddhist position regarding homosexuality, although as a whole evidence suggests Buddhism has been for the most part neutral on the subject.

This fundamental neutrality has allowed more flexibility for Buddhism to adapt to various cultural norms. "However, because of the essential neutrality of the Buddhist tradition in this regard, it has adapted to particular sociocultural norms, so that throughout its history we find a wide gamut of opinions concerning homosexual activity, ranging from condemnation (never to the point of active persecution) to praise. Were Buddhist doctrine not neutral in this regard, it would be difficult to see how such disparate opinions regarding homosexuality could have emerged throughout Buddhist history" (Cabezon, "Homosexuality and Buddhism"). Before we move on to the various Buddhist cultures and their views on homosexuality, sexuality in Buddhist ethics must be understood.

Sexuality Issues

In matters of sexuality, the primary issue is not heterosexuality versus homosexuality but sexuality versus celibacy. Also, there are distinctions between what is expected of monastics and lay people. Though celibacy was revered, the sexual, military, and social prowess of the heterosexual male was also of obvious cultural value. The flexibility of Buddhist teaching to adapt to non-celibacy among heterosexuals also allows similar flexibility in other sexual expressions. Scholar Jose Ignacio Cabezon comments, "What this means, of course, is that there is a flexibility to Buddhist ethics that takes for granted certain practices that are proscribed at the level of theory. Therefore, despite the ideal of monastic celibacy, the Buddhist tradition as it has manifested itself in various societies and times has been tolerant of diverse forms of sexual expression, especially at the lay level, but at times in the monasteries" (Cabezon).

Various Buddhist Cultures

In India there have been mixed views toward homosexuality. The Buddhist condemnation for homosexual acts is based on breaking celibacy vows or on male homosexuals taking on a sexually passive role as culturally prescribed for women. The evidence of eloquent prose suggests an acceptance of homoerotic feelings. One story about Buddha tells of a loving relationship that he had with one of his disciples, Ananda. In one tale they are depicted as two deer. The Buddha and Ananda "always went about together...ruminating and cuddling together, very happy, head to head, nozzle to nozzle, horn to horn." In another story, they are "two handsome young sons of Brahmin parents who refuse to marry so that they may remain with each other" (Conner et al.).

Very little scholarly work has been done on Chinese Buddhist views on homosexuality or the practice of it in monasteries. "If, as stated by Louis Crompton, it is the case that the Chinese 'perceptions of homosexuality were primarily aesthetic, literary and anecdotal, not moral, social, religious or scientific,' then scriptural and other data...may not be forthcoming" (Cabezon). Since there was a general acceptance of homosexual love in classical Chinese culture, it is thought that the same acceptance was mirrored in Chinese Buddhism. One account tells of a Buddhist nun who, sometime between the sixteenth and nineteenth centuries, founded the "Ten Sisters" society, "which embraced resistance to heterosexual marriage, passionate friendship and lesbian intimacy and held ceremonies of same-sex union" (Conner et al.). A similar group developed later named the Golden Orchid Association. Also known is a drama revolving around a lesbian love story written in the seventeenth century by Li Yu entitled "Lian Xiangban" ("Pitying the Fragrant Companion"). The present hostility toward homosexuality in China seems to have had a Western Christian influence.

In medieval Japan, homosexuality was "extolled and praised as a secret and mysterious practice that was the greatest source of sexual pleasure available to man" (Cabezon). It was traditionally thought that homosexuality was brought to Japan by Buddhist monks after returning from China. Some think that this account explains why homosexuality became the "preferred form of expression among the Buddhist priesthood" (Conner et al.).

According to Cabezon, Tibetan homosexual practice was seen primarily in a group of "working monks"—the *lDab ldob*—in the larger monasteries and did not meet with public disapproval. Other scholars such as Heinrich Harrar, E. Schafer, and E. Kawaguchi report that same-sex relationships were also prevalent in the Gelug monasteries. These relationships seem to have been particularly noted at the Gelug monastery at Sera, where they were celebrated during the "festival of Lights" held in wintertime (Conner et al.).

Contemporary North American Buddhism

In North American Buddhism, homosexuality is openly practiced and accepted. "Buddhist institutions within North America seem neither to marginalize their lay homosexual constituents, impede their full participation, require their abstinence, nor deny them ordination; and the Dalai Lama has publicly expressed acceptance of same-gender relationships" (Comstock). One well-known Zen-Buddhist temple that serves the gay and lesbian population of San Francisco is the Hartford Street Zen Center (Comstock and Henking). Two recent books reflect gay and lesbian Buddhist experiences: Gavin Harrison's *In the Lap of the Buddha* and Diane Mariechild's *Lesbian Sacred Sexuality*.

HOMOSEXUALITY AND AMERICAN INDIAN RELIGIONS

The Berdache Tradition

In order to examine homosexuality in American Indian religions, it is crucial to understand gender as more fluid than the typical Western perception. In many cultures, an alternative role to male or female has existed. In numerous American Indian societies, this role was referred to by anthropologists as berdache. Because of the vast diversity of tribes, the berdache was of course known by different names and given varying roles. Clearly, no generalization can be made about cultural traditions of North American Indians, although loose patterns can be examined (Williams, *The Spirit and the Flesh*).

"Briefly, a berdache can be defined as a morphological male who does not fill a society's standard man's role, who has a nonmasculine character. This type of person is often stereotyped as effeminate, but a more accurate characterization is an androgyny. Such a person has a clearly recognized and accepted social status, often based on a secure place in the tribal mythology" (Williams). Berdaches were generally known to take on a nonmasculine role, such as being a passive sexual partner with other men. The berdache, in some cultures, became a wife to a man.

Berdaches have special ceremonial roles in many Native American religions. They serve a mediating function between men and women because they are seen as something separate from each. Berdaches also serve a role as mediator between the physical and the spiritual. "In many Native American communities, berdache were regarded as sacred people, chosen by gods and given special powers that could benefit the community" (Swidler). These divine summonses, which were not to be ignored, came through dreams, visions, or experiences later clarified in ceremonies. In some communities, parents guided their child toward an alternative gender role.

The lives of two well-known berdaches, the Zuni We'wha and the Navajo Hastiin Klah, are described by Will Roscoe in an essay entitled "We'wha and Klah: The American Indian Berdache as Artist and Priest" (Comstock and Henking). Jonathan Katz, in *Gay American History*, provides excellent source documents on the berdache tradition as well as gay and lesbian Native American life in general from 1528 to 1976.

The Amazon Tradition

Information about lesbians or female parallels to the berdache is sparse. Among the Lakota there were women called Koskalaka, whose relationships with women were understood to derive from Spirit-direction (Duberman et al.). "The Lakota have a word for some of these women, ksoskalaka, which is translated 'young man' or 'woman who doesn't want to marry,' in our terms, 'dyke.' These women are said to be the daughters (the followers/practitioners) of a Spirit/Divinity who links two women together making them one in Her power" (Duberman et al.). In his book *The Spirit and the Flesh*, Walter Williams uses the word *amazon* to refer in general to the female counterpart to berdache. The amazon's role is distinct from the berdache, although similarities exist: cross-dressing, taking on nontraditional economic roles, and serving a religious ceremonial function.

Destruction of Native Traditions

With the European conquests of the Americas in the sixteenth century began the destruction of entire Indian communities. Consequently, the European rejection of homosexuality also arrived on North American shores. The Spanish conquistadors judged the berdache tradition as barbaric and something to be eradicated. More attacks on the berdache tradition came once Native Americans were confined to reservations, when many religious traditions were banned (Swidler).

Contemporary Traditions

The 1960s saw the reaffirmation of Native American traditions and the 1970s a growing tolerance of homosexual relations in the Euro-American culture, all of which set the stage for a renewal of the berdache tradition (Swidler). "In 1978, 250 *nadle* (Navajo berdache) held a meeting to discuss their role in Navajo religious and community life" (Swidler).

In 1975, Barbara Cameron (Lakota) and Randy Burns (Northern Paiute) founded the Gay American Indian organization (GAI), an event that signaled the modern emergence of gay American Indians (Thompson, *Gay Spirit*). What does the *berdache* have to do with gay people today? Burns responds, "We are living in the spirit of our traditional gay Indian people.... The gay Indian person is probably more traditional and spiritual and more creative than his or her straight counterpart because that was the traditional role we played. The old people, women especially, will tell you that" (Thompson). Ten years after the GAI formed, it had 600 members nationwide. In the late 1980s, "gay Indians gathered under the umbrella name 'Two Spirited People' and spawned the formation of other groups in San Diego, Toronto, and New York City" (Comstock).

OTHER SOURCES OF SPIRITUALITY

Many lesbians and gays have sought out less-traditional religions and other forms of spirituality out of a desire to pursue a spiritual life free of outright discrimination. These alternatives range from relatively new groups to ancient religions or religious practices. A few are profiled below. Often these spiritual paths—directly or indirectly—foster a unique integration of lesbian and gay life. In this way, being homosexual offers a distinctive view of life and thus a special perspective on spirituality. One's sexuality informs one's spirituality, and the lesbian and gay person becomes a spiritual teacher. This view is similar to the view of the berdache in that lesbians and gays offer unique insight because they are on the margins of society.

Queer Spirit

Queer Spirit came out of Queer political activism and seeks to highlight the unique spirituality of lesbians, gays, bisexuals, and transgendered persons. "Many lesbians, gay men, bisexuals, and transgendered individuals living at the end of the twentieth century have begun to (re-) claim the ancient association of same-sex eroticism, transgenderism, and sacred experience or role" (Conner et al.). The process of coming into one's own queer spirit is the personal path of coming out as lesbian, gay, bisexual, or transgendered, finding a political voice, and wrestling with one's spirituality as a queer. This may lead one to stay in traditional religions or to find one more accepting. The key is to remain identified as queer even in traditional religions. "Queer Spirit refers primarily, however to an eclectic movement based in the beliefs that the divine source embraces homoeroticism, lesbianism, bisexu-

Randy Burns

ality, and transgenderism and that persons enacting these behaviors or holding these identities have served in many cultures as spiritual functionaries, which include the role of (ritual) artist or craftsperson as well as that of (spiritual) warrior" (Conner). Queer Spirit honors same-sex and transgendered relationships, emphasizes communion with nature and expression through art, and furthers the ancient role of healer.

Radical Faeries

The Radical Faeries is another group that stemmed from the founders' personal and political journeys. Founded in 1979 by Harry Hay (also founder of the 1950s gay rights group the Mattachine Society), his companion John Burnside, and a small circle of friends, the Radical Faeries sprang from a common need to create a new inner vision, one that would recognize the unique and historic role of gay people as those who mediate between worlds as well as one that would honor the strength of "a circle of loving companions" (Thompson).

The Radical Faeries is not an organized religion per se, with established doctrines or governing bodies. From the Radical Faerie Mailing List on the World Wide Web comes this definition: "The radical Faerie Fellowship is a diverse and unorganized group of Gay men who center their spiritual lives around various and sundry pagan doctrines. While no doctrine predominates, the movement is deeply rooted in the precepts of Native American spirituality. Nonetheless, there are druids, wiccans, taoists, shamans, hindus, and any number of other recognized or unrecognized beliefs present among Radical Faeries. We embrace life in its entirety, yin and yang, drag and mufti. We create rituals meaningful to us in our lives, pagan rituals that validate and celebrate our lives as Gay men."

This openness and preferred lack of organization was evident from the beginning, when 200 men gathered in the Arizona desert on Labor Day weekend in 1979. "A spontaneous theme of paganism emerged.... Invocations were offered to spirits.... (Hay) called on the crowd to 'throw off the ugly green frogskin of hetero-imitation to find the shining Faerie prince beneath'" (Conner et al.).

The Radical Faeries, also referred to as The Faerie Circle, has become an international movement. Its primary publication is the *RFD* (*Radical Faerie Digest*), which lists contacts and various gatherings around the country.

Women-Centered Spirituality

Many lesbians as well as gay men find a spiritual home with Wicca, Goddess Reverence, or Women's Spirituality. All three are based on ancient practices.

Wicca, also known as Witchcraft (though not to be confused with Satanism), is "a matrifocal, earth-centered religion or spiritual tradition with roots in Goddess Reverence and in the ancient belief systems of the Greeks, Celts, and numerous other cultures" (Conner et al.). One Wiccan practice associates with the classical

Harry Hay

goddess Diana, who is often linked with lesbian desire. Because of this association, Dianic Witchcraft is especially viewed as lesbian affirming. "Contemporary Dianic Witches draw upon this rich heritage, infusing it with feminist and lesbian-feminist theory and practice" (Conner et al.).

Goddess Reverence refers to "ancient and tribal worship of a female deity or deities as well as to a contemporary spiritual movement or tradition which is Goddess-centered" (Conner et al.). Women's Spirituality—similar to Queer Spirit in its political birth—is described as "a celebration of the lives, lifestyles and values of women, women's participation in the cycles of the earth and the universe, and women's working toward a better world" (Conner et al.).

All three of these women-centered spiritualities implicitly challenge patriarchy by honoring women's experience and worshiping the Divine Feminine. Though this shift from dominant patriarchal traditions does not necessarily lead to full acceptance of lesbians and gays, it does provide a critical view of sexism and traditional gender roles that so often foster homophobia. In addition, these groups value the body and sexuality rather than maintaining a dualism between sexuality and spirituality, leading to more openness toward sexual diversity.

Lillian Faderman provides a historical sketch of lesbian spirituality in the 1970s in her book *Odd Girls and Twilight Lovers*. She writes, "The witch has particular appeal for lesbian-feminists as a spiritual-political model.... Witches stood for life-oriented, women-oriented values." Then, quoting Z. Budapest, founder of the first feminist coven in 1971, Faderman continues, "Women lost their power through religion. We were determined to gain it back again through a religion that had always belonged to women."

Yoruba

The Yoruba religion has its roots in Nigeria but developed as an African-diasporic tradition in the Americas as Africans were brought over as slaves. Many of the twelve million Africans were of Yoruba ancestry. "In the Yoruba religion there exists a Supreme Being, Olodumare, from whom all other *orisha* (divinities) emanate. Practitioners hold that the *orisha*, as well as the/our ancestors, provide spiritual guidance and imbue those who believe with spiritual energy, called *ashe*" (Conner et al.).

Primarily in the Americas, the Yoruba religion has created a niche for gay, lesbian, bisexual, and transgendered people. In fact, there are more than 25 terms—most of African origin—for such persons, showing their definite presence (Conner et al.). Some of the *orisha* are associated with same-sex eroticism. The Yoruba religion thus is appealing to gays and lesbians in that there are deities who will defend them and mirror their stories, there is an acceptance of homosexual behavior, the temples provide refuge and community, and there is appreciation for the distinct gender variant role of lesbians and gays (Conner et al.).

Twelve-Step Groups

While not a religion, twelve-step groups based on the principles of Alcoholics Anonymous provide spiritual sustenance to lesbian and gay alcoholics and their friends and families. One enters the program out of a desire to quit drinking or other compulsive behaviors (Overeaters Anonymous, Sex Addicts Anonymous, Narcotics Anonymous to name a few) and quickly finds that the twelve steps lead one through a spiritual journey, relying on a

Higher Power—as well as the group—for strength and wisdom. There are now numerous lesbian and gay twelve-step groups, which are open to all people but specifically foster a safe atmosphere for lesbians and gays. Here people tell their stories and find strength and hope not only for their addictions but also as lesbians and gays.

HOMOSEXUALITY AND CHRISTIANITY IN RECENT AMERICAN HISTORY

When we turn to modern history, we see some of the same threads of ancient history in the discrimination of homosexuals on the grounds that it is "unnatural" and breaks from prescribed gender roles. The Bible is often cited and thought to give outright direction to condemn and persecute gays and lesbians. This biblical view seeps into government legislation, which otherwise seeks to keep religion and state matters separate. Of course, the cultural climate fosters various religious views and vice-versa—religion informs culture. As we will see through American history in the last 50 or so years, a growing cultural tolerance has begun to influence gay and lesbian tolerance within various religious bodies. Conversely, at times it has been liberal religious leaders who have stood with gays and lesbians and called for tolerance and compassion and thus helped moved society further towards acceptance of sexual diversity.

Fueling the gay and lesbian civil rights movement have been countless courageous gay women and men who have risked their jobs, families, and lives to further equality for all people. This movement began to take shape after World War II, when significant gay and lesbian populations remained and grew in various cities. As these neighborhoods developed, so did the image of gay and lesbian life appear. Bringing together gays and lesbians in new numbers socially revealed shared stories of oppression and discrimination and thus engendered the momentum to fight for change.

Several decisive moments stand out in this history. Among them, the Stonewall Riots in New York City in 1969 was a watershed incident. In addition, in San Francisco four years earlier an incident involving the newly formed Council on Religion and the Homosexual (CRH) was instrumental in leading to public policy changes in regards to police activity in the gay and lesbian community.

Council on Religion and the Homosexual

The Council was formed by homosexual activists (including members of the gay rights groups The Mattachine Society and the Daughters of Bilitis) and Protestant ministers to promote a continued dialogue between the church and homosexuals. Its roots were in the efforts of the Reverend A. Cecil Williams and the Reverend Ted McIlvena of Glide Memorial Methodist Church in San Francisco to begin a ministry in 1962 with homosexuals in the "Tenderloin" area of the city (Comstock).

"On the eve of 1 January 1965, the Council, along with SIR (Society for Individual Rights), Mattachine, and DOB (Daughters of Bilitis), sponsored a fund-raising ball at California Hall. When the sponsoring ministers met with police before the ball, the police first tried to get them to cancel the event; after the ministers refused, the police then promised not to interfere" (Miller, *Out of the Past*). The police did intervene. In fact, many described what seemed like a war zone. "The police lit up the entrance with klieg lights and photographed each one of the six hundred people who entered, many of whom were in costume" (Miller). The police made constant supposed "inspections" of the building. Anyone interfering was arrested. One gay lawyer, Herb Donaldson, who returned to the site after he was arrested and released, recalled of the scene, "For all intents and purposes, the police were just running roughshod, walking in and out across the dance floor like they had taken over the place.... Some of the people were just terrified" (Miller).

On 2 January, a group of ministers with CRH held a news conference and angrily denounced the police. "The liberal ministers insisted on fighting the charges and exposing abuse by the police. For once, the judge, jury, and news media took the side of the homosexual because, as historian John D'Emilio notes, 'the ministers provided a legitimacy to the charges of police harassment that the word of a homosexual lacked.' The long-standing complaints of homosexuals were finally believed; police practices in bars actually changed; and the CRH felt encouraged to fight on for the freedom of homosexuals" (Comstock).

The Council established chapters in other cities and became the leading organization to educate clergy about homosexuals. It was instrumental in getting discussions going about homosexuality in many mainline denominations. The First National Conference on Religion and the Homosexual was held at the Interchurch Center in New York in 1971 (Comstock).

Publications on Christianity and Homosexuality

Starting in 1943 with the publication of *On Being a Real Person* by the Reverend Harry Emerson Fosdick, founding minister of the Riverside Church in New York, there have been significant volumes published on issues surrounding Christianity and homosexuality. Fosdick's book initiated a conversation about pastors being trained to minister to homosexual people. Though he still referred to homosexuality as a disease, he did not name it as a sin. In 1948, Henry Van Dusen, president of Union Theological Seminary in New York, published *Christianity and Crisis,* in which he decried the findings of the Kinsey Report as proof of the growing moral decadence in American society. These two approaches— one of condemnation, the other of acceptance and concern—came to typify the struggle within Christian circles (Comstock).

The 1955 book *Homosexuality and the Western Christian Tradition*, written by Britain's Derrick Sherwin Bailey, proved to be a foundational work. The importance of this work lies in its groundbreaking scholarly effort "to challenge traditional interpretations of allegedly antihomosexual biblical passages and to examine the European church's historical persecution of homosexuals" (Comstock). Another pioneering book was *Christ and the Homosexual* by the Reverend Robert W. Wood, a United Church of Christ minister; it was the first religious book written about homosexuality by an openly gay person. In addition to books of the times, one leading Christian magazine published an article on homosexuality in 1968. "The influential *Christian Century* magazine, for instance, found merit in proposals for law reform, equal employment opportunity, and an end to police abuses, even as it described as 'highly dubious' the notion that homosexuality might be morally desirable" (D'Emilio, *Sexual Politics, Sexual Communities*). Other publications followed throughout the 1960s and to the present and have provided much needed insight into theological and biblical understandings as well as into the lives of lesbian and gay Christians. Some of these more recent publications include Tom Horner's *Jonathan Loved David* (1978); Letha Scanzoni

Reverend Troy Perry

and Virginia Ramey Mollenkott's *Is the Homosexual My Neighbor?* (1978); John Boswell's *Christianity, Social Tolerance, and Homosexuality* (1980); Carter Heyward's *Touching Our Strength* (1989); and Robert Goss's *Jesus Acted Up* (1994).

Gay and Lesbian Churches

The first known gay and lesbian congregation was organized by George Hyde in 1946 on Christmas Eve in Atlanta. There were 85 people present that first night. A forerunner to other gay churches, it was named the Eucharistic Catholic Church.

In Los Angeles in 1968, the Reverend Troy Perry held a worship service for 12 people and thus began what is now the Universal Fellowship of Metropolitan Community Churches. This is the first Christian denomination whose primary outreach is to lesbians and gays. Its largest congregation in this now-worldwide denomination is the Cathedral of Hope MCC in Dallas, Texas, which boasts a membership of more than 2,000. The Samaritan Institute for Religious Studies, the denomination's educational arm, also resides in Dallas. The denomination has twice applied for membership in the National Council of Churches, in 1983 and 1992. Although it met all qualifications, its application and admission were denied.

Other gay and lesbian churches have formed over the years. One that focuses on outreach to lesbian and gay African Americans is the Unity Fellowship. Also known as Unity Fellowship of Christ

Church, the movement was founded in 1985 in Los Angeles by Bishop Reverend Carl Bean. The Fellowship's motto is "God is Love and Love is for Everyone." Today there are a total of nine churches located in California, New York, New Jersey, Michigan, Georgia, Washington, and Washington D.C. The church's website is: http://members.aol.com/UnityNY/index.html.

Actions by Religious Bodies

With the rise of the gay rights movement after Stonewall and the increased visibility of gays and lesbians, discussion in the church began to intensify. The civil rights movement in society was reflected in mainline denominations.

In the early 1970s, three religious bodies made significant decisions. "In 1970, the Lutheran Church of America and the Unitarian Universalist Association became the first denominations to adopt formal statements opposing discrimination against homosexuals and encouraging education about homosexuality within their churches. In 1972, the United Church of Christ became the first denomination to ordain an openly gay candidate for ministry, Reverend William Johnson" (Comstock).

In the years that followed, the discussion of homosexuality increasingly became a topic for debate in all denominations. Fourteen made public statements within five years time. Many of these supported gay civil rights yet held to their traditional teachings

551

on the incompatibility of homosexuality and Christian virtue (Comstock). These same debates continue within the Christian church. Several of the denominations have conducted surveys and studies of homosexuality. Gary David Comstock in *Unrepentant, Self-Affirming, Practicing* devotes an entire chapter to these studies.

Rise of Gay and Lesbian Organizations within Christianity

During the 1970s, lesbians and gays within mainline denominations began to organize for change. Many groups formed for the purpose of advocacy, education, and support. As debate on homosexuality increased and antihomosexual rhetoric was being advanced where before the issue had not appeared at all, these lesbian and gay advocacy groups were there as spokespersons for the homosexual community. Though many denominations conducted studies of homosexuality, few actually put any weight on the experience of gay women and men themselves. At various national denominational meetings, gay and lesbian speakers were often refused the right to speak for themselves. These groups thus were crucial to educating the church at-large, outside of official meetings and studies. They were also a rallying point and refuge for many closeted gays and lesbians remaining in the church.

There continues to be debate about the best form of political maneuvering within Christian denominations. Robert Goss in *Jesus Acted Up* proposes two types of resistance: reformist and transgressive. The reformists work toward transforming "existing cultural and political institutions" while transgressives aim to create "a new language around which to construct gay/lesbian lives, to articulate their identities, to express freedom, and to resist oppression." Transgressives would be against assimilating to the dominant heterosexist culture in order to find acceptance. In reality, over the years, both strategies have been utilized within lesbian and gay advocacy groups in mainline denominations—if not on a national level, at least on an individual basis.

The following is a list of the most well-known groups within mainstream Christian denominations. Many of their Internet websites are noted in the reference section. Louie Crew, founder of Integrity, has published a concise and informative historical outline of the Episcopal Church and Lesbigay Issues on the Integrity website. Other historical material, contact names, as well as listings of upcoming events are available on these websites.

GROUP NAME / DENOMINATION AFFILIATION

Affirmation / United Methodist
Affirmation / Mormon
Brethren Mennonite / Brethren, Mennonite Council
Dignity USA / Catholic
Emergence International / Christian Scientist
Evangelicals Concerned / Evangelical Christians
Friends for Lesbian and Gay Concerns / Quakers
GLAD Alliance / Disciples
Honesty / Southern Baptist
Integrity / Episcopal
Interweave / Unitarian
Lutherans Concerned North America / Lutheran
Walk Away / Ex-fundamentalists

Two groups in particular that are doing gay and lesbian interfaith advocacy are the Interfaith Alliance and the Interfaith Working Group. The Interfaith Alliance has been described by gay magazine *The Advocate* as "a national organization of clergy and lay

people who argue to school board members and Congress members alike that the religious right doesn't speak for all people of faith." They have a membership of 60,000 people in 112 chapters. The mission of the Interfaith Working Group, according to their website, is to "inform the public of the diversity of religious opinion on social issues where it is not widely recognized by providing a voice and a forum for religious organizations, congregations and clergy in the Philadelphia area who support gay rights, reproductive freedom, and the separation of church and state."

Christian Lesbians Out or CLOUT is a movement for Christian lesbians, who often experience a two-fold coming out—as a lesbian in Christian circles and as a Christian in lesbian circles. CLOUT began in 1991 as an intercultural, multiracial, solidarity movement organized by 113 lesbian clergy and laywomen from across the United States and Europe representing 14 Christian denominations. They now have a quarterly newsletter and regional and national gatherings.

Another group providing crucial support is Presbyterian Parents of Gays and Lesbians, which was founded by Jane Loflin—the mother of a gay son—in 1994 in Dallas, Texas. It has now expanded to other cities and is working with other denominations to begin plans for similar organizations.

Welcoming Congregation Movement

Various denominational advocacy groups have long thought that education about gay and lesbian issues needed to be presented at the local church level. This would create a grass roots movement for change in the church. Starting in the late 1970s in the Presbyterian Church with the More Light Churches Network and continuing into the early 1990s, various denominational groups have developed to interact with local churches wanting be inclusive of gay and lesbian people. This network of programs has now become known as the Welcoming Congregation Movement. They have helped hundreds of churches to take a public stance against homophobia and heterosexism and for openness to all people of diverse sexual orientations.

The following numbers and list come from the Winter 1997 issue of *Open Hands*, a quarterly publication of four programs of the Welcoming Congregation Movement. These figures were based on findings as of 1 February 1997.

"Since 1978, 735 local churches, 36 campus ministries, 29 judicatories, and 4 national ministries have publicly declared themselves welcoming of all people, including gay men and lesbian women. This represents an increase of 25 percent over last year! These 804 welcoming communities are found in ten denominations in 46 states, plus the District of Columbia and Canada."

No.	NAME OF PROGRAM	DENOMINATION
7	Affirm United	United Church of Canada
75	More Light Churches Network	Presbyterian
39	Oasis	Episcopal
217	Open and Affirming	United Church of Christ
34	Open and Affirming	Disciples
147	Reconciled in Christ	Lutheran
142	Reconciling Congregation	United Methodist
13	Supportive	Brethren/Mennonite
26	Welcoming and Affirming	American Baptist
107	Welcoming	Unitarian Universalist

The Winter 1993 issue of *Open Hands* gives a brief history of the Welcoming Congregation Movement. Each *Open Hands* issue presents news of various congregations and rulings from key denominations as well as informative articles centered on topical themes.

Three other groups not on the above list are the National Gay Pentecostal Alliance, begun in 1980; The Supportive Congregations Network, which is a network of Mennonite, General Conference Mennonite, and Church of the Brethren congregations; and AWARE, started in 1983 by a few people in the Christian Reformed Church in Toronto, Ontario.

By and large, these groups are not endorsed by their respective denominations. Two exceptions are the United Church of Christ and the Unitarian Universalist Association, the two most pro-gay denominations. Gary David Comstock in *Unrepentant, Self-Affirming, Practicing* provides a list of religious groups' general stance on homosexuality from the most accepting to the least accepting. He also goes into more detail and outlines four different categories of official positions: rejecting, semirejecting, semiaccepting, and accepting. He lists which religious bodies fall under which category.

One belief that is shared by some members of these mainline denominations is the fear that accepting homosexuality will divide their denominations. Many of these religious bodies were already seeing declining numbers, although there is disagreement about the reasons for the decline. Some believe that it is the church's lag behind modern science and culture that has led to the decline; the church is viewed as irrelevant to life today. However, those denominations that have taken accepting stances toward gays and lesbians have not seen massive declines in their memberships.

The Roman Catholic Church

In the 1980s the Roman Catholic Church, under the leadership of Pope John Paul II, cracked down on dissent from church teaching on homosexuality. Several officials writing or speaking in opposition to the church were stripped of their orders or severely sanctioned. In 1986, the Vatican toughened its stance even further through a document issued by the Congregation for the Doctrine of the Faith. This letter declared that "even an inclination toward homosexuality was 'an objective disorder.'" The letter further stated that "'special concern and pastoral attention should be directed towards those who have this condition, lest they be led to believe that living out this orientation in homosexual activity is a morally acceptable option. It is not.... It is only in the marital relationship that the use of the sexual faculty can be morally good. A person engaging in homosexual acts therefore acts immorally'" (Miller).

This statement also directed that all support should be withheld from groups that undermined church teaching on homosexuality. This of course led to the expulsion of Dignity chapters from Roman Catholic Churches where they held mass. At that time there were 100 chapters nationwide with 5,000 members (Miller).

On 30 September 1997, U.S. Catholic bishops issued a groundbreaking statement, entitled "Always Our Children," directed toward parents of gays and lesbians. The document was approved by the Administrative Board of the National Conference of Catholic Bishops. In the form of a pastoral letter, the bishops advised parents to put love for their gay children before church doctrine that condemns homosexuality. They also counseled parents not to reject their children and affirmed that homosexuality is not chosen but is an orientation.

CNN News Service reported excerpts of the letter, "All in all, it is essential to recall one basic truth. God loves every person as a unique individual. Sexual identity helps to define the unique person we are. God does not love someone any less simply because he or she is homosexual.... This child, who has always been God's gift to you, may now be the cause of another gift: your family becoming more honest, respectful and supportive." The letter also encouraged priests to be open to lesbians and gays in their parishes, help with support groups for their parents, and speak from the pulpit about the priest's willingness to discuss homosexual issues.

The U.S. bishops made a distinction between homosexual orientation and sexual activity, and urged parents to encourage their children to lead chaste lives. The letter did not abandon church doctrine, as it reiterated that genital sexual activity between same-sex partners is immoral. The point of the document, then, was to support parents of gay and lesbian children in loving their children no matter their sexual orientation.

Christian Conservatives

A backdrop to the struggle for lesbian and gay rights within mainline Christian denominations has been the rise of what is called the Religious Right. Starting in the 1970s during a backlash to the gay rights movement, several conservative Christian spokespeople came on the scene to denounce homosexuality.

In Miami in January 1977, the Dade County Commission joined other cities—about 40 in number—in enacting gay rights protection. In response to that decision, pop singer and born-again Christian Anita Bryant announced that she would lead a campaign to repeal the ordinance. "Bryant had testified at commission hearings, claiming that gay rights protections would 'violate my rights and the rights of all decent and morally upstanding citizens.'... Within six weeks, Bryant's organization, Save the Children, Inc., had collected sixty-five thousand signatures on a petition to force a county-wide referendum on the ordinance. Suddenly, organized opposition to the gay rights movement had emerged" (Miller). Bryant was instrumental in fostering the notion that homosexuals recruit by repeatedly stating, "Homosexuals cannot reproduce, so they must recruit."

In the 1980s, with the election of Ronald Reagan as president, the Religious Right now had an ally in office. Jerry Falwell and his group the Moral Majority typified the political agenda of the conservative Right. Homosexuality was one of several key issues; but, counting on (and fueling) the antihomosexual public fervor, these groups found that homosexuality was a lucrative way to fill their bank accounts. "A 1981 fund-raising letter from Jerry Falwell, echoing Anita Bryant, went, 'Please remember, homosexuals do not reproduce! They recruit! And many of them are out after my children and your children'" (Miller).

During the 1980s, conservative Christians evolved into the most-vocal critics of gay and lesbian rights. Using their well-organized grass-roots network, conservative Christians began pressuring politicians and corporations on matters of gay rights.

By the 1990s, the Religious Right had effectively entered mainstream politics, especially the Republican Party. At the 1992 GOP Convention, speaker after speaker expressed antigay messages. Pat Robertson, a key figure for the Religious Right and well known for his antihomosexual rhetoric, was perhaps the most outspoken in his attacks on gay and lesbians, but even President George Bush and Vice President Dan Quayle, vying for conservative votes, spoke against gays and lesbians. Outside of party politics, the Religious Right turned its attention to overturning gay rights ordinances in Portland, Maine and Tampa, Florida. They also pushed to forbid ordinances designed to protect gays against discrimination.

Mainline Denominations in the 1990s

The two issues at the top of the debate on homosexuality and the church in the 1990s are ordination of openly gay and lesbian persons and same-sex wedding ceremonies. Though many denominations support civil rights for gays and lesbians, their support wanes when it comes to job discrimination or church rites.

Many gay and lesbian persons have been ordained throughout history. However, as previously mentioned, the Reverend William Johnson in 1972 was the first openly gay person to be ordained. Much of the denominational debate and study of homosexuality is about allowing gays and lesbians to be ordained. In essence, many denominations today have a general practice similar to the military's "Don't Ask, Don't Tell" policy.

Through the years, openly gay and lesbian clergy have had their ministerial credentials threatened or withdrawn. In the 1980s, Rose Mary Denman, a United Methodist clergywoman in New Hampshire, was forced to undergo an ecclesiastical trial because of her lesbianism. The result was a suspension from performing ministerial duties. In another more recent trial with an interesting twist, Episcopal Bishop Walter Righter was brought up on heresy charges for ordaining an openly gay man, the Reverend Barry Stopfel. The trial was thrown out by an Episcopal court that ruled that church doctrine does not prohibit ordaining gays and lesbians in committed relationships. The court said that they were not ruling on the morality of homosexual relationships but on the issue of whether or not a bishop can ordain persons living in a committed gay or lesbian relationship. Stopfel published his story in his book, *Courage to Love*.

The *Dallas Morning News* reported Bishop Righter's comment: "We're making too much out of bedrooms. The question isn't gay. It's what kind of relationship do they have? Is it monogamous? Is it faithful?" Bishop John Spong of Newark—longtime supporter of gay rights and author of numerous books including *Living in Sin?* and *Rescuing the Bible from Fundamentalism*—also commented: "It means we take seriously our baptismal vows that we respect the dignity of every human being. The real issue is not sexual orientation. It's the holiness of a person's life."

The most recent ruling of mainline denominations has involved the Presbyterian Church (U.S.A.). Meeting in June 1997, the General Assembly moved to send a less-restrictive amendment for ratification to its presbyteries. This new amendment "would require those seeking ordination to 'demonstrate fidelity and integrity in marriage or singleness, and in all relationships of life' rather than living 'in fidelity within the covenant of marriage of a man and a woman or chastity in singleness,'" as in the previous amendment (*Open Hands*, Summer 1997). In the *New York Times*, one pastor responded to the compromise amendment. "'This is a way into the future,' said the Rev. John Lohr of Palisades, N.J. 'It's an interim step. It doesn't resolve the issue, but it gives us space for grace'" (*New York Times*, 21 June 1997).

Same-sex unions have been another important issue in the church, especially as the state of Hawaii considers legalizing these marriages. The concern revolves around questions of whether or not the church should hold these ceremonies as well as if pastors should officiate at them.

One church that struggled toward a decision to hold a holy union for two of its gay male members was Pullen Memorial Baptist Church in Raleigh, North Carolina, which in 1992 decided to endorse same-gender holy unions. Its move incensed Baptist officials, who "excommunicated" the church from the Raleigh Baptist Association and the North Carolina Baptist State Convention. After Pullen's 109 years of membership, the Southern Baptist Convention voted them out of the organization. One member gave a detailed account of the decision process and the aftermath in *Que(e)rying Religion*. She ended with these words, "It was, for all the pain it has caused before and since, a joy. Lesbians and gay men were being affirmed by a predominantly straight congregation. It wasn't just that we are capable of being Christian. It was that our deepest love has the potential to be a holybond. And this affirmation was from my own family of faith. Five years ago I could not have imagined such a gift."

Other Issues

Many important issues still face Christian denominations, especially in regards to pastoral care. For gay and lesbian youth, some of whom are growing up in the church, the suicide rate is 30 to 40 percent higher than for straight youth (U.S. Department of Health, "Report of the Secretary's Task Force on Youth Suicide"). Coming out, reevaluating one's life image, and mending damaged self-esteem are only a few of the issues that need to be seen in a spiritual light. For many religious gay people, coming out can be a faith crisis as well as an identity crisis. Pastors also need to be aware of the concerns of the parents, siblings, children, and other loved ones of gays and lesbians. They too receive the brunt of homophobia and heterosexism and are forced to deal with their own painful coming out process.

The church must also deal with sexuality issues in general. Some of the hardest work may come as American society begins to unpack gender issues, especially as gender studies begin to elaborate on new thinking on the fluidity of gender. Many courageous transgendered men and women have already begun to challenge the church.

Mainline churches will also need to look at their theological witness of exclusion rather than acceptance of gay and lesbian Christians in light of their baptismal theology. Baptism is a symbolic ritual, exemplifying God's love for all. In a book on this subject, South African Anglican Archbishop Desmond Tutu writes in the foreword, "We reject them (lesbians and gays), treat them as pariahs, and push them outside the confines of our church communities, and thereby we negate the consequences of their baptism and ours. We make them doubt that they are children of God, and this must be nearly the ultimate blasphemy" (Alexander and Preston).

PROMINENT PEOPLE

Christie Balka and Andy Rose

Christie Balka and Andy Rose published the anthology *Twice Blessed: On Being Lesbian or Gay and Jewish* in 1989. Balka is an activist who has written and spoken on the Middle East, feminism, and lesbian and gay issues. Rose is a social worker and community activist.

Derrick Sherwin Bailey (1910-1984)

Derrick Sherwin Bailey wrote *Homosexuality and the Western Christian Tradition*, which was the first scholarly work to challenge in detail traditional interpretations of biblical passages ostensibly related to homosexuality.

Nadean Bishop (1932-)

Nadean Bishop was the first openly gay minister to be hired by a local congregation within the American Baptist Churches in the United States. This historical event occurred in 1992 at the University Baptist Church in Minneapolis.

John Boswell (1947-1994)

John Boswell was the A. Whitney Griswold Professor of History at Yale University. His books include two groundbreaking scholarly pieces on Christianity and homosexuality: *Christianity, Social Tolerance, and Homosexuality* and *Same-Sex Unions in Premodern Europe.*

Malcolm Boyd (1923-)

Malcolm Boyd, Episcopalian priest and longtime social activist, has been one of the most successful gay Christian writers. His books include *Are You Running with Me Jesus, Take Off the Masks, Look Back in Joy: A Celebration of Gay Lovers, Gay Priest: An Inner Journey,* and *Half Laughing/Half Crying.* In 1981 he was appointed chaplain of Integrity, the gay and lesbian organization within the Episcopal church.

Randy Burns and Barbara Cameron

Randy Burns and Barbara Cameron founded Gay American Indians (GAI) in 1975 in San Francisco. Burns, with Will Roscoe, edited *Living the Spirit: A Gay American Indian Anthology.*

Rosemary Curb (left) and Nancy Manahan

Rosemary Curb (1940-) and Nancy Manahan (1946-)

Rosemary Curb and Nancy Manahan edited the groundbreaking book of essays *Lesbian Nuns: Breaking Silence,* published in 1985. Both have published various articles on lesbian spirituality.

Rose Mary Denman

Rose Mary Denman, a United Methodist minister, was tried by an ecclesiastical court in New Hampshire and suspended from performing ministerial duties because of her lesbianism. Her bishop started the formal proceedings to void her ordination after she wrote about being gay in a gay newspaper. She is the author of *Let My People In: A Lesbian Minister Tells of Her Struggles to Live Openly and Maintain Her Ministry,* published in 1990.

Issan Dorsey (1933-1990)

Issan Dorsey was certified by the Zen Center in San Francisco in 1989 as an authentic teacher and living representative of Buddha's lineage. The Gay Buddhist Club of which he was the abbot then became the Hartford Street Zen Center (also known as One Mountain Temple). He also started an AIDS hospice. His life story is presented in *Street Zen: The Life and Works of Issan Dorsey,* written by David Schneider.

Antonio Feliz

Antonio Feliz was a Mormon bishop who came out publicly about his homosexuality. He is the author of *Out of the Bishop's Closet: A Call to Heal Ourselves, Each Other, and Our World.*

James Ferry

James Ferry had his license to exercise his duties as a priest of the Anglican Church of Canada withdrawn because of his homosexuality. He is the author of *In the Court of the Lord: A Gay Priest's Story.*

Chris Glaser

Chris Glaser is a well-known gay activist in the Presbyterian Church. His books include *Uncommon Calling: A Gay Man's Struggle to Serve the Church, Come Home, Coming Out to God,* and *The Word Is Out.*

Harry Hay (1912-)

Harry Hay founded the Radical Faeries, a gay men's spirituality network with its first gathering in the Arizona desert on Labor Day weekend in 1979. He also founded the Mattachine Society, a male homosexual rights group in Los Angeles, in 1948.

Carter Heyward (1945-)

Carter Heyward was among the first group of women ordained priests within the Episcopal Church. She is a professor of Theology at Episcopal Divinity School in Cambridge, Massachusetts, and author of several books, including *Our Passion for Justice, Touching Our Strength: The Erotic as Power and the Love of God,* and *Staying Power.*

George Hyde

George Hyde started the first gay congregation in 1946 in Atlanta while he was a minister in the independent Catholic movement. Services were held in a gay bar on Christmas Eve for 85 people. They formed the Eucharistic Catholic Church, which was the forerunner of the gay church movement.

Jane Adams Spahr

William Johnson

William Johnson was the first openly gay person in the history of the Christian church to be ordained. He was ordained by The Golden Gate Association of the Northern California Conference, United Church of Christ, in 1972. He went on to found the UCC Gay Caucus.

Lucy Ann Lobdel (1829-1891)

Lucy Ann Lobdel published her 48-page autobiography called "The Narrative of Lucy Ann Lobdel, the Female Hunter of Dela-

ware and Sullivan Counties, New York" in 1855. In 1883, she entered an insane asylum as Rev. Joseph Lobdel. Her case was one of the earliest reports on lesbianism. She declared that she was a man, a Methodist minister, and married to a woman. The complexities of her life connected feminist protest, transvestitism, and lesbianism. Her story is documented in Jonathan Katz's *Gay American History.*

Phyllis Lyon (1924-) and Del Martin (1921-)

Phyllis Lyon and Del Martin were two of eight founders of the

Daughters of Bilitis, a lesbian rights group. They were also found-ing members of the Council on Religion and the Homosexual.

John McNeill

John McNeill is a gay Roman Catholic priest who was silenced by the Vatican and expelled from the Jesuit Order. He was sanc-tioned for arguing for the acceptance of monogamous homosexual relationships as a lesser evil than promiscuity in his article "The Christian Male Homosexual," published in the Catholic clerical journal *Homiletic and Pastoral Review* in 1970. Later, he pub-lished *The Church and the Homosexual.*

Troy Perry (1940-)

Troy Perry, a former Pentecostal minister, founded the Univer-sal Fellowship of Metropolitan Community Churches in Los An-geles in 1968. He continues to head this now-international denomi-nation whose outreach is primarily to lesbians and gay men. He is the author of *The Lord Is My Shepherd*, published in 1972, and *Don't Be Afraid Anymore: The Story of Reverend Troy Perry and The Metropolitan Community Churches,* published in 1990.

Michael Piazza

Michael Piazza is the senior pastor of the Cathedral of Hope Metropolitan Community Church in Dallas, Texas, the world's largest gay and lesbian congregation, with a membership of over 2,000. He is the author of *Holy Homosexuals: The Truth about Being Gay or Lesbian and Christian* and *Rainbow Family Values.*

Jane Adams Spahr

Jane Adams Spahr was called to be associate pastor for the Downtown United Presbyterian Church in Rochester, New York, as an open lesbian. Her call was later challenged and blocked by the National Church Court. She then served as National Evange-list Educator in order to help people understand the need for ac-ceptance of gay/lesbian/bisexual persons and their right to serve the church. Two videos based on her experiences have been pro-duced, "Maybe We're Talking About a Different God" and "Your Mom's a Lesbian, Here's Your Lunch, Have a Nice Day."

We' wha (1849-1896)

We' wha was a Zuni lhamana (in the general anthropological term, a berdache) who served as spiritual guide, dressing in tradi-tional female dress and excelling at sacred arts and crafts. One of the most renowned two-spirit leaders, lauded by President Grover Cleveland and others, We' wha is the subject of Matilda Coxe Stevenson's "The Zuni Indians," published in 1901-1902, and of Will Roscoe's 1991 acclaimed anthropological treatise *The Zuni Man-Woman.*

Mel White (1940-)

Mel White, former speech writer for leaders of the Christian Right, is currently Minister for Justice for the Universal Fellow-ship for the Metropolitan Community Churches. He has written numerous books and produced various video documentaries, in-cluding one on survivors of the Jonestown Massacre, a grisly mass suicide of a 1970s religious cult. He published his coming out story and challenge to the Christian Right in the book *Stranger at the Gate: To Be Gay and Christian in America.* He continues to work for justice for lesbian, gay, bisexual, and transgendered people by confronting the Christian Right through letters, protests, and at least two hunger strikes.

Mel White being arrested after a demonstration at the White House in 1996.

Nancy Wilson (1950-)

Nancy Wilson is the senior pastor of Metropolitan Commu-nity Church of Los Angeles. An elder in the UFMCC, she pub-lished her most recent book, *Our Tribe: Queer Folks, God, Jesus, and the Bible,* in 1995.

Robert Wood

Robert Wood, a United Church of Christ clergy, published *Christ and the Homosexual* in 1960. This was the first book to claim that one need not be heterosexual to be Christian. He was the first homosexual to use his real name and church affiliation in writ-ing.

REFERENCES:

Books

Alexander, Marilyn Bennett and James Preston. *We Were Bap-tized Too: Claiming God's Grace for Lesbians and Gays.* Lou-isville, Kentucky: Westminster John Knox Press, 1996.
Allen, Paula Gunn. *The Sacred Hoop: Recovering the Feminine in American Indian Traditions.* Boston: Beacon Press, 1986.

Bailey, Derrick Sherwin. *Homosexuality and the Western Christian Tradition*. London: Longmans, Green, 1955.

Balka, Christie and Andy Rose, eds. *Twice Blessed: On Being Lesbian, Gay, and Jewish*. Boston: Beacon Press, 1989.

Beck, Evelyn Torton, ed. *Nice Jewish Girls: A Lesbian Anthology*. Watertown, Massachusetts: Persephone Press, 1982.

The Bible, New Revised Standard Version. Division of Christian Education, National Council of the Churches of Christ. Thomas Nelson, Inc., 1990.

Boswell, John. *Christianity, Social Tolerance, and Homosexuality: Gay People in Western Europe from the Beginning of the Christian Era to the Fourteenth Century*. Chicago: University of Chicago Press, 1980.

———. *Same-Sex Unions in Premodern Europe*. New York: Villard, 1994.

Bosworth, C. E. et al. *The Encyclopedia of Islam*. Leiden: E.J. Brill, 1983.

Bouhdiba, Abdelwahab. *Sexuality in Islam*. London: R.K.P. Inc., 1985.

Boyd, Malcolm. *Are You Running With Me, Jesus? Prayers*. New York: Holt, Rinehart and Winston, 1965.

———. *Look Back in Joy: A Celebration of Gay Lovers*. San Francisco: Gay Sunshine Press, 1981.

———. *Take Off the Masks*. Philadelphia: New Society Publishers, 1984.

———. *Half Laughing, Half Crying: Songs for Myself*. New York: St. Martin's Press, 1986.

———. *Gay Priest: An Inner Journey*. New York: St. Martin's Press, 1986.

———. *Are You Running With Me, Jesus?: A Spiritual Companion for the 1990s*. Boston: Beacon Press, 1990.

Boyd, Malcolm and Nancy Wilson, eds. *Amazing Grace: Stories of Lesbian and Gay Faith*. Freedom: Crossing Press, 1991.

Brooten, Bernadette J. *The New Testament and Homosexuality: Contextual Background for Contemporary Debate*. Philadelphia: Fortress Press, 1983.

———. *Love Between Women: Early Christian Responses to Female Eroticism*. Chicago: University of Chicago Press, 1996.

Buchanan, Kimberly Moore. *Apache Women Warriors*. El Paso: Texas Western Press, 1986.

Budapest, Zsuzsanna. *The Holy Book of Women's Mysteries*. Berkeley, California: Wingbow Press, 1989.

Bullough, Vern L. *Sexual Variance in Society and History*. Chicago: University of Chicago Press, 1976.

———. *Homosexuality: A History*. New York: New American Library, 1979.

Butler, Becky, ed. *Ceremonies of the Heart: Celebrating Lesbian Unions*. Seattle: Seal, 1990.

Cabezon, Jose Ignacio. *Buddhism, Sexuality and Gender*. Albany, New York: SUNY Press, 1992.

Carstairs, Morris G. *The Twice-Born*. Bloomington: Indiana University Press, 1967.

Cherry, Kittredge and Zalmon Sherwood, eds. *Equal Rites: Lesbian and Gay Worship, Ceremonies, and Celebrations*. Louisville, Kentucky: Westminster John Knox Press, 1995.

Comstock, Gary David. *Unrepentant, Self-Affirming, Practicing: Lesbian/Bisexual/Gay People within Organized Religion*. New York: Continuum, 1996.

Comstock, Gary David and Susan E. Henking, eds. *Que(e)rying Religion: A Critical Anthology*. New York: Continuum, 1997.

Congregation for the Doctrine of the Faith. "On the Pastoral Care of Homosexual Persons." Rome: Vatican Polyglot Press, 1986.

Conner, Randy P., David Hatfield Sparks, and Mariya Sparks, eds. *Cassell's Encyclopedia of Queer Myth, Symbol, and Spirit*. London: Cassell, 1997.

Curb, Rosemary and Nancy Manahan, eds. *Lesbian Nuns: Breaking Silence*. Tallahassee, Florida: Naiad, 1985.

D'Emilio, John. *Sexual Politics, Sexual Communities: The Making of a Homosexual Minority in the United States 1940-1970*. Chicago: University of Chicago Press, 1983.

Denman, Rose Mary. *Let My People In: A Lesbian Minister Tells of Her Struggles to Live Openly and Maintain Her Ministry*. New York: Harper and Row, 1990.

Duberman, Martin, Martha Vicinus, and George Chauncey, Jr., eds. *Hidden from History*. New York: Meridian, 1990.

Edwardes, Allen. *The Jewel in the Lotus: A Historical Survey of the Sexual Culture of the East*. New York: The Julian Press, Inc., 1959.

Edwards, George R. *Gay-Lesbian Liberation: A Biblical Perspective*. New York: Pilgrim Press, 1984.

Eskridge, William N. Jr. *The Case for Same-Sex Marriage: From Sexual Liberty to Civilized Commitment*. New York: Free Press, 1996.

Faderman, Lillian. *Odd Girls and Twilight Lovers: A History of Lesbian Life in Twentieth-Century America*. New York: Penguin Books, 1991.

Fang Fu Ruan. *Sex in China: Studies in Sexology in Chinese Culture*. New York: Plenum Press, 1991.

Feliz, Antonio A. *Out of the Bishop's Closet: A Call to Heal Ourselves, Each Other, and Our World*. San Francisco: Aurora, 1988; Alamo Square, 1992.

Ferry, James. *In the Court of the Lord: A Gay Priest's Story*. New York: Crossroad, 1994.

Fewell, Danna Nolan and David M. Gunn. *Gender, Power and Promise: Stories of Desire and Division in the Hebrew Bible*. Nashville, Tennessee: Abingdon Press, 1993.

Furnish, Victor Paul. *Moral Teachings of Paul: Selected Issues*. Nashville, Tennessee: Abingdon Press, 1985.

Glaser, Chris. *ComeHome*. San Francisco: Harper San Francisco, 1990.

———. *Coming Out to God: Prayers for Lesbians and Gay Men, Their Families and Friends*. Louisville, Kentucky: Westminster John Knox Press, 1991.

———. *The Word Is Out: The Bible Reclaimed for Lesbians and Gay Men*. San Francisco: Harper San Francisco, 1994.

———. *Uncommon Calling: A Gay Christian's Struggle to Serve the Church*. Louisville, Kentucky: Westminster John Knox Press, 1996.

Gomes, Peter J. *The Good Book: Reading the Bible with Mind and Heart*. New York: William and Morrow, 1997.

Goss, Robert. *Jesus Acted Up: A Gay and Lesbian Manifesto*. San Francisco: Harper San Francisco, 1994.

Gottwald, Norman K. *The Hebrew Bible: A Socio-Literary Introduction*. Philadelphia: Fortress Press, 1985.

Grahn, Judy. *Another Mother Tongue: Gay Words, Gay Worlds*. Boston: Beacon Press, 1984.

Gramick, Jeanine and Pat Fure, eds. *The Vatican and Homosexuality*. New York: Crossroad, 1988.

Harrison, Gavin. *In the Lap of the Buddha*. Boston: Shambhala Publications, 1994.

Hartman, Keith. *Congregations in Conflict: The Battle over Homosexuality*. New Brunswick, New Jersey: Rutgers University, 1996.

Hasbany, Richard. *Homosexuality and Religion*. New York: Haworth Press, 1990.

Helminiak, Daniel. *What the Bible Really Says about Homosexuality*. San Francisco: Alamo Square Press, 1994.

Heyward, Carter. *Our Passion for Justice*. Cleveland, Ohio: The Pilgrim Press, The United Church Press, 1984.

———. *Touching Our Strength: The Erotic as Power and the Love of God*. San Francisco: Harper San Francisco, 1989.

———. *Staying Power: Reflections on Gender, Justice and Compassion*. Cleveland, Ohio: The Pilgrim Press, The United Church Press, 1995.

Hilton, Bruce. *Can Homophobia Be Cured? Wrestling with Questions That Challenge the Church*. Nashville, Tennessee: Abingdon Press, 1992.

Horner, Tom. *Jonathan Loved David: Homosexuality in Biblical Times*. Philadelphia: Westminster Press, 1978.

Hunt, Mary E. *Fierce Tenderness: Toward a Feminist Theology of Friendship*. San Francisco: Harper and Row, 1992.

Jordan, Mark. *The Invention of Sodomy in Christian Theology*. Chicago: University of Chicago Press, 1997.

Katz, Jonathan. *Gay American History: Lesbians and Gay Men in the U.S.A.* New York: Thomas Y. Crowell Company, 1976.

Leckie, Will and Barry Stopfel. *Courage to Love*. New York: Doubleday, 1997.

Lorde, Audre. *The Black Unicorn*. New York: W.W. Norton and Co., 1978.

———. *Uses of the Erotic: The Erotic as Power*. Trumansburg, New York: Out and Out Books, 1978.

———. *Zami: A New Spelling of My Name*. Freedom, New York: Crossing Press, 1983.

———. *Sister Outsider: Essays and Speeches*. Trumansburg, New York: Crossing Press, 1984.

———. *Undersong: Chosen Poems Old and New*. New York: W.W. Norton and Co, 1992.

Marcus, Eric. *Making History: The Struggle for Gay and Lesbian Equal Rights 1945-1990*. New York: HarperCollins, 1992.

Mariechild, Diane and Marcelina Martin. *Lesbian Sacred Sexuality*. Oakland: Wingbow Press, 1995.

McNeill, John J. *The Church and the Homosexual*. Kansas City, Missouri: Sheed, Andrews and McMeel, 1976.

Miller, Neil. *In Search of Gay America: Women and Men in a Time of Change*. New York: Atlantic Monthly, 1989.

———. *Out of the Past: Gay and Lesbian History from 1869 to the Present*. New York: Vintage Books, 1995.

Nelson, James B. *Body Theology*. Louisville, Kentucky: Westminster John Knox Press, 1992.

O'Neill, Craig and Kathleen Ritter. *Coming Out Within: Stages of Spiritual Awakening for Lesbians and Gay Men*. San Francisco: Harper San Francisco, 1992.

Parrinder, S. Geoffrey. *Sex in the World's Religions*. London: Sheldon Press, 1980.

Perry, Troy D. *The Lord Is My Shepherd and He Knows I'm Gay*. New York: Bantam, 1972.

———. *Don't Be Afraid Anymore: The Story of Reverend Troy Perry and the Metropolitan Community Churches*. New York: St. Martin's, 1990.

Pharr, Suzanne. *Homophobia: A Weapon of Sexism*. Inverness, California: Chardon Press, 1988.

———. *In the Time of the Right*. Berkeley, California: Chardon Press, 1996.

Piazza, Michael. *Holy Homosexuals*. Dallas: Sources of Hope Publishing, 1995.

———. *Rainbow Family Values*. Dallas: Sources of Hope Publishing, 1996.

Plaskow, Judith and Carol P. Christ, eds. *Weaving the Visions: New Patterns in Feminist Spirituality*. San Francisco: Harper and Row, 1989.

Rampal, S. N. *Indian Women and Sex*. New Delhi: Princtox, 1978.

Raphael, Lev. *Journeys and Arrivals: On Being Gay and Jewish*. Winchester: Faber and Faber Inc., 1996.

Ratti, Rakesh, ed. *A Lotus of Another Color: An Unfolding of the South Asian Gay and Lesbian Experience*. Boston: Alyson Publications, 1993.

Roscoe, Will, ed. (with Gay American Indians, including Randy Burns). *Living the Spirit: A Gay American Indian Anthology*. New York: St. Martin's, 1988.

Roscoe, Will. *The Zuni Man-Woman*. Albuquerque: University of New Mexico Press, 1991.

Samshasha (Xiaomingxiong). *History of Homosexuality in China*, Chinese edition. Hong Kong: Pink Triangle Press, 1984.

Scanzoni, Letha and Virginia Ramey Mollenkott. *Is the Homosexual My Neighbor? Another Christian View*. New York: Harper and Row, 1978.

Schmitt, Arno and Jehoeda Sofer, eds. *Sexuality and Eroticism among Males in Moslem Societies*. New York: Haworth Press, 1992.

Schneider, David. *Street Zen: The Life and Works of Issan Dorsey*. Boston: Shambhala, 1993.

Sheek, G. William, ed. "A Compilation of Protestant Denominational Statements on Families and Sexuality," 3d ed. New York: National Council of Churches, 1982.

Siker, Jeffrey S., ed. *Homosexuality in the Church: Both Sides of the Debate*. Louisville, Kentucky: Westminster John Knox Press, 1994.

Spong, John Shelby. *Living in Sin? A Bishop Rethinks Human Sexuality*. San Francisco: Harper and Row, 1988.

———. *Rescuing the Bible from Fundamentalism: A Bishop Rethinks the Meaning of Scripture*. San Francisco: Harper San Francisco, 1992.

Starhawk. *The Spiral Dance: A Rebirth of the Ancient Religion of the Great Goddess*. San Francisco: Harper and Row, 1979.

Swidler, Arlene, ed. *Homosexuality and World Religions*. Valley Forge, Pennsylvania: Trinity Press International, 1993.

Thompson, Mark. *Gay Spirit: Myth and Meaning*. New York: St. Martin's Press, 1987.

———. *Gay Soul: Finding the Heart of Gay Spirit and Nature*. San Francisco: HarperCollins, 1994.

Tuli, Jitendra. *The Indian Male: Attitude Towards Sex*. New Delhi: Chetana Publications, 1976.

Walker, Benjamin. *Hindu World: An Encyclopedic Survey of Hinduism*. London: George Allen and Unwin, 1968.

White, Mel. *Stranger at the Gate: To Be Gay and Christian in America*. New York: Simon and Schuster, 1994.

Williams, Walter L. *The Spirit and the Flesh: Sexual Diversity in American Indian Culture*. Boston: Beacon, 1986.

Wilson, Nancy. *Our Tribe: Queer Folks, God, Jesus, and the Bible*. San Francisco: HarperCollins, 1995.

Wood, Robert W. *Christ and the Homosexual (Some Observations)*. New York: Vantage, 1960.

Woods, Richard. *Another Kind of Love: Homosexuality and Spirituality.* Garden City, New York: Doubleday and Co., 1978.

Chapters in Books

Cabezon, Jose Ignacio. "Homosexuality and Buddhism," in *Homosexuality and World Religions,* edited by Arlene Swidler. Valley Forge, Pennsylvania: Trinity Press International, 1993.

Carmody, Denise and John Carmody. "Homosexuality and Roman Catholicism," in Swidler.

Duran, Khalid. "Homosexuality and Islam," in Swidler.

Ellison, Marvin M. "Homosexuality and Protestantism," in Swidler.

Eron, Lewis John. "Homosexuality and Judaism," in Swidler.

Furnish, Victor P. "Some Perspectives on the Bible and Homosexuality," in *Christian Argument for Gays and Lesbians in the Military: Essays by Mainline Church Leaders.* Lewiston, New York: Edwin Mellen Press, 1993.

Hill, Anita C. and Leo Treadway. "Rituals of Healing: Ministry with and on Behalf of Gay and Lesbian People," in *Lift Every Voice Constructing Christian Theologies from the Underside,* edited by Susan Brooks Thistlethwaite and Mary Potter Engle. San Francisco: Harper and Row, 1990.

Mollenkott, Virginia Ramey. "Overcoming Heterosexism—To Benefit Everyone," in *Homosexuality in the Church: Both Sides of the Debate,* edited by Jeffrey S. Siker. Louisville, Kentucky: Westminster John Knox Press, 1994.

Sharma, Arvind. "Homosexuality and Hinduism," in Swidler.

Periodicals

Allen, Paula Gunn. "Lesbians in American Indian Cultures," in *Connections,* no. 7, 1981.

Caldwell, Deborah Kovach. "Ex-bishop Spared Heresy Trial in Ordination of Gay Man," in *Dallas Morning News,* 16 May 1996: 1A.

Dossani, Shahid. "Gay by the Grace of Allah," in *Trikone: Gay and Lesbian South Asians,* July 1994: 1, 7.

Gomes, Peter J. "Homophobic? Re-Read Your Bible," in *New York Times,* 17 August 1992.

Grippo, Dan. "Why Lesbians and Gay Catholics Stay Catholic," in *U.S. Catholic,* September 1990: 18-25.

Hays, Richard. "Relations Natural or Unnatural: A Response to John Boswell's Exegesis of Romans 1," in *Journal of Religious Ethics,* vol. 14, 1986: 184.

Hunt, Mary E. "You Do, I Don't," in *Open Hands,* Fall 1990: 10.

Kahn, Joel. "Judaism and Homosexuality: The Traditional-Progressive Debate," in *Journal of Homosexuality,* 1989.

"Mark Smith, 29, religious freedom activist," in *Advocate,* 19 August 1997: 64.

Milgrom, Jacob. "Does the Bible Prohibit Homosexuality?" in *Bible Review,* December 1993.

Osterman, Mary Jo, ed. "Birth of a Movement," in *Open Hands,* Winter 1993: 8.

Osterman, Mary Jo. "Good News from Presbyterian General Assembly," in *Open Hands,* Summer 1997: 30.

———. "Our Welcoming Movement Grows," in *Open Hands,* Winter 1997: 27.

"Presbyterian Vote Eases Rule on Homosexuals in Pulpit," in *New York Times,* 21 June 1997: 11.

Umansky, Ellen M. "Jewish Attitudes Towards Homosexuality: A Review of Contemporary Sources," in *Reconstructionist,* vol. 51, 1985: 9-15.

Williams, Bruce. "Homosexuality: The New Vatican Statement," *Theological Studies,* vol. 48, 1987.

Yohalem, John. "Coming Out of the Broom Closet," in *Advocate,* 5 November 1991: 70.

Zwilling, Leonard. "Homosexuality in Pre-Muslim India," paper presented at the Conference on South Asia, Madison, Wisconsin, 1978.

———. "Sanskrit Terminology of Sexual Variation and Dysfunction with Special Reference to Homosexuality," paper presented at the annual meeting of the American Oriental Society, Boston, 1981.

———. "Homosexuality as Seen in Indian Buddhist Text," paper presented at the annual meeting of the American Academy of Religion, Boston, 1987.

Internet Sites

http://qrd.rdrop.com/qrd/religion/orgs/. This website is a good first start for information on religious organizations relating to the topic of homosexuality, as the site provides a direct link to many of these organizations. Many of the groups provide an article on their history, including Louie Crew's "The Episcopal Church and Lesbigay Issues" and Andy Lang's "United Church Actions on Lesbian and Gay Rights 1969-1994."

http://qrd.rdrop.com/qrd/religion/judeochristian/protestantism/. This website is filled with information specifically on Protestant Christian organizations.

http://world.std.com/~rice/q-light/links.html. This website provides information on the Universal Fellowship of Metropolitan Community Churches with links to specific churches such Cathedral of Hope MCC in Dallas, the world's largest gay and lesbian congregation.

http://www.lesbianbooks.com/relig-spirit.html. This website contains information on various lesbian and gay religious support groups.

http://www.intr.net/tialliance/links.htm. This website links to Interfaith Alliance Chapters on the Internet.

http://www.liberty.org/~iwg/. This is the website for the Interfaith Working Group.

http://www./wcgljo.org/wcgljo. This is the web page for the World Congress of Gay and Lesbian Jewish Organizations.

http://www.vidaviz.com/~geewhiz/adpages/gbf/gbf.html. This is the web page for the Gay Buddhist Fellowship.

http://www.qrd.org/qrd/religion/other/. This website is linked to various websites that provide information on the topic of homosexuality and other religious traditions outside of Christianity. Some of the groups included are The Radical Faeries, Metro'on (transgender priestesses), Rainbow Wind (lesbigay/transgendered pagans), and dharma dykes (Lesbian Zen Discussion Group).

Other

"Bishops to Parents: Love Thy Gay Children." CNN interactive, CNN.com, 30 September 1997, http://www.cnn.com/US/9709/30/catholic.gays.ap/index.html.

CLOUT-REACH, CLOUT Newsletter, P.O. Box 3234, Madison, Wisconsin 53704-0234.

Presbyterian Parents of Gays and Lesbians. P.O. Box 781591, Dallas, Texas 75378.

"Report of the Secretary's Task Force on Youth Suicide." U.S. Department of Health and Human Services. Washington, D.C., 1990.

—Marilyn Bennett Alexander

20

Science

- **What We Know**
- **The Biological Basis for the Research**
- **The Biological Research of Sexual Orientation**
- **Prominent People**

The biological research of sexual orientation is one of the most exciting, and cutting edge, bodies of current biological research. A relatively new field of research—the origins of the trait human sexual orientation has only recently become the object of serious, modern biological investigation—this body of work may well be seen in the future as historic; many biological traits that are expressed behaviorally, such as IQ, violence and aggression, gender, and so on, are of interest to scientists, but the research on sexual orientation is farther along than on any of those, and homosexuality, heterosexuality, and bisexuality may be the first behavioral trait in the history of biology that we will understand on the level of genes, hormones, and neurons.

This chapter will discuss, in order, Part 1) what we know now about human sexual orientation, which means all the empirical data we have assembled from decades of clinical research; this section will also explain why the popular media and the public misunderstand the political meaning of this work; Part 2) the biological research on which, historically, the investigation of sexual orientation is based; Part 3) the endocrinological, neuroanatomical, and genetic work.

WHAT WE KNOW

The Clinical Data for the
Trait Profile of Human Sexual Orientation

Before examining the biological research of sexual orientation, it is important to understand one of the great ironies of this well-known body of work, with its very high profile in the mainstream media: while the media's reporting on the details of the research—what genetic locus was found, what hormone was studied—is usually entirely accurate, what the media says the work means—politically, socially, religiously—is wrong. The reason reporters get this wrong is that they are unfamiliar with, or ignore, a vast body of empirical, clinical research that has been done on this trait, which is crucial to the biological research, and on which the biologists' work is based.

When ABC and the *New York Times* and CNN and National Public Radio report on the biology, they are trying to fit the science into the political debate, and thus they usually use a headline that says, more or less: "Homosexuality: Is it Genes or Choice?" This headline, short and moderate-seeming, means in essence, "If we find a gene for homosexuality, then people don't choose to be gay, but if we *don't* find a gene, people *do* choose to be gay." It says we need to find a gene to know whether homosexuality is a choice. This is what is entirely incorrect. The biology does not mean anything as far as choice is concerned.

Like it or not, whether people "choose" to be gay is the most politically important question in the national American debate over homosexuality. It's not really logical: Catholicism is a chosen alternative lifestyle, and nobody says it's bad for that reason, so why should homosexuals suffer even if they did choose to be gay? Logic aside, however, the fact is that homosexuals don't choose to be gay, and homosexuality is not a lifestyle, it's an orientation. That is the answer to the choice question. Furthermore, biological research is not needed to answer that question, because it was already answered, decades ago, by different means: empirical observation—otherwise known as clinical research.

We have an almost unending list of traits we want to understand biologically: eye color, height, cystic fibrosis, cancer, intelligence, Tay Sachs, athletic ability, resistance to some viruses and susceptibility to others, skin tone, muscle mass, allergies, sexual orientation, and more. Some traits can be defined simply by looking at the person, such as hair color or height. Some cannot, such as cancer or blood type (A, B, or O). Some human traits are behavioral, such as manual dexterity, sexual orientation, hand-eye coordination, and schizophrenia, and some are not, such as blood type (A, B, or O), race, or baldness. Some are disease traits: hemophilia, schizophrenia, cancer, color blindness. Some traits are politically and religiously charged, such as gender. Some are not politically and religiously charged: the hardness of the enamel on your teeth, which is controlled by a single gene, whose location is known and whose functioning we understand.

We have observed many of these traits empirically, which means we have measured them, evaluated and assessed them, and watched them trickling down through generations. We don't know what created them biologically, but we do know if, for instance, they're chosen or not. We don't know how some people have perfect pitch, but we certainly know they don't choose it. One such trait that interests us—human handedness—has been the object of decades of empirical observation, and researchers have compiled in the scientific literature a fairly complete external description of the trait, what is sometimes called a "trait profile." We do not know what

Two Trait Profiles:	Human Handedness	Human Sexual Orientation
Trait Description	**Stable bimodalism, behaviorally expressed**	**Stable bimodalism, behaviorally expressed**
Distribution[1]	Majority and Minority orientations	Majority and minority orientations
Population distribution:	Majority orientation: 92% Minority orientation: 8%	Majority orientation: 95% Minority orientation: 5%
Population distribution of orientations according to sex:	Male: 9% Female: 7%	Male: 6% Female: 3%
Male/Female ratio for minority orientation	1.3/1 Minority orientation @ 30% higher in men than women	2/1 Minority orientation @ 50% higher in men than women
Correlation Data: with		
race?	No	No
geography?	No	No
culture?[2]	No	No
pathology,[3] mental/physical?	No	No
Age of appearance of trait	@age 2	@age 2
Is either orientation chosen?	No	No
Can external expression be altered?	Yes	Yes
Can interior orientation be altered?	No	No
Is trait familial (run in families)?	Yes	Yes
Pattern of familiality:	"Maternal effect"–implies X-chromosome linkage	"Maternal effect"–implies X-chromosome linkage[4]
Parent-to-child segregation:[5]	Little to none: handedness of adopted (ie non-biological) children shows no relationship to that of adoptive parents, indicating a genetic, not social, origin.	Little to none: sexual orientation of adopted (ie non-biological) children shows no relationship to that of adoptive parents, indicating a genetic, not social, origin.
Among the children who have the minority orientation, is there an increased incidence of siblings who also share the minority orientation?	Yes. Elevated rate of left-handedness in families with other left-handed children.	Yes. Elevated rate of homosexuality in families with other homosexual children
Twin Data:		
Are monozygotic (identical) twins more likely to share minority orientation?	Yes	Yes
MZ concordance for minority orientation[6] (vs. background rate:)	12% (vs 8%, so MZ rate is 1.5 times higher)	50% (vs 5%, so MZ rates is 10 times higher)

Sources: I.C. McManus, "The Inheritance of Left-Handedness," *Biological Asymmetry and Handedness*, Ciba Foundation Symposium 162. John Wiley & Sons (Chichester): 1991, 251-267; J. Michael Baily and Richard Pillard, "A Genetic Study of Male Sexual Orientation," *Archives of General Psychiatry* 48 (December 1991): 1089-1096; Dean Hamer et al., "A Linkage Between DNA Markers on the X Chromosome and Male Sexual Orientation," *Science* 261 (16 July 1993): 321-327.

Trait profiles for human handedness and human sexual orientation.

genes and hormones make some people right-handed and other people left-handed—that is now the question to be answered, research that biologists are just beginning—but we have completed for this trait the standard first stage of biological research: determining what handedness is. Because this trait portrait bears striking similarities to the portrait for sexual orientation, examining the clinical profile is useful in helping us understand the clinical profiles for homosexuality and heterosexuality.

Footnotes for "Chart: Two Trait Profiles"

(1) Both traits show a very small number of humans are ambi-oriented. Handedness shows almost none for both men and women–McManus: "Measures of handedness usually show a bimodal distribution with few subjects appearing truly ambidextrous." Sexual orientation, likewise, shows almost none for men but a still small through significant number for women.

(2) However, may highly influence <u>expression</u>.

(3) There is currently fierce debate over the existence of a correlation between left-handedness and certain pathologies, most notably schizophrenia. Some researchers assert that handedness, thought to reflect one aspect of brain lateralization, may be a result or a cause–in some manner a concomitant–of schizophrenia's etiology or pathophysiology. A study done by Charles Boklage ("Schizophrenia, brain asymmetry development, and twinning," *Biol. Psychiatry* 12, 19-35, 1977) powerfully developed the hypothesis, and Nancy Segal ("Origins and implications of handedness and relative birth weight for IQ in monozygotic pairs," *Neuropsychology,* 27, 549-561, 1989) also supports some form of correlation. On the other hand, Luchins et al. (1980) and Lewis et al. (1989), in their respective replication attempts of Boklage's work, found little support, and Gottesman et al. ("Handedness in twins with schizophrenia: was Boklage correct?" *Schizophrenia Research,* 9, 83-85, 1993) conclude that there does not appear to be an association between handedness and schizophrenia. (See Gottesman for a more complete bibliography.) The point, however, is the distinct difference between the trait profile of handedness and that of sexual orientation: while there is clinical debate in scientific and research circles over whether handedness correlates in some way with psychobiological abnormalities, no such debate exists regarding sexual orientation, and neither heterosexuality nor homosexuality are implicated in any mental or physical pathology.

(4) A subset of gay men show the maternal effect. It does not appear in women.

(5) "Segregation" is a genetic term of art meaning the way the trait appears in individuals down through generations.

(6) Indicates that genetics play a significantly greater role in sexual orientation than in handedness.

Trait Profile for Human Handedness

1)   The trait is referred to by biologists as a "stable bimorphism (of two forms), expressed behaviorally."

2)   Its exists in the form of two basic internal, invisible orientations, with more than 90 percent of the population accounting for the majority orientation, right-handedness, and under 10 percent (one reliable study puts the figure at 7.89 percent) for the minority orientation, left-handedness, although there is still debate about the exact percentages.

3)   Only a very small number of people are truly equally oriented both ways, an orientation called ambidexterity.

4)   Evidence from art history suggests the incidence of the two different orientations has been constant for five millennia.

5)   A person's orientation cannot be identified simply by looking at him or her; those with the minority orientation are just as diverse in appearance, race, religion, and all other characteristics as those with the majority orientation.

6)   Since the trait itself is internal and invisible, the only way to identify an orientation in someone else is by observing in them the behavior or reflex that express it.

7)   The trait itself, however, is not a "behavior." It is a neurological orientation expressed, at times, behaviorally. A person with the minority orientation can engage, usually due to coercion or social pressure, in behavior that seems to express the majority orientation—several decades ago, left-handed people, particularly children, were frequently forced to behave as if they had the majority orientation, in other words, forced to write with their right hands—but internally the orientation remains the same. As social pressures have lifted, the minority orientation has become more commonly and openly expressed in society, and today virtually all left-handed people write with their left hands, the natural expression for them of the trait human handedness.

8)   Neither orientation is a disease or mental illness. Neither is pathological.

9)   Neither orientation is chosen.

10)   Signs of one's orientation are detectable very early in children, often, researchers have established, by age two or three, and one's orientation has probably been defined at the latest by age two, and quite possibly before birth.

These first intriguing observations began to catch the attention of biological researchers. They began to press ahead systematically with their inspection, fleshing out the answer to the first question biologists always ask of a trait: "What is it?" It is a question that in the chronology of research must be answered before a scientist can pursue the second, quite different question, "Where does it come from?" The data that began flowing back to them indicated that handedness might well have a genetic source:

11)   Adoption studies show that the handedness orientation of adopted children is unrelated to the orientation of their parents, demonstrating that the trait is not environmentally rooted.

12)   Twin studies show that pairs of identical (monozygotic) twins, with their identical genes, have a higher-than-average chance of sharing the same orientation compared to pairs of randomly selected individuals; the average (or "background") rate of the trait in any given population is just under 8 percent,

while the twin rate is just over 12 percent—more than 30 percent higher.

But the most startling and intriguing clues came from studies that began to reveal the faint outlines of the genetic plans that underlay the trait of human handedness:

13) The incidence of the minority orientation is strikingly higher in the male population—about 27 percent higher—than it is in the female population, a piece of information that gives indications to the biological conditions creating the trait.

14) Like the trait eye color, familial studies show no direct parent-offspring correlation for the two versions of handedness, but the minority orientation clearly "runs in families," handed down from parent to child in a loose but genetically characteristic pattern.

15) This pattern shows a "maternal effect," a classic telltale of a genetically loaded trait. The minority orientation, when it is expressed in men, appears to be passed down through the mother.

Handedness is interesting in relation to the trait we will be looking at in this section, sexual orientation, because of the striking similarities between the two. The trait profile for sexual orientation does differ from that of handedness in several ways: the population ratios for each trait's two orientations vary somewhat (while left-handed people comprise 8 percent of the population, the current figures for homosexuals is between 2 and 6 percent), and identical twin (MZ) concordance figures are radically different: twin concordance for left-handedness is 12 percent against a background rate of 8 percent, whereas for homosexuality MZ concordance is 50 percent against a background of only around 5 percent, indicating that homosexuality has a much higher purely genetic component than does left-handedness. (Also, and more subtly, the telltale "maternal effects" that both traits display are expressed somewhat differently.)

But these are the exceptions highlighting the fact that the trait profiles of the two are extraordinarily alike, and virtually everything we know about the one, we know about the other. Neither left and right-handedness nor hetero- and homo-sexual orientation can be identified simply by looking at a person. Since both are internal orientations, the only way to identify them is by the respective behaviors that express them: motor reflex and sexual response. Handedness shows up in children starting at age two or before, and John Money of Johns Hopkins University puts the age of the first signs of sexual orientation at the same age. Neither left-handedness nor homosexuality correlates with any disease or mental illness (although there are studies showing a higher correlation between left-handedness and, for example, schizophrenia). The grammar school coercion of left-handed children to use their right hands was ended years ago.

The two traits also function well as working analogies. If you are right-handed, take a pen in your left-hand and try to write your name. With some effort, you can probably get it down semi-legibly, but the fact that you have engaged in left-handed behavior does not make you a left-handed person. Behavior is irrelevant; the orientation you have is what counts. And you are just as right-handed sitting still watching a movie as when swinging a tennis racquet with your right-hand. Did you choose to be right-handed?

No? Then prove it. (You cannot; as one clinical researcher noted tersely, "Science can't 'prove' you don't choose to have appendicitis.") Just as obviously, an interiorly heterosexual person is not homosexual even in the midst of homosexual intercourse, behavior (when it does not reflect the interior orientation) is irrelevant, and a homosexual is equally homosexual during the sex act and when driving a car.

Another biologically significant similarity between the two is their ubiquitous and consistent presence across populations. "Of particular interest," researcher I. C. McManus writes of handedness, "is the absence of geographical differences, a finding compatible with handedness being a balanced polymorphism present in all cultures." There is one interesting difference between handedness and sexual orientation, and that is that we actually know less about the biological origins of handedness than about those of sexual orientation.

And this is why the media's idea—that you have to find a homosexuality gene before you know whether or not homosexuality is a choice—is inaccurate. ABC's science journalist, David Marash, reported that a genetic locus linked to homosexuality "suggests that homosexuality may not be a choice." This is the same as saying that only when we find a left-handedness gene—and we have not found one yet—will we be able to "suggest that left-handedness may not be a choice." But of course we know left-handed people do not choose to be left-handed because we have asked them and we have observed them over decades, young and old, in various cultures and situations. And it's clear they do not choose it. You do not need a left-handedness gene to tell you this; this is a question that has been resolved by empirical observation.

What would account for the baffling illogic, the failure to grasp this elementary aspect of biological research? Perhaps it is simply the refusal to recognize the evidence before our eyes, since that recognition would ruthlessly change so much of what so many people desperately believe. But then, empirical observation has been upsetting people since it began.

Contemporary Research into Sexual Orientation

Contemporary research into sexual orientation started, essentially, in the 1940s, when Alfred Kinsey launched his study of human sexuality. Kinsey's work was entirely clinical; he asked only "What is the trait?" and not "Which genes or hormones does it come from?" His methodology was appropriate to his purpose: he posed questions. Part of his research involved simply tracking down what most social scientists and psychoanalysts presumed would be a few isolated homosexual individuals. Since homosexuality was presumed caused by faulty parenting and psychological stress, or by bad moral example in unsavory quarters, it probably would only be found irregularly. Historian John D'Emilio wrote of the shock caused by what Kinsey actually discovered:

Kinsey's findings on homosexuality departed so drastically from traditional notions that he felt compelled to comment on them. In his male study Kinsey acknowledged that he and his colleagues "were totally unprepared" for such incidence data and "were repeatedly assailed with doubts" about their validity. Checking and cross-checking their tabulations only widened the distance separating their results from the estimations of others. "Whether the histories were taken in one large city or another," Kinsey wrote, "whether they were taken in large cities, in small towns, or in rural areas, whether they came from one college or from another, a church school or a state university or some private institution, whether they came from one part of the country or from another, the incidence data on the homosexual have been more or less the same.... Persons with homosexual histories are to be found in every age group, in every social level, in every conceivable occupation, in cities and on farms, and in the most remote areas of the country."

Kinsey was also the first systematically to observe homosexuality's immutability. Psychiatrist Richard Isay, with reference to attempts to change sexual orientation, has written of Kinsey's experience:

Kinsey and his co-workers for many years attempted to find patients who had been converted from homosexuality to heterosexuality during therapy, and were surprised that they could not find one whose sexual orientation had been changed. When they interviewed persons who claimed they had been homosexuals but were now functioning heterosexually, they found that all these men were simply suppressing homosexual behavior ... and that they used homosexual fantasies to maintain potency when they attempted intercourse. One man proclaimed that, although he had once been actively homosexual, he had now "cut out all of that and don't even think of men—except when I masturbate."

Recalling the Victorian reaction to Darwin, the head of Union Theological Seminary, Henry Van Dusen, said at the time of Kinsey's work that it reflected "degradation in American morality approximating the worst decadence of the Roman era." Research into human sexuality seems to be perpetually alarming, as much at the end of the 20th century as its middle.

Another major aspect of the clinical research was the battle over the question of "pathology," specifically, the notion that a homosexual orientation was itself a pathology or, alternatively, that people with homosexual sexual orientations were more likely to have other mental pathologies such as schizophrenia, pedophilia, and so on.

Psychiatrist Robert Spitzer of Columbia University points out that homosexuality is hardly the only trait that has suffered from distorted use of the label "disorder." The history of science is riddled with such cases, notes Spitzer, in part because of how hard it is to define "disorder." "We really don't have a satisfactory definition of what is a 'disorder' or 'disease,'" he says. "And we probably haven't had one in the history of medicine. Is baldness a disorder? ... Is nearsightedness a disease? Uncorrected, it impairs your ability to do a job, corrected it doesn't, but it doesn't in and of itself cause distress. Is depression a disease? Is anger? (It impairs your ability, causes stress, and can be healed.) Is left-handedness? Is a disease something that causes a natural, evolutionarily evolved function to stop functioning? Then how about having an appendix, which has no evolutionary function we can figure out? Basically, a disorder has been whatever people want it to be because of their prejudices, which leads to all sorts of ridiculousness."

Therefore, scientists have to be rigorous in their definitions. Spitzer says, "If you want a definition of disease or disorder that's going to be even somewhat useful, start with the precept that your

definition can't be a tautology: 'Left-handedness is a disorder because left-handedness is a disease' or 'because I say so.' Or 'because God says so,' which is fine in theology but not in science. Next, there has to be some objective mark, maybe that the thing impairs a person's ability to perform a job. By virtually any definition, homosexuality doesn't fit. Physical or mental impairment, suffering (other than from outside prejudice), deterioration of function—none apply."

The battle over the psychiatric classification of homosexuality as a disorder began in 1940 with a man named Harry Stack Sullivan. The beginning of the battle's end was brought about in 1957 by a woman named Evelyn Hooker.

Sullivan, who described himself as a "slight, bespectacled mild-looking bachelor with thinning hair and mustache," was a psychiatrist who had long sought a way to elevate psychiatry, derided by many as a half-science, to mainstream medical respectability. World War II provided the way. In May of 1940, President Roosevelt asked Congress to expand the American military, and Sullivan convinced the Selective Service Director that psychiatry was uniquely capable of weeding undesirables and potential mental casualties from the thousands of fresh inductees, as Allan Berube has written in *Coming Out Under Fire.*

Almost immediately, things went out of control. Although Sullivan himself believed sexual orientation played only a minor role in mental disorder and had not included homosexuality in his initial plan, the screening process became increasingly designed to identify homosexuals. And psychiatry's dominant theory of the time—that homosexuality was a mental disorder—was increasingly implemented in practice. In November of 1941, only a year after the process had begun, Sullivan bitterly resigned. The military hardened its screening procedures against homosexuality, and by the war's end, psychiatry had won newfound respectability, due in large part to its having exploited a false theory of homosexuality. The only problem was that psychiatry not only consistently failed to demonstrate that homosexuality was a pathology, it actively demonstrated the opposite.

In the early 1950s, Evelyn Hooker, a young psychologist teaching at UCLA, got to know one of her students, Sam From, who was homosexual. Hooker, a tall, common sense midwesterner, was intelligent, curious, and quite unintimidated by the unknown—she had wanted to study at Yale, but her professor had told her he felt he couldn't recommend a woman. When Sam said to her, "Now Evelyn, it is your scientific duty to study people like us," she demurred until a fellow scientist remarked to her, "He's right, we know nothing about them."

So Hooker applied to NIMH for a grant, got it (to her amazement), and began putting the study together. "I was prepared," Hooker said later, "if I was so convinced, to tell these men they were not as well adjusted as they seemed on the surface." At the same time, she added, "I didn't put too much credence in what the books said because I knew no one had really studied [homosexuality]."

Hooker took thirty homosexual men and thirty heterosexual men, and administered to them identical psychological tests. She removed all identifying marks including sexual orientation and, to eliminate her own biases—this is standard practice—gave the profiles to three well-known psychologists to interpret, the first being the nationally renowned Bruno Klopfer, famous for claiming he could easily identify homosexuals by their Rorschach Tests.

In fact, Klopfer could not distinguish any of the homosexuals from the heterosexuals, nor could any of Hooker's colleagues. In side-by-side comparisons, the heterosexual and homosexual men were indistinguishable, demonstrating an equal distribution of pathology and mental health irrespective of sexual orientation. Another psychologist was so incredulous that he insisted on reevaluating the entire test a second time, arriving at the same result.

In 1956 Hooker presented her paper, "The Adjustment of the Male Overt Homosexual," (overt meaning openly gay, not hidden) at a meeting of the American Psychiatric Association in the ballroom of the Sherman Hotel in Chicago. It generated furious debate, which would continue for almost two decades, but it was also the beginning of the end for the belief that the minority orientation was a disease. Hooker observed tartly and would continue to observe throughout a long career that for psychology and psychiatry to be even minimally scientific, pathology must be defined in a way that was objective and empirically observable through the scientific method. In 1973, the APA removed homosexuality as a disorder from its official *Diagnostic and Statistical Manual.* Perhaps the great irony of the entire, long episode is that Henry Stack Sullivan was himself gay and lived a comfortable and relatively open life in Bethesda, Maryland, with his devoted male partner.

More clinical data on sexual orientation in humans comes from cross-cultural research. Sociologist Fred Whitam compared the childhood experiences of 375 homosexual men in Guatemala, Brazil, the Philippines, Thailand, Peru, and the United States, and found in them "culturally invariable" characteristics that remained stable across geography, class, and time zone: playing with toys of the opposite sex, being regarded as a sissy, and preferring the company of girls and older women. "There can be little doubt," Whitam wrote, "that this [early childhood] behavior is linked to adult sexual orientation."

In his paper "Culturally Invariable Properties of Male Homosexuality," Whitam delineates six phenotypic aspects of homosexuality remarkable across cultures:

1) Homosexuality as a sexual orientation is universal, appearing in all societies.
2) The percentage of homosexuals in all societies seems to be the same and remains stable over time. Everywhere in the world, homosexual populations appear to comprise no more than 5 percent of the total population.
3) Social norms neither impede nor facilitate the emergence of homosexual orientation. Homosexuals appear with equal frequency in societies that are repressive of homosexuality and in societies that are permissive. Repression simply reduces the expression of a homosexual orientation, not its existence.
4) Homosexual subcultures appear in all societies, given sufficient aggregates of people.
5) Homosexuals in different societies resemble each other with respect to certain behavioral interests and occupational choices.
6) All societies produce similar continua from overtly masculine to overtly feminine homosexuals.

Although all six clinical observations are relevant to biologists, to whom they constitute strong evidence of sexual orientation's biological etiology, the third point is most relevant to political debate, specifically the notion that one or the other sexual orienta-

tion can be "promoted" or "encouraged." Whitam is careful to note that cultural considerations determine to a degree the way an individual's homosexuality or heterosexuality will be *expressed* behaviorally, but in no way does culture or environment determine whether an individual will *be* homosexual or heterosexual. His conclusion: "It does seem clear from the cross-cultural perspective that societies do not create homosexuals. Their emergence appears to be beyond the power of any society to control."

The clinical research of sexual orientation on the level of a human trait—what we can see and experience of heterosexuality, homosexuality, and bisexuality in people—is today quite extensive, and we now have a detailed, relatively complete trait description. What this has left us with is a "black box," a trait we know well on the clinical level but whose interior biological workings are still a mystery. The biologists have now stepped in and begun their work.

What this means ultimately is identifying homosexuals and heterosexuals biologically. We have presently no medical test, no CAT scan, no radioactive counter, no X ray, no blood workup, no biopsy that can identify either a left-hander or a homosexual. If they do not voluntarily or inadvertently reveal themselves, each is indistinguishable from their majority counterparts. They can hide their behavior, mask their true natures for their entire lives in societies that repress it. Because of social strictures, in many Arab cultures there appear to be no left-handed people at all. But they are there, hiding. There is only one way to determine if a person is left-handed: he or she states it. The same is true of homosexuals. The spectral, phantom quality of sexual orientation has been its overwhelming feature throughout history. The bioethicist Leonard Glanz noted: "The only reason there could be a closet is that gay people *aren't* different from everyone else and that coming out is revealing the only difference."

By the time the biological research is complete, we may have a chemical or genetic test revealing the differences that make some of us homosexual. The biological research means that when a child registers for elementary school, or a woman enters the army, or a man gets an annual physical, and blood is drawn, someone in some laboratory may extract from the blood some pure, whitish DNA and pour it into a bed of electrified gelatin, leaving that person's sexual orientation written clearly in the streaks of an autorad. It means that when a woman is pregnant, a few stray cells from her womb may tell her, or someone else, this aspect of her child. It means that gay people will no longer have the option of hiding.

Biologists have asked, "What is the black box, this trait?" They are now asking, "How does this box, this trait, work? What genes or hormones or neurons make it tick?" We are just now entering the second half of the process of biological research. Scientists have begun to open the lid of this black box and stick their hands down into the genes and dendrites and hormones that create human traits to try to solve this mystery, the creation of human sexual orientation.

THE BIOLOGICAL BASIS FOR THE RESEARCH

Once the Trait Profile of sexual orientation had been established by clinicians, the biologists turned from empirical observation to active investigation of hormones and neurons. Like all scientific work, the sexual orientation research would rest on what had come before: several discoveries had been made, and these are divided among three fields: endocrinology, the study of hormones; genetics; and neuroanatomy, the study of the structure of the brain.

The Endocrinological Basis

In 1977, UCLA neurobiologist Roger Gorski, peering through his laboratory microscope at tiny gray-pink slices of rat brain, discovered a nucleus in part of the rat brain called the hypothalamus that was five times larger in males than females. The nucleus is so huge one can tell the sex of the animal as easily from looking at this nucleus in the brain as by looking at the rats' genitals—but then from a biological point of view, rat brains and genitals are the same thing: features related to gender and sex that are physically molded by sex hormones. This was the concept of the "sexual differentiation of the brain," a difference according to sex. And Gorski, logically, called the nucleus he'd found the Sexually Dimorphic Nucleus, or SDN. This neuroanatomical feature—the nucleus—was created, it turned out, by endocrinology—hormones.

Gorski's work had precedent. In 1959, a UCLA researcher named Dr. Charles Barraclough had found that if you injected a female rat shortly before or just after her birth with testosterone, a male hormone, it would sterilize her, and she would be unable to ovulate. And Geoffrey Harris, a researcher at Oxford University, had then made another, stranger discovery: it was possible to make *male* rats ovulate, at least in the biochemical sense, by castrating newborn males to take away their source of precious male testosterone and then in adulthood injecting them with female estrogen, which kicked on ovulation. Scientists realized that to become male, males had to have testosterone because testosterone, it turned out, actually *physically alters* the developing brain. Gorski had found the testosterone-created nucleus that gendered the brains, exactly the same way testosterone gendered genitals, giving males their penises and testes.

Gorski then did a series of behavioral studies, and he showed that by castrating XY male rats just before birth (taking away their testosterone in utero as the brain was developing), in adulthood their sex behavior is decidedly female; they not only mount less, they let themselves be mounted by other males. Give a female testosterone, and not only does she show less "lordosis" (the receptive female mating posture where she curves her back and lifts her genitals for mounting by the male) but she exhibits typical male sex behavior and begins mounting other females.

Next to the rat research, there was another body of endocrinological work on sexual orientation. This was conducted on humans, and it was rather horrific, but as horrific scientific experimentation frequently does, it gave us important data about sexual orientation in humans. If the psychiatric theory of homosexuality was that it was a pathology created by environment, the endocrinological theory was that people were homosexual because they had a deficit or surplus of sex hormones. In the 1950s, in an effort to turn lesbians into heterosexuals, American doctors bizarrely forcibly removed the uteri of perfectly healthy homosexual women and cut off their breasts. Other lesbians were made to undergo injections of estrogen, a female sex hormone. None of these hormonal procedures ever altered their sexual orientations; the women all remained lesbian. Medical authorities in the United States routinely castrated gay men (one particularly enthusiastic doctor is known to have castrated more than 100) and lobotomized them. Other gay people were forced to undergo aversion therapy—both men and women were wired to machines that jolted them with electricity every time they were shown an arousing picture of someone of the same sex—and electroshock. One of the attending doctors, curious about the process he was administering, recalled that

he once grasped an electrode and turned on the machine. He reported, rather queasily, that the shock threw him across the room. Despite this "direct experimentation on the organism," the gay men's sexual orientations remained universally homosexual.

The procedures, however, continued even after this became apparent. The documentary *Changing Our Minds,* about Dr. Evelyn Hooker, contains medical film footage of these experiments. One film of the late 1940s records the lobotomization of a young gay man with a kind of double-bladed ice pick, ordered by his doctor to alter his homosexuality. Yet, the young man's sexual orientation remained homosexual, despite the fact that the ice pick-like tool had destroyed the thinking part of his brain. In a grainy black and white clip from a 1950s naval research film, a gay man covered with electrodes lies in a metal hospital bed. When they turn on the electricity, his body whiplashes violently and he begins to scream. Despite this radical treatment, his homosexual orientation was unaltered.

This work is an example of the worst abuses of science and medicine. As scientists have since pointed out, the hormonal theory of sexual orientation was absurd on its face; if, for example, women were lesbian because they had too much testosterone, the excess testosterone would have shown in their bodies, made them grow facial hair and other male characteristics. Yet lesbians are, physically, completely female and gay men, physically completely male. In the end, however, this work did have at least one positive outcome: it firmly established that homosexual orientation was neither chosen nor mutable, and that its biological roots must lie rather deep.

There has been one other great example of biological experimentation on sexual orientation, but this experimentation was both unintended and unharmful. It has been the explosion in the use of psychopharmaceuticals, the best known of which is Prozac but versions of which have been used for decades. The profound, almost unnerving changes in personality that are created with seratonin-reuptake inhibitors are well known, but all these drugs create remarkable transformations in personality and thus behavior. Lithium erases the depression that has been a life-long character mark and replaces it with (it almost seems) someone else, Effexor suddenly lightens mood and Prozac turns a dour person sunny, Haldol returns sanity and logic and perspective to someone always characterized by a very different temperament, and Clozaril and Risperdal not only cure apathy but alter reality itself. They change sexual drive and desire. But no Prozac capsule, no psychopharmaceutical, no hormone, no drug, no surgical procedure has ever changed anyone's sexual orientation. It seems that our sexual orientation is an even more deeply rooted part of us than our personality.

The Genetic Basis

In 1963, Kulbir Gill, a visiting Indian scientist at Yale, was looking in organisms for the genetic causes of female sterility in the fruit fly, *Drosophila melanogaster,* and discovered, to his surprise, genetically homosexual fruit flies.

Gill noticed one day that he had a strain of sterile male flies on his hands. The question was, *why* were these flies sterile? Observing them, he noticed that the mutant males were courting other males, following them and vibrating their wings to make characteristic and unmistakable courtship "songs." Gill tracked down the mutant gene responsible: it sits on the right arm of the third chromosome at position 91. He called it *fruitless.*

In the 1990s, geneticists discovered what the fruitless gene does. The physical sex of the fly—whether it has a male or female body—is controlled by one set of genes. But the gender of the fly's brain—whether it has a male or female brain—is controlled by a completely different set. The fruitless gene is one of the control genes for creating the gender of the brain, and it is apparently making the gay male fly by creating a partly female brain in a male body.

The Neuroanatomical Basis

While it had been established that rat brains were gendered, three later discoveries indicated that humans, too, had gendered, or sexually dimorphic, brains. First, in 1982, the British team of cell biologist Christine de Lacoste and physical anthropologist Ralph Holloway claimed that, like rats, men and woman have a differently shaped corpus callosum, a part of the brain that transfers information. Second, in 1990, a Dutch researcher in Amsterdam named Dick Swaab announced that a human brain nucleus, called the suprachiasmatic nucleus, or SCN, was also dimorphic—but not with sex, with sexual orientation. The nucleus was twice as large in homosexual men as in heterosexual men. And finally, Laura Allen, a post-doctoral candidate in Roger Gorski's lab, provided the last clue. Allen had wondered if, like rats, we humans had an SDN, a sexually dimorphic nucleus. She gathered some human brains, opened them to the hypothalamus, and eventually identified four nuclei, each the size of the tip of a pin. She and Gorski

gave them the hefty names "interstitial nuclei of the anterior hypothalamus 1, 2, 3, and 4"—or INAH (pronounced "EYE-nah") 1 through 4 for short. Allen had found that both INAH 2 and 3 were sexually dimorphic in humans, significantly larger in men than women.

All of this research was like an open invitation to biologists, as if it were saying to them: "Take a closer look at human sexual orientation; it appears you can uncover its workings."

THE BIOLOGICAL RESEARCH OF SEXUAL ORIENTATION

Neuroanatomy

In the late 1980s, a young neuroanatomist named Simon LeVay found this data intriguing, particularly (since it was his field) the neuroanatomical data. The hypothalamus is, LeVay knew, a regulatory authority monitoring information from the nervous system, constantly evaluating and controlling (among other things) thirst, body temperature, and sex drive; it has the job of turning on and off the pituitary, the all-important gland whose hormonal products set off ovulation in rats and humans. So LeVay began his paper with the logical hypothesis that "A likely biological substrate for sexual orientation is the brain region involved in the regulation of sexual behavior." Because the hypothalamus affected sex, Allen's "two [INAH] nuclei could be involved in the generation of male-typical sexual behavior." In other words, LeVay conjec-

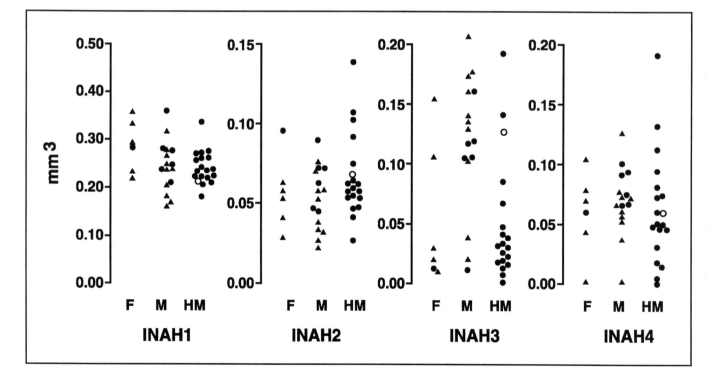

Volumes of four hypothalamic nuclei from Simon Levay's study. Volumes of the four hypothalamic nuclei studies (INAH 1, 2, 3, and 4) for the three subject groups: females (F), presumed heterosexual males (M), and homosexual males (HM). Individuals who died of complications of AIDS (solid circles), individuals who died of causes other than AIDS (solid triangles), and an individual who was a bisexual male and died of AIDS (open circles). For statistical purposes this bisexual individual was included with the homosexual men.

tured that a part of the brain regulating sex drive might according to different drives. Therefore, he wrote, "I tested the idea that one or both of these nuclei exhibit a size dimorphism, not [only] with sex, but with sexual orientation. Specifically, I hypothesized that INAH 2 or INAH 3 is large in individuals sexually oriented toward women (heterosexual men and homosexual women) and small in individuals sexually oriented toward men (heterosexual women and homosexual men)."

LeVay got brain tissue from 41 subjects who died at seven hospitals in New York and California. Among his subjects were 19 gay men, all of whom had died of AIDS; 16 presumed straight men (the 6 of these who died of AIDS had a history of IV drug use); and 6 presumed straight women. No lesbian brain tissue was available because, LeVay explained, there was no disease he could use to identify lesbians. In his study, LeVay used "sections," slices of the brain itself. He carefully extracted the anterior hypothalami, which gave him 41 tiny blobs of grayish pink brain matter, and with a machine called a microtome that resembles a precision meat-slicer sliced those portions into razor-thin sections. LeVay meticulously described his methodology:

> The [sections of the] brains were fixed by immersion for 1 to 2 weeks in 10 or 20 percent buffered formalin and then sliced by hand at a thickness of about 1 cm.... Tissue blocks containing the anterior hypothalamus were dissected from these slices and stored for 1 to 8 weeks in 10 percent buffered formalin. These blocks were then given code numbers; all subsequent processing and morphometric analysis was done without knowledge of the subject group to which each block belonged.... The sections were mounted serially on slides, dried, defatted in xylene, stained with 1 percent thionin in acetate buffer.

LeVay's study led to a four-page paper entitled "A Difference in Hypothalamic Structure Between Heterosexual and Homosexual Men." Published in *Science* magazine in August of 1991, these four pages exploded into world news.

"INAH-3 did exhibit dimorphism," LeVay wrote. "[T]he volume of this nucleus was more than twice as large in the heterosexual men ... as in the homosexual men.... There was a similar difference between heterosexual men and the women."

Endocrinology

The endocrinological search for sexual orientation in humans has so far produced only ambiguous results. The theory that differing hormone levels create sexual orientation, championed in the late 1960s by German scientist Gunther Dorner, has been thoroughly discredited by scientists such as Heino Meyer-Bahlburg and others. One of the current theories is that homosexuality is created by in utero fetal exposure to certain opposite-sex-typical hormones, but this has proven difficult to test. Dr. John Money and other scientists have looked at the sexual orientation of people exposed in utero to atypical sex hormone levels, but again the results are hard to interpret.

What is clear endocrinologically is that steroids—the sex hormones refined from raw cholesterol—have a clear role in creating male and female physical and behavioral differences. "The connection between steroids and aggression," Carl Sagan and Ann Druyan have written in *Shadows of Forgotten Ancestors,* "applies with surprising regularity across the animal kingdom. Remove the

principal source of sex hormones, and aggression declines, not just among the mammals and birds, but in lizards and even fish." In species from pit vipers to primates to certain African fish, losing in ritual battles for leadership means a marked decrease in testosterone, a sort of biochemical loss of self-esteem. In contrast, give males testosterone and aggression jumps. The more macho the androgens make males, the more they neglect their family responsibilities; raise the testosterone levels of male birds, and they decline to feed their hatchlings.`

Give an animal estrogen, and aggression falls; administer progesterone, and the female inclination to care for young increases. (The words *estrogen* and *progesterone* mean, respectively, "estrus-maker" and "gestation-promoter.") From rats to dogs, virgin females ignore or avoid newborn pups, but prolonged treatment with progesterone and estradiol that bring their hormone levels up to those typical of late pregnancy results in maternal behavior. Rats who have high levels of estrogen are less anxious, less fearful, and less likely to engage in conflict. This is not, Sagan and Druyan point out, the universal case. Male and female wolves, short-tailed shrews, ring-tailed lemurs, and gibbons are almost equally aggressive, but these are the exceptions. We humans are the rule. Males are more aggressive than females, and blood plasma testosterone is about ten times greater in men than in women. Compare levels of male sex hormones circulating in our bodies, and you find these figures (from McEwen, "Circulating Levels of Sex Hormones in Humans." Measurements in nanograms of hormone per milliliter of plasma per person):

	Men	Women
Testosterone	22	2

Compare estradiol, an estrogen, and progesterone, which is associated with maternal behavior, and the difference is monumental:

	Men	Women
Estradiol	.15	1.7
Progesterone	.7	32

It is this hormonally influenced male-typical, female-typical behavior that beckons toward a hormonal mechanism for sexual orientation. (The following is also part of the clinical data for sexual orientation.) Many have studied the question of when typical male-female behavior and evidence of heterosexual-homosexual orientation show up in humans, and the answer, it has long been known, is: very young. Richard Green, a UCLA psychiatrist, studied effeminate and masculine boys over a period of 15 years. Often from the age of two or three, a certain percentage of children clearly behave atypically for their gender, boys behaving markedly like girls from such a young age that there was no possibility of their having learned the behavior, no role models, no environmental inputs.

> *Mother:* (Speaking of her seven-year-old son) The first thing I noticed, one day at a friend's house—she has four little girls, he likes to go back in their room and play with their dolls. He went back there and grabbed a doll.... He took Kleenex and ... folded them and poked holes in them and made a very attractive dress for those dolls ....

Green: How old was he?

Mother: He was four, four-and-a-half.... He would tie aprons around himself ... to make a nice long skirt.... It got so that we were taking aprons and just sticking them places.... Even today I go around and find aprons wadded clear back on the closet shelves where we had tried to hide them, just in a fit of panic.

Or from a different interviewee:

Mother: He was playing with dolls, playing dress-up, playing school in nursery school at the age of three. By the time he was four it didn't diminish.

Green found a striking correlation between this gender atypical behavior—boys who display female-typical traits and instincts, such as sensitivity, cooperativeness, and less aggressiveness, and girls who display the male-typical traits of athleticism and greater aggressiveness—and sexual orientation. Interviewing his subjects as adults in their late teens and early twenties, he found that 75 percent of the men who had been effeminate boys had homosexual sexual orientations; other researchers have seen similar correlation with girls who behaved like boys. So homosexuals clearly have, in general, a degree of gender reversal. (It is important to note, however, that homosexuality—a same-sex sexual and romantic attraction—is completely clinically distinct from transsexualism—a profound feeling that one's psychic gender is the opposite of one's physical gender. Transsexuals are in no way homosexuals and vice versa, and this is demonstrated by the fact that a tiny number of people actually are born with *both* traits: a person with an XX female body who in her psyche feels herself inalterably male and who is attracted sexually and romantically to other men.) These gender atypical children were not "taught" their behavior. They behaved (because they felt) like no one they had ever seen, and persevered despite harsh, constant social pressure to change. The inescapable conclusion is that they are born with both their gender behavior and their sexual orientation.

Genetics

The first question for geneticists researching any trait is: how much of a contribution are genes making to this trait in humans? The answer for sexual orientation came in December of 1991, four months after the appearance of LeVay's work, in a twin study done by Dr. Michael Bailey, a psychologist at Northwestern University, and Dr. Richard Pillard, a psychiatrist at Boston University. Entitled "A Genetic Study of Male Sexual Orientation" and published in the *Archives of General Psychiatry,* it operated on a simple principle.

Identical twins are natural clones, two human beings with the exact same genes, while fraternal twins are just like usual siblings; they share half their genes. If a gene creates a trait, or creates part of a trait, then looking at twins helps you see this: the more genes you share with someone, the more genetic traits you both will have in common. You should see a pattern: identical twins should share that trait most frequently, fraternal twins and non-twin siblings next, and adopted siblings, who share no genetic material, least frequently. This pattern was exactly what the study found for homosexuality.

Bailey and Pillard compared 56 "monozygotic" twins (identical twins, from the same zygote or fertilized egg), 54 "dizygotic" (fraternal) twins, and 57 non-genetically related adopted brothers. The results lined up in exactly the way expected for a genetic trait. Eleven percent of the adoptive brothers were both gay, which is fairly close to the average or "background" rate in the general population, 22 percent of the dizygotic twins, and 52 percent of the monozygotic twins. Another way of describing the finding is that identical twins, who share the same genes, are twice as likely to share a homosexual sexual orientation as fraternal twins, who share only half their genes, and *five* times as likely as adopted brothers, who were raised in the same family by the same parents—the same environment—but share no genes at all. So the difference must come from genes.

A year later, Bailey and Pillard published a similar study of lesbian women. The results were virtually identical. Forty-eight percent of the twin sisters of lesbians were also lesbians, and, as predicted, as genetic relatedness fell so did the frequency of lesbianism; for fraternal twins the figure was sixteen percent and for adopted sisters, only six. One very important point—and a quite common misperception—arises here: when in identical twin pairs one twin is gay, the other is also gay only 50 percent of the time, but this fact does *not* mean that homosexuality is "50 percent a choice" or "50 percent environmental." What it means is that homosexual orientation is apparently somewhere between 50 percent and 70 percent heritable and the rest is due to non-genetic but biological—endocrinological? neuroanatomical?—factors. What many people fail to recognize is that while homosexuality is 50 percent concordant in identical twins, the trait auto-immune diabetes is only 30 percent concordant. And yet no one would argue that auto-immune diabetes is 70 percent a "chosen lifestyle." And left-handedness is only 12 percent concordant. Which means that while both homosexuality and left-handedness are probably 100 percent biological, genes probably play a much greater role in creating homosexuality than left-handedness.

This study was followed by an actual attempt at locating the genes involved. Dr. Dean Hamer and Dr. Angela Pattatucci, both molecular geneticists at the National Institutes of Health, set out to find the genes for homosexuality in men. At the outset, Hamer and Pattatucci faced three preliminary issues, all clinical.

The first was to confirm that what the clinical clues seemed to be saying, that there was indeed a gene influencing sexual orientation, was true. They wanted to be sure sexual orientation had real genetic roots and was not merely an environmentally or culturally created mirage, something that looked genetic but was not. The second issue was a conceptual one: how to narrow down the trait to its essence to get the clearest, most solid target for the team. And third, on a practical level, the team had to answer the basic question of just how they would go about the search, a question of methodology.

The first task meant defining as exactly as possible the trait profile for sexual orientation. "As you live in the world, you notice that people have lots of different traits," Hamer said. "You might notice, for instance, that lots of people speak English and lots speak Chinese. So if you're a geneticist and you're kind of already professionally obsessed with this stuff, you might say to yourself, 'My gosh, they're *everywhere,* people speaking one of these two languages. There must be a gene!' If you then were to say, 'I'm going to study the genetic basis of speaking English or Chinese,' the odds are that the first 100 Chinese speakers you found would be Asians and the first 100 English speakers you

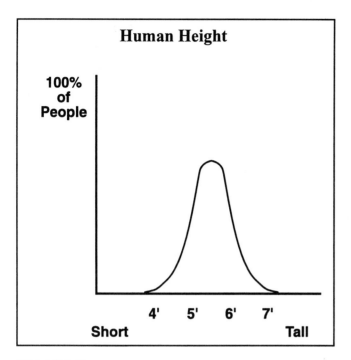

"Height" bell curve

got would be Caucasians. And you would hurriedly look in their DNA and say, 'Look! White guys and Asian guys have a genetic difference right here in this gene that makes them speak these two different languages. And then you'd spend years writing your grant proposals and figuring out your methodology and conducting interviews and searching genes. At the end, you'd announce, 'I've studied one million people, and 99 percent of the Chinese speakers have this version of the gene and 99 percent of English speakers have this one. I've found the language gene which makes some people speak English and some Chinese.' And you'd sit back and wait for the phone call from Sweden.

"And of course you'd be *totally* wrong, because obviously there are lots of genetic differences between Asians and Caucasians. The reason our eyes are different shapes and our hair is different colors is because of these genetic differences. What you would have done is taken the genes that form these traits and mis-assigned them to language. Obviously the ability to speak language is genetic, but the language you speak, Chinese or Ukrainian or Farci or whatever, is not. And you'd see this the moment you raised an Asian genotype—an Asian kid—in an English-speaking environment and found you'd gotten an English speaking person who was genetically Asian. It's easy to mis-assign genes, which is why you have to be very careful when you do genetics that your work is based on more than just associations because you can confound one trait you see in a person with another." He added, "Whenever you have a gene that you *think* is associated with a trait—any trait from hair color to speaking Chinese to sexual orientation— you'd better be able to prove that in some scientifically reasonable way."

In working on this problem, Hamer's team set out to determine whether sexual orientation was a "continuous" trait, expressed across a range, or "bimodal," divided into two expressions with few or no fine gradations in between. This is called the distribution curve of the trait, how the trait is distributed in populations.

"A good example of a continuous trait is height," Hamer explained. "People have all different sorts of height from very short to very tall, so you know there are a lot of genes affecting this trait, and that it's genetically very complex. Which makes studying the genetics of height—and all continuous traits—really tough. You can draw a picture of this idea, by the way."

Say you pick 100 women at random. The women would be all sorts of heights, which would be roughly distributed along this curve, most of them in the middle where it's highest, but some on the ends where there are a few very tall women and a few very short.

Bimodal traits, on the other hand, are either-or propositions. Diabetes in rats is controlled by around four or five genes, a relatively simple genetic etiology, and its distribution curve is pretty much simply bimodal: either the rat has diabetes or it doesn't. Albinism is controlled by only one. Again, you have albinism or you don't. "The distribution curve of handedness," said Hamer, "is basically the bimodal curve, right or left, although we haven't found the genes yet."

This is a J curve, where the trait is either one thing or another, and any geneticist is going to recognize it instantly. It's pretty much the opposite of the curve you get for a continuous trait, where the trait is distributed along a spectrum. Geneticists generally "like" bimodal traits simply because it makes them experimentally attractive: if you want to try to study a trait, isolate individual genes and figure out how they work, which is what genetics is about, then purely and only as a matter of practicality you would prefer to be researching a trait that's bimodal, like handedness, because it's probably caused by one or a small number of genes, each with a decent share of influence that you can actually measure. A continuous trait such as height is probably controlled by a number of genes, each with tiny, difficult-to-detect influences that can lead a lab off on a frustrating wild goose chase, too complex to track down with current genetic technol-

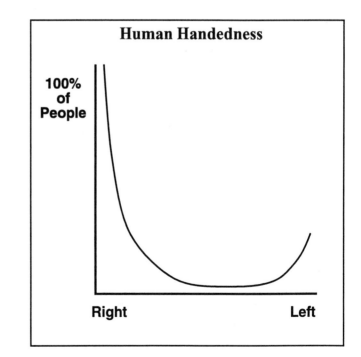

"Handedness" J curve

Human Sexual Orientation

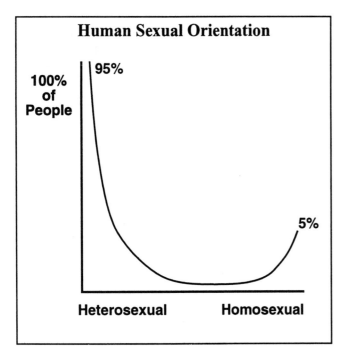

"Human Sexual Orientation" J curve

straight, and asking questions: was the person sexually attracted or oriented to men or women or both? Romantically? Had they always felt this way? How consistently had they felt this orientation? Along with distribution, they established seven indices to measure sexual orientation: self identification, fantasy, sexual behavior, sexual attraction, romantic/emotional attraction, social attraction ("with whom do you prefer to socialize"), and "lifestyle." Questions designed to assess these indices were carefully drawn up and put to the subjects. The results were quite clear: sexual orientation is a bimodal trait distributed along a J curve.

Hamer confirms this. "It's bimodal. That's what our data and the data of others tells us. This was a major debate in sexology that began with the creation of the field. Kinsey's rather vague notion was that everyone is born essentially bisexual, and if that were true, human sexual orientation should be a bell curve, a continuously distributed trait. He created a scale from 0 to 6, heterosexual to homosexual, and assigned the population to it in a bell shaped distribution. This was incorrect. In fact, we now know that the Kinsey scale—at least as far as it decrees a bell curve distribution—is basically a dead model because it doesn't reflect reality. Sexual orientation isn't a continuous bell. It is, particularly for men, a bimodal J."

This J curve was just a rough first assessment. When they completed analyzing the data, they found the trait actually had not one but *two* markedly different curves, yet these curves were not, as many would expect, of gays on one side and straights on the other. Actually, the two distribution curves for sexual orientation are divided between men and women, and they differed in three significant ways.

The first way was the shape of the curves. "Sexual orientation in men," Richard Pillard once joked, "isn't really a J curve. It's more like an 'L.'" The distribution of sexual orientation among men, Hamer and others have found, is essentially a standard J curve, like handedness, but with such an extreme distribution that

ogy. "We were sort of holding our breath at that point," Hamer said, "because this would give us a big clue up front as to whether or not we'd be able to pull this off—which one of these distribution curves matched sexual orientation, the trait we were looking for."

Hamer and Pattatucci began the painstaking job of sketching sexual orientation's distribution curve by finding subjects, gay and

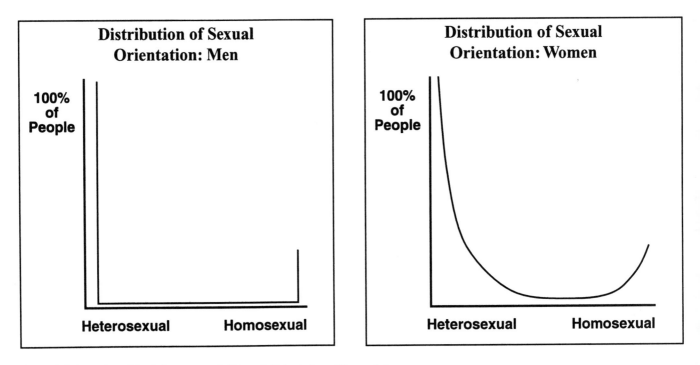

"Sexual Orientation: Men" L curve and "Sexual Orientation: Women" J curve

it is almost completely bimodal, either/or, gay or straight. Women, on the other hand, have "a real J"; although sexual orientation is clearly bimodal among women as well, there are more bisexual women than there are men—more 2s, 3s, and 4s—so the curve has more of a curve. Side by side, they look like the Modified J curve for "Sexual Orientation: Women" on the following page.

The second way the curves differed was in the percentage of gays to straights. Hamer and Pattatucci found that approximately 2 percent of all men were gay (and 98 percent straight) but the percentage of lesbians was roughly half that, around 1 percent. These figures are almost certainly low. Research on the population percentages for homosexuality has only recently begun, and the figures are still inexact since political, social, and religious pressure have always dissuaded homosexuals from identifying their sexual orientation. In addition, the low figures may in part result from scientific stringency in assessing the data, and Hamer and Pattatucci themselves believe that the numbers are actually around 4 to 5 percent for men, 2 to 2.5 percent for women, or slightly higher, although these too are only estimates. During the 1992 presidential elections there was a fascinating illustration of the change that is occurring in the establishment of an accurate phenotypic picture of sexual orientation as social pressures recede and more accurate data comes forward as a result. In those elections, a consortium of CBS, ABC, NBC, and CNN did a nationwide voter exit poll, conducted by Dr. Murray Edelman of Voter News Service in New York, and found that only 3 percent of all voters identified themselves as gay and lesbian. The story, however, lay underneath the 3 percent figure: for voters older than 60, only 1 percent self-identified as gay, but for those between ages 18 and 29, more than 5 percent did so. Pattatucci and Hamer, in trying to measure a trait subject to social censure, are made constantly aware of this problem.

But the third difference between the sexes was perhaps the most striking, and this was a difference of expression. Pattatucci conducted the interviews with the women in the study, evaluating, as she said, "tons of letters, tons of conversations on the phone, tons of interviews." She confirmed in the end that women do something men virtually never do: they move between straight, bisexual, and lesbian.

While the vast majority of women are stable in their orientation, Pattatucci determined that it is not unusual for a small portion of women to report feeling themselves to be straight at age 16, perhaps lesbian at age 24, maybe bisexual at age 38, and straight again at 55. With men, says Hamer flatly, "This sort of movement is very, very rare. It's pretty much a phenomenon we see only in women." Hamer tells of an interview he conducted with a woman in her sixties. "She's been happily married to a man, married her whole adult life, but he had died. Her answers to all the questions are down-the-line straight: never slept with a woman, never fantasized about sleeping with a woman, never *thought* about sleeping with a woman, always attracted to men, never thought of herself as lesbian, et cetera. So the interview's over, I've marked her down the line heterosexual, and I ask her if she has any questions about the study. She looks at me and comments matter-of-factly, 'You didn't ask me about the future.' My very eloquent response was, basically, 'Huh? What are you talking about?' She says calmly, 'Well, you know, I'm only in my sixties. My sex life isn't over, and who knows if in the future I won't be with a woman.'" Hamer noted, "Erotically, men never report experiencing even having the interest. You never, ever get a sixty-year-old straight guy who reports, 'I've slept with women

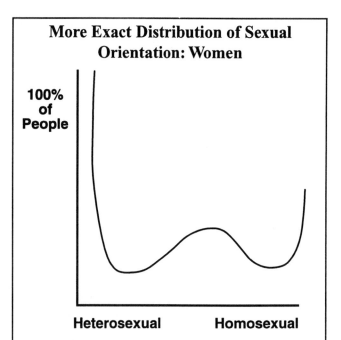

More Exact Distribution of Sexual Orientation: Women

100% of People

Heterosexual   Homosexual

Modified J curve for "Sexual Orientation: Women"

all my life, was married happily to my wife forty years, never had the slightest sexual attraction to any man or even *thought* about a guy romantically, but hey, who knows! Maybe next month I'll start doing it with men!'"

Pattatucci concurs. "If you track 100 men, after a few years, maybe—*maybe*—one will have moved. Just a little. Maybe. With 100 women, it's almost certain a number will move. Although," she adds, "women are actually more stable than we thought they would be." In fact, Pattatucci found that bisexual women are just as anchored in their bisexuality as straight and gay women in theirs. "More often than not, women identifying as 0 or 1 or 5 or 6 say they are fixed in that position," she said, "but even bisexual women at 2, 3, or 4 responded at a fairly high rate that their sexual orientations were fixed at 2, 3, or 4. I've found virtually no evidence that 2s, 3s, and 4s are any less stable in their categories than 0s or 6s. When women *do* move, they tend not to go drastically from 6 to 0 but maybe from 6 to 3 or 2 to 4. They don't make large movements. And I saw just as much movement from outside of the scale to inside as vice versa." Pattatucci learned that there is less to movement than meets the eye. "Sometimes a woman will identify as a 2 and then a year later will say she's a 4. At first I thought, 'Ah! her orientation has shifted. Now let's look into this.' Well, then I find that when I ask why she's telling me she's now a 4, she'll respond that in fact *nothing* has changed for her as far as her desires and feelings—the biological definition of sexual orientation—go. What has changed is the way other people react to her. Last year she had a boyfriend and went more to straight bars and places, but they broke up and so this year she has more access to the lesbian community. The orientation hasn't changed, just the social situation. So in fact, her orientation is quite stable."

Aside from the complications of movement with women, Pattatucci found a number of women identifying in the 0 and 1 and 5 and 6 range, and quite a few as 3, but less as 4 and 2, which gives this subtle variation in distribution.

"The distribution curve for women is more intellectually arresting," says Pattatucci, "but more methodologically problematic. It's basically a J, but with these variations."

Between men and women, she observed another fairly spectacular difference. Pattatucci explained "When you ask men, gay or straight, if they have ever wondered about their sexual orientation—if for example a straight guy has wondered, after a break-up with a girlfriend, if he's gay or a gay guy, if he meets a beautiful woman, if he's straight—they almost invariably say no. It's extremely rare to hear that they have, and in the few instances when you do hear it it's usually the result of some major event and goes away the instant the event is resolved. Yet it's not at all rare for us to have women say they've wondered. A large number of straight women and almost as large a percentage of lesbians have wondered about their sexual orientations."

Pattatucci found that the clinical part of their genetic study revealed, it sometimes seemed, more about the sexes than about sexual orientation. Although their work as molecular geneticists was nailing down the trait profile of sexual orientation, she and Hamer found themselves doing more than a little male/female sociological research. Pattatucci observed, "Men seem to be able to average their experiences—any experiences, not just sexual—with ease. You ask them about something, and they are able without pondering it too much to say decisively 'I guess that overall, although I'd say no in a few instances, in general the answer is yes.' For example, when you ask men about their lives—'Were you a good student in high school?'—you find they'll either give a yes or no. Experience is evaluated bimodally without undue effort or concern. You ask women, and they'll say 'Well, it depends.' Women look more at the details: 'Do you mean English or biology or algebra?' They separate it into categories and they focus on each category instead of giving you a clear general answer—and are, in fact, generally averse to a yes-or-no division of experience. As a clinical researcher, I'm not able to pull a general answer out of that.

"If I ask, 'Did you have sex in high school?' women will respond, 'Well, what do you mean by "sex?" Petting? Making out? One time or five times?' If I ask a man, he'll give me an almost immediate response, yes or no. I think that for men, having sex is a more narrowly defined phenomenon than for women. That is a striking difference in my opinion, and it speaks to a difference people have been talking about for a long time, that women's sexuality is expansive, that we need to have more things fulfilled than just erotic desire. On average, men get satisfaction purely from eroticism. If you ask women about their fantasies, they typically are very situationally oriented. It's not just sex, it's sex culminating from a series of attractive romantic but not necessarily sexual circumstances. As a biologist and clinician, that makes my asking the same question for men and women a different enterprise. Women are more informative, but women's responses can therefore be frustrating for me as a researcher because there are questions to which I need a general answer. It's easier to get to the core of a man since they tend to define things more narrowly. If I ask men a specific question, they'll give me a specific answer, and if I ask a general question, they'll give me a general answer. On the other hand, if I ask women a general question, they will often give me a specific answer, filled with detail, interspersed with political views and personal experiences, and contingent on conceptual arguments. And within women, there is a subset of women who seem to have so blended their uncontemplated desires and emotions with their politics and their feminist consciousness that I'm not able from their answers to separate the two."

This is, Pattatucci notes, an example of a fascinating, frustrating process crucial to the team's research: the separation of the biological definition of sexual orientation from the cultural definitions. It is a process common to all biological research of traits expressed behaviorally. Pattatucci faced it in one of the measures that she and Hamer were using to ascertain sexual orientation: "lifestyle."

She grimaced. "I hate the word 'lifestyle.' It's idiotic when applied to sexual orientation—would you refer to left-handedness as an 'alternative lifestyle?'—but the problem is that through misuse by the media and in political rhetoric it's become ubiquitous now, and there's nothing we can do about that. When reporters use it, it is simply intellectual laziness. But some people adore that word, and the reason is probably in many cases, I'm very sorry to say, that it is such an inaccurate description of homosexuality, implying that sexual orientation is something one chooses, something frivolous or faddish, determined by what you do as opposed to an internal orientation that is a component of what you are. It's gotten to the point that when your proposed study protocol gets reviewed, they nitpick you to death. 'Why didn't you include "lifestyle" as one of your criteria?'" The team put in the term originally because of politically formed expectations, but they did not include data gained through it in linkage analysis because it is a substantively meaningless and fundamentally inaccurate term for sexual orientation in a biological context.

In fact, in contrast to the popular misuse of "lifestyle" as synonymous with "homosexuality," Pattatucci and the NIH team used the word "lifestyle" for the express purpose of identifying and weeding out from the study those who are *not* homosexual. A relatively small number of women, Pattatucci found, said in the interview, "I'm not a lesbian, I just fell in love with this one woman." It was apparent that their feelings are, by pretty much every measurement, basically heterosexual. They perceive themselves as having had a serendipitous experience. They fell in love and committed to this one particular woman, and sex became part of the relationship. "We've noticed," said Pattatucci, "that one of the consistent identifying characteristics of this phenomenon is that these women will describe their relationship as living a '*lifestyle.*' They're quite comfortably certain that they are attracted to men *except* for this one woman."

Pattatucci did not include these women in the study. "Simply as a matter of good methodology and effective research, we have to study people most likely to have a genetic influence, and if you're assuming there's a genetic influence for homosexuality, then it stands to reason that it behaves like a lot of other traits. The way traits behave is that the same trait might show a strong genetic influence in some people, some weak, and some virtually none. Obviously the people who are in this last group won't be good candidates for a genetic study. That's axiomatic. We only have so many dollars to allocate, and we put our resources into clearer possibilities. People in the first group are the best candidates. We're not doing anything different from what biologists do for any other trait. Obviously if you're looking for a needle in a haystack and there's twenty-three haystacks, you'd better narrow your field as much as you can. The best place to look is at people who show the greatest amount of expression."

(A short time after beginning the study, Hamer and Pattatucci dropped "lifestyle" and settled on four criteria: self-identification, behavior, and, most importantly, sexual fantasy [for example, "when you masturbate, do you think about men or women?"] and attraction ["when you walk down the street and pass people ... do your eyes jump automatically to men or women?"].)

Another category of subjects that Pattatucci excluded from genetic analysis was what she referred to as "political lesbians." "These are women," she said, "who identify themselves as lesbian for political and ideological reasons with little or no evidence of a romantic or sexual attraction to women. If we had set up a large study of the genetics of left-handedness, got it funded, took blood, done the gene assays, and found that we were working on subjects who had identified themselves as left-handed simply in solidarity with the political and social oppression of left-handers but were actually right-handed, it would be scientifically pointless; of course you're not going to find a gene for left-handedness in these people's DNA. You're looking at right-handed people who don't have the trait you're researching."

Pattatucci added, "One of the basic political positions of these women is opposing discrimination against people who are gay and support for ideas such as women's equality. Am I sympathetic to those goals on a purely political level? I absolutely am. I'm a woman, and I'm a lesbian. But I am also a geneticist, and that is the context in which I operate here. I'm researching a scientific question, not a political one."

Pattatucci and Hamer both note that this is one more illustration of the difference between men's and women's sexuality. "With women," says Pattatucci, "we ask the question: Is this person a lesbian for political reasons? This is a question we never have to ask of men because it simply has never occurred." Hamer concurs. "There are no 'political gay men,' and you virtually never see a straight man fall in love and have sexual relationships with 'one special guy.'"

The profound differences between male and female sexuality, of which sexual orientation is only one component, have been observed by scientists for centuries. The most fundamental dividing line runs not between gays and straights but between men (both straight and gay) and women (both straight and lesbian). As Dr. Simon LeVay commented, "A major question that's been raging for years is, 'Is homosexuality really just "reversed sexuality?" Are lesbians just straight men in women's bodies?' In a word, no. The fact is that gay people are sex reversed in some ways, but in most ways, lesbians and straight women are, in the ways they view and experience sex, fundamentally the same. And gay men and straight men, who in just about all the various aspects of their sexuality resemble each other almost exactly, are most appropriately grouped not in opposition but together. There is the one obvious reversal everyone concentrates on and makes a fuss about: Gay men like men, straight men like women. But—and this is in a sense even more interesting—aside from the gender to which they are attracted, virtually all the typical sex behaviors, responses, desires, and fantasies of straight men are identical to those of gay men."

There is the well-known story about Mrs. Coolidge who, on a Presidential tour of a chicken farm, noted approvingly a rooster copulating with a hen. "Does he do that often?" she asked. "Oh, several times a day," said the farmer. "Please tell that to the President," she directed pointedly. President Coolidge turned to the farmer. "Always with the same hen?" he asked. "No, all different," was the response. "Please tell that," Coolidge said, "to the First Lady." The male-typical trait of being sexually aroused by diversity can be seen in the reproductive products we manufacture. Having two sexes is a popular, though by no means univer-

sal, mode of reproducing. Some lower plants have only one sex, making reproductive cells and mixing them up at random to create the genetic blend that results naturally from the two-sex method. Fungi have hundreds of sexes. Humans, with two, are specialized into making eggs or sperm, and our sexual behaviors originate from our respective specializations. Form and behavior, in a sense, follow function.

While all other human cells have a full complement of the 23 pairs of chromosomes, sperm and eggs are haploid, carrying exactly half a full complement. Each sperm only gets half of a man's chromosome pairs, and the same is true for a woman's eggs. As Hamer put it, "Basically sperm and egg both carry 23 single socks out of 23 pairs of socks in the wardrobe." But the similarity between sperm and egg ends there.

A man releases roughly 100 million sperm each time he ejaculates. Sperm are marvelous studies in minimalist design. Tiny even by cellular standards, they are the most stripped down, quick and dirty biological contraptions imaginable, purely functional delivery systems. Sperm are essentially just flimsy warheads packed with genetic material. This DNA payload is strapped to an expendable engine (the tail) that contains only enough stored-up energy to reach the target. By contrast, a woman's eggs, 85 thousand times larger than the sperm, are large, solid machines. They are resistant to drying and, with their own emergency food ration of yolk, self-sufficient. A woman puts a great deal of energy into making each egg. She will produce only about 400 in her lifetime, and at most only around 20 of those will become children. (A man could easily fertilize a lifetime's worth of 400 eggs with a single ejaculation.)

Given what they have to work with, men and women have evolved conflicting sexual modi operandi, which operate on the instinctual level. As sociobiologist E. O. Wilson has said of mating, "It pays for males to be aggressive, hasty, fickle, and undiscriminating [while] it is more profitable for females to be coy, to hold back until they can identify males with the best genes."

"How many sex partners a person wants is clearly different not between gays and straights but between men and women," concurs LeVay. "Men, both straight and gay, and all male animals want to have more sex partners than females do. Women, gay and straight, and all female animals want fewer sex partners. This is rooted relatively simply in biology and has to do with strategies for reproduction. Males try to have more sex partners than females because it's so 'cheap,' in biological terms, for males to inseminate females. Sperm is not, relatively speaking, a scarce resource. By contrast, it's very 'expensive' for females to get inseminated because then they have to go through pregnancy, childbirth, nursing, and care-taking, and they can only have a limited number of offspring. If you're a male, you are free, if you're powerful enough, to have a virtually unlimited number of partners and offspring, which is great for you. If you're female, your interests are very different, and you're going to be as choosy as you possibly can. This biological phenomenon is clearly visible in our behavior."

Researchers Bell and Weinberg, points out LeVay, record in one study that the number of sex partners that gay men reported averaged thirty-three times what lesbians reported. Straights report a number of partners lower than gay men and higher than lesbians. "But," asks LeVay, "is that what straight men and women really wanted?" Not really. He notes that as is frequently the case, behavior taken at face value can be misleading. "Lesbians present you with an opportunity—under controlled, laboratory conditions in a sense—for studying female sexuality in its purest, most un-diluted form, and gay men for studying pure male sexuality. With heterosexuals, if you're trying to distinguish how men feel and how women feel sexually, the waters are muddied because per-force you're mixing the two. There's a sort of battle of the sexes there because of the clash of biological interests and strategies. Straight men are limited in their sexual activity by the number of straight women who want to have sex with them. So with hetero-sexuals, behavior misleads. With gay people, however, the drive is the same in both partners, so they have a much better chance of finding partners interested in the same frequency of sex and the same variety of partners as themselves, and the data are clearer. This is why lesbians report fewer sexual partners than straight women and gay men report higher numbers than straight men. Of course," adds LeVay, "as we've seen in the age of AIDS, that is a drive that can lead to an epidemic."

Pattatucci commented, "In our studies we're showing that when you ask people how many sexual partners they have over their lives, most lesbian women will say 1-5 or 6-20 and less will say 21-40 and almost none 40-100. But when you ask gay men how many partners they've had over their lives, it's reversed: the num-bers are typically high, 40-100 is not rare, and the atypical ones are 1-5. But what is interesting is that when you pose the same questions to straight men and straight women, and you get ex-actly the same answers: The straight men want more variety—men like big numbers—and seek that, and the straight women want less." Aside from all that it says about disease and infection, the epidemiological data from the AIDS epidemic and the infection pattern of the disease, particularly in Africa, demonstrate with cruel clarity the biological point that males desire a far greater num-ber of sex partners than women. Male-typical sexual desire added to a common medical observation—that because the lining of the anus is more easily torn than that of the vagina or mouth, giving viruses easier access and resulting in higher viral infection rates from anal sex—equals the simplest explanation of the epidemio-logical demographics of the AIDS epidemic, which has spread pri-marily in the United States through men who are also homosexual. It is thought that the reason that in Africa AIDS is primarily a heterosexual disease is because 1) heterosexual anal intercourse is a common means of preserving virginity and practicing birth con-trol and 2) the rates of STD, which greatly facilitate transmission of HIV by creating open sores on the genitals, are much higher in Africa.

Another important sex-related trait that is not reversed in ho-mosexuals is gender identity. If gay men are the opposite of straight men in terms of the gender to which they're sexually at-tracted, they are completely like them in terms of their sense of themselves *as* men. "The feeling of what sex you are, in my view, has deep biological roots," says LeVay. "It's not just that you look down and see you have a penis, and your parents tell you you're a boy, and you say, 'Oh, I'm a boy, OK, great, that's my identity.' In fact, I think there must be some internal representa-tion of what sex you are independent of things like the appear-ance of your body. My evidence for saying that is simply the existence of transsexuals, people, male and female, who, in the face of every possible evidence of their anatomy and what soci-ety is telling them, are absolutely, irrevocably convinced that they are of the opposite sex."

LeVay has commented, "Transsexuals attest to gender orienta-tion being as real a phenomenon as sexual orientation. What's in-teresting is that homosexuality and transsexuality are distinct but

perhaps biologically parallel phenomena, one a reversal of the gen-der of the people to whom you're sexually attracted, the other a reversal of the gender that you feel you are. Gay men are aware of some degree of femininity in themselves, and gay women some degree of masculinity, yet there is no reversal of gender identity. Drag demonstrates this. There's a thousand jokes about this, which gay people enjoy as much as—actually, I think more than—any-one. But this is completely and notably different from the sense that you *are* a woman or a man. Even for gay men who dress up in the wildest women's clothes, the *point* of the whole thing is that it is parody, which is why it's funny. Gay men are abso-lutely convinced they are men, lesbian women are absolutely con-vinced they are women, and if you ask gay men, they respond, 'I have a firm, inner sense that I am a man. And *this* is a show.' Frankly the very essence of what makes camp camp is the con-scious tongue-in-cheek aspect. At the point at which it is taken seriously—at which one says that the inside and the outside match—it stops, by definition, being drag."

With distribution and expression nailed down, Hamer and his team had three more aspects of sexual orientation to determine before he could begin looking for a gene, but they were crucial. During the 1980s, researchers had been turning up data suggesting that homosexuality ran in families like any genetic trait. They knew that, if there were a gene that influences sexual orientation in men, then male homosexuality should run in families, and gay men should have more gay men in their families than on average. Genes go from parent to child, so you'd see familial aggregation of the trait.

After collecting 114 families, it became abundantly clear that the trait ran in families. Hamer marked off the first critical point on his "Seems To Be Genetic" checklist:

1)   Being gay runs in families. He characterized the finding in the extremely careful wording of the scientist: "Having the trait run in families is necessary but not sufficient to show a genetic influence on a trait."

Using the same data, he then looked at a second crucial question, and was able to check off a second important checklist point:

2)   "There were increased rates of gay people among family members genetically related to each other even when raised apart in different households." This finding filtered out "environmental influences"—the homosexual subjects had only genetics in common—and highlighted the biological correlation between related genes and homosexuality. "Again," said Hamer, "this is consistent with the genetic theory, but doesn't prove it."

The third and last question was the most important. Hamer ex-plained, "The question becomes the scatter of the trait: Do these family members show a random distribution, as if you'd taken the family tree and randomly sprinkled the trait over it like salt from a shaker. That's what would happen if there were no genes. Or do you see a pattern, a pattern that looks genetic?" If a trait is truly genetic, examining family after family in a pedigree analysis will be like repeatedly throwing a pair of loaded dice and watch-ing the patterns emerge: everything seems normal at first, but if you are careful, patient, and tenacious, after a time you will no-tice that certain sides turn up more often than others. The pattern of the orientations, the way they turn up over and over in family members as they cascade down through generations, is called "genetic loading." To the geneticist's eye, these patterns are as characteristic as a fingerprint.

Hamer finally found the pattern. He noticed that in some of the families, most of the homosexual members were aligned on the maternal side. Not only that, there were extra gay male cousins and uncles, and they, too, were on the maternal side. And yet all the other gay people, all the lesbians, all the gay male cousins and uncles on the paternal sides of the family, were randomly distributed. The fingerprint had leaped out from nowhere, narrowing the search in a single moment from the entire human genome to 1/20th of it: the X chromosome. The reason is simple: men have only one X, every gene that they carry on their X coming from their mother, which means that X-linked traits (as these traits are called) show up in men through generations on the maternal side of their families. And so Hamer crossed off the third and last point on his checklist:

3)   More male relatives on the mother's side were gay. "*Only* this pattern, called a 'maternal effect,' was consistent with the theory that there might be a gene on the X chromosome," said Hamer. "It is necessary for the theory—but doesn't prove it."

What proves it is finding the gene. And this is what Hamer and Pattatucci set out to do. Selecting 40 pairs of non-twin brothers, both of whom were gay, and using a technique called "linkage analysis," they conducted what is in a sense an elaborate coin toss, measuring the heads-or-tails results against random chance. If two brothers share a homosexual sexual orientation, and if there are genes on their Xs for that homosexual orientation, then the team was asking whether the brothers shared any single region of their Xs more times than one would expect by random chance alone. If they did, and if it were at rates significantly higher than random chance would dictate, they could assume there was a gene weighting the results (like tossing a quarter in the air 40 times and getting 30 heads in a row; if that happens, you can bet the quarter is weighted, the analogous situation to having a gene).

This is what they did. What they found was that the brothers shared the marker genes of their twenty-eighth region of the X chromosome between 81 percent and 85 percent of the time. This is much, much higher than chance alone would indicate, and when the figures are evaluated according to standard statistical models, it means there is 99.5 percent probability that the finding is "real," that there is in this region a gene for homosexuality. Measuring for "p value" or "significance," the fundamental scientific measure of a study's solidity, the value needs to be at least .05 or lower; the smaller the number, the stronger the finding. The p value for the study was .00001. This finding became the paper, written by Dean Hamer, Angela Pattatucci, et al. and published in *Science*, called "A Linkage Between DNA Markers on the X Chromosome and Male Sexual Orientation."

Methodological Problems

As scientists should, biologists have noted a number of methodological problems with the various studies that have been done.

In the LeVay study, Dr. Evan Balaban has pointed out that Nissl stain, which LeVay used, might be a standard neuroanatomical tool, but it is also a century-old technology. It is not known exactly what material Nissl is staining, whereas other, newer stains such as connection stain or antibody stain are known, respectively, to color very active brain cells or identify groups of cells that all perform the same function. Is a Nissl stain evidence of a coherent structure with a cognitive or instinctual purpose or is it simply of a group of cells sharing some chemical that attracts Nissl? Is the nucleus that LeVay found *causative*—is it creating a homosexual orientation in the brains of these men—or is it rather a *result* of having a homosexual orientation that was created by something entirely different? We don't know.

Dr. William Byne has pointed out that a number of LeVay's subjects—the presumed homosexuals—had clinical AIDS, and both AIDS and the drugs used to fight AIDS can decrease testosterone production. Testosterone has an effect on the brain, so what LeVay might have been measuring is a nucleus made smaller than normal simply because of a deprivation of testosterone, not because of a homosexual orientation.

On the conceptual side, Byne notes—and Roger Gorski readily agrees—that the rats who demonstrate same-sex sexual activity are not "homosexual" but rather closer to a human model for transsexuality; manipulating their hormonal levels has apparently made the male rats think of themselves as female and vice versa for the females. And Anne Fausto-Sterling, a developmental geneticist at Brown University, has noted that the studies of sexual dimorphism in the human brain, one of the basic conceptual theses on which the research is built, has not been firmly established; the results of the many replication attempts have been ambiguous, and ignorance, rather than knowledge, of the brain and its incredibly complex functions is the current preponderant state of neurology.

In the Bailey/Pillard sibling genetic study, the central problem is being certain of the relative numbers of homosexuals and heterosexuals both in populations and within families: are the numbers truly representative? In a society that subjects homosexuality to significant disapproval, can we obtain accurate responses about it from people? Michael Bailey has acknowledged, "I think that the most troubling methodological problem with the twins study is the 'ascertainment bias' problem: these were volunteers, and we don't know what went into their decision to volunteer. So your data can be skewed."

There are counter-responses to these critiques. LeVay has double checked his data against non-AIDS homosexual brains and achieved the same results. But a replication of the hypothalamus study is needed before the data can be generally accepted. Laura Allen replies to Anne Fausto-Sterling that there have been successful replications of the human sexual dimorphism studies (although here again there are questions of histology (tissue preparation) and whether the measuring methods were truly identical and simply the amount that we don't know about the function of the structures we are measuring). As for the sibling genetic study, the sibling data has been confirmed by numerous other studies, and the ascertainment bias question shrinks every day: it is, most fundamentally, a problem of social pressure, and as anti-gay discrimination continuously wanes, the data becomes more and more trustworthy.

The principal criticism of the Xq28 genetic study was the bimodal distribution curve dictated by Hamer and Pattatucci's data. The fact that sexual orientation is clearly "either-or" for men is

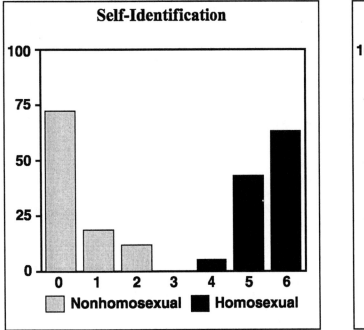

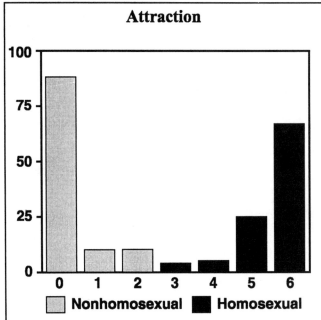

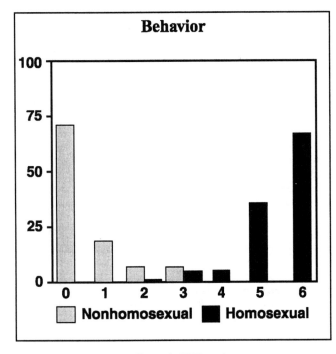

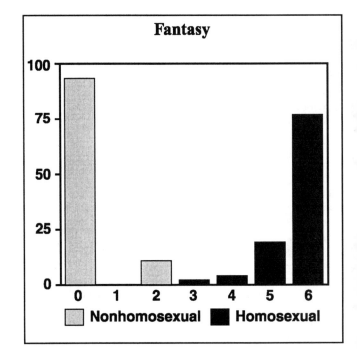

Four charts from Dean Hamer's NIH study

still a relatively new concept to many scientists, several of whom expressed doubts about the data. One college genetics professor insisted that the trait sexual orientation was "continuous"—that is, a bell curve—adding, "I don't really have any evidence for it, but it just makes sense."

However, Hamer points out accurately that his distribution curve has been confirmed by numerous studies, from Bailey to Pillard to Martin to Schwartz to Weinrich and so on. One of these, he notes, was conducted at a military hospital where the military's strict ban on homosexuality biases strongly against a response of

6, or homosexual. "You'd expect to get a large number of 'bisexual' responses in the military," explains Hamer, "2's, 3's, and 4's, because bisexuality would be a convenient way of shading the answer and protecting yourself. But again almost all of the men answered 6 or 0." The latest study was conducted in Australia by Michael Bailey and Nick Martin and had a sample size of more than 2,000 respondents.

One professor criticized the NIH study, writing: "Although the probands reported a wide range of sexual behaviors, identities, and fantasies, the experimenters [divided] the men into homosexual and heterosexual." In fact, this is a bias on the part of the professor. The four raw-data charts on page 1 of the Hamer study from which the distribution curve was derived are shown on the previous page as "Four charts from Dean Hamer's NIH study."

The numbers clearly indicate bimodal distribution in men. The irrelevant measurements, behavior and self-identification, are the least bimodal because they are the most subject to the non-biological filters of social and cultural influence, and the two relevant measurements for defining biological sexual orientation—fantasy and attraction—are the most bimodal.

Asked if he had anticipated this striking bimodality for male sexual orientation, Hamer says, "I have no theoretic argument with bisexuality. It's just that of the men we've interviewed, most identify themselves as either gay or straight. A handful identified themselves as bisexual, and we did not include them in the DNA analysis because of the possible genetic complexity in their cases and our need, at this stage, for simplicity. But of the few who said—even insisted—they were bisexual and made their case with the fact that they were also sleeping with women—which is behavior, and therefore irrelevant to us—it would become clear with most of them after just a couple of casual questions that they were really only attracted to men, that inside, their orientations—which *is* relevant to us—were homosexual. But they were in the process of coming out and felt more at ease at that point calling themselves 'bisexual' than 'gay,' which was a more radical term for them. They were still sleeping with increasingly fewer women for the same reason. Besides, as a geneticist, to be blunt about it, I don't really care what label anyone uses, or even what they do, or with whom. I care about what they feel, inside."

Quite important was the bias of the clinical questions Hamer and Pattatucci were using: they were *against* a bimodal distribution and *for* a range of sexual orientations. Hamer notes that when he started researching this question systematically, he was asking "continuous" type questions—that is, instead of asking, "Are you gay or straight," which would bias toward a bimodal model, he asked, "How do you ID yourself on this scale, who do you fantasize about, who do you have sex with?" and so on, which would tend to produce, if it would produce anything, a bell-shaped distribution. The Hamer team even based their data charts on Kinsey's four measurements, which were biased in favor of bisexuality. If anything, the whole Hamer methodology biased the answers in favor of a continuous distribution. And yet when they looked at the responses to these continuous-type questions, the responses were clearly bimodal, not continuous, despite the pro-continuous methodology.

There is one quite important final note to make in this section. Again, the popular media and popular culture have a completely incorrect understanding of the meaning of the biological critique of the research: many people, those who are most politically and religiously anti-homosexual among them, believe that scientific criticism of a biological study of sexual orientation—LeVay's study, for example—is equivalent to assertions that 1) homosexuality is not biological, 2) homosexuality is chosen, and 3) homosexuality is bad or wrong. This is false. Legitimate methodological criticism is standard in all scientific work, and the critique of the research from *scientists* (as opposed to religious or political figures, whose views on the research have expressly not been included here because they are not scientifically based) is entirely concerned with methodology, histology (preparation of tissue), correct control groups, and other aspects of the scientific process, and not at all with the clinical research which has established what homosexual-

ity is: an unchosen, non-pathological orientation. In fact, the three most avid and informed critics, Balaban, Fausto-Sterling, and Byne, are not at all opposed to the idea that homosexuality is biological, do not believe homosexual orientation is chosen, and specifically reject the idea that homosexuality is in any way "bad" or "wrong." They simply want to see the research done in the most scientific way possible, as do LeVay, Hamer, Bailey, and Pillard.

The best example of this misunderstanding involves Dr. William Byne. Because Byne is one of the most tenacious of critics, during the spring 1993 battle over Colorado state's Amendment 2 (which sought to forbid legal protections to homosexuals), the State of Colorado, supported by the anti-gay, conservative Colorado for Family Values and the Family Research Council, introduced Byne's critical work in its brief to the state's Supreme Court. These groups believed that because Byne was critiquing the studies, he too was anti-gay. They imagined that with Byne they were getting an expert who was asserting that homosexuality was a "lifestyle," not a sexual orientation; that homosexuality was a chosen, alternative behavior and/or a mental pathology unworthy of civil rights protections; and that homosexuality was not immutable but, rather, easily changeable. (Journalists who report on Byne, sexual orientation research, and Amendment 2 thought they were getting the same thing.)

What they actually got was this.

Byne didn't realize he was being cited as evidence for choice, lifestyle, and behavior. He was informed in a phone call by Dr. Dean Hamer, who had been subpoenaed as an expert witness by those attempting to halt Amendment 2. Hamer was sent the briefs of the case and was stunned to see Byne cited since he knew that Byne did not, in fact, think that homosexuality was a choice and, furthermore, that Byne was completely opposed to the idea of legal discrimination against gays and lesbians. Hamer had already been upset with Byne for making statements that the press, in its confusion, reported as anti-gay. At a meeting of the Academy of Sex Research at Asilomar near Carmel, Hamer had commented acerbically (and with clear reference to Byne, who was sitting in the audience) that given the political aspects of the research, scientists had a responsibility to make themselves understood.

Byne acted. When the State of Colorado officially asked Byne to be a pro-Amendment 2 (anti-gay) witness, he not only declined vehemently, he wrote a letter, dated 2 July 1993, and addressed to Hamer, to be used in the Amendment 2 case on the pro-gay side. "Dear Dean," it began, "This letter is in response to your statement at the Academy meetings that I must take responsibility for the misuse of my work by the anti-gay political and religious right."

Byne proceeded to reverse everything that Colorado for Family Values and the Family Research Council believed he was saying. "Some have apparently misinterpreted my recent [critique] with Bruce Parsons as disproving the biological hypothesis for the [origin] of homosexuality," he wrote. "Then, because they have been duped into believing the false dichotomy presented in news media headlines such as 'Homosexuality: Biology or Choice,' they erroneously interpret my review as supporting the view that homosexuality is a chosen lifestyle."

First of all, Byne stated, he did not reject even the simplest hypothesis that homosexuality was out-and-out biological. Quoting from his own writing (which the Family Research Council had been mailing out to conservatives), Byne noted with precision that he had merely concluded that "there is no evidence at present to substantiate a biologic theory." He was not claiming that homosexuality *is not* biological; all he was saying, he pointed out, was that as of yet we do not know. And, he noted, the anti-gay side and the press should have noticed that he was equally critical of all existing environmental theories, concluding that "there is no compelling evidence to support any singular psychosocial explanation."

Second, according to Byne, "[I would never] imply that one consciously decides one's sexual orientation. Had I been able to foresee how the paper would be misinterpreted and misused, I would have amplified that last statement." He mentioned a *New York Times*/CBS News Poll showing that people who believe homosexuality "is a choice" are less tolerant than those who believe it "cannot be changed." "No one who has spoken in depth with a number of homosexuals," Byne continued, "could conclude that they ... choose their orientation. Moreover, a survey of the literature on attempts to change sexual orientation leads inevitably to the same conclusion. Very few of even the most highly motivated to change sexual orientation have been able to do so despite investing tremendous emotional effort, many years, and many thousands of dollars in psychotherapy. In fact, the legitimate literature on attempts to redirect sexual orientation suggests that not only is sexual orientation not chosen, it is, by and large, immutable."

In response to Hamer's comments at Silomar, Byne also stated that the idea that only biological traits are immutable was completely incorrect, chiding "those ... responsible for the dissemination of this sloppy logic to the public through the news media. If I am to be held responsible for the misuse of my paper (which has occurred through misinterpretation), then you must also hold those ... responsible who have participated in the popularization of the view that if homosexuality is not biologically determined, it is chosen. They set the stage for my criticisms of the biological research to be misinterpreted."

Indeed, Byne amplified yet another quite important point about yet another common misunderstanding; the fact is that even if homosexuality were environmentally created, it would still be 1) unchosen, 2) non-pathological, and 3) immutable. Why was "Biology or Choice?," the central idea in the *Washington Post*'s reporting on the research, an incorrect headline? Scientists have long known, noted Byne, that many traits purely social in origin are immutable, such as a person's native accent, which can never be removed once it has been implanted in the brain. You don't choose it, your biology didn't create it, but most people retain accents throughout their lives despite their best efforts. Environment— the accents of West Texas or Shanghai or Odessa—have changed the brain, and these changes remain there forever, unchosen and unchangeable. And the converse of this is that just because something is a biological given does not automatically mean it is "good." Huntington's and Tay Sachs are both biological givens.

"In closing," wrote Byne, "I would suggest that the most responsible message that we can relay to the public is that we do not know what causes sexual orientation—but whatever the causes are, sexual orientation is not a matter of choice. To present a simple dichotomy—that sexual orientation is either biologically determined or a matter of choice—may recruit political activists to each side of the debate, but it will not advance science."

None of the participants in the scientific battle—LeVay, Allen, Byne, Fausto-Sterling, Balaban, Hamer—disagree on any of the "political" questions. Anne Fausto-Sterling has trenchantly critiqued the social and cultural biases that can skew the scientific process, but, appalled by the media's misinterpretation and mis-

use of her critique, she has also warned, "Don't make this more than it is. All I'm saying is that at *this* point in time in *this* culture and *this* political climate, researching things like gender and sexuality... is going to be so difficult to do objectively that it approaches the impossible. Look at history. Whenever these things have been done, they've been biased by sexism, racism, homophobia, classism, and every other prejudice.... I'm saying that it would be tough to do right. [However], if the study were done right, then you do the science and you find what you find, of course. I'm a scientist. I'm not opposed to science."

How Biology Might Create Homosexuality

The question facing biologists now is: how might genes, hormones, and neurons work together to create human sexual orientation?

Geneticist Fran Lewitter has commented, "Hamer's was a very good study. I have no doubt that he found something here. But remember that Dean's been quite careful and conservative in saying this is a gene which may act only in a very, very specific group of men, not 'the gene' for all homosexuals."

Lewitter's point is that while homosexuality may present itself to us as one, unitary thing—a same-sex sexual attraction—it, and heterosexuality, might actually be the result of different genes in different people. It is entirely possible, for example, that if two men are gay, one might be gay because of one gene on, say, chromosome 16, and the other might be gay because of several genes working together—and the man must have all of them, the full combination—on various chromosomes. Lewitter notes that there are ten different kinds of a disease called retinitis pigmentosa, and they are caused by genes on several chromosomes: autosomal dominant retinitis pigmentosa is caused by a gene on any of chromosomes 7, 8, 17, or 19; the gene for another kind, autosomal recessive retinitis pigmentosa, can be on the first or sixth; and so on. In other words, the gene or genes in Xq28 may account for 10 percent of all male homosexuality or they may account for 90 percent of it. It might be one gene that works alone, or it might be one gene that must work with others; the genes that make hemoglobin are on chromosome 11 (beta locus) and 16 (alpha locus), and both must be fully functional to produce hemoglobin.

Also, Hamer's subjects were mostly white males, and certain mutations are more frequent in certain ethnic populations. So Xq28 might be the gay gene for some ethnicities and not for others.

Indeed, Hamer himself has been careful to point out that in the original 1993 study, 18 percent of the gay brothers did not inherit the same portion of the Xq28 region from their mothers. It is possible the discordance arises from the mother's having a copy of the gay allele on both of her X chromosomes, but most probably, as with Lewitter's first example—retinitis pigmentosa—the source of these brothers' homosexual orientation is a completely different gene or endocrinological etiology. Hamer and other researchers are now looking for loci that influence sexual orientation on chromosomes other than the X. Dr. Angela Pattatucci has proposed that, given several profound differences between men and women— there are in general half as many gay women in a given population as men, for example—male homosexuality and female homosexuality may actually originate from completely different biological processes.

At the same time, the genetics of homosexuality may be, in fact, extremely uncomplicated. One of the commonest misperceptions of sexual orientation is that it is a "complex" trait, probably with a complex biological origin. In fact, researchers who understand sexual orientation believe that it may be biologically relatively simple. Dr. Cassandra Smith says, "I expect sexual orientation will come down to just one or two genes. Why? Sexual orientation is a simple trait. Everyone says it's complex, but it's not complex at all. *Sexuality* is complex. But don't confuse sexuality ... with sexual orientation."

"Sexuality" is not, Smith explains, "a trait" but rather "a common inheritance," like race, which is a composite of traits from eye color to hair color to eye shape and so on. Each of those relatively simple traits is controlled by genes, and it is only when they are added together that they become "race." The difference between sexual orientation and sexuality is the difference between a baseball and a baseball game. "Sexuality" is a huge rubric under which fall a vast number of traits from sex drive to the age of puberty to physical build to the preferred age or race of sexual partners one finds sexually attractive to the size of one's genitals to one's moral, political, and religious attitudes towards sex and the ways they create and govern ideas of romance and desire to sources of erotic stimulation and response to everything from money to power to education to the number of desired partners: one a day, one a year, one a lifetime.

Sexual orientation, by contrast, is simple: a sexual and romantic attraction to a gender—men or women or both.

Variety of preferences within the gender may be enormous, but that is not sexual orientation, which is, again, simply about the gender. A gay man can be attracted to tall men or short men. He may prefer dark men or masculine men. But these tastes and preferences are aspects of sexuality, not sexual orientation. Sexual orientation is the constant: he is always attracted to men. "Such a trait may easily be just a few genes," says Smith. "Maybe just one."

Sexual orientation is simply a directional marker pointing toward one or the other gender. (Richard Pillard's informal definition of sexual orientation, both simple and practical, underlines the "directional marker" definition. "Sexual orientation is when you pass people on the sidewalk on your lunch hour," Pillard says, "which sex do your eyes involuntarily flick on: men or women.") Philip Reilly, who agrees with Smith, does so for evolutionary reasons. "I imagine it comes down closer to one gene," he says. Why? Sexuality, in all its aspects, is one of the most fundamental phenomena subject to evolution, and in Reilly's view there has to be basic biological wiring that controls all the various traits that make it up, established at an early point. "I'd speculate that sexual orientation is linked to a very early event in embryogenesis and thus possibly could involve just a few fundamentally important genes that start that process unfolding. I really would be surprised for example if we were to learn that the gene turned on late in fetal development."

Because a genetically simple trait will, obviously, be worked out sooner than a complex one, most scientists seek to perpetuate the myth that sexual orientation is "complex." Dean Hamer admitted, "Originally, we used 'sexuality' and 'sexual orientation' almost synonymously, but the more work we do, *really* looking at exactly what you're trying to find, the more it becomes clear the original 'complexity' of the trait was due to that confusion. I'd say sexual orientation will probably be the same order of genetic complexity as handedness."

He adds that this analogy must be understood clearly. Handedness, the neurological ability to move the arm and fingers in a way that allows writing, swinging a racquet, or opening a jar, almost

certainly involves hundreds or thousands of genes. The *direction* of that handedness, however—left-handed or right-handed—may be determined by simple biological factors. "The overall machine," he notes, "which you could call sexuality, may be, genetically, incredibly complicated, but the directional switch for that machine, straight or gay, may be incredibly simple."

One of Hamer's colleagues, who would not allow himself to be identified, was much more frank. "Look, you'll never get me to say it publicly, but I think it's clear that this is really a pretty simple trait. It's just not politically wise for us working in this field to say it yet. It makes people nervous and upset; the simpler a trait is, the easier it is to research, and that's threatening to a number of different types of people on all political sides for a number of very different reasons. We'll say it when we get more evidence, which is as it should be, but if you look at where the data are going, there's not much question."

In fact, some of the so-called complex traits, such as the bell-curve-distributed height, turn out in certain circumstances to be not only not complex but, we now know, controlled by a single gene. One case in the literature where a single gene has a major effect on a "complex" trait is found in pygmies. If a pygmy has a child with an African of average height, all the children are either of average height or of pygmy height. The trait is one or the other, clear cut, and the reason is that the trait is controlled by one gene. What does the gene do? The most logical thing in the world: it helps manufacture the receptor molecule for growth hormone. Without the receptor, the hormone cannot dock, and it floats helplessly outside its destination, ineffectual, till it disappears. So this is a trait that appears to be complex but is, actually, genetically quite simple.

Here is one way a gay gene might operate: epigenesis, a genetic influence that interacts with an environmental input to create an effect. Richard Lewontin, a highly respected population geneticist, suggested that the gay gene may be a gene that controls the way a human embryo perceives heat. Explains Lewontin, "This is speculative, but once you've found a locus, your next step is to conceptualize what this gene's modus operandi might be. It might be a developmental gene that turns on in utero, that determines your response to heat stimuli that comes into the womb, that molds one person's neural architecture differently from another's. That creates a different sexual orientation." This epigenetic effect is well known, and Lewontin gives an example. Because of epigenesis, biologists will need to make sure that when they find a gay gene it is actually a gay gene. He points out that there are what scientists call "maze dull" and "maze bright" rats that do, respectively, poorly and well in mazes, and rats can be selected and bred for these traits, because there is a gene for running a maze. What is this gene? It turns out that the maze bright rats are partly blind. The reason they do so well in the maze is that they don't get distracted by other cues due to having genes that interfere with their perception of eye color. Lewontin imagines that human IQ is a similar story, that certain people are less distracted because they are less genetically sensitive to sights and smells when they're taking IQ tests. "We think of genes as 'making you smart,'" he says, "as if genes were little units inside us labeled 'High IQ.' In reality, these so-called IQ genes could be labeled 'Bad Eyesight, Needs Glasses.' Saying that there's a gene for sexual orientation is like saying there's a gene for running a maze well. What I'm saying is that there is a difference between saying that a gene causes sexual orientation or raises IQ or the ability to run a maze well, and a gene that has an epigenetic effect, a direct effect on one thing with a side effect on something else."

Here is a second way a gay gene might operate. If there is any popular near-universal misunderstanding of biology as applied to homosexuality, it is the notion that a gay gene could not be selected for by evolution. "If homosexuality were genetic, it would have died out by now" is the way it is usually expressed. This comes from the popular, superficial reading of Darwin, the assumption that genes that directly decrease reproduction are selected against and die out. The key word is "directly." "Many people," points out Eric Lander of the Whitehead Institute, "who have a gut reaction against homosexuality will express their feeling by saying that it is 'against nature'—that's the way they generally put it—because nature only selects alleles that enhance reproduction, and thus homosexuality, which is non-reproductive, must be a perversion of the natural order. This is based on a fundamental misunderstanding of evolution. People assume that a gay gene would lower reproduction. You can't assume that at all."

Biological theorist. E. O. Wilson of Harvard, the father of sociobiology, hypothesizes that nature has selected for the gay gene because it brings with it an indirect reproductive advantage. Suppose, says Wilson, that it is a million years ago, and there is a gene that stops some members of *Homo erectus* from reproducing because it directs their sexual desire to members of the same sex: a gay gene. And say this group makes up maybe around 5 percent of the population of each tribe. Wilson observes that since they do not produce their own offspring, these tribe members are available, if their brothers or sisters are killed on a hunt or in an accident, to help raise their sibling's children and assure their survival, a sort of natural safety net—which means, because the homosexual aunts and uncles share on average 50 percent of their siblings' genes, that they are assuring the perpetuation of their genes through these offspring, the most natural, Darwinian instinct in the world and a good reason why nature would actively select for and maintain a gay gene in populations. Wilson called this "kin selection."

Not only is this a powerful theory, it is supported by a quite well known real-life example. There is a gene for a trait, evolutionarily selected for over millennia, which directly decreases reproduction but indirectly increases it. And *this* gene does it by actually killing those who carry it. "There's this apparent conundrum," says University of California, Berkeley's Jasper Rine, "which is how come gene alleles that kill you or decrease reproduction in individuals don't die out of the population? Isn't natural selection supposed to select for genes that help you? The answer is 'Well, yes—but there's a catch.' The catch is that nature works on averages, not on individuals. Natural selection picks the genes that help more people on average than they hurt." This lethal gene sits on the 11th chromosome. It is a gene that, if you have two copies, gives you the disease sickle cell anemia. But if you only have one copy, it protects you from malaria. And on average, nature has found that while thousands are killed by this gene, more thousands are protected for it, and so the gene is selected for, perfectly natural even though it can be lethal. The gay gene may operate exactly like the sickle cell/anti-malaria gene, perpetuated by heterosexuals who carry it invisibly.

Here is a third way the gay gene might work: penetrance. Genes have something called "penetrance," which simply refers to the action of *other* genes or the environment on this gene's ability to express itself. "There's actually a pretty easy way to think about penetrance without a lot of genetic jargon," says Eric Lander, of the Whitehead Institute for Biomedical Research in Cambridge, Massachusetts. "The penetrance of an allele is basically its seniority in the corporate hierarchy of the genome. The question is simply how many genes can it override and how often can it get to do what it wants—and how many can override *it*. Penetrance is about power."

An allele that's 100 percent penetrant, says Lander, is 100 percent powerful. "The allele that gives you Huntington's is 100 percent penetrant. If you've got that allele, it gives you the trait, period, and no other genes can overrule it. Now, let's take a hypothetical. Say this gay allele [Hamer] is looking for in Xq28 has 5 percent penetrance. This means it has only a 5 percent chance of getting its way and making you gay. Not a lot of leverage, this gene. Even if two brothers inherit this gay allele from Mom, its low penetrance ensures that 90 percent of the time neither brother will be homosexual, about 10 percent of the time one brother will be, and only about one quarter of one percent of the time will both be gay. The reason is that homosexuality is created by a weak allele with very little political influence in the genetic decision making process." This means there could be hundreds of millions of straight men walking around with this gay allele but who are straight simply because it didn't penetrate. But they pass it on, and on average, in a certain percentage of their kids, the right combination of genes makes it so the gay gene can penetrate and produce a homosexual person.

Epigenesis as illustrated by Lewontin's gene for heat, Wilson's kin selection with Rine's example of net versus individual reproduction, and penetrance are all possible genetic models for the operation of a gay gene. The fourth is pleiotropy.

Pleiotropy occurs in genetics the way side effects occur with drugs. Homosexuality, one researcher theorizes, could be a genetic side effect.

The classic example of pleiotropy is found in an article by Richard Lewontin and Harvard paleontologist Stephen Jay Gould titled *The Spandrels of San Marco*. It's an architectural example of the biological question, 'Why is this thing—this effect, this trait—here?' Spandrels are triangular panels created when arches are placed next to each other, such as the arches holding up the dome of San Marco church in Venice. Painters took advantage of these triangular spaces to paint beautiful frescoes. The confusion of a gene's primary with its secondary effects would be like a researcher of sexual orientation going to San Marco and saying, "Look! Evolution has produced these spandrels as a place to put these beautiful paintings." And she would be completely wrong because the spandrels were created as by-products of the architectural structures called arches whose primary purpose is to support the building. Miss this fact, and the spandrel is misinterpreted. Pleiotropy thus poses the tricky question: is homosexuality the arch, selected according to kin selection to create a small number of non-breeders who will help breeders increase their reproduction, or is it the fresco-adorned spandrel, merely a secondary by-product?

It is ridiculously easy for genes to create secondary effects. Some scientists believe genes work not linearly, each exclusively on its own job, but in parallel, double- triple- and quadruple-teaming their workloads by joining up with different groups of genes to do different jobs. These scientists argue that without such cooperation, we would not have enough genes to create ourselves. With millions of overlapped jobs, it would be unusual if unintended, pleiotropic effects were not generated. So a gay gene could easily be the side-effect of another gene selected for a completely different, unrelated reason.

There is also what biologist William Rice calls "sex antagonistic pleiotropy," side effects that benefit one sex and hurt
the other. Hemochromatosis, a recessive genetic disease in which
excessive amounts of iron are deposited in the liver and skin,
may be an example of sex antagonistic pleiotropy because it is
more damaging to men than women. The allele responsible is
of a gene at 6p21 which, passed down through thousands of
generations, spends half its time in women and half in men.
The primary job of the allele (and the reason evolution has conserved it) is to enhance the ability to pick up iron from the
intestine. Biologist Jared Diamond argues that since women lose
iron when they menstruate, this allele might, as a secondary
effect—a pleiotropic effect—help women who are anemic and
lacking iron to maintain good iron levels. Since men don't lose
iron to the same degree, the secondary effect in men—the male
pleiotropic effect—is to leave them with an excess of iron,
which starts settling into their tissue and making them sick. Is
the gene good or bad? The fact that it has been conserved shows
that its average benefits to women outweigh its average costs
to men. And this is due to the fact that genes segregate randomly, spending on average 50 percent of their time in men
and 50 percent in women.

But there is one glaring exception to this 50/50 rule: any gene
on the X chromosome—which just happens to include Hamer's
gene somewhere inside Xq28. "The cool, and somewhat bizarre,
thing about a gene on the X," Hamer has remarked, "is the math."
Because men carry only one X but women carry two, an X gene
will spend two-thirds of its time in women and only one-third in
men. This strongly skews natural selection's interests and gives
X genes a decidedly different perspective on things. Given their
"female point of view," the good things X genes do for women
can be much less than the harm (decreased reproduction) they do
to men and still—from the gene's position—come out ahead. Why?
The beneficial effects for women are, essentially, being multiplied
by two.

What this means is a dramatic suspension of the normal math-
ematical rules of natural selection. In fact, the break even point
isn't even close to equal. Hamer points out that gay men and lesbians have always had children, but it's not unreasonable to suspect that they have somewhat fewer than their heterosexual counterparts. If an X-linked gene reduced the number of children men
have by, say, 50 percent, it would only have to increase the number of children women have by 25.1 percent—half that number
plus a tiny little bit—in order to tilt the balance scales and convince nature to select for it. It could increase reproduction in women
through any number of possible beneficial effects. Perhaps the
gene changes sex hormone metabolism in a way that makes men
gay (the pleiotropic side effect) but makes women go through puberty a little early or menopause a little late (the gene's primary
effect). This means the gene would be an "increased childbearing
gene" in women that on balance caused increased reproduction,
and only secondarily a "gay gene." Nature would concentrate on
the first trait, selecting the gene for it, while it would be only the
secondary trait that we would notice.

If the gene's "primary effect," the reason nature is selecting for
it, is to increase reproduction in women, it could do just about
anything to men, including killing them. Nature wouldn't care.
Most people, Hamer knows, assume he is tracking a gene whose
primary effect is homosexuality. It may actually be a gene that
creates homosexuality as a secondary effect. The problem with
the effects is deciphering which is which.

The Implications of the Research

The impact of the biological research of sexual orientation is in
some ways quite predictable and in others truly surprising.

One of the obvious implications is genetic testing for homosexuality, coupled with abortion and genetic surgery to change
sexual orientation, either in utero or even, eventually, in adulthood.
The viability of testing and surgery depends on the outcome of
all the data and theoretic work noted above. It may be difficult
and it may be easy. But the fact is that the more we know about
any trait, the closer we are to being able to manipulate and control it.

Another obvious implication involves a prevalent political debate over the research: should it be used in the battle for gay rights?
The answer to this debate, if one looks at it from a purely pragmatic point of view, is evident. There are certainly legitimate concerns over such use. Dr. Angela Pattatucci has noted the conceptual problems with using data showing homosexuality to be a natural, inborn, immutable trait: "The media is always insinuating that
because I'm a lesbian I'm leaning toward the genetic explanation.
There's always an assumption I have a vested interest in things
turning out a certain way. I find this amusing. I don't. I'm not
convinced. From a political standpoint, I'm not sure that even if a
strong genetic component for sexual orientation is demonstrated
beyond a shadow of a doubt that that will make things any better
for us. Pass non-discrimination legislation on those grounds, and
you not only limit coverage to people whose sexual orientations
has a genetic basis, but by that standard someone who is mulatto,
has black blood but doesn't look black, would not be covered because he or she is insufficiently biologically black. You don't make
laws against discrimination based on biology. You make them based
on principle, regardless of the origin."

But at the end of the day, political reality is quite clear: of Americans who believe homosexuality is a chosen lifestyle, most are
unwilling to support gay rights; of Americans who understand
that it is an inborn orientation, most are likely to support them.
A recent *US News* poll, confirming ABC and the *New York Times*
and on and on, found that only 45 percent of Americans favored
gay rights, but of Americans who believe homosexuality is biological, the figure is almost 70 percent. It is simply the way Americans think; 54 percent of us favor mental illness research, but 63
percent of us do who think it genetic.

The corollary argument against using the research politically,
"the fact that being black is biological didn't help black people so
homosexuality being biological won't help homosexuals," is also
nonsensical for an obvious reason: every hatred of every group
has its own particular, specific profile—anti-black and anti-
Jewish people never believed black people or Jews chose to be
black or Jewish, instead they believed other false things, which
blacks and Jews respectively had to demonstrate were false—and
"choice" and "promotion" simply happen to be the specific falsehoods anti-gay Americans have for whatever reason fixated on.
They are the falsehoods gay people must, like every other minority group before them in American history, show to be false.

This is exactly what the clinical and biological research does.

However, from a somewhat less directly pragmatic point of
view, political use of the research is much more complex and problematic, and this is because it has a surprising political effect: it is
empirical ammunition in the greater political war between conservatism and liberalism. For the past 400 years, since the beginning
of the modern age, the Right and Left have fought over the ques-

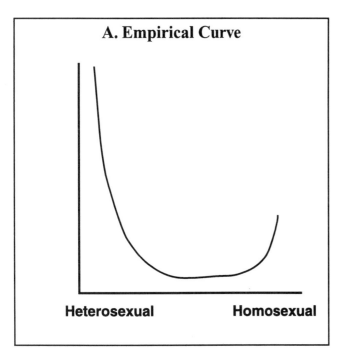

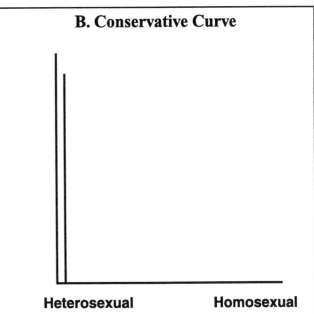

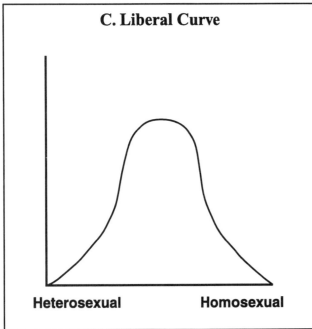

Empirical (top-l), conservative (top-r), and liberal (bottom) curves for sexual orientation.

tion of human nature: why are we human beings what we are? The two competing answers, the answers on which all policy prescriptions are based, are: born or made.

The conservative side has maintained that human beings are born with certain instincts and abilities. (The ultra-conservative Victorian social Darwinists, who told the lower classes to stay in their places because they were born to them, women to accept a secondary role that was natural, and non-whites that nature had made them the colonized, are the best example of

this.) They see an inherent, biological difference, even inequality, between people.

The liberal side believes that biology delivers us to the world as equal creatures with nothing inherent and society and environment make us what we are. (Marxists, who hold that if only we could change society and equalize all education and wealth we will create equality between people, are the best example here.) Since people are made, equal environments make for equal people. How one views laws and governmental policies is determined by how one views human nature.

The idea that sexual orientation is inherent is ammunition on the conservative side. In this way, it is equal to the biological research of IQ or gender or violence, which also says that these things are inborn and which is also strongly opposed on ideological grounds by liberals. And it creates a severe divide within the gay community between those who are conservative, and who like both the positive effect that the research has on gay rights and the supportive effect it has for the conservative point of view, and those who are liberal, who want gay rights and perhaps recognize the research's efficacy in getting them but cannot countenance its deeper, broader implication that liberalism's basic assumption is at least partly wrong.

In the end, however, the debate over ideology appears moot. The research will reveal what it will reveal. And if the modern era has taught us anything, it is that factual, empirical reality will prevail and ideology both of the Right and the Left will adapt to it. The research is having a disruptive political effect, but the disruption is symmetrical. Both the Right and Left, based on the ways they want to see human nature, have cherished notions about the trait human sexual orientation. The Right believes that everyone is "born naturally heterosexual," and homosexuals are merely heterosexuals who, for perverse reasons, choose to indulge in same-sex sexual behavior. The Left, which believes in social forces shaping human outcomes, believes that the great majority of people are born with a capacity for bisexuality and only society pushes us into becoming heterosexual or homosexual. Both of these are contradicted by the empirical data, specifically the Empirical Distribution Curve of Sexual Orientation in Humans. To be scientific about it, all three distribution curves can be graphed. They look like the "Liberal, Conservative, and Empirical distribution curves for sexual orientation" on the previous page.

Ultimately, the research contradicts cherished notions on both sides of the political fence. This is the role of science.

PROMINENT PEOPLE

Mike Bailey (1957-)

J. Michael Bailey was born on 2 July 1957, in Lubbock, Texas. He earned a B.A. in Mathematics in 1979 from Washington University in St. Louis and a Ph.D. in Psychology in 1989 from the University of Texas at Austin. Bailey is currently a professor in the Department of Psychology at Northwestern University. One of the central focuses of his research has been the genetics of sexual orientation—he is co-author with Richard Pillard of two of the best-known clinical studies in this area—and he has published extensively on the subject. With Nicholas Martin of the Queensland Institute of Medical Research, he has recently conducted the largest twin study of sexuality to date on nearly 5,000 Australian twins, and he is currently working on several other studies regarding the biology of sexual orientation. Those interested in participating in these studies can contact Bailey at his web site at http://www.psych.nwu.edu/psych/people/faculty/bailey/bailey.html.

Dean Hamer (1951-)

Dean Hamer was born in 1951 in Montclair, New Jersey. He received his B.A. from Trinity College, Connecticut in 1972 and his Ph.D. from Harvard Medical School in 1977. He has worked at the National Institutes of Health for 20 years, where he is currently the Chief of the Section on Gene Structure and Regulation in the Laboratory of Biochemistry of the National Cancer Institute. Dr. Hamer is a leading researcher in the recombinant DNA, drug and vaccine production, and gene regulation. For the past three years he has been studying the role of inheritance in human behavior and personality traits, including sexual orientation. His book *The Science of Desire* (Simon and Schuster), co-authored with journalist Peter Copeland, was a 1994 *New York Times* "Notable Book of the Year."

Simon LeVay (1943-)

Simon LeVay was born in Great Britain in 1943. He is the cofounder of the Institute of Lesbian and Gay Education as well as the author of numerous books, including *The Sexual Brain, Queer Science: The Use and Abuse of Research into Homosexuality,* and *Albrick's Gold,* a medical thriller.

Richard Pillard

Richard Pillard is a Professor of Psychiatry at Boston University Medical School. He was one of the first openly gay psychiatrists in the United States as well as one of the first openly gay physicians, and he worked with the American Psychiatric Association to eliminate homosexuality as a disease in the diagnostic nomenclature. Dr. Pillard's interests focus on biological aspects of sexual orientation, especially how and why homosexuality runs in families.

Angela M. Pattatucci (1951-)

Angela Pattatucci was born in 1951. She received her B.S. from Northeastern Illinois University in 1987 and her Ph.D.

Richard Pillard

from Indiana University in 1991. The focus of her work, she notes, "is in sexual and gender identity development within the broader fields of developmental and social psychology and how they potentially interface with biology. I also have a compelling interest in how public policy and social and cultural issues affect discriminatory attitudes based upon gender and sexual orientation." Among her writings are the book *Women in Science: Meeting Challenges and Transcending Boundaries* (Sage Publication) as well as numerous articles and book chapters.

References:

Books

Burr, Chandler. *A Separate Creation: The Search for the Biological Origins of Sexual Orientation.* New York: Hyperion, 1996.

Green, Richard. *The "Sissy Boy Syndrome" and the Development of Homosexuality.* New Haven, Connecticut: Yale University Press, 1987.

Hamer, Dean and Peter Copeland. *The Science of Desire: The Search for the Gay Gene and the Biology of Behavior.* New York: Simon and Schuster, 1995.

Le Vay, Simon. *Queer Science: The Use and Abuse of Research on Homosexuality.* Boston: MIT Press, 1996.

———. *The Sexual Brain.* Boston: MIT Press, 1993.

McManus, I. C. "The Inheritance of Left-Handedness," in *Biological Asymmetry and Handedness, Ciba Foundation Symposium 162*. Chichester, United Kingdom: John Wiley & Sons, 1991: 251-67.

Money, John and A. Ehrhardt. *Man, Woman, Boy, Girl*. Baltimore: Johns Hopkins University Press, 1972.

Whitam, Frederick and Robin M. Mathy. *Male Homosexuality in Four Societies: Brazil, Guatemala, the Philippines, and the United States*. New York: Praeger, 1986.

Periodicals

Allen, Laura, Melissa Hines, James Shryne, and Roger Gorski. "Two Sexually Dimorphic Cell Groups in the Human Brain," in *Journal of Neuroscience*, vol. 9, no. 2, 1989: 497-506.

Allen, Laura. "Sex Differences in the Corpus Callosum of the Living Human Being," in *Journal of Neuroscience*, vol. 11, no. 4, April 1991: 933-42.

Bailey, J. Michael and Kenneth Zucker. "Childhood Sex-Typed Behavior and Sexual Orientation: A Conceptual Analysis and Quantitative Review," in *Developmental Psychology*, vol. 31, no. 1, 1995: 43-55.

Bailey, J. Michael and Richard Pillard. "A Genetic Study of Male Sexual Orientation," in *Archives of General Psychiatry*, vol. 48, December 1991: 1089-96.

Bailey, J. Michael and Richard Pillard, et al. "Heritable Factors Influencing Sexual Orientation in Women," in *Archives of General Psychiatry*, vol. 50, March 1993: 217-23.

Byne, William and Bruce Parsons. "Human Sexual Orientation: The Biological Theories Reapprised," in *Archives of General Psychiatry*, vol. 50, March 1993: 228-39.

de Lacoste, Christine and Ralph Holloway. "Sexual Dimorphism in the Human Corpus Callosum," in *Science*, vol. 216, 25 June 1982): 1431-2.

Dorner, Gunther. "Hormonal Induction and Prevention of Female Homosexuality," in *Journal of Endocrinology*, vol. 42, 1968: 163-64.

Gorski, Roger, et al. "Evidence for a Morphological Sex Difference within the Medial Preoptic Area of the Rat Brain," in *Brain Research*, vol. 148, 1978: 333-46.

Goy, R. W. and J. A. Resko. "Gonadal Hormones and Behavior of Normal and Pseudohermaphroditic Nonhuman Female Primates," in *Recent Progress in Hormonal Research*, vol. 28, 1972: 707-33.

Hamer, Dean and Angela Pattatucci, et al. "A Linkage Between DNA Markers on the X Chromosome and Male Sexual Orientation," in *Science*, vol. 261, 16 July 1993: 321-27.

———. "Linkage Between Sexual Orientation and Chromosome Xq28 in Males But Not in Females," in *Nature Genetics*, vol. 11, November 1995.

Hooker, Evelyn. "The Adjustment of the Male Overt Homosexual," in *Journal of Projective Techniques*, vol. 21, 1957: 18.

LeVay, Simon. "A Difference in Hypothalamic Structure Between Heterosexual and Homosexual Men," in *Science*, vol. 253, 30 August 1991: 1034-7.

Money, John, M. Schwartz, and V. G. Lewis. "Adult Erotosexual Status and Fetal Hormonal Masculinization and Demasculinization: 46XX Congenital Virilizing Adrenal Hyperplasia (CVAH) and 46XY Androgen Insensitivity Syndrome (AIS) Compared," in *Psychoneuroendocrinology*, vol. 9, 1984: 405-15.

Myer-Bahlburg, Heino. "Psychoendocrine Research on Sexual Orientation: Current Status and Future Options," in *Progress in Brain Research*, vol. 61, 1984: 375-98.

Swaab, D. F. and M. A. Hofman. "An Enlarged Suprachiasmatic Nucleus in Homosexual Men," in *Brain Research*, vol. 537, 1990: 141-48.

Whitam, Frederick. "Culturally Invariant Properties of Male Homosexuality: Tentative Conclusions from Cross-Cultural Research," in *Archives of Sexual Behavior*, vol. 12, no. 3, 1983.

Other

Gill, Kulbir. "A Mutation Causing Abnormal Mating Behavior." Drosophila Information Service, 1963.

Whitam, Frederick and Christopher T. Daskalos. "Male Sexual Orientation, Femininity, and Childhood Cross-Gender Behavior in Four Societies: Brazil, Peru, Thailand, and the United States," presented at the Society for the Scientific Study of Sexuality. Miami: November 1994.

Web page for the research of sexual orientation: www/aol.members.com/gaygene.

—Chandler Burr

21

Sports

Gay and lesbian athletes have always contributed to amateur and professional sports, but only since the 1970s have a small but significant number of professional American athletes come out. The most general reason for such restraint can be found in the generally homophobic atmosphere of sports. Historically, homophobia has manifested itself in the locker room jeering of effeminate boys as "faggots"; the insinuation that overt lesbianism in women's sports presents a troubling image to spectators; and the speculation that an openly gay or lesbian athlete may never latch onto successful commercial endorsements.

This chapter examines the achievements of gays and lesbians in the sports world and highlights the underlying reasons for the traditionally hostile atmosphere of the sports world to openly lesbian and gay athletes. Because of the special obstacles women athletes have historically faced owing simply to their gender, the chapter devotes additional space to chronicling the evolution of women's sports in America. The "Prominent People" section provides information on the handful of openly gay and lesbian athletes who have emerged in the sports world since the 1970s, while the "References" section points the reader to further information about lesbians and gay men in the sports world. Finally, readers should note that this chapter focuses primarily on professional athletics as well as serious amateur athletic competition. Additional information about sports-related leisure activities for gay men and lesbians can be found in the "Travel and Leisure" chapter.

INTRODUCTION

The lack of openly gay athletes, along with other factors, traditionally discouraged many gay men from engaging in any amateur sports, or if they did compete they usually concealed their homosexuality. Homosexuality and male super-athletes seemed a contradiction in terms; the public generally assumed its most visible and hyper-masculine jocks (particularly the ones in contact sports) were straight. Rumors to the contrary could mar or even destroy any male athlete's career. Of course, some closeted gay male athletes feigned heterosexuality, although they did not always go to

great lengths to pretend. They were usually presumed to be straight in the first place.

The public's perception of its most successful female—gay or straight—athletes was quite different. Regardless of their true sexual orientation, they were not necessarily assumed to be heterosexual; this was certainly the case with "butch" women with masculine mannerisms (or mannish women, as they were known in the first half of the twentieth century). Given this psychology, many female athletes and physical educators found subtle means to project heterosexuality. For example, in interviews, they played up real or imagined boyfriends/fiances and talked about such traditionally feminine tasks as cooking or sewing.

The Significance of the University of Amsterdam Survey

In light of the above, a paper entitled "Survey on Discrimination on Sexual Preference in Sports" is especially relevant. Conducted by the University of Amsterdam (Netherlands) in the early 1990s, the survey focused on three general questions: to what extent discrimination because of homosexuality is reported in organized sports; which forms it has taken if it existed; and what discrimination meant for the participation of gays and lesbians in sports. To answer these questions, the researchers interviewed gays and lesbians about their experiences in organized sports.

While there is not a great deal of scholarly literature on gays and lesbians in sports, what has been written (Sabo and Runfola, 1980) suggests gay men who are perceived as effeminate have a very tough time finding a secure niche in amateur/professional sports, because sports are considered a masculine domain. Lesbians with a butch image are better represented in sports (sports are not considered a traditionally feminine domain), although they often encounter prejudice and discrimination. Hence, the inversion of gender roles has had different effects on gays and lesbians.

That only 185 men and 98 women (12 of that total considered themselves bisexual) participated in the survey can be partly explained by the tendency of gay and lesbian organizations in the Netherlands to recruit more males than females. And since the survey focused on gays and lesbians generally out of the closet, it cannot be said to be representative of the total gay and lesbian population. Finally, to what extent the results of the research generalize to American sports is debatable.

Still, given the dearth of research on the topic of sexual discrimination in sports, the University of Amsterdam survey is an important one, and its results are generally discouraging for gay and lesbian athletes. In summary, gays and lesbians in sports face many risks that have been somewhat resolved in women's soccer, but apparently in no other sport. Hence, a very small percentage of gay men and a somewhat higher percentage of lesbians in the survey came out in their respective sports. Many of the athletes who exposed their homosexuality (as well as many who did not) experienced some sort of discrimination, not atypical of the discrimination that pervades society.

Many gays and lesbians in the survey simply did not feel at home in sports, which, of course, does not constitute discrimination. Survey participants often witnessed verbal abuse (e.g., references to "faggots" and "dykes"), some of which was not directed at them or anyone else in particular, but it understandably contributed to a hostile atmosphere. In the most extreme cases of discrimination, gays and lesbians were brutally threatened and/or dismissed from their teams because their homosexuality was discovered. Lesbians more often than gays suffered more frequent instances of outright discrimination, in keeping with a greater percentage of lesbians being "out" in sports.

Lesbians have thrived in soccer to such an extent that the male president of one European soccer club once said of that sport, "Formerly half of the women were lesbians, now it is 90 percent." While no other sport has so many openly gay women, soccer has also been the battleground for the most blatant forms of discrimination. Second, many parents worry about their daughters playing soccer, for fear they will become lesbians. Still, the overall picture of lesbians in soccer is quite promising.

The University of Amsterdam survey also focused on sports bringing together people of different sexual orientations in a physical and potentially erotic situation. That eroticism may arouse any athlete, but for gays and lesbians it poses some risks. Unfortunately, many straight athletes do not believe they can trust gays and lesbians in physically intimate circumstances; unless this prejudice is eradicated, discrimination for gays and lesbians in sports will persist.

THE EVOLUTION OF THE GAY GAMES

Although there are still relatively few openly gay and lesbian professional athletes in America, the number of amateur sports organizations available to gays and lesbians has steadily expanded. Opportunities have abounded since the middle 1970s, among them bowling, tennis, football, softball, volleyball, wrestling, and even rodeo; what all these organizations offer is an environment for gays and lesbians to engage in sports for a variety of reasons without the burden of sexual self-consciousness.

The Gay Games has also furthered the spirit of amateur sports. The Games, a quadrennial international sports event, was created by Dr. Tom Waddell, a decathlon competitor in the 1968 Olympic Games. Despite his own athletic prowess, Waddell did not envision gay and lesbian athletes competing for their country or to win above everything else; rather, he conceived of an event in which all participants—regardless of their sexual orientation—aspired to contribute their personal best. Essentially, anyone who supported the spirit of the occasion could participate.

The evolution of the Gay Games, as we know it today, began in 1980 with the formation of the San Francisco Arts and Athletics organization. Its purpose was to conceive an event unofficially known as the Gay Olympic Games. However, the United States Olympic Committee (USOC) did not approve of this plan and got a temporary restraining order against the use of the word "Olympics." Waddell's original vision proceeded, albeit under the name of the "Gay Games." Over the next six years, USOC spent millions of dollars in legal efforts to prevent "The Gay Games"

from turning into "The Gay Olympic Games." In 1987, the United States Supreme Court, in a landmark decision, resolved the issue by ruling the USOC had proprietary rights to the word. To date, there have been "Special Olympics," "Police Olympics," "Nude Olympics," and "Dog Olympics," among other organizations that got permission to use the prestigious term for their purposes.

Despite the USOC's opposition and homophobia, the first Gay Games opened on schedule on 28 August 1982, in San Francisco. Approximately 1,350 athletes from about 180 cities in 12 nations participated in 14 athletic events. With a relatively small budget of $125,000, the event proceeded fairly smoothly, with about 600 volunteers on hand.

Since the Gay Games are a quadrennial event, Gay Games II occurred in 1986, also in San Francisco. In the interim between Gay Games I and Gay Games II, AIDS had evolved from a mysterious threat to the gay community to a full-blown epidemic, and Gay Games II provided an infusion of enthusiasm just when many gays and lesbians desperately desired it. The second occasion also expanded on the first by including a gay-related "Procession of the Arts," comprised of concerts, exhibits, plays, dances, films, and cabarets. San Francisco's gay-friendly mayor, Dianne Feinstein, also spoke at the opening ceremonies. Gay Games II comprised about 3,500 athletes (about 40 percent of whom were women) from 19 nations, 17 athletic events, and a budget of $350,000 ($30,000 of which was provided by the City of San Francisco).

In keeping with the patterns of growth, Gay Games III, which occurred in Vancouver, Canada, expanded on Gay Games II. In addition to drawing Vancouver's largest volunteer effort in history, the occasion included 7,500 athletes from 39 countries, 23 athletic events, and about 2,000 cultural participants. Its budget multiplied roughly six-fold, from $350,000 in Gay Games II to $2.1 million, the latter partially funded by the Canadian government. Sadly, three years prior to Gay Games III, Thomas Waddell, the man who had conceived the inspiration for the sports event, died of AIDS-related complications.

Gay Games IV, held in New York City's Yankee Stadium, not only simply surpassed Gay Games III in scope, it also surpassed the Olympics in size. Coincidentally, Gay Games IV overlapped the twenty-fifth anniversary of the New York Stonewall Riots, a milestone that in many ways solidified the contemporary gay liberation movement in the United States. In keeping with the spirit of gay rights, organizers of Gay Games IV convinced U.S. Attorney General Janet Reno to sign a blanket waiver permitting HIV-infected persons to enter the United States to participate in the Games. Gay Games IV attracted about 11,000 athletes and cultural participants from 2,000 cities in 45 countries; it included 31 sporting events and 7,000 volunteers. Its $6.5 million budget—more than three times that of the previous Gay Games—reportedly produced an economic impact of more than $150 million, according to the Games' organizers.

Although the Gay Games emphasize personal achievement—as evidenced by the tradition of all participants receiving a medal simply for partaking in the event—the event has drawn a fair number of gay and lesbian professional athletes, including former Olympian swimmer Bruce Hayes and the late professional baseball player Glenn Burke. At Gay Games IV, 12 world masters records and 4 U.S. records were achieved.

Gay Games V was held in August 1998 in Amsterdam. It was anticipated that the event would draw about 15,000 participants and as many as 200,000 visitors.

Ice skaters winning gold at the Gay Games.

HOMOPHOBIA IN THE NATIONAL FOOTBALL LEAGUE

While Martina Navratilova, Greg Louganis, Rudy Galindo, Muffin Spencer-Devlin, and Patty Sheehan are all openly gay athletes, they are also all participants in individual sports. Contact and team sports are a far less likely realm for an athlete to come out, and the National Football League is no exception. In the middle 1970s, Dave Kopay became the first openly gay professional football player, but by that time, he had retired from the game. Not that Kopay, a former NFL running back, lacked courage then, especially in light of the fact that he had a wife—who knew Kopay's sexual orientation. While Kopay remains the only athlete in his sport to admit his homosexuality, there have been endless rumors and innuendo about many others. (Kopay's friend and teammate Jerry Smith, a tight end for the Washington Redskins, never came out but died of AIDS in 1986. Since then, much innuendo and gossip over his homosexuality have ensued. Interestingly enough, David Slattery, the general manager of the Redskins, was a closeted gay man until he came out in 1993.)

Many gossipmongers—both pro-gay and homophobic—have speculated that certain football players are secretly gay. However, these rumors may have arisen out of simple professional infighting. In an *Advocate* article, NBC sports commentator Bob Costas

has speculated that an openly gay football player would not get as many offers to do endorsements, nor would the endorsements be as lucrative.

In the same *Advocate* article, ABC Sports reporter Dick Schaap echoed Costas's view to some extent. "People have been surprised enough by who is and isn't gay, so that they'll be less surprised in the future." However, Schaap also said that he did not personally know any gay football players.

Gay baiting occurs to some extent in every sport, but in football it sometimes seems more virulent and frequent. In 1997's spring predraft scouting combine, Jim Druckenmiller, quarterback of Virginia Tech, told reporters that he lifted weights with his offensive lineman because "I think it gives them a feeling that I'm not a pansy back there in the pocket."

In August 1997, in the Washington Redskins training camp, a running back named Stephen Davis supposedly mocked wide receiver Michael Westbrook as a "fucking faggot" to his face. Westbrook, known for his explosive temper, pummeled Davis with his fists, leaving Davis badly bruised with a black eye. In the publicity that ensued, Davis emerged looking a rose; his acceptance of Westbrook's apology qualified Davis as a "gentleman" in the eyes of his buddies. Westbrook, by comparison, appeared an uncivilized brute and was fined $50,000. That Davis had viciously

David Kopay

provoked Westbrook in the first place was forgotten or ignored by many.

Still, the possibility of a David Kopay-like football player announcing his homosexuality is not inconceivable. At a National Lesbian and Gay Journalists Association (NLGJA) panel discussion in August 1997, sports columnist Rick Telander said, "I think a top player will come out in the next decade. But it's got to be a courageous male in a team sport who's ready to be the martyr for the larger cause because it will cost him" [in endorsements].

SOFTBALL: A GAY AND LESBIAN PASTIME

Invented by the Chicago Farragut Boat Club on Thanksgiving Day 1887, softball soon became a very familiar part of the American sports landscape. By the 1930s, softball carried the distinction of being the game in which the most Americans participated. The Amateur Softball Association (ASA), formed in 1934, encouraged the development of recreational leagues for both sexes. In 1935, more than two million people in the United States played some softball; by the late 1990s, that figure had increased to 27 million, of whom 5 million were women.

While softball transcends gender and sexual orientation, many gays and lesbians have a particular affinity for the sport, which occupies a sacred niche at the Gay Games. For gay men and especially lesbians, softball teams evolved into a popular alternative to the often seedy, out-the-way gay bars that began in the 1940s.

Working class-women, who often labored under tough factory circumstances in the early twentieth century, also developed a par-

ticular passion for softball. The sport, whether played competitively or recreationally, was relatively inexpensive to organize, and it gave its female participants a chance to temporarily escape the dirty, often unsafe conditions of their employment. Many of the single women who played softball were lesbians. [See "Travel and Leisure" chapter for more information about softball in the lesbian community.]

The National American Gay Amateur Athletic Alliance (NAGAAA), created in 1977, provided another outlet for amateur sports. A nonprofit, international organization representing men and women, NAGAAA was specifically formed to encourage the participation of gay men and women in organized softball competition.

By the middle 1990s, about 30 cities in the United States and Canada belonged to NAGAAA, which is comprised of two divisions: Open Division and the Women's Division. Only all-women's teams may belong to the Women's Division, whereas the Open Division has teams of both sexes. The Open Division has three subdivisions: "A," "B," and "C." The "A" group represents the most competitive subdivision, while the "C" group is classified as recreational. Each year, NAGAAA has its Gay Softball World Series (GSWS) in a different city.

Some Reverse Discrimination

The popularity of softball for gays and lesbians grew in the 1980s and 1990s, but new complications have also cropped up. Brenda G. Pitts, a sports administration professor at the University of Louisville, explored some of them in her paper, "Leagues of Their Own: Organized Responses to Sports Homophobia." Her research bore out that the gay softball leagues had become more popular and more competitive than ever before, and those trends sometimes created a kind of reverse discrimination.

For example, the National Gay Softball Association had originally attempted to impose a 20 percent "quota" on the number of straight participants permitted to play on a gay team. The Community Softball League of San Francisco had always prided itself on its mixed teams, but in 1978 the San Francisco team was disqualified from the Gay Softball World Series for having too many straights on its teams. In the aftermath of this incident, the National Gay Softball Association replaced its original quota plan with a total ban on heterosexuals in gay softball.

At the Thirteenth Annual Gay Softball World Series in 1989, another sexually charged incident erupted. Rumors that heterosexuals were participants in the event surfaced, and NAGAAA attempted to quash them. But when New York's Break Falcons massacred Atlanta's Bulldog Lushpuppies by 17-1, the losing team cried foul because the Break Falcons supposedly had a straight player. NAGAAA ruled in Atlanta's favor, and New York forfeited the game. That the allegedly heterosexual player was married with two kids and would not admit to being gay heavily figured into NAGAAA's final decision.

It would be misleading to generalize that the aforementioned occurrences are typical in the realm of gay and lesbian sports. Only in team sports have such incidents happened at all, and most gay and lesbian organizers of sports are increasingly wary of provoking any discrimination charges. For example, the International Gay Bowling League—one of the largest gay sports groups—has had many nongay chairpersons. The Arcadia Bodybuilding Society makes a point of not discriminating against anyone, regardless of age, race, or sexual orientation.

THE EVOLUTION OF WOMEN'S SPORTS IN AMERICA

The Nineteenth Century

Traditionally, most American girls and women—gay, straight, or bisexual—were discouraged from seriously engaging in athletics. Even in the twentieth century, if a young girl chose to professionally pursue any of the traditionally male sports she might be branded a "tomboy," a term of endearment only up until a certain age. If the girl grew into a moderately attractive woman and successfully pursued a career in any sport, her chances of being stigmatized a lesbian or dyke were less than that of a plain, mannish woman in similar circumstances, all other things being equal. But generally, women were not encouraged to pursue careers in sports.

One needs some historical perspective to understand the evolution of women's sports in America (and lesbian participation in women's sports) in the twentieth century. Medical science in the nineteenth century generally purported that women were the physiologically weaker sex, burdened by their reproductive systems. In light of this theory, many doctors as early as the 1830s advocated moderate exercise for women to compensate for what they perceived as females' generally weak health characterized by mood swings, menstrual difficulties, and chronic fatigue.

As the nineteenth century proceeded, upper- and upper-middle-class women participated more often in certain sports, including croquet, horseback riding, swimming, golf, archery, and tennis. For women with much leisure time, these sports offered exercise and sociability. Bicycling also offered an outlet for middle-class women; it is believed that as many as 30,000 American women took up the sport in the 1890s. Frances Willard, a leader of the Women's Christian Temperance Union, was one of these women. What distinguished her from most of the others was that she was 53 years of age when she took her first bike ride. Willard recalled that although the first female cyclists were perceived as freaks, by the 1890s, much of that stigma had abated.

Women were not allowed to compete in the Olympics of 1896. Four years later, the Olympics permitted females in three sports: archery, golf, and tennis.

The Twentieth Century

With more women than ever participating in sports by the early twentieth century, many people began speculating on what effect sports would have on female sexuality. From roughly 1900 to 1930, many American scientists applied the term "mannishness" to anything that might be construed as female masculinity. But more specifically, the term implied three negative threats: that excessive exercise would mar a woman's reproductive system and so lessen her chances of having children; that female athletes would demonstrate masculine speech and mannerisms (i.e., become too sexually aggressive); and that female athletes would become overly passionate about sports, precipitating some kind of physical, moral, or emotional collapse.

Perhaps these three scenarios also thinly conceal a fearful, unspoken link between female sports participants and lesbianism. As early as 1883, P. M. Wise, in his article "Case of Sexual Perversion," wrote about a lesbian who "preferred masculine sports and labor; had an aversion to attentions from young men and sought the society of her own sex."

But as the United States struggled economically with the Great Depression of the 1930s, another pseudo-scientific school of thought emerged: the possibility that female athletes might also fail to live up to the traditionally heterosexual standards set for most American women. So the woman who pursued sports too seriously might have two strikes against her: not only would she be deemed unattractive to men, she might also prefer her own sex. Writer Fred Wittner, in his *Literary Digest* article, "Will the Ladies Join Us?," may have hinted at that scenario when he speculated that inevitably, "girls trained in physical education to-day may find it more difficult to attract the most worthy fathers for their children."

The Transformation of Babe Didrikson

In the light of the persistent debate about the sexuality of female athletes, it is worth examining the phenomenal track and field and golf careers of Mildred ("Babe") Didrikson, arguably the greatest female athlete of the twentieth century. Only 18 years of age, Didrikson won the Amateur Athletic Union (AAU) national team championship in 1932 when she competed as the only member of Employers Casualty Company "team." Less than a month later, she bulldozed the competition at the Los Angeles Olympics, taking home three medals—golds in the javelin and hurdles, and a silver in the high jump.

Didrikson emerged an overnight celebrity, but her wiry physique, "butch" haircut, oversized sweatshirts, and no-nonsense demeanor projected nothing remotely feminine about her. Consequently, the sports media treated her with a combination of fascination and disdain.

In reeling off an extensive list of accomplishments including track and field, basketball, football, and baseball, a journalist asked Didrikson, "Is there anything at all you don't play?" She supposedly responded, "Yeah, dolls." In interviews, Didrikson said she preferred horsing around with men to making love with any of them. That she could not even feign the slightest romantic interest in men for the benefit of her public presented a problem for reporters who wanted to show her as something other than a lesbian or a freak of nature. Some of them attempted to portray her as a sort of aging tomboy, albeit one who supposedly knew how to cook and sew. Despite these feeble attempts at rendering her at least potentially feminine, anyone who did not think mannish women should compete in track and field in the 1930s could use Didrikson as a case in point.

After giving up track and field in the middle 1930s, Didrikson plunged into the more socially acceptable (for women) game of golf. She further feminized her image by marrying George Zaharias, a burly professional wrestler, in 1938. With her transformation into a married—presumably heterosexual—woman, Didrikson now appeared well groomed and wore dresses and makeup for her public's benefit.

By the late 1940s, she had made the transition from an amateur to professional golfer and was back in the celebrity limelight. But the press often emphasized her achievements as a housewife over her athletic endeavors. For example, in his *Saturday Evening Post* article, "Whatever Became of Babe Didrikson," Frank Fawley gushed about Didrikson's cooking, curtain making, and interior decorating.

When Didrikson died of cancer in 1957, her early 1930s reputation as a wisecracking, man-hating, Amazonian lesbian had mostly faded from the public's consciousness. By that time, even some of her most visible critics, such as the writer Paul Gallico, mourned the loss of Babe Didrikson Zaharias.

Lesbian Baiting after World War II

Perhaps Babe Didrikson's transformation can be taken as a metaphor for America's post-World War II decreased tolerance for non-traditional sexual expression of any kind. As the United States emerged from its victory in World War II, the incidence of gay and lesbian baiting multiplied. While many gay and lesbian bars began and flourished in the early 1940s, homophobia came full force in the post-war atmosphere, partly explained by America's desire to return to traditional family values, which had supposedly been interrupted by World War II.

Among lesbians, college women who pursued careers in physical education suffered tremendous prejudice in this new climate. For example, the 1952 University of Minnesota yearbook teased, "Believe it or not, members of the Women's Athletic Association are normal ... at least one of WAA's 300 members is engaged."

Given the prevalence of lesbian baiting—whether implicit or explicit—at the time, it is not surprising that many female athletes took pains to at least appear traditionally feminine in their interests and mannerisms. For example, those athletes fortunate enough to get some media coverage now worked into their interviews such topics as cooking, sewing, and boyfriends or fiances.

Many physical education departments at colleges and universities also combated the image of their students as man-hating lesbians. For example, in a paper entitled "Desirable Objectives in Post-War Physical Education," Mildred Schaeffer wrote that physical education classes should help women "develop an interest in school dances and mixers and a desire to voluntarily attend them." Some physical educators also imposed dress codes, which forbade women to sport "boyish haircuts" or to wear men's shirts, pants, or socks on campus.

While many white female athletes continually combated malicious gossip and innuendo regarding their sexual orientations, their African-American counterparts suffered less homophobia in the 1940s and 1950s. Part of the explanation could be that white female athletes simply received a greater share of the media's attention, but semipro softball player Gloria Wilson (not her real name) provides another perspective. As reported in Susan K. Cahn's *Coming on Strong: Gender and Sexuality in Twentieth-Century Women's Sport*, Wilson recalled in a 1988 interview that she witnessed much less concern about lesbianism on her black softball team than she experienced when she taught at mostly white colleges. Wilson believed the expectation of heterosexuality among her African-American softball team players—most of whom were married—was simply a given, and anything outside of that norm was too bizarre to merit discussion.

Still, as African-American women received greater recognition for their athletic accomplishments in the late 1950s, the press occasionally hinted that some of the more Amazonian representatives might be lesbians. For example, Althea Gibson, the pioneering black tennis player who won both Wimbledon and the U.S. Championships in 1956 and 1957, appeared about as unfeminine to her public and press as Babe Didrikson had in the early and middle 1930s. In 1957, the black newspaper *Baltimore Afro-American* portrayed Gibson as a "tomboy" who "in later life ... finds herself victimized by complexes." While the nature of such "complexes" was not explained in the article, a between-the-lines reading might suggest lesbianism.

Title IX: A Boost to Women's Sports

A milestone piece of legislation paved the way for the acceptance of all female athletes, regardless of their sexual orientation. In 1972, Congress passed the Educational Amendments of 1972, one section of which, Title IX, prohibits sex discrimination in federally funded athletic programs. In effect, this means schools, colleges, and universities receiving federal funds in any part of the institution must offer equivalent sports opportunities, equipment, and funding for female sports. Hence, Title IX pertains to nearly all American colleges and universities and a smaller percentage of American high schools. In the aftermath of this legislation, more women have received college athletic scholarships, and some female Olympic athletes believe that without Title IX, they would not have reached the pinnacles of their sports.

Despite the impact of Title IX, many colleges and universities still discriminate against women in funding and opportunities to participate in sports. Female athletes and physical educators have filed dozens of lawsuits with the Office of Civil Rights at the Department of Education, many of which have been settled in their favor. In one of the most publicized cases, *Cohen et al v. Brown University*, the U.S. District Court found Brown in violation of Title IX, and ordered the reinstatement of women's varsity gymnastics and women's volleyball. In another case, *California Chapter of National Organization for Women v. California State University System*, the defendant settled with a consent decree that necessitates compliance with Title IX by 1998-99.

In the aftermath of Title IX, female athletes take themselves more seriously and, consequently, are taken more seriously. Studies in the 1990s bear out that girls who participate in sports generally demonstrate more self-esteem, better grades, fewer body image troubles, and a lesser likelihood of abusing drugs. In keeping with the above, more girls have ventured into the sports arena. According to the Women's Sports Foundation, in 1971 less than four percent of girls took part in high school sports; by 1994, roughly one third of high school girls participated. Hence, the mainstream media has devoted more attention to coverage of girls' and women's sports.

Still, even in the late 1990s, women are often discouraged from entering careers in sports for many reasons other than the prejudice that many, if not most, female athletes are lesbians.

Low salaries are one such deterrent. A National Collegiate Athletic Association (NCAA) report indicated that 75 percent of women college athletes wanted a career that offered a higher average salary than either coaching or administration of intercollegiate athletics. Indeed, coaches of women's teams earn considerably less than coaches of men's teams. For example, in basketball, men's head coaches averaged $71,511 annually, while their female counterparts received only $39,177.

Female Athletes and Coaches Discuss Homophobia

While some obstacles in women's sports pertain to all participants, others single out lesbians or women presumed to be lesbians.

At a 1996 panel discussion sponsored by the Women's Basketball Coaches Association (WBCA) and the National Collegiate Athletic Association (NCAA) Women's Final Four, panelists addressed the topic of homophobia in women's sports.

Linda Hill-MacDonald, women's basketball coach at the University of Minnesota, Twin Cities, and WBCA president, observed that many in the sports arena had been "putting our heads in the sand when it comes to the topics of homophobia. It certainly is a real issue, one that no longer can or should be avoided."

Pat Griffin, a professor of social justice education at the University of Massachusetts—Amherst, has frequently spoken about homophobia in female college sports in her lectures. While she has witnessed many lesbians discriminated against in sports, Griffin believes that prejudice extends to "all women in sports, because women are afraid of being associated with the lesbian label because of all the stereotypes. Women lose their jobs, they're not hired for jobs, athletes are dismissed from teams, coaches use negative recruiting."

According to Sandra L. Vivas, executive director of the American Volleyball Coaches Association (AVCA), certain athletic directors consider perceived sexual orientation when screening applicants for coaching and other positions. Some directors give considerable hiring preference to married women or male coaches to avoid the stigma of any team having a lesbian label. Other directors won't even consider hiring an openly lesbian coach, although few admit publicly to such discrimination.

Even in the late 1990s, some parents are still apprehensive about sending their daughter to a college or university with a reputation for many lesbian athletes and coaches. And some recruiters will not offer scholarships to young women whom they suspect of lesbianism. As Linda Hill-McDonald observed: "I know of people who say they will not have gay athletes in their program. They probably have had them, but they do not know about it. That's what we have to break through."

Some coaches suspect a double standard for lesbians and straight men. For example, Jacquie Joseph, the women's softball coach at Michigan State University and president of the National Softball Coaches Association, remarked: "What never is an issue is if the male coach sleeps with the female athlete. It's accepted. If a female coach sleeps with a female player, fire her tomorrow." While Joseph believes both situations are "horribly wrong," she cannot reconcile the unfairness of the male coach usually receiving a mild reprimand for his indiscretion, while the female coach is dismissed.

Joseph also challenges the stereotype that says women's sports attract a disproportionately higher percentage of lesbians than gays in men's athletics. She maintains that the oft-quoted 10 percent figure—one in 10 Americans are gay—applies equally to all sports for both genders, whether it is baseball, basketball, softball, etc.

Women's Basketball

Because of its status as one of America's most-popular sports for women, and also because of the longstanding, stereotypical association between lesbianism and women's athletics, women's collegiate basketball has always come under close scrutiny from the public. In the early 1980s, a sensational case at the University of South Carolina highlighted many of the issues surrounding lesbians who choose to come out in the arena of women's basketball.

Halfway through the 1981-82 college basketball season, Pam Parsons, coach of the women's team at the University of South Carolina, was thriving; her team ranked number two nationally and was undefeated. Then *Sports Illustrated* reported that Parsons was involved in an ongoing love affair with one of her athletes, Tina Buck. As the scandal progressed, Parsons resigned, but she and Buck continued to deny the relationship as portrayed in *Sports Illustrated*. They even sued the magazine for libel, demanding $75 million in damages. Ultimately, however, Parsons and Buck did admit to having an intimate relationship and were convicted of perjury and sentenced to four months in prison.

While the consequences continue to be dire for lesbians who are open about their sexuality in all women's team sports, these sports continue to attract lesbians, both as participants and as spectators. The latter phenomenon became especially apparent with the creation in the 1990s of two successful women's pro basketball leagues, the American Basketball League (ABL) and the Women's National Basketball Association (WNBA). Both leagues attracted devout lesbian followings in the communities in which franchises were located.

A Case of Sports Homophobia Fought and Won

While homophobia seems to exist in most sports to some extent, it has not always gone unpunished. A case in point: Ben Wright, the British-born, veteran sportscaster who was dismissed from CBS in January 1996. Wright was in Wilmington, Delaware, during the McDonald's LPGA Championship in May 1995, when he supposedly told *News Journal* reporter Valerie Helmbreck that "lesbians in the sport hurt women's golf" and "women are handicapped [in the golf swing] by having boobs." Gay and women's rights groups were in an uproar over these remarks, and Wright claimed that he never made them. Although CBS proceeded to renew Wright's contract, his problems continued after *Sports Illustrated* reported in December 1995 that at least some of Helmbreck's quotations were accurate. *Sports Illustrated* also quoted Wright as saying that Helmbreck was "a lesbian ... possibly with a gay-rights agenda."

CBS reacted to Wright's charge by suspending him—with pay— on 9 January 1996. Wright apologized to the network, LPGA, and Helmbreck, but also claimed that he had been "widely misquoted." USA Network and Intersport Television, which had also employed Wright as a broadcaster, responded by saying they had no desire to assign him further golf coverage. In April 1996, Wright checked himself into the Betty Ford Center in Rancho Mirage, California, for treatment of alcohol addiction.

PROMINENT PEOPLE

Profiles of several openly gay and lesbian sports figures follow. While the celebrities featured below have demonstrated an extraordinary range of achievements in sports, they cannot necessarily be classified as gay role models, although all qualify, in varying degrees, as gay activists.

Two have died of AIDS (Glenn Burke and Thomas Waddell); a third is living with the virus that causes AIDS (Greg Louganis); one probably killed himself (Justin Fashanu). Many have suffered, in varying degrees, problems of substance abuse, self-esteem, homophobia, and depression. Most did not receive significant opportunities to do lucrative endorsements, even those who dominated their sports (Louganis, Martina Navratilova, Patty Sheehan). A few have been involved in satisfying, long-term relationships; others experienced short-term, abusive relationships. One (Renee Richards) became a pioneer in American sports as the first—and to this day only—transgendered pro athlete. Of course, not all of their personal and professional situations revolve around their sexual preference.

Despite these misfortunes and obstacles, the profiled figures eventually gathered up the courage and self-esteem to come out in an atmosphere not particularly conducive to openly gay athletes. In fact, they drew from the heart of their personal and professional experiences (often with humor) to expose homophobia in American sports either taken for granted or ignored. Their individual and collective experiences perhaps illustrate why so few American athletes have come out.

Before the 1990s, many gay and lesbian athletes were outed, as opposed to coming out voluntarily (e.g., Navratilova), or came out in the twilight of their careers (e.g., David Kopay, Glenn Burke). In the 1990s, a positive trend has emerged, in that gay athletes at the height of their success (e.g., Rudy Galindo, Sheehan, Muffin Spencer-Devlin) have come out voluntarily, without the shame or awkwardness of their predecessors. While these recent voluntary outings pertain to athletes in individual sports, they may have ramifications elsewhere.

Glenn Burke (1952-1995)

Even as an adolescent, Glenn Lawrence Burke demonstrated great athletic promise. Named Northern California's High School's Basketball Player of the Year in 1970, 17-year-old Glenn could run the 100-yard dash in 9.7 seconds and dunk a basketball using both hands—the latter a particularly impressive feat for a player who stood just slightly over 6 feet tall.

Having grown up poor, black, and fatherless, Burke won a scholarship to the University of Denver. In 1972, the Los Angeles Dodgers recruited him to play in the minor baseball leagues in Utah, Washington, Connecticut, and New Mexico. In 1977, after Los

Glenn Burke

Angeles Dodgers teammate Dusty Baker achieved his thirtieth home run for the year in a game against the Houston Astros, Burke conceived the now-famous "high five" greeting.

Shortly after playing outfield in the World Series with the Dodgers, he was traded to the Oakland Athletics. The Dodgers' management may have authorized the trade because Burke wouldn't enter into a "marriage of convenience" to hide rumors about his homosexuality. After experiencing some homophobia from Billy Martin, the new manager of the Athletics, and injuring his knee, Burke was relegated to the minors. (Martin at one point had supposedly looked Burke straight in the eye and said "I don't want no faggot on my team.") In his 225 games in the major leagues, he had batted .237 with two home runs, 38 RBIs, and 35 stolen bases. In the early 1980s, he retired from professional baseball.

Burke, who continued in amateur competition, disclosed his homosexuality in the 1980s and was the first major league baseball player to do so. Like David Kopay, who came out about five years earlier, Burke was at the end of his professional career when he disclosed his sexual orientation. Burke participated in the 1986 Gay Games in basketball. Unfortunately, an addiction to cocaine and a car accident marked his financial and physical decline. Toward the end of his short life, Burke expressed pleasure that he had defied a stereotype as a gay baseball player; he also believed that being black and gay had made him a tougher person. He died of complications from AIDS on 30 May 1995.

Justin Fashanu (1961-1998)

The first million pound ($1.67 million) black soccer player in Great Britain and one of the very few openly gay professional athletes in contact sports, Justin Fashanu broke through two barriers. In his brief life of 37 years, Fashanu's trajectory swung from child abandoned by Nigerian parents, to superstar footballer, to openly gay icon, to fugitive on the lam from the police in the United States.

White, middle-class foster parents brought up Fashanu in a rural English environment, where he was one of few blacks. His soccer fame began in his teens, when as a striker for Norwich he scored an extremely impressive goal against Liverpool. Nottingham Forest manager Brian Clough seized on the moment to sign Fashanu to a one million pound contract. However, any rapport that Fashanu had developed with Clough was later dissolved when Fashanu came out to a tabloid newspaper. That disclosure and a severe knee injury that required endless surgery marred his athletic career, although he played soccer in many countries, including Canada, New Zealand, and Scotland.

Another complication in Fashanu's life occurred in his twenties: at the same time that he was exploring his gay orientation, he also became a born-again Christian. According to some friends, the pursuit of both goals rendered Fashanu confused and unhappy. While declaring Christian celibacy, he also pursued a secret gay sex life without ever achieving a long-term, secure relationship.

Ironically, as Fashanu's star declined, his brother John's ascended in the same sport. At one point in their relationship, John admitted to Justin that he disapproved of Justin's homosexuality. He also advised Justin not to disclose it publicly. At the time of Justin's death, the brothers had supposedly not spoken for about seven years.

In the middle 1990s, Fashanu made headlines again not for his athletic achievements but for telling a British newspaper that he had had homosexual affairs with two British government ministers. Later, he withdrew those allegations, admitting that he had invented the affairs to sell the story to newspapers.

In April 1998, a real scandal erupted in Fashanu's life. He had been in Maryland in the United States to coach a U.S. minor league soccer team called Maryland Mania. Fashanu spent the night of 24 March 1998, drinking alcohol and smoking marijuana with five other people in his apartment. Later, a 17-year-old high school dropout at the party told the police that he had awakened the following morning to find himself in Fashanu's bed with Fashanu performing a sexual act on him. The police interrogated Fashanu the next day and later put out a warrant for his arrest for second-degree sexual assault, first-degree assault, and second-degree assault. By that time, he had fled the United States.

On 2 May 1998, Justin Fashanu's body was found hanging in a lock-up garage in one of London's slums. Scotland Yard assumed that he had committed suicide.

Peter Tatchell, speaking on behalf of the London activist group OutRage!, told *The Washington Post* that Fashanu "showed that gay people could succeed even in tough macho sports, like football [soccer]. It helped undermine some of the stereotypes about gay men." But Tatchell, who was a friend of Fashanu in the 1980s, also remembered a man "destroyed by homophobia, Christian fundamentalism, and a lack of support from fellow football players and managers."

Rudy Galindo (1969-)

In a wry self-description, figure skater Rudy Galindo once called himself "openly gay, Mexican trailer trash." Winner of the U.S. National title in men's singles competition in 1996, Galindo, then 26, had previously made his mark in pairs skating with Kristi Yamaguchi. As a duo, Galindo and Yamaguchi defied skating tradition in a number of ways. Both were excellent solo skaters in an era when most members of pair teams did not thrive as solo skaters. Siblings or spouses of similar racial background and different physiques (i.e., the robust male skater usually looms well above his seemingly dainty female counterpart) often predominate in this sport. However, Galindo was not particularly tall, nor was Yamaguchi typically petite; he was of Mexican-American descent and she of Japanese-American background. Galindo once referred to them as a "rice and taco" combination.

Of course, much more unusual than the disparity between Galindo and Yamaguchi was the former's image as an openly gay athlete, in fact, the first openly gay man to win the title in the men's figure skating competition. Even though such sports as men's figure skating, diving, and gymnastics have acquired some reputation for being gay-friendly sports, many of the athletes in these sports firmly remain in the closet. To come out always increases the risk that they will be thought of as "unmasculine."

However, based on Rudy Galindo's biography *Icebreaker*, being gay at times may have been the least of his problems. Born into a poor family in San Jose, California, Galindo was five years old when the police took his psychologically unstable mother away from him, and he and his siblings spent two years living with another family in Los Angeles. Often teased as effeminate by his peers, Galindo witnessed his brother, George, coming out to the family—and being thrown out of the family trailer home for the disclosure. Having an openly gay brother did not embolden Rudy to come out himself; in fact, it had the opposite effect, and he stayed in the closet for many years. Rudy's brother eventually died of complications from AIDS, as would two of Rudy's skating coaches.

Not all of Galindo's childhood was Dickensian. Although his family had little money, they managed to set aside enough for Rudy to buy skates, hire coaches, and pursue competitions. And Rudy developed a particularly close relationship with his sister, Laura, who sacrificed her own skating career to become Rudy's coach.

Rudy's transition from teenager to adult was difficult; in his twenties, he suffered a cocaine addiction; a particularly abusive relationship with his former boyfriend, Kurt; the death of his father; a well-publicized drunken driving arrest; and the professional separation between him and Yamaguchi. But throughout it all, he has projected a refreshing candor about these obstacles and maintained his sense of humor.

Billie Jean King (1943-)

In 1970, 26-year-old Billie Jean King became the first female tennis player to make more than $100,000 in a single year. However, Rod Laver, the top male tennis player of that year, earned almost three times what King did, while he won only about one-third as many tournaments as she did. Given such male-female pay inequities that characterized so many sports, King began a boycott to protest what she perceived as another form of sexism on the pro tennis tour. In the early 1970s, she helped to initiate a separate women's pro circuit sponsored by Virginia Slims, and, along with other feminists, convinced the United States Lawn Tennis Association to equalize prize money at the U.S. Open for men and women.

Although King would break a record by winning 20 different singles and doubles titles at Wimbledon, she would receive as much media coverage for her "Battle of the Sexes" tennis match against the self-described "male-chauvinist pig" Bobby Riggs in 1973. While Riggs had once ranked as the number-one male tennis player, he had been retired from the men's tour for many years and was more than two decades older than King. Still, the concept of competing against a man violated King's sensibilities, because as she once said, "I was brought up a girl in a man's world, and an awful lot of attitudes—prejudices—are locked within me." Nonetheless, she gradually adjusted to the idea and trained well enough to easily beat Riggs in one of her best publicized—if not necessarily her most significant—victories. Their match remains probably the best-attended and most-watched tennis match in history.

In the late 1970s, King met a blonde hairdresser named Marilyn Barnett, and the two became lovers, although at the time, King was still married to her husband-manager, Larry King (not the television talk show host). King and Barnett's affair lasted two years, during which time they lived together in King's Malibu, California, beach house. King and Barnett had exchanged many love letters during their affair; after they broke up, Barnett threatened to turn over these letters to the media if King did not let her live in the Malibu house and pay her $125,000 in cash. Soon after, Barnett reneged on that threat and sued King for palimony (the term legally meaning a "divorce" between unmarried long-term lovers).

Ultimately, the judge ruled in King's favor, saying Barnett's actions bordered on extortion. However, her legal victory did not immediately compensate for the damage done to her reputation. Partly, King suffered as a victim of the homophobic climate that had permeated women's sports for decades. Still, she may have compounded her problems by acknowledging publicly that she had, indeed, engaged in a lesbian affair but did not consider herself a lesbian. Many of her fans found this disclosure a contradiction in terms, a disappointment from a tennis superstar with a longstanding reputation for candor and directness.

The disclosure of King's brief affair took a monetary, as well as psychological, toll on her; she once estimated that she lost more than $1.5 million in contracts for endorsements. In one extreme response to the scandal, Avon cosmetics even considered withdrawing its complete sponsorship of the women's professional tennis tour. King also claimed her husband lost about $400,000 in his business promotions, due to negative publicity over the affair.

Not content to rest on her laurels, King gradually overcame the stigma of the affair. In 1981, she founded World Team Tennis and has served as its commissioner since 1984. She won her last title, the Edgbaston Cup, in 1983 at the age of 39, which qualified King as the oldest woman to win a women's tour singles event. In 1987, she was inducted into the International Tennis Hall of Fame. She ranked No. 5 on the *Sports Illustrated* Top 40 Athletes List. King has also worked as a tennis analyst for CBS, ABC, NBC, CTV, and HBO. In 1998, she returned as the Federation Cup captain of the United States team.

David Kopay (1943-)

In 1997, David Kopay celebrated his fifty-fifth birthday and began collecting his National Football League pension; 22 years earlier, the football running back openly declared his homosexuality to the public. At the time, he was the only major North American athlete in team sports to come out, and that distinction has lasted into the late 1990s. By coincidence, his autobiography, *The David Kopay Story,* was published in March 1977, around the time that singer Anita Bryant was combating Dade County's human rights ordinances for including protection for homosexuals.

In his 10 years as a professional American football player, Kopay played for the San Francisco Forty-Niners, the Detroit Lions, the Washington Redskins, the New Orleans Saints, and the Green Bay Packers. In a 1997 *New York Times* article, "For Gays in Team Sports, Still a Deafening Silence," Kopay remembered, "I didn't put up big numbers, but I protected the passer and cracked the linebacker in the jaw."

After Kopay came out, he experienced many problems in locating employment. Large corporations thought he might make a good sales representative, but they weren't willing to hire him for fear of being perceived as a gay organization. Kopay now works in a family-owned business, Linoleum City, a supplier of flooring to movie studios. Reflecting on his football career, he remembers disclosing his homosexuality to many of his black teammates, because they seemed less apt to judge him in light of his sexual orientation. As a generalization, Kopay suspected management and coaches were more uncomfortable with openly gay football players than the actual players, although one homophobic Redskins teammate once nearly provoked Kopay into a fistfight.

Not in favor of outing gay athletes (although he knew many, including his friend and Redskins teammate, the late Jerry Smith), Kopay told the *New York Times* that he would approve of the National Football League issuing a human rights statement in support of gay athletes. Although Kopay believes much homophobia still remains in the world of professional sports, he would not be averse to coaching a college team if the opportunity presented itself.

Greg Louganis (1960-)

As arguably the most famous gay athlete of the 1990s, diver Greg Louganis has emerged as a popular, albeit complex, role model for many gays and lesbians worldwide. In February 1995, he publicly disclosed his HIV-positive status, although he had actually tested positive for HIV about seven years earlier. In 1988 during the Olympic Games in Seoul, South Korea, Louganis bashed his head on the diving board in an attempt to execute a complicated dive. After bleeding very slightly into the pool, Louganis, who knew he was HIV-positive, faced the conundrum of whether to inform the Olympic authorities of his virus. Having been assured that the chlorine in the pool would eradicate any HIV, Louganis said nothing at the time; the attending doctor, Jim Puffer, subsequently sutured his wound without wearing gloves.

A well-publicized controversy ensued when Louganis eventually revealed his HIV status in 1995: had Louganis in his silence exposed his doctor (and others) to the possibility of contracting HIV/AIDS? While Dr. Puffer has not tested positive for AIDS to date, the question of whether HIV-positive athletes pose a health threat to teammates or competitors remains unresolved in the minds of many.

From the media circus over the blood-in-the-pool incident, some have overlooked many of Louganis's accomplishments. In the course of his diving career, he acquired four Olympic gold medals, six world championships, and 47 U.S. titles. He is also the only male diver to have won the springboard and platform events at successive Olympics. He has sometimes spoken out against homophobia; for example, in his 1994 acceptance of the Robert J. Kane award, Louganis protested some of the anti-gay laws in Cobb County, Georgia.

After retiring from international diving competition, Louganis raised pedigree dogs, became a dancer, and published the autobiographical *Breaking the Surface*. In the latter, he revealed many of his misfortunes, including difficult relationships with his father and a former lover, a history of dyslexia, and the homophobia that he has experienced firsthand.

Martina Navratilova (1956-)

When Czech-born American tennis player Martina Navratilova retired from singles tennis, she had acquired 167 singles titles—nine of which were at Wimbledon—and cemented her reputation as perhaps the greatest woman tennis player in history. With her victory in the 1995 Wimbledon mixed doubles, her total number of Wimbledon titles reached 19, one short of Billie Jean King's record.

Born in 1956 in Prague (then the capital city of Czechoslovakia), Navratilova had good "tennis genes"—her grandmother and mother had both been local tennis champions. When the Communists captured power in Czechoslovakia in the late 1940s, Martina's fairly affluent family lost most of their wealth. Navratilova recalled a somewhat traumatic childhood in which well-intentioned adults often mistook the tomboy for an actual boy.

To compensate for her lack of femininity, Navratilova poured tremendous energy in excelling in tennis. The Czechoslovakian authorities recognized her exceptional talent and allowed the 13-year-old to make trips outside the country to compete in tournaments. Even then, she had hopes of settling permanently outside of Czechoslovakia, preferably in the United States. In 1973, the Czech Government allowed Navratilova to play on the U.S. winter circuit; two years later and still a teenager, she applied for and was granted political asylum in the U.S. In 1978, she won her first Wimbledon championship, and the Women's Tennis Association ranked her the top women's player in the world.

Although Navratilova had had a few lesbian experiences at this point, tennis remained her all-consuming passion; the possibility of becoming a lesbian activist seemed highly remote. Then she met Rita Mae Brown—the lesbian author of *Rubyfruit Jungle*—after a tournament in Virginia, and the two became romantically

Martina Navratilova

involved. Brown opened a world beyond tennis to Navratilova, and they lived together in a mansion in Charlottesville, Virginia.

Soon after, Navratilova became increasingly worried about her inconsistent tennis game, broke up with Brown, and became involved with Nancy Lieberman, an accomplished basketball player who later became head coach of the Detroit Shock in the Women's National Basketball Association (WNBA). The breakup with Brown was one of the most acrimonious scenes in Navratilova's life, and she feared her lesbianism would be exposed, as had Billie Jean King's in 1981. Navratilova's situation had additional complications; at this time, she was not yet an American citizen and feared being sent back to Czechoslovakia permanently. She decided to apply for citizenship in the State of California, where the potential matter of her sexuality might be treated more leniently. When the examiners did indeed inquire about her sexual orientation, she said she was bisexual. She took the citizenship exam in May 1981 and two months later learned that she had passed.

Soon after Navratilova became a U.S. citizen, she received a phone call from a *New York Daily News* reporter, to whom she had given an interview within the last year. In their talk, Navratilova had admitted to the possibility that her sexual orientation would be exposed and the negative impact it would have

on her tennis career. She also spoke candidly about her relationship with Rita Mae Brown. Now, the reporter said he had no choice but to publish the interview.

On the one hand, the timing was good for Navratilova: there had already been endless innuendo about her private life, and many people simply assumed that she was a lesbian. On the other hand, the 1980s were not a time in which gay American athletes came out, and Navratilova would remain the only prominent, openly lesbian athlete for many years to come.

While Navratilova's lesbianism undoubtedly cost her millions of dollars in potential endorsements, several of her sponsors stuck by her. What she lacked in commercial appeal, she made up in winning tournaments; by her retirement in 1994, she had won more singles titles than any other player, male or female. She had also earned more than $20 million in career prize money, not including the few endorsements she did garner.

By the 1990s, Navratilova had turned into a gay and lesbian rights activist. In 1992, she spoke out against Colorado's Amendment 2, which disallowed city ordinances protecting homosexuals from discrimination. In 1993, she spoke at the Gay and Lesbian March on Washington, and one year later, she served as a spokesperson for the 1994 Gay Games in New York.

Since her last match on the professional women's tennis circuit in November 1994, Navratilova has pursued a variety of endeavors, some of which focus on gay and lesbian themes. For example, she initiated the Rainbow Card (a Visa program to raise funds for gay and lesbian civil-rights groups). In the September 1997 issue of *The Pink Paper*, she ranked third in its listing of the top 500 lesbian and gay heroes.

Dave Pallone (1951-)

In 1970, 18-year-old Dave Pallone knew that he wanted to be an umpire. Soon after he completed his training at the Ted Williams Baseball School, Pallone was umpiring in the minor baseball leagues. By 1979, he had graduated to the major leagues and made a decision to conceal his homosexuality (which he had realized since his late teens) for fear of losing his job. With his dark, finely chiseled looks and masculine mannerisms, Pallone defied the stereotype of the effeminate homosexual and decreased his chances of exposure. However, by the middle 1980s, Pallone had come out to a few friends—and to then-President of the National League Bart Giamatti. By 1988, Pallone's sexual orientation was made public when the National League fired him for supposedly having sex with a minor, although the charges against Pallone had been dismissed. Pallone has always contended the real reason for his firing was his homosexuality.

By the 1990s, Pallone had a thriving second career as a gay activist, often drawing from his personal experience as a closeted man in the sports realm. Often speaking at schools and corporations, he confronts issues such as gays in the workplace; the increasing diversity of gays and lesbians in professional, college, and high school sports; and gay teen suicide. In his well-received autobiography, *Behind the Mask*, he also revealed a three-year relationship with his lover, Scott, who was killed by a drunk driver in 1982.

Renee Richards (1934-)

Born Richard Raskind in 1934, Renee Richards became the world's most famous transgendered person when she burst onto the women's professional tennis scene in 1976. Richards was an accomplished amateur tennis player as a man, good enough to compete at Wimbledon and at the U.S. Championships at Forest Hills. Rather than pursuing a career as a tennis pro, however, Richards became a respected ophthalmologic surgeon in New York State. In 1975, Richards underwent sex reassignment surgery, and then moved to California to start a new life.

In 1976, at the age of 41, Richards entered a women's professional tournament in La Jolla, California. Unbeknown to Richards, a former acquaintance who witnessed her victory recognized her and contacted a local television station. After the media firestorm that developed, Richards acknowledged her identity and decided to suspend her medical practice in favor of a full-time stint on the women's pro tour.

Her decision was greeted with tremendous opposition by the United States Tennis Association (USTA) and numerous women pro players, who feared that Richards would have an unfair advantage on the court. The USTA then enacted a policy declaring that all players would have to pass a chromosome test to determine their gender before they would be allowed into tour events. Richards refused to take the test and was denied admission into the U.S. Open that August. However, she filed suit over the matter; when a judge ruled in her favor in 1977, she was allowed to play in tour events. She stayed on the tour for five years, winning one singles title and reaching a high of #22 in the world rankings.

In contrast to other players' fears that Richards would dominate with physical strength, she made her mark as an expert strategizer on court. After her retirement from the game, she assisted Martina Navratilova as a coach in the early 1980s. She remains the only transsexual pro athlete in U.S. history.

Patty Sheehan (1956-)

In the 27 March 1997, issue of *Golfworld* magazine, Hall of Fame golfer Patty Sheehan came out as a lesbian, although her sexual orientation had already been generally known among her colleagues.

Sheehan wrote: "I've accomplished just about everything I set out to do in my career, including winning the U.S. Women's Open twice [in 1992 and 1994] and qualifying for the Ladies Professional Golf Association (LPGA) Hall of Fame. But the hard work and focus it took to fulfill those goals required that I make sacrifices in my personal and social life." However, as Sheehan explained, her personal life is no longer on hold. As a matter of fact, she and her lover/manager, of a dozen years, Rebecca Gaston, adopted a little girl, Bryce in 1997. With two dogs rounding out Sheehan's family, she described her life as "never ... more content or happy."

Sheehan, who was born on 27 October 1956 in Middlebury, Vermont, joined the LPGA Tour in 1980. She collected her first victory at the 1981 Mazda Japan Classic, and she captured four tournaments in 1983, including her first major title at the LPGA Championship. Her earnings exceeded the $1 million mark in 1985, and four years later, she became the sixth player in LPGA to surpass $2 million in career earnings.

In 1990, Sheehan earned $732,618 in season earnings—the second player in history to exceed the $700,000 mark. In 1993, Sheehan became the thirteenth player to be inducted into the LPGA Hall of Fame. In that year, she also won the LPGA Championship, and her total career earnings exceeded $4 million.

In 1996, Omnitrition International, Inc. hired Sheehan as a spokesperson for Omni Aqua, a bottled spring water product. It remains to be seen what effect coming out will have on Sheehan's potential to endorse other products.

Muffin Spencer-Devlin (1953-)

When Muffin Spencer-Devlin came out in the March 1996 issue of *Sports Illustrated*, she became the first openly lesbian player in the history of the Ladies Professional Golf Association (LPGA). Spencer-Devlin has said that a relationship with Lynda Roth, her lover of four years, motivated her decision more than political correctness did. While she has compared coming out to "a huge weight being lifted from my shoulders," she has also combated the image that some people have of her as "the head lesbian of the LPGA." In fact, Spencer-Devlin has claimed that lesbians are a minority in the LPGA, despite many rumors to the contrary.

The tall, blonde golfer was an aspiring actress and model before she joined the LPGA tour. In 1985, she captured the Mastercard International, and for the first time in her golfing career, Spencer-Devlin's single season earnings exceeded $100,000. She went on to capture the 1986 United Virginia Bank Classic, again topping $100,000 for the season.

By the late 1980s, however, a severe lower back injury limited her participation in tournaments. By 1990, a recurrence of manic depression forced Spencer-Devlin to take several months off from the tour. A holistic regimen, including vitamins and amino acids, gradually improved her health; today, Spencer-Devlin occasionally lectures on manic depression in conjunction with the Depression and Manic Depression Association of America. In 1995, Spencer-Devlin tied for 7th at the ShopRite LPGA Classic, tied for 9th at the Youngstown-Warren LPGA Classic, and tied for 10th at the Jamie Farr Toledo Classic. In that year, she also recorded her lowest scoring average (72.62) in 10 seasons.

Bill Tilden (1893-1953)

The first American to win Wimbledon, William Tatem ("Bill") Tilden, Jr., did not show a great deal of early tennis promise. Tilden, a slender adolescent who came from a wealthy family, was the team captain—not the top player—at the posh Germantown Academy. He completed only one year at the University of Pennsylvania, where he ranked at the lowest rung of the varsity tennis team. He was still a teenager when both his parents and his brother died of various illnesses within three years of each other, and he moved in with his only surviving relatives—an aunt and a cousin. Understandably depressed, he spent most of his time listening to opera records in his room before he decided to become a professional tennis player.

While in his twenties, Tilden once ranked as just the seventieth best tennis player in the United States. But in 1920, the 27-year-old Tilden took his first major title, winning at Wimbledon. An overnight celebrity, Tilden went on to win virtually every significant tennis title within the next six years.

But Tilden's arrogance worked against him. Although not openly gay, Tilden did not go to great lengths to conceal his sexual orientation and activities. His enemies in tennis knew the innuendo and were not above subtly exploiting it to Tilden's disadvantage. The American Lawn Tennis Association (ALTA) attempted to suspend Tilden in 1928, supposedly for taking money for writing newspaper articles about tennis. Since tennis was an amateur sport then, taking money for competition belied the "gentlemen atmosphere" of the game. But it was quite possible that ALTA in its attempt to suspend Tilden was surreptitiously reacting to rumors of his homosexuality.

The attempt to suspend Tilden occurred shortly before he was to play one of his foremost rivals, the French player Rene LaCoste, in a key Davis Cup match. Through the intervention of President Calvin Coolidge and a French ambassador, ALTA reneged on its decision. Tilden went on to beat LaCoste in a very close match.

During the Great Depression of the 1930s, Tilden continued to play professional tennis and live very well, often fraternizing with such movie stars as Charlie Chaplin and Joseph Cotton. Although still mostly closeted, he would occasionally discuss his sexual preference with friends; that he often fooled around with the ball boys of professional tennis gradually became common knowledge in the industry. He also became one of the oldest professional tennis players on record.

On 23 November 1946, the 53-year-old Tilden was arrested for driving his car erratically down Sunset Boulevard in Hollywood, California. With him in the car was a 14-year-old boy. Tilden, without showing any embarrassment, told the police that he had had "indiscretions" with the youth the night of the arrest. Charges were filed against Tilden, and in the courtroom he behaved haughtily, without an iota of remorse. Outraged by his lack of humility, the judge sentenced Tilden to a year of hard labor in jail. By this time, nearly all of Tilden's friends and remaining family had deserted him.

Less than two years after Tilden completed his sentence, he violated his parole by being alone in his apartment with another young man. Again, he was sentenced to a year of prison. Ironically, around the time he completed his second sentence, the National Sports Writers Association completed a poll in which Tilden was voted the most outstanding athlete of the first half of the twentieth century. In fact, Tilden received 10 times the number of votes as his runner-up.

Although his career, reputation, and financial standing were mostly ruined by this time, Tilden was too self-assured to entertain the notion that he was through with tennis. He died of a heart attack in his sleep on the night of 5 June 1953. Although 60 years of age, he had recently packed a suitcase to travel to the U.S. Professional Tennis Championship in Cleveland, where he hoped to compete.

Thomas Waddell (1937-1987)

The founder of the Gay Games and a gay sportsman, Dr. Thomas Waddell violated many of the stereotypes associated with the status of a gay sportsman. In addition to having finished sixth in the 1968 Olympic decathlon, he was also a husband and father, war veteran, photographer, and painter. Dr. Waddell's most famous achievement, The Gay Games, occur every four years and cover such sports as billiards, bodybuilding, swimming, and many others. The first Gay Games took place in San Francisco in 1982 and featured about 3,500 athletes from 37 states and 17 nations; the 1994 Gay Games, held in New York City, included 15,000 athletes and 500,000 spectators.

Born in 1937 to poor working-class parents who separated when he was a teenager, Waddell was eventually cared for and adopted

Thomas Waddell holding his daughter, Jessica.

by another couple who gave him his last name, Waddell. He became an M.D. in 1965 and was drafted into the Army the following year. After his achievement in the 1968 Olympics, he traveled on track and field exhibition tours in South America and Africa.

Throughout the late 1960s and early 1970s, in addition to his work as a doctor, Dr. Waddell contributed increasingly to lesbian and gay activism; in 1976, he and his lover were the first gay couple photographed for *People Magazine*.

Having always wanted a child, Waddell married a friend, Sara Lewinstein, who was herself a lesbian; their daughter, Jessica, was born in 1983. Waddell died of AIDS in July 1987.

REFERENCES:

Books

Cahn, Susan K. *Coming On Strong: Gender and Sexuality in Twentieth-Century Women's Sports.* New York: Free Press, 1994.

Collins, Bud and Zander Hollander. *Bud Collins' Modern Encyclopedia of Tennis.* Detroit: Visible Ink Press, 1994.

Griffin, Pat. *Strong Women, Deep Closets: Lesbians and Homophobia in Sport.* N.p.: Human Kinetics, 1998.

Sabo, Donald F. and Ross Runfola. *Jock: Sports and Male Identity.* Englewood Cliffs, New Jersey: Spectrum, 1980.

Young, Perry Deane. *Lesbians and Gays and Sports.* New York: Chelsea House, 1995.

Periodical Articles and Book Excerpts

Alienist and Neurologist, vol. 4, 1883: 88, as quoted in *Coming on Strong: Gender and Sexuality in Twentieth-Century Women's Sports*, by Susan K. Cahn, New York: Frees Press, 1994: 166.

Baltimore Afro-American, 29 June 1957: magazine section, p. 1.

Davis, Bryon Bradley. "Wimbledon Champs, Past and Future," in *Christian Science Monitor,* 1 July 1997: 15.

Fawley, Frank. "Whatever Became of Babe Didrikson," in *Saturday Evening Post,* vol. 216, 20 November 1943: 91.

Galvin, Peter. "Dennis the Menace," in *The Advocate,* 21 January 1997: 26-34.

University of Minnesota Archives. *Gopher* yearbook, 1952: 257.

Horn, Miriam. "New York's Week to Be Gay," in *US News & World Report,* 27 June 1994: 18.

Kamp, David. "The NFL's Closet Case (Part 1)," in *Gentleman's Quarterly,* January 1998.

Lidz, Franz and John Walters. "And the Band Plays On," in *Sports Illustrated,* 12 June 1995: 15.

Lipsyte, Robert. "For Gays in Team Sports, Still a Deafening Silence," in *New York Times,* 7 September 1997: Section 8, p. 15.

Longman, Jere. "After Glare of Victory, Galindo is at Peace with Himself," in *New York Times,* 22 June 1997: Section 8, p. 2.

Price, Deb. "On Deck for Success: When Girls Participate in Sport, They're More on the Ball," in *Detroit News,* 27 October 1995.

Reibstein, Larry, et al. "Public Glory, Secret Agony," in *Newsweek,* 6 March 1995: 48.

Schaeffer, Mildred A. "Desirable Objectives in Post-war Physical Education," in *JOHPE,* vol. 16, October 1945: 446-47.

Stockwell, Anne, and J.V. McAuley. "Tackling the NFL Closet," in *The Advocate,* 24 December 1996: 51, 52, 55.

Wittner, Fred. "Shall the Ladies Join Us?" in *Literary Digest,* vol. 117, 19 May 1934: 43.

—David Levine

22

Travel and Leisure

This chapter discusses travel and leisure options for lesbians and gay men, both historically and in the present. The chapter divides the discussion by gender, opening with a section about lesbian travel and leisure and closing with a section devoted to gay men. However, the "References" section at the close of the chapter combines resources for both lesbians and gay men.

LESBIAN TRAVEL AND LEISURE: OVERVIEW

In the 1990s, lesbians can choose from a myriad of leisure activities and travel adventures. The 1940s were quite different, with public socializing limited to bar rooms and softball fields. A historical view of leisure and travel illuminates the significant changes in lesbian life, pre- and post-Stonewall. A contemporary look at leisure and travel opportunities reflects the remarkable diversity of the lesbian community.

"Lesbian travel" encompasses vacations to such popular destinations as San Francisco and Provincetown and to events such as the Dinah Shore Golf Weekend. Women's tour companies such as Olivia Cruises and Resorts and lesbian bed and breakfasts are also discussed in the travel section.

"Lesbian leisure" is here considered to be those social activities in which one participates within or near one's home environment that display a lesbian cultural character. Certainly, lesbians watch TV for leisure, and garden and sew and play an instrument and read news magazines, like heterosexual Americans.

But lesbians also engage in activities and sports that are lesbian-focused, lesbian-representative, and lesbian-promoting. These are the activities discussed in this essay, exemplified by lesbian bar socializing, lesbian softball, lesbian clubs, and also women's music and music festivals, choruses, coffeehouses, and bookstores. From the 1940s through the 1990s, these activities have alternated in popularity for different kinds and classes of lesbians, but throughout this last half century, altogether they comprise the main leisure elements of "lesbian culture."

Women, generally speaking, have minimum amounts of expendable income, and they often, in addition, carry parenting responsibilities that stress their financial means. These social conditions have consequently caused women to build a larger leisure subcul-

ture than travel subculture. Bars, softball teams, music concerts, festivals, and other activities outlined in the leisure section have offered entertainment within greater fiscal reach of average lesbians. Thus, these leisure activities have touched hundreds of thousands of women over decades, while it is only in the 1990s that the number of women's tours, tour companies, and B&Bs have been measurable.

LESBIAN TRAVEL

When you ask a lesbian what comes to mind when you say "lesbian travel," a few answers are predictable. "Provincetown!" "San Francisco!" "Key West!" "A bed and breakfast!" "Michigan Music Festival!" Lesbians with more expendable income answer with: "Olivia Cruises!" "Dinah Shore Golf Weekend!" If the woman is thinking locally, she answers: "Russian River!" if she's Californian, "Rehoboth!" if she's from Delaware, "Northhampton!" is she's an easterner.

What these places all have in common is freedom—the freedom to be "out," to hold one's lover's hand in public, to be in the majority for a few days and not be harassed, to "fill up" with lesbian culture. Even if lesbians plan vacations to heterosexual spots such as Disneyland, they'll often plan a few days in San Francisco. Getting away is the chance to be with other lesbians, which is important to a still-oppressed subculture.

Below are descriptions of some popular destinations and events. Music festivals have been discussed previously in the Leisure section.

Provincetown

"P-town," at the tip of Cape Cod, Massachusetts, is the country's largest lesbian and gay resort. For lesbians, it is the preferred resort, because it is heavily populated with lesbians year-round and thus strongly reflects lesbian culture in its amenities, entertainment offerings, and shops. Provincetown counts 17 women's guesthouses among its 65 gay-friendly B&Bs. There are a half dozen women-owned restaurants and two popular lesbian bars, The Vixen and The Pied Piper, for evening socializing and dancing. Womencrafts, a women's bookstore and vendor of lesbian culture for over twenty years, is a fount of information about women's venues or events in Provincetown.

In the peak summer season, there are clubs many nights that offer women's bands, and increasingly women comedians. The Fabulous Dyketones, a rock and roll band that rewrites 1950s and 1960s classic hits with lesbian lyrics, took up residence in Provincetown and recorded a live performance there in 1988. Theatrical stages present lesbian and gay plays.

On the outskirts of town, there is a lesbian and gay beach in Herring Cove, where some women risk nude bathing. There are several cruise lines for getting out on the waters, and one woman-owned whale watching boat. Because of all the women-owned and lesbian-focused businesses and services in Provincetown, women on vacation here feel a euphoria being amongst "their own." Provincetown goes one step further in October, designating a "Women's Week." Approximately 5,000 women enjoy the special activities, which include a traditional Wednesday night community dinner and a Saturday night prom, offering the chance to don tuxedos.

Provincetown started out early in the century as a summer resort for artists and playwrights. Certain famous gay/bisexual writers—Eugene O'Neill, Tennessee Williams, Truman Capote, and Jane Bowles—vacationed in Provincetown, lending a gay tradition to the area. Provincetown never became a primarily male resort, as did Key West.

Key West

In contrast to Provincetown, Key West offers one lesbian-owned guest house, one lesbian-owned restaurant, and one mixed bar. Key West is primarily a men's resort, but one week in July the town throws a lesbian party. They call it "Women Fest," and they offer women's entertainment, women's dances, and a street fair.

Even though this tropical paradise is mostly male, the openness and freedom to be lesbian or gay affects the entire atmosphere, and lesbians feel a comfort level in Key West that they don't experience throughout heterosexual society. Thus women still consider Key West a lesbian vacation destination.

There are several women-captained sailing operations that offer all-women snorkeling trips and sunset sails off the island shores. Whether exploring the coral reef with other women or simply enjoying lesbian camaraderie on board a sunset cruise—both activities make for memorable reflections of this sunny paradise.

Palm Springs

Palm Springs is another largely male resort except for one week in March, when lesbians flock to Dinah Shore Weekend festivities. An LPGA major championship called the Nabisco Dinah Shore Golf Tournament is the excuse for partying. This first "major" of the year celebrated its twenty-fifth anniversary in 1996. The tournament attracts thousands of women who relish watching the professional women players.

Lesbian parties have grown up around the event in the last decade. A kind of lesbian "spring break," the weekend offers contests, dance parties, cocktail parties, pool parties, and celebrity entertainment. One special event is the "White Party," where hundreds of women gather, dressed in white.

The Desert Women's Association publicizes events. Two women's bars, one located in Los Angeles and one in San Francisco, are the primary supporters of the weekend events. They book two hotels in their entirety so that women's villages, so to speak, are created in these buildings. Lesbians are at ease this weekend, holding hands with their lovers, flirting, and in other ways publicly displaying affection.

There are so many activities associated with the weekend that a lesbian newspaper in Los Angeles has to print special editions to keep up with all of the activities. There are several women-owned bars in Palm Springs and three women's inns that work

overtime this weekend. The numbers of revelers for this informal lesbian festival are still growing.

Russian River

Sixty miles north of San Francisco lies another California resort area, Russian River. This get-away is in the redwood forests, close to the ocean. Russian River is known for having a casual atmosphere. One can camp or park one's RV at any of several commercial accommodations, some of which are gay/lesbian owned, and stay for awhile. Or one can drive up to the area for the day, enjoying the scenic drive and checking out the gay-owned antique stores and eateries in Guerneville. Hiking in the redwoods, canoeing the river, or absorbing the sun's rays from the river bank are typical daytime activities. Fishing in the Russian River offers bass in the summer and steelhead in the winter. Some women tour the countryside and stop in at vineyards for tastes of the region's wineries. There are 17 golf courses in the entire Sonoma County. A day at the coast offers seal watching and occasionally whale watching. If one gets the urge to dance, one can join a nighttime crowd at a Guerneville gay/lesbian bar.

Russian River is a resort area used to handling special weekend festivals, like the ones offered for jazz lovers, blues lovers, and rodeo lovers. There are two weekends a year, one in May and one in September, set aside especially for women to enjoy the area. Shuttles transport women between the venues presenting special "Women's Weekend" dances and entertainment shows.

San Francisco

Not only heterosexuals leave their hearts in San Francisco. A mecca in North America for gays and lesbians, the San Francisco Bay area boasts the largest lesbian and gay population in the country. Consequently, the area supports hundreds of bars, social organizations, and businesses that cater specifically to lesbians and gays. The turnout for the gay pride festival numbers more than 500,000 marchers and spectators. The Dyke Parade held that same weekend is also the largest in the country, numbering more than 40,000.

San Francisco has such a large lesbian population that one can divide the city into four neighborhoods typifying four different kinds of lesbians. Young activist lesbians call the Mission District home; yuppie lesbians and couples inhabit Bernal Heights; trendy wealthy lesbians frequent the Castro District, usually associated with gay males; and lesbian feminists settle in the East Bay area, especially Oakland and Berkeley.

For lesbian tourists, the entire Valencia Street strip between Market and Twenty-Fourth is the place to dyke-watch, where punk-dykes, sports-dykes, lesbian feminists, and lesbians of color patronize the lesbian and gay stores and cafes or take in a lesbian-themed movie at The Roxie. The adjacent Mission District offers two notorious businesses: a women's bathhouse (Osento) and a women's store for sex-toys (Good Vibrations). Of special interest to women who live in San Francisco is The Women's Building, which has been around since the 1970s. Originally a resource center just for women, it now takes bookings by mixed and male groups. Its spaces have seen poetry readings, film screenings, political rallies, conferences, and benefit shows.

There are so many women-owned B&Bs, restaurants, cafes, boutiques, and night spots that, on a vacation here, lesbians need never "matronize" a heterosexual or even a gay male business. Of course, a visitor would have to be connected to the lesbian com-

Lesbian-owned bed-and-breakfast hotels have become very popular with lesbian travelers.

munity, as dance events for women only are single nights once a month or once a week at otherwise straight and gay male establishments or at community centers. The choices, however, can be extensive, as the area offers salsa nights, swing dance and West Coast swing dance nights, lindy hop nights, in addition to rock and country-western dance nights.

Events one wouldn't find anywhere else in the country are found in San Francisco, such as a national gay/lesbian bodybuilding championship, a Women's Philharmonic, and an annual women's soccer tournament. Enough lesbians of color live in San Francisco that they can hold dances periodically for just Asian, Black, and/or Latina women. Because of the size of San Francisco's community, bars, support groups, parades, and publications promoting all types of sexual proclivity are readily available. Transgenderism and sado-masochism sexuality are conspicuous in the culture, and the country's first women's sex club is found in San Francisco. This town more than any other reflects the ideological diversity of lesbigay culture.

Bed and Breakfast Hotels

Bed and breakfasts (B&Bs) are attractive elements of vacations because of their romantic atmospheres and relative inexpense. A night or two in a Victorian three-story, a mountain log home, or a western ranch are effective ways to get away without spending too much time or money.

B&Bs are such intimate lodgings that lesbian or gay establishments are preferred in order to obtain the highest level of comfort. Being served breakfast in elegant surroundings and meeting lesbian guests from elsewhere in the country is a special treat.

Lesbian accommodations advertise in lesbian magazines and newsletters as much as they advertise in travel guides such as Ferrari's Inn Places. Lesbians also find out about them through word-of-mouth. Enchanting names such as The Ruby Slipper, Sophie's Comfort, and Innamorata lure women to the doorsteps. Lesbians generally regard B&Bs to be "special occasion" experiences, places to spend anniversaries or a special night on a vacation.

Olivia Cruises and Resorts

Olivia Cruises and Resorts started in 1990 as an off-shoot of Olivia Records, when the president of the record company took an off-hand suggestion seriously. A concert-goer remarked, "Wouldn't this [womyn's music] be wonderful on the water!" Thirty-plus cruises later, this arm of the company has been a financial success. Cruises have added a whole other realm to lesbian travel.

Olivia has sailed to islands in the Caribbean, the Galapagos, Africa, Greece and Turkey, Alaska, and Hawaii. The all-women passenger ships present lesbian cultural opportunities ranging from entertainment by women musicians who are stars of the womyn's music circuit (see "Music" in the "Leisure" section) to watching lesbian films to playing the favorite lesbian games of pool and volleyball. Of course, "girl-watching" is a prominent leisure activity.

Olivia also leases resort areas for a week at a time. These relaxing Club Med-type vacations, with all accommodations, food, and activities arranged, are popular. Again, the main attraction of these cruises and resort vacations is the all-lesbian environments, where women can feel free to publicly display their affections. (See "Profile: Judy Dlugacz and Olivia" for historical information on the company.)

Other Tour Companies

A book called *Adventures in Good Company* lists 98 tour operators that are either women-owned and run or companies known for organizing frequent women-only trips. Most are based in the United States, though there are a few in other countries. All kinds of trips are represented: ocean kayaking, river running and canoeing, African safaris, walking holidays, hiking and backpacking treks, bicycling and fishing trips, llama packing, ranch vacations, surfing

and skiing trips, whale watching expeditions, and more. All levels of adventurousness and physical activity are offered.

Some of these women's companies market to lesbians only. But most are simply women-centered, where both lesbians and other women are invited. For instance, Woodswomen has been an outdoor adventure company for women since 1977. Many lesbians over the years have participated in this company's treks, and often the guides have been lesbians, yet more heterosexual women than lesbians over the years have been served by this company. Robin Tyler Productions and Tours is a well-known lesbian-owned company that has been operating since 1980. Tyler has been an activist all her life, so many of her trips are associated with political events such as the World Conference on Women in Beijing. Being a comedian, Tyler also has a special interest in organizing trips to comedy festivals such as the International Lesbian and Gay Comedy Festival in Australia. Club Le Bon advertises upscale vacations at island resorts, while Skylink makes a point to reach out to lesbians of color. As these examples show, there are enough companies that different focuses are possible, offering greater opportunities for traveling lesbians. Some gay male and straight tour companies also occasionally offer all-women trips.

There are individual travel agents who organize special women's trips, upon their own initiation or at the behest of a group. One

A river rafting trip organized by Mariah Wilderness Expeditions.

Robin Tyler (left) with Wanda Henson.

noted example is Estilita Grimaldo-Smith. She is known by many as the first feminist travel agent in Los Angeles. For more than 20 years, she organized tours to special women's gatherings. In 1975, she organized a trip to the first UN Conference on Women held in Mexico City. She later organized trips to the second, third, and fourth world conferences in Copenhagen, Nairobi, and Beijing. In the mid-1970s, she organized an impressive tour of China for 100 feminist medical doctors, psychologists, and therapists. Eventually she developed her individual trips into her own company, Womantours, which also trekked to the Amazon, to Macchu Picchu, and to the Brontés environs in England. Estilita's Los Angeles-based company, sold in 1997, was the precursor to the ones that exist today.

Internet-organized Vacations

The Internet is a new way that women are finding each other and sharing time together. Through web pages and electronic discussion lists, women are sharing vacation stories and recruiting sister-participants for future adventures. Some trip-designers are charging for their efforts, while others are organizing trips for fun. One web page, Maiden Voyages Online (http://maiden-voyages.com/ventures.html), is a large directory of women-owned

touring companies or companies that offer women-only trips. Another web site, In the Company of Women (http://www.companyofwomen.com), was organized out of the web owners' dismay at the high prices and poor organization of some of the well-known travel companies. Just for fun, not for profit, they are finding women from across the country to share reasonably priced adventures.

Electronic discussion lists are other Internet means for lesbians to find one another and eventually travel together or organize a trip. Some discussion lists are focused around an activity, such as outdoor recreation, travel, square dancing, or singing. Other lists are general interest but geographically focused, such as queer lists in a state or region. Through all kinds of lists, individuals electronically meet one another, and many of them go on to meet each other in person. Making a friend through a European or Australian discussion list has been an entrée to a country. Some of the web pages listed in the "References" section point to discussion lists and subscription information.

LESBIAN LEISURE

Constituting the first representations of lesbian and gay "community" in the United States, bars have played major and multiple roles in lesbian culture in the last half of the twentieth century. As well as being leisure social spots, offering settings for congeniality and fun, bars have also offered space for self-discovery and identity affirmation. Unfortunately, bars have also had to be refuges from a hostile heterosexual world. Because of their important roles in lesbian life and their longevity in lesbian culture, much needs to be said about bars and bar life.

Although the Stonewall Rebellion in 1969 affected lesbian bars much the way it affected gay male bars by increasing individuals' militancy in their resistance to society's heterosexist beliefs, lesbian bars have an origin, history, and style of culture uniquely their own. Economic, sexist, and heterosexist oppression have forged a special social environment for women. The following details the development and community-building roles of lesbian bars in this special environment.

Conditions for a Subculture

Successful, stable lesbian bars originated in the 1940s. Prior to those years, most lesbians lived as isolated individuals with few lesbian acquaintances. Some adventurous women discovered public socializing opportunities in gay male bars, "friendly" heterosexual bars, short-lived all-women night spots, and private house parties. Three conditions promoted the building of a lesbian subculture, and ironically, the war era provided these conditions: money, confidence, and lesbian self-identification.

During World War II, women acquired money and confidence through their work filling the vacancies left by men in factories, offices, salesrooms, and farms. In "running the country" and in "doing men's work," women gained not only financial autonomy, but also a sense of importance. Women came to see their place in the world in a new light—one in which they were actors in the public realm. With more women working throughout and after the war years, lesbians acquired more anonymity and therefore more safety in making a living among men. Previously, a single working woman was eventually suspected of lesbian leanings.

The third condition that helped lesbians create their own subculture was lesbian self-identification. Part of that self-identification included the ability to dress as one wanted. Because of factory and industrial work environments, the dress code for all women changed during the war years to include pants. Liberalization of the dress code was not of small consequence to women. In the gender-stratified 1940s, pants were associated with male power, and women wearing pants prior to World War II represented an unacceptable presumption of that power. The strength of this symbolism is evidenced in the harassment, beatings, and arrests encountered by lesbians who dared wear pants publicly in pre-war times. With more women wearing pants, the lesbians who always preferred this attire now had "cover"—they could walk the streets day or night and not immediately be targeted as lesbians "needing to be put in their place."

Along with the ability to dress as they wanted came the opportunity for lesbians to get a glimpse of what all-women working and living environments could be like. Lesbian factory women found that they relished working side-by-side with women and socializing after work. Military women saw examples of women loving women in their barracks, units, and in the "off-limits" lesbian and gay bars. Gradually, lesbians came to see themselves as "not the only ones," as legitimately "different," and as people with a right to exist.

The Early Bars

By the end of the war, lesbian bars could survive economically because enough working-class women identified as lesbians, possessed discretionary monies, and concentrated in urban areas. Many of the first bars sprang up in port cities, where ex-military women settled. Factory and office women who had worked in or near cities throughout the war chose to remain in the cities, where anonymity offered them a degree of safety. They, like military women, looked forward to the prospects for community. Few of these women felt they could return to their hometowns due to society's general intolerance of lesbianism.

Some of the early bars, however, were miserable places. Part of a legally tainted subculture, they were seedy affairs, difficult to find, sometimes run by organized crime, and sometimes sharing space with prostitutes. Other early bars were decently managed or located in better neighborhoods, but these too had to pay off the police to prevent raids and harassment. These pay-offs were not always protective, especially when elections came around, giving cause for moral grandstanding on the part of politicians.

The relative freedom lesbians had found through the war years disappeared in the wake of McCarthyism. Gay men and lesbians were driven from the State Department and other government agencies. Politicians gay-baited in order to get elected, and psychologists tried to "cure" people of their homosexuality. Notes Faderman, "The 1950s were perhaps the worst time in history for women to love women" (Faderman, *Odd Girls and Twilight Lovers*).

One's life in the early bars was thus subject to restrictive behaviors and possibilities for arrest. If women touched, they could be arrested by undercover agents, so many of the early bars prohibited dancing. With arrests could come beatings, rapes, unwanted newspaper headlines, and bar closings. Women arrested in a "house of ill repute" automatically lost their jobs.

Despite the risks, women patronized the bars, as these were the only public places that offered a contact point for women to meet other lesbians. Women now knew they were not the only ones who felt same-sex attractions, and they were intent on finding others. Bars played a major role in helping women find friends of like mind as well as sexual partners. It was much too dangerous to approach a woman in the heterosexual world. In lesbian bars, women could act and be seen as lesbians, to whatever limited degree. Lesbians dropped their straight covers in the bars and scouted for friends and mates.

In their better moments, bars offered relaxation and fun. Besides drinking and conversing, women played pool, and ping-pong, and volleyball. In the 1950s and 1960s, bars were not unlike community centers, many developing a core group of patrons. Women held birthday parties for one another, and organized bar anniversary parties and holiday parties. Lesbians established softball teams through the bars, playing women from other bar-sponsored teams in the city. Over time, as it became safe for lesbians to dance with one another, different types of bars came into existence—neighborhood bars, piano bars, country-western bars, ethnic bars, and rock-and-roll bars.

Bar Culture

Working-class lesbians created a unique sexual and cultural dynamic known as butch-femme. Women who adopted the trousers and posturing associated with heterosexual men were called "butches." Women who embraced the feminine dress and less-assertive mannerisms associated with heterosexual women were called "femmes."

The butches made the overtures, romantic or sexual. They lit the cigarettes, opened the doors, and otherwise performed the chivalrous role. Sometimes this meant fighting a hostile straight man on the streets to protect the right to be with her femme. Butch-femme roles could be conformed to so rigidly that some bars were divided as if by an invisible line, with butches on one side of the bar and femmes on the other—until a butch was attracted to a femme and crossed the line. Butch-femme role playing would even be taken into the bedrooms.

Kennedy and Davis in *Boots of Leather, Slippers of Gold* studied the butch-femme culture of a post-war Buffalo working-class community. They found that the butch-femme relationship offered lesbians three kinds of liberation: a visible way to resist the cultural dominance of heterosexuality; a way to proclaim sexual autonomy; and a way to self-identify and create community. Though derived from heterosexual models, butch-femme role playing "transformed those models and created an authentic lesbian lifestyle" (Kennedy and Davis, p. 6).

Women who would not or could not accept either the "butch" or "femme" label were regarded as "kiki." Often these were middle- or upper-middle-class lesbians who had no tolerance for defined role-playing. Strict butches and femmes used the term "kiki" derogatorily, implying "confused" or "betraying the culture."

Butch-femme role playing has carried through to the 1990s for some lesbians. Some women still conform to the strict expressions of this dynamic, while other butch-femme couples have incorporated feminist concepts of equality into their relationships. Higher-educated women are likely to act the roles to honor lesbian history or to have fun with the roles. Some lesbians simply like the aesthetics of butch and femme. Lesbian visibility is still a valued outcome of butch-femme dress and mannerisms.

Stonewall and Its Effect

Researchers call the 1950s and 1960s the "pre-political era," where women and men individually strengthened their beliefs in their own human rights, practiced everyday rebellions, but generally did not form political groups. A lesbian and gay consciousness emerged through these decades that was necessary for the quick and solid takeoff of the liberation movement following the 1969 Stonewall Riots. It is logical that the ignition for the contemporary movement took place at a bar—bars being the primary places where lesbians and gays for decades had been publicly resisting society's censure. Without these two decades of civil rights fermentation and self-conscious community-building, Stonewall would have been a mere incident.

The Stonewall Rebellion in Greenwich Village, New York, extended over six nights. Lesbians and gays fought the police with beer bottles, bricks, and mockery. On 28 June 1969, police had attempted to carry out one of their frequent trumped-up inquiries into "selling liquor without a license," which usually included arresting bar patrons for likewise trumped-up "disorderly conduct" charges. This night, however, the police victims mouthed off and struck back. Lesbians and gays made it clear they were no longer going peacefully into the paddy wagons.

This fairly minor riot became a watershed event. After Stonewall, gays and lesbians became increasingly adamant about their right to exist in whatever style suited them. Police harassment-at-

will did not immediately cease everywhere in the country, but it started to turn around. The overt surveillance of bars soon stopped. In some places, fairly quickly, community relations officers were assigned to gay communities. Gradually across the country, the media stopped their alarmist treatment of the lesbian and gay issue.

Between 1975 and 1980, society-at-large made great strides in accepting, or at least tolerating, lesbians and gays. Consequently, bar life became increasingly free from fear. By 1980, throughout the country, police had reversed their earlier harassment; lesbians could now expect some amount of protection from their previous intimidators.

Other Lesbians

During the 1950s, 1960s, and 1970s, middle-class, upwardly mobile, and wealthy lesbians patronized higher-class bars, if they patronized bars at all. Only a few of these bars were lesbian bars. Many women either had too much to lose to be seen in bars, or they were so wealthy they could be themselves in their own elite worlds without suffering economic consequences, and thus didn't need bars.

The few stories, however, of middle-class lesbians in bars show that these women were not into role-playing. Nor was community-building a concern of theirs. Keeping their middle-class jobs as school teachers and social workers, for example, was of primary importance. Middle-class and wealthy lesbians cannot be credited with helping establish a public lesbian subculture in the United States.

Another form of socializing for lesbians in the 1940s, 1950s, and 1960s were house parties. All economic levels of lesbians seemed to host these kinds of open house gatherings, but African-American lesbians socialized in these ways to the greatest extent. For them lesbian house parties were a natural extension of their culture's rent parties and buffet flat parties. Black women did not patronize white lesbian bars until the mid-1960s, and then infrequently. Black women sometimes patronized white gay male bars, which black gay men also patronized. For the most part, the public venues that black women liked were the entertainment clubs, which were downtown or uptown spots tolerant of all races, sexes, classes, and gender preferences.

Lesbian Bars Today

Lesbian bars are no longer the centers of community they were in more-oppressive times. As society's acceptance of lesbians and gays has increased, lesbians have been able to publicly organize numerous clubs, groups, organizations, and businesses that serve their communities. Newsletters and newspapers advertise these activities and can be picked up in non-lesbian places, as well as gay and lesbian venues. Bars are not the only places any more to meet people, to exchange information, and to enjoy other lesbians.

Bars still fill the pages of lesbian travel guides. Some are doing well financially, but many are borderline, and others that used to exist have closed. In a documentary titled *Last Call at Maud's*, which explores the community-building roles that a lesbian bar played over twenty-three years in San Francisco, interviewees suggest reasons for its closure in 1989. Some of these speakers had been regular customers in Maud's heyday, and they had not missed Maud's as a socializing place for years.

The various reasons given for Maud's closing are likely to apply to other bars across the country: women don't go out as much; women are doing different things; women are into sobriety and healthier activities; women are focusing on their careers more; women are not into groups and community as much; and because change is constant.

At present, lesbian neighborhood bars seem to be struggling. Bars that pull crowds from a broad geographic base seem to be doing better. It is surprising, and perhaps indicative of the future of lesbian bars, that San Francisco, with the largest lesbian population in the country, in the late 1990s offers one-night-a-week or one-night-a-month all-women's nights at otherwise straight or gay male clubs, rather than offering seven-day-a-week lesbian bars.

Still, lesbian bars will probably continue to open and close as there are still some important roles they play in lesbian communities. Softball teams are still sponsored by bars. Dancing is still found in bars on a regular basis. Special nights, like those for Halloween and Gay Pride, and other nights set aside for comedians, touring singers, and for benefit shows, all bring lesbians together, providing a sense of community. Lesbian bars offer an entree to the community for those women trying to decide about their sexual orientation. Lesbians planning to relocate to a city can visit the bars and scope out the town as a place to live. Lesbians on vacation can visit a town's bar and feel connected to their subculture while far from home.

Softball

Softball is a national lesbian pastime. In large cities, teams composed entirely of lesbians frequently play other all-lesbian teams. Lesbians are also found in small towns, playing on mixed teams of gay and straight or male and female. If one scans the ball fields throughout America, it is likely one will meet lesbians, as it is a tacit understanding in the lesbian culture that softball fields are "where the girls are."

History of Softball

Softball has been a part of women's lives, lesbian or not, since 1887, when upper-class members of a boat club in Chicago invented the game. A modified form of baseball, softball quickly gained popularity among the masses, because the game fit within the dimensions of city-block playground areas.

For women, softball was one of the few acceptable sports they could play. As opposed to men's baseball, it was perceived that the softer ball, the lighter bats, and the shorter distances between bases in softball presented less of a risk of injury and caused less physical stress than baseball.

Working-class women who worked under harsh conditions in early twentieth-century factories and mills were encouraged to play softball by their employers. Companies underwrote the costs of facilities for softball because the industrial recreation movement pressured employers to counterbalance the hardships of employees' work lives with opportunities for healthy physical exercise. Softball fields were an antidote to the polluted indoor air and physically static work conditions of factories. Because of softball's connection with the workforce, it has always been the sport of working women. Many of those working women were lesbians, because as single women, lesbians had to support themselves.

The Depression brought about enforced leisure for many unemployed individuals. Softball being inexpensive, it added mem-

Softball has served as a unifying social activity for many lesbians.

bers quickly in these financially tough times. The Works Progress Administration, which employed people in public projects, created many city parks and playgrounds that in turn contributed to softball's growth.

The Amateur Softball Association encouraged the development of recreation leagues for men and women during the 1930s. This organization held its first national tournament in 1933, when 15 women's teams competed.

Unlike other sports for women in physical education programs in schools, softball evolved out-of-sight of educational administrators. The Softball Association had no educational or "female-appropriate" philosophy guiding it that caused it to establish separate rules of play for men and women on the public playing fields. Thus, women in softball were allowed to be coached by males, were allowed to be publicized for their accomplishments, were allowed to entertain spectators and charge admission, and were allowed to be competitive. Without arbitrary restrictions limiting them and their aspirations, women could play all out when they played softball.

The game was quite a physically challenging and sex role-challenging sport. Going against the social norms for women, it was thus an attractive game to the kind of woman who was already familiar with non-conformity and independence of spirit. Women softball players needed to excel in passionate intensity, strength, aggressiveness, toughness, physical ability, and competitiveness. In many instances, women softball players were lesbians.

Today, 5 million of 27 million softball players in this country are women. *Sports Illustrated* conducted a poll in 1986 that showed softball to be the number one team sport played by women in general. Similarly, the prevalence of softball in lesbian culture proves softball to be the number one sport of lesbians.

Softball's Accessibility

Softball is accessible in many senses. Geographically, softball fields are found easily. In big cities, women's bookstores, coffeehouses, bars, and lesbian and gay information phone lines can quickly lead one to the night's games. In small towns, one can simply drive around and find the ball fields. The rules of the game are easy to learn and similar across the country.

Not only is softball everywhere, attracting large numbers of lesbians, it attracts every kind of lesbian as well. From office clerks and delivery workers to dentists and lawyers, all kinds of lesbians make up softball teams. There are all levels of play available too, so one can find teams for super athletes, for average ball players, and for women who play "for fun."

Softball is also accessible economically. It does not require lots of equipment or have high playing fees. Therefore, women, who generally have less discretionary income than men, can participate readily in this sport.

Softball's Role in Lesbian Life

The socializing aspect of softball, whether playing, cheerleading, or going out afterwards, is as important to lesbians as the physical and competitive aspects of the game. Watching or playing softball is a primary way that women meet women. There are prospects for lovers, as well as friends, among the players and among the fans in the stands.

For women who avoid bars, softball is a social lifeline. For women who frequently patronize bars, softball is an additional social outlet. In either case, softball is a congealing force in the lesbian community. Friendships and partnerships are formed through the teamwork and cooperation demanded by the sport, as well as through the accompanying socializing rituals.

Lesbian and gay bars are often sponsors of softball teams, sometimes sponsoring more than one. Traditionally, players patronize these bars after the games, in appreciation for the bar's sponsorship and at the same time furthering the camaraderie begun on the field. There is an integral historic relationship between lesbian bar life and lesbian softball life.

Because of softball's universality, accessibility, and social catalyzing, it earns its number one spot as the leading lesbian sport.

Clubs

Clubs existed before Stonewall, but not in the large numbers, variety, and visibility that are common in the 1990s. Women's "Lavender" Pages and gay/lesbian organization directories are published in almost all large cities. Through these directories, through gay and lesbian newspapers and magazines, and increasingly through the Internet, lesbians discover many types of clubs to join.

Women play all kinds of sports, as is evidenced at the quadrennial Gay Games. But sports activity clubs for softball, rugby, and soccer are particularly popular with lesbians, as is golf (see "Palm Springs" in "Travel" section). Women's outdoor organizations are numerous, with mountain area clubs emphasizing skiing, hiking, and river running, coastal organizations emphasizing water sports, and Midwest organizations emphasizing hiking, camping, biking, and canoeing.

Other leisure groups include square dance clubs, which are often mixed groups of men and women. Book groups are common. Dining clubs are popular, but they are not as traditional as lesbians hosting potlucks at their homes. Lesbians have also invented non-musical festivals, which are country settings for camping and relaxing with other lesbians.

The Internet is the newest form of leisure for lesbians, at the same time as being a method for lesbians to find one another. Cyberdykes are meeting through discussion lists, chat lines, bulletin boards, and web pages and later meeting each other in person at potlucks and parties. Some of the interesting discussion lists found on the queernet web page (http://www.queernet.org) are: "crockdykes," a list for sharing recipes; "ba-filmdykes," a list for Bay area film/video makers, critics and students; "owls," a list for "lesbians over 40"; "ba-cyberdykes," a list for Bay area lesbians and bisexual women chatting about any topic; and "boychicks," a list for discussing butch-femme identity and gender issues. The first stop for lesbians looking for lesbians on the Internet is Lesbian.org (http://www.lesbian.org), a web site that points to all kinds of lesbian discussion lists, newsgroups, bulletin boards, chat rooms, and web sites. Other queer web resources are listed in the References section.

One additional and separate channel that women use to find each other for recreation is through sober dyke groups. These can be Alcoholics Anonymous groups for lesbians, or they can be unaffiliated grassroots-organized "clean and sober" groups. For some women, recreation is a big part of staying away from alcohol and drugs. Thus, many sober dyke groups are activity-focused, offering dancing, camping, game nights, softball, volleyball, as well as potluck socializing, dining out, and cultural evenings. The ground rule behind all of these group activities is abstinence from drugs and alcohol by all participants, which is a social atmosphere that women cannot rely on in any other club mentioned previously.

The Creation of a Women's Culture

The women's liberation movement flowered in the 1970s. For political women, leisure gatherings were suffused with the politics of the times, which announced women's strength, independence from men, and reliance on one's sisters. Thus, entertainment spots were also centers for organizing. Heterosexual and lesbian women found each other in coffeehouses and bookstores and formed groups to organize for women's right to reproductive freedom, women's campaigns for political office, women's equal rights, as well as educational opportunities exploring sexism, racism, heterosexism, and classism.

The liberation movement also took the form of building a women-only culture. Individuals created and organized publications, publishing houses, theater groups, concerts, recording companies, production companies, music festivals, coffeehouses, urban collectives, and even rural land communes—run in the closest semblance of equality and inclusiveness the groups could manage. These cultural creations offered a wealth of leisure activities. Many still exist in the 1990s, although many have changed face, looking more like traditional businesses. The political foundations are detectable, but not so overriding as when originally conceived.

The Music Scene

"Womyn's music" was a response to a political movement. Initially, musicians filled the gaps between speakers at political rallies. Meg Christian, Chris Williamson, Holly Near, and Alix Dobkin were four early musicians who performed at lesbian, feminist, and political left rallies and who eventually became "stars" on the womyn's music circuit. Listeners to their woman-identified music finally felt their lives reflected in lyrics detailing women's daily struggles in a male world and lesbians' dreams of being accepted by society. The music was "womyn's music" because it embraced all women's concerns in the building of the feminist movement.

Women overcame the male-dominated record industry's refusal to produce their works by producing their own records and forming their own record companies. The first-known womyn's music records were two 45 rpms produced in 1971: Maxine Feldman produced her openly lesbian "Angry Atthis," and Madeline Davis produced her song of gay and lesbian liberation, "Stonewall Nation." The first womyn's music album, Mountain Moving Day, was jointly issued in 1972 by two women's liberation rock bands, one from Chicago and one from New Haven, Connecticut.

In 1972 and 1973, two separate groups of performing women started their own companies—Redwood Records and Olivia Records, respectively. Redwood Records initially was Holly Near's effort to have her own anti-Vietnam, anti-imperialist, feminist songs produced. Olivia Records was launched by a group of lesbian-feminists wanting to make a living and carry out their feminist activism at the same time. These women faced the monumental tasks of learning the technicalities of sound studios and album production at the same time as learning the intricacies of marketing and financing.

Speaking in a 1974 interview about Olivia's goals, Ginny Berson, a founding member, said the group wanted to establish an "alternative economic institution" that was "completely controlled by women," which would eventually free women from "the male political system." They wanted to "produce a product that women want[ed] to buy," in order to "affect large numbers of women" with the feminist message. While doing this, they wanted to "employ women in a non-oppressive situation."

Another member, Meg Christian, spoke about the group's strategy:

> We are not going to focus on political or obviously feminist music because we want to reach women who are not yet in the women's movement. We want to bring women into some sort of feminist consciousness. Music is such an incredible vehicle for slipping in under people's blocks, under the walls that people have built—their defenses (Crow, et al., "The Muses of Olivia").

Christian further explained that there were two ways of being feminist about music, and she was concerned with both: the lyrics and the performance style. The feminism of lyrics was self-evident, but she saw a big difference in "performers who related to the audience as if they were there and women who got up and pulled a shell around them and performed, which is essentially your male performing trip" (Crow, et al., "The Muses of Olivia").

As these statements show, early womyn's music was politically driven. As these and other women's recording companies succeeded, heterosexual women and lesbians across the country heard powerful liberating music. This worthy result continually re-energized the musical pioneers, helping them face continuing monumental obstacles.

Distribution and production companies sprang up across the nation—some professional; most non-professional. The non-professional production companies were local women working voluntarily, learning about venues, contracts, advertising, and ticket-selling, in order to bring womyn's music to their towns. Women with no previous skills in technical and business areas nevertheless had the courage and feminist commitment to undertake a rapid learning curve in order to promote womyn's music. They made possible the development of local concerts into regional and national performances. Womyn's music concerts became popular "doings" in major and medium-sized cities in the late 1970s and 1980s. These were such exhilarating times that a woman who lived two hours away from a performance didn't think twice about getting friends to join her for a "concert outing."

Thus, womyn's music became a primary source of leisure activities. The peak years offered big-city women at least one major concert per month to attend. Gradually, women comedians added diversity to the music concerts. The music itself, originally dominated by acoustic folk style, gradually incorporated rock, punk, new wave, popular, new age, jazz, reggae, and classical sounds. More recording companies developed. Amateurs grew into professionals. Local concerts developed into regional and national music festivals. A sizable subculture of womyn's music lovers developed, influencing the womyn's music world just as the music world influenced the subculture.

The height of the womyn's music movement was the 1970s and 1980s. In the late 1990s, womyn's music as an art form is being threatened by both the waning of feminist audiences and by the mainstreaming of womyn's artists. Some women argue that the mainstreaming will only be partial and that women should not let the hard-earned subculture of womyn's music disappear. Others are finding it too difficult to run these feminist businesses in times of acculturation. Olivia Records, for instance, the longest-running womyn's record company, no longer promotes new artists, though they are still selling from their extensive backlog.

Ladyslipper Music, out of Durham, North Carolina, is an independent music label and a distribution company. For more than 20 years, it has sold womyn's music products; its present catalog runs to 88 pages. Its web page (http://www.ladyslipper.org) indicates how a large music and performance subculture by and for women has been developed over the past several decades. As a music label, Ladyslipper has produced more than half a dozen musicians. Ladyslipper has such faith in the future that it has just paid a downpayment on a building of its own. Though the future of womyn's music is uncertain, it is clear that changes are underway.

Music Festivals

Lesbians sometimes approach one another, asking "'been to Michigan?" They refer not to the state itself, but to a "happening" in that state—an event that began in 1976 and still occurs every August. If the woman answers affirmatively, a bonding occurs, as this week-long music festival in the countryside of Michigan is now a lesbian tradition. Michigan is a camping extravaganza, offering live music, topical workshops, arts and crafts, drumming and dance sessions, massage, volleyball, and films. Whatever engaging activity one might want at a festival, it's available.

Some women trek to Michigan every year. They see it as a reservoir of woman-identified energy that they refuel with before re-

The Michigan Womyn's Music Festival is a popular annual destination for lesbian travelers.

turning to straight society. Other women check out the festival once or several times to see what it's all about.

The Michigan festival creates a women's village every year. Activities are totally run by women for women. First-time participants find it consciousness-raising just to see a totally woman-run scenario. Women build the stages, set up the sound systems, buy the food for 5,000-plus women, schedule crews of hundreds, do upkeep on trails, organize shuttles transporting participants into the women-owned land, and organize healing/nursing tents, women-of-color tents, children's play areas, RV areas, chemically free sections, and areas for hearing-impaired and differently abled women. Over the past 20-plus years, every possible need has been expressed by the various participants, and the festival organizers (WWTC—We Want The Music Collective) have continuously adapted the festival to meet these needs. The collective holds an unshakable belief in inclusiveness.

Michigan was founded upon feminist principles of a new kind of women-only space, where all women are welcome to share in a self-affirming event that celebrates women. Cooperativeness and sharing are lauded. All women are expected to work four-hour shifts helping with the festival's operations. A shift could be security duty, protecting the festival from intruders. It could be cooking or serving the vegetarian meals. It could be offering one's nurs-

ing skills or counseling skills. The festival stays reasonably priced because everyone works. More importantly, the work arrangement promotes the idea of women throwing the festival for themselves, rather than passively being consumers.

There have been rifts for years over political issues, ranging from racist accusations to the inclusion of male children or transgendered participants in the festival. Many of the educational or skills-sharing workshops focus on political issues. National organizations gain members through Michigan workshops, and letter-writing campaigns get added bulk from Michigan signatures. Many causes, including domestic abuse, sexism, animal rights, and anti-nuclear activism, are actively campaigned for throughout the festival.

Music is a primary focus of the festival, however. Most of the women on the womyn's music circuit have played at Michigan. The festival is a tremendous opportunity to hear many music stars in just a few days. It's also an opportunity for up-and-coming musicians to gain exposure. The size of audiences can range from several hundred at a day stage to thousands at a night stage. But many other musical moments occur between non-professional women at Michigan, some planned, some spontaneous. Classical string players or jazz musicians might find each other in a workshop area, play for a solid two hours, and plan to meet the next two days. There are open drumming sessions daily. And there have been choruses and concert bands organized from among the festival participants in different years.

Michigan has been an inspiration to women all over the country. Regional festivals such as the West Coast Womyn's Music and Comedy Festival, the Southern Womyn's Music and Comedy Festival, the Gulf Coast Women's Festival (one of the newer ones), and more locally focused festivals such as Wiminfest in Albuquerque and Campfest in Pennsylvania, and other festivals in Texas, Virginia, Iowa, and Ohio—all sprouted from the mother festival at Michigan.

The festivals are very similar in structure, but sometimes enough different that they become known for that difference. The Southern Festival and Campfest are known as the "comfortable" women's festivals. The facilities rent cabins as well as offer camping, and they also feature a lake, a pool, and a roofed theater (with chairs) for the concerts. Ruggedness being the norm at Michigan, cabins and chairs are comfortable by comparison. The Southern event is also called the "Live and Let Live" festival because politics is not a front-line presence, though it still offers political speakers.

Some festivals make concerted efforts to attract minorities. Others offer music and games, but not workshops. Some festivals heavily promote spirituality, and another one focuses on writers and writing. Some are held in urban settings, such as the historically important National Womyn's Music Fesitval in Bloomington, Indiana. This festival was initially accompanied by womyn's music industry conferences, which were important gatherings in the building of the national womyn's music network. A major purpose of the Bloomington festival was to discover and showcase new talent. Eventually, the music industry conferences split off from the Bloomington music festival, and the latter, newly simplified event carried on for several years before moving to a different town in Indiana.

All the festivals give lesbians and other women the opportunity to celebrate themselves away from a homophobic and sexist society. The safety of festival spaces allows women to explore different ways of being and acting, to explore lesbianism without constraints, and to "come out" for some individuals. Michigan is notorious for displays of nudity, since festival attendees feel safe to express themselves this way in the women-only environment. Festivals are women's ways of creating different forms of lesbian nations. Being multi-faceted, music festivals offer unique, inexpensive, celebratory activities for lesbians on vacation.

Coffeehouses

Women-only spaces were a novel, though controversial, idea in the 1970s. Believers in women's right to their own spaces prevailed, however, and a whole range of women-only spaces developed. These spaces, including coffeehouses, were so safe and affirming that many women felt free to examine their life choices—resulting in some women leaving their families, others "coming out," and others going back to school.

The early women's movement depended on coffeehouses as places for women to connect with one another. Heterosexual as well as lesbian women created the coffeehouse scene, though it was lesbian-intensive. Church basements provided spaces for the weekly or monthly gatherings. Performers played for donations. Children were entertained in separate child-care rooms. Volunteers, working in collectives, planned events, advertised to communities, and tracked balance sheets.

Giving space to women's voices was one of the important purposes behind coffeehouses. Feminism dictated that performance stages present all women, whether they were professionals, aspiring artists, or simply women expressing themselves on issues or reading poetry. Speakers on issues, perhaps alcoholism or women's right to reproductive freedom, also took the stages. Storytelling evenings were popular, as were variety shows, which spotlighted the range of a community's talents. Oftentimes the stage was put away in favor of the dance floor, or screens were raised to show women's films.

Besides bolstering a local community's women, coffeehouses were vital in cheerleading national performing artists. In the 1970s, feminist artists could not get booked by mainstream nightclubs or theaters. Because coffeehouses existed eventually in most large towns and cities, a national circuit of performance places became available. This circuit allowed aspiring professionals to hone their arts.

Not only musicians but also comedians benefited from the coffeehouse circuit. Kate Clinton, now the best-known feminist comedian, advanced her career through coffeehouses, as did Robin Tyler, Mimi González, Marga Gómez, and Suzanne Westenhoefer.

Mountain Moving Coffeehouse in Chicago, as a single example, demonstrates the history of women's coffeehouses. Begun as a crisis phone service for women, the service was moved from a woman's home phone to a storefront early in its history. The storefront space was too large, however, for just a phone service, and by happenstance, the volunteer counselors decided to create a coffeehouse in the rest of the space. Its purposes were twofold: to provide a place for women to celebrate womanness and to provide a performance place for artists.

Mountain Moving Coffeehouse has continuously implemented its goals for more than 20 years. It has hosted innumerable musicians, comedians, actors, and poets—professional and amateur. It has offered space for plays, for dances, and for women's bands, most notably The Chicago Women's Liberation Rock Band. Empowerment of women and children has been an overriding theme behind all activities. Other feminist principles have also been prominent, such as catering to all women regardless of ability to pay, skin color, physical ability, or sexual preference. Coffeehouses have been healthy alternatives to bars—healthy in the sense of providing non-alcoholic beverages, smoke-free environments (usually), vegetarian fare, and most importantly, space to "be oneself."

Coffeehouses still exist all over the country, though to a lesser degree than in the peak years of the 1970s and 1980s. Sometimes coffeehouses operate out of gay/lesbian community centers and bookstores. Mama Bears in San Francisco is a long-standing bookstore/coffeehouse. A wall separates each business function, allowing the bookstore to be securely closed off when the coffeehouse stays open to present women comedians, poets, and musicians. Women discover coffeehouses through travel guides, community publications, and word-of-mouth.

Women's Choruses

In 1975, with the formation of Anna Crusis Women's Choir in Philadelphia, lesbians began singing together publicly. Within a few years, choruses started up in Washington, D.C., Madison, Wisconsin, and Minneapolis, Minnesota. Singing groups were another way to form community in the face of societal oppression against women and lesbians.

Choruses sang the feminist songs of the womyn's music movement, and also American popular songs re-written with strong-women lyrics. For instance, the song "What Are Little Girls Made Of?" was changed, with one choral section singing "Sugar and spice and everything nice" and another section singing "Gloria Steinem, Susan B. Anthony, and Janis Joplin." Over the years, all kinds of music about or by women have been presented in concerts, including folk, jazz, blues, classical, ethnic European, Latin American, and African. Singing groups have ranged in size from 5-person ensembles to 300-person choruses.

If one could carry a tune, one could join these inclusive, collective, feminist choruses. Many members felt that the importance of a chorus to them was as much the offering of sisterhood, political action, and women's culture-building, as it was the opportunity to sing music. Much of women's culture was exhibited through choral productions. Sometimes slide shows of women's art were shown on side screens at concerts. Sometimes women's poems were interspersed between songs. Humor skits and dramatic monologues have been known to vary the presentations. Political and community announcements were expected at intermissions.

Politics supported the culture and the culture supported the politics. These were not just lesbian politics, these were women's politics, as choruses were open to all women. Even deaf women were encouraged to attend the concerts by the inclusion of a new style of American Sign Language interpretation, which mixed dance movements with traditional sign language.

The Sister Singers Network was formed in 1980 to facilitate communications between the choruses. The network has published a directory of all the choruses and the contemporary composer-arrangers and has disseminated musical arrangements to choruses, a vital need in the early years. A newsletter enhanced communications, making regional concerts possible. By the late 1990s, approximately 55 choruses, including some in Canada and Europe, comprised the loosely organized network.

Individual choirs that can afford the expenses participate in national women's choral festivals sponsored by Sister Singers Network. There have been seven so far, with an eighth one planned for 1998 in Portland. Different choruses host these approximately three-day, 500-person vocal celebrations of women's lives, strengths, dreams, and accomplishments. Accompanying the concerts are workshops on all manner of topics, from drumming techniques to Balkan singing to greater multicultural awareness through music. Sometimes "stars" of womyn's music offer workshops, adding a pinch of glamour to the already compelling events.

Mixed gay and lesbian choruses also exist throughout the country, as well as all-men choruses. In a network separate from Sister Singers, GALA Choruses (Gay and Lesbian Association of Choruses) represents 160 vocal groups and holds annual conferences for choral directors, and also periodic choral festivals. Sometimes all-women's choruses join gay male choruses or mixed choruses for special events, such as a Christmas or Gay Pride concert. Electronic resources in the 1990s have greatly facilitated communications between choruses. GALA Choruses on the Web (http://www.tde.com/~dwc/galaweb.html) is an impressive web directory, and a discussion list exists for GALA Choruses members.

Whether through all-women choruses or mixed choruses, lesbians find political and spiritual community, artistic fulfillment, and leisure fun through their choral involvement.

Women's Bookstores

The first women's bookstores began as literature tables at women's conferences, demonstrations, and concerts. Women vol-untarily produced political literature out of their homes and just as committedly traipsed with the pamphlets, position papers, and newspapers to all the different gatherings of women.

The move to permanent quarters, such as storefronts, came about as materials and business increased. Tradition has it that Amazon Bookstore in Minneapolis, the oldest continuously operating feminist bookstore, started on a front porch in 1970 and moved inside when the harsh winter set in. In the 1960s, lesbians could barely find a book, story, or article that reflected their lives. By the late 1970s, women could actually walk into physical bookstores and find their literature. A quiet revolution had occurred because of the women in print movement. A count in 1978 showed there to be 60 women's bookstores in the U.S. and Canada.

"Feminist bookstore" is synonymous with "women's bookstore." Lesbians have always been major players in the women's bookstore movement. The feminist world that women were creating envisioned minorities, gays and lesbians, poor and working class equally participating in a newly constructed non-discriminatory society. The bookstores offered non-sexist, non-racist, non-classist, non-homophobic reading materials to further that ideal.

Written works reflecting women's and lesbians' lives, which had been rejected by mainstream publishers, finally reached their audiences through women's publishers and bookstores. These works educated women about their oppression and helped them grow into a sense of wholeness and legitimacy. Women's literature, of course, also offered mysteries, novels, and poetry for pleasure reading. The bookstores were also the primary outlets for all the records being simultaneously produced by the womyn's music movement.

Bookstores have always played a major communication role in women's culture. The early stores, in fact, were barely distinguishable from women's centers. The book stock was minimal in the early days, and the bookstore workers were so involved in the feminist movement that a visit to a store could easily find a bookstore worker helping a battered woman find shelter for the night, just as likely as selling a woman's publication.

The early bookstore decor of coffee pots, plants, kids' corners, and large bulletin boards all indicated the significant community functions of the bookstores. These bulletin boards have been a continuing presence throughout the last two decades, signifying the ongoing role of bookstores as community centers. Women's culture and gay culture are promoted through sidelines—bumper stickers, jewelry, greeting cards, women's crafts, and calendars. Feminist bookstores are hooked into the national scene as well as the local scene, specifically through national magazines, but also through Feminist Bookstore Network. Organized in 1976, this network supports feminist bookstores with an annual book catalog, a bi-monthly magazine called *Feminist Bookstore News*, and a staff that organizes annual meetings and strategic planning conferences and performs other network needs.

Bookstores sell tickets to concerts and plays, lectures, and conferences. They support community events. They sponsor support-groups, dances, softball teams, and book discussion clubs. They offer meeting space for community groups. They advertise for individual women and their businesses. Women moving to town or just visiting a town call bookstores to find out what's going on that weekend and what the community is like. Bookstores have been the hubs of women's communities. Through a bookstore's well-informed staff and volunteers, women get connected to community and leisure activities.

Bookstores have undergone an interesting history, not unlike the music business. Collectives ran the early stores, putting into practice the socialist ideals of group efforts. By the mid-1980s, the stress of these ideals had taken its toll, as had the financial difficulties, and bookstores were more likely being run by individuals or partners. This change to single proprietorships or partnerships happened to women's production companies and record companies also.

Though many bookstores closed their doors over the years, other ones sprang up. A count in 1997 totaled more than 100 women's bookstores, and a significant number of these had survived two decades. Total sales figures for the years 1981-91 showed an increase from $4 million to $30 million. A web page, Feminist Bookstores Index (http://www.igc.apc.org/women/bookstores/booknets.html), lists feminist bookstores worldwide.

Increasingly in the late 1990s, articles are being written about long-time women's (and other independently owned) bookstores closing due to their inability to compete with bookstore chains. These chains are intentionally and avidly going after the women's market. The same problems with mainstreaming that are diluting the womyn's music scene are diluting the women's bookstore industry as well. Major U.S. recording and publishing companies have taken notice of the popularity of certain authors, singers, and topics, have moved into those markets, and are selling those "products" at prices the women's businesses cannot compete against, eroding the women's bookstore and music customer bases.

Carol Seajay, publisher of *Feminist Bookstore News*, calls all of the elements of women's publishing a feminist "ecosystem." Feminist authors, publishing companies, periodicals, bookstores, womyn's music labels, and the readership all depend on one another. The whole is healthy only when all parts are healthy, and with parts of that ecosystem in jeopardy in the late 1990s, the entire system is in jeopardy.

The older supporters of women's culture are holding on against the assault from big business and weakening interest on the part of younger women. The danger is that the country stands to lose the intellectual diversity that independent booksellers provide. Big business booksellers do not exist to promote the voices of minorities. Concentrating on the "bottom line," they tend to sell the diluted messages of women and lesbians, those that will be bought by the masses, not the brazen, confrontational, women- and lesbian-identified writings and lyrics that have bolstered women's self-image and helped pull them out of the acquiescence of previous decades. Finally, without women's bookstores, women's communities would find it much harder to experience solidarity, a sense of community identity, and progress toward full liberation in society.

Profile: Judy Dlugacz and Olivia

Judy Dlugacz has been involved with the lesbian feminist movement all of her adult life. She worked with a political activist group in Ann Arbor, Michigan, called Radicalesbians, even before she participated at age 20 in an early music collective, for which she is best known. This collective became the well-known Olivia Records.

It was 1973, the energetic early feminist days. Ten women were determined to spread "womyn's music" all over the country. They began with a 45 rpm, presenting two of the collective members. Meg Christian cut side one with Carole King's "Lady." Chris Williamson recorded her own "If It Weren't for the Music" on the other side. Over time, these two composer/singers became the two most successful and favorite musicians of the early era of womyn's music.

"We had a vision of creating a musical cultural movement back when we started," says Dlugacz. Through Olivia's feminist organizational structure and operational principles, the group hoped to model the ideal way to collectively make and market a product. Their ideals incorporated non-hierarchical structure; consensus decision-making; racial and class diversity in artists and production workers; all-women technicians, sound engineers, album producers, and salespeople; and a socialistic pay schedule of "each according to their needs." Olivia reached many of these goals to some extent, though the latter one was fairly impossible to achieve. Deciding who needed more than another was quite an ethical dilemma. Financial difficulties, also, continuously strained the early company, increasing the doubtfulness of reaching their ideals.

Olivia started out in Washington, D.C., but eventually settled in Oakland, California. The collective chose the name Olivia from a 1940s pulp novel title. The name appealed to them phonetically, but they also liked the idea of taking an item representative of lesbians' difficult history and transforming it into something beautiful.

Dlugacz tells a funny story of early on when the company was incorporating and someone had to be named "president" for the incorporation papers. Even though she was the youngest member of the founding collective and had absolutely no business knowledge, Dlugacz raised her hand and that was that. That gesture would become fateful.

Olivia recorded its first album in 1974, *I Know You Know*, by Christian. The album sold 12,000 units in its first year, shocking the collective, which had anticipated selling 5,000 total units. Along Christian's tours women were requesting the original 45 record they had heard about. The Olivia pioneers now knew their record company idea was golden. They produced a second album a year later by Williamson, *The Changer and the Changed,* which sold 45,000 its first year. That record went on to become the best-selling womyn's music album in history.

Meg Christian, Chris Williamson, Margie Adam, Holly Near (Redwood Records), and other early Olivia artists had been playing at coffeehouses, women's center basements, dormitory hallways, and YWCAs—the only places that unknowns could be heard. Olivia Records changed that. These four artists toured the country together in 1975 to audiences four times larger than their usual audience-size.

In the early 1980s, the founding members started leaving the company. Dlugacz, 28 years old and Olivia president, was soon the only remaining founder. Two of her stated regrets about how she entered the recording business are that she wished she had had a background in business and that she "hadn't had to grow up doing the job." Dlugacz stayed with Olivia through all its changes because the ideas behind the company were "absolutely irresistible" to her. The lesbian visibility that Olivia promoted was too important for Dlugacz to forsake.

The company changed structure from a collective to what Dlugacz called "a humanistic hierarchy." In this transition, Dlugacz had to deal with both the losses of her feminist sisters and also the losses of certain company ideals. She also had to learn how to handle criticism without others to share it. She spent several years in low profile adjusting to this new role.

In a historical reflection on Olivia's development, as told to the editor of *Hot Wire*, a major womyn's music and culture publication, Dlugacz spoke about a turning point for her with the company. It was 1983, the tenth anniversary for Olivia. Dlugacz had the self-confidence, the respect for women's culture, and the out-

Judy Dlugacz, founder of Olivia Cruises and Resorts.

rageous vision to push for booking the revered Carnegie Hall for a Meg/Chris anniversary concert. When Dlugacz saw her faith vindicated—the seats sold out three months in advance, women traveling from Europe to attend, and exceptional fanfare created by the audience and even women across the country not attending the concert—she knew her decision to stay with Olivia had been the right one.

Dlugacz carried Olivia Records through the remainder of its production years. Through the artists she chose to produce, she continued the ideal of diversity. She organized concerts, tours, and festival appearances for her artists. By the company's fifteenth anniversary, 31 albums total comprised the record catalog, and over a million albums had been sold by a dozen artists. Part of those sales came about through a subsidiary rock label, called Second Wave, that Olivia had developed.

Dlugacz took a turn with the company in 1990 when she saw a market for a women's cruise business. She launched a new arm of the company, calling it Olivia Cruises & Resorts. The recreation line was successful and by 1994 was bringing in half the income for Olivia. Offering "Unique Vacations for Women," Olivia Cruises organizes all-women trips that sail to Nassau, Tahiti, Hawaii, and other exotic places. Many of Olivia's music stars over the years have entertained the guests on these sapphic ships.

By 1997, 12 employees were bringing musical sounds and leisure travels to the lesbian subculture. Olivia Records no longer finds it profitable to produce new musical artists, though the company continues to sell from its extensive catalog. The cruise and vacation resort business is still increasing in 1997, with 33 trips completed and 6 to 8 offered every year. Annual company sales are between $2.5 and $4 million.

At Olivia's twentieth anniversary in 1993, Dlugacz made opening remarks at a celebration concert that made it clear she has always viewed Olivia as one of the major instruments of lesbian liberation:

> It's an amazing time, isn't it? A time I had not expected to see in my lifetime. Lesbians on the cover of *Newsweek*? Clinton appointing Roberta Achtenberg? k.d. lang coming out? And Olivia turning twenty.
>
> Twenty years ago, we had a vision that spoke of changing the world. We believed that lesbianism was not only a lifestyle, but an incredibly positive choice women could make in their lives, to change their lives, to liberate their lives....
>
> Olivia—with her artists—has reached more lesbians than any other institution in the world ... has removed the isolation and stigma for so many more who thought they were the only ones....
>
> In the past year, things have changed dramatically. k.d. lang, Melissa Etheridge, the Indigo Girls, and Janis Ian joined Chris Williamson, Teresa Trull, Meg Christian, Linda Tillery, Lucie Blue, Deidre McCalla, Dianne Davidson, Tret Fure, Nancy Vogl, Kate Clinton, Karen Williams, Marga Gomez, Suzanne Westenhoefer, JoAnn Loulan, and all the other women and gay men who came out of the closet to help create visibility so that our lives could change through our own liberation movement....
>
> Do not for one minute underestimate the part we all have played in changing the world. For we are the ones who first opened the closet doors as lesbians and feminists (Armstrong, "Olivia Turns Twenty").

GAY MALE TRAVEL

According to a poll conducted by Overlooked Opinions in Chicago, gay men had an average annual household income of roughly $51,000 in the middle 1990s, while their lesbian counterparts made somewhat less: almost $43,000 a year. In turn, the average heterosexual household income for the same period was almost $38,000.

Of course, these and similar statistics reveal only part of the reason why gay and lesbian services have evolved into a massive growth market. Generally speaking, gays and lesbians who identify themselves as such—whether single or in a committed relationship—have much more disposable income than straights because most aren't bringing up children. The acronym DINKS (double income, no kids) also applies to gay and lesbian couples much more often than not. (According to the aforementioned poll, 5 percent of gay men and 10 percent of lesbians were raising kids, as compared with more than 34 percent of heterosexual couples, respectively.)

Whether it is called another form of mainstreaming, increased tolerance, or anything else, the point is that corporate America is relentlessly pursuing gay dollars in a multitude of ways. According to the Mulryan Nash advertising agency, businesses committed more than $61.6 million in 1995 to woo gay and lesbian customers. By 1997, advertising sales in 128 gay-themed newspapers and magazines increased 16 percent from the year before. At the 1997 National Gay & Lesbian Business and Consumer Expo held in New York City, roughly 50 percent of the 225 exhibitors represented mainstream companies (including IBM, American Express Company, and Metropolitan Life Insurance Company), up from one third in the previous year.

In light of the above, opportunities for gay male travel and leisure have multiplied. While nobody can accurately gauge the actual number of gay and lesbian people in the United States, there seem to be enough with disposable income to qualify as a market niche. By the 1990s, the gay travel industry in particular had stretched far beyond the traditional confines of modest, specialty shops. This transformation may reflect more on economics in the United States than ideology.

This cover of *One* magazine from 1958 shows that certain gay male travel destinations have been popular for decades.

Some statistics pertaining simply to gay travel services follow:

As reported in the *Philadelphia Business Journal*, a survey revealed that gay men and lesbians ventured on a staggering 162 million trips in 1996, with 127 million devoted to business trips and the remaining 35 million on vacations. More than 11 percent of gay men and about 9 percent of lesbians went on domestic vacations 10 or more times between 1992 and 1995.

The International Gay & Lesbian Travel Association (IGLTA) is a network of travel industry businesses and professionals dedicated to the support of its members who encourage gay and lesbian travel worldwide. First started in the early 1980s, its travel agent/agency members do more than $1 billion in travel businesses per year. Its guest house/hotel members transact more than $75 million annually in room revenue. By the middle 1990s, IGLTA totaled approximately 1,250 members, up from 300 in the late 1980s and 25 in 1983.

According to IGLTA, gays and lesbians spent approximately $17 billion on travel in 1996; IGLTA anticipates that figure will increase about 10 percent each year for the next several years. Gays and lesbians are also three and one half times more likely to be frequent-flyer club members than heterosexuals.

A study commissioned by *The Advocate*, a national gay magazine, reported that 72 percent of gays averaged 5.8 domestic trips in 1996. According to John D'Alessandro, president of IGLTA, "as little as three years ago we never had any special airline promotions being offered to us (IGLTA). Now we have lots of them: American Airlines, USAir, United, British Airways, Northwest...."

One more indication that many gays have much disposable income: A survey by the travel publication *Out & About* polled 1,000 of its readers at random. The results revealed that the average subscriber is 43 years old, takes an average of 8.3 business trips and 8.3 personal trips a year, and has a household income exceeding $121,000. In terms of education, 94 percent hold Bachelor degrees, 51 percent have Masters, and 22 percent have a Ph.D. or M.D. The most desired destination characteristics were relaxation potential, physical beauty, the gay scene, and arts/culture. In terms of sexual habits, nearly 60 percent of those surveyed said their amount of sexual activity did not change when traveling; 36 percent reported an increase; and 5 percent reported a decrease.

In light of such statistics, Joshua Kay, the owner of Pacific Ocean Holidays, reflected: "The one big change in the 90s is the explosion in the number of straight travel companies attempting to get into the gay market. While this has opened up a whole new plethora of choices for the gay traveler, it remains to be seen how well these companies will do, and how well served the gay traveler will be by this."

An example of the above can be found in Deborah Cloutier's Gay Adventure Travel. As Ms. Cloutier said in a 1996 *New Hampshire Business* Review, "You need a niche market. Gays, particularly male gays, often don't have kids. They usually consist of two-income, highly-educated couples with some disposable income. They also often can't go anyplace to relax and hold their partner's hand without getting an ugly stare."

Wedding Travel

As reported by Maria Torres-Kitamura in 1997 in *Hawaii Business,* law professor Jennifer Brown of Quinnipac College in Connecticut anticipated that the first state in the United States to le-

galize same-sex marriage could reap $3.4 billion in related benefits spread over the first five years of legalization. (Professor Brown's forecast speculates that only 3 percent of all Americans are gay or lesbian, gays and lesbians would marry at only one third the rate of heterosexuals, and such couples would shell out an average of $6,000 on a wedding and honeymoon.)

In light of President Clinton's signing of the Defense of Marriage Act (DOMA) in 1997 (an act of legislation that stated that no state, territory, or possession of the Untied States or Indian tribe was required to give effect to any marriage between persons of the same sex), the likelihood of nation-wide legalized same-sex marriage is remote, although a few individual states may recognize gay marriage.

Gay Marketing Expanding

Gay men in the 1990s have many new or formerly under-utilized leisure options other than travel. They include professional or recreational sports that cater to gay men at all levels of ability; literature portraying gays in flattering or at least realistic terms; and gay bars, clubs, and restaurants where patrons can openly eat, drink, and socialize.

While some of these choices existed before the Stonewall Riots of 1969, they were not generally available to gay men who did not actively seek them out. In 1997, not only have the variety of such diversions expanded, gay marketing is itself an ever-increasing niche. And with the most visible gay men typically childless, well-educated, and financially secure with much disposable income, that niche seems in no danger of extinction.

Different Hotels Treat Gays Differently

In light of the above statistics, it is easy to forget that gay and straight travelers are alike in many respects. First, most gays (whether traveling alone, in a couple, or in a group) appreciate many of the same traveling privileges that straights have taken for granted: the comfortable, double (or king-sized) bed if requested; a hotel clerk treating them with civility and discretion, not hostility or indifference; and renting a car and not needing to pay for an extra driver. (In regard to the latter: Until the middle 1990s, Avis and National Car Rental charged "Additional Driver Fees" when they applied to domestic partners, but not to legal spouses. Given the many complaints from gays and lesbians, both companies now treat gays and lesbians and married couples the same in this regard.)

By the 1990s, some hotel chains in the United States also realized that acquiring a reputation as insensitive to gays could cost them business and/or bad publicity. Conversely, a gay-hospitable hotel could increase its revenue and image. As reported in an *Out & About* article, some hotel chains, such as Outrigger, Hilton, ITT-Sheraton, Marriott, and the Kimpton Group realized that it was not enough to treat their gay guests respectfully, so they updated their own Equal Employment Opportunity clauses to include sexual orientation. Others, such as Hyatt, Ritz-Carlton, and Holiday Inn, had not. By the 1990s, Outrigger, Hilton, ITT-Sheraton, Marriott, and Hyatt all had some type of sensitivity training sessions for employees in which alternative lifestyles were addressed, among other topics.

The Gay Male Traveler with HIV/AIDS

It is reasonable to assume that there are more gay male travelers with AIDS than there are straight men, straight women, or lesbians with AIDS. With more people with AIDS living longer, healthier lives (in large part due to safer sex and protease inhibitors), there are more people traveling with AIDS.

As reported in *Out & About*'s website (http://www.outandabout.com), gay travelers have learned through their own experiences and observations that some insurance plans do not cover "pre-existing conditions." Many plans consider HIV or HIV-related illness in this category if a person has a condition that is not "stable" 60 days before the purchase of insurance. Insurers have traditionally often cited changes in medication, treatment, or illness to deny coverage to persons with HIV/AIDS.

One fortunate trend in the middle 1990s is that some major travel insurers dispensed with their pre-existing condition restrictions if the insurance had been bought within a week of first payment on a trip, and as long as the full value of the trip was covered.

Many travelers with HIV/AIDS have utilized the services of an emergency medical history and assistance company to deliver their medical history, medication, insurance information, and emergency contact information to medical care providers anywhere in the world. Such services, which usually charge a small annual fee, include: EMX Global Emergency Services, MedPass Global Emergency Medical Services, Traveler's Emergency Network, and International SOS Assistance.

Many travelers with HIV/AIDS take along intravenous paraphernalia and various medications. Domestic travelers may choose from a wide assortment of home IV therapy companies that supply medication, supplies, and nursing support at isolated locations. Some gays have spared themselves a legal nightmare by having handy a doctor's note documenting their medical needs; about two thirds of the states have either prescription or paraphernalia laws concerning possession of syringes or needles.

By the 1990s, many tourist destinations, including Chicago, Honolulu, Los Angeles, Miami/Fort Lauderdale, New York City, San Francisco, and Provincetown had started hotlines and other services to address AIDS and other health-related questions and/or provide medical referral services.

Popular Gay Tourist Destinations

The following locations represent a cross-section of preferred gay male tourist destinations. Some of them, such as Provincetown and San Francisco, have been perennial favorites for several decades; others, such as Rehoboth Beach and Denver, encountered a certain amount of homophobia in the 1980s and 1990s. In one community, Fire Island (consisting of Cherry Grove and the Pines for the purpose of this essay), some infighting among gays of different cultural dispositions culminated in the middle 1990s.

Philadelphia

Philadelphia hosted the International Gay & Lesbian Travel Association's (IGTLA) 14th Annual Convention in May 1997, a choice that might have astounded W. C. Fields, the comedian who spoke ill of the city. That Democratic, gay-friendly Mayor Ed Rendell was on hand for the festivities and more than 200 travel executives (including Virgin Atlantic, Northwest Airlines, American Airlines, United Airlines, and US Airways) attended the convention indicates how things have progressed since Fields openly disparaged Philadelphia, dogs, and babies.

Like New York and San Francisco, Philadelphia had a relatively active gay community before the Stonewall Riots of 1969. As early as 1960, the Mattachine Society (one of the first gay organizations in the United States and a forerunner of the contemporary gay liberation movement) had meetings in the Philadelphia suburb of Radnor, for which the police once arrested more than 80 people for viewing "gay films." By the middle 1960s, the Mattachine Society had formed a chapter in Philadelphia, and historian Marc Stein believed that the city then had "the most militant female and male wings of the national homophile movement."

For the latter half of the 1960s, Philadelphia gay activists protested in front of Independence Hall every July 4th. In 1975, the state of Philadelphia became the first governmental body in the nation—and worldwide—to initiate an organization to study the problems of sexual minorities. In 1976, Pennsylvania became the first state to start a Gay Pride Month. In the spirit of these milestones, Philadelphia in the early 1980s broadcast the United States' first public-service, gay-rights TV messages.

In keeping with this recent history, Philadelphia has wooed gay tourists in a multitude of ways in the 1990s. Since spring 1996, The Philadelphia Convention and Visitors Bureau has published Philadelphia Gay and Lesbian Travel News, a travel newsletter distributed to more than 1,200 IGLTA travel agents. This publication may be the first travel newsletter issued by a municipal convention and visitors organization.

Since 1996, the Philadelphia Convention and Visitors Bureau has offered two packages for gay travelers: the Philadelphia Phrolic tour and Philadelphia Phantasy. As *Out & About* travel newsletter editor Billy Kolber-Stuart commented, "Very few mainstream, big-city tour packagers do gay tours."

In 1996, The Philadelphia Museum of Art hosted a unique Cezanne retrospective exhibit. In an article from *Au Courant*, Deidre C. Wright, the Philadelphia Convention & Visitors Bureau communications associate, commented on these and other local cultural events: "These are not gay specific, certainly, but we figured the kind of audience we are targeting is a more sophisticated, more educated group who would be interested in those kinds of things, such as gourmet foods and the fine arts."

Miami

South Florida, particularly Miami, weathered (both literally and figuratively) much in the 1990s. A high rate of crime, storms and hurricanes, and Andrew Cunanan's probable murder of fashion superstar Gianni Versace in 1997 all conspired to hurt Miami Beach's reputation as a hot tourist destination. However, while the number of tourists to Dade County decreased, the number of gay male visitors swelled. And since many of them did not conceal their abundant wealth, no one visibly objected that much. In fact, one South Beach Business Guild brochure heralded Miami Beach as "the gay and lesbian destination of the nineties!"

In this climate, it's easy to forget (in fact, some gays may be too young to remember) singer Anita Bryant's well-publicized, successful effort in 1977 to repeal Dade County's gay rights ordinance. At that time, a lot of the area was economically depressed, in need of a financial and aesthetic facelift.

In large part, that facelift occurred in the 1980s and 1990s. Many gay northerners came to an area known as South Beach and gradually gentrified it. The Ocean Drive area, with its multitude of Art Deco buildings, came first; hoteliers refurbished many properties, some going back to the 1930s. Fashionable restaurants and discos followed; by the 1990s, photographers, models, and others had flocked to South Beach to unwind. Madonna spends much time in South Beach, and so do plenty of gays who worship her.

Miami Beach is the only gay resort near a major international city. With its close proximity to Miami International Airport, travel from Latin America, Europe, and the rest of the United States is quite convenient. Hence, wealthy gay foreigners, many from South and Central America, recently visited or settled in Miami Beach in record numbers.

The 1970s homophobia of Dade County has mostly subsided. A human rights ordinance was passed in 1992; Miami Beach has a gay-friendly mayor, and there are gays on the city council and on many city commissions. All of this has contributed to an atmosphere of general tolerance and informality. As Bob Guilmartin, the owner of the South Florida Hotel Network, a Miami Beach reservation service, said in a *Time* article: "People will call me and ask if we have gay hotels. I tell them, 'What do you need a gay hotel for? Everyone who works in the hotels is already gay.'"

For some, there is a downside to South Beach's vitality. For example, nightclubs often contribute to earsplitting noise and some lascivious behavior. Some Orthodox Jews have relocated elsewhere, making the atmosphere less traditionally Jewish than it once was.

Regardless, this geographical area should remain a solid gay tourist spot. As Billy Kolber-Stuart, editor of *Out and About*, says, "I would rank Miami just behind San Francisco and New York City [as a travel destination]."

Key West

Key West, Florida, the southernmost point of the continental United States, is considered a foremost domestic gay travel spot. With more than 30 guest houses on a two-mile by four-mile island, with its disproportionately large percentage of writers and artists, it's easy to forget that as late as the 1970s Key West wasn't always such a gay-friendly place to live or visit. Tennessee Williams lived there much of his adult life but often complained of homophobia and was gay-bashed at least once in Key West. However, Key West, at any time in its history, was probably less homophobic than most metropolitan areas in the United States.

Today, Key West is one of the most gay-friendly places in America, in large part because of its large gay population and because gays contributed to the lion's share of the restoration of its historic district. That gays and lesbians also contribute handsomely to Key West's tourism revenue cannot be underemphasized in this context.

AIDS has diminished much of the island's joie de vivre of the 1980s. That many gay male residents of Key West became HIV-positive and died of AIDS in the 1980s and 1990s is common knowledge. What is less well known is that scores of gay men already infected with HIV/AIDS relocated to Key West to resume their battle for survival. By the middle 1990s, the rate of HIV/AIDS infection in gay men in Key West had waned somewhat.

The silver lining in this tragedy is that many gays and lesbians—as well as gays and straights—have developed a certain affinity for each other. Key Westers seem less sexually self-conscious today, and lesbians are a much more visible force than ever before. Gays with more boisterous tastes love Key West's annual FantasyFest, always held in the last week of October. This weeklong gala includes a succession of parades, street fairs, and parties, and the infamous "Madness Ball." Another annual event that has surprisingly attracted some gay men: "Hemingway Days," which occurs in July. Here, beer guzzling, arm wrestling, and ex-

aggerated macho behavior are the norm in a celebration of Key West's favorite son.

Rehoboth Beach, Delaware

Rehoboth Beach, Delaware, may not be as obviously popular a gay tourist destination as San Francisco, but in the 1990s thousands of gay men summered there again and again. With slews of gay-owned and gay-friendly businesses, restaurants, bars, and house parties, this formerly vacant mile of oceanfront has emerged as one of the most frequented gay resorts located on the East coast.

In the late 1940s, gay men from the Mid-Atlantic states informally claimed the dunes of Whiskey Beach (later known as North Shores) as a good, secluded place for sexual encounters. Situated just north of Rehoboth in Cape Henlopen State Park, Whiskey Beach's reputation for public sex grew after the Chesapeake Bay Bridge opened in 1954.

In the late 1960s, a small gay bar called the Pink Pony opened in the vicinity. Given the emerging climate of gay liberation, many gays began frequenting it as the first bar of its kind in the area. The bar soon closed its doors, but many gays who found Rehoboth Beach enjoyed their visit and frequently came back.

In the 1970s, many more gay establishments developed, including the Nomad Village Bar and Resort and the Boathouse. The former represented the first exclusively gay business situated on the Delaware coast; the latter capitalized on the national disco craze starting in the middle 1970s.

Although such popular gay establishments as The Renegade (a dance club and hotel) and The Blue Moon (a bar and restaurant) thrived there in the 1980s, Rehoboth was hardly free from homophobia. With the increasing visibility of gays, a straight backlash began; throughout that decade, the Rehoboth Board of Commissioners considered many suggestions to keep gays from vacationing there. Cars with bumper stickers trumpeting "Keep Rehoboth a Family Town" were common. Rocks and other foreign objects were sometimes hurled at gay men who patronized The Blue Moon and The Renegade.

Despite such homophobia, more gays spent at least part of their summers in Rehoboth, and more gay-owned restaurants and dance clubs emerged in the 1980s and 1990s. Gay volleyball players and sunbathers discovered the deserted Carpenter's Beach. In 1991, Rehoboth's gay community organization, CAMP Rehoboth, began. By 1995 there were three gossip columns targeting the gay social scene.

Despite the increasing gay-friendly atmosphere of Rehoboth, there were some turbulent incidents in the 1990s. For example, in 1991, a gay man went into the ocean naked. Lifeguards reacted by radioing the police, who arrested the man as many gay bystanders observed the scene. The police anticipated violence from the gays who had witnessed the arrest and ordered everyone off the beach. Some men who refused to do so were arrested, but charges were dropped. To prevent similar incidents from happening, the police department's new chief offers gay sensitivity training.

In a June 1994 incident, police arrested a gay man outside a local gay bar for making too much noise. The gay community took offense. That year, the city council candidate who actively courted the gay vote won by the largest margin. In 1995, the five candidates who ran for city council all wooed the gay population. In light of the speculation that Rehoboth is only 10 percent gay, these developments attest to the pervasive influence of gays in the area.

Santa Fe/Taos, New Mexico

In the early years of the 20th century, affluent fathers often sent their homosexual and/or effeminate sons to Santa Fe to develop whatever artistic/literary talents they might possess. Sometimes the families had an ulterior motive: to keep their offspring away. In Santa Fe's dry, clean climate offering tremendous privacy, it was a relaxed lifestyle for most of the sons; some of them even turned into genuine artists. Gradually, Santa Fe attracted more talented persons and fewer dilettantes—unless the latter had great wealth at their disposal.

While Santa Fe tempted gay, artistic men over the course of the 20th century, lesbians, New Agers, hippies, and athletes more often explored its neighbor, Taos. As late as the early 1980s, the stereotype dictated that lesbians who visited New Mexico usually ended up in Taos, and their male counterparts settled on Santa Fe. Since then, there has been more intermingling between gays and lesbians. Both cities have much in common: large Hispanic and Native American populations; ample opportunities for hiking and skiing; high desert; authentic Southwestern restaurants; and upscale art galleries.

What neither city has, despite their many gay and lesbian visitors and permanent residents, is a reputation as a genuine gay resort. However, their respective omissions from that category do not render them homophobic hotbeds of activity. Simply, many of the tourists who visit Santa Fe and/or Taos (as well as much of the gay population there) enjoy the seclusion of the environment and are not necessarily there to carve out a gay niche.

To some extent, it is a matter of economics. While places such as Key West and Provincetown have numerous business establishments that cater almost exclusively to a gay and lesbian clientele, Taos and Santa Fe's relatively high cost of living makes them more dependent on mainstream tourism. A case in point: Santa Fe, which is a more costly place than Taos, had one gay disco, The Edge, which began marketing itself as a "straight" business in April 1995 to make enough money to stay in business. In the fall of 1995, a new gay disco opened.

No bed and breakfasts in the downtown vicinity classify themselves as "gay," a tradition that doesn't seem likely to change anytime in the near future. Owners of these establishments may not be homophobic at all; it's more likely that if their business were thought of as "gay-friendly," they would risk alienating straight customers with families. However, a few guest houses opened on the outskirts of town in 1997. In 1995, Santa Fe had its first lesbian, gay, and bisexual film festival.

An apolitical atmosphere characterizes much of Taos. For example, in the early 1990s, a gay pride rally occurred on the Plaza in Taos. Although some gays and lesbians volunteered stories about their sexual orientation, the audience largely reacted with apathy. Why? People in Taos generally take diversity and tolerance for granted but don't choose to talk about it.

Denver

In the 1980s, gays visited Denver, Colorado, for many of the same reasons that straights did—primarily the skiing, secondarily the art museums and galleries, and theaters. That this city of more than two million people also had several gay bars, gay-owned restaurants, and Cheeseman Park for car cruising were gravy to gay tourism. While Denver never developed into a gay resort town of Provincetown or Key West proportions, neighborhoods around

Capitol Hill and South Broadway acquired a certain reputation for gay hospitality.

On 3 November 1992, Colorado voters passed the explosive Amendment 2 to their state constitution. This amendment forbade all levels of government from enacting any statute giving homosexuals or bisexuals as a class "minority status, quota preferences, protected status or claim of discrimination." Essentially, Colorado became the first state in the United States to legalize discrimination against gays, lesbians, and bisexuals at the ballot box. Amendment 2 drew extensive national coverage, a lawsuit was filed on behalf of opponents to the amendment, other states considered passing similar amendments, and the "Colorado Boycott" began.

The organizers of "Boycott Colorado" committed to the repeal of Amendment 2 and advocated a complete ban of the state, including travel, tourism, goods, and services. At the suggestion of New York City Council member Thomas K. Duane, then New York City mayor David N. Dinkins issued an official ban on all city travel to Colorado while Amendment 2 was in effect. By June 1993, more than 60 companies had canceled conventions or meetings in Colorado, and more than 100 groups nationwide had signed the boycott. An article in *Modern Times* placed the minimum amount of monetary damage due to canceled convention business within Denver at $45.7 million by October 1993. Countless gays and lesbians canceled their leisure trips to Colorado, and a smaller number ceased all business with Colorado companies.

By 1994, much Colorado business had returned to normal. In part, that can be attributed to Colorado judge Jeffrey Bayliss's decision to put a restraining order on the state of Colorado, preventing it from enforcing Amendment 2. Although Colorado continued to have impressive skiing seasons in the aftermath of the boycott, its convention bookings dropped.

In May 1996, The U.S. Supreme Court struck down Amendment 2. While its memory lingers in Denver, the Colorado boycott is over and a relative tranquility has permeated the gay community there. To a gay visitor, Denver in 1997 may seem more like Denver in the 1980s than in the early 1990s.

Provincetown

Provincetown, Massachusetts, is arguably America's gayest resort town, and in fact may have earned that distinction long ago. By the 1920s, Provincetown (or "P-town," as it is commonly known) no longer commanded a solid fishing or whaling niche. However, at least six art schools dominated this relatively small locale (one of the farthest eastern points in the United States), and the Provincetown Art Association opened its first exhibits. On the theatrical front, the Provincetown Players, America's first theater company, produced some early plays of Eugene O'Neill and Edna St. Vincent Millay.

By this time, Provincetown had acquired a reputation as a refuge for artistic folk, and tourism became a considerable source of revenue. Gay men also discovered the dunes as a great place for public sex. Hundreds of painters, writers, musicians, and others rented rooms on Provincetown, and their presence contributed to a thriving arts (and gay) community.

Over the course of the next several decades, many of the most creative Americans visited Provincetown at least periodically, including Truman Capote, Tennessee Williams, Norman Mailer, Charles Demuth, Edward Hopper, Paul and Jane Bowles, Robert Motherwell (who died there), Hans Hofman, and Mark Rothko.

Provincetown gradually acquired a reputation for unconventional, even bizarre, people and behavior; however, gays and straights mixed well in the climate of sexual diversity and tolerance. And while many gays still escape to Provincetown to pursue creative endeavors, many arrive to relax part of the time. Although Provincetown's year-round population was about 3,500 in 1997, as many as 50,000 tourists may spend a weekend there.

As lesbian comedian Suzanne Westenhoefer wrote in a column for *The Advocate*, "But to get a good community mix (including straight folks) and more value for your gay dollar, you can't beat the tip of the cape."

She continues: "Every summer I watch literally tens of thousands of gays and lesbians come into P-town and leave their closeted lives behind them. In a matter of hours, you can watch people who normally wouldn't even look at their lovers a certain way while in public strolling down Commercial Street."

As Westenhoefer points out, Provincetown gays and lesbians outnumber straights by a wide margin. Hence, the vast majority of restaurants, bars, and businesses service gays and are gay-owned. In this atmosphere, gay-bashing happens very infrequently; when it does, the police react without bias for or against gays.

Another indication of how Provincetown is more gay-friendly than nearly every other gay resort town in the United States: as early as 1978, the Provincetown Business Guild (PBG) was formed to promote gay and lesbian tourism. By 1997, more than 200 businesses belonged to it. While Provincetown locals often perceive gays who visit the Cape as wealthier than lesbian tourists (in keeping with national trends), businesses there generally treat both—and straights—equally.

Fire Island, New York

Cherry Grove and The Pines, for most practical purposes, comprise "gay Fire Island." The evolution of Cherry Grove can be traced back to 1869, the year in which Archie Perkinson purchased a mile of East End beach for 25 cents a foot. Perkinson named this stretch of land "Cherry Grove" for its seemingly endless expanse of wild black cherry trees. He and his wife relocated to a cabin there; its former occupant was supposedly a pirate.

Cherry Grove's population remained fairly stable until the hurricane of 1938 wreaked havoc, rendering many mainland families unable or unwilling to rebuild their homes. In the aftermath of the destruction, wealthy Manhattanites of all sexual orientations, many of whom worked in the theater in some capacity, discovered Cherry Grove. Some of them were Greta Garbo, Paulette Goddard, Pola Negri, Earl Blackwell, and Arlene Francis.

For many years, Duffy's Hotel, built in 1930, symbolized the heart of social life in Cherry Grove. Catering to locals and visitors who enjoyed good cuisine and dancing to a nickelodeon's music, the Duffy Hotel was once the only place on Cherry Grove with electricity and a phone. The Hotel, destroyed in a fire in 1956, periodically resisted some of Cherry Grove's increasingly gay flamboyance; for example, at one time it banned same-sex dancing in the hotel until after midnight. Even so, for several decades, Cherry Grove may have been the only resort town in the United States with a substantial gay majority.

At exactly which point Cherry Grove acquired its reputation as a world-famous gay resort is impossible to pinpoint. However, one milestone in the development occurred when the English writers Christopher Isherwood and W. H. Auden in the late 1930s attended a masquerade party as Dionysus and Ganymede.

Fire Island has been a gay male gathering place for decades.

Since the middle 1940s, the Arts Project of Cherry Grove (APCG) has symbolized the spirit of gay pride, creativity, and camaraderie. Comprised of both locals and tourists, the APCG sponsors three productions each season. In collaboration with the Cherry Grove Property Owners Association (CGPOA), the APCG turns over the revenue from its fundraising events to the Cherry Grove community for such purposes as painting boardwalks, shoring up the dunes, and subsidizing the community doctor.

While Cherry Grove's population is and has been predominantly gay for some time, it is diverse in other ways—gender, race, age, and lifestyle. Generally, its residents and tourists are less muscled, less fashion-conscious, and older than those of its neighbor, the Pines. Another crucial distinction: roughly half the population of Cherry Grove has been lesbian in the middle 1990s, whereas the Pines is mostly gay male. Given such longstanding traditions as the yearly crowning of the (often male) Homecoming Queen, Cherry Grove has also attracted many drag queens since the 1960s. Since the 1980s, Cherry Grove has sponsored many small-scale AIDS and gay-rights benefits.

While Cherry Grove and the Pines are physically separated by a modest expanse of forest and a stretch of white beach, the two communities appeal to very different populations for reasons elaborated above. As a rule of thumb, the Pines seems fairly homogeneous: white, wealthy, gay male, athletic. The following superficialities have characterized the Pines for quite a while: cutoff denims; work boots; Armani sunglasses; shirtless, often hairy chests; and shopping bags from upscale food shops such as Zabar's.

Since the 1980s, the Pines has also acquired a reputation for hot sex, cruising, and marathon partying—sometimes to the disapproval of Cherry Grove. In August 1995, Hurricane Felix's wrath threatened to cancel The Gay Men's Health Crisis (GMHC) Annual Morning Party, to be held in the Pines. In the aftermath of its destruction, Felix had washed about $500,000 worth of sand back into the Atlantic Ocean. It seemed there was no real beach in the Pines to have one of the wildest, most awaited gay dance parties in the United States, an occasion that drew gays from as far away as West Hollywood, California, and Switzerland.

The National Park Service at the Fire Island National Seashore issued a permit to have the party in Cherry Grove that year, because Hurricane Felix had done less damage to Cherry Grove's drier, more expansive beach than to the Pines' beach. The Cherry Grove Property Owners' Association board also approved the change of location. However, many Cherry Grove residents who knew firsthand of the Morning Party's reputation for rampant drug use and unsafe sex were enraged. They confronted the GMHC volunteers in the midst of party preparation, many threatening to vandalize the occasion if it did not move back to the Pines. Some protesters said they would cut the cables for the electric generators if the party took place on Cherry Grove.

As reported by David Groff in *New York* magazine, Lyn Hutton, chief of the Cherry Grove volunteer fire department, said that she opposed the party for environmental reasons, not ideological ones. Given the delicate condition of the Grove's dunes, she said, "The last thing we needed was 8,000 feet walking around on our dunes and beach."

In the end, the Morning party relocated to the Pines. About 4,500 gay men and a minuscule number of straights and lesbians attended. In the wake of the party, the National Park Rangers issued only ten citations, one for walking in the dunes, five for urinating in the dunes, four for drug use.

Since the Morning party incident, many residents of the Pines and Cherry Grove have been on shaky terms. On a bright note, the Morning Party grossed about $350,000, some of it earmarked for GMHC's Substance Use Counseling and Education Department.

New Orleans

Gay tourists have long popularized New Orleans for its large and fairly open gay population, its relatively gay-friendly climate, and, certainly, its festive Mardi Gras tradition. (Literally meaning "Fat Tuesday," Mardi Gras is the day before Ash Wednesday, the first day of Lent.) However, starting in the 1980s, a series of new festivities lured large numbers of gay travelers into the city of many nicknames ("the Big Easy," "Crescent City," and "The Northernmost Coast of Central America").

One of the most successful gay-themed events is the New Orleans Annual Halloween Party, which started in the early 1980s as a one-night fundraiser for Lazarus House, a local AIDS hospice. By 1997, the Halloween Party had expanded into a large-scale event, beginning the weekend before Halloween, culminating in a Saturday night costume ball, and ending the following Sunday with a typically enormous New Orleans brunch.

In 1994, the Halloween Party raised about $160,000; in 1996, it brought in about $240,000. In addition to benefiting Lazarus House, the Halloween Party contributes to the revenues of hotels, restaurants, nightclubs, and retail businesses in New Orleans. However, it is difficult to quantify its impact.

Another gay-themed event, Southern Decadence, also focuses on a costume party theme. The evolution of Southern Decadence can be traced back to the early 1970s, when a group of persons from different backgrounds living in the French Quarter of New Orleans partied together, sometimes in drag, the Sunday before Labor Day. By the 1980s, Southern Decadence's theme was similar, but the occasion attracted many more people (mostly gay men) in even more outrageous garb.

Ironically, despite the long-term success of both events, many straight people in New Orleans hardly knew of their existence. However, both occasions have captured national attention among many gay organizations outside New Orleans.

Given that trend of increasing gay recognition, Larry Bagneris, Jr., of the Louisiana Lesbian & Gay Political Action Caucus (Lagpac) and other gay activists in New Orleans want the city to start spending some of its annual $3 million tourism marketing budget on local gay events. As reported by Keith Darce in *New Orleans City Business*, Lagpac, in collaboration with the Lesbian, Gay & Bisexual Life at Tulane University, surveyed about 2,000 gay tourists who visited New Orleans. The survey asked tourists such questions as why they came to New Orleans and how much money they planned to spend on their trip. Initial results indicated that gay tourists from many different economic and geographical backgrounds come to New Orleans to enjoy such gay-sponsored events as the Halloween Party and Southern Decadence.

Given the normally festive ambience of New Orleans, it is not surprising that many straights in New Orleans at one time perceived gay men as party ornaments and figures of camp. One such stereotype was the bachelor uncle: overly articulate, fussy, giddy, maybe a secret cross-dresser. Since New Orleans always celebrated people and things outside the norm, straights could accept gays if they camped it up on appropriate occasions.

But with so many gay men in New Orleans having died from AIDS in the 1980s and the 1990s, the number of gay krewes (secret societies that thrive on parties and parades during Mardi Gras) receded. Some of the city's joviality—and stereotyping—also diminished. In light of the AIDS epidemic, many straights in New Orleans started to understand the serious side of gays as normal people capable of suffering with dignity, not simply the products of swish and self-mockery.

San Francisco

For many gay men, San Francisco will always represent America's gay mecca. Of course, many of the city's greatest pleasures—splendid restaurants, roller coaster terrain, breathtaking architecture, and excellent and varied shopping opportunities—are open to people of any sexual orientation. What makes San Francisco one of the gayest places on the planet is its loose, vibrant atmosphere. It is also possibly the American city with the most adult-oriented enticements.

During World War II, San Francisco exploded with naval men, and the Polk Gulch neighborhood accommodated many of them with male prostitutes and hidden gay clubs. By the 1950s, the Mattachine Society was making a name for itself in the city, and

Events like the Folsom Street Fair, which attracts leather-bound revelers like the two men pictured here, help San Francisco maintain its reputation as a gay male mecca.

some fairly covert gay bars were in operation, although their owners (in pre-Stonewall times) usually bribed the police to stay in business.

During the 1960s, the San Francisco Police Department (SFPD) and the swelling gay population were frequently at odds. To justify their strong-arm methods of dealing with often-flamboyant gays, the SFPD once claimed that about 70,000 gays and lesbians lived in San Francisco and threatened the orderliness of the city. The police's speculation had the opposite effect of what it intended: now many gays and lesbians elsewhere came to San Francisco because it was suddenly the best place to show one's gayness.

By the 1970s, the formerly working-class Castro area became one of the most visible and flamboyantly gay ghettos in the world. By the end of the decade, mostly gay, middle-class men settled there; one of the most famous was the gay activist and camera shop owner Harvey Milk, who eventually was elected San Francisco's first openly gay supervisor.

In 1978, former city supervisor Dan White assassinated San Francisco's gay-friendly mayor George Moscone and supervisor Milk. In May 1979, White was sentenced to a prison term of only eight years, with parole possible after five years. Immediately following this verdict, countless enraged gays rioted in the streets, causing roughly one million dollars in damage, which included burning eleven police cars.

AIDS took an extremely heavy toll in San Francisco in the 1980s and 1990s, and no neighborhood suffered more psychologically and in terms of numbers than Castro. While the devastation of the epidemic is apparent throughout San Francisco, the city has retained much of its vitality and charm from the 1970s.

What distinguishes gay San Francisco in the late 1990s from gay San Francisco of the 1970s is its heterogeneity, particularly in the Castro neighborhood. Once comprised predominantly of middle- and upper-middle-class gay men, Castro now has persons of many socioeconomic classes, including lesbians. There are many more women-owned businesses in San Francisco today, and countless lesbians and straight women have devoted themselves to combating AIDS through their volunteer work, rallies, and fundraising. Ironically, many San Francisco neighborhoods that did not have a lot of visible gays and lesbians in the 1970s do today.

GAY MALE LEISURE

Gay Bars

Gay bars have occupied a fairly prominent niche as one aspect of gay life since the 1940s. For many gay men coming out in the 1970s and earlier, there were a limited variety of places (e.g., bars, nightclubs, discos, and bathhouses) where men could pick up or socialize with other gay men. These environments often revolved around alcohol and/or drugs, cruising, and casual sex.

To some gay men and straights, gay bars represent the worst stereotype of gay culture: a metaphor for promiscuous, self-destructive, irresponsible behavior. To others, they seem an invaluable part of gay life: an obvious place to meet and/or pick up men, a refuge from the straight-dominated culture, a place to be yourself or to pretend to be someone else.

With so few places where gay men could openly congregate until the 1970s, countless gay men frequented gay bars for picking up men, and many became infected with HIV/AIDS in the 1980s. Although gay men today have more leisure options, gay bars are still a popular choice, partly because they cover such a kaleidoscopic range: leather bars; dance bars; hustler bars; yuppie bars; piano bars; bars that cater to ethnic groups (e.g. Black, Latino, Asian).

During World War II, gay soldiers, sailors, and other servicemen on leave found bars and parks where men cruised each other; among the most famous American cities for such behavior were New York, San Francisco, New Orleans, and San Diego. Allan Berube, in his book *Coming Out under Fire*, wrote about New York City's Astor Bar as one example of such a place that fueled endless one-night stands and relaxed the tension of the war for many gay soldiers and civilians. (Supposedly, gays and straights coexisted nicely at the Astor Bar, with one side of the room holding the straights, the other side lined up with gays.)

Berube believes that in the early and middle 1940s, gay bars (although not usually labeled that then) had turned into the nucleus of gay life in America. More establishments accommodating gay GIs and civilians opened, and "a process of multiplication and specialization developed," in which, according to Berube, different bars enticed different personalities. Novelist John Horne Burns once said that the bars in Washington, D.C., included "the Brilliant Crowd, the Swishy Crowd, the Empire Builders, and the Drugstore Cowboys."

However, it would be erroneous to assume that gay bars operated openly before the New York City Stonewall Riots. It would be equally erroneous to assume that gay men did not put themselves at a certain amount of risk by frequenting them. Neil Miller, in *Out of the Past: Gay and Lesbian History from 1869 to the Present,* provided one of many examples: In the aftermath of the 1959 mayoral campaign, the San Francisco police began a three-year campaign of harassment against gay bars in the city. In the mayoral election, the challenger, city assessor Russell Wolden, claimed that incumbent mayor George Christopher had turned San Francisco into "The national headquarters of the organized homosexuals in the United States." Wolden's attacks failed, and he lost the election.

But after Christopher was re-elected, he did not want to appear "soft" on "sex deviates," so he instructed the police to ferret out as many gay bars as they could. By October 1961, the California Alcohol Beverage Commission had revoked the licenses of a dozen San Francisco gay bars. Misdemeanor charges against men and women caught in raids on gay bars often averaged as many as 60 per week.

Officially, in New York City in the middle 1960s, the State Liquor Authority was authorized to close bars and other establishments that served homosexuals. As reported by Miller, to test these regulations, Dick Leitsch and Craig Rodwell, two Mattachine members, invited some members of the press on a "sip-in" of Greenwich Village, a neighborhood in New York City with gay residents and tourists. Leitsch, Rodwell, and other Mattachine members went to a Howard Johnson restaurant, told a manager that they were gay and wanted service; he responded "How do I know you're homosexuals?" Since the manager thought they seemed like "perfect gentlemen," he told a waiter to bring them drinks.

But things turned out differently at the gay bar Julius, in which the bartender refused to serve the men drinks after they announced their sexual orientation. Mattachine filed a complaint with the State Liquor Authority against the bar for discrimination. About a year later, the state appellate court finally ruled that the State Liquor Authority could only revoke a bar's license if some evidence of indecent behavior was verified. An establishment could not deny a drink to a gay man or lesbian just because of his/her sexual orientation.

Stonewall and Disco

These are just two incidents out of hundreds, maybe thousands, of similar incidents for gay men and lesbians who patronized gay bars. But then the Stonewall Riots occurred. This occasion for many people marked the start of gay liberation, and the mood of gay festive defiance quickly spread to other cities. Exactly what caused so many gays (many of them drag queens) to physically and mentally explode at this point in history may never be completely understood, but one thing is clear: after so many decades of oppression and silence, gays and lesbians had finally reached a breaking point.

Like the Stonewall Riots, disco music also transformed the realm of gay bars and clubs in the 1970s. It originated in some of New York City's small black gay clubs; according to Anthony Thomas in an *OUT/LOOK* article, deejays in these clubs "overlapped soul and Philly (Philadelphia International) records, phasing them in and out to form uninterrupted soundtracks for non-stop dancing." Before the middle 1970s, white gay bars had relied more on popular black music for atmosphere than on the rock and roll music that white straight bars favored. By 1975, the disco fever phenomenon overtook most white gay bars, fewer black gay bars, and very few straight bars of any variety. A few years later, some disco songs by such singers as Gloria Gaynor and Donna Summer became mainstream hits.

While disco did not have complicated lyrics, seldom tackled real social issues, and often ignored gay-related topics, the music struck at the sensibility of many gay men who worshiped such divas as Billie Holiday, Diana Ross, Gloria Gaynor, and Donna Summer. (Summer later lost her gay following after she became a born-again Christian and supposedly said that God had infected gays with AIDS to punish them for their promiscuous behavior.) A successful musical group called the Village People, consisting of six male performers, contributed some fairly gay-specific music, including "YMCA" and "Macho Man."

By the late 1970s, some straights patronized white gay bars for their disco music—a trend formerly unknown in the world of dingy, hidden-away gay establishments. Gays had become trendsetters in music and dance.

Dancing, including the country-and-western line dancing variety, continues to be a popular gay male leisure activity.

The Gay Party Scene

As reported by Alan Brown in an *Out & About* article from 1997, the variety of new dance music (e.g., house, techno, rap, disco) since the movie *Saturday Night Fever*'s release had fused into a national—and international—gay party circuit. Since 1992, many gay party fundraisers have been held, including Steel Party (Pittsburgh, Pennsylvania), Cherry Jubilee (Washington, D.C.), and Fire & Ice (Phoenix, Arizona). The Black and Blue Party (Montreal, Canada) attracted 8,000 visitors in 1996, a record.

However, the nonprofit groups that sponsor such events are concerned with the increasing amount of recreational drug usage, particularly among young men, at these occasions. While criticism of this trend could force cancellation of some dance parties, demand for smaller, private parties (e.g., LAone, Afterglow, Phoenix Rising) may also increase. Some party promoters are working out guidelines for safer, less-crowded daytime gatherings. Brown in his article anticipates that less sexual homogeneity and more diversity will dominate these parties.

Since the 1970s, gay bars, other clubs, and the gay party circuit as openly run establishments have existed as a staple feature of gay life in the United States. Many young men who frequent them don't realize that earlier generations of gays either did not have access to them or took risks to enjoy them. While these establishments represent only one aspect of gay life and many gays are not drawn to them, that so many establishments have been transformed from covert, seedy places into thriving, visible businesses cannot be taken for granted.

Public Sex

According to Allan Berube in *The Guide*, the awareness that American men were having sex in semi-public spaces can be traced back to the 1880s. Many different sources—including medical, legal, and military—document these encounters. Among the endless locations in the United States that attracted this kind of activity were: Lafayette Square in Washington, D.C.; Central Park and Riverside Drive in New York City; The Common, Public Garden, and Esplanade in Boston; Bughouse Square and Union Station in Chicago; Ferry Building and Union Square in San Francisco; and YMCAs in most cities.

Bathhouses as generally asexual institutions can be traced back to the 1890s. Early gay bathhouses started in the 1920s. In the latter, sex was allowed in closed cubicles. Vice squads occasionally raided these places; if their owners were wealthy enough they could bribe the police not to reveal their patrons' identity. Many of the men who frequented gay bathhouses found them preferable to cruising in parks and other public places.

By the 1950s, the modern gay bathhouses that catered to an exclusively gay clientele emerged. After the Stonewall Riots of 1969, more bathhouses opened their doors in the spirit of gay liberation. Also, in the post-Stonewall mood, these institutions did not always conceal their whereabouts; many operated openly. By the late 1970s, numerous bathhouses included video rooms where patrons could masturbate while viewing sex videos.

While gay bathhouses became known for their availability of sex, many also included some social activities. For example, the Continental Baths in New York City included entertainment from such luminaries as Bette Midler, Barry Manilow, John Davidson, and Tiny Tim. Some bathhouses regularly showed such campy movies as *The Women* to its patrons. Gymnasiums and workout rooms were built into some bathhouses. The St. Marks Baths in New York even had a voter registration drive on its premises in the 1980s.

Somewhat ironically, in the 1970s, some bathhouses provided confidential testing for venereal disease (nobody had heard of AIDS then). By the 1980s, many bathhouses also distributed safe sex paraphernalia.

Throughout the rest of the 1980s and into the 1990s, however, cities began cracking down on bathhouses, in large part because of AIDS and often with the support of many gays and lesbians. In 1995, the New York City Council passed an anti-sex zoning law without precedent. Republican Mayor Rudolph Giuliani also has sworn to enforce New York's health code, which forbids any sexual activity—or anything that a health inspector could construe as sexual activity—in public spaces, including porn theaters, bar backrooms, and sex clubs. The bathhouses that survive this transformation will probably need to monitor the behavior of their patrons much more severely than they did formerly.

Not all gay activists disapprove of New York City's tougher sex laws. Michelangelo Signorile and Gabriel Rotello, both of whom have written for *The Advocate* and other publications, believe bathhouses, backroom bars, and similar sexually charged environments are unhealthy climates—physically and psychologically. The somewhat radical gay activist group ACT UP disagrees.

Gay Sports

Traditionally, many sports had a heterosexual connotation to gay men; in this arena, they had few, if any, visible role models. Some gays took the extreme position of not participating in or watching any sports, because they had painful high school memories of being taunted for their lack of athletic prowess. Many other gay men engaged in some recreational or professional sports but remained firmly closeted in that environment. If such restraint sounds excessive by the standards of the 1990s, we must remember that both Glenn Burke, a major league baseball outfielder, and Dave Pallone, an outstanding umpire, both lost their positions when rumors of their homosexuality surfaced.

The first professional gay male athlete to come out voluntarily was David Kopay, a professional running back who played for such teams as the San Francisco Forty-Niners, the Detroit Lions, the Washington Redskins, the New Orleans Saints, and the Green Bay Packers. He announced his sexual orientation in a *Washing-*

ton Star article in 1975. For the next two decades, virtually all professional gay male athletes remained closeted, but amateur gay male athletes increasingly found outlets for their sports interests. By the early 1990s, when Olympic diver Greg Louganis came out as both a gay man and a person infected with the AIDS virus, there were many organized sports for gay men to engage in or watch. Gay bowling leagues, hiking, rodeos, skydiving, baseball, football, and soccer were just a few of the choices.

The Gay Games, founded by Dr. Thomas Waddell (a former Olympic decathlete) in 1982, opened up possibilities that most gay men had enjoyed only vicariously. The Games occur every four years and cover such sports as billiards, bodybuilding, swimming, and many others. The first Gay Games took place in San Francisco in 1982 and featured about 3,500 athletes from 37 states and 17 nations; the most recent Gay Games was held in New York City and included 15,000 athletes and 500,000 spectators.

The U.S. Olympic Committee sued the Gay Games to prevent the latter from using the name "Gay Olympics." In 1987, the U.S. Supreme Court ruled 5 to 4 to forbid the Gay Games from the use of the term "Gay Olympics."

Gay Rodeo

One of the more unusual of the gay alternatives to straight sporting is gay rodeo. In October 1976, the National Reno Gay Rodeo began as a means to raise funds for muscular dystrophy. In 1981, the Colorado Gay Rodeo Association started. By 1985, the umbrella group International Gay Rodeo Association (IGRA) was formed.

By the early 1990s, there were 12 gay rodeos in 11 states, with roughly 36,000 daytime spectators and more than 70,000 evening spectators. The Miller Brewing Company was impressed enough with these numbers to become IGRA's first corporate sponsor. Later in the 1990s, IGRA became a genuinely international organization when the Northwest Gay Rodeo added British Columbia, Canada, as a member.

Gay Literature

Gay writers writing on gay topics is, in and of itself, nothing new in the 1990s. Since the 1940s and even earlier, many extremely talented gay writers—Tennessee Williams, Truman Capote, Edward Albee, James Baldwin, Edmund White, John Rechy, Gore Vidal, Lanford Wilson, and countless others have dominated the literary scene. Some directly targeted homosexual topics in their work, others referred to them obliquely, others did not tackle them at all.

However, as a generalization before the 1980s, when gay or straight writers included some discussion of homosexuality in their work, they seldom conveyed a tone of pride: homosexuality was a problem, an embarrassment, a lingering sense of guilt, a shame. Gore Vidal's *The City and The Pillar*; James Baldwin's *Giovanni's Room*; Truman Capote's *Other Rooms, Other Voices*; and many plays of Tennessee Williams, in varying degrees, conveyed aspects of the above. These works, at the time they were published and long after, often did capture the despair and confusion of many gay men; what they didn't do much was communicate the potential for pride and fulfillment.

But by the early 1980s, with such novels as Andrew Holleran's *Dancer from the Dance* and Edmund White's *A Boy's Own Story*, the gay literary landscape changed somewhat. Publishers now realized that a considerable gay male population enjoyed gay fiction about subjects familiar to them. This market also wanted something more: stories that conveyed the positive end of the gay spectrum: the pride, boldness, joie de vive, and casualness without guilt. In this atmosphere, writers such David Leavitt, Armistead Maupin, Stephen McCauley, and Christopher Bram thrived. And editor George Stambolian in his popular *Men on Men* anthologies often published the stories of talented gay authors who had not become famous yet.

For many gay men, reading had become a less-passive activity by the 1990s, in that gay community centers now had book clubs to discuss gay and other books.

More Options in the 1990s

In the late 1990s, gay men still rely on many of the same places for safe or unsafe sex, and most now understand, to some extent, that certain types of gay sex (most often, anal transmission) increase the chances of being infected with HIV/AIDS. What distinguishes the 1990s from the 1970s (and to a lesser extent the 1990s from the 1980s) is the endless assortment of gay leisure activities that do not rely on sex or drugs.

REFERENCES:

Lesbian Travel and Leisure: Books

Cruikshank, Margaret. *The Gay and Lesbian Liberation Movement.* New York: Routledge, 1992.

Damron Women's Traveller 1997. Damron: San Francisco, 1997.

Faderman, Lillian. *Odd Girls and Twilight Lovers*. New York: Penguin, 1992.

Ingram, Gordon Brent, Anne-Marie Bouthillette, and Yolanda Retter. *Queer in Space: Communities/Public Places/Sites of Resistance*. Seattle: Bay Press, 1997.

Inn Places: Worldwide Gay & Lesbian Accommodations Guide. Phoenix: Ferrari, 1997.

Kennedy, Elizabeth Lapovsky and Madeline D. Davis. *Boots of Leather, Slippers of Gold: The History of a Lesbian Community*. New York: Routledge, 1993.

The Lesbian Almanac. Berkley Books: New York, 1996.

Penelope, Julia, and Susan J. Wolfe, eds. *Lesbian Culture—An Anthology: The Lives, Work, Ideas, Art and Visions of Lesbians Past and Present*. Freedom, California: The Crossing Press, 1993.

Witt, Lynn, Sherry Thomas, and Eric Marcus, eds. *Out in All Directions: A Treasury of Gay and Lesbian America*. New York: Warner Books, 1995.

Zepatos, Thalia. *Adventures in Good Company: The Complete Guide to Women's Tours and Outdoor Trips*. Portland: The Eighth Mountain Press, 1994.

Zipter, Yvonne. *Diamonds Are A Dyke's Best Friend*. Ithaca: Firebrand Books, 1988.

Gay Male Travel and Leisure: Books

Berube, Allan. *Coming Out under Fire.* New York: The Free Press, 1990.

Collins, Andrew. *Fodor's Gay Guide to the USA*. New York: Fodor's Travel Publications, 1996.

Miller, Neil. *Out of the Past: Gay and Lesbian History from 1869 to the Present.* New York: Vintage Books, 1995.

Lesbian Travel and Leisure: Periodical Articles

Armstrong, Toni, Jr. "Redwood Records: More than Just 'Holly's Label,'" in *Hot Wire,* vol. 2, July 1986: 26-35.

———. "National Women's Music Festival: Showcase 1988," in *Hot Wire,* vol. 5, January 1989: 26-27, 58.

———. "Anniversary Weekend: Olivia Turns Twenty," in *Hot Wire,* vol. 10, January 1994: 24-26, 46-47, 62.

Armstrong, Toni, Jr., Sara Cytron, Harriet Malinowitz, Laura Post, Sandy Ramsey and Suzanne Westenhoefer. "The Mainstreaming of Women's Music and Culture," in *Hot Wire,* vol. 10, May 1994: 32-35, 44-46; vol. 10, September 1994: 42-43, 68-69.

Brody, Michael. "Mountain Moving Coffeehouse: Twenty Years of Entertainment for Women and Children," in *Hot Wire,* vol. 10, September 1994: 56-57, 61.

Corrigan, Theresa. "Feminist Bookstores: Part of an Ecosystem," in *WLW Journal,* vol. 16, Winter 1993-94: 3-5.

Crow, Margie, Margaret Devoe, Madeline Janover, and Fran Moira. "The Muses of Olivia: Our Own Economy, Our Own Song," in *Off Our Backs,* vol. 4, August/September 1974: 2-3.

Dlugacz, Judy. "If It Weren't for the Music: 15 Years of Olivia Records," in *Hot Wire,* vol. 4, July 1988: 28-31, 52; vol. 5, January 1989: 20-23.

Edelman, Sue. "Olivia Records Celebrates 15 Years," in *Sojourner,* vol. 13, April 1988: 33-34.

Elias, Ellen. "West Coast Women's Music & Comedy Festival," in *Hot Wire,* vol. 2, March 1986: 36-37.

Guse, C. W. "The Music Industry Conference: Third Annual Gathering at National Women's Music Festival," in *Hot Wire,* vol. 6, September 1990: 40-42.

Harper, Jorjet. "Southern: The 'Live and Let Live Festival,'" in *Hot Wire,* vol. 6, September 1990: 40-42.

———. "The 1990 AWMAC Conference," in *Hot Wire,* vol. 6, May 1990: 34-35, 48.

Hochberg, Marcy J. "One Producer, One Comfortable Festival: Campfest 1988," in *Hot Wire,* vol. 5, January 1989: 28-29.

Post, Laura. "The First Olivia Cruise: Maiden Voyage," in *Hot Wire,* vol. 6, September 1990: 26-27, 58.

Seajay, Carol. "20 Years of Feminist Bookstores," in *Ms.,* vol. 3, July/August 1992: 60-65.

Gay Male Travel and Leisure: Periodical Articles

Andriette, Bill. "Policing Public Sex," in *The Guide,* November 1997: 74-76.

Belden, Tom. "Phila. Makes Pitch to Gay Travel Group," in *Philadelphia Inquirer,* 12 April 1995: C1.

Berube, Allan. "Gay Baths," in *The Guide,* November 1997: 77-79.

Brown, Alan. "Forever Young: Five Years on the Dance Floor," in *Out & About,* September 1997: 108.

Cushman, Jennifer. "Tucson Businesses Court Gay Market," in *Tucson Citizen,* 4 March 1996: A1.

Darce, Keith. "Tourism Industry Discovering There's Gold in the Gay Market," in *New Orleans City Business,* 4 November 1996: 11.

"Dover Travel Agency Tries the Latest in Target Marketing: Vacations for Gays," in *New Hampshire Business Review,* 13 September 1996: 4.

Drummond Tammerlin. "Not in Kansas Anymore," in *Time,* 25 September 1995.

Groff, David. "Gay vs. Gay," in *New York,* 4 September 1995: 14-16.

Grossman, Cathy Lynn. "Philadelphia Freedom Offered in a Gay Package Deal," in *Daily Journal Vineland Edition,* 15 July 1996.

Kahan, Hazel and David Mulryan. "Out of the Closet," in *American Demographics,* May 1995: 40-47.

Kasrel, Deni. "Conference of Gays Travels to Philadelphia," in *Philadelphia Business Journal,* 14 March 1997: 3.

Keaney, Maura. "Colorado Hears the Amendment 2 Blues," in *Modern Times,* 20 October 1993.

Mullins, Joyce. "Convention & Visitors Bureau Wants Gays," in *Au Courant,* 23-29 April 1996.

"1997 Subscriber Survey Results," in *Out & About,* October 1997: 121.

Ricklefs, Roger. "Big Business Boosts Effort to Win Share of Gay Market Trade Show Signals Change in What Has Been a Field for Small Concerns," in *Wall Street Journal,* 1 May 1995.

Thomas, Anthony. "The House That Kids Built: The Gay Black Imprint on American Dance Music," in *OUT/LOOK,* Summer 1989.

Torres-Kitamura, Maria. "Out and About," in *Hawaii Business,* April 1997: 23.

Vasiliev, Ren. "Road Trip: Provincetown, Massachusetts," in *American Demographics,* October 1996: 26.

Westenhoefer, Suzanne. "Same Thing in Reverse," in *Advocate,* 9 July 1996: 41.

Lesbian Travel and Leisure: Videos

The Changer: A Record of the Times. Prod. and dir. by Frances Reid and Judy Dlugacz. Olivia Records, 1991.

Last Call at Maud's. Prod. by Karen Kiss. Dir. by Paris Poirier. 77 min. Water Bearer Films, 1993.

Lesbian Travel and Leisure: Internet Sites

http://www.igc.apc.org/women/bookstores/booknets.html. Feminist Bookstores Index. Impressive directory of feminist bookstores worldwide.

http://www.tde.com/~dwc/galaweb.html. GALA Choruses on the Web. A directory of 160 gay and lesbian choruses worldwide.

http://www.companyofwomen.com. In the Company of Women. Web site of two women who organize adventure trips "at cost."

http://www.ladyslipper.org. Ladyslipper Music. Web site of the womyn's music label and distributor, including sizable sales catalog for music recordings, videos, books; plus links to other women's web pages.

http://www.lesbian.org. Lesbian Org. The starting point for finding lesbian web sites, discussion lists, bulletin boards, newsgroups, chat rooms, and more.

http://maiden-voyages.com/ventures.html. Maiden Voyages. A directory of adventure and tour guide companies owned by women or that offer women-only tours.

http://oliviatravel.com. Olivia. Web site of Olivia Cruises and Resorts.

http://www.qrd.org/Qrd. Queer Resources Directory. A list of over 20,000 Internet files on every GLBT topic imaginable.

http://www.queernet.org. Queernet. A site that points to dozens of electronic mailing lists, including subscription information.

http://www.glweb.com/rainbowquery. Rainbow Query. A search engine to access queer web pages through either free text searching or subject categories.

Gay Male Travel and Leisure: Internet Sites

http://www.FireIslandcc.org/fires.html. This web site has much information about the history of Cherry Grove.

http://www.geocities.com/WestHollywood/1328/beach.html. Despite its title, this web site also has interesting information about Rehoboth Beach, Delaware.

http://www.outandabout.com. The travel publication, *Out & About,* maintains this publication and has some articles from its back issues here. Particularly helpful are its articles on HIV-Positive Travel Primer, Rating Hotel Chains, and Editor Choice Awards.

—Lesbian Travel and Leisure by Colleen Nunn
—Gay Male Travel and Leisure by David Levine

23

Local and Regional Views

The history of any particular segment of a national population will be affected by factors unique to its individual group experience and by overall forces of demography. The manner in which each group chooses to recall, codify, and preserve its past will also affect corporate memory. For gay and lesbian Americans since World War II, this has chiefly meant the construction (through both political theory and practical application) and diversification of a basic concept, the idea of the existence of a gay and lesbian "community," an abstract uniting force for isolated individuals scattered throughout the country.

The history of the local gay and lesbian communities of the United States has traditionally been passed along from one generation of its members to the next by word of mouth, an oral record shared in private homes and public settings, and, until recently, seldom written down in any form. Although research studies such as George Chauncey's 1994 work *Gay New York* and the detailed array of original records reprinted by Jonathan Katz in his compilations *Gay American History: Lesbians and Gay Men in the U.S.A., A Documentary* (1976) and the *Gay/Lesbian Almanac: A New Documentary* (1983) have begun to document the origins and existence of social networks of gay men in many cities of the United States during the nineteenth century, the recovery of such local and regional history has not proceeded uniformly. This is due in part to the difficulty in identifying pertinent materials in the holdings of existing historical societies and archives, the exclusion of gays and lesbians from the collecting scope of most such institutions until recently (a change tied to establishment recognition and acceptance of the idea of this constituency as a legitimate ethnic community), and the formation of independent gay and lesbian historical collections such as New York's Lesbian Herstory Archives, Chicago's Gerber-Hart Library, and the Bay Area Gay and Lesbian Historical Society of San Francisco. Recovering homosexual history thus requires the use of sources ranging from print media through oral accounts to films. This essay presents a picture of local and regional community histories from the East, the South, the Midwest and Great Plains, the Southwest and Intermountain region, and the Pacific states.

THE EAST

Broadly defined as consisting of the region extending south from Maine to the District of Columbia, and west to the eastern border of Ohio, the East has become in popular mythology about homosexual history the location "where it all began." This perception is due in part to the prominence of the three days of riots in New York City in June 1969 following a police raid on a gay bar, the Stonewall Inn, during which patrons fought back, refusing to submit tamely to harassment and arrest. The public spectacle (unprecedented in America) of homosexuals being militant and openly confrontational with figures of designated authority stimulated members of the homosexual population of New York's Greenwich Village to come together for political and social change, a concept that quickly became known as "gay liberation." The perception that the gay liberation movement was birthed into the universe as a new and unique creation without historical antecedents has also been perpetuated by a general (until recently) unawareness in the historical record of the presence and activity of homophile organizations in the area and the deliberate rejection of the homophile groups by the newer radicals as being too cautious and assimilationist to be effective in bringing about necessary changes. In addition, the absence of detailed local histories of the gay and lesbian communities of the various cities and urban areas of the East has, until recently, permitted the existence of older versions of such communities in the cities of the seaboard during the nineteenth century to remain relatively undocumented.

The true history of homosexuality in the lands that were to become the eastern United States begins with the initial setting up of European colonies during the seventeenth century. The legal codes adopted by the colonists were often either wholesale transplants of law systems in force in their nations of origin or abbreviated versions adapted to the challenging realities of the new land and its peoples. All were based in some fashion upon the strictures of both accepted custom and limits defined by scriptural writings of the Christian religion. Sexuality was considered a socially taboo subject except for such public affirmations as marriage and pregnancy, which provided validation of the colony's prosperity and future. Same-sex attractions and behaviors, to the extent that their existence was recognized at all, were universally condemned, with legal prohibitions drawing heavily upon texts from the Old Testament Book of Leviticus in prescribing execution for such individuals as having offended against the divine order established at the creation of the world. In locales as diverse as Virginia, the Massachusetts Bay Colony, New Netherland, Maryland, Rhode Island, and Pennsylvania, court records and minutes of councils reveal summary judgments upon individuals (both male and female) convicted of same-sex behaviors, referred to under the generic headings of "sodomy," "buggery," or "the crime not to be named." While a shift away from actual execution is evident by 1650, public opinion remained unalterably set in regarding such individuals as acting outside acceptable limits. The significance of this era for the later homosexual citizens of the region is that in some cases these laws remained on the books well into the twentieth century, such changes as were made only serving to update language without greatly diluting condemnation. The seventeenth and eighteenth centuries also saw the growth of the first major urban centers of the region as ports such as Philadelphia, New York, Baltimore, and Boston expanded into cities where homosexual activities were less likely to be remarked upon. These new cities also provided an expanded social framework admitting of the public discussion of homosexuality, an example being a printed broadside issued in Boston on 25 April 1826, speaking out against intergenerational same-sex activities in the prisons of "the New England States and New York" (Katz, *Gay American History*, p. 27). The changes necessary for the maintenance of public order in larger populations, in particular the organizing of formal police forces, set the stage for later confrontations with and systematic repression of homosexuals through such mechanisms as the twentieth century's notorious vice squads. By the time of the Civil War, poet Walt Whitman could write powerfully of same-gender bonding both on the battlefield and in the hospital wards of Washington, D.C., as well as comment upon the working men of his own city of New York. This association of homosexual behavior with particular social classes or occupations was greatly expanded in the later nineteenth century, as waves of immigrants poured into eastern cities. While most were in transit to the newly opened western territories, others chose to stay, among whom were homosexuals. By 1892, an underground world of clubs catering to persons seeking same-gender sex had emerged in New York City, a situation well known to the police (and thoroughly documented in George Chauncey's pioneering work *Gay New York*), with specific manners, customs, and identifying markings. The noted German physician and advocate of legal equality for homosexuals Dr. Magnus Hirschfeld, on a visit to Philadelphia and Boston in 1893, noted that "homosexual life in the United States is somewhat more hidden than in the United Kingdom" (Katz, *Gay American History,* p. 50). The pattern of homosexuals forming discrete, underground communities in expanding urban areas would remain a feature of most eastern (if not American) cities well into the twentieth century, increasing greatly during the mobilizations for the two World Wars.

The beginnings of change for homosexuals in this region came with the formation of social organizations separate from the saloon and bar venues that many individuals chose not to frequent. While the earliest documented example in the United States was Chicago's short-lived Society for Friendship and Freedom (1924-25), similar groups formed in New York City and elsewhere during the 1950s and 1960s. Chapters of the Los Angeles-based Mattachine Society (founded in 1950) and the lesbian group the Daughters of Bilitis appeared as the ideas behind them spread across the country. New York City, Buffalo, and Washington, D.C., Mattachine chapters (the last founded in 1961 by Dr. Franklin Kameny, who would later figure in a lawsuit overturning federal employment discrimination against homosexuals) gradually came into being, although they made no noticeable impact on the region. Two of the first three initial chapters of the Daughters outside their home city of San Francisco—Rhode Island and New

York City—were chartered in 1958, with Boston and Philadelphia following their example. The latter city would also become the site of a public demonstration, picket line, and leafletting at Independence Hall during the Fourth of July celebrations between 1965 and 1969. Known as the "Annual Reminder," it was intended to call attention to the fact that, for homosexuals, true liberty had not yet been gained. These groups provided secure spaces within which the first discussions of equal civil rights for homosexuals were held in the East. In 1963, ECHO (the Eastern Conference of Homophile Organizations) was founded, with "Regional" added to the title after 1964. This organization represented the first attempt at bringing together the homophile activists scattered across the area to agree on a common agenda of problems and strategies for change.

The police raid on the Stonewall Inn in New York City on 21 June 1969, and the unprecedented refusal of the patrons to submit quietly to incarceration and harassment sparked several days of unrest that became known as the "Christopher Street riots." For the first time in twentieth-century America, New York gays and lesbians took to the pavements in mass demonstrations to publicly affirm their orientations and their pride in identity. Out of this unrest came a new organization, the Gay Activists Alliance (GAA), and a new philosophy of "gay liberation" that would sweep from Manhattan across the entire country within five years. Its impact on the older homophile groups and their more sedate approach to working for change is exemplified by the events at the ERCHO conference held in Philadelphia on 1-2 November 1969. With the seating of the New York City Gay Liberation Front and three Student Homophile League delegations, newer radical positions were adopted, among them abandoning the Independence Hall picketing for a new celebration on the last Saturday of June in New York City. Initially known as "Christopher Street Liberation Day," this was the birth of the idea of annual "Gay Pride" parades, which swiftly became an established feature of all local homosexual communities. Even more important than this was the rejection of the clinical term "homosexual" for the defiantly blunt "gay" as the adjective of choice.

The immediate focus of many of the local gay liberation fronts in the East was the challenging of prejudicial treatment and representation, whether by public officials, police, the federal government, or the media. Examples of this new militancy included public confrontations with Mayor John Lindsay of New York over bar raids, the Joseph Acanfora case in Pennsylvania challenging employment discrimination against openly gay teachers, attacks on television show host Jack Paar for homophobic remarks (and on the networks in general for broadcasting episodes of popular shows such as *Marcus Welby, M.D.* depicting negatively stereotyped gay and lesbian characters), and the attempted introduction of bills across the region aimed at reforming relevant sections of county, city, and state legal codes. These latter actions laid the foundation for both the appearance of open homosexuals in politics (such as Representative Elaine Noble of Massachusetts) and the eventual passage of comprehensive protective legislation in the next decade.

The passage of civil rights bills aimed at protecting gay and lesbian citizens from discrimination (in fields as varied as employment, housing, and public accommodations) by the eastern states began in 1989 in Massachusetts. With the endorsement of then-Governor Michael Dukakis and Senator Edward Kennedy, this law was followed by passage of similar legislation in Connecticut (1991), Vermont and New Jersey (1992), Rhode Island (1995),

New York Gay Pride Day, 1989. Christopher Street was the birthplace of the annual gay pride parades that now occur across the United States.

and New Hampshire and Maine (1997). While a federal gay civil rights bill was first introduced in Congress on 25 March 1975, by Representative Bella Abzug of New York and 23 co-sponsors (with the goal of amending the Civil Rights Acts of 1964 to prohibit discrimination on the basis of affectional or sexual preference), the measure made no progress. Successive efforts in 1977 and 1979 in both the House and the Senate eventually failed due both to a decline in the number of legislators willing to address the issue and an increasingly conservative national political climate.

While the necessity of taking gay and lesbian political issues to a wider stage than one city or region was recognized almost from the beginning of gay liberation rhetoric, it was not until four years after Stonewall that the National Gay and Lesbian Task Force (NGLTF) formed in New York City. Among its goals were securing greater involvement of professional men and women in the movement (thereby expanding the available base of connections and expertise), setting a national media alert to monitor homophobic portrayals, and surveying candidates for office on their positions on gay rights. The question of becoming an effective organi-

zation for presenting homosexual issues to Congress was noted as vital but eventually took the form of involvement by successive Task Force leaders on specific issues and pieces of legislation. The unacceptability of this situation was recognized in November 1975 at a conference on "Gays and the Federal Government." Citing the then-current dilemmas posed by the newly introduced homosexual civil rights bill, a full-time permanent presence in the capital was viewed as essential. The national gay news magazine *The Advocate* sponsored a leadership conference in Chicago in the spring of 1976 at which a new body, the Gay Rights National Lobby, was created. Following the failure of broad-based protective legislation at the federal level, the Lobby focused on opposing employment discrimination, obtaining platform representation from both the Democratic and Republican parties, and attempting to document anti-gay discrimination as a basis for legislative action. In 1986, it merged with a third organization, the Human Rights Campaign Fund, founded in Washington in 1980 with the aim of officially supporting pro-human rights candidates at the federal level.

The East was also the region in which the first cases of what would later become known as AIDS (Acquired Immune Deficiency Syndrome) were identified, beginning in the hospitals of New York City in 1981. That city, together with Los Angeles and San Francisco, had in the years since Stonewall become identified as one of the national centers of the urban gay community, a place carefully observed for trends both political and cultural. With the appearance of this new health threat, such identification altered so that, along with San Francisco, Manhattan and its adjacent boroughs acquired a new and terrible significance. The need for organized and timely public health education about the symptoms and possible treatment regimens quickly became urgent within the gay community, as the fragmentary, imprecise (and often contradictory) information provided by the federal health care system was seen as inadequate. New York's network of public hospitals, already under severe strain due to aging facilities and inconsistent funding, was agreed to be incapable of planning and mounting the sustained campaign necessary. Alarmed by the situation, a group of 80 men gathered in playwright Larry Kramer's apartment in late 1981 to hear a physician present the facts available about what was popularly termed "gay related immunodeficiency disorder (GRID)" or "gay cancer." Following an informal fundraising appeal, this group maintained contact, and in January 1982 Kramer and five other men—Paul Popham, Nathan Fain, Larry Mass, Paul Rapoport, and Edmund White—met again to officially found a new organization, the Gay Men's Health Crisis (GMHC).

Fitting into the longstanding tradition of community clinics with an awareness of gay health needs, the GMHC was nevertheless an entirely new phenomenon. It swiftly came to be regarded as a model for local gay and lesbian communities in all parts of the United States attempting to create an infrastructure of care, support, and effective education for persons with AIDS. By 1987, GMHC had expanded its array of offerings from the initial information hotline to include direct patient services, ranging from a newsletter covering data on new drugs and therapies to a network of volunteer home visitors assisting with daily tasks. The first lawsuit involving AIDS-based discrimination was funded by GMHC as well, while the campaign of health outreach was so successful that the Centers for Disease Control requested its assistance in planning regional conferences to educate the general public on the threat posed by the growing epidemic. The GMHC also became known for its insistence on educating individuals on alternative forms of sexual expression that did not offer opportunities for the transmission of HIV. This concept, termed "safer sex," quickly became controversial (due to the constantly changing level of clinical information available about the retrovirus) and remained a constant point of debate among AIDS educators.

The speed with which the new disease appeared to be spreading, together with a constantly evolving epidemiology, created widespread fear within local homosexual communities nationwide throughout the early and mid-1980s. A perception that major pharmaceutical firms were exploiting this new market added resentment and anger to the emotional mix, a situation that called for resolution. The trigger for the next phase of AIDS organizing and activism came at a meeting on 10 March 1987, at New York's Gay and Lesbian Community Center featuring an address by Larry Kramer of the GMHC. He began by recalling for his listeners a piece he had written in 1983 for the *New York Native* detailing the apathetic reaction of national and local health care providers to AIDS at a time when slightly more than 1,100 cases of the syndrome had been diagnosed. Current numbers of known AIDS pa-

tients then stood at some 32,000, a figure cited by Kramer as he challenged the audience to answer "What are we doing ... to save our own lives ?" (Kramer, *Reports from the Holocaust*, p. 128). This open statement served to begin the coalescence of accumulated emotion into a determination to act. There was so much unresolved discussion that a second meeting was held two nights later, attended by more than 300 people alerted by informal channels. Out of this second gathering was born a new organization whose agenda quickly became identified by its acronym: the AIDS Coalition To Unleash Power, or ACT UP.

The goal of ACT UP, as stated in publicity materials, was to be "a diverse, non partisan group of individuals, united in anger and committed to direct action to end the AIDS crisis. We meet with government officials, we distribute the latest medical information, we protest and demonstrate. We are not silent." This last comment relates to the chosen insignia of the organization, a pink triangle underscored by the slogan "Silence equals death." A degree of militancy not seen in New York since the first days of gay liberation reappeared with a vengeance on 24 March 1987. In its first public demonstration, more than 600 protestors blocked all traffic on Wall Street to challenge the Reagan administration's lack of response to AIDS and the refusal of the Food and Drug Administration to release experimental drugs to HIV-infected individuals. The success of this event was swiftly followed by similar organized eruptions of anger, including a demonstration at the United Nations. Perhaps the most controversial action taken by ACT UP came in December 1989 at St. Patrick's Cathedral in Manhattan. Angered at statements opposing the use of condoms and safe sex education issued by Cardinal John O'Connor, more than 5,000 people blocked Fifth Avenue before the church. A small contingent also made their way into the sanctuary and deliberately disrupted the celebration of High Mass. Six activists were arrested and later prosecuted for this tactic. By 1990, ACT UP chapters had been established as far afield as Chicago, Los Angeles, and San Francisco, the last experiencing a schism over the inclusion of non-AIDS issues in its agenda.

The streets of New York City's Greenwich Village had over several decades become a sort of national homeland for gays and lesbians aware of their history, with the story of the 1969 raid on the Stonewall Inn rapidly taking on the status of a defining myth. Another aspect of the early American gay liberation movement was also present as a part of both political strategy and community activism—the image of angry and openly militant gays and lesbians taking to the pavements to command attention from an indifferent society. This tradition was reborn in March 1990 in New York City at a community meeting called by four men, two of whom had recently been beaten up for being openly homosexual. At that meeting, a decision was taken to create a new organization, whose purpose was "to be to homophobia and heterosexism what the AIDS Coalition To Unleash Power ... is to AIDS ... a grass-roots direct action response ... fighting homophobia and promoting visibility" (Podolsky, *The Advocate*, p. 52). Its immediate focus was on hate crimes targeted at homosexuals, a topic recognized as being opposed by but beyond the mandate of existing groups such as ACT UP. The group's choice of name, Queer Nation, reflected the changing self-image of a new generation of gays and lesbians for whom being visible and demanding recognition had taken the place of targeting specific political goals. This more general approach was a part of what was termed "queer consciousness," one of whose popular phrases, "being in your face," was to become virtually synonymous with the actions of

Queer Nation. From its beginnings in New York City, the organization spread to other eastern cities, including Boston and Philadelphia, and established chapters outside the region in many large urban areas with substantial gay and lesbian populations.

THE SOUTH

Reaching from Virginia to Florida and west to Kentucky, Tennessee, and the Mississippi, the lands of the South possess the longest recorded history of repressive measures against homosexual behaviors, beginning with the execution of a French interpreter in 1566 in Spanish Florida. The colonial era in the South emphasized the development of a predominantly agricultural civilization, with coastal cities such as Charleston, Savannah, and New Orleans serving as centers of exchange for imported manufactured goods. The basis of this massive regional economy was human slavery, a factor that laid the foundations for conflicts in philosophy and outlook that would later lead to the devastation of the Civil War. In a fashion similar to the New England colonies, the southern colonies undertook to provide legal prohibitions against same-gender sexual activities. Beginning with a provision of the Virginia legal code of 1610 that mandated the death penalty for "the horrible and detestable sins of Sodomie" (Katz, *Gay/Lesbian Almanac*, p. 68), the general pattern in this region was the utilization of the English law against "buggery," although its language was not usually explicitly adopted. An exception to this was South Carolina, where the English text was incorporated into local statute in 1712, remaining on the books unaltered until 1873, when its provision of the death penalty was repealed (Katz, *Gay/Lesbian Almanac*, p. 128). Such draconian measures did not, as local leaders hoped, extinguish such activities in their colonies, as a public whipping (with a sentence of 300 lashes) in Savannah on 25 March 1734, of a man convicted of sodomy indicates.

The general patterns of southern culture formed in colonial times continued unaltered until they were shattered in the 1860s by the upheavals of the Civil War and the chaotic years of Reconstruction. The relevance of this era to local gay and lesbian history lies in the fact that the types of discrimination targeted for criticism and later protest, all rooted in racial division, had their beginnings in these turbulent years. The elimination of slavery as a legal option for social control led to the formation of such groups as the Ku Klux Klan and the evolution of an unwritten social code wherein black people were dismissively assigned an inferior status. The pervasive focus on race segregation (including limitation of access to opportunity and equal treatment under the law) created a world within which same-gender behaviors were virtually invisible or, at best, tolerated as isolated natural eccentricities of the local "town fairy," a creature never taken seriously in any fashion.

During the 1950s, the homophile movement organizations that successfully established a presence in many cities of the Midwest and the East coast were not able to achieve similar success in the South. The only exception to this was the establishment of a chapter of the Daughters of Bilitis in New Orleans.

The situation of gay and lesbian individuals throughout the South was deeply affected by the civil rights movement of the 1960s, which laid a foundation for long-term social change and in itself challenged the continued existence of institutions basic to southern culture, most chiefly the "invisible caste" system that accorded the "Negro" an inherently second class status. The eyes of the United States became focused on this region by such events as the murder of civil rights workers in Mississippi, boycotts of historically segregated venues such as lunch counters and buses, and the killing of movement leaders Malcolm X and Martin Luther King, Jr. The relationship of this series of exceedingly public social crises to the future of gay and lesbian southerners lies in two areas: institutional sources and supporters of change, and the public demonstrations against racism themselves.

The civil rights effort across the South found forums for debate on many, if not all, university campuses, even where such discussion took the form of condemning the very existence of such activities. In these settings, gay men and lesbians of all colors were involved in questioning the immovable nature of doctrines such as "separate but equal" and in raising open challenges to the social methods and systems of conduct (including the well-known "Jim Crow" laws) that assigned and maintained a marginalized status to human beings. These heated exchanges presented gay individuals a chance to participate in consciousness-raising actions regarding the possibility of overturning entrenched prejudices while providing a model for the later construction of their own organizations and emergence.

While specific local marches and rallies against racism left little or no time or energy for the consideration of gay rights issues, the events themselves were of great significance to the hidden homosexual communities of the South, in that they offered practical lessons on the range of possible protest tactics available (and their effectiveness within local social limits). The most spectacular of these was the famous March on Washington in 1963, an event that commanded national attention and forced America to take seriously the civil rights movement and its goals. It also would serve as a standard against which later mass protests in the capital would be measured, including the three gay and lesbian gatherings of 1979, 1987, and 1993. A more direct connection lay in the fact that the organizer of the March, activist Bayard Rustin, was known to be gay by leading civil rights workers, a fact made public only years afterward.

The inspiration of the 1969 Stonewall confrontation in New York led to the formation in some southern urban areas of local gay liberation groups in the early 1970s. Significant organizing was begun with the formation of the Southeastern Region Gay Conference at the University of Georgia in Athens in November 1972, whose first goal was "to gain repeal of state laws oppressing homosexuals" (Ridinger, *Gay and Lesbian Movement*, p. 287). It was followed by the creation in the University of North Carolina, Chapel Hill, of the Southeastern Conference for Lesbians and Gay Men in 1976. These meetings mark the true coming of age of intellectual dialogue on the place gay and lesbian southerners would shape for themselves. Outside the universities and major cities, very little influence was exerted by news of events in New York City and other leading sites of liberation activity. An article discussing Atlanta as a center for gay and lesbian life, published in 1973, laments that "there is virtually no interest in the Gay Liberation Movement throughout the states of Louisiana, Mississippi and Alabama" (Doyle, *The Advocate*, p. 11).

Another aspect of southern life utilized by gay and lesbian individuals to advance their cultural politics and proclaim the reality of their lives was the field of literature. From colonial times onward, the genteel craft of the writer had been regarded as an acceptable channel for the voicing of social protest, the most notable examples being Virginia planter Thomas Jefferson's text of the Declaration of Independence and the numerous pamphlets and books whose authors defended the institution of slavery as part of the natural order. One of the earliest post-Stonewall novels about growing up lesbian, *Rubyfruit Jungle*, appeared in 1973 from the pen of Rita Mae Brown, establishing a tradition of lesbian feminist literature followed in the 1990s by the poetry and essays of Minnie Bruce Pratt. Perhaps the quintessential gay writer of the South is the playwright Tennessee Williams, many of whose works included the topic as a subtext.

It was in the South, paradoxically, that the second rejuvenation of the gay and lesbian movement was triggered. By the middle years of the 1970s, many United States cities had passed ordinances of various kinds guaranteeing homosexuals civil rights in various fields. In late 1976, an activist group formed in Miami calling itself the Dade County Coalition and taking local politicians to account for certain campaign promises, among which had been the enactment of a gay rights ordinance for the local community. This was the first such piece of local legislation in any major city of the South and immediately roused conservative opposition. By June 1977, singer and Christian activist Anita Bryant (known in the region through advertisements for the Florida citrus industry) had formed an organization called Save Our Children to challenge the new law, claiming that employment discrimination rights of this kind would permit local school districts to hire and retain openly gay teachers, who would then corrupt and recruit their students to become homosexuals. Her massive lobbying campaign culminated on 7 June 1977, when a referendum overturned Miami's law by a margin of two to one. This defeat spawned a flurry of similar repeal efforts across the country in cities such as Wichita and St. Paul, galvanizing the American gay and lesbian community out of a complacency generated by a succession of civil rights victories in the years since Stonewall.

The creation of an alternative press to serve the gay and lesbian communities across the southern states did not take place until approximately a decade after Stonewall, due in part to the adequate distribution of regional news through national media such as *The Advocate*. Publications such as Atlanta's *Southern Voice* (1988—) and the Tennessee paper *Dare* (later the *Nashville Query;* 1988—) thus mark a coming of age of gay and lesbian awareness and public presence in their respective cities. The appearance of the AIDS pandemic in 1981 also thrust the South into national consciousness in a totally unexpected manner. Federal publicity about ongoing research at the Centers for Disease Control in Atlanta (among whose public health duties was the dissemination of prevention information) and the National Institutes of Health in Virginia placed these facilities at the core of official debates over potential cures and effective strategies of mass sex education.

THE MIDWEST AND GREAT PLAINS

The regions of the central United States, stretching from Ohio to Nebraska and the Dakotas to Missouri, present a unique framework within which gay and lesbian identities would evolve. Characterized by a highly varied demographic pattern, ranging from several large metropolitan areas per state to smaller communities that functioned as social and educational centers for a widely scattered and predominantly rural population, it has served as witness to some of the most significant developments in modern gay and lesbian history.

For the majority of the nineteenth century, this geographical region was in the process of being opened up for settlement and agricultural development, with population centers emerging at natural transfer points along the river systems and on the Great Lakes.

Despite complications posed by political factors associated with the slavery debate, organization of the new territories into fully integrated members of the United States was in large part based upon the existing federal and state models. This included adopting versions of existing sodomy law and legislation into the new legal codes, a situation that would last in some cases for more than a century.

In the privately published 1908 volume by Edward Stevenson, *The Intersexes: A History of Similisexualism* (the first extended discussion of homosexuality by an American who belonged to that group), Chicago, St. Louis, and Milwaukee are noted as being among the "homosexual capitals" of the United States (Katz, *Gay/Lesbian Almanac,* p. 300). This description is corroborated in a report entitled *The Social Evil in Chicago* (see p. 55*)*, issued in 1911 by that city's Vice Commission, which makes extensive mention of female impersonation and soliciting of men for "pervert practices" (Katz, *Gay/Lesbian Almanac,* p. 336). In light of this, it is ironic that the formal history of gay and lesbian organizing in the United States prior to 1950 begins not on either coast, but in the Midwest.

During World War I, a young recent immigrant named Henry Gerber was stationed in Coblenz from 1920 to 1923 as part of the American contingent of the army of occupation. During this time, he made several trips to Berlin and was exposed to the active (and at that time fairly successful) German homosexual rights movement led by Dr. Magnus Hirschfeld and others. Having the example of the numerous German organizations before him, upon his return to the United States Gerber determined to attempt to emulate their success. On 10 December 1924, an application was filed with the State of Illinois requesting recognition of the Society for Human Rights as a bona fide organization. Its goals included educating homosexuals about society's attitudes towards them (and their bases) and reforming Illinois laws that prohibited same-gender sex. The Society in fact lasted less than one year, dissolving in the summer of 1925 following the arrest of Gerber and several other people.

In the era following 1950, the Daughters of Bilitis was the first national homophile group to establish a presence in either the Midwest or Great Plains states, with chapters appearing in Chicago, Detroit, and Cleveland. A far more significant development affecting this region began in 1953 with a grant to the American Law Institute from the Rockefeller Foundation to address the need for massive revision and unification of the United States penal code. The provisions of this model code were widely discussed in legislative circles during the 10 years of the project, and addressed virtually all behaviors classed as criminal, including homosexual relations. It was in this atmosphere that the Illinois General Assembly voted in 1961 to decriminalize homosexual relations between consenting adults in private, the first state to do so.

In June 1965, the Mattachine Society made its appearance in the region with the formation of Chicago's Mattachine Midwest. The body quickly became a highly active presence on the national homophile scene, acting as one of the sponsors of the second Annual Reminder demonstration in Philadelphia and sending delegates to the National Planning Conference of Homophile Organizations held in Kansas City in February 1966. This gathering adopted a statement calling for equal legal protection for homosexuals, the right to serve in the armed forces, and an end to police harassment. A second conference there in November 1968 (hosted by the Phoenix Society) drew homophile groups from Cincinnati, Dayton, Cleveland, Omaha, and Chicago. In what would prove to

Scene from the 1993 March on Washington.

be the final local event of this era, the North American Confer-ence of Homophile Organizations met on 25-29 August 1969, with 12 groups sending 30 delegates to Kansas City.

The birth of the new radical gay movement in June 1969 had a somewhat delayed impact in the central United States, with most local gay liberation fronts coming into being in 1970 and 1971. A feature unique to the region is the importance of gay and lesbian student organizations, as the large number of state-related and pri-vate university campuses in many instances provided a safe at-mosphere within which consciousness raising about homosexual-ity could occur.

The idea of enacting comprehensive legislation at the state level outside the criminal code to explicitly safeguard the civil rights of gay and lesbian citizens against discrimination (an objective that would be adopted across the United States) originated in Wiscon-sin. In 1974, State Representative David Clarenbach of Madison co-sponsored Assembly Bill 269, an omnibus bill aimed at sexual law reform. Among its provisions were the recognition of same-sex marriages and the repeal of all laws pertaining to consensual sex. Although unsuccessful in its initial form, this bill provided the basis for a subsequent eight-year political and educational ef-fort, culminating in the signing into law on 18 February 1982, of a measure adding "sexual orientation" to all Wisconsin state laws prohibiting discrimination. The Wisconsin law provided activists elsewhere in the country with both an example upon which to model their own drafts and an effective strategy for change in this area, that being the presentation of the issue of securing civil rights for homosexuals as an extension of provisions of already effective

legislation. Similar legislation was enacted in Minnesota in 1993, although a 1997 effort in Illinois was unsuccessful.

THE INTERMOUNTAIN REGION AND THE SOUTHWEST

The complex physical topography of the Intermountain and Southwestern states (Texas, New Mexico, Arizona, Colorado, Utah, Nevada, and Idaho) is matched in the turbulent history and growth of their gay and lesbian communities. In this region as no-where else in the United States, opportunities for community for-mation of any kind during the years of nineteenth-century settle-ment were initially severely limited by harsh landscapes and scarce resources. The relatively brief history of most political structures in the region (the Hispanic heritage of New Mexico, Texas, and Arizona excepted) coupled with the emphasis on ultramasculine values retained from frontier society made being homosexual here an uncertain matter at best. Although some cities were known dur-ing the nineteenth century as places where homosexuals could be found (Denver being the best documented case), there was little or no sense of belonging to a distinct population. Prior to the ar-rival of gay liberation in the 1970s, the surge of homophile orga-nizing and publishing originating on the Pacific coast that created centers of potential change across the United States had little ef-fect on this area, with Daughters of Bilitis chapters in Denver and Reno only.

The area did, however, receive national publicity in 1955 for a spectacularly tenacious witch hunt against homosexuals that took place in Boise, Idaho. Fully documented in John Gerassi's *The*

Boys of Boise: Furor, Vice and Folly in an American City, this event illustrated an atmosphere of legal repression nearly as severe as that of seventeenth-century New England. State sodomy laws were strongly worded and strictly enforced, with civil rights for those arrested a minor consideration. This created a situation similar to that on the East coast, in that some of the first confrontations over homosexuals and their public identity had as their goal the overturning of specific pieces of legislation.

Gay liberation movements in this region first began to appear in the early 1970s through attempts by students at such institutions as the University of Texas and the University of New Mexico to achieve formal recognition. The virtually complete absence of older organizational models at the local level permitted the newly emerging organizations in Phoenix, Houston, Dallas, Austin, Fort Worth, Denver, and elsewhere a freedom to experiment with locally effective strategies without conflicts with an older homophile "establishment." Two goals emerged early on: the elimination of state laws against sodomy and the passage of civil rights laws. While neither of these aims was unique to this region, the protracted nature of the struggle (due in large part to a combination of conservative politics and the opposition of organized religion, in particular the Church of Jesus Christ of Latter-Day Saints) would absorb much of the activist energy until well into the 1980s. A notable challenge to repressive legislation came in 1981 with the case of *Baker v. Wade*. The plaintiff, an elementary school teacher employed by the City of Dallas (and therefore a licensed public employee, said licensure being extended only to individuals deemed to be of good moral character) attempted to overturn Section 21.06 of the state penal code, which forbade homosexual conduct and deviate sexual intercourse of any kind. Recognition of gay political clout came slowly, with the exception being the 1982 mayoral campaign of Kathy Whitmire in Houston.

By the end of the 1980s, modest political gains had been made, frequently taking the form of protective ordinances enacted by municipalities. Such laws became the core of one of the most controversial attempts to limit homosexual civil rights. On 3 November 1992, 54 percent of the voters of Colorado approved a resolution designed to eliminate protection for gays and lesbians. Introduced by the conservative group Colorado for Family Values, its aim was to specifically prohibit the state or any local jurisdiction within it from passing laws treating homosexuality as the grounds for any legal "minority status, quota preferences, protected status or claim of discrimination" (Ponnuru, *National Review*, p. 22). "Amendment 2," as it was popularly known, also repealed existing measures on the books in Denver, Boulder, and Aspen, all of which allied with the American Civil Liberties Union in challenging its constitutionality in federal court. Regional public opinion on the matter was sharply divided, while the local gay populations were galvanized into action by anger and outrage.

The legal challenge to Amendment 2 began with the issuing of an injunction in January 1993 by a Colorado judge preventing its implementation pending clarification of possible constitutional questions through the courts. After hearing testimony from representatives of all concerned parties, state judge Jeffrey Bayless ruled in December 1993 that the proposed measure was in violation of the equal protection clause of the Fourteenth Amendment to the United States Constitution. This finding was appealed to the Colorado Supreme Court (which declared Amendment 2 unconstitutional on 11 October 1994) and eventually to the United States Supreme Court, as *Romer v. Evans*. That body stated in a six to three opinion on 20 May 1996, that the state of Colorado did indeed possess the right to grant homosexuals civil rights protections, the first time the high court had ruled in favor of a gay rights issue. By overturning Amendment 2, the argument that homosexuals were not entitled to "special rights," a favorite claim of opponents, lost its legal underpinnings.

The precedent of Amendment 2 spawned a flurry of copycat legislation across the United States, even within the mountain states themselves. The Idaho Citizens Alliance (an organization influenced by the unsuccessful example of Oregon's Measure 9) filed the "Idaho Civil Rights Act" on 4 March 1993, triggering a statewide debate over the definition of "civil" versus "special" rights. Following extensive campaigning by the Alliance, the measure was placed on the November 1994 ballot, where it failed to pass by 3,098 votes.

THE PACIFIC STATES

Taken together, the Pacific coast regions that would become Washington, Oregon, Alaska, Hawaii, and California formed the end of the frontier for the expanding United States. Their settlement came late enough in the transcontinental expansion for an environmental ethic to have evolved, resulting in the sequestering of large areas of land in national parks and reserves. In part, this limited the possibilities for the formation of large settled rural populations such as that of the Midwest or Texas, creating (with the exception of California) an area characterized by numerous small towns and only a few large urban centers. For the gay and lesbian communities of these states, this has meant an emphasis on initial networking at a state level as well as within specific cities, an example being the Dorian Group of Washington.

The first attempt at organizing American homosexuals since the demise of Chicago's Society for Human Rights (1924-25) began in Los Angeles shortly after the end of World War II. On 10 August 1948, Harry Hay first wrote down his thoughts on the creation of "a service and welfare organization devoted to the protection and improvement of Society's Androgynous Minority" (Timmons, *The Trouble with Harry Hay*, p. 136). Originally named the Society of Fools, the group dropped this in favor of the Mattachine Foundation (later Society), after the masked secret societies of the fifteenth century that parodied accepted customs. In addition to Los Angeles, Mattachine chapters spread out across California, appearing in San Francisco, Monterey, Laguna, Fresno, and San Diego, before expanding to the East and Midwest. A notable feature of the Society was its sponsorship of discussion groups on homosexual-related issues that met in private homes around Los Angeles. It was at one such meeting on October 15, 1952, that the idea of creating a magazine for the homophile community was proposed, anticipating the appearance of the *Mattachine Review* by more than two years. The first issue of *ONE Magazine: The Homosexual Viewpoint* appeared in 1953, taking its title from a quote from Thomas Carlyle that stated that "a mystic bond of brotherhood makes all men one." This periodical was the first publication for homosexuals in America to receive fairly wide distribution, and its production sparked the creation of a legal entity, ONE, Inc., whose other goal was to "aid in the social integration and rehabilitation of the social variant" ("How *ONE* Began"). Although the organization would exist until the late 1960s, its most memorable contribution to homosexual rights lies in the lengthy lawsuit it pursued with the U.S. Post Office between 1953 and 1958. The case began when the August 1953 issue of *ONE* was impounded on grounds of possible obscenity, resulting in a legal battle over this issue and that of October 1954 that eventually reached the United States Supreme Court. On 13 January 1958, the Court reversed both lower court rulings (which had upheld interdicting the mailings), thus establishing a precedent under which the later explosion of gay and lesbian journalism could occur.

While these groups were concerned with the rights of homosexuals in general, their membership was predominantly male. The first step at redressing the balance in favor of awareness of lesbian concerns as an independent subject was taken on the evening of 21 September 1955. That night (the first of what would be four weekly discussions) saw the meeting in San Francisco of a number of women who envisioned what they viewed as a secret lesbian club. This idea would grow into the first national organization devoted to lesbians and their welfare in the United States, the Daughters of Bilitis. Its agenda mirrored that of the male groups to a certain degree, emphasizing education as a mechanism for influencing public opinion, but its organizing and publishing efforts were far more successful. *The Ladder*, a monthly magazine that swiftly became America's first widely distributed lesbian publication, was in its sixth issue when the Daughters were granted official recognition from the State of California as a nonprofit corporation in January 1957. As word of the new activists spread through publicity in *ONE Magazine*, other local chapters were set up in Los Angeles, Portland, and San Diego as well as in urban centers across the country.

Scene from Christopher Street West parade in Los Angeles, 1972. During the 1970s, a large gay population settled in the city's West Hollywood district.

An alteration in the tradition of homophile publishing established by *ONE Magazine* had also begun in Los Angeles in September 1967 with the appearance of the first issue of *The Advocate*. Initially limited to covering such local controversies as police harassment and entrapment, it would within several years emerge as the national periodical of record for the gay community, wielding such a degree of influence that it was termed "the *New York Times* of gay America," a position it would retain well into the 1980s.

The de facto leadership of the homophile movement centered in Los Angeles and San Francisco served more as a focus for a widely scattered and hidden body of people, few of whom as yet had the temerity to think of themselves as a distinct community with civil rights. While writers, editors, and activists such as Harry Hay, Morris Kight, Phyllis Lyon, Del Martin, and Barbara Gittings were able to articulate a self-positive viewpoint for American homosexuals (in part to combat the numerous cultural sources of devaluation such as psychiatry and religion), another chief emphasis of the homophile philosophy was validation by outside experts and promoting social change through education. With the creation of a more militant "gay liberation" approach after 1969, the two philosophies were sure to collide.

The inevitable confrontation between the two factions took place at the 25-28 August 1970, meeting of the North American Conference of Homophile Organizations (NACHO) in San Francisco, somewhat fitting, given California's role as the home of the largest number of homophile groups in the country. For the first three days, established homophile leaders found themselves sharply challenged for using methods that the new liberationists viewed as ineffective. Calls for more radical political positions and debate over such issues as sexism within gay men's groups and identifying with the women's liberation movement punctuated the discussions, as did demands by the newcomers that they be allowed to vote on floor issues. This turbulent unrest culminated on 29 August 1970, when gay liberation delegates succeeded in passing a resolution mandating "one man, one vote" and gained control of the conference. Their first action (in keeping with the counterculture politics of the day) was the introduction and endorsement of several militant resolutions, among them statements of solidarity with all oppressed peoples, support for the Black Panther Party, and a proposal for a National Gay Strike Day. Older homophile activists' unwillingness to alter their political tactics (or to recognize these initiatives as valid NACHO opinion), coupled with the rapid formation of local gay liberation fronts, marked this as the end of the NACHO as an attempted national presence for America's homosexuals, who would henceforth reject this clinical term for the self-chosen and defiant "gay."

The decade of the 1970s saw an unprecedented growth and visibility of the gay community within the Pacific region. Notable events ranged from the election of the first openly gay city official, Supervisor Harvey Milk in San Francisco (assassinated along with Mayor George Moscone in 1978), to the development of Los Angeles as the home of the national gay and lesbian news magazine *The Advocate*. Taking the idea of community to its logical conclusion, unique heavily gay populations crystallized in the Los Angeles district of West Hollywood and in San Francisco's famous Castro Street neighborhood, acquiring both political presence and influence in civic affairs. The chief importance of the region, however, lies in its role as the site of experimentation with a wide range of alternative cultural models of being homosexual, whose results were monitored closely by smaller cities and towns across the country. What was to become a distinctive national symbol of gay culture, the rainbow flag, was also developed here, appearing first in San Francisco's Pride Parade in 1978.

The advent of AIDS in 1981 marks a transition period in local politics, mirroring in many ways the events taking place in New York City. Activist energies became divided between maintaining those civil rights gains achieved and creating new social channels to address the demands of the pandemic. San Francisco in particular became identified with the disease, both providing effective examples of community health care and creating a unique memorial to the dead through the NAMES Project Quilt.

By the 1990s, the conservative political shifts generally witnessed across America began to have an effect on the coastal states, most notably in Oregon. In 1991, the Oregon Citizens Alliance proposed and introduced for voter consideration Measure Nine (modeled in part upon the similar Amendment 2 being campaigned for in Colorado). This piece of legislation defined homosexuality as "abnormal, wrong, unnatural and perverse" (Witt and McCorkle, *Anti-Gay Rights,* p. 18) and would have amended the state constitution to prohibit "all governments in Oregon" from recognizing sexual orientation or sexual preference as a factor in its deliberation. Its initial defeat in 1992 was followed by the reintroduction of Measure Thirteen in 1994, whose provisions centered on equating homosexuality with race or other protected classifications and included bans on spousal benefits, the granting of marital status, and a limitation of library access to books on the subject to adults only. This and two subsequent attempts at limiting civil liberties for homosexuals in 1996 were rejected by Oregon voters. The local gay community as a result remains in a highly politicized state.

One of the premier issues of the queer activism of the 1990s was an increasing demand that same-sex unions be recognized both legally and culturally, a topic generally referred to under the label "gay marriage." The Pacific region served as the stage for what would become the first serious test of the constitutional acceptability of this through the case of *Baehr v. Lewin,* filed in Hawaii in 1991. That suit, brought by three same-sex couples—two lesbian, one male—was generated following the denial of marriage licenses to them by the state of Hawaii. The argument of the plaintiffs was that such action constituted gender discrimination, although the trial court supported the existing prohibitions. An appeal to the Hawaii Supreme Court resulted in a decision on 5 May 1993, that the law on marriage licenses appeared to violate the state constitution's ban on sex discrimination. The case was remanded to the trial court, which was instructed to examine the Hawaii marriage statute and determine whether "a compelling state interest" was involved. The ensuing series of testimonies by witnesses for both sides provided United States society as a whole with a detailed education on this subject, a factor involved in the drafting and passage of the Defense of Marriage Act by the U.S. Congress in 1996. On 3 December 1996, Circuit Judge Kevin Chang released his ruling in what was now known as *Baehr v. Miike,* rejecting the state of Hawaii's arguments and finding for the plaintiffs. This controversial decision was stayed the next day, pending a return appeal to the state Supreme Court, the latter expected to rule by the end of 1997.

COMMON GROUND

A notable development in the literature of gay and lesbian America during the 1980s and 1990s was the appearance of research aimed at retrieving varied aspects of local and regional community history. Perhaps the best example of this type of historical writing is the influential biography of Harvey Milk, gathered after his assassination by journalist Randy Shilts and published in 1982 as *The Mayor of Castro Street.* An earlier volume of interviews, entitled *The Gay Crusaders,* provides valuable information on the lives and viewpoints of many individuals active in the gay liberation movement in New York City. A longstanding stereotype was formally challenged by the 1996 collection edited by Will Fellows, *Farm Boys: Lives of Gay Men from the Rural Midwest,* while women's studies expanded to embrace the legacy of radical lesbian separatists, treating it as part of local history. Among the works of this kind are Elizabeth Kennedy's *Boots of Leather, Slippers of Gold: The History of a Lesbian Community* (1993) on Buffalo, New York; Floyd Galvin's history of the Dallas community, *The Lavender Shingle* (1996); and *One in Ten: A Profile of Alaska's Gay and Lesbian Community* (1986). Local filmmakers have also begun to generate documentaries, an excellent example being the audiovisual record *There Is No Such Thing as a Private Moment,* covering Madison, Wisconsin, from 1969 to 1982.

Another phenomenon seen in gay and lesbian communities across the United States beginning in the 1970s was the creation of local archival collections and the initiation of efforts to collect and preserve both printed and oral records. While the earliest began as private collections (such as New York's Lesbian Herstory Archives, founded in 1973), the most significant period of development occurred during the early 1980s, stimulated by a heightened sense of historical awareness generated by the premature deaths of many local community leaders from AIDS. Examples of such are Chicago's Gerber-Hart Library and Archives, The Quatrefoil Library of St. Paul, and the Gay and Lesbian Archives of the Pacific Northwest in Portland, Oregon.

The most basic commonality of all local gay and lesbian communities across the United States is struggle—for political recognition, for equal employment opportunities and retirement benefits, for due process and protection under the law, and for the right to have life partnerships formally sanctioned by the larger society. A second bond uniting widely separated populations lies in the philosophies of liberation espoused by regional and local leaders of both genders (whether home grown or adaptations of approaches successful elsewhere) and the direct action tactics chosen to implement them. This feature of national community also has a hidden historical dimension, in that those areas that possessed a chapter of the Mattachine Society, the Daughters of Bilitis, or ONE, Inc. are more likely to have developed gay and lesbian populations aware of the possibility of creating change within local cultural limits. While the homophile groups never numbered more than several hundred nationwide, the mere fact (or memory) of their existence in a city, coupled with the presence of older veteran activists, provided proof that local institutions could be created, an obvious if necessary realization basic to beginning any coherent program of planned revolution. Areas that did not participate in the homophile era (such as much of the South and the mountain West) were thus forced to synthesize by experiment tactics applicable to their unique settings. Targets of liberation activity were inevitably shared, given the legal, moral, and political underpinnings of American society. Limits such as sodomy laws, "victimless crime" legislation, police harassment, employment and housing discrimination, and stereotypes in both print and electronic media were all selected for challenge by the post-Stonewall generation of activists.

One area in which disparity exists lies in the visibility of gay and lesbian individuals as citizens who have chosen to affirm their presence and culture. The larger urban regions (whether coastal ports or interior capital cities and industrial centers) offered an environment whose relative anonymity provided a harassed minority with the option of blending in, or "passing." Although much of the activism during the first five years of the gay liberation movement stressed "coming out of the closet" and celebrating existence with visibility, this tactic was only sporadically adopted in smaller cities, many groups preferring to eschew a radical identification in hopes of increasing their political acceptability. The idea that homosexuality per se is a bicoastal phenomenon is rooted in this period of deliberate choices. Kept informed of marches and street demonstrations through the burgeoning gay and lesbian press (and later via the global connections of the Internet), most local community leaders pursued selective activism, rather than transplanting one strategy intact. A third difference at the local level observable since 1969 is the emergence of gay and lesbian "communities" made up of widely scattered individuals linked via a single issue (such as same-sex marriage) or a particular forum of communication. This last ranges from newsletters serving rural Wisconsin to the intricacies of the World Wide Web. Instantaneous transmission of data and debate has further made possible the formation of many "virtual" spaces with a homosexual character, to an extent that geographic location is no longer as powerful a defining factor as before. Open access to the plans and programs of those bodies concerned with a focused subtext of liberation (as with the Human Rights Campaign's lobbying work) allows for the coalescence of community public opinion outside of the immediate locale of issues with broad implications, such as Colorado's Amendment 2. The diversity of gay and lesbian America is both a fact to be celebrated and a political principle powerful enough to unify a people.

PROMINENT PEOPLE

Virginia Apuzzo (1941-)

The daughter of a working-class family in the Bronx, Virginia Apuzzo early on showed both an aptitude for learning and a deep interest in justice and civil rights. Following completion of her Catholic high school years, she acquired a bachelor's degree in history and education from the State University of New York, College of New Paltz, in 1963, and shortly thereafter became chair of the social studies department for the local school district in Marlboro, New York. Inner questions about the direction of her life (and a need to explore her already recognized lesbian identity) prompted her to enter the Sisters of Charity in the mid-1960s, where she remained for three years, pursuing a master's degree and teaching in two Catholic schools. In 1969, she left the Order to accept a position at Brooklyn College, where she remained until 1986. From this base, she expanded her civil rights interests, working first with the Manhattan Women's Political Caucus and later serving as assistant commissioner for operations for the New York City Department of Health.

Her connection to gay and lesbian activism began in the 1970s with her coordinating role in the effort to obtain a gay rights plank in the national platform of the Democratic party as a member of its platform committee, to which she was appointed after an unsuccessful election campaign for the New York State Assembly. From this post, she also became involved in organizing lesbian and gay political support for the Carter/Mondale presidential campaign. By 1982, she was one of the few openly gay delegates to attend the midterm Democratic party convention in Philadelphia, and had become director of the Fund for Human Dignity, the fundraising arm of the National Gay and Lesbian Task Force. In November 1982, she was appointed to succeed Lucia Valeska as executive director of the Task Force, a post she retained until 1985. In that time, she quickly became one of the most visible and articulate spokespeople for the American homosexual community and its issues, traveling widely and achieving a degree of national recognition not previously possessed by any gay community leader.

Her interests expanded quickly to focus on the then-emerging AIDS pandemic, beginning with a press conference in January 1983 attended by 50 gay community groups in an attempt to define a national policy for blood donations, while in May she appeared before a House appropriations subcommittee to urge that $100 million be allocated to AIDS research. In September 1984, she collaborated with the Lambda Legal Defense and Education Fund and the American Association of Physicians for Civil Rights to design a model consent form for participants in AIDS-related laboratory trials. Her appointment in 1985 by then-Governor Mario Cuomo as deputy of the New York State Consumer Protection Board enabled her to investigate the array of drugs and natural products being touted as possessing an effect on the AIDS virus. Perhaps the most notable of Apuzzo's state jobs has been her work since 1994 with New York's Civil Service Commission, among whose issues she has included the coverage of same-sex domestic partnerships by the state health insurance program.

Don Baker

Born and raised in Dallas, Don Baker became an activist by invitation. Having completed service in the United States Navy and professional training as a teacher, he had returned home and was working in the city schools system when he was approached in 1979 by the Texas Human Rights Foundation with a request to serve as plaintiff in a class-action lawsuit against all city attorneys in the state. The objective of the suit was to challenge the legality of section 21.06 of the Texas state penal code, which prohibited homosexual conduct and made anyone engaging in such behavior a de facto criminal. His qualifications (in addition to being elected president of the Dallas Gay Alliance in 1980 and service as a lobbyist on gay issues with the legislature in Austin) lay in his status as a licensed public employee, which under Texan statute automatically assumed him to be "of good moral character," an attribute homosexuals were automatically denied by existing law. The suit, presented under the title of *Baker v. Wade*, had completed testimony by June of 1981, with the state being able to offer few grounds to support its prohibition of private sexual activity.

Melvin Boozer

On 14 August 1980, the historic invisibility of gay people at the national level of American politics came to an end in New York City. Speaking to the assembled delegates at the Democratic Party's convention, African-American activist Melvin Boozer, head of the District of Columbia Gay Activists Alliance, became the first open homosexual to be formally nominated as a candidate for the office of Vice President. In his address, he cited the past involvement of the Democrats with opposition to discrimination and called upon the delegates to acknowledge the situation of gay and lesbian Americans who "hide in the twilight of fear

Harry Britt

and oppression." He received only 49 votes, and his unprecedented address was ignored in network news coverage. In 1981, he joined the staff of the National Gay Task Force and was involved with the organization in various capacities (including serving as a board member) until his replacement in 1983 by Jeff Levi.

Harry Britt (1939-)

Born and raised in Port Arthur, Texas, in a traditional Methodist setting, Britt chose early on to involve himself heavily in church fellowship activities as an alternative to the regional macho ideal. Winning a National Merit scholarship, he attended Duke University and subsequently wed the daughter of his local minister, entering the Methodist clergy. Among his first postings was a parish on the south side of Chicago (where he witnessed firsthand the rage and grief at the assassination of Martin Luther King, Jr.). Acknowledgement of his sexual orientation led to divorce, followed in 1971 by a move from Dallas to San Francisco, the city whose political life he would come to affect.

His first sighting of an openly gay activist came with the televised coverage of liberationist Jim Foster's address to the 1972 Democratic National Convention, an example which stimulated his curiosity about practical efforts for change. While working as an auditor for a major hotel, he met then-businessman Harvey Milk and became involved with the Alice B. Toklas Democratic Club, a forum which inadvertently made him part of the burgeoning group of gay and lesbian po-

liticos within the San Francisco neighborhoods. Following Milk's assassination by former Supervisor Dan White in 1977, Britt was named in his taped will as one of four individuals who could succeed him, and spoke at the mass memorial service. Mayor Dianne Feinstein named Britt to serve out the remainder of Harvey Milk's term on the Board of Supervisors in January 1979, an event which marked his formal entry into the civic government structure. In his inaugural speech, Britt stated that "decisions about gay people must be made by gay people," a continuation of the community-based approach characteristic of his mentor. This apprenticeship was followed by successful independent election in 1980, 1984, and 1988. In 1992, he retired from public service.

David Clarenbach (1953-)

Openly gay member of the Wisconsin State House of Representatives and sponsor of Assembly Bill 70, a measure adding the phrase "sexual orientation" to extant state legal protections against discrimination in employment, housing, and public accommodations. The bill passed both houses of the legislature and was signed into law on 25 February 1982, becoming the first such measure at the state level in the United States.

Brian Coyle (1944-1991)

Achieving a visible gay and lesbian presence in local government at the city and county level has long been an activist's goal.

In 1983, former university instructor Brian Coyle entered the race for the aldermanic seat from Minneapolis's Sixth Ward. His successful election marked the beginning of a seven-year presence as the first openly gay man ever to sit on the Minneapolis City Council, a position from which he resigned in 1991 due to AIDS. His political experience reached back to the 1960s, beginning with involvement with the New Left (including anti-Vietnam War activism) and progressing through membership in the New American Movement to work as a tenant's rights counselor. Work for the 1972 McGovern campaign both prepared him for his own later 1978 and 1981 runs for city office and served as background to his assistance to state legislators Allen Spear and Karen Clark, whose open lesbian and gay presence in Minnesota public life served as an example of realizing his dream. Among his priorities while in office were the sponsorship of a domestic partnership ordinance, addressing the problem of anti-gay violence in the Twin Cities area, and AIDS prevention and treatment.

Sarah Craig (1955-1994)

From the mid-1970s to the early 1990s, activist issues often found an articulate voice through Sarah Craig. Born in the Midwest, she attended Vassar College and the University of Illinois, thereafter supporting herself by involvement in gay and lesbian liberation. She joined the staff of Chicago's *GayLife* newspaper in the late 1970s (eventually becoming co-editor with Stephen Kulieke) and founded a typesetting business which produced much of the local gay and lesbian organizational literature of the time. In 1987, she joined *Windy City Times* as an associate editor, winning a Peter Lisagor Award in 1990 for news reporting. But to many people, it was her cohosted radio program "Horizons," first aired on WFYR-FM in July 1980, that established her as a familiar presence in the city's homosexual communities. Her premature death from an aneurysm left a distinct void in Chicago gay and lesbian politics and communications.

Jon-Henri Damski (c. 1939-1997)

Although a native of Seattle, writer and columnist Damski is most closely identified with his adopted city of Chicago. Following completion of a doctorate at the University of Washington, he was hired in the early 1970s by Bryn Mawr College as a professor of Latin and classics as part of an effort at expanding the inclusivity of their faculty. Arriving in Chicago in 1973 with a teaching position in the adult education division of Truman College, he quickly made a name for himself as the observer, recorder, and pundit of the weekly magazine *Gay Chicago*, initiating a career which ended only with his retirement from public journalism in the autumn of 1997 due to cancer. Beginning with his column "Nothing Personal," over a period of some 25 years he wrote nearly 1,000 columns for almost every gay newspaper and publication issued in Chicago, moving from his initial home to *GayLife* and its successors *Windy City Times, OUTlines,* and *Nightlines,* making him the longest running feature writer anywhere in the American gay press. On 4 June 1997, he was honored with a proclamation issued by the Chicago City Council recognizing his contribution to the drafting and passage of the city's gay and lesbian civil rights bill. He died on 1 November 1997.

Tim Drake (1953-)

A native of Gary, Indiana, Tim Drake took an early interest in Republican politics, working for the 1972 campaign of Richard Nixon. Moving to Chicago in 1974, he acquired practical experience through an unsuccessful run for the Illinois legislature. Backing the candidacy of John Anderson in the 1980 presidential primary, Drake became the first openly gay person to win a delegate spot to a meeting of the Republican National Committee. On 12 May 1980, at its convention in Chicago, the Committee refused to hear Drake's testimony, citing scheduling difficulties while granting time for a delegate representing religious interests. A longtime involvement with the Illinois Gay and Lesbian Task Force culminated in 1990 with his rise to co-chair of the organization. The same year also witnessed a second unsuccessful try for election to state office.

Jim Foster

Veteran San Francisco political activist Jim Foster was born in New York and raised in a conservative Republican household. He arrived in San Francisco in 1959 after receiving a dishonorable discharge from the army on grounds of homosexuality. By 1969, he was the political chairperson of the Society for Individual Rights, and he served as the first president of the Alice B. Toklas Democratic Club upon its founding on 8 February 1972. Later that year, he became the first openly gay delegate ever to address the Democratic National Convention. By 1975, he was serving as a director of the Whitman-Radclyffe Foundation and state chair of the Gay Caucus of the California Democratic Council. These activities made him a prominent figure in San Francisco gay political circles, a position he maintained during and after the election of Harvey Milk, including assisting the campaign of Milk's successor Harry Britt through fundraising. On 28 February 1981, he attended the meeting held in Washington, D.C., at which a national organization of gay and lesbian Democratic clubs was formed.

Gilberto Gerald (1950-)

Born in Panama and raised in the Caribbean, activist Gilberto Gerald immigrated to the United States in 1967 shortly before his seventeenth birthday. Although he had accumulated enough legal residency time to apply for full citizenship by 1972, he did not begin to take action on this matter until 1978, after completing a degree in architectural science from Pratt Institute. By that time, he had become active in several social and political organizations within the gay community of the District of Columbia (including the National Coalition of Black Gays), all of which he listed on his citizenship application as required by law. This honesty and compliance with federal regulations marked the beginning of what would eventually become a four-year battle to gain citizen status, a rank not achieved until January 1982. Gerald was a member of the delegation of Third World lesbians and gays of color which met with Carter presidential aide Anne Wexler at the White House in June 1979, an event organized by the Coalition, which requested him to address the issue of inequality and exclusion in American immigration laws on the basis of sexual orientation from his own personal experience. From 1983 to May 1987, Gerald served as the Coalition's executive director, challenging gay, lesbian, and African-American leaders to recognize and address the consequences of racism within the homosexual community on issues ranging from civil rights to access to AIDS care. He resigned in January 1987 to join the National AIDS Network.

Henry Gerber (1892-1972)

Born in Bavaria, Gerber immigrated to the United States at the age of twenty-one. Arriving in his new homeland in 1914, he enlisted in the Army the following year under a provision which permitted aliens to serve. Interned during World War I, he was able to serve in the Army of Occupation from 1920 to 1923 and was stationed in Coblenz. It was only upon his return to Germany that Gerber became aware of the organizations working for legal equality for homosexuals, such as Dr. Magnus Hirschfeld's Scientific Humanitarian Committee. Completing his service, Gerber took a job with the U.S. Postal Service and settled in Chicago. Having read German homosexual periodicals during his service, he was aware of the then-chaotic state of American sex law and legislation, but noted that "the homosexuals themselves needed nearly as much attention as the laws pertaining to their acts.... What was needed was a Society" (Katz, *Gay American History,* p. 338). Borrowing in translation the name of a German group, Gerber drew up a "Declaration of Purpose" for the new organization, the Society for Human Rights. Its application for legal recognition by the state of Illinois, filed on 10 December 1924, marks the earliest documented body in the United States devoted to the area of homosexual rights. Two issues of a now-lost periodical, *Friendship and Freedom,* also were published, marking a first attempt at establishing a gay journalism. The Society's stated object was "to promote and protect the interests of people who by reasons of

mental or physical abnormalities are hindered in their legal pursuit of happiness ... and to combat the public prejudices against them by dissemination of facts according to modern science" (Katz, *Gay American History,* p. 387). This last endeavor was to occur through a series of public lectures similar to those being mounted by Hirschfeld's organization in Berlin. These lofty aims were, however, never realized. In 1925, Gerber and several others were arrested by the Chicago police without warrants following a complaint from one of the members' wives. After three lengthy and rather bizarre court appearances, charges against the accused were dismissed for violation of due process, but Gerber's employment was ended for "conduct unbecoming a postal worker" (Katz, *Gay American History,* p. 393).

Leaving Chicago, Gerber moved to New York and wrote three articles which were printed in German homosexual publications between 1928 and 1930 on subjects ranging from attacking critics of Radclyffe Hall's *The Well of Loneliness* to a survey of American state laws covering sodomy and "the crime against nature." Between 1930 and 1939, working as a proofreader for the U.S. Army, Gerber produced *Contacts,* a pen-pal newsletter which

Franklin Kameny (in front of banner) in a 1979 march.

served as a discreet means for male homosexuals to find each other. Through it he initiated a lengthy correspondence with Californian Manuel Boyfrank (who was also interested in creating a society for homosexuals), which lasted until 1948. His activism in the 1940s took the form of writing letters to periodicals such as the *American Mercury* and the *Washington Post* opposing the prevailing clinical opinions about homosexuals and protesting prejudiced editorials. By early 1949, Gerber had completed translations of several chapters from Magnus Hirschfeld's mammoth work *Homosexuality in Men and Women;* the translations were then published in the *ONE Institute Quarterly*. While a short unsigned letter describing the fate of the Chicago effort appeared in *ONE Magazine,* and several essays were sent to the New York City Mattachine chapter for their newsletter, Gerber's involvement with the homophile movement was that of a persistent advocate who believed that organization and opposition to poor treatment would be the key to improving homosexual life. In September 1962, a lengthy, signed article expanding on his earlier piece about the Society for Human Rights appeared in *ONE Magazine*. Gerber died in the Washington, D.C., Soldier's Home on 31 December 1972, having lived long enough to witness the birth of the gay liberation movement.

Darrel Hildebrant (1947-)

Born and raised on a sheep ranch near Beach, North Dakota, librarian and puppeteer Hildebrant's significance for the gay and lesbian community lies in his role as creator of The Coalition, the first AIDS activist organization in North Dakota, at a time when that state had the fewest AIDS cases of any location in the United States. He traveled the state speaking to numerous groups ranging from professional associations to church congregations in isolated prairie towns, putting a human face on the pandemic and becoming the most prominent gay man in the state. He later moved to Minneapolis and worked for the Minnesota AIDS Project as an outreach educator, contributing articles to the local gay and lesbian newspaper *Equal Time*. He also participated in the program "AIDS Education: Meeting the Challenge" at the 1990 American Library Association annual convention in Chicago.

Franklin Kameny (1925-)

Born in Queens, New York, Dr. Franklin Kameny decided at the age of six that he wanted to become an astronomer. In 1941, he began study at Queens College but left to serve in World War II, eventually seeing hazardous combat as part of an armored infantry battalion in Germany. Returning to civilian life in 1946, he took a B.S. degree in physics and continued his interest in astronomy, graduating with a doctorate from Harvard in 1956.

His career as an activist began at the end of 1957, when he was discharged from his position as an astronomer for the Army Map Service (despite an excellent evaluation record) on the grounds of being homosexual. Over the next four years, Kameny contested this action through every legal venue then available, including presenting a petition to the United States Supreme Court (which refused to hear the case). In response, Kameny and a few friends in 1961 founded the Mattachine Society of Washington, whose stated purpose was to be a "civil-liberties, social-action organization dedicated to improving the status of the homosexual citizen." In 1968, taking inspiration from popular rhetoric of the time which celebrated various ethnic identities, he coined the phrase "Gay Is Good," which was first adopted by the North American Conference of Homophile Organizations and subsequently became a ral-

Morris Kight with the ashes of Harvey Milk.

lying cry during the earliest years of the gay liberation movement. Among the direct actions Kameny initiated was an article for the February 1971 issue of *Psychiatric Opinion* which attacked that discipline's position that homosexuality was a treatable mental illness and called upon the profession to remove it from its list of pathologies, an action finally taken in 1973. His visibility outside of the gay and lesbian community was heightened by his entry into the 1971 race for the non-voting seat in the House of Representatives occupied by the delegate for the District of Columbia. This unsuccessful campaign marked the first time an openly gay man had ever stood for election to the United States Congress, and foreshadowed the later presence on Capitol Hill of Gerry Studds and Barney Frank. The area of employment discrimination against gay and lesbian individuals by the federal government in non-classified grades was also a major target of his activism, an effort which eventually resulted in a decision of 3 July 1975, by the Civil Service Commission to drop homosexuality as grounds for termination. He also drafted the text of the legal measure enacted on 13 September 1993 repealing the District of Columbia's sodomy law.

Morris Kight (1919-)

Born in Texas, Kight became a pacifist as a young man after reading the works of Gandhi. During the 1940s and 1950s, he also did volunteer work against venereal disease in Arkansas and New Mexico. After moving to Los Angeles in 1958, he began his career as a homosexual activist in 1969, when he founded the Gay Liberation Front of Los Angeles. Subsequent work included helping with the establishment of the Gay Community Center, the Stonewall Democratic Club, and Christopher Street West.

Elaine Noble (1944-)

A native of New Kensington, Pennsylvania, Elaine Noble moved to New England in pursuit of a degree in fine arts, which she obtained in 1966 from Boston University. She swiftly became involved in the gay and lesbian political life of the city, joining the local chapter of the Daughters of Bilitis and the Homophile Union of Boston. In 1971, she founded (and, for several years, co-hosted) "Gay Way," a weekly radio show broadcast on station WBUR-FM. In 1974, she successfully ran for a seat in the Massachusetts legislature as representative for Boston's Fenway district as an open lesbian, becoming the first openly gay person to be elected to state office anywhere in the United States. During her two terms in office, she attempted unsuccessfully to pass a statewide job protection bill for gays and lesbians and served to shatter many stereotypes of lesbians. In 1978, with the redrawing of district boundaries, Noble found herself in the same jurisdiction as then-closeted gay legislator Barney Frank. Rather than split the gay vote over the race, she entered the Democratic primary for the United States Senate, losing to future presidential candidate Paul Tsongas.

Craig Rodwell (1940-1993)

Growing up in Chicago during the 1950s, Craig Rodwell had a clear sense of himself as different, and he discovered the city's gay subculture at the age of thirteen. After graduating from a public high school, he came to New York on a scholarship to study at the American Ballet School. Finding the meetings of the local Mattachine chapter too tame, he joined the newly formed Homosexual League of New York and participated in the first gay picket line in the United States. This action, held at the Whitehall Street Induction Center in 1963, was aimed at protesting the violation of confidentiality of draft records for gay men. By 1965, he had helped to bring Mattachine to a more activist stance, although the group was unwilling to create the type of storefront center he envisioned. Using his own capital, he stocked and opened the first gay bookstore in America, the Oscar Wilde Memorial Bookstore, in 1967.

David Scondras

David Scondras (1946-)

In the autumn of 1983, Northeastern University mathematics professor and veteran community activist David Scondras entered the race for the Boston City Council, running against another openly gay candidate. His election that October marked the first time the city had ever elected an openly gay public official, and Scondras quickly became one of the most articulate voices for improving the legal condition of gay and lesbian citizens. In November 1996, he was attacked in a Boston mall theater and severely beaten.

Allen Spear (1937-)

Born in Michigan City, Indiana, Allen Spear completed his undergraduate education at Oberlin College and later did masters and doctoral work at Yale prior to his appointment to the history faculty of the University of Minnesota in 1964. A longstanding involvement with the civil rights and anti-war movements, penal reform, and civil liberties issues is evident in his 1967 book *Black Chicago: The Making of a Negro Ghetto, 1890-1920*. A redrawing of political districts provided an opportunity for him to successfully seek election from a largely university-based district in Minneapolis. He was inspired to go public with his homosexuality by the success of Elaine Noble's political campaign in Massachusetts. Spear came out by granting a front-page interview to the *Minneapolis Star-Tribune* confirming his homosexuality. While many of his colleagues in the state senate viewed his admission as political suicide, Spear successfully won re-election in 1976. He was a major sponsor of the proposed state gay civil rights bill for Minnesota, which was finally enacted in 1993. By that time, Spear had risen to the rank of senate president, a post he held into 1996.

Urvashi Vaid (1958-)

Born in New Delhi, India, Urvashi Vaid immigrated to the United States at the age of seven. A transcultural childhood in the academic world of Potsdam, New York (where her father, an accomplished poet, was a member of the English faculty) was marked by an early interest in politics and civil rights. Graduation from high school in 1975 was followed by years at Vassar, which she credits as having taught her how to organize through experience planning four feminist conferences. College also enabled her to crystallize a lesbian identity, which she actively pursued in 1979 by moving to Boston after graduation. Her most important engagement with her new city was becoming a member in 1980 of the volunteer group that met to assemble *Gay Community News*. Northeastern University provided training as a lawyer, a career incorporating many aspects of her activist interests. By 1983, she was living in Washington, D.C., and working as an attorney for the American Civil Liberties Union's National Prison Project. Lobbying work brought her into contact with the National Gay Task Force staff and director Virginia Apuzzo.

Her full-time involvement with gay political work began in 1986 with her appointment as the Task Force's public information director and, eventually, executive director, the first lesbian of color ever to lead a national gay rights organization. During her six years in that position, she focused on media organizing, creating and strengthening links with grassroots homosexual rights advocates, planning and guiding direct action protests, and clarifying strategy and policy positions. She resigned in 1992 for personal reasons, among them the writing *of Virtual Equality: The Mainstreaming of Gay and Lesbian Liberation*, which was published in 1995. This influential work both summarized the politi-

Urvashi Vaid

cal strategies taken by the gay and lesbian movement to that point and set forth the steps necessary to alter what Vaid saw as a continuing second-class status of homosexual Americans. Vaid defines the title phrase in her preface as "a state of conditional equality based more upon the appearance of acceptance ... than on genuine civic parity." By 1997, she had resumed activist work, directing the Policy Institute of the Task Force.

REFERENCES:

Books

Beam, Joseph, ed. *In The Life: A Black Gay Anthology*. Boston: Alyson Publications, 1986.

Button, James W., Barbara A. Rienzo, and Kenneth D. Wald. *Private Lives, Public Conflicts: Battles over Gay Rights in American Communities*. Washington, D.C.: Congressional Quarterly Inc, 1997.

Chauncey, George. *Gay New York: Gender, Urban Culture and the Making of the Gay Male World, 1890-1940*. New York: Basic Books, 1994.

Katz, Jonathan. *Gay American History: Lesbians and Gay Men in the U.S.A., A Documentary*. New York: Thomas Crowell, 1976.

———. *Gay/Lesbian Almanac: A New Documentary*. New York: Harper and Row, 1983, new edition, 1994.

Kramer, Larry. "The Beginning of ACTing UP," in *Reports from the Holocaust: The Making of an AIDS Activist*. New York: St. Martin's Press, 1989: 127-39.

Marcus, Eric. *Making History: The Struggle for Gay and Lesbian Equal Rights, 1945-1990, An Oral History*. New York: HarperCollins, 1992.

Murphy, Lawrence R. *Perverts By Official Order: The Campaign Against Homosexuals by the United States Navy*. New York: Haworth Press, 1988.

Musbach, Tom. "Frank Kameny," in *Gay and Lesbian Biography*, edited by Michael Tyrkus. Detroit: St. James Press, 1997: 261-62.

Ridinger, Robert B. Marks. *The Homosexual and Society: An Annotated Bibliography*. Westport, Connecticut: Greenwood, 1990.

———. *The Gay and Lesbian Movement: References and Resources*. New York: G. K. Hall, 1996.

Sears, James T. *Growing Up Gay in the South: Race, Gender and Journeys of the Spirit*. New York: Haworth Press, 1991.

———. *Lonely Hunters: An Oral History of Lesbian and Gay Southern Life, 1948-1968*. Boulder, Colorado: Westview Press, 1997.

Shilts, Randy. *The Mayor of Castro Street*. New York: St. Martin's Press, 1982.

Sullivan, Andrew, ed. *Same-Sex Marriage: Pro and Con, A Reader*. New York: Vintage, 1997.

Timmons, Stuart. *The Trouble with Harry Hay: Founder of the Modern Gay Movement*. Boston: Alyson Publications, 1990.

Tobin, Kay and Randy Wicker. *The Gay Crusaders*. New York: Arno Press, 1975.

Vaid, Urvashi. *Virtual Equality: The Mainstreaming of Gay and Lesbian Liberation*. New York: Anchor Books, 1995.

Witt, Stephanie L. and Suzanne McCorkle. *Anti-Gay Rights: Assessing Voter Initiatives*. Westport, Connecticut: Praeger, 1997.

Periodicals

Doyle, Patrick. "Atlanta: Gay Pearl in Stolid South," in *Advocate*, 25 May 1973: 11.

"How ONE Began," in *ONE*, February 1995: 8-15.

"The Lessons of Miami: Four Perspectives of Dade County," in *Advocate*, 24 August 1977: 7-10.

"Personal Statement of Gerald E. Studds, 14 July 1983," in *Bay Windows*, August 1983: 7.

Podolsky, Robin. "Birth of a Queer Nation: Activists Say There's More To Do Than Just Act Up," in *Advocate*, 9 October 1990: 52-53.

Ponnuru, Ramesh. "Kennedy's Queer Opinion," in *National Review*, 17 June 1996): 22-23.

"Text of Mel Boozer's Speech," in *Washington Blade*, 21 August 1980: 6.

—Robert B. Marks Ridinger

GENERAL BIBLIOGRAPHY

Abelove, Henry, Michèle Aina Barale, and David M. Halperin, eds. *The Lesbian and Gay Studies Reader*. New York: Routledge, 1993. Explores sexuality from a variety of perspectives in many essays, some hard to find.

Adam, Barry D. *The Rise of a Gay and Lesbian Movement*. Boston: Twayne Publishers, 1987. Targets periods of persecution throughout history worldwide.

Alyson, Sasha, ed. *The Alyson Almanac: The Fact Book of the Lesbian and Gay Community*. Boston: Alyson Publications, 1993. Includes biographical information, historical highlights, slang, hotlines, and books, among many other gay-themed topics.

Bawer, Bruce. *A Place at the Table: The Individual in American Society*. New York: Poseidon Press, 1993. A gay writer reflects on the nature of homosexuality and his desire to discourage stereotypes.

Beam, Joseph, ed. *In The Life: A Black Gay Anthology*. Boston: Alyson Publications, 1986.

Beemyn, Brett, ed. *Creating a Place for Ourselves: Lesbian, Gay, and Bisexual Community Histories*. New York: Routledge, 1997. Eleven essays look at such communities as San Francisco, California; Detroit, Michigan; Buffalo, New York; and Birmingham, Alabama, before the birth of gay liberation.

Beemyn, Brett, and Mickey Eliason, eds. *Queer Studies: A Lesbian, Gay, Bisexual, and Transgender Anthology*. New York: New York University Press, 1996.

Bell, A. P. & Weinberg, M. S. *Homosexualities*. New York: Simon & Schuster, 1978.

Blumenfeld, Warren J., and Diane Raymond. *Looking at Gay and Lesbian Life*. Boston: Beacon Press, 1988. Explores a wide assortment of topics from law to biology.

Boykin, Keith. *One More River to Cross: Black and Gay in America*. New York: Anchor Books, 1996. From his own personal experience and that of other black gays and lesbians, Boykin, who once served as President Clinton's liaison to the minority press, explores such subjects as racism and homophobia.

Bremmer, Jan, ed. *From Sappho to de Sade. Moments in the History of Sexuality*. London/New York: Routledge, 1989.

Bronski, Michael. *Culture Clash: The Making of a Gay Sensibility*. Boston: South End Press, 1984.

Browning, Frank. *The Culture of Desire: Paradox and Perversity in Gay Lives Today*. New York: Crown, 1993. Author ponders whether an American gay culture actually exists in terms of sexual orientation, not from an ethnic or religious perspective.

Bull, Chris, and John Gallagher. *Perfect Enemies: The Religious Right, the Gay Movement, and the Politics of the 1990s*. New York: Crown, 1996. A balanced exploration of the political concerns of both the gay and evangelical movements, taking into account their similarities and differences.

Bullough, Vern, L. *Homosexuality: A History*. New York: New American Library, 1979.

Butler, Judith. *Gender Trouble: Feminism and the Subversion of Identity*. New York: Routledge, 1990. Purports, among other theories, that gender is more something one performs than something one possesses, and that the war between the sexes reflects culture more than anatomy.

———. *Bodies That Matter: On The Discursive Limits of "Sex."* New York: Routledge, 1993. Feminist theory centered on the philosophical exploration of the status of the body.

Button, James W., Barbara A. Rienzo, and Kenneth D. Wald. *Private Lives, Public Conflicts: Battles over Gay Rights in American Communities*. Washington, D.C.: Congressional Quarterly Inc, 1997.

Chauncey, George. *Gay New York: Gender, Urban Culture, and the Making of the Gay Male World, 1890-1940*. New York: HarperCollins, 1994. Argues that prior to World War II gay men and to a lesser extent lesbians were quite visible and respected in many aspects of the New York City landscape.

Comstock, G. D. *Violence against Lesbians and Gay Men*. New York: Columbia University Press, 1991. Argues for democraticizing sexual ethics and includes a discussion of HIV/AIDS.

Cruikshank, Margaret. *The Gay and Lesbian Liberation Movement*. New York: Routledge, 1992. From a feminist point of view.

D'Emilio, John. *Sexual Politics, Sexual Communities: The Making of a Homosexual Minority in the United States, 1940-1970*. Chicago: University of Chicago Press, 1983. Examines gay life in America before Stonewall.

———. *Making Trouble: Essays on Gay History, Politics, and the University*. New York: Routledge, 1992. Twenty essays written over almost two decades by one of the earliest gay historians.

D'Emilio, John, and Estelle B. Freedman. *Intimate Matters: A History of Sexuality in America*. New York: Harper and Row, 1988. Discusses such topics as the relationship between McCarthyism and gay baiting in the 1950s; Victorian pornography and prostitution; and the often-ignored lustiness of American Puritans.

Doty, Alexander. *Making Things Perfectly Queer: Interpreting Mass Culture*. Minneapolis: University of Minnesota Press, 1993. Discusses, among other topics, queer cultures, queer auteurs, and such television sitcoms as *Laverne and Shirley* in relation to the gay and lesbian realm.

Duberman, Martin. *Stonewall*. New York: Plume, 1993. Six different perspectives on the impact of Stonewall.

Duberman, Martin, ed. *A Queer World. The Center for Lesbian and Gay Studies Reader*. New York: New York University Press, 1997.

Duberman, Martin, Martha Vicinus, and George Chauncey, Jr., eds. *Hidden from History: Reclaiming The Gay and Lesbian Past*. New York: Penguin Books, 1989. Twenty-nine essays with perspectives ranging from historical to modern.

Duggan, Lisa, and Nan D. Hunter. *Sex Wars: Sexual Dissent and Political Culture*. New York: Routledge, 1995. Covers such topics as feminist antipornography legislation, censorship, and the Sharon Kowalski case.

Dynes, Wayne R. *Homosexuality: A Research Guide*. New York: Garland Publishing, Inc., 1987. Comprises more than 4800 citations (from many languages) under 24 main topics.

Dynes, Wayne R., ed. *Encyclopedia of Homosexuality*. Vols. 1-2. New York/London: Garland Publishing, 1990. More than 750 articles covering all facets of homosexuality, including a reader's guide.

Faderman, Lillian. *Surpassing the Love of Men: Romantic Friendship and Love between Women from the Renaissance to the Present*. New York: William Morrow and Company, Inc., 1981. Argues that loving companionships between middle-class women were common in the eighteenth and nineteenth centuries.

———. *Odd Girls and Twilight Lovers: A History of Lesbian Life in Twentieth-Century America*. New York: Penguin, 1991. Examines lesbian subcultures and how feminism and gay liberation promoted female, same-sex relationships.

Feinberg, Leslie. *Transgender Warriors: Making History from Joan of Arc to RuPaul.* Boston: Beacon Press, 1996. A compendium of transgender history.

Foucault, Michel. *Histoire de la sexualité/The History of Sexuality.* Vol. 1: *La Volenté de savoir.* Paris: L'editions Gallimard 1976 (trans.: *An Introduction,* New York: Pantheon 1978). Vol. 2: *L'usage des plaisirs.* Paris: L'editions Gallimard 1984 (trans.: *The Use of Pleasure,* New York: Pantheon 1985). Vol. 3: *Le souci de soi.* Paris: L'editions Gallimard 1984 (trans.: *The Care of the Self,* New York: Pantheon 1986).

Foucault, Michel. *The History of Sexuality. Volume I: An Introduction.* Translated from the French by Robert Hurley. New York: Random House, 1978. Foucault develops a political critique of sexual liberation.

Grahn, Judy. *Another Mother Tongue: Gay Words, Gay Worlds.* Boston: Beacon Press, 1990. Examines use of language in terms of gay and lesbian culture.

Greenberg, David F. *The Construction of Homosexuality.* Chicago: University of Chicago Press, 1990. From a cross-cultural and transhistorical perspective, Greenberg explores how different cultures have responded to homosexuality across time.

Greenblatt, R. Ellen, and Cal Gough, eds. *Gay and Lesbian Library Service.* Jefferson, NC: McFarland and Company, Inc. 1990. Focusing on the needs of librarians and library school students, this work includes such topics as collection development, services issues (reference, access, user-friendliness, exhibits, and censorship), descriptions of special collections, and bibliographic control.

Highleyman, Liz A. *A Brief History of the Bisexual Movement.* Cambridge: Bisexual Resource Center, 1993. Traces the evolution of the bisexual movement from the early 1970s to the 1990s.

Hogan, Steve, and Lee Hudson. *Completely Queer: The Gay and Lesbian Encyclopedia.* New York: Holt, 1998.

Irvine, Janice. *Disorders of Desire: Sex and Gender in Modern American Sexology.* Philadelphia: Temple University Press, 1990.

Jagose, Annamarie. *Queer Theory : An Introduction.* New York: New York University Press, 1996.

Katz, Jonathan Ned. *Gay/Lesbian Almanac.* New York: Harper and Row, 1983.

———. *Gay American History: Lesbians and Gay Men in the U.S.A.* New York: Penguin Books USA Inc., 1992. Study of gay and lesbian American history covering the years 1528 to 1976.

Katz, Jonathan Ned. *The Invention of Heterosexuality.* New York: Penguin Books USA Inc., 1995. An scholarly exploration of one distinct sexuality.

LeVay, Simon, and Elisabeth Nonas. *City of Friends: A Portrait of the Gay and Lesbian Community in America.* Cambridge: MIT Press, 1995. A discussion of the diversity of the gay and lesbian community in the U.S.

Likosky, Stephan. *Coming Out: An Anthology of International Gay and Lesbian Writings.* New York: Pantheon Books, 1992. Collection of gay and lesbian nonfiction since 1969.

Lorde, Audre. *Sister Outsider: Essays and Speeches.* Trumansburg, NY: Crossing Press, 1984. Among other topics, Lorde writes about her personal struggle with cancer, sex, poetry, racism, and being part of an interracial lesbian couple bringing up a son.

Malinowski, Sharon, ed. *Gay and Lesbian Literary Companion.* Detroit: Visible Ink Press, 1995. Biographies of 45 authors, mostly American and contemporary.

Marcus, Eric. *Making History: The Struggle for Gay and Lesbian Equal Rights.* New York: HarperCollins Publishers, Inc., 1992. Covers 1945 to 1990 as seen through the perspectives of many individuals with diverse experiences.

Marotta, Toby. *The Politics of Homosexuality.* Boston: Houghton Mifflin Company, 1981. Traces evolution of gay politics in the U.S. from the 1940s to the 1970s.

Miller, Neil. *In Search of Gay America: Women and Men in a Time of Change.* New York: Atlantic Monthly, 1989.

———. *Out of the Past: Gay and Lesbian History from 1869 to the Present.* New York: Vintage Books, 1995.

Morton, Donald, ed. *The Material Queer. A Lesbigay Cultural Studies Reader.* Boulder, CO: Westview Press, 1996. An anthology offering a materialist comprehension of marginal sexualities by providing a variety of classic and contemporary perspectives.

The National Museum & Archive of Lesbian and Gay History. *The Lesbian Almanac: The Most Comprehensive Reference Source of Its Kind.* New York: The Berkley Publishing Group, 1996. A thorough resource on lesbian history and culture, including chapters on notable North American lesbians; quotable quotes by and about lesbians; and a glossary of sayings, slang, signs, and symbols for lesbians.

———. *The Gay Almanac: The Most Comprehensive Reference Source of Its Kind.* New York: The Berkley Publishing Group, 1996. Companion to above title, but focusing on gay male culture rather than on lesbian culture.

Ochs, Robyn, ed. *The Bisexual Resource Guide.* Second Edition. Cambridge: Bisexual Resource Center, 1996.

Pharr, Suzanne. *Homophobia: A Weapon of Sexism.* Inverness, CA: Chardon Press, 1988. Explores the link between patriarchal heterosexuality and homophobia.

———. *In the Time of the Right.* Berkeley, CA: Chardon Press, 1996.

Ridinger, Robert B. Marks. *The Homosexual and Society: An Annotated Bibliography.* New York: Greenwood Press, 1990. Covers topics ranging from gay adoption to police attitudes to homosexuality and includes citations from the *Advocate,* the *Ladder,* and *Mattachine Review,* among other publications.

———. *The Gay and Lesbian Movement: References and Resources.* New York: G. K. Hall, 1996.

Roscoe, Will, ed., (with Gay American Indians, including Randy Burns). *Living the Spirit: A Gay American Indian Anthology.* New York: St. Martin's, 1988.

Rutledge, Leigh W. *The Gay Book of Lists.* Boston: Alyson Publications, 1987.

———. *The Gay Decades.* New York: Penguin Books, 1992. A daily chronology covering social, political, legal, and cultural gay-related occurrences from 1969 to 1990.

———. *The New Gay Book of Lists.* Los Angeles: Alyson Publications, 1996.

Sears, James T. *Growing Up Gay in the South: Race, Gender and Journeys of the Spirit.* New York: Haworth Press, 1991. Organized within five vantage points: Homosexuality and the Religious South; Homosexuality and Southern Communities; Homosexuality and the Southern Families; Gender and Sexuality; and Sexuality and Adolescence.

———. *Lonely Hunters: An Oral History of Lesbian and Gay Southern Life, 1948-1968.* Boulder, Colorado: Westview Press, 1997. The first oral history of homosexual Southerners in the U.S. combating racism, homophobia, and sexism.

Sears, James T., and Williams, Walter, L. *Overcoming Heterosexism and Homophobia: Strategies That Work.* New York: Columbia University Press, 1997. A resource for educators, social workers, psychologists, and community activists, this work offers suggestions for promoting diversity and overcoming both heterosexism and homophobia in such fields as politics, education, and the helping professions.

Stein, Arlene, ed. *Sisters, Sexperts, Queers: Beyond the Lesbian Nation.* New York: Plume, 1993. A free-spirited anthology reflecting on the diversity of the lesbian community.

Sullivan, Andrew. *Virtually Normal.* New York: Knopf, 1995. An examination of contemporary gay culture and an argument against those who oppose gay liberation.

Sullivan, Andrew, ed. *Same-Sex Marriage: Pro and Con, A Reader.* New York: Vintage, 1997. Offers opinions spanning 2000 years, from Plato to Melissa Etheridge.

Thompson, Mark, ed. *Long Road to Freedom: The Advocate History of the Gay and Lesbian Movement.* New York: St. Martin's Press, 1994. A compilation of interviews, photos, news, and cartoons from the *Advocate*, covering the years 1969 to 1994.

Tucker, Naomi, ed. *Bisexual Politics: Theories, Queries, and Visions.* New York: Harrington Park Press, 1995. An anthology of 35 interviews, essays, and poems focusing on the realm of bisexuality from the 1970s to the 1990s.

Tyrkus, Michael J., ed. *Gay and Lesbian Biography.* Detroit: St. James Press, 1997. Biographies of 275 notable gays and lesbians from all time periods and from many parts of the globe.

Vaid, Urvashi. *Virtual Equality: The Mainstreaming of Gay and Lesbian Liberation.* New York: Anchor Books, 1995. Discusses how the gay community has become in recent years a more visible presence, not an entirely positive development according to Vaid.

Vance, Carole S., ed. *Pleasure and Danger: Exploring Female Sexuality.* Boston: Routledge and Kegan Paul, 1984.

Weeks, Jeffrey. *Sex, Politics and Society: The Regulation of Sexuality since 1800.* London: Longman, 1981.

———. *Sexuality.* London/New York: Tavistock Publications, 1986.

Witt, Lynn, Sherry Thomas, and Eric Marcus, eds. *Out in All Directions: The Almanac of Gay and Lesbian America.* New York: Warner Books, 1995. Explores a multitude of topics, including the presence of the gay population, the gay press, coming out, sexuality, travel and leisure, and workplace issues.

NOTES ON ADVISORS AND CONTRIBUTORS

ALEXANDER, Marilyn Bennett. Writer, lecturer, and consultant on issues of spirituality, sexuality, and empowerment. She is the co-author of *We Were Baptized Too: Claiming God's Grace for Lesbians and Gays,* published by Westminster John Knox Press. **Chapter:** Religion and Spirituality.

BEEMYN, Brett. Assistant professor of African American Studies at Western Illinois University. He is co-editor with Mickey Eliason of *Queer Studies: A Lesbian, Gay, Bisexual, and Transgender Anthology* (NYU Press, 1996); editor of *Creating a Place for Ourselves: Lesbian, Gay, and Bisexual Community Histories* (Routledge, 1997); and author of *A Queer Capital: A History of Lesbigay Life in Washington, D.C.* (Routledge, forthcoming). He also serves as the queer theories and cultures reviewer for *The Year's Work in Critical and Cultural Theory.* **Chapter:** Chronology.

BENNETT, Lisa. Fellow at Harvard University's Shorenstein Center on Press, Politics, and Public Policy, where she is writing about "The Role of Prejudice in the Coverage of Gays and Lesbians." A former newspaper journalist, and currently a freelance writer, Bennett has written for numerous magazines, books, and organizations. She also is a faculty member at New York University, where she teaches about the coverage of minorities in the media. **Chapter:** Coming Out.

BETTINGER, Michael. Ph.D., M.F.C.C., marriage and family therapist in private practice in San Francisco working primarily in the queer community for the past 26 years. When not working, he spends time with Bob, his husband and the love of his life for the past 11 years, or he can be found raising hell riding his Harley Davidson motorcycle. **Chapter:** Family.

BRONSKI, Michael. Author of *Culture Clash: The Making of Gay Sensibility* and *The Pleasure Principle: Sex, Backlash, and the Struggle for Gay Freedom,* and the editor of *Taking Liberties: Gay Men's Essays on Politics, Culture, and Sex* and *Flashpoint: Gay Male Sexual Writing.*

BURR, Chandler. Contributor to the *Atlantic Monthly, US News & World Report,* and *Poz.* He has written for the *New York Times Magazine* on AIDS and is the author of *A Separate Creation: The Search for the Biological Origins of Sexual Orientation.* **Chapter:** Science.

COLEMAN, Bud. Assistant professor in the department of theatre and dance at the University of Colorado at Boulder. He has a Ph.D. from the University of Texas at Austin and is a former dancer with Les Ballets Trockadero de Monte Carlo, Fort Worth Ballet, and Austin Ballet, and co-director of Kinesis. **Chapter:** "Gay Male Theater and Dance" in Performing Arts.

CONERLY, Gregory. Assistant professor of history at Cleveland State University, where he teaches courses on sexuality, black culture, and gender. Currently, his research focuses on discourses by and about African-American gays, lesbians, and bisexuals. His work has been featured in such publications as *Queer Studies: A Lesbian, Gay, Bisexual, and Transgender Anthology* and *The Greatest Taboo: Perspectives on Homosexuality in the African Diaspora.* **Chapter:** Chronology.

DOLKART, Jane. Associate professor of law at Southern Methodist University School of Law. She teaches and writes in the areas of law and sexuality and employment law. Prior to embarking on a teaching career, she was a civil rights lawyer in Washington, D.C., with an extensive practice representing lesbian and gay clients and non-profit organizations. She is also a past board member of Lambda Legal Defense and Education Fund. **Chapter:** Law.

FEIL, Ken. Received his Ph.D. in 1995 from the department of radio-TV-film at the University of Texas at Austin. Currently, he teaches film studies courses at Emerson College and writes and delivers movie reviews for the radio show, "1-in-10." **Chapter:** Film.

FORMO, Dawn M. Assistant professor of literature and writing and of women's studies at California State University, San Marcos. Her research interests include feminist rhetoric and girl theory. **Chapter:** Literature.

GAGE, Carolyn. Lesbian-feminist playwright. Her collection *The Second Coming of Joan of Arc and Other Plays* (HerBooks, 1994) was a national finalist for the Lambda Literary Award in drama, and her lesbian musical *The Amazon All-Stars* was the title work in the first mainstream anthology of lesbian plays (Applause, 1996). She has written the first book on lesbian theatre production and direction, *Take Stage!* (Scarecrow Press, 1997). **Chapter:** "Lesbian Theater" in Performing Arts.

GARBER, Linda. Author of *Identity Poetics: Lesbian Feminism, Diversity, and the Rise of Queer Theory* (Columbia University Press, forthcoming) and *Lesbian Sources: A Bibliography of Periodical Articles 1970-1990* (Garland 1993), and the editor of *Tilting the Tower: Lesbians/Teaching/Queer Subjects* (Routledge, 1994). She is assistant professor of women's studies at California State University, Fresno.

GILLASPY, Mary L. M.S., M.L.S., manager of the Learning Center, a consumer health information resource at the University of Texas M. D. Anderson Cancer Center, Houston, Texas. She has a particular interest in HIV disease in women. **Chapter:** AIDS.

GONZALES-DAY, Ken. Artist and writer living in West Hollywood, California. Gonzales-Day was awarded a B.F.A. from Pratt Institute in Brooklyn in 1987. He received an M.A. in art history from Hunter College, C.U.N.Y., in 1990. In 1993, Gonzales-Day was a Van Leer fellow in the Whitney Museum of American Art's Independent Study Program (studio art), and in 1995 he received an M.F.A. from the University of California, Irvine. In 1996, Gonzales-Day received a WESTAF/NEA award in New Genres. His writing has been featured in *Art Issues, Art Papers*, and *NYQ* magazine. His own artwork has been exhibited nationally, most recently at Post and the Municipal Gallery in Los Angeles, and White Columns and Cristinerose Gallery in New York. Gonzales-Day currently teaches art, photography, and humanities at Scripps College (Claremont Colleges). **Chapter:** "Art and Photography" in Visual Arts.

GOUGH, Cal. Adult materials selection specialist for the Atlanta-Fulton Public Library system, where he worked for the previous 16 years as a reference librarian. He is co-author, with Ellen Greenblatt, of *Gay and Lesbian Library Service* (McFarland,

1990), which he and Ellen are currently revising. A member of the American Library Association's Gay, Lesbian, and Bisexual Task Force since 1986, Cal is also involved with a group of Atlanta volunteers working to document and publicize that city's lesbigay history.

GREENBLATT, R. Ellen. Currently assistant director for technical services at Auraria Library, University of Colorado at Denver. She has been active in lesbian and gay librarianship for a dozen years and is co-editor with Cal Gough of *Gay and Lesbian Library Service*.

HUBBS, Nadine. Assistant professor of music theory at the University of Michigan, and serves as member-at-large of the gay and lesbian study group of the American Musicological Society. Her critical essays on issues of gender, culture, and semiotics in classical and popular music appear in edited collections and in journals including *Perspectives of New Music, Theory and Practice,* and *Genders.* **Chapter:** "Classical Music and Opera" in Music.

HUBER, Jeffrey T. Ph.D., assistant professor in the School of Library and Information Studies at Texas Woman's University. He specializes in HIV/AIDS and contributes regularly to the body of knowledge concerning the disease. **Chapter:** AIDS.

JOHNSON, David K. Ph.D. candidate and instructor in the history department of Northwestern University, where he is completing his dissertation, "The Purge of the Perverts: Gays and Lesbians in the Federal Civil Service, 1945-1975." His writings on gay and lesbian history have appeared in the *Washington Blade, Washington History,* and the anthology *Creating a Place for Ourselves.* **Chapter:** Significant Documents.

LEVINE, David. Freelance writer and contributor to many publications, including *Novels for Students, Gay and Lesbian Biography, Exploring Law and Society,* and *Encyclopedia of American Industries.* He has a B.A. in journalism from the University of Wisconsin-Madison and currently lives in Brooklyn, New York. **Chapters:** Sports, "Gay Male Travel and Leisure" in Travel and Leisure, and General Bibliography.

MORITZ, Marguerite. Associate dean and head of the electronic media sequence at the University of Colorado School of Journalism and Mass Communication. She helped establish a gay studies certificate program on the Boulder campus and is on the national board of directors of the Gay and Lesbian Alliance against Defamation (GLAAD). She has written extensively on media representations of gays and lesbians. Before joining the faculty in 1986, she was a radio and television news and documentary producer at NBC in Chicago. **Chapter:** Media.

NUNN, Colleen. Reference librarian at the University of Colorado, Denver. She is also a freelance writer, a member of the GLBT History Project, Denver, and editor of a lesbian outdoor club newsletter, *Out and About.* **Chapter:** "Lesbian Travel and Leisure" in Travel and Leisure.

PETERSON, K. Jean. D.S.W. and associate professor of social welfare at the University of Kansas. She is the editor of *Health Care for Lesbians and Gay Men: Confronting Homophobia and Heterosexism* (Haworth Press, 1996) and a consulting editor of

Social Work, Smith College Studies in Social Work, and *Journal of Gay & Lesbian Social Services.* **Chapter:** Health.

RABEN, Robert. Democratic Counsel on the House Judiciary Committee, focusing on intellectual property and constitutional law, and has been counsel to Congressman Barney Frank (D-MA) since 1993. He is an adjunct professor of sexual orientation and the law at Georgetown and a co-founder of the Lesbian and Gay Congressional Staff Association. **Chapter:** Politics.

REICH, June L. Ph.D. candidate in the department of performance studies at New York University. She has published articles on lesbian performance in *Discourse* and *Women & Performance.* She is currently working on a short independent film with friends in New York City. **Chapter:** "Lesbian Performance Art" in Performing Arts.

RIDINGER, Robert. Electronic information resources librarian at Northern Illinois University and has been engaged in gay-related research for more than 15 years. His works include *The ADVOCATE Index, 1967-1982* and, most recently, *The Gay and Lesbian Movement: References and Resources.* **Chapter:** Local and Regional Views.

RIMMERMAN, Craig A. Professor of political science at Hobart and William Smith Colleges in Geneva, New York. He is a past American Political Science Association Congressional Fellow and is the author of *Presidency by Plebiscite: The Reagan-Bush Era in Institutional Perspective* (Westview, 1993), *The New Citizenship: Unconventional Politics, Activism, and Service* (Westview, 1997), and the editor of *Gay Rights, Military Wrongs: Political Perspectives on Lesbians and Gays in the Military* (Garland Publishers, 1996). Rimmerman teaches courses in American politics, environmental and urban policy, democratic theory, and gay and lesbian politics. **Chapter:** Military.

ROACH, Thomas J. Graduate student in the comparative studies in discourse and society department at the University of Minnesota. He also plays in the rock band Lifter Puller. **Chapter:** "Pop/Rock Music" in Music.

SILVERSTEIN, Sharon. M.B.A. from the Harvard Business School. Together with her partner Annette Friskopp, she is the co-author of *Straight Jobs, Gay Lives,* published in 1995 by Simon & Schuster. **Chapter:** Labor and Employment.

TATTELMAN, Ira. Independent scholar, architect, and artist. With degrees from Columbia University and Harvard University's Graduate School of Design, he has been able to combine his interests by writing a series of articles about Queer Space. They have or will soon appear in *Harvard Gay & Lesbian Review, Journal of Architectural Education, Public Sex--Gay Sex, Queers in Space: Communities, Public Places, Sites of Resistance,* and *This Vast Land: Creating Place in North America.* His photographs and design work have been exhibited at galleries and museums in Boston, New York, and Washington, D.C. **Chapter:** "Architecture" in Visual Arts.

TAYLOR, Darrell. Performance and intermedia artist from Nashville, Tennessee, currently residing in Iowa City, Iowa. He is completing his M.F.A. in intermedia art at the University of Iowa, where he also serves as 1997-98 director of the UI Fine Arts Council. Darrell is currently working with NEA recipient Mark McCusker on a series of bodywork pieces and is preparing for an engagement in Dortmund, Germany, with six other intermedia artists from the UI department of art and art history. **Chapter:** "Queer Male Performance Art" in Performing Arts.

TOWNSEND, Julie. Doctoral student in comparative literature at UCLA. She has written on sexual imagery in the work of Loie Fuller and is preparing a doctoral thesis on images of dancers in modernist literature. **Chapter:** "Lesbian Dance" in Performing Arts.

TRICE, Elliott. Graduate student in the department of English and comparative literature at Columbia University. He works on early modern drama and culture as well as queer theory and activism. **Chapter:** Organizations.

VAN BUSKIRK, Jim. Program manager of the James C. Hormel Gay & Lesbian Center at the San Francisco Public Library, and the co-author of *Gay by the Bay: A History of Queer Culture in the San Francisco Bay Area* (Chronicle Books, 1996). His reviews and essays have appeared in *James White Review, Lambda Book Report, Library Journal*, and other publications.

WIDMANN, R L. Instructor in the English department at the University of Colorado at Boulder. The first chair of the CU academic planning committee for a program in lesbigay studies, she has developed and taught courses in queer theory; she also teaches Shakespeare and courses in women writers. She conducts her research chiefly at the Folger Shakespeare Library in Washington, D.C.

YOUNGER, John G. Professor of classical archaeology at Duke University and director of the undergraduate program in the study of sexualities. He has written numerous studies of ancient Greek art, many of which concern gender and sexuality, and is a campus activist for LGBT and other minority rights. **Chapter:** Education and Scholarship.

INDEX

Barr, James, 365
Barrett, Ellen Marie, 100
Barrie, Dennis, 524
Barriga, Cecillia, 341
Barrymore, Ethel, 437
Baryshnikov, Mikhail, 452, 479
Bars in gay male culture, 626
Bars in lesbian culture, 2-3, 607-10
Barthes, Roland, 478
Bartlett, Neil, 443
Basile, Vic, 40, 287
Bassae, Antony, 467
Bastard Out of Carolina, 380
Bates, Katherine Lee, 373
Bathhouses, 185, 627-28
Bausch, Pina, 482
Baum, Terry, 450
Bauman, Robert, 284
Bawer, Bruce, 43, 260, 266
Baxt, George, 367
Bay Area Gay and Lesbian Historical Society, 631
Bazell, Robert, 190
Beach Boys, 412
Beam, Joseph, 6, 21
Bean, Carl, 7, 551
Bean, Terry, 40
Beardsley, Aubrey, 491
Beautiful Room Is Empty, The, 370
Beauty of Men, The, 382
Beck, Evelyn Torton, 22
Becoming a Man: Half a Life Story, 371, 383
Bed and breakfast hotels, 605
Beethoven, Ludwig van, 428
Beglarian, Eve, 428
Bellamy, Ralphy, 328
Bellas, Bruce Harry. *See* Bruce of Los Angeles.
Ben, Lisa, 402
Benecke, Michelle M., 42, 261
Bennett, Allen, 100
Bennett, Michael, 453
Benning, Sadie, 348-49, 351
Ben-Shalom, Miriam, 100, 255-56, 268
Bent, 441, 444
Bentley, Gladys
Berdaches, 273, 547
Berdemphl, William, 49
Berg, Vernon "Copy", 255-56
Bergalis, Kimberly, 177
Berkowitz, Richard, 192
Berle, Milton, 326, 390
Bernhard, Sandra, 399
Bernhardt, Sarah, 453
Bernstein, Leonard, 421, 422, 424-25, 427, 452
Berube, Allan, 254-55
Berson, Ginny, 612
Besecker, Joe, 443
Best, Paul, 461, 468
Beth Chazim Chadashim, 8, 100, 545
Betsky, Aaron, 505
Bianco, David Ari, 266

Biblical views of homosexuality, 541-44
Bikini Kill, 414
Bi-Net U.S.A., 15, 21
Biological origins of homosexuality. *See* Science.
Birch, Elizabeth, 37, 163, 201-02, 246, 295, 296
Biscardi, Chester, 428
Bisexual identities and issues, 21, 25, 68, 156, 244, 277, 411, 443, 581
Bishop, Elizabeth, 377
Bishop, Nadean, 555
Black Is, Black Ain't, 339
Black Panther Party, 8, 9, 280, 281, 639
Black Power movement, 331, 332, 345
Blackwell, Earl, 623
Blake, Nayland, 508-09
Blechman, Bert, 367
Bleckner, Ross, 509
Blitzstein, Marc, 422, 424, 425
Bloom, Alan, 409
Blue, Lucie, 618
Boesing, Martha, 451
Bolan, Marc, 412
Bond, Brian, 40
Bookstores, 615-16
Boorstein, Jonathan, 505
Boozer, Melvin, 284, 296-97, 641-42
Borden, Lizzie, 351
Bordowitz, Gregg, 351
Bornstein, Kate, 444, 464
Borrowed Time: An AIDS Memoir, 371, 383
Boswell, John, 22, 213, 540-41, 555
Bottoms, Sharon, 108, 125
Boulanger, Nadia, 426
Bound, 336
Boutte, Duane, 330
Bowers, Michael, 313-14
Bowers v. Hardwick, 14, 19, 81-85, 87, 89, 125, 208, 235, 275, 281, 285, 286, 306-07, 308
Bowie, David, 18, 332, 412, 415, 417
Bowles, Jane, 376-77, 381, 425, 622
Bowles, Paul, 376, 424, 425, 622
Boyce, Johanna, 455
Boyd, Malcolm, 462, 555
Boy George, 419
Boy in the Basement, The, 437
Boykin, Keith, 38
Boynton, Peter, 368
Boys in the Band, The, 331, 440, 468
Boy's Own Story, A, 385
Bradley, Marion Zimmer, 369
Brady Bunch Movie, The, 333, 334-35, 336
Bram, Christopher, 371, 629
Brando, Marlon, 437
Branner, Djola Bernard, 446
Braschi v. Stahl Associates, 317-18
Brause v. Alaska, 317
Bratmobile, 414
Breaking Open, 377
Breaking the Surface, 399
Breton, Andre, 525
Brett, Philip, 423